The Encyclopedia of
LIBERTARIANISM

Augustus was sensible that mankind is governed by names; nor was he deceived in his expectation, that the senate and people would submit to slavery, provided they were respectfully assured, that they still enjoyed their ancient freedom.

—Edward Gibbon, *The Decline and Fall of the Roman Empire*

The Encyclopedia of
LIBERTARIANISM

Editor-in-Chief

Ronald Hamowy

Professor Emeritus of History, University of Alberta

Assistant Editors

Jason Kuznicki

Research Fellow, Cato Institute

Aaron Steelman

Director of Research Publications, Federal Reserve Bank of Richmond

Consulting Editor

Deirdre McCloskey

Professor of Economics, University of Illinois, Chicago

Founding and Consulting Editor

Jeffrey D. Schultz

A project of the Cato Institute

Los Angeles • London • New Delhi • Singapore

A SAGE Reference Publication

For information:

SAGE Publications, Inc.
2455 Teller Road
Thousand Oaks, California 91320
E-mail: order@sagepub.com

SAGE Publications Ltd.
1 Oliver's Yard
55 City Road
London EC1Y 1SP
United Kingdom

SAGE Publications India Pvt. Ltd.
B 1/I 1 Mohan Cooperative Industrial Area
Mathura Road, New Delhi 110 044
India

SAGE Publications Asia-Pacific Pte. Ltd.
33 Pekin Street #02-01
Far East Square
Singapore 048763

Printed in the United States of America.

Library of Congress Cataloging-in-Publication Data

The encyclopedia of libertarianism / editor Ronald Hamowy.
        p. cm.
Includes bibliographical references and index.
ISBN 978-1-4129-6580-4 (cloth)
    1. Libertarianism—Encyclopedias. I. Hamowy, Ronald, 1937-

JC585.E53 2008
320.51'2—dc22   2008009151

This book is printed on acid-free paper.

08   09   10   11   12   10   9   8   7   6   5   4   3   2   1

Publisher:	Rolf A. Janke
Acquisitions Editor:	Jim Brace-Thompson
Production Editor:	Tracy Buyan
Copy Editor:	Heather Jefferson
Typesetter:	C&M Digitals (P) Ltd.
Proofreader:	Penelope Sippel
Indexer:	Julie Sherman Grayson
Cover Designer:	Ravi Balasuriya
Marketing Manager:	Amberlyn Erzinger

Contents

List of Entries

Reader's Guide

The Reader's Guide is provided to assist readers in locating articles on related topics. It classifies articles into three general categories: Biographical, Policy, and Topical.

Biographical

Acton, Lord
Adams, John
Aquinas, Thomas
Aristotle
Bastiat, Frédéric
Bauer, Peter
Becker, Gary S.
Bentham, Jeremy
Böhm-Bawerk, Eugen von
Branden, Nathaniel
Bright, John
Brown, John
Buchanan, James M.
Buckle, Henry Thomas
Burke, Edmund
Burlamaqui, Jean-Jacques
Cantillon, Richard
Childs, Roy A.
Chodorov, Frank
Cicero
Clark, Ed
Coase, Ronald H.
Cobden, Richard
Coke, Edward
Comte, Charles
Condorcet, Marquis de
Constant, Benjamin
Dicey, Albert Venn
Diderot, Denis
Douglas, Frederick
Dunoyer, Charles
Emerson, Ralph Waldo

Epstein, Richard A.
Ferguson, Adam
Fisher, Antony
Foucault, Michel
Friedman, David
Friedman, Milton
Garrison, William Lloyd
Gladstone, William Ewart
Godwin, William
Goldwater, Barry
Harper, Floyd Arthur "Baldy"
Hayek, Friedrich A.
Hazlitt, Henry
Heinlein, Robert
Herbert, Auberon
Hess, Karl
Hobbes, Thomas
Hodgskin, Thomas
Hospers, John
Humboldt, Wilhelm von
Hume, David
Hutcheson, Francis
Jacobs, Jane
Jefferson, Thomas
Jouvenel, Bertrand de
Kant, Immanuel
Kirzner, Israel M.
Knight, Frank H.
La Boétie, Étienne de
Lane, Rose Wilder
Lao Tzu
Las Casas, Bartolomé de
LeFevre, Robert
Leggett, William

Policy

About the Editors

Ronald Hamowy is Professor Emeritus of Intellectual History at the University of Alberta. He is the editor of Trenchard and Gordon's *Cato's Letters*, and the author, among other works, of *The Scottish Enlightenment and Spontaneous Order* and *The Political Sociology of Freedom: Adam Ferguson and F. A. Hayek*, and of numerous articles on 18th-century British and American political theory and on public health during the Progressive Era.

Jason Kuznicki earned a PhD in history from Johns Hopkins University in 2005. His work there specialized in early Modern France and Britain, with a particular interest on religion, government oversight, and the Enlightenment. He is currently a Research Fellow at the Cato Institute, where his ongoing interests include censorship, church–state issues, and civil rights in the context of libertarian political theory.

Aaron Steelman is director of research publications at the Federal Reserve Bank of Richmond.

Contributors

AC	Andrew Coulson *Cato Institute*	AV	Alexander Volokh *Georgetown University*	CB	Clint Bolick *Goldwater Institute*
AdJ	Anthony de Jasay *Author of* The State, Against Politics, *and* Justice and Its Surroundings	BAS	Bradley Smith *Capital University Law* *School*	ChB	Charles Baird *California State* *University, East Bay*
		BBG	Bettina Bien Greaves *Foundation for* *Economic Education*	CD	Christie Davies *University of Reading*
AeS	Aeon Skoble *Bridgewater State* *College*	BC	Bryan Caplan *George Mason* *University*	CH	Charles Hamilton *The Clark Foundation*
AF	Antony Flew *University of Reading*			CMS	Chris Sciabarra *Co-Editor,* Journal of
AK	Alan Charles Kors *University of* *Pennsylvania*	BDo	Brian Doherty *Senior Editor,* Reason magazine *Author of* Radicals for		Ayn Rand Studies *New York University*
			Capitalism	CoB	Colin Bird *University of Virginia*
AlC	Alejandro A. Chafuen *Atlas Economic* *Research Foundation*	BJW	Bart Wilson *George Mason* *University*	CP	Christopher Preble *Cato Institute*
AM	Andrew Morriss *University of Illinois*	BK	Bill Kauffman *Author of* Look	DAH	David Harper *New York University*
AMP	Allen M. Parkman *University of New* *Mexico*	BL	Homeward America Brink Lindsey *Cato Institute*	DB	David Boaz *Cato Institute*
AmS	Amy Sturgis *Belmont University*	BLB	Bruce Benson	DBa	Doug Bandow *Competitive Enterprise* *Institute*
AS	Aaron Steelman		*Florida State University*	DBK	Daniel Klein
	Federal Reserve Bank *of Richmond*	BP	Benjamin Powell *Suffolk University*		*George Mason* *University*

DBR	Douglas B. Rasmussen *St. John's University*	DMK	Douglas MacKenzie *State University of New York Plattsburgh*	GH	Gene Healy *Cato Institute*
DC	David Conway *Civitas: The Institute for the Study of Civil Society*	DNM	David Mayer *Capital University Law School*	GHS	George H. Smith *Author of* Atheism, Ayn Rand, and Other Heresies
DD	Detmar Doering *Friedrich Naumann Stiftung*	DRL	Dwight R. Lee *Southern Methodist University*	GMAG	Gregory Gronbacher *Acton Institute*
DDU	Douglas Den Uyl *Liberty Fund*	DRS	David Ramsay Steele *Author of* From Marx to Mises	GR	Gabriel Roth *Independent Institute*
DFM	Dario Fernández-Morera *Northwestern University*	DS	David Schoenbrod *New York Law School*	GWC	George Carey *Georgetown University*
DG	David Gordon *Ludwig von Mises Institute*	DT	David Trenchard *Cato Institute*	HLE	Hans Eicholz *Liberty Fund*
DJB	Donald Boudreaux *George Mason University*	DTB	David Beito *University of Alabama*	IDA	Imad-ad-Dean Ahmed *Minaret of Freedom Foundation*
DJM	Daniel J. Mahoney *Assumption College*	DTG	Dan Griswold *Cato Institute*	IK	Israel Kirzner *New York University*
DK	David Kelley *The Atlas Society*	EF	Edward C. Feser *Pasadena City College*	IV	Ian Vásquez *Cato Institute*
DLP	David Prychitko *Northern Michigan University*	EFP	Ellen Frankel Paul *Bowling Green State University*	JAD	James A. Dorn *Cato Institute*
DM	Daniel Mitchell *Cato Institute*	EM	Eric Mack *Tulane University*	JaK	Jackson Kuhl *Freelance Journalist*
DMC	Deirdre McCloskey *University of Illinois, Chicago*	EO	Eric O'Keefe *Americans for Limited Government*	JAS	Jeffrey A. Schaler *American University*
DMF	David Fitzsimons *University of Rhode Island*	ES	Edward Stringham *San Jose State University*	JB	James Buchanan *George Mason University*
DMH	David Hart *Liberty Fund*	FM	Fred Miller *Bowling Green State University*	JD	Jarett Decker *Public Company Accounting and Oversight Board*
		GC	Guy Calvert *Oxford University*	JGH	Guido Hülsmann *Université d'Angers*

JH   Jim Harper
      Cato Institute

JHA   Jonathan Adler
      *Case Western Reserve
      University*

JK   Jo Kwong
      *Atlas Economic
      Research Foundation*

JKT   Joan Kennedy Taylor
      Manhattan Institute

JM   John Mueller
      Ohio State University

JMB   John M. Brady
      *San Jose State
      University*

JN   Jan Narveson
      University of Waterloo

JoH   John Hasnas
      Georgetown University

JoN   Johan Norberg
      Cato Institute

JoR   Jonathan Rowe
      *Mercer County
      Community College*

JR   Jeff Riggenbach
      Liberty *Magazine*

JRH   Jeff Hummel
      *San Jose State
      University*

JSa   John Samples
      Cato Institute

JSh   Jeremy Shearmur
      *Australian National
      University*

JSo   Jason Sorens
      University of Buffalo

JT   John Tooby
      *University of California
      at Santa Barbara*

JTK   Jason Kuznicki
      Cato Institute

KB   Karol Boudreaux
      *George Mason
      University*

KZ   Kate Zhou
      *University of Hawai'i
      at Manoa*

LC   Leda Cosmides
      *University of California,
      Santa Barbara*

LE   Lee Edwards
      *The Heritage
      Foundation*

LH   Lester Hunt
      University of Wisconsin

LHW   Lawrence H. White
      *University of Missouri
      at St. Louis*

LL   Leonard Liggio
      *Atlas Economic
      Research Foundation*

LT   Louis Torres
      Editor, Aristos

LWR   Lawrence W. Reed
      *Mackinac Center for
      Public Policy*

LY   Leland Yeager
      Auburn University

MaS   Mark Skousen
      Grantham University

MC   Michael Chapman
      Cybercast News Service

MFC   Michael Cannon
      Cato Institute

MI   Malou Innocent
      Cato Institute

MK   Maureen Kelley
      *University of Alabama
      at Birmingham*

MLS   M. L. Schut
      University of Chicago

MM   Michael Munger
      Duke University

MP   Mark Pennington
      University of London

MR   Matt Ridley
      Author of The Origins of
      Virtue *and* Nature via
      Nurture

MT   Michael Tanner
      Cato Institute

MV   Michiel Visser
      *Edmund Burke
      Foundation*

MZ   Michael Zuckert
      Notre Dame University

NA   Nigel Ashford
      *George Mason
      University*

NB   Norman Barry
      *University of
      Buckingham*

NL   Nelson Lund
      George Mason University

NS   Nick Slepko

PB   Patrick Basham
      Democracy Institute

PDA   Paul Dragos Aligica
      *George Mason
      University*

PJB   Peter Boettke
*George Mason
University*

PKK   Peter Kurrild-Klitgaard
*University of
Copenhagen*

PTL   Peter Leeson
*George Mason
University*

RA   Richard Adelstein
Wesleyan University

RBo   Richard Boyd
Georgetown University

RE   Richard Epstein
University of Chicago

REB   Randy Barnett
*Georgetown University
Law Center*

RGH   Randall Holcombe
*Florida State
University*

RH   Ronald Hamowy
University of Alberta

RL   Roderick Long
Auburn University

RMB   Ralf Bader
*University of Saint
Andrews*

RMD   Robert McDonald
U.S. Military Academy

RoB   Robert Bannister
Swarthmore College

RoE   Rod L. Evans
*Old Dominion
University*

RoH   Robert Higgs
Independent Institute

RoW   Robert Whaples
Wake Forest University

RW   Richard Wagner
George Mason University

RWP   Robert W. Poole
The Reason Foundation

SBP   Stephen B. Presser
Northwestern University

SC   Stephen Cox
Senior Editor, Liberty
*University of California,
San Diego*

SD   Stephen Davies
*Manchester
Metropolitan University*

SFR   Sigrid Fry-Revere
Cato Institute

SH   Steven Horwitz
St. Lawrence University

SI   Sanford Ikeda
Purchase College

SMS   Stephen M. Sheppard
University of Arkansas

SP   Sharon Presley
*California State
University at East Bay
Co-Founder of Laissez-
Faire Books*

SRCH   Stephen Hicks
Rockford College

SS   Solveig Singleton
*Competitive Enterprise
Institute*

TB   Tom Bethell
Senior Editor, The
American Spectator

TC   Tyler Cowen
*George Mason
University*

TGC   Ted Galen Carpenter
Cato Institute

TGP   Tom G. Palmer
Cato Institute

TLP   Terry Price
*University of
Richmond*

TM   Tibor Machan
*Chapman
University*

TMH   Thomas M. Humphrey
*Senior Economist,
Federal Reserve Bank
of Richmond*

TMS   Timothy Sandefur
*Pacific Legal
Foundation*

TPB   T. Patrick Burke
Temple University

VLS   Vernon L. Smith
Chapman University

WAN   William A. Niskanen
Cato Institute

WD   Wayne Dynes
Hunter College

WME   Wendy McElroy
*Independent
Institute*

WO   Walter Olson
Manhattan Institute

WW   Will Wilkinson
Cato Institute

Editor's Introduction

In preparing this encyclopedia, our hope has been to offer a general guide to the social and political philosophy that today goes by the name of *libertarianism*. Although the title is comparatively new, the doctrine is not. Libertarianism is the heir to 19th-century classical liberalism and to the Whig ideology in the period prior to that. Indeed, its roots can be traced back to the earliest discussions of the nature of freedom in Western philosophy. At its most general, it embraces the view that men should be treated as autonomous individuals, free to make their own decisions regarding how to live their lives and how to determine their own salvation without being constrained to act against their wishes. Of course, this is not to suggest that their decisions will invariably conduce to their greatest happiness, nor that they will never be hurtful to others. But so long as their decisions were made freely and do not directly harm their fellow men, the only option open to others in trying to divert them from their chosen path is moral suasion and not force.

It is for this reason that libertarians are so distrustful of government, not because they fear the behavior of all collectivities, but because governments rest on law and all law is ultimately based on the threat of force. All law seeks to alter behavior, either by preventing people from acting in ways that, in the absence of law, they would freely choose to engage in or by inducing them to behave in manners foreign to their more agreeable wishes. These modifications in behavior are in every instance brought about by the government's threat to use force or by its actual use. Thus, fines, imprisonments, and even death itself are attached to engaging in certain actions or dissuading us from doing others. This aspect of law is seldom, if ever, considered. We often encounter distasteful conduct that we feel can be eradicated by the passage of some law or another. However, we seem unaware of the fact that, although we might benefit from the law's effectiveness, it has as its corollary that numbers of people will be punished for disobeying the law and even greater numbers will be thwarted from engaging in activities they would freely choose under pain of punishment. It is a basic principle of libertarian politics that no one should be forcibly prevented from acting in any way he chooses provided his acts are not invasive of the free acts of others. John Stuart Mill's justifiably celebrated words in the first chapter of *On Liberty*, written almost a century and a half ago, give eloquent testimony to this view:

> The object of this Essay is to assert one very simple principle, as entitled to govern absolutely the dealings of society with the individual in the way of compulsion and control, whether the means used be physical force in the form of legal penalties, or the moral coercion of public opinion. That principle is, that the sole end for which mankind is warranted, individually or collectively in interfering with the liberty of action of any of their number, is self-protection. That the only purpose for which power can be rightfully exercised over any member of a civilized community, against his will, is to prevent harm to others. His own good, either physical or moral, is not a sufficient warrant. He cannot rightfully be compelled to do or forbear because it will be better for him to do so, because it will make him happier, because, in the opinions of others, to do so would be wise, or even right. These are good reasons for remonstrating with him, or reasoning with him, or persuading him, or entreating him, but not for compelling him, or visiting him with any evil, in case he does otherwise.

This noble principle has, since the dawn of civilization, found itself at war with the notion that private decisions are not solely the prerogatives of individuals who are immediate parties to their outcome, but by groups of experts or committees representing the wishes of the larger population who claim to have some interest, however tenuous, in the consequences. This approach is predicated on the perception that nothing is totally private, that all acts affect the general public in some way or another, and that the entire collectivity has a legitimate interest in the results of any decision we make, whether it is what we read, what we ingest, whom we choose as our sexual partners, indeed any and everything that touch our lives that might be viewed as harmful to the community or ourselves. What is truly remarkable about the millions who support extensive governments is that they seem to have lost sight of the fact that those whom we empower to write and enforce the laws are no more moral and decent than the rest of us. Indeed, they are no less unethical and corrupt; in fact, there is substantial evidence that they are often more so than those over whom they govern, that for the most part their overriding interest is their own immediate welfare and their concerns extend no further than the next election. Yet we constantly rely on them to correct the evils we see around us and express surprise when no improvement occurs.

The facts are that ultimately we are either autonomous individuals empowered with primary control over ourselves and the property we create, or we are not. There are those who would claim that we are a mix of both, but these philosophers have been unable to locate the point at which individuals have surrendered their autonomy to some sovereign entity or in what that entity consists, whether an individual sovereign or a collectivity, or who is empowered to determine when the decisions of the sovereign take precedence over the wishes of the individual. Perhaps the most compelling of these theories of political obligation, however, and one embraced by almost all libertarians is that put forward by John Locke and that formed the theoretical underpinnings of Jefferson's Declaration of Independence. "We hold these truths to be self-evident," Jefferson wrote,

> that all men are created equal, that they are endowed by their Creator with certain unalienable Rights, that among these are Life, Liberty and the pursuit of Happiness. That to secure these rights, Governments are instituted among Men, deriving their just powers from the consent of the governed. That whenever any Form of Government becomes destructive of these ends, it is the Right of the People to alter or to abolish

> it, and to institute new Government, laying its foundation on such principles, and organizing its powers in such form, as to them shall seem most likely to effect their Safety and Happiness.

Despite attempts by some political theorists to translate these words into a defense of an all-pervasive government, their intent is clear. The crucial test of all government, no matter how constituted, lies in whether it respects the inalienable rights with which all men are endowed. These rights, Locke and Jefferson maintained, owe their existence neither to convention nor to the presence of a sovereign who both created them and made their exercise possible. They are rooted in man's very nature and are unconditional and nontransferable. Men do not, nor can they, compromise them by entering into civil society, nor can these rights be modified in some way to conform to the dictates of the magistrate. The transcendent purpose of government is the preservation of these rights. The rights to which Jefferson refers—and here he clearly follows Locke—are to be understood not as mandating individual or collective acts of any kind, but rather as restraining men from acting in certain ways. Put more simply, my right to something, say my liberty, entails only prohibitions on others and not positive commands. To the extent that I am free, I am "let alone," not "forced," "required," "commanded" by others to do (or not to do) something that I "can," "am able," "have the capacity" to do. The only boundaries limiting the actions of other men are those prohibitions against others that extend around my liberty.

The protection of this sphere constitutes the legitimate boundary of state action. When rights are understood in this manner, the rights of individuals cannot conflict because their rights do nothing more than constrain others from acting toward rights possessors in certain ways. The notion that rights are forever competing with each other arises when one includes in an enumeration of rights those that impose obligations on others and afflicts most contemporary discussions of the subject. We commonly speak of the rights of members of a community as in perpetual conflict, but this is in large part due to the fact that politicians and others who have vulgarized the language of political theory have found it to their ideological advantage to encourage the view that such conflicts are an invariable part of political life. Thus, my right to smoke directly conflicts with your right to a smoke-free environment and my right to spend my wages as

I alone see fit conflicts with your right to a superhighway. For once it is conceded that rights, of necessity, compete, there can be only one referee, and that is the modern democratic state.

In the past 100 years, the language of politics has become so mutilated by politicians and their ideological henchmen that no principled position makes sense, and we are reduced to a war of all against all in which the battlegrounds are our periodic elections. The result is the creation of a leviathan state that attempts to cater to an increasingly broad spectrum of more specialized interests. Even with the end of a world conflict to which the federal government had dedicated the blood and treasure of its citizens, the various levels of American government currently expend no less than 32% of all the goods and services produced in the nation. This scenario is hardly what the Founders had in mind when it limited the functions of government to securing the lives, liberties, and estates of its citizens. Nor is there any truth to the vicious canard, so often broadcast without the least evidence, that in the absence of a massive government apparatus the charity and compassion of private individuals would be insufficient to help the needy.

What this volume seeks to do is to offer a series of brief articles on the historical, sociological, and economic aspects of libertarianism and to place them within their broader context. They offer a commentary on the unending attempts of countless individuals to emancipate themselves from the control of an oppressive and overweening state, whether one is controlled by a despot or one is acting in the name of the wishes of the people. What these articles have in common is the search for a world in which man's subjection to the will of others is brought to a minimum. We do not seek, as those who would malign us claim, emancipation from the laws of God or the forces of nature, to which we are all, depending on our beliefs and our circumstances, more or less subject. Rather, we wish an open and divergent society, in which each may act as he thinks best, despite the consequences of his actions. We may exhort others from acting in ways that we feel may harm them, but we cannot use the police power of the state to punish them from so acting. This open society, to which Periclean Athens inclined, was, we are told, an education to all of Greece. So there was a time when America was an education to the world, and it is to this time to which we seek to return.

Ronald Hamowy
Rockville, Maryland

General Introduction

Libertarianism is a major feature of intellectual and political life as we enter the first years of the new century. It is at one and the same time a movement in politics, a recognized philosophy, and a set of distinctive policy prescriptions. As such, libertarianism, and the individuals who espouse it, play a prominent role in intellectual and political arguments in several countries. In disciplines such as philosophy, political science, jurisprudence, and economics, there is a recognized and substantial libertarian position and body of literature. All of that is in marked contrast to the situation that prevailed 30 or 40 years ago. At that time, libertarian ideas and analyses had little public visibility. This recent growth might lead one to conclude that libertarian ideas and politics are a phenomenon of the late 20th and early 21st centuries and should be placed in some kind of post or late modern category.

In fact, that is untrue. Contemporary libertarianism is only the latest manifestation of an intellectual, cultural, and political phenomenon that is as old as modernity, if not older. It is the movement earlier described as liberalism. The great problem with contemporary usage of the term *liberal*, at least in the Anglo-Saxon world, is that in the United States (and to a lesser extent in the British Commonwealth), it has come to refer to a body of ideas known in the rest of the world as social democracy or even simply as socialism. It is this shift in terminology that has led to the term *libertarianism* being used in English-speaking countries for what elsewhere is still called *liberalism*. The important thing to realize, however, is that contemporary libertarianism, in the United States and elsewhere, is only the most recent chapter in a long story that, in the Anglo-Saxon world, traces itself back to classical liberalism.

In what does libertarianism consist? This question is more difficult and profound than one might at first suppose. It is easy to think of political philosophies as

concrete, reified entities handed on from one generation to another like the baton in a relay race. The reality is more complex. The major ideologies of modernity—the most prominent of which are liberalism, socialism, conservatism, and nationalism—can be thought of differently, and each can be analyzed in distinct ways. One approach might look at the various political movements that share similar goals or have some other form of affinity, which would involve focusing on the history of political parties, on pressure groups, and on political biography. A second approach might concentrate on the development of philosophical concepts and abstract ideas. A third approach might center on the exploration of distinctive vocabularies or languages in which public affairs are discussed and debated. Yet another might examine the texts central to the specific ideology and try both to unearth the original meaning or intention of the authors and to relate them to their social and political contexts. Finally, one can explore the distinctive cultural content and consciousness, or *mentalité*, associated with a particular political label.

The intention of all such approaches is to construct a cogent analysis that explains how ideas, movements, and philosophical systems that exist in the present have come about and how they have changed over time. These analyses trace the origins of ideas, movements, and philosophical systems and relate them to other historical phenomena that they have influenced and by which they have been shaped. The aim is to avoid the problem of anachronism, of reading the present into the past and so misunderstanding both past and present. We should be careful to avoid the Whig form of intellectual history, which interprets past ideas only in terms of their connection to the present. What emerges, with libertarianism as much as any other system of thought, is a narrative in which we discover neither a timeless, ahistorical object, nor a progressive discovery of truth, but the slow growth and unfolding of a particular way of thinking. We also discover, in the case of libertarianism/liberalism, a pattern of elaboration in which these ideas flourished, followed by a period in which they were disregarded, only to revive again more recently.

The word *liberalism* refers to a distinctive set of beliefs and an associated political movement that appeared in the early 19th century. The first recorded occurrence of the term was in Spain in 1823 when the term *liberales*, or freedom lovers, was used to describe supporters of the constitutional regime established after the Napoleonic wars. (The liberals' opponents, supporters of the absolute rule of the Bourbons, were known as the *serviles*, or servile ones.) In France, the economist Jean-Baptiste Say and his followers began to use the adjective *liberal* to mean "in favor of freedom" following the Restoration of the Bourbons in 1815. In England, the word entered popular discourse at about the same time; one prominent early example was the name given to the journal *The Liberal*, published by Leigh Hunt and Lord Byron. The term *liberal* was well known in the 18th century, but was generally associated with its older meaning of "generous, open hearted" and so referred only to qualities of character. However, to adapt an expression of Byron's, although the word had not yet taken on its later meaning, the thing it came to describe had already come into existence.

Beginning with the later 17th century, the West has witnessed the gradual appearance of a way of thinking about the world and human society that has provided a perspective radically different from the providential approach that preceded it. This change grew partly out of intense political conflict and generated a particular political program. All of those developments came together in the later 18th century and the early part of the 19th century. Conservatism was to appear at the same time, as a reaction to the emerging liberal worldview, whereas socialism, both the word and the phenomenon, appeared only later.

The origins of classical liberalism lie in the great turmoil and upheaval of the period 1549 to 1688. In that terrible century and a half, Europe was torn by a series of wars larger and more devastating than anything experienced since the 14th century. Two forces had worked to produce that state of affairs. The first was the clash of Reformation and Counter Reformation, which had a profoundly destabilizing effect on the politics of every European state. The second was the "military

revolution," a transformation in the nature and scope of war that took place in the first part of the 16th century, which made war vastly more expensive and damaging than it had ever been in the Middle Ages. The result of both developments was the rise of absolutism, both as it was explicated in the philosophies of authors such as Jean Bodin and Thomas Hobbes and in the practice of government. During this period, a weakening of representative institutions and the growth of central power occurred, not least in the area of taxation. This growth of centralized power did not happen without resistance. Throughout Europe, scholars defended the older ideas of mixed or limited government, and rebels took up arms to uphold established constitutional settlements against the innovations of reforming monarchs and their ministers. The military power of the new monarchies was such, however, that any opposition to the growing power of strong central governments was defeated throughout Europe, with two exceptions: the Dutch Republic and Britain. There, constitutional government survived and became the established form of government. In Britain, the climactic event was the Glorious Revolution of 1688–1689.

The clash of ideas in those years led to a change in the arguments used to defend limited government against absolutism. As a consequence, new ideas emerged and were vigorously articulated. These ideas were then advanced in new ways by some authors to yield surprising conclusions. Two issues had emerged as central by the later 17th century: (1) constitutional versus absolute government, and (2) religious toleration, or freedom of conscience, versus the confessional state. Originally, the case for constitutionalism and (relative) toleration had been made on the basis of tradition and conservative, or historical, arguments. Those arguments proved inadequate, and there was a gradual shift toward arguments based on autonomy and ideas of natural right. Such new formulations were expressed in England during the Civil War, between 1637 and 1653. A political faction known as the Levellers emerged in London and became a significant minority in the New Model Army. In a series of essays, manifestos, petitions, and other documents, the Levellers argued the case for a constitutional government with strictly limited powers and complete religious toleration. The argument used to support their program was partly historical, but rested in the main on the connected ideas of property in one's own person (or self-ownership) and natural rights. Individuals, they argued, were sovereign, and government derived its powers by delegation from the individuals over whom it ruled—hence, a strict limitation on its powers. Those ideas did not disappear with the restoration of the monarchy in 1660, but remained alive—among exile circles on the Continent, particularly in the Netherlands, and in underground groups in London.

The unresolved political crisis in Britain came to a head in the later 1680s and led to the creation of a political settlement usually known by the name contemporaries gave it—the Glorious Revolution. This settlement involved the creation of a consensus between the two main political factions of the time, Whigs and Tories, so as to avoid the prospect of a second Civil War. The outcome was a limited constitutional government and a limited (and contested) degree of religious toleration, supported by a mixture of arguments, some of which incorporated both progressive and more conservative and retrospective elements. The more radical ideas that had appeared in the 1640s had not disappeared, however, and found expression in what was to become one of the key texts of liberal thought, *Two Treatises of Government* by John Locke. In that and other works, especially *Letter on Toleration* and *On the Reasonableness of Christianity*, Locke put forward an argument for a system of government withdrawn from most religious matters and dedicated to the protection of individual rights, or *property*—a term that then had a different and wider meaning ("Lives, Liberties, and Estates, which I call by the general Name, Property") than it has today.

For about 100 years, Locke's ideas remained somewhat marginal. They were taken up and developed by the so-called true Whigs or Commonwealthmen, including such figures as John Trenchard and Thomas Gordon, who jointly published a series of essays under the pseudonym Cato, which were to have a great impact on the thinking of colonial America. The Commonwealthmen constructed a critique of the emerging modern state as it appeared under Walpole and the Old Corps Whigs. Walpole, the British prime minister from 1721 to 1742 and the first holder of that office, was responsible for several of the institutions of the modern state, particularly the cabinet government and modern public finance. His followers, the Old Corps Whigs, remained in office after he fell from power.

The arguments put forward by the Commonwealthmen also drew heavily on the ideas and language of civic humanism, or classical republicanism, which were a central medium of public argument at that time. Early American thought also drew on ideas

circulating on the Continent. The author who played the greatest part in transmitting those ideas over the Atlantic was the Swiss writer Jean-Jacques Burlamaqui, now almost forgotten, but at one time a best-selling author.

In retrospect, the 18th century can be seen as the formative period of liberalism. Although a self-conscious movement and associated set of ideas did not yet exist, a number of intellectual developments took place that, when combined with the ideas that had come out of the earlier period in Britain, produced a distinctive style of reasoning. That, in turn, led to the appearance of an intellectual and, increasingly, political movement for reform of existing institutions in a number of countries. Two important sets of ideas took shape that played a central part in the gradual emergence of the liberal worldview. The first centered on the critical rationalism that grew out of both the Newtonian revolution in science and the skeptical reaction against religious enthusiasm of the 17th century. This way of thinking found expression in deism, Unitarianism, and even atheism, all of which were commonly, although not invariably, associated with the earlier ideas of a limited contractual state and freedom of opinion and expression. When critical reason was applied to existing institutions and beliefs, many—among them slavery, an established church, and the existing systems of law and government— were subjected to radical criticism and analysis (in today's language, deconstructed). The second was the gradual emergence of a new way of thinking about wealth, production, and exchange, which came to be called *political economy*. It involved a more abstract way of thinking about economic relations, rather than limiting itself to the more concrete and specific notions of trade and manufacture. It led to an emphasis on the beneficial effects of trade and commerce and stressed the connection between them and a civilized way of life. This view of commerce was in sharp contrast to the republican notion that luxury led to a corruption of the manly qualities and a degradation of manners. Political economy also produced, in the writings of Adam Smith and others, the belief that it was possible to expand wealth and output almost indefinitely, thus undermining the traditional view of economic life as a zero-sum game in which the greed of the few was the cause of the poverty of the many.

As the 18th century progressed, the British constitution became an object of admiration and envy for the growing critical philosophical movement on the continent. The government and politics of Britain were increasingly used as a point of contrast with the defects of the systems found elsewhere in Europe. After Britain's decisive victory over the French, ratified by the Peace of Paris in 1763, continental observers increasingly saw Britain as more advanced than her rivals. The irony, of course, was that the British constitution was more medieval (i.e., limited) than those on the Continent. By being more old-fashioned, the British were more modern. Not everyone saw emulation of British models as the way forward, however. A rival strategy focused on the way an enlightened ruler could reform and modernize the state. By the late 18th century, European thinking had been overtaken by the ideal of improvement, not quite the same thing as the later belief in progress but a related notion, deriving from the belief that it was possible to both discover what was best for human beings and bring about beneficial change by conscious action.

The apparently stable world of the *ancien régime* was torn apart in the great crisis of what the historian R. R. Palmer has called *the age of the democratic revolution*. The central events in this process were the two contrasting revolutions of France and America. For some, the events of 1776–1783 were not a revolution at all, but the secession of 13 self-governing colonies from the British Empire and their combining together to establish a common government with delegated powers. Others see the same events differently, as a Lockean revolution in which the political bonds of obligation were severed and a new contract and government established. This division of views was present from the beginning, as the near-contemporaneous historiography of the event reveals. In either case, however, the American Revolution did not seek to reshape the entire social, legal, and political order. Rather, the participants aimed to protect an established order and traditional liberties from the innovations of a British government facing a fiscal crisis as a result of the Seven Years' War. One result was to give fresh expression to the more radical individualist ideas of the Levellers, Locke, and the Commonwealthmen both in the writings and publications of the time, such as Paine's *Common Sense*, and in the principles articulated in the Declaration of Independence and, more debatably, the Constitution. There was no question, however, of overturning the entire social order partly because many of the institutions of the European *ancien régime* did not exist in the American colonies.

What did emerge in the writings of both the Federalists and Anti-Federalists was a much more elaborate version of the older ideas, of a constitutional regime with a government having limited and enumerated powers. The controversy over ratification of the new Constitution also led directly to a specific enumeration and protection of rights held by individuals in a free state, in the first eight amendments to the Constitution, whereas the 9th Amendment made explicit the doctrine of unenumerated rights—"The enumeration in the Constitution of certain rights shall not be construed to deny or disparage others retained by the people"— and the 10th Amendment unequivocally expressed the doctrine of enumerated powers—"The powers not delegated to the United States by the Constitution, nor prohibited by it to the States, are reserved to the States respectively, or to the people."

Events took a different course in France. An attempt to reform and restructure the government of the kingdom led to a sudden unraveling of the entire political fabric and a political and social revolution of a kind the modern world had not previously seen. Even now, more than 200 years later, there is a good deal of controversy regarding why the French Revolution developed as it did. The view that commands increasing acceptance is that it sprang from a combination of fortuitous circumstances, the influence of particular ideas, and the impact of war on internal French politics. Among the most significant events were two decisions taken by the Constituent Assembly—to nationalize the property of the Church as a solution to public debt, followed by the rapid printing of new money. The acute political crisis of 1791–1792 witnessed the appearance of a new political phenomenon, the attempt to sweep away all of the existing social and political institutions and replace them with something fundamentally different from what had gone before. Even more significant for the future history of Europe was the appearance of the modern nation-state, single and indivisible, along with its ideological offspring, the mass army. The period also saw the terror and, in the shape of the Napoleonic regime, the first modern despotism.

If the period before 1789 was a formative one in the history of liberalism, the mid-19th century was its classical period. During this period, most of the political vocabulary we now use came into being, with new terms created and the meanings of older ones altered. It was then that liberal ideas were fully worked out and a consistent set of ideas were created.

Much of this work was in response to the intellectual and political challenge posed by the events of 1789–1815. For those who neither supported the reactionary or conservative policies of Metternich and the Holy Alliance nor espoused the revolutionary ideals of Jacobinism, it was necessary to work out a more explicit understanding of what it was they believed and sought to achieve. By that time, it also had become apparent that a process of profound social change was underway in Britain, and by 1830, that process had already started to spread outside its country of origin. These events were later to be misleadingly referred to as the Industrial Revolution.

Its central phenomenon was the appearance of sustained, long-term economic growth and a rapid rise in the total amount of wealth and the living standards of the great mass of the people. This material progress was accompanied by rapid and widespread urbanization that brought about an alteration in the nature of society that still continues and is more profound in its nature than anything since the rise of agriculture in the later Neolithic period. The great intellectual challenge for 19th-century thought was to explain and understand this revolutionary process. Classical liberalism came about by building on the ideas already developed in the 18th century, which provided the language to both give an account of what was happening and to advocate a specific kind of society, government, and public policy.

By the 1830s, there were recognizable liberal political movements in every European state except Russia, and the term had widely entered the political discourse of the great European languages. In the United States, in reaction to the Federalist period, we can discern a series of movements that pushed for greater liberty: Jeffersonian Republicanism, the Jacksonian movement of the 1820s and 1830s, and the growing abolitionist and "free soil" movements after 1840. In Britain, the 1820s saw the appearance of a new generation of reformers, men such as Henry Brougham, Sydney Smith, James Mill, Jeremy Bentham, and the Philosophic Radicals. Richard Cobden and John Bright, the great figures of a growing liberal movement, became prominent in the 1830s, and in 1846, liberalism gained perhaps its greatest triumph with the repeal of the Corn Laws and the conversion of the British state to a policy of free trade. A recognizable British Liberal party came into being in 1857, which included among its ranks the man who was to be the dominant figure of 19th-century British liberalism,

William Ewart Gladstone. In France, there were politicians such as François Guizot and the "Doctrinaires" and intellectual figures such as Antoine Louis Claude Destutt de Tracy, Benjamin Constant, and Madame Germaine de Staël. Germany had perhaps the most active and successful liberal movement outside Britain, including individuals such as Karl von Rotteck, Karl Welker, and Friedrich Dahlman. Much of that movement was influenced by such great figures of the Enlightenment as Immanuel Kant and Wilhelm von Humboldt. Italy, Spain, Hungary, and the Netherlands each had its own leading figures and movements. This proliferation was not a matter of separate, distinct, national movements. Rather, there was a genuinely transnational movement with a flourishing exchange of ideas among writers in the three major linguistic cultures, English, French, and German. The existence of a "transatlantic persuasion" in Britain, the United States, and Canada is well known, but many of its ideas and arguments came from France or Germany via multilingual scholars such as J. S. Mill and Lord Acton. British liberalism, in turn, had a powerful effect on continental Europe.

What set of beliefs and arguments united those individuals and movements? Some authors, examining the robust arguments among liberals over issues such as land ownership, the franchise, intellectual property, and education, have argued that there was no coherent liberal political movement, nor a systematic set of beliefs and arguments. Liberalism, in their view, amounted to little more than a style of argument or vocabulary, which could be used to advocate a bewildering variety of ends. Undoubtedly, there was great diversity, but this point should not be overstated: The ideas of classical liberalism were not so diverse as to be incoherent. In fact, despite much variation (such as the importance of utilitarianism for British liberals and romanticism for Germans), there was a marked degree of agreement regarding a number of common themes, even when those were given a distinctively American, French, or German accent. Many of these ideas figure prominently in contemporary libertarian thought; others, although still of marginal concern, have faded in importance.

In the first, although not always the most important, place are a set of ideas about economic life and public policies conducive to prosperity and harmony. The conventional intellectual genealogy of those ideas regards them as having been originally formulated by Adam Smith and developed by classical economists such as David Ricardo, Thomas Malthus, and J. S. Mill. In fact, in much popular and public argument, a second line of descent from Smith was equally important, including such figures as Jean-Baptiste Say. The underlying idea was that the economic life of the community is a dynamic yet self-regulating system that, given the correct framework of laws and then left to itself, will produce wealth and convert the pursuit of individual, self-regarding ends into public benefits. A number of principles for public policy followed, notably a general principle of noninterference by the state in the outcome of private decisions (laissez-faire), the abandonment of protectionism and other restraints on trade, and support for free trade, low taxation, and government frugality, hard money, and freedom of contract. All of those principles are interconnected and were often summarized under the general heading of *free exchange*. It is significant that, although these are economic arguments, they were not generally advocated solely or even primarily on the grounds of economic efficiency. The usual arguments were moralistic and emphasized such themes as autonomy, personal responsibility, and the connection between free exchange—particularly free trade across national borders—and peace.

Another significant point is that these ideas were not in any sense conservative. Instead, they were profoundly radical and had implications reaching far beyond the straightforwardly economic, including implications for the relation between the sexes and the status of different races and ethnic groups. In particular, they combined with, and led to, a sharp attack on state-sanctioned privilege, social inequality, and unjust class divisions.

An almost forgotten element of classical liberalism is its theory of class and social divisions. Nowadays, this kind of analysis is associated primarily with Marxism, but it actually originated in the writings of liberal thinkers—something that Marx freely acknowledged. Classical liberal class theory was, however, different from that put forward by Marx and his epigones. Its fundamental premise is that there are only two ways to obtain wealth: either through production and exchange or by plunder (i.e., by using force). It followed that the basic division in society is that between the industrious or productive classes, on the one side, and the parasitic or exploitative classes, on the other. Classes are defined by their relation to the coercive institutions of political power, rather than productive or exchange relations. The exploitative ruling classes

are those who use their access to political power and force to enrich themselves at the expense of the industrious classes who create wealth. The former group includes, according to most liberal accounts, aristocrats, the clergy of established churches, state bondholders and rentiers, slaveholders, and also able-bodied paupers who are on relief. The exploited class includes peasants, artisans, proletarians, merchants, middlemen of all sorts, and entrepreneurs. Liberal class theory originated in Scotland, in the writings of authors such as James Millar, but it found its fullest expression in France, where it was developed and refined by Charles Comte, Charles Dunoyer, and Augustin Thierry. Their analysis involved a theoretical account of the origins and nature of the state and political power leading to the formulation of a historical sociology. Their analysis also was intimately connected with a distinctive theory of historical development, which originated in the writings of the Scottish Enlightenment authors, among them Adam Smith, but which was more fully elaborated by Comte and Dunoyer. According to this theory, history consisted of a succession of stages or levels of economic and social development, culminating in the final stage of commercial or industrial society. Each stage was marked by distinctive kinds of social and political relationships. The English liberal Herbert Spencer elaborated this historical account as the movement from militant societies, dominated by relations based on force, exploitation of the productive classes, and hierarchy, to industrial society, marked by voluntary, contractual relations. This evolution was described by another classical liberal, Sir Henry Sumner Maine, as the movement in social relations and law "from status to contract." All these thinkers agreed that as society progressed, the sphere of compulsion, and hence of the state and power, would shrink, just as the area of voluntary cooperation expanded. The end result would be a minimal state or even, according to some radical thinkers such as the economist Gustave de Molinari and the young Herbert Spencer, no state at all.

Classical liberals had a clear set of ideas about political arrangements. Their main goal was to reduce the scope of power and compulsion in society. Political power, they maintained, should be used only to protect and sustain individual rights. The two central political ideals of liberalism, constitutional government and the rule of law, were limited. These ideals were combined in Germany in the idea of the *Rechtsstaat* (the term *Recht* in German means both "law" and "right"), an idea influential throughout Europe. This conception implied that the law would recognize and protect a whole range of personal rights, such as the rights of assembly, free association, contract, and conscience and belief. Perhaps most important, it implied that the state was governed by law.

A compelling reason for restraining or reducing the scope of government was the intimate connection between state power and war. A major goal of most liberal movements and politicians was the replacement of war by arbitration as a means of settling international disputes. The abolition of identification papers and restrictions on the free movement of individuals was, therefore, an important goal.

Another important idea was the privatization of religious belief, or the separation of church and state. Religious persuasion, it was argued, is a matter of private choice and of no more concern to the government than one's choice of clothes or food. Living as we do in a largely secular age, it is difficult to realize how radical this demand was and what a revolutionary change it would produce. It remains, in some parts of the world, particularly in many Islamic countries, a controversial issue. Its underlying contention, that the state has no business in promoting a particular vision of the good life, continues to find expression in a whole range of intense political debates. It is often said that anticlericalism and secularism were features of continental European or Latin American liberalism, as opposed to the Anglo-Saxon variety, but that interpretation is not sustained by a reading of the writings of both American and British authors of the 1820s and 1830s. One should not think, however, that, because these thinkers wished to separate church and state, classical liberalism was intimately linked with atheism or free thought. Although some liberals were atheists, the majority were not, and indeed the connection between organized liberalism and certain religious denominations was close in some countries.

Another complex idea, often related to particular religious beliefs, was voluntarism, which refers both to a theory of social action and an account of the ideal form of social organization. Voluntarism implied that the only appropriate form for collective action was the free association of individuals, all of whom enjoyed a right of withdrawal. In the Protestant countries of Europe and in the United States, this idea derived from the form of church governance espoused by dissenting Protestant churches: The Church was a free association of self-governing congregations, each of which was, in turn, a free association of believers. However, the idea also was to be found in certain sections of Catholic Europe and was perhaps most fully elaborated in Spain, where its advocates looked back to the brotherhoods of medieval Spain. This way of thinking had radical implications for the political arrangements compatible with liberalism and implied a marked degree of decentralization. Its other principal application was in the area of social policy. Here it led to support for mutual aid or collective self-help as the solution to social problems, such as the need for protection against loss of income or ill health and old age. This notion found expression in a wide variety of mutual or friendly societies throughout Europe and North America, most of which have now been destroyed by the rise of the welfare state. Another application that has shown greater powers of survival was that of "people's banks," or credit unions, which were advocated by one of the great theoreticians of voluntarism, the German liberal Hermann Schulze-Delitzsch.

The last main element of classical liberalism, which in many ways united the other ones, was a particular conception of human individuality and the value and uniqueness of each human being. This individualism led to great emphasis on a particular kind of culture and human character compatible with one's full humanity. The idea of character was in fact central for most 19th-century liberals; Acton's famous remark about the corrupting effect of power referred to its impact on the character of those who held it. Although this notion played a central role in liberal thought throughout Europe and North America, as an element of liberal discourse it came in the first instance from Germany and the idea of *Bildung*, variously translatable as *formation*, *development*, *cultivation*, or *self-realization*. It led to strongly libertarian conclusions about the impropriety of restricting individual choice by coercion or even through social pressure. The two classic works in this area are Wilhelm von Humboldt's *The Limits of State Action* and, later, John Stuart Mill's *On Liberty*, which was strongly influenced by Humboldt's work. A further aspect of this element of liberal thinking was its emphasis on personal responsibility, independence, and self-help, expressed in a multitude of works, of which Samuel Smiles's *Self-Help* was one of the best known.

Democracy, understood in terms of an extreme franchise and majority rule, is prominently absent from the basic tenets of liberalism. Certainly, as the 19th century progressed, many classical liberals came to stress the need for a democratic form of government and the extension of the franchise. Some had advocated this idea even earlier, as was the case with the Jacksonians and the British Philosophic Radicals. The attitude of classical liberals toward democracy was always ambivalent, however. They were aware of the potential in an unbridled democracy for oppression of minorities by majorities. The franchise was seen not so much as a right as a responsibility, bringing duties and obligations, one reason that many, among them J. S. Mill, opposed the secret ballot. The main argument used by liberals in favor of extending the franchise was that governments exercised only a delegated authority (this idea had been put forward as early as 1647 by one of the Levellers, Thomas Rainborough) and that democratic political institutions served as a protection against the use of political power by exploitative minorities. Rousseauian arguments of popular sovereignty and the general will were not generally used by liberals. Moreover, 19th-century liberals, precisely because they had an elevated vision of politics, argued that certain preconditions must prevail for democracy to function properly: a wide diffusion of property, economic independence, education, independence of mind on the part of voting citizens, and an elevated public culture. Those considerations, rather than disdain for the masses, led them to advocate that the franchise only be gradually extended and that it be linked to economic independence and, frequently, the bearing of arms.

These liberal arguments were partly defined by what they opposed or sought to refute. Until the last third of the 19th century, the main opponents of classical liberalism were conservatives of various sorts: royalists and "ultras" in France, traditional Tories in Britain, Federalists and Whigs in the United States, and defenders of "throne and altar" in most parts of Europe. A persistent locus of opposition to liberalism does not clearly describe this category of conservative; they are best described as *populist* or *republican*. This group included such figures as Thomas Carlyle, John Ruskin, Orestes Brownson, and Jean Simonde de Sismondi, and political movements such as Chartism. What all of those thinkers and movements had in common was a critical or hostile view of modernity. Whereas liberals saw the economic and social transformations of modernity as on balance beneficial, their critics saw them as darkly destructive. Against liberal values of reason, liberty, individualism, and cosmopolitanism, they upheld tradition, authority, and

particularism. Socialism is best understood as a middle-way doctrine; its central thesis, especially in its Marxist variety, was that while accepting the populist critique of modernity it was not necessary to abandon modernity in its entirety. The contradictions and tensions could be resolved by advancing to a higher level of social and political organization in which it was possible to have the benefits of modernity without the perceived costs, understood as economic exploitation, alienation, social disruption and distortion, and loss of community.

Two other significant doctrines appeared in the 19th century that had a complex relationship with classical liberalism. The first was nationalism. Although national consciousness had existed from an early date, it had few political implications until the French Revolution. The political doctrine of nationalism— that each nation should have its own state and that the nation was the only proper basis for the state— appeared in fully fledged form soon after 1815. Initially, there was a close relationship between liberalism and nationalism, whereas conservatives, committed to upholding dynastic states, were generally hostile. Some figures such as Giuseppe Mazzini fall in both the nationalist and the liberal traditions. In the United States, nationalism, which tended toward a particular view of the nature of the American state and the constitutional compact, was first formulated and articulated by Alexander Hamilton and further developed by Whig politicians such as Henry Clay and Daniel Webster. Generally speaking, classical liberals embraced national self-determination as a part of their ideology. It was consonant with their opposition to imperialism and colonialism, and national self-determination was seen as the collective counterpart to individual liberty. In Germany and central or eastern Europe, national self-determination was regarded as a prerequisite for the achievement of liberty. Increasingly, classical liberals became aware of the practical problems inherent in nationalism, but saw the solution as lying in minimal government, individual rights, and autonomy for minorities through some form of federalism. There was a minority view among liberals that was hostile to conventional nationalism. It was put forward by Lord Acton and by the Hungarian liberal Jozsef Eötvös. As both of those authors realized, nationalism became problematic for liberals when coupled with the idea that there could be only one sovereign power within a state. Unfortunately, their warnings were not heeded, and the combination of nationalism with the sovereign territorial state was to prove deadly to liberal ideals and hopes. That proved to be the case in many places, but particularly in Germany and the United States.

The other doctrine that occasioned theoretical problems for liberalism was feminism. "The woman question," as it was called, became one of the central debates of the 19th century. The critical rationalism and individualism associated with liberalism entailed questioning the traditional views of women, as did liberalism's emphasis on individual rights and choice. When an organized feminist movement appeared by the mid-19th century in Europe and America, some organizations were hostile to liberalism. However, the majority were strongly committed to liberal ideas on the grounds that the adoption of liberal goals would lead to the liberation of women. An almost forgotten fact is that many prominent 19th-century feminists such as Harriet Martineau, Elizabeth Cady Stanton, and Josephine Butler were, in some respects, militantly individualist.

In the period up to 1860, liberal movements gained a series of victories. Free trade was progressively extended, its high point being the Cobden–Chevalier trade treaty between Britain and France in 1860. Generally speaking, there was a movement everywhere from mercantilism and government control to market economy, from absolutism toward representative constitutional government, from confessional monopoly toward freedom of expression and conscience, and from hierarchy toward social and legal equality. Slavery, until then widespread, was abolished, as were serfdom and other forms of unfree labor. There was a reaction against colonialism and imperialism, which were now seen as backward relics and part of the old system. A true world economy came into being through the free movement of goods, capital, and labor and through technological advances such as the transoceanic cable, the steamship, and the railway. It was at precisely that moment of triumph that classical liberalism suffered a series of critical defeats, which were to lead, in another generation, to a sharp reversal in its fortunes.

Some of the setbacks took the form of apparent victories. The year 1861 saw the final triumph of the movement for Italian unification, the *Risorgimento*, a long-standing liberal cause, under the leadership of Camillo di Cavour, one of the century's great liberal statesmen. However, the outcome was not solely the unification of the rapidly developing, liberal, northern half of Italy, as Cavour had intended, but the creation of a state including the backward and reactionary south due to Giuseppe Garibaldi's conquest of the Kingdom of the Two Sicilies. The result was to reduce Italian liberals to the status of a permanent minority in a population deeply hostile to liberalism, and liberal politicians were able to remain in power only by increasingly corrupt and desperate expedients. Cavour died immediately after the unification, and there was no one of his quality to replace him.

More significant in both the short and long run were contemporaneous events in Germany. After 1815, Prussia was the great hope of German liberals—the Rhenish provinces of Prussia were the heartland of liberalism. However, the 1850s saw a policy of reaction by the increasingly insane King Frederick William IV. Nevertheless, in 1859, the liberals gained a clear majority in the Prussian parliament, or *Landtag*. The liberal goal of *Kleindeutschland*, a united, liberal Germany excluding reactionary, absolutist Austria, seemed about to be realized. Then in 1862, the new Prussian ruler, William I, appointed his arch-conservative ambassador to Paris as Prussia's minister president. Otto von Bismarck gained a crushing victory over the Austrians in the Seven Weeks War of 1866. This military success united northern Germany under Prussian control and completely outmaneuvered and divided the Prussian liberals. They split into two parties, one of which supported Bismarck, and liberalism in Germany suffered a defeat from which it never recovered. In 1871, Germany was indeed united, but under Bismarck's terms and in a way that marked the total defeat of his liberal opponents.

The same period also saw critical turning points in the Anglo-Saxon countries. In 1874, Gladstone's first great reforming government suffered an unexpected electoral defeat, with the conservatives gaining a parliamentary majority for the first time since 1846. The liberals had run on a platform that included abolishing the income tax—they opposed it on the libertarian grounds that government had no right to know how much people earned—and its replacement by a duty on alcohol. The Tories owed their success to a revived imperialism, symbolized a short time later by Benjamin Disraeli's proclamation of Queen Victoria as Empress of India in 1876. Even more significant were events in America. The Civil War led to the long-sought emancipation of slaves, but at a terrible cost, not only in terms of casualties of war, dreadful though those were in the first "total war," but in the transformation of the nature of the American republic. The view of the state articulated by Hamilton, Clay, and Webster had triumphed completely, and although there was a considerable "rollback" of government power in the aftermath of the war, a whole range of precedents had been set, including the rudiments of the welfare state in the form of Civil War pensions. The common thread uniting all of those defeats for liberty—in Germany, Britain, and the United States—was nationalism, the idea of a sovereign, national state acting to achieve a collective national purpose or destiny.

The last third of the 19th century saw the decline of classical liberalism as both a body of ideas and a political movement. The period, described variously as the Gilded Age or La Belle Epoque, appears in retrospect as a kind of Indian summer of liberal civilization. In reality, the foundations of that civilization were being steadily eroded. Many states saw a movement in policy away from liberal prescriptions that had been instituted earlier—a crucial event in Britain was the first Gladstone government's creation of compulsory state education in the Education Act of 1870. By the 1870s, the growth of interventionist legislation had become marked enough for Herbert Spencer to mount a vigorous attack in *The Man versus the State*, declaring that "those now passing as liberals are tories of a new type" and forecasting "the coming slavery." After 1870, liberal arguments lost much of their radical content and cutting edge and became increasingly defensive and conservative. Liberal ideas no longer set the agenda. One aspect of this development was an ever-growing focus on economic matters and arguments at the expense of other areas of debate. Another was a dramatic change in the content of culture. Most early and mid-19th-century artists, composers, and writers had been sympathetic to classical liberalism, and these views were reflected in their work. Verdi, Stendahl, Hugo, Trollope, Beethoven, Brahms, and Manzoni were all ardent liberals. The major artistic figures of the later part of the century, including Zola, Ibsen, and Wagner, were almost without exception hostile to liberalism and bourgeois civilization.

One aspect of the decline of classical liberalism as a doctrine was a change in the content and form of much of what passed as liberal argument. In every country, liberalism bifurcated into two distinct but related discourses, described variously as *moderate/radical* as in Italy and Scandinavia or *classical/new* as in England and North America. The 1890s saw the rise of new liberalism in Britain and progressivism in the United States. In Germany, the new variant of liberalism, articulated by authors such as Friedrich Naumann, almost completely replaced the older form put forward by Eugen Richter and Ludwig Bamberger. New liberalism was a collectivist variant of liberalism that retained the commitment to freedom as the highest political good, but redefined the term as *positive liberty* or *capacity*, rather than *negative liberty*, which referred only to the absence of coercion. New liberalism gave a much larger role to the state in both economic and social matters and defined social development not in terms of increasing freedom, but as growing sociability and collective cooperation. This change did not go unchallenged. The 1880s and 1890s saw a vigorous debate in all countries, but particularly in Britain and the United States, between self-styled individualists and collectivists. In Britain, the case for limited government was put by organizations such as the Liberty and Property Defense League and the Personal Rights Association, ably supported by the older generation of feminists such as Helen Blackburn, Jessie Boucherett, and Josephine Butler. In the United States, a major individualist liberal was William Graham Sumner, a severe critic of the move to imperialism after 1896 in essays such as "The Conquest of the United States by Spain." The debate is best understood as centering on the meaning of key terms such as *liberty* and *progress*. The shift in the meaning of these ideas was described in 1900 by E. L. Godkin in *The Nation*:

> In the politics of the world, Liberalism is a declining, almost defunct force. The condition of the Liberal party in England is indeed parlous. There is actually talk of organizing a Liberal-Imperialist party; a combination of repugnant tendencies and theories as impossible as that of fire and water. On the other hand there is a faction of so-called Liberals who so little understand their tradition as to make common cause with the Socialists. Only a remnant, old men for the most part, still uphold the Liberal doctrine, and when they are gone it will have no champions.

The outcome of this debate was a decisive victory for the collectivists. In the United States, the turning point was probably the depression that followed Grover Cleveland's second victory in 1892. It led to the crushing defeat in 1894 of the Democrats, at that time the party of free trade, limited government, and laissez-faire, and the start of a prolonged period of Republican domination of Congress. One feature of the later 19th century was the appearance of a new kind of conservatism, founded on an alliance between government and big business. It was that alliance, forged in the United States by Republican "fixer" Mark Hanna, that lay behind much of the move toward a more collectivist and interventionist state. The Progressive Era saw further significant moves in the direction of statism in 1913, with the ratification of the 16th and 17th Amendments, which introduced a federal income tax and the direct election of senators. In Britain and Europe, the defeat of classical liberalism cannot be so clearly dated, but there is no doubt that by the 1890s, a definite movement away from its ideas and programs occurred.

The last 3 decades of the 19th century saw a sudden upsurge of a wide range of antiliberal ideas. Socialism, formerly a minor doctrine with limited support, suddenly became a major political force. Imperialism was revived on a massive scale; militarism grew and gave rise to an unprecedented arms race that turned Europe by 1900 into an armed camp of mutually hostile states. Other ideas that gained ground at the time were eugenics and racism. Socialism, nationalism, racism, and imperialism were all closely connected and frequently supported by the same people. There also was a marked growth in movements for the use of compulsion to reform people's behavior, particularly sexual activity and drinking. The leaders in those campaigns for social purity and prohibition were often leaders of feminist movements, which had moved away from their earlier libertarianism.

The most significant change, however, was in the economic and social policies of governments. The pacesetter here was Germany. In 1879, Bismarck abandoned free trade and instituted a policy of economic nationalism based on the ideas of the German economist, Friedrich List. This program involved large-scale government support for and encouragement of industrialization, a pattern soon imitated throughout the world, notably in Russia. The United States, which had already pursued a policy of protection before the Civil War, also adopted it wholesale after 1860, abandoning the argument that tariffs were merely a revenue-raising device. Government support for the railroads led to the Interstate Commerce Act of 1887, the first significant piece of regulatory legislation, passed under the guise of protecting consumers. Imperial Germany led the way in social policy as well with the adoption by Bismarck of the policy of *sozialpolitik*, or state welfare, in 1883, providing yet

another model that was to be emulated throughout Europe and, ultimately, America. The protectionist policies of the major states, together with a mistaken monetary policy, caused the Panic of 1893, but, as so often happens, that actually redounded to the benefit of interventionists. More serious was the impact of the changed economic policies of major states on international relations. The growing economic and fiscal problems of imperial Germany led the German elite to adopt increasingly risky policies until, in 1914, they took the insane gamble of fighting a war on two fronts.

The Great War of 1914–1918 destroyed the liberal civilization that had been built in the previous century. Among its consequences were not only 10 million dead, but the collapse of the international monetary system, a communist revolution in Russia, and, a short while later, a national socialist revolution in Germany, and ultimately a Second World War that saw even greater and more terrible suffering. The totalitarian regimes that grew out of the world war killed millions of their own subjects and millions of others who fell under their yoke. The years between 1914 and 1945 were truly the dark night of liberalism in all its forms. There were some brave individuals who continued to argue for liberty, toleration, free trade, limited government, and peace, but in one country after another, they were defeated by the advocates of collectivism and statism. In Britain, the decisive turning point was the move toward a welfare state by the liberal government in 1909, followed by the massive restrictions on civil liberties contained in the Defense of the Realm Act of 1914. In 1931, Britain finally abandoned free trade. In the United States, there was a sharp move toward statism under President Herbert Hoover, a move that accelerated after 1932 with the introduction of President Franklin D. Roosevelt's New Deal.

These two examples demonstrate that, although liberalism faced a mortal challenge from radical socialism, fascism, Nazism, and communism, the political agenda in the surviving democracies was increasingly set by collectivist new liberals and social democrats. Political scientists and economists came increasingly to demand widespread action by government to guide the economy, with the result that liberalism underwent a change of meaning. By the 1950s, liberalism had come to refer almost exclusively to its collectivist variant. Following the defeat of fascism in World War II, the challenge from communism, radical socialism, and fascism was successfully contained in most Western countries, and collectivist social liberalism became the dominant political discourse—as it still is today. The surviving classical liberals were increasingly driven to ally themselves with conservatives to oppose the predominant statist forms of politics. For various reasons, that was much easier in the Anglo-Saxon countries, to such a degree in fact that after 1945 classical liberals were commonly described as conservative, a label many of them adopted. However, the underlying differences between the two doctrines of conservatism and liberalism remained, and increasingly in English-speaking countries classical liberals turned to the term *libertarian* to define their identity in a way that distinguished them from both conservatism and collectivist liberalism.

In the late 1940s, the remaining libertarians were, in the words of one of their number, Albert J. Nock, a "scattered remnant." Their ideas had little purchase in academic and political debate, and many of the policies they had advocated were lost to sight entirely. This marginalization also reflected the dramatic narrowing of the scope of political debate and the range of ideological options that took place after about 1930. Yet it was at this point that the ideas and the movement that embraced them began to revive. The intellectual revival emerged largely as a result of the work being done in the discipline of economics. One intellectual development that took place in the late 19th century that lent support to liberal policies was the transformation of the science of economics by the "marginal revolution," which removed a number of fundamental weaknesses in economic analysis and put liberal ideas in this area on a much sounder footing. In the 1920s and 1930s, the Austrian School of Economics, especially its leading figures Ludwig von Mises and Friedrich A. Hayek, made two vital contributions to liberal thought. The first was Mises's demonstration that a pure socialist economy was literally impossible because of its inability to engage in effective economic calculation. Mises and Hayek both contributed to the second, the development of an explanation for the business cycle and the origins of economic depression in government monetary policy.

Following World War II, libertarian economists based at the University of Chicago and elsewhere developed an effective critique of the policy of demand management put forward by John Maynard Keynes and his followers, which had become the central policy of the postwar social democratic consensus. The figure most associated with this school is Milton Friedman, who was to become an effective popularizer of free markets in general. During the prolonged economic boom that followed the Second World War, Keynesian ideas remained predominant, but by the later 1960s, it had become clear that policies based on these conclusions led to severe problems. By the end of the 1970s, they were entirely discredited in the minds of all but a few diehards. Even more spectacular was the vindication of Mises's original analysis with the collapse of Soviet communism and the "revelation" of just how incredibly wasteful, exploitative, and cruel the Soviet economy had actually been.

After surviving and then flourishing in economics, libertarian analysis began to infuse other academic areas. Hayek became one of the 20th-century's most important social and political philosophers, well known for his elaboration and application of the notion of spontaneous order and his study of institutional solutions to the problem of knowledge. James Buchanan and Gordon Tullock used economic reasoning to explain the political process and, with other scholars, created the new discipline of public choice analysis. Buchanan's work built on the foundations laid before the Great War by liberals such as Vilfredo Pareto, Luigi Einaudi, and Knut Wicksell, while Hayek's arguments were in many ways an elaboration of the ideas originally formulated by Scottish enlightenment figures in the 18th century. Murray Rothbard extended and elaborated the ideas of Mises and Hayek, pushing them to radical conclusions. In philosophy, Lockean ideas became a part of debate once more mainly because of the work of Robert Nozick, especially *Anarchy, State and Utopia*. Perhaps the biggest impact on popular culture came through the work of Ayn Rand, who made the case for individualism through her best-selling novels and essays.

This revival constitutes a continuation and development of longstanding classical liberal thinking. That is not to say, however, that contemporary libertarianism is simply classical liberalism risen unchanged from the dead. The events of the last 150 years have left their mark on libertarian discourse. Most notably, the belief in the inevitability of progress, which was such a prominent feature of 19th-century liberalism, is now muted: What survives is something much more like the older notion of improvement. The understanding of politics and the nature of the political process is now much deeper. On the other side, there has been little revival yet of classical liberal ideas in such disciplines as history, sociology, or anthropology, although there are signs that this is starting to change.

The years after 1945 also saw the reappearance of an organized libertarian movement. Perhaps the most important initiative was the formation of the Mont Pelerin Society in 1948, which was followed by the growth of a plethora of organizations, societies, think tanks, and research institutes. There has not been a revival of organized politics to compare with the intellectual revival, but liberal ideas and analysis have had a growing impact on public debate and policy. The three major areas where libertarian arguments have once again emerged as important are, first, the old question of free trade versus protectionism, nowadays apostrophized as "the globalization question," second, the welfare state, currently in the ascendant politically but facing an acute fiscal crisis in the near future, and, third, environmental matters where libertarians are confronting the intellectual descendants of 19th-century antimodernists such as John Ruskin and William Morris. Alongside those areas lies the central question for anyone who is concerned about liberty: What is the role of political power and how can it be effectively limited? In fact, despite all of the changes that have taken place in the last 250 years, the underlying intellectual and political issues are still the same: What is the nature of modernity and what kind of civilization is it to be?

Stephen Davies
Manchester Metropolitan University

Further Readings

Bailyn, Bernard. *Ideological Origins of the American Revolution*. Cambridge, MA: Belknap, 1992.

Barry, Norman P. *On Classical Liberalism and Libertarianism*. New York: Palgrave Macmillan, 1987.

Berman, Harold J. *Law and Revolution: The Formation of Western Legal Tradition*. Cambridge, MA: Harvard University Press, 1983.

Bramsted, E. K., and K. J. Melhuish, eds. *Western Liberalism: A History in Documents from Locke to Croce*. London: Longman Group, 1978.

Brooks, David L., ed. *From Magna Carta to the Constitution: Documents in the Struggle for Liberty*. San Francisco: Fox & Wilkes, 1993.

Buchanan, James, and Gordon Tullock. *The Calculus of Consent: Logical Foundations of Constitutional Democracy*. Ann Arbor: University of Michigan Press, 1962.

Coase, Ronald H. *The Firm, the Market, and the Law*. Chicago: University of Chicago Press, 1988.

Friedman, Milton. *Capitalism and Freedom*. Chicago: University of Chicago Press, 1962.

Halevy, Elie. *The Growth of Philosophical Radicalism*. 3 vols. Preface by John Plamenatz. London: Faber & Faber, 1972 [1901].

Hayek, Friedrich A. *The Constitution of Liberty*. Chicago: University of Chicago Press, 1960.

Higgs, Robert. *Crisis and Leviathan: Critical Episodes in the Growth of American Government*. New York: Oxford University Press, 1987.

Jones, Eric L. *The European Miracle*. New York: Cambridge University Press, 1981.

Leoni, Bruno. *Freedom and the Law*. Princeton, NJ: Van Nostrand, 1961.

Lindsey, Brink. *Against the Dead Hand: The Uncertain Struggle for Global Capitalism*. New York: Wiley, 2002.

Macaulay, Thomas Babington. *History of England*. New York: Penguin Books, 1986 [1848].

Mises, Ludwig von. *Liberalism: The Classical Tradition*. Indianapolis, IN: Liberty Fund, 2005 [1927].

Nozick, Robert. *Anarchy, State, and Utopia*. New York: Basic Books, 1974.

Oppenheimer, Franz. *The State*. New York: Free Life Editions, 1975 [1914].

Rosenberg, Nathan, and L. E. Birdzell, Jr. *How the West Grew Rich*. New York: Basic Books, 1986.

Rüstow, Alexander. *Freedom and Domination: A Historical Critique of Civilization*. Princeton, NJ: Princeton University Press, 1980.

Spencer, Herbert. *Social Statics*. New York: Robert Schalkenback Foundation, 1970 [1851].

ABOLITIONISM

Abolitionism is the term used to describe the radical wing of the American antislavery movement during the 19th century. In the United States, the leading abolitionist was William Lloyd Garrison, a tenacious speaker, writer, organizer, and publisher who launched his influential periodical, *The Liberator*, in January 1831.

Abolitionism is distinguished by its opposition to *gradualism*. Thomas Jefferson and other gradualists, although condemning slavery as a horrendous evil, believed it should be phased out over many years so as to lessen the harmful effects on southern agriculture. Moreover, many gradualists believed that African Americans could not be successfully assimilated into American society. They supported a policy known as colonization, which called for freed slaves to be transported to colonies overseas.

Garrison and his followers, such as Wendell Phillips, were fierce critics not only of gradualism and colonization, but also of the racial prejudices that were endemic among many proponents of these schemes. They accordingly called for equal civil and political rights for African Americans.

The significance of abolitionism in the history of libertarian thought lies in its stress on self-ownership. The right of the slave to himself, Garrison argued, is "paramount to every other claim." Hence, utilitarian considerations, such as the impact that abolition might have on the southern economy, should not override the moral right of the slave to his or herself. This moral argument was essential to the call for immediate abolition. Abolitionists knew the eradication of slavery would take time, even under the best of circumstances, but they insisted that no pragmatic considerations should take precedence over the moral claim of self-ownership.

This stress on self-ownership is illustrated by the label *manstealer*, which was often applied to the owners of slaves. Abolitionists viewed slavery as theft on a grand scale because the slave owner expropriated from the slave that which was properly his own—namely, his body, labor, and their fruits. This argument also was called on during the many debates about the biblical view of slavery. When abolitionists (many of whom were deeply religious) were pressed to cite biblical injunctions against slavery, they frequently appealed to the commandment, "Thou shalt not steal."

Although abolitionists constituted a small minority even in those northern states where slavery had already been outlawed, their influence was considerable. Although all abolitionists were firmly opposed to slavery, there were a number of currents and cross-currents in this relatively small movement, some of which retain their theoretical interest today.

A major internal debate among abolitionists concerned the constitutionality of slavery. Garrison argued that, because the U.S. Constitution sanctioned slavery, it was "a covenant with death and an agreement with hell." That is why the Garrisonians opposed any strategy that involved electoral politics as a means of ending slavery. In their view, a conscientious abolitionist could not hold political office because this would require the swearing of an oath to uphold and defend the Constitution.

A different view was expressed by the radical libertarian and abolitionist Lysander Spooner, who wrote numerous tracts defending the position that the U.S. Constitution, as interpreted within the framework of natural law, provides no legal warrant for slavery. Although Spooner opposed political strategies to end slavery on other grounds—he was essentially an anarchist in substance, if not in name—his arguments influenced Lewis and Arthur Tappan, Gerrit Smith, and other abolitionists who were active in the Liberty Party (which had been organized in 1839). Garrison, in addition to rejecting political strategies, was a pacifist who did not approve of violence as a means of combating slavery. Spooner and other abolitionists disagreed with Garrison on this issue as well; they believed that violence could legitimately be used in self-defense. Indeed, in 1858, Spooner published a broadside—"A Plan for the Abolition of Slavery"—that encouraged armed abolitionists to infiltrate the South, liberate slaves, and foment insurrections. After attaining their freedom, slaves were to receive restitution from the property of their former owners. Some historians believe that Spooner's plan may have influenced John Brown's unsuccessful raid on the armory at Harper's Ferry, Virginia, in October 1859. Another interesting split in the abolitionist movement was occasioned by Garrison's argument that free states should secede from the Union and thereby make it easier for slaves to escape from the South. (The motto "No union with slaveholders" graced the front page of *The Liberator* for many years.) However, as Garrison later explained, when he put aside his pacifism to support the North during the Civil War, the right of secession applied states motivated by a just cause, so the South did not have this right and could be compelled to rejoin the Union.

Here again it was Lysander Spooner who proved to be the maverick among abolitionists. In three pamphlets bearing the title, "No Treason: The Constitution of No Authority," Spooner defended the right of southern states to secede despite his vehement opposition to slavery. Spooner also gave an economic interpretation of the causes of the Civil War while downplaying the role of slavery in bringing about that conflict.

GHS

See also Brown, John; Civil War, U.S.; Douglass, Frederick; Garrison, William Lloyd; Slavery in America; Slavery, World; Spooner, Lysander; Thoreau, Henry David; Wilberforce, William

Further Readings

Garrison, William Lloyd. *Documents of Upheaval: Selections from William Lloyd Garrison's "The Liberator," 1831–1865.* Truman John Nelson, ed. New York: Hill & Wang, 1966.

Jaffa, Harry. *A New Birth of Freedom: Abraham Lincoln and the Coming of the Civil War.* Lanham, MD: Rowman & Littlefield, 2000.

Ruchames, Louis, ed. *The Abolitionists; A Collection of Their Writing.* New York: Putnam, 1963.

Spooner, Lysander. *No Treason: The Constitution of No Authority.* Boston: L. Spooner, 1867.

ABORTION

Abortion is the deliberate termination of a pregnancy. This procedure generally occurs through one of three methods:

"Morning after pills" can prevent implantation of a fertilized egg; during the first trimester, drugs such as RU486 or mifepristone can cause spontaneous abortions; or a surgical procedure can remove a fetus from the womb.

The debate over abortion is polarized, with the most vocal advocates, both for and against, tending to assume extreme positions in the belief that they are enunciating a principle that allows for no compromise.

On one extreme, prochoice advocates—those who champion abortion rights-have advanced various arguments, including the need of poor women to control the number of their offspring to escape poverty. The most common argument, however, derives from a woman's right to control her own body. The abortion issue gave rise to the feminist slogan, "a woman's body, a woman's right." By this logic, the fetus is an aspect of the woman's body, and she is properly free to continue the pregnancy or remove the fetus—the tissue within her body—at her sole discretion.

On the other extreme, pro-life advocates—those who seek to prohibit all forms of abortion—usually employ religious arguments, among them that the soul exists at the moment a male sperm cell and a female ovum fuse to form a zygote. A significant minority of pro-life advocates, however, argues on the basis of basic human rights. That is, once a zygote is formed, a human being with full human rights comes into existence. By this logic, the humanity and rights of the fetus are equal to those of the mother, and thus abortion is an act of murder.

The beliefs of most people fall between these extremes. For example, many pro-choice advocates wish to prohibit partial-birth abortion, a late-term procedure in which a fetus is partially delivered before being killed, usually by having its skull punctured. On the other side of the debate, many pro-life advocates sanction abortion if the pregnancy threatens the life of the mother or if the fetus is discovered to have a serious deformity or is diseased.

The history of abortion varies from nation to nation depending largely on the culture, the level of technology, and the role and importance of religion in society. Within predominantly Catholic nations, for example, abortion has generally been prohibited. The issue of abortion—or, more broadly, birth control—has been intimately linked with the role of women within each society. The United States exemplifies abortion's evolution within a largely secular and technologically advanced nation.

Until the 1820s, abortion was legal—or at least unregulated—across most of the United States. In the 1820s, a number of states began to prohibit abortions after the fourth month, which coincided with "quickening"—a point between 16 and 18 weeks following gestation, at which fetal movements can be felt. Nevertheless, abortion continued as a widespread practice, with midwives prescribing herbal "remedies."

The rise of the American Medical Association (AMA), founded in 1848, had a profound impact on the laws and attitudes governing reproduction. Composed almost entirely of males, the AMA sought to establish its control over medical matters, including childbirth, an area of medicine almost entirely female in terms of both patients and caregivers (midwives). The AMA lobbied for laws that restricted the practice of medicine to those who were licensed by the state. Thus, law and physicians soon took control of reproduction, and abortion became less tolerated.

Social factors contributed to the decline of abortion. The heavy death toll of the Civil War (1861–1865) led to a call for a population increase. Immigration could have solved the depopulation problem, but many Americans feared that "foreign stock" would overwhelm that of native "Yankees." The disruption of war had left post–Civil War society awash with programs of social reform. Some blamed sexual promiscuity for social ills and called for "purity" legislation; others demanded the elimination of government from private matters, such as reproduction. This scenario pointedly illustrates how, in the history of American social life, abortion can become inextricably entangled with other social concerns, especially those involving purity.

In 1873, Congress passed the Comstock Act. Aimed at preventing obscenity, the act prohibited and severely punished the publication, distribution, and possession of information or devices connected to abortion. If the post office was used to distribute these materials even harsher penalties applied.

Decades of conflict ensued between antiabortion purity advocates and pro-choice freedom-of-speech zealots. An early victim of the Comstock Act was the libertarian Ezra Heywood, publisher and editor of *The Word,* who was arrested for the publication and distribution of a birth control booklet titled "Cupid's Yokes," in which he advocated sexual restraint. His wife, Angela Heywood, published an early defense of abortion as "a woman's body, a woman's right" in *The Word.*

By the late 19th century, abortion and related information became *de facto* illegal. Around the turn of the century, the fight for abortion was led by Margaret Sanger, a midwife in the poorer sections of New York City. The next decades saw state-by-state battles to legalize all forms of birth control, including abortion. (The struggle was conducted on a state level because, by virtue of the constitutional separation of powers, abortion was under state jurisdiction.)

In 1970, California, New York, Alaska, Hawaii, and Washington State legalized abortion. But the watershed event occurred in 1973, with the U.S. Supreme Court decision in *Roe v. Wade.* The Court's ruling invalidated most state laws against abortion because they violated the privacy rights guaranteed by the 14th Amendment. The *Roe v. Wade* decision separated the abortion of a fetus into three stages and recognized state interests in the last 2 trimesters. During the first 3 months, it held that abortion was a private matter, whereas during the second 3 months, it permitted the states to exercise some control. Finally, during the last 3 months, states were allowed to ban the procedure entirely.

Early abortion became legal and has remained so despite a growing number of restrictions that revolve around such issues as parental consent. In recent years, pro-choice advocates have claimed that abortion is being banned by increments through a series of restrictions that erode the core "right" to reproductive choice. They offer as an example the Partial Birth Abortion Ban Act of 2003. The act makes no exemption for women whose health is at risk or for the diseases or deformities the child may suffer in life. Pro-choice advocates view this Act as a signal for a second American crusade for reproductive rights.

Abortion may be the most difficult of contemporary social issues because it invokes complex theoretical questions, including privacy, self-ownership, and women's liberation. To these and other related questions, there are few definitive or satisfying answers.

Consider privacy: Pro-choice advocates maintain that the government should not intrude into a mother's personal decision as to whether to bear a child. Intrusions of this kind lead to state control of medicine and make doctors an arm of the state. Doctors would have to judge whether a miscarriage were natural or induced and report the latter as a possible crime. Women might well eschew medical help even if it were desperately needed. Some pro-choice advocates warn of pregnant women becoming state-monitored "wombs."

In contrast, pro-life advocates argue that privacy rights do not permit the murder of another human being, which they consider the fetus to be. A pregnant woman must be prohibited from harming her "child" by law or force, if necessary. Whether a woman who willfully aborts should be charged with premeditated murder, along with any caregiver who aids her, is rarely addressed.

Abortion is an issue of international concern. In the latter part of the 20th century, many nations liberalized their laws on reproduction partly due to pressure from world organizations like the United Nations. Currently, abortion is legal in most developed nations. According to estimates from the Alan Guttmacher Institute, 46 million women have abortions every year, with legal abortions accounting for over half of the total.

The same questions that haunted 19th-century America now dominate the international debate. If women cannot control their own bodies, how can they be truly liberated? Does uncontrolled reproduction produce poverty as well as unwanted children? If abortion is prohibited, will desperate women be driven to obtain unsafe abortions that endanger their lives?

Similar counterarguments also arise. Appealing to morality, pro-life advocates claim that accessible abortion will encourage promiscuity. Appealing to a theory based on the right to life, they maintain that no consideration outweighs the life of an innocent human being—the fetus. The battle over reproductive rights and wrongs will continue especially in developing nations.

WME

See also Bioethics; Feminism and Women's Rights; Sexuality

Further Readings

Alan Guttmacher Institute. *Sharing Responsibility: Women, Society & Abortion Worldwide*. New York: Author, 1999.

Gordon, Doris. "Abortion and Rights: Applying Libertarian Principles Correctly." *International Journal of Sociology and Social Policy* 19 (1999): 97–127.

Mohr, James C. *Abortion in America*. Oxford: Oxford University Press, 1978.

Sears, Hal D. *The Sex Radicals: Free Love in High Victorian America*. Lawrence: The Regents Press of Kansas, 1977.

Tabarrok, Alexander. "Abortion and Liberty." *Liberty for Women: Freedom and Feminism in the Twenty-First Century*. Wendy McElroy, ed. Chicago: Ivan R. Dee, 2002.

Thomson, Judith Jarvis. "A Defense of Abortion." *Philosophy and Public Affairs* I no. I (1971): 47–66.

ACTON, LORD (1834–1902)

John Emerich Edward Dalberg-Acton, First Baron Acton of Aldenham, was born in Naples, Italy, on January 10, 1834. Harold Laski, the eminent British socialist, wrote of Acton that, together with Alexis de Tocqueville, "a case of unanswerable power could, I think, be made out for the view that [they] were the essential liberals of the nineteenth century." His father, Sir Richard Acton, was descended from an established English line, and his mother, Countess Marie Louise de Dalberg, came from a Rhenish family that was considered to be second in status only to the imperial family of Germany. Three years after his father's death in 1837, his mother remarried Lord George Leveson (later known as Earl Granville, William Gladstone's foreign secretary) and moved the family to Britain. With his cosmopolitan background and upbringing, Acton was equally at home in England or on the Continent, and he grew up speaking English, German, French, and Italian.

Barred from attending Cambridge University because of his Catholicism, Acton studied at the University of Munich under the famous church historian, Ignaz von Döllinger. As the formidable influence of his life, Döllinger inspired Acton to pursue the study of history—and, in particular, the

history of liberty. As a historian living in the wake of the French Revolution and the Napoleonic wars, Acton came to believe that history had to be judged on how human freedom was safeguarded by institutions of authority, such as the church and the state. Acton has been known as the "Magistrate of History" precisely because of how he judged historical events and underscored the relationship between religion and liberty.

Acton saw the history of liberty as the unfolding resolution of the tension that exists between moral conscience and corruption. Liberty, he professed, is the only appropriate context for religious virtue, but without religious values as an ultimate orientation and guide, liberty would inevitably disintegrate into license. Acton claimed that "liberty is not a means to a higher political end. It is itself the highest political end." His penetrating insights into the nature of liberty situated him comfortably within the classical liberal tradition.

Convinced that an authentic history of liberty could only be known through exposure to primary sources, Acton spent a good portion of his life combing through historical archives. Consequently, his search for historical truth disposed him to extensive travel. He prescribed a scientific approach to historical research that sought to establish true objectivity in the field. By reading the actual letters, personal papers, and correspondence of history's many personalities, Acton believed that the truth of history would transcend the biases and coverups so characteristic of historical writing up to his own day. Because he sought to master the field of history prior to publishing, he was never able to finish his life's work, *The History of Liberty*.

Acton's Catholic faith nurtured within him a great love for the Church, but a love that refused to turn a blind eye to the many human weaknesses and follies that littered Church history. His often-critical appraisal of Church history more than once placed him in tension with ecclesiastical authorities. One such occasion was during the First Vatican Council, when he and others spoke out publicly against the formal definition of papal infallibility. Cardinal Manning, a staunch infallibilist at the Council, had Döllinger, his teacher, excommunicated. However, due to the testimony of his local bishop concerning his orthodoxy, Acton remained for the rest of his life in communion with the Church.

Acton identified himself in a long line of Christian liberals, including Cordara, Montalembert, and Tocqueville. Acton, although being a firm believer in limited government and freedom from unnecessary external restraint—in essence, a negative liberty—also shared the Christian view of a positive liberty, which he summed up with one of his more famous quotes, "Liberty is not the power of doing what we like, but the right of being able to do what we ought." This view of freedom was not only compatible with a support for limited government, but in a sense required limited government for the sake of religious and moral liberty.

The 1870s and 1880s saw the continued development of Lord Acton's thoughts on the relationship among history, religion, and liberty. Acton spoke of his work as a "theodicy," a defense of God's goodness and providential care of the world. In 1895, Lord Acton was appointed Regius Professor of Modern History at Cambridge University. While serving in this position, he deepened his view that the historian's search for truth entails the obligation to make moral judgments on history, even when those judgments challenge the historian's own deeply held opinions.

When he died in 1902, Lord Acton was considered one of the most learned people of his age, unmatched for the breadth, depth, and humanity of his knowledge. He has become famous to succeeding generations for his observation—learned through many years of study and first-hand experience—that "power tends to corrupt, and absolute power corrupts absolutely."

GMAG

See also Liberalism, Classical; Religion and Liberty; Tocqueville, Alexis de

Further Readings

Acton, John E. E. D. *The History of Freedom.* Grand Rapids, MI: The Acton Institute for the Study of Religion and Liberty, 1993.

Chadwick, Owen. *Professor Lord Acton: The Regius Chair of Modern History at Cambridge, 1895–1902.* Grand Rapids, MI: The Acton Institute for the Study of Religion and Liberty, 1995.

Hill, Roland. *Lord Acton.* New Haven, CT, & London: Yale University Press, 2000.

ADAMS, JOHN (1735–1826)

John Adams, American statesman and political philosopher, played a leading role in the American Revolution and served as the nation's first vice president and second president. He wrote a number of important works in constitutional and political philosophy, in which he argued for a balanced, moderate form of representative democracy to safeguard liberty. Adams, a Harvard-educated lawyer from a Puritan family, wrote the Constitution of Massachusetts, sat on the committee that drafted the Declaration of Independence, and served for a decade as a diplomat in Europe, which resulted in his not being able to attend the Constitutional Convention.

In 1776, Adams was urged to write a short pamphlet, *Thoughts on Government*, that proved to be the most influential of his writings. It is a guide for "forming a plan for the government of a colony." Social happiness, he argued, depends entirely on the constitution of government, "institutions that last for many generations." Just as the happiness of the individual is the end of man, the happiness of society should be the end of government. Hence, it follows that the form of government that results in happiness to the greatest number of people, to the greatest degree, is the best. That form of government is a republic, "an empire of laws, not men." *Thoughts on Government* is a warning against both direct democracy and unicameral unbalanced government. Human nature cannot be trusted with power, and the legislature must therefore be balanced by a strong executive, with the legislature split into a Senate, whose members should come from the socially powerful and serve longer terms, and a popular lower house. The executive should be given veto power over the actions of the legislature, and both legislative chambers must agree on any legislation. Adams wished to grant voting rights to all but the very poor, whom he considered "too dependent upon other Men to have a Will of their own." His recommendations were largely followed by most of the states that drafted constitutions in 1776. The most important exception was Pennsylvania, where the Quakers, under the influence of Thomas Paine, instituted a unicameral system with combined executive and legislative power. That experiment failed and was reformed in line with Adams's precepts in 1790.

While in Europe, Adams worked on his "chief political testament," a three-volume *Defence of the Constitutions of Government of the United States of America* (1787–1788), followed by a fourth volume separately published as *Discourses on Davila* (1791). The work preceded the new federal constitution, which was in the process of being drafted when the first volume appeared, and was directed against the French *philosophe* Turgot, who had accused the new American states of uncritically and unnecessarily copying the British constitutional structure, with its division among Crown, House of Lords, and House of Commons. The *Defence* is an unpolished book that might be best read as a lawyer's brief seeking to demonstrate that a coherent, reasonable political philosophy undergirds the American state constitutions. In the *Defence,* Adams surveyed the history of republicanism because he believed history is but philosophy by example. He concluded that most ancient republics had collapsed because they failed to achieve the right constitutional structure. Just as civilized man must control the maelstrom of swirling, raging passions inside him through reason and conscience, so should the makers of a commonwealth rule the passions within society by building constitutions that are compatible with human nature. Recognizing that men will not be ruled by reason and that an education in moral virtue does not secure good government, Adams sought to achieve balance by giving the various factions of a society stakes in its constitutional system.

Had Adams distilled his arguments into one, organized volume, the *Defence* could well have become a classic. Instead, he produced a repetitive work weighed down by long, often unattributed quotes cribbed from works in history and political philosophy. Therefore, although the *Defence* is unattractive reading, it was circulated at the Constitutional Convention and remains a treasure trove for students of the American constitutional regime.

Adams saw two major threats to a free republic: the envy of the people and the ambition of the elites. He believed that a nation's "natural aristocracy" posed a potential social problem. A society must give those who excel room to exercise their talents; otherwise their resentment will be turned against the system. In contrast, unchecked democracy leads to calls for the redistribution of property, that "absurd figment of the mind." Therefore, the rule of law must protect the "sacred" property rights of rich and poor alike. According to Adams, only a balanced constitution can protect the lives, liberties, and properties of the people by securing a stable and free government.

MV

See also American Revolution; Declaration of Independence; Jefferson, Thomas; Rule of Law; Washington, George

Further Readings

Handler, Edward. *America and Europe in the Political Thought of John Adams.* Cambridge, MA: Harvard University Press, 1964.
Haraszti, Zoltan. *John Adams and the Prophets of Progress.* Cambridge, MA: Harvard University Press, 1952.
Thompson, C. Bradley. *John Adams and the Spirit of Liberty.* Lawrence: University Press of Kansas, 1998.

Affirmative Action

Affirmative action is a term drawn from the American experience with racial discrimination. It refers to public policies and private efforts designed ostensibly to help individuals overcome the effects of past discrimination. As typically practiced in the United States and elsewhere, affirmative action usually involves preferential treatment for members of specified groups. Affirmative action practiced in that manner shares common ideological premises and goals, but often different rhetoric, with efforts to promote racial and ethnic diversity.

To understand the contemporary debate over affirmative action, one must have knowledge of competing concepts of equality and of the history of discrimination in America.

The Declaration of Independence proclaimed that "All men are created equal." The equality to which the Declaration refers is the fact that each person is equally possessed of certain inalienable rights, theirs by virtue of their birth, and thus each stands equal before the law.

The key attributes of that understanding of equality are universalism and individualism: All individuals should enjoy equality under law. As Thomas Paine argued, that principle is "plain and simple" for "where the rights of man are equal, every man must finally set the necessity of protecting the rights of others as the most effectual security for his own."

Libertarians argue that such equal treatment by the law should be distinguished from equal outcomes. As F. A. Hayek points out, "From the fact that people are very different it follows that, if we treat them equally, the result must be inequality in their actual position, and that the only way to place them in an equal position would be to treat them differently." That requires what Hayek calls "discriminatory coercion." As Hayek observes, "Equality before the law and material equality are therefore not only different, but are in conflict with each other; and we can achieve either the one or the other, but not both at the same time."

Libertarians have traditionally insisted that the principle of equality before the law must be absolute. In Thomas Paine's words, "Whenever we depart from the principle of equal rights, or attempt any modification of it, we plunge into a labyrinth of difficulties from which there is no way out but by retreating. Where are we to stop? Or by what principle are we to find out the point to stop at, that shall discriminate between men of the same country, part of whom shall be free, and the rest not?"

Sadly, for a nation founded on the claim that "All men are created equal," even the United States of America failed from the outset to honor the principles of equality under law. The institution of human slavery—the subjugation of individuals by making them the property of others—represents the most profound nullification of equality under law.

Hence, when the Civil War was won, the Reconstruction-era Congress, imbued with classical liberal ideals, not only abolished slavery (the 13th Amendment to the U.S. Constitution), but also passed the 14th Amendment, which provides that, "No State . . . shall deny to any person within its jurisdiction the equal protection of the laws." Senator Jacob Howard, a principal author of the amendment, declared that its goal was to "abolish all class legislation and do away with the injustice of subjecting one caste of person to a code not applicable to another." The authors of these amendments embraced equality of opportunity, not equality of result. Representative Benjamin Butler observed, "Equality—and I will embody it in a single phrase, as the true touchstone of civil liberty—is not that all men are equal, but that every man has the right to be the equal of every man if he can."

Still, for the next century, governments across the United States engaged in discrimination in access to employment, business opportunities, education, voting, and public accommodations. Against blacks, those policies were called "Jim Crow Laws," and these ostensibly were designed to achieve "separate but equal" opportunities. The separate but equal doctrine was upheld by the U.S. Supreme Court in *Plessy v. Ferguson* in 1896. State-sanctioned discrimination also was visited on other groups, particularly women and Asian Americans.

Separate but equal finally was repudiated by the U.S. Supreme Court in 1954 in the case of *Brown v. Board of Education.* In 1963, President John F. Kennedy asked Congress "to make a commitment that it has not fully made in this century to the proposition that race has no place in American life or law." Congress responded by enacting the Civil Rights Act of 1964, which forbade discrimination on the basis of race, color, national origin, sex, or religion in employment, education, housing, or public accommodations. The law's sponsors were emphatic that it would not lead to preferential treatment.

Around the same time, the concept of *affirmative action* arose. As originally conceived, affirmative action would provide human resource investment for people who were disadvantaged by discrimination so that they could compete on a level playing field. As President Lyndon B. Johnson explained, for a person previously in shackles to win a race, it is not sufficient merely to remove the shackles.

Even with such efforts, equality under law did not, of course, produce equality in results. Therefore, some began to embrace equality of result as the definition of equality. "Equality can be measured. It can be turned into numbers," proclaimed Jesse Jackson. Whitney Young was even more explicit, declaring that the "measure of equality has to be group achievement: when, in each group in our society, roughly the same proportion of people succeed or fail, then we will have true equality."

The new definition of *equality* was implemented in public policy in two principal ways. Executive Order 11246, issued on September 28, 1965, instructed all federal agencies to engage in affirmative action, which was to be measured by "goals and timetables" expressed through racial percentages. Meanwhile, courts began measuring compliance with civil rights laws in terms of racial parity. Before long, governments at every level, along with colleges and private businesses, began implementing race and gender preferences. The 1978 U.S. Supreme Court decision in *Regents of the University of California v. Bakke* struck down the most explicit quotas, but left less-rigid preferences intact. Justice Harry Blackmun exemplified the prevailing ideology by declaring, "In order to get beyond racism, we must first take account of race. And in order to treat persons equally, we must first treat them differently."

Race-based affirmative action fueled a predictable backlash among whites, Asians, and others passed over for employment, education, and contracting opportunities. Moreover, it left intact serious underlying problems, such as unequal educational opportunities, that contribute to racial disparities in income. For instance, the black/white educational gap actually widened in the 1990s, from 2.5 years at time of high school graduation to 4 years. Social scientist William Julius Wilson found that affirmative action benefits the most-advantaged members of preferred groups while leaving the problems of the truly disadvantaged unaddressed.

Starting in the mid-1980s, the U.S. Supreme Court began applying strict scrutiny to affirmative racial classifications and repeatedly struck them down in areas of public employment, contracting, and voting.

In 1996, California voters enacted Proposition 209, the California Civil Rights Initiative, which abolished race and gender classifications in public employment, education, and contracting. Two years later, Washington State voters did the same. In California, following Proposition 209, and in Texas, where preferences in higher education were abolished by court order, a new form of affirmative action has been implemented based on disadvantage rather than race, designed to improve the ability of disadvantaged individuals to more effectively compete. A similar initiative, called "One Florida," was implemented by Florida Governor Jeb Bush. Polls consistently find that most Americans support affirmative action, but oppose preferences. Those findings suggest that efforts to redefine affirmative action may reap public support.

Libertarians favor market institutions to eradicate racism and therefore tend to take a critical view of affirmative action when it is initiated by the government. In a system where economic incentives are allowed to work, libertarians believe that racist policies in the private sector will tend to disappear. For instance, refusing to hire blacks or women places the discriminator at a competitive disadvantage in the labor market, denying him a pool of talent to which he might otherwise have access. Only when discrimination is enshrined in law can discriminators indulge their irrational prejudices without economic penalty.

Unquestionably, competing conceptions of equality will persist. Libertarians argue that the only stable conception of equality, however, is equality under the law, because history teaches that serious racial and ethnic division—and ultimately inequality of results—are fostered by substituting legal guarantees of equality of results for equal treatment by the law.

CB

See also Equality; Racism

Further Readings

Bolick, Clint. *The Affirmative Action Fraud: Can We Restore the American Civil Rights Vision?* Washington, DC: Cato Institute, 1996.

———. *Changing Course: Civil Rights at the Crossroads.* New Brunswick, NJ: Transaction, 1988.

Eastland, Terry, and William J. Bennett. *Counting by Race.* New York: Basic Books, 1979.

Glazer, Nathan. *Affirmative Discrimination: Ethnic Inequality and Public Policy.* New York: Basic Books, 1975.

Graham, Hugh Davis. *The Civil Rights Era: Origins and Development of National Policy.* New York: Oxford University Press, 1990.

Lynch, Frederick R. *Invisible Victims: White Males and the Crisis of Affirmative Action.* Westport, CT: Greenwood Press, 1989.

Sniderman, Paul M., and Thomas Piazza. *The Scar of Race.* Cambridge, MA: Belknap Press of Harvard University Press, 1993.

Steele, Shelby. *The Content of Our Characters: A New Vision of Race in America.* New York: St. Martin's Press, 1990.

Thernstrom, Stephan, and Abigail Thernstrom. *America in Black and White: One Nation, Indivisible.* New York: Simon & Schuster, 1997.

Wilson, William Julius. *The Truly Disadvantaged.* Chicago: University of Chicago Press, 1987.

AMERICAN REVOLUTION

The American Revolution stands out as one of modern history's few major political and philosophical movements that resulted in an increase in liberty. It asserted, through words and deeds, the equal rights of all individuals to governments dedicated to the protection of their lives, liberties, and pursuits of happiness. As Thomas Jefferson, one of the Revolution's leading statesmen, wrote in 1826, the American independence movement advanced "the free right to the unbounded exercise of reason and freedom of opinion." The era of the American Revolution embraces three overlapping phases. In the first phase (1763–1776), colonists in British North America rediscovered a rich ideological tradition that emphasized freedom from coercion. In the second phase (1775–1783), self-proclaimed citizens of the new United States waged a war for independence that asserted this principle, yet also tested it. The third and final phase (1781–1791) witnessed attempts to reconcile the principles for which the war had been fought with the lessons that it and ensuing events seemed to teach. The success of this long-term struggle owes much not only to the ideas from which it emerged, but also from the commitment of the individuals who thought, fought, and acted in its behalf.

In 1763, few American colonists contemplated independence. Most exulted in their connection with Britain, which they had recently helped in the defeat of French forces in North America. Britain stood preeminent as the nation possessing the most global power and, more important, enjoying the most freedom. Ever since the Glorious Revolution of 1688, Britons had claimed the collective right of self-government. In addition, as John Locke famously asserted in his *Two Treatises of Government* (1690), Britons maintained that the only legitimate object of their laws was to protect the rights of each individual "to life, liberty, and estate." The English Bill of Rights of 1689 guaranteed these rights and placed limits on the purposes and powers of government. France, meanwhile, with its powerful monarchy and hierarchical Roman Catholic Church, struck the British Americans of 1763 as freedom's defeated oppressor.

The war with France set in motion a chain of events that undermined the optimism of American colonists and caused them to question the British government's commitment to their rights. Britain's debt doubled during the conflict, which drove the French from the North American continent, but merely humbled their American Indian allies. To help soothe tensions with Indians and reduce the costly need for the stationing of British troops along the frontiers of settlement, King George III issued the Proclamation of 1763, which prohibited the growing colonial population's expansion west of the Appalachian Mountains. Even more disturbing to most colonists, in March 1765, Parliament passed the Stamp Act, which aimed to help compensate the British government for the cost of maintaining soldiers in the colonies. It required that colonists pay for official seals affixed to documents such as newspapers, legal contracts, diplomas, and customs records.

American colonists responded with anger tempered by principle. Previously, Parliament had claimed authority only over the colonies' external trade and appealed to colonial assemblies for revenue. In levying the Stamp Act, however, Parliament for the first time taxed colonists directly and without the consent of their elected representatives. The colonists protested the law through public demonstrations, harassment of tax collectors, and a boycott of British goods. In 1765, a Stamp Act Congress was called to formally protest the tax, to which nine colonies sent delegates. Responding to these measures, Parliament repealed the Stamp Act a year after its passage. However, Parliament then enacted a Declaratory Act, asserting its legislative authority over the colonies "in all cases whatsoever."

The Stamp Act crisis served to rehearse the patterns of protest that characterized the colonists' responses to subsequent British legislation, including the 1767 Townshend Acts, which taxed imported products such as glass, lead, paint, and tea. In this instance, Parliament again reacted with partial capitulation. In 1770, it repealed all the duties except for the one on tea. The December 16, 1773, Boston Tea Party, however, provoked not retreat by Parliament, but a renewed commitment to punish colonists who engaged in extralegal activities. Although the men who had dumped 342 chests of taxed tea did so as anonymous private citizens, the Coercive Acts, passed in 1774, punished all the people of Massachusetts by closing Boston Harbor and provided that trials of British soldiers and officials accused of crimes in Massachusetts would be held in England, thus effectively shutting down local and colonial government. Parliament also passed a law that permitted British troops to be billeted in private homes throughout the colonies. The earlier assertions by radical colonists that the British government was conspiring to enslave colonists by taking away their rights to freely trade, negotiate voluntary contracts, govern themselves, and control their own property now seemed confirmed.

In response, colonies sent representatives to the First Continental Congress, which convened in Philadelphia in the fall of 1774. The Congress called on each colony to strengthen its military defenses and coordinate economic sanctions against Britain with the other colonies. It further recommended that Massachusetts form an independent government. After petitioning the king and Parliament to redress their grievances, the Congress resolved to reconstitute itself the following year if its complaints had not been addressed. When the Second Continental Congress gathered in May 1775, skirmishes between British troops and colonists at Lexington and Concord, Massachusetts, had already touched off what would become a War for Independence.

The Second Continental Congress quickly formed the Continental Army and designated George Washington as its commander. In July, it issued a final Olive Branch Petition to George III, which he rejected the following month. Diplomatic efforts seemed doomed as the war intensified. These facts, combined with the January 1776 publication of Thomas Paine's influential pamphlet, *Common Sense,* spurred the Continental Congress to adopt the Declaration of Independence in July. The Declaration, written principally by Jefferson, reflected Americans' broad agreement with the philosophies of Locke, George Mason, and other advocates of limited government and individual rights. It listed in detail Britain's abuses of power and bolstered the legitimacy of the independence of the American states, the citizens of which had already begun to form autonomous governments under new constitutions.

The most fundamental innovation of these political charters was that they claimed sovereignty not for a monarch, but for the people. In addition, all of the state constitutions incorporated measures designed to deny excessive power to the new governments and the men who held office within them. During the imperial crisis of 1763–1776, royal governors had used their authority to silence the voices of colonial legislatures. Now, however, the new states' chief executives commanded little independent power. Yet these constitutions generally checked even the power of popular legislatures by dividing them into an upper house, the members of which (depending on the state) were entrusted to 1- to 3-year terms, and an annually elected lower house. The few exceptions to this general pattern selected different means to achieve similar ends. Pennsylvania's 1776 constitution, for example, provided for a unicameral assembly elected annually; laws required the approval of two successive assemblies in order to take effect. Other provisions also acted as checks on government

power. The state constitutions opened the franchise to large numbers of citizens who owned enough property to render themselves economically independent. Others, according to their republican beliefs, might too easily yield to the influence of powerful neighbors or seek to use government to profit at others' expense. All of the constitutions included declarations of rights, and all of the states maintained their independence. Even after the 13 states ratified the Articles of Confederation in 1781, the Congress to which they sent delegates had little power to compel them to act or contribute funds.

In practice, this framework proved somewhat problematic, especially in time of war. Quick action was sometimes needed, yet the structure of the national government hampered decision making. It also occasionally failed to facilitate the reconciliation of the various states' short-term interests. Washington and other Continental Army leaders frequently complained of poor equipment and supplies, lack of pay for soldiers, and—after the initial enthusiasm of 1775–1776 waned—low enlistment levels. To pay the army, Congress printed money that possessed little real value. Despite a few victories, the war progressed slowly for Americans, who, after the Battle of Saratoga in New York, gratefully welcomed the assistance of their former French enemies. Their assistance proved crucial at Yorktown in 1781, when the French helped to defeat British troops in the final battle of the war. Two years later, Britain ratified the Treaty of Paris, which officially ended the conflict and recognized American independence.

Throughout the 1780s, additional factors caused some Americans to fear that initial impulses to limit the authority and power of government had gone too far. In 1782–1783 in Newburgh, New York, for example, officers whispered that the last vestiges of the army might revolt if Congress failed to satisfy officers' demands for pensions. Only after Washington reminded his men of the need for subordination to proper civilian authority did thoughts of conspiracy recede. Then in Massachusetts, in 1786–1787, indebted farmers led by former Army Captain Daniel Shays revolted after their state's government refused to alter contracts with their creditors.

Spurred by these and other threats to civic order, the states sent delegates to Philadelphia in 1787 to set up a new national government. Both James Madison and Alexander Hamilton, among others, persuaded other members of the Constitutional Convention to adopt a new constitution that created a national government with taxing powers and a strong executive. Most delegates expected Washington, possessed of a selflessness required of republican officeholders, to assume the role of chief executive. For some, however, not even Washington's reassuring presence was enough. In 1791, the First Congress proposed 10 amendments, the Bill of Rights, to the Constitution, which were duly ratified. These amendments in some respect reflected the English Bill of Rights and aimed to guarantee the liberties for which the War for Independence had been fought.

RMD

See also Adams, John; Cato's Letters; Declaration of Independence; Jefferson, Thomas; Locke, John; Paine, Thomas; Revolution, Right of; Washington, George; Whiggism

Further Readings

Bailyn, Bernard. *The Ideological Origins of the American Revolution.* Cambridge, MA: Harvard University Press, 1967.

Colbourn, Trevor. *The Lamp of Experience: Whig History and the Intellectual Origins of the American Revolution.* Chapel Hill: University of North Carolina Press, 1965.

Higginbotham, Don. *The War of American Independence: Military Attitudes, Policies, and Practice, 1763–1789.* New York: Macmillan, 1971.

Maier, Pauline. *From Resistance to Revolution: Colonial Radicals and the Development of American Opposition to Britain, 1765–1776.* New York: Alfred A. Knopf, 1972.

Rakove, Jack N. *Original Meanings: Politics and Ideas in the Making of the Constitution.* New York: Alfred A. Knopf, 1996.

Royster, Charles. *A Revolutionary People at War: The Continental Army and American Character, 1775–1783.* Chapel Hill: University of North Carolina Press, 1979.

Wood, Gordon S. *The Creation of the American Republic, 1776–1787.* Chapel Hill: University of North Carolina Press, 1969.

ANARCHISM

Max Weber famously defined *government* as an organization with a geographic monopoly on legitimate coercion. Libertarianism puts severe limits on morally permissible government action. If one takes its strictures seriously, does libertarianism require the abolition of government, logically reducing the position to anarchism? Robert Nozick effectively captures the dilemma: "Individuals have rights, and there are things no person or group may do to them (without violating their rights). So strong and far-reaching are these rights that they raise the question of what, if anything, the state and its officials may do."

Libertarian political philosophers have extensively debated this question, and many conclude that the answer is "Nothing." Even a libertarian minimal state is morally prohibited from (a) imposing taxes, or (b) granting itself a legal monopoly. By the standard Weberian definition, any government that respected these strictures would cease to be a government.

In isolation, this conclusion would probably be taken as a *reductio ad absurdum* of libertarianism. But upon consideration, libertarian economists, most notably Murray

Rothbard and David Friedman, concluded that the practical viability of anarchism is underrated: At least once established, so-called anarcho-capitalism would work better in pragmatic terms than a libertarian minimal government.

Libertarians' interest in anarchism is complicated by anarchism's historic association with the radical left. The most famous 19th-century anarchists, such as Peter Kropotkin and Michael Bakunin, are routinely described as anarcho-socialists or anarcho-communists. Anarchist mass movements—most famously, the CNT-FAI in pre-Franco Spain—were based on militant anarcho-syndicalist labor unions. Profoundly isolated from mainstream economics, left-wing anarchists rarely explain how their preferred society would function. If they favor voluntary egalitarian socialism, what will they do with people—especially abler people—who opt out? If all must join, does it not follow that a government is necessary to enforce participation? If people get to choose their commune, would not inequality reemerge among the more and less prosperous communes?

The territory controlled by anarchists during the Spanish Civil War elegantly illustrates these dilemmas. In the cities, anarchist workers took over their places of employment. However, because membership was voluntary, abler members demanded unequal shares, and workplaces with high capital-labor ratios refused to share. As many anarcho-socialists lamented, capitalism spontaneously reemerged. In contrast, in the country, anarchism took an Orwellian turn. Anarchist revolutionaries imposed forced collectivization at gunpoint, with—at best—token rights to opt out, producing small-scale Stalinism in all but name.

Despite anarcho-socialists' denials, anarcho-capitalism has 19th-century antecedents. The most clear-cut example is Belgian economist Gustave de Molinari, whose controversial 1849 article, "The Production of Security," forcefully argued "that no government should have the right to prevent another government from going into competition with it, or to require consumers of security to come exclusively to it for this commodity." Individualist anarchists, especially Lysander Spooner and Benjamin Tucker, likewise maintained that the free market could and should take over the functions of the nightwatchman state. Spooner and Tucker held stereotypically socialist economic theories about interest, rent, and wages, but insisted that laissez-faire was the solution for these supposed evils, not their cause. It was primarily Murray Rothbard and David Friedman, however, who rescued anarcho-capitalism from modern obscurity. In their respective 1973 classics, *For a New Liberty* and *The Machinery of Freedom,* they laid the groundwork for modern anarcho-capitalist literature.

Almost all anarcho-capitalists were at one point advocates of a libertarian minimal or nightwatchman state, in which government limits itself to the monopolistic provision of police, courts, criminal punishment, and national defense. The easiest way to grasp the anarcho-capitalist position is to start with the minimal state and then imagine what would happen if the free market absorbed its remaining functions.

A government police force supported by taxes would be replaced by police firms supported by paying customers. When disputes arose, police firms would turn to private courts for adjudication. Private courts, in turn, would strive to attract more subscribers by crafting judge-made law to prevent disputes from arising in the first place. Many rulings would be enforced by ostracism, bonding, or other nonviolent means. However, for violent offenders with few liquid resources, it would probably be necessary to have a private prison industry to extract restitution.

Anarcho-capitalism is often dismissed as utopian, but Rothbard rejects the charge: "In contrast to such utopians as Marxists or left-wing anarchists . . . libertarians do *not* assume that the ushering in of the purely free society of their dreams will also bring with it a new, magically transformed Libertarian Man." Indeed, anarcho-capitalists are deeply concerned about what economists call *incentive compatibility*: Would private firms in a defense services industry find it in their self-interest to behave as described?

Anarcho-capitalists predictably identify *competition* and *reputation* as the mechanisms that link selfish motives and socially beneficial results. Why would police firms do a good job for a reasonable price? If they fail, consumers would switch to a competitor. If Client A of Firm X accuses Client B of Firm Y and infringing his rights and B denies the charge, what would happen? A shoot-out between X and Y is possible, but unlikely. It would be more profitable for both sides to negotiate rather than fight. After all, the policemen work voluntarily and would have to be paid far more if bloodshed were a daily occurrence. In fact, business leaders would predict that such problems would likely occur and write contracts to handle them before they arose. Why would police agencies turn to a judge instead of defending their clients to the death? Agencies pursuing this strategy would counterproductively attract the high-risk clients. Why would judges give honest rulings instead of selling themselves to the highest bidder? A judge with a reputation for corruption would find it difficult to attract clients. How would one extract restitution from an indigent criminal? Convicted criminals would be sold to private prisons as indentured servants and released after they paid off their debt. Why would private prisons treat inmates humanely? Because a safe and healthy indentured servant is a productive indentured servant.

Even many libertarians find anarcho-capitalism outlandish and frightening. Therefore, it is worth pointing out that the market already plays a larger role in the defense services industry than is generally recognized. There are currently more security guards in the United States than government police. In many respects, private arbitration now resolves more disputes than the public courts. The market has created an array of nonviolent punishments—from credit reports to bonding to eBay feedback ratings—to deter offenses the government fails to prosecute. Despite the private sector's large current role in the defense services industry, dangerous side effects have yet to materialize.

Even libertarians are often given to hasty rejection of anarcho-capitalism. Ayn Rand, to take the most famous example, asserted that warfare would erupt as soon as the client of one police firm became embroiled with the client of another police firm. She did not explain why profit-maximizing businesses would prefer bloodshed to arbitration. The young Roy Childs won notoriety in libertarian circles by pointing out the internal inconsistencies of her critique of anarchism in his "Open Letter to Ayn Rand."

Critics are on firmer ground when they doubt the ability of the free market to repel foreign invaders. How would it be in anyone's financial interest to shoulder this burden? Standard economics suggests that defense is a public good; competing firms would free ride off the efforts of others, leading to a suboptimal supply. Austrian economists like Murray Rothbard unconvincingly reject this conclusion on methodological grounds. David Friedman has a less ideological response. Friedman agrees that defense against foreign invaders is a public good. However, the total cost of this public good is only a fraction of the current level of charitable giving. It is not unrealistic to suggest that national defense could be funded by redirecting existing charitable impulses. Many would also add that even if a tax-funded minimal government is better equipped to repel foreign aggressors, it also is more likely to engage in foreign aggression, provoke foreign attacks, or stage a coup d'état against domestic liberty.

Libertarians are normally skeptical about the extent and effectiveness of business conspiracies to push prices above the competitive level. These conspiracies are plagued by an array of difficulties—most fundamentally, new entry. However, this risk seems markedly greater in the market for defense services. A cartel of defense firms might collude to raise prices and then short-circuit the market's usual checks by threatening to attack new entrants who dare to undermine the agreement.

Is this possible? Yes, but is it likely? That depends on the equilibrium number of firms in the industry. As David Friedman puts it, "If there are only two or three agencies in the entire area now covered by the United States, a conspiracy among them may be practical. If there are 10,000, then when any group of them starts acting like a government, their customers will hire someone else to protect them against their protectors." The number of firms, in turn, depends on the level of demand and the extent of scale economies. If demand is low and scale economies are substantial, there might only be a couple of rival police firms, just as a small town sustains only a couple of grocery stores. But neither of these conditions is likely to hold in the defense services industry. Physical security is not a niche product; almost everyone would want to buy some, so overall demand for defense services would be fairly high. Although we must extrapolate with caution, the existing security industry does not exhibit substantial scale economies. Because privatization would sharply increase demand, a privatized police industry would probably be even more atomistic than it currently is.

Tyler Cowen advances a novel variation on the collusion theme. According to Cowen, defense services is a network industry, the defining characteristic of which is that competing firms must cooperate with each other to deliver an attractive product. For example, MCI competes with AT&T, but they also cooperatively interconnect their systems so MCI's customers can call AT&T's, and vice versa. If MCI users were only able to dial other MCI users, their phone service would be far less valuable. By the same logic, competing defense firms would want to interconnect so customers of Firm X could peacefully resolve disputes with customers of Firm Y.

In Cowen's view, this scenario gives rise to a special dilemma. If transaction costs are low enough to allow firms to interconnect, they also would probably be low enough to allow firms to cheaply collude to seize power. However, if transaction costs are too high for collusion, they also would prevent interconnection, leading to chaos and warfare. Either way, then, anarcho-capitalism will not work well. Cowen's thesis has been criticized for ignoring the fact that—in contrast to collusion—there is no incentive to cheat on an interconnection agreement.

In *Anarchy, State, and Utopia* (1974), the most famous modern work of libertarian political philosophy, Robert Nozick argues against the anarcho-capitalists that a minimal state could arise without violating libertarian rights. He begins by assuming that economies of scale in the defense services industry are so large that a single dominant firm would naturally emerge from the competitive process. This firm would then have the power to ban competing firms. More important, from a philosophical standpoint, Nozick maintains that the dominant firm would have the *right* to do so because rival judicial procedures would impose an illegitimate risk on the dominant firm's clients. Finally, Nozick maintains that the dominant firm would be morally obliged to compensate individuals who lose as a result of the ban, and the most natural form of compensation would be free defense services.

Anarcho-capitalists have heavily criticized every step in Nozick's thesis. Descriptively, Nozick provides little evidence of significant economies of scale. Normatively, Nozick's critics deny that a dominant firm could justifiably ban rivals merely because it felt that their procedures were too risky. At minimum, the dominant firm could not put its rivals out of business if they were to mimic the dominant firm's own procedural safeguards. Furthermore, if a ban is justified to

protect individual rights, there is no obligation to compensate those who lose as a result. Above all else, actual states did not arise in Nozick's rights-respecting manner, so, as Murray Rothbard put it, "it is incumbent upon Nozick to join anarchists in calling for the abolition of all States, and then to sit back and wait for his alleged invisible hand to operate."

Although dissenters remain, the consensus view of anarcho-capitalism held by libertarian scholars can be fairly summarized.

First, it is impossible to reconcile the minimal state with morally absolute individual rights. In terms of rights theory, only the anarcho-capitalist position is internally consistent. However, libertarians have become increasingly reluctant to embrace theories of absolute individual rights; in philosophical terms, consequentialism has gained considerably over deontology.

Second, there is at least a moderate risk that an anarcho-capitalist experiment would have poor consequences. Although it is more likely to be practically viable than usually believed, predictions about anarcho-capitalism's performance remain speculative. All we have are isolated historical examples, most notably David Friedman's account of medieval Iceland. Nevertheless, the modern industries of security, arbitration, credit rating, and the like could plainly play a much larger role without in any way endangering civilization. As these industries expand, it should be possible to slowly and safely learn whether anarcho-capitalists' optimism is justified.

BC

See also Anarcho-Capitalism; Childs, Roy A. Friedman, David; Hobbes, Thomas; Individualist Anarchism; Minimal State; Nozick, Robert; Rothbard, Murray; Spooner, Lysander; State; Tucker, Benjamin R.

Further Readings

Benson, Bruce. *The Enterprise of Law: Justice without the State.* San Francisco: Pacific Research Institute for Public Policy, 1990.

———. *To Serve and Protect: Privatization and Community in Criminal Justice.* New York: New York University Press, 1998.

Bolloten, Burnett. *The Spanish Civil War: Revolution and Counterrevolution.* Chapel Hill: University of North Carolina Press, 1991.

Caplan, Bryan, and Edward Stringham. "Networks, Law, and the Paradox of Cooperation." *Review of Austrian Economics* 16 (2003): 309–326.

Childs, Roy. "The Invisible Hand Strikes Back." *Journal of Libertarian Studies* 1 (1977): 23–33.

———. "Objectivism and the State: An Open Letter to Ayn Rand." *Liberty Against Power: Essays by Roy A. Childs, Jr.* San Francisco: Fox and Wilkes, 1994. 145–156.

Cowen, Tyler. "Law as a Public Good: The Economics of Anarchy." *Economics and Philosophy* 10 (1992): 249–267.

Friedman, David. *The Machinery of Freedom: Guide to a Radical Capitalism.* LaSalle, IL: Open Court, 1989.

Molinari, Gustave de. "The Production of Security." New York: The Center for Libertarian Studies, 1979.

Nozick, Robert. *Anarchy, State, and Utopia.* New York: Basic Books, 1974.

Rand, Ayn. "The Nature of Government." In *The Virtue of Selfishness: A New Concept of Egoism.* New York: Signet, 1964. 107–115.

Rothbard, Murray. *Man, Economy, and State.* Los Angeles: Nash Publishing, 1962.

———. "Robert Nozick and the Immaculate Conception of the State." *Journal of Libertarian Studies* 1 (1977): 45–57.

ANARCHO-CAPITALISM

Anarchism is a theory of society without the state in which the market provides all public goods and services, such as law and order. Although most anarchists oppose all large institutions, public or private, anarcho-capitalists oppose the state, but not private actors with significant market power. For evidence that this system is workable, anarcho-capitalists point to the 19th-century American West, medieval Iceland, and Anglo-Saxon England.

Because anarcho-capitalism is predicated on a capitalist economic system, it requires markets, property, and the rule of law. (Many anarchists reject one or more of these elements. Some of those objections are discussed later.) Anarcho-capitalists believe that private entities will provide those goods and services necessary for society to function in peace and good order without the existence of a state that coerces individuals into paying for or obeying legal institutions.

Consider the anarcho-capitalist solution to the need for law and order. We can decompose *law and order* into a set of discrete services: rule production, protection (deterrence of rule violations), detection (capture of rule violators), adjudication (determination of guilt), and punishment. In most modern societies, these services are bundled together by the state, which requires all taxpayers to purchase the bundle. All of these services are economic goods. Bruce Benson discusses the issues surrounding the market provision of legal systems in detail, including descriptions of the extent to which many law services are already market-based.

Anarcho-capitalists often point to the commonwealth period of Icelandic history (930–1264 A.D.) as the best example of an anarcho-capitalist society. Economist David Friedman, for example, concluded his description of medieval Iceland by saying: "One might almost describe anarcho-capitalism as the Icelandic legal system applied to a much larger and more complicated society." (Benson also relies on the Icelandic example.) The Icelandic commonwealth had a flourishing society with remarkably little government. The Icelandic sagas or epic histories recently collected in *The Sagas of Icelanders,* although subject to some scholarly debate as one might expect with 1,000-year-old folklore, present a fascinating example of a virtually stateless society.

Medieval Iceland's government had no executive, no criminal law, and no bureaucracy, and its system of chieftainships was based on markets. What we think of as criminal laws, against crimes like assault, murder, or theft, were resolved through tort-based civil law. As a result, there were few victimless crimes, and all penalties were monetary.

The key figures in this system were chieftains, called *goðar* (singular *goði*). The crucial feature of chieftainships was their market-based nature. The bundle of rights that constituted being a chieftain, called *goðorð*, was private property. As Friedman describes it, "if you wanted to be a chieftain, you found one who was willing to sell his *goðorð* and bought it from him." Allegiance to a chieftain was purely voluntary. The followers freely contracted with the *goði* for services. Even more important, switching allegiance to a different *goði* was possible and straightforward because Icelanders were not geographically limited in their choice of chieftain.

To see how this system functioned, consider the reliance on private entities to provide protection against violence. In the absence of police and courts, how did Icelanders prevent violent members of society from harming them? Physical harm to another required payment of damages, fixed according to a schedule that provided so much for loss of an eye, so much for loss of an arm, and so much for a killing. (Friedman estimates that the price of killing someone was between 12.5 and 50 years of income for an ordinary man.) Thus, an individual who harmed another would be required to pay the victim (or his heirs) for the harm caused. This payment system prevented the wealthy from abusing the poor, a frequent complaint by critics of anarcho-capitalism. If a wealthy individual harmed a penniless person, that person would receive enough funds as compensation to allow him to purchase retribution if the victim desired. Alternatively, the victim could sell or assign his claim to a stronger rival of his attacker and thus contract out collection.

The Icelandic commonwealth eventually came to an end in 1262–1263, when Icelanders voted to ask the king of Norway to take over the country. The reasons for this development remain obscure. Friedman speculates that Norwegian meddling; increased violence, which he calculates as roughly equivalent to our highway death rate today; or increasing concentrations of wealth and power made the system vulnerable and less stable.

Social anarchists, those anarchists with communitarian leanings, are critical of anarcho-capitalism because it permits individuals to accumulate substantial power through markets and private property. Noam Chomsky, for example, argued that anarcho-capitalism "would lead to forms of tyranny and oppression that have few counterparts in human history. . . . The idea of 'free contract' between the potentate and his starving subject is a sick joke, perhaps worth some moments in an academic seminar exploring the consequences of (in my view, absurd) ideas, but nowhere else."

For these anarchists, the key issue is the existence of power, not who wields it. By rejecting any meaningful role for market forces and private property, however, social anarchists leave unresolved the mechanism for coordinating the economic activity necessary to sustain human existence and generally retreat into evocations of the need for community.

Some libertarians reject anarcho-capitalism and argue instead for a government limited to dispute resolution and preservation of order. They object to the variance in standards of justice and procedure likely to occur when law depends on market forces—law will vary among places and persons, just as the varieties of breakfast cereals do. The problem with this argument, as Friedman has observed, is that it assumes the government is controlled by a majority that shares a taste for similar principles of law. If such a majority exists, market mechanisms also will produce a uniform set of legal services. If such a majority does not exist, however, anarcho-capitalism better serves to produce a diversity of legal services that would satisfy diverse tastes.

A further libertarian criticism of anarcho-capitalism is its failure to limit the types of law that will be produced by market forces. If almost everyone desires restrictions on some particular behavior, an anarcho-capitalist society might impose such restrictions, whereas a libertarian one will not. Some anarcho-capitalists (e.g., Murray Rothbard and his followers) have made similar criticisms of the analyses of other anarcho-capitalists (e.g., David Friedman). Andrew Rutten uses game theory to explore various problems with an anarchist society, including this one. Given the potential for abuse of power even in anarchy, these critics argue, it is not necessarily clear that anarchy will be better at protecting rights than the state. A related libertarian criticism is that an anarchist system will break down as the result of collusion between the firms providing law and order so that eventually something like a state emerges, but without constitutional limits on state power.

AM

See also Anarchism; Friedman, David; Minimal State; Rothbard, Murray

Further Readings

Benson, Bruce. *The Enterprise of Law: Justice without the State.* San Francisco: Pacific Research Institute for Public Policy, 1990.

Cowen, Tyler. "Law as a Public Good: The Economics of Anarchy." *Economics and Philosophy* 8 (1992): 249–267.

Friedman, David D. *The Machinery of Freedom: Guide to a Radical Capitalism.* 2nd ed. LaSalle, IL: Open Court, 1989.

Kellogg, Robert, and Jane Smiley. *The Sagas of Icelanders.* New York: Viking Penguin, 2000.

Morriss, Andrew P. "Miners, Vigilantes & Cattlemen: Overcoming Free Rider Problems in the Private Provision of Law." *Land & Water Law Review* 33 (1998): 581–696.

Rutten, Andrew. "Can Anarchy Save Us from Leviathan?" *The Independent Review* 3 (1999): 581–593.

ANTI-CORN LAW LEAGUE

In 1815, following the Napoleonic Wars, Great Britain imposed import duties on a large array of agricultural goods from abroad. Known collectively as the "Corn Laws," these laws prohibited the importation of foreign agricultural goods until the domestic price of wheat reached 80 shillings per quarter. In 1828, the laws were amended to allow a sliding scale of import duties—the duties fell as the prices at home rose. Still the measures remained highly protectionist and were condemned by liberal thinkers and statesmen around the British Isles. Some 11 years later, in 1839, the Anti-Corn Law League was founded to lobby for the repeal of these laws. The leaders of this group were Richard Cobden and John Bright, both of whom served in Parliament. They argued for a comprehensive liberal agenda, but at the forefront of their efforts were the causes of international trade and peace. Their efforts proved successful. In 1846, the Corn Laws were effectively repealed (although modest tariffs on some farm goods remained), and the league was disbanded.

Libertarians have long praised the efforts of the Anti-Corn Law League, arguing that it serves as a model for modern-day interest groups wishing to enact libertarian—indeed, radical—reform. Historians and economists, however, continue to debate whether the league was, indeed, fundamentally libertarian in orientation. Some have claimed that the league was composed primarily of self-interested manufacturers who believed that lowering domestic tariffs on agricultural goods would open markets for their industrial products. Foodstuffs would enter Britain from the continent, and, in exchange, manufactured items would flow abroad. These manufacturers, it is argued, had the same goals as libertarian free-traders, but their reasons were far from ideological. The efficacy of the league also has been debated at length. The league, to be sure, saw its goal achieved. But was it crucially instrumental in ending the Corn Laws? Or, instead, were the tariffs repealed primarily as a matter of simple economic necessity? On both points, the evidence is mixed.

There were, no doubt, members of the league who had little interest in a broader liberal agenda. But, in the main, the league was indeed a radical group comprising people who believed deeply in the principles of free trade. Historian Norman McCord put it succinctly:

> The leaders of the League were well aware that they were fighting for a great deal more than the repeal of a fiscal regulation. For them repeal of the Corn Laws and the adoption of a Free Trade policy by this country were only the first steps along a path which was to lead to international interdependence and a lasting peace, with the nations linked together by economic ties of self-interest.
>
> . . . These arguments were more than a mere trick of propaganda; the sincerity with which they were held is shown by the way in which they appear naturally in the private letters of the Leaguers, often cheek by jowl with references to unscrupulous political expedients which make it quite clear that the letters concerned were meant to be strictly private.

As for the league's effectiveness, it is unlikely that its members would have been able to repeal the Corn Laws in the absence of changing economic conditions. For instance, in the mid-1840s, Great Britain's farming sector suffered, and food was relatively scarce—especially in Ireland, which was experiencing famine conditions. In addition, many members of the landed classes, which had an interest in keeping tariffs on foreign competitors' goods high, began to diversify their holdings into the industrial sector and stood to benefit from freer trade in manufactured goods. Together these economic factors led Tory Prime Minister Robert Peel and Parliament, which disproportionately represented landed aristocrats, to support the repeal of the Corn Laws. That said, there can be little doubt that the league's near-constant campaigning for repeal—especially the tireless efforts of Cobden and Bright—created a far more favorable intellectual environment for repeal and perhaps even helped to convince Peel himself of the desirability of reform. Political scientist Cheryl Schonhardt-Bailey of the London School of Economics, arguably the leading modern analyst of Corn Law repeal, maintains that changing economic conditions and interests were the most important factors behind Great Britain's move to freer trade. But she also concedes that the league's efforts were the political culmination of "forty years . . . of remarkable activity among political economists, which contributed to an upsurge in the ideological argument for free trade."

Libertarians who view the efforts of the Anti-Corn Law League as an important model—even an inspiration—for liberal reform have good reason to do so. Certainly, its leaders, Richard Cobden and John Bright, belong in the pantheon of classical liberal heroes for their principled and indefatigable work on behalf of peace, free trade, improved living conditions, and individual liberty.

AS

See also Bright, John; Cobden, Richard; Price Controls

Further Readings

Anderson, Gary M., and Robert D. Tollison. "Ideology, Interest Groups, and the Repeal of the Corn Laws." *Journal of Institutional and Theoretical Economics* 141 no. 2 (June 1985): 197–212.

Irwin, Douglas A. "Political Economy and Peel's Repeal of the Corn Laws." *Economics and Politics* 1 no. 1 (Spring 1989): 41–59.

McCord, Norman. *The Anti-Corn Law League.* London: Unwin University Books, 1958.

McKeown, T. J. "The Politics of Corn Law Repeal and Theories of Commercial Policy." *British Journal of Political Science* 19 no. 3 (July 1989): 353–380.

Pickering, Paul A., and Alex Tyrrell. *The People's Bread: A History of the Anti-Corn Law League.* London: Leicester University Press, 2000.

Schonhardt-Bailey, Cheryl. *From the Corn Laws to Free Trade: Interests, Ideas, and Institutions in Historical Perspective.* Cambridge, MA: MIT Press, 2006.

———, ed. *The Rise of Free Trade.* 4 vols. London: Routledge, 1997.

ANTITRUST

Antitrust ostensibly aims to keep markets competitive. Such regulation is justified, it is claimed, because markets too frequently become monopolized in the absence of government intervention to ensure competition. Using both civil and criminal sanctions, antitrust statutes seek to prevent the three classes of behavior, all thought to be anticompetitive and, thus, harmful to consumers: collusion among rivals, mergers that threaten to create excessive monopoly power, and any number of exclusionary practices—such as predatory pricing—that allegedly hamper rivals' ability to compete.

The longstanding and still-popular explanation for the enactment of antitrust legislation in the United States holds that, starting in the 19th century, Congress sought to protect consumers from the increasing monopolization of the American economy. Judge Richard Posner's summary statement of the origins of the world's first national antitrust statute makes the point: "The basic federal antitrust law, the Sherman Act, was passed in 1890 against a background of rampant cartelization and monopolization of the American economy."

Economic history contradicts this popular understanding. The Gilded Age was not one of increasing monopolization. It was, much like the 1990s, an era of exceptionally vigorous competition and rapid growth.

In a ground-breaking study, Thomas DiLorenzo compiled price and output data on industries singled out, during congressional debates over the Sherman Act, as monopolized. He found that between 1880 and 1890, outputs in these industries increased an average of seven times faster than the increase in outputs for the booming American economy as a whole. Real prices in these industries also generally fell significantly during this same decade. Increased outputs and lower prices are not consequences of monopoly. For the record, it also should be noted that real, nonfarm wages were 34% higher in 1890 than in 1880.

In part prompted by DiLorenzo's findings, recent research into the history of antitrust legislation reveals that these statutes were supported by producers who lost market shares to newer, more entrepreneurial, and more efficient firms—such as Swift & Co. and Standard Oil. These newer firms were indeed generally bigger than their rivals—a fact explained by their success in using railroads, telegraphy, and innovative managerial and marketing techniques to serve wider geographic markets. Serving wider markets allowed these firms to capture economies of scale (lower per-unit costs made possible by spreading fixed costs over larger outputs) and economies of scope (lower costs of developing and producing new products).

Although surprising to most modern economists unfamiliar with economic history, the fact that the American economy in the late 19th century was highly competitive was widely understood by economists a century ago. Representative of the views of late-19th-century American economists were those of Richard T. Ely, founder of the American Economic Association (and no fan of laissez-faire). Writing in 1900, Ely recognized that, "when large-scale production without any special favors conquers a position for itself in any portion of the industrial field, it is because it carries with it advantages for society." Ely went on to accuse antitrust legislation of being "faulty and indeed deplorable" because it undermined the property rights necessary to direct enterprise into productive channels.

Although more research must be done to uncover the full panoply of political forces at work behind antitrust legislation, accumulating evidence supports DiLorenzo's thesis that producers whose customer bases were sharply reduced by new and dynamic rivals sought antitrust legislation to thwart this competition. That is, antitrust is anticompetitive. The collection of essays assembled by Fred S. McChesney and William F. Shughart II supports this claim. By pointing to the increasing average size of firms in many industries ("bigger is badder") and by inciting fear over the future consequences of today's low prices ("predatorily" low prices allegedly enable a price cutter to rid itself of rivals), firms seeking protection from competition fashioned sufficient public support for antitrust regulation.

The other major antitrust statutes—the Clayton Act of 1914, the Federal Trade Commission Act of 1914, and the Robinson–Patman Act of 1936—also were enacted without any real evidence of monopolization. The passage of antitrust legislation is simply not the outcome of legislators working selflessly to restore competition to an economy shackled by monopolists.

Of course, questionable origins alone do not prove that antitrust regulation is undesirable. Perhaps most contemporary economists and nearly all policymakers are right to assert that markets do not, on their own, remain competitive. Perhaps competitive markets can be adequately assured over the long run only by active antitrust oversight by government.

Perhaps. But there is surprisingly little economic theory to suggest that competition is unsustainable. Save for work done by scholars in the Austrian tradition, economists have no theory of competition. As Harold Demsetz explains, modern economists' theories of competition are really just theories of price and output determination under certain assumed conditions conventionally labeled *competitive* or *monopolized*. Nothing in these models explains how or why markets become competitive or monopolized.

One of the few economists to outline a genuine theory of market competition is Joseph Schumpeter. His explanation of the entrepreneur-driven dynamic market process is as valid today as it was when it was first written:

> The fundamental impulse that sets and keeps the capitalist engine in motion comes from the new consumers' goods, the new methods of production or transportation, the new markets, the new forms of industrial organization that capitalist enterprise creates. [The capitalist process] incessantly revolutionizes the economic structure from within, incessantly destroying the old one, incessantly creating a new one. This process of Creative Destruction is the essential fact about capitalism.

Entrepreneurial creativity, combined with the freedom of consumers to spend their wealth as they choose, exposes all firms to the unremitting threat that their customers will tomorrow switch their patronage elsewhere. This creativity and freedom keep markets competitive. Evidence supports Schumpeter's thesis that free markets robustly protect consumers from monopoly power. For example, size does not shield firms from competition. Only 11 of America's 20 largest firms (measured by market capitalization) in 1987 were among America's 20 largest firms in 1997, and only 8 of America's largest firms in 1967 were in this group in 1997.

Taking a broader perspective yields the same conclusion that markets are inherently dynamic—and becoming even more so. According to W. Michael Cox and Richard Alm (1999):

> Of today's 100 largest public companies, only five ranked among the top 100 in 1917. Half of the firms in the top 100 are new comers over just the past two decades. Although flux is a constant for the economy, the process seems to be taking place faster. In the 60 years after 1917, it took an average of 30 years to replace half of the companies in the top 100. Between 1977 and 1998, it took an average of 12 years to replace half of the companies, a near tripling in the rate of replacement.

Nor are firms protected from competition by large market share. For example, Sears, Roebuck was the nation's largest retailer in 1987. Less than 10 years later, that distinction belonged to Wal-Mart Stores. Likewise, Digital Equipment was the tenth-largest firm in America in 1987, enjoying the dominant market share in minicomputers. But the advent of workstations (principally by Sun Microsystems) and the increasing computing power of personal computers all but destroyed this market—and, along with it, Digital's preeminent market position.

Of course, the precise ways that entrepreneurial creativity unfolds in light of consumer choices cannot be prophesied by antitrust officials. Even the best-intentioned administrators and judges cannot foresee products, industries, and organizational and contractual forms yet to be created and tested in the market. Unequipped with this knowledge—and unavoidably judging innovations by standards set by existing and familiar practices—antitrust interference in markets today will too likely derail emerging competition and distort the competitive process.

The best that regulators can do is to try to improve the efficiency of existing industrial structures. A classic study of actual antitrust cases by William Long, Richard Schramm, and Robert Tollison found, however, that regulators at the Department of Justice are not guided by a concern for economic efficiency or competition when pursuing antitrust actions. A follow-up study by John Siegfried reached the same conclusion. Similarly, empirical research on predatory-pricing cases consistently reveals that the vast majority of such cases are economically unjustified. Indeed, even antitrust actions against firms accused of colluding to raise prices appear to be either pointless or often harmful to consumer welfare.

If economic and consumer welfare considerations do not motivate actual antitrust investigations, it is plausible to suspect that political considerations are ultimately the driving force behind antitrust's application. This conclusion is borne out in a study by Faith, Leavens, and Tollison, in which politics, not economics, was found to drive the decisions of antitrust authorities. Their data show that the principal determinant of Federal Trade Commission (FTC) aggressiveness is determined by the geographic location of specific firms. Firms located in districts represented by members of Congress who serve on the FTC oversight committees or on committees that control the FTC's budget are more likely to receive favorable FTC treatment than are firms whose political representatives are not on such committees.

Similarly, Malcolm Coate, Richard Higgins, and Fred McChesney found that much FTC litigation is driven by staff attorneys' self-interest in filling their resumes with litigation experience regardless of the economic merits of the litigation. (Such experience better ensures that these attorneys will successfully pursue lucrative careers in private practice.) These researchers also found that an FTC decision on whether to challenge any particular merger is strongly influenced by that merger's likelihood of driving resources and votes from the districts of powerful politicians.

Summarizing these and other findings on antitrust's remarkable failure (in the United States and abroad) to be guided by proconsumer considerations, economist Louis De Alessi wrote that, "regardless of their ideological orientation, few economists today would defend the historical record of antitrust."

It is apparent that antitrust owes its survival to the same forces that created it—namely, interest groups using antitrust to further their own narrow agendas at the expense of the public welfare. The proven capacity of the market to protect consumers from monopolistic exploitation, combined with the proven proclivity of antitrust regulation to be used against consumers, argues strongly in favor of a repeal of all antitrust statutes.

DJB

See also Capitalism; Interventionism; Posner, Richard A.; Regulation; Rent Seeking

Further Readings

Asch, Peter, and Joseph J. Seneca. "Is Collusion Profitable?" *Review of Economics and Statistics* 58 (February 1976): 1–12.

Bittlingmayer, George. "Decreasing Average Cost and Competition: A New Look at the Addyston Pipe Case." *Journal of Law and Economics* 25 (October 1982): 201–230.

Coate, Malcolm B., Richard S. Higgins, and Fred S. McChesney. "Bureaucracy and Politics in FTC Merger Challenges." *Journal of Law and Economics* 33 (October 1990): 463–482.

Cox, W. Michael, and Richard Alm. *Myths of Rich & Poor.* New York: Basic Books, 1999.

De Alessi, Louis. "The Public Choice Model of Antitrust Enforcement." *The Causes and Consequences of Antitrust.* Fred S. McChesney and William F. Shughart II, eds. Chicago: University of Chicago Press, 1995. 189–200.

Demsetz, Harold. *Efficiency, Competition, and Policy.* Cambridge, MA: Blackwell, 1989.

DiLorenzo, Thomas J. "The Origins of Antitrust: An Interest-Group Perspective." *International Review of Law and Economics* 5 (January 1985): 73–90.

Ely, Richard T. *Monopolies and Trusts.* New York: Grosset & Dunlap, 1900.

Faith, Roger L., Donald R. Leavens, and Robert D. Tollison. "Antitrust Pork Barrel." *Journal of Law and Economics* 25 (October 1982): 329–342.

Long, William F., Richard Schramm, and Robert D. Tollison. "The Economic Determinants of Antitrust Activity." *Journal of Law and Economics* 16 (October 1973): 351–364.

McChesney, Fred S., and William F. Shughart II. *The Causes and Consequences of Antitrust.* Chicago: University of Chicago Press, 1995.

Posner, Richard A. *Antitrust Law.* Chicago: University of Chicago Press, 1976.

Schumpeter, Joseph A. *Capitalism, Socialism, and Democracy.* New York: Harper, 1942.

Siegfried, John J. "The Determinants of Antitrust Activity." *Journal of Law and Economics* 18 (October 1975): 559–574.

AQUINAS, THOMAS (C. 1225–1274)

Thomas Aquinas was born of an aristocratic family in the town of Aquino in northern Italy. He early entered the Dominican order and received his doctorate in theology at the University of Paris in 1257. His contributions to scholastic philosophy were of such significance that his philosophical views were to dominate Catholic thinking and continue to do so even today, some three quarters of a millennium later. He was canonized in 1323. Lord Acton dubbed Aquinas "the first Whig" owing to his emphasis on the rights of conscience. If conscience tells us that human laws are unjust, then such laws "do not bind in conscience" and may be disobeyed.

Equally important for the development of libertarian theory was Aquinas's distinction between a good citizen and a good man. One can possess the virtues necessary for citizenship (e.g., one can abstain from theft) while being morally deficient in other respects. Although Aristotle was the source of this distinction, Aquinas drew conclusions from it that Aristotle had not. It became the foundation for a sphere of individual autonomy, in which the state is forbidden to interfere.

The proper purpose of human laws is to preserve social order. Such laws, he held, are necessary to regulate external behavior, but they cannot affect man's moral agency. As Aquinas put it in his *Summa Contra Gentiles,* human laws cannot create virtuous men "since the main thing in virtue is choice, which cannot be present without voluntariness to which violence is opposed." Similarly, in the *Summa Theologica*, Aquinas argues that "human laws do not forbid all vices, from which the virtuous abstain, but only the more grievous vices . . . without the prohibition of which human society could not be maintained; thus human law prohibits murder, theft and the like."

Individuals, therefore, have a private "sphere of action which is distinct from that of the whole." This private sphere should be left to voluntary choice, although vice may be the consequence. In the words of one commentator, for Aquinas, human laws "did not make men good but rather established the outward conditions in which a good life can be lived." Rather than prescribe a uniform goal for everyone, human laws should prescribe rules of external conduct that enable individuals to pursue their separate goals.

GHS

See also Acton, Lord; Aristotle; Natural Law; Scholastics/School of Salamanca

Further Readings

Acton, John Edward Emerich Dalberg-Acton, Baron. "The History of Freedom in Christianity." *The History of Freedom and Other Essays.* John Neville Figgis, ed. London: Macmillan, 1907.

Aquinas, Thomas. *On the Truth of the Catholic Faith.* Garden City, NY: Image Books, 1957.

———. *Summa Theologica*, Vol. 28 (1a2ae, 90–97). Dominican Fathers, trans. London: R&T Washbourne, 1923–1925.

ARISTOTLE (382–322 B.C.)

Aristotle of Stagira was a Greek philosopher, logician, and scientist and one of the most influential ancient thinkers. As a young man, Aristotle entered Plato's Academy in Athens, where he studied for 20 years. Subsequently, he was invited by Philip of Macedon to tutor his son, the future Alexander the Great. Aristotle later returned to Athens to found his own school, the Lyceum, and write some of his most important treatises. After Alexander's sudden death, Aristotle had to flee Athens because of his Macedonian affiliation, and he died soon after. Although many of his writings are lost, a substantial corpus survives, consisting of treatises probably compiled from his lecture notes. These works influenced Roman, Byzantine, Arab, and Jewish philosophers, and their rediscovery in Western Europe during the Middle Ages triggered the rise of scholasticism and contributed to the rise of modern science.

Aristotle's philosophical system consists of numerous specialized sciences. He holds that each science must be adapted to its own subject matter with distinctive problems, methods, and first principles. All the sciences presuppose a theory of logic, language, and knowledge, which Aristotle set forth in a set of treatises called the *Organon*. These common elements include a system of syllogistic logic that prevailed largely unchallenged until the 20th century. Aristotle formulated and defended the law of noncontradiction and the principle of identity, and he maintained (against his teacher Plato) that knowledge must be based on sense perception, that reality ultimately consisted of individual substances, and that substances belonged to natural kinds (e.g., human being or horse) with distinctive natural ends or functions. Aristotle distinguished three branches of science: (1) The theoretical (contemplative) sciences were devoted to knowledge or truth for its own sake. These sciences included the natural sciences (corresponding to physics, chemistry, biology, and psychology), mathematics, and metaphysics (the study of being qua being, culminating in theology). (2) The practical sciences (e.g., ethics, politics, and economics) are concerned with human action (praxis). (3) The productive sciences aim at some product, either useful (e.g., architecture or medicine) or imitative (e.g., poetry).

Aristotle's practical treatise, the *Nicomachean Ethics,* argues that the human good consists of happiness, understood as rational and virtuous activity; that moral virtue involves achieving a mean (or intermediate condition) between extremes (e.g., courage is a mean between cowardice and foolhardiness); and that this mean is attained through practical wisdom, a deliberative excellence cognizant of the human end. Although concerned with individual excellence, the *Ethics* describes itself as a work of "political science." The basis for this self-description is evident from Aristotle's *Politics,* which begins by arguing that human beings are by nature political animals, that the city-state (or polis) exists by nature, and that the city-state is prior by nature to individual human beings. Because the city-state is necessary for individual human perfection, ethics is a part of political philosophy.

Although the city-state represents, in Aristotle's view, the outgrowth and perfection of human nature, it also requires a lawgiver whose function it is to apply the science of politics in order to fashion a constitution, laws, and system of education for the citizens. The *Politics* expounds this theory, distinguishing between just constitutions that promote the common advantage of all citizens and unjust constitutions that seek the private advantage of the ruling class. The best constitution will assign political rights on the basis of civic virtue. Aristotle described a constitution that fulfills this ideal, including a system of public education aimed at producing virtuous citizens. He also discussed how political science should address problems of political change, revolution, and faction. Aristotle viewed revolution as a disease of the city-state that has injustice as its leading cause: The ruled become rebellious when they perceive the rulers treating them unjustly. Aristotle offered political remedies based on this analysis.

Aristotle's overall political position was conservative rather than libertarian. He held that social order must always be imposed by a single ruling element, so that he tended to favor authoritarian systems. He deprecated the view, which was popular among the democrats of his day, that freedom consisted of living as one wishes. Instead, from his perspective, freedom was the right to do what one should do. He advocated compulsory public moral education, and he endorsed the rule of men over women and of free persons over "natural" slaves.

Yet he also contributed to libertarian theory, especially through his theory of political justice. He criticized Plato's collectivist ideal, arguing that the best constitution promotes the interests of each and every citizen—and, hence, protects individual rights. Aristotle's constitutional theory also had an indirect, but important, influence on European classical liberals and on the founders of the American constitution. Indeed, some recent American libertarian political theorists explicitly acknowledge their debt to Aristotle.

FM

See also Aquinas, Thomas; Constitutionalism; Liberty in the Ancient World; Natural Law; Rand, Ayn

Further Readings

Barnes, Jonathan, ed. *The Complete Works of Aristotle.* 2 vols. Princeton, NJ: Princeton University Press, 1984.

Keyt, David, and Miller, Fred D., Jr. *A Companion to Aristotle's* Politics. Oxford: Blackwell, 1991.

Miller, Fred D., Jr., *Nature, Justice, and Rights in Aristotle's* Politics. Oxford: Oxford University Press, 1955.

Newman, W. L., ed. *The Politics of Aristotle.* 4 vols. Oxford: Oxford University Press, 1887–1902.

Rasmussen, Douglas B., and Den Uyl, Douglas J. *Liberty and Nature: An Aristotelian Defense of Liberal Order.* LaSalle, IL: Open Court Publishing, 1991.

Shields, Christopher. *Aristotle.* London: Routledge, 2007.

ARTS AND PUBLIC SUPPORT

Advocates of public support of the arts claim that the arts improve the overall quality of human life, stimulate economic growth, and confer on individuals and communities a host of other benefits and are, therefore, worthy of underwriting by government. Libertarians, in contrast, tend to oppose such support on the principle that the arts, like religion, are too much entwined with our deepest personal values. For most people, the subject is of little pressing concern. When contemporary work perceived as blasphemous, obscene, or otherwise politically charged is supported by the National Endowment for the Arts (NEA), however, public outcry inevitably ensues. Often the question is also raised as to whether the work exhibited is, in fact, art. Most arts professionals today subscribe to the notion that *anything* can be considered art even if it makes no sense or is intended primarily as political or social protest. The importance of such matters is magnified when they relate to public support of the arts at the local level, through art education in our public schools.

In *Visual Shock: A History of Art Controversies in American Culture,* historian Michael Kammen notes that ambiguity of purpose and meaning in contemporary art is often deliberate, and that the ordinary person finds it troubling when not "utterly baffled" by it. He reports that, by the 1970s, new kinds of "art"—most notably conceptual art, installation art, and performance art—had attained such legitimacy that they became eligible for public funding. As a result, possibilities for "political provocation" dramatically increased, and artists began to create objects as *art* while clearly intending them as instruments of social criticism and political activism. Similarly, conservative cultural critic Lynne Munson has observed in *Exhibitionism: Art in an Era of Intolerance* that, in the mid-1960s, the idea that "anything could be art was on the rise" (although neither she nor Kammen cites or proposes a definition of the term *art*).

The NEA has contributed to that trend. The original legislation establishing it in 1965 eschewed a formal definition of *art.* Instead, it stipulated a list of diverse forms—including, but not limited to, the traditional fine arts, as well as industrial and fashion design, photography, and the "media arts" of film, radio, and TV. Further, to avoid the appearance of government control, the NEA has from its inception depended, in its decisions regarding grant awards, on the advice of peer panels consisting mainly of members of the arts community. Although the panel system was intended to ensure both artistic freedom and a maximum diversity of creative expression, it has resulted in a *de facto* entrenchment of avant-gardism because the members of the arts community sought for the panels have tended to share the art world's dominant assumptions. In the absence of a clear definition of *art*, much less of "artistic excellence" (a criterion stipulated in NEA legislation), NEA grants related to new work, particularly in the area of the visual and "media" arts, have often favored new forms scarcely recognizable as art to the ordinary person.

During the 1990s, the NEA was continually embroiled in controversy. At the start of the decade, the director of the Contemporary Arts Center in Cincinnati was placed on trial for pandering obscenity and child pornography in connection with *The Perfect Moment*—an exhibition of photographs by Robert Mapplethorpe for which the NEA had provided support. At issue were five photographs of men engaged in homoerotic acts (characterized as "sadomasochistic" by the exhibition's curator) and two nude photographs of young children with their genitals exposed. All were certified as genuine works of art by experts who testified for the defense. Jurors were skeptical of such a claim, but were forced by the weight of testimony to conclude that the photographs met the legal requirement of possessing "serious artistic value."

In succeeding years, public and congressional outcry over sexually and politically charged "performance art" by Karen Finley and others who had received NEA support further sullied the endowment's reputation. Denial of additional grants to them led to litigation that eventually ended in a Supreme Court ruling in favor of the NEA. As a result of the protracted controversy, however, the NEA eventually abandoned its practice of making direct grants to individuals, instead channeling all its support through arts organizations, such as museums and theater companies.

Although the NEA's slogan is "A Great Nation Deserves Great Art," and its public face is largely defined by such high-minded national initiatives as "Shakespeare in American Communities," political and social activism barely disguised as art continues to receive support. Although not discernible from grant descriptions on the NEA's Web site, such activism is evident from information on Web sites of the grant recipients. A 2007 grant in the category "Access to Artistic Excellence" in "Visual Arts," for example, was awarded to an organization with the innocuous name "Art in General." The grant was for a project in which two individuals critical of U.S. policy regarding the terrorist detention camp at Guantanamo Bay, Cuba, traveled across the country in a van, conducting interviews and holding public discussions on security and terror, citizenship and

statelessness, and human rights. A grant in "Media Arts" for that year was for a short film titled *Twisted Truth*, produced by 10 teenagers "confronting some of the deeper issues surrounding the root causes of migration" in light of the national debate on immigration reform. NEA grants have supported numerous documentary films and other projects dealing with a wide spectrum of controversial topics, ranging from the death penalty to ecology. Regardless of whether such undertakings have any artistic or even informational value, they highlight a major libertarian concern— namely, that taxpayers who do not subscribe to their messages are nonetheless forced to support them.

A neglected area in studies relating to public support of the arts is art education in the public schools, which has long been influenced by avant-garde views. In 1990, for example, under the auspices of a program called Artists in the Schools, partly supported by the NEA, elementary classes in Portland, Oregon, were engaged in discussions about the meaning of art by a visiting professor. Regarding the lesson learned, one fifth grader wrote in a note to her mentor: "Art can be anything in the world. Anything is art. Thanks for coming to teach us about art." More recently, a little-known movement called "social justice art education," led by prominent scholars in the National Art Education Association (an organization whose members generally promote federal support of the arts and art education), explicitly advocates "political engagement and dialogue" in K–12 art classrooms. The implications of such activism are doubly urgent for libertarians, who not only oppose public support of the arts, but also seek to replace the present educational system with independent private schools. If anything can be art, and if art can receive public funding, then anything—including political indoctrination— can receive public funding under the guise of art education. This notion is clearly unacceptable to libertarians. It is also doubtless unacceptable to parents of whatever political stripe who expect that in their children's *art* classes they will be taught just that.

LT

See also Public Choice Economics; Rent Seeking

Further Readings

Benedict, Stephen, ed. *Public Money and the Muse: Essays on Government Funding for the Arts.* New York: W. W. Norton, 1991.

Boaz, David. "The Separation of Art and State." Cato Institute. Accessed August 14, 1997, from http://www.cato.org/pub_display.php?pub_id=6102.

Desai, Dipti, and Graeme Chalmers. "Notes for a Dialogue on Art Education in Critical Times." *Art Education* 9 (September 2007): 6–12.

Kamhi, Michelle Marder. "Where's the *Art* in Today's Art Education?" *What Art Is Online.* Accessed November 2002 from http://www.aristos.org/whatart/arted-1.htm.

Kammen, Michael. *Visual Shock: A History of Art Controversies in American Culture.* New York: Knopf, 2006.

Munson, Lynne. *Exhibitionism: Art in an Era of Intolerance.* Chicago: Ivan R. Dee, 2000.

Torres, Louis. "Blurring the Boundaries at the NEA." *Aristos* (January 1991).

———. "The Interminable Monopoly of the Avant-Garde." *Aristos* (January 2008).

Torres, Louis, and Michelle Marder Kamhi. *What Art Is: The Esthetic Theory of Ayn Rand.* Chicago: Open Court, 2000.

ASSURANCE AND TRUST

Many transactions involve promises of quality and safety that cannot be fully verified before the fact. In these situations, one party decides whether to trust the other to deliver what is promised. A consumer decides whether to trust the grocer, pharmacist, or mechanic to deliver a good or service of a certain quality. A bank decides whether to trust a prospective borrower. A landlord decides whether to trust a possible tenant.

Both the promiser and the person relying on him gain when the promiser keeps his promise (in the same way as prisoners gain by cooperating in the prisoner's dilemma). Society flourishes when people can trust each other. But those who act on the promises of others must have grounds for their trust. They value not only the quality and safety of a good or service, but, in the first instance, the assurance of quality and safety. Trust depends on assurance.

Many public policies are predicated on the belief that the free enterprise system (including a functioning tort system) cannot adequately provide quality and safety assurance. Numerous federal regulatory bodies, among them the Food and Drug Administration, the Consumer Product Safety Commission, the Securities and Exchange Commission, the Occupational Safety and Health Administration, and the National Highway Traffic Safety Administration, in addition to state and local licensing and housing bodies, all issue restrictions on citizens' freedom of contract in the name of ensuring quality and safety (popularly described as *consumer protection*). Research establishes that these restrictions bring significant social losses. If they do not achieve quality and safety assurance beyond what would be achieved by the free enterprise system, they are unredeemed.

The free enterprise system provides numerous ways of extending assurance. It may be impossible to verify the quality of the upcoming transaction, but one can often verify those of past transactions. Assurances of one kind or another circulate in various forms—as informal gossip or as carefully monitored databanks—which provide information regarding the reputation of the promiser. *Reputation* may be defined as the relevant current opinion of the promiser's trustworthiness.

Promisers gain by providing assurance, so they seek to build, expand, and project their good reputations. They create and display brand names, which serve as umbrellas under which their transactions are grouped in the minds of those who need to rely on them. Promisers manage the extent and scope of their products and services to generate the repetition and pattern of dealings that give their name and reputation cogency. Once established, a good reputation can be extended to other lines of service where trust had previously been limited. A promiser's failings or misdeeds, in contrast, damage his reputation and induce others to shun him.

With respect to services such as medical therapies, those who are dependent on the promises of others and those who extend promises interact infrequently and the possibility of repeat dealings is small. In these cases, the demand for assurance creates opportunities for the emergence of middlemen to serve as a bridge of trust between the participants. Consumers do not buy pharmaceuticals directly from Pfizer or Merck, but rather from established retail stores. The consumer's local drug store, which acts as a middleman, has extensive dealings with both the consumer and the manufacturer. In addition, the middleman often shares some of the expertise of the promiser and serves as an agent of those who, of necessity, rely on these promises. A nexus of reputation then links the parties. To the consumer, the manufacturer is like a friend of a friend. One of the important functions of all retailers, hospitals, clinics, dealers, brokers, and firms is to generate the reputational nexus that brings assurance to parties who would otherwise meet only infrequently or in isolation.

All promisers put on their best face and tend to conceal their failings. Again this problem creates opportunities for its own remedy. A parallel industry of third-party record keeping, evaluation, and certification will likely emerge to deal with these contingencies. Practitioners range from the amateur expert to industry inspectors to professional product raters to medical schools. These agents, in any of their varieties, may be called *knowledge possessors.*

Sometimes it is those who must rely on others that pay knowledge possessors for supplying information on promisers. Consumers pay the Consumers Union for its ratings, patients pay doctors to recommend drugs, employers pay agencies to screen prospective employees, home hunters pay agents and inspectors to evaluate properties, and creditors, landlords, employers, and insurers pay credit bureaus for credit reports.

Sometimes it is the promisers who pay knowledge possessors. Electronics manufacturers pay Underwriters' Laboratories to evaluate the safety of their products, corporations and governments pay Moody's or Standard & Poor's to evaluate the securities they issue, corporations pay accounting firms to conduct an audit of their financial statements, kosher food manufacturers pay rabbinical authorities to certify their preparations, and students pay universities, institutes, and training programs to certify their abilities. In all such cases, promisers apply to the knowledge possessor in the hope that they receive a seal of approval that can be shared with prospective consumers of their good or service. These consumers (or their agents) recognize such seals of approval and are thus assured by the trustworthiness of the promiser. After a fashion, the knowledge possessors rent out their own good reputation to promisers and have strong incentives to do so responsibly. (The principle of specialization or division of labor applies even to reputation.)

In addition to these practices, five other paths to assurance exist:

1. Promisers demonstrate quality and safety and make the content of promises clear and publicly understood by such means as advertisements, displays, sales assistance, labeling, packaging, and try-out periods.

2. Traders ensure the quality of their good or service by such means as warranties, guarantees, return policies, security deposits, and withheld payment.

3. Those who trust and their agents test and monitor promisers and third-party knowledge possessors using unannounced inspections, decoys, undercover operatives, and second opinions.

4. Promisers' failures are exposed by rival promisers in competitive advertising, product comparisons, and contests.

5. By making visible investments that would be profitable only for a high-quality product, promisers signal quality by advertising, obtaining accreditation, and making long-term investments in design, facilities, and so on.

The Internet is vastly expanding all forms of information exchange and reputation building. As soon as critics find some fault in e-commerce (such as doubts about privacy, security, or trust), entrepreneurs invent an e-solution, which usually takes the form of a service provided by middlemen or knowledge possessors.

The supply of assurance (or grounds for trust) takes myriad forms. Although regulators sometimes suggest that government restrictions are necessary to protect consumers, such suggestions never seem to seriously consider how resourceful middlemen, expert knowledge possessors, trustworthy promisers, and wary consumers function to achieve trust.

DBK

See also Anarcho-Capitalism; Externalities; Restitution for Crime; Voluntarism; Voluntary Contract Enforcement

Further Readings

Beales, Howard, and Steven Salop. "Selling Consumer Information." *Advances in Consumer Research* 7 (1980): 238–241.

Calkins, Earnest Elmo. *Business the Civilizer.* Boston: Little, Brown, 1928.

Klein, Daniel B. *Assurance and Trust in a Great Society.* Irvington-on-Hudson, NY: Foundation for Economic Education, 2000.

———, ed. *Reputation: Studies in the Voluntary Elicitation of Good Conduct.* Ann Arbor: University of Michigan Press, 1997.

O'Driscoll, Gerald P. "The American Express Case: Public Good or Monopoly?" *Journal of Law and Economics* 19 (1976): 163–175.

Scherman, Harry. *The Promises Men Live By: A New Approach to Economics.* New York: Random House, 1938.

Smith, Adam. "On the Influence of Commerce on Manners." *Lectures on Jurisprudence.* R. L. Meek, D. D. Raphael, and P. G. Stein, eds. New York: Oxford University Press.

B

BANKING, AUSTRIAN THEORY OF

The fundamental issue arising in banking and monetary policy is whether governments can improve the monetary institutions of the unhampered market. All government intervention in this field boils down to schemes that increase the quantity of money beyond what it otherwise would be. The libertarian case for the abolishment of government intervention in money and banking rests on the insight that the latter serves only redistributive purposes.

Banking and monetary policy are concerned with modifications of the quantity of money and money titles. Although policymakers might ultimately seek to control interest rates, unemployment, or the stock market index, attempts to realize any of these goals through monetary policy presupposes the ability to modify the quantity of money. For example, to reduce short-term interest rates, policymakers must be in a position to produce additional quantities of money and offer them on the so-called money market; without controlling these factors, they could not exercise any downward pressure on rates at all. Hence, the crucial question is: Who should be allowed to produce or destroy money and which goals should be pursued?

Banking policy is concerned with analogous questions. Rather than dealing with the production of money, it deals with the production of money titles, which can be instantly redeemed into money—as opposed to credit titles or IOUs, which can be redeemed into money only at some future point of time. A bank, in the sense that is relevant for banking policy, is a firm that issues money titles, which include bank notes, checks, credit cards, Internet accounts, Smart Cards, and so on. The crucial questions in banking policy concern who should be allowed to issue these money titles, for which purposes, and in which quantities.

In a completely unhampered market, every individual would have the right to invest his labor and property in the production of money and to sell or give away his product as he sees fit. Thus, every money producer would be in a position to pursue his own monetary policy, just as each shoe manufacturer in selling his products pursues his own "foot fashion policy." The two main questions of monetary policy are thus answered by the organizing principle of the market: private property. Each individual is a policymaker, making policy with his own property, and each individual pursues the goals that he would like to pursue.

Historically, different sorts of commodities (gold, silver, copper, shells, tobacco, cotton, etc.) have been used as money. Yet gold and silver have tended to drive out the other monies from the currency market because of their superior qualities for various monetary functions: They are homogenous, durable, easy to recognize, easy to shape, and so on. Their production is subject to the same laws that rule the production of other commodities. Hence, the "monetary policy" of mine owners and of each mint is strictly oriented toward consumer satisfaction, the quantities produced depending only on consumer demand.

Because paper currencies are the dominant type of money today, there has been some speculation about the possibility of a free market in paper or electronic money. However, there is no historical evidence to support this possibility; noncommodity monies have at all times and places been creatures of the state. In modern times, the state has introduced paper money by endowing a privileged note-issuing bank (the national Central Bank) with the authority to suspend the redemption of its notes. Although the historical record does not prove that a noncommodity money is incompatible with a free market, a number of economists have argued that, by its nature, money must ultimately be translatable into a commodity.

In a totally free market, every individual would possess the right to become a banker. Everybody could offer to store other people's money and issue money titles, which in turn would document the fact that money had been deposited with him and could be redeemed at any time.

Conceivably, bankers also would propose investment schemes that bear a certain resemblance to the business of storing money and issuing money titles. For example, they could offer to issue IOUs for money invested in their bank and try to make these IOUs more attractive by promising to liquidate them on demand at face value. They might even issue them in forms that are virtually identical with the forms in which money titles appear: "bank notes," "smart cards," "credit cards," and so on. This, in turn, might induce some market participants to accept these IOUs as payment in market exchanges, just as they occasionally accept mortgages or stock-market paper as payment.

Some economists think that such investment schemes have been realized in the past and call them *fractional-reserve banking*. They also use the term *bank notes* to describe these IOUs. Still it is important to be aware of the essential differences that exist between these IOUs and money titles. Despite these resemblances in appearance and use, money titles entail claims to money, while the promise to redeem an IOU entails claims to the efforts of a banker. Although all money titles can be redeemed at any time, only a part of these IOUs can be liquidated as promised by the banker, only a limited number of receipt owners can obtain such liquidation at the same time, and so on.

Identical names and the identical outer appearance of both money titles and liquid IOUs are not a mere coincidence. Historically, in most cases, bankers issuing liquid IOUs took pains to hide the real differences distinguishing their product from genuine money titles. Insofar as such efforts are meant to deceive other market participants, fractional-reserve banking is a fraudulent scheme that violates the principles of the free market and merely serves to enrich some individuals (the bankers and their customers) at the expense of all others.

The great issue in monetary and banking policy is whether free-market banking and the free-market production of money can be improved by schemes relying on coercion. The history of monetary analysis and policy has been the history of debates on the insufficiencies of the unhampered market and on how to remedy them with statist monetary schemes. Virtually all these discussions have revolved around problems of alleged money shortages, and the essence of all institutions designed to overcome these problems is to produce more money than could possibly be produced on the unhampered market.

Mercantilist writers traditionally argued that more money meant higher prices and lower interest rates, and that these in turn invigorated commerce and industry. Moreover, it was much simpler to levy taxes in a monetary system than in a barter economy. Thus, the mercantilists urged that imports of gold and silver be stimulated through tariffs on foreign goods and export subsidies for domestic

products, endorsed fractional-reserve banking to the benefit of the Crown, and supported special monopoly privileges for national or central banks.

They had a point: The kings profited from increased monetary circulation, which made looting their subjects far easier. However, the French physiocrats and the British classical economists were able to entirely destroy the intellectual underpinning of the mercantilist scheme. Tariffs and export subsidies, they pointed out, cannot permanently increase the domestic money supply, and the amount of money circulating in the economy has no positive impact on trade and industry considered as a whole. The great contribution of classical economics to the theory of monetary policy was to show that increasing the quantity of money could never increase the amount of services that money can render to the nation as a whole. A higher money supply merely leads to higher money prices, but it does not affect aggregate industry and aggregate real output. This principle is what classical economists had in mind when referring to money as a veil that is superimposed on the physical economy.

Later economists further refined this analysis by giving a more sophisticated account of the impact of money on the real economy. They showed that increases in the money supply brought about two forms of redistribution of income. On the one hand, increasing the money supply entailed that the purchasing power of each money unit is diluted. If this loss of purchasing power was not anticipated, the effect would be that borrowers would benefit at the expense of lenders. On the other hand, and independently of the market participants' anticipations, new money first reaches some market participants before others, and these people can now buy more out of an unchanged supply of real goods. All others will buy less at higher prices as the less valued money circulates throughout the economy because spending the additional money units raises market prices. Hence, although variations in the quantity of money bring no overall improvement for the national economy, they benefit some persons, industries, and regions at the expense of the other market participants.

For more than 100 years, the idea that a community could promote its well-being by increasing the money supply beyond what would exist on the unhampered market was discredited among professional economists, although the influential J. S. Mill undermined this monetary orthodoxy by various concessions.

Then John Maynard Keynes almost single-handedly gave new life to the old mercantilist policies. The charismatic Keynes was the most famous economist of the best-known economics department of his time. In his writings, public speeches, and private conversations, he used his personal and institutional prestige to promote the idea that multiplying money could achieve more than simply redistributing income in favor of the government and the groups that control it.

Keynesianism has vastly increased government control over the economy. It has given modern states the justification to engage in social engineering on an unheard-of scale and to deeply transform social relations and the geographical allocation of resources. However, Keynes's greatest legacy is that his ideas keep guiding present-day research in monetary economics. Today, virtually all publications in academic journals take it for granted that Keynes was right and monetary orthodoxy was wrong. Based on the tacit assumption that government can improve money and banking, thus increasing aggregate output, mainstream debates tend to turn around issues of interest for government policymakers. Such issues are, for example, the definition of various monetary aggregates, signaling through the behavior of central-bank officials, various insurance schemes for financial intermediaries, and indicators to predict the impact of monetary policy on prices, interest rates, production, and employment.

There are some free-market economists who discard monetary orthodoxy and try to make the case for a free market in money and banking on mercantilist-Keynesian premises. These economists argue that the supply of money has to be constantly adapted to match the needs of trade, to bring about monetary equilibrium, and so on. Yet they think that the institutions needed to ensure this permanent adaptation are most likely to emerge on the unhampered market.

It is difficult to predict which course the mainstream thinking in banking and monetary policy will take. For libertarian monetary economists who embrace Austrianism, there are ample and largely unexplored research opportunities dealing with the impact of a government-controlled money supply on the economy and on society at large and with the best ways to abolish government intervention in money and banking.

JGH

See also Böhm-Bawerk, Eugen von; Economics, Austrian School of; Hayek, Friedrich A.; Mises, Ludwig von; Money and Banking; Rothbard, Murray

Further Readings

Anderson, Benjamin. *The Value of Money.* Reprint. Spring Mills, PA: Libertarian Press, 1999.
Hayek, Friedrich August. *The Denationalisation of Money.* 2nd ed. London: Institute for Economic Affairs, 1977.
Hazlitt, Henry. *From Bretton Woods to World Inflation.* Chicago: Regnery Gateway, 1984.
Mises, Ludwig von. *Theory of Money and Credit.* Indianapolis, IN: Liberty Fund, 1980.
Paul, Ron, and Lewis Lehrman. *The Case for Gold.* Washington, DC: Cato Institute, 1982.
Rothbard, Murray N. *What Has Government Done to Our Money?* 4th ed. Auburn, AL: Mises Institute, 1990.
Selgin, George. *The Theory of Free Banking.* Totowa, NJ: Rowman & Littlefield, 1988.
Sennholz, Hans. *Money and Freedom.* Spring Mills, PA: Libertarian Press, 1985.
White, Lawrence H. *The Theory of Monetary Institutions.* Oxford: Blackwell, 1999.

BASTIAT, FRÉDÉRIC (1801–1850)

Claude Frédéric Bastiat, economist, popular writer, and statesman, made seminal contributions to the advance of libertarian principles and policies. His influence has been enormous and is especially evident in the fields of public choice, international trade, and law and economics. His work continues to inspire scholars to improve our understanding of how both states and economies function.

Virtually all of Bastiat's books and essays were written in the last 6 years of his life, from 1844 to 1850. Before then, he lived in relative seclusion in his native southwestern France, where he dedicated himself to the administration of his landed property and to the quiet and intense study of political economy, especially the works of Adam Smith, Jean-Baptiste Say, Antoine-Louis-Claude Destutt de Tracy, Charles Dunoyer, and Charles Comte.

In 1844, inspired by the success of the British Anti-Corn Law League under the leadership of Richard Cobden and John Bright, Bastiat joined the French classical-liberal *économistes* with an article devoted to "The Influence of English and French Tariffs." There he argued that the Anti-Corn Law League's abolition of tariffs would spur economic and cultural development in England to such an extent that it would overtake the hitherto dominant France—unless the French too abolished their tariffs.

Bastiat went on to produce a stream of articles, pamphlets, and books making the case for free trade and laissez-faire in a series of original and compelling arguments. In the last months before his death, he wrote *Economic Harmonies,* his (unfinished) magnum opus, and two of his most important essays, "The Law" and "What Is Seen and What Is Not Seen." Many of Bastiat's writings were translated into a number of foreign languages, including English, German, Spanish, Russian, and Italian, and have inspired classical-liberal movements all over Europe and in the United States. By the 1870s, virtually all who endorsed the classical-liberal tenets of political economy did so under Bastiat's impact.

Bastiat propounded the view that in a natural society, one based on private property, the interests of the various social groups would become harmonious. For example, although debtors and creditors seem to have conflicting interests, a more careful examination would show that in fact a debtor has an interest in the well-being of his creditor, who may be the source of further credits. Similarly, a creditor has an interest in the well-being of his debtor because only a prosperous debtor would be capable of paying interest. Bastiat discussed countless similar relationships, such as those between consumers and producers, workers and capitalists, landlords and tenants, and so forth.

Unlike some later economists, who have argued that laissez-faire would produce economic equilibrium (in the sense of a state of perfect balance), Bastiat contended more modestly that men's interests are harmonious, provided every man confined himself to his rightful sphere, and provided goods and services are exchanged freely and voluntarily. He contrasted that with the view that the interests of human beings, either individually or in groups, are necessarily antagonistic.

Bastiat's primary contribution consists not in a description of the natural order itself, but in a sophisticated analysis of the sources and the effects of disruptions of that order. Bastiat starts from the observation that a private-property order is safeguarded by the law, which he understands to mean those rules that determine how physical force may legitimately be used to protect property rights. In his essay "The Law," Bastiat argues that the whole point of this artificial institution, the law, is to protect the private property of each member of society: "It is not because men have enacted laws that personality, liberty and property exist. On the contrary, it is because personality, liberty and property already exist that men make laws." The law is "the collective organization of the individual's right to legitimate self-defense." Only insofar as man-made law supports nature-given private property is it just, and from the maintenance of justice a harmonious social order results.

Bastiat's writings on the relationship between law and economics and social order make him an important forerunner of today's academics who have married law and economics into a new discipline. Bastiat argued that law, as a man-made institution, also can be perverted by those who use it for purposes other than the defense of liberty and property. Protectionism, that is, special-interest policies established under the mantle of law, disrupts the natural harmony of interests and creates conflicts over privileges. For example, a tariff on wine benefits domestic wine producers at the expense of domestic consumers and foreign wine producers. This disruption also exists for subsidies and other schemes of redistribution, which in Bastiat's classification all fall under the broad category of protectionism inasmuch as one group is "protected" by a special privilege that has to be paid for by other individuals.

In 1927, economist Ludwig von Mises wrote in *Liberalism* that, although the science of economics had advanced greatly since Bastiat's time, "[Bastiat's] critique of all protectionist and related tendencies is even today unsurpassed. The protectionists and interventionists have not been able to advance a single word in pertinent and objective rejoinder. They continue to stammer: Bastiat is 'superficial.'"

Many people cannot see beyond the benefits to those protected by the legislation Bastiat condemns; they cannot appreciate the costs to those who have been plundered. Because the logic of plunder leads all to seek such benefits, Bastiat concluded in his essay "The State" that, "The state is the great fictitious entity by which everyone seeks to live at the expense of everyone else." Once protectionism is accepted as a principle, it sets in motion a process that progressively undermines the harmonious private-property order, the logical end point of which is full-blown socialism.

Perhaps Bastiat's central analytic contribution was his insight that political economy involves counterfactual comparisons of observed achievements of the real world with alternative (but unrealized) achievements. Contemporary economics expresses that idea in the concept of opportunity cost, according to which the cost of a choice is the most highly valued opportunity forgone in the act of choice. Thus, cost is what is *not* realized because something else *is* realized. It is only by comparing what is realized to what would have been realized that we can know whether there is a net addition to or a net subtraction from wealth.

Bastiat's most brilliant expression of that insight is found in his essay "What Is Seen and What Is Not Seen." After a boy breaks a pane of glass, some onlookers offer the owner of the window the consolation that, after all, some good will come of it because "Such accidents keep industry going. Everybody has to make a living. What would become of the glaziers if no one ever broke a window?" Along the same lines, it could be argued that wars are economically advantageous, that natural disasters such as hurricanes and floods lead to economic growth, and that public works increase employment and income in economic slumps. As Bastiat points out, the error in such reasoning is to focus exclusively on the observable events: the production of windows and cannons, people employed in producing such things, and the income that those people receive. Yet one does not see that, had the window not been broken, had the war not been started, and had the hurricane not destroyed houses, other goods would have been produced, and those goods would have added to preexisting wealth. Breaking windows does not add to the aggregate of wealth.

Military armament, public works, and subsidies, merely by keeping people busy, do not bring about a net increase in wealth because, although some are employed by the expenditure of tax monies, others are unemployed by the corresponding taxes, and net additions to wealth that would have been produced are not produced. Costs as well as benefits must be considered. That basic lesson inspired the economic journalist Henry Hazlitt to write his highly influential 20th-century work, *Economics in One Lesson*.

Although Bastiat's writings have won praise in later generations, his pioneering activities as a libertarian organizer and agitator have been unduly neglected. Bastiat drew his inspiration from the success of Cobden and Bright, and his book *Cobden and the League* was crucial for inspiring others on the European continent. However, in distinct contrast to his British predecessors, Bastiat placed the French free-trade movement within an all-encompassing libertarian theory. Whereas the Anti-Corn Law League pursued the rather narrow objective of unhampered trade in corn, the French movement offered a wide program for a truly free society that would realize an ideal of justice. Bastiat campaigned tirelessly for freedom of trade, respect for property, peace and opposition to imperialism, limited government, and economy in government.

Bastiat's strategy for the establishment of a free society merits careful analysis by present-day libertarians because he confronted the same problems that they face today. First, he sought to enlighten free-market campaigners through the campaign. (He once declared that he loved the spirit of the free market more than the free market itself.) Second, he always took care to generalize his discussion of specific political problems to link them to first principles. Bastiat consistently argued from principle, rather than merely pointing out some favorable consequence of a policy that he advocated. Finally, he sought to accustom his free-market colleagues to apply their principles consistently.

Shortly before his death, Bastiat put those principles into practice by becoming a leader of the liberal wing in the French Parliament during the short-lived Republic of 1848–1849 and was instrumental in saving France from the imposition of a totalitarian socialist state. He died in Rome on December 24, 1850, while campaigning for free trade.

JGH

See also Classical Economics; Comte, Charles; Dunoyer, Charles; Free Trade; Laissez-Faire Policy; Rent Seeking

Further Readings

Bastiat, Frédéric. *Economic Harmonies.* New York: Van Nostrand, 1964.
———. *Economic Sophisms.* New York: Van Nostrand, 1964.
———. *The Law.* Irvington-on-Hudson, NY: Foundation for Economic Education, 1996.
———. *Oeuvres complètes.* 7 vols. 3rd ed. Paris: Guillaumin & Co, 1881.
———. *Selected Essays on Political Economy.* New York: Van Nostrand, 1964.
Baudin, L. *Bastiat.* Paris: Dalloz, 1962.
DiLorenzo, Thomas. "Frédéric Bastiat: Between the French and Marginalist Revolutions." *15 Great Austrian Economists.* R. G. Holcombe, ed. Auburn, AL: Mises Institute, 1999.
Dolet, Bernard. *Bastiat—au-dessus de la mêlée.* Paris: Calman-Lévy, 1977.
Mises, Ludwig von. *Liberalism.* 3rd ed. Irvington-on-Hudson, NY: Foundation for Economic Education, 1985.
Roche, George Charles III. *Frederic Bastiat—A Man Alone.* New Rochelle, NY: Arlington House, 1971.
Rothbard, Murray N. *Classical Economics.* Aldershot, UK: Edward Elgar, 1995.
Russell, Dean. *Frédéric Bastiat: Ideas and Influence.* Irvington-on-Hudson, NY: Foundation for Economic Education, 1969.

BAUER, PETER (1915–2002)

Peter Bauer was a central figure in the 20th-century debates over economic development, foreign aid, and the role of institutions. He made significant contributions to political economy and the relationship between economic freedom and prosperity. The son of a Budapest bookmaker, he went to Britain in 1934 to study economics at Gonville and Caius College, Cambridge, where he later became a Fellow. His pioneering work in development economics, which began with his study of the Southeast Asian rubber industry in the 1940s and his classic 1954 book, *West African Trade,* led him to question and later overturn many of the beliefs held by mainstream development experts. His path-breaking work was primarily carried out while at the London School of Economics and Political Science, where he taught from 1960 to 1983. In 1982, he became a life peer and a Fellow of the British Academy. Just days before his death on May 2, 2002, Lord Bauer was named the first recipient of the prestigious Milton Friedman Prize for Advancing Liberty, awarded biennially by the Cato Institute.

Bauer's work is characterized by careful observation of how countries move from subsistence to exchange economies, an application of simple economic principles, and a sound understanding of the role of noneconomic variables in promoting material advance. As he noted in his book *Dissent on Development,* "Economic achievement depends primarily on people's abilities and attitudes and also on their social and political institutions. Differences in these determinants or factors largely explain differences in levels of economic achievement and rates of material progress."

Bauer observed that people in poor countries respond to price incentives just as in rich countries. He also took note of the fact that when people have the freedom to own property and to trade, and when government is limited to the protection of those rights, they will have a better chance of achieving prosperity.

The intellectual climate in the late 1950s was not hospitable to Bauer's critique of state-led development policy. In 1956, Swedish economist Gunnar Myrdal, later a Nobel laureate, wrote, "The special advisers to underdeveloped countries who have taken the time and trouble to acquaint themselves with the problem . . . all recommend central planning as the first condition of progress." That view persisted well into the 1960s and has only recently been supplanted by a more market-friendly view. It was not until after the collapse of communism in Eastern Europe and the Soviet Union that the World Bank admitted, in its 1997 development report, "State-led intervention emphasized market failures and accorded the state a central role in correcting them. But the institutional assumptions implicit in this world view were, as we all realize today, too simplistic."

In his book *Reality and Rhetoric*, Bauer recognized that

the critics who propose replacing the market system by political decisions rarely address themselves to such crucial matters as the concentration of economic power in political hands, the implications of restriction of choice, the objectives of politicians and administrators, and the quality and extent of knowledge in a society and its methods of transmission.

By observing economic reality and adhering to the logic of the price system, Bauer refuted key propositions of orthodox development economics, the most basic of which was the idea of a "vicious circle of poverty." Poor countries were said to be poor because people had low incomes and could not generate sufficient savings to allow for capital accumulation, which was widely viewed as a key determinant of economic growth. Bauer observed that many people and many countries had moved from poverty to prosperity and that large-scale capital investment is neither necessary nor sufficient for material advance. His study of small holdings in the Malayan rubber industry and his observation of the importance of small-scale traders in West Africa convinced him that the reality of the development process was considerably different from the rhetoric of development experts.

Bauer also questioned the widely held belief that poor countries cannot become rich without external aid. He found that underdeveloped countries have become rich without access to foreign aid, whereas those that have received substantial external aid have failed to escape poverty. He therefore argued that foreign aid is more likely to perpetuate poverty than to alleviate it, a claim that now has substantial empirical support.

Bauer also strongly disagreed with the widely held view that population growth is a drag on development. In his essay "Population Growth: Disaster or Blessing?" he wrote, "Economic achievement and progress depend on people's *conduct* not on their *numbers*." Unlike many of the development experts who wanted to use government to "help the poor," Bauer thought that poor people could lift themselves out of poverty through their own efforts if only governments would safeguard both economic and personal freedoms.

Bauer was one of the first economists to argue that state-led development policies and the quest for "social justice" would politicize economic life, impair individual freedom, and fail to achieve long-run prosperity for the majority of people. He also noted that those countries that had the fewest commercial contacts with the West were the least developed. He focused attention on the dynamic gains from free trade. In his last book, *From Subsistence to Exchange and Other Essays*, he wrote, "Contacts through traders and trade are prime agents in the spread of new ideas, modes of behavior, and methods of production. External commercial contacts often first suggest the very possibility of change, including economic improvement."

Bauer's emphasis on individual merit, character, culture, property rights, and markets, and his distrust of big government, foreign aid, and the welfare state place him squarely in the classical liberal tradition. His life's work rests squarely in the broader context of political economy, not in the narrow technical confines of modern development economics or the even narrower space of formal economic modeling. As Nobel laureate economist Amartya Sen stated in his introduction to Bauer's last book, "The indispensability of Bauer's analysis is a reflection of the reach and profundity of his political economy."

JAD

See also Development, Economic; Interventionism; Wealth and Poverty; Welfare State

Further Readings

Bauer, Peter T. *Dissent on Development*. Cambridge, MA: Harvard University Press, 1972 [rev. ed., 1976].
———. *Equality, the Third World, and Economic Delusion*. Cambridge, MA: Harvard University Press, 1981.
———. *From Subsistence to Exchange and Other Essays*. Princeton, NJ: Princeton University Press, 2000.
———. "Population Growth: Disaster or Blessing?" Cato Institute Distinguished Lecturer Series, Cosponsored with the Institute for Political Economy. Washington, DC: Cato Institute, 1995.
———. *Reality and Rhetoric: Studies in the Economics of Development*. Cambridge, MA: Harvard University Press, 1984.
———. *West African Trade: A Study of Competition, Oligopoly and Monopoly in a Changing Economy*. Cambridge: Cambridge University Press, 1954.
Dorn, James A., Steve H. Hanke, and Alan A. Walters, eds. *The Revolution in Development Economics*. Washington, DC: Cato Institute, 1998.
Yamey, Basil S. "Peter Bauer: Economist and Scholar." *Cato Journal* 7 no. 1 (Spring/Summer 1987): 21–27.

BECKER, GARY S. (1930–)

Gary S. Becker is a professor of economics and sociology at the University of Chicago. He was awarded the Nobel Prize in economics in 1992 for "having extended the domain of microeconomic analysis to a wide range of human behavior and interaction, including nonmarket behavior."

Becker received his undergraduate degree in 1951 from Princeton University and his PhD in 1955 from the University of Chicago. He was an assistant professor at Chicago from 1954 to 1957, before moving to Columbia University and the National Bureau of Economic Research. "I felt that I would become intellectually more independent if I left the nest and had to make it on my own," Becker has written. "I have always believed this was the correct decision, for I developed greater independence and self-confidence than seems likely if I remained at Chicago." Becker spent 12 fruitful years at Columbia, but ultimately returned to Chicago in 1969, where he has taught ever since.

As the Nobel Prize committee stated, if there is a defining characteristic of Becker's work, it is method. He has applied rational choice theory rigorously and ingeniously to topics that were once thought beyond the purview of economics. At the heart of Becker's approach is the idea that people, in all areas of their lives, maximize their utility subject to the constraints with which they are faced. In short, they act purposefully—rationally—not only in choosing a job, but also in choosing a mate. These actions are not always "selfish." Instead, Becker models behavior in a way that allows individuals to "maximize welfare *as they conceive it,* whether they be selfish, altruistic, loyal, spiteful, or masochistic." At first, his work was often viewed with skepticism by economists, who considered his choice of subjects odd and far afield from more well-trodden territory as, say, money and banking, and by sociologists, political scientists, and anthropologists, who viewed him as an interloper or, worse, an "imperialist" aiming to apply methods wholly unsuitable to their disciplines. Over time, however, his work has become widely accepted by economists, and, increasingly, social scientists across related fields have come to appreciate it as well.

Becker's work has spanned a wide variety of topics, but his influence arguably has been the greatest in four broad areas: racial discrimination, crime, human capital, and the family. When Becker first examined the economics of discrimination in the 1950s, much of American society was still segregated. Becker suggested that this fact implied that the employer who refused to hire African-American workers had a taste for discrimination. However, that taste, as Becker demonstrated, is not necessarily costless. In a competitive market, employers who systematically discriminate against specific racial or ethnic groups may suffer because the more productive workers from those groups will likely be hired by competing firms looking to gain an advantage. The more competitive the market, the more intense is the bidding for skilled workers regardless of their race or ethnicity.

Becker followed this analysis with discussions of individual skill-building or human capital. His conclusions were straightforward: that skills are, in fact, augmentable, and individuals face an economic choice about whether and how to build them. The fundamental issue is opportunity cost. Suppose one goes to college for 4 years to learn new skills and ultimately obtain a degree. There are often obvious costs involved, most significantly tuition. But there are less obvious costs, such as the time spent pursuing education—time that could have been spent in the labor market instead, thus earning wages. Individuals must assess whether the building of such skills will help them enough over their lifetimes—through improved earnings as well as cultural and other nonmonetary gains—to more than offset the time and effort spent acquiring them. This idea is now one of the most standard in labor economics—indeed, all of economics—which was quite novel at the time Becker began his work. Subsequent empirical studies have shown that the building of skills has become increasingly important in modern economies, both at the individual and macro level. High-skilled workers tend to receive a wage premium, and the economies of countries with relatively well-educated workforces tend to grow more quickly than those with relatively poorly educated workforces. As a result, human capital—specifically, how to most efficiently encourage investment in the building of skills—has become an important public policy issue.

Becker's work on crime overturned some long-held beliefs. As he put it: "In the 1950s and 1960s, intellectual discussions of crime were dominated by the opinion that criminal behavior was caused by mental illness and social oppression, and that criminals were helpless 'victims.'" Becker was critical of these assumptions. Most criminals, he argued, were rational, just like noncriminals. He acknowledged that, in general, people are constrained by moral and ethical considerations and would not commit crimes even when those crimes could be quite lucrative and the chances of being caught are quite low. But for those who do become criminals, many carefully assess their alternatives. Given the likelihood of being caught, is crime more profitable than pursuing work that is legal? If so, they may choose crime. It is important here to note the linkage with human capital. Those who have spent time improving their skills are less likely to pursue crime because their legal workplace alternatives tend to be better. In addition, they have more to lose, in both future earnings and social status.

Of all of Becker's research projects, his work on the family is perhaps the most controversial. It also has been the most mentally taxing. "Writing *A Treatise on the Family* is the most difficult sustained intellectual effort I have undertaken," Becker wrote. Despite its complexity, there are some key themes that run throughout his work. First is the idea that the household can be modeled as a small factory, where decisions about the distribution of work and the allocation of time are determined by largely economic factors. For instance, as family members' real wages increase, there is less incentive for home production and greater incentive to work outside the household. This fact explains, in part, the increase in female labor-force participation. Also, more women entering the workforce may have contributed to higher rates of divorce, as they become increasingly able to earn the income necessary to live independently. For those couples that remain married, earnings can have a significant effect on the number of children they have and how much they invest in their offspring's education. In general, as wages rise, Becker argued, families will tend to have fewer children and to invest more in each child's human capital. This theory has been borne out by the experience of the United States, Western Europe, and Japan, where fertility has generally fallen as wage rates and per capita incomes have risen.

Becker, like most members of the Chicago School, regards economics as a value-free, positive science. As such, his views on public policy issues are generally determined by empirical results. Still, on most matters, Becker is strongly supportive of the free market and skeptical of government intervention.

From 1985 to 2004, Becker wrote a monthly column for *BusinessWeek* magazine, the final article of which was titled "A 19-Year Dialogue on the Power of Incentives." He noted there:

> Along with many others of my generation, I was a socialist when I started my university studies. But my first few economics courses taught me the power of competition, markets, and incentives, and I quickly became a classical liberal. That means someone who believes in the power of individual responsibility, a market economy, and a crucial but limited role of government.

Many of those columns are collected in the 1996 volume, *The Economics of Life,* coauthored with his wife, Guity Nashat Becker. Since December 2004, Becker and Richard Posner—a member of the faculty at the University of Chicago Law School, a federal circuit court judge, and a founder of the law-and-economics movement—have maintained a blog, where they each publish a short weekly essay on a timely policy issue.

Those heavily influenced by Becker include Steven Levitt, professor of economics at Chicago and coauthor of the best-selling book, *Freakonomics: A Rogue Economist Explores the Hidden Side of Everything*. According to Levitt, "the science of economics is primarily a set of tools, as opposed to a subject matter," which means that "no subject . . . need be beyond its reach." Levitt, appropriately, is director of the Becker Center on Chicago Price Theory.

Becker is arguably the most ambitious and creative economist of his generation. Although not as famous as his mentor, Milton Friedman, Becker's influence may ultimately rival Friedman's. As the late George Stigler noted, "Gary Becker may well go down in history as the chief architect of a truly general science of society."

AS

See also Economics, Chicago School of; Family; Friedman, Milton; Posner, Richard; Racism

Further Readings

Becker, Gary S. *The Economic Approach to Human Behavior.* Chicago: University of Chicago Press, 1976.
———. *The Economics of Discrimination.* Chicago: University of Chicago Press, 1957.
———. *Human Capital.* New York: Columbia University Press, 1964.
———. *A Treatise on the Family.* Chicago: University of Chicago Press, 1981.
Becker, Gary S., and Guity Nashat Becker. *The Economics of Life.* New York: McGraw-Hill, 1996.
Febrero, Ramón, and Pedro S. Schwartz, eds. *The Essence of Becker.* Stanford, CA: Hoover Institution, 1995.

BENTHAM, JEREMY (1748–1832)

Jeremy Bentham is known today chiefly as the father of utilitarianism. During his lifetime, Bentham was famous as the proponent of a scientific approach to social reform. Born in London, the son of an attorney, Bentham was a precocious child. He studied at Westminster school and Queen's College in Oxford, England. In 1763, he began the study of law at Lincoln's Inn, but spent much time carrying out chemical experiments in his chambers. In December of that year, he attended the Oxford lectures of England's most famous lawyer, Sir William Blackstone, author of the celebrated *Commentaries on the Laws of England*. He remarked later that he had immediately detected the fallacies in Blackstone's arguments. In 1776, he fiercely attacked the *Commentaries* for being hostile to reform in his first published book, *Fragment on Government*. In *A Defence of Usury* (1787), he argued that it was a mistake for governments to prohibit high interest rates because individuals are the best judges of what will benefit them. His major work, *An Introduction to the Principles of Morals and Legislation*, was published in 1789. Other significant publications include *A Catechism of Parliamentary Reform* (1817, written in 1809), *The Rationale of Reward* (1825), *The Rationale of Punishment* (1830), the *Book of Fallacies* (1824), and the *Rationale of Judicial Evidence* (1827). Several of Bentham's writings were first published in French, and he was made an honorary citizen of France, with which he had close ties.

In Bentham's time, law, judicial procedures, and life in general were governed, to a much greater degree than in our own, by historical precedent and beliefs not subjected to critical examination. We owe much of the difference between his time and ours to Bentham. Bentham was a man of the Age of Reason; his models were such figures as John Locke (especially Locke's *Essay Concerning Human Understanding*), Claude Adrien Helvetius, and Voltaire, and his principal goal was to replace the traditional reliance on custom with rational analysis. Bentham argued that a policy or procedure was in accordance with reason when it maximized utility, understood as human happiness. One must judge a program in the light not of unproven assumptions, no matter how venerable, but of its consequences for people.

The model of rational analysis for Bentham was science. He aimed to occupy the same role with respect to society and law that Newton had to physics, by reducing the multiplicity of phenomena to unity through the discovery of a single basic principle: the principle of utility. The fundamental concepts of the law, he maintained, must be concrete and observable by the senses, not abstract, and they are two: pleasure and pain. The ground of the law is physical sensibility; everything men do is motivated by the desire to avoid pain or obtain pleasure, which are just two sides of the same coin. "Nature," he tells us,

> has placed mankind under the governance of two sovereign masters, pain and pleasure. It is for them alone to point out what we ought to do, as well as to determine what we shall do. On the one hand the standard of right and wrong, on the other the chain of causes and effects, are fastened to their throne.

An action or policy is rational to the extent that it possesses utility, that is, contributes to human happiness. The measure of right and wrong is the greatest happiness of the greatest number. Bentham fleshed out the concept of happiness by reference to four subordinate goals: security (from aggression by others), subsistence, abundance, and equality. The first two goals are more essential to happiness than the second two. Government can do much to provide security, through law, but little to provide subsistence, which must come from the efforts of the individual. Although equality is psychologically satisfying, it should not be achieved by measures that reduce security, such as coercive redistribution of property. Bentham was committed to equal treatment by the law, and "equal treatment of unequal individuals produces only inequality."

Both the American and French revolutions appealed for support to the ideas of natural law and natural rights. Bentham had no sympathy with these views and was initially hostile to American independence because of what he considered its poor arguments. Given his emphasis on observability, for Bentham, law could refer only to what was enacted by a legislature, and a right likewise was only something created by law. Genuine laws and rights were observable by the senses. A law is "an assemblage of words." A natural law or right could only be an imaginary one or at most what should be a law or right—and that question could rationally only be decided on the basis of utility. Natural rights, he stated in a famous phrase, were not merely nonsense, but "nonsense upon stilts." They were mere fictions, "sounds without meaning," of a kind with the many fictions indulged in by writers on law, which for the most part he considered pernicious. He maintained that "real entities alone can be the subject of true propositions," and "Abstracted from all relations to real entities, a proposition having for its subject a fictitious entity has neither truth nor meaning."

Liberty, for Bentham, if properly understood, also is a fiction, that is, an unobservable abstract concept. Liberty is simply the absence of external constraint. The liberty to do a certain action is nothing more than the fact that no law prohibits it and no physical force prevents it. Bentham was willing to concede that there could sometimes be useful fictions, and liberty was one of those fictions. However, it has importance for him not as a value in itself, but only insofar as it contributed to happiness, and that depended entirely on circumstances. The liberty that Bentham thought valuable was just a form of security, the law-given freedom from the encroachments of others. Such liberty makes it possible for us to peacefully pursue our own goals. Property is just a form of liberty, namely the freedom to dispose of a certain item as one wishes.

In his discussions of concrete issues, Bentham in general supported a laissez-faire economic policy, as can be seen in his *Defence of Usury*. There he takes issue with Adam Smith, whom he otherwise looked up to as a hero, because Smith was willing to support government in its attempts to keep the rate of interest down. In addition to economic freedom, Bentham especially espoused the cause of intellectual freedom and freedom of speech. Because individuals are usually the best judges of what is good for them, and because a regime of liberty provides the individual with the greatest freedom to follow his own goals, there is a presumption in favor of it, and the burden of justification is on those who would make exceptions.

Bentham's impact on libertarianism was profound. His pragmatic support for laissez-faire has continued to be influential, and his formulation of utilitarian criteria for evaluating policies is the foundation of much of the contemporary economic defense of free markets. His scorn for natural rights, however, remains controversial and is frequently blamed for providing a key conceptual foundation for the modern welfare state. Traditional advocates of natural rights have accused Bentham of undermining liberty by entrusting to legislators the power to rearrange legal rights whenever doing so might lead to more utility, thereby undermining the stability of rights necessary for generating the very utility Bentham thought the only proper goal of law.

TPB

See also Consequentialism; Mill, John Stuart; Rights, Natural; Utilitarianism

Further Readings

Bentham, Jeremy. *In Defence of Usury*. London: Payne & Foss, 1818.
———. *An Introduction to the Principles of Morals and Legislation*. Laurence J. Lafleur, ed. New York: Hafner, 1948.

Hamburger, Joseph. *Intellectuals in Politics: John Stuart Mill and the Philosophical Radicals.* New Haven, CT: Yale University Press, 1965.

Harrison, Ross. *Bentham.* London: Routledge & Kegan Paul, 1983.

Mill, John Stuart. *Utilitarianism.* Oxford: Oxford University Press, 1998.

Bill of Rights, U.S.

The first 10 amendments to the U.S. Constitution are commonly referred to as the Bill of Rights. These 10 articles resulted from the clash between those who supported replacing the Articles of Confederation with the Constitution, drafted by the convention in Philadelphia, and those who opposed the new document. Opponents of the Constitution—dubbed Anti-Federalists by its proponents—argued that the Constitution created a consolidated or national government. As evidence for that charge, they cited the lack of a Bill of Rights, which, in Thomas Jefferson's words, was "what the people are entitled to against every government on earth, general or particular, and what no just government should refuse, or rest on inference." Anti-Federalists were not so much interested in obtaining a Bill of Rights as they were in using its absence as a reason to reject the Constitution altogether.

Supporters of the Constitution, who called themselves Federalists, argued that a Bill of Rights was both unnecessary and dangerous. It was unnecessary because the general government was one of limited and enumerated powers and was not given the power to violate such rights as the right to freedom of the press. As Alexander Hamilton wrote, "Why declare that things shall not be done which there is no power to do? Why, for instance, should it be said that the liberty of the press shall not be restrained, when no power is given by which restrictions may be imposed?"

Federalists also argued that a Bill of Rights would be dangerous because the enumeration of any rights would inevitably be incomplete, but would nevertheless imply that those rights not enumerated had been surrendered to the general government and were thereby lost. Later, James Madison summarized this objection in noting that,

> by enumerating particular exceptions to the grant of power, it would disparage those rights which were not placed in that enumeration; and it might follow by implication, that those rights which were not singled out, were intended to be assigned into the hands of the General Government, and were consequently insecure.

Although ingenious, those arguments were ultimately unpersuasive. Opponents of the Constitution pointed to the few rights that were already explicitly protected in the text and replied that, even if an incomplete enumeration were dangerous, the danger already existed, and it could only improve matters to lengthen the list. When it became clear that the Constitution would not be approved by the necessary number of state legislatures, Federalist supporters turned the tables on the Anti-Federalists by pledging to propose to the states a Bill of Rights after the Constitution was ratified. That promise tipped the balance, and the Constitution was narrowly approved. Along with their ratification, several states submitted to Congress long lists of amendments they wished adopted. Some of those proposed changes in the structure or powers of the general government, whereas others were explicit protections of rights.

Getting the first Congress to consider a Bill of Rights, however, was not easy. The *Annals of Congress* show Representative James Madison repeatedly urging the House to take up the matter, only to be opposed by other members who were more interested in enacting taxes than in drafting a Bill of Rights to protect against "speculative" abuses that might occur in the future. Madison persisted and eventually offered his own list of proposed amendments. He was named to a select committee of the House that considered his and other proposals. The first Congress ultimately proposed 12 amendments to the states, the first 2 of which were not ratified. (One of those first two amendments, which concerns when increases in compensation for members of Congress may take effect, was ratified in 1992; it is now the 27th Amendment.) What is now the 1st Amendment was actually the 3rd of those originally proposed. What we now call the Bill of Rights consists of a few of the natural or inherent rights of the people—such as the rights to freedom of speech, freedom of the press, freedom of assembly, and the free exercise of religion—and some enhanced procedural restrictions on the exercise of governmental power, such as the right to be free from unreasonable searches and seizures and the right to a jury trial in civil cases. The 9th and 10th Amendments affirm that the rights of the people extend beyond those that were singled out for enumeration and that the national government was limited to its enumerated powers. In his speech to the House, Madison described what later became to the 10th Amendment as "superfluous" and "unnecessary" in light of "the whole of the instrument." However, because several states had requested this language, he thought "there can be no harm in making such a declaration." Madison was much more adamant about the 9th Amendment, considering it his response to "one of the most plausible arguments I have ever heard urged against the admission of a bill of rights into this system"—viz., that an incomplete enumeration was dangerous because it implied that all rights not enumerated had been surrendered to the general government—"but, I conceive it may be guarded against." Madison then referred his audience to what eventually became the 9th Amendment.

Historical accounts of the Bill of Rights are revealing in a number of ways. First, they support the view adopted by the U.S. Supreme Court in *Barron v. Mayor of Baltimore*

(1833) that the Bill of Rights only applied to the national government and not the states. That became a bone of contention in the years leading up to the Civil War and set the stage for the 14th Amendment, which was intended by its authors to reverse *Barron* by extending federal protection of the "Privileges or Immunities" of citizens against infringement by their state governments.

Second, scrutiny of the debates makes it clear that the Bill of Rights was not intended to change anything. It was generally agreed that it was not strictly necessary to add those rights because they were already protected. They were added only out of a sense of caution. But that implied that those rights were protected both before and after they were enumerated. It further suggested that unenumerated rights deserved the same protection as had been accorded enumerated rights, an inference made explicit in the 9th Amendment. The Amendment reads, "The enumeration in the Constitution of certain rights shall not be construed to deny or disparage others retained by the people."

Somewhat surprisingly, none of the enumerated rights received much, if any, attention in the early years of the United States. Indeed, the first time that a federal statute was held to be an unconstitutional violation of the 1st Amendment was in the 1965 case of *Lamont v. Postmaster General.* The most likely reason for the early neglect of the Bill of Rights by the courts was that, in the early years of the Republic, as was already noted, the Bill of Rights did not apply to state laws, and the national government largely kept within its enumerated powers. Even where Congress or the president did claim broader implied powers, those powers did not usually restrict the liberties of the people. The early history strongly suggests that a Bill of Rights is of greatest functional importance when governmental powers are not properly limited.

This question thus arises: Who was more prescient, the Federalists, who declared a Bill of Rights to be unnecessary and dangerous, or the Anti-Federalists, who insisted on having one? Clearly both were right. The Federalists' warning that a Bill of Rights would be dangerous has largely come true. With few exceptions, such as the right of privacy or the right to travel, only the enumerated rights have received any protection. Notwithstanding the 9th Amendment, in practice, almost every right that was not enumerated has been considered to have been surrendered to the general government. However, the Anti-Federalists accurately foresaw that the scheme of enumerated powers was inadequate to protect the rights retained by the people. Thanks to their insistence, the Bill of Rights has served as an essential, although incomplete, safeguard to limit the powers of government.

REB

See also Constitution, U.S.; Declaration of the Rights of Man and of the Citizen; Federalists Versus Anti-Federalists; Jefferson, Thomas; Madison, James; Magna Carta

Further Readings

Amar, Akhil Reed. *The Bill of Rights: Creation and Reconstruction.* New Haven, CT: Yale University Press, 1998.

Barnett, Randy E., ed. *The Rights Retained by the People: The History and Meaning of the Ninth Amendment.* 2 vols. Fairfax, VA: George Mason University Press, 1989–1993.

Bodenhamer, David J., and James W. Ely, Jr., eds. *The Bill of Rights in Modern America: After 200 Years.* Bloomington: Indiana University Press, 1993.

Cogan, Neil, ed. *The Complete Bill of Rights.* New York: Oxford University Press, 1997.

Hickok, Eugene E., Jr., ed. *The Bill of Rights and Current Understanding.* Charlottesville: University Press of Virginia, 1991.

Veit, Helen E., Kenneth R. Bowling, and Chalene Bangs Bickford, eds. *Creating the Bill of Rights: The Documentary Record from the First Federal Congress.* Baltimore: Johns Hopkins University Press, 1991.

BIOETHICS

There can be no libertarian bioethics without libertarian ethics. Once a libertarian approach to ethics is identified, resolving questions in bioethics involves little more than applying those principles to the sphere of human interaction specific to medicine and scientific innovation. For this reason, we must first touch on libertarianism as it relates to general theories of ethics before moving on to ethical theory with specific reference to bioethical questions.

Like the pursuit of liberty, bioethical questions have existed since the dawn of civilization, but the term *bioethics* and its emergence as an academic and clinical discipline first occurred in the 1970s. Then as now, some of the more theoretical topics include defining illness, patients' rights, medical professional integrity, human dignity, competency, research ethics, self-ownership, medical resource allocation, and social responsibility.

All ethical theories, of course, are intended to provide practical guidance for human interaction. A complete theory of ethics must do two things. First, it must provide a framework of rules intended to ensure peaceable interaction within a community; this framing is the purview of theories of justice. Second, it must provide guidance for individuals who wish to become morally better people; this guidance is the purview of theories of personal morality. Libertarian theories of justice are well documented and do not need further explanation. Suffice it to say that, unlike many theories of justice, libertarian theories are procedural rather than prescriptive in nature. The libertarian principle of equal freedom is illustrative: "Everyone has the right to live their life as they choose as long as in so doing they do not violate another's equal right to do the same."

Unfortunately, little attention has been given to libertarian theories of personal morality, particularly not from the perspective of ethical theory. At the end of the 19th century, Herbert Spencer, in his book, *The Principles of Ethics*, tried to provide a scientific foundation for a libertarian ethics. However, since then, there has been no such comprehensive effort. Both Murray Rothbard in *The Ethics of Liberty* and H. Tristram Engelhardt, Jr. in *The Foundations of Bioethics* provide fundamental theories of justice, not comprehensive theories of ethics. Others, such as Tibor Machan in *Generosity* and Ayn Rand in *The Virtue of Selfishness*, focus on analyzing a particular moral principle and do not provide a theoretical foundation for an entire libertarian theory of personal morality, although Rand clearly thinks she does.

What, then, would the theoretical foundations of a libertarian personal morality look like? First, like libertarian theories of justice, liberty would have to occupy a place of paramount importance. Several well-known ethical theorists, albeit not libertarians, make liberty central to their theories of personal morality. Aristotle, John Stuart Mill, and Immanuel Kant are among the most famous moral philosophers to stress that, without freedom, including the freedom to make mistakes, there can be no true moral conduct. Without choice, there is no morally blameworthy or praiseworthy actions, no good or bad conduct, no good or bad people. There is only more or less determined action, with little room for the intentional internalization of a moral code or personal moral growth. In addition, each of these great philosophers also stipulated what they believed that personal code should be.

Aristotle put forward a theory known as "virtue ethics." In the *Nicomachean Ethics*, written as a practical guide for his son, Aristotle stressed both that human beings naturally strove to better themselves and that virtue was the path to moral goodness. Aristotle argued that the good person is one who intentionally chooses to make practical wisdom and virtue habitual. The virtues at issue were temperance, courage, pride, truthfulness, fairness, and friendliness, among others.

John Stuart Mill, the most famous proponent of utilitarian ethics, argued that actions should be judged as right or wrong based on how well they contributed to the aggregate good of society, usually expressed in terms of the maximization of happiness. As he contended in *On Liberty*: "I regard utility as the ultimate appeal on all ethical questions; but it must be utility in the largest sense, grounded on the permanent interest of man as a progressive being. . . ."

Immanuel Kant is known as the father of rationally based deontological theories of ethics. Most deontological or duty-based systems of ethics are theological, but Kant's Enlightenment version claims its foundation in reason. Kant held that ethics provided the laws of freedom, the way physics provided the laws of nature. "Nothing in the world—indeed nothing even beyond the world—can possibly be conceived which could be called 'good' without qualification except a *good will*."

Kant proffered a rule, a categorical imperative, in which he argued that appeals should be made to common human reason: "Can I will that my maxim becomes a universal law?" This one simple sentence is the rational foundation of all moral conduct, Kant argued. Morally correct actions are conduct that one would find reasonable for everyone. The nonaggression axiom, embraced by libertarians, fits Kant's categorical imperative perfectly. It is logical not to aggress against others because, were everyone to do so, there would be chaos. With the help of Kant's categorical imperative and its corollary maxim of "respect for persons" as a precondition of liberty, an individual is set to cultivate a good will and become a better person. Although controversial, this assertion is all but self-evident given the history and theoretical foundations of libertarianism.

Many argue that there is something fundamentally unlibertarian about the concept of the *aggregate good*, which is inherent in all utilitarian theories, from the utilitarian theory of Mill to the social contract theories of Rousseau and Rawls. Individual freedom is not something that should be tolerated (or extolled) because of its utility, nor is it something to be traded for a promise that basic material needs will be met. Liberty is important in and of itself, not simply as a means to an end. For many libertarians, individual freedom is of such paramount importance that, even if it could be proven that liberty did not further the general interests of society, they would not be willing to give it up.

One way out of this utilitarian dilemma is to root the primacy of liberty in an Aristotelian ethics or a Lockean notion of natural rights. Aristotelian ethics has rightfully been criticized as subjective and culture-bound and can really only be redeemed by grounding it further in either natural law or reason.

Under natural rights theories, freedom is either a God-given right or an inherent aspect of human nature. The problem with this type of theory is that some libertarians do not believe in God or God-given rights, and others have misgivings about the scope of natural rights. Who is to say what qualifies as a natural right and on what grounds? Perhaps the answer lies in what is reasonable. If that is the case, then we need not rely on natural rights at all—and can simply make reason the foundation of liberty. We are thus brought back to the Enlightenment notion that reason can lead to right action in the same way that it can lead to a just system of government.

One theory that grounds liberty in reason was put forth by Kant in his book, *Foundations of the Metaphysics of Morals*. Libertarians who embrace this approach argue that rational beings do not want others interfering in their decision making, either public or private, economic or moral. In short, respect for others necessitates the primacy of liberty. Once it is clear that liberty is a necessary precondition of any libertarian theory of ethics and that reason is the only sufficient guide for libertarian moral conduct, it becomes all but self-evident what a libertarian theory of bioethics would look like.

Not uniquely libertarian, but important to any theoretical discussion of bioethics, are the four fundamental principles of bioethics described by Tom Beauchamp and James Childress in *Principles of Biomedical Ethics*, first published in 1979. These principles are respect for autonomy, nonmaleficence, beneficence, and justice. Beauchamp and Childress argue that it is the balancing and prioritizing of these four principles that is at the heart of bioethics.

Three other important concepts that touch on ethics as it relates to medical questions are paternalism, human dignity, and informed consent. Paternalism has reference to the principle at work when, in a conflict between beneficence and autonomy, beneficence takes precedence. From a libertarian perspective, paternalism is ethically suspect unless there is definitive proof that a person is mentally compromised. Unfortunately, the phrase *human dignity* in many bioethics discussions does not include respect for autonomy, but rather implies the imposition of one group of individuals' values on others. Finally, informed consent is a concept essential to autonomous decision making. It requires that a person be mentally competent, that he gives consent and does so voluntarily, and that he comprehend what is being decided. To help ensure comprehension, the person must have received a legally determined minimum amount of information necessary to make a well-reasoned decision and must be given an opportunity to request additional information. Finally, the information provided must be directed to the questions asked and do so accurately.

It should not be surprising that "respect for autonomy" and "informed consent" play crucial roles in a libertarian theory of bioethics. The other principles are generally only relevant to libertarian bioethics insofar as they relate to autonomous consent.

Consider how a libertarian theory of ethics would resolve a current-day bioethical dilemma. Is it ethical to let people sell their organs? The sale of organs is currently illegal in the United States, in part because legislators were swayed by concerns that the commodification of body parts is an affront to human dignity. The libertarian approach to this problem emphasizes that competent adults can make their own determinations as to what is an affront to their dignity and that they have the right to enter informed voluntary agreements for the sale of body parts if they so choose. In a libertarian society, the law should be concerned that such agreements are voluntary, that no fraud or deception is involved, and that, once legally entered into, contracts are upheld. But unlike current law, such arrangements would be legal.

A libertarian might well recognize the rights protected by law, but nevertheless suggest that certain motives for entering such arrangements are more or less praiseworthy and that certain conduct is more or less required by the imperative of respect for others. Value judgments are inherent to personal moral theory. Consider the moral status of the following motives: the gift of an organ simply to save a life, the sale of an organ to benefit the donor's children, the sale of an organ to rectify some wrong committed by the donor (e.g., to repair a borrowed car that was destroyed), and the sale of an organ to purchase something the donor desires. Libertarians would argue that all of these motives should be equally legal, but are not necessarily equally praiseworthy. In descending order, from the first to the last, they reflect a diminution of moral self-awareness, good will, virtue, and/or respect for persons.

Prescriptions for conduct also are inherent to personal moral theory. Consider the following questions: Would it be appropriate for an organ recipient, realizing that the donor is in great financial need, to offer barely more than the donor's cost associated with the donation? In other words, would it be moral to take advantage of a donor's weak economic bargaining position? Conversely, assuming a scarcity of organs available for transplantation, should the donor set a price so high that the recipient ends up alive but destitute? In other words, is it moral to exploit the recipient's desperate situation? Should organ recipients pay contractually unanticipated transplant-related expenses incurred by donors? Finally, should organ donors notify recipients if sometime after the transplant they develop an illness that may affect the ultimate success of the transplant even if not obligated by law or contract to do so? Arguably, the application of the categorical imperative and the principle of respect for persons would necessitate answering the first two sets of questions in the negative and the latter two in the affirmative.

A libertarian system of justice would not obligate the actors in any of these scenarios in one way or another. However, a libertarian theory of personal morality would provide both a means of judging the morality of conduct and prescriptions for being moral.

SFR

See also Abortion; Euthanasia; Feminism and Women's Rights; Genetics; Paternalism; Psychiatry; Rights, Theories of

Further Readings

Aristotle. *Nicomachean Ethics. Introduction to Aristotle*. Richard McKeon, ed. New York: Random House, 1947.

Beauchamp, Tom L., and James F. Childress. *Principles of Biomedical Ethics*. 3rd ed. New York: Oxford University Press, 1989.

Engelhardt, H. Tristram, Jr. *The Foundations of Bioethics*. New York: Oxford University Press, 1986.

Kant, Immanuel. *Foundations of the Metaphysics of Morals and What Is Enlightenment?* Lewis White Beck, trans. Indianapolis, IN: Bobbs-Merrill Educational Publishing, 1981.

Machan, Tibor R. *Generosity: Virtue in Civil Society*. Washington, DC: Cato Institute, 1998.

———. *Individuals and Their Rights, a Primer on Ethics*. Chicago: Open Court Publishing, 1989.

Mill, John Stuart. *On Liberty*. New York: W. W. Norton, 1975.

Rand, Ayn. *The Virtue of Selfishness: A New Concept of Egoism*. New York: Penguin, 1964.

Rothbard, Murray N. *The Ethics of Liberty*. New York: New York University Press, 1998.

Spencer, Herbert. *The Principles of Ethics*. Indianapolis, IN: Liberty Fund, 1978.

BLACK MARKETS

The black market is a complex and multifaceted phenomenon known and discussed under many different names: the informal, unofficial, irregular, parallel, second, underground, subterranean, hidden, invisible, unrecorded, and shadow economy. Its underlying feature is a set of activities that evade the regulatory and administrative standards of the formal or official economy, are not reported to the government, are unrecorded by the system of national income accounting, avoid the taxation system, and, in some cases, involve straightforward criminal products and services. The black market economy, when trading decisions are not the result of coercion, is a free market because, by definition, it lacks government intervention.

Libertarians interpret the emergence of the black market sector in two coextensive ways. First, they view this sector as a natural outcome of the fact that "the market embodies the sum of all human wishes," irrespective of how the general public or the government judges some of those wishes. Thus, black markets exist in certain goods and services that remain strongly in demand despite the fact that governments may prohibit them entirely (i.e., narcotics, pornography, and prostitution). Second, libertarians view such markets as an indicator of an unhealthy government policy that forces its citizens to take their activities underground. Among those policies are government price controls, rationing schemes, discriminatory taxation, governmental attempts to monopolize products, and extreme rates of taxation on otherwise perfectly legitimate wages, salaries, and small business profits. In addition to that, black markets also emerge in temporary service and low-capital occupations, where government detection and enforcement is unlikely (freelance handymen, household servants, temporary day laborers, etc.).

The Prohibition Era of the 1920s is a classic example of black market activity. Yet given that the size of the black market economy grows with the size of the governmental intervention, the ultraregulated socialist economies, such as those of Nazi Germany, Soviet Russia, and Eastern Europe, offer the most striking example of this phenomenon. There, massive regulatory and police establishments, and even the frequent imposition of the death penalty aimed at containing economic crimes, coexisted with a thriving underground economic sector. Nowadays, it can be argued that the "war on drugs" waged in many countries has created a situation similar to the one during the Prohibition period.

The diversity of facets and nuances of a black market economy complicates its discussion or analysis. For instance, underground activities and tax evasion are related, but not identical. No taxes are paid on underground activities, yet above-ground activities also are subject to tax-avoidance schemes. Nor should the underground economy be identified with criminal activity. Some activities are perfectly legal, but escape measurement in official statistics or taxation. In this context, some authors make a distinction between the *black* and the *underground* economy. The *underground economy* consists of all trade that occurs without detection by government and thus is not taxed, whereas the term *black market* is used to refer to trade in stolen goods or other theft-related activities. Part of the same family of concepts that mirror aspects of the black market is the *informal economy*, which has reference to local systems of exchange that fall outside state-controlled or money-based economic activities. These systems of exchange consist of barter, mutual self-help, odd jobs, allotment farming, street trading, and other similar activities. Finally, it is important to clarify the notion of the *gray market*—the circulation of goods through distribution channels other than those authorized by the manufacturer or producer. Gray market goods are not illegal. Instead, the process by which they are brought to market avoids the legal or standard distribution channels. Frequently this process occurs when the price of an item is significantly higher in one country than another. Hence, the existence of the gray market is an example of economic arbitrage.

The efforts to measure the size of the black market economy seek to relate the underground activity to officially measured national income and to determine its size relative to it. The most common method is the indirect or discrepancy approach. The assumption is that the effects of the underground economy are reflected in traces visible in the labor, money, and product markets. For instance, if spending in individual households and aggregate national accounts is higher than is officially recorded income, this result indicates black market activity. The size of black markets varies from one country to another and from one historical period to another. In general, the degree of government intervention and regulation is a good predictor of black markets' size. In many Third World countries, black market activity is believed to produce well over half of the gross national product. Informed estimates put the size of black markets at nearly 10% of the Gross Domestic Product for countries like the United States.

Both the general perception and much scholarly research regard the underground economy and its effects on the official economy mostly in negative terms that call for counteractive measures. But libertarians tend to look at the positive side of the black market economy: The black market economy is a spontaneous response to the demand for services and goods; it is a reservoir of innovative spirit and entrepreneurial talent. Further, it increases the competition and efficiency of the economy, challenges the authority and boundaries of government activities, contributes to the creation of markets, ensures financial resources for the poorest of the poor, and imposes beneficial changes on legal, social, and economic institutions. The choice between deterrence as a method of dealing with it (more regular and intensive controls, higher fines and prison sentences) as opposed to the positive approach (reducing regulation, reducing the tax burden, decriminalizing certain activities) is sometimes a difficult policy decision. Yet it is no surprise that libertarians consistently favor the second.

PDA

See also Drug Prohibition; Illicit Drugs; Private Property; Prohibition of Alcohol

Further Readings

de Soto, Hernando. *The Mystery of Capital: Why Capitalism Triumphs in the West and Fails Everywhere Else.* New York: Basic Books, 2000.
———. *The Other Path: The Invisible Revolution in the Third World.* London: Tauris, 1989.
Lippert, Owen, and Michael Walker, eds. *The Underground Economy: Global Evidence of Its Size and Impact.* Vancouver, BC, Canada: The Fraser Institute, 1997.

BÖHM-BAWERK, EUGEN VON (1851–1914)

Eugen von Böhm-Bawerk was a professor of economics at the Universities of Innsbruck and Vienna, a finance minister of Austria for many years, a major contributor to the "Austrian School" of economic thought, and an important critic of Marxism. Building on the work of Carl Menger, he developed a theory of capital and interest centered on "the relation between present and future in economic life." His analysis, in turn, provided the starting point for the theory of business cycles developed by his student Ludwig von Mises and by Friedrich A. Hayek. Böhm-Bawerk also pointed out internal contradictions in the value theory of Karl Marx's *Das Kapital,* a critique with which Marxists continue to struggle today.

Böhm-Bawerk is best known for his three-volume work, *Capital and Interest,* the first volume of which, *History and*

Critique of Interest Theories (1884), argued that previous attempts to explain the phenomenon of interest, particularly those by Marx and other socialist economists, were inadequate in ways that slighted the relation between present and future. In the second volume, *The Positive Theory of Capital* (1889), he offered his own explanation of interest. The third volume collected replies to various critics.

For Böhm-Bawerk, the "nub and kernel" of the phenomenon of interest was that "present goods are as a general rule worth more than future goods of equal quality and quantity." Thus, the fact that capitalists normally sell the product of labor for more than they pay the workers, and thus receive a "normal rate of profit" (interest) on investment in wages, does not represent an exploitation of the workers. Rather, it represents the discounting of future sums relative to present sums. Capitalists pay factory workers in advance of sales. The workers prefer to get wages today, equal to the present (time-discounted) value of the future sales revenue their work will generate, rather than wait for the larger (but later) sum that will arrive only when the output is sold. Socialist critics have naturally decried this as an apology for the capitalist's income (in Marxian terms, *surplus value*).

LHW

See also Banking, Austrian Theory of; Economics, Austrian School of; Hayek, Friedrich A.; Marxism; Mises, Ludwig von; Money and Banking

Further Readings

Böhm-Bawerk, Eugen von. *Capital and Interest.* 3 vols. South Holland, IL: Libertarian Press, 1959.
———. *Karl Marx and the Close of His System.* Paul M. Sweezy, ed. Clifton, NJ: Augustus M. Kelley, 1975.

BRANDEN, NATHANIEL (1930–)

Nathaniel Branden (born Nathan Blumenthal) is known to many as "the father of the self-esteem movement." Branden is the author of 20 books that explore the philosophical, psychological, and cultural foundations of individualism and the free society. Having developed a close personal relationship with novelist and philosopher Ayn Rand (whom he met as a college student in 1950), in 1958 Branden started Nathaniel Branden Lectures, in which he addressed and expanded on the psychological issues raised by Rand. These lectures were later formalized into the Nathaniel Branden Institute (NBI). The NBI disseminated Rand's Objectivist philosophy internationally through live lectures and audiotaped courses. Although his personal and professional relationship with Rand came to an end in 1968, his pioneering work on the psychology of self-esteem contributed to the renaissance of modern individualist and libertarian thought.

A defender of *voluntarism* as a moral concept and of *libertarianism* as a political concept, Branden argued, in *Taking Responsibility*, that "[t]he defining principle of libertarianism is the abolition of the initiation of physical coercion from human relationships." Like Rand, Branden celebrates individualism and personal autonomy as foundational to human freedom. For Branden, a free society cannot be sustained without certain psychological, ethical, and cultural prerequisites.

Among the psychological requirements of a free society are the six pillars of self-esteem—practices essential to the achievement of human authenticity: living consciously, self-acceptance, self-responsibility, self-assertiveness, living purposefully, and personal integrity. Branden sees the need for self-esteem as biological, as furthering human life, and constituting an aspect of an objective ethics that views such life and happiness as the standard of morality.

In *The Six Pillars of Self-Esteem*, he emphasizes the role of culture in both nourishing and suppressing self-esteem, and he challenges the "*forms* of culturally encouraged servitude" that reciprocally reinforce the political forms. Therefore, the struggle for a free society is a struggle for the values of the integrated individual self against groupthink and the entitlement mentality of the welfare state. Such authoritarian and statist political forms draw sustenance from implicit cultural beliefs that sanction conformity, dependence, and self-immolation.

In his clinical practice, Branden stresses a variety of techniques "[t]o honor the self—to honor mind, judgment, values, and convictions" as "the ultimate act of courage" and the ultimate prerequisite for human freedom.

CMS

See also Individualism, Political and Ethical; Rand, Ayn; Voluntarism

Further Readings

Branden, Nathaniel. *The Psychology of Self-Esteem*. 32nd anniversary ed. San Francisco: Jossey-Bass, 2001 [1969].
———. *The Six Pillars of Self-Esteem*. New York: Bantam, 1994.
———. *Taking Responsibility: Self-Reliance and the Accountable Life*. New York: Simon & Schuster, 1996.

BRIGHT, JOHN (1811–1889)

John Bright was a British radical, statesman, and advocate of free trade. With Richard Cobden, Bright successfully agitated for the repeal of Great Britain's Corn Laws, which were import tariffs on grain. Bright also was a proponent of a peaceful, noninterventionist foreign policy, arguing, for instance, against British involvement in the Crimean War, a position that briefly cost him his seat in Parliament. In addition, Bright argued passionately against the Established Church and slavery, as well as for greater independence for Britain's colonies. Indeed, during his life, Bright was best known as an orator, fiery and radical in speech, whereas Cobden, his associate in the Anti-Corn Law League, was considered more pragmatic and measured.

Bright was born in Rochdale in the north of England to a Quaker family. His father, Jacob, owned a cotton mill, where John worked as a young man and eventually became a partner. In 1839, he married Elizabeth Priestman, with whom he had a daughter, Helen. Elizabeth died shortly after Helen's birth, and Bright later married Margaret Elizabeth Leatham, with whom he would have seven children.

Bright was precocious, but had little formal schooling, his father believing that practical experience to be more valuable than academic training. Following a long trip through Europe and the Middle East, Bright returned to Rochdale and soon became involved in politics. The cause that concerned him most, and with which he would forever be associated, was trade. He believed that Britain's tariffs on agricultural goods were impoverishing a large share of its citizenry while benefiting only the landed aristocracy. In 1839, he joined with Cobden, already a well-established statesman, to found the Anti-Corn Law League, tirelessly arguing across the British Isles for free trade. In their near-constant tours on behalf of the cause of liberalized trade, Cobden would speak first, giving the reasoned case for reform, with Bright to follow with a more polemical appeal. In 1843, Bright joined Cobden in Parliament, representing Durham and, later, Manchester and Birmingham.

In 1845, in a speech before the league, Bright made the case against the protection of Great Britain's agricultural sector from foreign competition. He argued that,

> by withdrawing the stimulus of competition, the law prevents the good cultivation of the land of our country, and therefore diminishes the supply of food which we might derive from it. It prevents, at the same time, the importation of foreign food from abroad, and it also prevents the growth of supplies abroad, so that when we are forced to go there for them they are not to be found. . . . The most demoniacal ingenuity could not have invented a scheme more calculated to bring millions of the working classes of this country to a state of pauperism, suffering, discontent, and insubordination than the Corn-law which we are now opposing.

The same year that Bright delivered this speech, Ireland suffered a tragic famine, which eventually cost the lives of well over 1 million people (about 15%) of its population and drove roughly the same number abroad. The famine also led the Tory Prime Minister Robert Peel to introduce a bill to phase out the Corn Laws over a 3-year period. On June 25, 1846, the bill passed the House of Lords. Bright wrote George Wilson, another prominent member of the league, that "we have not seen the last of the Barons, but we have taught them which way the world is turning." In fact, during the ensuing decades, Great Britain as well as much of continental Europe moved toward a general program of freer trade. In July 1846, with the Corn Laws repealed, the league was disbanded.

Bright's commitment to liberalism extended beyond foreign affairs. When Peel proposed to reintroduce an income tax, Bright expressed his outrage in a letter to Cobden. "No government," he wrote, "can have a right to make me state the amount of my profits and it is a vile system of slavery to which Englishmen are about to be subjected." Cobden died in 1865, with Bright at his side. Although he would continue to push for liberal reforms until his own death more than 20 years later, Bright will forever be best known for his efforts to repeal the Corn Laws and bring peace and free trade to Great Britain.

AS

See also Anti-Corn Law League; Cobden, Richard; Free Trade

Further Readings

Ausubel, Herman. *John Bright: Victorian Reformer*. New York: Wiley, 1966.
Bright, John. *Speeches on Questions of Public Policy, Vols. I-II.* James E. Thorold Rogers, ed. New York: Kraus Reprint Co., 1970 [1869].
Robbins, Keith. *John Bright*. London: Routledge, 1979.

BROWN, JOHN (1800–1859)

John Brown, an American abolitionist leader, dedicated his life to the struggle against slavery. His willingness to employ violent tactics set him apart from many of his fellow white abolitionists, as did his support for full legal and social equality of the races and his own personally egalitarian relations with blacks.

Sternly religious, Brown regarded slavery as an affront against God's law and felt he had a divine mission to bring about its abolition. Although Brown's Calvinist Puritanism has often been regarded as essential to his motivation, neither his followers nor his backers were predominantly Calvinist; in fact, most—including his own sons—were freethinkers of various stripes. A student of the history of guerrilla warfare and slave insurrections, Brown was convinced that concerted private action against slavery could topple the system. In

1851, he helped organize a black self-defense league to resist the Fugitive Slave Law, and he personally assisted escaping slaves in the Underground Railroad.

Brown first came to national attention through his participation in the 1855–1858 strife over slavery in "Bleeding Kansas," where he and his followers were involved in a number of antislavery operations, including raids to free slaves (at least 11 people were liberated and smuggled into Canada), standard military battles, and, most controversially, the "Pottawatomie Massacre," in which five proslavery (but not slaveholding) men were taken from their homes and hacked to death with broadswords on the grounds that they "had committed murder in their hearts already." Although Brown, unlike his sons, never expressed regret for this latter targeting of noncombatants, he also never repeated it.

In 1857, Brown traveled to New England to meet with prominent abolitionists and raise money for his cause. Out of these meetings grew the "Secret Six," a clandestine group of wealthy abolitionists who would finance Brown's next antislavery operation—likewise in Kansas, they assumed. In the following year, radical abolitionist Lysander Spooner published a circular, *A Plan for the Abolition of Slavery*, proposing an alliance of blacks and antislavery whites to wage guerrilla war against slaveholders in the South. The authorship of the pamphlet was later mistakenly attributed to Brown. In fact, while agreeing with Spooner's proposals, Brown asked Spooner to stop circulating the *Plan* because it might deprive his own forthcoming project of the element of surprise. In the meantime, Brown had been drafting a provisional constitution intended to govern his own military forces and the territory they should succeed in liberating. A true "social contract," to which no adult was to be bound without his or her express consent, Brown's constitution included suffrage for all adults regardless of race or sex.

On October 16, 1859, Brown led 18 men—13 white and five black—to Harper's Ferry, Virginia, and seized the federal armory. His plan was to use it to arm local slaves and lead them on an insurrectionist campaign. However, Brown, evidently underestimating local resistance and overestimating the readiness of slaves and antislavery whites to flock to his banner, lingered too long and soon found his position besieged first by the local militia and then by U.S. troops under the command of Robert E. Lee. Brown was captured, and over half his force, including two sons, were killed.

Spooner attempted to organize a plot to rescue Brown by kidnapping the governor of Virginia, but the plan fell through owing to lack of funds and Brown's own preference for martyrdom. On December 2, 1859, Brown was hanged for treason.

Brown's raid electrified the nation, terrifying slaveholders and emboldening abolitionists. Ever since, Brown has found demonizers and beatifiers as scholars and activists continue to debate both the moral and strategic merits of Brown's plan. Some give Brown the credit or blame for helping to trigger the Civil War, whereas others speculate that if emancipation had come through Brown-style slave insurrection rather than Union occupation, the freed blacks might have been spared a century of Jim Crow and the country as a whole spared the federal centralization consequent on Union victory.

RL

See also Abolitionism; Civil War, U.S.; Revolution, Right of; Slavery in America; Spooner, Lysander; Thoreau, Henry David

Further Readings

Abels, Jules. *Man on Fire: John Brown and the Cause of Liberty.* New York: Macmillan, 1971.

Carton, Evan. *Patriotic Treason: John Brown and the Soul of America.* New York: Free Press, 2006.

Oates, Stephen B. *To Purge This Land with Blood: A Biography of John Brown.* 2nd ed. Amherst: University of Massachusetts Press, 1984.

Renehan, Edward J., Jr. *The Secret Six: The True Tale of the Men Who Conspired with John Brown.* Columbia: University of South Carolina Press, 1997.

Reynolds, David S. John Brown. *Abolitionist: The Man Who Killed Slavery, Sparked the Civil War, and Seeded Civil Rights.* New York: Vintage, 2005.

Sanborn, Franklin B., ed. *The Life and Letters of John Brown, Liberator of Kansas, and Martyr of Virginia.* Boston: Roberts Brothers, 1891.

Shively, Charles. "Critical Biography of Lysander Spooner." *The Collected Works of Lysander Spooner in Six Volumes; Volume One: Deist, Postal, & Anarchist Writings.* C. Shively, ed. Weston, MA: M&S Press, 1971. 15–62.

BUCHANAN, JAMES M. (1919–)

James M. Buchanan is one of the originators of public choice theory and among the foremost economists of the 20th century. Together with Gordon Tullock, Buchanan revolutionized the way economists view political economy by introducing motivational symmetry between public and private actors. Before Buchanan's contributions, it was standard practice to view market failures as prima facie evidence of the need for government intervention. Public choice theory forced scholars to confront the fact that government failures may be worse than the market failures the government is introduced to correct.

James Buchanan was born in October 1919. After serving in the U.S. Navy, he enrolled in the economics doctoral program at the University of Chicago, where he received his doctorate in economics in 1948. When he started at Chicago, Buchanan considered himself a "libertarian socialist." A price theory course taught by his mentor, Frank Knight, convinced Buchanan that the market was the most appropriate means to the ends he desired as a libertarian. In addition to having been exposed to Knight's work while at Chicago, Buchanan also became familiar with the writings of Knut Wicksell and the Italian school of public finance, all of which would have a profound influence on his contributions to political economy.

Between 1956 and 1969, Buchanan taught at the University of Virginia and Virginia Polytechnic Institute (VPI). While at VPI, Buchanan created the Center for the Study of Public Choice. In 1983, he was prevailed on to move with the Center to George Mason University, where he has remained since. In 1986, Buchanan was awarded the Nobel Prize in Economic Science. Among his most important books are *The Calculus of Consent* (1962), coauthored with Gordon Tullock, and *Cost and Choice* (1969). He later turned his attention to questions of social philosophy, publishing the *Limits of Liberty* (1975), *Liberty, Market and State* (1986), and *The Economics and Ethics of Constitutional Order* (1991). In these works, he laid out a contractarian theory of political philosophy that emphasized the need for establishing "rules of the game" to constrain self-interested political actors where their interests do not align with those of the public.

Buchanan is best known for *The Calculus of Consent,* which was coauthored with Gordon Tullock. This work opened up the theory of public choice, still in its infancy, and refocused the profession's attention on a realistic versus a romantic conception of politics. Against the prevailing tendency in political economy, Buchanan and Tullock argued that private costs and benefits guide individuals' decision making in politics just as they do in markets. Simply moving from the private sphere to the public does not transform interests from those that are self-concerned to those that are devoted to the public good. Depicting politicians as benevolent despots is therefore foolhardy. Realistic political analyses must start with the same assumptions about rationally self-interested behavior as economic ones.

Buchanan's "economics of politics" transformed political economy on several fronts. Implicit in its conclusions were questions relating to, among others, problems of functional finance, the theory of rent seeking, and democracy's short-sighted policy bias. Perhaps most important for advocates of the market, his theory provided a powerful warning against government intervention. To believe that government can correct market failures, we must first assume that political agents charged with this task desire to pursue the public good. Buchanan also argued against the ability of political actors to identify the public good. Furthermore, we tend to assume that, when confronted with a choice between using power for private ends and using it for public ends, politicians will choose the latter. But if political actors are as self-interested as private actors responsible for market failure, why should this notion be true?

The logic of Buchanan's insight suggests that calls for state intervention will often suffer from the fallacy of the "Emperor's Singing Contest." According to an ancient tale, the king wished to determine which of two singers was superior. He thus held a contest in which each would sing for him. On the day of the contest, the king listened to the first singer and was horrified by what he heard. He then declared the second singer the victor because she was clearly the better of the two. The problem, of course, was that, in reality, the second singer may have been even worse than the first. The tale suggests that those who observe market failure are prepared to automatically respond by calling for government correction without first considering what that "correction" entails. Allowing for symmetry between individuals' motivations in politics and the market means that there may be good reason to think that in many cases government failure will be worse than that of the market. This reasoning is especially true if the constraints on undesirable behavior that decision makers face in the political sphere are weaker than those faced by decision makers in the market.

As a consequence of these conclusions, Buchanan is concerned with how to effectively design rules that bind rulers and prevent them from pursuing personal ends at the expense of society. He sees constitutions as a crucial mechanism for political constraint and distinguishes between two levels of rules. The first level establishes the overarching rules of the game. It establishes the "rules about the rules," so to speak. This level is the realm of constitutions. The second level concerns the strategies that individuals pursue within the bounds of the rules established at the first level. This level is the realm of policy. Establishing constitutions to devise proper rules at the meta level will shape the incentives that guide rule making at the second level, where policies that directly affect citizens are implemented.

Buchanan's insights have had a profound effect on the way political economists view the government's relationship to the market. It is now largely true that the "public choice costs" of government activity are considered in deciding the desirability of proposed interventions. At the least, Buchanan's work has forced political economists to reconsider how they model the behavior of political actors and to evaluate government actions not as if they were being undertaken by angels, but instead as if they are undertaken by real people.

PTL

See also Constitutionalism; Market Failure; Public Choice
  Economics; Tullock, Gordon; Wicksell, Knut

Further Readings

Boettke, Peter. "Hayek, Arrow, and the Problems of Democratic Decision-Making." *Journal of Public Finance and Public Choice* 20 no. 1 (2002): 9–21.
———. "James M. Buchanan and the Rebirth of Political Economy." *Against the Grain: Dissent in Economics.* Steve Pressman and Ric Holt, eds. Aldershot, UK: Edward Elgar Publishing, 1998.
Boettke, Peter, and Peter Leeson. "Liberalism, Socialism and Robust Political Economy." *Journal of Markets and Morality* 7 no. 1 (2004): 99–111.
Mitchell, William, and Randy Simmons. *Beyond Politics: Markets, Welfare and the Failure of Bureaucracy.* Boulder, CO: Westview Press, 1994.
Wagner, Richard. *To Promote the General Welfare: Market Processes vs. Political Transfers.* San Francisco: Pacific Research Institute, 1989.

BUCKLE, HENRY THOMAS (1821–1862)

Henry Thomas Buckle was an eminent British historian. He was born at Lee, in Kent. Despite having had no formal education, he was to become one of the most celebrated British historians of the 19th century. Traveling widely, he taught himself 19 languages and devoted himself to writing an extensive and detailed history of English civilization.

The vast extent of this project can be gauged by Buckle's book, *Introduction to the History of Civilization in England* (originally published in two volumes, 1857 and 1861), which became an international best seller. The definitive critical edition of this work, edited by J. M. Robertson, consists more than 900 pages in small type, and this edition was merely intended to be an introduction to additional volumes. Buckle never lived to complete his project. Always in frail health and having worked himself to exhaustion, he died in Damascus at age 42.

Buckle's *Introduction* is usually remembered for its defense of the thesis that history is governed by deterministic laws of mental development, most notably the progress of knowledge. Also significant is its strident defense of laissez-faire liberalism.

The *Introduction* is a comparative intellectual history—richly detailed and meticulously documented—of four countries: England, Spain, France, and Scotland. Buckle traces the development of individual liberty in each country and attempts to isolate the factors that explain why freedom was more prevalent in some countries than in others. The result is a masterpiece of libertarian literature, but also a work that is virtually unknown to modern readers.

GHS

See also Liberalism, Classical; Progress; Whiggism

Further Readings

Buckle, Henry Thomas. *Introduction to the History of Civilization in England.* J. M. Robertson, ed. New York: Albert and Charles Boni, 1925.

Huth, Alfred Henry. *The Life and Writings of Henry Thomas Buckle.* New York: Appleton, 1880.

BUREAUCRACY

Although the term *bureaucracy* was used before Max Weber's elaboration of the notion and his well-known analysis of the phenomenon, his work and theories framed all subsequent approaches to the subject. From this perspective, the bureaucratic organization is a professional corps of officials organized in a pyramidal hierarchy characterized by a rational, uniform, and impersonal regulation of inferior–superior relationships. That hierarchy is based on the specialization of tasks and division of labor, with clear and specific supervision and appeal systems. The officials are not elected, and they cannot appropriate their offices. A derivative, popular usage of the term has the pejorative meaning of organizational pathology, functional rigidity, excessive formalism, abuse of official influence, and even corruption.

The libertarian perspective focuses mainly on political bureaucracy. It takes as its starting point the Weberian notion, but enlarges the picture by taking a systemic and comparative view. The comparative standpoint emphasizes the fact that the real nature of bureaucracy and bureaucratic management can be fully understood only when compared to profit and market-oriented management. When the ultimate organizational goal is profit, the method by which success or failure is assessed is clear: the assessment of profit or loss. The operational principle is unambiguous, and the degree of its application is measurable for the whole business and for any of its parts. Therefore, the structure and management of the organization are guided by it. However, organizations that do not have profit as an objective and cannot use market-oriented operational principles must find some method to ensure that they are performing their intended functions adequately. Thus, these organizations develop rules, procedures, and monitoring and control systems. The result is bureaucratic management, whose operational principle is compliance with detailed rules and regulations fixed by a hierarchical authority. Consequently, bureaucracy must be seen as a response to the absence of the sanctions provided by profit and loss.

This comparison of bureaucratic organizations with those based on profit maximization reveals just a part of the phenomenon. We are provided an even more comprehensive picture when we consider the systemic aspect of bureaucracies. Bureaucracy is intrinsically connected to the political system; it is part and parcel of its structure and functioning. Thus, the growth of bureaucracy is a symptom of a specific dynamic associated with political systems and not something that can be studied in isolation. The main cause of the bureaucratization of a society is the appropriation of economic and social functions by the government. As Ludwig von Mises put it, "The culprit is not the bureaucrat but the political system." Officials and bureaucratic structures are just the tools or agents for "exercising whatever powers have been acquired by government." Once these functions are centralized and are to be exercised by the government, instead of by private enterprise, the need for bureaucratic tools increases. Thus, the number of bureaucrats and offices increases with the volume of decisions entrusted to the government.

There are several noteworthy corollaries that follow from combining both the systemic and comparative approaches to bureaucracy. One corollary is that an organization is not bureaucratic unless it can evade the sanctions of the market. The farther away from the market, the more bureaucratic an organization is. The second corollary is that the analysis of bureaucracy is clearly distinct from an indictment of bureaucracy per se. Bureaucracy and bureaucratic methods are old and they are present in every system of governance of a certain level of complexity. In some cases, some amount of bureaucracy is even indispensable. The problem is not bureaucracy as such, but the intrusion of government into all spheres of private life.

Even if they were to accept the existence and, in some cases, even the necessity of bureaucratic management, libertarians have a rather pessimistic view of its internal workings. Public choice literature initiated by Gordon Tullock is a reliable guide in this respect. First of all, the literature questions the measures by which a bureaucratic organization is able to accomplish its declared objectives. It also notes the significant slippage between what the ostensible function of such an organization is and what actually goes on. Incentives and operating procedures are rarely structured so that individual interests intermesh to achieve whatever explicitly formulated organizational goals have been set. Moreover, certain goals cannot be realized by hierarchical organizations at all. The more complex the coordination of activities needed to achieve the objective, the more inefficient the bureaucratic instrument to achieve it will be. Coordination requires supervisory relationships, and each such relationship results in slippage. In addition, the errors of one supervisory level are accumulated at each subsequent level. The more levels of coordination are necessary, the greater is the amount of cumulative error. Thus, such supervision is costly and difficult to implement, and the costs of achieving organizational objectives get higher and higher. In the end, supervision becomes completely inadequate, and the organization is totally inefficient. Nonetheless, in a bureaucracy, the tendency of the bureaucratic superior is to build ever-larger bureaucratic structures, which fail to achieve their goals while growing increasingly inefficient. Thus, as Tullock put it, "the inefficiency of the over-expanded bureaucracy leads to still further expansion and still further inefficiency," so that "most modern governmental hierarchies are much beyond their efficient organizational limits." Finally, the ways in which bureaucrats advance in the bureaucratic world are structurally adversarial to the organization's objectives. In most cases, the incentives are set up in such a way that, to secure promotion, the situation requires actions contrary to the attainment of the objectives of the organization, and the bureaucrat will never choose a course of action detrimental to one's own advancement.

In summary, bureaucratic forms of organization have deep structural problems in effectively and efficiently accomplishing their tasks. It rests with decentralized modes of decision making, such as the market, to accomplish such tasks. That is the reason that libertarian literature considers the analysis of bureaucracy a good laboratory for the study of capitalism and socialism as forms of social organization. In thoroughly investigating the problems of bureaucracy, one is likely to discover some of the most fundamental social mechanisms and organizational pathologies that make socialist utopias entirely impracticable.

PDA

See also Mises, Ludwig von; Public Choice Economics; Spontaneous Order; Subsidiarity; Tullock, Gordon

Further Readings

Mises, Ludwig Von. *Bureaucracy*. New Rochelle, NY: Arlington House, 1969.
Niskanen, William A. *Bureaucracy and Public Economics*. Brookfield, VT: E. Elgar, 1994.
Tullock, Gordon. *The Politics of Bureaucracy*. Washington, DC: Public Affairs Press, 1965.
Weber, Max. *The Theory of Social and Economic Organization*. New York: Oxford University Press, 1964.
Wilson, James Q. *Bureaucracy: What Government Agencies Do and Why They Do It*. New York: Basic Books, 2000.

Burke, Edmund (1729–1797)

Edmund Burke, an Irish-born British politician and philosopher, served in the House of Commons for almost 30 years and authored an extensive and influential body of speeches and books. Conventionally held to be the "father of conservatism," Burke was a Whig whose influence on classical liberalism was considerable. Although his rich oeuvre spans four decades, Burke has become most famous for a series of works written in the last 7 years of his life in vehement opposition to the French Revolution, beginning with *Reflections on the Revolution in France* (1790) and followed by publications with a similar theme, such as *An Appeal from the New Whigs to the Old Whigs* (1791) and *Letters on a Regicide Peace* (1796).

Burke never wrote a theoretical treatise systematically spelling out his philosophy of government. Although his *Vindication of Natural Society*, published in 1756, offered a deft defense of anarchism, Burke later claimed it was solely a satire. His writings were often motivated by political crises and, therefore, were tentative and occasional. As a result, later commentators have accused Burke of inconsistency. However, it is not difficult to see that Burke adhered to a core philosophy centered on his concept of *ordered liberty*.

As a Whig, Burke defended the political settlement of 1688, when the English had rebelled against a king who had refused to have his power curtailed by either by Parliament or England's "ancient constitution." The Whigs' belief in limited, constitutional government emerged most clearly in Burke's position on three great political causes—his opposition to attempts by George III to limit the power of Parliament; the arbitrary power exercised by Britain over its colonies in America, Ireland, and India; and the overthrow of the old order during the French Revolution.

Burke rejected all abuse of power that resulted from ignoring the limits placed on political authority by constitutions—"the distribution by law of powers of declaring and applying the law." Burke, moreover, acknowledged the existence of an "unalterable constitution of things," from which one could derive a concept of natural law. In India, the corrupt governor general, Warren Hastings (who was impeached on accusation by Burke, but ultimately acquitted), may have had the letter of the law on his side, but he maintained that Hastings had violated the fundamental demands of natural justice.

In his antirevolutionary works, Burke attacked radical French Enlightenment philosophy, which he regarded as having inspired the French Revolution. Influenced by Scottish Enlightenment writers such as David Hume and Adam Smith, Burke warned that society is of an order of complexity such that no one mind, no matter how refined, could fully comprehend all its interlocking parts. Tradition, customs, and manners that form our social institutions are invaluable because they are the products of countless interacting minds, representing the past and the present, depositories of the wisdom of the ages. The French rejected this implicit knowledge as superstition and instead sought to reorder society in accordance with abstract theories, what Burke's intellectual heir, F. A. Hayek, would later call *constructivism*.

Burke believed in the rights of men, but not in absolute "natural rights," rights that antecede the institutions under which we live. In his view, the rights we possess by nature are only those that men have in the state of rude nature—the prepolitical, primitive state wherein each man is his own judge and executioner. In civil society, men have rights that are derived from actual, historical circumstances, including the right to justice between their fellows, to the fruits of their industry, and, indeed, to do whatever they can separately do without trespassing on others.

In economics, as Adam Smith contended, Burke and he thought exactly alike. Burke's main economic work, *Thoughts and Details on Scarcity* (1795), was written for Prime Minister William Pitt in opposition to a proposal that the government subsidize agricultural wages. The work was published posthumously in 1800. In it Burke saw no role whatever for the state in economic life. He believed it is not prudent for the state to provide for the necessities of the people because the government can do "very little positive good in this, or perhaps in anything else." State redistribution of wealth harms the rich without doing the poor any good. He defended freedom of contract against "the zealots of the sect of regulation" and argued for unregulated trade and commerce. The laws of commerce are the laws of nature, wrote Burke, and they are broken at man's peril. Disturbing the balance of the market would lay the "axe to the root of production itself."

Although he has been hailed by historians of political thought as the father of modern-day conservatism, Burke's conclusions often reflected prevailing Whig doctrine, especially in his opposition to the policy of the government in its quarrel with the American colonies.

MV

See also American Revolution; Conservatism; French Revolution; Spontaneous Order; Whiggism

Further Readings

Canavan, Francis. *The Political Economy of Edmund Burke: The Role of Property in His Thought*. New York: Fordham University Press, 1995.

Mansfield, Harvey C. *Statesmanship and Party Government. A Study of Burke and Bolingbroke*. Chicago: University of Chicago Press, 1965.

Raeder, Linda C. "The Liberalism/Conservatism of Edmund Burke and F. A. Hayek: A Critical Comparison." *Humanitas* 10 (1997).

Stanlis, Peter. *Edmund Burke and the Natural Law*. Ann Arbor: University of Michigan Press, 1957.

Wilkins, Burleigh Taylor. *The Problem of Burke's Political Philosophy*. Oxford: Clarendon Press, 1967.

BURLAMAQUI, JEAN-JACQUES (1694–1748)

Jean-Jacques Burlamaqui was a legal and political theorist who played an important part in intellectual history as the popularizer and transmitter of ideas more fully developed and articulated by others. The nature of these ideas and their influence, through his mediation, on several important historical figures accords Burlamaqui an important place in the history of classical liberal thought and politics. Born in Geneva, Switzerland, he grew up in the early years of the Enlightenment and became a professor of ethics and natural law at the University of Geneva at the early age of 25. He taught there for 15 years with great success before having to retire due to ill health. He also maintained a voluminous correspondence with many other intellectuals, both on the Continent and in Britain. After retiring, he was active in local politics, but he seems to have spent much of his time writing the two works for which he was best known, *Principles of Natural Law* (1747) and *Principles of Political Right* (1751).

These two books are, in the main, compendia or digests of the thoughts of other legal theorists, notably Cumberland and Grotius, and are written in an expository style. As such, they were popular and were soon translated into many languages, including English, as well as being read in the original French. They were the main vehicle by which ideas of natural law and its application to politics entered the English-speaking world, above all the American colonies. The work of Bernard Bailyn showed that Burlamaqui was one of the most widely read and cited authors among the founding generation and the immediate source of much of what we now regard as the politics embraced by the founding fathers. As such, although now largely forgotten, he deserves considerably wider notice.

SD

See also American Revolution; Locke, John; Natural Law

Further Readings

Baylin, Bernard. *The Ideological Origins of the American Revolution*. Cambridge, MA: Harvard University Press, 1992.

Burlamaqui, Jean-Jacques. *The Principles of Natural and Politic Law*. Thomas Nugent, trans. Indianapolis, IN: Liberty Fund, 2006.

Harvey, Ray Forrest. *Jean Jacques Burlamaqui: A Liberal Tradition in American Constitutionalism*. Chapel Hill: University of North Carolina Press, 1937.

CAMPAIGN FINANCE

Prior to the late 19th century, there were no laws governing campaign financing. Candidates were free to raise and spend any amounts of money from any source. However, over the last 100 years, state and federal regulation of campaign spending and contributions has proliferated. While limited in its effectiveness by the creative talents of political consultants and campaign managers, and checked in scope by the courts on 1st Amendment grounds, and at that only irregularly, these regulations now play a major role in shaping American politics, and campaign finance litigation has become an important campaign strategy.

The earliest campaign finance laws, which banned corporate contributions, were passed in the plains states in the wake of the 1896 presidential election, when corporate support helped fuel William McKinley's victory over farm-state favorite William Jennings Bryan. Federal regulation began with passage of the Tillman Act in 1907, which prohibited contributions by federally chartered banks and corporations. Congress proceeded to pass legislation closing "loopholes" or otherwise expanding the reach of campaign finance regulation in 1910, 1911, 1925, 1939, 1940, 1943, and again in 1947. Along the way, contributions from general corporate and union treasuries to federal candidates were barred, a prohibition that remains a cornerstone of campaign finance law.

In 1971, Congress completely overhauled the law with the passage of the Federal Elections Campaign Act (FECA), which underwent major changes in 1974. In addition to the ban on direct corporate and union contributions, the 1974 Amendments to the FECA limited individual contributions to candidates to $1,000 per election and limited the contributions of political action committees (PACs) to $5,000 (PACs are a mechanism allowing like-minded citizens to pool their small contributions in order to increase

the impact of their efforts). Individuals' contributions to political parties and PACs also were limited, as was the total amount of contributions one could make to all parties and candidates for federal office. The amendments also put a ceiling on total spending in House and Senate races, to just $75,000 in the case of races for the House and to an amount based on state population in Senate races. Additionally, individuals and groups were prohibited from spending more than $1,000 on any communication "related to" a candidate for federal office. Other provisions required the disclosure by a candidate or political committee of any contribution or expenditure in excess of $100. Finally, the act provided for government financing of presidential campaigns at both the primary and general election stages.

The 1974 amendments to the FECA were immediately challenged in federal court on 1st Amendment grounds by a broad coalition of plaintiffs, including the American Civil Liberties Union, the Libertarian Party, former Democratic Senator Eugene McCarthy, and Conservative-Republican Senator James Buckley. In *Buckley v. Valeo*, 424 U.S. 1 (1976), the Supreme Court recognized that the limits included in the FECA infringed on 1st Amendment rights of political association and free speech inasmuch as publishing a newspaper or taking out an ad in a newspaper, operating or advertising on a radio station, renting a hall for a speech, and printing leaflets all cost money. Recognizing this infringement of the 1st Amendment, the Court struck down the FECA's various spending limits, rejecting "the concept that the government may restrict the speech of some elements of our society in order to enhance the relative voice of others," as "wholly foreign to the First Amendment." However, the Court concluded that the government did have a compelling interest in "the prevention of corruption and the appearance of corruption spawned by the real or imagined coercive influence of large contributions on candidates' positions and on their actions." It then held that this interest was sufficiently compelling to justify limits on campaign contributions, despite the resulting infringements on constitutionally protected liberties.

Significantly, however, the Court interpreted the statutory phrase "related to" a candidate for office to be restricted to "communications that in express terms advocate the election or defeat of a candidate. . . ." A footnote explained that this category would include only political ads using phrases such as "vote for," "elect," "support," "defeat," and "vote against." Any broader interpretation, the Court held, would be so vague as to unduly burden all discussion of political issues. Thanks to this interpretation, political discussion, including the discussion of candidates for office, has remained largely beyond the reach of regulation so long as the speaker avoids such "express advocacy" of the election or defeat of a candidate. Furthermore, the Court held that even expenditures using such terms of express advocacy could not be limited if they were made independent of a candidate's campaign, on the grounds, first, that truly independent expenditures did not pose a danger of quid pro quo corruption, and, second, that even if they did, the ban would not eliminate that danger because "it would naively underestimate the ingenuity and resourcefulness of persons and groups desiring to buy influence to believe that they would have much difficulty devising expenditures that skirted the restriction on express advocacy of election or defeat but nevertheless benefited the candidate's campaign."

Finally, the Court also held that forced disclosure of campaign contributions made for express advocacy and the government funding system for presidential campaigns were constitutional. A substantial majority of states, and many local units of government, have passed legislation similar to the FECA, although usually without providing government funding of campaigns.

Buckley v. Valeo has been widely criticized by both those who think it gave too much protection to campaign giving and spending and those who think it gave too little protection to such political activities. However, the Supreme Court has rejected several opportunities to overrule *Buckley* and at the same time extended its reasoning to strike down, on 1st Amendment grounds, a number of limitations that had been imposed by various levels of government: limits on corporate contributions and spending in noncandidate races in *First National Bank of Boston v. Bellotti*, 435 U.S. 765 (1978); limits on contributions to ballot issues and petition drives in *Citizens Against Rent Control v. City of Berkeley*, 454 U.S. 290 (1981) and *Meyer v. Grant*, 486 U.S. 414 (1988); limits on spending by nonprofit, "ideological" corporations in *Federal Election Commission v. Massachusetts Citizens for Life*, 479 U.S. 238 (1986); and bans on independent expenditures by political parties in *Colorado Republican Federal Campaign Committee v. Federal Election Commission*, 518 U.S. 604 (1996).

Even as the courts adhered to *Buckley*, political scientists, economists, legal scholars, and activists engaged in a long-running debate over the empirical effects of efforts to control political spending and contributions. Critics of regulation point to a growing body of evidence showing that, whatever their intention, in practice contribution and spending limits favor incumbents over challengers, unduly burden grassroots political activists, and benefit powerful interests that have an institutional presence in the capital over broader, more diffuse interests. Moreover, studies by political scientists and economists indicate that campaign contributions have only minimal effects on legislative behavior, threatening to undercut the anticorruption rationale that justifies such limitations. These studies find that contributors tend to give to candidates who already agree with them, and that ideology, party affiliation, and constituency demands play a far greater role in determining voting patterns than do campaign contributions. Proponents of greater regulation have responded that these studies fail to capture the extent of contribution-related corruption because they focus on measurable activities such as voting records, ignoring less measurable forms of "corruption" such as "the speech not given." However, others argue that if contributions are corrupting, such corruption should show at the final stage of the process, where the contributor is most interested in the result.

In any case, the changes that occurred in campaigning strategy, many in direct response to contribution limits, have made those limits less and less effective. By the elections of 2000, an increasingly large percentage of total campaign spending took the form of unregulated "issue advocacy" ads paid for by parties and interest groups that praised or criticized candidates, but stopped short of specifically urging the election or defeat of given candidates. By avoiding such "express advocacy," the ads remained outside the regulatory reach of the FECA or similar state laws. The money expended in this way was dubbed "soft money." Many critics argued that issue ads funded by soft money were more negative, less informative, and less accountable than traditional campaign ads. But others point out that, in addition to the 1st Amendment issues involved, the growth of such issue ads was the result of limits on direct contributions to candidates and especially the failure to raise such limits to keep pace with inflation and population growth.

In 2002, Congress passed the Bipartisan Campaign Reform Act, more commonly known by the names of its Senate sponsors as the McCain–Feingold Act. The law prohibited political parties from receiving or spending soft money on noncandidate ads and activities. Additionally, it prohibited any corporation, including nonprofit membership corporations, from spending more than $10,000 to air broadcast ads mentioning a candidate within 30 days of a primary or 60 days of a general election. These controversial provisions were upheld by the Supreme Court in *McConnell v. Federal Election Commission*. These restrictions did little to prevent corruption of the political system, however.

Rather, during the first 5 years of the McCain–Feingold regime, the practice of "earmarking"—in which Congress marks spending for specific projects, often to the benefit of narrow special interests—grew rapidly, and Congress was rocked by a series of ethical scandals.

Despite the failure of past "reforms," many reform advocates continue to urge that the government pay for campaigns with tax dollars, either in addition to or in place of private financing. However, polls have consistently shown that the public is strongly opposed to expanded government financing of political campaigns, and at the federal level, fewer than 10% of taxpayers take advantage of the opportunity, provided on tax forms, to divert $3 of their taxes to the presidential election campaign fund. Further, assuming corruption exists, whether government financing would actually address this alleged corruption is in dispute. Few observers think that government financing has made presidential campaigns and elections superior to privately financed congressional campaigns and elections. Additionally, critics of government financing argue that it is immoral or unconstitutional to require taxpayers to fund political speech with which they may disagree.

Had the Supreme Court, in *Buckley* and later cases, not ruled as it had, there is little doubt that political speech would be much more heavily regulated than it currently is. Nevertheless, a substantial and well-financed lobby exists that advocates greater regulation, and the news media, which is exempted from most regulatory proposals, remains highly supportive of limits on paid political speech. Thus, until and unless the Supreme Court extends *Buckley* to protect all political speech and strikes down limits on contributions, campaign finance reform will remain a source of controversy on the national political agenda.

BAS

See also Corruption; Freedom of Speech; Regulation; Rent Seeking

Further Readings

Anderson, Annelise G., ed. *Political Money: Deregulating American Politics; Selected Writings on Campaign Finance Reform.* Stanford, CA: Hoover Institution Press, 2000.

BeVier, Lillian. "Money and Politics: A Perspective on the First Amendment and Campaign Finance Reform." *California Law Review* 73 no. 4 (July 1985): 1045–1090.

Corrado, Anthony et al., eds. *Campaign Finance Reform: A Sourcebook.* Washington, DC: Brookings Institution, 1997.

Malbin, Michael J., and Thomas Gais. *The Day after Reform: Sobering Campaign Finance Lessons from the American States.* Albany, NY: Rockefeller Institute Press, 1998.

Miller, James C. *Monopoly Politics.* Stanford, CA: Hoover Institution Press, 1999.

Palda, Filip. *How Much Is Your Vote Worth: The Unfairness of Campaign Spending Limits.* San Francisco: ICS Press, 1994.

Samples, John. *The Fallacy of Campaign Finance Reform.* Chicago: University of Chicago Press, 2006.

Smith, Bradley A. *Unfree Speech: The Folly of Campaign Finance Regulation.* Princeton, NJ: Princeton University Press, 2001.

CANTILLON, RICHARD (C. 1680–1734)

Richard Cantillon, born in County Kerry in Ireland and lived a substantial portion of his life in France, was regarded by many historians of economic thought as one of the truly great early economists. He has been praised in the highest terms: Edwin Cannan referred to him as "that extraordinary genius," W. S. Jevons has credited him with having written "the first treatise on economics," while F. A. Hayek wrote of him that he contributed more "really original insights of permanent value" to economics than any other writer before 1776.

Although born in Ireland, Cantillon early amassed a fortune as a banker in Paris largely because he foresaw the collapse of John Law's Mississippi scheme. Although his *Essai sur la nature du commerce en général* (*Essay on the Nature of Trade in General*) was published posthumously in 1755 (more than 20 years after Cantillon had been murdered in his London home), this book was originally written in English around 1730. After Cantillon translated his own book into French for the convenience of a friend, this version circulated in manuscript and influenced a number of French intellectuals, including François Quesnay, the founder of the Physiocrat School. Unfortunately, the original English version has not survived.

According to Cantillon, land (i.e., natural resources) is the "source" or "matter" of wealth, whereas labor is the "form" that produces it. Wealth "is nothing but the maintenance, conveniences, and superfluities of life."

Cantillon distinguishes between the "intrinsic" price of a commodity and its "market" price. The intrinsic price—or what Adam Smith would later call the "natural" price—is basically the cost of production, which is the minimum price that sellers must receive as an incentive to bring their goods to market.

Although there is a tendency for the market price of a good to gravitate toward the intrinsic price, "it often happens that many things which have actually this intrinsic value are not sold in the market according to that value." Rather, market prices, which are arrived at through bargaining, depend on the subjective "humors and fancies of men and their consumption."

Among Cantillon's many contributions to economic theory, three should be mentioned:

1. Cantillon developed an abstract model of a self-regulating free market. Throughout the *Essai*, Cantillon refers to the "natural" phenomena of the market; these

are cause–effect relationships that operate independently of the desires and intentions of particular individuals. F. A. Hayek has noted that Cantillon, in developing his theory of an economic system governed by natural laws, uses "the method of isolating abstraction," including "the device of the ceteris paribus clause," with "true virtuosity."

2. He was the first to examine the role of the *entrepreneur* (a term he apparently coined) in detail. An entrepreneur is a person who derives his profit from successfully dealing with the inherent "risk" and "uncertainty" in a free market.

3. Cantillon offered a detailed analysis of inflation. Although the "quantity theory" of money, according to which the injection of new money will cause a general increase of prices, was known to earlier theorists (e.g., John Locke), Cantillon was the first to explain the differential effects of inflation on the *structure* of prices. This differential impact, which depends on which segments of the economy are the earliest recipients of the new money, has become known as the "Cantillon effect." These contributions, among others, helped lay the foundation of modern economics and have ensured Cantillon's place as a theorist of the first rank.

GHS

See also Classical Economics; Entrepreneurship; Money and Banking; Physiocracy; Smith, Adam

Further Readings

Aspromourgos, Tony. *On the Origins of Classical Economics: Distribution and Value from William Petty to Adam Smith.* New York: Routledge, 1996.
Cantillon, Richard. *Essays on the Nature of Commerce in General.* Henry Higgs, trans. New Brunswick, NJ: Transaction, 2001.
Mark Blaug, ed. *Richard Cantillon and Jacques Turgot.* Brookfield, VT: Edward Elgar, 1991.

Capitalism

Capitalism as an economic system is the central feature of economic modernity. No other way of organizing a modern economy has proved successful. Libertarians broadly support and defend it against its critics while arguing for a purer, less compromised version.

Capitalism is a term widely used in contemporary economic and political debate. Originally pejorative, since the 1960s it has become a neutral term, employed by both supporters and critics of the phenomenon it describes. Broadly, *capitalism* is used to mean an economic system in which the means of production (accumulated assets or capital) are privately owned and in which the use made of those assets in the productive process is determined by the choices made by their owners. A second part of the definition, used more by supporters than critics, is that the choices should be voluntary, as reflected in exchanges and agreements entered into freely. Assuming that owners (those who offer goods and services to others) will generally seek to maximize their return from assets, economic activity will be largely market-driven (i.e., determined by the choices of consumers and producers in a system of free exchange or "market relations"). These relationships generate prices, which act as signals, and the choices made by the owners will, in the main, be responses to those signals.

This widely used and understood definition has a number of problems, however. It is to some extent an "ideal type" that does not reflect the messier and complicated reality. More seriously, it makes *capitalism* almost a synonym for *market economy*—that is, for any economic system based on private property and exchange. This near equivalence can be misleading and reflects a lack of understanding of the historicity of both the term and the phenomenon because the word did not come into widespread use until the later 19th century. Capitalism as an economic system is a specific kind of market economy, with certain distinctive features, that came into being during the 19th century and was, arguably, not fully realized until the 1920s.

The actual word *capitalism* is of comparatively recent origin. Rather surprisingly, Marx never used it in any of his published works and only employed it at all in some of his correspondence toward the end of his life. (He did of course use *capital* to mean productive resources and did sometimes refer to *capitalists*, although he more often referred to the *bourgeoisie*.) According to the *Oxford English Dictionary*, the first recorded use of the word in print was by William Makepeace Thackeray, in 1854, in his satirical novel, *The Newcomes*. However, it did not achieve widespread use until the 1890s, and its first extended use as a term of description and analysis came in 1902 in Werner Sombart's *Der Moderne Kapitalismus*. It was soon widely adopted, and by the 1920s it had become the normally used term for the status quo challenged by the new socialist system of the Soviet Union and by socialist parties everywhere. Until the 1920s, most people who opposed socialism or proposals for state intervention did not use the word *capitalism* to describe the kind of economic and social system they advocated. Instead, the term of choice was usually *individualism. Capitalism*, for authors such as Sombart, was a term of opprobrium, but, as so often happens, it was soon taken up by its targets as a badge of honor. One of the first examples of this was the book, *Confessions of a Capitalist*, by the English publisher and intellectual activist Sir Ernest Benn in 1925; it was soon followed by others. Even so, many preferred to use such terms as *free enterprise* or *the competitive system*; it is only since the 1960s that capitalism has come to be used by both sides of the argument in equal measure. One important milestone in this process was the publication in 1962 of Milton Friedman's *Capitalism and Freedom*, one of the first popular books to employ the term in an unabashedly positive way. Another important landmark was the 1969 collection of essays, *Capitalism: The Unknown Ideal*, by Ayn Rand and several other authors, including Alan Greenspan.

Since about the 1920s, *capitalism* has meant—in broad terms—a system that combines private property in the means of production with the shaping of economic activity by market exchange. This usage reflects its origins in the debate between advocates of various kinds of socialism (who argued for doing away with one or both of the two elements) and those who opposed socialism for a variety of reasons. However, this usage is deeply problematic. When not used simply to mean "the way things are," it makes capitalism the same thing as a market economy, and, indeed, many authors treat the two terms as synonymous. There are two problems with this implication. The first, relatively less important, is that the definition given earlier does not correspond to the actual messy reality of existing modern economic life. In particular, it ignores the frequently prominent role of the state and the ways in which the owners of resources capture and use political power for their own advantage and frequently respond to political signals as much as market ones. This is true, but it does not call into question the usual use of the term as a Weberian *ideal type*, contrasted to the equally abstract ideal type of *socialism* or *command economy*.

The much more serious difficulty is that the contemporary use of capitalism is largely ahistorical. This comment may sound strange given the now extensive historiography, but it is broadly true. If capitalism is the combination of private property and market allocation and thus much the same as *market economy*, then the problem is to locate it historically. Both private property and markets have existed in almost every period of recorded history; in fact, it is those episodes where one or both have been absent that stand out. The difficulty is that differences between, for example, the medieval or early modern European economy and today's are so great that to use the same term to describe them both makes that word almost meaningless. Marxists try to avoid this problem by using capitalism as the label for one of the successive stages of economic development in Marx's schema of history. They argue that primitive communism is followed by ancient economies based on slavery, then by feudalism, based on fealty relations, which in turn is succeeded by capitalism, which is based on market relationships. In each stage, there is a ruling class that controls the dominant factor of production (i.e., slave owners/landowners/capitalists). This schema makes capitalism a discrete stage in economic history. However, the escape is only apparent. Empirical research reveals that markets and privately owned accumulations of productive assets (capital) are found in most times and places, and it becomes almost impossible to give any kind of date to the periodization. Marxist historians, following Marx, have variously located the change from feudalism to capitalism in the 14th, 17th, and 18th centuries. Non-Marxist historians have attempted to distinguish between the industrial capitalism of the modern world and earlier variants, described as *agrarian* or *mercantile* capitalism. Again, it proves extremely difficult to locate these forms chronologically and this ambiguity makes capitalism no more than another term for *exchange-based economic activity*.

The solution to this conundrum, which gives the term capitalism a more precise meaning and also enhances our understanding of the modern world, is to distinguish among the categories of *market*, *market economy*, and *capitalism*. The best example of this kind of analysis is in the monumental three-part work of Fernand Braudel's *Material Civilization and Capitalism*. Economic activities that involve trade and exchange have existed throughout human history. However, they are not the only kind of economic activity. There also is the range of phenomena that are economic inasmuch as they involve manipulation of scarce resources to increase wealth, but that do not involve trade, exchange, or money. Such activity belongs to the sphere of domestic or everyday life and is the predominant feature of a subsistence economy, such as that of Carolingian Europe. An economy where trade relations are widespread or even dominant is a market economy. However, the class of market economies or, to put it another way, of market-based economic systems is large and diverse, both in theory and regarding real historical examples. Thus, the mercantile market economy of the classical Islamic world is different from both its ancient predecessor and the modern kind of market economy. In this way of thinking, capitalism is a specific kind of market economy with distinctive features. It also is historically located inasmuch as it appeared in a particular and identifiable time and place.

If all kinds of market economy feature private ownership and exchange, what then are the distinctive features of the capitalist variety? If we look at the modern economy as it has developed, initially in northwestern Europe but latterly more widely, certain institutions are prominent. It is these distinctive and historically specific institutions that define the kind of market economy that came to be called capitalism. The most important is the existence of a market for investment. It is historically common for there to be institutions that allow individuals to invest in an enterprise and so establish a fiduciary claim to a portion of the wealth or income created by that enterprise. In capitalism, these claims (shares or equities) are fully tradable, can be bought and sold like any other commodity, and are traded through sophisticated markets. This process creates a market in investment, which historically has led to much higher levels of investment and accumulation of capital than is the case in other forms of market economy. Closely related to this notion is another distinctive feature of capitalism, the organization of much large-scale production through large firms, which is based on the two principles of limited liability and perpetual succession. Again it is instructive to compare capitalism with the mercantile type of market economy that was predominant before the mid-18th century. There were large firms in medieval and early modern Europe (such as the Medici and the Fugger), but these were essentially large family businesses built around kinship connections and alliances between merchants. In capitalism, the firm increasingly becomes a structured and impersonal organization of the kind described by a number of authors, such as Peter Drucker and Alfred Chandler. These organizations may be run by actual owners/investors, but often it is professional managers who perform this function. The key figure in capitalism, either as a manager or an owner/investor, is the entrepreneur, who notices gaps in the market and by exploiting them both coordinates supply and demand and, more important, drives the process of "creative destruction" or constant innovation, which also is a marked feature of capitalism. The fourth feature of capitalism is mass consumption and production, made possible in part by the increased efficiency that results from the first two features. Finally, hugely important, but little noticed, the predominant part played in labor markets by wage labor constitutes another crucial aspect of capitalism. Historically, while paid employment was common, as opposed to slavery, serfdom, and other forms of unpaid labor, it usually took the form of indentured labor with long-term and highly prescriptive contracts between the employer and employee. Today, it is only highly paid professional athletes and entertainers whose work is organized in this way—European soccer players and American motion picture actors being prominent examples.

The capitalist form of market economy first developed in northwestern Europe between about 1720 and 1860. It grew out of the preexisting mercantile market economy, which was in a process of gradual change, but that nevertheless eventuated in a radical transformation of several existing economic institutions. Two crucial aspects were the appearance of capital markets from the 1690s onward and the emergence of the modern corporation after the 1720s and especially after passage of the British Companies Act in 1862. These changes were possible because of the earlier period of European history, which produced a range of institutions that favored economic innovation, saving, investment, and, above all, secure and enforceable property rights and a rule of law that bound and limited political power. However, the transition from a mercantile market economy to a capitalist one was not inevitable, and we should not think of the modern economy as a goal toward which all earlier European history was directed. Such a transition had not occurred in other market-based economies such as China's,

and one critical factor seems to have been Europe's continued political division in the face of several attempts by particular states to establish themselves as the predominant power. This political division led to competition among states, including institutional competition, and prevented one power from checking economic change, as happened in China.

One thesis, which has recently enjoyed a renewed popularity, holds that the emergence of capitalism involved a truly radical break with all previous social systems. This argument, which derives ultimately from Karl Polanyi's *The Great Transformation*, consists of two elements. The first is the claim that, before the late 18th century, the role of trade or exchange relationships (i.e., of markets) was limited, with all market exchange being "embedded in" (i.e., subordinate to) other kinds of social relations. In particular, this theory argues, land and labor were not freely traded commodities. Empirical research shows that this assumption is clearly untrue. As I have already indicated, markets and exchange relations have been a central feature of most of the world's cultures and civilizations for most of recorded history. Free exchange in both land and labor can be found in medieval England and the Low Countries, as well as in other parts of the world, such as Song China (960–1279 A.D.). The second claim is that the rise of a capitalist economy involved the appearance of a new kind of human rationality, of a way of thinking about and perceiving the world that had not existed before. According to this way of thinking, European society before the late 18th century (and by extension other societies elsewhere in the world) did not employ "economic rationality" and thought rather in terms of a "moral economy" dominated by noneconomic considerations. Again, this idea is contradicted by empirical research that suggests rather that people before the 19th century were more, rather than less, concerned with economic calculation. The novelty of the capitalist type of market economy should not lead us to exaggerate that novelty nor to believe that it somehow burst on the scene fully formed.

In general, libertarians are strongly supportive of capitalism. They hold this view in part because they see capitalism as superior to any of the alternatives on offer, but their support is more positive than simply regarding capitalism as "the worst system, apart from all the others." Libertarians regard modern capitalism as an essential or necessary condition of both liberty and a good life. They also argue that it is a virtuous and morally defensible economic system that articulates a body of moral values or virtues every bit as coherent and admirable as any other one. Some libertarians see support for a capitalist system as the necessary consequence of certain given axiomatic beliefs, such as the existence of a body of inherent natural rights. Others prefer to emphasize the beneficial consequences of capitalism. The most obvious is the remarkable increase in practical knowledge and wealth that has occurred since capitalism first appeared. Apart from leading to a huge improvement in the quality of life for ordinary people, capitalism has produced clear benefits where liberty is concerned. It greatly increases the capacity or agency of individuals, that is, their ability to realize goals. Along with other factors, such as increased mobility and the wider diffusion of knowledge, it also increases the range of options or life choices open to people who 300 years ago would generally have had their lives determined for them at birth. Capitalism also is associated with other changes in the modern world that libertarians welcome, above all the demise of slavery and other kinds of unfree labor, the emancipation of women, and the privatization of religious belief.

Despite these positive changes, there is a minority tradition within libertarian thinking that, while favoring capitalism over alternatives such as socialism or fascism, is critical of many features of actually existing capitalist economies. Almost all libertarians are hostile to the idea of a mixed economy and are highly critical of the often incestuous relationship between large firms and political power. Existing capitalism is criticized by contrasting it to an ideal type of pure laissez-faire. Some go further, however, and are critical of important features of capitalist economies that the more "mainstream" libertarians support. There is a persistent critique of the corporate form of business organization and some of its main features such as limited liability. Self-employment is often seen as superior to wage labor, and the growth of the latter is deprecated. The institution of intellectual property has attracted much criticism from libertarians over the years as a form of unjustified monopoly or privilege, and this line of argument is gaining support. There also is a strong undercurrent of hostility to the managerial class that has emerged as a key part of capitalism. Radical libertarians of this sort tend to advocate a different kind of market economy, one not dominated by large business organizations and with much less wage labor.

SD

See also Bastiat, Frédéric; Laissez-Faire Policy; Marxism; Material Progress; Private Property; Smith, Adam; Wealth and Poverty

Further Readings

Bastiat, Frédéric. *Selected Essays on Political Economy.* Irvington-on-Hudson, NY: Foundation for Economic Education, 1995.

Benn, Sir Ernest. *Confessions of a Capitalist.* London: Hutchinson, 1925.

Braudel, Fernand. *Material Civilization and Capitalism.* Baltimore: Johns Hopkins University Press, 1977.

Drucker, Peter F. *Concept of the Corporation.* New Brunswick, NJ: Transaction, 1993.

Friedman, Milton. *Capitalism and Freedom.* Chicago: University of Chicago Press, 2002.

Hayek, F. A. *The Road to Serfdom.* Chicago: University of Chicago Press, 1994.

Keayne, Robert. *The Apologia of Robert Keayne.* Bernard Bailyn, ed. New York: Harper & Row, 1965.

Polanyi, Karl. *The Great Transformation.* New York: Octagon Books, 1975.

Rand, Ayn. *Capitalism: The Unknown Ideal.* New York: Penguin/Putnam, 1986.

Smith, Adam. *The Wealth of Nations.* Indianapolis, IN: Liberty Fund, 1981.

CAPITAL PUNISHMENT

The issue of capital punishment divides libertarians just as it does other Americans. Debates among libertarians and others generally fall into two areas: the abstract question of whether the state may ever legitimately puts its citizens to death, and the more specific question of whether capital punishment is just and fitting as it is actually implemented in the American system of criminal justice.

Opponents argue that capital punishment is cruel and unnecessary, that juries in capital cases are almost inevitably unrepresentative of the community and skewed toward vengeance, that the risks of erroneous conviction and execution are unacceptably high, and that the breadth of discretion in charging decisions by prosecutors and sentencing decisions by juries renders capital punishment arbitrary and unfair, if not outright biased.

Proponents maintain that capital punishment is necessary to provide adequate retribution and vindicate the community's sense of decency in the face of particularly heinous crimes. For proponents, any complications or inequities in the application of capital punishment are manageable and similar to concerns that might be raised about other necessary aspects of the criminal justice system. In addition, some proponents also argue that capital punishment acts to deter crime.

Libertarians can be found on both sides of these disputes. But they tend to approach questions regarding capital punishment with a common language and sensibility, emphasizing the need to defend individual rights. A fundamental question that divides them is whether capital punishment should be viewed as an extreme exercise of state power in derogation of individual rights or, instead, as a vindication of the individual's right to retribution to be imposed in appropriate cases by juries as representatives of the community.

Some libertarians view capital punishment as an inherent abuse of state power. They argue that the execution of prisoners is never necessary to protect the public because the state can instead incapacitate them by imprisonment, for life if necessary. The use of capital punishment is therefore an overreach. If libertarians do not trust the government to handle tax dollars responsibly—so the argument goes—how can they entrust the government with the power of life and death over citizens?

The alternative view is that capital punishment is a legitimate and sometimes necessary vindication of the rights of victims, their families, and community norms of justice. In light of this understanding, the power to impose capital sentences may be entrusted to the state. As the philosopher Robert Nozick has argued, libertarians believe that individuals should entrust power to the state only for certain narrowly defined functions that would not be well handled through private agreements or self-help. Enforcement of laws against violence is the quintessential example of such a power that could be entrusted to government. In addition, with the important exception of self-defense, self-help in response to violence is inconsistent with well-ordered liberty and would lead to chaos, misdirected or disproportionate retaliation, and reverberating violence.

However, if individuals are to entrust the power to punish violence to the state and surrender their right to self-help, the state is obligated to provide justice that would satisfy widely shared norms and provide adequate retribution. For some crimes, particularly premeditated murder, only capital punishment may satisfy those requirements. According to proponents, failure to apply capital punishment in such extreme cases undermines the legitimacy of the state and would lead to self-help.

David Bruck, a lawyer who specializes in defending prisoners on death row, has aptly summarized much of the sentiment in favor of capital punishment:

> To those who spend their time thinking about civil liberties, the death penalty is the greatest possible intrusion of governmental power into the individual human personality. But I think to many Americans, perhaps to most, the death penalty actually appears as a *limitation* on governmental power. It is a limitation on the power of irresponsible and insensitive officials to release dangerous criminals back into society to resume their depredations. Seen in that light, the death penalty is a populist, anti-government measure. . . .

Some proponents argue that, in addition to affording necessary retribution, capital punishment deters crime. That argument has intuitive appeal, but, in the minds of many, has never been conclusively established through empirical evidence. On close examination, the apparent logic of the argument also fades in some commonly posited scenarios. For example, economists Richard Posner and Gary Becker argue that capital punishment raises the "price" of murder and therefore should be expected—all other things being equal—to lower the number of murders through what they call "marginal deterrence." That reasoning appears strongest for scenarios in which a criminal may engage in cost–benefit analysis (e.g., in deciding whether to kill witnesses at the scene of an armed robbery). Without the fear of capital punishment, the criminal arguably has little

incentive to leave witnesses alive, particularly if he has a prior record and would likely face life sentences for either robbery or murder.

One problem with this line of reasoning, however, is that a murder would likely substantially increase the law enforcement resources devoted to apprehension of the criminal, when compared with an armed robbery. It is in fact a complex question whether and when a rational and well-informed criminal would conclude that killing witnesses would lower his risk of apprehension.

The evidence regarding deterrence is likely to remain too murky to persuade the unpersuaded either for or against capital punishment. Positions on capital punishment are more likely to be based on subjective values. For some libertarians who believe that capital punishment is justifiable in the abstract, practical and institutional complications may counsel against its use in the American criminal justice system.

One institutional complication with capital punishment was pointed out more than 150 years ago by the libertarian writer and lawyer Lysander Spooner. In the American system of justice, contested felony criminal cases must generally be decided by juries representing a fair cross-section of the community. However, within almost every community, there is strong (even if minority) sentiment against capital punishment. Therefore, the only reliable way for the state to implement capital punishment is to exclude opponents of capital punishment from juries in cases where capital punishment is sought. That was done in Spooner's time, and is done today, through a process now called *death qualification*, which allows the prosecution during jury selection to strike all prospective jurors who admit to serious qualms about capital punishment that might prevent them from implementing it. The result, according to Spooner, is that in cases where capital punishment is sought, punishment (and even guilt) is not decided by juries representing a fair cross-section of the community. Instead, juries will be unrepresentative, filtered to include only the portions of the community most bent on vengeance.

More than a century after Spooner wrote about this issue, the U.S. Supreme Court, in the 1986 case of *Lockhart v. McCree*, found no per se constitutional violation in using death-qualified juries to decide guilt and punishment in capital cases, despite some statistical evidence offered to show that such filtered juries are more likely to convict than more randomly selected juries. But concerns about the fairness of death qualification remain. In theory, it would be possible for a court to avoid death qualification for a jury deciding guilt in a capital case by impaneling two juries, one to decide whether the defendant was guilty, another to decide whether the penalty should be death. But even then, the jury deciding whether to impose capital punishment would represent a filtered cross-section of the community, so some of the concerns raised by Spooner would remain.

Proponents tend to see these concerns as hypertechnical and overblown. Even if death qualification were to filter some prospective jurors, that would not show that the remaining jurors would be unfair. Indeed, proponents argue, the ordinary process of jury selection, called *voir dire,* could still serve to weed out any jurors who might be unduly biased toward the prosecution or otherwise unfair.

Another practical concern for some libertarians with regard to capital punishment is the risk of erroneous convictions. This concern has provoked increasing interest since the recent advances in the use of DNA evidence have resulted in a number of exonerations of prisoners on death row, as well as others in noncapital cases. DNA testing can in some cases show, to a virtual certainty, who did or did not leave blood or other bodily residues at a crime scene.

To date, DNA evidence has not shown that an executed prisoner was innocent. But that could be in part because of state resistance to DNA testing in "closed" cases, where an execution has already occurred, and the lack of resources devoted by opponents of capital punishment in contesting cases where there was no longer a living client. However, some argue that exonerations through DNA show that the system is working and has the capacity to correct errors before they become fatal.

Some proponents of capital punishment argue that, even if the risk of erroneous conviction and execution cannot be entirely eliminated from capital cases, a rare wrongful execution would be an acceptable price to pay for the benefits of maintaining capital punishment as a sanction in the criminal justice system. Opponents maintain that capital punishment is not necessary to a well-functioning criminal justice system, as shown by the experience of other Western democracies, and therefore is unacceptable if there is any significant risk of executing the innocent.

Some oppose capital punishment because of concerns about possible arbitrariness in its application, in addition to possible racial or other biases. This purported arbitrariness led the U.S. Supreme Court to strike down all existing capital punishment statutes in 1972 in *Furman v. Georgia.* Up to that time, juries had often decided whether to impose the death penalty with no clear criteria or guidance. Justice Potter Stewart concluded that the rare and seemingly random applications of capital punishment were "cruel and unusual in the same way that being struck by lightning is cruel and unusual."

In 1976, the U.S. Supreme Court approved some state-level capital-sentencing schemes that were drafted in response to *Furman* to provide juries with more guidance. Since then, much jurisprudence regarding capital punishment has focused on refinements in the selection criteria provided to juries to ensure that their decisions somehow consider all mitigating circumstances relevant to the offender and the crime and at the same time are sufficiently structured through instructions from the judge to prevent

caprice. As Justice Clarence Thomas pointed out in the case of *Graham v. Collins* in 1993, this effort may be self-contradictory and ultimately doomed to failure. How can jury decision making "consider everything" in the case at hand and yet also be channeled and rationalized through guidance from the court? However, a majority of the U.S. Supreme Court continues these efforts through case-by-case decisions about the adequacy of the evidence and instructions provided to juries to decide whether to impose the death penalty.

Over the years, the Supreme Court also has confronted claims of systemic racial bias in application of the death penalty. In *Coker v. Georgia* in 1977, the Court held that capital punishment was an unconstitutional sanction for rape. Although the Court reasoned that the punishment was disproportionate to the crime, use of capital punishment for rape also had been widely condemned as disproportionately applied to black offenders who had attacked white victims. However, in *McCleskey v. Kemp,* decided 10 years later, the Court refused to overturn a death sentence despite evidence offered to show that capital punishment was more likely to be applied in cases where the victim was white. Without evidence of actual bias in the case at hand, the Court was unwilling to act on alleged systemic bias.

In 1965, more than half of the American public opposed capital punishment in all circumstances. Support steadily rose after that and peaked in the mid-1990s, when more than 75% supported capital punishment in at least some circumstances. Since then, support has declined, but not dramatically, to a fairly steady level of between 60% and 70% of the population over the last 10 years. The recent drop in support has been accompanied by drastic drops in death penalties imposed by juries and actual executions performed by the states. Death sentences by juries peaked at 276 nationwide in 1999, but were down to 114 in 2006. Executions peaked at 98 in 1999 and declined steadily to 53 in 2006.

Opponents attribute the drop in sentences by juries to waning support for capital punishment in general. They maintain that even if a majority of the country nominally supports capital punishment, far fewer are actually willing to impose it when confronted with the responsibility as jurors. Proponents attribute the drop in capital sentences to the overall decline in violent crime.

It is possible that that both sides are right, in that drops in violent crime may have caused a softening in public attitudes toward capital punishment, which may in turn have caused reluctance to impose the sanction even by death-qualified juries. If that is the case, then a future rise in violent crime may cause public support and juror imposition of capital punishment to increase again.

JD

See also Nozick, Robert; Retribution for Crime; Spooner, Lysander

Further Readings

Bedau, Hugo Adam, ed. *The Death Penalty in America: Current Controversies*. New York: Oxford University Press, 1998.

Bruck, David I. "Does the Death Penalty Matter? Reflections of a Death Row Lawyer." *Reconstruction* 1 no. 3 (1991).

Goertzel, Ted. "Capital Punishment and Homicide: Sociological Realities and Econometric Illusions." *Skeptical Inquirer* 28 no. 4 (July/August 2004).

Nozick, Robert. *Anarchy, State, and Utopia*. New York: Basic Books, 1974.

Scheck, Barry, Neufeld, Peter, and Dwyer, Jim. *Actual Innocence: Five Days to Execution, and Other Dispatches from the Wrongly Convicted*. New York: Doubleday, 2000.

Spooner, Lysander. *The Illegality of the Trial of John Webster*. Boston: Bela Marsh, 1850.

CATO'S LETTERS

Cato's Letters comprise a series of 138 letters originally published in the British press between 1720 and 1723 and written under the pseudonym "Cato," after Cato the Younger, the steadfast opponent of Julius Caesar and defender of Roman liberty. They offer a vigorous defense of freedom of speech and conscience and are implacable in their attacks on public corruption and unrestrained government. Most of the letters appeared in the *London Journal*; however, in the fall of 1722, the journal underwent a shift in editorial policy when the Walpole administration succeeded in bribing the journal's owner into supporting the government. As a result, beginning with Letter No. 94 dated September 15, 1722, subsequent letters appeared in the *British Journal*. Over the course of the 3 years that they were published, the letters dealt with a broad range of contemporary social and political issues, in addition to a number of theoretical discussions concerning the authority of the clergy, the idea of liberty, and the nature of tyranny.

The letters were originally occasioned by the bursting of the South Sea Bubble, which precipitated a financial crisis of huge proportions in the early autumn of 1720. In the 30 years following the accession of William and Mary in 1689, England had engaged in a series of wars that led to a spectacular growth in the nation's long-term debt. In seeking to relieve the government of the burden of servicing this massive debt, Robert Harley, Earl of Oxford, then Chancellor of the Exchequer under Queen Anne, conceived a scheme whereby a new company, the South Sea Company, would relieve the government of its debt by distributing its stock to those prepared to surrender their government annuities in return for South Sea stock. In return, the South Sea Company would be granted certain monopoly privileges. In this instance, the company was awarded the *Asiento* (a contract with the King of Spain to act as the supplier of 4,800 slaves per year to the Spanish possessions in America) and

was granted a monopoly of all trade "to the South Seas," that is, to Spanish America. Ultimately, both of these "privileges" proved of no value whatever; the Spanish colonial system effectively closed off English trade to the area, and the *Asiento*, during the brief period when the company was able to take advantage of it, lost money. In return for these worthless grants from the British government, the South Sea Company not only assumed the whole of the national debt of £31,000,000, but also agreed to pay the government an annuity of £550,000.

The company was empowered to issue one share of South Sea stock, at a par value of £100, for each £100 of debt converted. If the market share of the stock were higher than its par value, the company would be in a position to issue that much more stock. The directors of the company could, and regularly did, create stock on the company's books, which it then "sold" back to the company at inflated prices. The effect was that large profits could be made, some of which were distributed in the form of bribes to persons of influence. Inasmuch as the company possessed no tangible assets, the holders of government debt agreed to surrender their government annuities for South Sea stock solely because they expected to make large capital gains. Indeed, a few stockholders, including the company's directors, were able to make substantial fortunes, having sold their stock early enough. However, like all financial pyramids, the scheme's collapse was inevitable and its effects extensive. Between September 1 and October 14, 1720, the company stock fell from £775 to £170, and large numbers of people, including some of the leading families in England and Scotland, were wiped out or brought to the brink of bankruptcy.

Disclosures regarding the manipulation of stock, of bribery, and of other corrupt practices by the South Sea directors implicated not only government ministers and members of the Lords and Commons, but members of the royal household. It was this alliance between the manipulators of credit and a duplicitous Court that was the primary object of censure in *Cato's Letters,* whose authors saw the intervention of government in the marketplace as a sure source of political corruption. It is a mistake to read the letters as indicting commerce and the instrumentalities of finance that began to flower at the beginning of the 18th century. What Cato so fervently condemned was the dishonesty of our magistrates when they seek their private interests instead of the public welfare that has been entrusted to them.

Although the letters were originally published anonymously, it was fairly well known that they were written by John Trenchard and Thomas Gordon, Whig publicists of impeccable credentials. Indeed, when the letters appeared in book form some years after the death of Trenchard, Gordon confirmed the letters' authorship when he added his and Trenchard's names to the collection and marked each letter as to author. Trenchard and Gordon had earlier collaborated in writing and publishing an anonymous weekly titled *The*

Independent Whig, which dealt with the dangers posed to English liberty by Jacobites and papists and argued in ringing terms that the individual conscience had precedence over ecclesiastical authority. This theme was again taken up in several of Cato's letters, in which the authors maintained that our religious convictions were subject only to God himself and were immune from all governmental jurisdiction. Indeed, they held, freedom of conscience was the first of our natural rights. In an age of Jacobite plots and conspiracies following the Revolutionary Settlement of 1688, Trenchard and Gordon's Low Church sympathies were an integral element of radical Whig doctrine, when Popery was seen as an instrument for restoring Stuart despotism.

Gordon had originally met Trenchard at a London coffee house in 1719, when Trenchard, who was far older than Gordon, had already obtained a reputation as a defender of radical Whig views. Trenchard, who was extremely wealthy, was impressed with the style and wit that Gordon had displayed in several recently published essays attacking the pretensions of the clergy, and he offered to hire the younger man as his secretary. This relationship quickly led to their collaboration, first on *The Independent Whig* and then on *Cato's Letters*. Trenchard died in 1723 while Gordon survived for another 27 years, having soon after Trenchard's death abandoned his political beliefs in return for a substantial bribe from Prime Minister Walpole. He died rich and corpulent, having married Trenchard's widow, and he devoted his remaining days to a translation and commentary on Sallust and Tacitus.

The letters bear the unmistakable stamp of John Locke's political philosophy and constitute a vigorous libertarian defense of limited government and individual freedom. Natural law and natural rights play a critical role in the structure of Cato's argument respecting the nature of political society and the limits of political authority. The authors maintained that man is possessed of inalienable rights and that the liberty to which all Englishmen are entitled is theirs not solely by virtue of the historical development of English law and custom, but a product of man's nature. "All Men are born free," Cato writes. "Liberty is a Gift from God himself, nor can they alienate the same by Consent, though possibly they may forfeit it by Crimes." The authority of the civil magistrate rests on no foundation other than consent and derives from our inherent right to defend ourselves against those who seek to trespass against our lives, liberty, or property. It is this function alone that circumscribes legitimate political authority. Our liberty, which government is obligated to protect, consists in the right we have over our actions and over all our property of whatever sort and is limited only in that we are precluded from infringing on a similar right in others. The idea that the laws of nature and the contract by which civil society is established constrain the sovereign to safeguarding the lives and estates of his subjects, is the central legacy of

Lockean theory and pervades 18th-century radical Whig thought in general and the views reflected in *Cato's Letters* in particular.

The letters proved immensely popular, not only when they originally appeared, but throughout the 18th century. Of the more than 40 weeklies published in England in the 1720s, the *London Journal*'s circulation soon surpassed all its competitors in influence and importance as a consequence of Cato's contributions. They were so well received that even while new letters were appearing, groups of earlier letters were published in collected form by several London presses. In addition, the whole collection appeared in six separate editions by 1755. The letters appear to have been as well received in the colonies as in Britain. Selected letters were republished in the American press, and American newspapers frequently quoted from them. In 1722, even while the letters were still appearing in London, the *Philadelphia American Weekly Mercury* began reprinting them in defense of the rights of free men. They were so highly thought of in the colonies that, during their struggles with the Crown, they were constantly invoked in response to the whole range of depredations under which the colonists suffered. Freedom of speech and conscience, the rights possessed by Englishmen both by virtue of their traditional laws and by their nature as human beings, the benefits of freedom, the nature of tyranny, and, above all, the right of men to resist tyranny, all found an eager reception in the colonies. Indeed, as the American historian Clinton Rossiter has noted, *Cato's Letters* were "the most popular, quotable, esteemed source of political ideas in the colonial period." They continue to constitute one of the most eloquent disquisitions against despotism written in the English language.

RH

See also Corruption; Liberalism, Classical; Locke, John; Republicanism, Classical; Sidney, Algernon; Whiggism

Further Readings

Carswell, John. *The South Sea Bubble*. Stanford, CA: Stanford University Press, 1960.

Dickinson, H. T. *Liberty and Property: Political Ideology in Eighteenth-Century Britain*. London: Wiedenfeld & Nicolson, 1977.

Dickson, P. G. M. *The Financial Revolution in England: A Study in the Development of Public Credit, 1688–1756*. London: Macmillan, 1967.

Jones, D. W. *War and Economy in the Age of William III and Marlborough*. Oxford: Blackwell, 1988.

Speck, W. A. *Stability and Strife: England, 1714–1760*. Cambridge, MA: Harvard University Press, 1977.

Trenchard, John, and Thomas Gordon. *Cato's Letters*. Ronald Hamowy, ed. Indianapolis, IN: Liberty Fund, 1720–1723.

Williams, Basil. *The Whig Supremacy, 1714–1760*. Oxford: Clarendon Press, 1939.

CENSORSHIP

Censorship is the coercive silencing of dissenting views by political authorities generally in order to protect an official orthodoxy or to prevent the spread of ideas not authorized by the powers that be. As Alberto Manguel writes in *A History of Reading*, censorship "is the corollary of all power, and the history of reading is lit by a seemingly endless line of censors' bonfires." Censorship has been and remains a common feature of oppressive regimes. John Milton, whose *Areopagitica* (written in protest of the censorship of his writings on divorce) remains the most eloquent defense of the free press written in English, provided a history of censorship from 411 B.C., when the works of Protagoras were burned in Athens on the grounds that they taught agnosticism. In the *Republic,* Plato advocates censorship of poetry and music that fail to promote the state's interests. This tradition has continued in modern times. Beginning in 1933, Josef Goebbels oversaw mass book burnings, which became a trademark of the Nazi regime. In the Soviet Union, an agency called Glavlit oversaw all printed publications, including even food labels, to prevent the dissemination of unacceptable material. Today, officials in China, Saudi Arabia, Pakistan, and other countries have implemented censorship of books, periodicals, television, radio, and the Internet to ensure that political dissent, religious heterodoxy, or sexually provocative material are not disseminated to the general public.

The introduction of the printing press and the Protestant injunction for believers to read the Bible for themselves made censorship an increasingly important subject of debate in Reformation Europe. In 1559, the Catholic Church issued the first *Index Liborum Prohibitorum*, which lists books forbidden as dangerous to the faith; the *Index* was not eliminated until 1966. Protestant nations were no less censorious. Henry VIII ordered the burning of Reformation books prior to his own break with Rome, including English translations of the New Testament, and established the licensing requirement for publishing that Milton would protest a century later in *Areopagitica*.

In the ensuing decades, the English common law gradually developed a principle of free expression that barred the government from engaging in "prior restraint" (i.e., the forcible prevention of publication). But no rule protected authors from punishment after publication. Thus, although William Blackstone explained in his *Commentaries* that the prohibition on prior restraints was of the essence to English liberty, there was no "freedom from censure for criminal matter when published." Dissidents could print their views, but the threat of prosecution for "seditious libel" and other political crimes helped temper criticism of the government. In America, however, the famous 1735 acquittal of John Peter Zenger largely eliminated seditious libel as a threat to colonial printers. Prosecutions for the publication of indecent material did continue, however. The first book to be banned in the United States was John Cleland's pornographic novel, *Fanny Hill, or Memoirs of a Woman of Pleasure*, which was prohibited in Boston in 1821 and, when republished in 1964, was again banned, leading to an important Supreme Court decision defining *obscenity*.

Because the common law defined freedom of the press by the absence of prior restraints, the 1st Amendment to the U.S. Constitution, which protects the freedoms of press and speech, has been interpreted as an almost absolute prohibition on prior restraints. Some have argued that the 1st Amendment goes no further, whereas others contend that it goes further than common law and prohibits certain forms of postpublication punishment or other government actions intended to limit the dissemination of information. American courts have identified three broad categories of censorship other than prior restraint: (1) the punishment of those who produce material—such as obscenity or extraordinarily intimidating threats—which is determined not to qualify as "speech" or "press" as the terms were understood by the authors of the 1st Amendment, (2) the use of libel and slander to punish those who utter falsehoods or unflattering comments, and (3) the removal of books from public libraries.

It is widely conceded that certain material is so obscene that it contains no ideas or expression worthy of constitutional protection. However, defining the word *obscene* has proven extremely difficult for courts because too broad a definition might well threaten the dissemination of provocative, but serious, material. In 1973, the Supreme Court defined obscenity as material that, taken as a whole, appeals to the prurient interest in sex, that portrays sex in a patently offensive way, and that lacks serious literary, artistic, political, or scientific value. This definition has proved difficult to apply, and in recent decades, governments in the United States have largely given up the efforts to ban pornography. Worse, it can be dangerous to declare that certain forms of expression are not protected forms of speech. Prohibitions of "hate speech," or of expressive actions thought to be extraordinarily offensive, such as flag-burning, are similar in that they can often be justified on the grounds that such forms of expression communicate sentiments that are unworthy of legal protection. The dangers of such a rationale are evident in the area of sexual harassment laws, which in recent years have been expanded so as to intimidate some speakers or to prohibit some forms of expression that, whatever their merit, are clearly communicative and not obscene or threatening. In addition, this effort to define certain categories of expression as outside constitutional protections has spawned legal theories which seek to define certain categories of speech as deserving "lesser" constitutional protection. This regime of diminished protection prevails in the realm of *commercial speech*, defined to be speech that proposes a commercial transaction. Although the Constitution provides no warrant for such discrimination, the Supreme Court has found that commercial expression can be extensively regulated because it is not considered part of the political or cultural dialogue thought essential to democratic decision making. Likewise, campaign finance regulations, although often restricting the rights of individuals to express their political preferences, are frequently defended on the grounds that limiting the expressive opportunities of wealthy groups fosters broader democratic debate.

Libel and slander laws have regularly been abused to stifle criticism of political authorities, but in the United States these efforts were severely curtailed by the 1964 Supreme Court decision *New York Times v. Sullivan*, which held that "public figures," such as government officials or those who choose to partake in matters of public concern, can only rarely prevail in libel cases. Even publication of obviously false and obscene material about a public figure has been held protected by the 1st Amendment, as when pornographer Larry Flynt successfully defended his right to publish a counterfeit interview suggesting that minister Jerry Falwell had lost his virginity to his mother in an outhouse. Although public figures can virtually never succeed when suing media for such libel in the United States, European countries, particularly England, do not prohibit such suits. As a result, criticism of political figures in England is still often hampered. Worse, because publications produced in the United States are easily available in England, public figures who have been criticized have brought suit against American writers in English courts and recovered, although these suits would be constitutionally barred under American law. This "libel tourism" has become a matter of increasing concern in the age of the Internet.

One common source of debate over freedom of expression in the United States involves the removal of controversial books from public libraries and libraries in public schools. Although not strictly a form of censorship—because the publications remain legal and available elsewhere—such attempts to prevent reading are common and are monitored by the American Library Association's Office of Intellectual Freedom. The U.S. Supreme Court has never ruled that such removals are prohibited by the 1st Amendment, but in *Board of Education v. Pico*, a plurality of justices held that while school boards have broad discretion to choose what books are appropriate for curriculum or classroom use, and to choose what books may be placed in a library, they may not remove books that are already in the library on the basis of the ideas contained in those books or in an attempt to prescribe orthodox opinions.

TMS

See also Education; Freedom of Speech; Freedom of Thought; Milton, John; Pornography; Separation of Church and State

Further Readings

Beauchamp, Raymond W. "England's Chilling Forecast: The Case for Granting Declaratory Relief to Prevent English Defamation Actions from Chilling American Speech." *Fordham Law Review* 74 (2006): 3073–3145.

Bernstein, David E. *You Can't Say That!: The Growing Threat to Civil Liberties from Antidiscrimination Laws*. Washington, DC: Cato Institute, 2003.

Board of Educ., Island Trees Union Free School Dist. No. 26 v. Pico, 457 U.S. 853 (1982).

A Book Named "John Cleland's Memoirs of a Woman of Pleasure" v. Attorney General of Massachusetts, 383 U.S. 413 (1966).

Hustler Magazine v. Falwell, 485 U.S. 46 (1988).

Klosko, George. *The Development of Plato's Political Theory*. New York: Methuen, 1986.

Manguel, Alberto. *A History of Reading*. New York: Penguin, 1996.

Miller v. California, 413 U.S. 15 (1973).

Nelson, Harold L. "Seditious Libel in Colonial America." *American Journal of Legal History* 3 (1959): 160–172.

New York Times Co. v. United States, 403 U.S. 713 (1971).

CHARITY/FRIENDLY SOCIETIES

During the 19th and early 20th centuries, ordinary Americans erected formidable networks of individual and collective self-help for protection. These social welfare systems fell into two broad categories: hierarchical relief and reciprocal relief. Hierarchical relief was characterized by large, bureaucratic, and formalized institutions supported by donors who usually came from significantly different geographical, ethnic, and income backgrounds than did the recipients. Reciprocal relief tended to be decentralized, spontaneous, and informal. The donors and recipients were likely to be from the same, or closely related, walks of life, and today's recipient could well be tomorrow's donor.

Hierarchical relief appeared in such guises as tax-funded almshouses, usually at the county level, and organized private charities. Because Americans of all classes and ethnic groups attached great stigma to dependence on this form of relief, however, few applied for it. In 1880, for example, 1 in 758 Americans was in an almshouse, and by 1903, this number had been reduced to 1 in 920. This pattern of reduced dependence was not limited to almshouses. According to the U.S. Census, in 1904, 1 in 150 Americans (excluding prisoners) resided in public and private institutions, including hospitals, orphanages, and insane asylums. The numbers of Americans dependent on other forms of government relief also were small. As late as 1931, about 93,000 families received mothers' pensions, the state-funded antecedent to Aid to Dependent Children.

Reciprocal relief was far more prevalent than either governmental or private hierarchical relief. In the United States, it found its most visible expression in the numerous fraternal societies. These organizations were most often characterized by an autonomous system of lodges, a democratic form of internal government, a ritual, and the provision of mutual aid for members and their families. Some examples included the Odd Fellows, the Knights of Pythias, the Sons of Italy, the Polish National Alliance, and the Ladies of the Maccabees. Organizations of women that met these criteria generally embraced the label of fraternal rather than sororal.

The Order of Freemasons was one of the earliest fraternal societies in Europe and the United States. While Masonic legends and ritual claim great antiquity, often embellished with fanciful tales of King Solomon's temple, the order probably developed from the stone masons' guilds of England and Scotland in the early 18th century and had spread to the American colonies by the 1730s. The Revolution was a who's who of American Masonry, among them Benjamin Franklin, Paul Revere, John Adams, and George Washington. By the late 18th century, Masonic lodges, both at the local and state levels, had established relief programs to aid members and their dependents who were in need. Later fraternal societies of all types borrowed much from the structure and practice of Masonry. They imitated its system of decentralized, but affiliated, lodges and embraced key elements of the Masonic ritual, especially its emphasis on different degrees of membership.

With the possible exception of churches, more Americans by the mid-19th century belonged to fraternal societies than any other kind of voluntary association. In 1910, the combined membership of these organizations was at least 13 million. The proportion of Americans who were lodge members is more difficult to gauge. Many individuals belonged to more than one society, and large segments of the fraternal population, such as blacks and immigrants, were often undercounted. A conservative estimate in 1910 was that one third of all adult males over the age of 19 were members.

The Australians and the British developed their own version of the American fraternal society: the friendly society. The first friendly societies, most notably the Manchester Unity of Oddfellows and the Ancient Order of Foresters, appeared in the late 18th century and grew rapidly thereafter. The friendly societies specialized in health insurance, including direct medical care. More than half of all wage earners in Great Britain and Australia may have had access to doctors through friendly societies at the turn of the century.

In contrast to Great Britain and Australia, fraternal societies in America were more likely to focus on the provision of life insurance, rather than health coverage. By 1920, members of these societies carried over $9 billion worth of life insurance. After the turn of the century, however, American lodges increasingly dominated the field of health insurance. They offered two basic varieties of protection: (1) cash payments to compensate for income lost through illness and

(2) physician care. Some societies, such as the Security Benefit Association and the Modern Woodmen of America, founded tuberculosis sanitariums, specialist clinics, and hospitals. Blacks, especially in the South, established some of the most successful of these fraternal hospitals, most of which date from the period between 1920 and 1940. One example was the hospital of the Knights and Daughters of Tabor in Mound Bayou, Mississippi. Between 1942 and 1964, it cared for more than 135,000 patients, many of them sharecroppers. In 1944, annual dues of $8.40 entitled an adult to 31 days of hospitalization, including major or minor surgery.

Despite the spread of these black hospitals before and after World War II, the overall growth in fraternal membership had already leveled off by the 1920s and plummeted during the period of the Great Depression. The unprecedented length of the economic crisis made it difficult for members, many of whom were unemployed for long periods, to keep paying their dues. Despite the severity of the Great Depression, few societies suffered bankruptcy or reduced their benefits to members. Per-person benefits for social welfare services were in fact higher in 1935 than in 1929. The numbers of children in fraternal orphanages and homes for the elderly also increased during the worst years of economic decline.

While millions of Americans still belong to societies in the early 21st century, these organizations have shed most of their social welfare services. The sources of fraternal decline have included changing cultural attitudes, restrictive governmental insurance regulation, commercial and employer competition in the provision of services, and the opposition of medical associations that fought, often in league with state regulators, the efforts made by fraternal organizations to offer health care. Additionally, there was another, more subtle, factor at work: the rise of the modern welfare state. It is no coincidence that these societies began to significantly reduce social welfare services in the late 1930s after the introduction of governmental welfare programs such as Aid to Dependent Children and Social Security. Mutual aid throughout history has been a creature of necessity. Governments, by taking away social responsibilities that were once the purview of voluntary associations, seriously undermined these organizations' reason for being. In the process, much that transcended monetary calculations was lost.

DTB

See also Great Depression; Privatization; Social Security; Voluntarism; Welfare State

Further Readings

Beito, David T. *From Mutual Aid to the Welfare State: Fraternal Societies and Social Services, 1890–1967.* Chapel Hill: University of North Carolina Press, 2000.

Green, David G. *Working Class Patients and the Medical Establishment: Self-Help in Great Britain from the Mid-Nineteenth Century to 1948.* New York: St. Martin's Press, 1995.

Murray, Charles. *In Pursuit: Of Happiness and Good Government.* New York: Simon & Shuster, 1988.

Olasky, Marvin. *The Tragedy of American Compassion.* Washington, DC: Regnery Gateway, 1992.

CHILDREN

At first glance, classical liberal thought and contemporary libertarian politics might appear guilty of neglecting the issue of children. In discussions of freedom, rights, responsibility, and the formation of civil society, questions about children have not been at the forefront. Instead, political debates about issues that affect children, such as education and health care, and discussions regarding the nature of rights and the good life have focused on adult decision makers, the rights of parents, and the freedom of families to raise children without state interference. A more careful look at the broader classical liberal tradition, however, might well provide a foundation for a more developed libertarian position on the moral and political status of children. In what follows, I highlight the issues involving children that should concern contemporary libertarians, but that do not get as much attention as they deserve. They include the limits on parental control and abuse, the role of freedom in child development, the possibility of children's rights, and contemporary political issues such as the emancipation of minors and health care decision making.

Since Plato's *Republic*, children and the family have been part of the discussion of ideal political orders and the role of the family within political life. It was not until the Enlightenment that a shift in thinking occurred and the spheres of family and state were separated. Prior to the Enlightenment, it was natural to view the family as intimately connected with the *polis* or city-state. Similarly, in Confucian thought, the family consisted of a natural hierarchy with the father at its head, and paternal authority, like state authority, was viewed essentially unchecked. Fathers were not unlike feudal lords, with wide-reaching but presumably benevolent powers. Indeed, it is a uniquely Enlightenment idea that subjects should be protected from their rulers. So too within the family, the idea that a child should be protected from a parent, or in any way independent of parental authority, was a notion foreign to Eastern, Greek, and early Roman conceptions of family and state.

Classical liberal thinkers of the 17th and 18th centuries, among them John Locke and John Stuart Mill, challenged the standard view, inherited from Roman law, that children were the rightful property of parents. This view also marked a major shift from the religious teachings of earlier Christianity regarding the proper functions of a family and the appropriate upbringing of children. Children, in Locke's view, were not to be thought of as chattels—things to be owned—but rather as future persons who would develop toward full personhood and responsibility. Children in the Lockean sense are divine gifts, and as such they exact certain moral obligations from the parents. John Stuart Mill's *On Liberty* takes parental obligation a step further and argues for an important exception to the idea that the state is only justified in interfering with individuals to prevent harm to others. When Mill discusses the practical application of this principle, he considers the possibility that society may be justified in intervening in a family when there are concerns about child abuse or a failure to educate the child. Mill's is a significant and rarely discussed exception to the classic defense of individual freedom, an exception that has widespread implications for child welfare laws and public education.

Notions of equality and pluralism discussed in the context of the family do not appear in these early liberal writings. Mill does not apply his idea of "experiments in living" or the marketplace of ideas to family life. Nor do we find the notion of a "contract" suggested when dealing with the family, otherwise a central idea used to justify political and social institutions in Locke and other classical liberal thinkers. There appear good reasons for this absence because the idea of a contract seems strained when applied to the rich and complicated relationships within a family, particularly the obligations between parents and children. Pediatrician and philosopher Lainie Ross has suggested that we view the complex interrelationships within a family as one of "balancing interests." Among these are (a) parent-serving interests, (b) child-serving interests, and (c) family-serving interests. There is no need to rely on a conception of rights because each of these interests is of equal moral standing and must be balanced against one another. This model captures the idea that family members are tied to each other in ways that members of a business or political community are not. Human beings are relational beings, and, as such, their autonomy, especially within a family, has its limits. These relationships are not ones of equality. Instead, we find even in the classical liberal tradition the notions of stewardship, development, and protection.

It is generally assumed that parents are usually in the best position to judge what is in a child's best interest. However, this idea obviously cannot be maintained when there is evidence that the child is being abused or neglected. If libertarians follow Mill's argument, when a parent fails in his or her obligations, others, including people with political authority, may be morally obliged to intervene. The crucial question of course is what is involved in being an acceptable parent. Current evidence in developmental psychology also supports the view that different children within a family can have totally different needs. Any assessment of a "child's best interests" would need to take this variability into account.

Children pose a problem to various justifications of basic human rights. The notion of natural self-ownership, central to Locke's conception of individual rights, cannot provide a foundation for the rights of children. Natural rights presuppose certain capacities (such as rationality), and rights that are the outcome of convention presuppose the ability to participate to some degree in public deliberation. Thus, whether the starting point is rationality or agreement, the capacity for the full range of human rights in children is only potential inasmuch as they are only in the *process* of developing these capacities. On what basis, then, can we ground children's rights becuse children are not full moral agents? The first formal statement regarding children's rights was put forward by the United Nations in 1989 and was followed by heated international debate. The scope of the rights it granted to children was broad and included not only protection from abuse, but also guarantees of health and education. In the course of the heated public debate that surrounded this statement, little was said about the philosophical grounding of children's rights.

It might be argued that children should be granted a series of positive rights while they are in the process of developing the capacities necessary for full moral agency. It would follow that parents or guardians have certain duties to attend to the needs of the child. On this account of rights, parental duties would not be contingent on the agency of the child, but rather on the needs and interests of the child. In the case of orphans, libertarians face a difficult policy question regarding the obligations of social institutions to meet the needs of vulnerable children who cannot rely on parents or guardians for support. Similarly, difficult questions remain in assessing social responsibility: When does a child or young adult become a full member of a moral community? If a teenager is violent, should we consider him a person without rational capacities, or a moral agent fully responsible for his actions and worthy of punishment, or some combination of these? Juvenile law typically looks to the child's demonstrated capacity to behave responsibly in other contexts.

Another challenge for a rights-based account in the context of families is how to determine whether mature children and adolescents have any rights against their parents. What importance should we attach to an adolescent's decision or preferences in making future plans? Imagine an adolescent child of Christian Science parents who wishes to become a doctor, against her parents' wishes and religious beliefs. Should a libertarian regard the child's personal decision regarding her future differently than if she had wished to drop out of school, hang out with her friends, and become a heroin addict? Both adolescents are presumably asserting a "right" to lead their own lives against parents' wishes. Most American states in fact allow minors to leave home under certain conditions, such as choosing to marry or if they are financially independent. Significant freedom also is granted to adolescents in health care decision making. There is a strong movement in pediatrics and pediatric research to encourage greater involvement of older children and adolescents in health care treatment decisions and to allow refusals to participate in research. The American Academy of Pediatrics has argued that adolescents who demonstrate the capacity to make health care decisions should be empowered to give strict consent for treatment and should be allowed to refuse unwanted treatment. The most difficult question raised by the academy guidelines is how to deal with those children and adolescents who refuse needed treatment. If we allow minors to be involved in the decision-making process, must we honor their refusals even if it causes them harm? The standard libertarian position is to respect an adult's choices even if those choices are self-destructive as long as others are not harmed in the process. For young adults, who still require guidance and development, it is not clear that libertarians should take a laissez-faire stance.

Whether we accept the arguments for or against children's rights, an important set of questions remain about the role of freedom in a child's education and development. One might not accept the notion of children's rights, but might still think we are obliged to encourage the capacities that help them lead full, free, responsible lives as adults. There is an air of paradox to the idea that children must live unfree lives, lives controlled by parents and teachers, in order to better exercise their freedom as adults. Should freedom play an instrumental role in child development and education? If so, what kind of freedom? Is freedom an intrinsic good that children can be taught to appreciate and respect? How can such capacities be encouraged within families, in schools, and in government? All are questions worthy of further exploration by those interested in the role of liberty in children's lives.

One of the most influential contemporary defenses for freedom in child development was offered by the philosopher of education, Maria Montessori. In her book, *The Absorbent Mind*, Montessori defended the view that freedom to choose among certain learning tasks and environments is central to the flourishing of a child's creativity, imagination, and moral development. Contrary to popular perception, Montessori classrooms are not chaotic free-for-alls. Montessori believed that guidance and control from parents and teachers were necessary for children's proper moral development and socialization.

Free play is a central feature of childhood and a crucial context for learning and development. It also is a crucial component of Montessori's educational model. For Montessori, the goal of education is the autonomy and social development of the child, which includes the ability to make projects and plans, to make choices and carry them out, to embrace one's projects as one's own, and to engage in respectful social relationships with others. Central to this philosophy is the idea that the child is an individual with his or her own sense of imagination and curiosity. Although this view of education emphasizes the importance of reasoning, it also underscores the joys of childhood, including play and imagination.

Current work on child development shows that children differ in their learning styles and educational needs. Children with initiative and confidence may thrive on freedom in the classroom and will accomplish as much when given great latitude. Others need more structure and authority to perform well. For every child, there is an optimal amount of structure, which is not the same for all children. Recent data also show that siblings and peer groups may have an enormous effect on the formation of a child's personality, which suggests that the role that peers play in shaping a child's views may be more important than that of parents and teachers during adolescence. There also is conflicting evidence about the resiliency of children. To some degree, development is forgiving and plastic. Given these considerations, there would be much greater latitude for parents and educators to make mistakes because they are not quite so devastating. However, childhood trauma and deprivation have been shown to be of permanent effect. Experiments in orphanages indicate that, during a window from 4 to 10 months of age, a child must receive a substantial amount of direct human contact, especially touch, or he will develop serious behavioral disorders. So-called attachment disorders include the inability to form human bonds, to trust others, and to communicate honestly. A libertarian view that allows families and parents the freedom to raise children as they see fit, interfering only in cases of physical abuse, is less plausible if children are less resilient. If the success of a free society crucially depends on responsible citizens who respect the liberty of others, then it seems by this logic that libertarians should be more concerned with children who are irretrievably stunted by emotional and physical neglect as well as poor education. An even greater challenge arises in illiberal communities that do not hold freedom in high regard and believe that constraining a child in every way possible to accept certain values is the optimal way in which children should be raised. Given the concerns raised here, libertarians may need to carefully consider the appropriate limits for protecting "experiments in living," especially if the very human capacities at stake are central to a libertarian vision of social and political life.

MK

See also Bioethics; Education; Family; Rights, Theories of

Further Readings

American Academy of Pediatrics. "Informed Consent, Parental Permission, and Assent in Pediatric Decision-Making." *Pediatrics* 95 (February 1995): 314–317; 96 (November 1995): 981–982.

Blackstone, Sir William. "Of Parent and Child." *Commentaries on the Laws of England*. Book I, chap. 16. Chicago: University of Chicago Press, 1979.

Brennan, Samantha, and Robert Noggle. "The Moral Status of Children: Children's Rights, Parents' Rights, and Family Justice." *Social Theory and Practice* 23 no. 1 (1997): 1–26.

Grisso, Thomas, and Linda Vierling. "Minors Consent to Treatment: A Developmental Perspective." *Professional Psychology* 9 (1978): 412–427.

Kipnis, Kenneth. "Parental Refusals of Medical Treatment on Religious Grounds: Pediatric Ethics and the Children of Christian Scientists." *Liberty, Equality, and Plurality*. Larry May, Christine Sistare, and Jonathan Schonsheck, eds. Lawrence: University Press of Kansas, 2007. 268–280.

Locke, John. "Of Paternal Power." *Two Treatises of Government*. Peter Laslett, ed. Cambridge: Cambridge University Press, 2005.

Lomasky, Loren. *Persons, Rights, and the Moral Community*. Oxford: Oxford University Press, 1987.

Montague, Phillip. "The Myth of Parental Rights." *Social Theory and Practice* 26 no. 1 (Spring 2000): 47–68.

Montessori, Maria. *The Absorbent Mind*. Claude A. Claremont, trans. New York: Holt, Rinehart, & Winston, 1967.

O'Neill, Onora. "Children's Rights and Children's Lives." *Ethics* 98 no. 3 (April 1988): 445–463.

Ross, Lainie Friedman. *Children, Families, and Health Care Decision-Making*. New York: Oxford University Press, 1998.

Scherer, David, and Dickon Reppucci. "Adolescents' Capacities to Provide Voluntary Informed Consent: The Effects of Parental Influence and Medical Dilemmas." *Law and Human Behavior* 12 (1988): 123–141.

Childs, Roy A. (1949–1992)

Roy A. Childs, Jr., a self-taught writer and speaker, was a major influence in the libertarian movement during the 1960s and 1970s. He is perhaps best known for his work as editor of *The Libertarian Review* (1977–1981) and as the primary reviewer for Laissez Faire Books from 1984 to 1992. Apart from these positions, however, he also played a role in determining the direction of contemporary American libertarian thought and is credited with popularizing the anarcho-capitalist movement through his "Open Letter to Ayn Rand," published when he was 20 years old.

He was born in Buffalo, New York, on January 4, 1949. His extensive reading led him to become a libertarian in high school. He graduated in 1966 and entered SUNY Buffalo, but from the late 1960s through the 1970s, even while still at college, he was fortunate in having a series of patrons and mentors within the movement who helped him in getting his essays published, created jobs for him, and promoted his speaking. Among these was Robert LeFevre, who discovered his talents when Childs was a college freshman, and, later, Murray Rothbard, Robert Kephart, Charles Koch, and Ed Crane. Childs also was involved with many of the organizations that gave the libertarian movement its shape during that period. He studied (and criticized) Ayn

Rand's Objectivist philosophy, he was a founding member of Rothbard's Radical Libertarian Alliance, and he was the Buffalo representative of the Society of Rational Individualists before its merger with the former Libertarian Caucus of Young Americans for Freedom to form the Society for Individual Liberty (SIL). In 1970, he left college to run SIL's book service.

Childs early on had the opportunity to speak and debate throughout the United States. One of his speeches so impressed Charles Koch that in early 1977 he bought a book review tabloid called *The Libertarian Review* from Robert Kephart and turned it into a magazine, with Roy as its editor; the magazine was originally located in New York, then moved to San Francisco, and finally to Washington, DC. While in San Francisco, Childs also became active in the Libertarian Party and became a research fellow at the Cato Institute. After *The Libertarian Review* was closed in 1981, Childs remained in Washington as a Cato policy analyst until 1984, when Andrea Rich invited him to New York to become a writer for Laissez Faire Books. During his last years, he struggled with obesity, which made it increasingly difficult for him to leave his apartment. He died in a hospital in Miami, Florida, where he had gone for a weight-loss program, on May 22, 1992.

Since then, the Cato Institute has established a Roy Childs Library in its Washington headquarters, and his personal papers are archived in the Hoover Institution for War and Peace Studies at Stanford University.

JKT

See also Anarcho-Capitalism; LeFevre, Robert; Rand, Ayn; Rothbard, Murray

Further Readings

Childs, Roy A. *Anarchism and Justice*. WTM Enterprises, 2004. Hosted at http://www.thornwalker.com/ditch/childs_aj_toc.htm.

Taylor, Joan Kennedy, ed. *Liberty against Power: Essays by Roy A. Childs, Jr.* San Francisco: Fox & Wilkes, 1994.

CHODOROV, FRANK (1887–1966)

Frank Chodorov, author and editor, was a lifelong individualist. Chodorov did not gain a position of prominence in the classical liberal movement until 1937, when he was appointed director of the Henry George School of Social Science at the age of 50. Prior to that time, he held a variety of jobs, including that of manager of a clothing factory and as an advertising agent.

Among Chodorov's intellectual heroes was Albert Jay Nock, who had been editor in the 1920s of a periodical titled *The Freeman.* Chodorov launched his own publication under the same title while at the Henry George School, and in its pages, he extolled the virtues of the free market and attacked President Franklin D. Roosevelt's New Deal. Soon after, however, much of Chodorov's attention turned from domestic to foreign affairs as he steadfastly opposed America's entry into World War II. Chodorov's writings caused consternation among some of the school's board members and forced his dismissal shortly following the bombing of Pearl Harbor. (The Henry George School continued to publish *The Freeman* for a short time before renaming it *The Henry George News.* Since the early 1950s, the Foundation for Economic Education has published its own magazine titled *The Freeman.*)

In 1944, Chodorov began publishing a four-page broadsheet called *analysis,* in which in nearly every issue he was the sole writer. He greatly valued his editorial independence, calling *analysis* the "most gratifying venture of my life." The publication's mission was straightforward: *"analysis,"* he wrote, "looks at the current scene through the eyeglasses of historic liberalism, unashamedly accepting the doctrine of natural rights, proclaims the dignity of the individual and denounces all forms of Statism as human slavery." Although *analysis* had a small circulation, it exerted great influence over many young conservatives and libertarians, including William F. Buckley, who later founded *National Review,* and Murray N. Rothbard, a leading economist of the Austrian School. "I shall never forget the profound thrill—a thrill of intellectual liberation—that ran through me when I first encountered the name of Frank Chodorov, months before we were to meet in person," Rothbard later wrote, adding,

> As a young graduate student in economics, I had always believed in the free market, and had become increasingly libertarian over the years, but this sentiment was as nothing to the headline that burst forth in the title of a pamphlet that I chanced upon at the university bookstore: *Taxation Is Robbery,* by Frank Chodorov.

In the end, however, such devoted readers were unable to save *analysis,* and, as a result, Chodorov was forced to merge his publication with the Washington-based *Human Events* in 1951.

Two years later, Chodorov and Buckley founded the Intercollegiate Society of Individualists (ISI), whose goal was to influence college students through a comprehensive series of publications, speaking engagements, and discussion clubs. (ISI was later renamed the Intercollegiate Studies Institute and is still in operation.) Such an approach was consistent with Chodorov's strategic vision that the current generation of policymakers might be difficult to influence, but young people—the policymakers of the future—could be reached with the message of classical liberalism. "What the socialists have done can be undone, if there is a will for it. But, the undoing will not be accomplished by trying to destroy established institutions. It can be accomplished only by attacking minds, and not the minds of those already hardened by socialistic fixations," Chodorov wrote. "Individualism can be revived by implanting the ideas in the minds of the coming generations. . . . It is, in short, a fifty-year project."

Chodorov suffered a massive stroke in 1961 while lecturing in Colorado and died in 1966 at the age of 79. A selection of his most important writings, *Fugitive Essays*, was published in 1980 and is still in print.

AS

See also Nock, Albert Jay; Rothbard, Murray; Taxation

Further Readings

Chodorov, Frank. *One Is a Crowd: Reflections of an Individualist.* New York: Devin-Adair, 1952.
———. *Out of Step: The Autobiography of an Individualist.* New York: Devin-Adair, 1962.
Hamilton, Charles H., ed. *Fugitive Essays: Selected Writings of Frank Chodorov.* Indianapolis, IN: Liberty Press, 1980.
Rothbard, Murray N. "Frank Chodorov: RIP." *Left and Right* 3 no. 1 (Winter 1967): 3–8.

CICERO (106–43 B.C.)

Marcus Tullius Cicero was one of history's most celebrated orators. He exerted a profound influence on the development of classical liberal and libertarian thought. In large measure because the beauty of his Latin prose led to its preservation into the modern age, Cicero's ideas about natural law and justice were preserved and transmitted to medieval Europe from classical antiquity. Cicero was born in Arpinum, a town about 70 miles south of Rome. As a youth, he studied rhetoric, jurisprudence, and philosophy. (His earliest work, *De Inventione,* is based on his study of the art of rhetoric.) He made his mark in law and politics as a *novus homo* (a "new man," not descended from one of Rome's great families).

Cicero was deeply involved in Roman politics. In 75 B.C., he was elected quaestor in Sicily and became a member of the Roman Senate. In 70 B.C., he successfully prosecuted Gaius Verres, former governor of Sicily, for corruption, a proceeding that made Cicero famous for his legal and oratorical abilities. In 66 B.C., Cicero was elected praetor, and in 63 B.C., he was elected to the consulship, in which office he prosecuted Catiline and the other conspirators for attempting to overthrow the Roman Republic. Cicero became known as a central defender of the institutions of the Roman Republic against those who sought to establish their personal rule. He made many enemies during his political career and was eventually murdered in 43 B.C.

on orders from Mark Antony; his severed head and hands were ordered nailed to the rostrum in the Roman Forum.

His philosophical writings transmitted to medieval writers and to the modern world many of the ideas that originated in the works of Aristotle, of the Stoics, and of other writers of Greek and Latin antiquity. Especially notable for their influence on political thought was the idea of a universal human nature and of a law of nature to govern mankind. In *De Officiis* (*On Duties,* 44 B.C.), he argued that,

> if nature prescribes that one man should want to consider the interests of another, whoever he may be, for the very reason that he is a man, it is necessary, according to the same nature, that what is beneficial to all is something common. If that is so, then we are all constrained by one and the same law of nature; and if that is also true, then we are certainly forbidden by the law of nature from acting violently against another person.

Such concern about the interests of other people extends not only to fellow citizens, but to all of mankind: "There are others . . . who say that account should be taken of other citizens, but deny it in the case of foreigners; such men tear apart the common fellowship of the human race." In *De Legibus* (*The Laws,* written between 52 and 43 B.C.), he affirmed that, "howsoever one defines man, the same definition applies to us all," and articulated the idea of a universal legal order. Those ideas, both directly and indirectly, deeply influenced the tradition of natural law that informed classical liberalism and libertarianism.

TGP

See also Liberty in the Ancient World; Natural Law; Republicanism, Classical; Stoicism

Further Readings

Cicero. *On Duties.* M. T. Griffin and E. M. Atkins, eds. Cambridge: Cambridge University Press, 1991.
———. *The Republic* and *the Laws.* Niall Rudd, trans. Oxford: Oxford University Press, 1998.
———. *Works.* 29 vols. Loeb Classical Library. Cambridge, MA, various dates.
Everitt, Anthony. *Cicero: The Life and Times of Rome's Greatest Politician.* New York: Random House, 2001.
Holland, Tom. *Rubicon: The Last Years of the Roman Republic.* New York: Doubleday, 2003.

CITIES

A city is, in its simplest definition, an urban settlement of more than a specific population. The size is ultimately arbitrary, but reflects the reality that a true city has features and qualities that smaller urban settlements lack. Legally, the concept usually implies that the entity has self-governing status, but this feature is not universal or necessary; there have been cities that have lacked this political status. Cities are an essential feature of human civilization. Indeed, the term *civilization* etymologically connotes the art of living in cities, rather than in other commoner forms of human settlement, such as the small town or village. The appearance and growth of cities is therefore perhaps the central element in the narrative of human economic, cultural, and intellectual development. For thinkers throughout the ages, the city has been a contested aspect of human life, for some the source of fine living and elevated thought and culture, for others the seat of moral and social corruption and danger. Those who embrace either side of this argument link cities to trade, wealth, and lavish consumption or "luxury," but differ in how these should be evaluated. Although there is a minority agrarian tradition within libertarianism, most libertarians have come to support the view that city and its role are beneficent. In the contemporary world, cities and urban planning are a major political issue in several countries, particularly in the United States, and libertarians have a distinctive position on these questions.

Cities first appeared during the so-called Neolithic revolution, which saw the appearance of agriculture and trade as well as large permanent settlements. The first cities appeared in the Fertile Crescent of the Middle East some 8,000 years ago. Later on, cities also appeared in the Indus valley and northern China. The traditional view was that cities were a consequence of the development of agriculture because these urban centers could only exist once there was a storable food surplus produced by farming. However, Jane Jacobs attacked this notion in her 1969 work, *The Economy of Cities*. She argued that, in fact, cities preceded agriculture and that farming and cultivation were first developed within urban settlements and then exported to the surrounding rural areas. In Jacobs's model, trade preceded large-scale agriculture and led to the appearance of large permanent settlements, which in turn encouraged agriculture. When this thesis was first put forward, it was treated with skepticism, but archaeological research has tended to confirm Jacobs's conclusions, and they now command wide support.

Jacobs went on to develop her argument in a later work, *Cities and the Wealth of Nations*. She argued that historically it is cities that are the source of economic growth and development and technological innovation due to a process of import substitution, by which the urban community discovers ways of reducing its dependence on its hinterland. She also argued that the true fundamental unit of economic analysis was the city region, consisting of a city and its hinterland, rather than the nation, and that the world or international economy is built up via the growth of trading links between such city regions. This thesis remains controversial, but again commands increasing support as an account of both the historic position and role of cities and as a way of thinking about the current world economy. (In this way of thinking, it makes more sense to think of the "U.S. economy" as actually consisting of some 200 city region economies, some of which have closer links to other parts of the world than they do to the rest of North America.)

Historically, cities have been and continue to be strongly associated with a number of other phenomena. Some are apparent, such as trade, commerce, and manufacture. In fact, although trade has always been associated with cities, a great deal of manufacturing in the past took place in rural areas, under the so-called putting-out system. The almost total domination of manufacturing by urban areas only really comes about during the last 200 years. Cities also are associated with phenomena such as government and administration, intellectual life, heresy and free thinking, elaborate and lavish consumption, fashion and style, the arts and high culture, ethnic and religious diversity and pluralism, and bohemianism or "experiments in living."

These various social phenomena all occur in cities to a much greater extent than outside them because of the essential features of city life, particularly of the great urban agglomerations. The presence of a large number of people in a relatively confined space creates all kinds of opportunities for human interaction at relatively lower costs in terms of time and effort, where the opportunity for economic specialization and enhanced division of labor is much greater. Thus, social life and human relations are more complex and varied, and ways of living can flourish that are not possible in a smaller community simply because of the lack of people with specific interests or tastes within a reachable geographical area. The proximity of large numbers of people with varied skills and tastes not only enhances productive specialization and output and the creation of a much denser and richer civil society, but also makes possible a much more diverse and varied pattern of consumption inasmuch as the costs of meeting peculiar or minority tastes are much less. The wealth and opportunities brought about by city life and the trade relations that connect flourishing cities to other, often distant, parts of the world mean that they are able to attract incomers from a wide range of ethnic, geographical, and religious backgrounds and have a diverse and varied population. (One of the signs of a city's decline is that its population becomes more and more homogenous—both a cause and an effect of that decline.) Most strikingly, the city offers something that is absent from life in smaller rural communities. It provides privacy and anonymity—the possibility of maintaining a substantially private and personal area of life that is not known to or is accessible to all of one's neighbors.

Historically, these qualities have brought both condemnation and praise, and they continue to do so. For some, the city is the locus of freedom and individualism, economic and cultural progress and innovation, and social and political diversity and independence. There is, however, a long tradition that sees the city as the source of impiety, moral and social corruption and breakdown, crime and disorder, and dangerous innovation. The city is here contrasted to the simple, pure, and secure life of the country. This kind of debate has gone on in the world's major civilizations since cities first appeared, as the Greek fable of the town and the country mouse shows. There is a close connection between this kind of antiurbanism and the antimodern and antiliberal ideologies over the last 300 years, which is still the case today.

Ever since the first cities appeared, their role has been varied. Frequently, one of its key functions has been to act as the central location for the apparatus of political power that extracts wealth from both the rural population and the commercial life of the city. Cities seen this way are the seat of government and administration, of religious hierarchy, and of royal and imperial courts. As a consequence of their intimate connection with the center of political institution, in certain cases cities may not even produce much. Examples of these cities are many and varied, including Rome, Constantinople, Delhi, Beijing, Baghdad, Moscow, Berlin, Paris, Madrid, London, and Washington, D.C. However, many of these cities also serve as examples of the other historic role of cities—as centers of trade, commerce, and investment. Here, in addition to Constantinople/Istanbul, London, and Baghdad, we might add Alexandria, Venice, Amsterdam, New York, Shanghai, Chicago, Tokyo, Mumbai, Cairo, Singapore, and Hong Kong. Until the 19th century, urban populations never constituted more than 20% of the population of any significant area. Before the great breakthrough in the productivity of agricultural labor in the early 19th century, no society could produce enough food to feed itself unless about 80% of its population was engaged in agriculture, and this constraint imposed fundamental limits on urban growth. Another constraint on the urban population was the difficulty of feeding more than a few large urban centers before the invention of the railroad and the internal combustion engine. In addition, the main drawback of city life before the 19th century was its lack of adequate sanitation and potable water. The result was that death rates, particularly for infants, were significantly higher in towns and cities than in rural areas.

All of these demographic considerations changed in the course of the 19th century with important breakthroughs in technology and medical knowledge leading to dramatic improvements in urban sanitation. A key event was the formulation of the germ theory of disease and the demonstration by John Snow of the way that diseases such as cholera were spread by contaminated water. The result was an explosive growth in both the absolute and, more important, the relative size of urban populations. In 1851, Britain became the first society in human history to have a majority of its population living in cities and large towns. This process has spread to other parts of the world and still continues. Indeed, rapid urbanization is one of the central phenomena of the modern world. Because of the profound differences between urban and rural life, this change constituted a social revolution as much as an economic one.

The libertarian view of the city is generally positive, and the move toward a predominantly urban life is generally welcomed. Historically, periods and episodes when cities were vibrant and influential, such as Ancient Greece, Song China, the Umayyad Middle East, medieval and Renaissance Italy, 17th-century Dutch Republic, and 19th-century Britain, are regarded with admiration by libertarians. The mercantile city-state and leagues of cities are often seen as the best kind of polity and as distinctly superior to the territorial state or empire. This preference for cities reflects the kinds of real-life connections and associations that promote a variety of voluntary interactions. For libertarians, the city and city life display the kinds of phenomena that they find admirable and worthy of encouragement. There is an older tradition of libertarian thought, however, that is hostile to the city and sees the independent farmer as the bedrock of a free society, with the city cast as the locus of corrupting political power. This notion goes back to the 18th century and earlier and the tradition of classical republican thought—"country" ideology as it came to be called—with its opposition to the court and royal power and government extravagance, both associated with the great metropolis. Later, with the French Revolution, the city became the scene of revolution and dangerous collectivist politics. This kind of agrarian libertarianism, with its republican antecedents, has effectively died out in Europe, but persists as a minority tradition within the United States, where it is articulated by authors such as Victor Davis Hanson, due to the continuing influence of Jeffersonian thought and ideas.

In contemporary intellectual and political debates about the city and urbanism, libertarians tend to adopt an unambiguous position with regard to two topics. The first is the historical and contemporary debate over the nature and consequences of urban growth during the revolutionary move from a predominantly rural society to one that has a city-dwelling majority. The orthodox view of this process as experienced in the 19th century regards it as a chaotic and disorderly development with significant market failure and the creation of massive slums and attendant social problems, which were only resolved by direct government action and the appearance of contemporary urban planning and zoning regulation. Libertarian historians argue that, in fact, the problems were much less severe than assumed, and that urban growth in places such as 19th-century Britain was a phenomenon of spontaneous order, with an orderly pattern of urban growth produced by the sophisticated use of property rights and contracts, above all the use of covenants. In the contemporary world, the massive growth of cities in places such as Mexico, Brazil, and parts of Asia and Africa is often thought of as both a social disaster and a chaotic phenomenon that requires massive action by government. The contrary view, put by authors such as the libertarian social commentator Hernando De Soto, is that the problems that do exist in such population centers are caused mainly by government action and above all by the lack of clear and transferable property rights for the inhabitants of areas, such as the *favelas* of Brazil. De Soto describes in detail the ways in which the conditions of urban life described earlier make possible the appearance of a wealth of voluntary institutions and private solutions to urban problems, which are held back by government regulations and inadequate property rights.

Similarly, the libertarian position on the nature of urban growth in the contemporary United States—and in Canada and Australia—opposes the planned and controlled development of cities. This approach has been a central part of the ideology and practice of the modern managerial state. Indeed, because the idea of the planned city appears at the foundation of the modern state in the Baroque Era, this approach is the earliest example of this kind of politics. A persistent theme in libertarian argument has been resistance to both the theory and practice of urban planning. A crucial event in this connection was the publication in 1961 of Jane Jacobs's *The Death and Life of Great American Cities*, written partly as a rejoinder to the policies of New York's urban planning supremo, Robert Moses. In this work, Jacobs put forward the view that the city and its neighborhoods were living spontaneous orders produced by the voluntary interaction of individual inhabitants, as opposed to the model of top-down rationalist planning as typified by Moses. Although Jacobs would not have defined herself as a libertarian, her ideas and analysis had a great impact on libertarian social critics. An early example was Martin Anderson, whose attack on 1960s "urban renewal" in *The Federal Bulldozer* pointed to the fact that contemporary urban planning and zoning regulations persistently and inevitably favored the rich and powerful over the poor and powerless.

More recently, libertarians have become involved in the debates over the nature of urban development in North America. Much contemporary literature has lamented the phenomenon of "urban sprawl" and the growth of suburbia. For many contemporary authors, the appearance of this kind of extensive, low-density urban environment has marked the crisis or even death of the city as historically understood and has been seen as a major threat to the natural environment, whereas the lifestyle of suburbia has been subjected to severe criticism as soulless and alienating. The libertarian response to this theory has been mixed. One frequent rejoinder has been to agree with much of the criticism, but to put the blame primarily on government and regulation. In particular, zoning laws are blamed for mandating extensive low-density housing, for creating socially homogenous neighborhoods by preventing low-cost housing alongside the more expensive variety, and for geographically separating different activities.

The federally funded Interstate Highway System and government funding of highways in general are blamed for urban sprawl because of the enormous hidden subsidy they represent to commuting and developers. The other response has been to welcome or defend many aspects of contemporary urban development. Many follow Joel Garreau's identification and defense of the "edge" city as the new form of spontaneously evolving city development and defend suburban life against its critics. One scholar whose work has become particularly influential for contemporary libertarians is Robert Nelson. He focuses on a phenomenon that libertarians welcome, the growth of privately governed communities or homeowner associations. Nelson points out that these communities make up the overwhelming majority of new housing in the United States and predicts a future in which these essentially private bodies have taken over most of the functions of local and even state government. This possible future is generally welcomed by libertarians, but sharply criticized by others.

The historical role of the city is generally seen by libertarians as positive, and most of them favor urban life over the alternatives. In the contemporary world, the analyses of scholars such as Jacobs and Nelson are leading libertarians to both articulate a distinctive position in current debates and envisage a future in which the city, reinvented as a congerie of self-governing private communities, is increasingly the main unit of both economic and political life.

SD

See also Cosmopolitanism; Culture; Jacobs, Jane; Spontaneous Order; Transportation; Urban Planning

Further Readings

Beito, David T., Peter Gordon, and Alexander Tabarrok, eds. *The Voluntary City: Choice, Community and Civil Society*. Ann Arbor: University of Michigan Press, 2002.

Garreau, Joel. *Edge City: Life on the New Frontier*. New York: Anchor Books, 1992.

Jackson, Kenneth T. *Crabgrass Frontier: The Suburbanization of the United States*. Oxford: Oxford University Press, 1987.

Jacobs, Jane. *Cities and the Wealth of Nations*. New York: Vintage, 1970.

———. *The Death and Life of Great American Cities*. New York: Vintage, 1992 [1st ed., 1961].

———. *The Economy of Cities*. New York: Vintage, 1970 [1st ed., 1966].

Mackenzie, Evan. *Privatopia: Homeowner Associations and the Rise of Residential Private Government*. New Haven, CT: Yale University Press, 1996.

Mumford, Lewis. *The City in History: Its Origins, Its Transformations and Its Prospects*. London: Harvest Books, 1968.

———. *The Culture of Cities*. London: Harvest Books, 1970.

Nelson, Robert H. *Private Neighbourhoods and the Transformation of Local Government*. Washington, DC: Urban Institute Press, 2005.

Sassen, Saskia. *Cities in a World Economy.* Thousand Oaks, CA: Pine Forge Press, 2006.

———. *The Global City: New York, London, Tokyo.* Princeton, NJ: Princeton University Press, 2001 [1st ed., 1991].

Weber, Max. *The City.* New York: Free Press, 1966.

Civil Society

The concept of civil society is a central one for most contemporary political theorists and social analysts. As such, it is of great importance for all political ideologies, including libertarianism. Essentially, the term *civil society* refers to the sphere of uncoerced collective action, as opposed to individual action, on the one hand, and government, on the other hand. In other words, it is the term used to describe the total range of voluntary social institutions that derive from the free association and cooperation of individuals in pursuit of a common interest, as opposed to the institutions of government, which ultimately rest on force. Thus, it includes clubs, unions and associations, firms, and a whole range of informal and ad hoc social institutions that are produced by repeated social interaction among individuals. The category of civil society is thus contrasted to that of government or the state, with the former deriving from voluntary choice and cooperation and the latter ultimately from coercion (however, this fact may be justified as necessary or desirable). It also has been contrasted, in much social theory since the 1890s, with the idea of a mass society that is a social order composed of unconnected individuals who lead essentially private and personal lives without participating or engaging in shared activities or cooperative endeavors.

The status of some institutions is ambiguous or may vary according to historical circumstances. Thus, churches are considered a part of civil society in places such as the United States, which have a strict separation of church and state, but would not fall under that rubric in most historical regimes where there was an established church that was intimately entwined with government and to which people were compelled to belong. Political parties are part of civil society in a pluralistic democracy, but not in an actual or de facto one-party state such as the Soviet Union, Nazi Germany, or Mexico for much of the 20th century because of the intimate connection between the party and the institutions of the state.

More problematic and difficult is the status and location of the family and larger kin groups such as the tribe or clan. For some, these groups count as part of civil society. However, many of the important theorists of the concept exclude them and make civil society something that fills the gap between the larger community of the state and the smaller level community of the family or household (e.g.,

Hegel adopted this position). This view also reflects the concrete reality that families and kin groups are not voluntary organizations in the way that clubs or associations are: As the well-known saying has it, you can choose your friends, but not your relatives. The idea of the family being part of civil society derives from the fact that marriage in some societies is the outcome of a voluntary choice, but this voluntarism is never the case for children and is often not true for spouses, both historically and in many contemporary cases.

As was the case with the notion of public opinion, the concept of civil society was formulated and developed in the later 18th and early 19th centuries. It was first articulated by the thinkers of the Scottish Enlightenment, the most important of whom were Henry Home, Lord Kames, and Adam Ferguson. Ferguson in particular worked out the outlines of the notion in his *Essay on the History of Civil Society*, published in 1767. As the title suggests, he saw civil society as having a history and, therefore, as being produced by a process of development in which society became more commercial and "polished," a development that was accompanied by greater complexity and variation in the connections and associations among individuals. Subsequently, the idea was elaborated and developed by Hegel, most prominently in his *Philosophy of Right*, in which he clearly distinguished the institutions of civil society from those of both the family and political realms. He also made the progressive development of civil society and its constituent institutions a central aspect of his dialectical model of historical development or unfolding. Subsequent German theorists coined the term *Zivilgesselschaft*, by which the concept became generally known in 19th-century Europe. Several other 19th-century thinkers made important contributions to the topic. Alexis de Tocqueville saw the existence and growing complexity of "intermediate institutions" between the individual and the state as one of the essential features of modernity. In *Democracy in America*, he argued that the strength of these institutions was a distinctive feature of the United States in particular and the Anglo-Saxon world in general, in contrast to his native France. Like Ferguson and Tocqueville, the French sociologist Emile Durkheim argued that the increasing density and variety of voluntary connections among individuals was a crucial aspect of modernity. However, he also introduced the idea of a mass society of atomized and deracinated individuals as another possible outcome of modern industrial society. Sir Henry Sumner Maine was responsible for the notion that an important part of the development of civil society was the gradual movement from a condition where most social relations were governed by status to one marked by contractual agreements, both formal and informal.

In the early 20th century, the idea of civil society was important for pluralists such as John Neville Figgis and the young Harold Laski, who employed it to criticize the orthodox doctrine of political sovereignty. However, during the first half of the 20th century, the notion was not as widely employed as was the case during the previous 100 years. With the advent of the cold war, however, it underwent a revival among both political scientists and sociologists. At this time, the concept of totalitarianism became increasingly important in social analysis, especially as an aspect of the critique of regimes such as those of Nazi Germany and communist Russia and China. It was argued that one of the distinctive features of such regimes was the lack of independent, voluntarist institutions and the total domination of every aspect of life by the party state. The idea of civil society was thus elaborated to explain what was absent in totalitarian regimes. Further, following Tocqueville and others, civil society was explicitly linked to both democratic politics and personal liberty. The last 50 years or so have witnessed a great deal of research and writing on the subject by a number of authors. Among the most important are Gabriel Almond, Sidney Verba, Robert Putnam, Elinor Ostrom, and Hans-Jürgen Habermas. The concept is a central one for the school of communitarian thinkers such as Charles Taylor, Michael Sandel, and Will Kymlicka.

This renewed interest among social theorists of all ideological views points to the fact that the concept is not peculiar to, or even strongly associated with, libertarians. Nevertheless, the notion is central to much libertarian thought. It provides one of the ideas that links libertarian thought to broader questions in social and political analysis, an area in which libertarians have drawn on and made use of arguments and ideas developed by nonlibertarians such as Ostrom, Habermas, and Putnam. At the same time, they have been critical of some of the analyses made by such theorists, in particular the positions adopted by communitarian writers such as Charles Taylor and Michael Sandel.

Libertarians, for the most part, accept the notion of civil society as described here and conceive it as beneficial and desirable. From their point of view, autonomous individuals pursuing their own ends or life projects do so not as isolated atomistic individuals—as the caricature of libertarianism would have it—but as social beings who can flourish and realize their full potential only through a net of relations with other people. What is important from the libertarian perspective is that the mutually beneficial relationships between individuals through which this flourishing takes place is voluntary and consensual, rather than coerced. These should not be the product of power- or status-based relations. The institutions of civil society are vital for human flourishing and are the product of the free action of individuals peacefully pursuing their goals while living peacefully with everyone else. As such, they are the embodiment of the spontaneous order of social cooperation produced by Adam Smith's "system of natural liberty," or the *great society* as Hayek termed it. Such voluntary cooperation also is the means by which shared or collective goals are realized without resorting to compulsion or

the coercion of dissenters or those who do not share the goal in question. This notion is particularly relevant in the case of social welfare, where libertarians have consistently favored resolving and addressing social problems through the medium of civil society via free cooperation and voluntary institutions such as mutual aid associations, rather than by government action. This view of civil society is not in conflict with that of theorists such as Habermas, but is distinct because it emphasizes voluntary cooperation and the way this cooperation creates institutions and practices, rather than the conversational or interactive aspect of the process, which Habermas stresses.

Moreover, for most libertarians, civil society as so understood is not only the product of liberty, of free choice, but also a defense of it. The institutions of civil society, they argue, provide a buffer against power and act as a protective cushion between the individual and the ruling groups in society, the state and state-linked institutions. Isolated individuals do not have the capacity to resist or withstand the power of the state, whereas the collective institutions of civil society make resistance to that power much easier. Libertarian intellectuals such as Albert Jay Nock noted that this pointed up the contrast between social and political power. Thus, not only are civil society and social power a protection against political power and force, but the growth of government and political power constitutes threats to civil society and peaceful social cooperation. For libertarians, a mass society of isolated atomized individuals, first diagnosed by Durkheim, was the product of the growth of government and the extension of political power inasmuch as these inevitably undermine and crowd out the private and voluntary means of realizing individual and collective goals. Massive government produces a situation where no collective yet voluntary institutions can exist, but only individuals on the one side and government on the other, with individual men and women in a position of childlike dependence and subservience. Thus, the threat posed to civil society by overweening political power becomes one of the principal arguments against that very power.

The experience of the last 100 years has led libertarians to reject the optimistic historical perspective of their 18th- and early 19th-century forbears, with civil society steadily becoming richer and more variegated. Rather, they tend to see an oscillating process in which the balance between civil society and government shifts one way and then another, often with a movement in one direction in one area of life matched by a shift in the opposite direction elsewhere. Thus, there are divergent responses from libertarians to the arguments of contemporary authors such as Robert Putnam. He has argued, in *Bowling Alone,* that there has been a decline in the institutions of civil society in recent years, with a consequent reduction in what he terms *social capital.* Some libertarians, while in the main agreeing with his diagnosis, also blame the growth of government as the underlying cause.

Others reject his analysis and argue that there has not been a decline in the richness and density of civil society of the kind Putnam identifies, but rather a transformation in its content and in the kind of personal relations of which it is comprised. This division among libertarians is partly a product of the difference between an optimistic and a pessimistic view of the present and in part due to differences over how to evaluate the new kinds of "virtual" community and civil society created by modern communications technologies.

Finally, while supporting and using the idea of civil society, libertarians are resistant to the kinds of arguments about it made by communitarians. Authors such as Charles Taylor have argued for a socially constituted self that is created by the institutions and practices of civil society and that, in reality, individual choices are and should be radically constrained by those collective institutions and conventions. Libertarians reject this notion both as a description and as a program largely on the grounds of methodological and ethical individualism. For them it is still the individual who is the primary component of social action and his or her choices and interactions that produce civil society. Normatively, they reject the notion that there is or should be a collective purpose or project embodied in the institutions of civil society in which individuals participate. Rather, civil society serves the interests of individuals and helps them to realize their personal life projects in a way that involves cooperation with others rather than conflict.

SD

See also Coercion; Family; Ostrom, Vincent and Elinor; Religion and Liberty; State

Further Readings

Eberly, Don E., ed. *The Essential Civil Society Reader: The Classic Essays.* New York: Rowman & Littlefield, 2000.

Edwards, Michael. *Civil Society.* London: Polity, 2004.

Ehrenberg, John. *Civil Society: The Critical History of an Idea.* New York: New York University Press, 1999.

Ferguson, Adam. *Essay on the History of Civil Society.* Cambridge: Cambridge University Press, 1996.

Hall, John A. *Civil Society: Theory, History, Comparison.* London: Polity, 1995.

Hodgkinson, Virginia, and Michael W. Foley, eds. *The Civil Society Reader: Historical and Contemporary Perspectives.* Boston: Tufts University Press, 2003.

Kaviraj, Sudipta, and Sunil Khilnani, eds. *Civil Society: History and Possibilities.* Cambridge: Cambridge University Press, 2001.

Keane, John. *Civil Society: Old Images, New Visions.* Stanford, CA: Stanford University Press, 1999.

Putnam, Robert. *Bowling Alone: The Collapse and Revival of American Community.* New York: Simon & Schuster, 2001.

———. *Making Democracy Work: Civic Traditions in Modern Italy.* Princeton, NJ: Princeton University Press, 1994.

Tocqueville, Alexis de. *Democracy in America.* London: Penguin, 2003.

CIVIL WAR, U.S.

The American Civil War raged between the northern and southern states from 1861 to 1865. The total number of dead on both sides—620,000—marks the conflict as the bloodiest in American history. However, the aspect of the war that is of particular concern to libertarians is its impact on liberty. The Civil War ironically represents the simultaneous culmination and repudiation of the principles of the American Revolution.

Before the war, the United States, already one of the world's most prosperous countries, possessed one of the most limited governments. There were only two sources of national revenue: a low tariff and the sale of public lands. These income sources had been more than adequate to cover the minuscule peacetime budgets, which peaked at $74.2 million in 1858. That amount translates into less than 2% of the economy's total output. The national debt stood at a modest $65 million, an amount less than annual outlays. Thus, most Americans paid no taxes whatsoever to federal officials directly, and their only regular contact with any representative of the central authority was the U.S. Post Office.

The one great blight on the American landscape was black chattel slavery. Although it was finally abolished during the Civil War—a triumph for free institutions that cannot be overrated—in other respects the American polity reversed direction. The war did not merely crush the aspirations of white Southerners for self-determination; it, like all wars, also brought in its train a massive increase in government power. Furthermore, postwar retrenchment failed to return the government's size and scope to prewar levels. Indeed, some argue that the Civil War, rather than the New Deal or some other watershed, marks the decisive turning point in American history with respect to the growth of government.

The war involved two central governments, Union and Confederate, whose policies were in many respects mirror images of each other. Both imposed internal taxes to cover the war's astronomical costs—the first such taxes Americans had paid to any central authority in nearly 40 years. By 1865, the Union budget had risen to more than 20% of the economy's total output. A vast array of national excise, sales, license, stamp, and inheritance taxes required an extensive Internal Revenue bureaucracy. More portentous was the first national income tax. Yet all the Union taxes combined were sufficient to cover no more than about one-fifth of the war's monetary cost.

The national debt consequently climbed to $2.8 billion, and the Treasury resorted to $431 million of fiat paper money, popularly known as Greenbacks, the first issued since the Constitution's adoption. The North's money stock approximately doubled, as did the price level. The Confederacy, having to depend still more heavily on paper money to finance the war, suffered a hyperinflation, with prices rising 2,676%.

To harness northern banking to war finance, Congress created a system of nationally chartered banks that is still in existence today. This system was just one part of a comprehensive wartime program of government subsidies and regulation that also included high protective tariffs, land grants and loans for transcontinental railroads, the first federal aid to higher education, and a new Department of Agriculture. In the North, the Civil War generally saw the triumph of a neomercantilist alliance between private businesses and governments at all levels, whereas in the much less industrialized South, it saw the emergence of full-blown war socialism, with governments directly owning factories and a variety of other enterprises.

The Civil War also brought with it the first centrally administered conscription in American history, initiated by the Confederacy in 1862, with the Union quickly following. Because of widespread resistance to the draft and other war measures, President Abraham Lincoln suspended *habeas corpus* and throughout the course of the conflict imprisoned at least 14,000 civilians without charges or trial. In addition, his administration monitored and censored both the mails and telegraphs, and it suppressed publication of more than 300 newspapers for varying periods.

After the Confederacy's defeat, national spending fell back to between 3% and 4% of total output, but this amount was still nearly twice the prewar level. Protectionism continued to dominate trade policy, the internal taxes were never fully abolished, and pork-barrel subsidies became scandalously common. Interest on the war debt commanded about 40% of federal outlays into the mid-1870s. To their credit, the postwar administrations ran surpluses for 28 straight years. Interest on the war debt, which had been the largest single budget item, was finally dethroned from its position in 1884 by yet another war-related expenditure: veterans' pensions. These pensions were so lavish that, in essence, they constituted a system of old-age and disability insurance that stands as a precursor to modern social security.

A contemporaneous surge in nationalism complemented the surge in actual government power. Northerners now viewed the United States as a single nation, rather than a union of states. Moreover, the war generated a proliferation of government activism at the state and local levels. The war accustomed the public to government solutions to a wide range of social problems, from public health measures to business regulations, from professional licensing restrictions to antiliquor and antivice controls.

This question inevitably arises: Could slavery have been abolished without these concomitant costs? The liberation of 4 million American slaves dwarfs all other emancipations in scale and magnitude, and the fact that it was an unintended consequence of the Civil War in no way gainsays the accomplishment. Although the fundamental reason for secession

was without a doubt the protection of what Southerners called their "peculiar institution," slavery had little to do with the northern refusal to let the South go. Federal authorities at the outset were quite explicit that the war was being fought solely to preserve the Union. Even Lincoln's final Emancipation Proclamation of 1863 was limited in its application, and only with the adoption of the Thirteenth Amendment in 1865 was chattel slavery totally eradicated within the United States.

No abolition of slavery throughout the world was totally peaceful, but the southern United States and Haiti were just 2 among 20-odd societies in the Western hemisphere where violence predominated during emancipation. The radical abolitionists, among them William Lloyd Garrison, had advocated northern secession from the South. They felt that this secession would best hasten slavery's destruction by allowing the free states to get out from under the U.S. Constitution, with its fugitive slave clause and other proslavery guarantees. At the time of Lincoln's inauguration in March 1861, the Union still retained more slave states than had seceded. Hence, letting the lower South go in peace in 1861 might have been a viable antislavery option. If Northerners had been sincerely interested in ending slavery, rather than maintaining the federal government's territorial integrity, alternate policies suggested by some abolitionists may have achieved this goal almost as rapidly and with far less loss of life and of other liberties.

JRH

See also Abolitionism; Conscription; Mercantilism; Money and Banking; Secessionism; Slavery in America; War

Further Readings

Bensel, Richard. *Yankee Leviathan: The Origins of Central State Authority in America, 1859–1877.* Cambridge: Cambridge University Press, 1990.

Fredrickson, George M. *The Inner Civil War: Northern Intellectuals and the Crisis of Union.* New York: Harper & Row, 1965.

Hummel, Jeffrey Rogers. *Emancipating Slaves, Enslaving Free Men: A History of the American Civil War.* Chicago: Open Court, 1996.

Rawley, James A. *The Politics of Union: Northern Politics during the Civil War.* Lincoln: University of Nebraska Press, 1974.

Stromberg, Joseph R. "The War for Southern Independence: A Radical Libertarian Perspective." *Journal of Libertarian Studies* 3 (Spring 1979): 31–53.

CLARK, ED (1930–)

Edward Emerson Clark is an attorney and the 1980 Libertarian Party presidential nominee. Ed Clark, a corporate attorney in New York and Los Angeles, opposed the Vietnam War while remaining a Republican, but when President Richard Nixon imposed wage and price controls in 1972, he joined the Libertarian Party and quickly became a member of its national committee and California State Chair. In 1978, he stood as the Libertarian candidate for governor of California, winning 377,960 votes, or about 5.5% of the total cast. That success led to his selection as the party's 1980 presidential nominee. Along with running mate David Koch, a businessman who made large contributions to the campaign, he appeared on all 50 state ballots and that of the District of Columbia, an unprecedented achievement for a third-party campaign. A close election between Jimmy Carter and Ronald Reagan and the presence on the ballot of independent John Anderson may have depressed the party's chances, and Clark received 920,000 votes (about 1.1%). Although the campaign was successful in some ways—it had gained respectful, if not plentiful, media attention, inspired some 300 Students for Clark organizations, distributed hundreds of thousands of copies of its campaign book, and placed no less than 47 five-minute ads on national television—the results were disappointing. Following the 1980 campaign, many of Clark's key supporters appear to have lost interest in the party, and a number of them drifted away. Clark remains an active Libertarian, and his wife, Alicia, served as national chairman from 1981 to 1983.

DB

See also Conscription; MacBride, Roger Lea; Peace and Pacifism; Price Controls

Further Readings

Clark, Ed. *A New Beginning*. Ottawa, IL: Caroline House, 1980.

Doherty, Brian. *Radicals for Capitalism: A Freewheeling History of the Modern Libertarian Movement*. New York: Public Affairs, 2007.

Kelley, John L. *Bringing the Market Back in: The Political Revitalization of Market Liberalism*. New York: New York University Press, 1997.

CLASSICAL ECONOMICS

Classical economics refers to a school of economics, the most famous proponents of which were Adam Smith, Jean-Baptiste Say, David Ricardo, and John Stuart Mill. Writing from the end of the 18th to the middle of the 19th centuries, they shared an approach to economic questions that embraced market-oriented principles that were to revolutionize and transform Western civilization. The classical model of free trade, limited government, balanced budgets, the gold standard, and laissez-faire shaped orthodox economic thinking and was accepted by all nonsocialist economists until the Keynesian revolution of the 1930s. Today, the economic model put forward by these thinkers is again gaining popularity.

Adam Smith (1723–1790), one of the most important figures of the Scottish Enlightenment, is considered the founder of the classical model. He dubbed it "the system of natural liberty" in his magnum opus, *The Wealth of Nations*. Published in 1776, *The Wealth of Nations* was a declaration of economic independence against the prevailing doctrines of protectionism and state interventionism. Little progress had been achieved over the centuries because of the entrenched system known as mercantilism. The commercial and political powers believed that one nation gained only at the expense of another and therefore favored government-authorized monopolies at home and supported colonialism abroad, sending agents and soldiers into poorer countries to seize gold and other precious commodities. Smith carefully delineated the host of high tariffs, duties, quotas, and regulations that aimed at restraining imports, production, and employment.

Smith denounced high tariffs and other trade restraints as counterproductive. Trade barriers hurt the ability of both countries to produce, he maintained. For example, by expanding trade between Britain and France, traditional enemies, both nations would gain: "If a foreign country can supply us with a commodity cheaper than we ourselves can make it, better buy it of them." Smith's solution to the economic nationalism and isolationism that then prevailed was regarded as particularly controversial. It involved the free movement of labor, capital, money, and goods. Milton Friedman has noted that "Adam Smith was a radical and a revolutionary in his time—just as those of us who preach laissez faire are in our time." Critics contended that Smith's radical suggestions would lead to economic disaster and instability. To the contrary, Smith promised that the dismantling of the state regulation of trade, prices, and employment would lead to "universal opulence which extends itself to the lowest ranks of the people."

His eloquent advocacy of natural liberty fired the minds of a rising generation. *The Wealth of Nations* literally changed the course of politics, dismantling the old mercantilist doctrines of protectionism and poverty. This revolution in economic policy was a fitting companion to the American Revolution of 1776 and accelerated the industrialization of Britain, then in its infancy.

The invisible hand, a term first used by Smith, best exemplifies his model of economic freedom. In *The Wealth of Nations*, Smith argued that if individuals were left to their own devices, pursuing their own self-interests, they would generate a self-regulating and highly prosperous society. George Stigler calls Smith's invisible-hand doctrine the "crown jewel" of economics. "Smith had one overwhelmingly important triumph," Stigler continued.

"He put into the center of economics the systematic analysis of the behavior of individuals pursuing their self-interests under conditions of competition."

The French laissez-faire school of Jean-Baptiste Say (1767–1832) and Frédéric Bastiat (1801–1850) advanced the classical model of Adam Smith by championing the boundless possibilities of open trade and a free entrepreneurial economy. J.-B. Say, known as the "French Adam Smith," developed Say's law of markets, which became the fundamental principle of classical macroeconomics. Say's law, often characterized as "supply creates its own demand," focused on the idea that savings, capital investment, and entrepreneurship—all elements of the supply side of the economy—are the keys to economic growth, and that rising consumption is the effect, not the cause, of prosperity.

Bastiat, a brilliant French journalist, was an indefatigable advocate of free trade and of laissez-faire policies, a passionate opponent of socialism, and an unrelenting debater and statesman. Bastiat was unrivaled in exposing fallacies, condemning such popular clichés as "war is good for the economy" and "free trade destroys jobs." In his classic essay *The Law*, Bastiat established the proper social organization best suited for a free people, one that "defends life, liberty, and property . . . and prevents injustice." Under this legal system, "if everyone enjoyed the unrestricted use of his faculties and the free disposition of the fruits of his labor, social progress would be ceaseless, uninterrupted, and unfailing."

The British economists Thomas Robert Malthus (1766–1834), David Ricardo (1772–1823), and John Stuart Mill (1806–1873) continued the classical tradition in supporting the virtues of thrift, free trade, limited government, the gold standard, and Say's law of markets. In particular, Ricardo vigorously and effectively advocated an anti-inflation, gold-backed British pound, as well as repeal of both the Corn Laws, England's notoriously high tariff wall on wheat and other agricultural goods, and the Poor Laws, England's modest welfare system.

Unfortunately, after Adam Smith, classical economics suffered from a serious flaw that provided ammunition to Marxists, socialists, and the critics of capitalism. Smith's disciples, especially Malthus, Ricardo, and Mill, promoted an antagonistic model of capitalism that gave classical economics a baleful reputation, leading English critic Thomas Carlyle to label it "the dismal science." Instead of focusing on Smith's creation of wealth and harmony of interests, they emphasized the distribution of wealth, the conflict of interests, and a labor theory of value.

In his famous *Essay on Population*, Thomas Malthus asserted that pressures on limited resources and a tendency for the population to constantly increase would keep most workers close to the edge of subsistence. His thesis underlines the gloomy and fatalistic outlook of many scientists and social reformers who forecast poverty, death, misery,

war, and environmental degradation due to an ever-expanding population and unbridled economic growth. Malthus remained true to Smith's laissez-faire roots by opposing government programs to alleviate poverty and control population growth, but he failed to comprehend the role of prices and property rights as an incentive to ration scarce resources. He also misunderstood the dynamics of a growing entrepreneurial economy through the creation of new ideas and technology. Medical breakthroughs, the agricultural revolution, and economic growth have postponed the Malthusian Armageddon, perhaps indefinitely.

Apart from his many positive contributions to economics, David Ricardo created an alternative "distribution" model, where workers, landlords, and capitalists fought over the economy's desserts. He endorsed a Malthusian "iron law of wages," where wages are constantly under pressure from an excess supply of labor. In Ricardo's fatalistic system, wages tend toward subsistence levels, there is a long-term decline in profits, and landlords reap unjust returns. Karl Marx and the socialists exploited Ricardo's hostile system of class conflict and labor theory of value, concluding that all interest and profit obtained by capitalists must be "surplus" value unjustly extracted from the true earnings of the working class.

John Stuart Mill perpetuated the classical model and the Ricardian system in his *Principles of Political Economy*, the standard textbook until Alfred Marshall's *Principles of Economics*. Mill wrote eloquently in support of Say's law, free trade, the gold standard, and individual liberty, especially in his classic work, *On Liberty*. Yet his textbook is thoroughly steeped in Ricardian economics, where prices are determined by labor costs, wages and profits vary inversely, and long-run wages tend toward subsistence levels. Most significant, Mill separated the "immutable" laws of production from the "arbitrary" rules of distribution, which led intellectuals to support grandiose tax and confiscation schemes aimed at redistributing wealth and income, convinced that such radical measures can be accomplished without disturbing economic growth. Friedrich Hayek has commented of Mill's economic conclusions: "I am personally convinced that the reason which led the intellectuals to socialism, was John Stuart Mill." Regarding the classical model, Murray Rothbard observed that, "economics itself had come to a dead end . . . having thus given hostage to Marxism."

It would not be until the subjectivist Marginalist Revolution in the 1870s, led by three theorists who had uncovered the theory of marginal utility at approximately the same time, Carl Menger in Austria, William Stanley Jevons in Britain, and Leon Walras in Switzerland, that the classical Ricardian system, especially the labor theory of value, was challenged and gradually replaced with a sounder model that became the core of neoclassical economics. Menger and the Austrians reversed the classical connection between value and cost. Prices, they maintained, are determined by the subjective evaluations of consumers, which in turn set the direction for productive activity. Furthermore, wage earners and producers of goods and services are paid according to the fruits of their labors based on their discounted marginal product. Thus, through the discovery of the principles of subjective value and marginal utility, the marginalists reversed the tide of Marxist socialism and restored the virtues of Adam Smith's invisible hand and harmony of interests.

The classical model of Adam Smith faced another serious challenge during the Great Depression of the 1930s. In his book *The General Theory of Employment, Interest, and Money*, British economist John Maynard Keynes claimed that Adam Smith's invisible hand only worked during times of full employment. During depressions, Keynes argued, the government should abandon free trade and the gold standard, run deficits, and engage in large public works and welfare projects. Effective demand and consumption became more important than supply and savings, contradicting Say's law. After World War II, the Keynesian Revolution took the economics profession by storm, and the classical model was viewed only as a special case.

However, Keynesianism's inability to deal with problems of inflationary recession and uncontrolled government spending and deficits during the postwar period led economists to reassess the classical model. Moreover, a theoretical counterrevolution—led by Milton Friedman of the Chicago School and Ludwig von Mises of the Austrian School—resurrected interest in the virtues of classical economics. Harvard's N. Gregory Mankiw, who began his career as a Keynesian, surprised the profession by beginning his textbook with the classical model. Mankiw wrote, "in the aftermath of the Keynesian revolution, too many economists forgot that classical economics provides the right answers to many fundamental questions."

MaS

See also Economics, Austrian School of; Economics, Keynesian; Marxism; Mercantilism; Mill, John Stuart; Physiocracy; Ricardo, David; Say, Jean-Baptiste; Smith, Adam

Further Readings

Bastiat, Frédéric. *The Law*. New York: Foundation for Economic Education, 1998 [1850].

Glahe, Fred R., ed. *Adam Smith and the Wealth of Nations: 1776–1976 Bicentennial Essays*. Boulder: Colorado Associated University Press, 1978.

Kates, Steven. *Say's Law and the Keynesian Revolution*. Cheltenham, UK: Edward Elgar, 1998.

Malthus, Thomas Robert. *An Essay on the Principle of Population*. New York: Penguin, 1985 [1798].

Mankiw, N. Gregory. *Macroeconomics*. 2nd ed. New York: Worth, 1994.

Mill, John Stuart. *The Principles of Political Economy*. New York: D. Appleton, 1884 [1848].

Ricardo, David. *On the Principles of Political Economy and Taxation*. Cambridge: Cambridge University Press, 1951 [1817].

Rothbard, Murray N. *Classical Economics*. Hant, UK: Edward Elgar, 1995.

Say, Jean-Baptiste. *A Treatise on Political Economy*. 4th ed. New York: Augustus M. Kelley, 1971 [1880].

Skousen, Mark. *The Making of Modern Economics*. New York: M. E. Sharpe, 2001.

Smith, Adam. *The Wealth of Nations*. New York: Modern Library, 1965 [1776].

Stigler, George J. "The Successes and Failures of Professor Smith." *Journal of Political Economy* 84 no. 6 (December 1976): 1199–1213.

COASE, RONALD H. (1910–)

Ronald H. Coase is a Nobel laureate economist from the University of Chicago. Coase was born in England and studied commerce at the London School of Economics. Coase's primary contributions to economics came from his work on the interface between law and economics and his emphasis on transaction costs.

In 1937, Coase published an article that demonstrated the importance of transaction costs in the formation of business organizations. Transaction costs refer to the costs of finding trading partners, negotiating terms of trade, and enforcing these terms. Coase argued that, to plan their production, entrepreneurs must choose between buying resources in markets or forming their own business organizations. Because transacting in markets is costly, entrepreneurs form business organizations with permanent employees and capital so they can avoid the costs of always using markets.

In 1959 and 1960, Coase published articles aimed at changing the way economists think about externalities and efficiency. *Externality* is a term that refers to the costs and benefits that people experience because of someone else's activities. An example of a positive externality would be when someone uses a private detective to catch a criminal, which prevents future crime on behalf of would-be victims who did not pay for this service. An example of a negative externality would be the noise heard by those who live near an airport. The airport pays for the costs of fuel, planes, and labor, but not necessarily for the cost of soundproofing walls. Before Coase's analysis, all economists thought of externalities as deviations from efficient resource allocation and argued that the only way to deal with these problems was through government taxes and subsidies.

Coase argued that externalities are the result of transaction costs. Coase reasoned that if there were no transaction costs, people would bargain over externalities and, in so doing, internalize them. According to the Coase theorem, if transaction costs are zero and property rights are well defined, people bargaining in markets will generate an efficient allocation of resources. For example, people who live in the vicinity of an airport or factory can bargain over local pollution. This is not to say that bargaining will eliminate the noise or other pollution. Rather, bargaining will force the factory or airport to take proper account of this cost.

There are several important implications of this theorem. First, markets can solve externality problems after courts resolve disputes over property rights, no matter which party wins. Second, market institutions that lower transaction costs are vital to the functioning of markets. Third, markets *and* governments cost something to operate, so resource allocation by *both* markets and governments fall short of perfection.

Some argue that Coase is unrealistic because transaction costs are never zero. This sort of criticism demonstrates the failure of many to appreciate Coase's arguments. Coase maintains that economists should focus on comparing alternative institutional arrangements, rather than comparing one set of imperfect institutions to an ideal situation where people enter into trades effortlessly. Coase's analysis assumed zero transaction costs not because they really are in fact zero, but because this assumption allows one to appreciate their importance.

In 1974, Coase wrote an important article titled "The Lighthouse in Economics." In this article, Coase challenged the idea that only governments can produce and operate lighthouses. Coase cited examples of privately owned and operated lighthouses in England. Coase saw both private and public lighthouses as imperfect ways of providing lighthouse services to ships.

Coase's work is unusual as a modern economist because he hardly used any mathematics or statistics. As the editor of *The Journal of Law and Economics*, Coase tried to move economists away from abstract modeling—what he referred to as *blackboard economics*. Instead, Coase used verbal logic and descriptive historical analysis to arrive at his conclusions.

Coase retired from the University of Chicago Law School in 1979 and stepped down as the editor of the *Journal of Law and Economics* in 1982. He was awarded the Nobel Prize in 1991. Coase succeeded in stimulating debate over a number of legal and environmental issues. However, there remain many subtle aspects of his economics that are relatively unknown or misunderstood.

DMK

See also Assurance and Trust; Economics, Chicago School of; Externalities; Law and Economics; Market Failure

Further Readings

Coase, Ronald. "The Federal Communications Commission." *The Journal of Law and Economics* 2 (October 1959): 1–40.
———. "The Lighthouse in Economics." *The Journal of Law and Economics* 17 (October 1974): 357–376 [Reprinted in *The Firm, the Market, and the Law*, 1988].
———. "The Nature of the Firm." *Economica* 4 (November 1937): 386.
———. "The Problem of Social Cost." *The Journal of Law and Economics* 3 (1960): 1–44 [Reprinted in *The Firm, the Market, and the Law*, 1988].
Ellickson, R. C. "The Case for Coase and against 'Coaseanism.'" *The Yale Law Journal* 99 (1989): 611, 613.
Glaeser, Edward, Simon Johnson, and Andrei Shleifer. "Coase Versus the Coasians." *The Quarterly Journal of Economics* 116 no. 3 (2001): 853–899.
Posner, Richard. "Ronald Coase and Methodology." *The Journal of Economic Perspectives* 7 no. 4 (1993): 195–210.

COBDEN, RICHARD (1804–1865)

Richard Cobden is best remembered for his partnership with John Bright in heading the movement in Britain to repeal the tariff on imported grain, known as the Corn Laws. Cobden also was a dedicated advocate of international peace and an uncompromising opponent of war. He was born at Dunford, in Heyshott, near Midhurst, Sussex. When Richard was 10 years old, his father was forced to sell his farm, and the family was reduced to straitened circumstances. However, his son went on to make a small fortune in the relatively risky calico-printing business in Manchester. In May 1840, Cobden married Kate Williams, who bore him a son who predeceased him and five daughters who survived him. He never enjoyed robust health, and in April 1865 died peacefully in London with his wife, his daughter Nelly, and his best friend, John Bright, at his bedside. Although he was a member of the House of Commons for 22 years, he refused higher office and remained a backbencher.

The Manchester Anti-Corn Law Association was organized in September 1838, and its successor, the Anti-Corn Law League, in March 1839, to seek repeal of the onerous duties on imported grain. This tax kept domestic prices high for the benefit of those who owned land, who thereby received much higher agricultural rents. However, this tariff impoverished consumers, particularly those poor households, for whom bread was a principal part of their diet. Richard Cobden, John Bright, and Charles Pelham Villiers became the league's most prominent spokesmen.

After 7 years of assiduous organization and unrelenting agitation both inside and outside Parliament, the league was finally successful in its campaign to repeal the "bread tax" and so deny the "breadstealers" further ill-gotten gains. On January 27, 1846, Sir Robert Peel, the prime minister and leader of the Conservative Party, announced that henceforth all grain from British colonies would be admitted upon the payment of a nominal duty, and foreign wheat would pay a much reduced duty on a sliding scale. All existing tariffs on corn were to terminate on February 1, 1849, and thereafter wheat, oats, and barley were to be subject to a nominal duty of one shilling a quarter.

As a consequence of this victory, in July 1846, the league council met to wind up its affairs. Cobden moved the formal resolution to dissolve the organizations, and Bright seconded it. Subsequently, it was decided that a special subscription would be raised for these two men. As a result, Cobden received £75,000, of which £40,000 had to go to paying business debts that Cobden had incurred as a result of his preoccupation with the league, and Bright received approximately £5,000.

The Anti-Corn Law League had a profound influence on advancing the cause of free trade in Great Britain. To this day, the league remains a splendid, but all too rare, example of how uncompromising dedication to a single, comprehensible objective, combined with sheer hard work and innovative propagandizing, can successfully accomplish that goal through peaceful means.

Cobden also was committed to constitutional reform; to the disestablishment of state churches; and to a series of social reforms, including the repeal of the primogeniture laws, entails in land, the game laws; and, most important, the abolition of slavery. He was a firm exponent of fiscal retrenchment and tax reform. He was a forceful proponent of universal free trade and, while in Parliament, negotiated the Cobden-Chevalier Treaty of 1860 with France. He also vigorously campaigned on behalf of international arbitration and disarmament and was an outspoken opponent of foreign adventurism and war.

Cobden and Bright devoted a great part of their public lives to the cause of international peace, but with much less success than attended their campaign to repeal the Corn Laws. They defied establishment and popular opinion on several occasions, most famously when they opposed British involvement in the Crimean War (1854–1856). They hated both the immoral loss of human life and the onerous financial burden entailed by Great Britain's unnecessary decision to support the Ottoman Empire against Russia.

Cobden, who was firmly committed to the liberal ideal, used his understanding of how the political process worked inside and outside of Parliament to secure reforms based on the principles he embraced. From all accounts, his private and public life exemplified the highest standard of personal morality. He also was a public benefactor without equal. British Prime Minister William Ewart Gladstone said of Cobden: "I do not know that I have ever seen in public life a character more truly simple, noble, and unselfish."

JMB

See also Anti-Corn Law League; Bright, John; Free Trade

Further Readings

Cobden, Richard. *The Political Writings of Richard Cobden.* 2 vols. Naomi Churgin Miller, ed. New York: Garland, 1973.

Edsalls, Nicholas C. *Richard Cobden: Independent Radical.* Cambridge, MA: Harvard University Press, 1986.

Hindes, Wendy. *Richard Cobden: A Victorian Outsider.* New Haven, CT: Yale University Press, 1987.

Hirst, Francis Wrigley, ed. *Free Trade and Other Fundamental Doctrines of the Manchester School.* New York: A.M. Kelly, 1968.

McCord, Norman. *The Anti-Corn Law League, 1838–1846.* London: Allen & Unwin, 1968.

Pick, Daniel. "Cobden's Critique of War." *War Machine: The Rationalization of Slaughter in the Modern Age.* Daniel Pick, ed. New Haven, CT: Yale University Press, 1993.

COERCION

In *The Constitution of Liberty*, F. A. Hayek defines *coercion* as occurring "when one man's actions are made to serve another man's will, not for his own but for the other's purpose." Thus, coercion must be distinguished from other potential threats to freedom. First, coercion involves intervention in the form of human agency. Although it is a fact of human nature that we are not free to do certain things, these limitations cannot be understood as coercive because they are not the products of human choice or human institutions. Second, we cannot understand the concept of coercion as applying to all instances in which the agency of others comes to bear on our choices. For example, it would seem to stretch the term beyond its meaning to say that an individual is coerced whenever he chooses other than he would have chosen but for the intervention of human agency. As Hayek puts it, "If, for instance, I would very much like to be painted by a famous artist and if he refuses to paint me for less than a very high fee, it would clearly be absurd to say that I am coerced." To set these conceptual difficulties aside, one might say that coercion is defined as the use or threat of force to get an individual to act in ways that are contrary to his own will. This understanding of coercion fits well with its common usage in political contexts.

Because the state exercises a relatively straightforward form of coercion, libertarian political theory views this threat to freedom as the particular moral peril of the state. In fact, the irreducibly coercive character of the state and its institutions generates the central issue for political justification: What justifies the state's use of force and the threat of force? It is commonplace to suggest that, at best, the coercive powers of the state lend themselves to justification as a necessary evil. Accordingly, a great deal of work in libertarian political thought is centered on questions regarding the justification of the state and the specification of the proper limits of state action. It leaves open the possibility that state coercion cannot be justified and, as a consequence, that the tenets of libertarianism support a commitment to some form of political anarchism. Historically, however, libertarian theory has subscribed to one of two basic sorts of justification for state coercion: (a) that the coercive apparatus of the state is grounded in consent, and (b) that the justification for its coercive nature is grounded in the ways in which our interests are advanced by political institutions. What both justifications have in common is the assumption that the coercive power of the state is necessary to prevent more worrisome forms of coercion among individual members of society.

The consent-based justification for the state's coercive powers takes the following form: On the condition that an individual gives consent to be bound by the laws of the state, no wrong is done him when the state uses force or the threat of force to get him to comply with these laws. John Locke articulates this condition in his *Second Treatise of Government*:

> The only way whereby any one divests himself of his natural liberty, and puts on the bonds of civil society, is by agreeing with other men to join and unite into a community for their comfortable, safe, and peaceable living one amongst another, in a secure enjoyment of their properties, and a greater security against any, that are not of it.

Locke recognized, of course, that it would not be accurate to say of future members of civil society that they were party to any such agreement, so he offered an alternative form of consent to justify their place under the coercive institutions of the state. He held that

> every man, that hath any possessions, or enjoyment, of any part of the dominions of any government, doth thereby give his tacit consent, and is as far forth obliged to obedience to the laws of that government, during such enjoyment, as any one under it. . . .

Members of society subject themselves to the political power of others, Locke thought, in order that they might secure "mutual preservation of their lives, liberties and estates, which I call by the general name, property."

The interest-based justification of the state's coercive powers finds expression in David Hume's essay, "Of the Original Contract." Hume criticized the Lockean justification of state coercion because it cannot account for the moral force that "the consent of each individual" plays in the argument. According to Hume, unless civil society has already been established on independent grounds, a "tacit promise to that purpose" cannot be binding. In lieu of any appeal to consent, Hume proposes that the state's justification turns on the fact "that men could not live at all in society, at least in a civilized society, without laws and magistrates and judges to prevent the encroachments of the strong upon the weak. . . ." In much the same way, F. A. Hayek relies on interest-based considerations in his claim that state coercion is justified "for the sole purpose of enforcing known rules intended to secure the best conditions under which the individual may give his activities a

coherent, rational pattern." The point of such arguments is that we must tolerate coercion with respect to some spheres of human action in order that a "protected sphere" free from such influences might be marked off for each individual.

John Stuart Mill's *On Liberty* makes a similar appeal to the "appropriate region of human liberty" in his defense of the proper limits of coercion. According to Mill, "the sole end for which mankind are warranted, individually or collectively, in interfering with the liberty of action of any of their number is self-protection." This principle is commonly referred to as the "harm principle," and it is to be distinguished from what Joel Feinberg calls other "liberty-limiting principles." In particular, this principle contrasts with claims that interfering with an individual's liberty of action can be justified because the action is offensive, harmful to the person engaged in it, or generally thought to be immoral. Feinberg ultimately rejects the extreme liberal position, arguing that both harm and offense serve as legitimate reasons for state coercion. Other advocates of modern liberalism defend the paternalistic view that the state can justifiably force an individual to act against his will for his own good. Some conservatives go so far as to say that state coercion is an appropriate tool for making people morally better or more virtuous. What distinguishes the libertarian position is a commitment to the idea that harm to others is the only plausible candidate for a justification of state coercion.

TLP

See also Contractarianism/Social Contract; Hume, David; Locke, John; Nonaggression Axiom; Positive Liberty

Further Readings

Feinberg, Joel. *Harm to Others*. New York: Oxford University Press, 1984.
Hamowy, Ronald. "Freedom and the Rule of Law in F. A. Hayek." *Il Politico* 36 (1971): 349–377.
Hayek, Friedrich A. *The Constitution of Liberty*. Chicago: Chicago University Press, 1978.
Hume, David. "Of the Original Contract." *Essays: Moral, Political and Literary*. Eugene Miller, ed. Indianapolis, IN: Liberty Classics, 1987.
Locke, John. *Second Treatise of Government*. Indianapolis, IN: Hackett, 1980.
Mill, J. S. *On Liberty*. Indianapolis, IN: Hackett, 1978.

COKE, EDWARD (1552–1634)

Sir Edward Coke was an English lawyer, judge, and royal advisor. Coke was a prominent Parliamentarian and author and was especially important in the creation of the early modern common law. His ideas about the ancient constitution of

England, derived from both history and the common law, concluded that common law was both integral to the evolution of the law's independence from royal power and served as a limit over administrative and official conduct. These ideas framed the understanding of the law among English colonists in North America as well as strongly influencing the modern ideal of the rule of law.

Edward Coke was born 5 years after the death of Henry VIII, in Mileham, a village in Norfolk, England. His father was a lawyer, and young Edward grew up in a literate household before attending Norwich cathedral school and Trinity College, Cambridge. Edward's father, Robert Coke, died when Edward was 7, and his mother remarried Robert Bozoun, a man of some property. Edward married twice to wealthy and powerful women—in 1582 to Bridgit Paston, with whom he had 10 children before her death in 1598, and then to Lady Elizabeth Hatton, with whom he had 2 more children.

He began formal law study at the age of 19, entering first Clifford's Inn and then the Inner Temple in 1572. Called to the bar in 1578, Coke quickly demonstrated great skill, and he soon appeared with the leading lawyers of his day arguing cases of national prominence. His arguments in these cases not only influenced his later opinions as a judge, but also have had an enduring influence in protecting liberty of conscience and the transferability of property. Appointed a reader, or lecturer, of Lyon's Inn while still in his 20s, Coke's first judicial appointment came in 1584.

Coke's talent and background made him a natural candidate for the political network orchestrated by William Cecil, Lord Burleigh, Elizabeth I's advisor, an association that led to his promotion through both Parliament and the courts. Coke served in Parliament in 1589 and 1593, when he served as Speaker. In the interim, he was appointed Solicitor General and was promoted to Attorney General, apparently as a result of Elizabeth's own preference—over Francis Bacon—in 1594. At times, Coke's zeal in the queen's service took him far beyond the limits of fact and law, as it did when he served as the Crown's attorney in the infamous trial of Sir Walter Raleigh.

With the accession in 1603 of Scotland's James VI to the English throne as James I, Coke was knighted and appointed Chief Justice of the Court of Common Pleas, the nation's most powerful judicial position. Following a string of opinions consolidating the power of the law courts, at the expense of the clergy, the nobility, and eventually the King, Coke was promoted to the less influential, if technically senior, position of Chief Justice of Kings Bench in 1613, from which he was removed in 1616, although he remained a royal advisor and held other Crown offices from time to time. Coke returned to Parliament in 1621 and 1628, where he was a principal drafter of the Petition of Right, the forerunner of the Bill of Rights of 1688. In the days before September 3, 1634, as Coke lay dying at his home in Stoke Pogis, Sir Francis Windebank, Charles I's Secretary of State, personally seized Coke's papers and manuscripts, including writings that would not be published until ordered printed by Parliament at the close of the English Civil War.

Throughout his professional life, Coke was a busy writer, copying and editing judicial opinions of his own and others, as well as writing commentaries on various points of law. In 1600, he published his first volume of the *Reports*, detailing the arguments and opinions in cases decided by the courts, replacing the traditional form of brief written conclusions summarizing each case with the modern form of judicial opinion and its report. Each of Coke's reports summarized the arguments before the court based on fact and on law, the judge's rationale, and the final decision, recording the whole in detail for later consultation. Reaching 13 volumes, including 2 following Coke's death, the *Reports* contained many of his most influential opinions. He also wrote several books for practitioners, but his greatest works were the four books of his *Institutes on the Lawes of England*, the first of which was his famous gloss on Littleton's property book, *Tenures*, and the second of which contained his commentary on Magna Carta, which influenced English, French, and American ideas of a constitution as a separation of powers and a source of rights.

No one single conception of law is articulated in Coke's books, speeches, and writings. Yet his ideas about the law are consistent over his long career, and they may be summarized as taking the form of four principles: as a measure of human conduct applied by professionals, as a set of rules common to all, as a limitation on officials, and as a source of rights.

With respect to the first, law as a principled measure of human conduct applied by professionals, Coke described the law as "artificial reason" arising from the study and practice of the law's precedents and customs. He saw this study as taking "new corn from old fields," relying on long-established principles of reason and right to govern new forms of conduct. Although criticized for a loose approach to history and precedent, Coke's approach allowed him to apply the ideas as he saw them in Magna Carta and other constitutional instruments to the modern Parliament and monarchy of his age. He was thus permitted to summarize complex notions of property law and to apply the results to administrators, monopolists, and corporations. It also allowed him to argue in the *Prohibition del Roi* that only those educated in its methods and practiced in the law's application could practice law or adjudicate cases, which would exclude the king from doing so. In the late 19th century, A. V. Dicey summarized Coke's approach in *An Introduction to the Law of the Constitution*, with a rhetorical flourish appropriate to Dicey's own project:

Nothing can be more pedantic, nothing more artificial, nothing more unhistorical, than the reasoning by which

Coke induced or compelled James to forego the attempt to withdraw cases from the Courts for his Majesty's personal determination. But no achievement of sound argument, or stroke of enlightened statesmanship, ever established a rule more essential to the very existence of the constitution than the principle enforced by the obstinacy and the fallacies of the great Chief-Justice.

With respect to the second principle, law as common to all, Coke developed a model of the law as a single national limit on all who would limit the freedom of others. The church, local barons, and specialized tribunals and corporations all claimed powers over individuals—powers that Coke successfully argued were reserved to the law courts of record. He issued countless orders of prohibition and praemunire, barring these extralegal institutions from arresting, imprisoning, or taking the property of ordinary individuals.

The third principle, law as a limit on officials, implied for Coke that law set standards of conduct for officials and ensured those subject to their authority that the procedures and rules of fairness embodied in the law could be enforced. Thus, in *Semayne's Case*, a person who barred a sheriff's man from entering his house without identifying himself committed no crime because "every man's home is his castle." In *Rooke's Case*, a landowner ordered to pay for a drainage ditch was entitled to a hearing and to apportionment of the costs among the others who benefited.

Coke held that law was a source of and a limit even the powers of Parliament and the King. The King, he argued, could hold property only according to and within the protections of law and could exercise powers that were limited by what Coke argued was the ancient constitution of England. Parliament could not, as he noted in *Bonham's Case*, enact a law against right and reason, by making a single entity both accuser and judge in its own cause. Judges, too, were governed by "what a judge ought to do," including to rule in cases before them only according to the reason of law.

The fourth principle inherent in Coke's legal theories is that law is a source of rights. Coke was pivotal in reframing the feudal common law into a law governing commerce and empire. In so doing, he took old ideas about property and recast them into new formulae that answered new questions. Chiefly, he protected what we would now call rights, but which he saw as those interests and privileges in property and offices that were understood as the result of long practice and custom, barring the King from taking privileges from Parliament, as in *Bates' Case,* and barring Parliament from limiting the prerogative of the King, as in the *Case of Non Obstante.* Overall, Coke's common law protected the customary rights of the subject from interference from all, whether from interference by a neighbor, a sheriff, the King, or Parliament.

SMS

See also Common Law; Constitutionalism; Dicey, Albert Venn; Judiciary

Further Readings

Bowen, Catherine Drinker. *The Lion and the Throne: The Life and Times of Sir Edward Coke (1552–1634).* Boston: Little, Brown, 1991.

Boyer, Allen D. *Law, Liberty, and Parliament: Selected Essays on the Writings of Sir Edward Coke.* Indianapolis, IN: Liberty Fund, 2004.

———. *Sir Edward Coke and the Elizabethan Age.* Palo Alto, CA: Stanford University Press, 2003.

Holdsworth, William S. "The Influence of Coke on the Development of English Law." *Essays in Legal History.* Paul Vinogradoff, ed. Oxford: Oxford University Press, 1914.

Hostettler, John. *Sir Edward Coke: A Force for Freedom.* Chichester, UK: Barry Rose Law Publishers, 1998.

Sheppard, Steve, ed. *The Selected Writings of Sir Edward Coke.* 3 vols. Indianapolis, IN: Liberty Fund, 2003.

Stoner, James R. *Common Law and Liberal Theory: Coke, Hobbes and the Origins of American Constitutionalism.* Lawrence: University Press of Kansas, 1994.

White, Stephen D. White. *Sir Edward Coke and "The Grievances of the Commonwealth," 1621–1628.* Chapel Hill: University of North Carolina Press, 1979.

COLLECTIVISM

Collectivism, as the political theorist Andrew Vincent has noted, was first used in the late 19th century to refer to those writers and intellectuals who sought to use the state and the apparatus of government to control or regulate the economy and other aspects of civil society. It also has been employed to refer to those who favor an organic view of society, as opposed to individualism. *Collectivism* is sometimes used to designate the same philosophical approach to social and political life as the term *socialism,* particularly in the sense of the favoring of the collective ownership of the means of production.

Collectivism may be contrasted with individualism in the areas of methodology and the explanation of social phenomena, and in terms of social philosophy and ethics.

Methodologically, the individualist emphasizes the actions of individuals and the consequences of these actions, whether intended or unintended. Individualists are of course prepared to acknowledge that the actions of individuals occur within a social context, and also that some of their actions may produce results that in turn affect us, as, say, in the case of interest rates or an economic depression. Yet for the methodological individualist, to understand the social world, it is necessary to conceptualize all phenomena in the social world as ultimately reflecting the actions and preferences of individuals. Nevertheless, there is some disagreement among methodological individualists as to what degree acting individuals should be looked at in social and cultural terms.

Methodological collectivism exists in both strong and weaker forms. Strong versions of methodological collectivism view the key explanatory factors in society and history as the product of social or other nonindividual forces, of which individual actors are merely the instruments. Examples of such collectivist views include the ideas that Divine Providence acts through history, which has been held by any number of religious philosophers; that the World Spirit realizes itself through history, as in Hegel; that individuals are merely the bearers of particular social positions, as in some interpretations of Marxism such as that of the French philosopher Louis Althusser; and that societies are possessed of certain mechanisms by which individuals can be imposed on to act in keeping with social needs, more or less willy-nilly. By contrast, some weaker forms of methodological collectivism, among them those that follow Durkheim in stressing the significance of the social or some interpretations of Marx, may, at bottom, be ultimately compatible with the view that it is individual actions that play the crucial role in shaping all social phenomena, although these views direct our attention to other things. Other views—such as, say, the noneconomic structuralism of Claude Lévi-Strauss and various kinds of poststructuralism, need to be considered on a case-by-case basis.

During the 1950s and 1960s, there was some broad discussion in the sociological literature of the relative merits of methodological individualism and collectivism, to which John O'Neill's collection, *Modes of Individualism and Collectivism*, is a useful guide. However, the reader of O'Neill's work might well conclude that the arguments for and against one view or the other would be better pursued by way of discussion of the relative merits of these contending theories.

With respect to questions of ethics and social philosophy, the situation is equally complex. The ethical individualist takes individuals to be the bearers of moral value. What is valued about them may differ, from an emphasis on the satisfaction of their preferences, their pleasures and pains, to ideas about self-development after the fashion of J. S. Mill's ideas about individuality and autonomy. In addition, there is debate among a range of egoist and eudaimonistic views, which focus on the particular individual, on the one hand, and views of a utilitarian kind, on the other hand. While valuing the happiness of each individual, these views allow for trade-offs within which the welfare of a single individual is sacrificed to that of a collectivity of other individuals (although what counts, in such a calculation, is the well-being of each individual).

The literature provides both stronger and weaker versions of ethical collectivism. Plato's *Republic* is a particularly dramatic version of the strong version. Plato's concern centers on the well-being of society and on the functional role that each individual should play within it. Although some have found these ideas attractive, others have taken strong exception to the fact that, in Plato's scheme, members of the society who appear to make no contribution are simply to be eliminated, and the welfare of slaves, although

they serve a social function, is "beneath consideration." Other theories of ethical collectivism have offered the view that societies, states, or particular nations may be accorded ethical priority over the individual, as was the case with various political regimes in the first half of the 20th century, whether fascist, national socialist, or communist.

Weaker forms of ethical collectivism tend to be those in which the values that underlie their collectivism are ultimately individualistic. Consider Marx's early writings, in which a picture of a fulfilled life is painted in terms of individual flourishing that is not all that dissimilar to Mill's ideas about individuality. However, Marx's substantive social theory, and his practical political impact, placed a priority on working-class solidarity in a manner that seems ethically collectivist. But if what underpins his social theory are his earlier ideas, there is a kind of ethical individualism at work here. Its form, however, is distinctive. For in Marx's account, the conditions for individual flourishing have reference to individuals being engaged in creative activities that meet the needs of other people. Ideals that depict an individual's happiness as intrinsically involving participation in some shared form of life—from Aristotle's view of us as political animals who flourish only when participating in civic life, through contemporary communitarianism—may likewise be ambiguous. These ethical views, which seem to be forms of collectivism strongly opposed to individualism, may rest on possibly mistaken ideas about the conditions for *individual* flourishing.

JSh

See also Communism; Individualism, Methodological; Individualism, Political and Ethical; Marxism; Nationalism; Racism; Socialism

Further Readings

Greenleaf, William H. *The British Political Tradition*. 3 vols. London: Methuen, 1983–1987.
Marx, Karl. *Karl Marx: The Essential Writings*. Frederic L. Bender, ed. Boulder, CO: Westview Press, 1986.
O'Neill, John, ed. *Modes of Collectivism and Individualism*. London: Heinemann, 1973.
Popper, Karl. *The Open Society and Its Enemies*. London: Routledge, 1945.
Vincent, Andrew. *Modern Political Ideologies*. 2nd ed. Oxford: Blackwell, 1995.

COMMON LAW

Law consists of the rules and mechanisms through which disputes are resolved. Although either can be provided privately, most modern societies rely, at least in part, on state institutions to provide both. The term *common law* has several meanings in describing those institutions. Libertarian writers in particular use common law to contrast, on the one hand, the body of judge-made legal rules developed through the resolution of disputes between private parties with, on the other hand, the statutes and regulations created by legislatures and enforced by state authorities. Many nonlibertarian legal scholars have expanded on this definition to include the legislative behavior of contemporary American courts. Common law also is frequently used to contrast legal systems with British heritage to those derived from French and Roman law, which are termed *civil law* or *civilian* systems.

Perhaps the most important meaning of the term *common law* is to describe the process of generating rules through judicial consideration of private disputes. Classical liberal and libertarian authors, including Bruno Leoni, Friedrich Hayek, and James C. Carter, have written about this aspect of the common law. More recently, authors like Bruce Yandle have shown common law to be a powerful means of addressing modern problems like pollution.

The common law process has several important characteristics. First, the common law relied on private parties to bring a dispute to a court. Relying on private actors substantially limits rent seeking by restricting the courts' ability to choose the issues they address. Second, the common law evolved rules incrementally. Change was thus largely on the margins and based on the specific facts of a dispute. Third, the substance of the common law to a substantial degree rested on the intent of the parties. To an extent surprising to a modern reader, the early common law was the law of contract. When the common law specified a rule, it most often did so in the form of a default rule, leaving the parties free to alter the rule in future transactions if they so chose. Finally, the common law developed out of a competitive market for dispute resolution in England where, during much of the early development of the English legal system, different court systems competed for litigants' business.

Statute law, by contrast, is the product of some legislative process subject to all the problems identified by public choice theory. Changes in statutes occur discontinuously. The passage of the federal Clean Air Act Amendments of 1970, for example, radically changed the rules governing air pollution. Statute rules are most often written as commands, rather than as suggestions, and so contracting around statutes is generally not permitted. Finally, statute law is typically the province of a state-monopoly legal institution.

An example can clarify the difference between the common and statute laws. Consider the problem of consensual behavior that is alleged to cause harm to third parties. A legislature is able to pass a statute making the activity the subject of severe penalties, as state and federal legislatures have at one time done with regard to everything from sodomy to interracial marriage. The legislature might hold hearings to gather information or might rely solely on its

members' beliefs about the appropriateness of the conduct. If hearings were held, respected experts or Hollywood stars might be the witnesses. Questions, if any, would be asked by politicians and legislative staff, not by interested parties. A vote of the legislature, likely cast with an eye toward how the issue would play out in the next election, would decide the issue.

How would the common law address a claim of harm from consensual third party behavior? First, a specific individual would have to allege and prove the claim of harm in court. Procedural safeguards like cross-examination would be available to weed out frivolous claims. Both sides would have an actual interest in the subject matter of the dispute, ensuring vigorous analysis of the strength of the claim. Second, even if a third party could prove harm from the behavior with respect to one individual, that precedent would be subject to further testing in future lawsuits if an attempt were made to extend it. Thus, for example, if an individual claimed and proved harm from his next-door neighbor's conduct, applying the precedent against someone living in the next town would be difficult. Finally, the issue would be determined by a neutral decision maker.

Most state courts in the United States, as well as government courts in many other English-speaking countries, continue to render decisions applying what they term *common law*. The modern understanding of the term differs significantly from the institution described earlier. Courts today tend to view a common law rule merely as a rule that the courts are free to alter at will. The development of legal theories under which gun manufacturers are sued by cities alleging the manufacturers' responsibility for illegal weapons sales, employers sued by employees alleging violations of an "implied covenant of good faith and fair dealing" in discharge, or McDonald's sued for serving coffee too hot are all examples of modern common law reasoning. In sharp contrast, courts applying the common law in the 19th and early 20th centuries felt constrained by not only their own prior decisions, but by the structure of the rules laid out in cases across jurisdictions. Recognizing that their function was primarily to ensure that the expectations of the parties were met, those courts rarely abandoned earlier precedent, but restricted legal remedies to cases of actual harm and demanded a causal link between the defendant's conduct and the alleged injury.

The world's legal systems are traditionally divided into two families: common law and civil law. The civil law system, derived in part from Roman law, is dominant in Latin America, continental Europe, and the former colonies of continental European powers. Civil law differs from common law in several important respects. Rather than relying on judicial opinions, civilian jurisdictions are centered on comprehensive codes of written laws. Unlike the collections of statutes Americans call *codes*, civilian codes are intended to be consistent, complete, and written at the highest possible level of generality. Definitions, for example, are (at least in theory) consistent across areas of the law. Instead of relying on court opinions as guidance, civilian lawyers rely more on commentators' analyses of the code and logical arguments based on code structure. Mexican court opinions, for example, become authoritative only when the court in question has made five identical rulings on the point at issue.

Neither system is inherently more libertarian in implementation. Supporters of civil law point to the constraints on judicial and legislative activism provided by the logical structure of the code (while lamenting the recent trend of legislatures to create exceptions to the code for favored groups). Common law advocates argue that the increased flexibility of legal rules and reduced opportunity for legislative tinkering make the common law superior. Despite that neither system of law is intrinsically more libertarian, it seems clear that the common law served as one of the pillars on which British liberty rested and played a crucial role in shaping a free society.

AM

See also Coke, Edward; Hayek, Friedrich A.; Judiciary; Spontaneous Order

Further Readings

Berman, Harold Joseph. *Law and Revolution: The Formation of the Western Legal Tradition.* Cambridge, MA: Harvard University Press, 1983.

Hayek, Friedrich A. von. *Law, Legislation and Liberty.* Chicago: University of Chicago Press, 1973–1979.

Leoni, Bruno. *Freedom and the Law.* 3rd ed. Indianapolis, IN: Liberty Fund, 1991.

Morriss, Andrew P. "Codification and Right Answers." *Chicago-Kent Law Review* 74 (1999): 355–391.

Rubin, Paul H. "Growing a Legal System in the Post-Communist Economies." *Cornell International Law Journal* 27 (1994): 1–47.

Yandle, Bruce. *Common Sense and Common Law for the Environment: Creating Wealth in Hummingbird Economies.* Lanham, MD: Rowman & Littlefield, 1997.

COMMUNISM

Communism as a political and economic ideology dominated the 20th century. In one way or another, it has affected nearly every nation and institution in the world—and it persists in some nations today. Communism claims that a materially abundant and peaceful world can be created by abolishing private property and allowing the collectivity, through the mediation of the state, to plan and direct all aspects of society along scientific and rational lines. It is a utopian idea that sacrifices individualism for the collective good. Ideologically, it is the antithesis of individualism and laissez-faire economics. During the preceding century, communist regimes arose in Russia, China, North Korea, Cuba, Vietnam, and elsewhere, capturing nearly one half of the world's population and landmass. Intellectually, communism also captured many of the hearts and minds of intellectuals worldwide. In human terms, more than 100 million people died as a result of communism. Communists still rule North Korea, Cuba, and a few other states, impoverishing millions of people. But indications suggest that these totalitarian states are dying or morphing into more liberal, capitalist nations.

Communism's philosophical roots can be traced to Plato. But for all practical purposes, the first detailed analysis of modern communism was offered by the German intellectuals Karl Marx (1818–1883) and Friedrich Engels (1820–1895). They presented their plan to the world in 1848, with the publication of the *Communist Manifesto*. Whereas Marx and Engels preferred the term *socialist* for the society toward which mankind was inevitably moving, they felt forced to use the term *communist* to distinguish themselves from the numerous utopian socialist theories that were then circulating and to underscore what they regarded as the scientific basis of communist philosophy.

The authors argued that all history was the history of class struggle, a struggle between those who owned the means of production and those who did not. "Freeman and slave, patrician and plebe, lord and serf, guild-master and journeyman, in a word, oppressor and oppressed," as they put it. Borrowing from Darwin's evolutionary theory and Hegel's dialectical materialism, Marx and Engels viewed this conflict as inevitable and integral to nature. Man and the social forces in which he found himself were progressing over time. By the 19th century, this struggle had evolved to its highest stage: a struggle between the bourgeoisie, who controlled society's productive facilities, and workers, who were exploited in the interests of the owning class.

Marx and Engels argued that workers, the proletariat, should unite and, with the communists as their vanguard, overthrow the capitalists and institute a socialist society, the end point to which all history led. In this new society, devoid of religion and other "false ideas," a new man—a selfless man—would emerge. As materialists, Marx and Engels believed that this new world would engineer a new humanity. No one would be oppressed, and, hence, there would be no more conflict. The State would ultimately wither away.

Sixty-nine years after Marx and Engels laid out their plan, Vladimir Lenin (1870–1924) and the Bolshevik Party attempted to put a version of Marx's theory into effect in Russia. In 1916–1917, Russia experienced extreme political, economic, and social turmoil primarily because of its involvement in World War I and the inept leadership of Tsar Nicholas II. Finally, agitation between liberal democratic and socialist groups put an end to the regime in

February 1917. Pressed by his military advisors, the tsar abdicated power and the Provisional Government was established, first under a liberal and then a social democratic prime minister. In November 1917, Lenin and Leon Trotsky, who headed the more radical wing of the Communist Party, seized control of Moscow and thereby effectively took control over the nation. A one-party dictatorship, led by Lenin, was established, and he and the communists quickly moved to nationalize all industry and build the new socialist nation based on the centralization of the economy.

Lenin and his aides issued streams of orders to eradicate all vestiges of the previous regime and construct their new world. Countless revolutionary tribunals were established, as was the Cheka, forerunner of the KGB, to enforce Moscow's dictates. As a result, bureaucracies and the entire state apparatus mushroomed. All public institutions, decrees, and laws were crafted to serve the state, the party, and the revolution. The courts and the laws changed to reflect the desires of the Party and particularly of its leader. In effect, individualism and individual rights were crushed. As British Prime Minister Margaret Thatcher said in 1991, under communism, "the state [is] everything and the individual nothing." All rights, in practice, belonged to the state and the Communist Party. Everyone was coerced into serving the state. At the same time, the millions of people running the government constantly maneuvered to protect their own interests.

Part of the overall plan was to harness Russia's economic and political strength to foster communist revolutions abroad, particularly in industrialized Europe. But the scope of the plan—managing the world's fifth largest economy and largest landmass—and the impossibility of setting prices by committee proved the scheme's undoing.

In communist Russia, as in other communist nations, the state owned and operated the means of production. By the early 1930s, large-scale private property did not exist. Farmers, for instance, no longer owned the land they farmed, and the price of the produce they sold was not set by the market, by supply and demand, but was "calculated" by a committee that oversaw farm production. However, in the absence of any means to calculate the costs of production, these committees had no real way to calculate what, for instance, a bushel of corn was worth.

It is impossible to determine the value of all the human actions involved in producing or buying anything in the absence of some price mechanism. Only when consumers and producers are involved in uncoerced exchanges can one arrive at a viable price, the result of the interaction between demand for a good or service and its supply. Yet Lenin and Joseph Stalin, his successor, thought they could do just that for an entire country and for every product and service. "Socialism is one of the most ambitious creations of the human spirit," said laissez-faire economist, Ludwig von Mises, but "socialism lacks the ability to calculate [prices]

and therefore to proceed rationally." Without private ownership of production, said Mises, "there could be no rational allocation of resources in the economy."

The economic system that dominated communist Russia lacked any sense. Because the committees empowered to set prices had no way of knowing the value of any good or service, they were unable to tell industries and workers which good to produce and how much of it, which led to countless miscalculations. Investment made no sense, nor did production or distribution. Quotas were established whose real purpose was to make the committees and the state look good. As a result, factories produced large numbers of things that people didn't want—5,000 left-footed shoes, and so on. In addition, the economy was plagued by never-ending shortages. More dramatically, the collectivization of the farms led to widespread famine in the 1920s and 1930s in which millions died.

These continual failures, caused by the government's irrational economic policies, were blamed on everyone and everything except the real culprits. As a result, arrests ballooned. A vast network of slave labor/concentration camps was built, launched by Lenin and expanded by Stalin. People were worked to death or starved in these camps while large numbers of inmates were executed. Centralized "planning" and quotas were applied to arrests, interrogations, and executions.

Following Joseph Stalin's seizure of power on Lenin's death in 1928, Stalin established several "5-year plans" to boost production of capital goods and armaments. As a result, "living standards declined precipitously because financing the industrialization drive called for reducing wages to a minimum," as Richard Pipes reported in his *Communism: A History*. "In 1933, workers' real earnings sank to about one tenth of what they had been on the eve of the industrial drive (1926–1927). According to Alec Nove, a specialist on the Soviet economy, "1933 was the culmination of the most precipitous peacetime decline in living standards known in recorded history."

In the early 1930s, Stalin also sought to industrialize the countryside through widespread collectivization of agriculture. "By this was meant that the peasants would supply food for the industrial labor force, cities, and armed forces at rock-bottom prices," says Pipes. This process led to more shortages and state recrimination. In addition, Stalin was able to use the policy to eliminate his personal enemies and entire classes of people he viewed as enemies of the state.

About the only industries in which Soviet Russia was to excel during its 70-year history were in the production of armaments, especially nuclear weapons, in space exploration, and in crude oil production. The Union of Soviet Socialist Republics was the first nation to launch a rocket that successfully orbited the moon. The Russian T-34 tank was the top in its class for many years. The Kalashnikov AK-47 rifle still sells well and is used by the armies of at least 50 nations.

Recent research by Richard Pipes at Harvard University and R. C. Raack shows that the Soviets encouraged Nazi success in Germany and were not averse to a war between Germany and the Western allies in 1939. Further, the Soviet Union, together with China and other communist nations, fomented numerous revolts in the 20th century, including those in Korea, Vietnam, Cambodia, Latin America, Africa, and the Middle East.

Soviet Russia's intervention in Third World countries, its costs in occupying Eastern Europe for 46 years, and its massive military spending all contributed to the regime's downfall. Largely because of its bureaucracy and inefficiency—and its failure in allowing free markets to set prices—the U.S.S.R. could not keep up with the more competitive and efficient West. The communist system in Russia collapsed in 1991 and is still in the process of recovering from its 70-year nightmare.

Soviet-style economic policies were implemented in China, North Korea, Cuba, Vietnam, and other communist nations and produced similarly dismal results. Mao Zedong, the communist leader of China, was successful in taking over the whole of China in 1949, following nearly 20 years of bloody insurgency that left 4 million dead. Like Lenin, Mao established a one-party dictatorship and sought to industrialize and communize an entire nation through the abolition of private property, the collectivization of agriculture, and a series of 5-year plans aimed at industrialization. As in Russia, these policies produced periodic shortages and several widespread famines. More than 20 million people died in the worst of these famines, during the "Great Leap Forward" of 1958–1960. As in the Soviet Union, a secret police force was established and an extensive system of prisons and concentration camps—the *laogai*—was erected. Mao, like Lenin and Stalin, periodically purged his alleged enemies, as happened, for example, during the Cultural Revolution (1964–1975), when nearly 8 million people were killed.

After Mao's death, less-militant leaders took over. In the last 25 years, China has introduced a series of promarket policies and tolerated an extensive black market that greatly benefited Chinese consumers. Expanded trade with the West has helped weaken communist rule, but there is a long way to go, as the 1989 Tiananmen Square massacre showed. Also, despite economic liberalization, the Chinese communists have killed an estimated 1 million people for political reasons since 1976. The *laogai* prison system still operates today with about 1,000 camps.

Under communist regimes, the arts (and education) suffered fates similar to that which befell the rest of society. Arts committees, for instance, were established in Soviet Russia and other communist states, staffed by bureaucrats charged with overseeing and directing the production of books, periodicals, paintings, architecture, dance, and music. Communist "planned" art was supposedly to serve the interests of the state and, in most cases, glorify its Communist Party leaders. These arts elevated Lenin, Stalin, Mao, Castro, Kim Il-sung, and Marx and Engels, among others, to the level of secular deities.

The following is a list of communist regimes and their longevity:

U.S.S.R. (Russia)	1917–1991
China	1949–present
Eastern Europe (satellites of the U.S.S.R.)	
Poland	1945–1990
East Germany	1949–1990
Hungary	1948–1989
Czechoslovakia	1948–1989
Romania	1947–1989
Yugoslavia	1946–1990
Albania	1944–1991
Bulgaria	1946–1990
North Korea	1948–present
Cuba	1959–present
North Vietnam	1954–1976
Vietnam	1976–present
Laos	1975–present
Cambodia	1975–1993
Ethiopia	1975–1991
Angola	1976–1993
Mozambique	1974–1994
Nicaragua	1979–1990
Afghanistan	1978–1992

Communism promised to liberate man and create a utopia on earth, where men would become as gods. Through the application of science and reason, man would conquer nature and create endless abundance. But in this "scientific" drive toward the point where history and class struggle end, the individual was viewed as mere matter—capital—to further the interests of the group, the state. The individual person was regarded as no more than "an element, a molecule within the social organism, so that the good of the individual [was] completely subordinated to the functioning of the socio-economic mechanism," said Pope John Paul II, who spent much of his life battling communism in Poland. "[T]he concept of the person as the autonomous subject of moral decisions disappear[ed]." As a result, people were thrown into the threshing machine of communist policy and killed by the millions—more than 100 million victims worldwide.

Lenin, Stalin, and Mao actually set execution quotas. They would decree that perhaps 5% of the people were counterrevolutionaries, so 5% percent of the population was ordered killed, people from all walks of life, wrote political science Professor Rudolph J. Rummel, a leading authority on government killings. Rummel estimates that the number of people killed worldwide because of communism is 110 million. Conservative estimates of the number of people killed because of communism, as provided in the highly acclaimed *Black Book of Communism* (Harvard University Press), are:

U.S.S.R.	20 million
China	65 million
Vietnam	1 million
North Korea	2 million
Cambodia	2 million
Eastern Europe	1 million
Latin America	150,000
Africa	1.7 million
Afghanistan	1.5 million
TOTAL	94.3 million

Communism, despite its pretensions about science, materialism, and rationalism, functions like a religion—a secular faith. Despite the economic success of capitalism and political and economic freedom that has accompanied it in Europe and the United States, Marx denied these successes, and Lenin sought to explain them away. Marx, Lenin, Stalin, and their intellectual supporters constructed an elaborate fantasy—a false idea that captured the emotions and then the minds of many people. Hatred of capital was a cause that provided for many a faith to believe in and fight for.

Communism, as a quasi-religion, promised man abundance and happiness. It had its saints, such as Marx, Lenin, and Mao. It had its Bible, the *Communist Manifesto*. It had its commandments, its theology, handed down by the Communist Party. It had its sacrifices on the altar of the state—all crafted to create a heaven on earth. In reality, Marx's philosophy has managed to create a hell on earth, its mass graves and gulags its legacy.

MC

See also Collectivism; Kleptocracy; Marxism; Privatization; Socialism; Socialist Calculation Debate

Further Readings

Conquest, Robert. *The Great Terror: A Reassessment*. Oxford: Oxford University Press, 1990.

Courtois, Stephane, Nicolas Werth, Jean-Louis Panné, and Andrzej Paczkowski. *The Black Book of Communism*. Cambridge, MA: Harvard University Press, 1999.

Kowlakowski, Leszek. *Main Currents of Marxism*. 3 vols. Oxford: Oxford University Press, 1978.

Lenin, Vladimir I. *Imperialism: The Highest Stage of Capitalism*. New York: International Publishers, 1969.

Marx, Karl, and Friedrich Engels. *The Communist Manifesto*. New York: Signet Classics, 1998.

Mises, Ludwig von. *Socialism: An Economic and Sociological Analysis*. Indianapolis, IN: Liberty Fund, 1981.

Nove, Alec. *An Economic History of the U.S.S.R.* New York: Penguin, 1993.

Pipes, Richard. *Communism, a History*. New York: Modern Library, 2001.

Solzhenitsyn, Alexander. *The Gulag Archipelago*. 3 vols. New York: HarperCollins, 1991–1992.

Volkogonov, Dmitrii. *Lenin: A New Biography*. New York: Free Press/Simon & Schuster, 2006.

COMPETITION

Competition refers to the set of actions that sellers take against each other as they each try to increase their own profits. In actual competition, sellers alter the prices and quality of their products as they try to win larger shares of the market for a good or service from each other. In contrast, cooperation between sellers is the set of actions that sellers take in concert as they seek greater overall profits. Sellers sometimes conspire against buyers to set prices above competitive levels, but at other times they cooperate in the development of new products and technologies.

Our understanding of competition has changed over time. Most early economists agreed that competition was a combative and open-ended process. However, modern economists disagree over competition's exact nature. Adam Smith argued that competition in free markets causes self-interested individuals to promote the welfare of others. He argued that individuals who wish to gain something for themselves by trading with others could only do so by agreeing to terms that also benefited their trading partners. Smith saw competition among buyers and sellers as a means of reconciling interests between the two groups. Smith also recognized the potential for sellers to conspire together with the government to raise prices above competitive levels.

In the 19th century, Antoine Cournot argued that sellers could first agree to divide market share among themselves and at that point act collectively to increase prices above competitive levels. However, some time later, Joseph Bertrand argued that because sellers could dramatically increase market share by cheating on their agreements, efforts between sellers to cooperate in setting prices above competitive levels would invariably end in failure. This argument is consistent with Smith's view that monopolies were nothing more than government-granted privileges.

During the early 20th century, the concept of perfect competition was put forward by economists; it referred to competition as it would exist under the following five conditions: first, that there were a large number of buyers and sellers trading a uniform product; second, that the market had free entry and exit; third, that all market participants were fully informed regarding all opportunities for trade; fourth, that bargaining and price changes cost nothing; and fifth, that enforcing the terms of a transaction is costless. Under these conditions, individuals will engage in trades that bring about perfection in the allocation of existing resources. This static view of competition treats it as an end state or goal, rather than an ongoing process.

Some economists have used the theoretical results of perfect competition as a standard in judging the performance of real-world markets and found the market system lacking. In this view, private businesses wield "market power" to set prices above perfectly competitive levels. These economists argued that governments could improve upon actual competition with policies that bring about perfectly competitive results.

Harold Demsetz has countered these conclusions by arguing that perfect competition is too high a standard for either real-world markets or the government to meet. This argument is true because there is a positive cost to operating any economic system. Because both competitive market systems and planned economies cost something to operate, neither will allocate resources perfectly. These operating costs create imperfections in both private markets and the public sector. Demsetz maintained that economists who condemn the free market on these grounds fail to account for the possibility that government intervention aimed toward correcting market imperfections is imperfect. Thus, when the government intervenes to correct the market, there always exists the possibility that it might make matters worse. Demsetz further demonstrated that abnormally high profit rates tend to disappear over time, thus negating the purposes of government intervention.

Similarly, Friedrich Hayek argued that the concept of perfect competition misconstrues the true nature of competition. According to Hayek, perfect competition represents a situation where actual competition has ended. To Hayek, competition is a procedure in which competitors search for opportunities for profit. Competitors begin this procedure with relatively little knowledge of the situations that they face in the markets in which they sell. Competition between sellers then amounts to a discovery procedure as sellers learn how to increase their profits and buyers discover new opportunities for consumption. This analysis directly contradicts the assumptions of perfect competition, which are predicated on the presence of perfect information. Hayek stressed that competition is important precisely because it drives individuals to improve on the limited knowledge that they possess. Consequently, attempts to condemn the market system because sellers lack perfect information make no sense.

Because competition involves the discovery of new opportunities for trade, the assumption of perfect information means that "perfect competition" would exist only in situations where all competition is over. Israel Kirzner extended Hayek's arguments in noting the crucial importance of alertness on the part of entrepreneurs in discovering new opportunities for profit.

Hayek and Kirzner emphasized that competition is an open-ended process and doubted the realism of perfectly competitive models. Under perfect competition, competition is an end state where all individuals know who their best potential trading partners are. By focusing on continuous discovery, Hayek and Kirzner demonstrated the importance of competition as a means of collecting the information that the perfect competition concept takes for granted.

The importance of advertising to competition was discussed by George Stigler and Lester Telser, who demonstrated that advertising acted as a means of reducing the costs of gathering information. To Stigler and Telser, advertising fosters competition by informing individuals about the opportunities that await them in markets.

Some economists have noted that in some markets natural barriers to entry and exit limit competition and may even result in the formation of private monopolies. Although this concern is legitimate, there are two important points to keep in mind. First, as economist William Baumol has argued, potential competition can work just as well as actual competition. In some cases, monopolies may form, although it is possible for other sellers to enter the market. In such instances, monopolists (in the sense of single sellers in the market) will price their products as if they in fact had competitors. In other words, monopolists who fear potential competition will charge competitive prices to prevent entry by competitors. Because the primary complaint about monopolies is that they charge prices above competitive levels, it makes little sense for anyone to worry about monopolies that use low prices as a barrier to entry.

Second, even if a monopolist secures another type of barrier to entry and sets prices above competitive levels, this fact does not imply that there is no competition. Instead, these situations generally imply that competition has moved to a different level. Barriers to market entry are seldom free and generally require maintenance. Demsetz points out that if some companies have higher profits than others, it may be because they have some uncapitalized asset, such as a trademark or goodwill. Some entrepreneurs create a barrier to entry through innovation. If an entrepreneur creates a new product or develops a new technology that reduces costs, then that entrepreneur is able to charge prices above competitive levels. Patent laws facilitate this process by enabling entrepreneurs to earn extra profits by patenting new products and technologies. Although it is true that these entrepreneurs can charge monopolistic prices, it also is true that they invest money in research and development (R&D). The money that entrepreneurs invest in R&D represents the cost of gaining monopoly status, and the extra profits they earn represent a return on the money that they invested in creating their monopoly. Because patents run out, these monopolists must reinvest in research and development to maintain their monopoly status over time. This reinvestment results in long-term technological progress and product innovation that Joseph Schumpeter described as *creative destruction.*

Edwin Chadwick distinguished between competition within a field and competition for a field. Chadwick's research drew a clear line between competition between sellers for customers and competition between sellers for the means to exclude each other. Gordon Tullock revived this issue by arguing that entrepreneurs lobby governments to construct artificial barriers to entry as a means of gaining monopoly control over prices. Labor unions and professional associations like the American Medical Association are examples of resource market monopolies that derive benefits from artificial governmental barriers. These monopolists pay for their privileges; however, in these instances, the resources that the monopolist invests in constructing and maintaining barriers to entry do nothing to enhance long-term progress and prosperity.

In competitive markets, entrepreneurs compete with each other for customers. In monopolistic markets, entrepreneurs compete with each other to either win or maintain monopoly status. In the absence of government-granted privileges, competition enables individuals to benefit from gains from trade and innovation. However, competition does become onerous when individuals compete for special privileges from the government that enable them to charge monopolistic prices without improving the quality of their products or services.

DMK

See also Antitrust; Capitalism; Hayek, Friedrich A.; Interventionism; Labor Unions; Laissez-Faire Policy

Further Readings

Baumol, William. "Contestable Markets: An Uprising in the Theory of Industrial Structure." *The American Economic Review* 72 no. 1 (March 1982): 1–15.

Chadwick, Edwin. "Results of Different Principles of Legislation and Administration in Europe; of Competition within the Field of Service." *Royal Statistics Society Journal* 22 no. 3 (September 1859): 381–420.

Demsetz, Harold. "Information and Efficiency, Another Viewpoint." *The Journal of Law and Economics* 12 no. 1 (April 1969): 1–22.

DiLorenzo, Thomas, and Jack High. "Antitrust and Competition, Historically Considered." *Economic Inquiry* 26 no. 3 (July 1988): 423–435.

Ekelund, Robert, Jr., and R. F. Hebert. "Uncertainty, Contract Costs, and Franchise Bidding." *Southern Journal of Economics* 47 no. 2 (October 1980): 512–521.

Goldschmid, Harvey J., H. Michael Mann, and J. Fred Weston, eds. *Industrial Concentration, the New Learning.* Boston: Little, Brown, 1974.

Hayek, Friedrich A. "Competition as a Discovery Procedure." *Quarterly Journal of Austrian Economics* 5 no. 3 (2002): 9–23.

———. "The Use of Knowledge in Society." *The American Economic Review* 35 no. 4 (September 1945): 519–530.

Kirzner, Israel. *Competition and Entrepreneurship.* Chicago: University of Chicago Press, 1973.

Stigler, George. "The Economics of Information." *The Journal of Political Economy* 69 no. 3 (June 1961): 213–225.

Telser, Lester. "Some Aspects of the Economics of Advertising." *The Journal of Political Economy* 41 no. 2 (April 1969): 166–173.

Comte, Charles (1782–1837)

François-Louis-Charles Comte was born in Sainte-Enimie in Lozère on August 25, 1782, and he died in Paris on April 13, 1837. He was a journalist; an academic (a professor of natural law); the author of works on law, political economy, and history; a member of the French Parliament; and a key participant in the classical liberal movement in France in the first half of the 19th century.

Comte met the man with whom his name is commonly linked, Charles Dunoyer, in Paris around 1807 when they were both studying law. They later coedited the influential liberal periodical, *Le Censeur* (1814–1815), and its successor, *Le Censeur européen* (1817–1819), which irritated both Napoleon and the restored Bourbon King Louis XVIII by criticizing the authoritarian nature of their regimes. Issues of the journal were seized by the police, and Comte was sentenced to a heavy fine and 2 months' imprisonment. He sought refuge in Switzerland, where he secured an academic post in Lausanne (1820–1823) and then in England (1823–1826). It was while in England that he met Jeremy Bentham. Comte eventually returned to Paris to turn his Swiss lectures on law and economics into the prize-winning book *Traité de législation* (1827), which was to have a profound impact on an entire generation of French liberals, including Frédéric Bastiat.

Comte, with Dunoyer, had discovered liberal political economy as a result of the closure of their journal in 1815. Temporarily without a job, Comte was able to spend his time reading voraciously, and he eventually came across a new edition of Jean-Baptiste Say's classic *Treatise on Political Economy.* As a result of this encounter with Say, Comte not only expanded his primarily political notion of liberty into one that included an economic and sociological dimension, but also ended up marrying Say's daughter. The new kind of classical liberalism jointly developed by Comte and Dunoyer informs Comte's *Traité de législation* (1827), where he explores, among other things, the class structure of slave societies and the nature of exploitation.

In the later 1820s, Comte became involved in a number of public debates, among them opposing government schemes to heavily subsidize public works to catch up with more economically developed countries such as Britain and defending the National Guard in the face of government efforts to dissolve the citizen militia.

After the July Revolution of 1830, Comte briefly served as the political representative of the Sarthe in the Chamber of Deputies. He resigned his political post to pursue an academic career in the reconstituted Academy of Moral and Political Sciences. Comte edited collections of the works of his father-in-law Say and Thomas Malthus for the liberal publishing firm of Guillaumin. His last substantial work before his death was a lengthy defense of property rights and a history of the evolution of property in *Traité de la propriété* (1834).

DMH

See also Bastiat, Frédéric; Dunoyer, Charles; Free Trade; French Revolution; Say, Jean-Baptiste; Slavery, World

Further Readings

Comte, Charles. *Traité de législation, ou exposition des lois générales suivant lesquelles les peuples prospèrent, dépérissent ou restent stationnaire* [Treatise on Legislation, Or, Exposition of the General Laws According to Which Peoples Prosper, Perish, or Remain Stationary]. 4 vols. Paris: A. Sautelet et Cie, 1827.
———. *Traité de la propriété.* 2 vols. Paris: Chamerot, Ducollet, 1834.
Hart, David M. *Class Analysis, Slavery and the Industrialist Theory of History in French Liberal Thought, 1814–1830: The Radical Liberalism of Charles Comte and Charles Dunoyer.* Unpublished doctoral dissertation, King's College, Cambridge, 1994.
Liggio, Leonard P. "Charles Dunoyer and French Classical Liberalism." *Journal of Libertarian Studies* 1 no. 3 (1977): 153–178.
Weinburg, Mark. "The Social Analysis of Three Early 19th Century French Liberals: Say, Comte, and Dunoyer." *Journal of Libertarian Studies* 2 no. 1 (1978): 45–63.

CONDORCET, MARQUIS DE (1743–1794)

Marie-Jean-Antoine-Nicolas Caritat, Marquis de Condorcet, was born in Ribemont, Picardy, in September 1743, and died in Bourg-la-Reine before reaching the age of 52. He was a mathematician, a philosophe, a friend of d'Alembert, Voltaire, and Turgot, a permanent secretary of the French Academy of Sciences from 1776, and a politician during the French revolutionary period. He was elected to the Legislative Assembly in 1791 and later appointed its president; he then became a member of the Convention in 1792. Condorcet was active in a number of committees that drew up legislation during the Revolution, especially laws relating to public education and constitutional reform. Alas, he became a victim of Jacobin repression when the liberal Girondin group was expelled from the Convention. After a period of hiding in late 1793, during which he wrote his most famous work, *Sketch for a Historical Picture of the Progress of the Human Mind*, he was arrested and died under suspicious circumstances. It is possible that he committed suicide or was murdered by the Jacobins.

Condorcet was educated at a Jesuit school in Rheims and received a rigorous scientific education at the College of Navarre of the University of Paris. His initial researches were in the areas of calculus and probability theory, and he later attempted to apply mathematics to the study of human behavior and to the structure of political organizations to create a "social arithmetic of man." His "Essai sur l'application de l'analyse de la probabilité des decisions rendues, la pluralité des voix" ["Essay on the Application of Probability Analysis to Decisions Made by Majority Vote"], published in 1785, was an attempt to show how probability theory could be used to make political decision making more rational and, hence, more enlightened. Condorcet wrote articles on this subject for a *Supplement* to Diderot's *Encyclopedia* several years later.

Condorcet lent his wholehearted support to the attempts by the new controller-general, Turgot, in 1774–1776 to free up the grain trade and deregulate the French economy. Turgot appointed him to the post of *inspecteur des monnaies* in 1774, and he wrote numerous pamphlets defending laissez-faire reforms, such as the abolition of forced labor (the *corvée*) and seigneurial dues. His "Vie de M. Turgot" (1786) is a spirited defense of Turgot and of the continuing need for free market policies despite Turgot's failure to overcome the entrenched vested interests that opposed reforms in the French economy.

Condorcet also advocated other enlightened reforms, such as a restructuring of the criminal justice system, the granting of civic rights to Protestants, and the abolition of slavery. With his wife, Sophie de Grouchy, whom he had married in 1786, Condorcet's home proved an important salon for the liberal elite of Paris where contemporary issues were discussed, as well as the progress of the new American republic and the future role of provincial assemblies in a politically reformed France.

During the early phases of the French Revolution, Condorcet joined other moderate liberal reformers in the

Society of Thirty, for whom he helped draw up *cahiers* or demands for liberal reform that were presented to the Estates General. He also was active in the Society of 1789, whose members included the marquis de Lafayette and Dupont de Nemours. Condorcet edited this group's journal, and it was here that he published his important essay *On the Admission of Women to the Rights of Citizenship* in 1790. Condorcet was elected to represent Paris in the Legislative Assembly in 1791, but broke with the moderate liberals over the issue of curtailing the power of the monarchy. He joined the moderate republicans Brissot and Thomas Paine in calling for the end of the monarchy and the introduction of a republican constitution. He served on the Legislative Assembly's Committee on Public Instruction and wrote their report in April 1792, a report that was not adopted until 1795, after Condorcet's death.

Condorcet's membership in the Convention, where he represented the Aisne, coincided with the trial and execution of the King. Condorcet, while supporting the abolition of the monarchy, opposed the King's execution. In February 1793, Condorcet presented a constitutional plan to the Convention's Constitutional Committee based on his idea of using mathematics to create a rational and representative elected body that would serve the interests of all the people and prevent a small group from seizing control. His constitutional plan fell victim to the power struggle going on in the Convention between the liberal Girondins and the radical Jacobins. When leading Girondins were expelled from the Convention, Condorcet protested and was forced into hiding to avoid arrest. Over the next few months, he wrote his best known work, *Esquisse d'un tableau historique des progrès de l'esprit humain* [*Sketch for a Historical Portrait of the Progress of the Human Mind*] (published posthumously in 1795), which demonstrated how human beings had been able to improve their situation over the centuries through the use of reason, technology, and liberty, and how in the near future a veritable liberal utopia might be created. He left his hiding place in March 1794 and was soon arrested, dying in prison after 2 days in captivity under suspicious circumstances.

DMH

See also Democracy; Enlightenment; Feminism and Women's Rights; French Revolution; Progress; Turgot, Anne-Robert-Jacques

Further Readings

Badinter, Elisabeth, and Robert Badinter. *Condorcet (1743–1794): Un intellectuel en politique*. Paris: Fayard, 1988.

Baker, Keith Michael. *Condorcet: From Natural Philosophy to Social Mathematics*. Chicago: University of Chicago Press, 1975.

Condorcet. *Oeuvres*. Stuttgart, Germany: Friedrich Fromman, 1968.

———. *Selected Writings*. Keith Michael Baker, ed. Indianapolis, IN: Bobbs-Merrill, 1976.

CONSCIENCE

Liberty of conscience, according to John Stuart Mill, was the "first of all the articles of the liberal creed," and Lord Acton agreed that the idea of conscience played a key role in the development of classical liberalism. A "reverence for conscience," which consists of "the preservation of an inner sphere exempt from state power," is essential to a free society. This "appeal to personal autonomy" is the "main protection against absolutism, the one protection against democracy."

The idea of conscience is deeply rooted in Western thinking about ethics, religion, and politics. Among ancient schools of thought, it was developed most fully by the Stoics, especially Epictetus, who spoke eloquently of an inner freedom that is immune to external coercion. We can, he held, achieve this independence only through the use of "right reason," a moral faculty that enables us to discern the precepts of natural law and thereby distinguish good from evil. Thomas Aquinas holds pride of place among medieval philosophers for his discussion of conscience—a fact that led Lord Acton to dub Aquinas "the first Whig." There are instances, Aquinas claimed, where a person is justified in acting according to his conscience even if his judgment is objectively mistaken. Although Aquinas did not pursue the logical implications of this theory, it left open the possibility of innocent error in matters of religious belief.

The expression "liberty of conscience" had become commonplace by the 17th century, and this sphere of inner liberty gradually developed into the notion of inalienable rights. A right that is inalienable is one that cannot be surrendered or transferred by any means, including consent, because it derives from man's nature as a rational and moral agent. For example, it is often argued that we cannot alienate our right to freedom of belief because our beliefs cannot be coerced. Similarly, we cannot surrender our right of moral choice because an action has moral significance only if it is freely chosen. Our beliefs and values fall within the sphere of inner liberty, the domain of conscience. This sphere is inseparable from our nature as rational and moral agents.

Thus, according to the 17th-century English clergyman, John Hale, "All the power in the world is neither fit to convince nor able to compel a man's conscience to consent to anything."

The inalienability of conscience has been defended not only by thinkers whose primary concern was religious belief, but by more secular thinkers, such as Spinoza, who wrote:

> Inward worship of God and piety in itself are within the sphere of everyone's private rights, and cannot be alienated. . . . No man's mind can possibly lie wholly at the disposition of another, for no one can willingly transfer his natural right of free reason and judgment, or be compelled so to do.

A significant development in the history of freedom occurred as the authority of conscience was applied to spheres other than religion. From the distinction between the inner sphere of liberty and the external sphere of compulsion, there emerged the distinction between the voluntary sphere of society and the coercive sphere of government. As Guido de Ruggiero wrote in *The History of European Liberalism*:

At first, freedom of conscience is considered essential to [man's] personality; this implies religious liberty and liberty of thought. Later is added all that concerns his relations to other individuals: freedom to express and communicate his own thought, personal security against all oppression, free movement, economic liberty, juridical equality, and property.

Herbert Spencer, who described the tradition of Protestant dissent in which he was raised as "an expression of opposition to arbitrary control," provides an excellent example of how later libertarians extended the argument from conscience to spheres other than religion. In one of his first articles, "The Proper Sphere of Government," published in *The Nonconformist* in 1842, Spencer maintained that the "chief arguments that are urged against an established religion, may be used with equal force against an established charity." He wrote,

The dissenter submits, that no party has a right to compel him to contribute to the support of doctrines, which do not meet his approbation. The rate-payer may as reasonably argue, that no one is justified is forcing him to subscribe towards the maintenance of persons, whom he does not consider deserving of relief. The advocate of religious freedom does not acknowledge the right of any council, or bishop, to choose for him what he shall believe, or what he shall reject. So the opponent of a poor law, does not acknowledge the right of any government, or commissioner, to choose for him who are worthy of his charity, and who are not.

The ultimate test of any society is whether it permits its dissidents to think freely. Regimes that seek to control the way people think are far more pernicious than authoritarian governments whose object is to enforce conformity in behavior. Demands that we all act in ways that meet the wishes of the state rob us of our bodies, but those that demand that we also think in certain ways, rob us of our souls.

GHS

See also Aquinas, Thomas; Freedom of Thought; Natural Law; Paternalism; Stoicism; Virtue

Further Readings

Aquinas, Thomas. *Summa Theologica,* 1a2ae, 90–97. The Dominican Fathers, trans. London: R&T Washbourne, 1923–1925.
Dalberg-Acton, John Emerich Edward, First Baron Acton. *The History of Freedom and Other Essays.* John Neville Figgis and Reginald Vere Laurence, eds. London: Macmillan, 1907.
De Ruggiero, Guido. *The History of European Liberalism.* R. G. Collingwood, trans. New York: Oxford University Press, 1927.
Epictetus. *Enchiridion.* George Long, trans. Amherst, NY: Prometheus Books, 1991.
Locke, John. "A Letter Concerning Toleration." *The Works of John Locke in Nine Volumes.* 12th ed. London: Rivington, 1824.
Mill, John Stuart. *On Liberty and Other Writings.* Stefan Collini, ed. Cambridge: Cambridge University Press, 1989.
Spencer, Herbert. "The Proper Sphere of Government." *The Man versus the State, with Six Essays on Government, Society, and Freedom.* Eric Mack, ed. Indianapolis, IN: Liberty Classics, 1981.
Spinoza, Benedict de. *Tractatus Theologico-Politicus.* Samuel Shirley, trans. Indianapolis, IN: Hackett, 1998.

CONSCRIPTION

Conscription, which is mandatory mass military service, served as an informal ancient tool. Service in war often was expected for men, whether as subjects of an aggressive empire, members of an embattled tribe, or citizens of a political community, such as the Greek city-states of Athens and Sparta. This form of military service differed greatly and varied over time. This most powerful empire, Rome, however, relied on a professional military.

Complex feudal rules governed military service in medieval Europe. Kings could call up troops, but often did not directly organize these forces. Men who were resident in free towns could be obligated to defend their communities when these cities were threatened, and even peasants sometimes were organized into local militias. In addition, soldiers could be impressed. Localities often were required to provide a certain number of troops for the military. Mercenaries also became a common staple of Western European warfare. The Ottoman Empire relied on a professional, hereditary force, the janissaries, as well as troops raised by provincial governors.

For a time, war was dubbed "the sport of kings," conducted with only limited forces and imposing only limited costs. Indeed, mercenaries had a distinct incentive to avoid undue bloodletting. However, concern about expense, loyalty, and efficiency eventually inclined courts and governments toward various forms of mandatory service. The consolidation of centralized state power led to practices more akin to modern conscription.

By the mid-16th century, militia service became obligatory in a number of countries when Sweden began the process of creating a standing military based on mandatory military service. In the 18th century, Russia inaugurated a system of lifetime conscription, although the draftees were selected by their local communities. With a smaller population, Prussia—informally known as an army that incidentally possessed a country—obligated all young men to serve, first in the active forces and then in the reserves.

It was revolutionary France that inaugurated the modern era of mass conscription, imposing a *levée en masse* in 1793. Only by impressing the entire population (and executing tens of thousands of regime opponents during the great Terror) did the government believe it could resist the invading forces of France's multiple hostile neighbors. It was in France during the revolutionary period that the notion of "the nation under arms" was born. Imperial France under Napoleon relied on a more systematic draft of young men. As a result, one-time limited dynastic struggles were turned into unlimited national wars. John Hackett, the military historian, has observed:

> What was new in a Europe in which war had recently been little more than the sport of kings was the enthusiasm of a revolutionary nation in arms. In this the impulse to defend the Revolution was fused with and then dominated by a passion to defend the country, just as in Soviet Russia in the Second World War.

By the end of the 19th century, conscription was pervasive. Among the continent's major military powers, only Great Britain maintained a volunteer military. Amid growing fear of war, nations such as France and Germany made their drafts more rigorous, expanding call-ups and lengthening service terms.

The vast carnage early in the "Great War" led Britain to institute conscription in 1916. The resulting controversy split the government and led to Lloyd George's ascent to the prime ministership.

Although America had long maintained a history of mandatory militia service of varying sorts, the nation's Founders were suspicious of a standing military. The Madison administration's proposal for a national draft during the War of 1812 was not well received even before it was obviated by the end of hostilities. For the most part, the national government relied on a small force of Regulars for defense and called up national volunteers and state militiamen during conflicts, such as the Mexican American and Spanish American wars. The first resort to national conscription in the United States was during the Civil War, when both the North and South drafted soldiers after casualties mounted and voluntary enlistments declined.

Following the end of the Civil War, America returned to a volunteer military, but attitudes toward government power and individual liberty shifted during the Progressive Era, leading to a well-organized preparedness campaign. Prior to America's entry into World War I, a strong movement emerged that promoted universal military training and service. Conscription was then almost immediately imposed shortly after Congress declared war on Germany in 1917. However, the United States ended conscription and rapidly demobilized after the end of hostilities.

The perceived virtues of war attracted some advocates of civilian service. For instance, shortly before World War I, William James wrote of the need for a "moral equivalent of war," in which all young men would be required to work for the community. He argued that "the martial virtues, although originally gained by the race through war, are absolute and permanent human goods," and that national service provided a method for instilling those same values in peacetime. "Our gilded youths would be drafted off," he wrote, "to get the childishness knocked out of them, and to come back into society with healthier sympathies and soberer ideas."

Anachronistic though his vision may seem today, his rhetoric has become the touchstone for national service advocates. In succeeding decades, a host of philosophers, policy analysts, and politicians proffered their own proposals for either voluntary or mandatory national service. Some smaller, voluntary initiatives were turned into law—the Civilian Conservation Corps as part of the New Deal, the Peace Corps and ACTION in the 1960s, and AmeriCorps under President Bill Clinton.

Military service, however, remained the only form of mandatory duty in America. After World War I, the United States maintained only a small, voluntary peacetime force, whereas most of the European states retained drafts. As part of the Versailles Treaty, a defeated Germany agreed to maintain only a small professional force; however, the Nazi regime reinstated conscription as part of its military buildup before World War II.

With Europe at war and tensions rising with Japan, the United States initiated peacetime conscription in December 1940, the first peacetime draft in American history. Like it had in World War I, the draft expired after the end of World War II. However, in 1948, while mired in the steadily chilling cold war and with garrisons still occupying the newly defeated Germany and Japan, America reinstated the practice. Conscription faced little opposition during the Korean War, but the lengthy and ever more unpopular Vietnam War led to increasing public criticism and sometimes violent opposition.

Defense Secretary Robert McNamara proposed tying civilian service to the draft in the early 1960s, but that idea died amid growing hostility to conscription. In 1969, President Richard Nixon appointed the Gates Commission, among whose members was the famed economist Milton Friedman. Named after its chairman, Thomas Gates, the Commission studied a return to voluntarism. Following its recommendations, Congress ended conscription in 1973 and created an all-volunteer force (AVF).

The AVF had a difficult birth because the Vietnam experience had tainted the idea of military service, making recruitment difficult. Advocates of a return to the draft remained active until the early 1980s, when Reagan administration policies led to a marked improvement in the AVF. In succeeding years, the U.S. military demonstrated its capabilities as the finest military in the world. In each of

America's wars, draft advocates made a brief appearance, but were quickly rebutted. Only as recruiting and retention proved increasingly difficult during the lengthy Iraq occupation did the argument for returning to conscription gain any resonance.

However, other nations were then following America's lead in moving toward voluntarism. France abandoned conscription, which was formally abolished in 2001. Russia debated professionalizing its force. China was downsizing its large and ill-trained volunteer army. In Germany, the draft remained, but its strongest supporters were not advocates of an efficient military, but rather social service agencies that benefited from cheap labor as young men chose "alternative" service to avoid the military.

America's experience with the AVF has demonstrated the clear superiority of volunteer military service, in which personnel choose to join and make the military a career. Professionals serve longer, are better trained, and desire to succeed. The fact that recruits choose to enlist and the military chooses whom to accept creates a much more positive institutional dynamic than conscription, in which draftees want to get out and the military must take and keep most everyone. The advantages of a professional force have grown more obvious as military technology has improved, putting a premium on education and training. The strongest supporters of the AVF now work in the Pentagon.

The most serious argument for conscription revolves around making military service a duty of citizenship. The claim that "everyone should serve" remains powerful motivation for conscription advocates today, although a draft military would be less effective than the AVF.

The libertarian response is that a military that is required to defend a society based on individual liberty should be raised in the manner most consistent with individual liberty (i.e., voluntarily). A system without the moral legitimacy to rouse its citizens in its own defense has little claim on the mandatory service of those same citizens. Moreover, weakening today's military by reinstating conscription would impose a high practical price on soldiers who would be at greater risk in combat—as a result of an unnecessary attempt at abstract social engineering. Indeed, treating military service as a citizenship obligation is demographically infeasible because barely 5% of today's 18-year-olds would be called to arms. Such a system would be inherently unfair and would generate far more resentment than patriotism.

The most serious threat to the volunteer military in America is today's foreign policy of global intervention. Some day young Americans might tire of being sent to fight conflicts and garrison countries that are irrelevant to U.S. security. Then Americans will have to choose between their military and their foreign policy. In such a case, one can only hope that they remember what America is supposed to be and choose wisely.

DBa

See also Foreign Policy; Slavery, World; Voluntarism; War

Further Readings

Anderson, Martin, and Barbara Honegger, eds. *The Military Draft.* Stanford, CA: Hoover Institution Press, 1982.
The Anthropo Factor in Warfare: Conscripts, Volunteers, and Reserves. Washington, DC: National Defense University, 1987.
Bandow, Doug. "Fighting the War Against Terrorism: Elite Forces, Yes; Conscripts, No." *Cato Institute Policy Analysis* 430 (April 10, 2002).
———. "The Volunteer Military: Better Than a Draft." *Cato Institute Foreign Policy Briefing* 6 (January 8, 1991).
Berryman, Sue. *Who Serves? The Persistent Myth of the Underclass Army.* Boulder, CO: Westview Press, 1988.
Chambers, John Whiteclay II. *To Raise an Army: The Draft Comes to Modern America.* New York: Free Press, 1987.
Corvisier, Andre. *Armies and Societies in Europe: 1494–1789.* Bloomington: University of Indiana Press, 1979.
Hackett, John. *The Profession of Arms.* New York: Macmillan, 1983.
O'Sullivan, John, and Alan Meckler, eds. *The Draft and Its Enemies: A Documentary History.* Urbana: University of Illinois Press, 1974.

CONSEQUENTIALISM

Consequentialism is the term employed to describe the view that consequences are what matter for moral, social, or political justification. The view can be applied to various objects of moral assessment (e.g., to individual actions or to the policies and institutions of the state). What consequentialist theories of justification have in common is that the objects of moral assessment are to be evaluated by appeal to the results to which they give rise. Put simply, the rightness of an action or a political policy or institution turns on its tendency to produce maximally good consequences. Hence, consequentialism takes the form of a general theory of rightness. The theory specifies the right-making criteria for actions, policies, and institutions. As such, consequentialism takes no position on the value of particular outcomes. The outcomes to which consequentialist theories aim might be as varied as trying to maximize profit, welfare, or virtue. Hence, consequentialism does not assume a particular view of what kinds of outcomes are good, but rather can be applied to competing theories of value. Accordingly, consequentialism must be combined with a "theory of the good" to constitute a substantive moral or political doctrine.

For good reason, consequentialism is most closely tied to the doctrine of utilitarianism. In its most traditional utilitarian version, consequentialism is paired with a hedonistic theory of the good. According to Jeremy Bentham, for example, right actions and policies tend simply to maximize pleasure or satisfaction over pain and dissatisfaction. Hedonistic utilitarianism was pointedly criticized by John

Stuart Mill, who referred to it as a "doctrine worthy only of swine." Mill's alternative utilitarian proposal introduces the distinction between "higher" and "lower" pleasures and assigns to the former, "the pleasures of the intellect, of the feelings and imagination, and of the moral sentiments, a much higher value as pleasures than to those of mere sensation." Mill's argument rests on the premise that anyone "competently acquainted with both" types of pleasures would prefer the higher to the lower pleasures. From this argument, he famously concludes that it is "better to be Socrates dissatisfied than a fool satisfied." Thus, Mill's alternative to hedonism aims to answer two perennial questions in the history of utilitarianism: (1) How should utility be characterized? and (2) To what extent is it possible to generalize across the utility functions of individuals?

In moral philosophy, consequentialism contrasts most sharply with deontological theories of morality. Deontological theories hold that the rightness of an action is determined by features of the action, not by the consequences to which the action gives rise. Immanuel Kant's moral theory is particularly representative of this approach. Kant argued that an action's consequences are ultimately irrelevant to its rightness or wrongness. The moral worth of an action depends "not on the realization of the object of the action, but solely on the principle of volition in accordance with which, irrespective of all objects of the faculty of desire, the action has been performed." It is the consistency between the principle of volition and the commands of reason that determines an action's rightness. According to Kant, the rationality of autonomous agents requires that our actions be "universalizable," that is, that it be possible for us rationally to conceive of and will a world in which our actions are generally done. Against consequentialism, then, Kant concludes that a particular action can be morally wrong despite the fact that, if carried out, it would lead to maximally good consequences.

Consequentialism has been charged with being morally lax in some circumstances and overly strict in others. It is commonplace to illustrate these charges by appeal to familiar types of examples. First, in some circumstances, it is relatively clear that violating commonsense moral prohibitions (e.g., prohibitions against lying and breaking promises) would lead to maximally good consequences. Generally speaking, consequentialist theories must hold that such circumstances would make these actions morally permissible or, more strongly, morally required. This fact prompts the charge of laxness aimed at consequentialist moral theories and, specifically, at utilitarianism. It is conceivable that there are cases in which, say, lying about an individual's guilt would lead to better consequences than would telling the truth. But critics of consequentialism charge that surely it would be wrong to punish an innocent person simply because so doing would lead to better consequences. One standard consequentialist reply has been to

claim that it is the consequences of *rules* not the consequences of *acts* that are relevant to moral assessment. The distinction between rule and act utilitarianism makes it possible to offer the moral argument that one should act on rules of the sort that, if generally followed, maximally good consequences would result. In line with ordinary morality, then, the rule utilitarian is in a position to claim that morality prohibits lying and promise breaking and, moreover, that it does so for good consequentialist reasons.

The second charge (viz., that consequentialism is overly strict) derives from the fact that this theory denies the moral relevance of intentions in assessing the morality of actions. By so doing, it risks winding up committed to a theory of blameworthiness and punishment on which individuals are held accountable for the results of their actions, even when these results were in no sense intended. In other words, some consequentialist theories hold individuals responsible for their actions when ordinary morality tells us that these individuals were not morally at fault. Such theories also stand accused of being overly strict on the grounds that they see all actions as being either morally required or forbidden. For example, if morality demands that our actions maximize utility, it will normally be the case that there is exactly one action that morality allows. All other actions will be prohibited.

As we might expect, the distinction between consequentialist and deontological theories has its parallel in political theory. As applied to this domain, consequentialism is most often set against theories of individual rights. Rights theorists claim that some ends, no matter how good, cannot be legitimately pursued because so doing would violate the rights of individuals. John Rawls put the point succinctly in his *A Theory of Justice*, claiming that utilitarian forms of consequentialism do not "take seriously the distinction between persons." But it is important to recall that not all consequentialist theories are utilitarian and, more interesting for our purposes, that consequentialist theories can be consistent with and, indeed, supportive of highly individualist understandings of justice. In fact, rights theorist John Locke makes explicit appeal to consequentialist considerations in his argument for property rights. Locke writes,

> he who appropriates land to himself by his labour, does not lessen, but increase the common stock of mankind: for the provisions serving to the support of human life, produced by one acre of inclosed and cultivated land, are (to speak much within compass) ten times more than those which are yielded by an acre of land of an equal richness lying waste in common.

David Hume similarly appeals to consequentialist considerations in his argument for a stable system of property "fix'd by general rules." Hume tells us that, "however single acts of justice may be contrary, either to public or private interest, 'tis certain, that the whole plan or scheme is highly conducive, or indeed absolutely requisite, both to the support of society, and the well-being of every individual." Both Locke's and Hume's arguments appeal to the benefits that we all receive from a system of justice and so do not lend themselves to the criticism that consequentialist arguments must sacrifice some individuals for the sake of others. As Hume puts the point:

> every individual person must find himself a gainer, on balancing the account; since, without justice, society must immediately dissolve, and every one must fall into that savage and solitary condition, which is infinitely worse than the worst situation that can possibly be suppos'd in society.

In fact, many consequentialist thinkers have suggested that the good of the individual and the good of society do not really conflict. Adam Smith, for example, held that the individual, "by pursuing his own interest . . . frequently promotes that of society more effectively than when he really intends to promote [society's good]." More recently, F. A. Hayek has argued in support of "property, in the wide sense in which it is used to include not only material things, but (as John Locke defined it) the 'life, liberty and estates' of every individual" on the grounds that property is necessary "in order to maximize the possibility of expectations in general being fulfilled." According to Hayek,

> the only method yet discovered of defining a range of expectations which will be thus protected, and thereby reducing the mutual interference of people's actions with each other's intentions, is to demarcate for every individual a range of permitted actions by designating (or rather making recognizable by the application of rules to the concrete facts) ranges of objects over which only particular individuals are allowed to dispose and from the control of which all others are excluded.

Admittedly, Hayek's argument, like all consequentialist arguments, relies on contingent, empirical considerations about the nature of human behavior under different social and political orders. Therefore, if the consequentialist argument is to be convincing, it must show that individualist institutions have the good results that they are purported to have.

TLP

See also Bentham, Jeremy; Hayek, Friedrich A.; Hume, David; Mill, John Stuart; Rawls, John; Rights, Natural; Utilitarianism

Further Readings

Bentham, Jeremy. *An Introduction to the Principles of Morals and Legislation*. Oxford: Clarendon Press, 1876.

Hayek, Friedrich A. *Law Legislation and Liberty*. Chicago: Chicago University Press, 1973.

Hume, David. *A Treatise of Human Nature*. Oxford: Clarendon Press, 1978.

Kant, Immanuel. *Groundwork of the Metaphysic of Morals*. New York: Harper & Row, 1956.

Locke, John. *Second Treatise of Government*. Indianapolis, IN: Hackett, 1980.

Mill, John Stuart. *Utilitarianism*. Indianapolis, IN: Bobbs-Merrill, 1957.

Rawls, John. *A Theory of Justice*. Cambridge, MA: Harvard University Press, 1978.

Smith, Adam. *An Inquiry into the Nature and Causes of the Wealth of Nature*. Indianapolis, IN: Liberty Classics, 1981.

CONSERVATISM

Although the roots of conservatism are firmly planted in classical political thought, the terms *conservative* and *conservatism* were not used in a political context until well into the 19th century. Credit for the emergence of conservatism as a sufficiently distinctive and coherent political philosophy, one that could assume a place alongside liberalism and socialism, is generally accorded to Edmund Burke. In his principal work, *Reflections on the Revolution in France*, Burke sought to repudiate as forcefully as possible the strands of Enlightenment thought that fueled the French Revolution. Although the character of his undertaking did not require the development of a systematic political theory, he was obliged nevertheless to articulate the principles and assumptions that prompted this repudiation. From this work—and to a lesser extent from his other writings and speeches—it is possible to extract the major principles, beliefs, and assumptions that constitute the core of modern conservative political philosophy.

Burke, consonant with the teachings of Aristotle, regarded society as a complex, organic whole characterized by a bewildering multitude of interrelationships. Each society, he believed, was unique, having evolved over time under different circumstances, thereby giving rise to distinctive traditions, beliefs, institutions, and relationships. Although at one point he pictures society in terms of a contract, the nature of this contract is markedly different from that postulated by Locke, Hobbes, or Rousseau. For Burke, the social contract takes the form of a "partnership in all science . . . in all art . . . in every virtue . . . and in all perfection." "As the ends of such a partnership cannot be obtained in many generations," he continues, the society also "becomes a partnership not only between those who are living but between those who are living, those who are dead, and those who are to be born."

These views constituted the grounds on which Burke challenged the basic presumptions and tenets of Enlightenment thought and provided the foundation from which modern conservatism takes its bearings. From

Burke's perspective, no single generation possesses either the wisdom or the right to remake a society to suit its transient wishes. To believe in "this unprincipled facility of changing the state as often, and as much, and in as many ways as there are floating fancies or fashions," Burke warns, is to sever the "whole chain of continuity of the commonwealth." "No one generation could link the other," rendering "Men . . . little better than flies of the summer."

Although Burke was aware that a state must possess the means to change in order to survive, he was careful to set forth a morality concerning the conditions and processes of change. Consistent with his understanding of the evolution and complexity of society, he held that reason by itself has limited utility in reforming or restructuring society, and that effective change must necessarily proceed slowly, largely through trial and error, with due attention accorded to the traditions, prejudices, expectations, and ways of life of the people. "If circumspection and caution are a part of wisdom when we work only upon inanimate matter," he writes in this regard, "surely they become a part of duty, too, when the subject of our demolition and construction is not brick and mortar but sentient beings." Accordingly, he wrote of the complexities involved in the "science" of "constructing," "renovating," or "reforming" a commonwealth. Such a science, he warned, is "not to be taught a priori." Rather, it is a "practical science" that requires long experience, "more experience than any person can gain in his whole life," primarily "because the real effects of moral causes are not always immediate." Thus, he admonished, "any man ought to" exercise "infinite caution" in "pulling down an edifice" or constructing one anew.

Likewise, Burke's organic conception of society allowed no room for the abstract, metaphysical rights in the form they were asserted by the French revolutionaries. These "pretended rights," he insists, "are all extremes; and in proportion as they are metaphysically true, they are morally and politically false." The metaphysical rights, he maintained, are difficult to apply in their pristine form to the society; they are like "rays of light which pierce into a dense medium" and "are by the laws of nature refracted from their straight line." Given man's passions and the highly complex nature of society, Burke held that it is "absurd to talk of them as if they continued in the simplicity of their original direction." These rights, he felt, had a middling status; they were "incapable of definition," but "not impossible to discern." Their application in society, he emphasized, involve prudential considerations that frequently involve balancing "differences of good," "compromises between good and evil, and sometimes between evil and evil."

Another aspect of Burke's thought central to conservatism was his belief in an objective and divinely ordained moral order. He embraced the position, critical to much of what he sets forth in *Reflections* and elsewhere, that "religion is the basis of civil society and the source of all good

and comfort." He remarked "that man is by his constitution a religious animal; that atheism is against, not only our reason but our instincts." Burke staunchly defended the union of state and religion on the grounds that those vested with power "ought to be strongly and awfully impressed with an idea that they act in trust, and that they are to account for conduct in that trust to the one great Master, Author, and Founder of Society." With this understanding, of course, Burke wrote with a keen appreciation of man's fallen nature and the need for restraints through law and tradition. Thus, he could write, "The restraints on men, as well as their liberties, are to be reckoned among their rights."

Other aspects of Burke's thinking are central to the understanding of modern conservatism. Hierarchy, he insisted, is an inherent attribute of society. "In all societies," he maintained, "consisting of various descriptions of citizens, some description must be uppermost." He observed that "those who attempt to level, never equalize," but only serve to "change and pervert the natural order of things." He defended the unequal possession of private property and regarded the "power of perpetuating our property in our families" as "that which tends the most to the perpetuation of the society." In this vein, among the "real" rights of individuals is that "to the fruits of their industry and to the means of making their industry fruitful." In various writings, he defended decentralized authority. Indeed, in the *Reflections*, he referred to the "love to the little platoon we belong to in society" as the "first principle of public affections," as "the first link in the series by which we proceed toward a love to our country and to mankind." He embraced as well a fundamental postulate of the subsidiarity principle, namely, "Whatever each man can separately do, without trespassing upon others, he has a right to do for himself."

These principles, articulated by Burke, provide the foundations for modern conservatism. Their application and operation vary from country to country so that conservatism lacks the inflexible characteristics of an ideology. However, they all share the view that social institutions are the product of evolutionary development, and this judgment holds as much for man's "rights," which are bound to differ from culture to culture, as for any other aspect of law and politics. Conservatives embrace the view that reforms must be made within the matrix of a society's social history, with due regard for its traditional rules and prejudices, whether they be libertarian or otherwise.

GWC

See also Burke, Edmund; French Revolution; Fusionism; Hayek, Friedrich A.; Meyer, Frank S.; Spontaneous Order

Further Readings

Burke, Edmund. *Reflections on the Revolution in France*. J. G. A. Pocock, ed. Indianapolis, IN: Hackett, 1987.

Carey, George W., ed. *Freedom and Virtue: The Conservative/Libertarian Debate*. Wilmington, DE: Intercollegiate Studies Institute, 1998.

Meyer, Frank S. *In Defense of Freedom and Related Essays*. Indianapolis, IN: Liberty Fund, 1996.

Oakeshott, Michael. *Rationalism in Politics and Other Essays*. Indianapolis, IN: Liberty Fund, 1991 [1962].

CONSERVATIVE CRITIQUE OF LIBERTARIANISM

Libertarianism and conservatism are frequently classified together as right-wing political philosophies, which is understandable given the content and history of these views. Both philosophies are hostile to the egalitarianism that has motivated socialists and modern liberals and to the statism with which egalitarians have sought to implement their program. Edmund Burke, the father of modern conservatism, was a Whig who sympathized with Adam Smith's economics, whereas John Locke, the intellectual ancestor of natural rights libertarians such as Robert Nozick and Murray Rothbard, gave his own doctrine of natural rights a theological foundation. Conservatives in the Anglo-American tradition have generally tended to follow Burke in endorsing the free market, and belief in Lockean natural rights has often been associated with the sort of religious worldview that most conservatives find congenial. Accordingly, some conservatives have drawn the conclusion that libertarianism and conservatism are complementary tendencies that are best understood as merely different aspects of the same basic political outlook (e.g., as representing, respectively, the freedom and order that are both grounded in the same natural law, and whose unique balance within Western civilization proves that both are the inevitable outcome of a process of cultural evolution). The most influential defender of this fusionist position was Frank S. Meyer, and his views did much to shape the contemporary conservative movement. But it also has been criticized by other conservatives, who tend to regard the similarities between libertarianism and conservatism as superficial, masking a deep philosophical divide that makes the two views ultimately irreconcilable.

Conservatives who hold this view generally regard libertarianism as merely one utopian modern ideology among others and as no less beholden to bloodless and rationalistic abstractions than socialism and fascism, even if the abstractions ("liberty," "rights," and "the market," rather than "class," "race," or "the people") are different and less dangerous. As Michael Oakeshott said disparagingly of F. A. Hayek's *Road to Serfdom*, "a plan to resist all planning may be better than its opposite, but it belongs to the same style of politics." Russell Kirk's criticism of libertarianism along similar lines is perhaps best known. His arguments are stated in, among other places, his essay "A Dispassionate Assessment of Libertarians" and are representative of conservative misgivings.

Kirk's first objection is that libertarians no less than Marxists deny the existence of the "transcendent moral order" to which conservatives are committed and "mistake our ephemeral existence as individuals for the be-all and end-all." In response, many libertarians would say that libertarianism does not necessarily deny that such a moral order exists, but holds only that it would be wrong and self-defeating to attempt to enforce it through the intervention of government. To do so would interfere with an individual's right of self-ownership, respect for which entails allowing for the possibility that individuals will sometimes abuse their rights by acting immorally. However, some conservatives argue that this reply misses the point of Kirk's objection. The sort of transcendent moral order Kirk has in mind, they would say, presumably involves something like the natural ends or purposes attributed to human beings by traditional Thomistic natural law theory or God's ultimate ownership of human beings as affirmed by Locke in his version of natural law. This sort of order puts definite constraints on the kinds of natural rights that human beings can coherently be said to have because the point of our having natural rights, according to these theories, is to facilitate the realization of our natural ends or purposes (according to traditional Thomists) or to safeguard God's property (according to Locke). For traditional Thomistic natural law theorists, this entails that there can in principle be no right to do what is contrary to our natural ends or purposes and, hence, no right to do what is intrinsically immoral (e.g., using illicit drugs or viewing pornography). For Locke, it entails that there can be no right to do what would violate God's rights over us (e.g., committing suicide). The thrust of Kirk's objection, then, would seem to be that, in insisting on a right to do many things that traditional natural law theories, whether Thomist or Lockean, would regard as immoral, libertarianism implicitly rejects the metaphysical foundations on which many conservatives take our moral obligations to rest.

Kirk's second objection is that order is prior to either liberty or justice because liberty and justice "may be established only after order is reasonably secure." However, he argues, libertarians "give primacy to an abstract Liberty" and thereby "imperil the very freedom that they praise." To this notion some libertarians reply that Kirk has things backward: Respect for individual rights to life, liberty, and property is in their view the foundation of order, because it makes possible the voluntary transactions out of which order—whether economic order, or indeed, for some libertarians, even legal and social order—spontaneously arises via an "invisible hand" mechanism. This disagreement brings us to Kirk's third criticism, which is directed at the libertarian view that "what holds civil society together . . . is self-interest, closely joined to cash payment." For Kirk, the market mechanisms appealed to by libertarians necessarily presuppose a moral framework within which the members of society view each other as more than merely potential trading partners with whom they might contract for mutual benefit. Society, he says—and in this comment he echoes Burke—"is a community of souls, joining the dead, the living, and those yet unborn." This line of thought has been pursued most systematically in recent years by Roger Scruton, who argues that the economic, political, and legal institutions of a free society can function only against a background of mutual trust between citizens, which requires a shared sense of membership in a community defined by social ties and loyalties—religious, ethnic, and cultural—that run far deeper than considerations of abstract right and rational self-interest.

Kirk's fourth objection alleges that libertarians "generally believe that human nature is good and beneficent, though damaged by certain social institutions," contrary to the conservative view that human nature is imperfect and imperfectible, at least in this life. Presumably, what Kirk had in mind here was the kind of celebration of man and of the power of human reason that one finds in writers like Ayn Rand, although not all libertarians have put the same emphasis on this theme that she did. Still there is a tendency in libertarian thinking to attribute the shortcomings of existing societies less to individuals than to institutions, especially governments. Kirk's fifth line of criticism takes more direct aim at this attitude, contrasting the libertarian view that "the state is the great oppressor" with the conservative view that "the state is natural and necessary for the fulfillment of human nature and the growth of human civilization." This idea is again inherited from the Thomistic natural law tradition, which regarded the state, no less than the family and the Church, as a social institution having an objective nature that does not arise from human convention or contract.

In the course of making this argument, Kirk also complains that "libertarians confound the *state* with *government;* in truth, government is the temporary instrument of the state." The state, he maintains, is the organic social whole of which government is but the executive organ, whose primary function is the restraint of those individual passions and interests that might threaten the common good. Some libertarians (such as adherents of the public choice analysis of governmental action) would object that government officials are motivated by selfish passions and interests no less than are private individuals. However, conservatives tend to argue that in the modern world this fact holds true largely because of the predominant individualist ethos, which models all human relations on market transactions and government on the private firm so that even the occupants of governmental offices inevitably regard them

as a means of personal advancement. The older ideals of *noblesse oblige* and of government as a sacred trust vouchsafed to men by God for the public interest rather than private gain were destroyed when the traditional view of the state as a divinely ordained natural institution gave way to the classical liberal view of the state as merely a human artifact created by a social contract entirely for the furtherance of private interests. From the conservative point of view, the libertarian critique of the pathologies of the modern state is analogous to a doctor's diagnosis of a disease that he has inflicted on his patient.

Kirk's final objection to libertarianism is that it "fancies that this world is a stage for the ego, with its appetites and self-assertive passions" and eschews the "duty, discipline, and sacrifice" on which the preservation of society depends. This view is "impious, in the sense of the old Roman *pietas;* that is, the libertarian does not respect ancient beliefs and customs, or the natural world, or love of country." These charges might seem unfair especially because many libertarians are religious and patriotic. Kirk's criticism, however, is presumably directed not at the personal motives of libertarians, but rather at the implications of their philosophy. What conservatives tend to object to in libertarianism is its insistence that we can have no enforceable positive obligations to others to which we do not explicitly consent. Most conservatives argue that we actually have many such obligations: to our parents, children, and other kin; to our country; and, at least in some circumstances, to those members of society who are in extreme need. These obligations are not based on an egalitarian conception of justice, to which conservatives would object no less vehemently than libertarians do, but rather on an organic and frankly inegalitarian view of society in which, to quote a line from Marcus Aurelius cited by Kirk, "we are made for cooperation, like the hands, like the feet." Not all of us have equal honor or equal duties, but each of us nevertheless plays an irreplaceable role in the overall social body with the strongest members having, if not a duty to renounce their strength, at least a duty to use that strength to help the weakest. Conservatives hold that this help should come primarily from families, churches, and other private agencies closest to those in need, but a role for government, especially at the local level, cannot be dogmatically ruled out.

Thus, Scruton objects to Nozick's claim that taxation amounts to forced labor, holding that "if we are to concede such an argument, then we abolish the conservative enterprise, and cease to acknowledge the web of obligations by which citizens are bound to each other and to the state." If, as many conservatives hold, the state is a natural institution that exists to provide for the common good, then it has a right to a portion of our income so that it will have the wherewithal to perform its proper functions. Although conservatives tend to favor strong private property rights, many of them regard property as having a social function that entails that at least under certain well-defined circumstances others can have a rightful claim to a part of our surplus wealth.

How a libertarian might reply to such conservative criticisms will probably depend, in large part, on whether he is attracted to Meyer's fusionism. A libertarian who is already sympathetic with the Burkean traditionalist and natural law premises to which conservatives appeal will find that he has to take conservative objections seriously and try to find some way of retaining these premises while avoiding the conclusions Kirk and others would draw from them. Those committed instead to a utilitarian or contractarian version of libertarianism will probably be unlikely to find such conservative premises attractive in the first place and are bound to be less troubled by the conservative critique.

EF

See also Burke, Edmund; Conservatism; Fusionism; Liberalism, Classical; Meyer, Frank S.; Progress

Further Readings

Carey, George W., ed. *Freedom and Virtue: The Conservative/ Libertarian Debate*. Wilmington, DE: Intercollegiate Studies Institute, 1998.
Hamowy, Ronald. "Liberalism and Neo-Conservatism: Is a Synthesis Possible?" *Modern Age* 8 (Fall 1964): 350–359.
Kirk, Russell. *The Politics of Prudence*. Bryn Mawr, PA: Intercollegiate Studies Institute, 1993.
Meyer, Frank S. *In Defense of Freedom and Related Essays*. Indianapolis, IN: Liberty Fund, 1996.
Oakeshott, Michael. *Rationalism in Politics and Other Essays*. Indianapolis, IN: Liberty Fund, 1991.
Scruton, Roger. *The Meaning of Conservatism*. 3rd ed. Basingstoke, UK: Palgrave Macmillan, 2001.

Constant, Benjamin (1767–1830)

Henri-Benjamin Constant de Rebecque was born in Lausanne, Switzerland, and died in Paris. He was a novelist, political theorist, journalist, and politician who, through his education and personal inclination, brought English and Scottish notions of liberal constitutional monarchy to France. It was unusual for members of his generation to study in Germany (Erlangen) and Scotland (Edinburgh), but his experience enriched classical liberalism by combining the theoretical French passion for liberty with an appreciation of English constitutional monarchism and the evolutionary and historical approach of the Scottish school of liberal thought.

In the late 1780s, Constant showed great promise as an original political thinker. However, he wasted a good deal of his time in a series of failed love affairs, excessive gambling, and duels. Fortunately, his family connections gained him a position as a chamberlain to the Duke of Brunswick in Paris, where he was a witness to the beginning of the French Revolution. The crucial turning point in his life occurred on his return from Switzerland in 1794, when he met with Germaine de Staël, the daughter of the one-time director of finance under Louis XVI and a political hostess of immense authority whose salon dominated Parisian social life. He became her lover and, under her guidance, began his career as a political pamphleteer and commentator. At her salon, Constant met many constitutional monarchists and aristocratic liberals. The two returned to Paris in 1795 after the fall of the Jacobins, and Constant supported the Directory (the successor government to the Convention) by writing pamphlets defending the coup that brought it to power, an act he was later to regret.

Constant began his political career in 1799, when he was elected a member of the Tribunate under Napoleon's Consulate. He served there until 1802. His criticisms of Napoleon's attempts to dismantle the representative system and to remove any checks on his power got him dismissed from the Tribunate and forced him into exile. He and de Staël spent their time traveling in Germany or at her estate at Coppet in Switzerland, where they produced a steady stream of pamphlets critical of Napoleon's regime. It was here that Constant wrote his famous romantic novel, *Adolphe* (1807, published 1816), and his scathing attack on Napoleon's militarism and political tyranny, "The Spirit of Conquest and Usurpation and Their Relation to European Civilization" (1814). In that essay, Constant made two important distinctions, one between ancient and modern notions of liberty and the other between ancient military society and modern commercial society. With regard to liberty, Constant argued that in ancient societies liberty was largely seen as political participation, whereas in modern societies liberty was seen as a private sphere protected from intrusion by the state. Constant argued that ancient societies acquired wealth primarily through conquest and exploitation, whereas modern commercial societies acquired wealth primarily through peaceful exchange and industry. With the defeat of Napoleon, Constant predicted that European society was on the eve of a new era of peace, industry, and prosperity—a view of history developed at much greater length by the economists Charles Comte, Charles Dunoyer, and Gustave de Molinari.

Surprisingly, Constant was invited back to Paris by Napoleon after his escape from Elba in 1814 to draw up a new constitution, the *Acte additionnel aux constitutions de l'empire*, or the "Benjamine" as it was known. Although it was never implemented, it proved an interesting design for a constitutional monarchy with a property-based but still quite extensive franchise. While advising Napoleon on constitutional reform, Constant published his first extensive statement of his own political views in "Principles of Politics Applicable to all Representative Governments" (1815), in which he argues that "constitutional monarchy offers us . . . that neutral power so indispensable for all regular liberty." When Napoleon fell from power again, Constant was once again forced into exile for his recent collaboration with the restored Napoleonic government—this time by the restored Bourbon monarchy.

After spending some time in England, Constant returned to France to resume his political career. He was elected to the Chamber of Deputies in 1819, where he served until his death in 1830, first representing Sarthe and then Paris. He also served as president of the Council of State. Constant combined his political duties with an active career in journalism and political pamphleteering. The main issues of the 1820s revolved around the constitutional limits to the King's power and the King's attempts to break free of them. Constant was a member of a group of liberals who wished to protect the constitution and to prevent the King from undermining it. Constant wrote pamphlets defending freedom of speech, ministerial responsibility, and religious toleration and supporting a number of oppressed groups, among them peasants against their aristocratic landlords, slaves in the French colonies, and the Greeks in their struggle against the Turkish Empire. His work was often censored by the regime, but he attempted to frustrate the censors by writing pamphlets more than 30 pages in length (shorter pamphlets were subject to prepublication censorship) and by putting his most critical comments in the footnotes, which he was confident the censors would never read.

While he was a member of the Chamber of Deputies, Constant continued to write more substantial theoretical works. He further developed his ideas on liberal constitutionalism in Course on Constitutional Politics (1818–1820). In his *Commentary on the Works of Filangieri* (1822), he advocated laissez-faire economic policies and the "night watchman state," and in his last major work, *On Religion Considered in its Source, Forms, and Developments* (1824–1831), he explored the relationship among religion, despotism, and liberty. He researched and wrote a substantial part of his monograph on religion when he was forced to temporarily retire from politics in 1822 after his arrest for engaging in a plot to overthrow the government. He was acquitted of this charge and returned to the Chamber of Deputies to represent Paris in 1824. At that point, the government tried to have this trenchant critic of its policies barred from the Chamber on the grounds that he was not a French citizen inasmuch as he was born in Switzerland. The government was not successful, and Constant resumed his seat to continue his struggle to defend liberty—opposing an Indemnity Bill to reimburse emigré aristocrats for property lost during the Revolution, opposing the Church's efforts to censor religious publications and to exclude Protestants

from teaching positions in schools and universities, and opposing a more restrictive press law. In the Chamber, Constant was a charismatic speaker and a somewhat eccentric figure. When he spoke on constitutional matters, he was authoritative and persuasive. He occasionally reverted to the excesses of his youth, however, such as when he fought a duel with an aristocrat from an armchair to which he was confined as a result of a knee injury.

In the late 19th and 20th centuries, Constant's reputation in France rested primarily on his authorship of the romantic novel, *Adolphe*, and of his diaries. His reputation as a political theorist has fared better in the English-speaking world, where his contribution to the theory of liberal constitutionalism has been long recognized, especially in the last three decades, where his political writings have undergone an intellectual renaissance among Anglo-American scholars.

DMH

See also Comte, Charles; Constitutionalism; Dunoyer, Charles; Enlightenment; French Revolution; Molinari Gustave de

Further Readings

Constant, Benjamin. *Oeuvres complètes*. Tübingen, Germany: M. Niemeyer, 1995.

Dodge, Guy Howard. *Benjamin Constant's Philosophy of Liberalism*. Chapel Hill: University of North Carolina Press, 1980.

Fontana, Biancamaria. *Benjamin Constant and the Post-Revolutionary Mind*. New Haven, CT: Yale University Press, 1991.

Holmes, Stephen. *Benjamin Constant and the Making of Modern Liberalism*. New Haven, CT: Yale University Press, 1984.

Kelley, George Armstrong. *The Humane Comedy: Constant, Tocqueville, and French Liberalism*. Cambridge: Cambridge University Press, 1992.

Wood, Dennis. *Benjamin Constant: A Biography*. New York: Routledge, 1993.

Constitution, U.S.

Adopted at a special convention that met in Philadelphia the summer of 1787 and then ratified by state conventions during the years 1787–1790, the U.S. Constitution is the second constitution of the national government of the United States and for over 200 years has provided the principal American model for limited constitutional government under the rule of law.

By the mid-1780s, many Americans had become quite unhappy with the first national constitution, the Articles of Confederation. The Articles had created a national government with limited powers, vested in a Congress, but the state governments retained most powers, including the power to levy taxes to pay the expenses of the national government.

The impetus for the Constitution arose from a 1786 conference in Annapolis, Maryland, where 12 delegates from 5 states met and adopted a resolution calling for a convention to meet the following year in Philadelphia to make the national constitution "adequate to the exigencies of the Union."

Between May 28 and September 17, 1787, the Constitutional Convention—with 55 delegates from 12 states, as Rhode Island boycotted the meeting—assembled in closed sessions. Although some prominent revolutionary leaders were absent—including Thomas Jefferson and John Adams, who were in Europe serving as American ambassadors—the delegates included such respected statesmen as Benjamin Franklin, James Madison, and George Washington (who was unanimously elected the Convention's presiding officer).

The framers of the Constitution incorporated into it various devices for limiting power and safeguarding against its abuse. Those devices included not only the new concept of enumerating powers, but also others that had been incorporated into early state constitutions, such as the separation of powers, checks and balances, and the amending process.

Some of its key structural features, however, resulted from political compromise. The most important of these centered on the bicameral nature of the federal Congress. The structure of Congress was a product of the "Great Compromise" between two competing plans offered early in the Convention: The Virginia Plan would have created a tripartite national government—an executive, a judiciary, and a bicameral legislature with the states represented by population; the third would be possessed of broad powers, including the power to veto state laws. The New Jersey Plan, in contrast, would have retained the basic structure of the Articles of Confederation government—including an equal vote for each state in Congress—but would have allowed the national government additional enumerated powers, including the power to tax imports and regulate trade. The compromise adopted by the Convention followed the structural design of the Virginia plan, but with the enumerated powers scheme of the New Jersey plan; it made Congress bicameral, with states represented by population in the House of Representatives, but of equal voting strength in the Senate.

The separation of powers emerges in the basic organization of the Constitution: Article I vests in Congress all legislated powers "herein granted"—in other words, the powers enumerated in Article I, Section 8 and in a few other provisions in the document; Article II vests in a single executive officer, the president of the United States, "the executive power" and others specifically enumerated in Article II, Section 2; and Article III vests in the federal courts (one Supreme Court and whatever "inferior" courts Congress may establish) "the judicial power," as defined in Article III, Section 2. The framers did not follow a pure separation-of-powers scheme, however; they supplemented it with the countervailing principle of checks and balances, assigning a portion of each functional power to another branch. Thus, for example, Congress was not given the exclusive power to make laws: The president was granted the power to either sign into law or veto bills passed by Congress. Similarly, two executive powers—the treaty-making power and the appointment power—are not held exclusively by the president, but are shared with the Senate, which is empowered to ratify treaties and to confirm presidential appointments.

Although the Convention rejected a plan to allow Congress to veto state legislation, which had been proposed in the Virginia Plan, in Article VI, it adopted language similar to that proposed in the New Jersey Plan, declaring that the Constitution, federal laws "made in pursuance thereof," and treaties "made . . . under the authority of the United States" are "the supreme law of the land" and that judges in every state shall be bound by them. Like the Articles of Confederation, the Constitution also imposed certain limits on the powers of the states—the Article I, Section 10 prohibitions—and in Article IV required each state to give "full faith and credit" to the public acts, records, and judicial proceedings of other states and to give its citizens "all privileges and immunities of citizens in the several states."

Anticipating hostility to the new constitution in many of the state legislatures, the Constitutional Convention decided to bypass them altogether by providing in Article VII that "the ratification of the conventions of nine states, shall be sufficient for the establishment of this Constitution between the states so ratifying." Ratification through special conventions whose delegates were chosen by the people of each state was thought not only politically expedient, but also accorded with American constitutional norms that, following the precedent set by the Massachusetts Constitution of 1780, required that constitutions derive their authority directly from the people to ensure they were superior to ordinary government.

Ratification of the Constitution was not easy; the "ordeal," as one historian has described it, was a hard-fought contest between its proponents (the Federalists) and its opponents (the Anti-Federalists) in many of the state ratifying conventions and in the public debates that preceded them. The Anti-Federalists argued that the Constitution transferred too much power from the states to a federal government. Among their many other objections to the Constitution, the most serious was the absence of a bill of rights.

Although the requisite nine states had ratified the Constitution by late June 1788, many of those states—along with the key states of Virginia and New York, which ratified in June and July 1788—also called for amendments, a bill of rights to the Constitution. When the first federal Congress under the Constitution met in New York in the spring and summer of 1789, it considered a series of amendments first proposed in the House of Representatives by James Madison of Virginia. By mid-September 1789, both houses of Congress had approved 12 amendments to be sent to the states for ratification. Only after that time was the Constitution ratified by North Carolina and Rhode Island, the last of the original 13 states to do so.

By December 1791, 10 of the 12 amendments proposed by Congress in 1789 had been ratified by the legislatures of three fourths of the states, as Article V requires, and so became the first 10 amendments, known popularly as the Bill of Rights. The first eight protect various individual rights, among them freedom of speech and press, religious freedom, the right to keep and bear arms, protections against unreasonable searches and seizures, property rights, the right to a jury trial in both civil and criminal cases, and various procedural safeguards for the rights of the accused. The 9th and 10th Amendments provide general rules of constitutional interpretation designed to solve the problems Federalists maintained would arise from the addition of a bill of rights to the Constitution: the 9th protects against the loss of unenumerated rights, while the 10th explicitly limits the national government to those powers enumerated in the Constitution.

In the 210 years since the ratification of the Bill of Rights, the Constitution has been amended only 17 times. By far the most significant amendments were added after the Civil War: the 13th Amendment, which abolished slavery; and the 14th Amendment, which redefined U.S. citizenship and imposed significant additional limits on state governments to protect the "privileges or immunities" of U.S. citizens, to ensure "the equal protection of the laws," and to prohibit the rights of "life, liberty, and property" from being denied without "due process of law." The most recent amendment, the 27th, which limits congressional salary increases, also is one of the oldest proposed, having been among the original 12 amendments recommended by the 1st Congress, and which finally was ratified in 1992 by the requisite three-fourths of the states.

Since the U.S. Supreme Court first declared unconstitutional an act of Congress in *Marbury v. Madison* (1803), the Court has exercised the power of judicial review, that is, the power to interpret the Constitution and to declare void any laws or governmental acts in conflict with it. Before the Civil War, that power was exercised sparingly. However, following the war and especially during the 20th century, the Court has sometimes aggressively used—and, in the eyes of many critics, abused—its powers of judicial review.

The Supreme Court has had an uneven record in enforcing the Constitution. Although the Court has expanded its protection of certain rights, such as the 1st Amendment protection of freedom of speech, the Court also has virtually eviscerated other constitutional provisions, such as the 14th Amendment's "privileges or immunities" clause. Since the late 1930s, the Court has followed a double standard of constitutional review under which it has given greater protection to certain preferred personal rights, but

less protection to property rights and economic liberty. Moreover, through its broad interpretations of congressional powers to spend money and to regulate interstate commerce, the Court in the late 20th century sanctioned the enormous growth of the national government, far beyond what the Constitution's framers ever intended or imagined.

DNM

See also Bill of Rights, U.S.; Constitutionalism; Federalists Versus Anti-Federalists; Freedom of Speech; Madison, James; Separation of Church and State

Further Readings

Barnett, Randy E. *Restoring the Lost Constitution: The Presumption of Liberty.* Princeton, NJ: Princeton University Press, 2004.

Cooke, Jacob E., ed. *The Federalist.* Middletown, CT: Wesleyan University Press, 1961.

Ely, James W., Jr. *The Guardian of Every Other Right: A Constitutional History of Property Rights.* New York: Oxford University Press, 1992.

Farber, Daniel A., and Suzanna Sherry, eds. *A History of the American Constitution.* 2nd ed. St. Paul, MN: West Group, 2005.

Farrand, Max, ed. *The Records of the Federal Convention of 1787.* Rev. ed. 4 vols. New Haven, CT: Yale University Press, 1966.

Kelly, Alfred H., Winfred A. Harbison, and Herman Belz. *The American Constitution: Its Origins and Development.* 7th ed. 2 vols. New York: W. W. Norton, 1991.

Kurland, Philip B., and Ralph Lerner. *The Founders' Constitution.* 5 vols. Chicago: University of Chicago Press, 1987.

Levy, Leonard W., ed. *Essays on the Making of the Constitution.* 2nd ed. New York: Oxford University Press, 1987.

McDonald, Forrest. *Novus Ordo Seclorum: The Ideological Origins of the Constitution.* Lawrence: University Press of Kansas, 1985.

Rutland, Robert Allen. *The Birth of the Bill of Rights, 1776–1791.* Rev. ed. Boston: Northeastern University Press, 1983.

———. *The Ordeal of the Constitution: The Antifederalists and the Ratification Struggle of 1787–1788.* Boston: Northeastern University Press, 1966.

CONSTITUTIONALISM

Constitutionalism is the effort to impose a higher level order on the actions of government so that officials are not the judges of the limits of their own authority. Just as law is a limitation on action, a constitution limits the government's actions and is therefore a "law for laws." In the absence of a constitution, a state's ruling power is ultimately arbitrary, and its decisions are matters of decree rather than of well-settled and generally understood principles. Such a society can provide little protection for individual rights, economic prosperity, or the rule of law.

Although some writers have defined the term *constitution* broadly enough to encompass any institution that helps constitute a society—including languages or religious traditions—the term is more precisely used to describe the political arrangements that set the terms under which a government operates. Constitutions can be written, as in the United States, or unwritten, as in England. Constitutionalism in the Western tradition began with ancient lawgivers such as Cleisthenes of Athens, who reorganized the city's tribes and set rules for membership in the legislative body. The earliest known written constitutions, such as the Iroquois Confederacy or the *Leges* of San Marino, were much more like treaties or statutory codes that placed limits on government officials. The first written constitutions in the latter sense were probably those of Commonwealth England and the American colonies. The latter took either the form of royal corporate charters or improvised agreements such as the Mayflower Compact.

Constitutional government can be contrasted with government by decree; law is to arbitrary power as reason is to will: The distinction rests on whether the government's action is based on some overriding and separately justified purpose or the product of simple *ipse dixit*; a mere assertion of power. Thus, there are three basic purposes for a constitution: (1) to impose stable and predictable limits on the state, (2) to ensure widespread understanding and debate concerning changes to those limits, and (3) to require that the government act on the basis of general public reasons, rather than arbitrarily for the private welfare of political insiders.

Nations with unwritten constitutions have often suffered from the fact that their ambiguity has allowed political authorities to expand their powers in novel and unpredictable ways—which, in turn, set precedents for future expansions of authority. For example, England suffered a major constitutional crisis in the early 17th century when James I and his successors asserted claims to absolute monarchy, including the power to rule without Parliament. This expression of royal power conflicted with the views of early Whigs, who believed that sovereign authority existed only when the King acted in conjunction with Parliament. The subsequent clash led to civil war, as well as to the adoption of many of the documents and principles that make up the present-day English Constitution, including the Petition of Right, the Bill of Rights, and the concept of parliamentary sovereignty.

Although the advent of written constitutions helps avoid or minimize such controversies, regimes where constitutions are frequently rewritten generally suffer the same or worse effects because the government becomes unstable and behaves unpredictably. This endangers individual rights and deters economic investment and innovation. Peru, for example, went through five constitutions in the 20th century—which is one reason for its well-documented political and economic woes. To avert this mutability, James Madison urged his countrymen to adopt an almost religious reverence for their Constitution.

If constitutionalism is to accomplish its purposes of limiting and stabilizing the political order, it is essential that the government actually comply with it. Regimes such as the Soviet Union had written constitutions that included explicit guarantees of certain individual rights, including freedom of speech. Yet the actual operations of the government were completely arbitrary, with no adherence to the constitution's terms. Thus, the Soviet Union was a lawless regime, lending credence to Friedrich Hayek's observation that a totalitarian state is one in which law has essentially been abolished.

In addition to predictability, constitutionalism helps to ensure that changes in the scope and nature of state power are subjected to widespread discussion before they are implemented and that such changes are as unambiguous as possible. Where the structure of government can be drastically altered without an orderly, openly discussed, and unequivocal change to the constitution, the legitimacy of such changes are open to doubt, and individual rights are threatened. Squealer's midnight alterations to the Seven Commandments in George Orwell's *Animal Farm* are a well-known dramatization of this principle. Another more recent example is the debate spurred by the contention of Bruce Ackerman and others that the expansion of federal power during the New Deal—and the Supreme Court's decisions upholding that expansion—amounted to an unwritten amendment to the Constitution. But such "amendments"—enacted without formal popular consent—cannot be legitimately ascribed to the will of the people and set a dangerous precedent for manipulation of the Constitution by unelected elites.

James Buchanan has contended that one important role for a constitution is to restrain the possibility of legislation that redistributes wealth and opportunities between interest groups in society. A requirement that laws be generally applicable would eliminate lobbyists' "incentive[s] for investment in efforts to secure differentially or discriminatorily favorable treatment." James Madison saw this role as essential for the Constitution—if not the very definition of constitutional government: "In a society under the forms of which the stronger faction can readily unite and oppress the weaker, anarchy may as truly be said to reign as in a state of nature, where the weaker individual is not secured against the violence of the stronger." Early in American history, the Due Process Clause was, in fact, read as a generality requirement under the theory of "substantive due process," and Cass R. Sunstein, otherwise unsympathetic to libertarian constitutionalism, has contended that it is "focused on a single underlying evil: the distribution of resources or opportunities to one group rather than another solely on the ground that those favored have exercised the raw political power to obtain what they want." However, as Anthony de Jasay has argued, such a requirement is insufficient because just as legislative majorities may seek to influence the legislature for their own benefit, so they will seek constitutional regimes that will maximize the possibility for such legislation. The New Deal's relaxation of Due Process requirements is best seen as a step in this direction.

Because different constitutional interpretations will yield different conclusions regarding the limits of government power, debates over interpretation are often highly charged political matters. In the United States, libertarian constitutionalism tends to emphasize *originalism* or *textualism*—the first referring to the view that the constitution should be interpreted consistent with the way it was understood at the time of its ratification and the latter having reference to the view that the constitution should be interpreted strictly according to its text, rather than through broad interpretations of its terms. "Living constitutionalism," by contrast, tends to be embraced by those who support an expanded government role that would allow it to reach beyond the Constitution's explicit limits. Expansive readings of the Commerce Clause, for instance—which was originally intended as a limited grant of federal authority—currently authorize the federal government to act virtually at will with respect to any matter connected with commercial enterprise in even the most attenuated way, thus replacing orderly constitutional government with a government that can determine the scope of its own powers. Hence, Roger Pilon has described such interpretive theories as "politics trumping law."

Libertarian constitutionalism descends from the theories of James Madison and other classical liberals, whose views were taken up by John Quincy Adams, his protégé Charles Sumner, and other abolitionists and Radical Republicans of the Civil War era, including Lysander Spooner, Gerrit Smith, and Frederick Douglass. These Republican constitutionalists embraced natural rights-based theories to argue that protecting individual freedom is the leading goal of the constitution's limitations. These thinkers tended to emphasize the Declaration of Independence as a reference point for interpretation—or even as a binding legal document—a theory that has recently been called *liberal originalism.*

Republican constitutionalism was explicitly adopted in the 13th, 14th, and 15th Amendments, although these were severely undermined by decisions of the contemporaneous Supreme Court, such as *The Slaughterhouse Cases.* Although writers such as Eric Foner and Paul Kens describe this Republican constitutionalism as a facet of "Free Labor Ideology" and contend that it was devised in the 19th century as an ideological rationalization for capitalism, it in fact descended directly from the views of Madison, James Wilson, and other prominent constitutional framers. What was truly innovative and a challenge to the natural rights understanding of the Constitution was the view that it was a treaty between sovereign states. This theory was pioneered by such thinkers as John Taylor and John C. Calhoun and later defended by paleo-libertarians,

who contended that state sovereignty would help check the expansion of federal power. The best primer on most aspects of modern libertarian constitutionalism is Randy E. Barnett's book *Restoring the Lost Constitution.*

The underlying premise of Republican, and later libertarian, constitutionalism is that liberty takes precedence over democracy. This notion is consistent with the Constitution's unambiguous description of liberty as a "blessing" and the fact that in many particulars it limits the power of democratic majorities. Democracy is regarded as an instrumental good, justified only insofar as it is consistent with liberty. Libertarian constitutionalism emphasizes natural rights, which are incorporated into the Bill of Rights, through the Privileges or Immunities Clause of the 14th Amendment and by the 9th Amendment's reference to "other" rights beyond those explicitly listed. Libertarians reject the view that government is the source of rights and contend that it is only a mechanism for protecting rights that arise from an independent source. Therefore, government may not simply cancel such rights or create new ones by fiat that conflict with natural rights. The fact that natural rights are innumerable and that the 9th Amendment forbids the reading of the Bill of Rights as exhaustive requires courts to presume in favor of individual freedom when lawsuits are brought challenging the constitutionality of laws. This view contrasts with currently prevailing jurisprudence, under which most laws are presumed to be constitutional until they are proven inconsistent with explicit constitutional rights.

Although originally retarded by hostile Supreme Court decisions, important parts of Republican constitutionalism managed to prevail in the form of "substantive due process," beginning with *Loan Association v. Topeka* decided in 1874, *Hurtado v. California* in 1884, and *Lochner v. New York* in 1905. These cases embraced the view that, because government exists to provide for the general public welfare, any law that promotes only the private welfare of particular groups, for no general public reason, is a mere act of force or will and, therefore, not a "law." Thus, any law that takes property from A and gives it to B simply because B has greater political power, or because the legislature wished to confer a benefit on B, cannot qualify as "due process *of law*" and violates the 14th Amendment.

By the early 20th century, the Progressive theories of living constitutionalism and legal positivism—which reject natural rights and see law as simply the will of the lawmaker—have become increasingly popular. During the 1930s, the Supreme Court conclusively adopted them, abandoning substantive due process and natural rights almost entirely. Instead, the Court today generally defers to legislatures to such a degree that they are often free to act as they will, with little or no constitutional constraint. On the present Supreme Court, only Justice Clarence Thomas has explicitly endorsed a natural rights understanding of the Constitution, but his defense of the view that the

Constitution is a league of sovereign states and his refusal to endorse substantive due process disqualify him as a true libertarian constitutionalist.

A constitution is sometimes said to represent the will of the sovereign. In the United States, where the people are sovereign and the Constitution is explicitly ordained by "the people of the United States," the Constitution represents the basic agreement of the whole people—as distinguished from mere legislation, which only represents the agreement of the members of a particular legislature at a particular time. Thus, according to *The Federalist*, the judiciary is actually *enforcing* the will of the people—not overriding it—when it annuls a law that exceeds constitutional limits.

If a constitution is a higher order law that limits the legislative powers of the state, it must be drafted or authorized by some power other than the legislature. In his *Notes on the State of Virginia*, Thomas Jefferson declared that one of the leading defects of the Virginia Constitution at that time was that it could be altered by the legislature. This idea was problematic because a legislature could not have power to "pass an act transcendent to the powers of other legislatures," such as a constitution. "The other states in the Union have been of the opinion that to render a form of government unalterable by ordinary acts of assembly, the people must delegate persons with special powers." It was in this spirit that the federal convention of 1787 prepared, and special ratification conventions later approved, the U.S. Constitution. Moreover, the fact that it was not ratified by state legislatures made the 1787 Constitution an agreement of the whole people of the United States, as opposed to a league of sovereign entities, as were the Articles of Confederation. For Madison, this distinction was essential because "one of the essential differences between a *'league'* and a *'Constitution'* was that the latter would prevent subunits from unilaterally bolting whenever they became dissatisfied." Thus, the fact that the Constitution is, in fact, a constitution and not a treaty is decisive in the question of whether secession is constitutionally permissible.

TMS

See also Constitution, U.S.; Madison, James; Magna Carta; Rule of Law

Further Readings

Ackerman, Bruce. *We the People: Transformations*. Cambridge, MA: Harvard University Press, 1998.

Amar, Akhil Reed. *America's Constitution: A Biography*. New York: Random House, 2005.

Barnett, Randy E. "The Original Meaning of the Commerce Clause." *University of Chicago Law Review* 68 (2001): 101–147.

Buchanan, James M. "Generality as a Constitutional Constraint." *The Collected Works of James M. Buchanan*. vol. 1. Geoffrey Brennan, Hartmut Kliemt, and Robert D. Tollison, eds. Indianapolis, IN: Liberty Fund, 1999. 427.

Cooley, Thomas. *A Treatise on Constitutional Limitations*. Boston: Little, Brown, 1868.

De Jasay, Anthony. *Justice and Its Surroundings*. Indianapolis, IN: Liberty Fund, 1998.

Douglass, Frederick. "The Constitution of the United States: Is It Pro-Slavery or Anti-Slavery?" *Frederick Doulgass: Selected Speeches and Writings*. Philip Foner and Yuval Taylor, eds. Chicago: Lawrence Hill Books, 1999.

Gerber, Scott. *To Secure These Rights: The Declaration of Independence and Constitutional Interpretation*. New York: New York University Press, 1996.

Hayek, Friedrich. *Law, Legislation and Liberty: Vol 2. The Mirage of Social Justice*. Chicago: University of Chicago Press, 1978.

Kens, Paul. *Justice Stephen Field: Shaping Liberty from the Gold Rush to the Gilded Age*. Lawrence: University Press of Kansas, 1997.

Pilon, Roger. "How Constitutional Corruption Has Led to Ideological Litmus Tests for Judicial Nominees." *Nexus: A Journal of Opinion* 7 (2002): 67–78.

Rosen, Gary. *American Compact: James Madison and the Problem of Founding*. Lawrence: University Press of Kansas, 1999.

Sandefur, Timothy. "How Libertarians Ought to Think about the U.S. Civil War." *Reason Papers* 28 (2006): 61–83.

Schor, Miguel. "Constitutionalism through the Looking Glass of Latin America." *Texas International Law Journal* 41 (2006): 1–37.

Sunstein, Cass R. "Constitutionalism after the New Deal." *Harvard Law Review* 101 (1987): 421–510.

———. "Naked Preferences and the Constitution." *Columbia Law Review* 84 (1984): 1689–1732.

Contractarianism/ Social Contract

The idea of a social contract as the basis for morality or political principles goes back a long way—there is, for example, a brief statement of it in Plato's *Republic*. More notably, the great writers on political and moral philosophy of the 18th century were contractarians. In our own time, John Rawls's work is regarded, both by him and those who are familiar with his writings, as falling within the general tradition of social contract theory, while David Gauthier's "morals by agreement" present an elaboration of the principles of contractarianism.

Inasmuch as contractarianism has specific reference to a theory about the foundations of moral and political philosophy, its relation to libertarianism is somewhat indirect. Libertarianism is a theory regarding the general principles of justice. The underlying support for these principles, in the contractarian view, is that such theories are rational only if all agree to it. Additionally, contractarianism has no direct connection to any actual historical event, such as a Constitutional Convention; the idea is more abstract than that.

Two features of contract are crucial. First, one who enters into a contract does so for reasons of his own, usually reasons of self-interest. We want to buy this car, we are willing to pay the proposed price, and we sign an agreement to that effect. Second, whereas self-interest provides the motivation, agreement provides the moral basis for holding the parties to it. Having signed the contract for the car, I am now obligated to pay the price specified; my obligation is a function of my having voluntarily signed the relevant agreement. The obligation is thus self-imposed. If we extend this notion to the project of founding a moral system, it follows that the "contract" is made between everyone and everyone else: We all agree with each other to do these things. However, in reality, such contracts have not been nor can be made. Rather, we can all understand that we are related to each other in such a way that agreeing with each other to act in certain ways is the thing to do: It is prescribed by reason—the reason that each person possesses.

What contractarian theory enables us to understand is why, given an initial situation in which there is as yet no morality and no law, people can nevertheless (a) see the need to have rules, and (b) shape the rules that will emerge in light of their own interests and their relation to all others. The contractarian idea is of enormous interest to libertarians because the theoretical project it envisages conceives of morality (and also government) as a set of restrictions that would be freely agreed to by people acting on their own without any antecedent constraints. By looking at how people stand in relation to each other and what kind of needs and problems their relationships entail, we can see what basic restrictions are needed.

The father of modern contractarian theory is Thomas Hobbes, who argued that any individual in a social situation where there were no rules imposing restrictions on anyone's behavior would have a life that was "solitary, poor, nasty, brutish, and short." The fundamental problem in a society without agreed-on rules is that of interpersonal violence, which all of us can engage in and from which all of us can suffer. Violence impedes or makes impossible the victim's pursuit of the good life as he sees it. Thus, the thing to do is agree on rules against such violence. All else requires agreement on particulars. So the basic contractarian rules are: nonviolence, which implies, in turn, that each is to have as much liberty as is possible for all, with no more for any individual or subset of individuals. Equal liberty implies that we are required to keep specific agreements of our own free making, subject to whatever restrictions and escape clauses may be built in.

Our incentive to live up to these agreements proceeds from our interests: We simply do better to live under these mutually advantageous rules than would otherwise be the case. We are constrained to obey these rules by two forces. The first is moral: We internally monitor our behavior to see to it that others have no complaint against us; and the second issues from whatever arrangements we may have made to help enforce these rules. Government, notoriously, is

widely thought to be justified and required for this purpose. A number of theorists, however, argue that the necessity is by no means clear. What is required is third parties engaged by the original parties whose function is to wield the necessary force against those who renege on their agreement.

Proponents of the theory of a social contract argue that contractarianism alone can provide a genuine sense of moral constraint among free people. All other moral theories appeal to intuition or axioms that cannot be explained, lacking any clear reason that these theories should be embraced. The social contract, however, supplies a reason: It is the interests of people, given the exigencies of social life, which provide both the motivation and a rational method of determining the substance of moral requirements.

There have been many variants of the social contract idea, all of which, to a greater or lesser degree, modify this description. By far the most prominent recent theory is the one put forward by John Rawls, who argues that the social contract must originate from behind a "veil of ignorance," in which the parties are unaware of what positions they will occupy after agreement. They then agree, he argues, to certain principles. However, it is unclear how a contract can exist that comprises only one party, albeit a supposedly universal one. It is more than unclear why real people would accept something that was made by "people" who don't know what positions they might occupy after the contract came into force. In the end, it appears that Rawls is imposing a scheme of values on people whose characteristics cannot possibly include the attributes he demands of them. Rawls's approach is in marked contrast to the contractarian idea that we must generate morals out of our separate, premoral interests.

The pure version of contract theory is of interest precisely because it proposes to derive and explain morals and politics from premises that merely reflect commonsense observations of what people are like, plus game-theoretical results concerning their options. Each individual acts in his own interests, but when the interests of different people conflict, then the way is open for them to accept mutual constraints that will enable each to do as well as socially possible, thus motivating a real interest in moral and political principles and in the creation of institutions to enforce them.

JN and DT

See also Constitutionalism; Hobbes, Thomas; Locke, John; Nozick, Robert; Rawls, John; Revolution, Right of

Further Readings

Binmore, Ken. *Game Theory and the Social Contract.* 2 vols. Boston: MIT Press, 1994, 1998.

De Jasay, Anthony. *Social Contract, Free Ride.* Cambridge, MA: Blackwell, 1989.

Gauthier, David. *Morals by Agreement.* New York: Oxford University Press, 1986.

Hobbes, Thomas. *Leviathan*. New York: Everyman Library, 1960 [1651].

Narveson, Jan. *The Libertarian Idea*. Peterborough, ON, Canada: Broadview Press, 2001.

Rawls, John. *A Theory of Justice*. Cambridge, MA: Harvard University Press, 1972.

CORRUPTION

The *Oxford English Dictionary* defines the verb *corrupt* as turning "from a sound into an unsound impure condition; to cause to 'go bad'; to make rotten or rotting." In public life, the verb *corrupt* means "to destroy or pervert the integrity or fidelity of (a person) in his discharge of duty; to induce to act dishonestly or unfaithfully; to make venal; to bribe." This definition is both more familiar and more problematic for liberty, and in this context the idea of corruption speaks to the proper relationship of private interests to politics and government.

The exchange of money for goods and services in private markets reveals individual preferences and contributes to human welfare. Paying money for goods or services provided by a public official constitutes bribery and often involves punishment for the parties to the transaction. Why is bribery invariably equated with corruption and condemned? It is not obviously inefficient. Indeed, in highly collectivized nations, paying public officials to allow what would otherwise be normal market exchanges may contribute much to human welfare.

Experts have condemned bribery for economic and political reasons. Economic studies have found that bribery of state officials is associated with poor economic performance. Susan Rose-Ackerman concludes that "it can reasonably be conjectured that corruption is one of the primary causes of the continued under-development in South Asia, Latin America and Africa and an important cause of the disappointing performance of the post-communist transition in the former Soviet Union." Critics also argue that bribery contravenes the normative basis of politics. In modern democracies, voters (principals) elect representatives (agents) who are trusted to act to advance the welfare of their principals. Most people see bribery as incompatible with this trust. The bribe payer seeks a benefit from the government that is provided by the bribe taker in exchange for the bribe. The private interests of both the bribe payer and the bribe taker seem incompatible with the broader interests of the voters who elected a representative. Thus, bribery corrupts the representative function of modern democracies.

These standard accounts of corruption and bribery involve efficiency and democratic accountability, not liberty. But bribery has implications for liberty as well. Bribes that purchase special tax preferences imply higher taxes for others given the same level of government spending. Bribes that obtain regulations to bar entry to a market coerce those who wish to do business in that market. In some cases, government actions that are particularly prone to bribery—like the licensing of economic activity—inherently restrict individual liberty.

It is possible that bribery might liberalize some parts of society, but such payments are unlikely to create a general liberty under the rule of law. The bribe payer seeks a series of private, individual benefits from government; he would have no reason to purchase a broad liberalization of a whole market. One would expect bribes to enlarge a coalition of rent seekers, but not to generally liberalize society. More empirical evidence on this question would be welcome.

In the United States, money, democracy, and liberty interact, not always happily, in the financing of election campaigns. Taxpayers pay for a relatively small proportion of the costs of election campaigns in the United States, whereas individuals and groups contribute to the campaigns of chosen candidates. The U.S. Supreme Court has recognized that such contributions and spending by candidates affect freedom of speech, holding that such contributions and spending are 1st Amendment rights. Therefore, Congress is prohibited from making any law restricting these liberties. However, Congress has enacted, and the courts have validated, many restrictions on donations of money in elections, including mandatory disclosure and contribution limits. Courts have justified such measures as ways to prevent corruption or the appearance of corruption in government. Contributions can be the equivalent of bribes if they are given implicitly or explicitly in exchange for official favors (often called quid pro quo corruption). But contributions most often are nothing more than expressions of support for a candidate or cause. Laws that restrict donations made for these purposes thus impinge on individual liberty without preventing corruption.

The problem here goes beyond the inevitable errors associated with all regulation. Most campaign finance regulation seeks to bias electoral struggles in favor of the majority party in a legislature or of incumbents in general. In both cases, campaign finance regulations complicate the entry of challengers into elections, thereby sustaining an existing partisan majority or increasing the probability of the reelection of the average incumbent. In short, campaign finance regulations do not accidentally violate freedom of speech; such violations are the primary reason for the regulation. Campaign finance regulations, like the corruption they seek to prevent, actually serve the narrow interests of parties and incumbents instead of the interest voters have in open competition for legislative seats. Thus, campaign finance restrictions may be deemed a kind of corruption.

The U.S. Supreme Court's "appearance of corruption" justification for regulating money in politics has little to do with actual bribery or corrupt dealing. The Court argued that if citizens came to believe that contributions bought political favors, they would lose confidence in the government. Thus, contribution limits and other restrictions are said to bolster confidence in government by mitigating this appearance of corruption. However, as Nathaniel Persily discovered, campaign finance appears to have no real relationship one way or the other to trust in government. In any case, public trust in government tends to reduce, rather than protect, individual liberty. Thomas Burke has identified two other conceptions of corruption in U.S. Supreme Court decisions. The conception of corruption centering on distortion assumes that official actions should closely reflect public opinion: "Campaign contributions are corrupting to the extent that they do not reflect the balance of public opinion and thus distort policymaking through their influence on elections." The Supreme Court has applied this concept of distortion to bless state restrictions on political activity by businesses whose wealth and campaign donations do not reflect public opinion. The "monetary influence" conception says public officials are corrupt if they perform their duties with monetary considerations in mind; sometimes contributions are said to create political debts that endanger the integrity of the system. Campaign contributions can thus corrupt governing even if no explicit deals are made.

Distortion as a corrupt practice assumes that policymaking should follow public opinion. This idea leaves little room for constitutional constraints on majorities or for intense minority views that might one day persuade a majority. In particular, the illiberal idea that existing public opinion should provide a standard for limiting participation in politics enshrines the status quo. Fortunately, this conception of corruption has been largely ignored by the Supreme Court. The "monetary influence" conception of corruption has been joined to ideals of deliberative democracy. Dennis Thompson argues that representatives should deliberate about the public good. Private interests are permitted in a deliberative democracy, but those who advance them must frame their interests in broader arguments about the public good. It is argued that money corrupts politics when contributions enable private interests to make policy or direct their energies for purely private reasons.

However, campaign donations have a legitimate place in a liberal republic. They may support speech and other political activities to advance an ideal of the public good. How then can citizens or public officials distinguish corrupt and laudable contributions? The motivations of the giver are difficult or perhaps impossible to discern, particularly when purely private interests become skilled at transforming their self-interest into arguments for the common good. The deliberative standard seems unworkable, especially given the important liberties that hang in the balance. Bruce Cain has objected that deliberative democrats misconstrue the nature of American politics and thus its corruption or integrity. The American founders did not create a deliberative republic in which representatives act as trustees of the public good. Instead, policymakers aggregate preferences

that citizens reveal through votes, campaign contributions, voluntary associations, and other ways. The representative in this pluralist republic is a delegate for the preferences of his constituents. Apart from bribery, the monetary conception of corruption makes no sense in this republic; donations are a weapon in political struggle and a way to better inform social choices.

Is this conception of pluralism compatible with a liberal government? Pluralism offers a justification for public power after constitutional constraints were abrogated with the New Deal. Groups struggle over policy in a world where government power over economic life observes few limits. Pluralists see themselves as the intellectual heirs of James Madison, but some differences should be noted. Madison believed in a liberal, constitutional republic in which group struggle helped sustain the limited nature of the government. Pluralists recognize no such restraints. Private interests organize and seek to win in policy struggles. The result can be rent seeking, which libertarians regard as corruption. Of course, the organization of groups also may constrain state power, but the limits here are only partially Madisonian. Madison's commitment to constitutions and liberalism has been lost to most writers who embrace the pluralist conception of politics. The deliberative democrat seeks to tame private avarice and abuses of government power through restrictions on money in politics. Thus, although it is true that the concerns of pluralists and the deliberative democrats at times intersect with those of libertarians, both differ in fundamental ways. As Bradley Smith argues, it is doubtful that reforms can constrain abuses of power in a postconstitutional regime like the United States.

Other approaches to corruption exist. Scholars have recently given much attention to classical republicanism. Their findings have sometimes deeply contravened liberal notions. Gordon Wood, for example, writes that "ideally, republicanism obliterated the individual" in early America. In recounting the American view of civic virtue in the 1770s, Wood writes of the "willingness of the individual to sacrifice his private interests for the good of the community." Individual liberty in this regard becomes something akin to corruption of the citizen. Similarly, contemporary communitarians seem to equate individual liberty with selfishness and social decline. Such characterizations assume that any conduct not directed to the common good of a society must be thought corrupt. This hope for a Spartan regime has little in common with liberty.

Yet the problem of private interests in politics lingers for the libertarian. Most libertarians blame the expansion of the state for corruption. Hence, if we reduce what the government does, we also will reduce corruption. But if voters are corrupt in a libertarian sense, liberty may foster corruption and the expansion of the state. Americans have the liberty to engage in politics. When they do, they form groups that seek redistributed wealth for their members or lobby for restrictions on the liberty of others that would benefit them.

Voters are hardly exempt from the desire for plunder. Gordon Tullock has noted that campaign contributions "are not actually for the purpose of buying votes. The votes are bought by the bills passed by Congress, or the Legislature, which benefit voters." In that exchange of votes for money, might one not discern a loss of integrity among average Americans? The "pure" libertarian citizen would support the rule of law and generality in public policymaking, as well as strong rights to life, liberty, and private property.

Although people create institutions, institutions also create people, so it is perhaps not surprising that voters expect government benefits in exchange for their votes. How might a nation escape this cycle of democratic corruption? Politicians need to be elected, and they are unlikely to attain that end by telling voters they cannot have what they want. But libertarians might recognize that corruption may be more than an excuse to limit liberty. It also may offer a way to identify and understand the moral decline that follows (and fosters) the continual expansion of the welfare state.

JSa

See also Campaign Finance; Madison, James; Public Choice Economics; Tullock, Gordon; Welfare State

Further Readings

Burke, Thomas F. "The Concept of Corruption in Campaign Finance Law." *Constitutional Commentary* 14 no. 127 (1997): 127–149.

Cain, Bruce E. "Moralism and Realism in Campaign Finance Reform." *University of Chicago Legal Forum* 111 (1995): 115–116.

Persily, Nathaniel, and Kelli Lammie. "Perceptions of Corruption and Campaign Finance: When Public Opinion Determines Constitutional Law." *University of Pennsylvania Law Review* 153 no. 1 (2004): 119–180.

Rose-Ackerman, Susan. *Corruption and Government: Causes, Consequences, and Reform.* New York: Cambridge University Press, 1999.

Smith, Bradley A. "Hamilton at Wits End: The Lost Discipline of the Spending Clause vs. the False Discipline of Campaign Finance Reform." *Chapman Law Review* 4 (2001): 117–145.

Thompson, Dennis F. *Ethics in Congress: From Individual to Institutional Corruption.* Washington, DC: Brookings Institution Press, 1995.

Tullock, Gordon. *Public Goods, Redistribution and Rent Seeking.* Northampton, MA: Edward Elgar, 2005.

Wood, Gordon. *The Creation of the American Republic, 1776–1787.* Chapel Hill: University of North Carolina Press, 1969.

COSMOPOLITANISM

The term *cosmopolitanism* is derived from the Greek word used to denote a "citizen of the world" (*kosmopolitês*). This notion of world citizenship is derived from the Greek terms for "universe" and "polis," which were understood as moral and legal order. The central libertarian claim that all human beings—indeed, all rational agents—have equal fundamental rights is rooted in the ancient tradition of cosmopolitan thought. (Another use of the term, which refers to a person of worldly or sophisticated tastes, is not directly relevant to its moral/political use; one could have parochial or unsophisticated tastes, but cosmopolitan political beliefs.)

Cosmopolitanism has deep roots in Western culture. About the year 420 B.C., the philosopher Democritus wrote, "To a wise man, the whole earth is open; for the native land of a good soul is the whole earth." According to the philosopher Diogenes Laertius, the following story was told of Diogenes the Cynic: "The question was put to him what countryman he was, and he replied, not 'Citizen of Sinope,' but 'Citizen of the world' (*kosmopolitês*)." The cosmopolitan idea was later articulated by such influential figures in the Roman world as Cicero, who in his *De Officiis* criticized those "who say that account should be taken of other citizens, but deny it in the case of foreigners; such men tear apart the common fellowship of the human race." A number of later Stoic figures underscored the importance of living in accordance with "nature" and therefore not merely in accordance with the conventions of this or that city or country.

The idea of a universal moral order and of a higher law by which all human actions might be judged was poetically expressed in the Sermon on the Mount:

> You have heard that it was said, "You shall love your neighbor and hate your enemy." But I say to you, Love your enemies and pray for those who persecute you, so that you may be sons of your Father who is in heaven; for he makes his sun rise on the evil and on the good, and sends rain on the just and on the unjust.

This passage was repeatedly cited in arguments for universal standards of justice, notably by the lawyer-pope Innocent IV about the year 1250 in a legal opinion governing the wars with Islam. Innocent IV defended the rights of non-Christians on the grounds that

> lordship, possession and jurisdiction can belong to infidels licitly and without sin, for these things were not made only for the faithful but for every rational creature as has been said. For he makes his sun to rise on the just and the wicked and he feeds the birds of the air. Accordingly we say that it is not licit for the pope or the faithful to take away from infidels their belongings or their jurisdictions because they possess them without sin.

As the notion of human rights developed throughout the medieval period, it too drew on the cosmopolitan tradition. Thus, in his arguments supporting the equal status of the American Indians, Bartolomé de las Casas, the Spanish Bishop of Chiapa, concluded his great defense of the Indians in 1552 by maintaining that "the Indians are our brothers, and Christ has given his life for them. Why, then, do we persecute them with such inhuman savagery when they do not deserve such treatment? The past, because it cannot be undone, must be attributed to our weakness, provided that what has been taken unjustly is restored." That speech (and the book based on it) influenced all later discussions of human rights and set the stage for the emergence of libertarianism in full form, notably among the Levellers in England, who campaigned for universal human rights, including the freedom to trade and travel.

Cosmopolitanism has been closely connected with the mutual enrichment of cultures that came with increasing contact as opportunities for trade and travel expanded, a freedom that had long been a central libertarian demand. Joseph Addison, writing in *The Spectator*, famously illustrated a cosmopolitan attitude in his description of his visit to the Royal Exchange of London in 1711:

> Sometimes I am justled among a Body of Americans; sometimes I am lost in a Crowd of Jews, and sometimes in a Group of Dutch-Men. I am a Dane, a Swede, or Frenchman at different times, or fancy myself like the old Philosopher, who upon being asked what country-man he was, replied that he was a Citizen of the World.

The theme was taken up again in the 20th century by such classical liberal figures as Ludwig von Mises, who wrote in *Liberalism* that, "for the liberal, the world does not end at the borders of the state. In his eyes, whatever significance national boundaries have is only incidental and subordinate. His political thinking encompasses the whole of mankind."

Libertarian thinkers have often been rebuked by nationalists for their cosmopolitanism. Max Hildebert Boehm, in his influential discussion of cosmopolitanism, asserted that, "by standing, or aiming to stand, in immediate communion with all men, an individual easily avoids the risks and sacrifices which in view of the perpetual conflicts between all particularistic groups beset a social life based on narrower solidarities." Boehm concluded that "it often exists among persons whom fortune has relieved from the immediate struggle for existence and from pressing social responsibility and who can afford to indulge their fads and enthusiasms." The contemporary British philosopher David Miller, an articulate champion of both nationalism and socialism, dismisses cosmopolitans who hold that people "should regard their nationality merely as a historic accident, an identity to be sloughed off in favor of humanity at large." Miller argues that anticosmopolitan nationalism is a necessary condition for the creation of socialism. Cosmopolitanism, according to Boehm, Miller, and other critics of libertarianism, undermines social justice.

Critics of libertarianism also assert that cosmopolitanism (often referred to as globalization) threatens cultural and, ultimately, personal identity. Communitarians such as Michael Sandel have argued that one's identity rests on constitutive understandings that comprehend a wider subject than the individual alone. Sandel argues on epistemic grounds that the relevant unit of political analysis is not the individual, but some wider group. In the modern world, that is identified with the nation state, which, he alleges, exhaustively encompasses one's identity. An alternative approach to understanding personal identity was articulated by the German legal historian Otto von Gierke, who noted that in the modern world no circle of association "encompasses the totality of a human being" inasmuch as the identity of each of us is formed by many overlapping commitments. The sociologist Georg Simmel characterized the modern liberal personality as emerging from an ever-expanding "intersection of social circles." To be sure, there are differences among groups, including national groups, but modern identity is not formed by a concentric series of circles, with the nation-state forming the hard outer shell, but by an ever-expanding series of intersecting circles, many of which cut across national boundaries, as anyone with foreign friends or religious or other attachments that transcend national borders will attest.

Moreover, many critics charge that global freedom of trade and travel threatens to destroy the individuality of cultures and to rob people of their unique cultural identities. The debate is a complex one and has been joined by any number of writers who have argued that cultures tend to flourish when they are open to the influence from other cultures. Many also challenge the assumption of those who criticize globalization that there are pure cultures that are more authentic than others and that that purity is threatened by allowing people contact with other cultures. Living cultures, as opposed to dead museum exhibits, maintain their continuity by processing and adapting to influences from outside.

Cosmopolitanism, understood as recognition of a universal set of moral and political obligations and rights, has long been a core commitment of libertarian political thought. It remains, through the contemporary debates over globalization, a central source of controversy in political and social thought.

TGP

See also Cicero; Civil Society; Culture; Las Casas, Bartolomé de; Nationalism; Natural Law; Stoicism

Further Readings

Cicero. *De Officiis [On Duties]*. M. T. Griffin and E. M. Atkins, eds. and trans. Cambridge: Cambridge University Press, 1991.

Cowen, Tyler. *Creative Destruction: How Globalization Is Changing the World's Cultures*. Princeton, NJ: Princeton University Press, 2002.

Harris, Hugh. "The Greek Origins of the Idea of Cosmopolitanism." *The International Journal of Ethics* 38 no. 1 (October 1927): 1–10.

Hayek, F. A. *Law, Legislation, and Liberty: Vol. 3. Mirage of Social Justice.* Chicago: University of Chicago Press, 1978.

Miller, David. *On Nationality.* Oxford: Clarendon Press, 1995.

Mises, Ludwig von. *Liberalism: The Classical Tradition.* Indianapolis, IN: Liberty Fund, 2005.

Palmer, Tom G. *Globalization and Culture: Homogeneity, Diversity, Identity, Liberty.* Berlin: Liberales Institut, 2004.

Schlereth, Thomas J. *The Cosmopolitan Ideal in Enlightenment Thought.* Notre Dame, IN: University of Notre Dame Press, 1977.

Tierney, Brian. *The Idea of Natural Rights.* Atlanta: Scholars Press, 1998.

Waldron, Jeremy. "Minority Cultures and the Cosmopolitan Alternative." *The Rights of Minority Cultures.* Will Kymlicka, ed. Oxford: Oxford University Press, 1995. 93–119.

CRIME

See RESTITUTION FOR CRIME; RETRIBUTION FOR CRIME

CULTURE

Culture contains so many elements that the term gives rise to many possible definitions. Most would stress the idea of a body of customary beliefs, social forms, and material traits constituting a distinct complex of traditions belonging to a racial, religious, or social group. Others focus on beliefs, morals, laws, customary opinions, religion, superstition, and expressions of art.

Culture is a system of meaning that plays a primary role in organizing society, from kinship groups to schools and states, and that extends from generation to generation. However, the relationship between what is taught and what is learned varies with different people, times, and environments. Thus, there arise negotiated agreements among members about the meanings of a word, behavior, or other symbol.

The ancient Latin word *cultura* carried the meaning of "cultivation," which focused on human improvement of some product or plant. Later on, according to the *Oxford English Dictionary*, culture took the meaning of "the training, development, and refinement of mind, tastes, and manners" or what we today call *high culture*. More recently, the influence of cultural anthropology and sociology has affected the way we understand the term. For example, the British anthropologist Edward Tylor defined *culture* as a complex whole that includes knowledge, belief, art, morals, law, custom, and any other capabilities and habits acquired by man as a member of society. American anthropologists A. L. Kroeber and Clyde Kluckhohn cited no less than 164 definitions of the word. Despite these differences, however, culture has been regarded as a socially patterned style of human thought and behavior.

This emphasis on the organized repetitive responses of society's members and social heredity suggests that culture is static. This characteristic might be due, in part, to the fact that anthropologists were in the habit of paying attention to comparatively stable primitive cultures and pre-state societies and did not usually examine modern cultures that have been rapidly changing. In addition, these same anthropologists tended to focus on general culture, rather than on specific cultures, notably Western culture, or those of Europe and the United States. As a result, many important questions have remained unanswered. For instance, the question of why only Western culture provided the necessary conditions for the rise of modern capitalism has yet to be satisfactorily answered. Although Max Weber attributed the rise of capitalism to a cultural phenomenon—the rise of Calvinist Protestantism—Edward Banfield discussed the roots of poverty and authoritarianism in southern Italy in cultural terms. Similarly, recent rapid economic growth in East Asia has been attributed to the culture of Confucianism. Recently, Samuel P. Huntington at Harvard has written two monographs illuminating the universal application of cultural analysis to political and economic development. All those theorists suggest that there are intrinsic cultural values that are linked to crucial civil values, prosperity, democracy, and a regime of justice. They believe that, because cultural values are a powerful force in shaping nations and the political, economic, and social performances of people, the primary reason that some countries and ethnic groups are better off than others is their culture, and the best way to achieve progress in these areas is to promote positive cultural values. From this view, it follows that governments can best promote prosperity by changing people's values. But why are the same Chinese people economically better off now than 20 years ago? What cultural change has occurred that accounts for this economic growth? The notion that cultural change is ultimately responsible for economic prosperity fails to tell us why Taiwan and Hong Kong are doing so much better than their counterparts in China, although they are culturally similar.

Because culture is usually difficult to alter, it may appear that the fate of the developing countries is sealed. Yet although culture and tradition do matter, culture and tradition do sometimes change. Why and how does such change occur? What is the origin of the change initiated by some and, over time, adopted by an ever-increasing number of other people? According to F. A. Hayek, the evolution of culture may come as a result of competition among traditions. The traditions, practices, and rules that make up the culture of a society were not deliberately chosen, he argued, but became established as the norm because they were the ones that most enhanced prosperity. This insight into the nature of culture has proved extremely useful to understanding how certain social patterns have spread.

This approach to culture differs fundamentally from the cultural relativism that holds that cultural differences are intrinsic and reflect basic differences between people. This emphasis on the relativistic nature of culture tends to lead one to believe that culture is not learned, but almost genetically determined. Each and every person is born and brought up in a certain culture and may seem as helpless before it as was an animal who attempted to alter its instincts. This view, of course, does not take into account that people can be swayed by their political inclinations or by their emotional commitments. They can misinterpret facts to fit preconceived notions or they can seek scientific justifications for their cultural prejudices.

Some other schools of thought (e.g., Marxism) downplay the importance of culture. For Marxist sociologists, culture is simply part of the superstructure that reflects the underlying basis of society, its economic substructure, and the relations between those who control the means of production and those who do not. Culture, Marxists have maintained, has been used by the ruling class to exploit the class differences among people. Culture is the effect, whereas economics is the cause. When people accept the dominant culture, they are tricked into accepting the economic conditions that prevail as natural and the ruling class as possessing a right to their position. When people abandon these cultural blinders, they will see their real interests. Marxists suggest that there is no such thing as shared culture.

Globalization has proved that culture is both flexible and adaptable. The consumer culture iconized by McDonald's, Sony, and Nike is accepted throughout the world. Although many local tastes are added to this new consumer culture, basic values such as good service and low prices are appreciated in most societies. Culture is adaptive and changing. When enough people in a society begin to adopt a new behavior in a way that challenges the old way of doing things, cultural change can take place.

To understand culture, we must understand how human beings operate because they create a society's culture. Human beings not only try to adapt themselves to the environment, but also try to adapt the environment to themselves. They have both social and personal needs. Unfortunately, most definitions of culture reject the dual nature of human needs.

KZ

See also Civil Society; Material Progress; Sociology and Libertarianism; Tocqueville, Alexis de

Further Readings

Bell, Daniel. *The Cultural Contradictions of Capitalism*. New York: Basic Books, 1976.

Clark, Henry C. *Commerce, Culture, and Liberty: Readings on Capitalism before Adam Smith*. Indianapolis, IN: Liberty Fund, 2003.

Harrison, Lawrence E., and Samuel P. Huntington. *Culture Matters: How Values Shape Human Progress*. New York: Basic Books, 2000.

Hayek, F. A. "The Three Sources of Human Values." *Law, Legislation and Liberty*. vol. 3. London: Routledge & Kegan Paul, 1979.

Llosa, Mario Vargas. "The Culture of Liberty." *Foreign Policy* 122 (February 2000): 66–71.

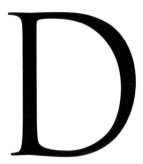

DECENTRALISM

"Small is beautiful," declared economist E. F. Schumacher in his 1973 book of the same title, and the epigram encapsulates the spirit of decentralism. There is a poetic quality to decentralism, rooted as it is in a love of the particular. The British writer G. K. Chesterton noted in his novel of local patriotism, *The Napoleon of Notting Hill*, that the true patriot "never under any circumstances boasts of the largeness of his country, but always, and of necessity, boasts of the smallness of it."

A decentralist believes that political power (and, in some but hardly all cases, wealth) should be widely dispersed. He or she believes that concentrated power is the bane of liberty; its remoteness insulates the wielder of power from the citizen—or, perhaps more accurately, the subject. As the most literary of modern decentralists, the Kentucky poet-farmer Wendell Berry has warned, "Everywhere, every day, local life is being discomforted, disrupted, endangered, or destroyed by powerful people who live, or who are privileged to think that they live, beyond the bad effects of their bad work." Decentralists would cite as specific examples the federal policy of requiring cities to bus children to schools outside their neighborhoods, which virtually destroyed cohesive ethnic enclaves in American cities; the siting of public housing projects and nuclear waste facilities over the objections of residents of the affected areas; and the deracinating effects of an interventionist foreign policy that sends young men (and now women) hither and yon, far from their home places.

From the founding, American political debate has pitted advocates of a strong central state against partisans of decentralism. Although James Madison, writing as Publius, assured readers in Federalist no. 45 that "The powers delegated by the proposed Constitution to the federal government are few and defined," the "Anti-Federalists," who opposed

ratification, saw in the Philadelphia compact the scaffolding of empire. Republican government "is only suited to a small and compact territory," argued Maryland Constitutional Convention delegate Luther Martin. Within a unitary government spread over a wide territory, citizens would have little opportunity to know those whom they might elect; lawmakers would govern in ignorance of local conditions, and tyranny would be necessary to enforce their laws.

This argument has continued throughout American history: Are liberty, property, and the integrity of small places best secured by local government or by national (or, increasingly in the age of globalization, international) authority?

In American politics, this argument has often been rendered in shorthand as the Jefferson–Hamilton debate. Although Thomas Jefferson's presidential administration sometimes overstepped constitutional bounds (e.g., with his Louisiana Purchase) and although he was essentially neutral on the matter of the Constitution's ratification, he is regarded as the founding father of American decentralism. Sketching his ideal in a letter from Monticello in 1824, Jefferson wrote that even the county was too distended a district for meaningful citizenship; he favored the creation of smaller "wards." In Jefferson's description,

> Each ward would thus be a small republic within itself, and every man in the State would thus become an acting member of the common government, transacting in person a great portion of its rights and duties, subordinate indeed, yet important, and entirely within his competence. The wit of man cannot devise a more solid basis for a free, durable, and well administered republic.

The wit of man, at least in the United States, had other plans. The centripetal force of three major wars—the Civil War and the two world wars—consolidated extraordinary power in the national government; decentralists were relegated to the political fringe because as the liberal historian Arthur Schlesinger, Jr., cautioned in his manifesto of cold war liberalism, *The Vital Center* (1949), "One can dally with the distributist dream of decentralization," but "you cannot flee from science and technology into a quietist dreamworld. The state and the factory are inexorable: bad men will run them if good abdicate the job."

The distributists whom Schlesinger dismisses as airy dreamers were the most visible decentralists in the years between 1930 and 1950. Drawing inspiration from Catholic social teaching and from such figures as G. K. Chesterton and Dorothy Day, founder of the anarchist Catholic Worker movement, the distributists promoted the Catholic principle of subsidiarity. That is, the management of affairs should devolve to the lowest possible level of society—individual, family, block, village, and, only in the rarest cases, the national government. In 1936, the American distributists, in league with agrarian and libertarian allies, published a widely heralded programmatic book, *Who Owns America?* The guide had little practical effect on the drift toward centralization.

In post–World War II American politics, decentralist themes can be found in such disparate groups as the New Left (especially Paul Goodman, Carl Oglesby, and Karl Hess), the libertarians, the Greens (see Kirkpatrick Sale's encyclopedic *Human Scale*), the Democratic left (former California Governor and Oakland Mayor Jerry Brown), Southern agrarian intellectuals (Thomas J. Fleming, Clyde Wilson, and Donald Livingston), and such Republican Party figures as Senator Robert Taft of Ohio and Vermont State Senator John McClaughry.

In 1975, Ronald Reagan declared, in words ghostwritten by McClaughry,

> I am calling for an end to giantism and for a return to the human scale—the scale that human beings can understand and cope with. . . . In government, the human scale is the town council, the board of selectmen, the precinct captain. It is this activity on a small human scale that creates the fabric of community, a framework for the creation of abundance and liberty.

If the Reagan administration seldom honored this vision—imposing a national drinking age of 21 and ordering state National Guard units to Central America over the objections of governors—recent years have seen a revivification of decentralist thought. The post–cold war fissioning of overlarge states is the realization of Leopold Kohr's exhortation in *The Breakdown of Nations* (1978): "Instead of union, let us have disunion now. Instead of fusing the small, let us dismember the big. Instead of creating fewer and larger states, let us create more and smaller ones."

Decentralism is a motive force in the early 21st-century secession movements in Quebec, Scotland, Northern Italy, and elsewhere, as well as in proposals to divide such American states as California, New York, and even Kansas into two or more states. The Nobel laureate Russian novelist Aleksandr Solzhenitsyn made a lyrical, if largely ignored, plea for a "democracy of small areas" in *Rebuilding Russia* (1991). In the 1990s, there also was a renewed emphasis in popular, if not yet in legal, circles on the 10th Amendment to the U.S. Constitution, which provides that, "The powers not delegated to the United States by the Constitution, nor prohibited by it to the States, are reserved to the States respectively, or to the people."

Decentralists insist that the love of the local and particular need not exclude a love of the national or even universal. In his essay "Provincialism," the early 20th-century philosopher Josiah Royce emphasized that "the tendency toward national unity and that toward local independence of spirit must henceforth grow together." The national culture of the United States was to be the sum of a thousand and one distinct and vibrant local cultures. (The cultural implications of centralized government should not be discounted: The two great flowerings of American letters, in the 1850s and 1920s, came during eras of much-derided "weak" presidents and a relatively inactive national government.)

In the formulation of the Iowa painter Grant Wood, "when the different regions develop characteristics of their own, they will come into competition with each other; and out of this competition a rich American culture will grow."

Political decentralists would extend the same principle to governance: permit each polity to adopt laws suited to local conditions, let San Francisco be San Francisco, and let Utah be Utah. Or in the remark of Supreme Court Justice Louis Brandeis, "The United States should go back to the federation idea, letting each state evolve a policy and develop itself. There are enough good men in Alabama, for example, to make Alabama a good state."

Critics of decentralism demur. They point to the numerous instances in which local authority has been exercised unwisely or even repressively, most notably in the Jim Crow laws and state-sanctioned segregation in the states of the Deep South. The federal government, through the Civil Rights Act of 1964 and the Voting Rights Act of 1965, secured the basic rights of American blacks—although decentralists would reply that the same government was sending those same young Southern black men across the world to fight and die in Vietnam. The central state giveth, and the central state taketh away.

Dorothy Day's Catholic Worker movement, which drew localist and anarchist lessons from Christianity, held that bigness "is not only impersonal, but also makes accountability, and, therefore, an effective political forum for redressing grievances, next to impossible." If my town council passes an ordinance that I regard as silly or oppressive, I can remonstrate, face to face, with men and women who are my neighbors. If the federal government enacts a law to which I object, I can do little more than write a letter to a federal office holder, who will respond with a computer-generated reply, or I may cast a vote in the next federal election: impersonal and probably futile acts.

The devitalizing, dispiriting effect of centralization was captured by novelist Norman Mailer, who in his 1969 campaign for the mayoralty of New York City proposed that the city become an independent state and that this new state devolve all political power to the neighborhood level. Mailer wrote:

> Our authority has been handed over to the federal power. We expect our economic solutions, our habitats, yes, even our entertainments, to derive from that remote abstract power, remote as the other end of a television tube. We are like wards in an orphan asylum. The shaping of the style of our lives is removed from us—we pay for huge military adventures and social experiments so separated from our direct control that . . . our condition is spiritless. We wait for abstract impersonal powers to save us, we despise the abstractness of those powers, we loathe ourselves for our own apathy.

From Thomas Jefferson to Norman Mailer, the faces change, the styles too, but decentralists endure.

BK

See also Federalism; Hess, Karl; Jefferson, Thomas; Subsidiarity; Urban Planning

Further Readings

Agar, Herbert, and Allen Tate, eds. *Who Owns America? A New Declaration of Independence.* Wilmington, DE: ISI Books, 1999 [1936].

Berry, Wendell. *Home Economics.* San Francisco: North Point Press, 1987.

Bryan, Frank, and John McClaughry. *The Vermont Papers.* Colchester, VT: Chelsea Green, 1989.

Chesterton, G. K. *The Napoleon of Notting Hill.* Mineola, NY: Dover, 1991 [1904].

Davidson, Donald. *The Attack on Leviathan.* Chapel Hill: University of North Carolina Press, 1938.

Hess, Karl. *Dear America.* New York: Morrow, 1975.

Jefferson, Thomas. *Writings.* New York: Viking, 1984.

Mailer, Norman. "An Instrument for the City." *Existential Errands.* Boston: Little, Brown, 1972.

Naylor, Thomas, and William H. Willimon. *Downsizing the U.S.A.* Grand Rapids, MI: Eerdmans, 1997.

Declaration of Independence

Adopted on July 4, 1776, by the Second Continental Congress, meeting in Philadelphia, the Declaration of Independence is the founding document of the United States of America. In addition to the Congress's official explanation of "the causes which impel" Americans to declare their independence from Great Britain, the document also identifies the founders' political philosophy of limited government dedicated to the protection of individual rights.

On June 11, 1776, anticipating a vote on Virginia delegate Richard Henry Lee's resolution calling for independence, Congress appointed a five-man committee to draft a declaration justifying that momentous step. The committee members were John Adams of Massachusetts, Benjamin Franklin of Pennsylvania, Roger Sherman of Connecticut, Robert Livingston of New York, and Thomas Jefferson of Virginia. Jefferson was assigned the task of drafting the document.

Late in life, Jefferson wrote that the purpose of the Declaration was "to place before mankind the common sense of the subject, in terms so plain and firm as to command their assent, and to justify" American independence. In drafting the document, he sought to express "the harmonizing sentiments of the day," the views of Americans' rights, and their violation by the British government—subjects, he maintained, on which "all American whigs thought alike." "Neither aiming at originality of principle or sentiment, nor yet copied from any particular and previous writing, it was intended to be an expression of the American mind."

In making the case for American independence, Jefferson employed the language of 18th-century logic and rhetoric. The argument of the Declaration is in the form of a syllogism, with a major premise, a minor premise, and a conclusion. Jefferson supplemented those basic components of the syllogism with corollary principles that reinforced the overall argument.

The second paragraph, which states the major premise, posed the greatest difficulty for Jefferson as the many changes he marked in his "original rough draught" attest. "We hold these truths to be sacred & undeniable," he originally wrote, "that all men are created equal & independent, and from that equal creation they derive rights inherent & inalienable, among which are the preservation of life, & liberty, & the pursuit of happiness." After Jefferson substituted the more precise term *self-evident* for the phrase *sacred & undeniable*, he made further changes suggested by Franklin and Adams, resulting in the familiar language: "We hold these truths to be self-evident: that all men are created equal; that they are endowed by their creator with certain unalienable rights; that among these are life, liberty, & the pursuit of happiness."

The concept that all men equally enjoyed certain natural rights was one of the "harmonizing sentiments of the day" to which Jefferson later alluded; it reflected the influence on Jefferson and other American Patriots of a variety of sources, including 17th- and 18th-century Enlightenment treatises and English radical Whig writings, particularly John Locke's *Second Treatise on Government.* Although much of the language in the second paragraph of the Declaration closely paraphrases passages from Locke's work, Jefferson departed from Locke's identification of "life, liberty, and property" as the three fundamental natural rights. Contrary to what some modern scholars have asserted, however, in substituting *pursuit of happiness* for *property*, Jefferson was not devaluing property rights. Rather, following the ideas of the Swiss natural rights philosopher Jean Jacques Burlamaqui, he understood that more fundamental than property itself was the right to pursue happiness, which included the rights of acquiring, using, and disposing of property, as many early American state constitutions affirmed.

The rest of the second paragraph identified the other "self-evident truths" that constituted the major premise of the Declaration's argument: "to secure these rights, governments are instituted among men, deriving their just powers from the consent of the governed"; and "whenever any form of government becomes destructive of these ends, it is the right of the people to alter or to abolish it, and institute new government." Those principles also derived from English radical Whig philosophy, and particularly from John Locke's *Second Treatise*, which identified the protection of individual rights as the essential purpose of government and also justified revolution against an existing government when it violated the ends for which it was established. Jefferson added the corollary principle that the right of revolution was not to be exercised by a people for "light and transient causes," but only when "a long train of abuses and usurpations . . . evinces a design to reduce them under absolute despotism." In such a case, however, "it is their right, it is their duty," to throw off such a despotic government and "to provide new guards for their future security."

The main body of the Declaration provides the minor premise of its argument: a long list of George III's "unremitting injuries and usurpations," showing the King's design to establish "absolute tyranny" over the American colonies. The first 12 counts against the King concerned abuse of executive power, including such offenses as dissolving colonial assemblies, making judges dependent on his will, keeping standing armies, and making the military superior to the civil power. The 13th count charged that the King had given his assent to various "acts of pretended legislation" passed by the British Parliament, including efforts to tax the colonists without their consent and to restrict their trade. Counts 14 through 18 charged that the King had "abdicated government" by declaring the colonies out of his protection and had made war on the colonies using not only British troops, but "foreign mercenaries," "merciless Indian savages," and the Americans' own black slaves. The 19th and final count against the King related the fact that, "in every stage of these oppressions," the Americans had petitioned for redress, but their "repeated petitions have been answered only by repeated injuries." The King, therefore, was shown to be "a tyrant" and "unfit to be the ruler of a people who mean to be free."

Although many of those charges against George III were recognized in English constitutional law as tyrannical acts that would justify rebellion against a king, others were

peculiar to the American quarrel with the British government, such as the complaints against Parliament taxing the colonists and regulating their trade. Significantly, the Declaration did not mention the British Parliament by name; it voiced these complaints in terms of the King conspiring "with others" to subject Americans to "a jurisdiction foreign to our constitutions and unacknowledged by our laws."

When Congress debated the text of Jefferson's draft on July 2–4, 1776, it made many changes in wording and two major deletions: a clause that blamed King George for slavery and the slave trade, and a clause that denounced the British people as "unfeeling brethren." With a few additional changes in the wording of the final paragraph—including the incorporation of the words of Lee's resolution declaring that the colonies "are, and of right ought to be, free and independent states"—Congress concluded the Declaration's argument for American independence.

The 56 men who signed the Declaration pledged their "lives," their "fortunes," and their "sacred honor," and many of them paid the price for this courageous act of principle that British authorities viewed as treason. Although Benjamin Franklin allegedly had encouraged his fellow delegates to sign the document by quipping, "If we don't hang together, we shall most assuredly hang separately," none of the signers was executed. Some, however, were captured by the British military and held as prisoners, including three of the four signers from South Carolina. Several died of wounds received or hardships suffered during the Revolutionary War, and many had their homes and property destroyed or lost their wives or children. Half of the signers held public office in the United States—Adams and Jefferson as president and others as members of Congress, governors, or state legislators—and a number of them helped adopt the U.S. Constitution.

Late in life, Adams and Jefferson took special pride in their roles in drawing up the Declaration of Independence. They kept track of the surviving signers, realizing they were among the last. Their final words concerned the document—Adams proclaimed, "Jefferson still lives," whereas Jefferson asked, "Is it the Fourth?"—on the day they both died, July 4, 1826, the 50th anniversary of the Declaration's adoption by Congress.

DNM

See also Adams, John; American Revolution; Burlamaqui, Jean-Jacques; Jefferson, Thomas; Pursuit of Happiness; Revolution, Right of

Further Readings

Becker, Carl L. *The Declaration of Independence: A Study in the History of Political Ideas.* New York: Vintage Books, 1958.

Boyd, Julian P., ed. *The Papers of Thomas Jefferson.* vol. 1. Princeton, NJ: Princeton University Press, 1950.

Cohen, I. Bernard. *Science and the Founding Fathers*. New York: W. W. Norton, 1995.

Eicholz, Hans L. *Harmonizing Sentiments: The Declaration of Independence and the Jeffersonian Idea of Self-Government*. New York: Peter Lang, 2001.

Hamowy, Ronald. "Jefferson and the Scottish Enlightenment: A Critique of Garry Wills' *Inventing America: Jefferson's Declaration of Independence*." *William and Mary Quarterly* 36 (1979): 503–523.

Machan, Tibor, ed. *Individual Rights Reconsidered: Are the Truths of the U.S. Declaration of Independence Lasting?* Stanford, CA: Hoover Institution Press, 2001.

Malone, Dumas, Hirst Milhollen, and Milton Kaplan. *The Story of the Declaration of Independence*. New York: Oxford University Press, 1975.

Mayer, David N. *The Constitutional Thought of Thomas Jefferson*. Charlottesville: University Press of Virginia, 1994.

Munves, James. *Thomas Jefferson and the Declaration of Independence*. New York: Charles Scribner's Sons, 1978.

White, Morton. *The Philosophy of the American Revolution*. New York: Oxford University Press, 1978.

Declaration of the Rights of Man and of the Citizen

On August 26, 1789, the Declaration of the Rights of Man and of the Citizen was adopted by the French National Assembly, which also was known as the Constituent Assembly, owing to its self-appointed task of framing a constitution for the French nation. This body began as one of three Estates, or orders, within the Estates-General, which had been convened in early May by King Louis XVI. The three orders of which the Estates-General consisted were the nobility, the clergy, and the Third Estate, made up of all other French citizens.

This remarkable event—the summoning of the Estates-General, the first since 1614—was precipitated by the bankruptcy of the French government and its desperate need to raise revenue. The crown's attempts to levy taxes on those who could afford them generated a power struggle with the nobility (especially the reform-minded *Parlement* of Paris), and both sides decided they had something to gain by convening an Estates-General. Events, however, soon took on a life of their own as both the King and the aristocracy found themselves unable to control the course of events.

The Third Estate first acted in a revolutionary manner on June 17, when, by a majority of 491 to 89, it renamed itself the National Assembly. Although deputies from the other two orders were invited to join the National Assembly—and were later ordered to do so by Louis XVI after he had lost a significant political battle—this assumption of political sovereignty by the Third Estate was a clear sign that a number of ancient legal privileges that the crown and nobility possessed would not be permitted to stand. Indeed, many members of the nobility and clergy strongly supported the abolition of feudal privileges and other radical reforms that were about to follow.

The Declaration was intended to serve as a preamble to the French Constitution of 1791, which established a constitutional monarchy. (A purely republican form of government awaited the Constitution of 1793, after the treason conviction of Louis XVI had led to his execution and the abolition of monarchy.) Historians continue to debate the extent to which the Declaration was influenced by American precedents, such as George Mason's Virginia Declaration of Rights (1776) and various state constitutions adopted during the 1780s. The Marquis de Lafayette, who emphasized the need for a Declaration of Rights and played a prominent role in its drafting, was among the 8,000 Frenchmen who had participated in the American Revolution. Moreover, key documents in the American struggle, such as Thomas Paine's *Common Sense* and various state constitutions, had been translated into French and were widely read.

Some historians maintain that this situation is more a case of correlation than of causation. As the historian George Rudé observed, "both Americans and Frenchmen acknowledged a common debt to the 'natural law' school of philosophy, in particular to Locke, Montesquieu, and Rousseau." At the least, however, the American experience provided an inspiration and example, if not an exact model, for the French Declaration of Rights. According to John-Joseph Mounier, a member of the National Assembly who contributed to the Declaration, the American Revolution had instilled in the French "a general restlessness and desire for change." Americans had shown that it was possible to begin anew and construct a government on rational principles.

The Declaration, which contains 17 articles, is a short document. The preamble describes it as a "solemn declaration [of] the natural, inalienable, and sacred rights of man." Failures to protect these rights, it notes, are the "sole causes of public misfortunes and the corruption of governments." By codifying the basic rights and duties of citizens, the Declaration's intent was to legitimize the new French government and to encourage respect for the legislative and executive powers by providing citizens with "simple and incontestable principles" that could be used to evaluate the justice and social utility of governmental institutions and actions.

Article 1 begins with the statement: "Men are born and remain free and equal in rights." It should be noted that the words *man* and *men*, when used in this context, referred to all individuals, male and female alike. Both men and women were viewed as possessing equal *natural* rights in the Lockean tradition. Gender inequalities, such as the inability to vote—which the Constitution of 1791 did nothing to rectify—were viewed as an issue of *civil* rather than natural rights.

Unlike some versions of social contract theory, in which natural rights are irrevocably transferred or surrendered to government, this passage suggests that (a) the power to enforce rights, rather than the rights themselves, is delegated to government; and (b) this "executive power" (as Locke called it) may be reclaimed by individuals in those cases where a government becomes despotic or tyrannical.

The purpose of government is to preserve the "natural and imprescriptible rights of . . . liberty, property, security, and resistance to oppression." "The natural rights of individuals" are limited by the equal rights of other individuals. "Liberty consists in being able to do anything that does not injure another," and the primary function of law is to define and specify these limits. Thus, natural rights constitute a standard of public utility that determines the common good. The law may forbid only those actions that are "harmful to society." All actions not expressly forbidden by law are permitted, and no one may be compelled to do anything that is not mandated by law.

Although much of the Declaration may be broadly described as Lockean, another influence—that of J. J. Rousseau—also is evident at various points, particularly Article 3, which holds that "the source of all sovereignty resides essentially in the nation," and Article 6, which reiterates the Rousseauian notion that "the law is the expression of the general will."

Conservative critics of the French Revolution, such as J. L. Talmon, have focused on these elements to denounce the Declaration, following on the argument first proposed by Edmund Burke in his *Reflections on the Revolution in France* (1790). According to these critics, the references to national sovereignty and the "general will" contain the seeds of totalitarian democracy—a tendency that would later manifest itself in events such as the Reign of Terror and Jacobin one-party rule. However, this criticism is misplaced. The claim that sovereignty resides in the nation was intended to rebut the doctrine of absolute monarchy, according to which sovereignty resides solely in the king. To state that no body or individual "can exercise authority that does not explicitly proceed" from this source is merely to affirm, if in a somewhat roundabout fashion, the Lockean principle that all legitimate political authority must be based on the consent of the governed.

The "general will," an expression that appears only once in the Declaration, was closely associated with Rousseau, who failed to make its meaning clear. But we at least know what Rousseau did not mean because he explicitly cautions against confusing the "general will" with the will of the majority.

Although many deputies in the National Assembly were familiar with Rousseau's writings, it is unlikely that these practical men—many of whom were lawyers—intended to inject his abstruse notion the "general will" into the Declaration. It is more plausible that their understanding was based on the argument put forward by the Abbé Sieyès, an active member of the assembly, in *What Is the Third Estate?* Throughout this highly influential tract, published early in 1789, Sieyès expressly equated the "general will" with majority rule. Although Rousseau, who had died 11 years earlier, would not have been happy with this simplistic interpretation of his theory, majority rule is possibly all that most members of the National Assembly understood by the "general will."

When viewed in this light, this mention of the "general will" becomes far less sinister than its many critics would have us believe—especially when we keep in mind that the Declaration was drafted specifically to establish limits on government power. The government envisioned in the Declaration is far closer to the limited constitutional State described by Locke than to the totalitarian democracy that is often attributed, whether rightly or wrongly, to Rousseau. Indeed, Article 16 states that a "society in which the guarantee of rights is not secured, or the separation of powers not clearly established, has no constitution." This emphasis on the separation of powers is not something we find in Rousseau, whereas it is essential to Locke's theory.

The rule of law is a recurring theme in the Declaration; 9 of the 17 articles refer to it. This insistence is understandable given the many legal privileges and inequities of the Old Regime. All citizens, it proclaims, have the right to participate in the making of law, whether personally or through their representatives. All citizens are equal in the eyes of the law, which should be applied impartially regardless of social distinctions. The holding of public offices should be determined solely on the basis of "virtues and talents."

No person may be accused, arrested, or detained except under the forms prescribed by law, and those public officials who abuse their power should be held accountable. Those legal punishments are alone justifiable, which are "strictly and evidently necessary" for the protection of rights, and no one may be tried for violating a law that was not in effect at the time of the offense. Moreover, "Every man is presumed innocent until he has been found guilty," and only the minimal amount of force necessary to secure an arrest is warranted.

Freedom of religion is guaranteed, "provided [religious] expression does not trouble the public order established by law." This proviso probably owed its inclusion to the Catholic clergy. The Constitution of 1791 did not abolish laws against blasphemy, nor did it establish a separation of church and state.

A similar proviso is attached to "one of the most precious rights of man" (i.e., "the free expression of thought and opinions"). Every citizen is free to speak, write, or print what he pleases, "subject to accountability for abuse of this freedom in those cases determined by law." This broad qualification, however troublesome it may seem, may have been intended merely to accommodate libel laws and similar measures that are found even today in countries that pride themselves on free speech.

The Declaration concludes by stressing the importance of property rights: "Property being an inviolable and sacred right, no one can be deprived of it, unless legally established public necessity obviously demands it, and upon condition of just and prior indemnity." The Declaration proved to be one of the great documents in the history of freedom. It was translated and published in all the countries of Europe, and served it as the basis of countless demands throughout the continent for a society based on liberal principles.

GHS

See also Declaration of Independence; Enlightenment; French Revolution; Rights, Theories of; Rousseau, Jean-Jacques

Further Readings

Acton, John Edward Emerich Dalberg, Lord. *Lectures on the French Revolution*. John Neville Figgis, ed. Indianapolis, IN: Liberty Fund, 2000.

Burke, Edmund. *Reflections on the Revolution in France*. Francis Canavan, ed. Indianapolis, IN: Liberty Fund, 1999.

Locke, John. "Second Treatise on Government." *Two Treatises on Government*. Peter Laslett, ed. Cambridge: Cambridge University Press, 2005.

Mason, George. "Virginia Declaration of Rights." *The Papers of George Mason 1726–1792*. Robert A. Rutland, ed. Chapel Hill: University of North Carolina Press, 1970.

Paine, Thomas. *Paine: Political Writings*. Bruce Kuklik, ed. Cambridge: Cambridge University Press, 2000.

Rousseau, Jean-Jacques. *"The Social Contract" and Other Later Political Writings*. Victor Gourevitch, ed. Cambridge: Cambridge University Press, 1997.

Sieyès, Emmanuel Joseph. *Political Writings: Including the Debate between Sieyes and Tom Paine in 1791*. Michael Sonenscher, trans. Indianapolis, IN: Hackett, 2003.

Van Kley, Dale. *The French Idea of Freedom: The Old Regime and the Declaration of Rights of 1789*. Stanford, CA: Stanford University Press, 1997.

DELEGATION

A legislature delegates its legislative power when it authorizes others to make rules of conduct in its place. Such delegation harms liberty and undercuts democracy because it permits legislators to largely escape responsibility for the rules that govern society. When legislators enact a rule of conduct by statute, they create rights and impose duties on voters. They are thus accountable at the polls for both the benefits and costs of the rule. When, however, they delegate lawmaking power to some executive agency, they instruct that agency to make rules of conduct to serve some high-minded purpose while imposing no duties. In this manner, legislators can claim credit for the benefits expected if it pursues vigorously the purpose announced by the legislature, but shift blame to the agency for the costs and disappointed expectations if it does not. In this way, delegation allows legislators to evade accountability for the costs and disappointments.

John Locke wrote in the *Second Treatise on Government* that "the legislative cannot transfer the power of making law to any other hands" because the electorate has indicated that they placed in those specific hands the power of making law. This concern for the delegation of legislative authority to others was to become an issue with the American colonists in their struggle with Great Britain. The colonists opposed not only taxation without representation, but also regulation without representation. James Madison understood the opening words in the first article of the U.S. Constitution—"All legislative Powers herein granted shall be vested in a Congress of the United States"—to mean that Congress alone was empowered to exercise those powers and this is, in fact, what prevailed for the first 100 years of the Republic. Indeed, according to both the early Supreme Court and Friedrich A. Hayek, the power to make law is the power to make the rules of private conduct. According to early Supreme Court decisions, the power to make law is the power to make the rules of private conduct. F. A. Hayek reached similar conclusions and pointed to the dangers of lodging what amounted to legislative power in the hands of administrative tribunals that were empowered to make ad hoc rulings.

During the Progressive Era, from about 1875 to 1920, social reformers unwittingly eroded the barrier against a conflation of these two functions. These reformers encouraged legislatures to enact statutes that authorized executive agencies, ostensibly staffed by experts, to achieve regulatory goals by overseeing private conduct. The Progressives wrongly held that the application of technical expertise by agencies would produce uniquely right answers. They also thought that such statutes authorized agencies to execute law, rather than to make it. So, although the Progressives strongly believed in the importance of the separation of powers, they did not view statutes of this kind as giving agencies lawmaking power.

Under the influence of the Progressives, Congress passed statutes establishing the Interstate Commerce Commission, the Federal Trade Commission, and other commissions and agencies. The Supreme Court approved them on the grounds that the Congress was empowering these agencies not to enact but, rather, to implement the law. By the time it became clear that this approach to solving regulatory problems through the application of specialized technical knowledge failed to produce uniquely right answers, a substantial number of lawmaking agencies had been created.

In 1935, the Supreme Court, in a unanimous decision, ruled that the National Recovery Administration constituted a delegation of legislative power to the executive that violated the provisions of the Constitution. The Court thus attempted to draw a line against the erosion of legislative authority, which had reached mammoth proportions under the New Deal. The Court's action provoked President Roosevelt to attempt to "pack" the court, thus ensuring that a majority of justices would sanction the creation of further agencies of this type. Although Congress did not support Roosevelt's court-packing scheme, the Court soon retreated on the issue of legislative delegation to the point where today the delegation of legislative power to expert agencies is generally approved.

The Court nonetheless remains concerned about delegation and has attempted to prevent its expansion into yet further areas. It has ruled against Congressional attempts to delegate legislative powers to one house of Congress, two houses of Congress acting without the president, the president acting alone, or to law enforcement officials or private persons. The Court also interpreted some statutes to minimize the degree of delegation. State courts have gone even further.

Concern for the problems posed by legislative delegation is not limited to the United States. For example, the German Constitution has a provision limiting delegation, and some opposition to increasing the power of the European Community has been provoked by fears that the Community's agencies would make laws for which no legislators would be directly accountable.

DS

See also Corruption; Democracy; New Deal; Progressive Era; Public Choice Economics; Regulation

Further Readings

Hayek, Friedrich A. *Law, Legislation and Liberty: Volume 1. Rules and Order*. Chicago: University of Chicago Press, 1978.

Lowi, Theodore J. *The End of Liberalism: The Second Republic of the United States*. New York: W. W. Norton, 1979.

Schoenbrod, David. "Politics and the Principle That Elected Legislators Should Make the Laws." *Harvard Journal of Law and Public Policy* 26 (Winter 2003): 239–280.

———. *Power without Responsibility: How Congress Abuses the People through Delegation*. New Haven, CT: Yale University Press, 1993.

———. "Symposium—The Phoenix Rises Again: The Nondelegation Doctrine from Constitutional and Policy Perspectives." *Cardozo Law Review* 20 (January 1999): 731–766.

Sunstein, Cass R. "Nondelegation Canons." *University of Chicago Law Review* 67 (Spring 2000): 315–343.

DEMOCRACY

Democracy refers to that form of government in which the people, either directly or through their representatives, determine the laws. In the 20th century, during a time of a deep ideological divide between authoritarian dictatorships and capitalist democracies, democracy was often associated with liberty and respect for the individual. Although there is a correlation between liberty and democracy, democracy refers to a particular type of political system that does not necessarily imply or lead to a society in which men are free. A democratic system provides that citizens exercise control over the government, whereas liberty refers to the limits of that power regardless of who exercises it. A popular view of democracy is that democratic government should act to further the will of the majority, but this vision is obviously incompatible with liberty. As Alexis de Tocqueville observed, a majority can be just as tyrannical as a dictator.

Democracy works well as a collective decision mechanism when there is a consensus of opinion within the decision-making group, but many other collective decision mechanisms would work equally well when there is widespread agreement among group members. When there is lack of a consensus, however, democratic decision making breaks down; so when evaluated as a mechanism for arriving at political decisions, democracy works worst when it is needed most. There are a number of reasons that democracy might not work well in the absence of a consensus among members of the decision-making group.

In a democracy, there are some cases where there will be no clear outcome supported by a majority. This case can be illustrated with an example in which majorities are cyclical. In the simplest of these cases, there are three voters, 1, 2, and 3, who choose by majority rule among options A, B, and C. Voter 1 prefers A to B and B to C, voter 2 prefers B to C and C to A, and voter 3 prefers C to A and A to B. If options A and B are the only political options, then a majority (voters 1 and 3) would prefer A to B. However, a majority also prefers C to A, and a majority prefers B to C. So by majority rule, A defeats B, C defeats A, and B defeats C. No one option can defeat all others by majority rule; in this example, there is no clear majority preference. Kenneth Arrow has shown that it is not possible to design a social choice mechanism that is able to produce a rational ordering of group preferences from the orderings of the preferences of the individuals in the group. In theory, democratic decisions must be imperfect reflections of the preferences of those in the decision-making group.

More significant problems may occur in democracies when there is a clear-cut majority that is able to use the political system to impose its will on the minority. Such instances make the conflicts between liberty and democracy readily apparent and reveal the wisdom of placing substantial constitutional restrictions on the ability of democratic governments to implement policies that are approved by a majority. Alexis de Tocqueville believed that once the majority realized that they could vote themselves benefits at the expense of the minority, democracy was in danger of collapse.

Minorities also pose a significant danger in democracies in the form of special interest groups. Because in democratic governments one citizen's vote is unlikely to have much impact on government policy, citizens in democracies tend to be rationally ignorant, as Anthony Downs emphasized. There is little benefit to becoming politically informed because one's vote counts for so little, so most people are unaware of most of what the issues before the voters entail. Rational ignorance provides the opportunity for special interest groups to lobby government for concentrated benefits directed at them at the expense of the general public. Politicians gain the support of the interest groups they help, whereas the general public remains rationally ignorant of the costs they bear to provide these interest group benefits. Mancur Olson observed that as democratic governments mature, special interest groups gain an increasing amount of power and ability to effect transfers to themselves, generating societies in which people substitute transfer-seeking activity for productive activity, which ultimately leads to social decline. Because democratic leaders always run the risk of being voted out of office, they often pursue more shortsighted policies, and they tend to favor special interests over the general interest more than would government leaders with more secure long-term prospects.

It is apparent that there are many problems with democratic government. As Winston Churchill observed, "Democracy is the worst form of government except for all those others that have been tried." The biggest advantage of democracy over other forms of government is that political leaders require a wide base of support to remain in office, so public officials cannot ignore popular opinion. In autocratic governments that are maintained by a small coalition of supporters, political leaders must provide benefits to those supporters to keep them from defecting to potential rivals, which leads to corruption, cronyism, and inefficient policies designed to benefit a small coalition, rather than the general public. Leaders of democratic governments also try to maintain political support by providing benefits to their supporters, but when most people are able to vote, officials sometimes attempt to provide benefits that appeal to a broad cross-section of the public. However, because democratic leaders try to gain the support of various special interest groups by targeting policies to their benefit, democratic governments still tend to favor special interests over the general public interest. The difference is that autocratic governments tend to favor only a few who are the leader's strong supporters, whereas democracies tend to spread special interest benefits to a larger group.

Democracies come in different forms, and the parliamentary democracies that govern Europe appear to have been less successful at controlling the size of government than American democracy because interest groups can wield more influence in parliamentary systems. Although every nation is different in its particulars, in parliamentary democracies, parties choose who will represent them in elections, in contrast to the system that prevails in the United States, where anyone can run for office. Additionally, voters in parliamentary systems almost always vote for parties, rather than individual candidates. After parliamentary elections, the winners form a government that has control over legislation as long as it remains in power. Because the parties choose representatives in parliamentary systems, representatives vote the party line and do not have the independence to vote against the party position, unlike in the United States. As a result, interest groups have more influence in parliamentary systems primarily for two reasons. First, special interests form relationships with parties, and those relationships can last beyond the terms of individual members, whereas in the United States interest groups must deal with individual representatives who may or may not vote with their parties. Second, once they are in power, parliamentary governments have less opposition because they control a majority of the legislature, whereas in the United States individual representatives often vote against their party leaders, so the leaders of the majority party in the United States have less power to dictate policy than they would in a parliamentary system. The larger point here is that there are differences among democracies, and the differences in the form of democracy can have a significant impact on government policy.

There are many problems inherent in democratic decision making. Recognizing these problems, the American founders were wary of the power of democracy and deliberately designed a government with constitutionally limited powers. The United States was not designed to be a democracy, in the sense of a government whose policies are determined by popular opinion. Rather, the founders fashioned constitutional limits on the government's powers and created a system of checks and balances to try to prevent abuse. In addition, they limited the ability of citizens to directly influence government decision makers. Despite the popular appeal of democracy, one must recognize that the success the United States has enjoyed in producing prosperity and freedom relative to other parts of the world is more due to the constitutional limits placed on government power than to democracy.

The American founders, as they originally designed the federal government, created institutions that were strongly insulated from popular opinion and the will of the majority. The judicial branch is insulated from democratic pressures because justices and judges are appointed by the president and confirmed by Congress and hold office for life. The founders intended the executive branch to be similarly insulated, with the president chosen by an Electoral College. The Constitution did not specify how the members of the Electoral College were to be selected, and early in the nation's history the most common way was to have presidential electors selected by the state legislators. The founders envisioned the Electoral College as a selection committee to choose the president, insulating the selection of the president from direct input from the citizens. The process never worked quite as they intended, and it evolved into a more democratic one by the 1830s, in which citizens nominally voted for the president. Similarly, the Constitution originally provided for Senators to be chosen by their state legislatures, and this process was altered only in 1913 when the 17th Amendment mandated their direct election. Yet as the government was originally designed, only members of the House of Representatives were to be directly accountable to the citizens. If each of the three branches of government were given equal weight, as would be required if a system of checks and balances were to work, then the government would only be one-sixth democratic, with only half of the legislative branch of government subject to direct popular control. However, with the popular election of the president and Senators, it is now two-thirds democratic. The U.S. government is much more democratic and its leaders are much more immediately accountable to its citizens than when the nation was founded.

The 20th century was characterized by a deep ideological divide between oppressive communist dictatorships led by the Soviet Union and freer capitalist democracies, the most prominent of which was the United States. This war of ideologies led many people to equate democracy with freedom. Yet democracies have the potential to be as tyrannical as dictatorships, and the road to freedom is not to move from dictatorship to democracy, but from bigger to smaller government. Although democracies tend to be freer than dictatorships, democracy and freedom are by no means the same thing, and more democracy does not necessarily bring more freedom with it.

RGH

See also Buchanan, James M.; Condorcet, Marquis de; Constitution, U.S.; Public Choice Economics; Tocqueville, Alexis de

Further Readings

Arrow, Kenneth J. *Social Choice and Individual Values*. New Haven, CT: Yale University Press, 1951.

Black, Duncan. *The Theory of Committees and Elections*. Cambridge: Cambridge University Press, 1958.

Buchanan, James M., and Gordon Tullock. *The Calculus of Consent*. Ann Arbor: University of Michigan Press, 1962.

Bueno de Mesquita, Bruce, Alastair Smith, Randolph M. Siverson, and James D. Morrow. *The Logic of Political Survival*. Cambridge, MA: MIT Press, 2003.

Downs, Anthony. *An Economic Theory of Democracy*. New York: Harper & Row, 1957.

Hamilton, Alexander, John Jay, and James Madison. *The Federalist*. Washington, DC: National Home Library, 1937.

Holcombe, Randall G. *From Liberty to Democracy: The Transformation of American Government*. Ann Arbor: University of Michigan Press, 2002.

Hoppe, Hans-Hermann. *Democracy, the God That Failed*. New Brunswick, NJ: Transaction, 2001.

Olson, Mancur. *The Rise and Decline of Nations*. New Haven, CT: Yale University Press, 1982.

Tocqueville, Alexis de. *Democracy in America*. New York: Knopf, 1963 [1835].

Development, Economic

Economic progress is a modern phenomenon. For most of human history, growth was stagnant or low, calculated on a per-person basis. Mass poverty was the norm. According to the World Bank, in 1820, about 75% of the world's population lived on the equivalent of $1 a day or less. Today, that figure is about 15% according to the bank and even less according to leading independent economists.

The modern era of economic growth that began in Western Europe in the mid-18th century and that has since spread unevenly around the world has produced a diverse record of economic development. Western Europe, its offshoots, and Japan have experienced sustained increases in wealth; poorer countries have gone through erratic growth cycles; some have seen declines in income or have merely stagnated; and at least one country—Argentina—went from developed country status in the early 20th century to developing country status. In recent decades, a minority of poor countries have enjoyed economic success by achieving and sustaining high growth.

The varying growth paths, including the West's initial escape from poverty, have prompted a diversity of explanations about what causes prosperity. As far back as 1755, Adam Smith cited the importance of policies and institutions as key determinants of economic progress, factors he would highlight later in his monumental work, *An Inquiry into the Nature and Causes of the Wealth of Nations*. "Little else," he wrote, "is requisite to carry a state to the highest degree of opulence from the lowest barbarism, but peace, easy taxes, and a tolerable administration of justice; all the rest being brought about by the natural course of things."

Smith focused mainly on Europe and the Western world, as did other classical economists. It was not until the closing years of World War II and the postwar era that a strong interest arose among economists and policymakers in the development of what came to be known as the Third World. It was during this period that the field of development economics, a subfield of economics, was born. The promotion of economic development as a policy objective of rich countries became institutionalized through various foreign aid programs.

The early development economists were influenced by the experience of the Great Depression, which they interpreted as a failure of the free market, and by Keynesian economics, which emphasized macroeconomic stimulation of national demand to reduce unemployment and spur growth. The apparent success of the Soviet Union at industrialization also influenced policy prescriptions for rapid growth. From the beginning, the orthodoxy in this field viewed industrialization and capital accumulation—characteristics associated with advanced economies—as policy goals. The lack of capital was seen as a major cause of poverty. Paul Rosentstein-Rodan and Hans Singer wrote about the "vicious circle" of poverty, in which the lack of savings and investment perpetuated underdevelopment as small markets and limited resources made it unlikely that private investment would rise to a level sufficient to raise growth. Theorists assumed a direct relationship between investment levels and growth rates, and growth models calculated the "financing gap" said to exist in poor countries. Foreign aid was used to fill that gap.

Trade pessimism also dominated the thinking of development economists and Third World governments. Ragnar Nurkse believed that the conditions that helped developed countries increase exports in the 19th century no longer held and that trade would stimulate unnecessary consumption and reduce savings rates in poor countries. Raul Prebisch argued that developing countries faced deteriorating terms of trade—the price of their exports, mainly primary products, fell in relation to the price of their imports, mainly industrial goods from rich countries. Thus, free trade favored rich countries and condemned poor nations to poverty.

The policy response to these analyses was protectionism and development planning. Poor nations erected trade barriers to encourage the growth of domestic industry. The contribution of agriculture to development was considered to be limited, and the rural poor were thought to be unresponsive to price signals in a market economy. Because private capital was seen as unable or unwilling to invest in poor countries, government planning became widespread. Policies included reliance on price and wage controls, state-owned enterprises, agricultural marketing boards, government-directed credit, capital controls, and extensive regulation of the private sector. Gunnar Myrdal recommended "central planning as a first condition of progress." Countries such as India and Pakistan adopted Soviet-style 5-year plans.

Such planning was supported and encouraged by the World Bank and other aid agencies, which were thought to provide a "big push" to poor nations and, in the view of Walt Rostow, lead to an economic takeoff. The idea that modernity had to be forced on backward societies pervaded the development orthodoxy. Myrdal wrote approvingly about compulsion to make planning succeed.

Dissent against the development consensus arose, but was limited to a few voices in the wilderness. Peter Bauer, the most articulate of the dissenters, criticized the disregard of individual choice, reliance on extensive state interventionism, and the obsession with capital accumulation. Bauer explained, "To have money is the result of economic achievement, not its precondition." Thus, he noted that the notions of a vicious circle of poverty and of foreign aid as essential to development were absurd as is evidenced by rich countries that were once poor but developed without outside aid. In Bauer's view, decentralized decision making in the market led to the best use of resources and limited an increase in "man's power over man." Economic progress depended on the complex interaction of policies, institutions, and values, not all of which were easily susceptible to measurement or manipulation.

It would take decades of development experience, however, before some of those views became more widely shared. By the 1960s, inward-looking development strategies were already failing. Protection of domestic industries increased production costs on agriculture and prices on consumer goods, but failed to produce quality products. Agricultural goods also often faced export taxes. The bias against agriculture depressed that sector, perpetuating poverty in rural areas, and reduced its export earnings. Imports of capital goods and even food increased, exchange rates became overvalued, and countries began having balance of payment problems.

Highly protected industrialization turned out to discourage exports and lead to macroeconomic distortions. But not all developing countries followed that model. In the 1960s, South Korea and Taiwan began turning away from import substitution industrialization and toward the open trade policies that characterized Singapore and Hong Kong. In 1979, Ian Little documented the four nations' reliance on comparative advantage:

> The major lesson is that labor-intensive export-oriented policies, which amounted to almost free-trade conditions for exporters, were the prime cause of an extremely rapid and labor-intensive industrialization, which revolutionized in a decade the lives of more than 50 million people, including the poorest among them.

As the four tigers advanced economically, wages rose, poverty fell, and their economies became modern, more service-oriented, and dependent on higher skills and higher technology. Japan's postwar rise from devastation to First World country within a matter of decades also set an example. Labor-intensive production then shifted to other countries in Asia as, among others, Thailand, Malaysia, Indonesia, and China began opening their economies.

The development orthodoxy, meanwhile, went through various fads and adjustments, emphasizing, for example, government support for agriculture and redistribution to the poor. However, it was not until the outbreak of the Third World debt crisis in the early 1980s and the subsequent collapse of central planning that the failure of state-led development became widely acknowledged.

The debt crisis revealed that a lack of capital was not a problem for the Third World. Rather, economic mismanagement and the domestic policy environment were at fault. Highly indebted South Korea did not experience economic crisis as did highly indebted Latin American countries. Thus, by the early 1980s, Deepak Lal was moved to declare "the poverty of development economics." A worldwide move to the market slowly began and by the early 1990s accelerated in pace and scope, including most of the formerly socialist countries.

The early liberalizers set a pattern of development that other countries have emulated with varying degrees of success. From 1960 to 2000, the four Asian tigers maintained average annual per-person growth rates of more than 5%, increasing their income by at least seven times, with Hong Kong and Singapore surpassing the United Kingdom. Likewise, reform pioneers Chile and China began liberalizing their economies in the 1970s with notable results. Chile's per capita income is now more than 3 times greater than in 1975, whereas China's income is nearly 10 times higher than when reforms began.

The era of globalization has produced other reform successes in countries as diverse as Vietnam, El Salvador, Ireland, and Estonia. Central European nations have succeeded in introducing policies of political and economic liberalization, putting them on a convergence path with Western Europe. Yet other countries—in Latin America and in the former Soviet Union, for example—have had a more difficult time implementing coherent reforms and sustaining high growth. Most of sub-Saharan Africa and much of the Middle East have yet to see significant economic reform. Mainly because of their economic policies, Africans are poorer today than they were 30 years ago.

The era of globalization has also renewed an interest in domestic institutions, such as the rule of law, and other factors that could explain widely different reform experiences. The International Monetary Fund estimated, for example, that if institutions in Africa were brought up to the level in emerging Asia, African long-term per capita income would nearly double. The Fraser Institute's annual *Economic Freedom of the World* report—the most systematic long-term study measuring policies and institutions consistent with personal choice, voluntary exchange, protection of private property, and freedom to compete—finds a strong empirical relationship between economic freedom and prosperity. Countries that are more economically free tend to be wealthier and grow faster. That relationship remains even after taking into account other factors such as education or demographic indicators.

Poor countries that move in the direction of economic freedom in a significant way, as China and India have done, tend to enjoy fast growth and are thus catching up to rich countries. Annual per capita growth rates of more than 8% since the early 1980s and about 5% since the early 1990s in China and India, respectively, have pulled hundreds of millions of people from poverty and reversed the centuries-long growth of world income inequality.

Greater economic freedom also is strongly related to improvements in the range of human development indicators—longevity, access to safe drinking water, infant mortality rates, environmental quality, and so on. During the past several decades, the gap in human well-being between poor and rich countries has been closing dramatically and at a faster pace than the gap in incomes. The advantage of underdevelopment today is that poor countries can grow at much faster rates than was the case for rich countries when they were at similar stages of development. Moreover, for a given income level, countries enjoy notably higher standards of living than was the case even 30 years ago. More economic freedom in the world appears to be benefiting even those countries that have done little to reform.

The development consensus now generally favors market-oriented policies and institutions that constrain political power and support market exchange. Although we know that institutions matter, there is no consensus on *how* to promote the right institutional or policy environment. The difficulty that countries as different as Russia, Argentina, and Malawi have had in successfully introducing reforms has generated an awareness of institutional inertia and the role of institutions in shaping political behavior and seemingly enduring power structures.

Development appears to be more a political than an economic challenge. The recognition that institutional change is more complex and occurs at a slower pace than policy change has led to pessimism among some observers about the prospects of development in many parts of the world. Yet precisely because institutional change takes time, such conclusions may be premature. It took about eight centuries for the institutions supportive of market exchange and the rule of law to develop in the West. By contrast, the current era of liberal reforms is still only a few decades old and may already be leading to incipient institutional and cultural change in countries that have recently begun opening their economies. The 21st century will tell whether the case for optimism is stronger than the case for pessimism.

The thinking regarding economic development has matured and has involved a rediscovery of classical liberal insights into the causes of prosperity. Experts have a greater appreciation of the limits of development economics and its ability to forcibly promote growth; of the relevance of the development path of advanced economies to developing countries; of the role of local knowledge and of incentives on individual and entrepreneurial behavior; and of the complex influence that institutions, culture, geography, history, political regimes, and other factors exert on each other and on growth. As such, the study of development has become qualitative and multidisciplinary, drawing on work from economic historians, legal scholars, anthropologists, and political scientists.

Despite those advances, a political push led by international organizations such as the United Nations and the

World Bank and a minority of economists continue to call for massive increases in aid for the poorest countries, especially in sub-Saharan Africa. Old and bankrupt ideas from the 1950s and 1960s have been revived, including the notion of poverty traps, the need for planning, and an aid-financed "big push" that would lead to economic takeoff. Unlike the early postwar period, however, skepticism of such grandiose plans is widespread among academics and development practitioners.

In practice, the rise of aid is likely to continue, but so is globalization and its modernizing effects. In most of the world, where the latter is more predominant than the former, we can expect to see more enduring progress even if it occurs in fits and starts. Liberal advocates of economic progress would do well to promote the ideas of human freedom and keep a modest view of their own influence. The complex process of economic development will continue to be unpredictable and influenced by unique factors, including, as Peter Bauer and Milton Friedman used to remind us, chance events.

IV

See also Bauer, Peter; Friedman, Milton; Globalization; Interventionism

Further Readings

Acemoglu, Daron, Simon Johnson, and James Robinson. "Institutions as the Fundamental Cause of Long-Run Growth." *Handbook of Economic Growth*. Philippe Aghion and Steve Durlauf, eds. Amsterdam: North Holland, 2005.

Bauer, P. T. *Dissent on Development*. Cambridge, MA: Harvard University Press, 1972.

———. *Economic Analysis and Policy in Underdeveloped Countries*. Durham, NC: Duke University Press, 1957.

De Soto, Hernando, Enrique Ghersi, and Mario Ghibellini. *El Otro Sendero*. Lima: Editorial El Barranco, 1986.

Easterly, William. *The White Man's Burden*. New York: Penguin, 2006.

Goklany, Indur. *The Improving State of the World: Why We're Living Longer, Healthier, More Comfortable Lives on a Cleaner Planet*. Washington, DC: Cato Institute, 2007.

Gwartney, James, and Robert Lawson. *Economic Freedom of the World: 2007 Annual Report*. Vancouver: Fraser Institute, 2007.

Lal, Deepak. *The Poverty of Development Economics*. London: Institute of Economic Affairs, 1983, 1997.

Smith, Adam. *An Inquiry into the Nature and Causes of the Wealth of Nations*. Chicago: University of Chicago Press, 1976.

Wolf, Martin. *Why Globalization Works*. New Haven, CT: Yale University Press, 2004.

DICEY, ALBERT VENN (1835–1922)

Albert Venn Dicey was an influential British professor of law whose book *An Introduction to the Study of the Law of the Constitution* organized ancient and modern theories of law into a single constitutional principle he termed the *rule of law*.

Dicey was born on February 4, 1835, the third son of the owner of *The Northampton Mercury*, a weekly newspaper. His middle name paid homage to the social reformer and logician John Venn, in whose Clapham Sect of reformers the Dicey family was quite active. Albert was taught at home before entering King's College School, London, and then Balliol College, Oxford, where he took a double first in classics and where he found a circle of friends, among them Algernon Swinburne, T. H. Green, and James Bryce, all of whom would prove influential both in Dicey's life and English thought. In 1860, Dicey wrote a college prize essay on the British Privy Council that sparked a lifelong interest in constitutional law, and he became a fellow of Trinity College, Oxford. The following year, he entered the Inner Temple and was called to the bar in 1863. In 1872, he married Elinor Mary Bonham-Carter, the daughter of an influential Member of Parliament.

Between 1861 and 1882, Dicey lived in London, practiced law, and wrote extensively, contributing articles to a number of newspapers, including his father's, in addition to writing two lawbooks. Although these books were not prominent, they led to his election as Vinerian Professor of English Law in 1882, which took him back to Oxford and to a fellowship at All Souls College. He held his fellowship for more than a quarter century, during which time he produced his greatest works. While a fellow and following his retirement, Dicey became prominent in public affairs. He was frequently in the public eye promoting traditionalist, conservative, and Unionist views. He died in Oxford on April 7, 1922.

While Vinerian Professor, Dicey wrote many articles and gave numerous lectures that placed him in the upper ranks of the Victorian intelligentsia. He wrote several books on legal practice, most notably *A Digest of the Law of England with Reference to the Conflict of Laws* and a half-dozen books presenting his political views, particularly arguing against Home Rule in Ireland.

Dicey's continuing influence comes from two other books, most important his *Introduction to the Study of the Law of the Constitution*, published in 1885, and, to a lesser degree, his *Lectures on the Relation between Law and Public Opinion in England during the Nineteenth Century*, written as a Harvard lecture 20 years later and updated in 1919.

Law and Public Opinion, his neo-Benthamite polemic on social and legal history, argued that the English law throughout the 19th century had been directly influenced first by toryism, then by individualism, and finally by collectivism. In broad terms, Dicey approved of the reforming influence of Jeremy Bentham, John Stuart Mill, and the economists, particularly Harriet Martineau, and he worried about the collectivist influence of Unionists (those who sought a constitutional union between Ireland and Great

Britain), suffragettes, and what we might now call socialists, all of whom he saw as a threat to the constitution of England. Although Dicey's historical methodology has been criticized, his summaries of the development, acceptance, and criticisms of laissez-faire ideology among intellectuals and in legislation, remain a useful study.

The Law of the Constitution, written at the height of Dicey's powers and after long study, endures as a masterpiece of exposition and jurisprudence, particularly its articulation of a theory of the rule of law. More fundamentally, Dicey's work presented a coherent argument for an unwritten British constitution that at once revived earlier discussions and refined them along new lines. Arguing that there existed a rich tradition of law protecting individual rights and freedoms under a framework of parliamentary sovereignty, Dicey succeeded in reinventing the arguments of both Edward Coke and Edmund Burke in a generally Whiggish history that had great resonance for the Victorian intellectual. It is true that Parliament had succeeded to the powers and the responsibilities once held by the monarch, but the law, he contended, persisted as an independent force. The purpose of the law was the security of the rights of the individual.

Dicey's basic principles for the rule of law were three: that no one can be punished or lawfully interfered with by the authorities except for breaches of law, which must be defined by the proper authority; that no one is above the law, and everyone is subject to the ordinary law of the land; and, finally, that no one should be possessed of the authority to interfere with the rights of a private person, which are defined and protected by the courts of law. Dicey saw the rights of English subjects as well protected by an unwritten constitution, better indeed than they would be by a written constitution or bill of rights, because the courts could ascertain rights as consequences of general protections of the law.

> So again the right to personal liberty, the right of public meeting, and many other rights, are part of the law of the constitution, though most of these rights are consequences of the more general law or principle that no man can be punished except for direct breaches of law (i.e. crimes) proved in the way provided by law (i.e. before the Courts of the realm).

Developing his idea of the Rule of Law as both a specially English creation and as a principle of universal appeal, Dicey both reinforced the Victorian certitude in the primacy of British law and governance (which had justified its imperial ambitions) and asserted a domestic political claim that would support a constitution that defended individual interests against collectivist change. Both aspects of his theory strongly contrasted the limits of English common law with the discretion of French *droit administratif*. Still, Dicey's idea of the constitution was conservative, not merely traditional. Among his arguments for constitutional reform was a defense of the referendum as a people's veto

over legislation that does not command public support. The allure of Dicey's *Law of the Constitution*, however, extended beyond national pride. Its clear prose presented a claim that lawyers accepted and nonlawyers could understand, that the law enshrined, indeed that English law had long confirmed, a special protection of individual freedom from state interference.

SMS

See also Burke, Edmund; Coke, Edward; Constitutionalism; Rule of Law

Further Readings

Cosgrove, Richard A. *The Rule of Law: Albert Venn Dicey, Victorian Jurist*. London: Macmillan, 1980.

Dicey, Albert Venn. *Introduction to the Study of the Law of the Constitution*. Indianapolis, IN: Liberty Fund, 1982.

———. *Lectures on the Relation between Law and Public Opinion in England during the Nineteenth Century*. London: Macmillan, 1919.

Ford, Trowbridge H. *Albert Venn Dicey: The Man and His Times*. Chichester, UK: Barry Rose Law Publishers, 1985.

Qvortrup, Matt. "A.V. Dicey: The Referendum as the People's Veto." *History of Political Thought* 20 no. 3 (1999): 531–546.

Rait, Robert S., ed. *Memorials of Albert Venn Dicey, Being Chiefly Letters and Diaries*. London: Macmillan, 1925.

Shinn, Ridgway F., Jr., and Richard A. Cosgrove, eds. *Constitutional Reflections: The Correspondence of Albert Venn Dicey and Arthur Berriedale Keith*. Lanham, MD: University Press of America, 1996.

DIDEROT, DENIS (1713–1784)

Denis Diderot was a philosopher and the chief editor of the *Encyclopedia, or Reasoned Dictionary of the Sciences, Arts, and Trades*, a key work of Enlightenment thought. He wrote extensively on religion and atheism, philosophical materialism, art, literature, and education. He is of particular interest to libertarians for his opposition to censorship, colonialism, slavery, sexual restrictions, and religious intolerance. Often he received no credit for his efforts because many of his works were not published until after his death, many were anonymous, and the authorship of still others remained long in dispute.

Diderot was born in Langres, Champagne, and received a Jesuit education. Although he prepared for a degree in theology, he abandoned Catholicism early in life and embraced an open, often strident atheism. His 1749 *Letter on the Blind* expanded on the empiricist philosophy of John Locke and argued that all ideas must originate with the senses and that, by implication, neither innate ideas, nor God, nor divine revelation was real.

Diderot's work earned him a stay in the Vincennes prison, an experience that solidified his hatred of censorship and arbitrary power. Although his most influential writings are in epistemology, metaphysics, and aesthetics, his political thought is likewise of great interest. Diderot used commentaries on both the ancient and contemporary worlds to expound a variety of ideas that have since become central to libertarian thinking. For example, in his *Essay on the Life of the Philosopher Seneca*, Diderot wrote,

> Tyranny imparts a brutish character on every sort of action; even language is not exempt from its influence. Indeed, is it really of no consequence for a child to hear around his cradle either the pusillanimous murmur of servitude, or the noble and proud accents of liberty?

The notion that control over language and education means control over the people has become important to the modern libertarian movement.

Yet just as often, Diderot's ideas are far removed from the classical liberal thinking of his era and are more akin to those of Jean-Jacques Rousseau, the 18th century's most significant exponent of what would later be termed *positive liberty* and whom some commentators regard as the period's most significant defender of collectivism.

An example of Rousseau's influence on Diderot can be found in his writings on Tahiti, which Europeans had only recently discovered and which Diderot imagined as a sexually liberated—albeit communist—utopia. His *Supplement to the Voyage of Bougainville* described a world free of coercion and even of most standards of modesty in dress and behavior. He implored Europeans not to interfere with the natural community of property and of women that were to be found on the island—which, critics have pointed out, Diderot never actually visited.

As head of the vast *Encyclopedia* project, Diderot struggled with the complex censorship of Old Regime France to produce a product that contained not only the distilled knowledge of his time, but also piquant commentaries on government, freedom of religion, and free expression. An enduring question in Diderot's thought lies in the tension between the *Encyclopedia*, with its praise of industry and material progress, and the *Supplement to the Voyage of Bougainville*, which instead glorifies a lost ancestral liberty. Diderot was, however, always critical of entanglements between church and state, and he remains famous for his quip that "Man will never be free until the last king is strangled with the entrails of the last priest."

JTK

See also Enlightenment; Material Progress; Positive Liberty; Rousseau, Jean-Jacques; Voltaire

Further Readings

Diderot, Denis. *Oeuvres*. Laurent Versini, ed. Paris: R. Laffont, 1994–1997.
Encyclopédie ou Dictionnaire raisonné des sciences, des arts et des métiers. Denis Diderot, Jean Le Rond d'Alembert, eds. CD-ROM version. Marsanne, France: Redon, 1999.
Furbank, P. N. *Diderot: A Critical Biography*. London: Secker & Warburg, 1992.

Division of Labor

The notion of the division of labor is central to classical liberalism and the theory of a market economy. The division of labor refers to the situation that obtains when different individuals perform different tasks and then trade with each other in order to get what they prefer. Instead of having John grow his own food and be his own doctor, John, who is primarily a farmer, trades his products for money, which he then uses to buy many diverse goods and services from others, among them medical care.

Discussions of the division of labor go back to Plato and have been dealt with by numerous writers over the centuries. However, it was not until 1776 and the publication of Adam Smith's *Wealth of Nations* that an extensive analysis of the division of labor against the backdrop of a modern economy was offered. Smith pointed out that the immense productivity advantages of the market economy rest on the division of labor. The example he offered of the manufacture of pins, which demonstrated how more pins are produced when tasks are divided across many individuals, has become a classical illustration of the benefits that follow from the division of labor. Yet Smith also understood that the division of labor is a far broader concept. Individuals pursue different avocations, regions grow different products, countries have different exports, and so on.

Smith coined the famous maxim that "division of labor is limited by the extent of the market," which meant that only large and well-developed markets could support a high degree of specialization. If we imagine 10 people stranded on a desert island, none of them will have the luxury of specializing. Such a small group cannot support a science fiction writer, a biochemist, and a writer of computer software. In reality, the group would have to spend almost all of its effort in gathering, hunting, or growing food. Populous and wealthy societies, however, are highly diverse, as evidenced by the numerous different occupations we find in any advanced society.

Thus, we can see that the market and the increasing division of labor hold a symbiotic and mutually reinforcing relationship. The division of labor boosts the productivity that drives the growth of the market. At the same time, a larger market enables more specialization and a greater division of labor. Thus, healthy economic growth creates feedback effects that lead to further economic growth. Contemporary economists refer to the concept of *increasing returns* to describe this feedback process.

Smith, it should be noted, also recognized some of the disadvantages to the division of labor, as did Adam Ferguson in Scotland and Jean-Jacques Rousseau in France. In some cases, it can lead individuals to perform the same tasks in an extremely repetitive and boring fashion. Many of the classical economists, among them John Ramsey McCulloch and Jean-Baptiste Say, otherwise strong defenders of a market economy, recognized that the division of labor could dull the faculties of many workers. This criticism, however, has become less persuasive over time. The widespread introduction of labor-saving devices has eliminated many repetitive jobs and increased the number that involve creative content, working with others, and idiosyncratic decision making.

The theory of comparative advantage, an essential element of classical economics, is connected closely to the idea of the division of labor. It makes economic sense for each person to produce what he or she can make most efficiently and then trade for other products. The relevant notion of advantage here is comparative, not absolute. If a lawyer is a better typist than her secretary, the lawyer may still have the secretary do the typing so that the lawyer's time can be employed in higher value activities. But comparative advantage suggests that some division of labor will always be present.

Marxist economists have led a frontal assault on the notion of division of labor because they find it destructive of individual initiative and independence of will. Marx, extending Smith's notion that the division of labor could alienate workers, argued that workers could never be truly happy or fulfilled while consigned to repetitive tasks, something that capitalism demanded. Communism, in contrast, would abolish most of the negative aspects that accompanied the division of labor. In place of the drudgery of mindless repetition of some minute task imposed on the worker in an advanced capitalist system, Leon Trotsky foresaw a future in which "man will become immeasurably stronger, wiser and subtler; his body will become harmonized, his movements more rhythmic, his voice more musical. The forms of life will become dynamically dramatic. The average human type will rise to the heights of an Aristotle, a Goethe, or a Marx."

The concept of the division of labor continues to command the attention of economists, sociologists, and other social scientists. It is perhaps most important to developing and emerging economies, in which a high proportion of the population is engaged in agriculture or staff the government bureaucracy. These economies often seek to increase their division of labor in a productive and sustainable manner. But the division of labor is both a cause and a symptom of growth. There is no magical recipe for a more effective

division of labor as distinct from the more general problem of how to stimulate economic growth and liberalize political institutions.

TC

See also Free-Market Economy; Marxism; Smith, Adam; Wealth and Poverty

Further Readings

Buchanan, James M., and Yong J. Yoon. *The Return to Increasing Returns.* Ann Arbor: University of Michigan Press, 1994.

Durkheim, Émile. *The Division of Labor in Society.* New York: Free Press, 1964.

Marx, Karl. *Economic and Philosophic Manuscripts of 1844.* New York: International Publishers, 1964.

Smith, Adam. *An Inquiry into the Nature and Causes of the Wealth of Nations.* New York: The Modern Library, 1937.

Trotsky, Leon. *Literature and Revolution.* New York: Russell & Russell, 1957.

DOUGLASS, FREDERICK (1818–1895)

Frederick Douglass was an abolitionist, a reformer, a statesman, and the author of the American classic *Narrative of the Life of Frederick Douglass, An American Slave.* Born into slavery in Maryland, Douglass was never certain of his exact birth date or the identity of his father, although some have speculated that his father was his first master, Aaron Anthony. Douglass, whose birth name was Frederick Bailey, moved at the age of 10 to the Baltimore household of Hugh Auld, where at an early age he learned rudimentary reading and writing thanks to Auld's wife and to the white children in the neighborhood, whom Douglass bribed for lessons in spelling. When he found a copy of the *Columbia Orator,* a schoolbook incorporating several antislavery passages as reading and writing exercises, Douglass devoured the idea of abolitionism. This concept made him rebel against his condition as a slave, and at 16 he was sent to Edward Covey, a "slave-breaker," whose job was to beat obstreperous slaves into submissiveness. Covey failed, and Douglass returned to Auld's household determined to escape. In September 1838, he finally managed to sneak out of Maryland disguised as a Navy seaman with forged papers obtained through the Underground Railroad. He moved to Rochester, New York, which with some interruptions was his home for the rest of his life. He took the name Douglass as a disguise to prevent recapture.

Shortly after moving to New York, Douglass attended a speech by William Lloyd Garrison, whose *Liberator* was the most notorious of abolitionist newspapers. Garrison called on Douglass to speak, and Douglass described slavery in such moving terms that Garrison asked him to join the Massachusetts Anti-Slavery Society. Douglass worked hard on his speaking and writing skills, but his eloquence and power caused some to doubt that he was actually an escaped slave. Douglass responded to this charge by writing his memoir, the *Narrative*, which he would revise twice during his life, first as *My Bondage and My Freedom* and, finally, as *The Life and Times of Frederick Douglass.*

Douglass broke with Garrison in 1851, when he rejected Garrison's views that the U.S. Constitution was an inherently proslavery document ("a pact with the devil," in Garrison's words) and that the North should secede from the South over slavery. Douglass objected that northerners, who had profited from and abetted slavery, owed slaves the duty of working to emancipate them, and must not "leave the slave to free himself." Moreover, Douglass was persuaded by such writers as Lysander Spooner and Gerrit Smith that the Constitution was actually an antislavery document. In one of his best-known speeches, "What to the Slave Is the Fourth of July?" Douglass declared that "interpreted as it ought to be interpreted, the Constitution is a GLORIOUS LIBERTY DOCUMENT," and he insisted that slavery was already unconstitutional even before the ratification of the 13th Amendment. Douglass's constitutional philosophy would today be described as "liberal originalism." He admired Justice John Harlan, whose dissents in *The Civil Rights Cases* and *Plessy v. Ferguson* led him to call on Harlan to run for president.

Douglass also repudiated Garrison's pacifism and enthusiastically recruited blacks to join the Union Army during the Civil War. Two of his own sons served in the 54th Massachusetts volunteers, the famous black regiment that suffered heavy casualties in a brave attack on Fort Wagner at Charleston, South Carolina. (Douglass's sons survived unharmed.)

Although early feminists like Elizabeth Cady Stanton had long been friendly to the abolitionist cause, they split with Douglass over his support of the 15th Amendment, which guaranteed the right to vote regardless of race but explicitly limited the right to men. Douglass supported female suffrage, but believed that holding out for a gender-neutral amendment would doom the chances of black suffrage.

In 1884, Douglass married a white woman, Helen Pitts, and 5 years later was appointed ambassador to Haiti by President Benjamin Harrison. The end of Reconstruction, however, brought on a national withdrawal from efforts at establishing racial equality, and Douglass would never again hold such a high office. He became increasingly embittered as the nation turned away from the cause of racial equality.

Douglass was a strong supporter of private property rights and free markets, although he did make some exceptions. He insisted that former slaves learn trades and become self-reliant, and he opposed Charles Sumner's plan to confiscate southern plantation lands for redistribution to former slaves. He fervently opposed labor unions that barred blacks from admission, and he denounced many proposals for government aid to former slaves because the aid would constitute a badge of inferiority. "The black man is said to be unfortunate," Douglass explained.

> He is so . . . but I affirm that the broadest and bitterest of the black man's misfortunes is the fact that he is everywhere regarded and treated as an exception to the principles and maxims which apply to other men. . . . Necessity is said to be the plea of tyrants. The alleged inferiority of the oppressed is also the plea of tyrants. . . . Under its paralyzing touch all manly aspirations and self-reliance die out and the smitten race comes almost to assent to the justice of their own degradation.

Blacks were "not only confronted by open foes, but [also] assailed in the guise of sympathy and friendship and presented as objects of pity." Government paternalism would undermine the self-respect blacks needed to break free of their second-class status. "No People that has solely depended upon foreign aid, or rather, upon the efforts of those, in any way identified with the oppressor . . . ever stood forth in the attitude of freedom." But Douglass did endorse some aid programs, including the Freedman's Bureau, and he objected to sharecropping arrangements and the payment of wages through certificates redeemable only in company stores. These, he complained, perpetuated a system worse than slavery, in which the rights of blacks were respected *de jure,* but ignored *de facto.* Late in his life, he complained that "so-called emancipation" was a fraud and that black sharecroppers were paid low wages, legally prohibited from moving away in search of higher pay, and frequently lynched with impunity.

In old age, Douglass took on a number of protégés, including antilynching crusader Ida Wells and educational reformer Booker T. Washington, who wrote the first biography of Douglass. A story tells of Douglass being approached by a young man who asked what he should do with his life. "Agitate, agitate, agitate," Douglass replied.

TMS

See also Abolitionism; Feminism and Women's Rights; Garrison, William Lloyd; Racism; Slavery in America

Further Readings

Foner, Philip, and Yuval Taylor, eds. *Frederick Douglass: Selected Speeches and Writings.* Chicago: Lawrence Hill Books, 1999.

Gates, Henry Louis, ed. *Douglass: Autobiographies.* New York: Library of America, 1994.

Martin, Waldo E. *The Mind of Frederick Douglass.* Chapel Hill: University of North Carolina Press, 1984.

Mayer, Henry. *All on Fire: William Lloyd Garrison and the Abolition of Slavery.* New York: St. Martin's, 1998.

McFeely, William. *Frederick Douglass.* New York: W. W. Norton, 1992.

Quarles, Benjamin. *Frederick Douglass.* New York: Da Capo, 1997.

DRUG PROHIBITION

Drug prohibition refers to policies that restrict access to and criminalize the sale and possession of certain mood-altering substances, such as marijuana, cocaine, and heroin. Intoxicants have been used in most societies throughout history, and for most of history, such use has been governed by social custom, rather than legal penalty. In the 20th century, however, Western nations adopted a series of increasingly restrictive policies on the use and sale of certain drugs, restrictions that have become almost universal. Libertarians have opposed such restrictions because of their harmful effects and because they violate individual rights.

The road to prohibition began with medicalization, with both the American and British governments restricting distribution by persons other than medical professionals before banning the substances outright. In 1868, the British Parliament enacted the Pharmacy and Poisons Act, and in 1914, the United States passed the Harrison Narcotic Act. Both restricted the sale of opiates and certain other drugs by anyone other than pharmacists. By the 1920s, America's Harrison Act, which had limited the consumption of opiates except by physician's prescription, had become a more general prohibition on their use when the courts interpreted the act to allow prosecution of physicians who prescribed drugs to addicts.

During the same period, America introduced alcohol prohibition. In 1920, the 18th Amendment to the Constitution and its enabling legislation, the Volstead Act, banned the manufacture, transportation, and sale of beverages containing more than 0.5% alcohol. The famed evangelist Rev. Billy Sunday greeted Prohibition ecstatically: "The reign of tears is over. The slums will soon be a memory. We will turn our prisons into factories. . . . Men will walk upright now, women will smile and children will laugh. Hell will be forever for rent."

The results of this "noble experiment" did not quite match the Rev. Sunday's expectations. Violent crime skyrocketed during Prohibition, with the murder rate going up every year from the passage of the Volstead Act until its repeal in 1933, after which the rate declined steadily for 11 years. Prohibition marked the start of the organized crime problem in America. By making alcoholic beverages illegal and turning tens of millions of Americans into scofflaws, the policy handed the trade in liquor over to ruthless groups willing to break the law and settle disputes with violence.

The notorious St. Valentine's Day Massacre—a 1929 gangland slaying orchestrated by Al Capone—was merely one battle in a turf war over alcohol distribution in Chicago, Illinois.

The Volstead Act also demonstrated what one drug policy scholar has termed *The Iron Law of Prohibition*, which holds that the greater the efforts to disrupt the distribution of a prohibited substance, the more potent that substance becomes. Thus, Prohibition saw a significant increase in the consumption of distilled spirits, which offered "more bang for the buck" to the consumer and less chance of interdiction for the supplier. Smugglers risking jail by bringing alcohol over the Canadian border wanted to minimize that risk by transporting a more compact and potent product— whiskey rather than beer or wine. Accordingly, although prices of all alcoholic beverages increased from 1920 to 1933, the increase in the price of beer was far sharper than that of distilled spirits.

Libertarians have emphasized the parallels between the effects of alcohol prohibition, on the one hand, and of drug prohibition, on the other hand. The drug war has proved as futile as the prohibition of alcohol and for the same reasons. Every effort to restrict supply raises prices, and those higher prices serve as a signal to criminal entrepreneurs that there are enormous profits to be made in the drug trade. For every supplier put out of business, more arise in his place, some as creative as—if far more brutal than—any entrepreneur in the above-ground economy. As with alcohol prohibition, drug prohibition provides dramatic profit opportunities for violent criminal distribution networks. By driving the trade underground, the drug war has given it over to gangs that fight over market share with bullets. The price increases spurred by prohibition also contribute to crime when addicts steal to support a habit whose costs have been artificially inflated.

The Iron Law of Prohibition that shifted consumption from beer and wine to distilled spirits has operated in similar fashion with the narcotics trade. It has led to the prevalence of drugs that are more concentrated, more potent, and less safe. As the drug war intensified in the late 20th century, the bulkiest and least harmful illegal drug, marijuana, was no longer the safest risk for cross-border smuggling to the United States, causing a shift to coca leaves and opium poppies in Latin American cultivation patterns. Prohibition, by raising the price of prohibited substances, also encourages their ingestion in more concentrated forms. Instead of chewing the coca leaf—as farmers in the Andes have done for thousands of years—Westerners under prohibitionist regimes snort or smoke the refined product. Instead of smoking opium, drug users under prohibition inject its derivative, heroin—at far greater risk of disease and overdose. Because of the drug war, proscribed substances have become black market products for which dosage is difficult to determine. In addition, there is an ever-present risk of impurities and dangerous additives in street drugs. When drug users are injured or killed, a products liability lawsuit is hardly an option.

Libertarians have opposed the drug war because of the futility and perverse effects attending drug prohibition. But they also have offered a complementary, rights-based critique of drug laws. This critique proceeds from the principle of self-ownership. If a person owns his own body, the decision about what substances to ingest is ultimately his alone. Drug use is a quintessentially self-regarding act that violates no one's rights and harms no one except, perhaps, the user. Prosecution of drug users and sellers is aggression, rhetoric about public health and the moral fiber of society notwithstanding.

Disrespect for individual rights in this area has led to the erosion of civil liberties in prohibitionist regimes. In the United States, the metaphorical "war" on drugs has increasingly taken on the aspects of a real war. Starting in the 1980s, the U.S. government passed a series of statutes encouraging the transfer of military equipment to domestic police departments and even the use of U.S. military forces on America's borders. Increased militarization has repeatedly led to the death of innocents in door-smashing "no-knock" raids gone awry. Protections against unreasonable searches and seizures have weakened to the point that one Supreme Court Justice in 1989 could speak ruefully of an emerging "drug exception" to the Constitution. By 2001, thanks in large part to its vigorous prosecution of drug offenders, the U.S. prison population had reached a record 2 million inmates—equaling Russia's rate of incarceration.

Despite—or perhaps because of—the drug war's effect on civil liberties, there has been significant evolution in public attitudes toward drug legalization since the peak of prohibitionist sentiment in the 1980s and early 1990s. During that period, the American drug czar, William Bennett, could talk casually about the possibility of beheading drug dealers. In 1990, legislation that would have allowed the military to shoot down American planes suspected of carrying drugs was almost passed into law. By 2003, several American states had passed initiatives allowing the consumption of marijuana for medical purposes, such as glaucoma or as an anti-nauseant for HIV sufferers and chemotherapy patients. Notwithstanding these laws, the federal government continued to prosecute marijuana users, including some who were desperately ill.

The trend toward liberalization in Western Europe began earlier and has gone further than in the United States. Today, in most of Western Europe, possession of small amounts of narcotics for personal use is not a crime, although drug trafficking remains a serious offense. Whether liberalization will continue to spread remains to be seen, although at the turn of the 21st century, there are reasons for cautious optimism.

GH

See also Bill of Rights, U.S.; Black Markets; Illicit Drugs; Prohibition of Alcohol

Further Readings

Duke, Stephen B., and Albert C. Gross. *America's Longest War: Rethinking Our Tragic Crusade against Drugs*. Los Angeles: Tarcher Putnam, 1993.

Hamowy, Ronald. *Dealing with Drugs: Consequences of Government Control*. Lanham, MD: Lexington Books, 1987.

Lynch, Timothy, ed. *After Prohibition: An Adult Approach to Drug Policies in the 21st Century*. Washington, DC: Cato Institute, 2000.

MacCoun, Robert J., and Peter Reuter. *Drug War Heresies: Learning from Other Vices, Times, and Places*. Cambridge: Cambridge University Press, 2001.

Sullum, Jacob. *Saying Yes: In Defense of Drug Use*. New York: Tarcher Putnam, 2003.

Woodiwiss, Michael. *Crimes, Crusades, and Corruption: Prohibitions in the United States, 1900–1987*. London: Pinter Publishers, 1988.

DUNOYER, CHARLES (1786–1862)

Barthélemy-Charles-Pierre-Joseph Dunoyer—journalist, academic, and noted economist—was born in Carennac in Lot and died in Paris at age 76. Dunoyer, a professor of political economy, authored numerous works on politics, political economy, and history, and he was a founding member of the Society of Political Economy in 1842. He occupies a crucial role in the history of the French classical liberal movement of the first half of the 19th century, along with Jean-Baptiste Say, Benjamin Constant, Charles Comte, Augustin Thierry, and Alexis de Tocqueville.

Dunoyer studied law in Paris, where he met Charles Comte, with whom he was to edit the liberal periodical *Le Censeur* (1814–1815), and its successor, *Le Censeur européen* (1817–1819). He became politically active during the last years of Napoleon's Empire and the early years of the Bourbon Restoration, when he strenuously opposed authoritarian rule, whether Napoleonic or monarchical. He was especially active in his opposition to censorship, militarism, the slave trade, and the extensive restrictions placed on trade and industry.

Dunoyer and Comte discovered the liberal political economy of Jean-Baptiste Say in 1815 after their journal had been closed down by the censors. This event was seminal in Dunoyer's intellectual development because it proved the catalyst for his fusion of three different strands of thought into a new and powerful theory of individual liberty. Dunoyer and Comte combined the political liberalism of Constant, whose main pillars were constitutional limits on the power of the state and representative government, the economic liberalism of Say (i.e., laissez-faire and free trade), and the sociological approach to history of Thierry, Constant, and Say, which was grounded in class analysis and a theory of the historical evolution of society through stages, culminating in the laissez-faire market society of industry.

Those views were further developed in numerous articles in *Le Censeur européen* and in two books that Dunoyer published during the 1820s. These monographs were based on his lectures at the Athénée Saint-Germain in Paris: *L'Industrie et la morale considérées dans leurs rapports avec la liberté* (1825) and *Nouveau traité d'économie sociale* (1830). He continued to expand and refine his ideas on the evolution of a free society in his three-volume magnum opus, *De la Liberté du travail* (1845).

After the Revolution of 1830 brought a more liberal-minded constitutional monarchy to power, Dunoyer was appointed a member of the Academy of Moral and Political Sciences and worked as a government official—he served as Prefect of L'Allier and La Somme. Dunoyer became a member of the Council of State in 1838; however, he resigned his government posts in protest against the coup d'état of Louis Napoléon in 1851. He died while writing a critique of the authoritarian Second Empire. The work was completed and published by his son, Anatole, in 1864.

DMH

See also Comte, Charles; Constant, Benjamin; Liberalism, Classical; Say, Jean-Baptiste

Further Readings

Dunoyer, Charles. *De la liberté du travail, ou simple exposé des conditions dans lesquelles les force humaines s'exercent avec le plus de puissance.* Paris: Guillaumin, 1845.
———. *Nouveau traité d'économie sociale, ou simple exposition des causes sous l'influence desquelles les hommes parviennent à user de leurs forces avec le plus de LIBERTE, c'est-à-dire avec le plus FACILITE et de PUISSANCE.* 2 vols. Paris: Sautelet et Mesnier, 1830.
Hart, David M. *Class Analysis, Slavery and the Industrialist Theory of History in French Liberal Thought, 1814–1830: The Radical Liberalism of Charles Comte and Charles Dunoyer.* Unpublished doctoral dissertation, King's College, Cambridge, UK, 1994.
Liggio, Leonard P. "Charles Dunoyer and French Classical Liberalism." *Journal of Libertarian Studies* 1 no. 3 (1977): 153–178.
Weinburg, Mark. "The Social Analysis of Three Early 19th Century French Liberals: Say, Comte, and Dunoyer." *Journal of Libertarian Studies* 2 no. 1 (1978): 45–63.

Dutch Republic

From the late 16th to the late 18th century, the United Provinces of the Netherlands, measured by libertarian standards, had perhaps the best government in Europe.

Although today we can easily find much to criticize about the Dutch Republic, it remains a crucial early experiment in toleration, limited government, and commercial capitalism.

The results were stunning: Even contemporaries noted the Dutch Republic's astonishing wealth and military power. "The United Provinces are the envy of some, the fear of others, and the wonder of all their neighbors," wrote Englishman Sir William Temple in 1673. The tiny state was then engaged in an all-out defensive war against both France and Britain, a war that the Dutch won, thus maintaining their territorial integrity. Despite its small size, the Dutch Republic was renowned for its military discipline and prowess. The skill of its navy was second to none, and the Dutch Republic repeatedly defended its home territory against several of the great powers of Europe.

Off the battlefield, the Dutch saw even greater accomplishments: The nation's cosmopolitanism, local autonomy, and sharply limited central state helped to create a commercial and cultural superpower. The enormous wealth that Dutch traders brought back with them proved to be more enduring than the prosperity produced by the precious metals of Spanish and Portuguese colonial ventures. Fabrics, spices, timber, and other consumer goods not only enriched individual traders, but also supplied raw materials for Dutch industry.

Dutch shipping, banking, commerce, and credit raised living standards for the rich and the poor alike and for the first time created that characteristically modern social phenomenon, a middle class. This middle class enjoyed unprecedented access to commercial goods, including spices, silk, porcelain, and other imported items formerly the reserve of the upper nobility. All in all, Dutch townsmen enjoyed the highest collective standard of living of any similarly situated group in Europe.

With these favorable conditions came cultural and scientific achievements. In only a few decades, this tiny country produced Baruch Spinoza, Hugo Grotius, Rembrandt van Rijn, Jan Vermeer, Christiaan Huygens, and Anton van Leeuwenhoek. The first modern bank, the first stock market, and the first multinational corporation were among the notable achievements of what has since been called the Golden Age of the Netherlands. Contemporaries were astonished at the paved streets, the clocks in ordinary homes, and the now-iconic windmills, which drove the country's manufacturing sector and also powered the elaborate network of drainage channels that kept much of the country above water.

The Dutch Republic was noted for its intellectual tolerance. It welcomed exiled thinkers René Descartes and Pierre Bayle, as well as Jews who fled religious persecution in Spain, Huguenots fleeing France, and dissenters leaving England. Dutch presses were famous throughout Europe for printing material that fell afoul of censorship laws elsewhere; indeed, in contemporary France, the "Dutch" book trade was virtually synonymous with subversive and forbidden literature. Much of it was merely pornographic, but some we now recognize as among the greatest literary works of the period.

The early modern Dutch experiments in religious tolerance and decentralized government were not undertaken deliberately or in any systematic fashion. They evolved piecemeal from many different sources, and, as such, they reflected the fragmentary and particular nature of Dutch society. Yet even in its haphazard and frequently imperfect state, Dutch social tolerance inspired political philosophers and propagandists such as John Locke and Voltaire, both of whom praised the confluence of religious tolerance, social peace, and wealth. Locke in particular had firsthand experience of Dutch society, and he composed his "Letter Concerning Toleration" while living in exile in the Netherlands.

Local autonomy and traditions were deeply ingrained in the Dutch political consciousness, and during the life of the Republic, no effort at stamping them out was ever quite successful. In the 15th century, the Dutch provinces, which then belonged to the dukes of Burgundy, fought an independent war against the Hanseatic League, and in 1477, their States General received the privilege of convening whenever it chose. Although short-lived, this "Grand Privilège" also set limits on the rulers' abilities to levy taxes and raise armies. This decree became, in historian Jonathan Israel's words, a key "political myth of how things should be." It established the precedent that no single person should hold too much power over the provinces, and for centuries, the Dutch fought to maintain this tradition.

Meanwhile, in confessional matters, the Dutch Reformation owed more to the tolerant, urbane humanism of Erasmus of Rotterdam than it did to the intolerant Luther and Calvin. The weakness of centralized authority in both State and Church also meant that the Dutch Reformed Church was incapable of making attendance compulsory; this limitation no doubt fueled religious diversity even further. William the Silent (1533–1584), the great leader of the Dutch revolt against Spanish rule, is thought to have earned his sobriquet through his refusal to indulge in religious controversy. Instead, William kept his religious views private and constantly advocated tolerance for all major faiths in the nascent Republic. During his lifetime, William met with little success in implementing religious toleration and ultimately was assassinated by a Catholic zealot. Yet his vision of a religiously tolerant society slowly gained ground in the subsequent decades, as trade, intellectual ferment, and religious experimentation fed a virtuous circle of increased acceptance of minority views.

The Dutch Republic was not, of course, undilutedly good. Indeed, a present-day libertarian might be tempted to find more faults than merits to the so-called Dutch Golden Age. The commercial empire, for example, depended to a considerable extent on military conquest and exploitation. Trading opportunities were in many instances state monopolies. The renowned toleration was fragile and often excluded significant, entirely peaceful sects. Libertarians value the Dutch Republic as a historical phenomenon not because it represented any sort of perfection, but above all because it demonstrated to several generations of intellectuals the practicality of allowing citizens greater liberties than were customarily accorded them, which in turn contributed to producing what we now know as classical liberalism.

JTK

See also Freedom of Speech; Free Trade; Locke, John; Material Progress; Religion and Liberty; Voltaire

Further Readings

Hsia, Ronnie Po-Chia, and H. F. K. Van Nierop, eds. *Calvinism and Religious Toleration in the Dutch Golden Age*. Cambridge and New York: Cambridge University Press, 2002.

Israel, Jonathan. *The Dutch Republic: Its Rise, Greatness, and Fall*. Oxford: Clarendon Press, 1995.

Schama, Simon. *The Embarrassment of Riches: An Interpretation of Dutch Culture in the Golden Age*. New York: Vintage Books, 1997.

Van Gelderin, Martin. *The Political Thought of the Dutch Revolt, 1555-1590*. Cambridge: Cambridge University Press, 1992.

E

ECONOMICS, AUSTRIAN SCHOOL OF

What is it about the Austrian School of Economics that attracts adherents even more than 100 years after the school's founding by Carl Menger in 1871? Many think the answer lies in the libertarianism that is so closely associated with this analysis of economic issues. No doubt in the case of many teachers and scholars, the libertarian conclusions reached by many Austrian economists go a long way toward explaining their interest in the subject. However, if one is primarily concerned with the conclusions drawn by libertarianism, which, after all, is primarily a political theory, it does not follow that one must adhere to the Austrian School's teachings on economics. Milton Friedman, probably the most notable of all libertarian economists, was methodologically and analytically at odds with the Austrian School, although he shared the normative conclusions of many Austrians. Friedman's long-time colleague, George Stigler, shared Friedman's views, as does Friedman's son, David. Indeed, non-Austrian libertarians within the economics profession have proven themselves much more successful in advocating the necessity of reducing the role of government in the economy. Austrian economists, however, insist that one must take issue with economic orthodoxy to arrive at a proper understanding of how markets really work, thus supplying a firm support to the underlying economic argument for freedom. Nor indeed does Austrianism necessarily imply a defense of an unrestrained market economy. Many of its most prominent spokesmen supported some, and in certain instances substantial, government intrusion in the economy. For example, Friedrich von Wieser, under whom Hayek studied in Vienna, advocated a fairly extensive welfare state. In the main, however, Austrian economists have embraced a free and unfettered market only minimally constrained by government.

Austrian analysis of economic phenomena rests on the methodological foundation comprising (a) methodological individualism, (b) methodological subjectivism, (c) methodological dualism, (d) an analytical focus on processes of adjustment to changing conditions, and (e) the study of spontaneous order by use of the composite method. These methodological foundations were forged in the context of the intellectual development of economic thought and, in particular, in response to two opposing intellectual forces—the Ricardianism of the late-classical economics and the historicism that defined the German School and the American Institutionalists. The Ricardians argued that economic outcomes are the product solely of long-run technological possibilities. Thus, they purged the human element from economic explanation. Historicism, in contrast, denies that universal economic explanations, valid at all times and in all places, are possible but argues that economic explanations hinge on the details of historical circumstance and culture. The Austrian School, beginning with the work of Carl Menger and continuing to this day, argues that a universal science of economics is possible and that man is the alpha and omega of economic life. In the Austrian conception of economic science, the individual is not an abstract being disembodied from his social environment. Instead, scholars working in the Austrian tradition understand man as embedded in social relations. Like the historicists, Austrians are critical of an economic science that models human actors as isolated automatons, yet they are sympathetic to other neoclassical economists who argue against those critics who insist that universal explanation on the basis of marginal utility analysis is possible. All economic outcomes, the Austrians insist, are filtered through the human mind. Our imagination gives rise to desires, which lead to actions and, in turn, economic outcomes. Human action can indeed be systematically studied and not merely described. But it must be underscored that human action in reality takes place in a world of uncertainty. Action is directed at an unknown future and logically must be; if the future were known, there could be no way in which human action could affect the outcome. As Mises puts it: "The uncertainty of the future is already implied in the very notion of action. That man acts and that the future is uncertain are by no means two independent matters. They are only two different modes of establishing one thing."

The market process emerges out of the interaction of human actors. We can conceive of the market process in a way best explicated by Israel Kirzner in his book *The Meaning of Market Process*. There are two sets of variables in economic life, Kirzner argues. There are the underlying variables of tastes, technology, and endowment of natural resources, and there are the induced variables of prices, profit, and loss. In competitive equilibrium, the induced variables of the market correspond perfectly to the underlying variables, such that all resources are utilized in such a way that the highest value is achieved and the least costly technologies are employed. When the market is in competitive equilibrium, it simultaneously realizes production efficiency, exchange efficiency, and product-mix efficiency. In short, given the conditions of the world, one could not better arrange these variables even were an omnipotent being to do so.

Critics of economics emphasize the highly specific conditions required for this simultaneous achievement of efficiency. These critics tend to deny that there is any relationship among the underlying variables of tastes, technology, and resource endowment, on the one hand, and the induced variables of monetary prices, profit, and loss, on the other hand. Without postulating an intimate relationship between the underlying and the induced variables, it is argued, the efficiency properties of the market cannot be sustained. The Austrians have mediated this debate between the perfect and imperfect markets by maintaining that, although induced variables do not perfectly map the underlying variables, nevertheless they are closely related. Economics is not a science about exact points, but instead a science of tendency and direction. A lagged relationship exists between the two sets of variables. To the extent that the induced variables of the market do not reflect the underlying variables, there will exist opportunities for pure profit for those who move in the direction of narrowing the gaps between the two. Ironically, if all actors knew of these opportunities, then no profit would be realized because profit opportunities that are known to all will be realized by none. Austrianism postulates that no knowledge is perfectly known to all. Instead, knowledge is divided among market participants and must be communicated through the activities of economic agents and through the institutions of the market system. In the absence of any change in the underlying variables, the induced variables of the market will move in the direction of dovetailing with them. However, because tastes and technology are constantly changing as

circumstances change, a perfect correspondence of economic variables and plans is impossible. Nevertheless, economic analysis is able to inform us on how any state of affairs outside of perfect correspondence will provide incentives and information for actors to move in the direction that would result in such perfection were it not for intervening changes in the underlying variables.

This emphasis on the mechanics that encourage adaptation to changing conditions requires not only a different way to do economic science, but also a different set of economic arguments that point to the benefits of markets. In the canonical general equilibrium model, for example, the plans of economic agents are prereconciled, such that the market is said to clear. This approach highlights the interconnectedness of all economic activities and represents one of the great intellectual achievements in the field of economics of the 19th and early 20th centuries. Yet the equilibrium approach tends to preclude from analysis the very activities that enable markets to emerge and work effectively to coordinate the plans of economic actors. The most obvious activity that must be eliminated in equilibrium analysis is the entrepreneurial discovery of pure economic profits because *economic profits*, by definition, are zero when all aspects of the economy are in equilibrium.

One of the implications of eliminating the entrepreneur as a central character in economic analysis is that competition is given a different meaning, as Frank Machovec has pointed out in his book *Perfect Competition and the Transformation of Economics* (1995). The economist's notion of competition differs from its common usage. In ordinary parlance, *competition* is a term used to connote an activity. Thus, *to compete* is used when we wish to refer to two teams vying to win a game. However, when an economist uses the term, it is more than likely used as a noun to describe a state of affairs. The contrast between these two meanings of the term is no more evident than it was in the antitrust case brought by the Justice Department against Microsoft. It is hardly the case that only Austrian economists have supported Microsoft against an overzealous government. Indeed, perhaps the most able critics of the government's case are Stanley Leibowitz and Stephen Margolis, whose book, *Winners, Losers & Microsoft*, argued the case in terms of equilibrium economics. However, a significant aspect of their analysis turns not on equilibrium economics, but on human imagination and entrepreneurial activity.

One of the primary reasons that the Austrians are so sensitive to these issues in ways that other economists are not is because of the debates these economists were embroiled from the 1930s to the 1950s. The Austrian economists, in particular Mises and Hayek, led the intellectual opposition to the new models of market socialism and Keynesian demand management. The Austrians were perceived by most economists and the general public to have lost both debates. However, both the market socialists and Keynesian models failed utterly as guides to enhance prosperity, as

Mises and Hayek warned. The reason that both models failed to achieve the level of economic prosperity promised was because of what these approaches—market socialism and Keynesian demand management—had assumed away. In both instances, the models were predicated on the assumptions that they sought to prove. Government officials were assumed to be both benevolent and to possess omniscience, which allowed the government to be employed as a corrective to perceived failures. It is almost certainly because of this intellectual history that Austrian writers have tended to focus their applied economics on issues of socialism and macroeconomics.

Macro models suffered the same problems as did models of market socialism and were plagued by unwarranted assumptions and excessive aggregation. Classic works in Austrian macroeconomics by Mises and Hayek were largely written before the Keynesian hegemony in economics, which lasted from the 1940s to the mid-1970s. A younger generation of Austrian economists, however, was inspired by these classics, the work on monetary theory, and the business cycle by Murray Rothbard, which sought to develop further the insights first offered by Mises and Hayek. They have pioneered work in the area of free banking and challenged the idea that unregulated banking would be chaotic. More recent work has challenged the theoretical coherence of the contending macroeconomic models and argued that, rather than a labor-based approach, macroeconomics should restructure its analysis to be capital-based. The most significant shortcoming of standard macroeconomics in all its varieties is the slight attention that is paid to capital theory. Roger Garrison has dubbed this *labor-based macro*, as opposed to the more Austrian style *capital-based macro*. The main issue here is not simply a focus on capital markets, but the way the capital markets are conceived. Austrian economists view capital not as a stream of financial resources, but as a structure of capital goods that must be coordinated in the process of production through time. Capital goods are heterogeneous and have multiple specific uses, and Austrians have traced in detail the important role of capital goods and capital accounting in a modern economy.

With respect to my original question regarding what continues to make Austrian economics a worthwhile approach to the study of the production and distribution of goods and services, several economists have attempted to answer this question by way of the biography of a set of ideas and by developing these ideas in the hope that they will transform economic scholarship. This approach springs from an honest commitment to the belief that the Austrian school provides us with a better opportunity to gain truth in economic understanding. It is an approach to economics that is grounded in the choices of human beings. It shies away from heroic assumptions, and it does not begin every analysis by postulating an asymmetry between private and public actors. Instead, the same foibles and weaknesses that might be attributed to people in the private sector are equally assumed in describing those in the public sector. The difference in the conclusions of the comparative analysis between private and public actors is a function of the institutional environment within which choices are made. In the absence of an institutional environment of secure private-property rights, freedom of price negotiation, accurate profit and loss accounting, and nondiscretionary politics, the promise of material progress and social cooperation will go unrealized.

The Austrian School of Economics provides a set of utilitarian arguments in support of a classical liberal order that are indispensable for those who place a high value on human liberty. However, it is important to stress that these arguments are a consequence of the analysis that Austrians undertake and not presumptions that they hold before the analysis. Austrian economics is not synonymous with libertarianism. Rather, it is a scientific body of thought that, when combined with some ethical precepts, leads to a strong argument for a libertarian society.

PJB

See also Banking, Austrian Theory of; Böhm-Bawerk, Eugen von; Hayek, Friedrich A.; Individualism, Methodological; Kirzner, Israel M.; Mises, Ludwig von; Praxeology; Rothbard, Murray; Socialist Calculation Debate; Spontaneous Order

Further Readings

Boettke, Peter. *Coordination and Calculation: Essays on Socialism and Transitional Political Economy.* New York: Routledge, 2001.

———, ed. *Socialism and the Market: The Socialist Calculation Debate Revisited.* 9 vols. New York: Routledge, 2000.

Hayek, F. A. *Individualism and Economic Order.* Chicago: University of Chicago Press, 1948.

Horwitz, S. *Microfoundations and Macroeconomics.* New York: Routledge, 2000.

Kirzner, I. *Competition and Entrepreneurship.* Chicago: University of Chicago Press, 1973.

Lachmann, L. *Capital and Its Structure.* Kansas City, MO: Sheed Andrews McMeel, 1977 [1956].

Lewin, P. *Capital in Disequilibrium.* New York: Routledge, 1999.

O'Driscoll, G., and M. Rizzo. *The Economics of Time and Ignorance.* 2nd ed. New York: Routledge, 1995.

Rothbard, Murray. *America's Great Depression.* Princeton, NJ: Van Nostrand Press, 1963.

Selgin, G. *The Theory of Free Banking.* Totowa, NJ: Rowman & Littlefield, 1988.

Economics, Chicago School of

The Chicago School of Economics refers to that group of economists associated with the University of Chicago and most closely identified with the work of Milton Friedman and George Stigler. Frank Knight and his protegé, Henry Simons, are commonly credited with having established this school of thought in the 1930s and 1940s. The Chicago School's approach to economics, as it developed under Friedman and Stigler in the 1960s and 1970s, rests squarely on the conclusions reached earlier by the English classical economists that the rational allocation of economic resources required free and unhindered markets and that capitalism alone was consistent with political and social freedom. This conclusion stood in sharp contrast to the prevailing neo-Keynesian orthodoxy at midcentury, which regarded government intervention in the economy as essential to economic stability and progress and as necessary to ensure a fair distribution of wealth.

The members of the Chicago School not only underscored the importance of free markets in achieving economic progress, but also placed great emphasis on the effect of the money supply, which they viewed as the most crucial determinant of economic stability. The most important spokesman of these monetarist views is Milton Friedman, who, following Henry Simons, has concluded that an intimate connection exists between the money supply and the business cycle and that, to avoid either inflations or depressions in the economy, it is vital for central banks to keep the money supply stable. In 1963, Friedman, together with Anna Schwartz, published the *Monetary History of the United States, 1867-1960*, among whose findings was that the 1929 Depression was brought about by a severe contraction in the money supply. Indeed, Friedman came to refer to the 1929 Depression as the Great Contraction. Thus, Chicago School economists differentiated themselves from economists of the Austrian School, among them Mises and Hayek, who argued that inflations and depressions are based on the misinformation provided investors by interest rates set by central banks that do not in fact reflect the true time preferences of borrowers and lenders.

Another common characteristic of the members of the Chicago School is the emphasis they place in their academic work on empirical research. Their views on the importance of empirical testing of economic propositions once again distinguish them from the economists of the Austrian School, who regard economics as a science whose propositions derive from first principles. In this regard, the Chicago School, in the minds of many economists, has much in common with the German Historical School of the last decades of the 19th century, whose proponents claimed that the only acceptable epistemological approach to economic questions was a historical one. Led by Gustav Schmoller, the Historical School took issue with the claims of Carl Menger and the other members of the Austrian School, who, although not denying the value of some historical analyses, maintained that these studies properly belonged to economic history. Nor would the Austrians have accepted the notion that historical conclusions could

say anything useful regarding the logical conclusions derived from economic axioms, which was the proper subject matter of economics. Thus, although a study of the effects of rent control in New York City in the decades following the Second World War might prove of interest and value to a historian, it ultimately can add nothing to the theoretical conclusion dictated by economic science that, should a ceiling be placed on the price of housing below its market price, there will be far more seekers than suppliers.

Although since the 1960s, Friedman and Stigler were its most prominent members, there are a number of other prominent economists associated with the Chicago School, among them no less than nine Nobel laureates who served as faculty members at Chicago when they received the prize and four other economists who shared their views: Friedman (1976), Theodore W. Schultz (1979), Stigler (1982), Merton H. Miller (1990), Ronald H. Coase (1991), Gary S. Becker (1992), Robert W. Fogel (1993), Robert E. Lucas, Jr. (1995), and Roger B. Myerson (2007) at Chicago; and Herbert Simon (1978), James Buchanan (1986), Harry Markowitz (1990), and Myron Scholes (1997) at other universities. The Chicago School's success is truly a remarkable achievement for an award that was first conferred in 1969. Some have interpreted this seeming preference for neoclassical economics as reflecting the biases of the committee awarding the prize and particularly of its chairman between 1980 and 1994, Assar Lindbeck. Lindbeck, professor of economics at the University of Stockholm, served on the Nobel Prize selection committee from its inception until 1994 and, as a result of his own research, had reached conclusions similar to those of the economists at Chicago School. However, this fact does not explain why most of the prizes were awarded by unanimous vote and that economists with sharply divergent views were equally honored. Nor does it account for the fact that two of the University of Chicago's nine Nobel Prizes were granted after Lindbeck retired from the committee.

The methodology and research interests of the Chicago School have left an indelible imprint not only on economics, but on a number of different areas in the social sciences.

The application of economic reasoning to a whole range of problems in law, sociology, history, and political science has had a far-reaching impact on the way social problems are currently investigated and has given rise to the Law and Economics movement and to Public Choice Theory. This procedure is best summarized by one of its most important practitioners, Gary Becker, who maintained: "The combined assumptions of maximizing behavior, market equilibrium, and stable preferences, used relentlessly and unflinchingly, form the heart of the economic approach as I see it." That almost any social problem is amenable to economic analysis (i.e., that is allows one to reach original and valid conclusions) does not, of course, preclude approaching these same problems in more traditional ways, as some critics of what has been called the Chicago School's "economic imperialism" have contended. It simply allows new and different insights into a particular set of social questions and permits conceiving of problems in terms of people attempting to maximize certain values. The economic approach of which Becker writes seeks not to dislodge the more traditional modes of analysis, but to supplement them. This approach, possibly more than anything else, is the defining characteristic of the modern Chicago School: its emphasis on price theory and its unrelenting application to problems of public policy. For all practical purposes, this approach was initiated by Friedman and extended and refined by Becker.

Libertarians are indebted to the proponents of the Chicago School for bringing to bear their analysis of economic phenomena on misguided political policies and for energizing political forces around the world in support of the free market.

RH

See also Becker, Gary S.; Buchanan, James M.; Classical Economics; Coase, Ronald H.; Economics, Austrian School of; Friedman, Milton

Further Readings

Becker, Gary S. *The Economic Approach to Human Behavior.* Chicago: University of Chicago Press, 1976.
Ebenstein, Lanny. *Milton Friedman: A Biography.* New York: Palgrave Macmillan, 2007.
History of Economic Thought Website. Available at http://cepa .newschool.edu/het/schools/chicago.htm.
Miller, H. Laurence, Jr. "On the 'Chicago School of Economics.'" *The Journal of Political Economy* 70 no. 1 (February 1962): 64–69.
Overtveldt, Johan van. *The Chicago School: How the University of Chicago Assembled the Thinkers Who Revolutionized Economics and Business.* Chicago: Agate, 2007.

ECONOMICS, EXPERIMENTAL

Experimental economics applies laboratory methods of inquiry to the study of motivated human behavior in social contexts governed by explicit or implicit rules. *Explicit rules* may be defined by experimental control and information, or the rules may be shaped by market institutions in which cash-motivated people buy or sell abstract rights to consume or produce commodities and services within some particular technological context. *Implicit rules* refer to the norms, traditions, and habits that people bring to the laboratory as part of their cultural and biological evolutionary heritage; they are not normally controlled by the experimenter. By devising and running markets and other

exchange systems in the laboratory, and through the use of actual people, experimental economics helps us better understand why markets and social exchange systems work the way they do.

Generally, we can think of experimental outcomes as the consequence of behavior governed by individual choice, driven by the economic environment, and mediated by the language and rules that govern interactions supplied by the institution. The economic environment consists of preferences, knowledge, skills, and resource constraints. Abstractly, institutions map the messages (e.g., bids, asks, acceptances, words, and actions) that give rise to our outcomes.

Under the operation of these rules or norms, people choose messages consistent with their economic environment. A well-established finding in experimental economics is that institutions matter because the rules matter, and the rules matter because incentives matter. However, the incentives to which people respond are sometimes not those one would expect based on the canons of economic theory. It turns out that people are often better, and sometimes worse, at achieving gains for themselves and others than is predicted by standard forms of rational analysis. These contradictions provide important clues to the implicit rules that people may follow and can motivate new theoretical hypotheses that can then be examined in the laboratory.

The design of experiments is motivated by two quite distinct concepts of a rational order. Rejecting or denying either of these should not lead one to assume that the actor's decision was irrational. Thus, if people in certain contexts choose outcomes yielding the smaller of two rewards, we ask why, rather than conclude that this choice is irrational. The first concept of a rational order derives from today's standard socioeconomic science model and dates back to the 17th century. This model is a product of what Hayek has called *constructivist rationalism*, which, in its modern form, stems from Descartes, who argued that all worthwhile social institutions were and should be created by conscious deductive processes of human reason. Cartesian rationalism provisionally requires agents to possess complete information—indeed, far more than could ever be given to one mind. In economics, the resulting analytical exercises, while yielding insightful theorems, are designed to aid and sharpen thinking in the form of "if–then" parables.

Yet these exercises may not approximate the level of ignorance that has given shape to real institutions. Our theories and thought processes about social systems involve the conscious and deliberate use of reason. Therefore, it is necessary to constantly remind ourselves that human activity is diffused and dominated by unconscious, autonomic, and neuropsychological systems that enable people to function effectively without always calling on the brain's scarcest resource: attention and reasoning circuitry. This property is an important one of the brain. These considerations lead to the second concept of a rational order, an undesigned ecological system that emerges out of cultural and biological evolutionary processes: homegrown principles of action, norms, traditions, and morality. Thus, "the rules of morality . . . are not the conclusions of our reason." According to Hume, who was concerned with the limits of reason, rationality was a phenomenon that reason discovers in emergent institutions. Context matters because experience matters, and our memory matters because cultural and biological evolutionary processes matter. Hence, context must be regarded as crucial in small-group experiments.

Adam Smith expressed the idea of spontaneously generated orders in both *The Wealth of Nations* and *The Theory of Moral Sentiments*. It is the antithesis of the Cartesian belief that, if an observed social mechanism is functional, somebody in the unrecorded past must have used reason consciously to create it to serve its currently perceived purpose. In experimental economics, the Scottish tradition is represented by the discovery of Smith's notion of order in numerous studies of existing market institutions, such as the double auction. To paraphrase Adam Smith, people in these experiments are led to promote welfare-enhancing social ends that are not part of their conscious intention. This principle is supported by hundreds of experiments whose environments and institutions exceed the capacity of formal game-theoretic analysis. But they do not exceed the functional capacity of collectives of incompletely informed human decision makers whose mental algorithms coordinate behavior through the rules of the institution—social algorithms—to generate high levels of measured performance. Acknowledging and recognizing the workings of unseen processes are essential to the growth of our understanding of social phenomena, and we must strive not to exclude them from our inquiry if we are to have any hope of understanding data inside or outside of the laboratory.

VLS and BJW

See also Classical Economics; Free-Market Economy; Hayek, Friedrich A.; Smith, Adam; Spontaneous Order

Further Readings

Hoffman, Elizabeth, Kevin McCabe, Keith Shachat, and Vernon L. Smith. "Preferences, Property Rights and Anonymity in Bargaining Games." *Games and Economic Behavior* 7 no. 3 (November 1994): 346–380.

Smith, Vernon L. "Constructivist and Ecological Rationality in Economics." *American Economic Review* 93 no. 3 (June 2003): 465–508.

———. "Markets as Economizers of Information: Experimental Examination of the 'Hayek Hypothesis.'" *Economic Inquiry* 20 no. 2 (April 1982): 165–179.

———. "Microeconomic Systems as an Experimental Science." *American Economic Review* 72 no. 5 (December 1982): 923–955.

———. "Two Faces of Adam Smith." *Southern Economic Journal* 65 no. 1 (July 1998): 1–19.

ECONOMICS, KEYNESIAN

Keynesian economics has reference to a set of theoretical explanations for persistent unemployment and to specific governmental employment policies. The general notion behind Keynesian economics is that persistent unemployment derives from decreases in total private sector spending. According to Keynesian economists, the government can alleviate unemployment by increasing the total amount of spending in the economy.

Keynesian economic policy began during the European Great Depression. Some economists blamed the Great Depression on private spending. The German economist Wilhelm Lautenbach published a spending theory of unemployment in 1929, and the Nazi government acted in accordance with this theory by increasing spending on public projects and on the military. One of Keynes's associates, Joan Robinson, remarked that "Hitler found a cure against unemployment before Keynes was finished explaining it." In fact, in the German edition of his book, Keynes noted that "the theory of aggregated production, which is the point of the following book, nevertheless can be much easier adapted to the conditions of a totalitarian state than . . . under conditions of free competition and a large degree of laissez-faire." The Polish economist Michal Kalecki also published a similar theory of unemployment in the mid-1930s.

In the early 1930s, Keynes debated the Austrian economist F. A. Hayek over the causes of the Great Depression. Hayek argued that the Depression was caused by the manipulation of interest rates by central banks. When Keynes published his *Treatise on Money* in 1930, Hayek wrote a devastating critique of this treatise. While Keynes continued to attack Hayek's theory, he also revised his own work in response to Hayek's criticisms.

In 1931, one of Keynes's students, Richard Kahn, developed an income-expenditure multiplier to explain the Depression in terms of total spending. Keynes adopted Kahn's theory of the income-expenditure multiplier into his system, and the aggregate spending theory of unemployment was often referred to as the Kahn–Keynes theory. Keynes rose to a position of prominence in 1936 with the publication of his book *The General Theory of Employment, Interest and Money*. Keynes's mentor, Alfred Marshall, had stressed the importance of prices and individual decisions, but Keynes downplayed the importance of incentives in structuring individual behavior. Keynes's rejection of the tenets of neoclassical economics followed from his belief that output and employment are determined by irreducible aggregate forces in the economy. Individual decisions concerning relative prices, wages, and interest rates did not matter to Keynes because he thought psychological factors would override personal incentives. Keynes pointed to three fundamental psychological propensities that shaped behavior: the propensity to consume, one's feelings regarding liquidity (i.e., money demand), and the psychological expectation of the future yield from capital assets. He concluded that the propensity to consume and the rate of new investment could cause total private spending (effective demand) to fall short of the level needed to produce full employment—two factors that hinged on psychology, rather than incentives and rational choice. In other words, if capitalists do not feel like investing and consumers do not feel like spending, then these psychological states of mind will result in mass unemployment.

Keynes was credited with developing a new theory of unemployment despite the fact that other economists had published similar work years earlier. Because many economists were already receptive to spending theories of unemployment, Keynes's *General Theory* soon became popular. Of course Hayek had previously countered Keynes's arguments, but for reasons that are unclear, Hayek neglected to review the *General Theory*.

The mainstream postwar version of Keynesian theory was not actually developed by Keynes. John R. Hicks published a paper in 1937 that laid out the standard IS/LM model for postwar Keynesian economics. IS/LM refers to a set of equations that sought to relate national income with the gross domestic product (GDP) and described how an economy could settle at a particular level of GDP that was below full employment. Some early Keynesians, like Joan Robinson, objected to the direction in which Hicks took Keynesian economics, and Hicks later admitted that he had deviated from what Keynes actually wrote. Yet Hicks's version of Keynesian economics was to become the mainstream of Keynesian theory.

Hayek offered an alternative to Keynes's theoretical conclusions with his 1941 book, *The Pure Theory of Capital*. Ludwig von Mises and Henry Hazlitt wrote critiques of Keynesian economics from the perspective of the Austrian School. Mises chided Keynes for popularizing an abundance theory that derived from the philosophy of the businessman, rather than sound economics. However, it was too late for the Austrians to replace the popularity of Keynesian theory in the profession. Indeed, most economists ignored the fundamental arguments of Austrianism.

As far as policy is concerned, Keynes rejected comprehensive central planning of production, but did endorse partial economic planning. Keynes suggested that government should plan investment in new capital goods and direct communal savings. It was Abba Lerner, one of the foremost British economists after Keynes, who actually developed what came to be known as Keynesian fiscal policy. Lerner developed a proposal for functional finance, whereby it was proposed that politicians should run deficits during recessions and surpluses during economic booms. These surpluses and deficits would cancel out over time. Politicians would be able to deal with recessions, he argued, simply by cutting taxes and increasing spending, and could raise taxes later to pay down previously accumulated debt.

Keynesian monetary policy was developed by a group of early Keynesians, including Arthur Phillips, who noticed a statistical tradeoff between unemployment and inflation. These early Keynesians suggested that central banks should exploit this tradeoff and that central banks could reduce unemployment simply by printing more money. They were prepared to concede that this policy would cause inflation, but it also would increase total spending and reduce unemployment. Early Keynesians thought that they could use an active fiscal and monetary policy to fine-tune the economy to permanently reduce unemployment while also controlling inflation and balancing the fiscal budget.

In the 1950s, the American economist, Milton Friedman, advanced several critiques of this postwar version of Keynesian economics. First, he cast doubt on the practicality of Keynesian policies and argued that activist fiscal policy can take years to formulate and implement. Given the time that it takes Congress to change spending and tax rates, the nation could not rely on fiscal policy to deal with economic crises. Second, Friedman developed what became known as his permanent income hypothesis, which holds that private spending is relatively stable, so there should be little need for Keynesian policies. It further suggests that Keynesian policies would have unpredictable effects. Finally, he proposed that the demand for money is stable and that a policy that seriously altered the money supply would have a strong impact on economic conditions. Indeed, an active monetary policy is uncalled for inasmuch as the alleged tradeoff between inflation and unemployment is temporary. If a central bank increases the supply of money, this action might reduce unemployment for a short time, but would ultimately result solely in higher inflation rates. Friedman recommended that politicians balance the budget in peacetime and that central banks expand the money supply at a slow and predictable rate. Thus, Friedman favored government policies and those of the central banks that constrained them to abide by strict rules, thus foregoing activist fiscal and monetary policies.

James Buchanan and William Nordhaus criticized Keynesian economics by calling into question the motives behind deficit and inflationary policies. Nordhaus claimed that politicians would use deficit spending and inflation to increase their popularity during election years. After wining office, politicians would try to run surpluses and reduce inflation. Such policies would result in a *political* business cycle. Similarly, Buchanan argued that Keynesian economics broke down the fiscal discipline of politicians and would result in ever-increasing public debt. Experience has confirmed the predictions of Buchanan and Nordhaus.

In the 1970s, Art Laffer and Jude Wanniski advanced yet another critique of Keynesian economics. According to this critique, which became known as *supply side* economics, the idea that higher taxes increased total revenue was wrong. According to supply side economics, confiscatory tax rates slow economic growth and reduce potential revenue. Keynesian tax policies work only as described if tax rates are low to start. The Reagan administration implemented supply side policies. Critics of supply side economics, however, have claimed that the Reagan deficits proved this theory wrong. The conclusions of supply side economics, they contend, do not indicate that tax cuts will reduce deficits. Although it is true that cuts in confiscatory tax rates might increase government revenue, deficit reduction requires spending control as well. It is true that both Warren Harding and Calvin Coolidge cut taxes and paid off the national debt, but they also reduced spending while revenue increased. Economists now all agree that confiscatory tax rates have serious supply side effects.

Robert Lucas carried Friedman's critique of Keynesian economics further. According to Lucas, the alleged tradeoff between inflation and unemployment did not really exist. According to Lucas, people would come to anticipate inflationary policies and, once having anticipated them, will demand higher money wages. The result will be that inflation will have no effect on employment. The Friedman–Lucas and Buchanan–Nordhaus critiques of Keynesian economics caused most Keynesians to abandon major elements of their paradigm. With regard to policy, few Keynesians still brag about being able to fine-tune the economy. Most Keynesians now claim that they can coarse-tune the economy provided that they learn about recession quickly enough. Some Keynesians have even admitted that Keynesian policy is too hard to implement and that Friedman's program is more practicable.

Most Keynesians have given up on aggregate analysis altogether. Economists like Greg Mankiw and Joseph Stiglitz developed "new Keynesian economics," which focuses on wages and prices, rather than total spending. However, there remain a minority of dissenting post-Keynesians, led by Paul Davidson and John Kenneth Galbraith, who follow Joan Robinson by adhering to the original version of Keynes's theory, along with other early writers.

Twentieth-century experience with Keynesian policies has caused most Keynesians to rethink their position. Keynesian policies were responsible for serious problems with inflation and the accumulation of large amounts of public debt. This debt accumulation was a function of public spending that was, for the most part, wasteful. Academic debate has revealed serious logical problems with Keynesian economics, especially in its earlier forms. Despite all of these problems, some economists persist in promoting Keynesian economics. However, because many Keynesian ideas have been overturned in the past, contemporary Keynesians are by no means certain to succeed in their efforts.

DMK

See also Great Depression; Hayek, Friedrich A.; Interventionism; Money and Banking; Taxation

Further Readings

Buchanan, James, and Richard Wagner. *Democracy in Deficit: The Political Legacy of Lord Keynes*. New York: Academic Press, 1977.

Friedman, Milton. "The Role of Monetary Policy: Presidential Address to AEA." *American Economic Review* (1968).

———. *A Theory of the Consumption Function*. Princeton, NJ: Princeton University Press, 1957.

Hayek, F. A. *The Pure Theory of Capital*. Chicago: University of Chicago Press, 1941 (2007 reprint).

Hazlitt, Henry. *The Failure of the New Economics*. Princeton, NJ: Van Nostrand, 1959.

Keynes, John Maynard. *The General Theory of Employment, Interest, and Money*. New York: Harcourt Brace, 1936 [1953].

Lucas, Robert E., Jr. "Expectations and the Neutrality of Money." *Journal of Economic Theory* 4 (April 1972): 103–124.

Mankiw, N. Gregory, and David Romer, eds. *New Keynesian Economics*. Vols. I and II. Boston: MIT Press, 1991.

Nordhaus, William. "The Political Business Cycle." *Review of Economic Studies* 42 (April 1975): 169–190.

EDUCATION

The term *education* refers to the systematic process through which students learn skills, values, knowledge, and customs. Preferences regarding the desired content and outcomes of education vary from family to family, although areas of significant consensus do exist. The origins of formal education in the West date back to the 5th century B.C., and a wide range of alternative funding systems have been employed over the institution's 2,500-year history. Tax-funded government schooling currently predominates in industrialized countries, with the level of government at which power is concentrated varying from nation to nation.

Since the inception of modern government school systems in the mid- to late 19th century, occasional proposals have been made to reintroduce market incentives and parental choice. Calls for such reforms increased steadily during the last decades of the 20th century, leading to a vigorous debate over the relative merits of alternative structures.

The public's educational expectations fall into two categories: the individual and the social. The first category includes things parents want for their own children; the second includes the broader social effects that citizens, as consumers, expect their educational system to produce. For parents, preparation for success in life and work is paramount, and specific goals include mastery of basic academic and job skills, moral and religious education, a safe and studious educational setting, and the wish that these goals can be achieved affordably. There is considerable agreement among parents on the importance of job skills and basic academics, but preferences vary dramatically in other areas, especially with respect to religious instruction. A sizable portion of the public in modern democracies views the goals of a good educational system as comprising the following: all children should have access to education regardless of income, schools should foster community harmony, schools should encourage parental involvement and responsibility, and schools should promote understanding of and participation in the democratic process.

Historically, systems of formal education have often taken shape through a gradual, evolutionary process. As economies have grown and trade has expanded, literacy has become increasingly valuable and parents are better able to do without their children's labor. These developments have provided both the incentive and the opportunity for education.

One of the earliest cases of formal education directed beyond a small ruling elite was found in the Greek city-state of Athens during the early 5th century B.C. The prevailing view of the role of women and the institution of slavery both contributed to the fact that only free male children were formally educated. Of the eligible child population, the majority attended school for at least a few years. Both elementary and advanced instruction was offered by independent teachers who competed with one another to attract students. Tuition was sufficiently modest as to make education affordable to all but the destitute, although poor children generally attended school for fewer years than their wealthier fellows. Government played no role in the provision, funding, or regulation of education in Athens.

The sophistication, scope, and diversity of Athenian education grew over the course of the 5th century, and at least one school for girls was opened in the latter half of that century by the philosopher Aspasia. By the last decades of the 4th century, the education of girls had become commonplace throughout the Greek-speaking world. It is not possible to draw too many conclusions regarding the pedagogical system adopted in Athens, but it can be said that, during its height, Athens was the most literate, the most economically successful, and one of the most culturally vibrant societies of its time.

Education under the Roman republic of the late 2nd century B.C. was structured similarly to that in classical Athens. Cicero wrote, "Our people have never wished to have any system of education for the free-born youth which is either definitely fixed by law, or officially established, or uniform in all cases." The most notable difference between the two systems was that Roman teachers were usually Greek slaves, whereas teachers in classical Athens had generally been free individuals. The educational control that parents enjoyed in Rome was gradually chipped away as the Republic gave way to the Empire in the 40s and 30s B.C. With the ascension of each new emperor, additional restrictions were placed on what could be taught and who could teach. Imperial authorities also began to offer sporadic subsidies to teachers during the 1st century A.D., particularly to those who spoke well of the imperial leadership and supported its policies.

With the dissolution of the Western Roman Empire in the 6th century, mass education disappeared in Europe, although isolated pockets of scholarship continued to exist, particularly around monasteries. However, just as popular literacy and learning were disappearing in the West, they began to take root in the East. By the 8th century, a vigorous market in education served families in Arab-controlled areas from northwestern India to northwestern Africa and across the Mediterranean. There existed no systematic government regulation, provision, or funding of the market in education, although many schools were privately subsidized, thus broadening access to education. For several centuries, the Muslim world enjoyed a level of literacy at least the equal of anything that had gone before. In poetry and philosophy it was immensely prolific, and in the sciences it was unsurpassed. As one historian has observed, however, the vibrancy of this educational system began to wane in the 11th century, when schools fell under increasing state control and were transformed into tools for promoting narrow political and religious aims.

The 14th-century European Renaissance had only a slight effect on the education of the great majority of the public, and it was not until the 16th century that literacy began to again extend beyond the ruling elite. Certainly the invention of movable type and the commercialization of the book industry did much to increase literary throughout Europe. Literacy in the German states was among the highest in Europe during the 17th and 18th centuries, although its growth was at times impeded by the divergent goals of the nobility and the common people. The nobles subsidized the education of a Latin-speaking bureaucracy, whereas the masses of the people chiefly sought education in their mother tongue.

In England and the United States, near-universal literacy was achieved by the mid-19th century. Up to that point, education in both nations chiefly operated as a free, competitive enterprise, with only limited government provision or funding. However, the latter half of the 19th century marked the rise of fully tax-funded state-run school systems. Scholars have shown that total enrollment rates were largely unaffected by this transformation, although the combination of increasing education taxes and decreasing government school tuition (which eventually fell to zero) was followed by a significant shift of students from the private to the government sector.

The effects of this shift from market to state provisioning of educational services are in considerable dispute. Critics of state schooling argue that student achievement has stagnated or declined; parental choice, control, and involvement have diminished; efficiency has fallen and costs risen; and that community conflicts over the content of government schooling have become commonplace. In fact, studies have shown that currently the cost of public school education is appropriately twice that of the average private school. Defenders of government-run school systems, however, dispute all of these allegations. They assert that the average student today completes many more years of schooling, their achievements have held constant or gone up, pedagogical experts make better educational decisions than do parents, cost increases have either been overstated or are justifiable, community conflicts over education are not attributable to the state operation of schools, and the level of parental involvement is a cultural phenomenon unrelated to school governance structures.

These different assessments have spurred a debate over the merits of market-run versus state-run education. No consensus has yet been reached, and there exist several occasionally overlapping viewpoints. At one end of the spectrum are those who feel that government schooling is the best, if not the only, mechanism for fulfilling the public's social goals for education. This group advocates improving educational outcomes through higher spending, reduced class sizes, enhanced teacher certification and training, leadership programs for administrators, and the like. A second group also sees the government operation and oversight of schools as indispensable, but believes that the system would improve if all families chose from among the available government schools, rather than having their children automatically assigned to a school. This practice is known as *public school choice*. A third group agrees with the need for parental choice, but feels that that choice is too confined by existing government school regulations. They recommend easing these regulations for state schools that promise to deliver a minimum level of student achievement. Government schools operating under this combination of eased regulations and contractual performance obligations are called *charter schools*. Charter schools, argues a fourth group, are good so far as they go, but do not go far enough. This group believes that government schools operating under charters have too many limitations compared with independent schools, among them the likelihood of reregulation and the inability to offer devotional religious instruction, set tuition levels, or control admissions. Their solution to these problems is to allow for state subsidization of education without government provision of schooling. In particular, they recommend that the state distribute the money it collects in taxes earmarked for education directly to families on a per-child basis. These disbursements, most famously proposed by economist Milton Friedman in the early 1950s, have come to be known as *vouchers*. A final group asserts that the pseudo-market policies advocated by the other groups would not produce a competitive, consumer-driven education industry. This last group further contends that genuinely free markets in education, when supplemented with means-tested

private or state subsidies, best meet the public's individual and social goals for education.

AC

See also Children; Family; Privacy; Privatization

Further Readings

Bowen, James. *A History of Western Education: Volume One. The Ancient World: Orient and Mediterranean.* New York: St. Martin's Press, 1972.
Cicero. "The Republic." *Cicero XVI.* London: Heinemann, 1988.
Coulson, Andrew J. *Market Education: The Unknown History.* New Brunswick, NJ: Transaction, 1999.
Marrou, Henri I. *A History of Education in Antiquity.* Madison: University of Wisconsin Press, 1982.
Nakosteen, M. *History of Islamic Origins of Western Education.* Boulder: University of Colorado Press, 1964.
West, E. G. *Education and the State: A Study in Political Economy.* Indianapolis, IN: Liberty Fund, 1994.

EMERSON, RALPH WALDO (1803–1882)

Ralph Waldo Emerson, a Massachusetts native, was one of the founders of Transcendentalism, a philosophical, literary, and cultural movement that stressed spiritual oneness with nature, reliance on inner experience, and rejection of social conformity. Other prominent Transcendentalists included Bronson Alcott and Henry David Thoreau.

Although Emerson began as a Unitarian minister, his increasing emphasis on feeling and conduct over creeds and external forms led him to resign the pulpit in 1832. Emerson insisted that a human life should be guided more by inner development than by traditions, institutions, or social expectations. This ethical individualism expressed itself in political liberalism, but grudgingly so. Emerson long opposed slavery, the mistreatment of American Indians, and the denial of the suffrage to women, yet he disliked political involvement and felt that social reform must begin with the reform of the individual. Despite an initial tendency to regard reformers as alienated busybodies, however, Emerson reluctantly became one himself, when passage of the Fugitive Slave Law in 1850 played a crucial role in radicalizing him. The eventual extent of his political engagement is, in fact, often underestimated by those who rely solely on his early works. Despite the philosophical complexities of his prose, Emerson also became a popular and influential lecturer. His popularity did not preclude his becoming a frequent target of attack as well, first for his heterodox religious views and later for his increasingly militant abolitionism.

For Emerson, the scope of political activism remained limited by his greater trust in individual self-transformation, rather than in collective action. Although he did not reject the latter, he insisted that to be effective or worthwhile it must be founded on, rather than substituted for, individual development. Stressing self-reliance in both the material and spiritual spheres, Emerson held that we should seek to direct our own lives and not those of others. Hence, he concluded that "the less government we have, the better," and he came to regard all states of whatever form as corrupt. Although not himself an anarchist, he expressed friendliness toward anarchy, opining that, "with the appearance of the wise man, the State expires." He pointed to various peacefully stateless episodes in American history (Massachusetts during the American Revolution, California during the gold rush) as evidence of the practicability of anarchism. For Emerson, social cooperation was not something that needed to be imposed on society by an alien force. On the contrary, he contended that each human being was "made of hooks and eyes, and links himself naturally to his brothers."

For Emerson, slavery was not only a wrong in itself but also harmful in its results, not only for the enslaved but also for the enslaver. He attributed the South's lower degree of economic development to its reliance on slave labor, rather than on free industry. Agreeing with the doctrine of such radical abolitionists as Lysander Spooner, Ainsworth Spofford, and his friend, Thoreau, that no statute contrary to human liberty can possess any binding legal obligation, Emerson expressed admiration for John Brown's attempt to spark a slave insurrection at Harper's Ferry. When the Civil War broke out, Emerson supported the Northern cause—but only on the premise that slave emancipation, not the mere preservation of the Union, would be the outcome of Union victory. Indeed, through his lectures and essays, Emerson has been credited with helping to make emancipation a Union aim in the war, as it had not obviously been at the start. Emerson also maintained that freed slaves should receive both suffrage and financial compensation.

In the area of economics, Emerson was critical of competitive capitalism for fostering materialism and plutocracy and worried that the division of labor made individuals less self-reliant. Nevertheless, he favored "free trade with all the world without toll or custom-houses" and was skeptical of the practicability of top-down, governmentally imposed solutions to social problems. Small wonder that individualist anarchists like William B. Greene and Bolton Hall, who sought to achieve socialist ends by free-market means, found Emerson a congenial spirit.

RL

See also Abolitionism; Feminism and Women's Rights; Free Trade; Individualism, Political and Ethical; Thoreau, Henry David

Further Readings

Emerson, Edward Waldo, ed. *Complete Works of Ralph Waldo Emerson: Vol. XI. Miscellanies*. Boston: Houghton Mifflin, 1904.

Ferguson, Alfred R., and Jean Ferguson Carr, eds. *The Collected Works of Ralph Waldo Emerson: Volume III. Essays: Second Series*. Cambridge, MA: Harvard University Press, 1994.

Gougeon, Len, and Myerson, Joel, eds. *Emerson's Antislavery Writings*. New Haven, CT: Yale University Press, 1995.

Richardson, Robert D., Jr. *Emerson: The Mind on Fire*. Berkeley: University of California Press, 1995.

Robinson, David M. *The Political Emerson: Essential Writings on Politics and Social Reform*. Boston: Beacon Press, 2004.

EMINENT DOMAIN/TAKINGS

Eminent domain refers to the legal power of a government or a private entity to which government has delegated this power to forcibly take private property from its owners. Under American law, the government's power to seize property is limited, most notably by the U.S. Constitution and state constitutions. The Takings Clause of the 5th Amendment of the U.S. Constitution reads, "nor shall private property be taken for public use without just compensation."

In the case of *Boom Co. v. Patterson*, the U.S. Supreme Court, in 1879, decided that eminent domain is an inherent power of government, "an attribute of sovereignty." However, this power was rarely exercised by the federal government until after the Civil War. Prior to the war, it was state governments who exercised their authority to seize private property—usually to build canals, harbors, highways, and other infrastructure. Many scholars have argued that governments would not have been able to complete such projects without this power of eminent domain. From the 1870s, however, the federal government has commonly made use of this power.

The Takings Clause and the doctrine of eminent domain are meant to restrict government's ability to take property to situations where seizure of the property is for public use. That is, government could confiscate property from a private owner only if the government planned to use the property for a public purpose whose goal was to benefit the whole citizenry. In such cases, governments were obligated to pay just compensation to each owner for the loss of their property. Just compensation has traditionally been interpreted to mean "fair market value."

When exercising eminent domain powers, the government was required to offer to purchase the private property for a fair price. If the owner accepted the offer, title to the property was formally transferred to government. However, if the offer was rejected and if subsequent good-faith negotiations did not lead to a voluntary sale, the government customarily began condemnation proceedings to force the transfer of title. In condemnation cases, private owners possessed the right to be notified of the taking and to respond or object to government evidence regarding the property's value. Whether property was condemned or transferred voluntarily, each private owner retained the right to just compensation.

In some situations, a government, whether state, local, or federal, has taken actions that clearly infringe the rights of a property owner to use and enjoy that property. If the government offers no compensation for this interference, property owners could sue the government for what was known as an "inverse condemnation" in order to compel the government to pay fair compensation for its taking.

When a government regulates and thus interferes with the use, development, and enjoyment of private property, courts have only rarely required it to pay owners for the losses that result from such regulatory (as opposed to physical) takings. Such takings often occur as a result of environmental, historic preservation, and zoning regulations. Courts are more likely to order compensation for a regulatory taking if the regulation has reduced the value of the property to near zero. Such a regulation would be considered to constitute a full, as opposed to a partial, taking. An example of the Supreme Court's reasoning in a case involving a regulatory taking can be found in the 1992 case of *Lucas v. South Carolina Coastal Council*. However, most regulatory takings are uncompensated, which means that private owners must bear almost all the costs of the regulatory action that, presumably, benefit many.

Granting any government the power to take private property for any use, even with compensation, is deeply problematic. The reasons are numerous. First, private property is an extremely effective bulwark against government tyranny. If politically powerful individuals can legally take property for public use and if the politically powerful can determine what uses are "public," then we can expect these interpretations to be quite broad. It is predictable that the politically weak will be more likely targets of eminent-domain actions than will the politically well connected.

This notion was particularly true following the Court's 5–4 decision in *Kelo v. City of New London*, that government entities possessed the authority to transfer land holdings from one private owner to another if it were thought that the transfer would further economic development. Justice Sandra Day O'Connor recognized this problem in her dissenting opinion to the case:

> The beneficiaries [of eminent domain] are likely to be those citizens with disproportionate influence and power in the political process, including large corporations and development firms. As for the victims, the government now has license to transfer property from those with fewer resources to those with more. The Founders cannot have intended this perverse result.

Justice O'Connor is surely right that the Founding Fathers did not intend government to have the legal power to take property from one private citizen and give it to another for the latter's enrichment, as was the case in *Kelo*. The restrictions of the Takings Clause, and similar restrictions in state constitutions, are evidence of attempts by the Framers and their successors to limit such redistributive actions.

Second, eminent-domain powers make the tenure of private citizens in their own property insecure and, therefore, less valuable. Third, government officials who pay "just" compensation are unable to take the subjective value of private property into account. As a result, private owners may be forced to transfer property at a price far below that which the owner would accept in a voluntary exchange. Given that American courts have traditionally been extremely deferential to legislatures when determining whether a use is public, governments now possess expansive powers to transfer property from the private to the public domain or, recently, from one private owner to another—powers that threaten individual liberty.

KB

See also Private Property; Regulation; Rent Seeking; Transportation

Further Readings

DeLong, James V. *Property Matters: How Property Rights Are under Assault—and Why You Should Care.* Albany: State University of New York Press, 1993.

Epstein, Richard A. *Takings: Private Property and the Power of Eminent Domain.* Cambridge, MA: Harvard University Press, 1985.

Pipes, Richard. *Property and Freedom: How through the Centuries Private Ownership Has Promoted Liberty and the Rule of Law.* New York: Knopf, 1999.

Sandefur, Timothy. *Cornerstone of Liberty: Property Rights in 21st Century America.* Washington, DC: Cato Institute, 2006.

Siegan, Bernard H. *Property and Freedom: The Constitution, the Courts, and Land-Use Regulation.* New Brunswick, NJ: Transaction, 1997.

English Civil Wars

The English Civil Wars had their immediate origins in the attempts of Charles I to impose elements of the Anglican liturgy, including use of the Book of Common Prayer, on the fiercely Calvinist Scottish Church. These attempts to conform the Scottish Kirk to English practices was naturally met with fierce resistance by the Scots, who, at a meeting of a large number of nobles, burgesses, lairds, and ministers held in Edinburgh in February 1638, endorsed a petition known as the National Covenant, which sought to abolish all forms of episcopacy in the Scottish Kirk. The petition was circulated and received wide support; it was endorsed by a General Assembly of the Kirk held in Glasgow in November 1638, which removed all bishops from office and asserted the power of the Scottish people over the authority of the Crown in matters of religion. As a result, Charles felt himself forced to raise an army to march on Scotland. He twice attempted to crush the Scottish Covenanter armies, in 1639 and again in 1640, but the Royalist armies were unsuccessful in fighting against a force that comprised men energized by a defense of their faith. Indeed, the Scottish armies were so successful that in August 1640 they were able to take both Newcastle and Durham. As a result, a temporary peace, the Treaty of Ripon, was signed in 1641 on terms extremely generous to Scotland. Among its terms were that Scottish armies would continue to occupy Northumberland and Durham while being paid £850 per day until a final settlement was reached.

Although Charles had no intention of permitting his Scottish subjects to continue in a state of rebellion, he was faced with the difficulty of raising funds for another army. In addition, he was confronted with the financial obligations imposed on him by the Treaty of Ripon. Attempts to borrow from his brother-in-law, the King of France, and even from the Pope proved unsuccessful. As a result, the King was forced to call Parliament into session in the fall of 1640. He had previously summoned Parliament in April 1640, prior to his second foray into Scotland, hoping that they would provide the necessary funds to prosecute the war. Although there is some evidence to support the notion that the Commons were prepared to eventually vote the requested subsidies even though they opposed the issues over which the conflict was fought, they refused to do so until Charles had first dealt with a number of grievances regarding the King's political and religious policies. Parliament had not been summoned for 11 years, and its list of complaints was lengthy and extensive. So unnerved was the King by Parliament's demands, however, that, against the advice of his favorite, the Earl of Strafford, he dissolved Parliament (later known as the Short Parliament) after only 3 weeks.

When Parliament again assembled in the fall, the strength of feeling against the Crown was truly intense; as a result, the Long Parliament (as the Parliament called in November 1640 was later known) was extremely hostile to the King's request for funds. They were outraged that he maintained that he ruled over Great Britain by divine right and that he had presumed to act independently of the wishes of his Parliament and his subjects. He persisted in levying customs duties without renewed Parliamentary consent. In 1634, he had extended his authority to collect ship money (previously levied only on port cities) to the whole kingdom. Additionally, there appears little question

that Charles had abused his authority by relying on the various prerogative courts, the most infamous of which was the Court of Star Chamber, to stifle political opposition. Finally, his High Church leanings and his flirtation with Roman Catholicism had successfully alienated the overwhelming portion of his subjects. Both the Independents and Presbyterians were particularly incensed at his attempts to impose his Anglo-Catholic views on both the Scots and the English dissenters.

The Long Parliament immediately enacted a series of sweeping reforms that radically altered the relation between the Crown and Parliament. It abolished the prerogative courts, among them the Court of Star Chamber, and freed those imprisoned by their verdicts. It enacted the Triennial Act, which mandated that no more than 3 years could elapse between Parliamentary sessions; by the terms of another act, it prohibited the dissolution of Parliament without its own consent. Customs duties and ship money were to be levied only with Parliamentary authorization. Both Thomas Wentworth, the Earl of Strafford, and William Laud, the Archbishop of Canterbury, favorites of the Crown whom the Parliamentarians particularly detested, were impeached; Laud was imprisoned and Strafford was executed.

Charles appeared prepared to suffer all these reforms; however, despite his seeming acquiescence, he was still distrusted by the Parliamentary party. When the Irish rebelled against English rule in October 1641 and it was felt necessary to raise an army to deal with them, the Parliamentarians refused to turn control of these forces to the King, fearing that he might use them against Parliament. Instead, under the leadership of John Pym, one of the most outspoken members of the radical Puritan forces, Parliament issued a Grand Remonstrance, indicting the King's political and ecclesiastical policies and assuming direct control of the army. In retaliation, in January 1642, Charles attempted to arrest five of its more outspoken members, including Pym. The attempt proved a failure, but it signaled the fact that a permanent breach between King and Parliament was inevitable. In March, the Long Parliament decreed that its own ordinances were valid even without royal assent. On August 22, 1642, after Charles raised his standard at Nottingham, civil war between the Crown and Parliament—at least those members of Parliament who had abandoned their Royalist sympathies—began.

The Parliamentary army, known as the New Model Army, was inspired and directed by Oliver Cromwell, a member of the gentry and a strict and zealous Puritan. Under his direction, Parliamentary forces (the Roundheads) were able to hold the Royalists (the Cavaliers) at bay and, at the Battle of Marston Moor in July 1644 and at Naseby in July 1645, imposed crushing defeats on the King's armies. The fate of the King, however, had been effectively sealed in September 1643 when Parliament formed an alliance, a Solemn League and Covenant, with the Scots, whereby Presbyterian ritual and church government would become mandatory in England. It was imposed by Parliamentary ordinance on everyone in England and Wales, and all those holding command or office under Parliament were required to sign it. Its provisions, however, were resisted by English Independents (Congregationalists) and by a substantial portion of the New Model Army.

In April 1646, when Charles's cause failed, he fled from Oxford and placed himself in the hands of the Scottish army, who in turn surrendered him to Parliament in exchange for being paid what was owed them for their participation in the war. A year later, the New Model Army, in disagreement with Parliament over its Presbyterian sympathies, managed to secure the King, who quickly entered into secret negotiations with the Scots to finally and securely establish Presbyterianism as the religion of England. The upshot was that Cromwell decisively defeated a Scottish army at Preston in August 1648 and in December occupied London, which the Army then purged of its Presbyterian members. On January 30, 1649, the King, found guilty of treason, was beheaded.

The events of 1640–1649 are often referred to as the Puritan Revolution. However, these events and their outcome were not solely—perhaps not even predominantly—religious in character. It is true that Parliament was successful in crushing Laud's attempts to impose religious uniformity throughout England, but the revolutionary religious reforms were to prove temporary. Indeed, conditions under the Commonwealth, which replaced the monarchy, were in some ways harsher than they had been earlier. Of greater significance were the long-term political changes that emerged during these years, which were far reaching. They included permanently laying to rest the notion that the sovereign ruled by divine right, which Charles and his father James I had so zealously embraced, limiting the appointment of ministers to those in whom Parliament had confidence, and reaffirming the provision of Magna Carta that the monarch may not impose any tax without the approval of the people's representatives. Equally important, the political and religious ferment through which England passed during that decade spawned a variety of political groups, one of which was clearly libertarian in character—the Levellers.

The Levellers, who strongly supported the establishment of a republic and the institution of universal manhood suffrage, adumbrated elements of the political philosophy of John Locke, including the notion that all men were born equally free and that they were all possessed of certain natural rights. Despite their demands that all men be treated alike, they were not, as some have claimed, early socialists who sought a redistribution of private property. Indeed, they called for increased safeguards for property and condemned the granting of monopolies by the government. John Lilburne, their chief spokesman, maintained that the

Levellers were "the truest and constantest assertors of liberty and propriety."

For a time, their movement was extremely popular, both in the New Model Army and among the residents of London. However, following the abolition of the monarchy, Lilburne and the movement's other leaders were arrested and confined to the Tower of London awaiting trial. Found innocent of supporting anarchism and the destruction of private property, they were freed. However, their movement, as just and noble as it was, soon faded, not to be resurrected until certain of its elements appeared a half century later.

RH

See also Levellers; Magna Carta; Private Property; Puritanism; Republicanism, Classical; Sidney, Algernon; Whiggism

Further Readings

Coward, Barry. *The Stuart Age: England, 1603–1714*. London: Longman, 1994.
Firth, C. H. *Oliver Cromwell and the Role of the Puritans in England*. Oxford: Oxford University Press, 1900.
Gregg, Pauline. *King Charles I*. Berkeley: University of California Press, 1984.
Hill, Christopher. *Some Intellectual Consequences of the English Revolution*. Madison: University of Wisconsin Press, 1980.
———. *The World Turned Upside Down: Radical Ideas during the English Revolution*. London: Penguin Books, 1973.
Kenyon, J. P. *The Stuarts: A Study in English Kingship*. London: Severn House, 1977.
Trevelyan, George M. *England under the Stuarts*. 2nd ed. London: Routledge, 2002.

ENLIGHTENMENT

The Enlightenment developed those features of the modern world that most libertarians prize—liberal politics and free markets, scientific progress, and technological innovation.

The Enlightenment took the intellectual revolutions of the early modern 17th century and transformed European and American society in the 18th century. At the beginning of the 17th century, Europe was largely feudal and prescientific. By the end of the 18th century, however, liberal democratic revolutions had swept away feudalism; the foundations of physics, chemistry, and biology had been laid; and the Industrial Revolution was at full steam.

The Enlightenment was the product of thousands of brilliant and hardworking individuals, yet two Englishmen are most often identified as inaugurating it: John Locke (1632–1704), for his work on reason, empiricism, and liberal politics; and Isaac Newton (1643–1727), for his work on physics and mathematics. The transition to the post-Enlightenment era is often dated from the successful resolution of the American Revolution in the 1780s—or, alternatively, from the collapse of the French Revolution and the rise to power of Napoleon Bonaparte in the 1790s. Between Locke and Newton at the end of the 17th century and the American and French Revolutions at the end of the 18th century, there occurred 100 years of unprecedented intellectual activity, social ferment, and political and economic transformation.

Fundamental to the achievements of Locke and Newton was confident application of reason to the physical world, religion, human nature, and society. By the 1600s, modern thinkers began to insist that perception and reason are the sole means by which men could know the world—in contrast to the premodern, medieval reliance on tradition, faith, and revelation. These thinkers started their investigations systematically from an analysis of nature, rather than the supernatural, the characteristic starting point of premodern thought. Enlightenment intellectuals stressed man's autonomy and his capacity for forming his own character—in contrast to the premodern emphasis on dependence and original sin. Most important, modern thinkers began to emphasize the individual, arguing that the individual's mind is sovereign and that the individual is an end in himself—in contrast to the premodernist, feudal subordination of the individual to higher political, social, or religious authorities. The achievements of Locke and Newton represent the maturation of this new intellectual world.

Political and economic liberalism depend on confidence that individuals can run their own lives. Political power and economic freedom are thought to reside in individuals only to the extent that they are thought to be capable of using them wisely. This confidence in individuals rests on a confidence in human reason—the means by which individuals can come to know their world, plan their lives, and socially interact.

If reason is a faculty of the individual, then individualism becomes crucial to our understanding of ethics. Locke's *A Letter Concerning Toleration* (1689) and *Two Treatises of Government* (1690) are landmark texts in the modern history of individualism. Both link the human capacity for reason to ethical individualism and its social consequences: the prohibition of force against another's independent judgment or action, individual rights, political equality, limiting the power of government, and religious toleration.

Science and technology more obviously depend on confidence in the power of reason. The scientific method is a refined application of reason to understanding nature. Trusting science cognitively is an act of confidence in reason, as is trusting one's life to its technological products. If one emphasizes that reason is the faculty of understanding nature, then the epistemology that emerges from it, when systematically applied, yields science. Enlightenment thinkers laid the foundations of all the major branches of science. In mathematics, Newton and Gottfried Leibniz independently developed the calculus, Newton developing his version in 1666 and Leibniz publishing his in 1675. The monumental publication of modern physics, Newton's *Principia Mathematica,* appeared in 1687. A century of investigation led to the production of Carolus Linnaeus's *Systema Naturae* in 1735 and *Species Plantarium* in 1753, jointly presenting a comprehensive biological taxonomy. The publication of Antoine Lavoisier's *Traité Élémentaire de Chimie* (*Treatise on Chemical Elements*) in 1789, proved to be the foundational text in the science of chemistry. The rise of rational science also brought broader social improvements, such as the lessening of superstition and, by the 1780s, the end of persecutions of witchcraft.

Individualism and science are consequences of an epistemology predicated on reason. Both applied systematically have enormous consequences. Individualism when applied to politics yielded a species of liberal democracy, whereby the principle of individual freedom was wedded to the principle of decentralizing political power. As the importance of individualism rose in the modern world, feudalism declined. Revolutions in England in the 1640s and in 1688 began this trend, and the modern political principles there enunciated spread to America and France in the 18th century, leading to liberal revolutions in 1776 and 1789. Political reformers instituted bills of rights, constitutional checks on abuses of government power, and the elimination of torture in judicial proceedings.

As the feudal regimes weakened and were overthrown, liberal individualist ideas were extended to all human beings. Racism and sexism are obvious affronts to individualism and went on the defensive as the 18th century progressed. During the Enlightenment, antislavery societies were formed in America in 1784, in England in 1787, and a year later in France; in 1791 and 1792, Olympe de Gouges's *Declaration of the Rights of Women* and Mary Wollstonecraft's *A Vindication of the Rights of Women*, landmarks in the movement for women's liberty and equality, were published.

Free markets and capitalism are a reflection of individualism in the marketplace. Capitalist economics is based on the principle that individuals should be left free to make their own decisions about production, consumption, and trade. As individualism rose in the 18th century, feudal and mercantilist institutions declined. With freer markets came a theoretical grasp of the productive impact of the division of labor and specialization and of the retarding impact of protectionism and other restrictive regulations. Capturing and extending those insights, Adam Smith's *Wealth of Nations*, published in 1776, is the landmark text in modern economics. With the establishment of freer markets came the elimination of guilds and many governmental monopolies, and the development of modern corporations, banking, and financial markets.

Science, when applied systematically to material production, yields engineering and technology. By the mid-18th century, the free exchange of ideas and wealth resulted in scientists and engineers uncovering knowledge and creating technologies on an unprecedented scale. The Industrial Revolution, underway for some decades, was substantially advanced by James Watt's steam engine after 1769. Items that were once luxuries—such as pottery, cotton fabric, paper for books and newspapers, and glass for windows in houses—soon became mass-produced.

When science is applied to the human body, the result is advances in medicine. New studies of human anatomy and physiology swept away supernaturalistic and other premodern accounts of human disease. By the second half of the 18th century, medicine was placed on a scientific footing. Edward Jenner's discovery of a smallpox vaccine in 1796, for example, provided protection against a major killer and established the science of immunization. Over the course of the century, physicians made advances in their understanding of nutrition, hygiene, and diagnostic techniques. These discoveries, combined with newly developed medical technologies, contributed to modern medicine. At the same time, advances in public hygiene led to a substantial decline in mortality rates, and average longevity increased.

The Enlightenment also was responsible for the establishment of the idea of progress. Ignorance, poverty, war, and slavery, it was discovered, were not inevitable. Indeed, Enlightenment thinkers came to be profoundly convinced that every human problem could be solved and that the human condition could be raised to new and as-yet unimagined heights. "The time will come," wrote the Marquis de Condorcet, a mathematician and social reformer who also translated Smith's *Wealth of Nations* into French, "when the sun will shine only on free men who have no master but their own reasons." Through science the world was open to being understood, to disease being eliminated, and to the unlimited improvement of agriculture and technologies. Every individual possessed the power of reason, and, hence, education could become universal and illiteracy and superstition eliminated. Because men possess reason, we are able to structure our social arrangements and design political and economic institutions that will protect our rights, settle our disputes peaceably, and enable us to form fruitful trading partnership with others. We can, they thought, become knowledgeable, free, healthy, peaceful, and wealthy without limit. In other words, the Enlightenment bequeathed to us the optimistic belief that progress and the pursuit of happiness are the natural birthrights of humankind.

Yet not all commentators regarded the Enlightenment as unrelievably progressive. Conservatives leveled three broad criticisms—that the Enlightenment's rationalism undermined religious faith, that the Enlightenment's individualism undermined communal ties, and that by overemphasizing the powers of reason and individual freedom the Enlightenment led to revolutions that instituted changes of such rapidity that they undermined social stability. Socialists also offered three criticisms—that the Enlightenment's idolatry of science and technology led to an artificial world of dehumanizing machines and gadgets; that the Enlightenment's competitive individualism and capitalism destroyed community and led to severe inequalities; and that the combination of science, technology, and capitalism inevitably led to technocratic oppression by the haves against the have-nots.

Contemporary debates over the significance of the Enlightenment thus have a threefold character—between those who see it as a threat to an essentially religious-traditionalist vision, those who see it as a threat to an essentially Left-egalitarian vision, and those who see it as the foundation of the magnificent achievements of the modern scientific and liberal-democratic world.

SRCH

See also American Revolution; Diderot, Denis; Industrial Revolution; Kant, Immanuel; Locke, John; Material Progress; Montesquieu, Charles de Secondat de; Smith, Adam; Voltaire; Wollstonecraft, Mary

Further Readings

Cassirer, Ernst. *The Philosophy of the Enlightenment*. Princeton, NJ: Princeton University Press, 1968.
Gay, Peter. *The Enlightenment*. New York: Knopf, 1966.
Horkheimer, Max, and Theodor W. Adorno. *Dialectic of Enlightenment*. New York: Continuum, 1994 [1944].
Kramnick, Isaac, ed. *The Portable Enlightenment Reader*. New York: Penguin, 1995.
Kurtz, Paul, and Timothy J. Madigan, eds. *Challenges to the Enlightenment*. Amherst, NY: Prometheus Books, 1994.
Rusher, William A., ed. *The Ambiguous Legacy of the Enlightenment*. Lanham, MD: University Press of America, 1995.
William, David, ed. *The Enlightenment*. Cambridge: Cambridge University Press, 1999.

ENTREPRENEURSHIP

Entrepreneurship has been an elusive phenomenon in much economics scholarship. It is typically subsumed under the managerial function as an organizing factor of production. Part of the difficulty in studying entrepreneurship is that standard economic methods focus on constrained optimization (i.e., economizing) within a given ends–means framework, whereas entrepreneurship is related more to people's discovering and creating new ends and new means. Entrepreneurship is intimately connected with the notion of economic change, and just as there are different conceptions of economic change, so too there are different conceptions of the entrepreneurial function.

Joseph Schumpeter's conception of the entrepreneur emphasized creative changes and heroic, large-scale innovations. (His later work, however, adopted a wider definition that embraced more humble acts of entrepreneurship.) Schumpeter's focus was on "new combinations" that are discontinuous with what has come before (e.g., the commercialization of the automobile). The Schumpeterian entrepreneur, by virtue of being an entrepreneur, engages in the creation of new products, the adoption of new methods of production, the discovery of new markets for outputs and new sources of supply of inputs, the development of new marketing methods, and the creation of new forms of business organization (e.g., the multinational corporation). Accordingly, entrepreneurship involves the creation of new production functions, either new products or new methods for creating existing products, rather than just an adaptive response to exogenous changes. With its emphasis on discontinuous innovation, Schumpeter's general approach emphasized the disequilibrating nature of entrepreneurship—that is, entrepreneurship disturbed previous states of economic coordination.

The conception of entrepreneurship offered by Israel Kirzner has received increasing attention from economists in the past few years. His approach built on ideas regarding competition and market processes earlier put forward by Hayek and Mises. Kirzner's analysis conceived of entrepreneurship in two related ways. On the one hand, his depiction focused on alertness to profit opportunities as its essential defining character. In this sense, Kirzner focused on the entrepreneurial element of human decision making. It is a propensity of human beings, he argued, to make spontaneous discoveries of opportunities (including new ends–means frameworks) that are somehow "staring them in the face."

The second way that Kirzner conceived of the entrepreneur was as someone who takes advantage of opportunities for arbitrage. In focusing on arbitrage, Kirzner emphasized the entrepreneur's economic function and the essential role that he plays in coordinating market activities. These two conceptions are clearly interwoven because together they alert individuals who discover hitherto undiscovered profit opportunities and engage in arbitrage.

The simplest version of Kirzner's approach is a single-period model for a single good. The entrepreneur is one who discovers two prices for the same good in the market; the price differential represents pure arbitrage profit that is available to the person who spots it. The entrepreneur knows exactly what to do and buys the good at the low price and sells it at a high price. The price discrepancy arises because buyers who buy at high prices in one part of the market are unaware of sellers who are selling at lower prices in other parts of the same market. Ignorance of opportunities for mutually beneficial exchange gives rise to a lack of coordination of buyers' and sellers' plans. In this model, entrepreneurship is instantaneous and involves no uncertainty or risk. (Schumpeter also excluded the bearing of risk from the entrepreneurial function; in his view, capitalists bear the risks.)

Kirzner's static model of interlocal arbitrage can be extended to a more dynamic setting, which includes intertemporal arbitrage—that is, speculation over time. In this case, the entrepreneur sniffs out differentials between prices today and expected prices tomorrow. For example, the entrepreneur might buy a good today at a low price in the expectation of selling at a higher price tomorrow—a price that would more than compensate for any temporary holding costs. In this capacity, the entrepreneur functions as a speculator. Of course, this type of entrepreneurial activity communicates information to other market players as well so that over time their ignorance of these particular opportunities diminishes.

Kirzner's model can be extended in other ways. Thus far, we have only been considering markets for a single (final) good. However, it is possible to imagine similar kinds of entrepreneurial adjustments being made between factor (input) markets and product (output) markets. In these cases, the entrepreneur discovers differences between prices in input markets and the price of the final good that those inputs produce. If the final good is a new type of product that does not yet exist, then the entrepreneur is engaged in innovation.

Kirzner's contribution is significant because it provides a unified analysis of all three forms of entrepreneurship—arbitrage, speculation, and innovation. The latter two activities are more sophisticated versions of arbitrage from an economic point of view. His approach has been criticized, however, for its relatively static treatment of time, its downplaying of the radical uncertainty involved in entrepreneurial decision making, and its consequent inattention to entrepreneurial errors and losses. In addition, there is no explicit treatment of firms in his theory of entrepreneurship.

Like Kirzner, Mark Casson emphasized the equilibrating role of entrepreneurship. His theory of entrepreneurship seeks to inject market-process ideas into conventional neoclassical economic theory. Casson defined the entrepreneur as someone who specializes in taking judgmental decisions about the coordination (i.e., the allocation) of scarce resources. According to Casson's approach, Kirznerian arbitrage and Schumpeterian innovation are special cases of a more general notion of entrepreneurial speculation based on self-confident judgment. The essence of entrepreneurship is having a superior perception of events and opportunities. Casson's entrepreneur is the one who has superior access to unique information that must be protected to exploit it fully. Because of the transaction costs of market-making, the entrepreneur often creates and manages new firms to undertake production rather than contracting with outsiders. Like Kirzner, Casson emphasized that most of the obstacles to trade emanate from ignorance of one sort or another.

Although having correctly emphasized the crucial role of entrepreneurship in the market process, neither Kirzner nor Casson adequately tackled the problem of how entrepreneurs improve their knowledge over time. To redress this need, the author of this article has applied Karl Popper's theory of the growth of knowledge to questions of how entrepreneurs learn from their experiences within the market. Seen in this light, entrepreneurs are constantly engaged in problem solving that involves forming conjectures about the latent demands of consumers and ways of satisfying them and then testing these conjectures in the market and exposing them to the possibility of refutation. Entrepreneurs test their ideas so as to eliminate their errors as efficiently as possible in the course of new ventures. This notion is important given that most entrepreneurial ideas, at least in their original form, turn out to be mistakes. This approach also inquires into the philosophical and practical difficulties that entrepreneurs encounter in determining whether their ventures are failing.

The determination of what the entrepreneurial function is has important implications for the design of institutions—the "rules of the game" that frame market processes. Thus, some economists have analyzed Kirzner's theory in terms of how institutions (e.g., constitutions, political structures, property rights, and contracts) affect people's perceptions of their own causal capabilities, the degree of their alertness, and the directions in which their entrepreneurial energies are channeled. Analyzing entrepreneurship in this way requires consideration of its economic, psychological, political, legal, and cultural dimensions from the perspective of the market. It attempts to explain the psychological mechanisms regarding why, when, and how some people and not others are quicker to discover profit opportunities. In contrast, previous economic approaches have ignored the role of culture and socializing forces on entrepreneurial behavior.

Entrepreneurship theory not only has relevance for high-level institutional analysis, but also can be applied to the development of public policy. Such a market-process approach identifies and explains the largely unintended consequences of public policies for entrepreneurial discovery and experimentation. It more accurately evaluates the hidden dynamic effects of government intervention, such as the stifling and misdirection of entrepreneurial energies. Thus, it is less likely than alternative approaches to understate the adverse consequences of regulatory interferences in the market and less likely to underestimate the potential beneficial effects of economic liberalization and deregulation.

Finally, the market-process approach underscores the fact that, because we cannot predict what entrepreneurs will discover in an unhampered market (i.e., we cannot predict what new products will be generated), the market process is inherently open-ended. By imposing regulations that seek to implement specific market outcomes in order to address some alleged market failure, we may be inhibiting the market's own self-corrective properties. This approach also requires us to examine how government interference in market processes gives rise to superfluous or redundant entrepreneurial opportunities that would not have existed without such intervention.

DAH

See also Free-Market Economy; Kirzner, Israel M.; Schumpeter, Joseph

Further Readings

Casson, Mark C. *The Entrepreneur*. Oxford: Martin Robertson, 1982.

Harper, David A. *Foundations of Entrepreneurship and Economic Development*. London: Routledge, 2003.

Hayek, F. A. *Individualism and the Economic Order*. Chicago: University of Chicago Press, 1948.

Ikeda, Sanford. *Dynamics of the Mixed Economy: Toward a Theory of Interventionism*. London: Routledge, 1997.

Kirzner, Israel M. *Competition and Entrepreneurship*. Chicago: University of Chicago Press, 1973.

———. *Perception, Opportunity, and Profit*. Chicago: University of Chicago Press, 1979.

Mises, Ludwig von. *Human Action. A Treatise on Economics*. 3rd rev. ed. San Francisco: Fox & Wilkes, 1966.

Sautet, Frédéric E. *An Entrepreneurial Theory of the Firm*. London: Routledge, 2000.

Schumpeter, Joseph A. "The Creative Response in Economic History." *Journal of Economic History* 7 no. 2 (1947): 149–159.

———. *The Theory of Economic Development: An Inquiry into Profits, Capital, Credit, Interest and the Business Cycle*. Cambridge, MA: Harvard University Press, 1934.

Environment

Environmental protection emerged as a major policy issue in the early 1960s, when public concern about the impact of human activity on our natural resources and their consequent impacts on human health became an important political issue. The result was the enactment of numerous laws designed to protect the environment through government regulation. Although there is broad public support for protecting the environment, there is increasing debate over whether government regulation is the best means of achieving environmental protection. Critics of environmental regulation point to its high costs and inconsistent results and also to its abundant weaknesses. Contemporary environmental regulation's greatest failing, according to many of its critics, is that its effects are equivalent to those of central economic planning. These critics argue that market institutions, such as property rights, voluntary exchange, and common-law liability rules, would do a better job of advancing environmental concerns in concert with individual liberty. This approach to the environment, known as free-market environmentalism (FME), has played an increasingly prominent role in the debate over environmental policy.

Most environmental regulations are predicated on the idea that market failures exist when the government does not intervene. In the simplest of terms, this perspective holds that markets fail to account for the external environmental costs—externalities—produced by economic activities. Such external effects range from the air and water pollution that accompanies industrial production and agriculture to the depletion of natural resources that are commonly owned. For example, if a factory were to emit untreated effluent into a river or stream without compensating those who are impacted by the pollution, the costs of the factory's actions are externalized. Whereas the factory must pay for the labor, capital equipment, and material inputs that it uses to make products, it need not pay for its use of the river for waste disposal. Such pollution externalities are presented as evidence that markets fail to account for environmental values, at which point, it is argued, government intervention is required. One problem with this paradigm is that it justifies government regulation of all human activities that have any measurable environmental impact. As a result, it provides an available pretext to regulate nearly anything.

Libertarian analysis of environmental policy rejects the market failure paradigm. In the broadest sense, libertarianism holds that environmental problems are instead the result of the absence of markets. Environmental problems, whether uncontrolled pollution or the unsustainable use of natural resources, result when resources are left outside of the market institutions of property rights, voluntary exchange, and the rule of law. Libertarian environmentalists note that privately owned resources are typically well maintained. In contrast, resources that are unowned or politically controlled are more apt to be inadequately and poorly managed. Proponents of FME would establish institutional arrangements so that more of the world would enjoy the same custody and protection as a home or yard owned by an individual or group. "At the heart of free market environmentalism is a system of well-specified property rights to natural resources," explain Terry Anderson and Donald Leal in *Free Market Environmentalism.*

FME's focus on property rights evolved from the work of Garrett Hardin, Harold Demsetz, and Ronald Coase, who demonstrated the importance of defining and defending property rights for the protection of resources. Hardin, in particular, explained that when a resource is unowned or owned in common, such as the common grazing pasture in a medieval village, there is no incentive for an individual to protect it. In such a situation, it is in every cattle owner's self-interest to have his herd graze the pasture as much as possible and before any other herd. Every cattle owner who acquires additional cattle gains the benefits of a larger herd, while the cost or overusing the pasture is borne by all members of the village. Inevitably, the consequence is that the pasture is overgrazed and everyone loses. Indeed, the cattle owner with foresight will anticipate that the pasture will become barren in the future, and this knowledge will give him an additional incentive to overgraze. To refuse to add another cow to one's own herd does not change the incentive of every other cattle owner to do so. The end result, according to Hardin, is a "tragedy of the commons."

Libertarian environmentalists argue that avoiding the tragedy of the commons requires the creation of property rights in the underlying resource so as to align the incentives of resource users with the sustainability of the underlying resource. Private ownership overcomes the commons problem because owners have strong incentives to protect and enhance the value of their properties. Property owners also can prevent overuse by controlling access to the resource. As Hardin noted, "The tragedy of the commons as a food basket is averted by private property, or something formally like it." Demsetz's work on the management of beaver by Native Americans reinforces these conclusions; the creation of de facto property rights in beaver populations led to their sustainable use. Other FME scholars, such as Terry Anderson and P. J. Hill, have shown how the value of unowned resources creates incentives for the establishment of property rights in the first place, but also for the development of technologies that allow such property rights to be defined and protected. This idea can be observed in the development of branding and barbed wire as technologies to protect cattle in the American West.

For property rights in a resource to provide the right incentive to its owner, these rights must be definable, defendable, and divestible. Owners must be free to transfer their property rights to others at will, which encourages property owners to consider the environmental concerns of other potential resource owners. Thus, for example, a timber company may take better care of its land if there is a prospect of selling or leasing that land to outdoor recreational users or others who also will care how the land is managed.

FME places the protection or property rights at the heart of pollution control as well. Common law liability rules, such as prohibitions on "nuisance" and "trespass," create liability for environmental harms. Where property rights are protected, an upstream polluter can be sued by a downstream property owner for money damages and injunctive relief because to harm someone's property by polluting it is no more acceptable than vandalizing it—and this result provides additional incentives for sound resource stewardship.

Although the common law liability approach to pollution has largely been abandoned in the United States and Canada in favor of administrative regulations, it is still in use in much of England. The prospect of litigation from downstream property owners discourages companies from polluting.

Litigation against polluters is not always possible. Proof of harm, identifying the source of a given pollution problem, and the costs of litigation can all discourage downstream property owners from taking action against an upstream polluter. Some argue that such problems can be overcome through the creation of associations and other entities that specialize in the protection of property rights from environmental harm. In England, for example, an association of fishing clubs is extremely active in policing the rights of its members and taking legal action against polluters.

Another element of the libertarian approach to environmental issues is a hostility toward government programs that cause environmental harm. Numerous environmental problems are caused or exacerbated by governmental actions that introduce inefficiencies or subsidize polluting activity. In the United States, government agencies are among the nation's largest polluters. Research by Mikhail Bernstam, published in his book *The Wealth of Nations and the Environment*, also documented that those nations with the most regulated and controlled economies, such as the former Soviet Bloc countries, also had the worst environmental problems. Without market institutions, there was little incentive for firms to reduce material use or improve productive efficiency, let alone engage in stewardship of environmental resources. The results, in many parts of the former Soviet Bloc, are environmental problems far more severe than anywhere in the West.

FME also applies the insights of economists such as James Buchanan and F. A. Hayek to argue that governmental agencies have neither the incentives nor the information to properly manage environmental concerns. Terry Anderson, among others, noted that the records of most governmental agencies entrusted with land management responsibilities are dismal. Lacking the price signals of profit and loss, public officials rarely have the information they need to plan complex systems and allocate resources. Even well-intentioned government managers are unable to anticipate how various institutional arrangements will affect the incentives that motivate individuals. Many economists also note that environmental agencies, no less than other governmental agencies, are subject to political pressure by economic interest groups engaged in rent seeking.

It is difficult to apply the FME paradigm to some environmental resources. Regional air pollution, for example, is difficult to address because of the inability to define and defend individualized property rights in air. Regional airsheds may well be unfenceable commons. To address this sort of problem, libertarian environmentalists endorse various policies that seek to replicate the institutional arrangements provided by markets. Two quasimarket approaches that are often discussed are the imposition of "pollution taxes" and the creation of quasiproperty rights in emissions, such as tradable emission permits that can be bought and sold. Another approach is the creation of an association or cooperative enterprise to manage the resource, much like a condominium association manages the common areas of a condominium. This property-based approach has been used for various land and water bodies and might be applicable to local or regional airsheds. Where pollution problems are the result of multiple small sources, such as individual automobiles, such aggregation can reduce the transaction costs involved with property-based approaches to environmental protection.

This market-based strategy is pervasive in discussions of environmental policy today. The benefits of FME approaches to environmental protection can be seen in many resources that are managed through property institutions. Examples include the creation of property rights in instream water flows in the western United States, which has empowered environmentalists to purchase water to protect fish; the establishment of property interests in wildlife in much of southern Africa; and the use of property rights in fisheries in New Zealand, Iceland, and parts of the United States. In each of these instances, the creation of property interests in environmental resources has created powerful economic incentives for sound resource stewardship and protection. The challenge for free-market environmental advocates is to develop creative means of extending market institutions to a broader range of environmental resources.

JHA

See also Coase, Ronald H.; Development, Economic; Externalities; Market Failure; Private Property

Further Readings

Adler, Jonathan H., ed. *Ecology, Liberty, & Property: A Free Market Environmental Reader*. Washington, DC: Competitive Enterprise Institute, 2000.

Anderson, Terry L. "The New Resource Economics: Old Ideas and New Applications." *American Journal of Agricultural Economics* 64 no. 5 (1982): 928–934.

Anderson, Terry L., and P. J. Hill. "The Evolution of Property Rights: A Study of the American West." *Journal of Law and Economics* 18 no. 1 (1975): 163–179.

Anderson, Terry L., and Donald R. Leal. *Free Market Environmentalism*. San Francisco: Pacific Research Institute for Public Policy and Westview Press, 1991.

Coase, Ronald H. "The Problem of Social Cost" and "Notes on the Problem of Social Cost." *The Firm, the Market and the Law*. Chicago: University of Chicago Press, 1988.

Demsetz, Harold. "Toward a Theory of Property Rights." *Journal of Law and Economics* 9 (1966).

Hardin, Garrett. "The Tragedy of the Commons." *Science* 162 (1968): 1243–1248.

Meiners, Roger E., and Andrew P. Morris, eds. *The Common Law and the Environment*. Lanham, MD: Rowman & Littlefield, 2000.

Smith, Fred L., Jr. "A Free-Market Environmental Program." *Cato Journal* 11 no. 3 (1992): 457–476.

Smith, Robert J. "Private Solutions to Conservation Problems." *The Theory of Market Failure: A Critical Examination*. Tyler Cowen, ed. Fairfax, VA: George Mason University Press, 1988. 341–360.

Yandle, Bruce. *Common Sense and Common Law for the Environment*. Lanham, MD: Rowman & Littlefield, 1999.

EPICUREANISM

Epicureanism has reference to a philosophical movement of some popularity in ancient Greece and Rome. It based itself on the teachings of the Athenian philosopher Epicurus (341–271 B.C.) and propounded an atomistic cosmology, a hedonistic ethics, and a contractarian social theory. Epicurus was a prolific writer whose collected writings are said to have run to 300 volumes. However, nearly all of his writings are lost and must be reconstructed from reports of other classical authors such as Cicero and Lucretius.

With regard to the natural sciences, Epicureans defended an empiricist methodology in which all appeal to supernatural causation or divine intervention was decisively rejected in favor of explanations invoking the interactions of atomic particles. Despite this apparently materialist approach, Epicureans affirmed human autonomy, arguing that those who embraced purely mechanistic accounts of human action were implicitly refuting themselves by the very act of freely and purposefully asserting their viewpoint.

In ethics, Epicureans enshrined pleasure as the supreme value, but regarded the pleasures of inner tranquility and freedom from mental turmoil as being of far greater importance than merely physical pleasures; they urged extirpation of unnecessary desires and urged men to be content with modest material wealth. Because human beings ceased to exist when their component atoms were scattered, and inasmuch as there was no survival of the spirit beyond death, death was not to be feared because only pain was something to be dreaded and death meant the cessation of all experience and, hence, was painless. In the meanwhile, however, Epicureans counseled that men withdraw from politics and public life to pursue the private goals of friendship and philosophical discussion.

Epicurean social theory anticipated many conclusions that later marked classical liberalism. They were thoroughgoing defenders of spontaneous order, in both the social and physical realms. Just as Epicureans developed a rudimentary theory of natural selection to explain the apparent teleology of natural phenomena without invoking a divine designer, so they attempted to account for the emergence of beneficial social institutions without hypothesizing wise prehistoric legislators. In modern terminology, they regarded such institutions as the result of human action, but not of human design. For example, Epicureans argued that language could not have been anybody's conscious invention because whoever invented it would have had no way of communicating his invention to others. Instead, language must have evolved out of the gradual refinement of natural cries and gestures.

Epicureans also were among the pioneers of social contract theory. Against the mainstream of ancient ethics, Epicureans maintained that moral virtue was valuable not for its own sake, but as a strategic means by which each individual could secure his own happiness. Justice was regarded as originating in a mutually advantageous agreement of rational egoists not to harm or be harmed by one another. Those who clearly saw the benefits arising out of such a contract were motivated to abide by it without need for the additional sanction of punishment. Indeed, some Epicurean writers looked forward to a day when enlightened self-interest would be so widely understood that laws, military defenses, and other means of coercive enforcement would no longer be necessary.

Epicureans were criticized by their contemporaries for taking a purely instrumental attitude toward other people, but they denied the charge and insisted that it was rational for us to care about others for their own sake because only by cultivating such an attitude in ourselves would we attain most pleasure in the long run.

Among the classical liberal thinkers to acknowledge Epicureanism as a major source of inspiration are David Hume, Thomas Jefferson, and John Stuart Mill.

RL

See also Cicero; Contractarianism/Social Contract; Hume, David; Jefferson, Thomas; Mill, John Stuart; Spontaneous Order

Further Readings

Long, A. A., and Sedley, D. N. *The Hellenistic Philosophers: Volume I. Translations of the Principal Sources with Philosophical Commentary*. Cambridge: Cambridge University Press, 1987.

Mitsis, Phillip. *Epicurus' Ethical Theory: The Pleasures of Invulnerability*. Ithaca, NY: Cornell University Press, 1988.

Nichols, James H. *Epicurean Political Philosophy: The De Rerum Natura of Lucretius*. Ithaca, NY: Cornell University Press, 1976.

EPSTEIN, RICHARD A. (1943–)

Richard A. Epstein, a law professor and legal theorist, teaches at the University of Chicago Law School and is a senior fellow at the Hoover Institution at Stanford University. He is one of the leading legal scholars in the United States and a prominent libertarian author.

Epstein's work on eminent domain brought him fame when Senator Joseph Biden held up a copy of Epstein's book *Takings* during the 1991 confirmation hearings of Clarence Thomas to the U.S. Supreme Court. According to Biden, judges who agreed with the central thesis of the book—that the federal government should be more vigilant about compensating people when their property is taken for public use—were unfit to sit on the Supreme Court. Epstein has said that he "took some pride" in being criticized for his position.

> But I took even more pride in the fact that, during the [Stephen] Breyer hearings, there were no such theatrics, even as the nominee was constantly questioned on whether he agreed with the Epstein position on deregulation, as if that position could not be held by responsible people.

Epstein also has challenged established wisdom on employment discrimination laws, arguing that government intervention in employment contracts is unnecessary and even undesirable. "Labor markets raise *neither* of the two problems on which a principled case for legal intervention may properly rest," he has written.

> There are neither the holdout, coordination, or public good problems that justify government coercion and control so long as compensation is paid to regulated parties; nor are there the problems with externalities in the use of force or fraud against strangers that justify the use of state force without compensation.

Moreover, if one is interested in redistributing income to groups that have traditionally suffered discrimination, then antidiscrimination laws are a blunt tool to use toward that end. A combination of tax and welfare systems, keyed to individual wealth, would be more simple and effective, Epstein argues.

Although Epstein's discussions of eminent domain and antidiscrimination laws may appear radical to some observers, they in fact reveal how his worldview differs from those libertarians who see themselves as more uncompromising in their views. Epstein is no anarchist, nor does he believe that government action should be confined to protecting people from violence. In other words, he is no advocate of a night watchman state. Instead, he argues that the state must intervene in the provision of key public goods, such as supplying the nation's infrastructure in transportation and energy to overcome coordination problems among private interests. "I do not think that 'free markets,' let alone 'capitalism,' supplies the answer to all the questions of social organization," Epstein writes. "Markets depend on governments; governments of course depend on markets. The key question is not to exclude one or the other from the mix, but to assign to each its proper role."

Epstein has made his consequentialist case for classical liberalism in three recent books: *Simple Rules for a Complex World, Principles for a Free Society*, and *Skepticism and Freedom.* He also has written extensively on health care, arguing that a less regulated system would provide better access and service to a greater number of people.

AS

See also Affirmative Action; Economics, Chicago School of; Eminent Domain/Takings; Health Care; Market Failure; Racism

Further Readings

Chapman, Stephen. "Takings Exception: Maverick Legal Scholar Richard Epstein on Property, Discrimination, and the Limits of State Action." *Reason* (April 1995): 36–42.

Epstein, Richard A. *Forbidden Grounds: The Case Against Employment Discrimination Laws.* Cambridge, MA: Harvard University Press, 1992.

———. *Principles for a Free Society: Reconciling Individual Liberty with the Common Good.* Reading, MA: Perseus Books, 1998.

———. *Simple Rules for a Complex World.* Cambridge, MA: Harvard University Press, 1995.

———. *Skepticism and Freedom: A Modern Case for Classical Liberalism.* Chicago: University of Chicago Press, 2003.

———. *Takings: Private Property and the Power of Eminent Domain.* Cambridge, MA: Harvard University Press, 1985.

EQUALITY

Within the libertarian tradition, equality has primarily signified an equality of individual rights. This idea, which took centuries to develop, owed a good deal to post-Renaissance interest in the ancient philosophies of Stoicism and Epicureanism.

Stoics, working from the premise that all human beings possess the faculty of reason, maintained that each individual had an equal ability to live a virtuous life. Epicurus and his followers were early proponents of a social contract, a hypothetical model in which every individual has self-interested reasons to respect the equal rights of every other individual. Also important, especially in Anabaptist, Quaker, and other radical offshoots of Reformation thought, was the Christian doctrine that all human beings are equal in the sight of God.

The democratic implications of a theory of equal rights came to the fore in England during the 1640s, the era of the English Civil Wars. Libertarians such as John Lilburne, Richard Overton, and William Walwyn defended religious freedom (in some cases even for atheists), free trade, the rights of private property, and government by consent. Ironically perhaps, these libertarians are still known as *Levellers*, originally a term of opprobrium given to them by their political enemies who accused them of wishing to level all differences of property.

In fact, the Levellers were opposed to any kind of egalitarian socialism. While defending private property, based on the natural right of self-proprietorship, they rejected the doctrine that substantial property holders—especially in land—should enjoy special political rights. As Colonel Rainborough put it during the "Putney debates," a public exchange between the Levellers and Cromwellians: "For I really think that the poorest he that is in England hath a life to live, as the greatest he . . . that the poorest man in England is not at all bound in strict sense to that government that he hath not had a voice to put himself under."

The most influential statement of what later became the libertarian theory of equal rights appeared in John Locke's *Second Treatise of Government.* According to Locke, "all Men are by Nature equal." The state of nature (that "State all Men are naturally in") is not only a "State of perfect freedom," but "a State also of Equality, wherein all the Power and Jurisdiction is reciprocal, no one having more than another. . . ." The most fundamental among these equal rights is the right of every individual "to his own Person, which no other man has power over, but the free Disposal of it lies in himself."

The import of Locke's notion of equal rights may be described as *political reductionism.* This theory states that all rights and powers claimed by government must ultimately be reducible to the equal rights and legitimate powers of individuals as they would exist in a state of nature. Equal rights can be transferred, delegated, or alienated only through consent, according to Locke. Therefore, no person can lay claim to a natural privilege of sovereignty, which supposedly entitles him or her to rule others without their consent. Nor (as Samuel Pufendorf and others had argued) can a government lay claim to special rights that no individual could possibly possess.

Locke's theory of equal rights had radical implications that would later manifest themselves in the American and French Revolutions. But even critics of these revolutionary tendencies would often defend some version of equal freedom with a distinctively Lockean flavor. For example, according to Edmund Burke,

> [Social] liberty . . . is that state of things in which liberty is secured by the equality of restraint. A constitution of things in which the liberty of no one man, and no body of men, and no number of men, can find means to trespass on the liberty of any person, or any description of persons, in the society.

Similarly, Immanuel Kant, after defining *freedom* as "independence from the constraint of another's will," argued that authentic freedom must be "compatible with the freedom of everyone else in accordance with a universal law."

This idea received one of its most influential formulations in Herbert Spencer's "Law of Equal Freedom" (in *Social Statics,* 1851). According to Spencer, "Every man has freedom to do all he wills, provided he infringes not the equal freedom of any other man." The "freedom of each must be bounded by the similar freedom of all," and "every man may claim the fullest liberty to exercise his faculties compatible with the possession of like liberty by every other man."

This approach to equal rights stands in stark contrast to various doctrines of *egalitarianism* as this term is commonly understood. For instance, in *Power and Market* (1970), the libertarian economist Murray Rothbard argues that "the diversity of mankind is a basic postulate of our knowledge of human beings," so "it can be shown that equality of income is an *impossible* goal for mankind." Egalitarianism is "a literally senseless social philosophy."

Another libertarian critique of egalitarianism, one that has profoundly influenced the course of contemporary political theory, appears in Robert Nozick's *Anarchy, State, and Utopia* (1974). Nozick criticizes "welfare economics" and other theories of egalitarianism that are defended in the name of "distributive justice," defending instead what he calls an "entitlement theory" of justice.

A libertarian theory of justice is not patterned or coercively imposed according to some notion of end results. According to Nozick, the "entitlement theory of justice in distribution is *historical;* whether a distribution is just depends upon how it came about." If property titles were originally acquired by just means and if they have since been transferred voluntarily, then the resulting state of affairs is just even if it does not conform to the moral ideal of social planners. Hence, "The entitlement conception of justice in holdings makes no presumption in favor of [material] equality, or any other overall end state or patterning. It cannot merely be *assumed* that equality must be built into any theory of justice."

GHS

See also Epicureanism; Levellers; Locke, John; Nozick, Robert; Rawls, John; Stoicism

Further Readings

Cicero, Marcus Tullius. *On Duties.* M. T. Griffin and E. M. Atkins, eds. Cambridge: Cambridge University Press, 1991.

Locke, John. *Second Treatise of Government.* Peter Laslett, ed. Cambridge: Cambridge University Press, 2005.

Lucretius. *On the Nature of Things.* Frank O. Copley, trans. New York: W. W. Norton, 1977.

Nozick, Robert. *Anarchy, State, and Utopia.* New York: Basic Books, 1974.

Rothbard, Murray. *Power and Market.* Kansas City, MO: Sheed Andrews & McMeel, 1970.

Sharp, Andrew, ed. *The English Levellers.* Cambridge: Cambridge University Press, 1998.

Spencer, Herbert. *Social Statics.* London: Chapman, 1851.

Vonnegut, Kurt. "Harrison Bergeron." *Welcome to the Monkey House*. K. Vonnegut, ed. New York: Dial Press Trade Paperbacks, 2006.

———. *The Sirens of Titan*. New York: Dial Press Trade Paperbacks, 2006.

EUTHANASIA

Euthanasia engenders debates over courage and cowardice, glory and defeat, and dignity and suffering. Ultimately, the euthanasia debate is about who we are as human beings. Are we masters of ourselves, if not of our universe, or are we more like subjects of a ruler whose reasoning we struggle to understand? Are we Prometheus or are we Job?

All concerns over end-of-life decision making ultimately are concerns about euthanasia. For those who follow in the footsteps of Job, *euthanasia* is a dangerous concept, and the word itself has only negative connotations. For those who follow in the footsteps of Prometheus, the word *euthanasia* harks back to its original meaning in the Greek: εὐθανασία: εὐ, eu, meaning "good," and θάνατος, thanatos, meaning "death."

In some major respects, the moral foundations of our culture are in direct conflict with each other. Joseph Campbell explains that "the ultimate loyalty of the Bible . . . is not to mankind but to God . . . , whereas the sympathy of the Greeks, finally, is for man; and the respect of the Greeks, for man's reason." Modern Western traditions are now a mix of these two diametrically opposed perspectives. Campbell continues: "Monday, Tuesday, Wednesday, Thursday, Friday, and Saturday, we are humanists with the Greeks; Sunday, for half an hour, Levantines, with the Prophets: and the following Monday, groaning on some equally troubled psychotherapist's couch."

No ethical debate in our culture exemplifies this fundamental philosophical contradiction more than the debate over end-of-life decision making. From Karen Ann Quinlan to Terri Schiavo, families, courts, legislatures, and society in general continue this ancient debate. When is it acceptable to allow individuals to hasten their own deaths or for them to request that others do it for them? Is it ever acceptable to hasten the death of another without their consent or even against their will? What if the person has left no indication of his wishes or is incapable of making this decision because of diminished capacity?

In all ancient cultures, it was thought that the gods held considerable influence over man's fate. However, in some cultures, like the Greek, humans took pride in challenging their deities, whereas in others, like the Judeo-Christian culture, humans took pride in unquestioning obedience. To the Greeks, *euthanasia* meant having the courage to control fate in the face of inevitable death, defeat, or indignity, and

to do so was merciful and/or honorable. To ancient Jews and Christians, euthanasia, regardless of the circumstances, was an affront to God, a challenge to his ultimate authority, and neither noble nor courageous. The modern-day confusion of these traditions has muddled our vocabulary and our laws with respect to end-of-life decisions in general and euthanasia in particular.

The terminology used to discuss euthanasia is constantly in flux. Usually, people signal their acceptance of some aspect of euthanasia by calling it something else (e.g., *letting die, letting nature take its course, assisted dying, death with dignity, mercy medication,* and *aid in dying*). Conversely, people signal their disapproval of forms of letting die or assisted dying by calling it *euthanasia*.

Broadly speaking, euthanasia is the killing of a person, including possibly oneself or an animal, in a merciful way for the purpose of relieving suffering or some other undesirable condition. Some of the most common limitations on what is considered euthanasia include the following claims: Euthanasia is distinguishable from suicide because in euthanasia someone kills another, whereas suicide is, by definition, self-inflicted. Euthanasia is not murder because the killing done in euthanasia is done with the intention of alleviating pain and suffering, not inflicting it. Treatment refusals that result in death are neither euthanasia nor suicide because in such cases nature or God is the direct cause of death. Similarly, cases where mercy medication results in death are not euthanasia because the death is only incidental to the primary goal of easing pain. Although each of these distinctions holds moral sway with those making them, they are of secondary importance to some more fundamental distinctions that need to be made.

There are five basic concepts that need to be understood and agreed on before any discussion of euthanasia or end-of-life decisions in general can proceed with coherent results.

1. *Voluntary euthanasia* is the term used for requesting to be killed or killing oneself to escape some inevitable ill fate. The killing is voluntary because either the person does it himself or requests that another do it for him. The ill fate that is usually at issue is intractable pain, a terminal illness (imminent death from an incurable disease), or an irreparable harm to one's dignity. For most people, the term *euthanasia* does not apply unless at least the first two of these conditions are met; killing another merely to preserve that person's dignity is usually considered murder, and to kill oneself under such circumstances is suicide.

Currently under U.S. law, ending one's own life is only allowed through the refusal of treatment and generally only if death is imminent even if treatment were continued. There are two exceptions: The first is that the termination of treatment is sometimes allowed in cases where death is not imminent (e.g., when a patient is in a persistent vegetative state). The second is that a person is sometimes, albeit rarely, allowed to end his own life by taking medication rather than refusing it (e.g., mercy medication and aid in dying). Mercy medication is allowed in several U.S. states. It refers to the use of dangerously high doses of pain medication to relieve the pain of dying patients. Aid in dying is currently allowed in only one state (i.e., in Oregon, competent adult citizens suffering from incurable diseases with a prognosis of 6 months or less to live may, if various additional conditions are met, legally obtain a deadly dose of medication for the purpose of killing themselves).

Voluntary euthanasia requires a voluntary act, decision-making capacity, and informed consent. A person must overtly express his wishes, usually to a health care provider, family member, or friend. Advance directives are a formal way of recording such wishes and/or appointing a surrogate decision maker for situations where patients cannot make decisions themselves. Under the Oregon Death with Dignity Act, patients must be capable of taking the lethal medication themselves; advance directives are not an option. Voluntary euthanasia can be either active or passive.

2. *Involuntary euthanasia* is the killing of someone against their will to help them escape some inevitable ill fate. When practiced on humans, involuntary euthanasia is generally considered murder and illegal. One exception is capital punishment, which some people consider a form of involuntary euthanasia. Involuntary euthanasia can be either active or passive.

3. *Nonvoluntary euthanasia* is killing someone who is incapable of giving consent to help them escape some inevitable ill fate. Both involuntary and nonvoluntary euthanasia are sometimes called *mercy killing*. Euthanizing animals is appropriately called nonvoluntary because animals cannot communicate their approval or disapproval, let alone understand what is happening. The same would be true of very young children or anyone who is permanently unconscious or sufficiently mentally incapacitated not to understand the ramifications of what is being considered. Currently under U.S. law, nonvoluntary euthanasia is legal under limited circumstances. Legally recognized surrogates are sometimes allowed to refuse or withdraw treatment from incompetent patients who either did not leave any indications of their end-of-life preferences or never had the capacity to make such decisions. Nonvoluntary euthanasia can be either active or passive.

4. *Active euthanasia,* which can be voluntary, involuntary, or nonvoluntary, involves an agent actively participating in hastening or causing death. Usually there must be a definitively identified physical action that is the cause of death. For example, swallowing deadly pills or giving oneself a lethal injection are examples of active voluntary euthanasia. Assisted suicide, if done with valid informed consent, is active voluntary euthanasia, while assisted "suicide" if done contrary to a person's wishes is active involuntary euthanasia. Assisted suicide, if done where no consent is possible, is active nonvoluntary euthanasia. Killings associated with genocides predicated on ridding society of what proponents described as *bad* or *useless* elements of society are a form of active involuntary euthanasia.

5. *Passive euthanasia,* which can be voluntary, involuntary, or nonvoluntary, involves allowing a predictable death to occur without intervening to stop it. Often passive euthanasia is called *letting die.* Voluntary passive euthanasia is legal in the United States if a patient's prognosis is hopeless. The refusal of treatment or request for withdrawal of treatment can be made directly by the patient at the time of treatment or in advance through a written directive. Involuntary passive euthanasia is illegal, but sometimes occurs (e.g., several health care professionals have been tried for mercy killings in cases where the patient or his or her surrogate clearly indicated a wish to continue treatment and the professional in charge of the patient's health care independently decided to let the patient die). Generally, withholding or not initiating life-saving treatment is illegal unless the patient or the patient's surrogate has consented. Thus, nonvoluntary, but not involuntary, passive euthanasia is only an option available to surrogate decision makers and even then usually requires a convincing argument for why hastening the patient's death is necessary to end some form of needless suffering.

In our society, the active/passive distinction is the focus of much of the euthanasia debate, but from a libertarian perspective, only the voluntary/involuntary distinction is of any great significance. Many courts have held that the withdrawal of a breathing or feeding tube is letting die (i.e., passive euthanasia) and therefore acceptable. Yet withdrawing treatment is clearly an overt action (the courts have extended the notion of acceptable passive euthanasia to this obviously active act because they do not want people to hesitate to initiate treatment for fear it will be impossible to stop it later). In contrast, some states that allow the withholding and withdrawing of other types of treatment have passed laws prohibiting the withholding and/or withdrawing of nutrition and hydration even if a patient has voluntarily expressed a wish to refuse such treatment. Some states never allow such decisions, and others only allow them of competent patients, but not formerly competent patients (i.e., the state will not accept any form of advance directive as justification for the withholding or withdrawing of nutrition and hydration).

These preferences for passive over active forms of euthanasia are carried over into discussions of voluntary, involuntary, and nonvoluntary euthanasia. Nonvoluntary or even involuntary euthanasia, brought about by treating a patient with large amounts of pain medication in an attempt to relieve suffering (i.e., mercy medication), is allowed in some states. In such cases, the killing is considered passive in the sense that the patient's death is incidental to the physician's attempt to control pain. Conversely, voluntary euthanasia is generally only allowed if passive. The one notable exception is Oregon, where physician-assisted suicide for terminally ill patients is legal.

Given these distinctions, it is logical, based on libertarian first principles of individual liberty and self-determination, that a libertarian society would support an individual's right to choose either passive or active euthanasia, regardless of whether he were terminally ill, and equally condemn any form of involuntary euthanasia whether passive or active and no matter how close to death a person may be. The only proper role of government would be to ensure voluntariness by creating safeguards to ensure that decisions regarding euthanasia be made by competent individuals who understand the consequences of their intended actions and give their full and informed consent freely. As long as these criteria are met, libertarian societies also would allow individuals to arrange for euthanasia while competent to be carried out at a later date should they become incapable of making their wishes known. For example, someone could have an advance directive requesting what could be understood as active nonvoluntary euthanasia (e.g., the advance directive requests active euthanasia should its author ever become permanently unconscious or ever advance to stage 3 of Alzheimer's disease).

Libertarian theory, however, does not provide clear guidance with respect to incompetent individuals. Temporary incompetence can be dealt with by emphasizing efforts to bring about competency. For example, under certain circumstances, it may be appropriate to wait for children to mature sufficiently to make their own decisions. Patients who are unconscious, paralyzed, or heavily sedated to facilitate treatment could, if at all possible, be revived to assess their end-of-life wishes. But what if it is impossible to get informed consent?

A presumption that someone close to the incompetent patient should make decisions for that patient provides a workable solution. Although not necessitated by libertarian theory, such surrogate decision making is not inconsistent with libertarian theory. Having someone close to the incompetent patient, usually a family member, make decisions is preferable to having a court, a committee, or some other governmental entity making the decision. There is no doubt that family responsibilities can cause conflicts of interest, and therefore it should be possible to challenge a surrogate's decision. However, anyone challenging a surrogate's motives should bear the burden of showing that the surrogate has no reasonable grounds for making the proposed decision. When the choice is letting the family, however defined, decide based on its own cultural and religious norms, as opposed to letting the government apply some generalized independent standard of what is in the patient's best interest, the choice should be clear: It is preferable to keep such personal and difficult decisions as private and as free of the interference of others as possible.

Whether you wish to live or die like Prometheus or like Job should be your decision or, barring your competence, the decision of those who love you, not a decision made by anyone else through government fiat or otherwise.

SFR

See also Bioethics; Health Care; Individual Rights; Paternalism

Further Readings

Arras, John D., and Bonnie Steinbock, eds. *Ethical Issues in Modern Medicine.* 5th ed. Mountain View, CA: Mayfield, 1999.

Campbell, Joseph. "Mythological Themes in Creative Literature and Art." *Joseph Campbell. The Mythic Dimension: Selected Essays 1959–1987.* Antony Van Couvering and The Joseph Campbell Foundation, eds. New York: HarperCollins, 1997. 189.

Engelhardt, H. Tristram, Jr. *The Foundations of Bioethics.* New York: Oxford University Press, 1986.

Foley, Elizabeth Price. *Liberty for All: Reclaiming Individual Privacy in a New Era of Public Morality.* New Haven, CT: Yale University Press, 2006.

Hall, Mark A., Mary Anne Bobinski, and David Orentlicher. *Bioethics and Public Health Law.* New York: Aspen, 2005.

Jonsen, Albert R., Mark Siegler, and William J. Winslade. *Clinical Ethics: A Practical Approach to Ethical Decisions in Clinical Medicine.* 6th ed. New York: McGraw-Hill, 2006.

EVOLUTIONARY PSYCHOLOGY

The goal of research in evolutionary psychology is to discover, understand, and map the human mind as well as to explore the implications of these new discoveries for other fields. The eventual aim is to map human nature—that is, the species-typical information-processing architecture of the human brain.

Like all cognitive scientists, when evolutionary psychologists refer to the *mind,* they mean the set of information-processing devices, embodied in neural tissue, that are responsible for all conscious and nonconscious mental activity and that generate all behavior. Like other psychologists, evolutionary psychologists test hypotheses about the design of these information-processing devices—these programs—using laboratory methods from experimental cognitive and social psychology, as well as methods drawn from experimental economics, neuropsychology, and cross-cultural field work.

What allows evolutionary psychologists to go beyond traditional approaches in studying the mind is that they make active use in their research of an often-overlooked fact: That the programs comprising the human mind were designed by natural selection to solve the adaptive problems faced by our hunter-gatherer ancestors—problems like finding a mate, cooperating with others, hunting, gathering, protecting children, avoiding predators, and so on. Natural selection tends to produce programs that solve problems like these reliably, quickly, and efficiently. Knowing this information allows one to approach the study of the mind like an engineer. One starts with a good specification of an adaptive information-processing problem and develops a task analysis of that problem. This process allows one to see what properties a program would have to have in order to solve that problem well. This approach allows one to generate testable hypotheses about the structure of the programs that comprise the mind.

Evolutionary psychology dates back to Darwin. It emerged in its present form during the 1980s and was motivated by new developments and insights from a series of different fields, among them,

- the cognitive revolution that, for the first time in human history, provided a precise language for describing mental mechanisms as programs that process information;
- advances in paleoanthropology, hunter-gatherer studies, and primatology, which gave access to data about the adaptive problems with which our ancestors were confronted regarding how to survive and reproduce and the environments that were most conducive of this notion;
- research in animal behavior, linguistics, and neuropsychology, which showed that the mind was not a blank slate passively recording the world. (Indeed, it was discovered that organisms come factory-equipped with knowledge about the world, which allows them to learn some relationships easily and others only with great effort, if at all, and demonstrating that Skinner's hypothesis—that learning is a simple process governed by reward and punishment—was simply wrong); and
- evolutionary game theory, which revolutionized evolutionary biology, placing it on a more rigorous, formal foundation of replicator dynamics. This theory clarified how natural selection works, what counts as an adaptive function, and what the criteria are for calling a trait an adaptation.

A number of scientists realized that if one were careful about the causal connections between disciplines, these four new developments could be pieced together into a single integrated research framework in a way that had not been exploited before because the connections ran between fields, rather than cleanly within them. They called this framework *evolutionary psychology*. The framework that emerged from these advances can be summarized in six points.

First, each organ in the body evolved to serve a function: The intestines digest, the heart pumps blood, and the liver detoxifies poisons. The brain also is an organ, and its evolved function is to extract information from the environment and use that information to generate behavior and regulate physiology. From this perspective, the brain is a computer (i.e., a physical system that was designed to process information). Its programs were designed not by an engineer, but by natural selection, a causal process that retains and discards design features on the basis of how well they solve problems that affect reproduction.

The fact that the brain processes information is not an accidental side effect of some metabolic process. The brain was designed by natural selection to be a computer. Therefore, if one wants to describe its operation in a way that captures its evolved function, one needs to think of it as composed of programs that process information. The question then becomes, what programs are to be found in the human brain? What are the reliably developing, species-typical programs that, taken together, comprise the human mind?

Second, individual behavior is generated by this evolved computer in response to information that it extracts from the internal and external environment, including the social environment. To understand an individual's behavior, therefore, one needs to know both the information that the person registered and the structure of the programs that generated his or her behavior.

Third, the programs that comprise the human brain were sculpted over time by the ancestral environments and selection pressures experienced by the hunter-gatherers from whom we are descended. Each evolved program exists because it produced behavior that promoted the survival of our ancestors in a way better than alternative programs that arose during human evolutionary history. Evolutionary psychologists emphasize hunter-gatherer life because the evolutionary process is slow—it takes tens of thousands of years to build a program of any complexity. The Industrial Revolution—even the Agricultural Revolution—are mere eye blinks in evolutionary time, too short to have selected for new cognitive programs.

Fourth, although the behavior generated by our evolved programs would, on average, have been adaptive to ancestral environments, there is no guarantee that it will be so now. Modern environments differ importantly from ancestral ones—particularly when it comes to social behavior. We no longer live in small, face-to-face societies, in semi-nomadic bands of 50 to 100 people, many of whom were close relatives. Yet our cognitive programs were designed for that social world.

Fifth, and perhaps most important, the brain must be comprised of many different programs, each specialized for solving a different adaptive problem our ancestors faced (i.e., the mind cannot be a blank slate).

In fact, the same is true of any computationally powerful, multitasking computer. Consider the typical desktop computer. So many people analyze data and write prose that most computers come factory-equipped with a spreadsheet and a text editor. These two separate programs each have different computational properties because crunching numbers and writing prose are very different problems: The design features that make a program good at data analysis are not well suited to writing and editing articles, and vice versa. To accomplish both tasks well, the computer has two programs, each well designed for a specific task. The more functionally specialized programs it has, the more intelligent the computer is and the more things it can do. The same is true for people.

Our hunter-gatherer ancestors were, in effect, on a camping trip that lasted a lifetime, and they had to solve many different kinds of problems well to survive under those conditions. Design features that make a program good at choosing nutritious foods, for example, will be ill suited for finding a fertile mate. Different problems require different solutions. Many of these solutions—these evolved programs—will be domain-specific: well designed for processing information about certain domains of human life (e.g., potential mates) but not others (e.g., potential foods). This idea can be most clearly seen by using results from evolutionary game theory and data about ancestral environments to define adaptive problems and then carefully dissecting the computational requirements of any program capable of solving those problems.

Last, if one wants to understand human culture and society, one needs to understand these domain-specific programs. The mind is not like a video camera, passively recording the world, but imparting no content of its own. Domain-specific programs organize our experiences, create our inferences, inject certain recurrent concepts and motivations into our mental life, give us our passions, educate our moral sentiments, and provide cross-culturally universal frames of meaning that allow us to understand the actions and intentions of others. They cause us to think certain specific thoughts; they make certain ideas, feelings, and reactions seem reasonable, right, interesting, and memorable. Consequently, they play a key role in determining which ideas and customs will easily spread from mind to mind and which will not. That is, they play a crucial role in shaping human culture.

The view that humans reliably develop a large number of functionally specialized, domain-specific programs that structure human learning, inference, and choice has stirred the most debate. Most research in the social sciences is implicitly guided by the *Standard Social Sciences Model* (SSSM), and a central tenet of the SSSM is that few, if any, programs of this kind exist. The SSSM assumes that the evolved architecture of the human mind is a tabula rasa equipped with a small number of content-free programs that operate uniformly across domains. If true, then all the content of our thoughts and feelings would derive externally from the social and physical environments. None would reflect the operation of a rich human nature.

During the 20th century, many failed experiments in social engineering, especially those implemented by communist regimes, were rooted in the SSSM assumption that human desires, emotions, and motivations are infinitely plastic social constructions that can be easily molded into any form.

Instincts are often thought of as the diametric opposite of reasoning. But the reasoning programs that evolutionary psychologists have been discovering are specialized for solving adaptive problems. In addition, they reliably develop in all normal human beings without any conscious effort and in the absence of formal instruction. These programs are applied without any awareness of their underlying logic and are distinct from more general abilities to process information or behave intelligently. In other words, they have all the hallmarks of what we usually think of as an instinct. In fact, one can think of these specialized circuits as *reasoning instincts*. They make certain kinds of inferences just as easy, effortless, and natural to us as humans, as spinning a web is to a spider or building a dam is to a beaver.

For example, evolutionary psychologists have found that the mind reliably develops programs that are functionally specialized for reasoning about social exchange, which include a subroutine for cheater detection. This latter program is neurally isolable: After brain damage, a person can have a deficit in their ability to detect cheaters, yet have a normal IQ and be able to successfully solve reasoning problems that are logically isomorphic to those that involve cheater detection (but deal with a different adaptive domain). This evolved competence also is found cross-culturally: It is as robustly present in nonliterate hunter-horticulturalists in remote areas of the Amazon as it is in college-educated individuals from market economies. When problems are constructed such that the correct answer for detecting cheaters violates rules of inference drawn from formal logics, people everywhere follow the adaptive logic of social exchange in preference to logical rules. Evolved social exchange mechanisms provide the cognitive foundations of trade.

Like many results in evolutionary psychology, research indicating that the mind has a system functionally specialized for cheater detection cuts to the heart of debates on the nature of human reasoning and rationality. It raises the possibility that the power of human intelligence comes from bundling together a collection of diverse mechanisms, each of which is specialized for reasoning about a different adaptive domain.

This position directly challenges the assumption that human rationality is accomplished by a small set of content-free inference procedures drawn from logic, mathematics, or rational choice theory. It also challenges the "heuristics and biases" school of thought, in which human reasoning is viewed as riddled with errors and biases that prevent good judgment and decision making. For this reason, evolutionary psychology has awakened interest and debate not only in the cognitive sciences, psychology, and neuroscience, but in economics, law, anthropology, and philosophy—in every field that concerns itself with human rationality.

Many political theories and public policies rest on strong assumptions about human nature. As empirical investigations of human nature proceed, some will have to be abandoned. The assumptions about human nature, on which certain political theories are founded, will turn out to be incorrect; some policies will fail because their success requires human nature to be other than it is.

The position most central to libertarianism—that human relationships should be based on the voluntary consent of the individuals involved—makes few if any assumptions about human nature. However, these assumptions do play a role in libertarian thought. They may be found in some philosophical justifications of the libertarian position, in particular public policy recommendations, and in arguments about how institutions should be created that will preserve liberty over time. Libertarian theorists—like the Founding Fathers before them—will need to take human nature into account in deciding the best ways to implement liberty, property rights, and the rule of law.

LC and JT

See also Assurance and Trust; Culture; Industrial Revolution; Natural Law; Progress; Voluntarism; Wealth and Poverty

Further Readings

Cosmides, Leda, and J. Tooby. *Universal Minds: Understanding the New Science of Evolutionary Psychology.* New Haven, CT: Yale University Press, 2004.

Gigerenzer, Gerd, Peter M. Todd, and the ABC Research Group. *Simple Heuristics That Make Us Smart.* New York: Oxford University Press, 2000.

Pinker, Steven. *How the Mind Works.* New York: W. W. Norton, 1997.

Tooby, J., and L. Cosmides. "Psychological Foundations of Culture." *The Adapted Mind: Evolutionary Psychology and the Generation of Culture.* J. Barkow, L. Cosmides, and J. Tooby, eds. New York: Oxford University Press, 1992.

Wilkinson, Will. "Capitalism and Human Nature." *Cato Policy Report* 27 no. 1 (January/February 2005).

EXISTENTIALISM

"That individual": When Søren Kierkegaard suggested this epitaph for himself, he unknowingly summarized a diverse collection of ideas and philosophies that would later become known as *existentialism*. It has become a truism to observe that *existentialism* is impossible to define with precision. Many philosophers who have traditionally been called *existentialists* either did not apply this label to themselves or repudiated it altogether. In his excellent overview of existentialism, Luther J. Binkley points out that every person, according to Kierkegaard, "is subjectively very much an individual and has the inalienable right to be himself." This emphasis on the "primacy of the individual" is something that Kierkegaard and Nietzsche have in common, despite their many differences, and this theme recurs throughout the writings of philosophers who are called *existentialists*. In the words of Edward Tiryakian, "existential thought quite early insisted upon the needs peculiar to the individual, and in fact viewed those needs as having primacy over the needs of society."

The links between existentialism and libertarianism are theoretical and hypothetical, rather than historical and concrete. That is to say, although the emphasis on individuality that we find in existentialism has clear libertarian implications in the field of political theory, few existentialists have explicitly made this extrapolation. "In politics," Alasdair MacIntyre notes, "existentialism appears to be compatible with almost every possible standpoint." Kierkegaard was a conservative, Jaspers was a liberal, Sartre was a heretical Marxist, Heidegger was sympathetic to Nazism, and Nietzsche's political beliefs defy classification.

This diversity is to be expected in a tradition that arose in opposition to the formal academic philosophy of an earlier era. Although many existentialists have expressed libertarian sentiments—as when Nietzsche characterized the state as "the coldest of all cold monsters" that "bites with stolen teeth"—we will look in vain for a systematic libertarian theory from an existentialist perspective, however much the key insights of existentialism cry out for such a development.

Existentialism is best known through the aphorism "existence precedes essence." This phrase underscores the role of individual choice in existentialist philosophy. Man, unlike a rock or tree, does not have a fixed essence or nature. Man is in a continuous process of creating himself, of *becoming,* and this process entirely depends on his or her subjective choices. People create their own natures through the choices they make, which are not necessitated by society or other deterministic factors. As MacIntyre puts it: "If any single thesis could be said to constitute the doctrine of existentialism, it would be that the possibility of choice is the central fact of human existence."

Thus, although existentialism is often criticized for its supposed nihilism, owing to its rejection of objective moral standards, it also is true that existentialists have typically emphasized that individual responsibility comes with the ability to choose. Indeed, to many commentators, nothing seems more antithetical to the existentialist notion of self-creation that the state's attempts to shape our wishes and our nature.

GHS

See also Foucault, Michel; Individualism, Political and Ethical; Nietzsche, Friedrich; Rights, Theories of; State

Further Readings

Camus, Albert. *The Plague*. Stuart Gilbert, trans. New York: Knopf, 1948.
Nietzsche, Friedrich. *Beyond Good and Evil*. Marion Faber, trans. New York: Oxford University Press, 1998.
Sartre, Jean-Paul. *No Exit, and Three Other Plays*. New York: Vintage Books, 1955.

EXTERNALITIES

There is no universally accepted definition for the term *externality*, but that put forward by Harvey Rosen adequately conveys the principle. He writes that an externality occurs when "the activity of one entity (a person or a firm) directly affects the welfare of another in a way that is outside the market mechanism." Externalities may be negative (as when industrial pollution injures people's health or positive (as when the presence of a security guard whose function is to prevent theft from a store serves to protect you as well). In both cases, someone's welfare must be directly affected incidental to another's activity. Thus, externalities differ from altruism or spite. Additionally, the effect must be "outside the market mechanism," that is, not mediated by prices. The pecuniary externality created when incoming residents drive up housing prices, benefiting local homeowners and hurting tenants, is not a proper externality.

The presence of externalities is often considered a prima facie argument for remedial government intervention. In *The Economics of Social Welfare*, A. C. Pigou distinguished between the *private net product* of an activity and the *social net product* (which takes into account all externalities). When private net product exceeds social net product, production is greater than is efficient, and vice versa. Pigou proposed using damage remedies or taxes and subsidies, set at the amount of the external cost or benefit, to bring about efficiency by making market actors internalize the externalities of their behavior.

Ronald Coase questioned Pigou's solution, on the same efficiency grounds, in a path-breaking article, "The Problem of Social Cost." Coase noted that all externalities are reciprocal. Suppose factory production, through its pollution, reduces the quantity of fish, so that any increase in production comes at the expense of fish, and vice versa. Then giving the factory the right to pollute would harm the fishery, but giving the fishery the right to be free from pollution would harm the factory. Coase further pointed out that if the parties can negotiate, they will, under certain assumptions, come to the efficient arrangement regardless of who holds the rights: Either the factory will compensate the fishery for its reduced catch or the fishery will pay the factory to produce less or to introduce pollution control devices. Even if the parties cannot negotiate because of high transaction costs—so that the initial allocation of rights determines the ultimate outcome—who should pay is not obvious on efficiency grounds alone; the factory should not pay if it is the highest valued use of the resources involved. Thus, even when externalities exist, the Pigovian "polluter pays" solution is not necessarily efficient.

Whether an externality even exists depends on prevailing institutions. For instance, common pastures tend to be overgrazed because each of many users can increase the size of his herd without taking into account the harm (i.e., crowding out) he imposes on the other users—in economics, this is known as "the tragedy of the commons." Private ownership of the pasture, which lets the owner exclude other users, eliminates these externalities. Similarly, the costs of unhealthy behavior are mainly borne by the individual. However, when the government subsidizes medical care, unhealthy behavior generates fiscal externalities, harm to the taxpayer that may be alleviated by regulating health risks or eliminated by removing the subsidy.

Externalities are ubiquitous. Some people's happiness depends on whether they live in a drug-free world, how income is distributed, or whether the Grand Canyon is developed. Given such moral or ideological tastes, any human activity can generate externalities; one may choose to ignore such effects for moral or political reasons, but they are true externalities nonetheless. Moreover, some behavioral economists have recently noted that when individuals are time-inconsistent (e.g., smokers who always want to quit "tomorrow"), their present selves impose costs, which one might call *internalities*, on their future selves. On this view, even if smokers impose no costs on others, taxes on cigarettes or restrictions on their sale may improve the well-being of smokers by their own standards—a form of utilitarian paternalism.

The libertarian concern with preventing harm to others customarily implies that most justifiable interventions by the government in a libertarian society can be characterized as remedies for externalities. But given the pervasiveness of externalities, the breadth of harms they encompass, and their potential implications for sweeping government measures, libertarian theory is loath to consider the presence of negative externalities to be a sufficient condition for even ideal government interventions, much less an intervention in the real world, where it may be inappropriate to assume that government is omniscient, omnipotent, or benevolent. Free expression, for instance, will inevitably offend some, but such offense generally does not justify regulation in the libertarian framework for any of several reasons: because there exists a natural right of free expression, because offense cannot be accurately measured and is easy to falsify, because private bargaining may be more effective inasmuch as such regulation may make government dangerously powerful, and because such regulation may improperly encourage future feelings of offense among citizens. Among some libertarians, even the possibility of conferring positive externalities is not sufficient for government intervention. Suppose a reduction in the work day would make everyone better off. Such an arrangement is unlikely to arise voluntarily because of the large number of people involved and because it would require policing owing to the high rewards to being the lone holdout. John Stuart Mill, a utilitarian, argued in his book *Principles of Political Economy*, that regulation conferring such positive externalities was acceptable. However, without actual consent by all parties, it is hard to see how such regulation would fit into the framework of libertarian theory.

AV

See also Coase, Ronald H.; Environment; Market Failure; Nonaggression Axiom; Utilitarianism

Further Readings

Browning, Edgar K. "The Myth of Fiscal Externalities." *Public Finance Review* 27 no. 1 (January 1999): 3–18.

Coase, R. H. "The Problem of Social Cost." *Journal of Law and Economics* 3 no. 1 (October 1960): 1–44.

Gruber, Jonathan, and Botond Köszegi. "Is Addiction 'Rational'? Theory and Evidence." *Quarterly Journal of Economics* 116 no. 4 (November 2001): 1261–1303.

Hardin, Garrett. "The Tragedy of the Commons." *Science* 162 (December 13, 1968): 1243–1248.

Mill, John Stuart. *Principles of Political Economy*. London, New York: Longmans, Green, 1909 [1987].

Pigou, A. C. *The Economics of Welfare*. 4th ed. London: Macmillan, 1932. (New York: AMS Press, 1978.)

Rosen, Harvey S. *Public Finance*. 6th ed. Boston: McGraw-Hill/Irwin, 2002.

FAMILY

The social institution of the family has not received a great deal of attention from libertarian theorists. Because it is primarily concerned with political ideas, libertarianism has emphasized the legitimate limits of the state and the ability of voluntary associations to help achieve social goals. Those associations have first and foremost been those connected with the market economy. However, in the last decade or two, libertarians have paid increasing attention to the crucial role played by other social institutions, among them, although less so, the family. The family presents at least two sets of issues for libertarians: the relationship between the family and the state in general, and the tension between parental rights and the rights and interests of children.

As they do with many other institutions, libertarians can find no rationale for the state to intervene in providing support for the traditional family or in helping shape the various forms that the modern family takes. Historically, the relationship between the family and the state has been a close one. The institution of the family was not created by the state, but rather emerged out of prehistoric needs for forging cooperative networks of extended kin in order to survive in the face of scarce resources and to provide for the needs of helpless infants. However, much of the family's evolution in the last several hundred years has been shaped by the state's attempts to support or punish various forms that the family might take. Examples include everything from coverture laws (the merger of a woman's rights into those of her husband at marriage) and other restrictions on women as individuals, to regulations on who could marry whom, to tax code incentives that punish secondary earners (usually women) or that reward having larger families.

Much discussion about the degree to which the state should encourage or prevent particular familial forms has obscured a question that is more important to libertarians, which is ensuring that families are able to perform their evolved functions and are allowed to continue to evolve within the economic, political, and social contexts in which they operate. Families are in this way part of an ongoing, unplanned, social evolutionary process that is driven by the wants of individuals and their own judgments about how to accomplish the various ends they are pursuing. Just as libertarians believe, in general, that the diverse economic wants of individuals can be best met by the unplanned coordination of millions of individual judgments made possible by the market, so they have argued that families need the same degree of freedom to create forms that address their own needs.

The state, libertarians argue, should strive to remove itself from issues involving the family (beyond any role it might have in protecting individual rights), and, where it cannot remove itself, should seek to make itself neutral with respect to the kinds of families people might wish to form. The contemporary debate among libertarians over same-sex marriage illustrates these two principles. The ideal solution from a libertarian perspective is to get the state out of the marriage business altogether and turn marriage contracts into private arrangements between the parties involved, with religious institutions having their own freedom to sanctify whatever marriages they might desire. The more contentious debate among libertarians has been over whether it is an appropriate second-best solution to allow the state to grant marriage licenses to same-sex couples. For some libertarians, in a world where the state is intimately involved in the marriage process, it is incumbent on government to treat all citizens alike; therefore, it should offer marriage on equivalent terms to any two adults. For others, the desire for equal treatment extends the state's reach into marriage even further, which is especially misguided given the first-best alternative of getting out of marriage altogether.

The question of parental rights is a particularly vexing one for libertarians. Clearly, libertarian doctrine suggests that parents should have the right to make decisions about their children rather than other adults or the state. In the United States, constitutional jurisprudence has, since the 1920s (in *Meyer v. Nebraska* and *Pierce v. Society of Sisters*), largely upheld this principle as a matter of substantive due process under the 14th Amendment. At the same time, it also has recognized arguments centering on the "best interest of the child" in 1944 in *Prince v. Massachusetts*. Recognizing the primacy of parental rights, however, raises more questions than it answers; it does not tell us at what point children are "adult enough" to begin making their own decisions, regardless of parental preferences, nor at what point the exercise of parental rights spills over into abuse and neglect that can justify intervention by the state or others.

With respect to the first question, a minority of libertarians strongly defends the rights of children and believes they should be able to make more decisions at an earlier age than is commonly thought. Whether this perspective is simply part of a philosophy of childrearing or a political statement about the individual rights of children is not always clear. Libertarians have no clear answer to the issue of neglect. However, inasmuch as libertarians embrace the view that the burden of proof for intervention in the affairs of individuals rests with the state, it follows that there is a presumption that parents have both the knowledge and incentive to do what is right for their children. Furthermore, the state must demonstrate that by subjecting the children to its actions it will not bring about a situation that is worse than that which obtains at home. Just as the existence of imperfections in the market does not ipso facto mean state intervention will improve upon them neither does an imperfect family mean that interference with parental rights, especially by removing children from a home, will lead to an improvement in the life of the children. It also should be clear that claims of "family privacy" (as distinct from "parental rights") that in earlier generations permitted men to use violence, including rape, as a way to "control" their wives, is utterly contradictory to libertarianism, inasmuch as no reasonable understanding of the marriage contract can override the libertarian prohibition on the initiation of physical force or the threat thereof against competent adults.

Libertarianism rests on the premise that consensual behavior between adults should be free from interference by others. However, this view is complicated by what constitutes "consent" and "adulthood," which are both challenged by the presence of children and the nature of the tacit understandings that comprise familial relationships. These questions do not lend themselves to simple solutions and provide ongoing areas of debate among the libertarians who address them. That said, libertarians generally agree that the state should remain either absent or neutral in its treatment of the multiplicity of family forms that humans can develop and maintain and that when it comes to issues of abuse and neglect, the burden of proof is on the state to show that interference with parental rights is warranted and that the alternative solution is superior to the status quo.

SH

See also Bioethics; Children; Education; Feminism and Women's Rights; Marriage; Paternalism; Sexuality; Welfare State

Further Readings

Becker, Gary. *A Treatise on the Family*. Chicago: University of Chicago Press, 1981.

Evers, Williamson. "The Law of Omissions and Neglect of Children." *Journal of Libertarian Studies* 2 no. 1 (1978): 1–10.

Horwitz, Steven. "The Functions of the Family in the Great Society." *Cambridge Journal of Economics* 29 no. 5 (September 2005): 669–684.

Long, Roderick. "Beyond Patriarchy: A Libertarian Model of the Family." *Formulations* 4 no. 3 (Spring 1997). Available from http://libertariannation.org/a/f4312.html.

McElroy, Wendy, ed. *Freedom, Feminism, and the State*. 2nd ed. New York: Holmes and Meier, 1991.

Peden, Joseph R., and Fred R. Glahe, eds. *The American Family and the State*. San Francisco: Pacific Research Institute for Public Policy, 1986.

FASCISM

Critics of libertarianism often regard it as a species of fascism. Libertarianism seems both "extreme" and "right-wing," and what is fascism if not "right-wing extremism"? Even conservatives have repeated the charge: In his review of Ayn Rand's novel, Whittaker Chambers wrote that, "from almost any page of *Atlas Shrugged,* a voice can be heard, from painful necessity, commanding: 'To a gas chamber—go!' "

Libertarians justifiably object that fascism advocates unrestrained government power, not laissez-faire. However, this response often raises more questions than it is taken to answer. Inasmuch as libertarianism is anathema to the left, how can it simultaneously be diametrically opposed to the fascism of the extreme right? The study of comparative politics is able to shed a great deal of light with respect to this question. To regard libertarianism as akin to fascism presupposes that all political ideologies occupy some point on a political spectrum, the poles of which are communism on the left and fascism on the right. Political moderates are understandably sympathetic to this view. More surprising was the Communist International, which officially defined *fascism* as the "overt, terrorist dictatorship of the most reactionary, chauvinist and imperialist elements of finance capital" and pioneered the strategy of calling all of its opponents "fascists."

The problem with this totalitarian model is that fascism and communism are in many respects quite similar. Most tellingly, both advocated and imposed a significantly larger role for government in the economy. This fact is frankly admitted by thoughtful socialists like Carl Landauer:

> In a history of socialism, fascism deserves a place not only as the opponent which, for a time, threatened to obliterate the socialist movement. Fascism is connected with socialism by many crosscurrents, and the two movements have some roots in common, especially the dissatisfaction with the capitalist economy of the pre-1918 type. . . . [F]ascism was ready to use forms of economic organization first suggested by socialists—and very likely that use of socialistic forms would have increased if fascism had not all but destroyed itself in causing the Second World War.

Observations of this sort underscore the totalitarian nature of both ideologies: The greater the power of the state, the more totalitarian it is. Richard Pipes has characterized both communism and fascism as comprising "an official, all-embracing ideology; a single party of the elect headed by a 'leader' and dominating the state; police terror; the ruling party's command of the means of communication and the armed forces; central command of the economy." Stalin's Russia and Nazism were near the totalitarian pole, and Italian Fascism was quickly approaching it.

Although political scientists who use the totalitarian model rarely draw attention to the fact, libertarianism—with its severe strictures on government power—plainly occupies the opposite end of the spectrum from all brands of totalitarianism. If the United States is less totalitarian than the Soviet Union because it has more personal and economic freedom, it is more totalitarian than a "capitalist economy of the pre-1918 type."

Although we regard fascism as a term of opprobrium, to understand it as a political ideology, we must study its theory and practice during the interwar period when millions proudly accepted the label. No one denies that fascism arose in opposition to orthodox Marxism. What is difficult for many to grasp is the source of the mutual hostility between these two political movements. The issues in dispute did not center on economics. Mussolini, Hitler, and the other fascist leaders were prepared to embrace the statism of their socialist rivals. The issue on which they fundamentally differed was nationalism. According to orthodox Marxism, the fate of the *nation* (defined as the political entity holding monopoly power over a specific geographic area) was of no interest to workers. The fascists, in contrast, strongly disagreed: Just as members of the same economic class had interests in common, they argued, so did inhabitants of the same country. Fascists accordingly replaced veneration of "the workers" with equally fanatical devotion to "the nation."

Mussolini's transition from orthodox Marxism to fascism is well known. In April 1914, he was, "in the judgment of sympathizers and opponents alike, the dictator of the Socialist Party." Yet after Mussolini switched his allegiances on the issue of war with the Central Powers, the Socialist Party expelled him. It was at this point that he began publishing his newspaper, the *People of Italy*, to promote his synthesis of nationalism and socialism:

> Mussolini insisted that the only socialism that would be viable in the twentieth century would be a socialism prepared to identify itself with the nation. . . . Mussolini's argument effectively identified traditional socialism as both antinational and antisocialist.

Unlike Mussolini, Hitler had never been a Marxist. Yet he eagerly accepted the socialist label despite suspicion that "we [Nazis] were nothing but a species of Marxism. . . . For to this very day these scatterbrains have not understood the difference between socialism and Marxism." What Hitler condemned most in Marxism was its internationalism. Hitler hated the Marxists not for their economics, but because they "stabbed Germany in the back" during World War I with their revolutionary activities. Indeed, he repeatedly claimed that Marxism was procapitalist and that it sought "only to break the people's national and patriotic backbone and make them ripe for the slave's yoke of international capital and its masters, the Jews."

From a libertarian perspective, the dispute between these rival brands of collectivism is, in many respects, cosmetic. Indeed, fascist economic policies, like those advocated by socialists, involved extensive government regulation, expansive public works, and generous social programs. Such policies had precedents in socialist legislation, but the fascists gave them a nationalist rationale: to heal internal class divisions, move toward economic autarchy, and prepare for war. As Hitler put it:

> [T]he task of the state toward capital was comparatively simple and clear: it only had to make certain that capital remain the handmaiden of the state and not fancy itself the mistress of the nation. This point of view could then be defined between two restrictive limits: preservation of a solvent, national, and independent economy on the one hand, assurance of the social rights of workers on the other.

The Italian fascists were consistently less radical than were the German Nazis, and the influence of national socialist doctrine on Italian economic policy was initially mild. However, government intervention in the economy accelerated in the mid-1930s. Public works, state-enforced cartels, and welfare spending expanded significantly. The state bought the assets of failing banks and corporations, eventually owning most of the banking sector and controlling "a greater portion of the national economy than in any other nation-state west of the Soviet Union."

Once having taken power, the Nazis were quicker to expand the role of government and cut ties with the world economy than the Italians had been. In their first 4 years, the annual increase in real private consumption in Germany was 2.4%, versus an astronomical 19.7% for public consumption. Rearmament had priority, but real nonmilitary government spending grew at an annual rate of 5.3%. Nazi trade policy reduced imports to below their Depression levels, particularly in agriculture, and regulation rapidly expanded throughout the economy. David Schoenbaum notes of the German economy under the Nazis,

> Wages, prices, working conditions, allocation of materials: none of these was left to managerial decision, let alone to the market. . . . Investment was controlled, occupational freedom was dead, prices were fixed. . . . [B]usiness, particularly big business, declined or flourished in direct proportion to its willingness to collaborate.

World War II brought more radical economic changes in Germany. The Nazis instituted state slavery, forcing millions of foreigners into involuntary—and often lethal—servitude. As the war progressed, Germany moved close to full socialism, ultimately conscripting women, the elderly, and even children for economic and military service.

Admittedly, the fascists avoided the radical socialist policies of economy-wide nationalization of industry and collectivization of agriculture. But this deviation from orthodox Marxism was hardly unique to fascism: Given these policies' devastating effects in the Soviet Union, every socialist with a modicum of common sense wanted to avoid them.

During World War II, Ludwig von Mises wrote,

> The Marxians are not prepared to admit that the Nazis are socialists too. In their eyes Nazism is the worst of all evils of capitalism. On the other hand, the Nazis describe the Russian system as the meanest of all types of capitalist exploitation and as a devilish machination of World Jewry for the domination of the gentiles. Yet it is clear that both systems, the German and the Russian, must be considered from an economic point of view as socialist.

Since the collapse of communism, many political scientists and historians have belatedly embraced Mises's perspective. Although they received little recognition for their contribution, libertarians like Mises and Hayek were pioneers of pointing to the similarities between these two brands of totalitarianism. It is unlikely that they will receive the credit they deserve, but, as their model takes root, comparisons between libertarianism and fascism look increasingly spurious.

BC

See also Collectivism; Nationalism; Racism; Socialism; War

Further Readings

Barkai, Avraham. *Nazi Economics: Ideology, Theory, and Policy.* New Haven, CT: Yale University Press, 1990.
Branden, Barbara. *The Passion of Ayn Rand.* New York: Doubleday, 1986.
Gregor, A. James. *The Faces of Janus: Marxism and Fascism in the Twentieth Century.* New Haven, CT: Yale University Press, 2000.
———. *Young Mussolini and the Intellectual Origins of Fascism.* Berkeley: University of California Press, 1979.
Hitler, Adolf. *Mein Kampf.* New York: Houghton Mifflin, 1971.
Landauer, Carl. *European Socialism: A History of Ideas and Movements.* Berkeley: University of California Press, 1959.
Mises, Ludwig von. *Omnipotent Government: The Rise of the Total State and Total War.* Spring Mills, PA: Libertarian Press, 1985.
Payne, Stanley. *A History of Fascism, 1914–1945.* Madison: University of Wisconsin Press, 1995.
Pipes, Richard. *Russia under the Bolshevik Regime.* New York: Vintage Books, 1994.
Schoenbaum, David. *Hitler's Social Revolution: Class and Status in Nazi Germany 1933–1939.* New York: W. W. Norton, 1980.

FEDERALISM

Federalism is a normative concept that emphasizes a diffusion of political authority among levels of government. Federal political systems are political organizations marked by shared power among their constituent units. Some examples of federal political systems include unions, constitutionally decentralized unions, federations, confederations, federacies, associated states, condominiums, leagues, and joint functional authorities. As Ronald Watts has written, a federation

> is a compound polity combining constituent units and a general government, each possessing powers delegated to it by the people through a constitution, each empowered to deal directly with the citizens in the exercise of a significant portion of its legislative, administrative, and taxing powers, and each directly elected by its citizens.

In contrast, a confederation is more dependent on its constituent governments, is composed of delegates from the member states, and relates directly to its constituent governments and only indirectly to the citizens of those member states. This section examines the contributions of federalism and confederation to liberty in theory and in practice.

The Articles of Confederation established the structure of the first national government for the 13 former English colonies. The proponents of the Confederation believed liberty required republican government, but, following Montesquieu, they argued that republics could only extend over a small territory. That implied that the states, not a national government that extended over a large area, would act as the foundation of liberty in the new nation. The intent was for the states to create a national government with powers that would affect only the states and not their citizens. As a creature of the states, this confederation would be controlled and limited by its constituent member states, each of whom had equal voting power. In this way, the size of the new American nation could be reconciled with the demands of liberty and republican government. Those who supported a confederation of this nature were concerned that the Constitution of 1787 would create what they called a consolidated government, a national government that wholly subsumed the powers and independence of the states.

One major stream of Federalist thinking begins with the arguments put forward in *The Federalist Papers* and runs through much of the political history of the English-speaking world. Notably, James Madison did not see a necessary relationship between republics and liberty. In Federalist no. 10, he noted that "popular government" is prone to factions. Factions comprising a majority are especially dangerous to "the public good and the rights of other citizens." Indeed, he continued, many had noted "that our [state] governments are too unstable; that the public good is disregarded in the conflicts of rival parties; and that measures are too often decided, not according to the rules of justice, and the rights of the minor party; but by the superior force of an interested and over-bearing majority." For Madison, a confederacy of republics would not do because majoritarian democracies governing a small territory would endanger the rights of the individual. The sheer size of the new nation offered some protections against the threat posed by the states. The states, in turn, would limit the national government.

The federal form of government defended in the pages of *The Federalist Papers* seems to be a compound republic comprising both national and state powers, a halfway point between confederacy and consolidation. In Federalist no. 39, Madison pointed out that each state, acting as a sovereign body, would ratify the new Constitution. The state governments would have representation in the national government both in the Senate and in the election of the president through the Electoral College. Madison noted one other federal element in the new Constitution. The power of Congress would extend only to "certain enumerated objects" while leaving "to the several States a residuary and inviolable sovereignty over all other objects." In operation, however, the powers of the national government would be such that it directly operated on individual citizens and not just on the state governments. To that extent, the new government was national and not federal. In summary, "the proposed Constitution . . . is in strictness neither a national nor a federal constitution; but a composition of both." Familiarity should not lead us to underestimate the novelty of this diffusion of authority. Prior to 1789, most theorists assumed that sovereignty required a unitary government. In federalism, as in many other matters, the framers of the Constitution saw the virtues of complexity and diffused authority, virtues that would serve the cause of liberty.

For a century and a half after the ratification of the U.S. Constitution, the states were the primary units of government in the nation. The concept of *dual federalism* governed the relationship between the states and the national government. Dual federalism meant that the states and national government had separate and proper spheres of authority. This notion was consistent with the founders' view that the states retained specific powers not delegated to the national government.

The New Deal brought a final end to dual federalism. In its place, the New Dealers promoted "intergovernmental relations," which focused on cooperation between the national and state governments "in providing an undifferentiated set of common governmental services." The new doctrine rejected constitutional limits on the national government that were based on a distrust of centralized power. After 1941, the national government had plenary powers constrained only by specific rights explicitly mentioned in the Constitution and unspecified political rights. The commerce clause, in particular, provided constitutional justification for sweeping regulatory control over the states by the national government. From the Great Depression, through World War II, to the Great Society and its aftermath, the authority of the national government subsumed that of the states as it relentlessly centralized authority. This centralization depended on several factors, including public faith in the benevolence and competence of the national government and dismay at the racial segregation legalized by several states.

Beginning in the 1990s, the pace of centralization of power in Washington slowed. The states became genuine "laboratories of democracy" that created and tested important new policy innovations like welfare reform. The states also began to shed their image as racial backwaters as a new generation of politicians, many African American, took office in the South. The Supreme Court's expansive reading of the commerce clause had encouraged expansion of the federal government's powers. In 1995, however, in the case of *United States v. Lopez*, the Rehnquist Court limited the reach of the federal government under the commerce clause. More generally, a majority of the Rehnquist Court appeared to respect the federal nature of government in the United States by imposing limits on the centralization of power. At the same time, as the states rose in influence, the public's trust of the federal government decreased, reaching bottom in 1994. As a consequence of these changes, a revitalized federalism seemed possible as the United States entered the 21st century.

European justifications for decentralizing government differed radically from Federalist theories embraced by Americans. Most European accounts of the state have concluded that sovereignty is indivisible and that the national state must be the source of all political authority and power. Thus, European theory precludes the possibility of more than one government in a nation. All subsidiary governmental bodies possess their authority and powers solely by delegation from the central authority. The result is that the European tradition of Federalist thought necessarily builds on the idea of subsidiarity. To the extent that lower levels of government can best perform certain governmental acts, the authority to do so must be assigned to them by the central authority. Decentralization of political power is tolerated in the interests of administrative effectiveness, rather than political liberty. Political power is unified, not diffused, and lower-level governments do not limit the power of the central authorities.

In recent years, the European Union has come to comprise a free trade area and an increasingly unified government. In 2003, the member states submitted a draft constitution for Europe for approval by the governments of the member states. Part I, article 9 of the constitution stipulates three principles that are to govern the powers of the new central government in relation to the member states: conferral, subsidiarity, and proportionality.

Part IV of the draft constitution includes a "Protocol on the Application of the Principles of Subsidiarity and Proportionality." Part I, article 9 states that "the Union shall act within the limits of the competences conferred upon it by the Member States in the Constitution to attain the objectives set out in the Constitution. Competences not conferred upon the Union in the Constitution remain with the Member States." This language recalls the American doctrine of delegated and enumerated powers enshrined in the 10th Amendment: "The powers not delegated to the United States by the Constitution, nor prohibited by it to the states, are reserved to the states respectively, or to the people." The 10th Amendment has proved to be at best a limited constraint on the consolidation of government in the United States, and there appears no reason to believe that political events in Europe will take a different course.

The exclusive competences of the new European government include monetary policy, common commercial policy, a customs union, and the conservation of marine biological resources. In time, the limits of the powers of the Union may be defined by the objectives of the Constitution, which include peace, the well-being of its peoples, freedom, security, justice without internal frontiers, a single market where competition is free and undistorted, sustainable development of Europe based on balanced economic growth, a social market economy, environmental protection, scientific and technological advance, equality between women and men, solidarity between generations, children's rights, economic, social and territorial cohesion, and solidarity among member states. The conferral principle seems unlikely to restrict the powers of the central European government of the future.

The European Constitution also lists many powers shared with the member states, including virtually all policy areas. The Union may exercise a shared power when "the objectives of the intended action cannot be sufficiently achieved by the Member States." The member states are free to object that a proposed action by the central government violates the principle of subsidiarity. If one-third of the member states object, the European Commission is constitutionally required to review its proposed act, after which it "may decide to maintain, amend or withdraw its proposal."

Thus, the constituent members possess no effective veto over the centralization of power in the new European state.

The principle of proportionality states that "the content and form of Union action shall not exceed what is necessary to achieve the objectives of the Constitution" (part I, article 9). This principle seems more a general aspiration for the new government than an effective limit on its powers.

The new European Constitution seems unlikely to sustain a form of government that can properly be called a European confederation. Like many of its member states, the European Union will have few legal barriers to consolidating political power and transforming its member states into efficient administrators of centrally determined policies. Of course, the member states in question may successfully resist their subordination to Brussels. If they do, their success will owe much to *realpolitik* and little to constitutional restraints.

The European Constitution explicitly refers to liberty, together with several other cardinal values. The first objective of the Union, we are told, is the promotion of peace and the well-being of its peoples. Indeed, the economic interests of the member states are a driving force toward union. Liberty is only one among many values pursued by the new Europe. Given the absence of effective restraints on the central government, it seems unlikely that the institutions of a united Europe will give much weight to individual liberty in the decades to come, especially if expansion of the central state serves the economic interests of some member states in the short term.

Federalism, as it has been understood in the United States, represents a balancing of objectives, not the least of which is occasioned by the fear of centralized power and a strong consolidated government. It has been suggested that our current concern with multiculturalism might revive this fear. Multiculturalists insist on protections for minority cultures and, at least theoretically, on limits on the uses of political power. Most multiculturalists, however, seem unlikely to embrace a renewed federalism. Where American federalism sought decentralized institutions as a way to protect liberty, multiculturalists aim at other values like diversity or recognition of a people or culture. Moreover, the multiculturalist aims at vindicating the cultural rights of peoples, rather than the right to liberty of individuals. Multiculturalists, like many contemporary critics of liberalism, see personal identity as collectively defined, rather than individually determined. Moreover, their efforts may contravene republican equality and the rule of law. That said, a least one political theorist has argued for a "multiculturalism of fear" aimed at preventing violence, cruelty, and institutional humiliation against disfavored groups. This multiculturalism bears a family resemblance to the traditional motivations of classical liberal theory.

In Europe, the question of consolidation depends on the willingness and ability of nation-states to constrain the new central government. In that struggle, the central government will have two major advantages: The new European Constitution does not effectively limit the central authority, and European tradition suggests sovereignty must be unitary. In the United States, the tragic attacks of September 11, 2001, made homeland security and war making, two responsibilities of the national government, the central concern of American politics. More generally, some scholars argue that Washington should take a larger role in redistributive policies like health care and welfare spending. Others continue to seek institutional changes that might protect liberty by reviving a federalism of mutual constraint between the national government and the states. The success or failure of that search may go some distance toward deciding the fate of liberty in the new century.

JSa

See also Constitution, U.S.; Decentralism; Federalists Versus Anti-Federalists; Judiciary; Limited Government; Subsidiarity

Further Readings

Conlan, Timothy J. *From New Federalism to Devolution: Twenty-Five Years of Intergovernmental Reform.* Washington, DC: Brookings Institution Press, 1998.

Derthick, Martha. *Keeping the Compound Republic: Essays on American Federalism.* Washington, DC: Brookings Institution Press, 2001.

Dinan, John J. "The Rehnquist Court's Federalism Decisions in Perspective." *Journal of Law & Politics* 15 (Spring 1999): 127–194.

Levy, Jacob. *The Multiculturalism of Fear.* New York: Oxford University Press, 2000.

Moravcsik, Andrew. *The Choice for Europe: Social Purpose and State Power from Messina to Maastricht.* Ithaca, NY: Cornell University Press, 1998.

Niskanen, William A. *On the Constitution of a Compound Republic* (Cato's Letter no.14). Washington, DC: Cato Institute, 2001.

Peterson, Paul E. *The Price of Federalism.* Washington, DC: Brookings Institution Press, 1995.

Pollack, Mark. "Theorizing the European Union: International Organization, Domestic Polity, or Experiment in New Governance?" *Annual Review of Political Science* 8 (June 2005): 357–398.

Samples, John, ed. *James Madison and the Future of Limited Government.* Washington, DC: Cato Institute, 2002.

Whittington, Keith. "Dismantling the Modern State? The Changing Structural Foundations of Federalism." *Hastings Constitutional Law Quarterly* 25 no. 4 (Summer 1998): 483–527.

FEDERALISTS VERSUS ANTI-FEDERALISTS

The Federalists and Anti-Federalists conducted a spirited debate over ratification of the U.S. Constitution beginning in late 1787 and continuing through the following year.

This momentous struggle about the nature of the American union and its future central government had its genesis in the American Revolution, which had ended 6 years earlier.

The Revolution succeeded by virtue of a temporary coalition of competing viewpoints and conflicting interests. At one end of the coalition stood the American radicals— men such as Samuel Adams, Patrick Henry, Thomas Paine, Richard Henry Lee, and Thomas Jefferson. The radicals objected to excessive government power in general and not simply to British rule in particular. Spearheading the Revolution's opening stages, the radicals were responsible for all the truly revolutionary alterations in the domestic status quo. At the other end of the Revolutionary coalition were American nationalists—men such as Benjamin Franklin, George Washington, Robert Morris, Alexander Hamilton, and James Madison. Representing a powerful array of mercantile, creditor, and landed interests, the nationalists went along with independence, but resisted the Revolution's libertarian thrust. They preferred an American central government that would reproduce the hierarchical and mercantilist features of the 18th-century British state, only without the British.

The Revolution had started out as a struggle against taxation. What passed among the newly independent American states for a central government did not have direct access even to this most basic and usual of political powers. The Articles of Confederation, a written constitution adopted in 1781, failed to give Congress any authority either to collect taxes or to regulate trade. The war, however, helped spawn various pressure groups that clamored for stronger government. Eastern land speculators agitated for a standing army that could protect their vast claims, and in this effort they were joined by many of the Continental Army's former officers.

One of the nationalists' most potent political weapons was the Revolutionary War debt, which provided an enduring rationale for national taxation and another special interest, those to whom the debt was owed, who supported such taxation. An equally popular justification for strengthening Congress was trade regulation. Subsequent accounts have painted a fanciful picture of competing trade barriers among various states that disrupted the American economy. The prevailing practice regarding interstate trade prior to the Constitution, however, was complete reciprocity among the states. What American merchants were actually after was uniform navigation laws discriminating against foreign shippers. At the same time, American artisans wanted nationwide protective tariffs, unmarred by competing state exemptions.

All direct efforts to strengthen the Articles of Confederation proved futile because proposed amendments required the unanimous ratification of the states. Consequently, Hamilton and Madison assumed leadership of the nationalists and attempted to bypass this bottleneck by calling for a special convention to meet in Philadelphia in 1787. Aiding this movement was a growing antidemocratic mood throughout the country brought on, in part, by Shays's Rebellion, which had erupted in western Massachusetts in 1786. According to the nationalist accounts, it represented an egalitarian assault on the property rights of creditors. In reality, the rebellion was more a tax revolt than a debtors' revolt. Prior to its outbreak, only Virginia, Pennsylvania, and New Jersey had chosen delegates to the Philadelphia convention. Subsequently, every state government except Rhode Island sent delegates.

The convention was officially charged with the task of proposing revisions to the Articles of Confederation, but the delegates, meeting in secret, quickly decided to violate their instructions and draft a totally new document. Of the 55 delegates present, only 8 had signed the Declaration of Independence. Most of the leading radicals were absent, and the convention was dominated by the coalescing nationalist factions. These groups wanted a consolidated government under which the states would be subordinate, like counties within the states. Madison's Virginia Plan, the basis for the convention's deliberations, essentially embodied this goal. But like the Revolution, the Constitution turned into a hybrid product, the result of disparate coalitions. The nationalist dream of a central government with plenary powers slowly eroded away. Some of this erosion occurred just as the orthodox interpretation of the making of the Constitution has it, through compromises worked out within the Philadelphia convention. But much occurred outside the convention, through a subtle process of reinterpretation, as the nationalists were compelled to defend their completed handiwork before the general public.

The new proposed Constitution probably did not have the support of a majority of Americans. Yet its framers enjoyed the support of General Washington, who had presided over the Philadelphia convention and whose prestige among the colonists was enormous. Supporters also were more tightly organized than their more provincial opponents. These advantages allowed the nationalists to force the Constitution through the first five state conventions in rapid succession. The Constitution's supporters furthermore pulled off a significant linguistic coup by successfully seizing the label "Federalist." They had, in fact, designed the Constitution to replace the federal system of government under the Articles of Confederation with a national system. The true defenders of federalism were therefore the Constitution's opponents. The misnamed Anti-Federalists weakened their own case by acceding to the need for some additional national power. This compromise permitted the Federalists to vigorously deny that the Constitution would create a national government in which the states would be subordinate. Instead, the document would establish a delicate balance of power between the national and state governments, each sovereign within its own realm. In other words, the much-touted federalism of the United States was not so much an intended consequence of the Philadelphia convention. Rather, it was an unintended and insincere concession that the Anti-Federalists wrenched from the Federalists during the ratification struggle.

This Federalist equivocation spilled over into the Constitution's most controversial feature—its omission of a bill of rights. This single issue united all Anti-Federalists and gained them the greatest support. The Federalists responded with the claim that the Constitution provided a government possessing only specifically enumerated powers. As a result, argued Hamilton in Federalist no. 84, a bill of rights would be positively harmful. "They would contain various exceptions to power which are not granted" and imply that the national government could do anything not specifically prohibited. The difficulty with this argument was that it contravened a second Federalist argument based on the explicit words of the Constitution. In the same Federalist paper, Hamilton maintained that the Constitution already contained a truncated bill of rights scattered throughout its clauses. This obvious contradiction cast justifiable suspicion on the underlying claim that the Constitution created a government of delegated, rather than plenary, powers.

By the time the Constitution was under consideration in the key states of Massachusetts, Virginia, and New York, the Federalists were in trouble. Earlier, at the Pennsylvania ratifying convention, the defeated Anti-Federalists had drawn up a proposed bill of rights, which circulated widely in other states. The Federalists had to draw up a series of recommended amendments to get the Massachusetts convention to join in ratifying the document, and they just barely avoided making Virginia's ratification conditional upon a series of 40 amendments passed by the convention. At New York's ratifying convention, the Federalists not only assented to a full slate of proposed amendments, but also to a circular letter calling for a second constitutional convention.

The prospect of amendments mollified enough radicals to allow the Constitution to squeak through. The aging Sam Adams was one such Anti-Federalist, finally voting for ratification at the Massachusetts convention. Jefferson, then serving as the American minister in France, urged ratification, but only by the requisite nine states. The remaining states should, he maintained, hold back until certain crucial amendments were added. Other radicals, such as the still fiery Patrick Henry and his fellow Virginian, Richard Henry Lee, remained implacably hostile to the Constitution. Five states overall coupled their ratifications with proposed amendments, whereas in two others, the minority urged passage of certain amendments they drafted. The North Carolina convention refused to ratify at all unless a bill of rights was added, and Rhode Island would have nothing to do with the Constitution whatsoever. The proposed amendments often went far beyond a simple bill of rights. In particular, a curb on the national government's taxing power found unanimous support among amendment proposals. Many Anti-Federalists had been consistently willing to permit the central government to collect import duties, but they insisted that all internal taxes be levied only at the discretion of the state governments.

The Anti-Federalists planned to enact these amendments, which would have stripped the central government of many of its new powers, through a convention called by two-thirds of the states. Unable to defeat the Constitution outright, they now pinned their hopes on this second constitutional convention. Virginia, North Carolina, and Rhode Island all promptly endorsed this recommendation, which originated in New York. However, because North Carolina and Rhode Island had not yet ratified the Constitution, their endorsement of a new convention could not technically count toward the total in calculating two-thirds of the states. Having made the tactical decision to function within the legal framework of the Constitution, the Anti-Federalists discovered that the resulting legitimacy they granted to the new government worked against them.

On the other end of the political spectrum, many ardent Federalists were prepared to renege on their solemn promises to amend the Constitution once the new national government began operations in 1789. However, the politically astute Madison had come to believe that the popular demand for a bill of rights should be placated. There also is some evidence that Madison had altered his views on the need for a federal bill of rights. Regardless of what served as the principal motivation for his change of heart, Madison carefully culled through the more than 200 state proposals. Diehard Anti-Federalists and even Jefferson felt that Madison's amendments were not radical enough. Nonetheless, Madison successfully steered the Bill of Rights through Congress. Although these widely publicized amendments would not be ratified for several years, they satisfied many opponents of the new government. North Carolina, for instance, finally joined the Union in November 1789.

Most of the Amendments comprising the Bill of Rights restricted the national government's direct authority over its citizens. Only one section dealt with the relationship between the state and central governments; the 10th Amendment "reserved" to the states or the people all powers not "delegated to the United States by the Constitution." Nothing better illustrates that, whereas the Anti-Federalists had lost on the ratification issue, they had won on the question of how the Constitution would operate. The Constitution had not established a consolidated national system of government as most Federalists had at first intended, but a truly federal system, which is what the Anti-Federalists had wanted. In simpler terms, the Federalists got their Constitution, but the Anti-Federalists determined how it would be interpreted.

JRH

See also American Revolution; Bill of Rights, U.S.; Constitution, U.S.; Federalism; Madison, James

Further Readings

Brown, Roger H. *Federalists, Taxation, and the Origins of the Constitution.* Baltimore: Johns Hopkins University Press, 1993.

Cooke, Jacob E., ed. [Alexander Hamilton, James Madison, and John Jay.] *The Federalist.* Middletown, CT: Wesleyan University Press, 1961.

Ferguson, E. James. *The Power of the Purse: A History of American Public Finance, 1776–1790.* Chapel Hill: University of North Carolina Press, 1961.

Jensen, Merrill. *The Making of the American Constitution.* Princeton, NJ: D. Van Nostrand, 1964.

———. *The New Nation: A History of the United States during the Confederation, 1781–1789.* New York: Knopf, 1950.

Kohn, Richard H. *Eagle and Sword: The Federalists and the Creation of the Military Establishment in America, 1783–1802.* New York: Free Press, 1975.

Main, Jackson Turner. *The Antifederalists: Critics of the Constitution, 1781–1788.* Chapel Hill: University of North Carolina Press, 1961.

McGuire, Robert A. *To Form a More Perfect Union: A New Economic Interpretation of the United States Constitution.* New York: Oxford University Press, 2006.

Storing, Herbert J. *What the Anti-Federalists Were For.* Chicago: University of Chicago Press, 1981.

Wood, Gordon S. *The Creation of the American Republic, 1776–1787.* Chapel Hill: University of North Carolina Press, 1969.

FEMINISM AND WOMEN'S RIGHTS

The term *feminism* refers to the belief that men and women are politically and morally equal and should be treated as such. The term is most often attached to various movements over the last two centuries that have acted to implement this vision of equality by embedding it in law and throughout the culture.

Diverse schools exist within the feminist tradition, however, and they often disagree on the definition of *equality*. For individualist feminists, equality means equal treatment under laws that respect the person and property of all human beings regardless of secondary characteristics such as sex, race, and ethnicity. For another school, known as radical or gender feminism, equality means socioeconomic equality, in which power and wealth are redistributed by law throughout society so that the historical privileges of men are erased. These two schools of feminism define the extremes within the movement.

Historically speaking, the form of feminism with which Western society is most familiar established itself in the 18th century as a protest against the laws and conventions that required women to function in a subordinate role. Two women pioneered this movement: Olympe de Gouges and Mary Wollstonecraft.

De Gouges was a French playwright and journalist at the time of the French Revolution. In 1791, in response to the famous Declaration of the Rights of Man and of the Citizen of 1789, she issued the Declaration of the Rights of Woman and the Citizen, in which she challenged the exclusion of women from citizenship and argued for equality between the sexes.

The British classical liberal Mary Wollstonecraft also responded to the French Revolution. Wollstonecraft first wrote the pamphlet *Vindication of the Rights of Men* (1790), in defense of the ideals of the Revolution, which had come under attack from the British statesman Edmund Burke. *A Vindication of the Rights of Women* followed in 1792. In this work, she argued that women are the equals of men and only appear inferior due to their poor education, which required them to focus on the domestic arts. The second *Vindication* is considered to be a founding document of feminism.

Thus, Western feminism was born in the claim that men and women are equal as moral and political agents who possess the same natural rights. Feminism gave voice to the broader demand that those rights be equally recognized and to its call that women be educated to think independently.

As an organized movement, American feminism arose from a different set of historical circumstances. In particular, it sprang from the abolitionist movement of the 1830s. Abolitionism was the radical antislavery movement that demanded an immediate cessation to slavery on the grounds that every man was a self-owner; that is, every man has moral jurisdiction over his own body.

Abolitionism fostered feminism in several ways. It was the first organized, radical movement in which women played leadership roles and were encouraged to speak from public podiums to mixed audiences of men and women. Many of the female abolitionists came from Quaker backgrounds, in which they were accorded far more education and equality than the general population. They soon became uncomfortable with one aspect of abolitionism: They seemed to be working only for men's self-ownership, not for women's as well. William Lloyd Garrison, the leading figure within abolitionism, shared feminists' discomfort and came to champion women's rights.

In the early 19th century, a married woman could not enter into contracts without her husband's consent, women lost all title to property or future earnings upon marriage, children were legally controlled by the father, and women were generally without recourse against kidnapping or imprisonment by husbands and other male relatives. Sarah Grimké's famous pamphlet, *Letters on the Equality of the Sexes and the Condition of Woman* (1837), compared the laws governing slaves with those governing women, which were remarkably similar even in wording. Thus, feminist demands focused on eliminating legal barriers to women, as well as acquiring the same rights to person and property as men enjoyed.

A pivotal moment came in 1840 when American female delegates to the World Anti-Slavery Conference in London were barred from sitting in the assembly. Two women who were so outraged—Lucretia Mott and Elizabeth Cady Stanton—returned home and organized the 1848 Seneca Falls Convention to discuss women's rights. There they drafted the Declaration of Sentiments. Arguably the most famous feminist document, the Sentiments paraphrased the Declaration of Independence to declare woman's independence from man's shadow. A woman's suffrage resolution also was introduced and narrowly passed.

From that point until the ratification of the 19th Amendment to the Constitution in 1920, mainstream American feminism focused on securing the vote for women with Stanton and Susan B. Anthony assuming leadership roles. Other feminists were active in three separate areas—social (especially labor) reform, reproductive rights, and education—but they tended to function as either as individuals or female voices within broader reform movements. The situation was similar in Britain, where "suffragettes" campaigned for universal suffrage for decades before the vote was extended to single women over the age of 30 in 1918 and then to all adults over 21 years of age in 1928.

After achieving the vote for women, feminism in America and Britain appears to have lacked a central issue to galvanize the movement. Again, individual women spoke out for women's rights. For example, in 1920, Suzanne La Follette's book, *Concerning Women*, defended free markets and opposed state intervention into women's lives. Women also spoke out from within broader movements; for example, Dorothy Day—founder of the influential periodical *The Catholic Worker*—was instrumental in the Catholic pacifist movement.

Nevertheless, feminism as a self-conscious and independent movement effectively disappeared from America until the 1960s, when Second Wave feminism, an expression that acknowledged their 19th-century forerunners as the First Wave, emerged. As with abolitionism, Second Wave feminism sprang from discontent with the treatment of women within a broader movement: in this instance, opposition to the Vietnam War. This revival sprang from left-wing or liberal ideology.

Second Wave feminism's call for women's liberation resonated with many women who were chafing at the sexual and social restrictions of the 1950s, restrictions that included abstinence before marriage, the assumption of domesticity rather than a career, prohibition against children out of wedlock, and attitudes against lesbianism. Betty Friedan's pathbreaking 1963 work, *The Feminine Mystique*, which argued that domesticity enslaved women, inspired a generation of women to pursue a career instead. Helen Gurley Brown, author of the best-selling book, *Sex and the Single Girl* (1962), expressed an emerging sexuality that accompanied both the rise of feminism and the new availability of effective birth control—the pill.

Second Wave feminism aimed at reform rather than at revolution; women demanded equal representation and fair treatment within the existing system. For example, one of the movement's major goals was affirmative action, through which women would be included in greater numbers within existing institutions such as universities. The Equal Rights Amendment (ERA) became the pivotal issue for liberal feminism. This proposed amendment to the U.S. Constitution aimed at guaranteeing equal rights under the law regardless of sex. It proved a stunning defeat for liberal feminism when the ERA's deadline for ratification passed in 1979.

Hitherto, radical feminism (also called gender feminism) had functioned as a minority and revolutionary voice within the Second Wave. In the early 1980s, radical feminism became ideologically dominant. Radical feminism defined current society and institutions as "the patriarchy"—a mixture of white male culture and capitalism through which men as a class oppressed women as a class. A key ideological theorist, Catharine MacKinnon, called the vision "post-Marxist feminism" because of its reliance on class or gender analysis and its anticapitalist approach.

This gender analysis view of sexuality was reflected in books like Susan Brownmiller's *Against Our Will* (1975), in which all men were portrayed as "rapists" because all men benefit from the "rape culture" of patriarchy. In a series of books, theorist Andrea Dworkin explained how virtually every aspect of society, from pornography to children's books, sexually exploited women and created violence against them.

Radical feminism's methodology is predicated on the notion of political correctness: a system of laws and policies that encourage proper expression and behavior while discouraging improper forms. For example, government funds are routinely allocated to programs that promote the expression of correct sexual attitudes in the workplace and on campus. Meanwhile, laws and policies against incorrect attitudes or behavior (e.g., comments viewed as sexist or sexually harassing) punish such expression, often through costly lawsuits.

Political correctness runs counter to the natural-rights origins of classical liberal and 19th-century American feminism, also known as individualist feminism or, by the present-day formulation "ifeminism." The punishment of speech, even with the intention of preventing harassment, would have undoubtedly alarmed the early feminists, who staunchly defended freedom of speech, especially speech on which society frowned. After all, censorship laws were used to silence abolitionist feminists from speaking out on both slavery and women's rights. Throughout feminist history, censorship has stifled discussion of controversial topics such as birth control and lesbianism. Thus, freedom of speech has been vital to the development of feminism and the well-being of women.

The assumption of class conflict that underlies political correctness also runs counter to feminism's individualist roots. Political correctness divides society into distinct classes defined by characteristics such as gender and race; the classes are deemed to have different and antagonistic political interests. Thus, government intervention is necessary to protect and promote disadvantaged classes in order to ensure a proper distribution of wealth and power throughout society occurs. In short, some classes receive governmental privileges to the disadvantage of other classes.

By contrast, individualist feminism advocates the elimination of all classes under law so that every individual has equal rights and an equal claim to person and property, regardless of characteristics such as gender or race. The proper role of government is to eliminate privilege and protect the rights of individual men and women equally.

Between the polar extremes of gender and individualist feminism lie a variety of other schools that either employ a different ideological approach or define themselves according to another standard. For example, equity feminism aims at equality under existing institutions without necessarily reforming the current system to reflect the natural rights of individuals. Ecofeminism links male domination of women to the destruction of the environment and so focuses on the role women must play in preserving nature.

Whatever the school or tradition, however, certain issues are considered to be feminist ones. Reproductive rights such as birth control and midwifery are of primary importance because they involve a woman's control of her own body in an area that is uniquely female. Indeed, abortion is often considered to be a litmus test of feminism; that is, those who oppose legal abortion cannot be feminists of any description.

Whatever consensus might exist between schools of feminism on reproductive rights, however, breaks down on other issues. Pornography highlights these differences. Radical feminists view pornography as the quintessence of man's sexual oppression of woman and wish to prohibit it as an act of violence in and of itself. Individual feminists may or may not like pornography, but they view it as a choice every woman (or man) has a right to make either as a participant or as a consumer. They wish to decriminalize pornography and other sex work as a matter of personal choice. So-called pro-sex feminists celebrate sex work as an ultimate expression of women's empowerment; they also seek decriminalization.

The future of feminism is problematic. In the Western world, most inequalities under the law and within the culture have been swept away so that women and men generally face the same basic choices. Indeed, to the extent that there is gender inequity, it lies in the privileges that women are granted through laws or policies such as affirmative action. Hence, both individualist and equity feminism argue for the removal of privileges for women in order to achieve true equality. Moreover, the rise of counterintuitive schools of feminism, such as conservative feminism that champions the traditional family and conservative values, has acted to blunt the historical mission and goals of feminism.

Outside the Western world (e.g., in Africa and Arab nations), women often endure second-class citizenship and widespread violation of their natural rights. The burqa has become a symbol of the oppression of such women, but it also reflects the division between Western and non-Western feminists. The all-concealing costume that women are often forced to wear, most notoriously by the Taliban in Afghanistan, is anathema to Western feminists. But many of their non-Western counterparts argue that wearing a burqa or adopting other allegedly antifemale practices of Islam are free choices and should be respected as such. As radical feminism expresses itself increasingly through global organizations, especially through the United Nations, it is not clear how its ideology and goals will reconcile with the deep cultural differences it encounters among women.

WME

See also Abolitionism; Abortion; Equality; Individualism, Political and Ethical; Islam; Pornography; Sexuality; Wollstonecraft, Mary

Further Readings

Brownmiller, Susan. *Against Our Will: Men, Women, and Rape.* New York: Simon & Schuster, 1975.

Hersh, Blanche Glassman. *The Slavery of Sex: Feminist Abolitionists in America.* Urbana: University of Illinois Press, 1978.

La Follette, Suzanne. *Concerning Women.* New York: Arno Press, 1972.

McElroy, Wendy. *Individualist Feminism of the Nineteenth Century: Collected Writings and Biographical Profiles.* Jefferson, NC: McFarland & Company, 2001.

———. *Liberty for Women: Freedom and Feminism in the Twenty-First Century.* Chicago: Ivan R. Dee, 2002.

Paglia, Camille. *Sexual Personae: Art and Decadence from Nefertiti to Emily Dickinson.* New Haven, CT: Yale University Press, 1990; New York: Vintage, 1991.

Taylor, Joan Kennedy. *Reclaiming the Mainstream: Individualist Feminism Rediscovered.* Buffalo, NY: Prometheus Books, 1992.

FERGUSON, ADAM (1723–1816)

Adam Ferguson was among the most original and important thinkers of the Scottish Enlightenment. He, together with Adam Smith and David Hume, contributed to shaping the philosophical underpinnings of British liberalism. Whereas Smith's contributions consisted mainly in examinations of the mechanism by which wealth is created and distributed, and Hume's lay in offering a theory of jurisprudence distinct from older notions of natural law, Ferguson's work was primarily in the area of sociology and conjectural history.

Adam Ferguson was born in Perthshire, the youngest son of the minister of the parish. After having attended his local parish school and the grammar school at Perth, Ferguson was enrolled in the University of St. Andrews in 1738, where he read classics. Some 4 years later, at the age of 19, he entered the university's divinity school, and in 1745, he obtained his license to preach. After having served a few years as a military chaplain, Ferguson was able to obtain the help of his good friend David Hume to succeed him as Keeper of the Advocate's Library in Edinburgh. Finally, in 1759, Ferguson was appointed to the faculty of the University of Edinburgh, where he held the chair of pneumatics and moral philosophy from 1764 until his retirement in 1785. It was during his tenure as professor of moral philosophy that three of his four most important works were published: the *Essay on the History of Civil Society* in 1767; the *Institutes of Moral Philosophy*, a synopsis of his lectures on moral philosophy, in 1769; and the *History of the Progress and Termination of the Roman Republic* in 1783. It was during the years of his retirement that Ferguson completed his major work in philosophy, a revision and expansion of his *Institutes*, titled *The Principles of Moral and Political Science*, which appeared in two volumes in 1792. Ferguson died on February 22, 1816, at St. Andrews in his 93rd year, and he was buried in the cathedral there.

Of Ferguson's principal writings, the *Essay on the History of Civil Society* is unquestioningly the most important and was regarded as such by both his contemporaries and political theorists writing today. In it Ferguson offers a conjectural history of social institutions, maintaining that societies naturally evolved from savagery to barbarism to civilization. Of these stages of development, the first, Ferguson maintained, was both prepolitical and lacked any real notion of private property. In barbaric societies, in contrast, property had ceased to remain communal, and private wealth, most often in the form of agricultural products and animal herds, had developed. Despite the existence of unequal possessions, however, a formal institutionalized system of laws regarding property had to await the development of civilized society. It was in response to the emergence of that complex of rules regarding the possession and transfer of property, and the permanent subordination of rank that follows upon it, that political institutions appeared. In summary, Ferguson argued, government was a creature of property, and property was an artifact of civilization.

Embedded in Ferguson's conjectural analysis of the historical development of societies is the notion that the institutions under which men live are not the product of deliberate contrivance, but take their form through a process of evolution. Indeed, these institutional arrangements are of such a high order of complexity that their structure and interconnections with each other are beyond the comprehension of any mind. Rather, they come into being and are shaped by numerous discrete individual actions, none of which aims at the formation of coherent social institutions. Society is not the result of calculation, but arises spontaneously, and its institutions are not the result of intentional design, but of men's actions, which have as their purpose an array of short-term private objectives. As Ferguson wrote:

> Every step and every movement of the multitude, even in what are termed enlightened ages, are made with equal blindness to the future; and nations stumble upon establishments, which are indeed the result of human action, but not the execution of any human design.

That conception, that social structures are formed spontaneously and that it is possible to have ordered arrangements of great complexity without a designer or coordinator, is possibly the single most spectacular contribution to social philosophy of the Scottish Enlightenment and is reflected in Adam Smith's description of the market as an "invisible hand" and in David Hume's discussions of the origin and nature of justice. It was via the Scottish Enlightenment that the theory entered British liberal thought and was employed to explain why social order and individual liberty are perfectly compatible. At the same time, the theory provided a powerful argument against *dirigiste* systems and added strength to the arguments, put forward most forcefully by F. A. Hayek in the 20th century, that institutional arrangements that operate under central direction are unable to coordinate the many diverse interests, bits of knowledge, and plans that make up what Adam Smith called "the Great Society."

RH

See also Civil Society; Enlightenment; Hume, David; Progress; Sociology and Libertarianism; Spontaneous Order

Further Readings

Hamowy, Ronald. "Progress and Commerce in Anglo-American Thought: The Social Philosophy of Adam Ferguson." *Interpretation: A Journal of Political Philosophy* 14 (1986): 61–87.
———. *The Scottish Enlightenment and the Theory of Spontaneous Order*. Carbondale and Edwardsville: University of Southern Illinois Press, 1987.
Kettler, David. *The Social and Political Philosophy of Adam Ferguson*. Columbus: Ohio State University Press, 1965.
Lehmann, William. *Adam Ferguson and the Beginnings of Modern Sociology*. New York: Columbia University Press, 1930.
Spadafora, David. *The Idea of Progress in Eighteenth-Century Britain*. New Haven, CT: Yale University Press, 1990.

Fisher, Antony (1915–1988)

Sir Antony Fisher, British philanthropist, launched an international network of independent, public policy think tanks to disseminate and popularize the ideas of liberty—the rule of law, free markets, property rights, individual responsibility, and limited government.

Born in London, Fisher served as a fighter pilot in the Royal Air Force during World War II. After the war, his odyssey in the world of ideas developed upon reading the condensed version of *The Road to Serfdom* by Friedrich Hayek. It crystallized Fisher's fears that the very freedoms he sought to protect in the war were increasingly at risk from growing support for collectivism. Fisher visited Hayek and shared his plans to enter politics. Instead, Hayek challenged him to find a way to change the long-term climate of opinion.

Exactly 10 years later, in 1955, Fisher responded to Hayek's challenge by creating an independent research organization to produce publications and seminars and otherwise engage opinion leaders in the ideas of free and open markets. He approached economists Ralph Harris and Arthur Seldon and together they launched the Institute of Economic Affairs in London.

Twenty years later, Fisher helped establish or advise several other think tanks in their early years, all of which remain highly influential today, including the Adam Smith Institute (London), Centre for Independent Studies (Australia), Fraser Institute (Canada), Manhattan Institute (New York), and the Pacific Research Institute (California).

In 1981, Fisher founded the Atlas Economic Research Foundation to institutionalize the process of assisting, developing, and supporting free-market public policy institutes. At present, Atlas continues in the tradition of its founder, working with a network of approximately 200 institutes around the globe.

JK

See also Development, Economic; Free-Market Economy; Hayek, Friedrich A.

Further Readings

Cockett, Richard. *Thinking the Unthinkable: Think-Tanks and the Economic Counter-Revolution, 1931–1983*. New York: HarperCollins, 1995.
Frost, Gerald. *Antony Fisher, Champion of Liberty*. London: Profile Books, 2002.

Foreign Policy

Throughout the first 150 years of America's independence, political leaders and the public alike sought to keep the country out of armed conflicts that did not have direct relevance to the nation's security. Two episodes in particular, the War of 1812 and the Mexican-American War, were major conflicts that in the minds of some historians directly threatened the security of the American homeland. America's casus belli for the War of 1812 was the British

Royal Navy's seizure of American merchant ships and the impressment of U.S. sailors, punishment for its continued trade with Napoleonic France, then Britain's adversary. The Mexican-American War commenced more than 30 years later, after Mexico attacked American troops following the American government's annexation of Texas, then an independent state. Despite these major conflicts, there was still an aversion in the United States to having the country involved in what were viewed as the cynical, amoral power politics of the international system. Fissures began to develop in that noninterventionist consensus in the 1890s, when the United States acquired a small but far-flung colonial empire following its victory in the Spanish-American War. An even greater departure from tradition occurred in 1917 when President Woodrow Wilson took it upon himself to lead the country into a full-scale European war. However, it was not until World War II destroyed any semblance of a global balance of power that the United States explicitly rejected its traditional policy of staying aloof from foreign quarrels.

During the subsequent cold war era, the federal government established a network of formal and informal alliances around the world. For the first time in its history, the United States undertook to defend a disparate assortment of allies, clients, and protectorates. The architects of this new policy argued that America's inability to stay out of World War II (a failure punctuated by the Japanese attack on Pearl Harbor) had effectively discredited America's traditional policy of isolationism. In addition, they contended that the severity of the threat posed by the Soviet Union, and the absence of any other great powers capable of balancing Soviet capabilities, gave the United States no choice but to play a globally activist role to contain the USSR.

However, despite the collapse of the Soviet empire, the policy of global interventionism has remained dominant. Indeed, in the post–cold war decade, the United States has undertaken additional security commitments. The United States has led the drive to expand the membership of NATO and supported that alliance's venture into "out-of-area" military missions, among them those in Bosnia and Kosovo. Many U.S. political leaders also have embraced the doctrine of humanitarian military intervention—a concept that could well involve the United States in a broad array of conflicts.

Proponents of the current policy insist that any retrenchment of Washington's global leadership role would create dangerous instabilities in Europe, East Asia, and other regions of the world. These increases in instability, they argue, would damage important U.S. economic and security interests and could even lead to a disastrous replay of the bitter nationalist rivalries that produced the two world wars. Advocates of a more restrained role of strategic independence for the United States counter that such a worst-case scenario is highly improbable. They also argue that a

global interventionist policy entails its own costs and risks, which can be quite severe. The United States was mired in two peacekeeping missions in the Balkans in the 1990s. Washington currently risks major tensions with China, an emerging great power, over America's commitment to defend the tiny client state of Taiwan.

Washington responded to the September 11, 2001, terrorist attacks with even more dubious foreign policy activism. In the wake of al-Qaeda's attack, the administration of President George W. Bush inaugurated a Global War on Terror, a campaign meant to root out Islamic extremism, bring terrorists to justice, and prevent terrorists from securing resources that would aid them in funding another attack on the American homeland.

The first battleground of this new campaign was in Afghanistan, a conflict fought with America's NATO allies against the Taliban regime for its harboring of al-Qaeda. The second battleground was Iraq, a war that has since been widely accepted as a misguided war of choice. The war in Iraq was meant to rid Ba'athist leader Saddam Hussein of his alleged weapons of mass destruction (WMDs) and convert Iraq into a democratic model for the entire Middle East, producing new regimes friendlier to the United States. The WMD allegations were unfounded, and Washington's regional plan to remake the Middle East proved hopelessly naive. Unfortunately, the war in Iraq precipitated a power vacuum in the region and the internal displacement of more than 2.5 million Iraqis. It also exacerbated the problem of Islamic extremism and shifted the region's balance of power in Iran's favor. The war has divided the American public, and, as of this writing, it has led to the deaths of more than 3,800 American troops and cost over $590 billion in American treasure.

America's global interventionist policy has had a pervasive and overwhelmingly negative impact on the Republic's domestic affairs, transforming the nation economically, socially, and politically. Waging the cold war led to the creation of a large and expensive military establishment; despite the end of that struggle, military spending remains at a lofty level—currently more than $650 billion dollars a year—including the wars in Iraq and Afghanistan. U.S. military outlays dwarf those of other industrialized countries, noninterventionists note. For example, Japan spends just $41 billion and Germany a mere $28 billion. Each American must pay more than $1,000 a year to support the military; the burden for each German is about $260, and for each Japanese it is about $310. Indeed, the United States now spends as much on the military as the rest of the world combined. That huge disparity is one tangible measure of the financial costs of sustaining a foreign policy based on maintaining U.S. global leadership.

The Global War on Terror also has had a deep and profound impact on domestic policies, including a substantial curtailment of civil liberties, a more intrusive federal government, and massive increases in deficit spending. The Global War on Terror vividly demonstrates that being a supporter of free markets and limited government precludes the advocacy of American interventionism abroad.

In addition, the government frequently manipulates the American economy in the name of national security. In marked contrast to the pre–World War II era, the national security apparatus wields considerable economic power. The emergence of multibillion-dollar defense firms whose principal (and, in some cases, sole) customer is the Pentagon is testimony to that fact. There also are restraints on commerce that would have been unthinkable only a few decades ago. Embargoes have been imposed on trade with several countries deemed to be adversaries of the United States. In addition to such formal sanctions, there exists a variety of restrictions on the export of technologies that the government has determined could have military applications or national security implications.

Not only has an interventionist foreign policy facilitated the expansion of federal governmental power at the expense of the private sector, opponents charge, it has produced ominous changes within the federal government. The conduct of foreign affairs during the cold war greatly enhanced the power of the executive branch. Fulfilling global obligations places a premium on the reliability of Washington's commitments as well as the speed (and often the secrecy) of execution. The procedural demands of an interventionist foreign policy conflict with the division of responsibilities and powers set forth in the Constitution. Extensive congressional participation in the foreign policy process, for example, raises the possibility of delay, the disruption of national unity, and the creation of doubts about America's constancy.

A number of observers have charged that maintaining a global interventionist policy has inexorably led to the emergence of an "imperial presidency." Chief executives have grown accustomed to using the military according to their personal definitions of the national interest. Harry Truman's unilateral decision to commit more than 300,000 U.S. troops to the Korean conflict was the most graphic episode of presidential war-making during the cold war, but it was hardly the only one. Nor has such executive displacement of the congressional authority over matters of war and peace abated now that the cold war is over. The Clinton administration's March 1999 decision to bomb Yugoslavia without seeking congressional authorization confirms that point.

This routine bypassing of the congressional war power is deeply alarming. The primary reason the Founders placed that authority in the legislative, rather than the executive, branch was to make certain that no one person would be able to take the republic into war. Such awesome power in the hands of a single individual (elected or otherwise), they concluded, was a characteristic of empires and absolute monarchies and was not appropriate for a constitutional republic.

In the Global War on Terror, the Bush administration has consistently overstepped its constitutional authority, claiming the power to designate even American citizens suspected of terrorist activity as "enemy combatants" and stripping them of their constitutional protection for the duration of the War on Terror.

Advocates of an activist U.S. role insist that America has an unprecedented opportunity and responsibility to, as Senator Richard Lugar put it, "manage the world." They dismiss calls for a less interventionist policy as a dangerous resurgence of isolationism that would have America, in the words of then–Secretary of Defense William Cohen, "act as if we could zip ourselves into a continental cocoon and watch events unfold on CNN."

Most proponents of noninterventionism or strategic independence are not suggesting that the United States become a hermit republic, however. They insist that there are many forms of engagement in world affairs and that the United States can and should be extensively involved economically, culturally, and even diplomatically. It is only the military form of engagement, they argue, that needs to be severely limited. America should recognize that the world has changed considerably since the early years of the cold war. There is no threat comparable to that posed by the Soviet Union, not even by al-Qaeda and other terrorist networks. There are now a number of prosperous countries capable of taking on far more responsibility for their own defense and for the security and stability of their region, rather than relying on the United States. Supporters of strategic independence contend that the United States could have a far smaller and less expensive military if Washington did not insist on being the global policeman and focused instead on countering major adverse developments that could pose a serious threat to the security of the American people. Even more important, the United States would reduce its risk by letting other powers handle problems in their neighborhoods. According to this logic, the countries of the European Union, not a U.S.-led NATO, should be responsible for dealing with squabbles in the Balkans. Similarly, Japan and other Asian powers should have primary responsibility for responding to a crisis on the Korean Peninsula or in the Taiwan Strait.

Moreover, the United States need not abrogate its position as the global economic powerhouse or disregard its extensive diplomatic influence. A libertarian foreign policy of noninterventionism holds that the execution of America's military force should be limited to instances when the territorial integrity, national sovereignty, or liberty of the United States is at risk, and also believes in reigning in the federal government and bringing it back to the constitutionally prescribed balance of executive and legislative power.

A wide-ranging and at times heated debate on the proper extent of U.S. security commitments is already beginning to take shape in the early years of the 21st century. The outcome of that debate will likely determine the nature of America's role in the world for many years to come.

TGC and MI

See also Military-Industrial Complex; Peace and Pacifism; War; War on Terror; War Powers

Further Readings

Bandow, Doug. *Foreign Follies: America's New Global Empire.* Longwood, FL: Xulon Press, 2006.
Carpenter, Ted Galen. *Peace and Freedom: Foreign Policy for a Constitutional Republic.* Washington, DC: Cato Institute, 2002.
Dempsey, Gary T. *Fool's Errands: America's Recent Encounters with Nation Building.* Washington, DC: Cato Institute, 2001.
Lynch, Tim, and Gene Healy. *Power Surge: The Constitutional Record of George W. Bush.* Washington, DC: Cato Institute, 2006.
Taft, Robert A. *A Foreign Policy for Americans.* New York: Doubleday, 1952.

FOUCAULT, MICHEL (1926–1984)

Michel Foucault was one of the most influential social theorists of the 20th century. He held a chair at the Collège de France; his studies on mental health, prison and penal reform, sexuality, and epistemology have profoundly influenced their respective fields. Particularly in academic humanities, Foucault's work enjoys widespread influence.

Much of Foucault's work drew on his personal experience. He was born in Poitiers, France, the son of a surgeon, and he spent a good part of his adult life critically reexamining the history of medicine, particularly its practitioners' troubling use of coercion. His early years in the rigidly structured elite French educational system seem to have deeply informed his analysis of institutionalized power relationships. In addition, his open homosexuality—and his embrace of its sadomasochistic subculture—led him to doubt the prevailing views regarding modern sexuality.

In each of these areas, Foucault questioned whether the accepted professional techniques, which were commonly coercive, could ever produce genuine, unbiased knowledge or, indeed, whether such knowledge was even possible. His influential book *Madness and Civilization* traced modern psychiatry's institutionalization of people whose behavior deviated from a set of increasingly stringent norms. He termed this process *the great confinement*, and he suggested that modernity had not increased liberty but reduced it.

A similar paradoxical approach runs throughout Foucault's work. The science of sexuality, Foucault argued, curtailed human freedom by insisting on rigid sexual identities, only some of which were normal. Likewise, modern epistemological categories, including the abstract numbering of populations and the scientific mapping of territories, increased state power and subjected the individual to the government in a profoundly dehumanizing manner. Foucault similarly argued that some of the worst cruelties of the civilized world could be found in the prison system, whose original purpose was to rehabilitate criminals and end the cruel punishments found before the Enlightenment. All that modernity had accomplished here, Foucault claimed, was to hide cruelty from public view, which helped it to continue.

Even outside his academic work, Foucault attacked modernity's darker side. He participated in the student uprisings of the 1960s, edited harrowing firsthand accounts of prison life, and even traveled to Iran in the ultimately vain hope of finding a genuine popular revolution against the modern state, exemplified by the Shah and his government. He was one of the leading inspirations of the modern gay rights movement, and he contributed often to the francophone gay press.

Although Foucault consciously rejected Enlightenment hopes for human betterment through liberty, he still has much to offer libertarians, and Foucault seems to have been aware of this possibility even while he always placed himself on the political left. In particular, his attacks on the way government conceptualized itself brought him to doubt the need for government at all and—surprisingly for some—to recommend to his students the works of Friedrich Hayek and Ludwig von Mises. In Foucault's words, they should be studied as examples of "the will not to be governed." His analysis of compulsory mental health has often been likened to that of libertarian psychiatrist Thomas Szasz, who discovered similar ideas independently and who also argued against forcible confinement.

Like many intellectuals of his era, Foucault joined the Communist Party, although he quickly abandoned both communism and Marxism. As recent scholars have agreed, Nietzsche was his most important intellectual ancestor. His mature works show a critical, antinomian libertarianism, rather than a rigid, class-based analysis of social phenomena. Particularly in his final years, as he grew ill from AIDS and contemplated his approaching end, his politics approached classical liberalism, tempered with a deep interest in Stoic philosophy. From attacking state coercion, Foucault had come to wonder what might replace it. Much of Foucault's work from these final years remains unpublished, and still more of it was destroyed, rendering much of Foucault an enigma in death as he was in life.

JTK

See also Bioethics; Coercion; Enlightenment; Government; Nietzsche, Friedrich; Psychiatry; Retribution for Crime; Sexuality

Further Readings

Burchell, Graham, Colin Gordon, and Peter Miller, eds. *The Foucault Effect: Studies in Governmentality: With Two Lectures by and an Interview with Michel Foucault*. London: Harvester Wheatsheaf, 1991.

Foucault, Michel. *Discipline and Punish: The Birth of the Prison*. Alan Sheridan, trans. New York: Vintage Books, 1995.

———. *The History of Sexuality Volume I: An Introduction*. Robert Hurley, trans. New York: Vintage Books, 1990.

———. *Madness and Civilization: A History of Insanity in the Age of Reason*. Richard Howard, trans. New York: Vintage Books, 1988.

Miller, James. *The Passion of Michel Foucault*. Cambridge, MA: Harvard University Press, 1993.

FREEDOM

There is little disagreement surrounding the claim that freedom is the central value of the liberal political order. However, there is little agreement regarding the proper understanding of this value and, more precisely, the kinds of constraints on individual freedom that the state would be justified in imposing. On this issue, proponents of freedom can be roughly divided into two basic camps: those who articulate the value of freedom negatively as "freedom from" interference, and those who understand it in a more positive fashion as "freedom to" live under certain conditions, participate in particular activities, or develop in a specified way. Simply put, advocates of negative freedom limit their focus to constraints that originate in the wills of other individuals or in state intervention. Freedom, in this sense, focuses on external human control over the decisions and actions of individuals, and it calls for respect for fundamental civil liberties. Accordingly, the function of the state is to maintain and enforce laws that protect this domain for individuals. In contrast, advocates of positive freedom point out that individuals also are constrained in other ways (e.g., by lack of opportunity or lack of resources). Some of the constraints may be material in origin, yet others political. Proponents of positive freedom appeal to certain desirable states of affairs for which negative freedom will not be a sufficient means.

Benjamin Constant drew the relevant distinction as one between the civil liberties exalted by modern theorists and the participation in public life that the ancients regarded as the essential component of being free. John Stuart Mill makes the classic argument for a modern notion of freedom in his book *On Liberty*. Mill defends freedom of conscience, freedom of the press, freedom of expression, freedom of association, and freedom to pursue "our own good in our own way, so long as we do not attempt to deprive others of theirs or impede their efforts to obtain it." As opposed to Mill's conception of freedom,

that of Jean-Jacques Rousseau more closely approaches that of the ancients, at least as Constant characterizes it. In *The Social Contract*, Rousseau famously identifies the most important kind of freedom as a constitutive element of democratic government. For Rousseau, freedom is not solely acting as we want without hindrance from other human agents. As Rousseau understands it, a person is free only to the extent that he participates in the political decisions that determine what he may or may not do. In this way, the state plays an active role in enhancing not only political freedom, but also moral freedom, "which alone makes [a man] truly master of himself." Political man trades the freedom of the state of nature for the freedom to be something much greater than he might otherwise have been.

It is clear that these differing conceptions of freedom arise from competing views of moral agency. Some conceptions of freedom give substantial weight to an individual's understanding of his own well-being. For example, Mill holds that, "with respect to his own feelings and circumstances the most ordinary man or woman has means of knowledge immeasurably surpassing those that can be possessed by anyone else." In marked contrast, as Isaiah Berlin points out in his seminal essay, "Two Concepts of Liberty," other accounts draw on notions of a

> dominant self . . . variously identified with reason, with my "higher nature," with the self which calculates and aims at what will satisfy it in the long run, with my "real," or "ideal," or "autonomous" self, or with myself "at its best"; which is then contrasted with irrational impulse, uncontrolled desires, my "lower" nature, the pursuit of immediate pleasures, my "empirical" or "heteronomous" self, swept by every gust of desire and passion, needing to be rigidly disciplined if it is ever to rise to the full height of its "real" nature.

Berlin's analysis can thus be read as a pointed warning against political orders committed to this view of human agency. In Berlin's words, "Enough manipulation with the definition of man, and freedom can be made to mean whatever the manipulator wishes. Recent history has made it only too clear that the issue is not merely academic."

In response to just this kind of argument, Charles Taylor claims that those who would have us reject positive freedom for "fear of the Totalitarian Menace" make us "incapable of defending liberalism in the form we in fact value it." Taylor's thesis is that freedom is not "just the absence of external obstacles *tout court,* but the absence of external obstacle to significant action, to what is important to man." We protect certain kinds of freedom (e.g., religious freedom) by appeal to their significance, not by appeal to the overall amount of freedom their exercise would allow. According to Taylor, no society would be considered more free simply because its members were permitted to carry out more acts all told, but fewer meaningful ones, say, fewer acts of religious worship. But if we concede that the objects of freedom can be more or less significant, it is hard to imagine how we might "maintain the incorrigibility of the subject's judgments about his freedom, or rule out second-guessing" with respect to these judgments. Taylor's argument urges a return to what he calls "the most inspiring terrain of liberalism, which is concerned with individual self-realizations," and it suggests "a view of freedom which sees it as realizable or fully realizable only within a certain form of society." Of course, this line of argument does little to ensure that such a society will not bring with it "excesses of totalitarian oppression in the name of liberty." Taylor's point, however, is that these worries must be taken up in their own right, not predetermined by a particular definition of freedom.

Challenges to conceptions of justice predicated on negative accounts of freedom extend beyond the objections posed by the proponents of positive accounts. In particular, critics of libertarian conceptions of justice have charged that appeals to freedom as understood in its negative sense do not provide the support that one might attribute to them in arguments for the minimal state. Critics contend that freedom-based justifications for the minimal state fail even when we assume that negative freedom would be determinative in such an argument. G. A. Cohen, for example, maintains that "it is quite unclear that social democratic restriction on the sway of private property, through devices like progressive taxation and the welfare minimum, represents any enhancement of governmental interference with freedom." Here it is important to notice that Cohen is concerned with negative freedom. His claim is that, without further argument, we cannot reject redistributive schemes on the grounds that they increase the total number of restrictions on negative freedom. For just as property rights constrain nonowners' actions to maximize negative freedom for property owners, "incursions against private property which *reduce* owners' freedom and transfer rights over resources to non-owners thereby *increase* the latter's freedom." Cohen concludes that "private property, like any system of rights . . . is a particular way of distributing freedom *and unfreedom*," even in its negative variety.

This species of critique leaves the advocate of libertarianism with several possibilities for response. First, the libertarian can offer the argument that the minimal state does indeed enhance negative freedom. This argument would be all the stronger for showing that strong property rights increase negative freedoms on the whole in society. A second line of response better attends to the fact that certain negative freedoms have more value than do others. The rights-based form of this argument draws on conceptions of negative freedom typically associated with John Locke. On Locke's account, the state should limit itself to a concern with those constraints on negative freedom that violate individual rights. Admittedly, the appeal to negative freedom cannot be foundational in an argument for the minimal state. Because the value of the negative freedoms protected by the minimal state is grounded in a particular set of individual rights, the rights must be grounded in something other than negative freedom.

One alternative to the rights-based defense of certain negative freedoms is consequentialist in nature. Here the work of F. A. Hayek is instructive. In his book *The Constitution of Liberty*, Hayek makes the argument that, "the case for individual freedom rests chiefly on the recognition of the inevitable ignorance of all of us concerning a great many of the factors on which the achievement of our ends and welfare depends." In other words, the negative freedoms identified with the minimal state allow individuals to "make use of this knowledge in their actions" for their own well-being and for the well-being of others. The consequentialist version of the argument thus allows one to defend a particular distribution of negative freedoms without an appeal to a particular set of individual rights.

TLP

See also Liberty in the Ancient World; Nonaggression Axiom; Paternalism; Positive Liberty; Rousseau, Jean-Jacques; Virtue

Further Readings

Berlin, Isaiah. "Two Concepts of Liberty." *Four Essays on Liberty*. Oxford: Oxford University Press, 1969.

Cohen, G. A. "Capitalism, Freedom, and the Proletariat." David Miller, ed. *Liberty*. Oxford: Oxford University Press, 1991.

Constant, Benjamin. "The Liberty of the Ancients Compared with That of the Moderns." *Political Writings*. Biancamaria Fontana, ed. Cambridge: Cambridge University Press, 1988.

Hayek, Friedrich A. *The Constitution of Liberty*. Chicago: Chicago University Press, 1978.

Kant, Immanuel. *Groundwork of the Metaphysic of Morals*. New York: Harper & Row, 1956

Locke, John. *Second Treatise of Government*. Indianapolis, IN: Hackett, 1980.

Mill, J. S. *On Liberty*. Indianapolis, IN: Hackett, 1978.

Nozick, Robert. *Anarchy, State, and Utopia*. New York: HarperCollins, 1974.

Rousseau, Jean-Jacques. *The Social Contract and Discourses*. London: J. M. Dent Ltd., 1973.

Taylor, Charles. "What's Wrong with Negative Liberty?" *The Idea of Freedom*. Alan Ryan, ed. Oxford: Oxford University Press, 1979.

Freedom of Speech

The emergence of freedom of speech as an essential value of Western civilization is inseparable from the emergence of individual religious liberty in the 17th and 18th centuries. For generations, following the Reformation of the

16th century, religious war, mutual fratricide, torture, hatred, and repression had rent the fabric of European society, which pointed to the increasing incompatibility of coercing inward belief and outward expression with the needs of civil and policy society. Further, the consciences of a growing number of Europeans were moved by the seeming contrast between the violence of such coercion and repression, on the one hand, and the claims of religion to be a source of peace and love, on the other hand. For reasons of practice and conviction, then, the call for liberty of belief and expression grew steadily more compelling for those who saw such spectacle as inconsistent with religion, creating a growing desire to find ways to live in societies of more mutual forbearance. The arguments on behalf of that mutual forbearance, however, led logically and in practice to freedom of speech being recognized as both a necessity of our living peacefully together and a moral end in itself.

Many of the calls for religious freedom initially were meant to apply only within limited but increasingly variegated communities of belief: to Protestants in general, for example; or, an extreme latitude at the time, to those who simply believed in God. As usually occurs with claims for liberty, however, the spirit of the arguments overflowed the initial boundaries envisaged. In societies that believed religion to be mankind's highest calling and whose members' greatest pain was occasioned by what they saw as heretical or impious expressions, winning the debate on behalf of liberty in religion—the area where restrictions on speech seemed the most reasonable—carried with it a victory on behalf of freedom of speech in general.

In the midst of the English Civil War, the Parliamentary party attempted to censor the book trade by means of the Licensing Order of 1643. In his *Areopagitica*, published in 1644, John Milton, although an ardent supporter of the Parliamentary cause, argued passionately on behalf of allowing the full force of free debate to sustain both liberty and truth. Although his opposition to censorship was intended for good Protestants alone, Milton's soaring defense of freedom of expression established more universal themes. One can choose truth and goodness, he wrote, only where there is "knowledge of evil": "I cannot praise a fugitive and cloistered virtue, unexercised and unbreathed, that never sallies out and sees her adversary." Confrontation with error, he wrote, is essential "to the confirmation of truth," and that confrontation depends on "hearing all manner of reason." Further, what men possibly could be trusted to regulate human discourse? When God gave man reason, Milton urged, "He gave him freedom to choose," which made human beings morally responsible. To "know" truth because of coercion was without merit, and Parliament would err grievously if it sought, even on behalf of the good, "to suppress all this flowery crop of knowledge and new light sprung up and yet springing daily in this city . . . to bring a famine upon our minds again." Any "free and

humane government" favored "free writing and free speaking." Liberty, he wrote, raises the human mind to rare heights: "Give me the liberty to know, to utter, and to argue freely according to conscience; above all liberties." We need not worry about the strength of truth: "Let her and Falsehood grapple; who ever knew Truth put to the worse, in a free and open encounter?" England, he urged, should be "the mansion house of liberty."

On the Continent, generations of religious warfare and persecution led many thinkers to believe that coerced uniformity and suppression of differences in belief were far more threatening to both the individual human soul and the stability and peace of society than diversity of opinion and freedom of expression. In many of his writings, the great critic, polemicist, and philosopher Pierre Bayle (1647–1706), a Huguenot living in exile in Holland after the revocation of even limited toleration of Protestants in France, argued that suppression of the outward expression of sincere belief, however false, corrupted the human spirit, leading men to a damnable cruelty and hypocrisy. Holland, finely balanced between Catholics and Protestants, permitted the most freedom of speech of any nation in Europe by the late 17th century, out of a prudential concern for what would follow if various claimants to truth had to fight for control of the state in order to have liberty of expression. In his *Tractatus-Theologico Politicus* (1670), Baruch Spinoza devoted his final chapter to the proposition that, "in a free commonwealth, every man may think as he pleases and say what he thinks." Because belief was a matter of "individual right . . . no man may surrender it even if he wishes to do so," and governments that sought to compel belief were "tyrannical" and therefore unstable and subject to violent overthrow. At the heart of such compulsion was the effort to control expression, and "the most tyrannical government will be that in which the individual is denied the freedom to express and to communicate to others what he thinks." The function of the state was not "to transform human beings from rational creatures into beasts or automatons," but, to the contrary, "to enable them to develop their mental and physical faculties in security" so long as they did not harm others in their liberty and security. In short, "the purpose of the state is, in actuality, freedom."

Shortly after his return to England from exile in Holland, the philosopher John Locke published *A Letter Concerning Toleration* (1689), in which he argued that "It is one thing to persuade, another to command" and "It is only light and evidence that can work a change in men's opinions." Locke did not intend that his arguments on behalf of toleration should apply in particular to atheists or Catholics, both of whom he believed represented a danger to the state and society. Yet as with the Declaration of Independence, whose "all men are created equal" and whose "life, liberty, and the pursuit of happiness" were far from inclusive claims in the author's mind, Locke had articulated a principle that had a power to expand human freedom in general.

The inseparability of the campaign for religious toleration from the emergence of claims on behalf of freedom of speech is seen clearly in the American experience, where the 1st Amendment of the Bill of Rights—ratified in 1791—first established freedom of religion as an essential right and only then established freedom of speech as such. Arguing in 1776 on behalf of religious liberty in the Commonwealth of Virginia, James Madison urged that "the opinions of men, depending only on the evidence contemplated by their own minds, cannot follow the dictates of other men." Madison's own bill declared that "all men shall be free to profess, and by argument to maintain, their opinion in matters of religion." With religion considered to be the most important set of truths, freedom there meant freedom of expression on virtually all matters of conscience and importance. Such freedom was, in Madison's view, among "the natural rights of mankind," and, thus, beyond the reach of any government.

Writing in support of the fullest possible freedom of belief and expression (absent direct harm to others), the English philosopher John Stuart Mill wrote in 1859, in his *On Liberty*, that, in order to establish freedom of expression, he would take the most difficult case of all, the right of those who dissented fundamentally in matters of religion, because if he could win the issue there, he had won it for all lesser instances. In making his plea for freedom of belief and expression, Mill essentially established the pole toward which both public opinion and jurisprudence gradually, fitfully, but powerfully would move.

Most people believe that they favor free speech, Mill argued, but, in fact, almost everyone sets limits at what they believe to be without value, or dangerous, or just obviously wrong. Why should we favor freedom of expression even to what we consider beyond the pale? For Mill, there were four ultimately compelling reasons, confirmed by history, for supporting "freedom of opinion, and freedom of the expression of opinion." First, the opinion might indeed be true, and "to deny this is to assume our own infallibility." Second, the opinion, although largely or almost wholly in error, most probably would "contain a portion of truth," and censorship would deny us the possible "remainder of the truth" that only could be gained by "the collision of adverse opinions." Third, even if prevailing opinion were the whole truth, if that truth were not "vigorously and earnestly contested," it would be believed by most not on "its rational grounds," but only "in the manner of a prejudice." Only freedom of expression would permit truth to be embraced by conviction, not by memorization. Fourth, if people were not obliged, by liberty of opinion, to defend their beliefs, truth would be "in danger of being lost, or enfeebled, and deprived of its vital effect on the character and conduct," becoming merely a formula repeated by rote, "inefficacious

for good . . . and preventing the growth of any real and heartfelt conviction, from reason or personal conviction." The negative consequences of the suppression of freedom of speech would fall both on the individual and the society deprived of strong and daring individuals. In Mill's celebrated formulation: "If all mankind minus one were of one opinion, and only one person were of the contrary opinion, mankind would be no more justified in silencing that one person, than he, if he had the power, would be justified in silencing mankind."

It was not until the 20th century that the U.S. Supreme Court, in a set of quite dramatic decisions, brought the interpretation of the 1st Amendment's speech clause— "Congress shall make no law . . . abridging the freedom of speech, or of the press"—closer to Mill's sense of such liberty. Originating in cases (and often in minority dissents) involving the rights of protestors opposed to American participation in World War I, a line of Supreme Court jurisprudence vastly broadened the meaning of protected free speech. In *Terminiello v. Chicago* (1949), writing for the Court, Justice William Douglas noted that the

> function of free speech under our system of government is to invite dispute. It may indeed best serve its high purpose when it induces a condition of unrest, creates dissatisfaction with conditions as they are, or even stirs people to anger.

In *Cohen v. Connecticut* (1971), the Court held that emotively powerful and offensive speech was constitutionally protected because outrage or anger "may often be the more important element of the overall message sought to be communicated." "One man's vulgarity," Justice Marshall Harlan opined, "is another's lyric." In *United States v. Eichman* (1990), the Court struck down the Flag Protection Act of 1989, ruling that, although "desecration of the flag is deeply offensive to many . . . the same might be said . . . of virulent ethnic and religious epithet . . . and scurrilous caricatures." In a free society, citizens were free, in the absence of direct harm, to be offensive and scurrilous in each other's eyes. In *R.A.V. v. City of St. Paul* (1992), the Court invalidated a city ordinance that sought to protect individuals from expression that "arouses anger, alarm or resentment on others on the basis of race, color, creed, religion or gender." Writing for the Court, Justice Antonin Scalia stated, "St. Paul has no such authority to license one side of a debate to fight freestyle, while requiring the other to follow Marquis of Queensbury rules."

The Court, however, has never taken the "no law" provision of the 1st Amendment literally. Obscenity, speech posing "a clear and present danger" of imminent violence, and disclosures of information (such as troop or naval movements) deemed threatening to national security all remain unprotected. Nonetheless, the Court has brought the law closer and closer to the spirit of John Stuart Mill's observation about not only freedom of speech, but also the freedom to act on the beliefs we hold and express:

> The only freedom which deserves the name, is that of pursuing our own good in our own way, so long as we do not attempt to deprive others of theirs, or impede their efforts to obtain it. Each is the proper guardian of his own health, whether bodily, or mental or spiritual. Mankind are greater gainers by suffering each other to live as seems good to themselves, than by compelling each to live as seems good to the rest.

The lessons learned during generations of religious fratricide have found a welcoming, although always threatened, home.

AK

See also Bill of Rights, U.S.; English Civil Wars; Locke, John; Religion and Liberty; Separation of Church and State

Further Readings

Bayle, Pierre. *Philosophical Commentary on These Words of the Gospel, Luke 14:23, "Compel Them to Come In, That My House May Be Full."* John Kilcullen and Chandran Kukathas, eds. Indianapolis, IN: Liberty Fund, 2005.

French, David A., Greg Lukianoff, and Harvey A. Silverglate. *FIRE's Guide to Free Speech on Campus.* Philadelphia: Foundation for Individual Rights in Education, 2005.

Madison, James. *James Madison on Religious Liberty.* Robert S. Alley, ed. Buffalo, NY: Prometheus Books, 1985.

Mill, John Stuart. *On Liberty.* New York: W. W. Norton, 1975 [1859].

Milton, John. *Areopagitica.* Eugene: University of Oregon, 1977 [1644].

Spinoza, Baruch. *Theological-Political Treatise.* 2nd ed. Samuel Shirley, trans. Indianapolis, IN: Hackett, 2001.

FREEDOM OF THOUGHT

Freedom of thought is a generic label that includes freedom of religion, speech, press, and artistic creation. It also was affiliated with a tradition of religious skepticism known as "freethinking" and "freethought." It is scarcely coincidental that 18th-century freethinkers were often associated with libertarian causes, such as freedom of speech and press. When dealing with an established church, such as the Anglican Church in England or the Catholic Church in France, to criticize the doctrines of Christianity also was to challenge the political status quo and render oneself vulnerable to potentially severe punishments for blasphemy.

The words *freethinking* and *freethinker* made their first appearance in English literature during the latter part of the 17th century, when they were applied to Pantheists, Epicureans, Pelagians, Socinians, Deists, and others who dissented from traditional Christian doctrines. Although *freethinker* began as a term of opprobrium because it described a person who preferred the judgments of his or her own reason over the dictates of a religious or secular authority, it was soon embraced by many proponents of intellectual independence.

The most influential defense of freethinking was written by Anthony Collins, a Radical Whig and literary executor of John Locke's estate. In *A Discourse of Free-Thinking* (1713), Collins wrote:

> By free-thinking I mean the use of the understanding in endeavoring to find out the meaning of any proposition whatsoever, in considering the nature of the evidence for or against it, and in judging of it according to the seeming force of the evidence.

As defined here, *freethinking* is synonymous with the critical investigation of a belief or doctrine. Collins was calling for more than the *legal* freedom to use one's mind; he was also challenging the widespread belief that some beliefs, whether in religion or politics, are sacrosanct and should therefore be immune to critical inquiry. In other words, Collins was defending the *moral* right to freedom of thought. As he put it, "we have a right to know or may lawfully know any truth. And a right to know truth whatsoever implies a right to think freely."

Arguments for freedom of thought were not confined to religious skeptics or to one particular religious group. The remarkable advances in science during the 17th century, which entailed the wholesale rejection of orthodox scholastic doctrines in physics and astronomy, illustrated the value of unrestrained critical inquiry. Equally important was the development of modern philosophy. René Descartes, for example, employed systematic doubt as a means of arriving at certainty. Although Descartes was careful to exempt essential moral and religious ideas from this methodical doubt, the Cartesian method—which was devoid of any appeals to authority—effectively communicated the message that freedom of thought is indispensable to the pursuit of truth.

The other great pioneer in modern philosophy in this period was Francis Bacon, a severe critic of orthodox doctrines in science and philosophy who called for a new "instauration" of knowledge. Perhaps the most lasting contribution of Bacon was his discussion of various "idols," or prejudices, of the human mind that hindered the pursuit of objective knowledge. The upshot was a stress on human fallibility and the innocence of error. There are various reasons that even well-intentioned people may disagree, according to Bacon. Dissent was not necessarily a result of the deliberate rejection of truth. Knowledge is cumulative; it advances as new information is discovered by empirical means. Intellectual progress (or what Bacon called "the advancement of learning") requires a continuous process of criticism, a willingness to examine accepted beliefs and of sorting the true from the false.

Arguments for freedom of thought appeared in various pleas for religious toleration and freedom of speech and press throughout the 17th century. One of the most influential was John Milton's book, *Areopagitica* (1644), which was cited as late as 1851 by Herbert Spencer in his *Social Statics* as presenting a definitive case for toleration. Milton's eloquent words—"Give me the liberty to know, to utter, and to argue freely according to my conscience, above all liberties"—would frequently be quoted by later libertarian writers.

Milton was a Puritan in his earlier years, but his fierce love of liberty caused him to repudiate the Puritan claim to a monopoly on religious truth. Thus, when the Puritan Parliament reinstated a law requiring the licensing of books in 1643, Milton responded with his *Areopagitica,* subtitled "A Speech for the Liberty of Unlicensed Printing, to the Parliament of England."

Although the *Areopagitica* defense of religious toleration did not extend to "Popery and open superstition," his forceful arguments transcended his own exceptions. Moreover, although his arguments specifically addressed prepublication licensing, they had much broader implications for freedom of thought. The inner logic of Milton's arguments would later be developed by libertarians and applied to areas other than freedom of the press.

Especially significant was Milton's statement that "here the great art lies, to discern in what the law is to bid restraint and punishment, and in what things persuasion only is to work." This attempt to draw a bright line between the proper spheres of state coercion and voluntary social interaction reflected a dominant theme in libertarian political theory.

Much of the *Areopagitica* is devoted to the idea that liberty is the best "school of virtue," a theme Milton was to take up in another essay. Milton contended that virtue and vice flowed from the same source, namely, the inner dispositions of the individual and that dispositions are ultimately determined by the judgments of reason. Because reason is "but choosing" (i.e., because reason is the seat of man's moral agency), an action can be deemed virtuous only insofar as it flows from a free, uncoerced choice. Hence, "They are not skilful considerers of human thing, who imagine to remove sin by removing the matter of sin. . . ." The "trial of virtue" requires a free society in which individuals are free to form their own judgments and learn from their mistakes. God does not "captivate [man] under a perpetual childhood of prescription, but trusts him with the gift of reason to be his own chooser."

During the 17th century, as arguments for free trade became increasingly popular, we find a number of analogies between freedom of thought and commercial freedom. In *Liberty of Conscience* (1643), the English merchant

Henry Robinson discussed "free trading of truth." Similarly, Milton compared the licensing of books to a commercial monopoly enforced by law, which "hinders and retards the importation of our richest Merchandise, Truth." By the early 19th century, British liberals explicitly defended freedom in religion (and of ideas generally) as one aspect of free trade. We commonly find expressions like "free trade in religion" and "free trade in Christianity" among foes of the Established Church.

This notion led to a theory of spontaneous order in ideas, one in which truth is most likely to emerge from uncoerced intellectual activity. According to Milton, truth "needs no policies, nor stratagems, nor licensing to make her victorious." The philosopher Spinoza agreed that "freedom is absolutely necessary for progress in science and the liberal arts: for no man follows such pursuits to advantage unless his judgment be entirely free and unhampered." John Locke was another who maintained that truth will fare well in the ideological marketplace: "Truth certainly would do well enough, if she were once made to shift for herself. . . . She is not taught by laws, nor has she any need of force to procure her entrance into the minds of men."

Even after the arguments for freedom of thought and expression had become widely accepted in Europe and America, there was a concern among those philosophers and social theorists who were proponents of freedom of thought that the absence of legal restraints was not sufficient to maintain the intellectual vitality required for a free society. This concern was expressed by Alexis de Tocqueville in his classic work, *Democracy in America*. Tocqueville's visit to America led him to arrive at a startling conclusion regarding its people: "I know of no country in which, generally speaking, there is less independence of mind and true freedom of discussion than in America." The majority in America has "enclosed thought within a formidable fence. A writer is free inside that area, but woe to the man who goes beyond it." Freedom of thought, which despotic monarchs had attempted in vain to suppress, was controlled in America by the power of public opinion. A dissenter with radical beliefs, although he may not have suffered legal punishment, could well find himself a social outcast, a person unable to hold political office and shunned by his neighbors.

A single despot, Tocqueville concluded, is able to strike the body, whereas a democracy "leaves the body alone and goes straight for the soul." "Thought," he wrote, "is an invisible power and one almost impossible to lay hands on, which makes sport of all tyranny." Even the most absolute of European sovereigns with an unlimited power to punish the body cannot prevent the spread of seditious and unorthodox ideas within their realms or even within the confines of their own courts. But American democracy, in which the will of the majority is invested with a quasi-sacred status, has been able to control public opinion to a degree that exceeds the power of the most despotic monarch.

This concern with the potentially deleterious effects of democratic opinion on freedom of thought also was expressed in J. S. Mill's "On the Liberty of Thought and Discussion," a seminal chapter in *On Liberty* (1859). In addition to legal freedom, Mill emphasized the need for "diversity of opinion" and the need for personal toleration of unorthodox beliefs in maintaining the social conditions of a free society.

GHS

See also Censorship; Conscience; Freedom of Speech; Religion and Liberty; Separation of Church and State

Further Readings

Bacon, Francis. *The Major Works*. Brian Vickers, ed. New York: Oxford University Press, 2002.

Collins, Anthony. *A Discourse of Free-Thinking*. New York: Garland, 1978.

Descartes, René. *Discourse on Method* and *Meditations on First Philosophy*. Indianapolis, IN: Hackett, 1998.

Locke, John. "A Letter Concerning Toleration." *The Works of John Locke in Nine Volumes*. vol. 5. 12th ed. London: Rivington, 1824.

Mill, John Stuart. "On the Liberty of Thought and Discussion." *On Liberty*. London: J. W. Parker and Son, 1859.

Milton, John. *Areopagitica and Other Political Writings of John Milton*. John Alvis, ed. Indianapolis, IN: Liberty Fund, 1999.

Orwell, George. *1984*. New York: Harcourt, 2000.

Spencer, Herbert. *Social Statics: or, the Conditions Essential to Happiness Specified, and the First of Them Developed*. London: John Chapman, 1851.

Tocqueville, Alexis de. *Democracy in America*. Harvey C. Mansfield and Delba Winthrop, eds. Chicago: University of Chicago Press, 2000.

Free-Market Economy

A free-market economy is a complex of voluntary exchange relationships. Some of these relationships are fleeting, as when someone buys a T-shirt from a street vendor, whereas others are more elaborate, as when a company agrees to supply to a customer certain specified cellular telephone services over the course of a year. Common to all voluntary exchanges is each party's belief that his participation in the exchange will make him better off. This conclusion follows from the fact that all exchanges on free markets are voluntary. Because every person has the right to refuse any offer of exchange, each person accepts only those offers that he believes to be in his interest.

All that is necessary for a free-market economy to exist is security of private property rights and its natural twin: contract law to ensure that exchanges of these rights are truly voluntary. Each owner of each bundle of rights can choose whether, when, and how to use or exchange his property in whatever ways he deems best. The only restriction is that this use or exchange not physically harm others' properties, nor obstruct others' equal rights to use their properties as they choose.

Even with no production, the voluntary exchange of property rights means that parties to these exchanges are made better off. But people go beyond simple exchange; they produce. Producers in a free-market economy assemble various inputs into outputs that are then offered to consumers. If consumers willingly purchase some output at a price sufficiently high to enable the producer to cover all of his costs, the producer makes both himself and his customers better off. The world is materially wealthier as a consequence of this production decision.

At first glance, this conclusion might appear odd because there is no centralized decision maker in a free-market economy. Consumption and production decisions are made individually by each property owner according to his own assessment of how his resources can best be used to promote whatever ends he chooses to pursue. It appears intuitive that the results would be chaotic. However, decentralization of decision making within a regime of private property rights not only does not lead to chaos, but, in fact, generates a coherent and prosperous economic order that would be impossible to achieve otherwise.

The great advantage of the free market is that it maximizes the amount of mutual accommodation at work to satisfy human wants. Mutual accommodation occurs whenever two or more people adjust their actions with respect to each other in ways that make each of them better off. Even if all human wants, resources, and production techniques were unchanging, the immense number of different wants and alternative ways of satisfying these wants implies that no single person or committee could possibly learn all that must be known to direct production as effectively as it is directed by the market. Decision making *must* be decentralized. Different bits of knowledge from literally millions of people are necessary to produce almost any products found in modern society.

Consider the ordinary pencil. No single person or committee can know what kind of wood is best used for the pencil shaft *and* where to find the trees that produce this wood *and* how to make the ax for felling the trees *and* where to find the graphite used for the pencil's center *and* how to build the machines used to extract the graphite from the earth *and* how to refine the graphite *and* where to find and how to mix the bauxite and alumina necessary to make the aluminum ferrule that holds the eraser on securely *and* how to extract the oil from the ground *and* how to refine it so that it serves as the base of the paint to coat the pencil *and* how to accomplish all of the other multitude of tasks necessary for the production of a pencil. A few moments of reflection reveal that the amount of knowledge required to produce an ordinary pencil is incomprehensibly vast.

Pencils are produced only because millions of people, each one with highly specialized knowledge of one of these countless different pieces of the process necessary to produce pencils, cooperate in ways that result in their production and sale. This cooperation is directed by market prices, which do a far better job at coordination than could possibly be achieved by a central planner. If, say, pencil retailers initially overestimated the number of pencils demanded by consumers, these retailers will, in the future, purchase fewer pencils from pencil manufacturers. Needing to supply fewer pencils, pencil manufacturers reduce their demands for the inputs used to manufacture pencils. Consequently, the price of each of these inputs falls. These falling prices tell producers of these inputs (paint for the pencil casing, lead-and-graphite shafts for the core, aluminum ferrules, etc.) to produce fewer of these inputs. The production of a larger volume of different inputs for other purposes becomes more attractive.

The price system informs each of the myriad producers along the way to reduce the amount of effort and resources devoted to making parts for pencils (and, hence, to shift this effort toward the production of inputs whose prices have risen relative to those of pencil parts). The Nobel laureate economist F. A. Hayek perceptively explained this communications feature of the price system:

> The most significant fact about this system is the economy of knowledge with which it operates, or how little the individual participants need to know in order to be able to take the right action. In abbreviated form, by a kind of symbol, only the most essential information is passed on only to those concerned. It is more than a metaphor to describe the price system as a kind of machinery for registering change, or a system for telecommunications which enables individual producers to watch merely the movement of a few pointers, as an engineer watches the hands of a few dials, in order to adjust their activities to changes of which they may never know more than is reflected in the price movement.

As essential as this system of decentralized decision making is when wants, resources, and production techniques are static, it is even more essential when these things change. In reality, constant change—change initiated by both consumers and producers—is the norm.

In light of what has so far been said, the reader can easily see that unexpected changes in consumer tastes, resource availability, and production techniques can be accommodated best by relying on people on the spot—each with a direct and personal stake in accommodating those changes—to arrive at ways to best respond to these changes. Relying on political authorities to accommodate these changes would be to rely on people who possess neither sufficient incentive nor the detailed knowledge necessary to respond appropriately.

What isn't as obvious is the advantageous role played by decentralization in promoting beneficial change. Although the current pattern of resource use might be better than all other known alternatives, the number of possible ways to use resources is so colossal that even the best currently known set of resource uses almost certainly can be improved upon. Israel Kirzner is surely correct to insist that "we live in an open-ended world, in which as yet unseen opportunities always exist for improving human well-being through the discovery of new resources or of new ways of deploying resources productively."

Discovering these unseen opportunities requires human creativity—creativity to produce heretofore unimagined goods and services, and creativity to devise and execute heretofore unknown means of producing outputs. If all production decisions are required to be made only centrally, by politically selected operatives, the amount of productive creativity at work will be minimal. The reason is that only people on the spot possess a sufficiently specialized knowledge of the myriad nuanced facts surrounding any particular piece of the economic landscape. The intimate familiarity of someone who is "on the spot" is likely to provide him with reliable hints about how that piece of the landscape might be improved. Such hints are reliable because they are the product of deep familiarity borne of specialization. Compared with a centralized decision maker, the on-the-spot person has a greater sense of both the possible (i.e., how the current way of doing things might be improved) and the impossible (i.e., the inevitable limitations pressing on his piece of the economic landscape).

Moreover, when decisions to experiment with new patterns of production are made by owners of private property, each experimenter bears the largest bulk of the costs—and receives a large part of the benefits—of such experiments. Internalizing the costs and benefits of economic experiments on those who actually decide which experiments to undertake and which to avoid is the best possible way of ensuring that we get the experiments necessary to generate progress without, at the same time, suffering waves of experiments that prove to be wasteful.

The great advantage of a free-market economy is that its foundation of private property rights means that decisions on resource use are decentralized; they are in the hands of people on the spot, each with unique knowledge of how best to use his resources to accommodate the wishes of other property rights owners within his purview. The prohibition against anyone coercing or defrauding another into accepting an offered exchange means that the resulting prices and other information generated by market transactions are reliable guides to how resources can effectively be used to satisfy human wants. The spur of profit prompts people not only to adjust to changes in familiar and predictable ways, but also to be alert to creative new ways to use resources. These market signals ensure that the countless instances of on-the-spot mutual accommodation that occur daily in markets coalesce into a vast productive order. If history is a guide, a free-market economy ensures continual improvement in humankind's material welfare.

DJB

See also Civil Society; Decentralism; Entrepreneurship; Laissez-Faire Policy; Private Property; Wealth and Poverty

Further Readings

Cox, W. Michael, and Richard Alm. *Myths of Rich & Poor*. New York: Basic Books, 1999.

Hayek, F. A. "The Use of Knowledge in Society." *Individualism and Economic Order*. F. A. Hayek, ed. Chicago: University of Chicago Press, 1948. 77–91.

Kirzner, Israel M. *How Markets Work*. London: Institute of Economic Affairs, 1997.

Lebergott, Stanley. *Pursuing Happiness*. Princeton, NJ: Princeton University Press, 1993.

Polanyi, Karl. *The Great Transformation*. New York: Octagon Books, 1975.

Rand, Ayn. *Capitalism: The Unknown Ideal*. New York: Penguin Putnam, 1986.

FREE TRADE

Free trade means the exchange of goods and services across international borders, unhindered by government tariffs, quotas, or other restrictions. Since the publication of *The Wealth of Nations* by Adam Smith in 1776, the debate over free trade has been one of the major battlegrounds in the broader controversy about economic freedom. Free trade is an essential component of globalization, which includes not only trade, but the international flow of capital and people and the resulting integration of national economies with each other.

Free trade has been a central tenet of the libertarian, or classical liberal, philosophy for centuries. The same philosophical and economic arguments for the freedom of exchange within a national economy apply equally to exchange across international borders. According to libertarian principles, workers should be free to voluntarily exchange the fruits of their labors with others for mutual benefit, whether the trading partner lives across the road or across an ocean. The increased competition occasioned by free trade can indeed result in some domestic industries losing market share and workers temporarily losing jobs, but advocates of free trade see this loss as a normal and healthy outcome of free-market competition.

Mankind has always engaged in trade. Even in the poorest societies, households have traded with one another, and rural farmers have traded with city dwellers. However, natural barriers, long distances, and government controls have hindered international trade throughout much of mankind's history. Despite those obstacles, trade flourished in the Mediterranean basin for centuries before the rise of the Roman Empire, reaching its height in the 2nd and 3rd centuries A.D., while during the late Middle Ages, the member states of the Hanseatic League were engaged in a burgeoning trade in the Baltic and North Seas. During that same time, Venice thrived as the center of the overland spice trade from Asia. Venetian traders pioneered foreign exchange, bank loans, accounting, and letters of credit. Spices and manufactured goods were the staple of trade in the Mediterranean, whereas lumber, fish, wool, and hides were the chief commodities of trade in Northern Europe.

The voyages of discovery in the 15th and 16th centuries opened new routes among Europe, the New World of the Americas, and the markets of South and East Asia, ushering in the Mercantilist Era. The discoveries and dramatic expansion of sea-going trade were made possible by the development of three-masted ships, called *carracks*, which could sail more sharply into the wind and made shipping less dependent on seasonal trade winds. The leading trading nations of that era, which lasted until about 1800, were Spain and Portugal, followed by the Dutch Republic and then France and Great Britain. As trade grew, so did government intervention. According to the prevailing mercantilist ideas at the time, exports were preferable to imports because they better enabled governments to acquire and accumulate gold, the universal currency of the day. As a result, a web of national laws evolved that hindered trade in a broad range of goods, but especially manufactured items.

Against this backdrop, Adam Smith published his magisterial work, *An Inquiry into the Nature and Causes of the Wealth of Nations*. Smith argued, with systematic logic and illuminating examples, that a nation's wealth is not measured by its stockpile of gold, but by the ability of its people to produce goods and services of value to others. Nations raise their productivity through the division of labor, with households, regions, and nations specializing in what they do best. Trade allowed the creation of more wealth by expanding the size of the market, thus allowing a finer division of labor among and within nations. As Smith famously observed in Book IV,

> It is the maxim of every prudent master of a family, never to attempt to make at home what it will cost him more to make than to buy. . . . What is prudence in the conduct of every private family, can scarce be folly in that of a great kingdom. If a foreign country can supply us with a commodity cheaper than we ourselves can make it, better buy it of them with some part of the produce of our own industry, employed in a way in which we have some advantage.

The intellectual argument for free trade was fortified in 1817 when British stockbroker David Ricardo first explained the theory of "comparative advantage." According to this theory, even if a nation's workers can produce everything more efficiently than workers in other nations, they can still trade profitably. What matters is what those workers produce most efficiently compared with whatever else they could produce. Hence, if workers in a rich country are twice as efficient at producing shoes as workers in a poor country, but five times more efficient at producing computer chips, it is still an advantage for both nations for the rich country to specialize in computer chips and import shoes from the poor country. By specializing in their comparative advantages, each country can shift resources—capital, labor, and land—to those sectors where gains in productivity and output are greatest. The final result is that workers in both nations can increase their consumption of both goods.

The ideas of Smith and Ricardo fueled the movement in Great Britain to repeal trade barriers and embrace free trade. Reformers Richard Cobden and John Bright led a successful effort in 1846 through the Anti-Corn Law League to the repeal of Britain's high tariffs on agricultural grains. For the rest of the 19th century, Britain engaged unilateral free trade. Cobden later joined Parliament and became an international advocate of free trade as an instrument of peace among nations.

Meanwhile, in a series of brilliant essays, French economist Frédéric Bastiat argued for free trade on the European continent. Through a combination of incisive analysis and devastating satire, Bastiat ridiculed the whole range of protectionist arguments. In "A Petition," for example, he used the protectionists' own logic to argue for a law requiring citizens to cover their windows during the day to protect France's candle-making industry from unfair competition from the sun. Like Cobden, Bastiat argued that international commerce promoted peace among nations and is widely credited with the saying, "When goods cannot cross borders, armies will."

Bastiat portrayed free trade as an essential human liberty. In an 1849 essay, "Communism and Protection," Bastiat noted,

> every citizen who has produced or acquired a product should have the option of applying it immediately to his own use or of transferring it to whoever on the face of the earth agrees to give him in exchange the object of his desires. To deprive him of this option when he has committed no act contrary to public order and good morals, and solely to satisfy the convenience of another citizen, is to legitimize an act of plunder and to violate the law of justice.

Although the benefits of free trade were soon accepted as economic orthodoxy, it was not universally practiced even during the height of the first wave of globalization in the 19th and early 20th centuries. Germany and the United States, in particular, used trade barriers to protect certain industries. But barriers to trade remained on average low compared with what they had been during the mercantilist era, and rapid industrialization, falling transportation costs due to steamships and railroads, and political stability fueled a dramatic rise in global trade and capital flows until World War I.

The global conflict from 1914 to 1918 disrupted trade and ushered in new economic controls that did not disappear when the war ended, and efforts to return to the economic policies of the more liberal prewar system were only partially successful. The Great Depression of the 1930s unleashed a vicious cycle of rising trade barriers, falling trade volume, and deepening economic misery and nationalism. The U.S. Congress and then-President Herbert Hoover compounded the crisis by enacting the Smoot–Hawley tariff in 1930, which raised tariffs dramatically on a broad swath of imports to the United States. The tariff bill did not cause the Great Depression, but it did prolong and deepen it, and it certainly did not protect domestic industry and jobs as its advocates claimed it would.

After the devastation of the Great Depression and World War II, the United States and its Western allies lowered trade barriers unilaterally and through the multilateral General Agreement on Tariffs and Trade (GATT), which 23 nations first signed in 1947. The reduction in trade barriers stimulated a dramatic rise in global trade flows and cemented peaceful ties among Western Europe, the United States, and Japan. Through engagement in the global economy, the "Tigers" of East Asia—South Korea, Taiwan, Singapore, and Hong Kong—transformed themselves from poor to rich countries. Beginning in the 1970s, Mainland China, India, Chile, Mexico, and less-developed nations lowered their previously high trade barriers, welcomed foreign investment, and dramatically increased their trade with the rest of the world. The collapse of global communism in 1989 and the growing disillusionment with protectionism as a tool of development have led to further reductions in trade barriers worldwide.

Despite more than two centuries of economic thought and empirical evidence in support of free trade, it continues to remain controversial today. Industries seeking relief from competition from abroad have been joined by environmentalists, antimarket activists, and some conservatives in opposing market-opening trade agreements. Others have argued that free trade spurs a "race to the bottom" as multinational companies seek locations where labor and regulatory costs are lowest. Supporters of free trade counter that the wealth that trade creates allows people in less-developed countries to raise their own environmental and labor standards and to reduce or eliminate child labor. They point out that most global investment flows between developed countries, where workers are more productive because of better education, capital, and infrastructure.

Today, people generally enjoy greater freedom to engage in mutually beneficial trade across international borders than they had been allowed in the past, but government controls still remain significant. Trade barriers in much of the less-developed world remain high, retarding development and restricting freedom. In rich countries, low average tariff levels are belied by stubbornly high barriers against imports of textiles, apparel, steel, and many agricultural goods, such as sugar, cotton, beef, citrus, and dairy products. So-called antidumping laws are used to impose tariffs on imports that are allegedly being sold at an unfairly low price, but in reality are being priced according to normal market conditions.

Libertarians agree on the desirability of free trade, but not always on how to achieve it. Some libertarians are skeptical of trade agreements between governments, such as the North American Free Trade Agreement, because such agreements can exclude politically sensitive sectors from liberalization or can create new bureaucracies to monitor environmental or labor standards. They see the World Trade Organization (WTO), the successor to the GATT, as an unnecessary governmental body and a potential threat to national sovereignty. Other libertarians argue that such agreements, including those negotiated through the WTO, restrain the power of governments to interfere in peaceful commerce, and that any flaws are usually outweighed by the trade liberalization they achieve. Debate also continues on whether trade promotes peace among nations, as Richard Cobden and others believed. A decline in international wars in recent decades, along with rising globalization, appears to support the connection, although some economists challenge whether there is any significant correlation.

Despite the political controversy it generates, free trade has become widely accepted by economists as the best trade policy for promoting a nation's prosperity. It is a genuine libertarian idea that has gained widespread acceptance in theory, if not in practice.

DTG

See also Anti-Corn Law League; Development, Economic; Globalization; Mercantilism; Taxation

Further Readings

Bastiat, Frédéric. *Economic Sophisms* and *Selected Essays on Political Economy*. Princeton, NJ: Van Nostrand, 1964.
Bhagwati, Jagdish. *In Defense of Globalization*. New York: Oxford University Press, 2004.
Hazlitt, Henry. *Economics in One Lesson*. San Francisco: Laissez Faire Books, 1996.
Hinde, Wendy. *Richard Cobden: A Victorian Outsider*. New Haven, CT: Yale University Press, 1987.
Irwin, Douglas. *Against the Tide: An Intellectual History of Free Trade*. Princeton NJ: Princeton University Press, 1996.
———. *Free Trade under Fire*. 2nd ed. Princeton, NJ: Princeton University Press, 2005.
Larsson, Tomas. *The Race to the Top: The Real Story of Globalization*. Washington, DC: Cato Institute, 2001.
Lindsey, Brink. *Against the Dead Hand: The Uncertain Struggle for Global Capitalism*. New York: Wiley, 2002.
Norberg, Johan. *In Defense of Global Capitalism*. Washington, DC: Cato Institute, 2003.
Sally, Razeen. *Classical Liberalism and International Economic Order: Studies in Theory and Intellectual History*. London: Routledge, 1998.
Smith, Adam. *An Inquiry into the Nature and Causes of the Wealth of Nations*. New York: Modern Library, 1982 [1776].
Wolf, Martin. *Why Globalization Works*. New Haven, CT: Yale University Press, 2004.

FRENCH REVOLUTION

The French Revolution, which usually dates from the meeting of the Estates-General in 1789 to the end of the Directory in 1799, or sometimes to 1815, was part of a more general movement for liberal reform that transformed Western Europe and North America in the late 18th century. This movement for liberal reform, whose aims included deregulation of the economy, constitutional limits on the power of the monarch, equality before the law, freedom of speech and of the press, and religious tolerance can be seen as originating in the American Revolution, continuing in several parts of Europe during the 1780s with the reforms of the "enlightened despots," among them Joseph II of Austria, and intensifying with the outbreak of the French Revolution in 1789. The historian R. R. Palmer has shown how reform ideas, money, and people flowed back and forth between America and Europe during those decades as the aptly named "trans-Atlantic" revolution swept away the old regime and created the foundations for the modern liberal, constitutional, and democratic societies that were to emerge in the 19th century.

The French Revolution not only transformed France by sweeping away the legal and political privileges of the ruling elites, but also triggered independent revolutions in other states, such as the French colony of Haiti, where ex-slaves created an independent state. More important, it carried the reformist ideals of democracy and republicanism via the French Civil Code to the neighboring European states as Republican and then later Napoleonic armies conquered much of Europe. One of the many paradoxes created by the French Revolution is the idea that all the people of Europe could be liberated from feudal oppression at the point of a French gun. Another paradox, which was hotly debated by liberal historians in the 19th century, was how to explain a movement whose original intentions were to increase individual liberty, deregulate the economy, and limit state power that yet produced the Jacobin Terror and the military dictatorship of Napoleon Bonaparte. It might well be that every revolution for liberty sows the seeds of an inevitable period of counterrevolution before more stable and workable political and economic institutions emerge in which liberty can flourish.

It is useful to view an event as complex as the French Revolution as a series of sometimes overlapping stages in which rival groups contended for control of the state, with various political groups having the upper hand at different times. Classical liberals were active at some of these stages and were able to implement many of their reforms, but at other times they were forced into exile, as was Benjamin Constant. Still others went into political retirement or even were arrested and killed.

The first of these stages was essentially prerevolutionary and took place between 1787 and 1789, when the fiscal crisis of the Old Regime forced Louis XVI to call a meeting of the Estates-General, the first since 1614, to enact new tax measures to stave off bankruptcy.

This meeting was followed by a stage marked by liberal reforms passed by the National Assembly, the parliamentary body created when the Third Estate (i.e., those who represented neither the nobility nor the clergy) declared itself, in June 1789, to be the National Assembly of France and invited the other estates to join it. The Assembly immediately proceeded to enact reforms that effectively ended the Old Regime. On the night of August 4, 1789, in one of the most dramatic moments of the Revolutionary period, one member of the nobility after another stood in the Assembly and renounced all feudal obligations owed them. Several weeks later, the Assembly proclaimed the Declaration of the Rights of Man and of the Citizen. In the form of a new National Constituent Assembly, it was the Third Estate that undertook the more difficult tasks of drawing up a new constitution, reforming the administration of the country, and reforming the judiciary. The result was the Constitution of 1791, which, for the first time in France, created a liberal constitutional monarchy.

The third stage saw a militarization and expansion of the Revolution. It began on September 20, 1792, with the declaration that France was a republic, and continued through the fall of Robespierre on 9 Thermidor Year II (July 27, 1794). It and the subsequent stages of the Revolution were generally marked by centralization, war, and expansion, until the final defeat of Napoleon in 1815. This constant warfare was partly a reflection of the pressing need for France to defend itself against a coalition of monarchical powers opposed to the Revolution, a coalition that was led and financed by Great Britain and that sought to restore the monarchy and the privileges of the clergy and nobility. It also was partly the result of the desire to liberate the rest of Europe from the burden of feudalism by force of arms if necessary.

Internally, the Revolution became more radical with the trial and execution of the King in January 1793. From then onward, the radical, antimarket Jacobins gained in political power, purged their enemies, and initiated the Terror, which was to characterize the remainder of the Revolution's third stage. During the Terror, the Jacobins suspended the rule of law in order to eradicate their enemies. For example, the "Law of Suspects" facilitated the arrest of anyone suspected of opposing the regime. During this period, any power previously in the hands of liberals was removed. Liberal policy,

which since 1789 was aimed at creating a free society in France, was replaced by an economic dictatorship whose primary goal was to fund the state and the army. Perhaps the most famous decree falling under this rubric was the Law of the Maximum, which introduced stringent price controls. In addition, the "Ventôse Decrees" allowed the state to confiscate the property of "enemies of the state." It is estimated that 17,000 people were officially executed during the Terror—many by the newly invented humane killing machine known after its inventor as the guillotine. A further 10,000 to 12,000 people were summarily killed without trial. That illiberal madness only ended when Maximilien Robespierre, the leader of the Jacobins, was arrested on the ninth of Thermidor (July 27, 1794) as a result of internecine struggles among the ruling elite. He was guillotined the following day.

The fourth stage reflects a period of relatively more moderate, liberal republicanism under a government known as the Directory (1794–1799). Under the Directory, the inflationary paper money, *assignats*, originally issued in 1790, was replaced by a more stable metallic currency, and the policy of massive economic interventionism came to an end. The wars of expansion, however, continued, especially in northern Italy, where a young general, Napoleon Bonaparte, was in the process of creating the foundations for a future political career as someone who could solve the problem of continuing political chaos with strong leadership. The hopes of many liberals for the Directory were dashed by persistent corruption, the threats of political coups from both the "left" (radical Jacobins) and "right" (royalists), the annulment of elections when royalists did better than expected, and an ongoing policy of anticlericalism.

The fifth and final stage of the Revolution began with the coup d'état on 18 Brumaire (November 10, 1799), which bought General Bonaparte to power, first as Consul and then as self-proclaimed Emperor. The Empire is marked by a curious amalgam of legislation that entrenched many aspects of the Revolution in French society—under the Civil or "Napoleonic" Code of 1804—and resurgent militarism and statism that were antithetical to the liberal ideals of 1789. When Napoleon was finally defeated at Waterloo in 1815, the French Bourbon monarchy was restored in name, but was forced to coexist with a new legal code and a constitution—the "Charter" of 1814—that realized many of the ideals of the liberal, constitutional monarchists who had begun the Revolution.

The role played by classical liberals in the French Revolution was significant, although they had to compete (not always successfully) with radical democratic Jacobins, militaristic Napoleonic imperialists, and unrepentant monarchists. During the last decades of the Old Regime, many prominent Enlightenment figures had argued for religious toleration (Voltaire), economic liberalization (Turgot), the abolition of slavery and the slave trade (the abbés Raynal and Grégoire), and other liberal reforms. They helped create a climate of opinion on the eve of the

Revolution that was reflected in the *Cahiers des doléances*—the books of complaint drawn up in each region for the Estates-General in 1789. These documents reflected the almost universal opposition to the unequal and heavy tax burden placed on ordinary citizens. Thus, like the American Revolution, the early phase of the Revolution can be understood, at least in part, as a tax revolt against the Old Regime. There were numerous classical liberals among the clergy and the nobility who were members of the Estates-General and who defected from their Estates to join the Third Estate in the National Assembly. There they introduced the reform legislation of the period 1789 to 1791, during which the liberalization of French society was most advanced. The classical liberals active at this stage of the Revolution tended to be supporters of the free market, among them Pierre Samuel Dupont de Nemours, and of constitutional monarchism—such as the members of the "Society of 1789," which included Lafayette, Sieyès, and Mirabeau. Their agenda was to abolish the legal privileges enjoyed by some groups, to free the economy, and to place constitutional limits on the powers of the King.

At a time when formal political parties did not exist, like-minded individuals formed loose and informal groupings or clubs to pursue a common political agenda. Prior to the Terror, the most liberal of the groups was the Girondins, so called because its most influential members represented the Gironde region around Bordeaux. The Girondins were active in the Legislative Assembly (1791–1792) and in the early National Convention (1792–1793), where they continued their liberal reforms. However, their position as defenders of individual liberty was severely weakened by their support for the war on those nations that supported the French monarchy. Their primary motive in doing so was to rally popular support for the Revolutionary regime, but it required spending vast resources on the army, resources that were not available to the government, but that were procured by inflating the newly issued currency, paper *assignats* supposedly backed by the expected future sale of land confiscated from the church and the nobility. The hyperinflation that followed did much to alienate the poorer classes from the liberal revolution and to radicalize the urban poor, thus paving the way for the political victory of extremist Jacobins. The war was used as justification for massive interventions in the economy, notably the Law of the Maximum, which imposed price controls on staple goods. The Girondins were further weakened by a split in their ranks over the trial and execution of the King. Some of them were radical republicans who voted for the execution and for the formation of a republic in order to protect the Revolution from aristocratic counterrevolution. Others were moderate republicans, such as the American Thomas Paine, who in the Convention opposed the execution and favored exiling the former Louis XVI to America. Still others were constitutional monarchists, who wanted only to chastise the King and to tighten the constitutional limits on

his power. Thus, weakened by internal disputes, the economic crisis brought on by hyperinflation, and military reversals, the Girondins were driven from power by the Jacobins in June 1793. The Jacobins forced many Girondins to flee, arresting some, including Paine, and executing others. The Jacobins reversed many of the liberal reforms that had been introduced since the Estates-General was first convened. The rule of law was suspended so that "enemies" of the revolution could be more easily arrested, tried, and executed; the currency was further devalued to finance the revolutionary armies; and extensive price controls and other government interventions in the economy were introduced to supply the urban crowds with cheap bread and the armies with materials.

Not all the liberals involved in shaping the Revolution were Girondins. The so-called *Idéologues* were influential during the period of the Directory and the early years of Napoleon's rule. The Directory reintroduced free markets and limited government and was thus naturally attractive to liberals recovering from the Terror. One notable liberal, Antoine-Claude-Laurent Destutt de Tracy, found a home in the newly created National Institute's Class of Moral and Political Sciences, where he pursued his study of human behavior and the nature of free institutions, a study he called "idéologie." Other classical liberals were active as journalists or in politics, among them Benjamin Constant and Jean-Baptiste Say. With Napoleon's rise to power, liberal criticism was less and less tolerated, and many Idéologues fell silent, retired, or were forced into exile. This state of affairs continued until 1814, when Napoleon belatedly rediscovered the virtues of liberal constitutionalism on his return from Elba.

It remains to evaluate the impact of the French Revolution on European society, especially its contribution to creating a free society, both in France and elsewhere in Europe. This assessment poses a difficulty for the classical liberal, in that some stages of the Revolution were marked by considerable liberal reforms, whereas others witnessed the reversal of those reforms and the reemergence of political and economic oppression in a variety of forms. The classical liberals of the early and mid-19th century generally held, given the refusal of the Old Regime to reform itself, that the Revolution was inevitable and was the only means whereby the old ruling elites could be dispossessed of their privileges. Despite its ups and downs, on balance it made a major contribution to individual liberty by creating the foundation for the free societies that were to emerge in the 19th century. As the liberal historian and politician François Guizot noted with some wisdom and insight in 1820:

> I will still say that the Revolution, brought on by the necessary development of a society in progress, founded on moral principles, undertaken with the design of the general good, was the *terrible* but *legitimate* battle of right against privilege, of legal liberty against despotism, and that to the

Revolution alone belongs the task of regulating itself, or purging itself, of founding the constitutional monarchy to consummate the good that it has begun and to repair the evil it has done.

When trying to draw up a "balance sheet," one needs to take into account the complexity and long duration of the Revolution and the short- and long-term changes brought about in European society. Many of the beneficent reforms took some years to emerge, which suggests that Edmund Burke's vigorous criticism of the Revolution in 1790 was somewhat premature. Some of the gains were short-lived and were overturned by later regimes, thus making an overall assessment of its achievements difficult. The positive achievements of the Revolution include the following: the abolition of the legal privileges of the ruling elites of the old order; the sale or privatization of church and émigré land that created a new, more diversified property-owning class; the abolition of slavery and the granting of many civic rights to women, such as divorce; the creation of the Civil Code—begun before Napoleon but completed under his rule—that provided legal guarantees for the protection of life, liberty, and property, but that unfortunately severely reduced the rights of married women; the spread of the idea that a constitution should spell out the rights and duties of citizens and limit the power of the monarch; and the spread of the ideas of individual rights, democracy, and republicanism.

The negative consequences of the Revolution also were quite numerous. They included the virulent anticlericalism of some of the radicals, which alienated potential supporters of the Revolution, such as the liberal-minded clergy and pious peasants; the hyperinflation of the *assignat* paper money that produced economic chaos, corrupted the state, and imposed a severe economic burden on the poor and thus radicalized and militarized the main constituency that helped bring the Jacobins to power; the Terror and economic dictatorship of the Jacobins whose violation of individual liberty on a massive scale brought the nation near to economic and social collapse; the conquest and annexation of neighboring countries in the name of liberating them from feudalism, which alienated potential supporters of the Revolution and stimulated the rise of nationalism, especially in Spain and the German states; the administrative and tax reforms of the Revolution that continued the centuries-old practice of centralizing state power in Paris at the expense of federalism and the autonomy of the regions; the demands of war, combined with unstable and corrupt governments that resulted in the rise to power of a military dictator who eventually proclaimed himself Emperor; and the more conservative and reactionary regimes that followed the radical phase of the Revolution, which led to the loss of freedoms that had been won earlier (especially for slaves and women).

In many respects, the most positive achievement of the Revolution was the creation of a new language of politics, natural rights, constitutionalism, democracy, and republicanism—which can be summarized in the revolutionary slogan of "liberty, equality, fraternity"—along with the expectation that the institutions of a free society would be built during the coming century on top of the precedents established during the liberal stages of the Revolution. But, like a two-edged sword, the Revolution did much the same thing for the enemies of individual liberty. For example, Marx and other socialists looked to the political violence and massive government intervention in the economy of the Jacobin Terror as a model for the future socialist revolution. Today, with the collapse of the Soviet Union and the discrediting of Marxism, it seems likely that the liberal aspects of the French Revolution will be its most enduring legacy.

DMH

See also Burke, Edmund; Constant, Benjamin; Declaration of the Rights of Man and of the Citizen; Paine, Thomas; Rousseau, Jean-Jacques; Say, Jean-Baptiste; Voltaire

Further Readings

Acton, John Emerich Edward (Lord Acton). *Lectures on the French Revolution*. London: Macmillan, 1910.

Burke, Edmund. *Reflections on the Revolution in France*. Conor Cruise O'Brien, ed. New York: Penguin, 1983.

Hobsbawm, E. J. *Echoes of the Marseillaise: Two Centuries Look Back on the French Revolution*. London: Verso, 1990.

Lucas, Colin, ed. *The French Revolution and the Making of Modern Political Culture*. Oxford: Oxford University Press, 1988.

Molinari, Gustave de. *L'Evolution politique et le Révolution*. Paris: C. Reinwald, 1884.

Paine, Thomas. *Rights of Man* (1791–1792). Henry Collins, ed. New York: Penguin, 1976.

Palmer, R. R. *The Age of Democratic Revolution: A Political History of Europe and America, 1760–1800: Vol. 1. The Challenge*. Princeton, NJ: Princeton University Press, 1959.

———. *The Age of Democratic Revolution: A Political History of Europe and America, 1760–1800: Vol. 2. The Struggle*. Princeton, NJ: Princeton University Press, 1964.

Tocqueville, Alexis de. *The Old Regime and the Revolution*. Alan S. Kahan, trans. Chicago: University of Chicago Press, 1998.

Van Kley, Dale, ed. *The French Idea of Freedom: The Old Regime and the Declaration of Rights of 1789*. Stanford, CA: Stanford University Press, 1994.

FRIEDMAN, DAVID (1945–)

David Friedman, like his late father Milton Friedman, is both an academic economist and a popular intellectual with an unabashed libertarian orientation. However, there are important differences between the views embraced by the two men. Academically, David Friedman is best known for his largely theoretical work in the economic analysis of law and his textbook-level writings on microeconomics. Politically, he is an advocate of the radical libertarian position known as "anarcho-capitalism," arguing that even the limited functions of the night-watchman state (police, courts, law, and punishment) can and should be privately supplied. Unlike other anarcho-capitalists, most notably Murray Rothbard, Friedman does not deny the theoretical cogency of the neoclassical literature on market failure, nor has he been inclined to attack economic efficiency as a normative benchmark. Instead, his replies normally take two forms. The first is to question the empirical evidence of market failure charges by noting that supposed monopolists in fact have acted competitively or else had extensive government assistance in securing their monopolistic position in the market. The second is to admit that market failure is real, but nevertheless less serious than comparable government failures. For example, Friedman points out that the democratic process is riddled with externalities. The costs of gathering political information, he contends, are private, whereas the benefits are social; the result is an inefficiently small supply of informed voting. Friedman's academic and popular interests interact in a number of ways. Most notably, his academic research on the political economy of medieval Iceland has provided anarcho-capitalists with arguably the best historical example of their preferred social system. At the same time, Friedman's interest in the economic analysis of law has led him to criticize various absolutist interpretations of libertarian principles with the aid of some creative counterexamples.

BC

See also Anarcho-Capitalism; Friedman, Milton; Market Failure

Further Readings

Friedman, David. *Hidden Order: The Economics of Everyday Life.* New York: HarperBusiness, 1996.
———. *Law's Order: An Economic Account.* Princeton, NJ: Princeton University Press, 2000.
———. *The Machinery of Freedom: Guide to a Radical Capitalism.* La Salle, IL: Open Court, 1989.

Friedman, Milton (1912–2006)

Milton Friedman was an American economist and leading representative of the Chicago School during the last half of the 20th century. Friedman received the Nobel Prize in 1976, having made significant contributions to several branches of economic theory, while also writing and speaking on public policy issues from a distinctly free-market perspective. His combination of technical acumen and policy advocacy made him one of the most influential economists and libertarians of his generation.

Friedman was born in New York City to immigrants from central Europe who moved to northern New Jersey when Friedman was a child. He graduated from high school just prior to his 16th birthday, and he attended Rutgers University on a scholarship. After graduating from Rutgers in 1932, Friedman pursued graduate studies in economics at the University of Chicago, which would become his intellectual home for the most productive period of his career. While at Chicago, he met a fellow graduate student, Rose Director, who would become his wife, lifelong partner, and frequent coauthor. In 1998, they published their memoirs, *Two Lucky People*.

Friedman received his MA from Chicago in 1933 and then accepted a fellowship at Columbia University. While at Columbia, he also held a position with the National Bureau of Economic Research, where he worked closely with future Nobel laureate Simon Kuznets on a study titled *Incomes from Independent Professional Practice*. Friedman recounted,

> That book was finished by 1940, but its publication was delayed until after the war because of controversy among some Bureau directors about our conclusion that the medical profession's monopoly powers had raised substantially the incomes of physicians relative to that of dentists.

It also served as his doctoral dissertation, which was approved by the Columbia faculty in 1946.

During the Great Depression and World War II, Friedman held several government positions in Washington, D.C. He also taught briefly at the University of Wisconsin and the University of Minnesota, before returning to the University of Chicago in September 1946, where he would spend the next 30 years, retiring in 1977. He and Rose then moved to California, where he accepted a position at Stanford University's Hoover Institution, which he held until his death.

Friedman's contributions to economics have been enormous and far reaching. In 1953, he published his *Essays in Positive Economics*. The introductory essay set forth his fundamental methodological position:

> the relevant question to ask about the "assumptions" of a theory is not whether they are descriptively "realistic," for they never are, but whether they are sufficiently good approximations for the purpose in hand. And this question can be answered only by seeing whether the theory works, which means whether it yields sufficiently accurate predictions.

In a 1996 interview, he elaborated: "The validity of a theory depends upon whether its implications are refuted, not upon the reality or unreality of its assumptions."

Friedman's methodological position, adopted by most of his colleagues at Chicago and eventually a good portion of the profession, laid the groundwork for important empirical work and elegant mathematical modeling that have helped economists better understand the world. It also placed the Chicago School squarely in opposition to the Austrian School, whose proponents embraced many of the same promarket positions as Friedman, but who argued that economists must base their work on a set of assumptions that can be demonstrated to be logically correct. Moreover, the Austrians argued that much empirical work was of limited value because social scientists cannot model human behavior in the same way that physical scientists model their objects of study. One can say, for instance, that a price control will lead to a shortage, but the magnitude of that shortage will be difficult, if not impossible, to predict.

Friedman considered his *A Theory of the Consumption Function*, published in 1957, as his "best purely scientific contribution" to economics. In it, he argues for the "permanent income hypothesis," which maintains that people make consumption decisions based on the permanent component of their income stream, not on transitory components. In short, people are forward-looking and act based on long-term income prospects. This hypothesis has several implications. First, people tend to smooth their consumption over their lifetimes. For instance, young people with high future earning power may rationally accumulate debt early in life, knowing that they will be able to pay it off as their incomes increase. Second, tax cuts may not spur consumption if the public believes those cuts to be only temporary. The permanent income hypothesis has become one of the cornerstones of modern macroeconomics.

Although Friedman considered *A Theory of the Consumption Function* to be his most significant contribution, his work in the area of monetary theory was surely his most influential. Inflation, Friedman famously argued, was "always and everywhere a monetary phenomenon." It is not fundamentally caused by unions demanding higher wages for their members, thus increasing labor costs and the prices of goods. Nor is it a product of companies wielding expansive market power and charging monopolistic prices. Instead, it is caused by too much money chasing too few goods. Central banks, Friedman concluded, should focus narrowly on maintaining price stability and adopt rules that would ensure such an outcome.

In 1963, Friedman, with Anna J. Schwartz, published *A Monetary History of the United States, 1867-1960.* The book spanned almost a century of monetary history, but its most important section dealt with what the authors called "the great contraction." Friedman and Schwartz argued that the Great Depression was not caused by the failings of the market system. Rather, they maintained, the Federal Reserve had pursued a monetary policy that

was excessively tight and that had led to a sharp decline in economic activity. *A Monetary History* was a rare scholarly achievement: It has had great influence among both the economics profession and policymakers.

In his 1967 presidential address to the American Economic Association, Friedman questioned the theoretical and empirical validity of the "Phillips curve," a statistical relationship that purportedly demonstrated a permanent tradeoff between unemployment and inflation. This tradeoff implied a set of choices for society. If you wanted greater employment, you simply had to increase the money supply. That in turn would produce higher inflation, which might be acceptable given current circumstances. Conversely, if inflation became too high, one could simply tighten the money supply and accept more unemployment. Not surprisingly, these ideas were popular with activist policymakers. Friedman challenged these conclusions, arguing that the tradeoff between unemployment and inflation was temporary and resulted only from *unanticipated* changes in inflation. The public, he claimed, was unlikely to be systematically fooled, and policymakers could not easily manipulate the economy. He later recalled,

> As employers and workers caught on to what was happening, any trade-off would disappear. I introduced the concept of a "natural rate of unemployment" to which the level of unemployment would tend whatever the rate of inflation once economic agents came to expect that rate of inflation. To keep unemployment below the natural level requires not simply inflation, but accelerating inflation.

Friedman's argument was later refined and expanded by economists Edward Prescott and Finn Kydland, and it would become increasingly accepted as stagflation gripped the American economy in the 1970s.

While Friedman was engaged in technical economic research at the highest levels, he also took an active interest in public-policy issues. In 1962, he published *Capitalism and Freedom*, the product of a series of lectures he gave at Wabash College in 1956. Although directed at a general audience, the book contains sophisticated and sometimes technical arguments for a number of free-market proposals, all presented in clear and accessible prose. For instance, Friedman called for the establishment of unilateral free trade and flexible exchange rates, introduced the idea of school vouchers, and argued for the privatization of social security. Also, as the title of the book suggests, Friedman argued that economic freedom is a necessary prerequisite for political freedom, a proposition that has been criticized by many political scientists. In *Capitalism and Freedom*, Friedman made it clear that he believed some state involvement was necessary if a stable and prosperous society were to function. "The consistent liberal is not an anarchist," he wrote. Yet he later rejected or greatly qualified his support for certain government actions that he defended in the book, such as antitrust laws to counter monopolies. Empirical work by his colleagues at the University of Chicago had demonstrated, Friedman argued, that antitrust laws were more often counterproductive than beneficial. His policy advocacy was based on an abiding belief in human freedom—in liberalism—as well as the findings of modern economic science.

Friedman was the author of a column for *Newsweek* from 1966 to 1983, as was Paul Samuelson, a long-time friend of the Friedmans and the leading Keynesian economist of the 20th century during most of this period. Some of Friedman's *Newsweek* articles were later collected in two anthologies, *An Economist's Protest* and *There's No Such Thing as a Free Lunch.*

Perhaps more than any other endeavor, *Free to Choose*, cowritten with his wife, brought the Friedmans' liberal ideas to a wide audience. In its preface, the authors compare *Free to Choose* to *Capitalism and Freedom*, noting that the new volume "is a less abstract and more concrete book. Readers of *Capitalism and Freedom* will find here a fuller development of the philosophy that permeates both books—here, there are more nuts and bolts, less theoretical framework." In addition, they wrote that much of the analysis in *Free to Choose* is informed by work done in the 1960s and 1970s by public choice economists who modeled the political system, like the economic system, as a market with self-interested actors. *Free to Choose* became a best seller, selling more than 400,000 copies in its first year. Perhaps even more important, however, was the 10-part PBS series that accompanied its publication. Each episode dealt with a chapter in the book, followed by debates in which Friedman took on his critics. The show was a huge success and brought liberalism into the living rooms of thousands of people who were unfamiliar with such ideas.

Friedman served as an economic advisor to Barry Goldwater during his 1964 presidential candidacy, as well as to Presidents Nixon and Reagan. Although he had their ear, they often did not follow his advice. The most grievous example was Nixon's imposition of wage and price controls in 1971, which Friedman widely criticized. Friedman also was a stalwart opponent of conscription, persuasively arguing that a volunteer army was both more just and more efficient. In addition, Friedman actively campaigned for tax and spending limitations on the state level; in fact, he was in Michigan speaking in favor of such a proposal when he was informed that he had won the Nobel Prize. He also spent much energy promoting school vouchers, establishing the Milton and Rose D. Friedman Foundation for Educational Choice in 1996.

Friedman died in 2006, survived by his wife Rose, his daughter Janet, and his son David, also an economist. "Milton Friedman was a giant," stated Paul Samuelson upon Friedman's death. "No 20th-century economist had his importance in moving the American economic profession rightward from 1940 to the present."

AS

See also Economics, Chicago School of; Friedman, David; Money and Banking

Further Readings

Friedman, Milton. *Capitalism and Freedom*. Chicago: University of Chicago Press, 1962.

———. *Essays in Positive Economics*. Chicago: University of Chicago Press, 1953.

———. "The Role of Monetary Policy." *American Economic Review* 58 no. 1 (March 1968): 1–17.

———. *A Theory of the Consumption Function*. Princeton, NJ: Princeton University Press, 1957.

Friedman, Milton, and Rose D. Friedman. *Free to Choose*. New York: Harcourt Brace Jovanovich, 1980.

———. *Two Lucky People: Memoirs*. Chicago: University of Chicago Press, 1998.

Friedman, Milton, and Anna J. Schwartz. *A Monetary History of the United States, 1867-1960*. Princeton, NJ: Princeton University Press, 1963.

Hetzel, Robert L. "The Contributions of Milton Friedman to Economics." Federal Reserve Bank of Richmond *Economic Quarterly* 93 no. 1 (Winter 2007): 1–30.

FUSIONISM

The resurgent American conservative movement of the 1950s embraced two conflicting schools of thought. The first, consonant with the principles of libertarianism, held that maximizing individual liberty should be the chief end of political society; the other took its bearings from the principles articulated by Edmund Burke and stressed the need for an organic community grounded in the precepts of an objective, divinely ordained moral order. In 1962, Frank S. Meyer, then on the editorial board of the *National Review* and a regular contributor to its pages, wrote *In Defense of Freedom*, in which he endeavored to resolve the apparent differences between these two schools the in hope of rendering American conservatism philosophically coherent and consistent. In the same year, L. Brent Bozell, also a member of *National Review*'s editorial board, portrayed Meyer's undertaking as an effort "to promote and justify modern American conservatism as a 'fusion' of the libertarian and traditionalist points of view." This characterization of Meyer's purpose as a "fusion" struck a receptive chord and soon thereafter the words *fusion* or *fusionism* were widely used to describe constructs designed to render libertarianism and traditional conservatism philosophically compatible. Over the decades, Meyer's efforts at this philosophical conciliation have attracted the most attention so that fusionism is closely associated with his writings, most notably *In Defense of Freedom*.

Meyer's fusionist philosophy rests on certain cardinal points, the most fundamental being that freedom is necessary for virtue; that an act or course of behavior that results from compulsion, coercion, or habituation cannot be virtuous. Accordingly, he held that individual freedom is the "central and primary end of political society," the realization of which, in turn, is the criterion by which to measure the goodness of the social and political order.

In his efforts to merge libertarianism and traditional conservatism, Meyer eschewed relativism. He agreed with the traditionalists that there are "good ends" or "absolute truths and absolute values towards which men should direct themselves" and also acknowledged that freedom, although indispensably necessary for virtue, does not guarantee virtuous decisions or behavior. Freedom, he maintained, is neutral with respect to virtue and vice and for this reason its exercise entails risks. Yet in his view, "without freedom no moral end can be achieved by the particular kind of being man is" nor would "spiritual and moral ends" have any meaning. Thus, he concluded, these risks had to be accepted, particularly for the purpose of realizing the virtues that traditional conservatives championed.

Another key element of Meyer's effort at conciliation attempted to show how these ends could be realized without invading or intruding on the domain of individual liberty. In practice, he found much to admire in the American constitutional order and tradition bequeathed by the Founding Fathers. This tradition, he argued, recognizes the primacy of freedom within the context of an objective moral order. Meyer believed that the writings of James Madison and John C. Calhoun are best interpreted as efforts to provide theoretical solutions for the simultaneous realization of freedom and virtue. In a more general vein, he argued that the maintenance and improvement of the social order, in keeping with the tenets of traditional conservatism, comes about through the noncoercive influences of intellectual and moral leaders who possess "the understanding and imagination to maintain the prestige of tradition and reason."

Throughout his effort to fuse libertarian principles with traditional conservatism, Meyer emphasized that institutions, associations, and communities played a vital role in creating conditions that would conduce individuals to opt freely for virtue. At the same time, he insisted, the "locus of virtue" is the individual person, not the society or the community. The inculcation of virtue through education, for instance, "depends upon the individuals persons who do the teaching and upon the beliefs and ideas they hold." Similarly, although he regarded religious institutions as supremely important in inculcating virtue, Meyer asserted that individuals must have the freedom to accept or reject their teachings.

At the level of everyday politics, Meyer's formulation was flexible enough to accommodate both the libertarian and traditionalist forces that composed the heart of the conservative movement during the 1960s. At the theoretical level, however, his fusionism came under severe attack. The most notable of these was L. Brent Bozell's extensive critique, which appeared in *National Review*. Writing from the perspective of Catholic natural law teachings, Bozell rejected both the priority Meyer assigned to individual freedom of choice and his understanding of the nature of man. Bozell argued that to accord primacy to the maximization of individual liberty means that "there is no point at which men are entitled to stop pulling down the 'props' [both state and social] which every rational society in history has erected to promote a virtuous citizenry." Consequently, Bozell continued, the net effect of according individual freedom priority is to render the realization of virtue "as difficult as possible." Without the help of props provided by the society and state, individuals would confront numerous and formidable challenges that only a few could meet with success. Whereas Meyer pictured man as capable of heroic choices, readily capable of overcoming the obstacles to virtuous decisions, Bozell pointed out that Christian teachings held otherwise. Man is unique "among created beings," he wrote, because he "has the capacity to deviate from the patterns of order—to, as it were, repudiate his nature, i.e., he is free. So viewed, freedom is hardly a blessing; add the ravages of original sin and it is the path to disaster."

Meyer's effort scarcely fared any better from the libertarian perspective. Murray Rothbard maintained that, in the last analysis, Meyer's political philosophy was essentially libertarian. Its minor deviations from libertarianism he attributed to Meyer's desire "to find a face-saving formula to hold both very different parts of the conservative movement together in a unified ideological and political movement." "Intellectually," he believed, fusionism "had to be judged a failure."

Rothbard's estimate is widely shared today by both libertarians and traditional conservatives. Nevertheless, although fusion seems to be impossible at the theoretical level, it is useful in explaining and understanding the sources of division among those who have consistently opposed the principles and policies of modern liberalism.

GWC

See also Conservatism; Conservative Critique of Libertarianism; Meyer, Frank S.

Further Readings

Carey, George, ed. *Freedom and Virtue: The Conservative/ Libertarian Debate*. Wilmington, DE: Intercollegiate Studies Institute Press, 1998.

Kirk, Russell. *The Essential Russell Kirk: Selected Essays.* George Panichas, ed. Wilmington, DE: Intercollegiate Studies Institute Press, 2006.

Meyer, Frank. *In Defense of Freedom: A Conservative Credo.* Chicago: Henry Regnery Company, 1962.

Nash, George H. *The Conservative Intellectual Movement in America.* Wilmington, DE: Intercollegiate Studies Institute Press, 1998

Schneider, Gregory, ed. *Conservatism in America since 1930: A Reader.* New York: New York University Press, 2003.

GAMBLING

Most Americans appear to enjoy gambling. Opportunities abound, ranging from state and interstate lotteries, to traditional contests of horses and greyhounds, to all manner of casinos, whether on land or water or on the Internet. However, although more and more consumers embrace this new freedom to wager, others insist that there is cause for serious concern. Fearing an outbreak of compulsive gambling, they have lobbied lawmakers to intervene to prevent a further proliferation of gambling outlets and to roll back those that currently exist. Their lobbying has raised a number of questions, among them: Should gambling be permitted at all? If so, which forms of gambling are acceptable? Finally, if gambling is to be tolerated, should it be regulated and how?

Legalized gambling has become one of those polarizing issues that drive many thoughtful individuals to examine their underlying beliefs regarding freedom of the individual. Some, such as the Cato Institute's Tom W. Bell, have argued that "our rights to peaceably dispose of our property include the right to gamble, online or off." Others, worried about personal corruption through compulsive gambling, have urged "a strategy of containment to minimize the moral risks of gambling for individuals and society." Fed up with the liberal attitude toward gambling adopted by many states, this group recently elevated their campaign to the federal level. Accordingly, in 1997, the 104th Congress established the National Gambling Impact Study Commission (NGISC) to "conduct a comprehensive study of the social and economic impacts of gambling in the United States." Two years later, the NGISC recommended a "pause in the expansion of gambling."

This controversy is nothing new. Both in America and throughout the world, gambling has a long and colorful history. Historians Lisa Morris and Alan Block have shown that, in the United States, gambling was legalized in the lower Mississippi Valley, and "until the 1840s professional, organized gambling was primarily carried out on steamboats plying the Mississippi and Ohio Rivers and the Great Lakes." By midcentury, the locus of organized gambling moved to the West and particularly northern California, where it was vitalized by the Gold Rush.

Later, despite Prohibition—or perhaps because of it—underworld gambling operations thrived on land, spawning "a series of infamous 'crime towns.'" Lotteries date back to ancient times, and in the 16th century, Queen Elizabeth I chartered the first English lottery. In colonial America and following independence, lotteries prospered as a much-promoted and voluntary means to supplement the public coffers. However, as a steady procession of public scandals took their toll, the 19th century witnessed a political backlash against lotteries that culminated in their universal prohibition. The legal lottery did not return until 1963, when New Hampshire introduced a state lottery. Between 1965 and 1993, no less than 35 states and the District of Columbia introduced state lottery monopolies.

The historical tug of war between gambling proponents and detractors continues. Today, an overwhelming majority of states enthusiastically promote homegrown lotteries, and a renewed interest in casino gaming is flourishing. According to a recent Harrah's survey, fully 32% of U.S. households gambled at a casino in 1996. Those households that did gamble averaged 4.8 visits, for an overall total of 176 million visits. This figure is up by 14% from 1995.

The rapid increase in popularity of gambling has led to a sense of emergency among its opponents, who have pressed their case on several fronts. The various state lotteries have been almost universally denounced as immoral and economically harmful. Although state officials undoubtedly enjoy the additional revenue, critics have argued that "losses fall disproportionately on some of the more vulnerable members of society." Meanwhile, casinos are accused of displacing—even cannibalizing—rival service and enter-tainment businesses, such as hotels, restaurants, and theme parks. Worse, it is alleged, this displacement is achieved by ruthlessly exploiting the addictions of compulsive gamblers, thereby causing financial distress, destabilizing families, and fueling welfare dependence and crime.

Many of these charges lack merit. *Cannibalization* appears to mean little more than *vigorous competition*. Additionally, many of the crime statistics that underlie the claim that gambling breeds crime have been based on dubi-ous measurements. For example, early analysis of Atlantic City crime figures shortly after the arrival of casinos sug-gested that per capita crime had markedly increased. However, these crime statistics failed to take account of the swelling local population due to casino-related tourism; the effect was that estimates of crime were heavily inflated. When the crime statistics for Atlantic City were readjusted to take account of this and other elementary crime-reporting errors, the resulting crime levels were unremarkable.

Still, nobody denies that there are those who, for what-ever reason, gamble in ways that have a negative impact on themselves or others. Although the severe cases are thought to be uncommon, the actual numbers are often elusive. Again, for the most part, measurement and classification problems haunt efforts to reliably estimate prevalence. Indeed, there is no clear consensus on what sort of behav-ior should be labeled *compulsive* or *problem* gambling. Nor is it clear that problem gambling, however it is defined, has been exacerbated by legalization. One study on gambling behavior in Connecticut found that "probable pathological gambling rates may actually have fallen . . . and have cer-tainly not risen, during a period [1991–1996] in which one of the largest casinos in the world [Foxwoods] was opened in the state."

Moreover, to the extent that compulsive gamblers behave badly toward others, it is not always due to gam-bling. Ronald A. Reno estimates that "one to three percent of the adult population are pathological gamblers," but notes, "about half of compulsive gamblers experience prob-lems with alcohol and substance abuse," which constitutes an important confounding factor.

However, from time to time, truly pathological gam-bling can result in genuine human misery. Of course, the same—or worse—is true of alcohol abuse and a number of other legal activities. As in the case of alcoholism, the ques-tion is whether problem gambling is better addressed on a voluntary basis, rather than through prohibiting the activity entirely. Self-help programs, such as Gamblers Anonymous (GA), insist that treatment, at least, must be voluntary. As the GA literature makes clear, the

> compulsive gambler needs to be willing to accept the fact that he or she is in the grip of a progressive illness and has a desire to get well. Our experience has shown that the

> Gamblers Anonymous program will . . . never work for the person who will not face squarely the facts about this illness.

In any case, lawmakers in a free society must ask not simply whether the choice to gamble is harmful solely to the gambler, but whether this choice clearly involuntarily harms others. Negative neighborhood effects may on occa-sion be just grounds for government to step in, at least in instances where the intervention can be shown to be effec-tive and where it does not lead to other, more harmful effects. But this is rarely the case. Historically, gambling prohibitions have done more harm than good. As Reuven and Gabrielle Brenner note, when

> a comprehensive law prohibiting all forms of gambling was passed in Nevada in 1909 . . . the result was that gov-ernment revenues from licensing were lost, a large number of games were played, and corruption and "protection" became widespread, bribes coming to seem like little more than a form of license.

The repeal of this law in 1930 changed all of that. The impact of legalization was that eventually the gambling industry in Nevada, which features a massive corporate structure, was characterized by honesty toward its customers.

In another example cited by Brenner et al., "New York's legislature in 1960 passed a series of new antigambling laws whose purpose was to facilitate convictions and, by increased penalties, to have a detrimental effect on gam-bling." But the results were disappointing. Gambling and the organized crime associated with it persisted, but few convictions were obtained. If it had a significant effect, it was on the police, for whom, the Knapp Commission found, gamblers' protection money was the main source of bribes. A typical policeman on the gambling squad was able to get $300 to $1,500 per month, and his or her superiors got additional sums.

That widespread gambling legalization has substan-tially decreased mob influence in the gambling industry is beyond dispute. Whether government oversight played an important role is debatable. This question is important because, naturally enough, industry representatives are eager to deal with any concerns the public might have about the honesty of their enterprises. Although concern about mob influence has led some to call for more strenuous gov-ernment licensure and oversight of the entire industry, such an approach is certainly not without cost nor is there any indication that it is needed. By artificially raising the cost of entry to the casino industry, licensure serves to protect cur-rent industry participants from new competition. Moreover, to the extent that a license becomes a valuable commodity, public officials overseeing the licensing process are easily put in a compromising position. If the intent of government licensure is to shore up the integrity of the industry, it is not doing a terribly good job, as critics of former Louisiana

Governor Edwin W. Edwards—convicted of taking gifts in exchange for casino licenses—would attest. But if not licensure, then what? One alternative, already adopted by many Internet casinos (understandably eager to assure Web surfers of their reputation for fair play), is to retain the services of a private, third-party accreditation agency.

A final word on the lotteries: In nearly all states, lotteries have been revived as jealously guarded government monopolies. Across America, they have been lauded as a secure and voluntary source of state revenue. But lottery players are generally older, poorer, and less educated than the average American, or even the average casino patron, leading to outcries of exploitation in some quarters. Lottery critics then divide into two camps—those who would do away with lotteries altogether and those who would open them up to competition from private operators. As one critic observed:

> For once, responsible politicians need not design new programs, draft new regulations, or create new bureaucracies to achieve some immediate progress—they need only terminate any involvement they may have as operators of state lotteries.

GC

See also Assurance and Trust; Black Markets; Corruption; Paternalism; Prohibition of Alcohol; Virtue

Further Readings

American Legislative Exchange Council. *Harrah's Survey of Casino Entertainment, 1997.* Available from http://www.harrahs.com/survey/ce97/ce97_index.html

Brenner, Reuven, and Gabrielle A Brenner. *Gambling and Speculation.* Cambridge: Cambridge University Press, 1990.

Detlefson, Robert R. *Anti-Gambling Politics—Time to Reshuffle the Deck.* Washington, DC: Competitive Enterprise Institute, 1996.

Galston, William A., and David Wasserman. "Gambling Away Our Moral Capital." *The Public Interest* 123 (Spring 1996): 69.

Goodman, Robert. *The Luck Business: The Devastating Consequences and Broken Promises of America's Gambling Explosion.* New York: Free Press, 1995.

Margolis, Jeremy. *Casinos and Crime: An Analysis of the Evidence.* Chicago: Altheimer & Gray, 1997.

Morris, Lisa, and Alan Block. "Organized Crime and Casinos: An International Phenomenon." *Gambling: Public Policies and the Social Sciences.* William R. Eadington and Judy A. Cornelius, eds. Reno, NV: Institute for the Study of Gambling and Commercial Gaming, 1997. 664.

Reno, Ronald A. "The Diceman Cometh." *Policy Review* (March–April 1996): 42.

Summers, Susan Robinson, David S. Honeyman, and James L. Wattenbarger. "The Resource Suppression and Redistribution Effects of an Earmarked State Lottery." *Gambling: Public Policies and the Social Sciences.* William R. Eadington and Judy A. Cornelius, eds. Reno, NV: Institute for the Study of Gambling and Commercial Gaming, 1997. 537.

WEFA Group. "A Study Concerning the Effects of Legalized Gambling on the Citizens of the State of Connecticut." Prepared for State of Connecticut, Department of Revenue Services, Division of Special Revenue, June 1997, 9.

GARRISON, WILLIAM LLOYD (1805–1879)

William Lloyd Garrison was the most prominent of the young, radical abolitionists who burst on the American landscape in the 1830s. Garrison attacked black slavery, prevalent throughout the southern states, with unparalleled vehemence. Exasperated at the betrayal of the Revolutionary promise that all forms of human bondage would disappear in this new land of liberty and marshaling all the evangelical fervor of the religious revivals then sweeping the country, Garrison demanded no less than the immediate emancipation of all slaves. He not only opposed any compensation to slaveholders and any colonization outside the country of freed slaves, but also demanded full political rights for all blacks, whether in the North or the South.

The son of a sailor who had abandoned his family, Garrison grew up in a poor but pious Baptist household in Newburyport, Massachusetts. He served as a printer's apprentice and then made his first notable mark on anti-slavery activism when he went to jail rather than pay a fine for libeling as a "highway robber and murderer" a New England merchant who shipped slaves between Baltimore and New Orleans. This near-sighted, prematurely balding, 25-year-old editor brought out the first issue of a new weekly paper, the *Liberator*, in Boston on January 1, 1831. He left no doubt about his refusal to compromise with the sin of slavery:

> I will be as harsh as truth, and as uncompromising as justice. On this subject, I do not wish to think, or speak, or write with moderation. No! No! Tell a man whose house is on fire, to give a moderate alarm: tell him to moderately rescue his wife from the hands of the ravisher; tell the mother to gradually extricate her babe from the fire into which it has fallen;—but urge me not to use moderation in a cause like the present. I am in earnest—I will not equivocate—I will not excuse—I will not retreat a single inch—AND I WILL BE HEARD.

Garrison conceded that the elimination of slavery would, in practice, take time. However, that should not, he felt, inhibit forthright condemnation of this moral evil. "Urge immediate abolition as earnestly as we may, it will alas! be gradual abolition in the end. We have never said that slavery would be overthrown by a single blow; that it ought to be we shall always contend."

The crusading editor, however, did not look to direct political action to eradicate slavery. Moral suasion and nonviolent resistance were his strategies. With agitation, he at first hoped to shame slaveholders into repentance. By early 1842, Garrison had gone so far as to denounce the U.S. Constitution for its proslavery clauses as "a covenant with death and an agreement with hell." He publicly burned a copy during one 4th of July celebration, proclaiming: "So perish all compromises with tyranny!" He now believed that, if anything, the North should secede from the central government. The slogan "No Union with Slave-Holders" appeared on the masthead of Garrison's *Liberator* for years.

The *Liberator* would continue to appear every week without interruption—despite recurrent financial straits, antagonism from respectable leaders throughout the North, and even an enraged mob that almost lynched its editor—until passage of the 13th Amendment abolishing slavery 35 years after the paper's founding. Garrison also helped organize the American Anti-Slavery Society in 1833. Although 2,000 local societies with 200,000 members had sprung into existence by 1840, abolitionists remained only a tiny minority of the American population. Hope for greater public sympathy helped splinter the movement into acrimonious, doctrinal factions. A primary source of discord was Garrison's early and hearty support of the movement for women's rights, which was a direct offshoot of abolitionism. Controversy also raged around Garrison's advocacy of disunion, denunciation of the Constitution, opposition to voting and to political parties, anarchism and pacifism, and disillusionment with and rejection of organized churches. The *Liberator* stood at the center of all these debates, which were conducted throughout its pages by all sides.

Often overlooked today is the extent to which abolitionism was a manifestation of 19th-century classical liberalism. Garrison denounced slavery as man-stealing, a violation of the principle of self-ownership, and praised the system of free labor. This worldview made him hostile to the fledgling trade-union movement and sympathetic to free trade and laissez-faire. Later, during the American Civil War, the prospect of finally ridding the country of human bondage seduced the *Liberator*'s editor into compromising his earlier principles by supporting Abraham Lincoln, the Republican Party, and the Union war effort. Yet without the foundation provided by Garrison's inflammatory but compelling writing, speaking, and organizing, there may have been no effective antislavery movement at all.

JRH

See also Abolitionism; Civil War, U.S.; Douglass, Frederick; Secessionism; Slavery in America; Spooner, Lysander; Thoreau, Henry David

Further Readings

Cain, William E., ed. *William Lloyd Garrison and the Fight against Slavery: Selections from* The Liberator. Boston: Bedford Books, 1995.

Foner, Eric. "Abolitionism and the Labor Movement in Ante-bellum America." *Politics and Ideology in the Age of the Civil War*. Eric Foner, ed. Oxford: Oxford University Press, 1980.

Kraditor, Aileen S. *Means and Ends in American Abolitionism: Garrison and His Critics on Strategy and Tactics, 1834–1850*. New York: Random House, 1969.

Mayer, Henry. *All on Fire: William Lloyd Garrison and the Abolition of Slavery*. New York: St. Martin's Press, 1998.

Perry, Lewis. *Radical Abolitionism: Anarchy and the Government of God in Antislavery Thought*. Ithaca, NY: Cornell University Press, 1973.

GENETICS

Genetics refers to that branch of biology that focuses on the mechanisms of heredity. Scientific knowledge about those mechanisms is rapidly increasing as we continue to uncover greater detail about the human genome. As we learn more and gain more control over the mechanism of heredity, the controversy surrounding genetics technology will increasingly take center stage in our politics. We may see government efforts to regulate or ban certain technologies or, more ominously, government efforts to coerce people to "improve the stock." In that regard, the tragic experience with eugenics in the 20th century in Western Europe and the United States is a cautionary tale for the 21st century.

By 1900, eugenics had caught the popular imagination. The focus soon shifted, however, from encouraging the eugenic breeding of the best to halting the dysgenic breeding of the worst. The *worst* soon came to refer to the feeble-minded, which included alcoholics, epileptics, and criminals, as well as the mentally retarded. Much of the American enthusiasm for eugenics stemmed from anti-immigrant feeling. At a time of rapid immigration from eastern and southern Europe, it was easy to encourage a sense of paranoia that the nation's supposedly better Anglo-Saxon stock was being diluted. Eugenic arguments provided a convenient cover for those who wished to restrict immigration for racist reasons. The Immigration Restriction Act of 1924 was a direct result of eugenics campaigning. For the next 20 years, it consigned many desperate European emigrants to a worse fate by denying them a new home in the United States, and it remained on the books unamended for 40 years.

Restrictive immigration was not the only legal success for the eugenists. By 1911, six states had enacted laws allowing the forced sterilization of the mentally unfit. Six years later, another nine states had joined them. Although at first the Supreme Court threw out many of these sterilization laws, in 1927, it changed its position; in *Buck v. Bell*, the Court ruled that the commonwealth of Virginia could sterilize Carrie Buck, a 17-year-old girl committed to a colony for epileptics and the feeble-minded in Lynchburg, where she lived with her daughter, Vivian. After a cursory examination, Vivian, who was 7 months old, was declared an imbecile, and Carrie was ordered to be sterilized. As Justice Oliver Wendell Holmes, a consistent supporter of every government intrusion into private life, famously put it in his judgment, "Three generations of imbeciles are enough." Virginia continued to sterilize the mentally handicapped into the 1970s. In America, a bastion of individual liberty, more than 100,000 people were sterilized for feeble-mindedness, in keeping with more than 30 state and federal laws passed between 1910 and 1935.

The governments of other countries also enthusiastically sterilized the allegedly unfit. Sweden sterilized 60,000. Canada, Norway, Finland, Estonia, and Iceland all enacted coercive sterilization laws. In the 1930s, Germany, most notoriously, first sterilized 400,000 people and in many cases followed this procedure with their murder. In just 18 months in the Second World War, 70,000 already sterilized German psychiatric patients were gassed just to free hospital beds for wounded soldiers. Britain, almost alone among Protestant industrial countries, never passed a eugenics law (i.e., a law allowing the government to interfere in the individual's right to procreate). There was never a British law preventing marriage of the mentally deficient, and there was never a British law allowing compulsory sterilization by the state on the grounds of feeble-mindedness. Why was Britain able to resist the direction in which the rest of the world was moving?

British scientists were certainly not responsible for Britain's decision to forego this kind of legislation. Scientists like to tell themselves today that eugenics was always seen as a "pseudoscience," frowned on by true scientists, but there is little in the written record to support this notion. Most scientists welcomed the flattery of being treated as experts in a new technocracy. They were perpetually urging immediate action by the government.

Nor could the socialists claim credit. Although the Labor Party opposed eugenics by the 1930s, the socialist movement in general provided much of the intellectual ammunition for eugenics before that. The works of H. G. Wells are especially rich in juicy quotes: "The swarms of black, and brown, and dirty white, and yellow people . . . will have to go." Socialists, embracing a belief in public planning and ready to confer on the state a position of blanket power over the individual, were ready-made for the eugenic message.

Conservatives and Liberals also were enthusiastic for this kind of legislation. Arthur Balfour, ex-prime minister, chaired the first International Eugenics Conference in London in 1912, and the sponsoring vice presidents included the Lord of Chief Justice and Winston Churchill. As Churchill put it, "the multiplication of the feeble-minded" constituted "a very terrible danger to the race."

One man deserves to be singled out for mounting Parliamentary opposition to the eugenics movement, especially with respect to a draconian bill put forward in 1918: the radical libertarian MP named Josiah Wedgwood. Wedgwood had been elected to Parliament in the Liberal landslide of 1906, but later joined the Labor Party and retired to the House of Lords in 1942. Wedgwood charged that the Eugenics Society was trying "to breed up the working class as though they were cattle." But his main objection was on the grounds of individual liberty. He was appalled that this bill gave the state powers to take a child from its own home by force and granted policemen the duty to act on reports from members of the public that somebody was feeble-minded. His motive was not social justice, but individual liberty, and he was joined by Tory libertarians such as Lord Robert Cecil. Their common cause was that of the individual against the state.

The clause in the eugenics bill that truly appalled Wedgwood was the one that stated it be "desirable in the interests of the community that [the feeble-minded] should be deprived of the opportunity of procreating children." This statement was, in Wedgwood's word, "the most abominable thing ever suggested" and in no way reflected "the care for the liberty of the subject [nor] the protection of the individual against the state that we have a right to expect form a Liberal Administration." His attack was so effective that the government withdrew the bill, and when it was represented in the following year, it was much watered down. Wedgwood had identified the central flaw in the whole eugenic project: not that it was based on faulty science, nor that it was impractical, but that it was fundamentally oppressive and cruel because it employed the full power of the state against the rights of the individual.

As our knowledge of the human genome increases, genetic screening and germ-line engineering—the manipulation of the genetics of egg or sperm to alter their issue— will become increasingly viable in the decades to come. Already calls for government restriction abound—some based quite openly on opposition to extending the human lifespan. One of the most quoted bioethicists of our time, Daniel Callahan of the Hastings Center, has said: "The worst possible way to resolve [the question of life extension] is to leave it up to individual choice. There is no known social good coming from the conquest of death."

Those with a more conventional view of social goods recognize that if government were to ban those technologies, it would doom many people to avoidable suffering. It would be just as cruel to outlaw screening or genetic engineering as to make them compulsory. These decisions are for the individual, not ones that can safely be left to theocrats or technocrats.

There is a world of difference between genetic screening and what the eugenists called for in their heyday, and it lies in this: Voluntary genetic screening is about giving private individuals private choices on private criteria, whereas eugenics was about nationalizing that decision to make people breed not for themselves, but for the state.

Many modern accounts of the history of eugenics discuss it in terms of the dangers of allowing science, genetics especially, to go uncontrolled. It is much more an example of permitting government the discretionary powers associated with a totalitarian state.

MR

See also Bioethics; Family; Immigration; Privacy; Racism; Sexuality; Social Darwinism

Further Readings

Avise, John C. *The Hope, Hype and Reality of Genetic Engineering.* New York: Oxford University Press, 2004.

Bailey, Ronald. *Liberation Biology: The Scientific and Moral Case for the Biotech Revolution.* Amherst, NY: Prometheus Books, 2005.

Kühl, Stefan. *The Nazi Connection: Eugenics, American Racism, and German National Socialism.* New York: Oxford University Press, 2002.

Ridley, Matt. *Genome: The Autobiography of a Species in 23 Chapters.* New York: HarperPerennial, 2000.

Rosen, Christine. *Preaching Eugenics: Religious Leaders and the American Eugenics Movement.* New York: Oxford University Press, 2004.

Wedgwood, C. V. *The Last of the Radicals, Josiah Wedgwood, MP.* London: Cape, 1951.

GLADSTONE, WILLIAM EWART (1809–1898)

William Ewart Gladstone was a native of Liverpool of Scottish descent. Between 1868 and 1894, he was four times prime minister of the United Kingdom and four times chancellor of the Exchequer. In office, Gladstone was largely successful in advancing his classical liberal vision of limited government, fiscal discipline, low taxation, free-market economics, free trade, devolution of power, and protection and expansion of political and religious liberties, both at home and overseas. When not in office, he became the most effective spokesman for these causes not least because he was widely and correctly expected to soon return to government. Any serious understanding of Gladstone's policies, life, and career must take account of his intense lifelong struggle with his deeply held Christian faith, as well as his immersion in Greco–Roman thought.

Gladstone graduated from Christ Church, Oxford, and became a member of important reforming governments, both Tory-Conservative, Whig-Radical, and Liberal. In addition to being chancellor and prime minister, Gladstone held numerous other prestigious positions in and out of government, such as vice president of the Board of Trade, president of the Board of Trade, Colonial Secretary, and Lord Rector of Edinburgh University. As chancellor, Gladstone improved Britain's financial system beyond recognition, creating the conditions for future prosperity. During his first premiership, free trade reached its apotheosis, and laissez-faire governed the workings of the domestic market. His political career finally came to an end in 1894, when his administration was unable to enact a bill supporting Home Rule for Ireland, which was defeated in the House of Lords.

Gladstone is generally considered to have become more left wing as he grew older, turning from a liberal Tory into a conservative Liberal leader of a Liberal Party that emerged around him. Nevertheless, it is questionable whether his political development from a self-described "out-and-out inequalitarian" into a backer of "the masses against the classes" reflected a fundamental shift in philosophy. Gladstone tended to favor reforms less for their own sake than in response to changing circumstances. He stayed ambivalent about extending the franchise, for example, making it difficult to conclude whether he was the enemy of the aristocracy or their savior, or whether his later populism was sincere.

Moreover, Gladstone continued to praise Aristotle, Augustine, Dante, Bishop Butler, and Burke as his guiding lights throughout the political and religious turmoil of his long life, while he maintained his dislike for the ideas of Bentham and J. S. Mill. Much like Lord Acton—his friend, advisor, and fellow Burkean Liberal—Gladstone believed in natural and divine law, as well as in the historical liberties of Englishmen, while remaining skeptical about abstract rights. Gladstone may have shared practical ends with the Liberal Party without identifying with the philosophical views of the majority of its supporters. "He is, and always was, in everything except essentials, a tremendous Tory," judged Arthur Balfour.

Colin Matthew, who edited Gladstone's diaries, also was his best biographer. Roy Jenkins's life of Gladstone, although much acclaimed, appears at best uninterested in Gladstone's guiding principles and, at times, condescending about his religious life. Lord Morley, a former member of Gladstone's cabinet, wrote a memoir of Gladstone that continues to fascinate.

MLS

See also Burke, Edmund; Free Trade; Liberalism, Classical; Whiggism

Further Readings

Jenkins, Roy, *Gladstone*. London: Macmillan, 1995.

Matthew, H. C. G. *Gladstone 1875–1898*. Oxford: Clarendon Press, 1995.

Morley, John. *The Life of William Ewart Gladstone*. 3 vols. New York: Macmillan, 1903.

GLOBALIZATION

Globalization is the term used to describe the condition that prevails when communication, people, goods, services, and capital move more freely across borders. Often globalization is the result of technological improvement that facilitates communication and transport and economic liberalization that gives people the freedom to make use of them. It is the most important international phenomenon of the early 21st century, touching almost all aspects of life, politics, and business.

Libertarians have traditionally promoted globalization because of its liberating effects on people's lives. Globalization is an international extension of free markets and open societies. In effect, it is capitalism without borders. In closed societies, people are limited to what is developed locally; they buy locally made products from a local supplier, they work for local employers, and they have to borrow money from the local bank. Globalization permits us to interact with whomever we choose, and to buy from, to work for, or to borrow from others than the local employers and suppliers. These greater horizons permit people the freedom to look for alternatives and the dignity to set their own terms for cooperating with others.

Globalization also increases material progress. When consumers are able to choose alternatives, domestic businesses are exposed to competition from the world's most efficient alternatives, which forces them to look for ways to make their products and services better and cheaper. It also means that each business and nation is in a position to specialize in producing what it does best, importing other goods from countries where they are more cheaply produced, thus increasing total world production. The corollaries to this material progress are that ideas and technologies are easily transferred across borders and capital is free to move to the places with the most promising ideas and innovations.

Globalization is particularly important for poor countries. In an open world, they can employ technical and business solutions that took richer countries generations and billions of dollars to develop, they can attract investment from richer nations, and they can sell goods in wealthier markets. This ability to leapfrog entire stages of industrial development explains why countries with open economies governed by the rule of law have grown faster as wealth in the rest of the world has increased. From 1780, it took England 60 years to double its national income. However, Sweden was able to accomplish the same feat in the 40 years following 1880, 100 years later. Yet another 100 years later, it took Taiwan and South Korea just 10 years to do the same.

One can make a reasonable argument that classical liberalism as a political movement was born in the campaign for free trade in the 19th century, which the liberals saw as a way of promoting international peace, individual freedom, and material progress. In the mid-19th century, liberalism was able to consolidate almost the whole of Europe into a free trade area, marked by freedom of movement for capital, goods, and people. Liberalism's success in this area accelerated the Industrial Revolution and caused an economic convergence among European nations. This first era of globalization was not completed inasmuch as the greater portion of the world was forced into monopolistic trade relationships through colonization. Unfortunately, the openness in trade that marked the last third of the 19th century collapsed under pressure from increased nationalism and protectionism that accompanied the period immediately prior to the First World War. The war, of course, marked the return of strong protectionist barriers between nations.

It was not until the end of the Second World War that globalization again reappeared. Trade barriers between the major trading countries were lowered, and technological breakthroughs in transportation and computer technology, combined with liberal reforms in the majority of countries in the 1980s and 1990s, allowed individuals greater freedom to travel, trade, and invest across borders. With the fall of communism at the end of the 1980s, one could again speak of a globalized world, made the more meaningful by the decision of developing countries like India and China to begin to participate in the global economy.

Libertarians disagree about the role of regional trade agreements like the North American Free Trade Agreement (NAFTA) and institutions such as the World Trade Organization (WTO), which promote free trade via multilateral negotiations and a system of rules regulating the use of trade barriers. The agreements that underpin these organizations follow a strange logic because nations agree to allow their citizens the freedom to buy from foreigners only on the condition that other countries extend the same rights to their citizens. However, these reciprocal agreements might be the only viable method of liberalizing trade in a world of illiberal governments, where influential special interests oppose imports. This notion is particularly true where protectionist sentiments predominate and where many voters want to repeal those liberalized policies that have already been enacted. However, the most important trade reforms in the last decades have occurred unilaterally by countries that have seen that it is in their best interest to reduce their barriers to trade regardless of what other countries do.

Today, about 3 billion people live in countries that can be said to be a part of the global economy. These countries have growth rates of about 5%, which means that their per capita incomes double every 15 years. Rich countries have growth rates of about 2% per capita, further evidence of the convergence of wealth among nations. Estimates are that, since the early 1980s, poverty in developing countries has been halved, child labor has almost been halved, and chronic hunger has been reduced by two-fifths. These improvements have been especially marked in countries that have opened their economies to world market forces.

Despite these clear indications of the economic improvement that follows freer trade, a strong antiglobalization movement emerged in the late 1990s—a movement that has staged several mass protests that have been given international publicity. Currently, thousands of influential organizations and pressure groups around the world continue to oppose various aspects of globalization. These groups are not homogenous, and some have incompatible views. A few who have participated in antiglobalization activities are protectionist corporations and unions who want to stop poor countries from exporting goods that would compete with home-grown manufactures. Other groups wish to stop richer countries from exporting their goods, thus forcing consumers to consume higher priced local products. In addition, nationalists and Luddites of all stripes want to shut the rest of the world out, and a few utopian socialists dream of a world government that will take control of all market forces. What they have in common is their opposition to globalization, which is often referred to as "neoliberal globalization" or "corporate globalization," thus revealing that their real animus is not toward globalization as such, but free markets.

These groups give voice to the same hostility against competition and free enterprise as has been seen in domestic debates about free trade since the Industrial Revolution. However, many opponents of globalization also complain that a liberalization of trade allows individuals and companies to escape government rules and regulations by choosing the location of their activities, the home residence of their firms, and the nature of their investments. Many politicians and international political institutions, like the United Nations, the European Union, and the Organisation for Economic Co-operation and Development, view globalization as a threat to political control. They have often tried to administer the globalized economy by harmonizing domestic policies (e.g., on taxes) and to regulate markets. This attempt to internationalize political control is often called "political globalization," but is in fact a movement that works against the spontaneous globalization led by voluntary decisions of individuals and businesses.

In many ways, the society in which we live is more globalized than ever. However, much remains to be done. In developing countries, the absence of the rule of law and property rights make it impossible for the majority to participate in large-scale economic activities. Even the policies in place in richer countries are far from ideal. Agricultural protectionism and multibillion-dollar subsidies make it impossible for poor countries to export their goods and develop their agriculture. Domestic government monopolies in health care and education prevent international competition and freedom of choice in those sectors. Finally, although goods and capital might flow fairly freely across borders, the restriction on the movement of people is still much alive.

JoN

See also Cosmopolitanism; Development, Economic; Free Trade; Material Progress; Simon, Julian; Tax Competition

Further Readings

Bhagwati, Jagdish. *In Defense of Globalization*. New York: Oxford University Press, 2004.

Cowen, Tyler. *Creative Destruction: How Globalization Is Changing the World's Cultures*. Princeton, NJ: Princeton University Press, 2002.

Irwin, Douglas. *Against the Tide: An Intellectual History of Free Trade*. Princeton, NJ: Princeton University Press, 1996.

Norberg, Johan. *In Defense of Global Capitalism*. Washington, DC: Cato Institute, 2003.

Sally, Razeen. *Classical Liberalism and International Economic Order: Studies in Theory and Intellectual History*. London: Routledge, 1998.

Wolf, Martin. *Why Globalization Works*. New Haven, CT: Yale University Press, 2004.

GLORIOUS REVOLUTION

The events of 1688–1689, during which James II was deposed by Parliamentary authority and force of arms in favor of his daughter Mary II and her husband William III of Orange, are collectively known as the Glorious Revolution, although, properly speaking, it was not so much a revolution as it was a *coup d'état*. The Stuart restoration of 1660, which placed Charles II, son of Charles I, on the throne, brought in its wake a resurgence of distrust in the Crown. Charles II, like his father and grandfather, was dismissive of Parliamentary concerns about his policies, both political and ecclesiastical. Although it had been firmly established that the appropriation of all monies was in Parliament's hands, control over how taxes were expended was still left to the King and his ministers. What particularly incensed Parliament was Charles's sympathies with Roman Catholicism, which was equated by most Englishmen with the most primitive levels of superstition and political oppression. Indeed, it was felt that inasmuch as Catholics owed their primary allegiance to the Pope, they would be prepared at any point to betray their country should they be ordered to do so by the Church. Under these circumstances, any movement toward the toleration of Catholics was politically impossible, and Charles's attempts in this direction were bitterly resented.

At the urging of a Royalist Parliament (the remnants of the Long Parliament) that had invited Charles to resume the throne, the King had agreed to enact a series of measures passed between 1661 and 1665, known as the Clarendon Code, that effectively reestablished the supremacy of Anglicanism in England and placed those who embraced Nonconformism on a par with Roman Catholicism. The first of these measures, the Corporation Act, which was aimed primarily at the large number of Presbyterians who held office in the cities and boroughs, provided that no one could be elected to municipal office unless he had in the previous 12 months received the sacraments according to the rites of the Church of England. Other statutes made the Book of Common Prayer compulsory in all religious services (the Act of Uniformity), prohibited meetings of more than five people for unauthorized religious purposes (the Conventicle Act), and forbade all Nonconformist ministers from coming within 5 miles of any incorporated town (the Five Mile Act). Although Charles appears to have had few compunctions about imposing these disabilities on Nonconformists, they conflicted with his Roman Catholic leanings, which grew in strength throughout his reign. Indeed, Charles attempted to suspend these statutes in 1672 by a Declaration of Indulgence, which would have extended toleration to both Catholics and Dissenters, but he was forced by Parliament to withdraw it in the following year.

In 1670, Charles entered into negotiations with Louis XIV of France, the outcome of which was the secret Treaty of Dover. When Charles ascended the throne in 1660, Parliament had agreed to supply the Crown with an annual payment of £1,200,000, but this amount was apparently insufficient because the Crown ran a persistent annual deficit of between £400,000 and £500,000. One of the principal aims of the Treaty was to free Charles from financial dependence on Parliament for additional revenues. The Treaty of Dover provided that Charles would receive a generous subsidy from France in return for joining an alliance against the Dutch. In addition, he promised that he would, at some convenient point, publicly declare that he had reconciled himself with the Church of Rome. Louis further agreed to loan Charles 6,000 French troops should the British rebel at the announcement of Charles's conversion. Even without knowledge of these treasonous provisions, Parliament regarded the alliance with France as repugnant and responded by enacting the Test Act, which compelled all government officials and military officers to receive communion according to the Anglican rite.

Anti-Catholic feeling was so widespread that when, in 1678, Titus Oates, an Anglican minister, claimed that he had uncovered a Catholic plot to assassinate Charles and establish Catholicism in England, panic ensued throughout the country. Anti-Catholic feeling was especially intense in London, where it was rumored that Jesuits had been responsible for the Great London Fire of 1666. Eighty people were arrested, among them five Catholic lords who were sent to the Tower. Sixteen men were tried and executed in direct connection with this "Popish Plot," in addition to eight Catholic priests, among them the Bishop of Armagh, whose only crime appears to have been that they were Catholic. Oates even implicated Catherine of Braganza, Charles's queen consort, of attempting to poison the King, but she was protected from the charge by Charles. The anti-Catholic party in Parliament (the Whigs) under Anthony Cooper, the Earl of Shaftesbury, seized the occasion to introduce an Exclusion Bill that was designed to bar Charles's Catholic brother, James, from succeeding to the throne, but the bill failed of passage when Charles dissolved Parliament. Oates himself, a repellent liar and cheat, was for a time lauded and granted an allowance by Parliament until it was proved that he had manufactured his charges out of whole cloth.

Although Charles had several children, none was by his wife. As a result, the succession would normally pass to his brother, James, Duke of York, a zealous Catholic. Parliamentary attempts to exclude James from the throne were frequent and gained in intensity over the last years of Charles's reign. Although Charles had apparently converted to Catholicism in 1670, the conversion was secret, and no attempts were made to overthrow him. What concerned most Englishmen, however, was that James had openly embraced Catholicism in 1669, had married a no less devout Catholic, Mary of Modena, and had no intention of denying his faith. When the Test Act was passed in 1673 barring Catholics from holding office, James chose to resign as Lord High Admiral and went abroad.

Parliament made several attempts, in 1680 and again in 1681, to pass an exclusion act that would change the order of succession should Charles not bear an heir, but they failed when Charles was able to dissolve Parliament before it had finally acted. In 1683, a conspiracy to assassinate both Charles and James as they passed Rumbold's Rye House, on the road between Newmarket and London, failed because the King had changed his travel plans. The facts of what became known as the Rye House Plot are somewhat cloudy, but it appears to have been related to several schemes discussed by the conspirators to foil the succession. Implicated in the plot were Arthur Capel, First Earl of Essex, at one point a high-ranking minister in Charles's cabinet; William, Lord Russell, one of the leaders in the Commons to exclude James from the throne; James, Duke of Monmouth, the illegitimate son of Charles II and Lucy

Walters; and Algernon Sidney, the great republican publicist. Essex committed suicide, Russell and Sidney were executed, and Monmouth was exiled and took refuge in the Netherlands. What the conspirators sought, indeed what was sought by all those who opposed the succession of the Duke of York, was that the throne would pass either directly to Mary, an unwavering Protestant, wife of William of Orange and daughter of James by his first wife, Anne Hyde, or to Charles's illegitimate son, Monmouth. These alternatives would have avoided the anomaly of having a Catholic as titular head of the Church of England.

On February 6, 1685, Charles II died, and the Duke of York ascended the throne. Evidence shows James to have been so totally inept a king that he managed to alienate almost all segments of the English population during this 3-year reign. Within a matter of months of his accession, the Duke of Monmouth led a rebellion to wrest the Crown from his uncle. Landing with only 82 followers at Lyme Regis in the west of England, where his popularity was strongest, he soon raised a ragtag army of almost 6,000 men, but these forces proved no match for James's troops, and he was routed at the Battle of Sedgemoor in Somerset. Monmouth was captured and beheaded at the Tower of London in July. James dispatched the Lord Chief Justice, George, First Baron Jeffreys, who had earlier sentenced Russell and Sidney to death, to the West Country to exact revenge against those who had rebelled against him. The "justice" meted out by Jeffreys was so savage that the trials over which he officiated became known as the Bloody Assizes. Between 150 and 200 rebels were executed, and several hundred others were ordered sold into slavery and shipped to the colonies. This despicable man was not above personally profiting from his position, regularly extorting money from his victims.

Time and again, James's policies rode roughshod over Parliament's directives. He raised Jeffreys to the position of Lord Chancellor; he appointed a number of Catholics to senior positions in the English armed forces and in the universities, contrary to English law; and he increased the size of the military and ordered elements of the army to camp on the edges of the capital, thus threatening the city. He reestablished the Court of High Commission, an ecclesiastical prerogative court that had been abolished by the Long Parliament in 1641. In 1685, he prorogued a hostile Parliament, and 2 years later, he issued a Declaration of Indulgence, lifting the disabilities under which English Catholics and Dissenters suffered. When seven bishops of the Anglican Church, including the Archbishop of Canterbury, petitioned that he reconsider, they were charged with seditious libel and sent to the Tower of London. Although they were acquitted by a sympathetic jury, the effect of James's actions was to shift the ministry of the Anglican Church from its earlier position of neutrality to open hostility to his reign.

On June 10, 1688, Mary of Modena gave birth to a male heir, whose claim to the throne took precedence over those of his half-sisters, Mary and Anne. Both Whigs and Tories were fearful that this birth would mark the beginning of an ongoing Catholic dynasty in England. As a consequence, on June 30, 1688, five peers and two commoners, acting on behalf of Parliament, invited Mary, James's eldest daughter, and her husband, William of Orange, to assume the throne. On November 5, the Prince of Orange landed at Brixham with an army of 15,000. Rather than take up arms in what would have clearly been a failing cause, James chose to flee the country in December, was captured, and was allowed to escape to France. On January 28, 1689, a Convention of Lords Spiritual and Temporal, and Commons declared that James had abdicated the throne, and he was succeeded by his daughter, Mary, and her husband, William of Orange.

The events of 1680–1690 were to have a profound effect on English politics. The Revolutionary Settlement of 1689 established once and for all that Parliament and not the Crown had precedence in all political matters up to and including the succession. These events produced a mass of political literature, none more powerful than Algernon Sidney's *Discourses on Government* and John Locke's *Treatises of Government*. With respect to Locke's *Treatises*, although the first and second treatises were published in 1690 as two distinct works, the second of which was to be taken as an apologia for the Revolutionary Settlement that had already occurred, current research has shown them to be two parts of a unitary essay with the middle missing. Evidence appears to indicate that the work was actually written in the early 1680s, during a period when the Whigs were plotting to alter the succession to the throne and that it was in fact a call for revolution. If this theory is true, then the middle sections of the work, composed before Locke left England for Holland in 1682 and destroyed before his departure, must have been explicit in this respect. It follows that the essay should be taken as a far more radical treatise than many commentators have suggested.

Sidney's essay, like Locke's *Treatises*, maintained that all mankind was, by virtue of their humanity, free beings possessed of certain rights that governments transgressed at their peril, that kings owed their authority to the consent of those over whom they governed, that this authority must be validated by the people, and that all members of society, including the king himself, were subject to the same laws. Should the sovereign contravene the law, the people have the right to replace him. Although Sidney was executed in 1683, his *Discourses* were not published until 1698. They became extremely popular and were regarded by the American colonists, along with Locke's *Treatises*, as providing the philosophical foundations of government and of the nature of political obligation.

RH

See also English Civil Wars; Locke, John; Religion and Liberty; Sidney, Algernon; Whiggism

Further Readings

Clark, G. N. *The Later Stuarts, 1660–1714*. Oxford: Clarendon Press, 1961.
Grell, Ole Peter, Jonathan I. Israel, and Nicholas Tyacke, eds. *From Persecution to Toleration: The Glorious Revolution in England*. Oxford: Clarendon Press, 1991.
Haley, K. H. D. *Politics in the Reign of Charles II*. New York: Blackwell, 1985.
Jones, J. R. *The Revolution of 1688 in England*. London: Weidenfeld & Nicolson, 1972.
Ogg, David. *England in the Reign of Charles II*. 2nd ed. Oxford: Clarendon Press, 1962.
———. *England in the Reigns of James II and William III*. Oxford: Oxford University Press, 1969.
Trevelyan, George M. *The English Revolution, 1688–1689*. Oxford: Oxford University Press, 1972.

GODWIN, WILLIAM (1756–1836)

William Godwin, the founder of philosophical anarchism and the author of *An Enquiry Concerning Political Justice* (1793)—one of the most significant political texts of its day—had a profound impact on a whole generation of writers, including the romantic poets Percy Bysshe Shelley and Lord Byron.

The son of a dissenting minister, Godwin briefly entered the clergy, where he became familiar with the radical politics of Richard Price, Joseph Priestley, Thomas Paine, and the French philosophers of the Enlightenment. His anarchist leanings emerged quite early in his career. A character in the first book Godwin published under his own name, *Sketches of History* (1784), declared, "God Himself has no right to be a tyrant." Godwin's best-selling book, *Political Justice*, published during the French Revolution, established Godwin's fame as a nonviolent anarchist and classical liberal. By *political justice* he meant the principles of morality and truth by which society properly worked. He believed that "government by its very nature counteracts the improvement of the human mind," leading mankind into ignorance and dependence. Emphasizing the crucial importance of individualism, he argued that people acting rationally could live without government or other institutions of society that limited man's freedom, such as marriage.

In 1794, Godwin's first novel, *The Adventures of Caleb Williams*, appeared to acclaim. It depicted the victimization of the individual by society. In the Preface, Godwin explained, "[I]t was proposed in the invention of the following work, to comprehend, as far as the progressive nature of a single story would allow, a general review of the

modes of domestic and unrecorded despotism, by which man becomes the destroyer of man."

Outraged by the government's treatment of radicals, Godwin penned several influential pamphlets, among them "Considerations on Lord Grenville's and Mr. Pitt's Bills Concerning Treasonable and Seditious Practices and Unlawful Assemblies," in which he attacked the government's view of treason. His pamphlets also attacked radical appeals to passion as damaging to both reason and human perfectibility. A collection of his essays, published as *The Enquirer. Reflections on Education, Manners, and Literature* (1797), was a proximate cause of Thomas Malthus's classic "Essay on the Principle of Population" (1798), in which Malthus disputed Godwin's trust in man and reason.

A key figure in London's intellectual circle, Godwin became reacquainted with the famed precursor of feminism, Mary Wollstonecraft, whom he married in 1797, despite his having attacked the institution. Wollstonecraft died some months later while giving birth to their daughter, Mary, who was later to marry Shelley and write the classic novel *Frankenstein* (1818). Grief-stricken, Godwin wrote a passionate tribute to Wollstonecraft: *Memoirs of the Author of a Vindication of the Rights of Women* (1798).

Among Godwin's most important and influential works in later life were *Of Population* (1820), in which he attacked Malthus; *History of the Commonwealth of England* (4 vols., 1824–1828); and *Thoughts on Man* (1831), a collection of political and philosophical essays.

WME

See also Anarchism; French Revolution; Marriage; Wollstonecraft, Mary

Further Readings

Clark, J. P. *The Philosophical Anarchism of William Godwin*. Princeton, NJ: Princeton University Press, 1977.
McElroy, Wendy. *The Debates of Liberty: An Overview of Individualist Anarchism*. Lanham, MD: Lexington Books, 2002.
Woodcock, George. *William Godwin: A Biographical Study*. Montreal and New York: Black Rose Books, 1989.

GOLDWATER, BARRY (1909–1998)

Barry Goldwater, senator from Arizona from 1953 to 1965 and 1969 to 1987, was the most libertarian of all the major candidates running for president in the 20th century. As the Republican nominee in 1964, he proposed a voluntary option for social security, termination of the farm subsidy program, privatizing parts of the Tennessee Valley Authority, and keeping welfare "a private concern." No one should have been surprised by his antigovernment crusade given what he had written in his 1960 best-selling manifesto, *The Conscience of a Conservative*. The turn to freedom in America will come, he maintained, when the people put in public office those who pledge to enforce the Constitution, restore the Republic, and proclaim: "My aim is not to pass laws, but to repeal them."

Goldwater's radical message in the 1964 campaign was not well received: He defeated his opponent in only six states, and he received only 38.5% of the popular vote. But his uncompromising stand for freedom at home and abroad laid the foundations of a political counterrevolution that led to Ronald Reagan's presidential victory in 1980 and Newt Gingrich's historic Contract with America in 1994. Barry Goldwater was, in fact, the most consequential loser in presidential politics.

He was an unlikely revolutionary: the grandson of a Jewish itinerant salesman who became a millionaire; a college dropout; a master mechanic and ham radio operator; a gifted photographer whose sensitive portraits of Native Americans have hung in galleries around the world; an intrepid pilot who flew more than 170 different planes in his lifetime, including the U-2. Goldwater was a fiercely independent Westerner who opposed Big Government, Big Business, Big Labor, and Big Media. He called himself a Jeffersonian republican with a small "r." He had deep-seated reservations about the Religious Right and its pro-life, antigay positions.

His presidential candidacy marked the beginning of a shift in modern American politics from liberalism to a more conservative economic philosophy that continues to this day.

LE

See also Conservatism; Fusionism; Taft, Robert A.

Further Readings

Goldwater, Barry M. *The Conscience of a Conservative*. Princeton, NJ: Princeton University Press, 2007.
Middendorf, J. William. *A Glorious Disaster: Barry Goldwater's Presidential Campaign and the Origins of the Conservative Movement*. New York: Basic Books, 2006.

GOVERNMENT

A group of people is said to be subject to "government" if there is among them a subset of people, acting in concert, who are purportedly authorized to impose requirements on the whole group using force if necessary. We must distinguish governments from (a) voluntary associations such as clubs and businesses, and (b) larger communities that share common traditions and values. Subjection to political authority stems solely from being born in a specific area; only occasionally are the subjects of a particular government immigrants. Nor need the subjects share common goals and interests. Those who exercise political power rule by force if necessary; the will of the rulers is expressed mainly in laws—general directives to all, more or less effectively enforced by the rulers.

This definition already suggests what libertarian concerns about government are likely to be. What, if anything, would justify government? What, if anything, could it legitimately be empowered to do? What are the best workable methods for selecting those individuals who are to wield governmental power? Historically, governments have typically had their origins in an imposition by force, which is just what libertarians object to. Even if governmental power were originally acquired peaceably, libertarians have raised questions about its legitimacy.

For present purposes, we may distinguish three general theories of government.

The first, cynical, view holds that governments act in their own interests, and the rulers tend to use their powers to line their own pockets and maximize their power over others. The other two views agree in opposing this description and hold that those who hold government positions must devote themselves to the well-being of the subjects, not themselves. However, they diverge in a crucial way.

The second view, which might be described as the conservative or Platonist version, holds that rulers should promote what is really good for people, and that this good can be known to government officials. Government, in short, should make people virtuous (Aristotle), should "fulfill their potential" (a host of thinkers, notably Marx), or perhaps "make people equal" (contemporary *liberals* in the now-familiar nonlibertarian sense of the term).

Finally, the third, liberal, view holds that people should be permitted to define their own good, and that the function of government is to enable each of us to pursue our own good in our own way.

Can political philosophy choose among these? Philosophy ideally should provide us with the answer to why government is or would be good for us. This view virtually rules out the first two. Rational people act on their own values, not anybody else's. If the Platonist thinks his view of government is correct, he must convince others that it is; if successful, then his also will be their view, and liberalism will embrace it. But if he fails, it would be irrational to hold that people will act on it. We do not act rationally on premises we think to be false.

Because people have their own interests and, for the most part, run their own lives, if government is to be justified, it must be shown that people are likely to confront insurmountable obstacles to their choices unless they surrender some of the freedom of action. In the case of voluntary associations, it is easy to show this is the case: We join such groups because we share a common interest, and we can best promote that interest by accepting some direction from others. But government is not a voluntary association, and there is no common purpose whose promotion requires that we must sacrifice our freedom. If government is to have a rational basis, it appears that only universal consent could provide it. However, there are problems in assuming the existence of universal consent. Theorists such as Locke, who appeal to implicit consent, have been attacked by critics such as Lysander Spooner, who argued that no contract can exist between two parties, one of whom is effectively compelled to consent to the agreement.

The alternative argument to universal consent is to predicate government on what is now known as public goods theory in order to demonstrate that the individual might be better off, even on his own terms, by submitting his judgment to that of a central body with respect to certain problems. When the effort by A to pursue his goods spills over onto B and C, and this situation is difficult to avoid, it appears as if some supraindividual authority may be needed to render A's efforts compatible with those of B and C. The public goods approach—made famous, if not in those words, by Thomas Hobbes and his successors—looks, at least at first sight, promising, but has been trenchantly criticized by authors such as Anthony de Jasay. It is clear that government can impose solutions, but it is not clear that government is needed to solve such problems as criminality, property distribution, public utilities management, or, the thorniest of these problems, defense against foreign invasion.

The most popular form of government among political theorists has been democracy for a variety of reasons. In democracies, all participants are consulted, and all act on their own view of what is good for them. However, democracy, as Mill has astutely noted, is not self-government, the government of each over himself. Instead, it is government of each by the rest, indeed by only a majority of others. Not only does democracy not solve this fundamental problem, but it generates serious problems of its own, including the possibility of an enormous expansion of government powers at the expense of individuals.

Given the libertarian ideal that only the prevention of force and fraud constitute legitimate uses of force against others, what then can government do to justify itself? The one obvious answer is that it would function only to keep people, in their pursuit of their own interests, from using violence or fraud. This view has been labeled *minimalist* (or *minarchist*). The panoply of contemporary regulations and agencies would be pared down to the bare minimum necessary to keep the peace—that is, to defend people and their property by suitable court procedures and policing.

That maintaining peace is the fundamental aim of government has been accepted by a host of classic political philosophers, among them Aquinas, Hobbes, Locke, and Kant. It is expressed in such formulations as John Locke's "Law of Nature," which calls on all "not to harm others in their life, health, liberty, or property." This notion constitutes the principal libertarian directive: All people are allowed to do as they please insofar as they do not aggress against others. In other words, governments may not use force against anybody for the purpose of supposedly promoting that person's own good, nor may they use it against any person to promote anybody else's good. This viewpoint sharply differentiates the libertarian view from modern welfarist views, according to which governments may tax people to provide education, health, welfare, or equal opportunity to all.

Even the least intrusive modern governments do far more than would be allowed were libertarians to have their way. Indeed, most libertarians would claim that governments as they are do not even perform their minimally legitimate functions very well. In contemporary Western societies, the criminal's chances of escaping from punishment for murder, rape, or robbery are excellent, and the peaceful citizen's chances of being left alone by government approach zero. If the libertarian view about the proper functions of government is correct, these likelihoods are major condemnations of modern government, and perhaps of any government.

JN and DT

See also Anarchism; Contractarianism/Social Contract; Minimal State; State

Further Readings

Aristotle. *Politics*. H. Rackham, trans. Cambridge, MA: Loeb Classical Library, 1932.

Calhoun, John C., and C. Gordon Post. *A Disquisition on Government: And Selections from the Discourse*. New York: Liberal Arts Press, 1953.

Hayek, F. A. von. *Constitution of Liberty*. Chicago: University of Chicago Press, 1960.

Hobbes, Thomas. *Leviathan*. Richard Tuck, ed. Cambridge: Cambridge University Press, 1996.

Locke, John. *Two Treatises on Government*. Peter Laslett, ed. Cambridge: Cambridge University Press, 2005.

Marx, Karl. "Manifesto of the Communist Party." *Marx: Later Political Writings*. Terrell Carver, ed. Cambridge: Cambridge University Press, 1996.

Mill, John Stuart. *On Liberty*. London: J. W. Parker and Son, 1859.

Paine, Thomas. "Common Sense." *Paine: Political Writings*. Bruce Kuklik, ed. Cambridge: Cambridge University Press, 2000.

Plato. *The Republic*. Allan Bloom, trans. New York: Basic Books, 1991.

Rand, Ayn. "The Nature of Government." *Capitalism: The Unknown Ideal*. New York: Signet, 1986.

Spooner, Lysander. *No Treason: The Constitution of No Authority*. Boston: L. Spooner, 1867.

Tullock, Gordon. *Autocracy*. Boston: Kluwer Academic, 1987.

GREAT DEPRESSION

The Great Depression was a worldwide economic collapse that struck the United States particularly hard. American economic output and prices fell dramatically from 1929 to 1933 while the unemployment rate reached an all-time high and stayed high for over a decade. Economic historians have concluded that the Depression was caused mainly by the flawed policies of central banks, including the Federal Reserve, in response to a malfunctioning international gold standard, although additional economic weaknesses and policy mistakes were involved. The response to the crisis was a permanently enlarged national government. If you body slam a physically fit economy, will it break? The answer from the Great Depression seems to be: Almost.

The U.S. economy grew strongly during most of the 1920s, spurred by robust productivity growth derived from recently introduced technologies, including electrification and the internal combustion engine. It reached a peak in August 1929 and then began an unprecedented contraction that lasted until March 1933. During the contraction, wholesale prices fell nearly 37%, whereas retail prices fell about 28%. Real gross domestic product (GDP), the value of all final goods and services produced in the economy (adjusting for changes in prices), fell about 26.5%, dwarfing the size of previous and subsequent economic downturns. Not surprisingly, the unemployment rate exploded, reaching 25% in 1933, meaning that one out of four would-be workers was jobless. The official unemployment rate subsequently exceeded 10% until 1940 (although these numbers are inflated by counting emergency workers in government programs as unemployed).

Agriculture, the construction industry, and manufacturing were particularly hard hit. Prices paid to farmers fell by half, dropping the ratio of the prices they received to the prices they paid by more than a third. Industrial production fell by 45% (with output of durable goods, such as automobiles, falling 70–80%), and new housing starts dropped 82%. Gross investment plummeted by more than 80%, meaning that the capital stock actually shrank because depreciation outstripped new investment, although personal consumption fell much less rapidly, only 18%. Although almost everyone suffered, the economic pain was not shared evenly; investors saw the value of the Dow Jones Industrial Average fall over 80%, and soup lines swelled with unemployed workers, but deflation-adjusted hourly earnings of those with jobs were virtually unchanged. All in all, the Depression hit harder in the United States than anywhere else. From 1929 to 1932, total industrial production fell by 11% in Britain, 23% in Italy, 26% in France, 32% in Canada, 41% in Germany, and 45% in the United States.

Contemporaries lacked good explanations of the causes of the Great Depression, which often led them to adopt policies that only worsened the situation. However, economic historians have done much to cast light on the matter. The general consensus is that policy mistakes and a malfunctioning international financial system converted an ordinary business downturn into the Great Depression. As Peter Temin and Barry Eichengreen put it, "central bankers continued to kick the world economy while it was down until it lost consciousness."

Traditional explanations of the Depression begin with the spectacular stock market crash of October 1929. The crash wiped out significant gains in asset prices and drove overleveraged investors into debt. It seems to have signaled a shift from optimism to pessimism in the economy, but most modern explanations see it as a secondary cause of the Depression. Another factor that may have played an important role in reducing aggregate demand is the dissipation of a home construction boom, which peaked in 1926. In addition, the enactment of the protectionist Smoot–Hawley Tariff has been blamed for exacerbating the recession, especially by inviting retaliatory tariffs among the country's trading partners. However, modern explanations of the Depression begin with Milton Friedman and Anna Schwartz, whose book, *Monetary History of the United States, 1867-1960*, carefully documented how disruptions in the financial sector harmed the rest of the economy.

Friedman and Schwartz argued that several waves of banking failures, beginning in October 1930, led to a drastic decline in the money supply, which caused considerable damage to the overall economy. As these bank failures unfolded, depositors became increasingly wary of keeping their assets in uninsured banks. Banks moved to reassure depositors by holding more of these deposits as reserves and in assets like government bonds that were easy to quickly convert into money. This scenario caused the supply of loanable funds to shrink, driving up interest rates and making it nearly impossible for many businesses and households to borrow. Deprived of credit, businesses and consumers were forced to curb their hiring and spending, reducing the overall demand for output and pushing other businesses and households to cut back as the crisis snowballed. This drop in aggregate demand caused prices to fall, but the deflation seems to have only worsened the problem because debt levels were higher than in previous downturns, so the drop in prices meant that it was harder for borrowers to pay back their loans. Many defaulted, making creditors even more wary to lend. Others paid back their loans, but were forced to cut back spending elsewhere to do so, exacerbating the problem. The extensive, fairly new automobile loan market seems to have played an important role because many of these loans were structured so that missed payments could easily result in repossession and loss of the built-up equity in the car, even if most of the loan had been paid off. In addition, rapidly falling prices meant that investors could come out ahead by simply sitting on their cash, which would appreciate in value by the fall in prices without the risk of default that lending brought.

Why were the bank failures of the Great Depression so persistent and widespread? Some of the weakness emanated from the rural banking sector, which was wracked by turbulent trends in agricultural commodity prices and land values in the aftermath of World War I. These weaknesses were exacerbated by state-level laws that often restricted banks to a single branch, making it difficult for them to diversify the risks in their loan portfolios. In earlier recessions, banking panics had been averted when deep-pocketed financiers, like J. P. Morgan, stepped forward to lend money to banks and when some banks temporarily suspended the ability of depositors to withdraw their money. The Federal Reserve was established, in part, to take the place of financiers as a "lender of last resort," and legislation ended the ability of most banks to close temporarily.

The traditional means of short-circuiting bank panics had been hamstrung by the federal government, and, critics argue, the Federal Reserve subsequently utterly failed in its duty to provide funds to the banking system as it began to crumble. The Fed's leaders seem to have seen the deflation and bankruptcies of the era as a *good* sign for long-term economic health. The administration of President Herbert Hoover and the staff of the Federal Reserve included many "liquidationists," who believed that overextended economic agents should be forced to rearrange their economic affairs and curb their speculative excesses. They viewed the bankruptcies, belt-tightening, and the entire downturn as an antidote, or even "penance," for the excesses of the 1920s. This theory is exemplified by a well-known quotation from Treasury Secretary Andrew Mellon, who advised Hoover to "liquidate labor, liquidate stocks, liquidate the farmers, liquidate real estate. . . . It will purge the rottenness out of the system. High costs of living and high living will come down. People will work harder, live a more moral life." Accordingly, the Federal Reserve didn't step in to add to the supply of loanable funds. Rather, in 1928 and 1929, it had acted to *decrease* the supply of credit available for stock market speculators and was slow to reverse course. Fed officials don't appear to have fully realized that credit had become tight because they observed that banks were carrying excess reserves (unloaned funds) and charging fairly low interest rates. Although these nominal interest rates were low and falling, they masked the high price that borrowers paid due to the fact that deflation made it harder to pay back loans. Real interest rates were at unusually high levels, reaching 20% or more after adjusting for deflation, and banks' excess reserves were a precautionary move, rather than a sign that there was plenty to lend.

Tellingly, when Britain left the gold standard in September 1931, the Fed *increased* its interest rate, rather than making credit easier to obtain, precipitating a new wave of bank failures. Barry Eichengreen, among others, has explained the Fed's seemingly perverse behavior in light of the contemporary understanding of the gold standard. From 1870 until World War I, the international gold standard had worked exceptionally well in providing a financial environment that made global investment and trade unusually stable and secure, allowing strong, widespread economic growth. At the conclusion of the war, it was obvious to most central bankers, businessmen, and policymakers that a return to the gold standard was a prerequisite for a return to renewed growth and stability. The hyperinflation in Weimar Germany shortly after the war emphasized the dangers of currency that was not backed by an inflexibly supplied commodity, such as gold. To make the gold standard work, each country convinced investors that it was committed to redeeming its currency for a specific amount of gold, to protecting them from a loss in their investment due to devaluation of the currency. To do so, it needed to hold enough gold. When it ran a trade surplus with other countries on the gold standard, it attracted more gold, which expanded its money supply and drove up prices, reducing exports of its goods and bringing the system back into balance. When it ran a trade deficit, the opposite occurred—it lost gold, shrinking the money supply, forcing its prices downward, and making them easier to export, closing up the deficit.

The system worked well when input prices, especially wages, were sufficiently flexible. Returning to the gold standard after World War I proved difficult because several countries, especially Great Britain, found their prices out of alignment with the prewar exchange rates, necessitating deflation. However, deflation no longer equilibrated the system because wages didn't fall enough, probably due to the rising power of labor unions in many European countries and the spread of internal labor markets and personnel departments in the United States. This shift in American labor market policies, designed in part to reduce turnover and increase the length of employment relations, has been attributed to a range of factors, including the reduction of immigration, technological changes, rising education and skill levels among workers, and diffusion of enlightened human resource policies. Thus, new political and economic realities meant that the traditional gold standard adjustment mechanism, deflation and wage cuts, no longer functioned as well as previously. Wages didn't fall much; instead, unemployment swelled. Moreover, the countries with the most gold, America and France, didn't adequately play by the rules of the game in the late 1920s, refusing to allow inflation to occur, thus creating a deflationary bias in the entire system. The United States didn't take the lead in replacing weakened Britain in ensuring that the system functioned properly.

Accordingly, when deflationary pressures emerged during the Great Depression, countries began to abandon the gold standard. Evidence shows that the sooner a country abandoned the gold standard, the quicker recovery commenced. Unfortunately for the U.S. economy, it clung to the gold standard longer than most other countries, suspending convertibility of the dollar after Franklin Roosevelt's inauguration in 1933. When Britain suspended the convertibility of the pound into gold in September 1931, the Fed knew that international investors feared the United States would soon join in abandoning the gold standard and thus devaluate the dollar in the process. Investors began to convert their dollar-denominated assets into gold, so the Fed acted to make the dollar more attractive through the sharpest increase in the rediscount rate in the system's history. Unfortunately, this interest rate hike worsened the domestic banking crisis, making it harder for shaky banks to obtain credit. In October 1931, more than 500 banks closed, and in the 6-month period starting in August 1931, banks with deposits totaling almost $1.5 billion suspended operations. A final banking crisis hit in the period between Roosevelt's election and his March 1933 inauguration. As bank runs spread from state to state and governors felt compelled to declare banking "holidays," depositors lost confidence in the entire banking system.

Between 1930 and 1933, more than 9,000 banks failed—more than a third of the initial total. Ben Bernanke argues that this situation helps explain the subsequent longevity of the Great Depression. The loss of these banks made the economy much less efficient than it had previously been, making it considerably harder for individuals and businesses who had built up relationships with the failed banks to obtain credit, forcing them to cancel plans to buy and invest. In addition, the length of the Depression has been explained by a series of policy missteps. In a recent survey of economic historians, half agreed that, despite many policies that helped to right the economy, "taken as a whole, government policies of the New Deal served to lengthen and deepen the Great Depression."

The policy they found most blameworthy was probably the National Industrial Recovery Act, enacted in June 1933, which aimed to rein in competitive forces, which many naively blamed for the economic collapse. The act allowed industries to draw up "codes of fair competition," which effectively cartelized production in many sectors, significantly boosting goods' prices and, thus, reducing the quantity of goods demanded and curtailing employment. The act was finally declared unconstitutional in May 1935. In addition, events suggest that the overall attitude of the Roosevelt administration and specific policies that threatened the security of property rights (such as the lack of response by government entities to sit-down strikes) discouraged investment, which jumped about 60% after the New Deal coalition suffered electoral defeats in 1938.

Amid the recovery, the economy suffered another steep downturn in 1937 when industrial production and wholesale prices fell by 33% and 11%, respectively, whereas unemployment rose 5%. This recession has been attributed to the Fed's deflationary overreaction in doubling banks' reserve requirements as a preemptive strike against inflation and the reduction in aggregate demand caused by the levying of social security payroll taxes several years before benefits were to begin being paid out.

Research concludes that this era might have been one of immense economic progress, as the years from 1929 to 1941 were, in the aggregate, the most technologically progressive of any comparable period in U.S. economic history. However, the scholarly consensus is that a series of policy mistakes and a malfunctioning international financial system made it an era of economic insecurity, opening the door to a permanently expanded economic presence of government.

RoW

See also Classical Economics; Friedman, Milton; Interventionism; Money and Banking

Further Readings

Bernanke, Ben S. *Essays on the Great Depression*. Princeton, NJ: Princeton University Press, 2000.

Eichengreen, Barry. *Golden Fetters: The Gold Standard and the Great Depression, 1919–1939*. New York: Oxford University Press, 1992.

Eichengreen, Barry, and Peter Temin. "The Gold Standard and the Great Depression." NBER Working Paper 6060, 1997.

Fearon, Peter. *War, Prosperity and Depression: The U.S. Economy, 1917-45*. Lawrence: University Press of Kansas, 1987.

Friedman, Milton, and Anna J. Schwartz. *A Monetary History of the United States, 1867–1960*. Princeton, NJ: Princeton University Press, 1963.

Hall, Thomas E., and J. David Ferguson. *The Great Depression: An International Disaster of Perverse Economic Policies*. Ann Arbor: University of Michigan Press. 1998,

Parker, Randall E. *The Economics of the Great Depression: A Twenty-First Century Look Back at the Economics of the Interwar Era*. Cheltenham, UK: Edward Elgar, 2007.

Romer, Christina D. "The Nation in Depression." *Journal of Economic Perspectives* 7 no. 2 (Spring 1993): 19–39.

Steindl, Frank G. *Understanding Economic Recovery in the 1930s: Endogenous Propagation in the Great Depression*. Ann Arbor: University of Michigan Press, 2003

Temin, Peter. *Lessons from the Great Depression*. Cambridge, MA: MIT Press, 1989.

Weinstein, Michael. *Recovery and Redistribution under the NIRA*. Amsterdam: North-Holland Publishing, 1980.

Wicker, Elmus. *The Banking Panics of the Great Depression*. New York: Cambridge University Press, 1996.

H

HARPER, FLOYD ARTHUR "BALDY" (1905–1973)

Floyd Arthur Harper, better known as Baldy Harper, is best remembered as the founder of the Institute for Humane Studies (IHS). The IHS, which Harper founded in 1961, is devoted to research and education in the classical liberal tradition and the promotion of libertarian ideals. An able economist and political theorist, Harper's main contribution was as a strategist of the libertarian movement, an institution builder, and a mentor to hundreds of classical liberal scholars.

Raised on a farm in Michigan, Harper attended Michigan State University as an undergraduate and obtained a doctorate in economics at Cornell University, where he taught for many years, ultimately as a full professor of marketing. In 1946, concerned about the future of liberal ideals in a world in which socialism was becoming dominant among the intellectual classes, Harper left the academy and joined the libertarian Foundation for Economic Education (FEE), then run by its founder, Leonard Read. A year later, Harper joined Ludwig von Mises, Milton Friedman, Karl Popper, and other present and future scholars at the founding meeting of Friedrich Hayek's Mont Pelerin Society at Mont Pelerin, Switzerland, to discuss the future of classical liberal ideas, which were then besieged by those who had embraced the social democratic orthodoxy.

While at FEE, Harper produced a number of significant works. In 1951, FEE published Harper's powerful antiwar pamphlet, *In Search of Peace*, in which he argued that the "problems of war—all conflict—are exclusively problems of abolished liberty. Thus the prevention of war, or of the threat of war, must take the form of cutting the bonds on liberty." In his 1957 monograph, *Why Wages Rise*, Harper lucidly explained the various causes of the gains in labor productivity that enable the growth of wages—labor unions and government intervention in the business cycle notably not among them. Harper's most remarkable work, however, was his earlier book, *Liberty: A Path to Its Recovery*, published by FEE in 1949, in which he laid out his comprehensive, natural law-tinged libertarian philosophy. In *Liberty*, Harper attempts to derive strong individual rights to property and free exchange as corollaries of a right to life. The most original aspect of the book was his emphasis on then-current empirical biological science to establish the biological basis of human individuality. Harper argued that individual variations in talent, together with the distinctively human "capacity for independent thought and action," were the source of all economic and cultural progress. Liberty, which exists "when a person is free to do whatever he desires, according to his wisdom and conscience," sustained the conditions under which diverse individual types could flourish and the progress of civilization could be realized.

Harper, who, according to Murray Rothbard, had arrived at an anarcho-capitalist position in the winter of 1949–1950, became increasingly disenchanted with FEE president Leonard Read, who, in a widely distributed pamphlet, had vigorously defended the government's power to tax.

In 1958, Harper decamped to become Senior Research Economist at the William Volker Fund near San Francisco, then the main source of financial support for libertarian scholars. Since his time at Cornell, Harper had dreamed of establishing an institute devoted to the interdisciplinary study of human action. In 1961, while at the Volker Fund, Harper, with the help of Murray Rothbard, Friedrich Hayek, and others, drew up plans for establishing the IHS, which was to be handsomely endowed with Volker money and to carry on the mission of discovering, sponsoring, and publishing the works of libertarian scholars while creating a community of libertarian thinkers through conferences and seminars. The idea was to revitalize the study of liberty by providing libertarian scholars an active, well-funded alternative to establishment sources of academic support. In 1962, however, the Volker Fund collapsed before it could fund IHS on a permanent basis. As a result, in 1962–1963, Harper became a visiting professor at Wabash College in Indiana. When he returned to Menlo Park, California, in 1963, he set up the IHS on a shoestring budget in his own garage. With the original idea of creating a center for libertarian scholarship fixed in his mind, over the next 8 years, Harper, as executive director, patiently built the IHS into a significant institution capable of holding conferences, publishing books, and supporting students and scholars. During that time, he carried out a vast correspondence while teaching and advising hundreds of students and succeeded in creating a large, far-flung network of scholars unified in a commitment to the study of classical liberal ideals that, in somewhat altered form, remains active to this day.

WW

See also Hayek, Friedrich A.; Mont Pelerin Society; Read, Leonard E.; Rothbard, Murray

Further Readings

Doherty, Brian. *Radicals for Capitalism: A Freewheeling History of the Modern American Libertarian Movement.* New York: Public Affairs, 2007.

Harper, F. A. *Liberty: A Path to Its Recovery.* Irvington-on-Hudson, NY: Foundation for Economic Education, 1949.

———. *The Writings of F. A. Harper: Volume I. The Major Works.* Menlo Park, CA: Institute for Humane Studies, 1978.

Rothbard, Murray. "Floyd Arthur 'Baldy' Harper, RIP." *The Libertarian Forum* (May 1973).

HAYEK, FRIEDRICH A. (1899–1992)

F. A. Hayek is quite possibly the most eminent free-market economist and social theorist of the postwar world. He was born in Vienna in 1899 and entered the University of Vienna immediately following the end of the First World War. Hayek took his doctorates in jurisprudence in 1921 and in political theory in 1923. Although his work in economics would earn him the Nobel Prize in 1974, Hayek's interests were far broader. Over the course of a long and productive life, he made significant contributions to a number of disciplines, including political and social theory, psychology, and the history of ideas.

In 1922, while Hayek was still completing his graduate studies, Ludwig von Mises published his devastating critique of a planned economy. In *Die Gemeinwirtschaft* (later translated into English as *Socialism*), Mises demonstrated that once markets are replaced by central planning, there

exists no way of determining the values of goods and services, thus making rational economic calculation impossible. Mises's essay was decisive in proving that without a genuine price system real costs cannot be calculated. As a consequence of reading Mises, Hayek abandoned his youthful socialist leanings and became a firm adherent of free markets and a regular participant at Mises's weekly seminars.

Hayek's early interest in the relation between bank credit and the business cycle led to his being appointed director of a newly established Austrian Institute for Business Cycle Research in 1927. While there he published his first important work in economics, *Geldtheorie und Konjunkturtheorie* (published in English in 1933 as *Monetary Theory and the Trade Cycle*), which sought to explicate the complex relationship between credit expansions and capital malinvestment and how these factors lay at the root of business cycles. As a consequence, Hayek was invited to deliver a series of lectures at the London School of Economics (LSE) by Lionel Robbins, who headed the economics department there. Those lectures, which appeared in book form as *Prices and Production,* took the economics profession by storm; as a consequence, Robbins offered Hayek the Tooke Professorship in Economic Science at the LSE, which Hayek took up in 1931.

It was from that period that Hayek's famous confrontation with John Maynard Keynes occurred. Keynes, at the time arguably the world's most celebrated economist, had published his *Theory of Money* in 1930, and Lionel Robbins, editor of the prestigious journal *Economica,* assigned the book to Hayek to review. In his critique, Hayek argued that Keynes's theory was fatally flawed by its failure to appreciate the importance of monetary factors in altering the structure of production and causing malinvestment. To that Keynes wrote a reply and, as editor of the *Economic Journal* at Cambridge, asked Piero Sraffa to review Hayek's book. Hayek in turn replied to Sraffa's review, to which Sraffa wrote a rejoinder. The debate between Hayek and Keynes, which dominated academic economics for a time, soon spread throughout Britain and came to include every important economist then writing.

It was while at the LSE that Hayek also first published his essays on knowledge and prices, which constituted one of his most original contributions to the field of economics and social philosophy. In "Economics and Knowledge" (1937) and "The Use of Knowledge in Society" (1945), Hayek maintained that the rational allocation of resources was dependent on the coordination of the dispersed bits of knowledge possessed by each actor in an economy and that only free markets could provide the necessary coordinating structure. Knowledge, he argued, takes a variety of forms and need not even be conscious. It is through the individual pursuit of private ends that bits of knowledge are transmitted to economic actors in the form of prices. The market, Hayek argued, can be understood as serving an essential epistemological purpose, as a discovery process, that is, as a vehicle for the generation of knowledge.

Hayek's insights into the market as a coordinating mechanism of otherwise dispersed knowledge served as the philosophical underpinning of his most important insight into social theory, the idea that complex social institutions, while the product of human action, are not the product of human design. Social institutions, Hayek contended, are so complex that their internal structure cannot be fully understood by any one mind or group of minds. They arise and take their shape not from conscious human invention, but through evolution as the product of countless human interactions, each aimed at some more immediate, private end. The notion that the social arrangements under which we live are the product of evolution and not of deliberate calculation had been earlier suggested by the thinkers associated with the Scottish Enlightenment, in particular Adam Smith, David Hume, and Adam Ferguson. Indeed, Adam Smith's conception of the invisible hand is one prominent instance of the broader idea of spontaneously generated orders. In his writings, Hayek maintained that language, law, morals, and social conventions were all instances of spontaneously generated orders. Hayek regarded the view that social arrangements required some central controlling authority, lest lawlessness and chaos ensue, as the entryway to totalitarian ideologies. Hayek regarded this rationalistic approach to social problems, predicated on the view that the methodology of the natural sciences was applicable to social questions, as inimical to a free society, and associated it with the French Enlightenment and continental political theory.

Alarmed by the prodigious growth of government in the 20th century, even in those nations ostensibly dedicated to personal liberty and private initiative, Hayek wrote *The Road to Serfdom* in 1944. The essay was directed primarily at a lay rather than an academic audience, and it warned of the dangers inherent in a planned economy, pointing to the similarities between the social and economic systems that had been embraced by National Socialist Germany and Fascist Italy, on the one hand, and by the Allied powers, on the other hand. Hayek had been alarmed by the prevailing orthodoxy that viewed an immense welfare state and extensive government intervention into the lives of its citizens as a compassionate response to unrestrained capitalism. In *The Road to Serfdom,* he hoped to show that those preconceptions were rooted in the same distrust of individual initiative and voluntary exchange as were the ideologies with which the West was at war, and that central planning, even should its intentions be benign, resulted in destroying the spontaneously generated order of the market, which in turn led to even more government planning.

The book was received enthusiastically in both the United States and Great Britain, to the point where the American publisher, the University of Chicago Press, was unable to print enough copies to meet the demand because of the wartime rationing of paper. However, the essay was able to reach a much larger American audience when the *Reader's Digest* published a 20-page excerpt of the book in April 1945. The American lecture tour that followed the appearance of the *Reader's Digest* excerpt whetted Hayek's appetite to spend more time in the United States, and he was prevailed on to accept an appointment to the Committee on Social Thought at the University of Chicago, which he took up in 1950.

While at the University of Chicago, Hayek published his most ambitious work in social and legal philosophy, *The Constitution of Liberty* (1960). In that work, Hayek attempted to set out nothing less than a treatise on the theoretical foundations of a free society. A work of immense erudition, *The Constitution of Liberty* outlines Hayek's views on the origins and nature of law in a liberal society, his conclusions regarding the nature of justice, and his conception of a free society. A free polity, Hayek contended, is one in which men are governed by abstract, general rules that are predictable in their application and apply to all, in contrast to systems of government based on the exercise of wide, discretionary powers by those in authority.

Among his final essays was the three-volume *Law, Legislation, and Liberty* (1973, 1976, 1979), in which Hayek elaborated on his earlier discussions of the nature of liberty and the political and legal framework of a free commonwealth. In that work, Hayek amplified his views on the nature of social evolution and described how the moral and legal rules that have proved themselves compatible with free societies emerged without the need of a lawgiver. In *The Fatal Conceit* (1988), Hayek took up a theme that he had dealt with earlier in a series of articles that first appeared in the British journal *Economica* and were later published in book form as *The Counter-Revolution of Science: Studies in the Abuse of Reason* (1952). Those earlier studies provided a persuasive defense of methodological individualism and criticized those who asserted that we may make meaningful statements about social collectivities independent of their constituent components. *The Fatal Conceit* was to be Hayek's last book. In it, he once again took issue with those who refuse to acknowledge the limitations of human knowledge and who are under the mistaken notion that reason alone is sufficient to shape the complex of rules and institutions that make up modern society and that, as a consequence, conscious social planning is possible and salutary.

Hayek died in 1992, having witnessed the total collapse of the socialist economies of Eastern Europe. More important, he was aware that his own work played a crucial role in the revolutions that swept the Eastern Bloc. That is certainly the highest tribute that can be accorded to someone who dedicated his life to the ongoing war against tyranny.

RH

Further Readings

Barry, Norman P. *Hayek's Social and Economic Philosophy.* London: Macmillan, 1979.

Boettke, Peter, ed. *The Intellectual Legacy of F. A. Hayek in Politics, Philosophy and Economics.* 3 vols. Cheltenham, UK: Edward Elgar, 2000.

Gissurarson, Hannes. *Hayek's Conservative Liberalism (Political Theory and Political Philosophy).* New York: Garland, 1987.

Gray, John. *Hayek on Liberty.* Oxford: Blackwell, 1984.

Hamowy, Ronald. *The Scottish Enlightenment and the Theory of Spontaneous Order.* Carbondale: Southern Illinois University Press, 1987.

Kukathas, Chandran. *Hayek and Modern Liberalism.* Oxford: Clarendon Press, 1989.

O'Driscoll, Gerald. *Economics as a Coordination Problem: The Contribution of Friedrich A. Hayek.* Kansas City, MO: Sheed Andrews & McMeel, 1977.

Sciabarra, Chris. *Marx, Hayek, and Utopia.* Albany: State University of New York Press, 1995.

See also Banking, Austrian Theory of; Common Law; Economics, Austrian School of; Mises, Ludwig von; Spontaneous Order

HAZLITT, HENRY (1894–1973)

Henry Hazlitt, a journalist, writer, and economist, was born in Philadelphia. His father died soon after his birth, and he attended a school for poor, fatherless boys. His mother remarried, and the family moved to Brooklyn, New York. When he graduated from high school, Hazlitt's ambition was to go to Harvard and write books on philosophy. But his stepfather died, and he started attending the no-tuition College of the City of New York. However, he soon left school to support himself and his mother. In those years, it was not hard for a young man to get a job. With no government-imposed obstacles to hiring or firing, no minimum wage laws, no workday or workweek restrictions, and no unemployment or social security taxes, employer and potential employee needed only to agree on the terms of employment. If things did not work out, the employee could quit or be fired. Hazlitt's first jobs lasted only a few days each.

When Hazlitt realized that with shorthand and typing skills he could earn two or three times the $5 per week he was being paid as an unskilled office boy, he studied stenography. Determined to become a writer, he looked for a newspaper job and soon took a job with the *Wall Street Journal,* then a small limited-circulation publication. Its executives dictated editorials to him, and reporters phoned in their stories. At first he knew nothing about Wall Street. On one assignment, Hazlitt was informed that a company had *passed* its dividend. Hazlitt thought this meant the company had approved it. But in stock market terminology, *passing* a dividend meant skipping it. Fortunately, in reporting the story, Hazlitt used the company's original verb. He was learning about the market.

Having missed out on college, Hazlitt determined to study on his own. He started reading college economics texts, but was not misled by their anticapitalist flavor. Experience had taught him that businessmen did not always earn profits; they sometimes suffered losses. Hazlitt's uncle had been forced to close his Coney Island enterprise when it rained heavily over a Fourth of July holiday and customers stayed away in droves. Hazlitt's stepfather lost his business making children's hats when this custom went out of fashion.

Hazlitt's real economic education began with his study of Philip H. Wicksteed's *The Common Sense of Political Economy,* which introduced him to the subjective theory of value, only recently developed by Austrian economists Carl Menger and Eugen von Böhm-Bawerk. Hazlitt continued his self-study program and persisted in his ambition to write. His first book, *Thinking as a Science,* appeared in 1916 before his 22nd birthday.

In 1916, Hazlitt left the *Wall Street Journal* for the *New York Evening Post.* He was forced to leave during World War I, serving in the Army Air Corps in Texas. However, when the war ended, the *Post* wired Hazlitt that he could have his job back if he was in the office in 5 days. He entrained immediately, went directly to the newspaper, and worked that day in uniform.

From the *Post,* Hazlitt went on to become either financial or literary editor of various New York papers. From 1934 to 1946, Hazlitt was an editorial writer for *The New York Times.* Hazlitt and the *Times* parted company over the Bretton Woods Agreement, against which Hazlitt had been editorializing. The *Times* supported the agreement, which had been endorsed by 43 nations, but Hazlitt claimed it would only lead to monetary expansion and refused to support it. Hazlitt secured a position with *Newsweek* and left the *Times.* From 1946 to 1966, he wrote *Newsweek*'s Business Tides column.

An analysis of Hazlitt's libertarian sympathies must mention his association with Ludwig von Mises, the leading exponent of the Austrian School of Economics. Hazlitt first heard of Mises through Benjamin M. Anderson's *The Value of Money,* published in 1917. Anderson criticized many writers on monetary theory, but said he found in Mises's works "very noteworthy clarity and power. His *Theorie des Geldes und der Umlaufsmittel* [later translated into English as *The Theory of Money and Credit*] is an exceptionally excellent book." Although Mises had been widely respected in Europe, he was little known in this country when he arrived as a wartime refugee in 1940. When Mises's *Socialism* appeared in English in 1937, Hazlitt remembered Anderson's remark about Mises and reviewed *Socialism* in the *Times,* describing it as "the most devastating analysis of socialism yet penned . . . an economic classic in our time." He sent his review to Mises in Switzerland and, 2 years later, when Mises came to this country, he phoned Hazlitt. Hazlitt recalled Mises's call as if coming from an economic ghost of centuries past. Hazlitt and Mises soon met and became close friends. Hazlitt's contacts helped establish Mises on this side of the Atlantic, enabling him to continue his free-market teaching, writing and lecturing. Hazlitt was instrumental in persuading Yale University to publish Mises's *Omnipotent Government* and *Bureaucracy* in 1944 and then his major opus, *Human Action*, in 1949. As a founding trustee of the FEE, Hazlitt also was responsible for Mises's appointment as economic advisor to that Foundation.

In 1946, Hazlitt wrote and published his most popular book, *Economics in One Lesson*. It became a best-seller, was translated into 10 languages, and still sells thousands of copies each year. Its theme—that economists should consider not only the seen but also the unseen consequences of any government action or policy—was adopted from 19th-century free-market economist Frédéric Bastiat. Thanks to *Economics in One Lesson*'s short chapters and clear, lucid style, countless readers were able to grasp its thesis that government intervention fails to attain its hoped-for objectives.

While still at *Newsweek*, Hazlitt edited the libertarian biweekly, *The Freeman*—as coeditor from 1950 to 1952 and as editor-in-chief from 1952 to 1953. When the left-liberal *Washington Post* bought *Newsweek*, Hazlitt became a columnist from 1966 to 1969 for the international *Los Angeles Times* syndicate.

At least two of Hazlitt's books made original contributions to libertarianism. *The Failure of the "New Economics"* contributed to a much more sophisticated understanding of the economics of the modern world. Chapter by chapter, he criticized John Maynard Keynes's *The General Theory of Employment, Interest and Money*, which explained why Keynes's politically popular inflationary recommendations would fail to solve unemployment, work against the revival trade, and even exacerbate the economic slump.

Hazlitt's second major contribution to libertarianism, *The Foundations of Morality*, elaborated on Mises's statement that "Everything that serves to preserve the social order is moral; everything that is detrimental to it is immoral." Hazlitt wrote, "Morality is older than any living religion and probably older than all religion." He noted a common denominator in law, ethics, and manners: They all rest on the same principles: sympathy, kindness, and consideration of others. The moral philosophy Hazlitt presents is "utilitarian . . . [i]n the sense that all rules of conduct must be judged by their tendency to lead to desirable rather than undesirable social results."

By the age of 70, Hazlitt had estimated he had written some 10,000 editorials, articles, and columns, plus a dozen books—six more followed later. Hazlitt's literary works were not mere potboilers. Each book on a special theme—government intervention, foreign aid, welfare, poverty, morality, and inflation—was based on sound libertarian principles. Each short piece analyzed some current event from a free-market perspective. Mises credited Hazlitt's repeated warnings of the dangers of inflation in *Newsweek* for possibly giving the government's monetary authorities a "guilty conscience" and dampening their political inclination to inflate.

Some dismiss Hazlitt as "just an economic journalist." But he was no ordinary economic journalist, no "secondhand dealer in ideas" in the sense used by economist F. A. Hayek. He was an original thinker who contributed to an understanding of economics and libertarian principles and to their dissemination among millions. He died on July 9, 1993.

BBG

See also Hayek, Friedrich A.; Mises, Ludwig von; Money and Banking

Further Readings

Bastiat, Frédéric. "What Is Seen and What Is Not Seen." *Selected Essays on Political Economy*. Seymour Cain, trans. Irvington-on-Hudson, NY: Foundation for Economic Education, 1995.

Ebeling, Richard M., and Roy A. Childs, Jr. *Henry Hazlitt: An Appreciation*. Irvington-on-Hudson, NY: Foundation for Economic Education, 1985.

Hazlitt, Henry. *Economics in One Lesson*. New York: Arlington House, 1979.

———. *The Failure of the "New Economics"; An Analysis of the Keynesian Fallacies*. Irvington-on-Hudson, NY: Foundation for Economic Education, 1995

———. *The Foundations of Morality*. Irvington-on-Hudson, NY: Foundation for Economic Education, 1998.

Hume, David. *An Enquiry Concerning the Principles of Morals*. J. B. Schneewind, ed. Indianapolis, IN: Hackett, 1983.

HEALTH CARE

Health care represents a special area of public policy for libertarians, although not for the reasons typically offered in support of government intervention. In limited circumstances, a substantial number of libertarians support state-sponsored coercion to prevent the spread of infectious diseases. In the absence of violence, theft, tortious injury, fraud, or breach of contract, however, libertarians reject the use of coercion in health and medicine as immoral and counterproductive.

People can do violence to each other by transmitting contagious diseases. Therefore, most libertarians sanction limited government efforts to identify and contain infectious diseases and punish those who infect others intentionally or negligently. They do so cautiously, however. A 2004 survey published in the journal *Health Affairs* hints at one way such powers could be abused. Amid widespread concern about bioterrorism, roughly equal shares of white and black Americans expressed support for quarantines to contain a serious contagious disease. When subsequently asked whether they would support a compulsory quarantine, where the authorities would have the power to arrest violators, 25% of whites changed their minds, whereas 51% of blacks did, indicating an awareness that these policies would not necessarily be fairly implemented. Just as libertarians advocate limits on government's ability to pursue criminals generally, they closely circumscribe the use of force to protect public health. For example, an outbreak must pose a serious health threat, there must be no feasible alternative to coercion, and the state must use the least coercive measures available. Libertarians reject government intervention to remedy private health problems, such as obesity, diabetes, or addiction.

There exist more unjustified uses of the state's coercive power in health and medicine than in nearly any other area. In the United States, governments routinely forbid competent adults from making medical decisions that affect no one but themselves. Libertarians maintain that such laws are unjust and ultimately counterproductive. For example, the government denies patients, including terminally ill patients, the ability to determine their course of treatment. Proponents argue that such laws exist to ensure the safety and effectiveness of medical products. Libertarians argue that those laws cause more morbidity and mortality than they prevent.

Licensing laws restrict entry into the medical professions, dictate what tasks each profession may perform, and deny patients the right to be treated by the practitioner of their choice. Libertarians agree with a quip that Mark Twain delivered before the New York General Assembly in 1901, as reported in *The New York Times*:

> I don't know that I cared much about these osteopaths until I heard you were going to drive them out of the State; but since I heard this I haven't been able to sleep. . . . Now what I contend is that my body is my own, at least I have always so regarded it. If I do harm through my experimenting with it, it is I who suffer, not the State.

Proponents of licensing argue that it enhances the quality of care, but libertarians point to the fact that low-quality care is widespread despite licensing, that licensing does not improve overall quality because it reduces access to care for the poor, and that the chief proponents of licensing are incumbent practitioners who profit by restricting entry. Meanwhile, unregulated markets are extremely likely to develop private quality certification.

Government prohibits the sale of human organs to transplant patients or organ brokers. Proponents of that ban consider it immoral to commodify the human body, but such a ban allows government to assert a property right in the body of every citizen. Further, it makes organs no less valuable a commodity, but merely imposes on them a zero price and consequently creates an artificial shortage that causes thousands of unnecessary deaths in the United States each year.

Governments infringe on the individual's ability to choose whether to purchase health insurance and what type of insurance to purchase. Targeted tax breaks penalize consumers for purchasing the wrong type of health insurance or no insurance. Libertarians note that these laws require adults to buy coverage they do not want and may even consider immoral. Legislatures enact these laws at the behest of the providers of the covered services, which increases the costs of health insurance and the number of uninsured.

Libertarians further object to the government's refusal to honor contracts limiting a provider's liability for malpractice in exchange for reduced-price or free medical care. Proponents of that rule argue that patients harmed by negligent providers might not be able to recover. Opponents say that such rules limit the right of consenting adults to engage in mutually beneficial exchanges that harm no one else and that they reduce access to care among those least able to pay. Finally, regulations of this sort reduce experimentation with malpractice rules that ensure both quality and access.

Government may do the greatest damage to health and personal liberty through its influence over the financing of medical care. Government programs such as Medicare and Medicaid finance nearly half of all medical expenditures in the United States. They devour private health insurance markets and deny adults the ability to choose whether and how to fund their health needs in retirement and how to assist the needy. These programs waste more than $60 billion per year on care that makes patients no healthier or happier. Targeted tax breaks divert even private spending from pursuing high-quality, affordable care and unnecessarily induce millions to become dependent on government. These targeted tax breaks deny workers control over their earnings and their health insurance. They encourage wasteful consumption of medical care and strip workers of their health insurance when they leave a job.

In 1963, Nobel laureate economist Kenneth Arrow wrote that licensure and other features of health care markets can be partially explained by uncertainty about the quality of medical care and the fact that physicians possess more certainty regarding quality than do patients. Many supporters of licensure cite Arrow's analysis when arguing for government intervention to correct the perceived market failures of imperfect and asymmetric information. With respect to Arrow's conclusions, however, health economist James C. Robinson has replied,

> The most pernicious doctrine in health services research, the greatest impediment to clear thought and successful action, is that health care is *different*. . . .
>
> To some within the health care community, the uniqueness doctrine is self-evident and needs no justification. After all, health care is essential to health. That food and shelter are even more vital and seem to be produced without professional licensure, nonprofit organization, compulsory insurance, class action lawsuits, and 133,000 pages of regulatory prescription in the *Federal Register* does not shake the faith of the orthodox. . . .
>
> The central proposition of [Arrow's 1963] article, that health care information is imperfect and asymmetrically distributed, has been seized upon to justify every inefficiency, idiosyncrasy, and interest-serving institution in the health care industry. . . . It has served to lend the author's unparalleled reputation to subsequent claims that advertising, optometry, and midwifery are threats to consumer well-being, that nonprofit ownership is natural for hospitals though not for physician practices, that price competition undermines product quality, that antitrust exemptions reduce costs, that consumers cannot compare insurance plans and must yield this function to politicians, that price regulation is effective for pharmaceutical products despite having failed in other applications, that cost-conscious choice is unethical while cost-unconscious choice is a basic human right. . . .

Libertarians do not dispute that health and medicine present unique challenges, but they argue that noncoercive measures are best able to address these challenges.

MFC

See also Bioethics; Paternalism; Regulation; Rent Seeking; Welfare State

Further Readings

Arrow, Kenneth J. "Uncertainty and the Welfare Economics of Medical Care." *American Economic Review* 53 no. 5 (December 1963): 941–973.

Cannon, Michael F., Daniel B. Klein, and Alexander Tabarrok. "Do Economists Reach a Conclusion on the Food and Drug Administration?" *Econ Journal Watch*, forthcoming.

Cannon, Michael F., and Michael D. Tanner. *Healthy Competition: What's Holding Back Health Care and How to Free It.* Washington, DC: Cato Institute, 2007.

Conover, Christopher J. "Health Care Regulation: A $169 Billion Hidden Tax." *Cato Institute Policy Analysis* 527 (October 4, 2004).

Epstein, Richard A. "Medical Malpractice: The Case for Contract." *American Bar Foundation Research Journal* 1 no. 1 (1976): 87–149.

———. *Mortal Peril: Our Inalienable Right to Health Care?* Reading, MA: Addison-Wesley, 1997.

Hamowy, Ronald. "The Early Development of Medical Licensing Laws in the United States, 1875–1900." *Journal of Libertarian Studies* 3 (Spring 1979): 73–119.

———. *Government and Public Health in America.* Northampton, MA: Edward Elgar Publishing, 2007.

Hyman, David A. *Medicare Meets Mephistopheles.* Washington, DC: Cato Institute, 2006.

Kling, Arnold. *Crisis of Abundance: Rethinking How We Pay for Health Care.* Washington, DC: Cato Institute, 2006.

Robinson, James C. "The End of Asymmetric Information." *Journal of Health Politics, Policy and Law* 26 no. 5 (October 2001): 1045–1053.

Starr, Paul. *The Social Transformation of American Medicine.* New York: Basic Books, 1984.

HEINLEIN, ROBERT (1907–1988)

Robert Heinlein, author and social critic, was born in 1907 in Missouri. He was one of the century's most important writers of science fiction. J. Neil Schulman said it best in his *Reason* article (later reprinted in "The Robert Heinlein Interview") when he drew this picture of Robert A. Heinlein's eclectic followers:

> His devotees range from freaked-out astrologers to coolly rational astronomers; from Goldwater-country conservatives to Greenwich Village anarchists; from atheists such as Madalyn Murray O'Hair to members of the Church of All Worlds who proclaim him a prophet and his novel, *A Stranger in a Strange Land*, a holy book.

Heinlein's award-winning science fiction spanned five decades and paved the way for a new era in the genre. Indeed, his works constitute some of the most commercially successful libertarian fiction of all time.

Writing science fiction was not Heinlein's original career goal. He served in the U.S. Navy, where he stayed until his health forced him into retirement at age 27. Engineering, politics, and other pursuits followed. He did not set pen to paper until 1939, when he wrote his first story and sold it to *Astounding*. After that, his ascent was all but immediate. Dozens of novels, novellas, and short stories followed, bringing Heinlein multiple awards, including the very first Grand Master Hugo Award. He continues to hold the record along with Lois McMaster Bujold for the most Hugo Awards won for science fiction novels. Chief among these works was *The Moon Is a Harsh Mistress*, written in 1966. Heinlein here offered a loose retelling of the American Revolution, with the revolt against tyranny set on the moon. The "Loonies" rebel against the iron control of the authorities on Earth and in the process learn the lesson that "there ain't no such thing as a free lunch" or, as Heinlein states it in the novel, TANSTAAFL. Ultimately, the Loonies, like the colonials after whom they were modeled, achieve an independence of sorts, but not without great cost.

Other works, such as *Stranger in a Strange Land* and *Revolt*, published in 2001, also carried similar messages centering on individuality, liberty, and sacrifice. Some of his most famous writings were aimed at a juvenile audience. *Starship Troopers* was one of these writings and one of his many works later adapted to film. Heinlein also scripted a few movies in the 1950s, including *Destination Moon*, the story of a privately funded space mission.

Heinlein also wrote nonfiction. His book, *Take Back Your Government*, bemoaned the runaway state and the uninvolved citizens that allowed it. Articles such as "The Last Days of the United States" and "How to Be a Survivor: The Art of Staying Alive in the Atomic Age" called for an end to nuclear proliferation. "The Happy Days Ahead" warned of "the cancerous explosion of government" and exhorted citizens to be active and vigilant. His works are pervaded by a concern for government bankruptcy, dictatorship, and a nuclear holocaust in the United States. His confession in "The Happy Days Ahead" was typically wry: "I don't claim to be altruistic. Just this pragmatic difference: I am sharply aware that, if the United States goes down the chute, I go down with it."

At different times, Heinlein was criticized for his ideas about politics, gender, race, and the military. The 1973 *Time Enough for Love: The Lives of Lazarus Long*, which was built on his 1941 novel, *Methuselah's Children*, was even touted by certain groups as pornographic. The author expanded on these themes in his new stories, and his calls to action continued even after death. His posthumous *Grumbles from the Grave* in 1989 carried on this tradition in Heinlein's most irascible manner.

Before his demise, Heinlein was interviewed by classical liberal author J. Neil Schulman about his publications and his overall philosophy. During this discussion, Heinlein boasted of the libertarianism embedded in his writings, remarking:

> I would say my position is not too far from that of Ayn Rand's; that I would like to see government reduced to no more than internal police and courts, external armed forces—with the other matters handled otherwise. I'm sick of the way the government sticks its nose into everything, now. . . . It seems to me that every time we manage to establish one freedom, they take another away. Maybe two.

In his 1980 collection, *The Expanded Universe*, Heinlein joked that "either I or this soi-disant civilization will be extinct by 2000 A.D." After more than a decade of poor health, Robert A. Heinlein died in 1988. His works continue to be reprinted and to find their way to the screen.

AmS

See also American Revolution; Rand, Ayn; Religion and Liberty

Further Readings

Heinlein, Robert A. *The Expanded Universe*. New York: Ace Books, 1982.
———. *The Moon Is a Harsh Mistress*. New York: St. Martin's Press, 1997.
Schulman, J. Neil, and Brad Linaweaver. *The Robert Heinlein Interview and Other Heinleiniana*. New York: Pulpless.Com, 1999.

HERBERT, AUBERON (1838–1906)

Auberon Herbert was a British writer and political theorist. He was the most consistent advocate of libertarian doctrines writing in late Victorian Britain. Among his systematic works on the role of politics in society were *A Politician in Trouble about His Soul* (1883–1884), *The Right and Wrong of Compulsion by the State* (1885), and *The Voluntaryist Creed* (1908). Herbert also played an important role in public life. He was a Liberal member of the House of Commons from 1870 to 1874 and from the 1880s onward strove to create a host of libertarian political associations. He organized public opinion against British intervention in Russia, Egypt, and southern Africa. Between 1890 and 1901, he published *Free Life,* a weekly, later monthly, journal subtitled "The Organ of Voluntary Taxation and the Voluntary State."

Herbert's moral and political views were largely inspired by the work of Herbert Spencer. However, they diverged at the foundational level and with respect to a number of policy recommendations. Spencer embraced the utilitarian principle of the greatest good of the greatest number as the bedrock standard of morality. He then argued that this standard required compliance with the law of equal freedom and implied equal rights. In contrast, Herbert regarded utilitarianism (i.e., the doctrine of convenience) to be inherently antithetical to the law of equal liberty and the rights of self-ownership. Herbert offered two main arguments for the proposition that each person possessed rights over his own person, faculties, and energy. First, each person should pursue happiness and moral development. To do so, each person must be left free to devote his faculties and energies as he judges will best promote that happiness and development. It was therefore crucial for each individual to enjoy a right to exercise his own faculties and direct his own energies. It follows, he argued, that no one can correctly ascribe this right of self-ownership to himself and not also ascribe it to everyone else. According to the second argument, morality must include some ascription of fundamental rights. The alternative is the unacceptable belief that no norms are sacred and that everything is merely a matter of convenience. These ascribed fundamental rights must be either rights of self-ownership or rights of mutual ownership.

There are, however, deep incoherencies in the idea of rights of mutual ownership. Hence, our fundamental rights must be rights of self-ownership.

Herbert defended property rights as extensions of the individual's rights of self-ownership. To deny an individual the right to the product of his faculties and energies is to deny him the right to those faculties and energies. Cultivated land is as much the product of one's labor as the crops that are cultivated. So, contrary to Herbert Spencer, rights to a certain portion of land are as well established as the rights to the crops that issue from that land. Individuals may not be deprived of their rightful possessions without their consent. For this reason, they may not be subject to force or fraud. An individual (or his agent) may use force only to resist the initial use of force (or fraud). Even the defensive use of force is morally problematic, but the necessity of self-preservation makes it "a justified usurpation."

Herbert regarded it as essential that one distinguish between true "direct" force and the "indirect" force that is involved when A takes advantage of B's situation by making B an offer that B "finds he cannot" refuse. If B finds himself in a difficult situation and A is not responsible for that situation, but merely offers B some way of improving on his current condition—by, say, becoming A's employee—B benefits from the interaction and cannot properly be said to be coerced by A. In contrast, genuine direct force is involved if A is forbidden to deal with B or if A is required to ameliorate B's difficult position. Impermissible direct force also is involved in governmental attempts to protect individuals from their own mistakes or vices. Moreover, any such use of force undermines the natural processes of discovery and moral self-improvement.

At the core of Herbert's position was the view he shared with Spencer and J. S. Mill—that individual autonomous judgment is the source and realization of what is most valuable in life. Any attempt to do good by circumventing or suppressing independent judgment will almost certainly be counterproductive. Herbert also pointedly criticized the neo-Hegelian trend in late Victorian thought that denied the ultimate reality and importance of the individual. He argued that this neo-Hegelian critique of individualism confused the simple fact that individuals continually influence one another's lives with the falsehood that only the collectivity is real.

Herbert maintained that all compulsory taxation involves morally unacceptable force. Thus, only voluntary taxation (i.e., fees that individuals freely agreed to pay in exchange for the service of having their rights protected) was permissible. Individuals should be free to purchase—or not to purchase—a rights-protection service from any vendor. Here Herbert endorsed the view of the young Herbert Spencer that each person has a right to ignore the state. However, Herbert distinguished his position from that of the "reasonable" individualist anarchists, such as Lysander Spooner and Benjamin Tucker, in that he held that individuals should and would freely converge on a single supplier of rights protection.

EM

See also Liberalism, Classical; Mill, John Stuart; Spencer, Herbert; Voluntarism

Further Readings

Harris, S. Hutchison. *Auberon Herbert: Crusader for Liberty.* London: Williams & Norgate, 1943.

Herbert, Auberon. *The Right and Wrong of Compulsion by the State and Other Essays.* Eric Mack, ed. Indianapolis, IN: Liberty Classics, 1978.

Mack, Eric. "Voluntaryism: The Political Thought of Auberon Herbert." *The Journal of Libertarian Studies* 2 no. 4 (Winter 1978): 299–309.

HESS, KARL (1923–1994)

Karl Hess, a libertarian author, activist, and publicist, was a popular libertarian speaker and movement personality in the late 1960s through his death in 1994. He edited the Libertarian Party's official newspaper, *LP News,* from 1986 to 1989, and he was the father of Karl Hess, Jr., who writes libertarian works on property rights and the environment.

Hess began his career as a reporter for the *Washington Star* and wrote for various D.C.-area newspapers in the early 1940s. He became an editor of various magazines through the 1940s and early 1950s, including *Aviation News, Pathfinder* (where he was religion editor), and *Newsweek* (where he was press editor). His first consuming political interest was anticommunism, which he pursued avidly while at *Newsweek.* He lost his job there for signing his name and *Newsweek* affiliation to an ad defending Senator Joseph McCarthy's anticommunist actions. Hess wrote in his posthumous autobiography, *Mostly on the Edge,* of his involvement in aborted schemes to run guns to a non-Castro enemy of Cuban dictator Batista and to enlist the Mafia's help in hijacking money en route from the Soviet Union to American communists.

Hess came to national political prominence with the Republican Party by helping to write their 1960 and 1964 platforms. He was a speechwriter for Barry Goldwater during his 1964 presidential campaign. Despite popular misattribution, Hess was not the author of Goldwater's famous "Extremism in the defense of liberty is no vice . . ." phrase, which was in fact contributed by Harry Jaffa. Hess wrote a book about the meaning of the Goldwater campaign, *In a Cause That Will Triumph* (1967).

After the Goldwater campaign, Hess went through personal and political changes that found him aligned more toward the culturally leftist end of the libertarian movement. Hess was not a theoretician or original political thinker. He believed that a defense of liberty could not rest on rationalist grounds, but ultimately was an aesthetic choice. He brought to the libertarian movement of the late 1960s and early 1970s, particularly its campus branches, a colorful Left-leaning revolutionary style that many found attractive, especially within the context of Vietnam War–era student unrest. He described himself as the "master of ceremonies" of the libertarian breach with the conservative youth group Young Americans for Freedom in 1969. He worked with the leftist Institute for Policy Studies from 1968 to 1970, and he was simultaneously an early partner with Murray Rothbard in the *Libertarian Forum*, a newsletter that chronicled and shaped the libertarian student activism of the period. However, he left abruptly due to conflicts with Rothbard.

Hess was known for an extraordinary personal charisma that won him admiration and friendship across both the libertarian and leftist spectrums. His 1975 book, *Dear America*, presented his post-Goldwater political philosophy, a libertarianism tinged with animus toward any large concentrations of money and influence, whether governmental or private. In the 1970s, Hess's interests turned to advocating neighborhood self-sufficiency as a solution to the centralizing government tendencies of the time. In his 1979 book, *Community Technology*, Hess wrote candidly of some of the successes and of the many failures that attended his efforts to turn his Adams-Morgan neighborhood in D.C. into a self-sufficient community through rooftop hydroponic gardens and trout aquaculture in basements.

After a series of break-ins, Hess and his second wife, Therese, moved to Kearneysville, West Virginia, where he built his own home and continued his experiments in self-sufficient neighborhoods in a rural setting. Hess's move to West Virginia led to his taking up commercial welding, and he employed his new skill in creating a number of sculptures. He regarded his new vocation as consistent with the view that human technologies have been more important to the spread of liberty than political philosophers or ideologues. From 1980 to 1985, he edited a newsletter titled *Surviving Tomorrow*, in which he emphasized small-scale alternative technologies over big centralized ones. In a fit of libertarian purity, in 1969, Hess refused to pay taxes and wrote a letter to the Internal Revenue Service telling them why. This move created legal problems for Hess for the rest of his life, and he was unable to have any legal income, which would have been immediately confiscated.

In his later years, Hess became involved with the Libertarian Party, editing its newspaper. For most of his waning years in West Virginia, he was ill with recurring heart disease; in 1992, he underwent a full heart transplant, which limited his productivity. He also was a founding editor of *Liberty* magazine, a still-surviving libertarian movement journal launched in 1987.

BDo

See also Goldwater, Barry; Left Libertarianism; Rothbard, Murray; Taxation; Urban Planning

Further Readings

Hess, Karl. *In a Cause That Will Triumph: The Goldwater Campaign and the Future of Conservatism.* New York: Doubleday, 1967.

———. *Community Technology.* New York: Harper & Row, 1979.

———. *Dear America.* New York: Morrow, 1975.

———. *Mostly on the Edge: An Autobiography.* Amherst, NY: Prometheus Books, 1999.

HOBBES, THOMAS (1588–1676)

Thomas Hobbes, an English philosopher and political theorist, was strongly influenced by the English Civil Wars and the beheading of Charles I, and by the growing interest in science. He hoped to set social philosophy on a firm scientific foundation, which, he thought, also would have the happy result of showing all rebellion against authority to be in the wrong. Hobbes's embrace of science consisted in trying to describe people as they actually were, rather than as the writer would like them to be. To this end, Hobbes began his investigation by attempting to determine how humans would behave in the absence of political institutions. This hypothetical state of society, in which no political institutions exist, Hobbes called the *natural condition of mankind* or the *state of nature*. If it can be shown what the condition of man in the state of nature was and why political institutions were essential if these conditions were to be improved, the result would be a strong justification for government. This demonstration is exactly what Hobbes attempts to do in his masterpiece, *Leviathan*, which was published in 1649.

Hobbes's analysis of man's state of nature led him to arrive at a series of conclusions. First, practical rationality consists of applying one's thinking ability to the situation in which one finds oneself with a view to realizing one's interests, whatever they might be. Men seek the best life possible, but our views of what *best* consists of vary enormously. Despite this variation, it is logical to presume that we all wish to avoid death.

Second, all men are equal in the sense that "the weakest has strength enough to kill the strongest." We are therefore all equally vulnerable. Thus, no one may pretend to social superiority solely by virtue of being who or what he is.

Third, although goods are scarce in man's natural state, this situation is rectifiable. However, nature is not generous. Men must work, indeed work in cooperation with others, to increase the supply of wealth at our disposal. Unfortunately, a shortcut to wealth is available; we can simply take what others have produced through their labor, rather than laboring ourselves. This ability to gain at the expense of others, not innate aggression, sets the stage for conflict between men.

Fourth, we are capable of love, at least in a limited way. Hobbes is widely thought to have espoused egoism, in that the only things we desire are those that conduce to our private good. Yet Hobbes is aware that love unites families, despite our having little general affection for strangers. In a contest between self and strangers, people are prone to act selfishly.

Finally, we are not naturally moral. Hobbes argued that, in the absence of moral or affectional restraint, opportunities to gain by violence will often prevail. At the same time, people will move to defend themselves, including engaging in preemptive warfare. No one trusts anyone, cooperative activity is impossible, and there is "continual fear, and the life of man, solitary, poor, nasty, brutish, and short."

The method by which men extricate themselves from this terrible state is morality. Hobbes provided a list of laws of nature, laws based exclusively on the use of our reasoning from our general interests and not on intuition or religion. The first and most fundamental law of morality requires us to confine ourselves to peaceful interchange with others except when attacked; at that point, we may defend ourselves. This moral law leads to several others, among them that we may claim only as much, but no more liberty, for ourselves as we are willing to grant others, and that we honor our agreements.

These laws of nature, Hobbes maintained, are "eternal and immutable." If so, why, then, is there a need for the State to enforce these laws? Hobbes argued that these laws of nature are weak and cannot be relied on to enforce themselves. One should refrain from making war on others, but only if they do not engage in warfare first. However, if one can gain from aggressive action of this sort, there is really nothing to stop us. Contracts, Hobbes noted, are "mere words" and "of no strength to bind a man." What man needs is security, without which we remain in the most awful of worlds, the state of nature. This security can only be obtained, Hobbes concluded, through the creation of a State, to which each of us concedes our power.

It is here that Hobbes blunders and blunders badly. First, there are many devices that might conduce to the security necessary to peaceful coexistence, not the least being parental training of the young. In addition, there are peer pressure, reputation, and the formation of voluntary defensive agencies such as security companies. Second, the idea of government by general consent was, on Hobbes's own assumptions, impossible. Consent is signified by words. If words do not bind, the agreement to create government is impossible, and we are stuck in the state of nature.

This problem gives rise to the most pervasive dispute among libertarians—whether it is in our interests to have a state, albeit limited in its extent, or market anarchism. The statist thinks the state is necessary to prevent chaos, but its activities can and should be confined to a narrow range—the minimal state (*minarchism*). Market anarchists argue that the free market is capable of doing everything, including protecting the free market. Nevertheless, both schools agree that Hobbes's political conclusions are wrong. Indeed, if he were right, all governments, including the worst in history—Stalin, Hitler, Nero—are legitimate because, however bad they are, they are better than the state of nature. Hobbes's singular contribution to the development of political theory is the clarity of his discussion of the general nature of morality, in which he shows what a proper state, if there can be any such, would do: namely, forbid interpersonal aggression and nothing else. Hobbes saw that peace, prosperity, and the possibility of each of us living the best life as we each understand it lies solely in the prevention of violence. Thus, he deserves pride of place as the founder of liberalism.

JN and DT

See also Coercion; Contractarianism/Social Contract; English Civil Wars; Liberalism, Classical; Locke, John; Natural Law; Revolution, Right of

Further Readings

Hobbes, Thomas. *Leviathan*. Richard Tuck, ed. New York: Cambridge University Press, 1991.

Locke, John. "Second Treatise on Government." *Two Treatises on Government*. Peter Laslett, ed. Cambridge: Cambridge University Press, 2005.

Oakeshott, Michael. *Hobbes on Civil Association*. Indianapolis, IN: Liberty Fund, 1975.

HODGSKIN, THOMAS (1787–1869)

Thomas Hodgskin was one of the most original libertarian theorists in Victorian England. His first major work was *Travels in the North of Germany* (1820). This two-volume travelogue, which is interspersed with political commentary on "the much governed countries of Germany," frequently discusses the inefficiency and waste of governmental projects. Hodgskin even suggests that police functions should be placed in private hands. In 1825, Hodgskin published *Labour Defended against the Claims of Capital*, a tract cited repeatedly by Karl Marx and later to cause historians to claim that Hodgskin was a "Ricardian Socialist." In fact, Hodgskin disliked Ricardo's theories, vastly preferring the insights of Adam Smith, and he hated socialism even more. Although *sui generis* in many respects, Hodgskin is best categorized as an individualist anarchist.

Hodgskin's *Popular Political Economy* (1827), in addition to its defense of free-market currency, banking, and other libertarian institutions, anticipates some later insights by F. A. Hayek and other Austrian economists, such as the role of prices in transmitting crucial market information in a spontaneous economic order. His greatest contribution to libertarian theory was *The Natural and Artificial Right of Property Contrasted* (1832), a vigorous defense of natural rights and a sustained critique of the utilitarianism and legal positivism of Jeremy Bentham and his followers.

In 1846, Hodgskin became senior editor for *The Economist*, where for many years he continued to defend libertarian causes, such as voluntary education and opposition to capital punishment. It was during his tenure with this influential publication that Hodgskin befriended Herbert Spencer, then a junior editor on the magazine.

GHS

See also Hayek, Friedrich A.; Individualist Anarchism; Liberalism, Classical; Private Property; Smith, Adam; Spontaneous Order

Further Readings

Hodgskin, Thomas. *Labor Defended against the Claims of Capital.* New York: A. M. Kelley, 1969.
———. *The Natural and Artificial Right of Property Contrasted.* Clifton, NJ: A. M. Kelley, 1973.
———. *Popular Political Economy.* New York: A. M. Kelley, 1966.
Marx, Karl. *Capital.* New York: International Publishers, 1967.
Smith, Adam. *An Inquiry into the Nature and Causes of the Wealth of Nations.* Indianapolis, IN: Liberty Classics, 1981.

Hospers, John (1918–)

John Hospers is a philosopher and the first presidential nominee of the U.S. Libertarian Party. Hospers is best known to philosophers for his work in aesthetics, especially his book *Understanding the Arts.* He is the author of two widely used textbooks, *Introduction to Philosophical Analysis* and *Human Conduct: Problems of Ethics.* He taught at the University of Minnesota, Brooklyn College, and, beginning in 1966, the University of Southern California, where he also served as chairman of the philosophy department. In New York, he became acquainted with Ayn Rand and helped introduce her work to professional philosophers as editor of *The Personalist* and *The Monist.* In 1971, he published a comprehensive work, *Libertarianism: A Political Philosophy for Tomorrow.* That book and his academic stature made him the first presidential candidate of the fledgling Libertarian Party in 1972. On the ballot only in Colorado and Washington, he and vice presidential candidate Tonie Nathan nevertheless campaigned widely in major cities and on college campuses. They received only 3,671 official votes plus an unknown number of write-ins and had their greatest success when Virginia elector Roger L. MacBride cast his electoral vote for Hospers and Nathan instead of Nixon and Agnew. Despite the lack of electoral success, Hospers's intelligent campaign did rally libertarians to the new party and lay the groundwork for greater success in the 1976 and 1980 elections.

DB

See also MacBride, Roger Lea; Nathan, Tonie; Rand, Ayn

Further Readings

Doherty, Brian. *Radicals for Capitalism: A Freewheeling History of the Modern Libertarian Movement.* New York: Public Affairs, 2007.
Hospers, John. "The First Time: I Run for President." *Liberty* (November 1992).
———. *Introduction to Philosophical Analysis.* Paramus, NJ: Prentice Hall, 1953, 1996.
———. *Libertarianism: A Political Philosophy for Tomorrow.* Los Angeles: Nash, 1971.
———. *Understanding the Arts.* Paramus, NJ: Prentice Hall, 1982.
Kelley, John L. *Bringing the Market Back In: The Political Revitalization of Market Liberalism.* New York: New York University Press, 1997.

Humanism

Humanism has been given a wide variety of often vague meanings. Two of these definitions have been more important than any of the others. In what was historically the first of these two meanings, it was employed to characterize the culture of Renaissance Europe. Renaissance students of the literature of classical Greece and Rome—especially Greece—were called *humanists.* They all would have agreed with the claim of the Greek tragic poet Sophocles: "Many are the wonders of the world but none more wonderful than man."

Such students of classical literature were optimistic about human possibilities, attended enthusiastically to human achievements, and eschewed what they wanted to dismiss as theological niceties. Humanism, in this sense of the word, was no doubt formally consistent with Christian religious belief and devotion. But Erasmus, perhaps the greatest of these Renaissance humanists, was embarrassed to be reminded by Luther, during their *Dialogue on Freewill and Predestination*, of the most appalling doctrine, divine predestination—that God predetermines all of us human beings to conduct our lives in the different ways for which He intends either to reward or to punish us eternally—would appear to have been very clearly taught by St. Paul himself in his *Epistle to the Romans*. In the same *Dialogue*, Luther also forestalled what has come to be called the Freewill Defense. He wrote,

> Now by "necessarily" I do not mean compulsorily . . . when a man is without the Spirit of God he does not do evil against his will, as if he were taken by the scruff of his neck and forced to do it . . . but he does it of his own accord and with a ready will.

In the 20th century, the label *humanist* was appropriated by people who rejected all religious belief and insisted that they were concerned only with human welfare in this world. By the middle of that century, it had become widely agreed that theism—what the philosopher Hume, rather than the mathematical physicist Laplace, was the first to describe as the religious hypothesis—could not either be proved to be true or proved to be false by reference to any facts of this world.

All such humanists are still atheists. But most now construe the letter "a" in the word *atheist* as having the same negative but unaggressive meaning as the "a"s in such words as *atypical* and *asymmetrical*. By at least the beginning of the 21st century, many of the countries of Europe and North America had become so completely secularized in their culture as to leave little room for specifically humanist organizations. Indeed, well before the end of the 20th century, the main secular humanist organization in the United States gave birth to a Committee for the Scientific Investigation of the Claims of the Paranormal (CSICOP) while its publishing arm had, well before September 11, 2001, produced more than one substantial scholarly work critical not of Christianity, but of Islam.

AF

See also Enlightenment; Religion and Liberty; Republicanism, Classical; Whiggism

Further Readings

Flew, Antony. *Atheistic Humanism*. Buffalo, NY: Prometheus Books, 1993.

Gaskin, J. C. A., ed. *Varieties of Unbelief: From Epicurus to Sartre*. New York and London: Macmillan, 1989.

Kurtz, Paul, and Timothy J. Madigan, eds. *Challenges to the Enlightenment: In Defense of Reason and Science*. Buffalo, NY: Prometheus Books, 1994.

HUMBOLDT, WILHELM VON (1767–1835)

Wilhelm von Humboldt was a German political theorist and a statesman. It is difficult to say when classical liberalism as a political philosophy fully emerged. In England, one usually thinks of John Locke and his *Two Treatises on Government* (1690) as the starting point of this philosophy of limited government. In Germany, the question cannot be answered as easily, although there is one major candidate for honors as its major early advocate: von Humboldt, whose famous treatise was titled *The Limits of State Action*. At the least, it is difficult to find another work of such outstanding relevance and quality within the German liberal tradition.

By the mid-18th century, liberal ideas had already made some advance within the various German principalities, but the French Revolution inspired the first wave of strict liberalism in the political world of the Old Empire. Thinkers such as Kant began to speak out for the rights of man, but there also were some conservatives and moderate liberals who expressed fears about the violent turn the French revolutionary movement would take. It was during this period that von Humboldt's political mind was shaped.

Born in Potsdam, near Berlin, von Humboldt was born into the Prussian lower aristocracy. Brought up with his brother, the explorer and scientist Alexander von Humboldt, von Humboldt began studying law and classical literature at Göttingen University in 1788. When the French Revolution broke out a year later, he undertook a journey to Paris on the invitation of the political essayist and statesman the Comte de Mirabeau to watch the "funeral ceremony of French despotism." He came back slightly disillusioned. As a result, in his *Thoughts on Constitutions* (1791), von Humboldt did not hesitate to declare his sympathy with the liberal ideals of the Revolution, but doubted whether these ideals could be maintained throughout its course. A more gradualist approach, he argued, would have been less dangerous.

The Limits of State Action outlined his political ideas most fully. Although today it is regarded as his masterpiece, von Humboldt felt uneasy about it, perhaps for fear of censorship. Only a few sections of the book were published during his lifetime, but it became an instant classic of political philosophy when it was published posthumously in 1851.

Von Humboldt's intellectual interests went far beyond that of political philosophy. A universally educated man, he wrote extensively about such diverse subjects as linguistics, natural history, and education. However, it was practical politics, rather than theory, that soon became the focus of his life. Prussia's defeats at the hands of Napoleon forced long-needed reforms within the Prussian state. A peculiar brand of liberalism came into existence that was typical of

Prussia: *Beamten-Liberalismus*, or civil servants' liberalism. Enlightened persons from the royal bureaucracy tried to modernize the country from the top down. Among them were Baron vom Stein, the father of German local self-government. Von Humboldt became minister for Public Instruction in 1809 and instituted a series of reforms that proved to be outstandingly efficient and durable. In fact, in Germany today von Humboldt is mainly remembered for these reforms. A multitiered system of educational institutions was introduced—from the elementary schools to the university level, all of which were aimed to encourage a sense of individual autonomy and independence of thought. As von Humboldt had already stated in his *The Limits of State Action*, self-development and individuality were the central goals of education.

Beginning in 1810, von Humboldt was the chief Prussian diplomat in Vienna; in 1813, he became ambassador to the British Court. In 1819, he became minister for Estate (Diet) Affairs, but soon resigned in protest against Metternich's Karlsberg Decrees, which introduced more censorship and other repressive policies. At that point, he decided to withdraw from politics and devoted his life to his family and to academic research until his death in 1835. His political thought can be found in *The Limits of State Action:* "The true end of Man," he wrote,

> or that which is prescribed by the eternal and immutable dictates of reason, and not suggested by vague and transient desires, is the highest and most harmonious development of his powers to a complete and consistent whole. Freedom is the first and indispensable condition which the possibility of such a development pre-supposes; but there is besides another essential—intimately connected with freedom, it is true—a variety of situations. Even the most free and self-reliant of men is hindered in his development, when set in a monotonous situation.

Thus, he concluded that only a minimal state that secured internal and external peace and security was legitimate. A state that provided for more would inevitably encourage conformism and uniformity. Von Humboldt's concept of self-education is distinguishable from similar traditional Aristotelian concepts. Aristotelian essentialism aimed at humans developing themselves as the realization of a general ideal of mankind, whereas von Humboldt believed in the development of the individual with all his individual peculiarities. Von Humboldt's views deeply influenced John Stuart Mill, who had read the first translation of *The Limits of State Action* when it appeared in 1854. In his famous treatise, *On Liberty* (1859), Mill often referred to von Humboldt as his intellectual inspiration who helped him to overcome his narrow utilitaristic philosophy.

There is little reason to doubt von Humboldt's liberal convictions throughout his life, despite his role in directing a system of state education. He never embraced

nationalism, like so many of his previously enlightened liberal contemporaries, and he always stayed in touch with liberal circles throughout Europe, especially in France. Indeed, Benjamin Constant continued to remain politically close to him. With respect to his educational reforms, Humboldt simply had to accept certain constraints. Although he was in no position to privatize the whole educational system, he managed to make it accessible to everyone and cleared it of privilege and patronage. The autonomy and freedom of all educational institutions was the cornerstone of his reforms.

His role as education minister was consistent with his early liberal ideas. These were radical in their final vision, but they also were gradualist and reformist in their practical outlook. Self-organization and voluntary cooperation to him were more desirable than compulsory state-dominated association. Von Humboldt's individualism was not atomistic. In the process of self-education, he maintained, one learns and rises to the level where such a cultivated voluntary self-organization is possible. Therefore, a liberal order could never be imposed on the people, but would grow with their capabilities.

This insight also is reflected in his later publications, such as the *Memorandum on the German Constitution* (1813), where he warned of the nationalistic enthusiasm for a centralized unitary state and advocated a decentralized constitution for all Germany that would secure freedom and cultural diversity to the citizens.

DD

See also Civil Society; French Revolution; Limited Government; Rights, Natural

Further Readings

Humboldt, Wilhelm von. *The Limits of State Action.* J. W. Burrows, ed. Indianapolis, IN: Liberty Fund, 1993.
Knoll, Joachim H., and Horst Siebert. *Wilhelm von Humboldt: Politician and Educationist.* Bonn: Inter Nationes, 1967.
Sweet, Paul R. *Wilhelm von Humboldt. A Biography.* Cleveland: Ohio State University Press, 1978.

HUME, DAVID (1711–1776)

David Hume, a Scottish philosopher, was one of the most highly regarded thinkers who wrote in the English language. Although his contributions to the theory of knowledge as well as to moral and political philosophy form the basis of this high opinion, he also was the author of a highly acclaimed *History of England* in six volumes and many essays on various literary, moral, and political topics.

Hume's first major work, *A Treatise of Human Nature* (1739), in the author's own account, "fell dead-born from the press," and its poor reception moved him to write two shorter and more popularly written essays: *An Inquiry Concerning Human Understanding* (1748) and *An Inquiry Concerning the Principles of Morals* (1752). The section devoted to morals in the *Treatise* and the whole of the *Inquiry Concerning the Principles of Morals*, together with some of the political essays, constitute the basis for his reputation as a moral and political philosopher. Among the most important and original of these essays was "Of the Original Contract" (1748), in which he sought to show that there could not have been a state of nature in which a contract to form society took place.

It is difficult to summarize Hume's philosophy, either with respect to his theory of morals or his political philosophy. In the *Principles of Morals*, he supports the general claim that utility is the foundation of justice, but he also maintains that moral virtue consists of those qualities of mind that are "agreeable or useful to self or others." He does not, as a more fully developed utilitarian theory suggests, propose that we should measure utility in the manner of Jeremy Bentham; that is, a scale that permits comparisons of utility from one person to another and by a measure that assumes all utilities of are of the same type and thereby measurable one against the other. Having failed to do so, it is not entirely clear how utility can be determined.

In "Of the Original Contract," Hume explores the notion that society or government was or could be founded on some historical meeting of minds among the original members, but he does not really address the far more challenging and relevant thesis that the general principles by which social and political affairs should be run should be the object of rational agreement by all. He does, however, offer a devastating critique of the idea that the foundation of all morals or politics ultimately rests on agreement by pointing out that the obligation to keep one's agreements is one of the primary principles of justice. Hume's utilitarianism once again emerges when he concludes that the true foundation of any and all such general obligations is the good of society.

Some scholars have attributed to Hume's views a fundamental conservatism, which, they claim, rests on two foundational aspects of his thought: his support of private property and his insistence that apparently arbitrary points of law should be adhered to regardless of their apparent uselessness. However, Hume's insistence that private property is essential to society in fact has little to do with conservatism as such, but is, in fact, fundamentally libertarian. The second idea, regarding obedience to law, may lend support to the idea that Hume can properly be regarded as what we would now call a *rule utilitarian*. Yet his conclusions here have more to do with his perceptiveness about the nature of public goods—that is, goods the consumption of which by some does not limit the amount of the goods available to others—than with his conservative leanings.

JN and DT

See also Contractarianism/Social Contract; Freedom of Thought; Rights, Natural; Smith, Adam; Utilitarianism

Further Readings

Gauthier, David. "David Hume: Contractarian." *Philosophical Review* 88 (1979): 3–38.

Hume, David. *An Inquiry Concerning the Principles of Morals.* Charles Hendel, ed. Indianapolis, IN: Bobbs-Merrill, Library of Liberal Arts, 1957.

———. *Treatise of Human Nature.* P. Nidditch, ed. Oxford: Oxford University Press, 1978.

Yellin, Mark E. "Hume's Indirect Utilitarianism." *Critical Review* 14 no. 4 (2002): 375–390.

HUTCHESON, FRANCIS (1694–1746)

Francis Hutcheson is considered a major figure in the Scottish Enlightenment. Born in Ireland, he spent the last 17 years of his life as a professor of moral philosophy at the University of Glasgow. Through his books and teaching at Glasgow, he exerted considerable influence on Adam Smith, David Hume, and other 18th-century moral philosophers.

Hutcheson, following the lead of the German political and legal philosopher Samuel von Pufendorf (1632–1694), distinguished between two categories of rights: perfect and imperfect. He regarded perfect rights as enforceable moral claims. If a person violated this kind of right, then the victim might legitimately use force to either protect himself or seek legal redress. In his *Inquiry Concerning Beauty and Virtue* (1725), Hutcheson wrote,

> Instances of *perfect Rights* are those to our *Lives;* to the *Fruits* of our *Labours;* to demand Performance of *Contracts* upon valuable Considerations, from men capable of performing them; to *direct* our own Actions either for *publick,* or innocent *private Good,* before we have submitted them to the Direction of others in any measure; and many others of a like nature.

In contrast to these enforceable rights to life, property, contract, and personal liberty—like John Locke, Hutcheson maintains that "each man is the original proprietor of his own liberty." Hutcheson also categorized some rights as imperfect. These rights consisted of moral obligations that, although they tended to promote the public good, could not justifiably be enforced, but must instead be left to the conscience and free choice of individuals. Among these imperfect rights were kindness, charity, gratitude, and so on.

Adam Smith, who studied under Hutcheson at the University of Glasgow, employed Hutcheson's terminology, as did many other moral philosophers. During the 19th century, as the term *imperfect rights* became less common (today these are simply called *moral virtues* or *obligations*), libertarian philosophers such as Lysander Spooner typically used labels like *crimes* and *vices* when making essentially the same point. Nonetheless, the distinction between perfect and imperfect rights was a crucial stage in the evolution of the libertarian doctrine that government should be confined to the protection and enforcement of individual rights.

Hutcheson is best known for his defense of moral sense theory, which bore the influence of the Third Earl of Shaftesbury. In Hutcheson's more systematic account, our approbation of moral virtue is a kind of perception that precedes rational analysis. The constitution of human nature is such that every normal person will feel pleasure and approval on observing a benevolent action. This moral sense, which is essentially a theory of conscience, is fundamental to Hutcheson's theory of the natural sociability of human beings. It also is central to his secularization of moral theory.

Hutcheson was charged by the Presbytery of Glasgow with teaching the heretical doctrine that one can possess knowledge of good and evil without knowledge of, or belief in, God. His argument that atheists can lead virtuous lives, although unpopular in his day, was an important step in the movement for religious toleration.

GHS

See also Freedom of Thought; Hume, David; Rights, Natural; Smith, Adam

Further Readings

Hume, David. *An Inquiry Concerning the Principles of Morals.* J. B. Schneewind, ed. Indianapolis, IN: Hackett, 1983.

Hutcheson, Francis. *Inquiry into the Original of Our Ideas of Beauty and Virtue.* Wolfgang Liedhold, ed. Indianapolis, IN: Liberty Fund, 2004.

Locke, John. "Second Treatise of Government." *Two Treatises of Government.* Peter Laslett, ed. Cambridge: Cambridge University Press, 1988.

Smith, Adam. *The Theory of Moral Sentiments.* D. D. Raphael and A. L. Macfie, eds. Indianapolis, IN: Liberty Classics, 1982.

I

ILLICIT DRUGS

Libertarians have consistently argued that individuals should be free to consume mind-altering substances such as heroin, cocaine, marijuana, alcohol, and tobacco given that others are not harmed. When we examine spillover harms that are allegedly caused by the consumption of these products, they cannot stand muster. Further, even if some spillovers occur, anticonsumption policies are not warranted because their implementation, it has been shown, invariably imposes even greater costs than drug use. Yet prohibitionist policies persist because they promote the interests of several powerful political groups.

Drug war advocates contend that drug cravings cause people to steal; thus, they argue, controlling drug markets will have the effect of reducing both drug consumption and property crime. However, substantial evidence shows that property crime is not caused by drug use. Surveys of jail inmates indicate that almost half of regular hard-drug users were employed full time before their drug offense was committed, and only 29% reported having had any illegal income, much of which originated as earnings from consensual crimes like prostitution and drug sales. More than half the jail inmates who admitted to regular drug use also said that their first arrest for a nondrug offense occurred an average of 2 years before their first drug use. Similarly, a study of prison inmates found that approximately half who had ever used a major drug and roughly three-fifths of regular users did not consume drugs until after their first arrest for some nondrug crime.

Notwithstanding these statistics, drug enforcement is, in fact, directly linked to property crime. Police resources are scarce, so increased efforts against drugs translates into less effort against other crimes. In Florida, for instance, an estimated 10% increase in property crimes in the period from 1984 to 1989 was due to reallocating police efforts to drug

control. Overcrowding of prisons and early release of convicted criminals also resulted from the drug war during this period. Grim consequences abound as violent criminals were released to carry out more violence.

Prohibitionists also argue that drugs cause violence, but research suggests that the causal link is between the criminalization of drugs and violence. Black markets generate violence because participants must enforce contracts using threats and physical harm, rather than the court system. Drug market participants carrying drugs or cash are relatively attractive robbery targets who are not likely to report the crime. Other factors are at work, too. Increasing drug enforcement disrupts local drug markets, causing dealers to seek other markets where violent confrontations with other dealers, one of the standard methods of competition in illicit markets, can erupt. Consider Quebec's experience when it increased cigarette taxes in excess of 60%. This increase probably caused a minor reduction in cigarette consumption, but also encouraged many smokers to break the law. Soon after the cigarette tax was raised, roughly half the cigarettes sold in Quebec were purchased on the black market, which in turn made smuggling so lucrative that the involvement of organized crime increased dramatically. Armed gangs of smugglers competed for shares of the market. Quebec's citizens recognized the futility of this war against tobacco, and cigarette taxes were eventually reduced. The events in Quebec followed the same pattern that had prevailed with alcohol prohibition in the 1920s.

The drug war has made Americans more vulnerable to attacks by police. Police corruption is an inevitable consequence of black markets, where so much wealth is at stake. In addition, courts, under intense prodding from drug enforcement officials, have relaxed search-and-seizure standards to facilitate the "war" on drugs. Similar reasons lie behind legislation that has undermined property rights by encouraging civil confiscations, which do not require proof of guilt. The 1984 Comprehensive Crime Control Act contains a section on asset forfeitures that allows local police to keep assets seized during drug investigations conducted with the cooperation of federal agencies, in contrast to many state laws directing such assets into general or special funds. The Department of Justice has gone even further, "adopting" seizures even if a local agency was not involved in a drug raid and passing the seized assets back to the local agency, less a "handling charge." This policy has had a dramatic impact on how police allocate their efforts. Civil seizures (many apparently from innocent citizens), as well as drug arrests and convictions, have risen sharply in light of these policies. A state law allowing police to keep seizures also has led to an increase in drug arrest rates by at least 18%, thus providing strong support for the hypothesis that the upsurge in drug enforcement after 1984 is a direct consequence of the federal seizure legislation.

For drug prohibition to prove a success, the laws of economics would have to be repealed. Large-scale interdiction of marijuana during the early 1980s had the predictable effect of increasing the price. Because the law of demand dictates that consumers will buy less when prices rise, it follows that they are more likely to turn to substitutes. One study found that young users drank more beer when the price of marijuana increased, which, in turn, led to more traffic fatalities. Another reported a precipitous increase in crystal methamphetamine use after a crop destruction program decimated Hawaii's marijuana supply. Similarly, states that had decriminalized marijuana during the 1970s had fewer hospital emergencies involving hard drugs. Sellers, looking for an alternative product to sell at the low-priced end of the drug market during the early 1980s, also turned to more easily concealed cocaine and introduced crack, adopting a technology in use in the Bahamas. Yet a further study shows that—when interdiction efforts are successful—marijuana farmers have developed increasingly potent varieties in their efforts to pack a greater punch in a smaller package that can be more easily hidden. Attempts to thwart the drug trade are no match for entrepreneurial creativity, so why do prohibitionist efforts continue? A number of self-interested political motivations have been identified. The demands of the American Pharmaceutical Association for limits on drug distribution have been a potent factor in keeping the war on drugs alive, as has the desire by some groups to control racial minorities, who allegedly employ illicit drugs to greater degrees than does the population at large. Law enforcement bureaucrats also have been a major source of demand for criminalization. These interest groups have interacted with others, among them temperance groups, to strengthen drug prohibition legislation. The 1984 asset seizure legislation was a product of agitation by law enforcement officials and others whose professional interests lay in keeping drugs illegal.

Bureaucrats advocate directly controlling "a source of blame," that is, the drugs themselves, for at least two reasons, despite the history of failure surrounding this policy. First, because opposition to these prohibitive policies always exists, when drug enforcement officials fail in their attempts to curtail drug use, opponents can be blamed for limiting expenditures to combat the problem. Second, because the results of current drug policy depend, in large measure, on the efforts of a number of groups and bureaus and the range of possible control methods is large, when the method selected fails, bureaucrats can argue that: (a) they advocated a different method of control, and/or (b) others (e.g., witnesses, judges, legislators who approve budgets, other law enforcement agencies) failed to do their part. Under prohibition, police incentives may be even more "perverted," however. When police focus on drug control, arrests and drug seizures rise, marking their effectiveness, while at the same time, reported property and violent crime rates will simultaneously increase, thus suggesting that there exists a greater need for even more police services.

The official publication of both true and false information, or "selective distortion," plays a significant role in all bureaucratic policy advocacy. Selective distortion has been especially notable with respect to the government's drug policy inasmuch as law enforcement has been the major source of antidrug propaganda. Indeed, given the continued advocacy of prohibition by police and in light of consequences of the drug war, police interests, not the "public interest," seems to be at the root of the drug war. Thus, whether considered from the perspective of liberty or efficiency, prohibitionist policies cannot be justified.

BLB

See also Black Markets; Corruption; Drug Prohibition; Prohibition of Alcohol; Rent Seeking

Further Readings

Benson, Bruce L. "Are Public Goods Really Common Pools: Considerations of the Evolution of Policing and Highways in England." *Economic Inquiry* 32 no. 2 (April 1994): 249–271.

———., Brent D. Mast, and David W. Rasmussen. "Deterring Drunk Driving Fatalities: An Economics of Crime Perspective." *International Review of Law and Economics* 19 no. 2 (June 1999): 205–225.

Coase, Ronald H. "The Problem of Social Cost." *Journal of Law and Economics* 3 (October 1960): 1–44.

Lindesmith, Alfred. *The Addict and the Law*. New York: Vintage Press, 1965.

Mast, Brent D., Bruce L. Benson, and David W. Rasmussen. "Beer Taxation and Alcohol-Related Traffic Fatalities." *Southern Economic Journal* 66 no. 2 (October 1999): 214–249.

———. "Entrepreneurial Police and Drug Enforcement Policy." *Public Choice* 104 nos. 3–4 (2000): 285–308.

Miron, Jeffrey A., and Jeffrey Zweibel. "The Economic Case Against Drug Prohibition." *The Journal of Economic Perspectives* 9 (Fall 1995): 175–192.

Rasmussen, David W., and Bruce L. Benson. *The Economic Anatomy of a Drug War: Criminal Justice in the Commons.* Lanham, MD: Rowman & Littlefield, 1994.

Thornton, Mark. *The Economics of Prohibition.* Salt Lake City: University of Utah Press, 1991.

Wisotsky, Steven. "A Society of Suspects: The War on Drugs and Civil Liberties." *Cato Policy Analysis*, No. 180. Washington, DC: Cato Institute, 1992.

IMMIGRATION

Immigration is the movement of people from one country to another where they are not native. Since the beginning of history, men and women have been crossing political borders to better their economic condition, reunite with their families, and escape the dangers they faced in their country of origin. In the late 1990s, an estimated 130 million people, or about 2% of the world's population, were living outside the country in which they were born. About 10% of these immigrants were refugees forced from their homes by war, persecution, or natural disaster. Immigration has played an important role in the settlement and development of the United States and, indeed, of the whole New World. Its defenders argue that not only does immigration enhance the freedom and well-being of those who have moved to their adopted country, but it also has benefited its natives by stimulating the economy and enriching the culture. Opponents claim that immigrants compete with native workers, thus lowering wages, and fragment the traditional culture.

Throughout history, freedom to travel and immigrate has been closely tied to freedom of commerce. In medieval England, immigration was seen as a basic right. Chapter 41 of Magna Carta asserts that, "All merchants shall have safe and secure exit from England and entry to England, with the right to tarry there and move about as well by land as by water, for buying and selling by the ancient and right customs." Throughout history, states that were the most open to trade and new ideas, such as Venice and the Dutch Republic, also tended to be the most open to immigrants. As trade and economic liberalization expanded in the 19th century, so, too, did immigration. The late 19th century, in particular, saw mass migrations from Europe to the Americas, Oceania, and Asia. The bulk of this immigration, however, was directed at the United States. The increased immigration of this era was spurred by the introduction of the steamship, which dramatically reduced the cost and risk of ocean travel, and by industrialization, which created new demands for labor that were met, in part, by voluntary, large-scale immigration. With few exceptions, governments allowed the free movement of people across borders during most of this period. In the century ending in 1920, 60 million people left Europe, three-fifths of whom came to the United States. The

other major destinations of European immigration were Canada, Australia, New Zealand, South Africa, and Argentina. During this same period, millions more left China, India, and other Asian countries, moving to East and Southern Africa, and nations surrounding the South China Sea, such as Malaysia and Indonesia, and, to a lesser extent, to the Americas. Economist J. Bradford DeLong of the University of California at Berkeley estimates that, by 1870, about 1 out of 10 people in the world lived in a country other than the one of their birth, five times as many as today. After the First World War, however, restrictions against immigration became more widespread, particularly in the United States. Motivating those restrictions were populist concerns that immigrants harmed natives by driving down wages, posed a national security threat, diluted native culture, and were of "inferior" racial or ethnic stock. Today, even as a growing number of nations are lifting barriers to international trade and investment, immigration remains far more tightly controlled than a century ago.

The United States is a nation founded by immigrants. Among the long train of abuses of which the Founding Fathers accused King George III was that he "has endeavored to prevent the Population of these States" by "obstructing the Laws for Naturalization of Foreigners" and by "refusing to pass others to encourage their Migrations hither." Between 1820 and 2001, 67 million immigrants officially entered the United States. The first wave of European immigrants to what is now the American colonies were from Great Britain, followed by a rising number from Germany in the later 18th century. Not all immigrants came willingly. From the early 1600s to 1820, about 8 million Africans were forcibly transported to the New World under indescribably squalid conditions to be sold into slavery. Immigration of all kinds was relatively attenuated from the period of American independence until the 1840s. At that point, the Irish Potato Famine of 1846–1847 was attended by the immigration of no less than 1.7 million Irish to the United States in the 1840s and 1850s, more than one-fifth the population of that island. Irish, German, and Scandinavian immigrants predominated through about 1890, to be eclipsed by Italians, Austro-Hungarians, and Russians during the Great Migration of 1900–1914. Immigration during this period was virtually unrestricted. Entrants were screened only for contagious diseases and obvious mental deficiencies at such facilities as Ellis Island in New York City. The only exception to free entry until then had been the Chinese Exclusion Act of 1882, a piece of clearly racist legislation, which virtually barred the immigration of Chinese laborers. After World War I, growing anti-immigrant sentiment led Congress to place quotas on immigrants based on the proportion of the population represented in the 1910 Census. This effort excluded almost all Asians and culminated in the Johnson–Reed Act of 1924, which favored immigrants from Northern Europe through a national-origins quota system. In the 1930s, the United States, Canada, and many Western European nations refused to accept Jews fleeing Nazi persecution.

These immigration regulations remained essentially unchanged until 1965, when Congress scrapped racial quotas in favor of a system that allocated visas more uniformly across nations, with a cap on total annual immigration. Since then, total annual legal immigration has been steadily rising, especially from Asia and Latin America. Although equal in absolute numbers to the first wave of immigration a century ago, currently, the number of immigrants is significantly smaller relative to the total U.S. population. The United States in the 1990s allowed entry to approximately four immigrants a year per 1,000 U.S. residents, compared with 10.4 per 1,000 during the peak of the Great Migration in 1901–1910. By 2000, about 11% of the U.S. population was foreign-born, compared with the previous peak of 14.7% in 1910.

Almost all legal immigrants entering the United States today fall into one of four categories. By far the largest comprise family members, who account for about two-thirds of the annual inflow. An American citizen may legally sponsor a spouse, child, parent, or sibling, whereas noncitizen residents with a work permit (known as a green card) can sponsor a spouse or child. The second largest category is employment-based immigration. U.S. law reserves about 140,000 green cards a year for immigrants hired to fill specific jobs by American companies. (Highly skilled foreign-born workers also can enter the country through temporary nonimmigrant visas.) In addition, in a typical year, the United States admits about 100,000 refugees and asylum seekers fleeing from war, persecution, or natural calamities in their home countries. Refugees are given approval before they enter the United States, whereas those seeking asylum enter the country first and then declare to authorities that they are fleeing persecution. Another 50,000 immigrants are issued green cards each year through a lottery system.

Advocates of immigration contend that newcomers stimulate the domestic economy by starting businesses; discovering new ideas, products, and production methods; and filling jobs that natives cannot or will not perform. Indeed, there appears to be no systematic evidence that immigration reduces the general wage level or raises unemployment among natives. Because immigrants tend to arrive at the beginning of their prime working years, they keep the nation demographically younger and actually reduce the dependency ratio of nonworkers to workers. Moreover, immigrants enrich the culture by diversifying the nation's art, folk traditions, and culinary choices. The large majority of immigrants, and virtually all of their children, have successfully assimilated into American society, learned the language, and absorbed American social and civic values. Even more important, free movement is among the basic rights of mankind. An immigrant who engages in private,

voluntary contracts for work, housing, and other provisions is not violating the basic rights of any other person. Indeed, by restricting immigration, the government also limits the freedom of native-born Americans who are denied the right to hire employees or direct their businesses as they see fit with people from other countries.

Opponents of immigration, especially opponents of the current level of inflow, contend that immigrants harm the economy by taking jobs that Americans would otherwise fill. They claim that immigrants drive down wages by competing with natives for jobs. Immigrants, they maintain, also are more likely to draw public assistance because of their lower incomes. In addition, they fear that the latest wave of immigration is changing the racial and ethnic character of America from a country comprised predominantly of whites of European ancestry to one with not only African American but sizeable Latino and Asian minorities as well. Thus, they view current immigrants as diluting and "Balkanizing" American culture and harboring divided loyalties between the United States and their country of birth. By raising the nation's population growth rate, immigration allegedly contributes to traffic congestion, air pollution, and crowded public schools. Surely, they argue, every government owns the right to "control its borders."

Most people who object to immigration, even when not avowedly racist, almost invariably betray a basic misunderstanding of economics. The fact is that, like free trade, immigration expands human liberty by increasing the choices people can make as consumers and producers. A free labor market directs immigrants to where their work is most in demand. Efforts by the government to manage the labor market are as apt to fail as similar efforts to protect domestic industries or orchestrate industrial policy. Any issue of welfare use should be addressed by reducing access to government programs, not by further reducing the liberty of immigrants and the native-born to cooperate for mutual advantage. Indeed, statistics indicate that immigrants take advantage of welfare programs at a rate only slightly higher than do native-born Americans. If an immigrant seeks to engage in peaceful, voluntary transactions that do not threaten the freedom or security of the native-born, the government should not interfere.

DTG

See also Cosmopolitanism; Free Trade; Magna Carta; Nationalism; Racism; Simon, Julian

Further Readings

Block, Walter. "A Libertarian Case for Free Immigration." *Journal of Libertarian Studies* 13 no. 2 (Summer 1998): 167–186.

Borjas, George J. *Heaven's Door: Immigration Policy and the American Economy*. Princeton, NJ: Princeton University Press, 1999.

Capaldi, Nicholas, ed. *Immigration: Debating the Issues*. Amherst, NY: Prometheus Books, 1997.

Handlin, Oscar. *The Uprooted: The Epic Story of the Great Migrations That Made the American People*. New York: Little, Brown, 1973.

Micklethwait, John. "The New Americans." *The Economist* (March 11, 2000): 1–18.

National Research Council. *The New Americans: Economic, Demographic, and Fiscal Effects of Immigration*. Washington, DC: National Academy Press, 1997.

Simon, Julian L. *The Economic Consequences of Immigration*. Ann Arbor: The University of Michigan Press, 1999.

———. *Immigration: The Demographic and Economic Facts*. Washington, DC: Cato Institute and National Immigration Forum, 1995.

U.S. Immigration and Naturalization Service. *2001 Statistical Yearbook of the INS*. Washington, DC: U.S. Government Printing Office, 2003.

IMPERIALISM

Imperialism refers to both a political practice and the set of arguments used to justify it. In the first sense, it means a state of affairs in which one nation, tribe, or political entity (or, actually, their ruling elite) exercises political power over others. The resulting polity is an empire. The term *empire* also can be used to describe a political order that unites all of a single civilization or culture, as in the case of historic China, but this scenario is less common. In its pure form, imperialism involves the direct rule of subordinate peoples and territories by the imperial power. However, it also can take the form of indirect or hegemonic control, in which the imperial power does not govern directly, but through clients.

Empires have been a feature of world politics almost since the first appearance of complex political orders some 6,000 years ago. In fact, by some calculations, the majority of human beings in most periods of history have lived within empires, rather than one of the other forms of polity. In most periods, the logic of interstate relations and the self-interest of ruling elites have driven states to expand and become empires by various means, until they were checked by an external force or by natural limits. The ancient world saw a whole series of empires rise and fall, including the Assyrian, Babylonian, and Achaemenid Persian Empires in the Middle East and the Mauryan, Kushan, and Gupta Empires in India. In China, the various competing states were united into a single inclusive empire by the state of Qin in 221 B.C. The best-known empire of the ancient world was, of course, the Roman Empire, which faced an equally large adversary in the neo-Persian empire of the Sassanians after 224 A.D. In the ancient world, one can already see the emergence of an ideology of empire as well as its practice. This ideological rationale takes two distinct, but not exclusive, forms. The first in essence is the argument that "might makes right," that the success of the dominant imperial power justifies and legitimates its rule. This argument suggests that the imperial power is simply the one that has come out on top through its own qualities or fortune. However, this justification is usually supplemented by the second argument—that the imperial state is favored by divine authority and is fulfilling some kind of providential destiny and that, in doing so, it benefits the world in general and its own subjects in particular. This view makes of imperialism a moral enterprise. The benefits always include peace, order, and good government.

The early Middle Ages saw a decline of empires in several parts of the world, but imperialism later reappeared, particularly in China and the Middle East. The 13th century saw the formation of the largest empire yet and the closest the world had come to a truly universal one, with the appearance of the Mongol empire created by Genghis Khan and his successors. However, the empires that shaped much of the history of the modern world came into being after the disintegration of the Mongol hegemony, as a result of the so-called *military revolution* of the late medieval and early modern period. By 1590, most of the Old World was dominated by a small number of large empires, in particular the Chinese, Ottoman, Iranian, Russian, and Mughal empires. Europe did not see the emergence of a single imperial hegemon in the way that China, India, Russia, and the Middle East did. However, the European advantage in long-distance oceanic travel and the conquest by European nations of most of the New World after 1492 led to the appearance of seaborne empires, in which European powers exercised imperial rule over territories in other parts of the world through naval power. The first such empires were those of Portugal and Spain, followed by the Dutch Republic, France, and Britain.

The 18th century was the first great age of world imperialism. The European empires that had come into being during the previous two centuries ruled large parts of the planet directly and increasingly dominated other areas, such as much of India. Meanwhile, the Chinese conquered Tibet and a large part of Central Asia while the Russians expanded overland across Northern Asia. At the same time, there was a rearticulation of the ideology of imperialism. Although it continued to be defended on the grounds of self-interest, imperial rule was further justified as spreading civilization and true religion and as reflecting the moral, cultural, and racial superiority of the imperial nation. The argument from self-interest rested on the connection of imperialism and its related phenomenon of colonial settlement with the economic doctrines of mercantilism. According to this view, trade was a form of competition or struggle between states for shares of an ultimately fixed amount of wealth. Thus, the way to prosperity was for a state to control a large area of the planet's surface and of the trade that took place among the people who lived on it and to capture the wealth that the trade created. This approach meant encouraging specialization and a division of labor within the empire, but not on a global basis. In particular, it implied that colonies should supply raw materials and cash crops in exchange for finished manufactured goods and high-value services, which would be produced by the core imperial territory. Nor would direct trade be permitted with people from outside the imperial sphere. This prohibition was enforced by tariffs or outright trading prohibitions. The effect was that, in practice, imperialism led to grants of monopoly trading rights within a given part of the world to specially privileged groups of merchants and investors, such as those involved in the Dutch and British East India companies.

Opposition to this kind of imperialism was a central feature of classical liberal thought and agitation from the beginning. Adam Smith made criticism of the "colonial system" a central part of the *Wealth of Nations*, and his arguments were extended and developed by subsequent economists and liberal activists. They maintained that imperialism and the associated economic policy of protectionism and special privileges were harmful to both the subaltern populations of the colonies and the overwhelming majority of the inhabitants of the imperialist territory. In fact, the only groups that were economically better off as a result of these imperialist ventures were those who gained from the special privileges that were part of the system. This economic critique was only one element in the case against imperialism made by classical liberal thinkers and politicians. It also was attacked because it was viewed as inherently associated with other things that they opposed, such as slavery and warfare. In particular, imperialism's opponents made the argument that imperialism was necessarily associated with extensive and oppressive government and a whole series of cultural values that they strongly condemned. Imperialism was inherently wrong, they contended, because it violated the political principle of consent, which, for most classical liberals, was the only legitimate basis for political authority. One important argument that combined political and social analysis with an economic one was that imperialism was a policy that served the interests not of the great bulk of society—the "industrious classes"—but of the parasitic groups that gained wealth through the exploitation of political power. Thus, this conclusion combined a critique of imperialism with the classical liberal theory of class conflict as articulated by thinkers such as Frédéric Bastiat, Charles Comte, and Charles Dunoyer.

Between 1776 and the 1850s, the intellectual and political tide moved in favor of the classical liberal critique and against imperialism. Movements such as the Manchester School of Richard Cobden and John Bright made opposition to British imperialism one of their central doctrines. Following the successful revolt of the American colonists against the first British Empire, most of the Spanish and Portuguese territories gained independence by the later 1820s, and after the Mackenzie rebellion in 1837, the Durham Report led to the granting of self-government to Canada, a model followed elsewhere in the British Empire. By 1850, there seemed to be a growing consensus that colonies and imperialism were morally disreputable and a waste of money. However, British rule in India through the East India Company became even more extensive and intrusive over this period, and anti-imperialism began to lose support in the 1860s. The last third of the 19th century witnessed a revival of European imperialism both in practice and theory with the extension of direct imperial rule to areas that had previously escaped it, such as most of Africa and parts of Asia and the Pacific. This renewed expansionism was justified partly by a revival of mercantilist thinking, but, more important, by the increasing popularity of the idea of empire as a civilizing mission of tutelary powers engaged in the uplifting of backward peoples, together with the newly formulated arguments of pseudoscientific racism. Classical liberals such as Herbert Spencer kept up a strong resistance to the idea of a civilizing empire, and to the racism it often entailed, but they were on the losing side.

The position of the United States in this argument was problematic. As a polity born of a successful revolt against imperial rule, the United States being an anti-imperial power was always an important part of its national self-image. However, during the first half of the 19th century, there was a vigorous internal debate between the advocates of territorial expansion and groups such as the Old Republicans and certain elements in the Democratic Party who saw episodes such as the Mexican War as imperialist and a threat to the republican and constitutional nature of the American regime. After the Civil War, the expansion of the United States to its natural boundaries—defined by the two oceans, the Rio Grande, and the 49th parallel—was seen by most Americans as inevitable and not an example of imperialism. However, arguments in favor of the United States adopting an imperialist policy in other parts of the world became stronger after 1880 and finally proved successful with the Spanish American War of 1898, which led to the annexation of the Philippines and Puerto Rico. This conquest was followed by a much more extensive interventionist policy in Latin America and the Caribbean under Theodore Roosevelt, leading to an informal empire in much of that region of the world. Classical liberals such as E. L. Godkin and William Graham Sumner strongly opposed this turn in policy and argued that as well as being wrong, it would be harmful to the cause of liberty and republican government within the United States.

During the 20th century, imperialism reached its height after World War I. However, the period since 1939 has seen the collapse of all of the European empires, as well as the demise of Russian, German, and Japanese imperialism and the final disappearance of the Ottoman Empire. The United

States played an active role in much of this ruin, and its hostility to the French and British Empires contributed to their demise. Critics, however, including some libertarians, have argued that this overtly anti-imperialist policy went along with the development of an informal American empire. Discussion of imperialism in the 20th century has been dominated by the analysis put forward in 1902 by J. A. Hobson in his book *Imperialism: A Study*, which was later taken over by Lenin in *Imperialism: The Highest Stage of Capitalism*. Hobson reiterated the classical liberal argument that imperialism reflected the interests of a small predatory class, but made this class financial investors, rather than a political elite. Lenin adopted this view and argued that imperialism allowed the capitalists to buy off their own working classes and so head off the supposedly inevitable proletarian revolution. Although disproved by a whole range of empirical evidence, this thesis has been and remains amazingly influential.

The last 10 years have seen a revival of the argument for imperialism as a broadly beneficial phenomenon. The case put forward by authors such as Niall Ferguson is that the world economy as a whole needs a single imperial power that will act as a global hegemon and provide public goods such as protection against predators and a framework of rules and laws for the global economy and society as a whole. In the 19th century, this service was provided by the British Empire, whereas the United States now finds itself with this role. The second part of the argument is an updated version of the notion of imperialism as a civilizing mission. The idea is that imperial powers can provide the goods of law and good government and social and economic development to parts of the world that would otherwise lack them. In general, most contemporary libertarians are as strongly opposed to this revival of imperialist thinking as their classical liberal forbears were to its antecedents 100 or 200 years ago.

SD

See also Cosmopolitanism; Liberty in the Ancient World; Nationalism; Racism; War

Further Readings

Armstrong, William M. E. L. *Godkin and American Foreign Policy, 1865–1900*. New York: Bookman, 1957.

Hobson, John A. *Imperialism: A Study*. New York: James Pott and Co., 1902.

Mises, Ludwig von. *Nation, State, and Economy*. New York: New York University Press, 1983.

Spencer, Herbert. *Facts and Comments*. New York: D. Appleton & Co., 1902.

Trask, H. A. Scott. "William Graham Sumner: Against Democracy, Plutocracy, and Imperialism." *Journal of Libertarian Studies* 18 no. 4 (Fall 2004): 1–27.

INDIVIDUALISM, METHODOLOGICAL

Although the term *methodological individualism* was coined by the economist and historian Joseph Schumpeter, he was not the first to identify this methodological device and principle of explanation in the social sciences. For example, prior to Schumpeter, the sociologist Max Weber referred to the *individualistic method*, and the intellectual historian Élie Halévy wrote of an *individualistic hypothesis*, which he defined as a "principle of explanation," in which the individual human being serves as the basic unit of analysis in the social sciences.

According to Ludwig von Mises, methodological individualism views "all actions [as] performed by individuals"— or, in the words of Karl Popper, that social phenomena "should always be understood as resulting from the decisions, actions, attitudes, etc., of human individuals, and that we should never be satisfied by an explanation in terms of so-called 'collectives' (states, nations, races, etc.)."

Methodological individualism does not claim that only the individual human being is real or that social phenomena do not exist. It simply holds that the individual human being alone is able to think, feel, and act. We can impute actions, purposes, and values only to individuals; when we apply these terms to society, we enter the domain of metaphor. But this does not mean that society cannot be said to exist in some fashion. Many things exist that neither think nor act nor feel.

Methodological individualism should not be confused with social nominalism. Nominalism is the doctrine that society and social phenomena exist in name only—that they are literally *fictions* (as Jeremy Bentham called them) that cannot be said to exist apart from individuals and their actions.

The writings of Herbert Spencer point up the differences between social nominalism and methodological individualism. To the question, is society "but a collective name for a number of individuals" whose existence is "merely verbal?" he replied, "no." He regarded society as an "entity" with identifiable properties. Although Spencer was clearly a methodological individualist, this notion did not prevent him from maintaining that society is real in some sense. According to Spencer, society is a system of individual relationships. Institutions are recurring patterns of interaction with definite characteristics that can be identified and studied by the sociologist, apart from their concrete manifestations in particular cases. Social institutions are "real" in the sense that they reveal themselves to human consciousness as objective features of the external world. It is this objectivity that makes sociology and other social sciences possible.

Methodological individualism is typically contrasted with social holism, according to which social institutions are unique wholes that cannot be reduced to, that is, cannot be completely explained in terms of, the actions, beliefs, values, and so forth of individuals. Holism, according to a popular if somewhat loose definition, is the doctrine that a social whole is "more" than the sum of its individual parts—or, alternatively, that the whole is in some sense logically prior to the individuals that comprise it.

Holists have often compared social phenomena to the emergent properties of a chemical reaction. According to this argument from analogy, individual human beings are "atoms" that, when combined in a particular manner through interaction, produce social "molecules" (institutions) with new and unique characteristics.

In criticizing this view, which he dubbed "the chemical method," John Stuart Mill wrote: "Human beings in society have no properties but those which are derived from, and may be resolved into, the laws of the nature of individual man." However, Mill has been criticized by other methodological individualists for his defense of *psychologism*, which is the label given by Karl Popper to the view that all social phenomena can be explained in terms of the intentions, purposes, and motives of individual human beings.

Although psychologism rightly insists that we must reduce the actions and behavior of collective entities to the actions and behavior of individuals, it erroneously maintains that such explanations must be psychological (i.e., that they must ultimately refer to the conscious states and dispositions of acting agents). According to Popper, Hayek, and other methodological individualists, this error is serious because many social institutions were not consciously designed, but instead are the unintended consequences of human action.

Hence, Mill's psychologism, although a species of methodological individualism, is but one variation of this approach. According to its critics, many of whom are methodological individualists, psychologism fails to take into account the many social institutions, such as money and language, that have developed spontaneously without conscious planning or foresight. To say that all institutions are the result of individual actions is not to say that these institutions are the product of deliberate planning or design. As Adam Ferguson put it in his book *An Essay on the History of Civil Society* (1767), many social institutions "are indeed the result of human action, but not the execution of any human design."

We are largely indebted to Adam Ferguson, David Hume, Adam Smith, John Millar, and other luminaries of the Scottish Enlightenment for our understanding of unintended consequences and their role in the development of spontaneous, unplanned social institutions. It is scarcely coincidental that these sociological pioneers were methodological individualists. None would have seriously entertained the notion that social phenomena are reducible to anything more than the actions of individuals and their recurring relationships.

Modern social theory arose with the desire to explain the origin and development of undesigned institutions. In 1882, Carl Menger phrased "the most noteworthy problem of the social sciences" as follows: "How can it be that institutions which serve the common welfare and are extremely significant for its development come into being without a common will directed toward establishing them?"

Karl Popper has noted that an "action which proceeds precisely according to intention does not create a problem for social science." In a similar vein, in *The Counter-Revolution of Science*, F. A. Hayek has argued that modern social theory grew from a desire to explain the origin and development of undesigned institutions: "It is only insofar as some sort of order arises as a result of individual action but without being designed by any individual that a problem is raised which demands a theoretical explanation."

The significance of the theory of spontaneous order for methodological individualism is that it offers a third alternative to the extremes of psychologism and holism. The methodological individualist can readily concede that some social institutions result from something more than individual actions—if by this we mean the intended outcome of such actions. We also may speak of institutions as possessing emergent properties—if by this we mean properties that emerged spontaneously, apart from the intentions or plans of individual actors.

It must be emphasized that methodological individualism is not a libertarian theory per se. It is simply a method of investigation in the social sciences. Although almost all ethical and political individualists have embraced methodological individualism, it also has been employed by philosophers and social theorists with different moral and political beliefs. Methodological individualism, however, is far more consistent with the economic, sociological, and political foundations of libertarianism than with any other social philosophy.

In modern sociology, the most influential proponents of methodological individualism have been Max Weber, Georg Simmel, Alfred Schütz, and other proponents of the interpretive and phenomenological schools of social theory. It also has been widely employed by modern economists, including Austrians such as F. A. Hayek and Ludwig von Mises, members of the Chicago School such as Frank Knight and Milton Friedman, and pioneers in Public Choice theory such as James Buchanan. Last, methodological individualism has been vigorously defended by Karl Popper and his followers, most notably J. W. N. Watkins.

GHS

See also Economics, Austrian School of; Individualism, Political and Ethical; Individual Rights

Further Readings

Hamowy, Ronald. *The Scottish Enlightenment and the Theory of Spontaneous Order*. Carbondale and Edwardsville: University of Southern Illinois Press, 1987.

Hayek, Friedrich. *The Counter-Revolution of Science: Studies on the Abuse of Reason*. Indianapolis, IN: Liberty Fund, 1980.

Menger, Carl. *Investigations in the Method of the Social Sciences with Special Reference to Economics*. New York: New York University Press, 1985.

Popper, Karl. *The Open Society and Its Enemies*. 2 vols. New York: Routledge, 2003.

Spencer, Herbert. *Social Statics*. Whitefish, MT: Kessinger, 2007.

Weber, Max. *Economy and Society: An Outline of Interpretive Sociology*. 2 vols. Los Angeles: University of California Press, 1978.

INDIVIDUALISM, POLITICAL AND ETHICAL

Individualism rests on the idea that the relevant units of political or ethical inquiry are the individual human beings in question, as opposed to a society, race, class, sex, or other group. Libertarianism is a quintessentially individualist political theory.

Ethical individualism holds that the primary concern of morality is the individual, rather than society as a whole, and that morality primarily concerns individual flourishing, rather than one's interactions with others. Contemporary Neo-Aristotelian philosophers such as Ayn Rand, Douglas J. Den Uyl, and Douglas Rasmussen are among those who articulate this view. Rand contended not only that morality is primarily a matter of psychic health, but that service to a group is not a proper moral goal. However, not all individualists are egoists. Plato, for example, while teaching that individuals owe ethical obligations to serve the state even to the point of death—as Socrates does in the *Crito*—nevertheless holds that the proper beneficiary of one's moral actions is oneself. Likewise, Jesus, while teaching a morality of self-sacrifice, nevertheless repeatedly states that each individual is precious in the eyes of God and that "the kingdom of God is within you." Other altruist philosophers, however, including Kant and Auguste Comte, contended that each person should devote himself entirely to the service of others without thought of personal reward.

Some forms of Protestantism placed a particularly heavy emphasis on the importance of the individual. Martin Luther's doctrine of the "priesthood of all believers" held that the clergy was not a spiritually distinct category of human beings, but that each person bears a direct relationship with God through Jesus. Thus, all persons are equal before God. Other Protestant sects emphasized the importance of an individual's religious duties and of his commitment to salvation. George Fox, the 17th-century founder of the Society of Friends, the Quakers, argued that each individual was guided by an "Inner Light" implanted by God; indeed, many Protestant persuasions taught the importance of individual devotion, including reading the Bible for himself. Many Renaissance thinkers also emphasized the centrality of the individual, and the combination of these trends in 17th-century England helped give rise to classical liberalism. Although religious individualism was one of many doctrinal issues that led to bloody clashes during this period, some figures—notably Sir Edward Coke and John Milton—gave voice to those political philosophies based largely on religious and secular individualism. Coke argued that Magna Carta's guarantees for *freemen* applied to all subjects, not just to the feudal class to whom that word originally applied. Milton held that government was created by individuals who chose to enter into society for the protection of the freedom that God had granted to each of them. This early Whig doctrine would evolve into the classical liberalism articulated by the American Founding Fathers.

Thus, political individualism holds that each person, and not the group, possesses rights and that the purpose of the state is to protect the individuals that comprise it, rather than that individuals should serve the purposes of the state. As Jefferson wrote, "What is true of every member of the society, individually, is true of them all collectively; since the rights of the whole can be no more than the sum of the rights of the individuals." Thus, the government is analogous to an individual and may only act in ways that also would be open to an individual, such as acting in self-defense on behalf of its citizens. Political individualism, therefore, stresses individual freedom, choice, and self-direction while rejecting the notion of victimless "crimes against society."

Anti-individualists, or "communitarians," criticize individualism on the grounds that an individual's identity is created by social forces and that one's social roles should be given some additional consideration or even take precedence over one's personal identity. John Dewey explained that the breaking point between classical and modern liberalism was the discovery "that an individual is nothing fixed, given ready-made[, but] is something achieved . . . with the aid and support of . . . cultural . . . economic, legal and political institutions," which government should provide. Amitai Etzioni echoes this idea when he excoriates individualism as "intellectually defective and morally misguided" because it fails to recognize "that our selves are, to a significant extent, culturally and historically constituted. We are born into communities and cultures that initially form us, including our conceptions of the good and our 'choosing' selves." However, individualists do not deny the powerful influences that communities have on people, nor do they dismiss the importance of social bonds or the benefits of group or family associations. Instead, they see these concepts as goods for the individual, and which the individual must choose to accept if they are to have any value as goods. Communitarians invert this structure and see society as the determining entity by which individuals should be judged as good or bad. Author Robert Putnam, for example, contends that networks of people create the social capital necessary for healthy democracy, and that a growing "disrespect for public life" has harmed American society. This notion assumes, however, that democracy or society are ends in themselves or agents capable of assigning value to things, which they are not. Only individuals can assign value to things, and it is for their sake that social interactions or democracy are goods, if they are goods at all.

Moreover, libertarians reject the notion that individuals are merely the creatures of their societies or that others can have a claim over the individual stronger than the individual's claim over himself. The libertarian contends that each individual has the primary right to control his body and mind for three basic reasons. First, from the beginning of his existence, each individual is in constant and indefeasible possession of himself so that no action short of death can sever his connection to his body or his mind. In this sense, his possession of himself is inalienable. Second, no individual can wholly escape the responsibility for his actions, either to himself or to others. If he fails to gain the goods necessary for life, he will suffer the consequences. Nor can any other person control his actions without his choosing to comply with that person's commands. He cannot, therefore, alienate the responsibility of choosing; if he injures others, they will (rightly) blame him even if he acts on the command of another. Ethical individualism and political individualism are thus connected in that no person can wholly alienate his own obligations or responsibilities. Finally, the first two obligations are equally true of each individual. Hence, no person is inherently entitled to rule another or, in other words, "all men are created equal." These three observations apply to all people, regardless of their culture, and they support the conclusion that each person, as a person, has the highest claim over his own mind and life. Thus, if another wishes to govern him, that other person must obtain his consent.

Given the principle that each individual has an indefeasible right over himself, his ability to cooperate depends on finding a social system that respects each individual's rights. Far from denying the importance of community, individualism lays the groundwork for creating communities that are truly responsive to the needs of the individuals who make them up, without intruding on that very individuality that makes society desirable. This groundwork is laid through the recognition of rights and respect for the principle of consent. The fact that a libertarian society permits, but does not compel, membership in social networks means that people who do join social networks are more motivated to make those networks excel. As David Conway has noted, a libertarian society "might still be capable of providing its members with greater scope for full-blooded community than does any other societal form." Collectivist systems, by contrast, treat individuals as interchangeable components of the social organism whose consent is irrelevant and whose rights are simply permissions created—and revocable—by "society as a whole." As a result, voluntary social networks in collectivist societies tend not to be as strong as those in free nations.

Another common critique of individualism is that it weakens the foundations of virtue. Alisdair MacIntyre, for example, contends that individualism teaches people to place the satisfaction of their personal whims above the pursuit of moral excellence. Libertarians do not deny that individuals might indeed make self-indulgent and immoral choices, but offer two points in response: First, any virtue, to be a virtue, must be consciously chosen by the individual in question. An act that is not a matter of choice is not an ethical good because such goods must be regarded as goods by that person's evaluation. Whatever a person is compelled to do, even if it accomplishes something that he should prefer, is not a value to that person without his belief that it is so. Second, all political systems are governed by fallible human beings who are just as likely to pursue irrational goals as other citizens. As Thomas Jefferson said, "Sometimes it is said that man can not be trusted with the government of himself. Can he, then, be trusted with the government of others? Or have we found angels in the forms of kings to govern him?" Limiting the power of the state will not make the citizens good, but will protect those who choose to pursue virtue from those who do not and from political leaders who are at least equally likely to err with regard to excellence and who might choose self-dealing rather than the real good of the subjects.

Individualism is an important part of American culture, not only as the result of the nation's Protestant heritage, but also because of its frontier experience. As H. W. Brands contended in *The Age of Gold*, the mid-19th century transformed the "American dream" from the vision that each person could enjoy a stable, agricultural community life to the vision that each person could set out on his own and strike it rich. "The new dream held out the hope that anyone could have what everyone wants: respite from toil, security in old age, a better life for one's children." In addition, as pioneers moved west, many anti-individualistic social taboos were gradually dropped, in large part because people confronting a hostile natural environment without the relative safety of established urban institutions found these traditions to be a waste of time and effort. Thus, perceptions of American women moved haltingly from fragile, Victorian figures of virtue to that of strong, self-sufficient frontier wives. During this era, individual initiative and critical thinking became magnified as American virtues, and to this day the cowboy remains a quintessential symbol of American individualism. Again, in the decades after World War II, individualism experienced a resurgence as the civil rights movement demanded that social stratification based on race and other immutable characteristics be abandoned and that, in Martin Luther King's words, people should be "judged by the content of their character." To this end, American popular culture tends to celebrate remarkable individuals, rather than classes or groups for their unique gifts and talents.

TMS

See also Collectivism; Conscience; Individualism, Methodological; Individualist Anarchism; Individual Rights; Rand, Ayn; Religion and Liberty

Further Readings

Brands, H. W. *The Age of Gold*. New York: Doubleday, 2002.

Bronowski, J., and Bruce Mazlish. *The Western Intellectual Tradition*. New York: Harper & Row, 1960.

Conway, David. *Classical Liberalism: The Unvanquished Ideal*. New York: Saint Martin's, 1998.

Dewey, John. "The Future of Liberalism." *Journal of Philosophy* 32 no. 9 (April 25, 1935): 225–230.

Etzioni, Amitai. "Individualism—within History." *The Hedgehog Review* (Spring 2002): 49–56.

Fitzpatrick, Sheila. *Everyday Stalinism: Ordinary Life in Extraordinary Times: Soviet Russia in the 1930s*. Oxford: Oxford University Press, 1999.

MacIntyre, Alisdair. *After Virtue: A Study in Moral Theory*. 2nd ed. London: Duckworth, 1985.

Palmer, Tom G. "Myths of Individualism." *Cato Policy Report* 28 (September/October 1996).

Peikoff, Leonard. *Objectivism: The Philosophy of Ayn Rand*. New York: Meridian, 1991.

Putnam, Robert. *Bowling Alone*. New York: Simon & Schuster, 2000.

INDIVIDUALIST ANARCHISM

Anarchism is the theory that there should be no ruling powers. Because libertarianism is a theory of limited government, some have argued that its logical extension (or reductio ad absurdum, depending on one's stance) is the absence of all government. Libertarian or individualist anarchism needs to be distinguished from socialist or collectivist anarchism. From the 1840s to the 1860s, anarchism was largely associated with the same social-revolutionary movements that produced Marxism. Although Pierre-Joseph Proudhon, in his 1840 work, *What Is Property?* maintained that all social arrangements should be based on voluntary contractual agreement, he also regarded property as theft.

This idea is hardly the answer one expects to hear from a libertarian. The differences between individualist and collectivist anarchists are sometimes difficult to determine with any specificity. Mikhail Bakunin advocated public ownership of the means of production, yet took issue with Marx over the issues of authority and liberty. In the 1890s, Peter Kropotkin echoed Marx's slogan "from each according to his ability, to each according to his needs" and saw the state as an agent of moral corruption. Max Stirner, in contrast, was a radical individualist. A contemporary of Marx and Bakunin, Stirner rejected the notion of society, instead advocating a loose union of egoists.

The crucial difference between the anarchism of the left and that of the right seems to rest on their understanding of the notion of rights and of man's nature. The left appears to view anarchism as the logical result of the social nature of man, freely joining into collective, yet decentralized, associations. The right sees anarchism as the extension of the priority of individual liberty. Perhaps unsurprisingly, the American anarchists tended to be of the individualist variety. From Josiah Warren in the 1850s to Lysander Spooner and Benjamin Tucker in the 1870s and 1880s, to Albert Jay Nock in the 1930s, the development of anarchism in America has been an integral part of libertarian history. The individualist ideals of these early writers formed part of an intellectual landscape where the ideas of liberty could be developed free from any neo-Hegelian notions of history's progress, giving rise to such modern individualist anarchists as Murray Rothbard and David Friedman. In American libertarian thought, the problem has not been so much whether individualism or collectivism formed the basis for anarchism, but whether the priority of individual liberty could be reconciled with a minimal state or if it required its absence.

Individualist anarchists argue that there are no functions of government that could not be handled by market arrangements. Minimal-state libertarians typically argue that individual liberty is the predominant value in the political realm, and therefore government intervention in the economy or in people's personal lives is unwarranted. If a person's conduct is not in violation of the rights of others, then the government should not regulate or prohibit it. Nevertheless, the government has a legitimate, if minimal, role in human affairs. Although these minimalists concede that most goods and services can more effectively be provided by the market, the government is needed to operate courts where disputes can be resolved and run police agencies to keep people safe. The individualist anarchist, in contrast, argues that these services too can be provided by voluntary market arrangements; hence, they sometimes prefer the label *anarcho-capitalists*. Among anarcho-capitalists, Proudhon's claim that property is theft is replaced with the notion that taxation is theft because tax money is collected coercively and used to fund the provision of goods and services for which at least some taxpayers are not prepared to pay. If all goods and services can be provided through voluntary market arrangements, then even the minimal state is rights-violating. The state becomes, in this view, a monopolist whose monopoly is secured through the use of force. Like the classical liberal or minimal-state libertarians, individualist anarchists see individual liberty as the paramount political value and agree that the market is the most efficient provider of goods and services. Having been convinced of the bankruptcy of central planning, they have concluded that all services, even those traditionally provided by the state, should be open to the competition of the market.

As an example, because the function of law courts is to provide the resolution of disputes, one can imagine more than one provider offering this service. Rather than being forced to pay taxes to the government as the sole provider of this service, one can imagine people having several dispute-resolution companies to choose from, which would be paid by those who use them. These companies would prosper by cultivating a reputation for fairness and efficiency, and they would presumably have agreements with each other to adjudicate interagency conflicts. Similar market arrangements are envisioned for policing services. Of course there already are private "police" services in shopping centers, universities, and the like. But these police services are currently additions to the state-run police agencies. Anarchists hold that there could be more than one such firm providing the services of protection and enforcement. Of course, the plausibility of privatizing these core functions of the minimal state is precisely the bone of contention between minimal-state libertarians and individualist anarchists. But these groups seem to have more in common ideologically (e.g., the priority of individual liberty, the importance of property rights) than do individualist anarchists and socialist or collectivist anarchists. A minimal-state libertarian might argue that the minimal state is necessary for the basic functioning of civil society, although its scope must be limited to preventing harm to others, whereas the individualist anarchist argues that no forcible monopoly is consistent with individual liberty, and hence all the state's functions must be voluntary.

AeS

See also Anarchism; Anarcho-Capitalism; LeFevre, Robert; Left Libertarianism; Nock, Albert Jay; Proudhon, Pierre-Joseph; Spooner, Lysander; Thoreau, Henry David; Tucker, Benjamin R.

Further Readings

Barnett, Randy. *The Structure of Liberty*. Oxford: Oxford University Press, 1998.

Benson, Bruce. *The Enterprise of Law*. San Francisco: Pacific Research Institute, 1990.

Friedman, David. *The Machinery of Freedom*. New York: Harper Colophon Books, 1973.

Nock, Albert Jay. *Our Enemy the State*. San Francisco: Fox & Wilkes, 1994 [1935].

Nozick, Robert. *Anarchy, State, and Utopia*. New York: Basic Books, 1974.

Rothbard, Murray. *For a New Liberty*. New York: Macmillan, 1973.

———. "Society without a State." *Nomos* 19 (1978).

Sanders, John T., and Jan Narveson, eds. *For and against the State: New Philosophical Readings*. Lanham, MD: Rowman & Littlefield, 1996.

Spooner, Lysander. *No Treason*. Larkspur, CO: Pine Tree Press, 1965 [1870].

Wolff, Robert Paul. *In Defense of Anarchism*. New York: Harper Torchbooks, 1970.

INDIVIDUAL RIGHTS

Individual rights provide moral protection for individuals against unchosen and characteristically harmful incursions carried out by other individuals or groups. Rights are normative signposts that tell us that such incursions are morally impermissible, that groups or individuals that engage in such incursions act wrongfully, and that such wrongful incursions may rightfully be suppressed. Individual rights are often described as moral fences or boundaries. An individual's rights specify the domain over which he rightfully exercises control; if others intrude on that domain, they trespass on him. As John Locke put it in *Two Treatises of Government*, rights allow individuals "to order their actions, and dispose of their possessions and persons, as they think fit . . . without asking leave, or depending upon the will of any other man." Morally speaking, individual rights divide the world—including, most fundamentally, the world of persons—into "mine and thine." Indeed, libertarian doctrines of individual rights are often cast in terms of a fundamental right of self-ownership. However, libertarian theories of individual rights also affirm individual rights to extrapersonal objects (e.g., to acorns, tractors, and software). Individual property rights radically expand the domains in which individuals may act as they see fit; without rights to extrapersonal objects, the outer boundaries of those domains would be the outer surfaces of our bodies. Individual rights—including property rights—protect persons in the private pursuit of their own preferred ends. They protect each individual's freedom to pursue his own conception of the good against all individuals and groups that might propose to subordinate the individual or his resources to another's purpose.

Although some libertarian thinkers eschew the vocabulary of rights, doctrines of individual rights have been fundamental in most libertarian theorizing. Most of the great figures in the history of political philosophy to whom libertarians appeal—such as John Locke, Immanuel Kant, and Herbert Spencer—placed doctrines of individual rights at the core of their political philosophies. Similarly, most of the recent theorists to whom libertarians appeal—such as Ayn Rand, Murray Rothbard, and Robert Nozick—have grounded their libertarian conclusions in robust affirmations of individual rights. That common appeal to individual rights is not surprising, because affirmation of individual rights manifests the core individualism of libertarianism and of the philosophical traditions on which libertarianism draws.

Indeed, among libertarian advocates of individual rights and among their philosophical predecessors, the ascription of protective individual rights reflects a deeper belief in the separate importance of each individual's person, life, happiness, or life projects. Advocates of significant protective rights do not think of persons and their lives (or their happiness or life projects) as important merely as a means to some collective end (e.g., the collective end of social happiness or social equality). Rather, those advocates think of each person and his life (or his happiness or life projects) as something that has its own independent importance. Advocates of individual rights take seriously the separate importance of persons (or their individual lives, happiness, or projects) by asserting the existence of moral fences that protect each person against incursions that treat the individual as a mere means to others' ends. It must be emphasized, however, that advocates of individual rights are divided among themselves about precisely which features of human existence give rise to persons' possession of rights. They also are divided about precisely how claims about the rights of individuals are grounded in the features of human existence that give rise to each person's possession of rights. Rather than pursue these philosophical controversies, we turn to a more precise delineation of individual rights and the role of individual rights within libertarian theory.

If an individual possesses some right against another moral agent, the second person is morally required to constrain his action toward the first in certain ways. For instance, if we possess a right to life, then others are morally required not to threaten or destroy it. On most accounts of rights, because we may demand that others act in accordance with our right, we may enforce our rights against others or we may authorize some third party to enforce those rights. Thus, part of what is distinctive about this dimension of morality is that it is legitimately enforceable. Rights are the heavy artillery of moral discourse. If I have a right to someone else's acting in a certain way, it is not merely praiseworthy that that person act in that way; morally speaking, he must act and may be made to act in accordance with my rights.

The fact that rights are morally demanding also may be appreciated by noting that, in general, rights and obligations are correlative. That means that, in general, if I have some right against you, then you have a corresponding obligation to me. If I have a right against you that you not take my life, then you have an obligation toward me not to take my life. Your forbearing to take my life is not merely praiseworthy; it is obligatory and properly subject to being enforced. However, to say that rights and the obligations correlative to those rights constitute the enforceable dimension of morality is hardly to say that that is the only dimension of morality. Indeed, a great part of the point and value of a regime of enforced individual rights is that it frees people to act on their broader moral understanding of what is good and virtuous and what is bad and vicious.

Because rights mark off those moral claims of individuals for which respect may be enforced, and because political and legal institutions are instruments of enforcement, rights provide guidelines for legitimacy in political and legal institutions. The use or threat of force by political and legal institutions will be morally acceptable—and those institutions will be legitimate—only insofar as force or the threat of force is used to secure respect for the rights of individuals. Insofar as political and legal institutions use force or the threat of force for ends other than securing the rights of individuals, they act wrongfully and lack legitimacy.

Because rights are the heavy artillery of moral discourse, rational fear of bombardment counsels us to be highly selective in which assertions of rights we accept. A too-ready acceptance of alleged rights leads to an oppressive list of enforceable obligations. As the list of others' rights grows, each of us is subject to a growing burden made up of the obligations correlative to those rights; correspondingly, the ability of rights to be protective of individual choice dissolves. Moreover, as the list of rights grows, so too does the legitimate role of political and legal institutions, and the libertarian case for radically limiting the scope and power of such institutions withers away. Libertarian theories of rights avoid generating an oppressive list of obligations through the employment of two crucial distinctions—the distinction between negative and positive rights and the distinction between general and special rights.

If an individual possesses a negative right against others, then others are merely required not to act in a certain way with respect to the rights holder. In contrast, if an individual possesses a positive right against others, then they are required to perform some action with respect to the rights holder. For instance, my right to life construed as a negative right is tantamount to a right not to have my life destroyed or threatened. All that an individual's negative rights can require of other people is that they leave that individual alone—that they leave him to the peaceful enjoyment of what is legitimately his. In contrast, my right to life construed as a positive right entails that I have a right to be provided with life (i.e., to be provided with the necessities of life). If I have positive rights against another, then his merely leaving me alone violates my rights.

General rights are rights that every individual has against every other individual. Those rights have often been referred to as natural rights or human rights because individuals possess them on the basis of some common natural feature of human existence (e.g., on the basis of the ultimate separate importance of each person and each person's life). The right of self-ownership and the right not to have one's life taken are examples of general rights. In contrast, special rights are rights that specific individuals possess on the basis of particular actions performed by other individuals—individuals who, through their particular actions, have incurred special rights-correlative obligations. For example, I may possess a right against another that he deliver a copy of this encyclopedia to me, and I may possess that right on the basis of his having contracted to deliver this tome. This right is specific—conferred on me alone and not on anyone else. Contract is only the most obvious type of action by which one person may confer a special right on another. A person also might, for instance, have conferred a right on me to be provided with a copy of the encyclopedia by way of the other person having destroyed my previously purchased copy.

Libertarian theorists hold that all general rights are negative rights. For all persons, the initial baseline rights and obligations are negative. We are, so to speak, each born free—morally free to do with our lives as we see fit, subject to the negative constraint that we leave others equally free to do with their lives as they see fit. That is to say that all individuals are born to full self-ownership, to self-sovereignty; no individual is born to servitude to others. Although each person is born to a negative obligation to leave others in the peaceful enjoyment of their persons and their own property, that baseline obligation is not oppressive. For fulfilling that general negative obligation leaves one entirely free to dispose of oneself and one's own property as one sees fit. Moreover, for each person, all others being subject to that negative constraint is essential to his own moral freedom, to his own right to do as he sees fit. Rights to a particular property (aside from property in one's own body) are obviously not general rights; no one is born to any particular rights to extrapersonal objects. Still, property rights—like general rights—are negative rights. In the absence of special complications, one's property rights only impose on others the duty not to trespass and to leave one free to do as one sees fit with oneself and one's own property. Moreover, for each person, the fact that others are bound to respect one's property rights is essential to one's own freedom to do as he sees fit with his person and property. Negative rights are nonoppressive.

In libertarian theories of individual rights, all positive rights are special rights. An individual can acquire positive rights against another—rights to another serving me in one way or another—only if that right is conferred on me by the other person. All of a person's positive obligations must arise from actions performed by that person, such as his entering into an agreement to provide another with a copy of the encyclopedia. That is the sense in which, on the basis of a libertarian theory of rights, there are no unchosen positive obligations. All positive obligations are chosen, most characteristically through the agreements into which individuals voluntarily enter. The world of interpersonal relations is indeed thick with a great variety of positive rights and obligations, but those special rights and obligations are the products of particular decisions made by the individuals who are bound by those obligations. They are not obligations to which individuals are born, nor are they obligations that are imposed by others' needs, desires, or decrees. Libertarian theories reject assertions of positive rights that cannot be traced to the specific obligation-incurring actions of the individuals who are subject to those rights. Thus, individuals control the positive obligations to which they are subject, and, accordingly, the list of recognized obligations remains nonoppressive.

All general rights (and property rights) are negative rights. Yet this scenario is not a recipe for a world in which all or even most individuals retreat behind their right to be left alone. For the right to be left to the peaceful enjoyment of oneself and one's own is the right to choose which socioeconomic relationships one will enter. Recognition and protection of everyone's baseline negative rights induce the formation of relationships that individuals willingly enter on the basis of their perception of the value of those relationships. The recognition and protection of the positive rights and obligations that arise within those voluntary relationships sustain and advance the complex and mutually beneficial social order that emerges from respect for individual rights. It is that complex and advantageous social order, not merely the right to be left alone, that the doctrine of individual rights serves.

EM

See also Freedom; Kant, Immanuel; Nozick, Robert; Positive Liberty; Private Property; Rand, Ayn; Rights, Theories of; Rothbard, Murray

Further Readings

Kant, Immanuel. *The Metaphysical Elements of Justice*. J. Ladd, ed. Indianapolis, IN: Bobbs-Merrill, 1964.

Locke, John. *Two Treatises of Government*. P. Laslett, ed. Cambridge: Cambridge University Press, 1967.

Lomasky, Loren. *Persons, Rights, and the Moral Community*. Oxford: Oxford University Press, 1987.

Machan, T. R., ed. *Individual Rights Reconsidered*. Stanford, CA: Hoover Institution Press, 2001.

Mack, Eric. "In Defense of the Jurisdiction Theory of Rights." *Rights, Equality, and Liberty*. G. Pincione and H. Spector, eds. Dordrecht: Kluwer Academic Publishers, 2000.

Nozick, Robert. *Anarchy, State and Utopia*. New York: Basic Books, 1974.

Rand, Ayn. *The Virtue of Selfishness*. New York: Signet Books, 1964.

Spencer, Herbert. *Social Statics*. New York: Robert Schalkenbach Foundation, 1970.

Steiner, Hillel. *An Essay on Rights*. Oxford: Blackwell, 1994.

Tuck, Richard. *Natural Rights Theories*. Cambridge: Cambridge University Press, 1979.

INDUSTRIAL REVOLUTION

The *industrial revolution*, a term under dispute but hard to avoid, refers to the economic transformation that began in northwestern Europe in the 18th century, accelerated in the 19th century, and then spread worldwide—with many diversions for war and socialism—in the 20th century. Such an industrial revolution was the cause in the world today of much of what is different from earlier times: poor people who are rich by historical standards, ordinary people in charge of their own politics, women with jobs outside the home, children educated into their 20s, retirees living into and beyond their 80s, universal literacy, and the flowering of the arts and sciences.

Fifteen or more is the factor by which real income per head nowadays exceeds that around 1700 in Britain and in other countries that have experienced modern economic growth. This increase in material wealth indeed is the heart of the matter. Economic historians in the 1960s have uncovered the fact that the average participant in the British economy in 2000 was 15 times better supplied with food, clothing, housing, and education than were her remote ancestors. If one's ancestors lived in Finland, the factor is more like 29; the average Finn in 1700 was not a great deal better off in material terms than was the average African of the time. If one's ancestors lived in the Netherlands, it is only a factor of 10 or so largely because in 1700 the Netherlands was the richest—and the freest and most bourgeois—country in the world, approximately 70% better off than the soon-to-be United Kingdom. If one were in Japan, the factor since 1700 is fully 35. If in South Korea, the factor is 18 merely in the past half century—since 1953—when income per head, despite access to some modern technology, was about what it had been in Europe 450 years earlier. The improvement has been crammed into 4 decades instead of, as in the British case, stretched out over 2 centuries.

These facts are not, in rough outline, controversial, although their magnitudes are not something that people suspicious of capitalism know on their pulse. The gigantic enrichment of all who allow capitalism and the bourgeois virtues to work—the average person as well as the captain of industry—is one argument to support them. The enrichment

is, so to speak, a practical justification for the sin of being neither soldier nor saint. You may reply, and truly, that money isn't everything. But as Samuel Johnson replied, "When I was running about this town a very poor fellow, I was a great arguer for the advantages of poverty; but I was, at the same time, very sorry to be poor." Or you may ask the inhabitants of India (average per capita income in 2007 in U.S. purchasing-power-corrected dollars of $4,720) or China ($9,700) whether they would like an American per capita income of $47,700. Or you can note the direction of permanent migration. Immigrants from the developing world reveal their preferences quite clearly by coming to the United States and other rich countries.

Britain was first to achieve industrialization. Britain also was among the first in the study of economics, from the political arithmeticians of the 17th century through David Hume, Adam Smith, T. R. Malthus, David Ricardo, John Stuart Mill, and the British masters of the subject in the early 20th century. "The bourgeoisie," wrote Marx and Engels in 1848, "during its rule of scarce one hundred years has created more massive and colossal productive forces than have all the preceding generations together." It was a prescient remark. But the classical economists from Adam Smith to Marx and Mill were writing before the upsurge in real wages of British and American working people in the last third of the 19th century and long, long before the explosion of world income in the 20th century. They imagined a moderate rise of income per person, perhaps at the most by a factor of two or three, such as might conceivably be achieved by Scotland's highlands becoming as wealthy as capital-rich Holland (Smith's view), by manufacturers in Manchester stealing savings from their workers (Marx's view), or by the savings generated from globalization being invested in European factories (John Stuart Mill's view). But the classical economists were mistaken.

Why did the economy do so much better than the classical economists believed? The answer lies in new thoughts, what the economic historian Joel Mokyr calls the *industrial enlightenment*. What made the modern world was, proximally, innovation in machines and organizations, such as the spinning jenny and the insurance company, and innovation in politics and society, such as the American constitution and the British middle class.

Of course, if you conceive of a waterpower-driven spinning machine, you need some savings to bring the thought to fruition. But another of the discoveries by economic historians is that the savings required in England's heroic age of mechanization were modest indeed, nothing like the massive "original accumulation of capital" that Marxist theory had posited. Early cotton factories were not capital-intensive. The source of the industrial investment required was short-term loans on inventories and loans from relatives, not savings ripped in great chunks from other parts of the economy.

The classical and Marxist idea that capital begets capital, "endlessly," is hard to shake. It has recently been revived even among some economists, in the form of so-called *new growth theory*, an attempt to present what the development economist William Easterly calls *capital fundamentalism* in mathematically spiffed-up form. You see capital fundamentalism in all the stage theories from Smith to Marx to Walt Rostow. "Accumulation, accumulation," wrote Marx, "That is the law and the prophets." The economic historians have discovered that it is not so.

One trouble is that savings, urbanization, state power to expropriate, and the other physical-capital accumulations that are supposed to explain modern economic growth have existed on a large scale since the Sumerians. Yet modern economic growth—that wholly unprecedented factor in the high teens—is a phenomenon of the past two centuries alone. Something happened in the 18th century that prepared for a temporary but shocking "great divergence" of the European economies from those of the rest of the world.

Changes in aggregate rates of saving, in other words, drove nothing of consequence. No unusual Weberian ethic of high thriftiness or Marxian anti-ethic of forceful expropriation started economic growth. East Anglian Puritans learned from their Dutch neighbors and co-religionists how to be thrifty in order to be godly, to work hard in order, as John Winthrop put it, "to entertain each other in brotherly affection." Although this philosophy is well and good, it is not what caused industrialization—as indeed one can see from the failure of industrialization even in the Protestant and prosperous parts of the Low Countries, or for that matter in East Anglia. The habits of thriftiness, luxury, and profit, and the routines of exploitation, are humanly ordinary and largely unchanging. Modern economic growth depends on ingenuity in crafting gadgets.

The gadgets—mechanical and social—appear to have depended, in turn, on free societies, at least when the gadgets need to be invented, not merely borrowed, as was later the case in the USSR and the People's Republic of China. Such innovations of the 18th and 19th centuries in Europe and its offshoots came ultimately out of a change in what Adam Smith called *moral sentiment*. That is, they came out of a change in the *rhetoric* of the economy. Honest invention and hopeful revolution came to be spoken of as honorable, as they had not been before, and the seven principal virtues of pagan and Christian Europe were recycled as bourgeois. Holiness in 1300 was earned by prayers and charitable works, not by buying low and selling high. The blessed were those people "poor of the faith," as the heretical Albigensians in southern France put it (i.e., they were rich people like St. Francis of Assisi who *chose* poverty). Even in Shakespeare's time, a claim of virtue for working in a market was spoken of as flatly ridiculous. Secular gentlemen earned virtue by nobility, not by bargaining. The very

name of *gentleman* in 1600 meant someone who participated in the Cadiz Raid or attended Hampton Court, engaging in nothing so demeaning as actual work.

The wave of gadgets, material and political, in short, came out of an ethical and rhetorical tsunami in the North Sea around 1700. This time was unique in world history, and the change had stupendous economic consequences. To put it in Marxian terms, a change in the superstructure determined a change in the base.

Away from northwestern Europe and its offshoots in the period around 1848, when revolution spread throughout Europe and when Marx and Engels published their *Communist Manifesto* and Mill's *Principles of Political Economy* appeared, the economic virtues were still not respectable in the opinion of the dominant classes. Right up to the Meiji Restoration of 1867, after which things in Japan changed with lightning speed, leading opinion scorned the merchant. More widely, in Confucian cultures, the merchant was ranked as the lowest of the classes: In Japan, for example, the order of precedence was the daimyo, the samurai, the peasant, the craftsman, and, last, the merchant. A merchant in Japan, China, and Korea was not a *gentleman*, to use the European word, and had no honor—likewise, everywhere from the caves onward, and, likewise, too, circa 1600 in England.

Why, then, did the period from 1600 to 1776 in England witness what Joseph Schumpeter called the coming of a *business-dominated civilization*? Two things happened from 1600 to 1776, and even more so from 1776 to the present. The material methods of production were transformed, and the social position of the bourgeoisie was raised. The two were connected as mutual cause and effect. If the social position of the bourgeoisie had not been raised, aristocrats and their governments would have crushed innovation by regulation or by taxes as they had always done. The *bourgeois gentilhomme* would not have turned inventor.

Yet if the material methods of production had not, therefore, been transformed, the social position of the bourgeoisie would not have continued to rise. Without honor to the bourgeoisie, there could be no modern economic growth. (This last point is, in essence, a thesis put forward by the late Milton Friedman.) Without modern economic growth, there was no honor to the bourgeoisie. (This last point is, in essence, a view embraced by the economist Benjamin Friedman.) The two Friedmans capture the essence of freed men, and women and slaves and colonial people and all the others freed by the development of bourgeois virtues. The causes were freedom, the scientific revolution (although not in its direct technological effects, which were postponed largely until the 20th century), and bourgeois virtue.

What we economic historians can show clearly is that the usual suspects do not work. The slave trade, colonial exploitation, overseas trade, rising thrift, improved racial stock—no such material cause works to explain the modern world. We must recur—as economic historians like Mokyr are doing—to ideas, the ideas about steam engines and about the standing of bourgeois men and women who make the steam engines and the ideas about liberty that allow other ideas to change. The change in ideas arose perhaps from the turmoil of 17th-century Europe experimenting with democratic church government and getting along without kings. It certainly arose with the printing press and the difficulty of keeping Dutch presses from publishing scurrilous works in all languages. It also arose from the medieval intellectual heritage of Europe, free universities, and wandering scholars. In short, it was newly freed people who innovated and kept their just rewards.

DMC

See also Capitalism; Development, Economic; Division of Labor; Marxism; Material Progress; Smith, Adam

Further Readings

Berg, Maxine. *The Age of Manufactures: Industry, Innovation and Work in Britain 1700–1820*. Oxford: Oxford University Press, 1985.

Easterly, William. *The Elusive Quest for Growth: Economists' Adventures and Misadventures in the Tropics*. Cambridge, MA: MIT Press, 2001.

Hudson, Patricia. *The Industrial Revolution*. Sevenoaks, Kent, UK: Edward Arnold, 1992.

Innes, Stephen. "Puritanism and Capitalism in Early Massachusetts." *Capitalism in Context: Essays on Economic Development and Cultural Change in Honor of R. M. Hartwell*. J. A. James and M. Thomas, eds. Chicago: University of Chicago Press, 1994. 83–113.

Macfarlane, Alan. *The Riddle of the Modern World: Of Liberty, Wealth, and Equality*. Basingstoke, UK: Palgrave. 2000.

Maddison, Angus. *The World Economy: A Millennial Perspective*. Paris: Organisation for Economic Co-operation and Development, 2001.

Mathias, Peter. "Credit, Capital and Enterprise in the Industrial Revolution." *Journal of European Economic History* 2 (1973): 121–144. Reprinted in Mathias, Peter. *The Transformation of England: Essays in the Economic and Social History of England in the Eighteenth Century*. New York: Columbia University Press, 1979. 88–115.

McCloskey, Deirdre N. *The Bourgeois Virtues: Ethics for an Age of Commerce*. Chicago: University of Chicago Press, 2006.

Mitch, D. *Education and Economic Development in England*. Princeton, NJ: Princeton University Press, 1992.

Mokyr, Joel. *The Lever of Riches*. New York and Oxford: Oxford University Press, 1990.

Pocock, J. G. A. "Virtues, Rights, and Manners: A Model for Historians of Political Thought." *Political Theory* 9 (August 1981): 353–368.

Pollard, S. *Peaceful Conquest: The Industrialization of Europe, 1760–1970*. Oxford: Oxford University Press, 1981.

Pomeranz, Kenneth. *The Great Divergence: China, Europe, and the Making of the Modern World*. Princeton, NJ: Princeton University Press, 2001.

Rostow, W. W. *The Stages of Economic Growth: A Non-Communist Manifesto*. Cambridge: Cambridge University Press, 1960.

INTELLECTUAL PROPERTY

Private property is the cornerstone of the market system. A well-functioning free-market economy requires that property rights be clearly defined and protected so that people can engage in trade. Most libertarians agree that such rights should be extended to physical property, but they differ about property rights in ideas (i.e., intellectual property). More specifically, they differ about whether patents and copyrights are legitimate.

Many market-oriented economists believe that intellectual property rights must be protected. In principle, they argue, people would have little or no incentive to invent and develop goods that they will ultimately bring to market. Consider prescription drugs, for instance. Such drugs have benefited millions of people, improving or extending their lives. Patent protection enables drug companies to recoup their development costs because for a specific period of time they have the sole right to manufacture and distribute the products they have invented. After that period elapses, these drugs may be sold in generic form. The copyright system works in a similar way and for similar reasons. Novelists, for example, have the exclusive right to profit from the stories they write as long as those works are under copyright. To libertarian supporters of patent and copyright, the key is to develop an optimal intellectual property regime, one that promotes both innovation and consumer welfare, not to abolish the system altogether.

But to other libertarians, abolition is indeed the proper goal. Intellectual property laws, they argue, cannot be ethically justified. Consider the position taken by libertarian philosopher Roderick Long. He writes:

> Ethically, property rights of any kind have to be justified as extensions of the right of individuals to control their own lives. Thus any alleged property rights that conflict with this moral basis—like the "right" to own slaves—are invalidated. In my judgment, intellectual property rights also fail to pass this test. To enforce copyright laws and the like is to prevent people from making peaceful use of the information they possess. If you have acquired the information legitimately (say, by buying a book), then on what grounds can you be prevented from using it, reproducing it, trading it? Is this not a violation of the freedom of speech and press?
>
> It may be objected that the person who originated the information deserves ownership rights over it. But information is not a concrete thing an individual can control; it

is a *universal,* existing in other people's minds and other people's property, and over these the originator has no legitimate sovereignty. You cannot own information without owning other people.

Some libertarian-minded critics of intellectual property laws maintain that, in many cases, such measures may simply be unnecessary. In the 1930s, the distinguished British economist Arnold Plant noted that many authors are not driven by the profit motive whatsoever. "For such writers copyright has few charms," wrote Plant. "Like public speakers who hope for a good Press, they welcome the spread of their ideas."

Still, Plant conceded that some "authors write books because copyright exists, and a greater variety of books is published." It is important to keep the incentive to produce intact, while doing a better job of protecting the book-buying public, which often has to pay artificially high prices because the copyright terms have been extended too long.

More recently, Michele Boldrin and David Levine of Washington University in St. Louis made a comprehensive case against intellectual property, arguing that it

> is not like ordinary property at all, but constitutes a government grant of a costly and dangerous private monopoly over ideas. We show through theory and example that intellectual monopoly is not necessary for innovation and as a practical matter is damaging to growth, prosperity, and liberty.

They give many examples of the development of new products and methods of production when intellectual property protection is either lax or nonexistent. One famous case is design—from fashion, to furniture, to architecture. In the United States and many other countries, a firm can ostensibly patent the design of, say, a dress, but other firms can quickly sell similar items at sharply lower costs. Meanwhile, the pace of innovation in the clothing industry remains robust. "The now worldwide phenomenon of the Spanish clothing company Zara (and of its many imitators) shows that one can bring to the mass market the designs introduced for the very top clientele with a delay that varies between three and six months," write Boldrin and Levine. "Still, the original innovators keep innovating, and keep becoming richer."

Indeed, most libertarians, whether they support or oppose intellectual property laws in theory, believe that, in practice, such laws have been manipulated beyond their intended purpose. Consider the Copyright Term Extension Act (CTEA), passed by Congress in 1998, which added 20 years to all copyright terms. The result is that copyrights are now protected for the lifetime of a work's creator plus 70 years following his death, and that copyrights held by corporations are good for 95 years. The CTEA, libertarians have argued, gave an unfair monopoly grant to a few copyright holders at the expense of millions of potential consumers. In other words, Walt Disney Co. benefits substantially from the CTEA because without it some of Disney's most famous images, such as Mickey Mouse, would have entered the public domain. However, people who would like to read, say, an out-of-print, but still copyrighted, poem by Robert Frost would be damaged because no one would be allowed to publish it online without charge.

The constitutionality of the CTEA was challenged in the courts. A group of economists, including many prominent classical liberals such as James Buchanan, Ronald Coase, and Milton Friedman, submitted a "friend of the court" brief urging the law be overturned. They maintained that extending copyright for existing works "makes no significant contributions to the author's incentive to create, since in this case the additional compensation was granted after the relevant investment had already been made." In other words, it is simply a windfall to the owners of the relatively small percentage of copyrighted works that remain commercially viable. The Supreme Court was not persuaded, however, and upheld the CTEA on a seven-to-two vote.

Ultimately, nearly all libertarians believe that the current system of intellectual property laws is too rigid and should be liberalized. How far we should go toward dismantling the system, and for what reasons, are the real points of contention.

AS

See also Censorship; Freedom of Thought; Posner, Richard A.; Private Property; Rent Seeking

Further Readings

Boldrin, Michele, and David K. Levine. *Against Intellectual Monopoly*. New York: Cambridge University Press, forthcoming. Available from http://www.dklevine.com/general/intellectual/againstnew.htm.

———."Perfectly Competitive Innovation." Federal Reserve Bank of Minneapolis Research Department Staff Report No. 303, 2002.

Landes, William M., and Richard A. Posner. *The Economic Structure of Intellectual Property Law*. Cambridge, MA: Harvard University Press, 2003.

Long, Roderick T. "The Libertarian Case against Intellectual Property Rights." *Formulations* 3 no. 1 (Autumn 1995): 10–13.

Plant, Arnold. "The Economic Aspects of Copyrights in Books." *Economica* 1 no. 2 (May 1934): 167–195.

———. "The Economic Theory Concerning Patents for Inventions." *Economica* 1 no. 1 (February 1934): 30–51.

INTERNET

The Internet is a communications medium that grew to prominence in the mid-1990s and has come to be an important worldwide information resource and conduit for expression and commerce. Its use has dramatically advanced liberty and prosperity by empowering individuals to disseminate communication and ideas as never before, as well as by improving competition and market processes in several areas. The widespread use of the Internet also has borne with it many challenges, among them in the areas of copyright law, individual privacy, and data security. Although the Internet is often regarded as offering hope of a utopian libertarian society, it is just as susceptible to use by governments to create extensive systems of surveillance and control.

Emerging from theoretical work on communications networks in the early 1960s, the Internet originated with ARPANET, a network designed at, and with funding from, the U.S. Defense Department's Defense Advanced Research Projects Agency. The core concept behind the Internet is packet-switched communication, the practice of converting sound waves and other data into digital form—sets of 1s and 0s—and then breaking the communication into "packets" that are then transferred by a distributed network to their destination. Packet "headers" contain numerical routing information that are read by routers all across the network. Each of them forwards the communication closer to its destination until it arrives and is converted back into analog form as text, sound, or video. The rules that govern the transmission of packets across the Internet are called the Transmission Control Protocol/Internet Protocol (TCP/IP).

A major step forward in the commercialization and growth of the Internet came in 1993 when the National Center for Supercomputing Applications (NCSA) at the University of Illinois at Urbana–Champaign released the Mosaic Web browser. This browser was the first popular graphical Web browser that used a protocol called Hypertext Markup Language (HTML) to display information on attractively designed "pages" containing text and images that could be embedded with links pointing to other pages. The intuitive presentation of HTML pages helped to popularize the Internet's "World Wide Web." NCSA's Mosaic browser was quickly overtaken in popularity by the commercial Netscape Navigator browser, which came out in 1994.

The Internet is often conceived of as having several "layers." At the bottom lies the physical layer—the wires, cables, fibers, and routers over and through which packet-switched communications travel. Next, there is the logical layer, which contains the routing and presentation rules such as TCP/IP, HTML, and other protocols that govern the transfer of packets of data and their display. Next comes the application layer—the computer programs that people use to create and communicate content such as e-mail, Web pages, video, and voice. Finally, there is the content layer, which is the e-mail, Web sites, video, and other information that actually traverses this communications system.

The growth of the Internet and the use of TCP/IP have prompted telecommunications convergence and competition. The infrastructure originally built and optimized for wired telephone, wireless telephone, radio, broadcast TV, and cable TV is more and more being reconfigured to carry any kind of communication using IP. At the same time, new infrastructure such as fiber optics is being installed for purely IP communications. This development has had profound procompetitive effects on the telecommunications industry and has brought substantial benefits to consumers. Formerly, distinct networks that had provided cable TV or telephone services exclusively, for example, are competing with one another to provide voice services, video services, and Internet access services to consumers. Internet applications and Web sites also provide voice and video directly over consumers' Internet connections. These developments have rendered separate regulatory regimes for each distinct service obsolete as the distinctions among them blur and as competition replaces public utility regulation in promoting consumer welfare.

The Internet and the World Wide Web also have spawned convergence and competition in news, entertainment, commentary, and the arts, which in turn has expanded the amount of information and the range of opinions that are available to the average person. Traditional media outlets have been pressed to provide their services in a new variety of formats, for example. Major newspapers have Web sites with equivalent or greater readership than their print editions, on which they also provide video and user-generated commentary and content. The Internet also has lowered barriers to competition in all forms of media. A variety of Internet applications and commercial Web-hosting services give almost anyone seeking to publish information nearly worldwide reach. An endless variety of commentators, reporters, artists, and activists use the Internet to distribute and promote information, some in competition with established media and some for altruistic purposes. The result is that an endless ocean of information and ideas is available to the public via the Internet, including those embraced by libertarians, such as ideas of liberty, free markets, and peace.

Compared to the distribution of information prior to the development of the Internet, the widespread ability to transfer information on the Internet is a major step forward for communication and free expression. Advocates for all political and social views can collaborate and communicate using the Internet, and on protected Web sites they can discuss and share information about sensitive topics. They can distribute information and advocate positions broadly, each contributing to the competition in the "marketplace of ideas" with greater or lesser success at persuading others of their views.

Blogging, for example, has become a prominent practice, used to disseminate ideas and opinion on every topic imaginable. Search engines "crawl" the Web to catalog the information that is available on it so they can guide their visitors to the subjects that interest them. Other uses of the Internet, such as peer-to-peer file-sharing networks, allow users to trade files directly among one another, disseminating information and entertainment quickly and cheaply. All of these things contribute to the wealth of ideas available to people and help empower individuals to improve their political and economic lives.

The Internet also is increasingly used for commerce. Many Web sites sell goods or services or carry advertising that supports their operations. This commercial activity has restructured economic life in several respects. Internet retailers like Amazon.com, for example, give consumers access to a huge variety of goods that no physical retailer can match. This phenomenon has increased the value of publishers' and artists' "back catalogs." Past publications and artworks, no longer found in retail stores or similar outlets, can often still be purchased online, which has given rise to the concept of "the long tail"—the long, diverse list of "unpopular" works and items that make up an increasingly significant part of society's consumption.

Online marketplaces like eBay also have wrung inefficiencies out of the economy. Millions of items that consumers want, out of season or out of stock in any particular store, may be found and purchased online. Millions of items once destined for the trash have found their way to consumers who want them, at low cost to discover and buy. Many specialty markets and stores have cropped up online to give more people access to things they want. A large number of people supplement their incomes or support themselves entirely by selling online.

By freeing people to create their own business enterprises, the Internet is improving the quality of life for millions of people. This dynamic is fostered somewhat in the United States by the rules with regard to taxation of goods sold in remote commerce. Under "dormant Commerce Clause" analysis, the U.S. Supreme Court has held that remote sellers of goods cannot be made responsible for the collection of taxes for the jurisdiction to which the goods are being sent. Thus, many sellers of goods online do not have to collect and remit taxes to the governmental jurisdictions where the purchasers live, relieving sellers of a significant regulatory burden. This restriction is a challenge to jurisdictions that would put sales tax collection burdens on sellers outside their states. But it is just one of many challenges that the benefits of the Internet create for a number of institutions and interests.

Beyond taxation, the robust communication enabled by the Internet represents a threat to governments in a variety of ways. Autocratic governments are menaced by the potential that the Internet may be used by political organizations aimed at seeking reform, which could topple existing regimes. China is the world's most notorious Internet monitor and censor. Its combined efforts to contain the power of the Internet have been called "the Great Firewall of China," although it is far from the only country to control Internet communications or use the Internet as a tool of political and social control.

The Internet also can be used for criminal planning and criminal deeds, and for such things as terrorism planning and promotion. The U.S. government has reportedly been aggressive in monitoring communications in the conduct of its "War on Terror." IP networks make data easy to collect, store, and analyze compared with the analog information on circuit-switched networks of the past. More information than ever is available to law enforcement and national security interests in the United States and around the world because of the Internet and digital communications, although some rarely used methods of encryption and routing can protect information from interception and collection.

In many ways, the Internet is like a giant copying machine, reproducing information time and time again as it flows from computer to computer. Many uses of the Internet challenge or violate copyright law, which vests the authors of creative works with rights to control the copying, and thus dissemination and use, of their works. Peer-to-peer file-sharing networks, for example, transfer a good deal of popular copyrighted material in violation of copyright law. The content industry, chiefly the recording and movie industries, have aggressively sought to stem the flow of their copyrighted content across the Internet. The Digital Millennium Copyright Act, passed in 1998, sought in various ways to limit the accessibility of copyrighted content online.

New business models in traditionally copyright-oriented sectors have begun to emerge, accommodating the difficulty of enforcing copyrights online. "Open source" software development, for example, makes a unique use of copyright law: Rather than controlling the making of successive copies, this model makes software available for copying and use subject to the caveat that any further copy or derivative work also be available for copying and use under the same terms. Creators in traditionally copyright-reliant industries are exploring business model options that allow them to profit from goods that are complementary to the expressive works they produce, instead of trying to profit directly from copyright control.

The Internet and online culture challenge individual customs and expectations, such as privacy, as well. Just as it carries copyrighted content, the Internet and Internet-connected computers prolifically create and distribute personal information about their users. Analog formats for communication of the past, such as printing on paper, naturally made information difficult to copy, transmit, and store. Societal expectations about privacy evolved consistent with that. The data collection and copying done by the Internet threaten the privacy expectations of older generations while leading younger generations to adopt expectations that are more permissive about personal information and privacy.

Another challenge that the Internet presents to both individuals and institutions is data security. The rapid emergence of online business, communication, and information-sharing over a decade or so caused rapid adoption of technical infrastructures like computers, routers, and software that are relatively insecure given the purposes to which they are being put. They are more susceptible to attack, from both outsiders and insiders, than real-world infrastructure like the buildings, pipes, safes, cabinetry, and fencing that secure tangible possessions. The methods used to secure things in the tangible world emerged slowly, and society has had hundreds of years of experience with securing physical infrastructure. Only a few short decades of work have gone into securing the "intellectual infrastructure" of the Internet, computing, and computers.

A great deal of security against crime or fraud could be added to transactions conducted over the Internet, and to the Internet generally, such as for national security purposes, if all users were required to be identified accurately whenever they use the Internet. This process would undermine important values like free speech and the benefits it offers for social and political change, but the possibility illustrates how easily convertible the Internet is to surveillance and use by governments for political and social control. Although many transactions do require the security offered by identification, anonymity also is an important protection for many other important uses of the Internet.

Packet-switched networks are relatively complicated, and the details of how they are managed as they carry more and more communications can be manipulated to affect the content that they carry and how well they carry it. With a small number of national Internet Service Providers (ISPs), some argue that there is insufficient competition among them to protect consumers against threats to their interests as Internet users. ISPs are in a position to degrade certain protocols; to throttle services that compete with their own offerings, such as voice or video; or even to censor communications based on its content. Proposals for prophylactic regulation of broadband Internet service have been put forward intending to prevent these problems from emerging. The capability of a legislature or regulatory body to successfully write and administer network management regulations without throttling innovation and competition, however, are drawn into doubts by opponents of such "'Net neutrality" regulation.

The Internet is a unique communications network based simply on packet-switching instead of continuous circuits, and its societal and political ramifications are enormous. Because it favors direct communication and organization among people, its use often favors liberty. However, the technical infrastructure of the Internet is easily convertible to surveillance and use by governments for political and social control. The meaning of the Internet for liberty will continue to play itself out as the Internet grows in prominence.

JH

See also Censorship; Freedom of Speech; Intellectual Property; Privacy; Regulation; Spontaneous Order

Further Readings

Anderson, Chris. *The Long Tail: Why the Future of Business Is Selling Less of More*. New York: Hyperion, 2006.
Center for Democracy and Technology. *Updating Privacy Protections to Keep Pace with Technology*. Accessed February 2006 from http://www.cdt.org/publications/digital-search-and-seizure.pdf.
Leiner, Barry M., Vinton G. Cerf, David D. Clark, Robert E. Kahn, Leonard Kleinrock, Daniel C. Lynch, Jon Postel, Larry G. Roberts, and Stephen Wolff. *A Brief History of the Internet*. Available from http://www.isoc.org/internet/history/brief.shtml.
Raymond, Eric. *The Cathedral and the Bazaar: Musings on Linux and Open Source by an Accidental Revolutionary*. Cambridge, MA: O'Reilly Media, 2001. Available from http://www.catb.org/~esr/writings/cathedral-bazaar/.
Searls, Doc, and David Weinberger. *World of Ends: What the Internet Is and How to Stop Mistaking It for Something Else*. Available from http://worldofends.com/.

INTERVENTIONISM

Interventionism refers to the doctrine of the limited use of political power to address the perceived shortcomings of laissez-faire capitalism. Thus, public choosers (i.e., persons such as voters, politicians, and public authorities with access to legitimized aggression) employ interventions to attempt to promote outcomes they prefer compared with those of the unhampered market process. After the delegitimization of communism in the 1990s, interventionism has become the dominant policy doctrine throughout the world.

The economist and social historian Murray Rothbard has classified interventions into three types: autistic, binary, and triangular. Autistic interventions are those that interfere with individual, nonexchange activities, such as speech and religious observances. Binary interventions force exchanges between private individuals, on the one hand, and the state, on the other hand, and include taxation and subsidies. Finally, triangular interventions refer to the state-mandating exchanges among two or more private individuals, examples of which are income redistribution, price and production controls, and environmental, health, and civil rights regulations.

Governments intervene for a variety of political, fiscal, and ideological reasons, although a particular kind of intervention may serve more than one purpose. A tax on cane sugar, for example, can raise tax revenues at the same time that it favors producers of corn syrup. The focus here is on interventions that have an economic rationale. The justification for economic interventionism is commonly called *market failure*, and, in principle, the kinds of market failure that interventions are claimed to solve range from income inequality and problems caused by the business cycle to monopolies and pollution. Among these failures are those relating to sexual and racial discrimination, urban sprawl, and climate change, and they encompass moral hazards and adverse selections due to lack of willpower and the systematic miscalculation of risk. Although these failures are often claimed to provide a theoretical basis for interventionism, in practice, political agents also use market-failure arguments merely to camouflage their opportunistic manipulation of the political process to further personal ends, a phenomenon known as *rent seeking*. In this case, there is a divergence between public choosers' announced and actual intentions.

Whatever the motive, it is important to note that interventionism does not advocate the complete abolition of private property or thoroughgoing central planning. Interventionism promises to combine the best elements of capitalism with those of collectivism while avoiding the shortcomings of each. Indeed, the principal attraction of interventionism is that it putatively retains the basic institutions and benefits of capitalism, especially its wealth-creating capabilities, while promising to draw on these productive forces to achieve the particular objectives of public choosers (e.g., more spending to end racism, poverty, or climate change). In this way, interventionism differs from socialism and other forms of collectivism, although at just what point interventionism shades into the latter is not well defined. The politico-economic system that results from interventionism is sometimes called the *mixed economy*. Problems arise, of course, when the political objectives of a mixed economy conflict or when different groups of public choosers cannot agree on how to rank ends that compete for the same resources.

Although historically the concept of interventionism was identified and analyzed by the Austrian School of political economy, in particular by Ludwig von Mises, the phenomenon to which it refers has been treated from a variety of ideological viewpoints. At one end of the political spectrum, there is the post-Marxian analysis of Claus Offe, whose discussion of the dynamics and ultimate crisis of legitimization of the welfare state, a form of interventionism, is remarkably similar to that of the Austrians. At the other end is traditional public choice theory, associated with James M. Buchanan and Gordon Tullock, which emphasizes the tendency under redistributive institutional "rules of the game" to generate economic inefficiencies as political opportunism crowds out market-based self-interest. A prime example of

this approach is their analysis of rent seeking, which is the expenditure of valuable resources to acquire government-created privileges that generate no net benefit.

Because of its historical link, however, the present discussion focuses on the Austrian School, which, in contrast to public choice theory, places a greater emphasis on knowledge problems than on incentive problems. It is possible to dichotomize assumptions about the knowledge that public choosers have as being either perfect (i.e., there is no possibility for their regretting their decision) or imperfect (i.e., genuine errors are possible) and about their motives as being either benevolent (i.e., aimed at promoting the general welfare) or opportunistic (i.e., involving gain at the expense of another). The public choice approach tends to assume that public choosers do not make systematic mistakes and that they are opportunistic, whereas Austrians have typically assumed, for methodological reasons, that public choosers are well meaning, but not particularly well informed. For Austrians, public policy fails when actual outcomes diverge from intended outcomes. Finally, in contrast to both public choice and Austrian political economy, supporters of interventionism perforce assume that public choosers not only act benevolently, but always do so with sufficient knowledge.

The defining characteristic of interventionism also is the source of contradictions that result in profound systemic instability. That is, the attempt to combine a decentralized private property order with elements of collectivism and central planning inevitably generates consequences that tend to frustrate the intentions of benevolent public choosers. The interventionist dynamics in such cases are therefore the result of unintended consequences and of public choosers' ill-informed responses to them—consequences that emerge at the interface of the market and governmental processes.

The market process consists of the exchange relations that form and dissolve dynamically under a regime of economic freedom and a framework of private property rights, free association, and the rule of law. Complex networks and social cooperation emerge from these relations without the need for central direction and as a result of the perceptions and decisions of an enormous number of individuals. This decentralized decision making is driven by profit seeking, constrained by both legal rules and ethical norms, and guided by relative prices that are generated through free exchange. The process is emergent and self-sustaining.

In contrast, the governmental process consists of a dynamic that takes place within the governmental apparatus, that is, the legislature and bureaucracy, which is typically hierarchical and where well-defined property rights are relatively problematic. Decision making is motivated by the desire to preserve or acquire political power, whether in the context of democratic or dictatorial institutions, rather than from profit seeking. Thus, although networks can and do emerge spontaneously in the governmental process in response to changing circumstances, the integrity of government requires maintaining a stable structure of command and rule-following that severely constrains its ability to adjust. Therefore, compared with the main adjustment mechanism of the market process, entrepreneurial profit seeking, the governmental process—voting and legislation, in the case of democracies; command and control under dictatorship—tend to be relatively sluggish. Finally, the governmental process is financed primarily through the redistribution, rather than the creation, of wealth. Although it is possible that these two processes can, to some extent, coexist, as their spheres of operation overlap, the mutually exclusive nature of their underlying principles generates cumulative contradictions.

A simple illustration of the dynamics of interventionism can be seen by analyzing the imposition of price ceilings on certain commodities, such as gasoline. The attempt here is to direct an impersonal adjustment process toward a preconceived outcome. Although the intent of regulators may be to help motorists by keeping prices low, the immediate result, as elementary economic theory conclusively shows, is to create a gasoline shortage. If the regulators attempt to cope with the shortage by intervening further and imposing price ceilings on the inputs that go into the production of gasoline, such as oil or labor, further shortages in those markets will ensue. Unless the authorities reverse course, which they can do at any step in the regulation process, the market process will ultimately break down and systemic failure will occur as centralized decision making displaces the decentralized decisions of the market. At some point, authorities will have to decide whether to abandon their interventionist policy in favor of more consistently collectivist planning methods or to dramatically disintervene in the direction of significantly greater economic liberty. One can find other examples of this dynamic at the macro level in the form of business-cycle policy and more locally in the history of large-scale urban planning.

There are at least two conceptual questions raised by this example. First, why would policymakers take so long to correct their errors? We may call this *policy myopia*. Second, if interventionism is so unstable a system (indeed, it is debatable whether it constitutes a system at all), why has it been so widespread and apparently enduring for at least a century? We may call this the *paradox of intervention*. One explanation for policy myopia is that politically connected agents opportunistically employ political means with full knowledge of the consequences. As already noted, rent seeking is an important part of the modern political landscape and can explain much of the 20th century's march toward statism. But even if agents do not engage in such opportunism—if they are, for example, benevolent—imperfections in knowledge can induce a myopia that handicaps their ability to realize that the consequences of their interventions may at some level contravene their intentions.

Under complete collective ownership of property, the "knowledge problem" of harnessing knowledge that is dispersed across society that is relevant to the successful completion of any given plan cannot be rationally solved. Agents will not have market prices and profits to reveal to them when they are or are not making errors. In the case of the mixed economy, although it is less-than-full collectivism, interventions tend to undermine the certainty and security that agents have in their property rights, rendering prices, profits, and losses to that degree less reliable guides to their decision making. As the public sector expands, this tendency to leave property rights less definite and enforceable makes it increasingly difficult for all agents, including benevolent policymakers, to learn whether their actions have been effective, even from their own point of view. Additionally, distortions in prices and profits will result from the interventions, as is the case with price controls. Therefore, interventionism affects the politico-economic system with respect to incentives and knowledge.

Interventionism also has what F. A. Hayek has characterized as a psychological impact that changes underlying norms of acceptable behavior, especially those that might constrain the use of political means. If an agent sees others using public policy to enrich themselves at the taxpayers' expense, that an increasing range of choices come to rely on political considerations, or that government is promising a growing number of persons job security and the like, it follows that the use of political means to achieve private ends becomes increasingly acceptable. This process reinforces the incentive- and knowledge-related tendencies toward government expansion.

The resolution to the "paradox of interventionism" rests on the observation that if the various politico-economic systems in the world pursue interventionist policies, most will tend to cycle between laissez-faire capitalism and complete collectivism—the realm of the mixed economy. First of all, minimal states will tend to be unstable for the same reason that interventionist ones are: Even minor interventions have negative unintended consequences that will likely set an interventionist dynamic into motion. As a result, minimal states will be rare. Second, once the scope of government begins to expand under an interventionist dynamic, it becomes increasingly difficult to detect and correct its underlying policy errors. The drift will be toward bigger government. Third, economic calculation and solving the knowledge problem is impossible under complete collectivism. Consequently, maximal states also will be rare.

At any given time, most systems will therefore be interventionist, and the dynamics of interventionism will tend to push them gradually toward collectivism, whereas the occasional systemic failure will plunge some either toward the minimal state or toward more thoroughgoing collectivism, where, however, they cannot remain for long. Thus, although interventionism is an unstable system (indeed, it is not really a coherent system at all), it does not mean that it is transitory, especially given the wide range of mixed economies.

SI

See also Collectivism; Laissez-Faire Policy; Minimal State; Regulation; Socialism; Social Security; Welfare State

Further Readings

Hayek, F. A. *The Road to Serfdom.* Chicago: University of Chicago Press, 1972 [1974].

Ikeda, Sanford. *Dynamics of the Mixed Economy: Toward a Theory of Interventionism.* New York: Routledge, 1997.

Kirzner, Israel M. "The Perils of Regulation." *Discovery and the Capitalist Process.* Chicago: University of Chicago Press, 1985.

Mises, Ludwig von. *Interventionism: An Economic Analysis.* Bettina Bien Greaves, ed. Irvington-on-Hudson, NY: Foundation for Economic Education, 1998.

Offe, Claus. *Contradictions of the Welfare State.* John Keane, ed. Cambridge, MA: MIT Press, 1984.

Rothbard, Murray N. *Power and Market: Government and the Economy.* Kansas City, MO: Sheed Andrews & McMeel, 1977.

Tullock, Gordon, Arthur Seldon, & Gordon L. Brady. *Government Failure: A Primer in Public Choice.* Washington, DC: Cato Institute, 2002.

ISLAM

Like other religions, Islam has been invoked to justify a variety of legal and political systems, in support of both liberty and authority. Today, we are in the process of witnessing libertarian and democratic Muslims struggle against their intolerant and authoritarian brothers.

Some libertarian Muslims are inspired by the Western secular enlightenment, but Islamic libertarians also draw inspiration from the Qur'anic affirmation of the direct responsibility of every individual to the Creator. According to the Qur'an, the Muslim holy book, even the prophets, including Muhammad, are only messengers sent to warn men of the Judgment Day, and any who attempt to evade responsibility for their choices by blaming their leaders (whether political or religious) will have their punishment doubled.

The nonaggression principle, at least with respect to faith, is explicitly stated in the Qur'an: "Let there be no compulsion in religion" (2:256). Because Islam is interpreted by its followers as a complete way of life, the scope of that commandment may be interpreted to include political action. It is not, however, a call for pacifism because the Qur'an permits war in response to aggression and specifies punishments for theft, fraud, and certain breaches of public order.

Islamic libertarians regard governments as subject to a fixed rule of law binding on all, including the civic magistrate, a position strongly rooted in Islamic jurisprudence. Abu Bakr, the first Caliph, declared on his election that, "if I do well in my job, help me. If I do wrong redress me. Truthfulness is fidelity, and lying is treason. . . . Obey me as long as I obey God and His Prophet. But if I disobey God's command or His Prophet, then no obedience is incumbent upon you." In the Islamic tradition, law is conceived of as based on human nature, founded on divinely revealed principles articulated in the Qur'an, put into practice by the Prophet Muhammad, and interpreted through a process of discovery engaged in by legal scholars, rather than through legislative enactments. These interpretations are adopted or rejected in the marketplace of ideas and are ultimately based on the community's respect for their authors.

Islam established a form of pluralism that, although not secular, was more extensive than anything before the American era. In exchange for a small tax in lieu of military service, Jews, Christians, Sabians, and—in practice—other religious minorities were allowed to follow their own religious laws in all matters internal to their own communities and in their private actions. Although some Muslim rulers violated the spirit and letter of this system, the prosperity and liberty it afforded to minority communities has been generally recognized in most of the 700-year history of Moorish Spain, but it also applied through most other times and places of Muslim rule.

The Qur'an and the Prophet strongly emphasize property rights and freedom of trade. The Prophet was a merchant, and trade is thus a respected profession among Muslims. One exception to the Qur'anic mandate for free trade, a product of its condemnation of usury, is that Muslim scholars have generally opposed fixed rates of return in commercial loans and have demanded that lenders share in the risk of any enterprise as venture capitalists.

The Mu'tazilla of 8th-century Iraq were the earliest Muslims to be called libertarian by Western scholars. They referred to themselves "the partisans of reason and justice" and believed that humans must be left free to succeed or fail in the exercise of their God-given free will. They died out as a coherent movement when, having acceded to power, they insisted that only people who shared this view should be allowed to hold positions in government, sparking a rebellion against their insistence that all participants in the political process take a "loyalty oath."

The most consistent of the many free-market economists in Islamic history is Ibn Khaldun. In his *Muqaddamah*, or "Introduction to History," he argued that civilizations rise and fall because of their adherence to or departure from principles of justice, including freedom of trade and protection of property. He anticipated what in recent years has been called "supply side economics" by asserting that, in their beginnings, dynasties raise large revenues from low tax rates and at their end raise small revenues from high tax rates. He warned that government intervention into commerce would bring the ruin of a dynasty.

Rose Wilder Lane, among others, has argued that Islamic ideas influenced the rise of Western liberalism. Aristocrats who returned from the Crusades, where they observed how the rule of law bound Saladin, imposed Magna Carta on King John. The influence of Muslims on Thomas Aquinas and Frederick the Great also is well established. Recently, the historian G. A. Russell has argued that John Locke's abandonment of pragmatism to embrace natural law theory was influenced by Pococke's translation of Ibn Tufayl's *Alive the Son of Awake.*

Muslim libertarian organizations today include the Association for Liberal Thinking (ALT) in Turkey, the Minaret of Freedom Institute (MFI) in the United States, and Making Our Economy Right (MOER) in Bangladesh. The ALT has been remarkably successful in influencing the discourse in Turkey to the point that the Justice and Development Party has implemented measures that have drastically cut inflation, freed up entrepreneurship, and reformed Turkey's human rights policies to the degree that Turkey is close to conforming with the European Union human rights standards. (However, they have not been able to reform Turkey's oppressively secular laws to the point of permitting women who wear an Islamic-style headscarf to attend university.) The power elites in Turkey have harassed the head of the ALT, who has been put on trial for allegedly "insulting Turkish nationalism" because of his statement that the Turkish Republic should not have been established as a one-party system.

The MFI has taken the position that the real conflict in the world today is not between civilizations, but within civilizations—that is, between the libertarian and authoritarian trends within both Islam and the West. Muslims were cut off from their heritage by the colonial experience and the secular-socialist states of the postcolonial era. The failure of secular socialism has sparked an Islamic resurgence that, in its political form, is called *Islamism.* Liberal and democratic wings, inspired by Islamic modernists like Jamal-ad-Din al-Afghani and Muhammad Abdu, contend against extremist wings, inspired by ultraconservatives like Muhammad ibn Abdul-Wahhab and radicals like Sayyid Qutb. The liberals have taken advantage of young Muslims' interest in the Internet to establish a "Muslim Students Liberty Network" on Facebook. Too often important issues like the status of women and tolerance for non-Muslims are not discussed substantively, but have become iconic proxies for the issues of Western imperialism and the plight of the Palestinians, a situation that liberal Muslims are working to change. A variety of academic and popular pieces from MFI have addressed such issues as female genital mutilation, the death penalty for apostasy, and the Iraq war.

Al-Afghani, Abdu, and Abdul-Wahhab are all examples of Salafi thinkers, meaning those who wished to return to original sources in order to reform Islamic thought from an ossified tradition. The liberals among such thinkers have had a limited influence, mainly on other intellectuals, whereas the conservative followers of Abdul-Wahhab have been so influential that recently commentators have used the broader term *Salafi* as if it applied only to the conservatives. This misnomer is largely due to the enormous influence Wahhab's thought has enjoyed due to the rise of Saudi Arabia. Muhammad ibn Saud, an Arab tribal leader, supported Abdul-Wahhab's interpretation of Islam and obtained Abdul-Wahhab's endorsement of his claim to kingship over the Arabs. Two initial attempts to establish a Saudi kingdom failed due to opposition from the Ottomans and from the local tribes, but the third attempt, backed by the British and dramatized in the movie *Lawrence of Arabia*, was successful. The Saudi state made ibn Abdul-Wahhab's interpretation of Islam the official one, and the enormous oil wealth subsequently allowed the Saudi view to be exported around the world. Many extremists, like those associated with al-Qaeda, have been influenced by both the Wahhabi interpretation of Islam and Egyptian radicals, who have appropriated the traditional Muslim concept of *jihad* (struggle) into service of a militaristic, even imperial, vision.

The essential framework of Islamic law is that all relationships are contractual. However, authoritarian modalities now dominate in many critical areas of the modern Muslim nation-states, including women's rights, religious tolerance, and freedom of expression. The status of women, much more advanced in early Muslim society than anywhere else at that time, has eroded severely. The hybridization between Islamic law and Western law implemented by the male founders of certain modern Muslim states in the postcolonial era has generally been disastrous for women. In Pakistan, for example, rape has been classified as a sex crime, following British law, rather than as a crime of aggression, following Muslim law. This classification has resulted in female victims of rape being punished, rather than their attackers. Due to considerations of privacy and dignity, Islamic rules of evidence are much stricter for sex crimes, like adultery and fornication, than for crimes of aggression, like robbery and rape. These higher standards, such as the requirement of four eyewitnesses, are usually impossible to meet in cases of rape, resulting in charges being dropped against the aggressor, while the victim is accused of having confessed to a sexual crime.

Advances in the status of women, such as the reinstitution of divorce rights for women in Egypt, have succeeded because of the participation of groups arguing within the Islamic paradigm. The traditional right of women to unilaterally divorce their husbands by returning the marriage gift (called a *khula*, divorce) was suppressed by the British during their occupation of Egypt on the grounds that the ease with which women could initiate a divorce was harmful to society. When feminists in the late 20th century attempted to restore this right, the religious establishment and a populace that had forgotten the Islamic origins of the institution resisted. Women's study circles rediscovered the Qur'anic verses on the subject while female sociologists have demonstrated how common the practice was when the Ottomans ruled Egypt.

The argument that Muslims have misinterpreted Islam in recent times has met with some successes in promoting reform. Meanwhile, those who have presented reform as a de-Islamization of society have not merely failed, but have provoked an intense and sometimes violent backlash. For example, the claim that whether Islam requires a woman to cover her hair is ultimately determined by the free choice of individual women has increased respect for individual rights among American and Turkish Muslims, whereas the claim that wearing a headscarf constitutes an undesirable symbol of Islam has only increased the number of women wearing the headscarf in Egypt and France and has intensified the politicization of the issue by turning a question of decorum into a symbol of identity.

A similar phenomenon can be seen with regard to religious intolerance. The normal standard of tolerance in Muslim society was most compromised when Muslims were under attack or occupation by foreign powers. When the Muslims took Spain in the 8th century, their indigenous Christian and Jewish clients held the lands taken from the previous Visigoth occupiers for the Muslims. During the Reconquista, there were periodic episodes of intolerance. Similarly, when Muslims struggled with the Christians over Jerusalem in the 8th and 12th centuries, they reopened the city to the expelled Jewish populations, but with the Zionist conquest of modern Palestine, anti-Jewish bigotry has appeared among those Muslims who are unable to make a distinction between Zionism and Judaism. Intrafaith tolerance is vulnerable in the same way, as exemplified by the deterioration of Sunni–Shia relations in Iraq. Before the American invasion, Sunni–Shia intermarriage was common and communal fighting rare. Since the invasion, differences between the communities regarding the occupation and the nature of the postwar state have resulted in the outbreak of sectarian violence.

IDA

See also Feminism and Women's Rights; Locke, John; Religion and Liberty; War on Terror

Further Readings

Ahmad, Imad-ad-Dean. "Islam and the Progenitors of Austrian Economics." *The Contributions of Murray Rothbard to Monetary Economics*. C. Thies, ed. Winchester, VA: Durrell Institute at Shenandoah University, 1996. 77.

———. "An Islamic Perspective on the Wealth of Nations." *The Economics of Property Rights: Cultural, Historical, Legal, and Philosophical Issues*. Vol. 1. S. Pejovich, ed. Cheltenham, UK: Edward Elgar, 2000.

al-Faruqi, Ismail Raji. *Tawhîd: Its Implications for Thought and Life*. Kuala Lumpur: Dicetak oleh Percetakan Polygraphic Sdn. Bhd., 1982.

Ali, Abdullah Yusuf. *The Holy Qur'an: Text, Translation and Commentary*. New York: Tahrike Tarsile Qur'an, 1988.

Black, Antony. *The History of Islamic Political Thought: From the Prophet to the Present*. New York: Routledge, 2001.

Haykal, Muhammad. *The Life of Muhammad*. Indianapolis, IN: North American Trust Publications, 1976.

Hodgson, Marshall G. S. *The Venture of Islam: Conscience and History in a World Civilization*. Chicago: University of Chicago Press, 1974.

Ibn Khaldun, Wali ad-Din. *The Muqqadamah: An Introduction to History*. Franz Rosenthal, trans. Princeton, NJ: Princeton University Press, 1967.

Lane, Rose W., and Ahmad, Imad-ad-Dean. *Islam and the Discovery of Freedom*. Beltsville, MD: Amana, 1997.

Rosen, Lawrence. *The Anthropology of Justice: Law as Culture in Islamic Society*. Cambridge: Cambridge University Press, 1989.

Russell, G. A., ed. *The "Arabick" Interest of the Natural Philosophers in Seventeenth Century England. Brill's Studies in Seventeenth Century England*. Leiden, Germany: E. J. Brill, 1994.

Sonbol, Amira El-Azhary. *The New Mamluks: Egyptian Society and Modern Feudalism*. Syracuse, NY: Syracuse University Press, 2000.

Wahbah, Mourad, and Mona Abousenna, eds. *Averroës and the Enlightenment*. Amherst, NY: Prometheus Books, 1996.

ITALIAN FISCAL THEORISTS

It is appropriate that an encyclopedia devoted to libertarianism should have an entry on "Italian Fiscal Theorists." An essential first step toward an appreciation of and adherence to libertarianism requires that we shed all vestiges of the romantic vision of how politics works. Profound skepticism about politics and politicians is a characteristic feature of the Italian culture, and it is not surprising that this feature has a profound impact on political economy at the intersection between analyses of the market sector (economics) and analyses of the government sector (political science).

The Anglo-American tradition of economics can properly claim credit for preeminence in developing the economic theory of markets, stemming from its classical roots in the 18th century through its 19th-century neoclassical and 20th-century postclassical developments. No comparable claim could possibly be advanced for the theory of politics or government. English-language scientific discourse over the better part of these centuries was dominated by a mixture of Platonic idealism and naive utilitarianism. Politics was modeled on a continued search for the "good," whereas little or no attention was paid to politics as it was practiced and as carried on by ordinary persons, whether as putative rulers, willing or unwilling subjects, or as participants in cooperating or conflicting interactions in democratic institutions.

With Machiavelli and Guicciardini as precursors, we could scarcely have expected Italian scholars to remain blindfolded to the reality of politics. As the classical economics of Adam Smith, David Ricardo, and J. S. Mill entered Italian thought through the intercession of Francesco Ferrara in the 1850s, we find the origins of a specific tradition in fiscal theory that extended over most of a century. That tradition embodied analyses of politics that were both more comprehensive and more sophisticated than anything published by English-language scholars before the mid-20th century. Works in that tradition also were more "scientific" than their English-language counterparts in the sense that normative elements were deliberately excluded.

The contributions of the fiscal theorists in that tradition are easily summarized. Beyond Ferrara, the important names here include those of de Viti de Marco, Pantaleoni, Einaudi, Barone, Puviani, Fasiani, Cosciani, Griziotti, and Montemartini, a partial listing, with Pareto looming as an indirect influence in the background.

First and foremost, the Italian tradition incorporated the elementary recognition that some model or theory of politics must inform any discourse about taxing and public spending if that discourse is to have any impact on prospects for ultimate reform. Analyses of this or that tax in terms of the economists' orthodox efficiency criteria are meaningless until and unless the processes and institutions through which taxes are levied are specified. Relatedly, and equally important, one side of the fiscal account cannot be analyzed separately from the other. Taxes raise revenues which governments spend, either to finance goods or to make transfers, and this spending side of the account exerts effects comparable to those on the taxing side.

Italian scholars examined politics in two parallel models: that of the monopoly or coercive state and that of the cooperative or democratic state. The basic treatises of de Viti de Marco and Fasiani explicitly presented this dual approach. As the coercive authority of the state is confronted, the taxpayer necessarily reacts privately within the limits of the constraints exogenously imposed. At the same time, however, in any political setting purporting to be democratic, the individual may sense, at least indirectly, a role as a potential participant in the collective decision processes that ultimately determine the allocation of fiscal constraints.

The contrasting models of state authority may be separately developed. How would the monopoly state, freed from the effects of direct feedback from a representative democracy, behave fiscally? That is the question that prompted Amilcare Puviani to develop his concept of fiscal illusion. Such a monopoly state, always aiming at securing general support from members of the public, would seek to minimize the felt burden of taxes and maximize the felt benefits of its outlays. Indirect and hidden taxes would be preferred over direct and explicit levies. Taxes would, when possible, be associated with pleasurable events, and

a multiplicity of small levies would be preferred to a consolidated imposition. Although not imagined by Puviani, withholding of taxes at source would almost ideally fit his criteria. Public outlay would be of the "bread and circuses" variety ("pork" in its modern form). Officials would spend much time in ribbon-cutting ceremonies. Opportunity costs would never enter the lexicon of political rhetoric.

It may perhaps seem paradoxical that, at the same time models of the coercive fiscal authority were treated as central elements in the Italian tradition, there was widespread recognition that collectively financed services were classified as sources of product value. De Viti de Marco reckoned that the services of the state should be placed alongside labor, land, and capital as factor inputs in the generation of valued output. The Italian fiscal theorists seem to have totally rejected Adam Smith's relegation of collective services to the category of the unproductive.

Luigi Einaudi (who became president of the Italian Republic after World War II) deserves special mention for his long-time advocacy of a completely general flat-rate tax on all units of income, without exception. His argument was straightforward. Each unit of earned income carries against it a claim by the state for the publicly supplied productive services that made the income possible. There is no justification for differentiation or discrimination among sources or uses of income. Implicit in Einaudi's proposal is recognition of the efficiency gains to be expected from the elimination of rent-seeking efforts to secure special treatment. Einaudi was foremost among those who criticized the practice of analyzing taxes independent of spending, referring to the *imposta grandine*, taxes treated as hailstorm damage.

The Italian fiscal theorists were systemic in their approach to the subject matter at hand, which was separately placed in university curricula. They were not writing as Marshallian neoclassical economists who used shifts in tax constraints to illustrate the basic logic of partial equilibrium theory. They were motivated to ask, and did ask the basic questions: What is the state? To what extent is the state separated from the citizenry? What are the motivations of those who act as decision makers for the collectivity? To what degree can collective action be factored down into participatory roles for individuals subject to such action?

It should not be surprising that those fiscal theorists were realists, rather than romantics in their evaluation of political processes. In the English-language literature, both academic and public attitudes have, almost literally, spent the half century after World War II "catching up" with their Italian peers.

JB

See also Classical Economics; Coercion; Taxation; Welfare State

Further Readings

Buchanan, James M. "La scienza delle finanze: The Italian Tradition in Fiscal Theory." *Fiscal Theory and Political Economy*. James M. Buchanan, ed. Chapel Hill: University of North Carolina Press, 1960.

Cosciani, Cesare. *Principii di Scienza delle Finanze*. Turin: Unione Tipografico Beditrice, 1953.

De Viti de Marco, Antonio. *First Principles of Public Finance*. E. P. Marget, trans. London: Jonathan Cape, 1936.

Einaudi, Luigi. *Opere di Luigi Einaudi: Vol. 1. Saggi sol Risparmio e L'Imposta*. Turin: Einaudi, 1958.

Fasiani, Mauro. *Principii di Scienza delle Finanze*. 2 vols. Turin: G. Giappichelli Editore, 1951.

Ferrara, Francesco. *Opera Complete*. Vol. 2B5. Rome: Banca Italia, 1955.

Musgrave, Richard A., and Alan T. Peacock. *Classics in the Theory of Public Finance*. London: Macmillan, 1958.

JACOBS, JANE (1916–2006)

Jane Jacobs, a pioneering urbanologist, social theorist, and activist, is best known for *The Death and Life of Great American Cities*, published in 1961. Her stated objective was to overthrow the rationalistic urban design theories and heavy-handed practices of the day, best illustrated by the "radiant-city" concept of the architect Le Corbusier and the municipal mega-development policies of the urban planner Robert Moses.

To Jacobs, a living city cannot conform to a single rational or aesthetic ideal because it poses a "problem of organized complexity" that emerges from the free interaction of millions of individuals. In this context, safety, trust, and economic development emerge in a spiral that depends on a spontaneous combination of population density and economic diversity. In other words, a diversity of primary uses, such as residential and commercial (an idea imperfectly captured today by "mixed uses"), attracts large concentrations of people, most of whom are strangers, to the public spaces in a given locale around the clock and provides a safe environment that encourages free and informal contact among them. This in turn forms the basis for social networks of trust that promote the utilization of local knowledge, entrepreneurial discovery, and serendipitous creative interactions—ideas that presage modern social-network theory. Although this dynamic is rare in small towns, it is characteristic of a living city, making it an incubator of new ideas. Such a city is capable of indigenously generated economic development.

While *Death and Life* discusses how a city depends on its neighborhoods and districts, her next book, *The Economy of Cities*, explains how cities depend on one another for economic development and expansion, and *Cities and the Wealth of Nations* argues that the global economy is a dynamic network of great but interdependent cities, some living and some dying. These books offer a consistent approach that takes the perceptions and actions of ordinary people as its starting point. She presents a distillation of this economic framework in *The Nature of Economies*, which overlaps, complements, and, to an extent, advances the ideas of the Austrian School of Economics.

Systems of Survival is perhaps her most libertarian book. It argues that the virtues appropriate to action in the market are fundamentally different from those guiding government. Confusion and dangerous contradictions arise when agents attempt to apply the moral system of one sphere while operating in the other.

Despite the libertarian nature of her writings, Jacobs disliked being ideologically pigeonholed. She advocated limited forms of government intervention at the local level, such as zoning for diversity. She also argued that large-scale projects, public or private, threatened to undermine local communities and that cities were vulnerable to endogenous, self-destructive processes. But she remained skeptical of planning at all levels of government because it is incapable of comprehending local knowledge and needs.

Jacobs dramatically changed the face of the urban landscape both through her ideas and her activism, which, among other things, helped to stop a federally funded project to bulldoze a freeway through what later became a vibrant district in Lower Manhattan. Her activism continued in her adopted city of Toronto, where she and her family moved as a consequence of the Vietnam War. Her life and work continue to inspire and appeal across the ideological spectrum.

SI

See also Cities; Civil Society; Natural Harmony of Interests; Spontaneous Order; Urban Planning

Further Readings

Jacobs, Jane. *The Death and Life of Great American Cities.* New York: Vintage, 1961.

———. *The Nature of Economies.* New York: Modern Library, 2000.

———. *Systems of Survival.* New York: Vintage, 1992.

JEFFERSON, THOMAS (1743–1826)

Thomas Jefferson was the author of the Declaration of Independence and other key documents of early American constitutionalism. He was almost certainly the founder most instrumental in developing the philosophy of limited government that dominated American political thought until the 20th century. Jefferson was a quintessential Renaissance man, with law and politics as perhaps the least favorite of his many interests, yet he was drawn into the political conflicts of his time because of his devotion to what he called "the holy cause of freedom."

Educated at the College of William and Mary and trained as a lawyer by Williamsburg attorney George Wythe, by the mid-1760s, Jefferson was well versed in the English radical Whig political tradition and its core principle that government, when its citizens are not vigilant, can threaten liberty. Like other radical Whigs, he was profoundly distrustful of concentrated power and intensely devoted to the ideals of limited government and the rule of law.

Jefferson's involvement in the colonists' disputes with the Crown began when, as a member of the Virginia House of Burgesses, he helped organize committees of correspondence with the other colonies. In August 1774, he wrote proposed instructions for the Virginia delegates to the first Continental Congress. Published under the title *A Summary View of the Rights of British America*, Jefferson's essay stridently defended Americans' rights against the British Parliament, which he maintained had no authority to legislate for the colonies.

In 1775–1776, Jefferson was a Virginia delegate to the Second Continental Congress in Philadelphia, where in June 1776 he drafted the Declaration of Independence, adopted by the Congress on July 4. As he later described his purpose, he sought "to place before mankind the common sense of the subject"—justification of American independence—"in terms so plain and firm as to command their assent." In doing so, he also defined the American philosophy of government, which was premised on the fact that each person, by virtue of his or her humanity alone, possessed inherent natural rights, among them the rights of "life, liberty, and the pursuit of happiness." These he identified as "self-evident truths." "To secure these rights," he wrote, "governments are instituted among men, deriving their just powers from the consent of the governed."

During the Revolutionary War, Jefferson sought to help establish new republican governments both in his home state of Virginia and in the United States. In the summer of 1776, he drafted a constitution for Virginia, but it was not adopted. As a member of the state's House of Delegates again during the years 1776–1779, he served on the committee to revise the laws of the Commonwealth and drafted several important bills, among them the one subsequently enacted as Virginia's Statute for Religious Freedom, which broadly prohibited government establishment of religion and protected its free exercise. From 1779 to 1781, he served two 1-year terms as governor of Virginia; following his retirement from that office, he wrote the draft of *Notes on the State of Virginia,* his only book-length publication.

After a brief return as a Virginia delegate to Congress in 1783–1784, during which time he helped draw the plan for settling the West that was later enacted as the Northwest Ordinance, Jefferson was appointed to succeed Benjamin Franklin as minister to France in 1785. While residing in Paris from 1785 to October 1789, Jefferson witnessed firsthand the early events of the French Revolution and advised his friend the Marquis de Lafayette on the formation of a French constitution.

Although Jefferson was absent from the United States when the Constitutional Convention met in Philadelphia to adopt a new Constitution to replace the Articles of Confederation, he played a critical role in the Constitution's ratification during 1787–1789. Jefferson maintained neutrality in the ratification debates—calling himself "neither a Federalist nor an Anti-Federalist"—although he generally supported the new Constitution. Through his trans-Atlantic correspondence with James Madison and others, however, he helped push for the addition of a Bill of Rights, which he considered "necessary by way of supplement," to ensure that the national government would not abuse the powers granted it under the Constitution.

During the 1790s, Jefferson served as secretary of state during the presidency of George Washington and then, after a brief retirement from politics, as vice president of the United States during the presidency of John Adams. With his friend and collaborator James Madison, Jefferson headed the Republican Party opposition to the Federalist administrations of Washington and Adams. Among his many political writings during that decade were his opinion on the constitutionality of the bank bill (1791), which advised Washington that the Constitution does not empower Congress to charter a national bank; and the Kentucky Resolutions (1798), which Jefferson drafted anonymously in protest against the constitutionality of the Alien and Sedition Acts.

In the election of 1800, Jefferson's Republican Party won control of Congress and he was elected president, although a peculiarity in the electoral system resulted in a tie vote between Jefferson and his running mate, Aaron Burr, which threw the election into the House of Representatives. Jefferson regarded the Republican electoral victory of 1800 as a vindication of his party's principles and "as real a revolution in the principles of our government as that of 1776 was in its form." In his first inaugural address on March 4, 1801, although he was conciliatory, Jefferson nevertheless affirmed Republican principles, among them "a wise and frugal government which shall restrain men from injuring one another, [but] which shall leave them otherwise free to regulate their own pursuits."

As the third president of the United States (1801–1809), Jefferson for the most part succeeded in following those principles. His administration pursued a policy of economy in government, drastically reducing the size of the federal payroll, while also repealing all internal taxes. Critical of his predecessors' failure to respect the "chains of the Constitution" that restrained presidential powers, Jefferson refrained from exercising the veto power (which he believed should be used only against clearly unconstitutional legislation) and, as commander in chief during the Barbary War in the Mediterranean, ordered the navy to engage in defensive operations only until Congress authorized war. In an important symbolic move that set a precedent that lasted until Woodrow Wilson's presidency, Jefferson refused to personally deliver his annual message to Congress, instead sending it in writing. He regarded a personal address as too reminiscent of the British monarch's speech from the throne opening a new session of Parliament.

Perhaps the most noteworthy event of Jefferson's first term as president was the Louisiana Purchase, which doubled the size of the United States. Although Jefferson's critics, both past and present, have decried the Purchase as in violation of his strict constitutionalism, Jefferson opened himself up to the charge of hypocrisy by questioning the constitutionality of the Purchase and attempting to validate it explicitly by constitutional amendment, and thus "to set an example against broad construction"—an effort that he abandoned when his political advisors told him it was unnecessary and might jeopardize ratification of the treaty. More troubling as a precedent for broad federal power, however, was the embargo policy that Jefferson pursued during his second term in order to avoid U.S. involvement in the war between Britain and France. That policy failed, and conflict came during the presidency of his successor, James Madison, with the War of 1812.

Following his presidency, Jefferson again retired to Monticello, his Virginia mountaintop home, where he continued his keen interest in political matters through a voluminous correspondence. He encouraged the "Old Republicans," a group of radical Jeffersonians in Virginia, in their protest against a series of decisions by the Supreme Court that they believed threatened to consolidate power at the national level. Jefferson also advocated a system of public schools in Virginia, believing it necessary for the preservation of republican government that all citizens be sufficiently educated, particularly in history, so they can "know ambition" in all its forms.

A lifelong slaveowner who nevertheless repeatedly stated his abhorrence of slavery, Jefferson had an ambivalent record regarding the institution that was so incompatible with the principles he articulated in the Declaration of Independence. In his draft of the Declaration—in a passage deleted by the Continental Congress—he condemned slavery and denounced the British king for allowing the slave trade to continue. His 1776 draft of a constitution for Virginia prohibited the importation of new slaves; his 1784 report for Congress on the government of the Western territories proposed a ban on slavery and involuntary servitude, a proposal finally adopted in the Northwest Ordinance of 1787; and as president he signed into law a bill ending the importation of slaves into the United States in 1808, the first year the Constitution permitted Congress to do so. In his retirement years, however, he refused to publicly oppose slavery, maintaining that he was too old to fight such a battle; largely because of his indebtedness, he failed to manumit more than just a few of his own slaves.

Before his death on July 4, 1826—the 50th anniversary of the American Revolution—Jefferson wrote the epitaph for his own tombstone, asking to be remembered for only three achievements: his authorship of the Declaration of Independence, his authorship of the Virginia Statute for Religious Freedom, and his founding of the University of Virginia, the favored project of his twilight years.

DNM

See also American Revolution; Declaration of Independence; Revolution, Right of; Separation of Church and State; Slavery in America; Whiggism

Further Readings

Cunningham, Noble E., Jr. *In Pursuit of Reason: The Life of Thomas Jefferson*. Baton Rouge: Louisiana State University Press, 1987.

Malone, Dumas. *Jefferson and His Time*. 6 vols. Boston: Little, Brown, 1948–1981.

Mayer, David N. *The Constitutional Thought of Thomas Jefferson*. Charlottesville: University Press of Virginia, 1994.

Peterson, Merrill D. *Thomas Jefferson and the New Nation*. New York: Oxford University Press, 1970.

———, ed. *Thomas Jefferson: Writings*. New York: The Library of America, 1984.

Yarbrough, Jean M. *American Virtues: Thomas Jefferson on the Character of a Free People*. Lawrence: University Press of Kansas, 1998.

JOUVENEL, BERTRAND DE (1903–1987)

Bertrand de Jouvenel was a prominent French political philosopher, social scientist, and essayist whose writings covered a wide range of political and social thought. Born into a cultivated milieu—his father, Henri, was a distinguished French politician, diplomat, and journalist, and his mother, Sarah Boas, ran a celebrated salon—the young Jouvenel experienced the intellectual dislocations characteristic of the generation that came of age after the First World War. A famous journalist, he traveled widely and interviewed many of the principal actors on the world stage, including David Lloyd George, Churchill, and Hitler. In the 1920s and early 1930s, he tirelessly worked to promote Franco–German reconciliation. At the time, he identified with moderate socialist political currents. In the aftermath of the Great Depression, he became increasingly disillusioned with and discouraged by the inability of the established French political parties to address the problem of mass unemployment and to overcome debilitating partisan conflict. In 1936, he joined a radical right-wing party, the *Parti Populaire Francais* (PPF), headed by the ex-communist Jacques Doriot, which promised to revitalize France and overcome the political "decadence" of the French Third Republic. Jouvenel left the PPF in the fall of 1938 because of its support for the Munich Pact—Jouvenel had longstanding personal as well as political ties to the imperiled Czechoslovakian democracy.

Jouvenel's political oscillations in the interwar period and some questionable friendships at the beginning of the war helped create the impression that he had been some kind of collaborator during World War II. In fact, he joined the resistance in his native Corrèze in 1942 and fled to neutral Switzerland in 1943 with his second wife, Hélène, when the Gestapo became aware of his underground activities. It was during his Swiss exile that he wrote his best-known book, *Du Pouvoir* (*On Power*). The book, published in French in 1945 and in English in 1948, has become a minor classic and remains in print to this day. *On Power* marked Jouvenel's conversion to the sober conservative-minded liberalism that would define his thought for the next three decades or more. Jouvenel was the first major 20th-century French political thinker to rediscover the political wisdom of 19th-century French liberals such as Benjamin Constant and Alexis de Tocqueville. The work is at once a powerful indictment of the progressivist rejection of natural and divine limits and an impassioned chronicle of the rise of the modern, centralized state. It also can be understood as an implicit self-correction, a reaffirmation of "old verities" that Jouvenel seemed to have forgotten in his prewar impatience to address pressing social problems and that he had to relearn through bitter personal experience. The modern Minotaur, as Jouvenel called the centralizing state, sought to devour all those "spiritual authorities and of all those intermediate social forces which frame, protect, and control the life of man, thereby obviating and preventing the intervention of Power." Jouvenel's classically liberal critique of collectivism is rooted in a more thoroughgoing conservative rejection of what he understood as a radical species of rationalism. Such a rationalism is marked by the reduction of the human world to the twin poles of the individual and the state. Jouvenel's twofold concern with limiting state power and recovering the moral foundations of liberty would inform all of his writings in the postwar period.

Sovereignty, published in French in 1955 and in English in 1957, is the direct sequel to *On Power*. Like all of Jouvenel's postwar writings, *Sovereignty* freely draws on the writings of Greek and Roman antiquity, Christianity, and classical liberalism. It is arguably Jouvenel's most penetrating work of political philosophy. In it he attempted to redirect political science away from a narrow focus on legitimacy, on who exercises power, to a broader reflection on the nature of authority within free political communities. In this connection, he hoped to liberate the indispensable notion of the "common good" from its historical identification with the small, homogenous political communities recommended by political philosophers such as Plato and Rousseau. The common good is not an a priori concept to be imposed from above, but rather entails an ongoing effort to sustain social friendship within an open, dynamic society. In this way and others, Jouvenel mediated between the insights of ancient and modern philosophers. He opposes the conceit that the human will can ever provide the foundation of a humane and free moral and civic order, even as he rejected every effort to petrify society by creating a timeless political order freed from conflict. Jouvenel envisioned a society open to multiple private initiatives, but one where statesmen self-consciously aim to preserve the framework of civic trust.

Jouvenel was a charter member of the Mont Pelerin Society, the worldwide organization of intellectuals and economists founded in 1947 by F. A. Hayek to defend the free market and free society against its collectivist critics. He left the society in 1960, however, because of philosophical objections to what he regarded as its excessively libertarian orientation. However, his 1952 book, *The Ethics of Redistribution*, remains widely admired by libertarians and classical liberals. That work established an integral connection between government efforts at the redistribution of income and the unprecedented centralization of state power. It also argued that large-scale efforts at redistribution would radically transform the tenor of society, transferring influence from old aristocratic and bourgeois elites to a new soulless managerial class. Jouvenel's opposition to redistributionist projects was never tied to moral relativism in public policy or "public choice." As he put it in a 1960 essay, "the judgments we pass upon the quality of life are not mere expressions of individual fancy but tend to objective value, however approximately attained." He harbored fundamental doubts about the identification of the good life with the endless expansion of wealth and the satisfaction of all subjective desires. He therefore increasingly directed his attention to sustaining the amenities of life amid the materialist preoccupations of modern society. At the same time, he had no illusions about the ability of collectivism to produce a humane and free alternative to what he called "the civilization of power." In his later years, he became a commonsensical environmentalist, friendly to market solutions, and concerned with preserving a "home" worthy of man. He also wrote widely on "prevision," as in his 1967 book, *The Art of Conjecture*, because informed reflection on the future was essential to exercising prudent judgment under conditions of modernity. His last major work, 1983's *Marx et Engels: La Longue Marche*, examined the economic, philosophical, and political thought of Marx and Engels. Jouvenel's surprisingly sympathetic engagement with the thought of Marx disconcerted some of his conservative and classical liberal admirers. This work, however, finally took Marx to task for failing to do justice to the intimate connection between initiative in the intellectual realm and freedom in the economic realm. Jouvenel put forward an unambiguously negative judgment about Marx's political legacy: Marx's thought, he contended, "opens the road to despotic regimes, involuntarily but logically."

Jouvenel's mature reflections are rich and varied, irreducible to today's familiar ideological categories. All of his writings are united by a deep concern for reinvigorating social and constitutional restraints on "power," for revivifying the "social authorities" that "enframe" and "protect" the life of man, and by a bracing philosophical reflection on the requirements of the "common good" within an open, dynamic society.

DJM

See also Civil Society; Conservatism; Mont Pelerin Society; State

Further Readings

Jouvenel, Bertrand de. *Economics and the Good Life: Essays on Political Economy*. Dennis Hale and Marc Landy, eds. New Brunswick, NJ: Transaction, 1999.

———. *The Ethics of Redistribution*. Indianapolis, IN: Liberty Fund, 1990.

———. *Itinéraire (1928–1976)*. Presenté par Eric Roussel. Paris: Plon, 1993.

———. *On Power: The Natural History of Its Growth*. Indianapolis, IN: Liberty Fund, 1993.

———. *Sovereignty: An Inquiry into the Political Good*. Indianapolis, IN: Liberty Fund, 1997.

Mahoney, Daniel J. *Bertrand de Jouvenel: The Conservative Liberal and the Illusions of Modernity*. Wilmington, DE: ISI Books, 2005.

JUDICIARY

The judiciary is that branch of government charged with interpreting the meaning of laws and applying them to particular circumstances. In the English common law system inherited by the United States, the judiciary was traditionally divided into (a) courts of law, which judged cases by strict conformity to rules and could require wrongdoers to pay money damages; and (b) courts of equity, which could take special circumstances of particular cases into account and could order people to do certain acts or to refrain from them—the power of injunction. Although these two systems have long been merged in the judiciaries of the United States and most states, remnants of the old division remain (e.g., litigants are not entitled to a jury in cases traditionally considered matters of equity).

The common law judiciary relies on the litigants themselves (through their attorneys) to present facts to a neutral decision maker. This system differs from the Roman-inspired civil law system, which relies on inquisitorial courts empowered to investigate as well as decide. The great English jurist Sir Edward Coke considered this difference important for distinguishing the civil law system (which he considered tyrannical) from the common law system, which he saw as the heart of English liberty. More important, common law prohibited torture of witnesses, whereas the civil law system did not, and common law courts provided defendants with the protection of habeas corpus, which civil law did not. These important protections for individual rights were, however, frequently disregarded in his time and later.

A more famous judicial institution for protecting individual rights is the jury, which historically evolved from a team of advisors assembled to aid judges. In the famous *Bushnell's Case*, the English courts established that juries could not be punished for refusing to convict defendants. This case firmly established the principle of "jury nullification," which remains the law in the United States. Some libertarian writers contend that juries should be made more familiar with this power and should refuse to convict defendants charged under unjust laws, including drug laws. Others, however, contend that jury nullification is more commonly used in the service of racism or other popular prejudices because white juries routinely refused to convict white defendants for injuries to blacks during the Jim Crow era, and that it is unlikely that nullification would make a significant difference in the war on drugs.

The common law judiciary tended to see its role as the discovery and application of legal rules implied by existing statutes and practices or by the requirements of logic and human nature. Many natural rights-oriented libertarians continue to abide by this view. During the early 20th century, however, theorists who embraced "legal realist" jurisprudence contended that the judiciary is a policymaking branch of the government that makes, rather than discovers, the law, and does so in the service of social progress. Modern realists, including law and economics scholar Richard Posner, have contended that judges should devise rules to accomplish economically efficient outcomes. Other realists, of a more moralistic bent, such as Robert Bork, have argued that the judiciary should enforce socially created mores. Friedrich Hayek's view of the judicial role was a confused attempt to strike a middle course between these extremes. Judges should "maintain and improve" the system of social rules that have evolved through practice, he argued, and to "cope with new problems by the application of 'principles' [that they] distill from the *ratio decidendi* of earlier decisions, and so to develop these inchoate rules . . . that . . . will produce the desired effect in new situations." Yet he also acknowledged that on occasion judges would have to "improve the existing system by laying down new rules." Hayek's attempt to accommodate the acknowledged need for the "deliberate efforts of judges . . . [to] improve the existing system by laying down rules" into his broader critique of "rationalist constructivism" and his belief that judges ought to "maintain and improve a going order" and to "enforce expectations" is among the weakest parts of his political philosophy.

Montesquieu's pioneering work on the separation of powers, *The Spirit of the Laws*, held it to be essential that the judiciary be separated from the executive and legislative branches because an independent judiciary is such a powerful check against unilateral power. Indeed, during the 17th century, the Stuart monarchs of England diminished the independence of the judiciary by choosing judges sympathetic to the crown, discharging those who were not, and creating independent legal systems staffed by royal cronies. The most infamous of these courts was the secretive one known as Star Chamber, after the colorfully painted ceiling in the room where it met. Star Chamber dragged political and religious dissenters before it and would cut off their ears, among other mutilations, as punishment. Its abolition in 1641 was a milestone in the development of the common law.

The U.S. Constitution requires the separation of powers and bolsters judicial independence by providing judges with indefinite tenure—now an almost unique feature among written constitutions. This independence has led many to criticize the judiciary as an undemocratic threat to popular government. However, this critique ignores two fundamental principles: first, that the judiciary, like the other branches, possesses only the powers delegated to it by the people in their Constitution, and second, that the judiciary is empowered to defend the Constitution—which represents the true will of the people—against the encroachments of legislatures that at most represent only a temporary consensus among particular legislators. Thus, as Hamilton wrote in Federalist no. 78, the judiciary is not nullifying, but *affirming* the will of the people, when it declares a law void for contradicting the Constitution. It was for this reason that Justice Stephen Field described the Supreme Court as "the most democratic" of the branches of government: because the people of the United States, through their Constitution, have entrusted that branch with the duty to ensure that their legislators act only within the boundaries of the Constitution. In addition, the legislative and executive have powerful checks against the judiciary inasmuch as they are empowered to limit the courts' jurisdiction and to refuse enforcement to their decisions. These factors led the authors of the Federalist to call the judiciary the "weakest" branch of government, and such checks have been used frequently, as when Congress barred courts from reviewing challenges to military tribunals in the War on Terror, or when the Jackson administration, by refusing to enforce the Court's rulings in favor of the Cherokee tribe, precipitated the Trail of Tears. Critics of so-called judicial activism routinely ignore these factors and even argue that legislatures should be free to override court decisions or that courts should be stripped of their power to declare laws unconstitutional. This, however, would lead naturally to the legislature being the sole judge of its own powers. Thus, the critique of "judicial activism" is often an attack on constitutional government.

Despite the constitutional requirement of the separation of powers, many administrative agencies, although officially regarded as parts of the executive or legislative branches, frequently exercise judicial powers—by interpreting regulations and holding hearings—as well as executive power—by enforcing regulations—and legislative power—by drafting and revising rules. This blending of powers has been blessed by the Supreme Court, however, on the grounds that if some form of appeal to the courts remains available, such proceedings are compatible with the Constitution.

Although judicial powers are exercised by the judicial branch of government, there are many private market alternatives for dispute resolution. This is a throwback to the origins of the judiciary, which is rooted in the Law Merchant of the European maritime states of the Renaissance. This privately operated system provided a comprehensive means for resolving disputes and rendering judgments with regard to commercial law, and it was particularly useful for disputes crossing jurisdictional boundaries. Today, dispute resolution by such private organizations as the National Arbitration Forum or the American Arbitration Association gives consumers a choice that tends to be faster, cheaper, confidential, and conducted in layman's language. Arbitration also allows consumers to choose the operating rules for dispute resolution in a way that government courts do not. The Federal Arbitration Act of 1925 authorizes courts to enforce the decisions of private arbitrators, and federal courts have held that arbitration is a preferred method of resolving contractual disputes. The advent of the Internet also has opened a new field for private arbitration of disputes; organizations such as Virtual Magistrate and Square Trade have created for-profit, online arbitration systems for settling disputes between Internet users. As one commentator has noted, these systems tend not only to be faster and cheaper than government courts, and to avoid complicated jurisdictional issues, but they also tend to be more legitimate to online users who "are more likely to accept a system of law that evolves from the community it governs."

TMS

See also Common Law; Law Merchant; Liability; Montesquieu, Charles de Secondat de; Voluntary Contract Enforcement

Further Readings

Amar, Akhil Reed. *America's Constitution: A Biography*. New York: Random House, 2005.

Bell, Tom W. "Polycentric Law in a New Century." *Cato Policy Report* (November/December 1998).

Benson, Bruce L. *The Enterprise of Law*. San Francisco: Pacific Research Institute, 1990.

Bork, Robert. *Coercing Virtue: The Worldwide Rule of Judges*. Washington, DC: AEI Press, 2003.

Field, Stephen J. *Letter of Retirement*, 168 U.S. 713 (1897).

Hang, Lan Q. "Online Dispute Resolution Systems: The Future of Cyberspace Law." *Santa Clara Law Review* 41 (2001): 856–866.

Hayek, Friedrich. *Law Legislation and Liberty: Volume 1. Rules and Order*. Chicago: University of Chicago Press, 1973.

Levin, Mark. *Men in Black: How the Supreme Court Is Destroying America*. Washington, DC: Regnery, 2005.

Sandefur, Timothy. "The Wolves and the Sheep of Constitutional Law: A Review Essay on Kermit Roosevelt's The Myth of Judicial Activism." *Journal of Law and Politics* 23 no. 1 (2007): 1–40.

Sturgis, Amy H. *The Trail of Tears and Indian Removal*. Westport, CT: Greenwood Press, 2006.

Ware, Stephen J. "Arbitration under Assault: Trial Lawyers Lead the Charge." *Cato Institute Policy Analysis* no. 433 (April 18, 2002).

K

KANT, IMMANUEL (1724–1804)

Immanuel Kant is generally considered to be one of the most important philosophers of all time. His philosophy is often described as the culmination of the Enlightenment, providing a synthesis of rationalism and empiricism. His work is highly systematic, spanning most areas of philosophy. Kant's theories had and continue to have a huge impact on many areas of philosophy. He is generally seen as a classical liberal, and he inspired and influenced many libertarian scholars, such as F. A. Hayek. Kant was much concerned with freedom and the prevention of coercion. His categorical imperative gives rise to a deontological ethical system. He argued that there are absolute constraints on what people are morally allowed to do. Certain kinds of actions are prohibited, and individuals have correlative negative rights that entitle them not to be interfered with in certain ways. These rights demarcate a sphere of noninterference and, hence, may be classified as absolute side constraints in the sense described by Robert Nozick. Although Kant's ethical system is congenial to libertarianism, his political philosophy, while assigning a significant role to freedom, is at times at odds with classical liberalism. However, arguably these aspects of Kant's political theory do not follow from his moral philosophy.

Kant believes that there is an objective standard of right and wrong that holds universally. His account of right and wrong, however, differs radically from most other ethical theories because it is not based on the commands of God, on some supposed teleological purpose of nature, on self-interest, on moral sentiments, or on a substantive conception of human nature. Rather, it is based on reason. For Kant, the moral law is a law of reason.

In the *Groundwork of the Metaphysics of Morals*, Kant sets out to identify the supreme principle of morality. That principle is the categorical imperative, which constitutes the centerpiece of Kant's ethical theory. Kant's argument begins with an analysis of the concept of the good will. According to Kant, the only thing that has unconditional worth is a good will. The worth of everything else is in some way dependent on the worth of a good will. Now a good will is understood as a will that acts out of duty. Acting out of duty has to be distinguished from acting in accordance with duty. The latter amounts to an action conforming to what duty commands, which, for Kant, is not sufficient for moral worth. Rather, for an action to be moral, the agent has to do the right action because it is right. That is, the rightness or morality of the action must feature in the motivation of the agent. It is not sufficient that he acts in a way that happens to be the right way. This argument would be too contingent and would make morality a matter of chance. Instead, there must be an internal connection insofar as the rightness of the action is the reason for the action. Kant then identifies acting out of duty with acting out of respect for universal law.

The most famous formulation of the categorical imperative is what is usually known as the "formula of universal law," which states: "I ought never to act except in such a way that I could also will that my maxim should become a universal law." The categorical imperative binds, as its name suggests, categorically and unconditionally. That is, its commands are binding on us in and of themselves. It tells us what to do, and its validity is not dependent on any desires or ends that we might have. There is no contingency involved. As such, it sharply differs from hypothetical imperatives that are only hypothetically binding, that is, binding on the condition that certain ends are willed. The commands of the categorical imperative also have categoricity, and the constraints that they impose are absolute. It does not admit of what has been called a *utilitarianism of rights* because the rights that it confers cannot be outweighed by the rights of other persons or by considerations of utility. Accordingly, it leads to a deontological moral system involving an understanding of rights as absolute side constraints on actions. The key idea that is embodied in the categorical imperative is the idea of universalization. It is a formal principle that tests maxims to assess whether they are universalizable, ruling out those maxims as inadmissible that fail this procedure.

Another formulation of the categorical imperative is the formula of humanity, which states: "so act that you use humanity, whether in your own person or in the person of any other, always at the same time as an end, never merely as a means." This variant emphasizes not so much the formal nature of moral maxims, but rather the value of rational beings. There is a natural equality of human beings, deriving from the fact that they all possess the faculty of reason and are all capable of moral action. There is no natural hierarchy. Instead, every rational being possesses dignity. This dignity places important constraints on how we can treat other people. We have to respect their dignity and rationality, which implies that we cannot use them as mere means toward the achievement of our ends. Rather, we have to respect their rationality and treat them as ends in themselves. That is, we have to respect that they are autonomous agents who have their own ends to pursue.

These formulae of universal law and humanity, taken together, give us the "formula of the kingdom of ends." "Act in accordance with the maxims of a member giving universal laws for a merely possible kingdom of ends." This formula represents the combination of both the form and matter of morality. Although the idea of a universal law captures the form of morality, namely that it holds universally and with necessity, the idea of humanity provides the matter or end of morality insofar as it is rational beings who possess value, can act morally, and impose constraints on the actions of others. The idea of a kingdom or realm of ends integrates these two elements to give us a complete specification of the moral law. Moreover, it provides an inspiring ideal that can be understood as the state of affairs that would arise if everyone were to follow the commands of morality and toward the achievement of which we should continuously strive.

In the *Metaphysics of Morals*, Kant identifies two aspects of practical philosophy, namely the "doctrine of right" and the "doctrine of virtue." The former is concerned with enforceable duties that are owed to other people and that bring with them correlative rights. Everyone to whom these duties are owed has a claim on us. Enforceability is restricted to negative duties. We have a narrow core of enforceable morality, combined with a wide base of ethical duties. Coercion can only be legitimately used when it comes to enforcing negative duties and upholding their correlative negative rights. Actions are assessed regarding their conformity to the laws, and external conformity is all that is demanded. Someone who follows the law purely out of self-interest without any regard to morality is behaving in a manner completely consistent with right. This notion is contrasted with virtue, which does not just require external conformity, but also takes into account the reasons for which we perform actions. Motivations matter for virtue, and an action is only virtuous if it was done because it was the right action.

Kant argues that the state exists to protect the freedom of the individuals, as well as to uphold right and property. There are no substantive ends that the state should achieve. Human interests and needs, and consequently socioeconomic factors, are not to be taken into consideration. Rather, the understanding of state activity is purely procedural and formal. It is lawfulness and universality that determine the concept of right. The state should only be concerned with the external sphere of action, with how people behave toward each other, ensuring that they do not interfere with each other's external freedom. Individuals should enjoy complete inner freedom. Anything that does not impact on the freedom of other people, such as a person's interests, needs, beliefs, and convictions, is to be left untouched by the state. Government has no business whatsoever in telling people what to do with their lives except insofar as it affects the freedom of others. Kant is strongly opposed to any form of paternalism. As we have noted, the distinction between acting in accordance with duty and acting out of duty is central to Kant's ethics. Only the latter way of acting has moral worth. Hence, morality is only possible through freedom; it cannot be imposed from the outside, but must be freely chosen. Virtuous behavior cannot and should not be coerced or enforced. Liberty, considered as the absence of coercion, is thus a precondition of autonomy and moral agency.

Kant provides a defense of private property rights while also critiquing Locke's theory that property arises from the mixing of one's labor with the natural world. According to Kant, anything that does not have a will can be treated as a mere means and can be utilized for achieving the ends of rational beings. Any limitations on human actions must derive from the formal law of reason. Thus, the private acquisition of external goods is justified or authorized to the extent to which it is universalizable. This universalizability requires that acquisition be such as to make general relations of property possible, which for Kant implies the need for an institutionalization of property. Authorized appropriation thus implies that the property rights must be confirmed by a judicial or legislative procedure in which the universal agreement of all those who are affected is given. Prior to such confirmation, property rights are only subjectively justified, but they are not yet objectively determined. Thus, there is a need for a state to render property rights determinate. Property rights must be given a fixed and determinate standard by positive law that is legislated by the state and that represents the agreement of the general will.

Although this theory of right is in general in broad agreement with some of the key tenets of classical liberalism, there are certain illiberal strands in Kant's thought. In particular, there is the noteworthy fact that Kant argues that there is no right to revolution. Individuals have rights against the rulers, but these are unenforceable. The prohibition on revolution is absolute, and reform is supposed to be peaceful and gradual. Active resistance against a political regime is not permitted under any circumstances. In this respect, Kant strongly diverges from Lockean and even Hobbesian political theory. Another feature that appears to contravene liberal doctrine is the restriction of full political membership to self-sufficient persons, that is, to property owners. This idea clashes with the universalism that is advocated by classical liberals and that features so strongly in Kant's ethical thought. This restriction is symptomatic of a more general clash between the radical conception of morality and human nature that Kant advocates in his ethical writings and his rather submissive attitude toward politics, which results from the fact that what happens in practice usually does not match up to Kant's highly rationalistic understanding of the state. Arguably, these illiberal tendencies do not follow from his philosophical system, but rather can be seen as personal prejudices and ad hoc additions that even conflict with his ethical commitments. That is, these problematic features partly derive from Kant's failure to consistently turn his ethical theory into a political theory, rather than being integral to his thought.

In his well-known pamphlet, *Toward Perpetual Peace*, Kant argues that the highest political good is perpetual peace. It is a utopian aim that we can and should try to approximate. States have a duty to leave the international state of nature and enter a world republic in the same way that individuals who find themselves in a state of nature have a duty to enter into a political state. Such a world republic is an ideal that is practically unattainable. Kant argues that it can nonetheless be approximated and that a pragmatic substitute for it consists in a free federation of states that submit to international laws to ensure a condition of permanent peace. Peace among nations requires, according to Kant, that certain internal conditions obtain within the different states. That is, lasting external peace between states presupposes certain political arrangements of states. In particular, Kant thinks that states should have a republican form of constitution because he believes that states are more likely to be peaceful if they have representative governments.

RMB

See also Enlightenment; Hayek, Friedrich A.; Individual Rights; Nozick, Robert; Peace and Pacifism; State

Further Readings

Allison, Henry E. *Kant's Theory of Freedom*. Cambridge and New York: Cambridge University Press, 1990.
Kant, Immanuel. *Practical Philosophy*. Cambridge and New York: Cambridge University Press, 1996.
Korsgaard, Christine. *Creating the Kingdom of Ends*. Cambridge and New York: Cambridge University Press, 1996.
Kuehn, Manfred. *Kant: A Biography*. Cambridge and New York: Cambridge University Press, 2001.
O'Neill, Onora. *Constructions of Reason: Explorations of Kant's Practical Philosophy*. Cambridge and New York: Cambridge University Press, 1990.
Williams, Howard, ed. *Essays on Kant's Political Philosophy*. Chicago: University of Chicago Press, 1992.
———. *Kant's Political Philosophy*. New York: St. Martin's Press, 1983.
Wood, Allen W. *Kant's Ethical Thought*. Cambridge and New York: Cambridge University Press, 1999.

KIRZNER, ISRAEL M. (1930–)

Israel M. Kirzner, a British-born economist and theorist, is associated with the Austrian School and was a student of Ludwig von Mises. He has been an important academic representative of the Austrian School of Economics in America, holding a professorship of economics at New York University from 1957 to the present. He is the author of many books, including *Competition and Entrepreneurship* (1973) and *The Meaning of Market Process* (1992).

Kirzner received an MBA from New York University (NYU) in 1955. While pursuing that degree, he came across Ludwig von Mises's seminar; under Mises's influence, he decided to pursue a career in academic economics instead of accountancy as he had originally planned. In 1957, Kirzner became one of a handful of students to pursue and receive his doctorate in economics under Mises.

Kirzner taught at NYU throughout the 1960s and early 1970s without any larger Austrian presence or program at the school. By the mid-1970s, however, with interest in Austrian theory growing—to a large degree thanks to seminars that Kirzner helped develop under the auspices of the Institute for Humane Studies—fellow Austrian School economist Ludwig Lachmann became attached to the department. Soon, with outside funding, an Austrian program developed at NYU and a series of weekly colloquia in Austrian economics held there has become a central gathering point for economists interested in the Austrian tradition. Under Kirzner's leadership, many other Austrians have taught at NYU, although only one other besides Kirzner, Mario Rizzo, has gained tenure.

Kirzner's first book, *The Economic Point of View*, was a work of intellectual history that traced the development of the concepts of economics as a human, praxeological science in the Misesian style. Kirzner also has written extensively explaining and extending Austrian capital theory. His essays, aimed at the mainstream of economic thought, tended to emphasize important differences between the Austrian tradition and the neoclassical mainstream, and how Austrian insights provided a more profound understanding of the real-world process of markets. In an edited collection called *The Crisis in Economic Thought* (1982), he wrote:

> [M]odern mainstream economics displays a number of related features which, for Austrians, appear as serious flaws. These features include especially: a) an excessive preoccupation with the state of *equilibrium;* b) an unfortunate perspective on the nature and role of *competition* in markets; c) grossly insufficient attention to the role (and subjective character) of *knowledge, expectations,* and *learning* in market processes; and d) a normative approach heavily dependent on questionable *aggregation* concepts and thus insensitive to the idea of *plan coordination* among market participants. Together these flaws represent very serious distortions, at best, in the understanding of market process in capitalist economies which modern neoclassical economics is able to provide.

Kirzner emphasized the market as a process, where individuals with differing knowledge pursuing their subjective values increased their knowledge and helped coordinate their plans and expectations. Much of his writing concerned the role of the entrepreneur, whom Kirzner noted was not simply a businessman, but any person trying to make the world conform to his hopes and expectations. Humans try to discover opportunities for profit, those areas where people have not yet come to realize they can buy low and sell high. New opportunities for entrepreneurs to profit by their alertness to things others have not noticed always arise. In doing so, they not only satisfy themselves but also help bring other people what they want, and they tend to move toward an equilibrium where everyone has what they want and there is no longer reason to trade. But because of the constantly shifting nature of reality and people's knowledge and desires, this equilibrium beloved by neoclassical economists is never reached. In the Hayekian tradition, Kirzner viewed the market "as a social instrument for mobilizing all the bits of knowledge scattered throughout the economy." The entrepreneurial role is to be alert to the relevant bit of information that will satisfy others' needs better and move toward equilibrating everyone's plans and expectations.

Kirzner was one of the least political of the Austrian economists, writing little on matters of public policy or political philosophy, despite having served for many years as a trustee of the libertarian educational organization, the Foundation for Economic Education, and considering himself a libertarian. But Kirzner thinks that entrepreneurial discovery gives property rights over any resultant profit in a Lockean homesteading sense—by first discovering an opportunity, you gain rightful property in it. He even extended this theory to one member of a group in a desert who is first to find a water hole—the first discoverer should have full property rights in the water, Kirzner believed.

Kirzner's emphasis on the entrepreneur's role in coordinating the market process and discovering relevant and useful information has its libertarian political implications. Kirzner's entrepreneur is most effective at finding profit opportunities (which are opportunities to satisfy others) through chance, undeliberate learning in a free economy. Free markets, in Kirzner's view, thus generate the greatest quantity of profit-generating and market-equilibrating entrepreneurial action.

BDo

See also Economics, Austrian School of; Entrepreneurship; Mises, Ludwig von

Further Readings

Kirzner, Israel M. *Competition and Entrepreneurship.* Chicago: University of Chicago Press, 1973.
———. *The Economic Point of View.* Princeton, NJ: Van Nostrand, 1960.
———. *Market Theory and the Price System.* Princeton, NJ: Van Nostrand, 1963.
———. *The Meaning of Market Process: Essays in the Development of Modern Austrian Economics.* London: Routledge, 1992.
———. *Perception, Opportunity, and Profit: Studies in the Theory of Entrepreneurship.* Chicago: University of Chicago Press, 1979.

KLEPTOCRACY

Kleptocracy is that form of government by which government officials routinely engage in theft or confiscatory policies. Although in familiar political discussions kleptocracies are taken to be corrupt versions of the range of acceptable variations of government forms, libertarian political science suggests that nearly all governments are, in fact if not in intent, much closer to kleptocracies than one would at first suppose. This conclusion is implied by "public choice" theory developed by James Buchanan and Gordon Tullock in their famous work, *The Calculus of Consent.* Buchanan, together with Tullock, were the prime movers in developing this area of economics. As a consequence, Buchanan received the Nobel Prize in economic science in 1986.

Public choice theory is predicated on the assumption that everyone pursues his or her own private objectives—sometimes problematically referred to as *self-interest*—and that when someone enters what is widely called *public service,* this assumption applies no less there than it does when someone enters the market place. The crucial difference is that in the marketplace, at least in nonmonopolistic enterprises, most of us meet with fairly stringent budgetary constraints—if our goods or services do not sell well, if our creditworthiness dries up, if our stored capital dissipates, we will need to discontinue the pursuit of our objectives and turn to different, profitable pursuits. In the public service, however, these standard constraints do not hold or, if they do, it is to a far lesser degree. Budgets can be increased by a variety of means—increased taxation, the borrowing and printing of money, and so forth—thus making it easy for public servants, so called, to pursue their objectives and follow their agendas, whatever these may be. (I hesitate to call these their private objectives *self-interest* because in some cases public servants actually pursue objectives that do not appear to be their own, but rather those of other parties, among them the goals of their constituencies. However, although some economists dispute that concerns directed toward other groups are even possible, there seems good reason to believe that in some cases this is likely.)

If we understand public choice theory correctly, it follows that nearly all governmental activities have a significant element of kleptocracy about them. They obtain their funds without the consent of those who generated or rightly own them. Although the term *thievery* is commonly used in descriptions of kleptocracy, a broader term from a libertarian perspective would be *extortion*.

There are many who dispute that such characteristics are inherent to government. They often argue that the libertarian idea that individuals have the right to private property and that all wealth in a free and just society should be privately held is misguided. Rather, they maintain, wealth is a social product that belongs to the society as a whole. Although private parties—individuals, companies, and organizations of all kinds—may hold society's wealth, they do not actually own it. They are permitted to hold it by government, but government has the proper authority to reclaim part of that wealth via taxation. This contention was espoused by Liam Murphy and Thomas Nagel in *The Myth of Ownership* and Stephen Holmes and Cass Sunstein in *The Cost of Rights*.

Libertarians dispute this attempted justification for the collective ownership of wealth and instead regard governments that pretend to own society's wealth as kleptocracies, wherein "the management of public funds is designed to primarily sustain the personal wealth and political power of government officials and their cronies." Libertarians argue that wealth is created by individuals, sometimes with ease, sometimes with great difficulty, and individuals have the right to hold and trade what they thus rightfully own. The theory of property rights is a fundamental tenet of libertarian thought. Although there is no complete consensus about how property should properly be originally allocated, most embrace Locke's view that it has its origin in mixing one's labor with the items found in nature. Libertarians also point to the fact that those who champion the idea that governments are the rightful holders of society's wealth as returning to the monarchical conception of ownership, wherein the monarch is the ultimate owner of everything in the realm. In this view, subjects merely rent whatever property they use either in their trade or as their residence. It is just this monarchical viewpoint, however, that was challenged during the American Revolution and rejected as a principle of the new nation.

Needless to say, the claim that nearly all governments are kleptocracies is a controversial one, and even some libertarians allow that a government, properly restrained via a well-crafted constitution, could avoid the evils of a kleptocracy. Indeed, many socialists have argued that, inasmuch as private property is a fiction, so only collective ownership of wealth is possible, and this collective ownership must be administered by a group of individuals who appear to be acting in their own interests, but are in fact making use of wealth they are entrusted to manage as they deem proper. If this management follows proper procedures, as specified in, say, a supposedly viable theory, such as democratic socialism, then what libertarians regard as kleptocratic is, in fact, simple ordinary macroeconomic public finance.

Probably the most brazen case of kleptocracy in the traditional sense, where government is in the hands of thieves, is evident in some postcommunist countries. Here there is hardly any pretense at following constitutional edicts or the rule of law. Instead, what is evident is widespread cronyism among those who possess sheer coercive power in light of having been in the employ or a chief in one or another of the enforcement agencies in the former communist regimes. Armed with their coercive power, such individuals can amass wealth that is not theirs (e.g., by nationalizing private enterprises). Sometimes the discovery of vast reserves of natural resources, such as oil, facilitates the kleptocratic nature of governments because they are able to establish monopoly power over such resources and trade them in the global economy as if they legitimately owned them. These states offer nothing more than an extensive system of improper takings by some in a society of the wealth of others without recourse to even the flimsiest of legal rationales.

TM

See also Communism; Corruption; Eminent Domain/Takings; Public Choice Economics; Welfare State

Further Readings

Conquest, Robert. *Harvest of Sorrow: Soviet Collectivization and the Terror-Famine*. New York: Oxford University Press, 1986.

Epstein, Richard A. *Takings: Private Property and the Power of Eminent Domain*. Cambridge, MA: Harvard University Press, 1985.

Meredith, Martin. *Mugabe: Power, Plunder, and the Struggle for Zimbabwe*. Philadelphia: Perseus Group, 2007.

Rose-Ackerman, Susan. *Corruption and Government: Causes, Consequences, and Reform*. New York: Cambridge University Press, 1999.

Tullock, Gordon. *Public Goods, Redistribution and Rent Seeking*. Northampton, MA: Edward Elgar, 2005.

KNIGHT, FRANK H. (1885–1972)

Frank Hyneman Knight was born in McLean County, Illinois, and was educated at small denominational colleges in Tennessee. Knight received a BS and an MA from the University of Tennessee in 1913, before going on to Cornell University to pursue a PhD in philosophy. After being rebuffed by the philosophy faculty, Knight enrolled in the department of economics, where he completed his doctoral dissertation titled "A Theory of Business Profit" in 1916. Published with significant revisions under the title *Risk, Uncertainty and Profit* (1921), this work develops the crucial distinction between rent, or the legitimate and predictable return on a business share, on the one hand, and profit, which is the product of entrepreneurial risk-taking in an environment of uncertainty, on the other hand. Although this book remains a classic of neoclassical economic theory, virtually all of Knight's subsequent work combines a respect for the legitimate explanatory power of economics with a philosopher's skepticism about its ethical and methodological limitations.

Knight also is remembered for two influential collections of articles and papers, *The Ethics of Competition* (1935) and *Freedom and Reform* (1947), reflecting two different periods of his career. The majority of the essays in the first volume were written during the 1920s while Knight was a professor of economics at the University of Iowa. In essays like "The Ethics of Competition" and "Ethics and the Economic Interpretation," Knight was highly critical of the "apologetic economics" of his day. Because the free-market system of prices rests only on the factual coincidence of supply and demand, which are products of the economic system, it can never be defended as ethical. His second, methodological complaint is that insofar as neoclassical economics treats preferences as static or given, it cannot speak to the pluralistic motivations and aspirations of real persons. In attempting to remedy what he saw as the reductionism of neoclassical economics, Knight turned to the writings of German institutional thinkers, particularly Max Weber. Knight's translation of Weber's *General Economic History* (1927) was the first of Weber's major works to appear in English.

Knight's interest in developing an American institutionalist economics was the primary motive behind his appointment as professor of economics at the University of Chicago in 1927, where he taught until his retirement in 1952. Along with his colleague, Jacob Viner, Knight is regarded as one of the formative influences on the Chicago School of Economics. Among Knight's students during his early years at Chicago were Milton Friedman, George Stigler, Henry Simons, Aaron Director, and, later, James Buchanan. Knight also was a major influence on the sociologist Edward Shils, who attended Knight's lectures on Max Weber while at Chicago. In addition to the profound influence he was to have on particular students, Knight's textbook, *The Economic Organization* (1933), was used as a basic text in the social sciences at Chicago for a number of years. Knight never endorsed the Chicago School's later positivism or the public choice application of rational actor models to political behavior, but he is widely cited as a major influence among American free-market economists in the latter half of the 20th century. In the aftermath of World War II, Knight gathered with F. A. Hayek and other postwar defenders of liberty at the first meeting of the Mont Pelerin Society. He also was one of the cofounders of the Committee on Social Thought at Chicago in 1945.

Knight's reputation as a classical liberal thinker stems mainly from his writings of the late 1930s and 1940s, many of which are collected in the volume *Freedom and Reform*. Knight objected just as strenuously to the New Deal's economic reforms as he had to the laissez-faire apologists of the 1920s. The essays comprising *Freedom and Reform* center on four main themes. The first concerned the vogue for social experimentation and economic planning, about which Knight complained bitterly. Even if we could agree on what should be done for the betterment of society, what he characterized as the insurmountable value problem, social reforms, Knight maintained, always come at the cost of some measure of human freedom, clearly a value worthy of respect. Second, he noted the implicit tension between the unchecked workings of the free market and the moral and sociological underpinnings necessary for the maintenance of democratic government, or what Knight called *government by discussion*. Third, Knight was simultaneously fascinated and repelled by the social ethics of Christianity. While acknowledging that the religious instinct was natural to human beings, he criticized attempts to derive social justice from the Christian gospels and dismissed natural law philosophies as the "last refuge of a bigot." Finally, rather than defending freedom for its anticipated benefits, whether economic or social, Knight's preference for limited government was based on a profound skepticism about the frailties of human nature and the "sickness of liberal society." He defended freedom for its own sake with no illusions about the uses to which flawed human beings might choose to put their liberty. Knight's other major works include a third collection of papers *On the History and Method of Economics* (1956), as well as *The Economic Order and Religion* (with Thornton W. Merriam, 1945) and *Intelligence and Democratic Action* (1960).

RBo

See also Economics, Chicago School of; Interventionism; Mont Pelerin Society; New Deal; Welfare State

Further Readings

Boyd, Richard. "Frank H. Knight and Ethical Pluralism." *Critical Review* 11 (Fall 1997): 519–536.

Emmett, Ross B. "Frank H. Knight (1885–1972): A Bibliography of His Writings." *Research in the History of Economic Thought and Methodology* (Archival Supplement 9): 1–100.

———. "'What Is 'Truth' in Capital Theory? Five Stories Relevant to the Evaluation of Frank Knight's Contribution to the Capital Controversy." *New Economics and Its History.* John B. Davis, ed. (Annual Supplement to *History of Political Economy*, vol. 29). Durham, NC: Duke University Press, 1997. 231–250.

Knight, Frank H. *The Ethics of Competition and Other Essays.* New Brunswick, NJ: Transaction Publishers, 1997.

———. *Freedom and Reform: Essays in Economics and Social Philosophy.* Indianapolis, IN: Liberty Press, 1982.

———. *Risk, Uncertainty, and Profit.* Boston: Houghton, Mifflin, 1921.

L

LA BOÉTIE, ÉTIENNE DE (1530–1563)

Étienne de La Boétie was a French political theorist and author of the *Discourse of Voluntary Servitude*. He received his law degree from the University of Orléans in 1553, and the heady atmosphere of free inquiry that persisted there provided an inspiring milieu for La Boétie, who wrote this essay there at the age of 21. The *Discourse* so impressed essayist Michel de Montaigne that he sought out La Boétie in 1559; they remained good friends until La Boétie's untimely death. Although La Boétie never penned another comparable political piece, he wrote poetry and was a distinguished judge and diplomatic negotiator. Like Montaigne, he did not apply the principles of the essay to his personal life, instead remaining a loyal subject of the French monarchy. When radical Huguenots published an incomplete version in 1574, Montaigne, who hated them, was incensed and tried to salvage La Boétie's reputation as a conservative. One scholar even claimed that it was Montaigne who really wrote the essay because of the similarity of style, but the evidence, according to the intellectual historian Nannerl Keohane, is not convincing.

The *Discourse* was unlike any existing political essay. A call for mass civil disobedience and defense of liberty, it not only questioned the legitimacy of authority over others, including elected rulers, but dared to ask why people consent to their own enslavement by political authority. Terror and force were not enough to enforce obedience, La Boétie argued. He called for people to resist oppression not through bloodshed, but by withdrawing their consent. "Resolve to serve no more and you are at once freed." The tyrant "has indeed nothing more than the power that you confer upon him to destroy you. . . . How would he dare assail you if he had not cooperation from you?"

Foreshadowing modern research in the social psychology of obedience, La Boétie asserted that people do not simply obey out of fear. Rather, people obey out of habit, short-sighted self-interest, greed, and love of privilege or through the influence of state tricks, propaganda, and symbols. "Let us therefore admit that all those things to which he is trained and accustomed seem natural to man." Stanley Milgram, author of the classic *Obedience to Authority*, concurs, considering La Boétie's thoughts on the psychological foundations of authority to be highly insightful.

La Boétie, the libertarian Murray Rothbard has argued, "was the first theorist of the strategy of mass, non-violent civil disobedience of State edicts and extractions." Although the *Discourse* is not an anarchist document, it was an important intellectual precursor to anarchism and civil disobedience, inspiring Tolstoy, German anarchist Gustav Landauer, and the writers of the French Revolution. Although Rothbard considers his tone pessimistic—La Boétie believed people have come to love their servitude—he sees a note of hope in the essay. People become used to servitude; once it is thrown off and the bulwark of habit removed, tyranny may be difficult to reestablish. The masses may not be willing, but a few clear thinking individuals may save it: "Even if liberty had entirely perished from the earth, such men would invent it."

SP

See also Coercion; Conscience; Montaigne, Michel de; Revolution, Right of

Further Readings

Keohane, Nannerl O. "The Radical Humanism of Étienne de La Boétie." *Journal of the History of Ideas* 38 no. 1 (January–March 1977): 119–130.

La Boétie, Étienne de. *The Politics of Obedience: The Discourse of Voluntary Servitude*. Introduction by Murray Rothbard. New York: Free Lifte Editions, 1975.

LABOR UNIONS

The libertarian principle on which the legitimacy of labor unions depends is freedom of association. Any person has a natural right to associate with any other person or group for any purpose that does not trespass against the natural rights of third parties and provided the relationship is voluntary. Conversely, any person has a natural right to refrain from association with any other person or group no matter how fervently the other parties may desire the association. Labor unions that respect each person's freedom of association are legitimate. American labor unions, formed and operated under the National Labor Relations Act (NLRA), are not. There are several reasons for this fact, but three are especially important.

First, the NLRA forbids workers individually to choose whether a union represents them in bargaining with employers about terms and conditions of employment. Instead, a union is granted monopoly bargaining ("exclusive representation") privileges over all the employees of an enterprise whenever a majority of those employees votes for monopoly bargaining. A union that wins such a "certification election" represents all the workers who voted for the union, which is legitimate. However, the union also represents workers who voted against the union as well as those who did not vote. Individuals are forbidden to represent themselves. If a union represents you, you are associated with it. If you do not consent to the association, your freedom of association is violated.

Defenders of monopoly bargaining justify it by appeal to democracy. We choose our congressional representatives by majority vote; so, the defenders claim by analogy, it is proper to choose our workplace representatives in the same manner. But this analogy is specious. Forcing a numerical minority to concede to the will of a numerical majority might be an appropriate decision in questions that are inherently governmental such as the election of congressional representatives. Such force, however, is never justified in the private sphere of human action, such as the purchase and sale of one's labor services. Moreover, the analogy is incomplete. Under the NLRA, a union that wins a certification election never has to stand for reelection.

Second, under the NLRA, a certified union can force all the workers it represents to pay fees for its representation services. These fees are called *union security*. It is legitimate for a union to charge those members who entered it voluntarily for its services, but it is not legitimate to force those who do not want the union to represent them to pay for its services. When you are forced to accept representation services you do not want, your freedom of association is denied. When you also are forced to pay for these services that you do not want, the trespass against you is compounded.

Defenders of union security justify these forced membership dues by appeal to the free-rider argument. They say

that the NLRA forces a certified union to represent all the workers who were eligible to vote in the certification election. Therefore, when a union is successful in bargaining for better terms and conditions of employment, all workers, not just voluntary union members, receive those gains. If the other workers are not forced to pay for the union's bargaining services, they would receive union-generated benefits for free, and that, the defenders argue, would be unfair. The counterargument is obvious. If unions represented only the members who voluntarily elect to be represented, there would be no free-rider problem. Union-generated benefits would accrue only to the workers they represent. This free-rider problem does not emerge from the inherent nature of employment relationships; it is an artifact of the NLRA.

Moreover, many workers consider themselves to be forced, not free, riders. A forced rider is one who receives net harms from some collective action and is nevertheless forced to pay the perpetrators for their activities. Whether a union bestows net benefits or net harms on a worker can only be revealed by the choices he makes as he exercises his freedom of association.

Third, under the NLRA, employers are forced to bargain in good faith with certified unions. The good-faith requirement means that an employer may not extend any take-it-or-leave-it offers. The only sure defense an employer has against a charge of failure to bargain in good faith is a record of making concessions. Parties to bargaining are associated with each other, thus forced bargaining is forced association. No one should be forced to bargain over any issue, and parties who agree to bargain should not be forced to make concessions during the process.

In summary, libertarians believe that each individual worker must be free to choose whether to be represented by a union prepared to represent him, by some other willing third party, or by representing himself. Each union must be free to choose which workers it agrees to represent, nor may any union, which represents only its voluntary members, force any union-free workers to pay any fees for any alleged services of any kind. Employers and unions representing voluntary members may choose to bargain and come to agreements based on mutual consent, but they may not be forced to bargain with each other. These relationships are the only ones consistent with a society of free individuals entering into free associations.

ChB

See also Capitalism; Charity/Friendly Societies; Civil Society; Rent Seeking; Voluntarism

Further Readings

Baird, Charles W. *Liberating Labor: A Christian Economist's Case for Voluntary Unionism*. Grand Rapids, MI: Acton Institute, 2002.
———. "Toward Equality and Justice in Labor Markets." *The Journal of Social, Political and Economic Studies* 20 (1995): 163–186.

Dickman, Howard. *Industrial Democracy in America.* LaSalle, IL: Open Court, 1987.

Epstein, Richard A. "A Common Law for Labor Relations: A Critique of the New Deal Legislation." 92 *Yale L.J.* 1357 (1983): 1357–1408.

Machan, Tibor R. "Some Philosophical Aspects of National Labor Policy." *Harvard Journal of Law and Public Policy* 4 (1981): 67–160.

Reynolds, Morgan O. *Power and Privilege: Labor Unions in America.* New York: Universe Books, 1984.

LAISSEZ-FAIRE POLICY

Modern economies can be categorized by three kinds of economic policies. The first is one in which the government owns the means of production, or socialism. The second is marked by substantial government regulation, or interventionism, where the government leaves production to the private sector, but tries to shape market outcomes with subsidies, taxes, licensing, price and quantity restrictions, standards of quality, safety, and health, nonwaivable worker and consumer rights, and other measures. The third is the free market, or laissez-faire, where private property rights and freedom of contract alone provide the framework for the interaction among the many firms, consumers, and workers that comprise the economy. The relationship between libertarianism and laissez-faire is a simple one: Laissez-faire is *the* libertarian position on economic policy. Although most who regard themselves as libertarians admit exceptions, even the most moderate embrace a laissez-faire economy as the benchmark of a free society.

There can be little doubt that a commitment to laissez-faire is the most distinctive and controversial aspect of the libertarian program, at least in the democracies of North America and Western Europe. Although support for civil liberties is hardly unanimous in these countries, libertarian positions on personal freedom have considerable support from nonlibertarians across the political spectrum, and particularly from the left. In contrast, even in the United States, with a political culture that has traditionally been most market-friendly, laissez-faire economic policy has few adherents. The politicians most critical of state ownership and regulation are primarily opponents of more state ownership and regulation, rather than proponents of the radical privatization and deregulation measures a true laissez-faire system would require.

Although laissez-faire has often been equated with disorder and even lawlessness, this equivalence is, in fact, a caricature put forward by its critics. As Ludwig von Mises observed, "The alternative is not plan or no plan. The question is whose planning? Should each member of society plan for himself, or should a benevolent government alone plan for them all?" Laissez-faire is as much defined by what it forbids as by what it allows. Under laissez-faire, it

would at once be legally permissible to use one's own property however one desires and legally forbidden to use that property to harm others or to employ the property of others without their consent. Similarly, it would be legal for parties to make almost any voluntary contract they desired involving their own property and illegitimate to violate such a contract. In summary, a policy of laissez-faire entails that individuals and voluntarily formed groups would have the liberty to use their own property, singly or conjointly, in any way they choose, always provided that they did not infringe these same rights of others.

Deontological arguments against laissez-faire are numerous and well known, appealing to the free markets' incompatibility with egalitarian and democratic principles. However, there also are deontological arguments in support of laissez-faire, most of which fall into three categories. The first rests on the fact that people are morally entitled to the fruits of their labor and that income redistribution and "positive rights" like the "right to an adequate pension when one reaches the age of sixty-five" amount to a politer form of slavery. The second is that economic freedom deserves the same respect as does personal freedom, consequences aside. Using the notion of sexual autonomy as a simile, Robert Nozick famously noted that, "The socialist society would have to forbid capitalist acts between consenting adults." The third argument is predicated on the fact that the deontological critics of laissez-faire are altogether inconsistent. Few egalitarians want to equalize incomes on the international level, and perhaps even fewer insist on equalizing friendship or sex.

Consequentialist cases for and against laissez-faire, for the most part in the form of cost-benefit analysis (or, in economic terminology, "Kaldor–Hicks efficiency") are remarkably well developed. The efficiency case against state ownership is now widely accepted, intellectually if not politically. Bureaucrats lack the financial incentives to satisfy consumers and minimize costs, they face severe knowledge problems, and they have low rates of innovation. Even if state funding has efficiency advantages, at best questionable, these advantages do not require state ownership. Admittedly, only a minority of economists would favor significant privatization in a country like the United States, but this view often stems from a bias in support of the status quo, rather than because they accept that the government operations are more efficient than are their private alternatives.

The primary efficiency debate is now between proponents of laissez-faire, on the one hand, and some form of intervention, on the other hand. Sophisticated critics of laissez-faire, such as Joseph Stiglitz, Paul Krugman, and Robert Frank, would agree that many forms of government intervention, among them price controls, entry restrictions, and high marginal tax rates, are typically inefficient. However, they would still insist that much government regulation is rational because of its efficiency, pointing to the commonly accepted list of market failures: externalities and public goods, monopoly and imperfect competition, and imperfect information.

Defenders of laissez-faire have offered four types of response to this criticism. The first is to deny that the critics are applying market failure concepts appropriately. The second is that markets are much more able to handle genuine market failures than critics realize. The third is that interventionist policies are almost invariably ineffective or even counterproductive ways to deal with market failure. The fourth is to draw attention to a parallel list of political failures to show that, even when promising opportunities for efficiency-enhancing intervention, governments customarily choose inefficient policies.

Externalities and public goods are probably the most misused of the arguments supporting market failure. Education has been widely classified as a public good, but it is not clear what benefits that accrue from one's education individuals cannot be internalized. Those people who acknowledge this point often make vague appeals to the benefits education has in sustaining a viable democracy. However, if these benefits exist, they are probably of only marginal significance. Public goods arguments for social security, worker safety regulations, and health care for noncontagious ailments are similarly strained.

Efficiency complaints about monopoly and imperfect political competition rest on particularly weak theoretical grounds. When economies of scale are large relative to the size of the market, efficiency requires imperfect competition. Moreover, in many oligopoly models, firms act no differently from perfect competitors, and the same holds for monopolists, who, although seemingly in a monopoly situation, in fact face potential competition.

To take a final case, markets can function well even with low levels of information. So long as information is symmetrically distributed, the standard results essentially still apply.

The market can often take care of market failures given time or in the absence of government restraint. Many externality problems stem from government ownership of lands, waterways, wildlife, airwave frequencies, and the like, and they could be readily solved by privatization. Other externalities can be handled with bargaining between affected parties, as Ronald Coase emphasized. Collusion and predation, the primary problems associated with imperfect competition, similarly face effective market checks and would probably be rare even if they were legal. Imperfect information problems can be solved by investing in firm reputation; simply allowing firms to adjust prices for observable risk can often eliminate inefficiencies associated with asymmetric information.

Government solutions to problems occasioned by externalities often intensify the problem: Drug laws, for example, amplify the crime and health externalities that supposedly

justify prohibition. Antitrust probably remains the best example of government policy with perverse efficiency effects. Antitrust laws provide a rationale for forbidding mergers with large potential cost savings and allow inefficient firms to sue more successful rivals for anticompetitive practices. In general, these policies act as a tax on market leaders. Most interestingly, as the antitrust laws have undergone interpretation, one of the few business strategies free of legal risk is often to charge high prices. Similarly, much insurance regulation that economists rationalize in terms of imperfect information intensifies the problem by making it more difficult to tailor prices to risk.

Even in the rare instances where efficiency-enhancing government policies are feasible, will they actually be implemented? Defenders of laissez-faire often appeal to "public choice theory," which emphasizes that politicians and bureaucrats are self-interested actors who respond to political clout, not economic efficiency. Democracy is a weak check at best: Political information and economic understanding are public goods that individual voters have little incentive to supply. Giving government the power to "subsidize goods with positive externalities," for example, sparks wasteful competition for government support (rent seeking) among rival lobbies. The winners tend to be the best-connected political players, not industries with particularly large externalities.

More generally, all of the problems that interventionists find in markets—externalities, monopoly, imperfect information, and so on—can and do also appear in the political arena. Combining this realization with other doubts about intervention yields a strong consequentialist presumption for simply accepting market failures, rather than trying to correct them through the political mechanism.

Efficiency is not the only consequentialist measure of interest. Most philosophers minimally would correct for the marginal utility of income. Here again, however, the consequentialist reply in favor of laissez-faire also applies. Many supposedly redistributive programs like spending on education, social security, and Medicare actually tend to increase income inequality. Redistributive programs aimed at the poor have large negative side effects: Aside from the obvious impact on work and family structure, welfare programs provide a rationale for harming the world's poorest with stricter immigration restrictions. Simple public choice considerations—in particular, that the poor are unlikely to be successful rent seekers—again bolster the case for simply accepting income inequality, rather than using state action to improve upon it.

There are cases where what constitutes a laissez-faire policy is difficult to ascertain. Air pollution can be understood as a property rights invasion, but human beings exhale carbon dioxide onto one another simply by living. Likewise, all "capitalist acts between consenting adults," as Nozick terms them, may be legal, but when does a person become an adult? In other cases, laissez-faire policy is clear, but proves disturbing, as a number of David Friedman's hypothetical scenarios show. Still occasional ambiguities and fanciful counterexamples are at most mild impediments to laissez-faire as a practical policy regime. The more important question is, what role for government is compatible with laissez-faire? If the literature concerning market failure is unable to make its case, the anarcho-capitalist position certainly should suggest itself as an alternative.

BC

See also Capitalism; Competition; Interventionism; Natural Harmony of Interests; Socialism

Further Readings

Friedman, David. *Hidden Order: The Economics of Everyday Life.* New York: HarperBusiness, 1996.
Friedman, Milton. *Capitalism and Freedom.* Chicago: University of Chicago Press, 1982.
Landsburg, Steven. *The Armchair Economist: Economics and Everyday Life.* New York: Free Press, 1993.
———. *Fair Play.* New York: Free Press, 1997.
Mises, Ludwig von. *Human Action.* New Haven, CT: Yale University Press, 1966.
Nozick, Robert. *Anarchy, State, and Utopia.* New York: Basic Books, 1974.
Rand, Ayn. *Capitalism: The Unknown Ideal.* New York: Signet Books, 1967.
Rothbard, Murray. *For a New Liberty: The Libertarian Manifesto.* New York: Libertarian Review Foundation, 1978.
———. *Power and Market: Government and the Economy.* Kansas City, MO: Sheed Andrews & McMeel, 1977.
Shleifer, Andrei. "State versus Private Ownership." *Journal of Economic Perspectives* 12 no. 4 (1998): 133–150.

LANE, ROSE WILDER (1886–1968)

Rose Wilder Lane was born in 1886, the first child of Almanzo and Laura Ingalls Wilder; the latter was the author of the *Little House on the Prairie* series. Her parents would later become famous thanks to the book series, originally written by her mother and vastly reworked and edited by Lane herself. Whereas her mother was known for provincial tales of wilderness family life, Lane became famous as a sophisticated world traveler and outspoken divorcée. As a reporter, columnist, and author, Lane became interested in the issues of free trade and individual rights, especially as viewed against the backdrop of world events. She was one of several highly visible libertarian women writing in the first half of the 20th century.

After a pioneer upbringing that included a cross-country trip in a horse-drawn hack from Dakota Territory to the Ozark Mountains of Missouri, Rose Wilder moved to California and began writing for the *San Francisco Bulletin*. There she met and married Claire Gillette Lane, whom she divorced 9 years later. By then she had published short stories and nonfiction articles in such magazines as *The Ladies Home Journal*, *Harper's Monthly*, and *The Saturday Evening Post*. She ghostwrote *White Shadows on the South Seas* for Frederick O'Brien, and penned the novel *Diverging Roads* and the book *The Making of Herbert Hoover* under her own name.

It was her work as a reporter for the American Red Cross that introduced Lane to the world beyond the United States. Following World War I, she visited the war-torn countries of Europe and wrote about the conditions she found there; her works from this era include *The Peaks of Shala* and *Travels with Zenobia*, about her experiences in Albania. Her beliefs about individual rights and limited government found full voice in her reports from overseas. Her political themes became more subtle and her subject far less exotic when she returned to the United States and helped her mother with *Little House in the Big Woods* and the resulting *Little House* series. Although Laura Ingalls Wilder sometimes chafed at her daughter's hands-on approach to editing, which included adding completely new passages at will, Lane midwifed the books to best-seller status. Today, the series is considered a children's classic as well as a clever study on the ideas of frontier individualism, morality, and liberty. Lane followed these books with her own novels such as *Free Land*.

Lane's personal manifesto, *The Discovery of Freedom: Man's Struggle against Authority*, appeared in 1943. The year was a noteworthy one, as it also heralded the publication of Ayn Rand's *The Fountainhead* and Isabel Paterson's *God of the Machine*. Together, Lane, Rand, and Paterson formed the first wave of libertarian women writing in the 20th century.

In *The Discovery of Freedom*, Lane sketched a historical and geographic overview of the cause of liberty from "The Old World" through "the third attempt" at freedom, namely the American experiment after the War of Independence. After indicting the communistic and feudal systems of the past, Lane explored the meaning of constitutionalism and republicanism, often returning to what she viewed as the fundamental right of property. "It is a legal right," Lane wrote of property, "absolutely essential to an individual's exercise of his natural rights." Lane argued that, in the "daring aim of the Revolution" or the defense of property rights, the colonials hit on the cornerstone of the later U.S. system and the reason for its success. Her views on the crucial importance of private property and a government circumscribed by strict limits were underscored by her visit to the Soviet Union, where, unlike so many writers of the period, she was appalled. She ended her passionate volume on a positive note, saying, "Americans are fighting a World War now because the Revolution is a World Revolution. Freedom creates this new world, that cannot exist half slave and half free. It will be free."

Lane not only touched the public with her writing, but she also cultivated minds with her friendship. For the 25 years following *The Discovery of Freedom*, Lane tested and expanded her political and economic thought through long correspondences with Ludwig von Mises, Robert LeFevre, Hans Sennholz, and Frank Meyer. In addition, Jasper Crane, the eminent businessman, also enjoyed a robust correspondence with Lane, and these letters were eventually published in 1973 under the title *The Lady and the Tycoon*.

Lane's political involvement continued throughout her life, from protests against the social security system to reports from Vietnam as a war correspondent. She died on October 30, 1968, while planning yet another trip to Europe. HarperCollins Publishers has immortalized her childhood in a spin-off series of *Little House* books. Those interested in libertarian ideas best remember her, however, as the author of *The Discovery of Freedom*. Scholar and author Albert Jay Nock attested to Lane's influence when he said of her most powerful work, "When it comes to anything fundamental, Mrs. Lane never makes a mistake. She is always right. In this respect her book is really remarkable."

AmS

See also Mises, Ludwig von; Nock, Albert Jay; Paterson, Isabel; Rand, Ayn

Further Readings

Holtz, William V. *The Ghost in the Little House: A Life of Rose Wilder Lane*. Columbia: University of Missouri Press, 1995.

Lane, Rose Wilder. *The Discovery of Freedom: Man's Struggle against Authority*. 50th anniversary ed. San Francisco: Fox & Wilkes, 1993.

MacBride, Roger Lea, ed. *The Lady and the Tycoon: The Best of Letters between Rose Wilder Lane and Jasper Crane*. Caldwell, ID: Caxton, 1973.

LAO TZU (C. 600 B.C.)

Lao Tzu (the "Old Philosopher") is thought to have been an older contemporary of Confucius and arguably the first libertarian. In the *Tao Te Ching* ("The Classic of the Way and Its Virtue"), Lao Tzu discusses the relations among the individual, the state, and nature. Like 18th-century liberals,

he argued that minimizing the role of government and letting individuals develop spontaneously would best achieve social and economic harmony.

In 81 short chapters (less than 6,000 words), Lao Tzu sets out his vision of good government and a good life. At the center of his thoughts were the principle of *wu-wei* (nonaction or nonintervention) and the notion of spontaneous order. In chapter 57, he sums up the core of his liberal views:

> The more restrictions and limitations there are, the more impoverished men will be. . . . The more rules and precepts are enforced, the more bandits and crooks will be produced. Hence, we have the words of the wise [the sage or ruler]: Through my non-action, men are spontaneously transformed. Through my quiescence, men spontaneously become tranquil. Through my non-interfering, men spontaneously increase their wealth.

This passage, written more than 2,000 years before Adam Smith's call for a "simple system of natural liberty," is a reminder that China's greatest legacy is not the oppressive state experienced under Mao Zedong's thought, but the potential for a free and open society embodied in Lao Tzu's thoughts. Although Lao Tzu did not fully develop a theory of the spontaneous market order, as did F. A. Hayek, he clearly recognized the importance of limited government and voluntary exchange for wealth creation. The manifest implication of his views is that an overly intrusive government necessarily politicizes economic life and increases what Frédéric Bastiat was later to call *legal plunder*.

The corruption that plagues China today stems from too much, not too little, intervention. When people are free to choose within a system of just laws that protect life, liberty, and property, socioeconomic harmony naturally follow, and this spontaneous order can only evolve from decentralized market processes.

Government, to be good, must be in harmony with each person's desire to prosper and to expand his range of choices. By emphasizing the principle of nonintervention, Lao Tzu recognized that when governments leave people alone, then, "without being ordered to do so, people become harmonious by themselves." Thus, he understood, at least implicitly, that central planning generates social disorder by destroying economic freedom. When coercion overrides consent as the chief organizing principle of society, the natural way of the Tao and its virtue (*Te*) will be lost to the heavy hand of the state and its power.

Disorder arises when government oversteps its bounds—that is, when it overtaxes and denies people their natural right to be left alone to pursue their happiness, as long as they do not injure others. Lao Tzu argued that taxes, not nature, were the primary cause of famine: "When men are deprived of food," he wrote, "it is because their kings [rulers] tax them too heavily." Likewise, he recognized that rulers could easily destroy the natural harmony that people cherish by destroying their liberty: "When men are hard to govern, it is because their kings interfere with their lives."

Mao's destructive policies during the "Great Leap Forward," which abolished private property, imposed central planning, and led to the imposition of crippling taxes on farmers in the form of compulsory grain deliveries, caused mass starvation between 1958 and 1962. The "Great Helmsman's" disregard for private property and human rights still haunts China. Conflicts between developers and farmers over land-use rights are the cause of much social turmoil in present-day China. Although land-use rights have been extended, the government has refused to allow full-fledged privatization, which would undermine the Chinese Communist Party's power. The internal passport (*hukou*) system also interferes with individual freedom and leads to economic inefficiency.

Freedom requires some boundaries or rules if it is to be socially beneficial and not lead to chaos. Lao Tzu understood the need for rules, but, unlike later liberals, he did not develop the ideas of private property and freedom of contract that undergird a liberal market order. Hong Kong's motto "Small government, big market" is in tune with Lao Tzu's conclusions. His advice to China's early rulers remains pertinent: "Governing a large country is like frying a small fish. You spoil it with too much poking."

China's present leaders are calling for a harmonious society, but, as Lao Tzu understood, such a society is impossible without widespread individual freedom and a rule of law that limits the power of government to the protection of persons and property.

JAD

See also Freedom; Liberty in the Ancient World; Limited Government; Natural Harmony of Interests; Spontaneous Order

Further Readings

Becker, Jasper. *Hungry Ghosts: Mao's Secret Famine*. New York: Henry Holt/Owl Books, 1998.

Chan, Wing-Tsit. *A Source Book in Chinese Philosophy*. Princeton, NJ: Princeton University Press, 1963.

Chang, Chung-yuan. *Tao: A New Way of Thinking*. New York: Harper & Row/Perennial Library, 1977.

Dorn, James A. "China's Future: Market Socialism or Market Taoism?" *Cato Journal* 18 (Spring/Summer 1998): 131–146.

Fung, Yu-lan. *A History of Chinese Philosophy: Vol. 1. The Period of the Philosophers*. 2nd ed. Derk Bodde, trans. Princeton, NJ: Princeton University Press, 1952.

Mitchell, Stephen. *Tao Te Ching*. New York: HarperCollins/HarperPerennial, 1991.

Schwartz, Benjamin I. *The World of Thought in Ancient China*. Cambridge, MA: Harvard University Press, 1985.

Las Casas, Bartolomé de (1474–1566)

Bartolomé de Las Casas, a historian and strong advocate of human rights, was born in Seville, Spain. He studied in Seville and at the University of Salamanca, and in 1502 he went to America. For a decade, he developed a large mining and agricultural operation in Hispaniola (the island shared by Haiti and the Dominican Republic) with labor from Indian slaves. He also was involved in the conquest of Cuba, for which he was awarded a large land grant. In 1512, he became a priest, but it was not until 1514, while he was preparing a sermon, that he changed his views. He decided to return his slaves and devote his life to the justice of the Indians.

Las Casas became the most famous propagandist of American Indian rights and a champion of human rights. He did not always champion objectivity, prudence, and truth. His lengthy *Apologetic History* attempted to show that American Indians were superior in virtue and reason not only to Spaniards but also to ancient Greeks and Romans. His utopian attempt to create a colony using free labor ended in dismal failure.

He achieved fame after his death with the publication of his *Destruction of the Indies*, an indiscriminate attack on a segment of the Spanish leadership. Soon after it first appeared as an appendix to his *Apologetic History*, the book was promoted by the enemies of Spain. During the following century, it was translated into six European languages in more than 50 editions. This widespread republication gave rise to the "Black Legend," which showed an exaggerated view of the negative aspects of the Spanish conquest of America. During the early part of the 19th century and at the end of the 20th century, his writings again became popular, for the most part employed as propaganda in support of certain social issues. In the 19th century, they were used to encourage the emancipation of native peoples, and at the end of the 20th century, in Chiapas, the region of Las Casas's bishopric, an insurgent movement encouraged a selective focus on Las Casas's writings. These writings were pushed by supporters of liberation theology, who, unlike Las Casas, favored socialism and neglected Las Casas's orthodox Christian doctrines.

Las Casas's views on economics are less known. The Dominicans who settled in Hispaniola were the first to call for free trade in the American colonies and also were great champions of private property. In 1537, in a response to the Dominicans, Pope Paul III affirmed the rights of the Indians to liberty and property.

Las Casas's struggle for the oppressed did not call for socialism, but for giving the natives the same rights to private property, free trade, and freedom of conscience that most Dominicans were seeking for the Spaniards.

Spaniards living in the New World could only trade with the motherland and also were banned from trading with other colonies.

Las Casas, in contrast, is an unlikely figure given his fame as a champion of individual rights inasmuch as he was an orthodox Catholic. He did not depart from his creed, which today would be regarded as radically conservative in values and religion, while his views on economics were close to those of classical liberalism. However, Las Casas's self-adulatory but engaging propagandist style and rhetorical skills, in addition to his indiscriminate attack on powerful figures of his day, lent his writings to those who later sought to manipulate the public. By manumitting his slaves and foregoing a search for economic or social power, he lent credibility to his popular, yet sometimes exaggerated, accounts.

AIC

See also Imperialism; Racism; Rights, Natural; Slavery, World; Scholastics/School of Salamanca

Further Readings

Hanke, Lewis. *All Mankind Is One: A Study of the Disputation between Bartolomé de Las Casas and Juan Gins de Sepulveda in 1550 on the Intellectual and Religious Capacity of the American Indians.* DeKalb: Northern Illinois University Press, 1974.

Watner, Carl. "'All Mankind Is One': The Libertarian Tradition in Sixteenth-Century Spain." *Journal of Libertarian Studies* 2 no. 8 (Summer 1987): 293–309.

LAW AND ECONOMICS

Economists have long offered insight into the law. With respect to libertarianism and the analysis of the market, Nobel laureate Friedrich von Hayek's definitive works *The Constitution of Liberty* and *Law, Legislation, and Liberty* applied crucial insights from the Austrian School of Economics to legal issues. On the left, John R. Commons of the University of Wisconsin, in his *The Legal Foundations of Capitalism* (1921) and other works, applied economic analysis to legal institutions. A number of other economists also have dealt with legal issues, among them Nobel laureate Gary Becker's pioneering work on issues centering on discrimination and family law. During the 1960s and 1970s, however, a group of scholars went beyond simply applying economic insights to legal issues and developed a body of work that became the known as the *law and economics* movement. The emergence of this movement was one of the most important developments in 20th-century legal thought. Indeed, Professor Ian MacNeil, despite being critical of many aspects of the movement, called law and economics

"the most powerful single monofocused discipline in American legal studies." Largely associated with the University of Chicago during its early days, scholars who have centered their study on the interrelationship between law and economics today apply a variety of methodologies to bring the tools of economic analysis to bear on legal issues.

Two individuals dominated this movement. Ronald Coase, who was awarded the Nobel Prize in 1991, and author of a pathbreaking article in the field, "The Problem of Social Cost," is often credited with initiating this approach in 1960. He was quickly joined by University of Chicago law professor Richard Posner, who is currently a judge on the U.S. Court of Appeals for the Seventh Circuit. Posner, through numerous articles and books and his definitive treatise, the *Economic Analysis of Law*, has played a major role in expanding the parameters of the field.

Coase's contribution cannot be understated. "The Problem of Social Cost," one of the most often cited articles in both economics and law, laid most of the intellectual groundwork for many of later developments in the field. Coase wrote the article as a response to the earlier work by A. C. Pigou, which was crucial in structuring modern welfare economics. In the 1920s, Pigou pioneered the analysis of market failures and focused on the most appropriate means of correcting these failures. For example, where a firm polluted a river with waste water, thus imposing costs on downstream users, the appropriate response had been to create a tax on waste water that brought the firm's private costs into line with the social costs of its behavior. Pigouvian solutions are correspondingly heavily reliant on central government intervention. Coase's analysis, in contrast, focused on the allocation of property rights. If downstream entities held a right to receive unpolluted water, they would be in a position to then use the legal system to force the upstream polluter to pay damages or stop to polluting. The solution to "market failures" thus lay with better definition of property rights, not corrective taxes.

Equally important, Coase took his analysis a step further by showing that, at least in economic terms, the precise allocation of property rights was irrelevant to the parties involved reaching a solution. Nor does it matter if property rights are allocated to the upstream polluter or to the downstream user because in either case having a clear property right would produce an equally efficient solution. If the gains from polluting the river outweighed the harms done to the downstream user, the two parties would be able to negotiate a transfer of the rights to the polluter regardless of where the right originated. If the costs of the pollution were to outweigh the gains, the inverse would hold true. The problem was thus reciprocal and not one-sided.

Finally, and most significant, Coase used these insights to argue that where transaction costs (e.g., the cost of hiring negotiators, drafting agreements, etc.) were zero, the same solution would result regardless of who was initially allocated the property right. Although Coase never explicitly formulated these conclusions in exactly this way, the fact that the assignment of property rights has distributional consequences is frequently referred to as the "Coase Theorem." Transaction costs are of course not zero in the real world, something of which Coase was fully aware. Nonetheless, the insight is significant because Coase's analysis pointed toward our understanding of transaction costs and how they may be reduced, in opposition to the Pigouvian preoccupation with calculating optimal taxes.

Richard Posner's contribution is no less significant than is Coase's. Drawing together the still relatively sparse body of law and economics scholarship in 1972, the first edition of the *Economic Analysis of Law* systematized thinking in the field and helped spark a dramatic increase in the breadth and depth of scholarship. Posner brought to the study of law and economics an emphasis on positive, theoretical analysis of individual behavior. Posner also can be credited with developing an explicit philosophical basis for the law and economics movement. Further, Posner has played a major role in developing the argument that the common law has proved itself economically efficient.

Like a new religion, the movement's success led to the development of distinct denominational subgroups. Three major subgroups warrant particular mention. One, often associated with a number of faculty members of the Harvard Law School, developed sophisticated mathematical models of legal issues. In many ways, this group of scholars mirrored developments in the economics profession in general, where increasing mathematicization brought both technical sophistication and raised concerns about the relevance of the work to real world issues. One of the most astute scholars in this group, Professor Steven Shavell, summarized their insights into tort law with his 1987 book, *The Economic Analysis of Accident Law*.

A particularly apt example is Shavell's identification of the problem of optimal activity levels in negligence cases. Traditional negligence tort rules hold a defendant liable only when the defendant failed to take a reasonable level of care to prevent harm. Because these rules do not take into consideration whether the defendant should have engaged in the risky activity at all, they tend to underdeter harm-causing activities. In contrast, strict liability rules require defendants to pay for all the harm they cause and so do not suffer from this problem.

Another group of scholars have employed econometric and other empirical techniques to examine the predictions of economic theory relating to legal institutions. For example, Brent Mast, Bruce Benson, and David Rasmussen have applied econometric techniques to criminal justice issues. In one article, they examined the impact of civil forfeiture laws on police activity. They found that, throughout the 1980s and 1990s, states increased the ability of law enforcement agencies to seize property in connection with allegations of illegal activity, most often in connection with drug prohibition. Using data on police activity and differences in state forfeiture laws, the authors demonstrated that when police departments were able to keep larger proportions of seized property, they increasingly diverted law enforcement activity into those areas. In another major work in this area, Yale Law School Professor Robert Ellickson used detailed examination of individual behavior among Shasta County, California, residents to test the Coase Theorem.

Finally, a third group draws on the Coasian tradition and emphasizes property rights in their researches. Often termed *new resource economists* or *free-market environmentalists*, this group has emphasized ways in which the creation and allocation of property rights can solve problems ranging from overgrazing of public lands to the inefficient allocation of water rights. Terry L. Anderson and Don R. Leal's *Free Market Environmentalism* epitomizes this approach. Work in this tradition tends to be less focused on the heavily mathematical models and more concerned with explaining how real institutions function.

Law and economics analysis often supports libertarian conclusions. Benson has taken a careful look at the economics of the criminal justice system and argues that market forces are capable of substituting for most state activity in this area. Despite conclusions of this nature, however, there are significant differences between rights-based libertarian thought and law and economics. The most prominent of these divergences is the strongly utilitarian basis that underpins the conclusions drawn by law and economics analysis. The research done by Posner and his followers particularly tends toward utilitarian justifications for legal rules. Both law and economics scholars and libertarians, for example, are likely to agree that freedom of contract promotes economic well-being. In cases where a model suggests that it does not, however, a law and economics adherent might be willing to trade liberty for prosperity, whereas a libertarian is unlikely to agree to this. This distinction is well illustrated by the differences in approach between Judge Posner and his University of Chicago colleague professor Richard Epstein. Epstein's work more consistently favors liberty over utility.

The impact of law and economics can be gauged by comparing it to a parallel development in law that arose on the left in the 1970s. The critical legal studies movement developed at roughly the same time and had considerable influence on the legal academy in its early years. By the mid-1980s, however, the "crit" movement had fractured into racial, sexual orientation, and gender subgroups (critical race theory, gay and lesbian legal theory, and feminist legal theory), none of which has managed to exert a serious influence on the development of legal studies.

AM

See also Coase, Ronald H.; Economics, Chicago School of; Externalities; Judiciary; Posner, Richard A.; Rule of Law

Further Readings

Anderson, Terry L., and Donald R. Leal. *Free Market Environmentalism*. San Francisco: Pacific Research Institute for Public Policy, 1991.

Barzel, Yoram. *Economic Analysis of Property Rights*. Cambridge: Cambridge University Press, 1989.

Benson, Bruce L. *The Enterprise of Law: Justice without the State*. San Francisco: Pacific Research Institute for Public Policy, 1990.

Coase, Ronald. *The Firm, the Market and the Law*. Chicago: University of Chicago Press, 1988.

Ellickson, Robert. *Order Without Law*. Cambridge, MA: Harvard University Press, 1991.

Mast, Brent D., Bruce L. Benson, and David W. Rasmussen. "Entrepreneurial Police and Drug Enforcement Policy." *Public Choice* 104 nos. 3–4 (2000): 285–308.

Posner, Richard A. *Economic Analysis of Law*. 5th ed. Boston: Little, Brown, 1998.

Shavell, Steven. *Economic Analysis of Accident Law*. Cambridge, MA: Harvard University Press, 1987.

LAW MERCHANT

Lex mercatoria, or the "Law Merchant," refers to the privately produced, privately adjudicated, and privately enforced body of customary law that governed virtually every aspect of commercial transactions by the end of the 11th century. Thus, the Law Merchant provides libertarians with an important example of effective law without coercive state authority.

Rapid expansion in agricultural productivity during the 11th and 12th centuries meant that less labor was needed to produce sufficient food and clothing for Europe's population. The effect of this increase in production was that individuals were able to specialize in particular crafts and population began to move into towns, many of which rapidly became cities. Specialization effectively functions only with trade and the class of professional merchants expanded to facilitate such trade. These merchants spoke different languages and came from different cultures. However, although geographic distances often prevented direct communication, let alone the building of strong personal bonds that would facilitate trust, the effect of this increased trade across large distances required numerous middlemen to move products from producers to their ultimate consumers. All of this activity generated mistrust among merchants. Internationally recognized commercial law arose as a substitute for personal trust. As one historian has pointed out, it was during this period "that the basic concepts and institutions of ... *lex mercatoria* ... were formed, and,

even more important, it was then that [this] ... law ... first came to be viewed as an integrated, developing system, a *body* of law."

The Law Merchant developed within the merchant community, rather than through government fiat; the police power was not the source of incentives to recognize its rules. Indeed, the Law Merchant was a voluntarily recognized body of law willingly embraced by its adherents. The reciprocity necessary for voluntary recognition arose, in part, from the mutual gains generated by repeated exchange. Furthermore, each merchant traded with many other merchants, so the spread of information about breaches of commercial conduct would affect a merchant's reputation for all his subsequent transactions. Indeed, the Law Merchant was ultimately backed by the threat of ostracism by the merchant community at large because individuals known to engage in illegal behavior would not have found trading partners.

Merchants also established their own courts. One crucial reason for doing so was that royal courts often were not prepared to enforce customary merchant practices and usage (e.g., royal courts would not recognize contracts that involved interest charges because these courts regarded all interest as usurious). In addition, merchant court judges were merchants chosen from the relevant trading community (whether from a fair or a market), whereas lawyers and royal judges often had no knowledge of commercial issues. The effect was that the risk of an inefficient ruling was substantially lower in a merchant court, particularly when highly technical commercial issues were involved. Additionally, merchants traditionally had to complete their transactions during a brief period, at one market or fair, and then quickly move on to the next. The need for speed and informality in settling disputes was unmet when confronting judges who had no knowledge of commercial issues.

Where the participants to a dispute found, because of conflicting local customs, that alternative rules might apply, those practices that proved to be the most conducive to facilitating commerce often supplanted those that were less effective. When new conditions arose that were not clearly covered by an existing rule, the scope of existing rules was expanded to encompass the new conditions or an entirely new rule was devised. The mechanism by which legal change was introduced was through agreement of the parties involved. Another mechanism for change was dispute resolution. In either case, the new rule only applied to the parties directly involved who had agreed to the rule. If others saw these changes as useful, they adopted them in future interactions. In this matter, rules spread through a process of voluntary acceptance.

The Law Merchant underwent considerable change in a relatively short time. One commentator has noted that, "a great many if not most of the structural elements of the modern system of commercial law were formed in this period." By the 12th century, commercial law in Europe provided foreign merchants with substantial protection "against the vagaries of local laws and customs," and by the early 13th century, the Law Merchant clearly was a universal, integrated system of principles, concepts, rules, and procedures. Indeed another reason for the use of merchant courts was that royal judges would not or could not adopt new rules as fast as the rapidly changing commercial system required. From 1000 to 1200, and especially from 1050 to 1150, the rights and obligations of merchants in their dealings with each other "became substantially more objective and less arbitrary, more precise and less loose." After all, no one would voluntarily recognize a legal system that was not expected to treat him fairly.

Kings gradually asserted authority over commerce, generally to tax it or to extract other types of revenues by selling monopoly franchises or other special privileges to politically powerful business interests. The Law Merchant became less recognizable as royal courts supplanted merchant courts and as statutes, precedents, and treaties supplanted or supplemented business tradition and practice. Nonetheless, the rules that were initiated in the Law Merchant have survived in varying degrees within nations and particularly in international trade. In fact, beginning in the mid-1950s, *lex mercatoria* also began to be applied to certain aspects of international commercial law, which largely remained customary law. The customary rules of international trade are still backed by the desire to maintain reputations and arrangements that would encourage repeated dealings with other traders. Furthermore, almost all international contracts involving trade expressly mandate arbitration rather than adjudication by national courts. International arbitration procedures are speedy and flexible, but they also are chosen because traders assume that national courts will not enforce obligations derived solely from commercial practice and usage, whereas arbitrators "do not hesitate to refer to international commercial custom, including contract practices in international trade, as a basis for their award." Detailed analysis has revealed that, with respect to arbitration, "the answer to every dispute is to be found *prima facie* in the contract itself. What did the parties intend, what did they agree and what did they expect?" When a contract does not reveal the intentions of the parties, arbitrators still do not refer to any nationalized system of law unless the parties have specified one in the contract. Instead, they apply a "non-national and generally accepted rule or practice" that the parties should have been aware of within their international business community. Thus, in international trade, the Law Merchant continues to govern.

BLB

See also Anarchism; Anarcho-Capitalism; Common Law; Friedman, David; Voluntarism; Voluntary Contract Enforcement

Further Readings

Benson, Bruce L. "An Exploration of the Impact of Modern Arbitration Statutes on the Development of Arbitration in the United States." *Journal of Law, Economics, & Organization* 11 (October 1995): 479–501.

———. "The Spontaneous Evolution of Commercial Law." *Southern Economic Journal* 55 (January 1989): 644–661.

Berman, Harold J. *Law and Revolution: The Formation of Western Legal Tradition.* Cambridge, MA: Harvard University Press, 1983.

Berman, Harold J., and Felix J. Dasser. "The 'New' Law Merchant and the 'Old': Sources, Content, and Legitimacy." *Lex Mercatoria and Arbitration: A Discussion of the New Law Merchant.* Thomas E. Carbonneau, ed. Dobbs Ferry, NY: Transnational Juris Publications, 1990.

Lew, J. D. M. *Applicable Law in International Commercial Arbitration: A Study in Commercial Arbitration Awards.* Dobbs Ferry, NY: Oceana, 1978.

LeFevre, Robert (1911–1986)

Robert LeFevre was a libertarian polemicist and an educator. LeFevre founded and operated the first modern school dedicated to libertarian education, called the Freedom School, later renamed Rampart College.

LeFevre, while an anarchist who did not believe in the morality or necessity of any government, rejected the term *anarchy* because he thought it embraced active attempts to eliminate government, which he thought was as immoral as government itself. He called his antistate philosophy *autarchism* after the Greek for "self-rule."

LeFevre worked as an actor, radio broadcaster, door-to-door salesman, real estate speculator and manager, TV newsman, and assistant to a pair of charismatic American cult leaders in a religious movement known as the Mighty "I AM." He then turned to political activism, originally aligning himself with anticommunist and antiunionist movements. In the early 1950s, he worked with such groups as the Wage Earners Committee, the National Economic Council, and the Congress for Freedom.

In 1954, he became an editorial writer for the *Colorado Springs Gazette-Telegraph*, part of R. C. Hoiles's libertarian Freedom Newspaper chain. He launched his Freedom School in 1957 in a rural setting in the Palmer Range of Colorado, where he hoped that F. A. Harper, later founder of the Institute for Humane Studies, would be the school's principle teacher. However, Harper declined.

The first graduating class of the school's intensive 2-week series of lectures on libertarian economics and philosophy comprised a mere four students, but by its 1968 closing, hundreds had gone through the program. Guest lecturers at the school included Frank Chodorov, F. A. Harper, Leonard Read, Rose Wilder Lane, Hans Sennholz, and Roy Childs.

From 1965 to 1968, he edited an academic journal called the *Rampart Journal of Individualist Thought*. In the mid-1960s, LeFevre began plans to turn the Freedom School into a 4-year degree-granting institution called Rampart College, and he hired W. H. Hutt to run the economics department and James J. Martin for the history department. Disagreements with Hutt and Martin, however, and an expensive and damaging flood and mudslide in 1965 scuttled those plans, and LeFevre was forced to close the school in Colorado in 1968. He then conducted a more truncated lecture series under the name Rampart School in Santa Ana, California, until 1975. A brief attempt to revive a Rampart Institute was made in 1980. LeFevre continued lecturing on libertarian thought until his death in 1986.

LeFevre's beliefs were similar to those taught by Murray Rothbard and F. A. Harper, a property-based libertarianism that saw any initiation of force or abrogation of property rights as crimes. But LeFevre's views on several subjects were more radical, even in libertarian terms. For example, he held even defensive force completely impermissible. He also was resolutely against any political action to spread libertarian ideas—in fact, against any action at all other than the education of others in libertarian principles and personal attempts to disengage from the state.

Despite his radicalism, he had a long record of attracting support and enthusiasm from successful businessmen, including billionaire libertarian financier Charles Koch, who attended the Freedom School courses twice, and textile magnate Roger Milliken.

BDo

See also Anarchism; Harper, Floyd Arthur "Baldy"; Peace and Pacifism; Voluntarism

Further Readings

LeFevre, Robert. *The Fundamentals of Liberty*. Santa Ana, CA: Rampart Institute, 1988.

———. *This Bread Is Mine*. Milwaukee, WI: American Liberty Press, 1960.

———. *A Way to Be Free: The Autobiography of Robert LeFevre: The Making of a Modern American Revolution*. 2 vols. Culver City, CA: Pulpless, 1999.

Left Libertarianism

Left libertarianism is a fairly recently coined term for a fairly old idea. Those people who embrace this view agree with other libertarians in holding that individuals should be free. They regard each of us as full self-owners. However, they differ from what we generally understand by the term *libertarian* in denying the right to private property. We own ourselves, but we do not own nature, at least not as individuals. Left libertarians embrace the view that all natural resources, land, oil, gold, trees, and so on should be held collectively. To the extent that individuals make use of these commonly owned goods, they must do so only with the permission of society, a permission granted only under the proviso that a certain payment for their use be made to society at large. In effect, left libertarians, although prepared to recognized private property in oneself, are socialists with respect to all other resources. We each have equal rights over nature.

A great many writers have subscribed to one or another form of this ideology. Even John Locke, the apostle of capitalism in the eyes of many, assumed that, in some respects, nature was a "commons" and devoted a portion of his *Treatises of Government* to the issue of how individuals can by rights become exclusive owners of bits of nature, such as farms or forests. Locke regarded this problem as soluble, however, and did not conclude that we are all bound to make payment to society at large for the privilege of making use of the natural resources. By contrast, the 19th-century American writer Henry George advocated a single tax on land, holding that land ultimately belonged to all in common and could not be the exclusive property of any individual—as was true of our bodies and our labor.

The question arises as to whether left libertarianism is both coherent and plausible. Defenders of libertarianism as we generally understand the term have offered two extremely strong philosophical objections to the left-libertarian view. The first centers on the distinction that left libertarianism makes between self-ownership and nature ownership. This distinction, on careful consideration, really makes no sense. The second objection is that left libertarians are unable to explain how it is that nature comes to be communally owned, as it must be if their claims that individual owners owe a rental or tax to the community for employing natural items. In addition to these two objections, the issue of which system is more efficient in the creation and distribution of wealth divides these two approaches.

It is an essential aspect of self-ownership that people are to be able to do with themselves as they please, that is, that they be allowed to engage in activity under their own guidance, in accordance with their own ideas. However, if they are prohibited from using anything outside themselves, it is hard to see that there is much that one is free to do. The Stoic philosophers taught that our minds are always free no matter how enslaved we may otherwise be. But most of us would find this stoic freedom at best impossibly confining, if not a fraud. We want to walk about, work as we like, play as we like—a "free" life inside our heads is not enough. Libertarians embrace the principle that we may do what we like, including using those things we find outside of our own bodies, up to the point where our use of those things imposes damages, costs, and losses on others. Within those limits, we should be able to appropriate whatever we can use. Owning an object means being able, reliably, to continue to use it in future, not just now. Why, the libertarian will ask, should we not be able to do so if the theory we all accept is that of general liberty for all?

The second point is closely related to the first. Left libertarians claim that humankind collectively is somehow the owner of nature. This notion raises the following question: How did humanity come by it? The left libertarian supplies no real answer: We are simply informed that it is "just ours." If this statement is asserted as a fundamental intuition, it is a highly disputable one. Surely, the obvious position on this matter is that nature, as such, is simply inert and not "owned" by anybody—it is just there, and what we do about it is up to us.

True, the property libertarian wants to say that our ownership of our own bodies also is in some way fundamental, and many libertarians assert this self-ownership as a natural right or intuited moral truth. But they need not do so. It is possible to hold, for example, as some libertarians do, that we claim ownership of ourselves as part of a social contract. The question then arises as to whether this contract extends to the ownership of things outside ourselves. Many theorists, including John Locke, have argued that it does. The left libertarian has an analogous problem: How can he distinguish between my ownership of myself—which, obviously, I cannot have made by my own labor, which is exactly like other natural resources in that respect—and my nonownership of everything else?

A less philosophical, but more practical, question concerns the efficiency of the social system in which natural resources are in principle excluded from private ownership. It is arguable that private ownership is simply more efficient and, as such, really better for all. Certainly most economic theorists have convincingly argued that socialism is certain to be inefficient (or, as Mises put it, in practice impossible). Why then should a system of resource ownership be any better? Indeed, there is every evidence that the socialist regimes this century have botched the job of efficiently producing and distributing wealth about as thoroughly as could be feared. When land, coal, and so on are used by individual people in such a way as to maximize those people's returns, resources will be used by those who can make the best use of them. In the end, this scenario makes the poor in private-property societies better off than the middle class in socialist societies. Surely it makes sense that this system of ownership should equally apply in the area of resources.

JN and DT

See also Locke, John; Private Property; Socialism

Further Readings

Gwartney, James, and Richard Stroup. *What Everyone Should Know about Economics and Prosperity.* Vancouver, BC, Canada: Fraser Institute 1993.
Lester, Jan. *Escape from Leviathan.* New York: St. Martin's Press, 2000.
Mises, Ludwig von. *Liberalism.* San Francisco: Cobden Press, 1985.
Vallentyne, Peter, and Hillel Steiner, eds. *The Origins of Left Libertarianism.* New York: Palgrave, 2000.

Leggett, William (1801–1839)

William Leggett was a New York newspaperman and the intellectual leader of the laissez-faire wing of the northern Democratic Party in the late 1830s. In his editorials, collected and republished in book form shortly after his death, he embraced libertarian principles to a greater and more consistent degree than did any previous American writer. Starting from a Jeffersonian belief in equal natural rights to liberty and property, and combining it with the Jacksonian view that expansion of government characteristically favors a few privilege seekers over the many, he railed against any expansion of government beyond minimal "night watchman" functions. He was an influential proponent of free banking and of replacing the system of special legislative charters with a general law of incorporation open to all businesses. Initially a moderate on slavery, he soon became a radical abolitionist. In an era sometimes seen as having minimal business regulation, he argued for eliminating existing state restrictions on entry, price, and quality in dozens of businesses, among them securities trading, gambling, butchering, baking, the sale of commodities like coal and flour, ferrying, medicine, and turnpikes and canals. He called for privatizing mail delivery, weights and measures, coinage, wharves and docks, and even the declaration of Thanksgiving Day.

Some historians have characterized Leggett as an opponent of economic development or even as an "agrarian" (despite that his readership consisted mostly of New Yorkers). However, his attack was confined to businessmen who sought government privileges, not business per se. He praised the "active spirit of enterprise," which he was sure would "not flinch from undertaking whatever works of internal improvement might be needed by the community, without the aid of exclusive rights and privileges." He favored a general law of incorporation and opposed monopoly charters as a means of "leaving capital to flow in its natural channels, and enterprise to regulate its own pursuits." If he wrote for workingmen rather than businessmen, it was because he viewed workingmen as the natural constituency for laissez-faire policies in a polity where government intervention was a means for the well-connected aristocracy to exploit the common man.

LHW

See also Jefferson, Thomas; Liberalism, Classical; Minimal State

Further Readings

Leggett, William. *Democratick Editorials: Essays in Jacksonian Political Economy*. Lawrence H. White, ed. Indianapolis, IN: Liberty Press, 1984. Available from http://www.econlib.org/library/Leggett/lgtDE.html.

White, Lawrence H. "William Leggett: Jacksonian Editorialist as Classical Liberal Political Economist." *History of Political Economy* 18 (1986): 307–324.

LEVELLERS

The Levellers were a heterogeneous group of English radicals, many of a quasilibertarian bent, who, as an organized movement, were briefly active during the tumultuous years of the English Civil War (1642–1649). The movement surfaced in the summer of 1645, became a vocal popular party in 1646, and, for all practical purposes, disappeared as an organized movement during the fall of 1649. Its most prominent spokesmen were John Lilburne (1615–1657), Richard Overton (1631–1664), and William Walwyn (1600–1681).

As a political movement, the Leveller party's initial concerns centered on religious issues, first and foremost the demand for religious freedom and separation of state and church. These demands were soon taken up by ordinary citizens and soldiers who opposed the Church of England, the House of Lords, and the government of Charles I. The Levellers were for a time associated with Oliver Cromwell, the Independents, and the Protectorate. However, as the Civil War progressed and it became evident that the new Commonwealth was turning itself into a tyranny, the Levellers quickly took on the role of Cromwell's most vocal and radical opponents.

The Levellers were not a uniform group sharing one common, clearly defined political ideology, but they did share a common viewpoint on a number of issues that proved to adumbrate modern libertarian ideology in a great many respects. Overton's writings particularly provide an overview of the Levellers' chief concerns. Overton was not only among the most colorful and remarkable of all the personalities thrown up by the English upheavals of 1640–1660, but also was an influential political pamphleteer and the most prominent ideologue of the movement. In clear and often satirical prose, Overton endorsed a radical voluntarist and secular version of natural law that centered on the "principles of right reason" and a semicontractarian limited government.

The "principles of right reason" espoused by Overton comprised an inalienable right of individuals, and indeed a duty, to seek their own self-preservation with whatever means necessary, and a requirement that all relationships with others be voluntary and based on the consent of the parties involved. These principles are mediated through one central analytical concept—namely, what Overton called *self-propriety*, which is quite similar to what many contemporary libertarians call *self-ownership*. This notion is best captured in this passage in Overton's pamphlet, *An Arrow against All Tyrants* (1646):

> To every Individuall in nature, is given an individuall property by nature, not to be invaded or usurped by any: for every one as he is himselfe, so he hath a selfe propriety, else could he not be himselfe, and on this no second may presume to deprive any of, without manifest violation and affront to the very principles of nature, and of the Rules of equity and justice between man and man; mine and thine cannot be, except this be: No man hath power over my rights and liberties, and I over no mans; I may be but an Individuall, enjoy my selfe and my selfe propriety, and may write my selfe no more then my selfe, or presume any further; if I doe, I am an encroacher & an invader upon an other mans Right, to which I have no Right. For by naturall birth, all men are equally and alike borne to like propriety, liberty and freedome, and as we are delivered of God by the hand of nature into this world, every one with a naturall, innate freedome and propriety (as it were writ in the table of every mans heart, never to be obliterated) even so are we to live, every one equally and alike to enjoy his Birth-right and priviledge; even all whereof God by nature hath made him free.

This self-propriety is inalienable, and any attempt to contravene it would violate what is both a command of God and a law of nature: "[F]or as by nature, no man may abuse, beat, torment, or afflict himselfe; so by nature, no man may give that power to another, seeing he may not doe it himself. . . ."

The second principle that Overton sets forth is that it is legitimate to seek self-preservation by all means necessary, irrespective of any context other than the limits set down by the self-propriety of others, so that "[n]o man hath power over my rights and liberties, and I over no mans." The right and duty of the individual to seek his self-preservation thus naturally entails a reciprocal duty to respect a similar right in all others—that is, "Liberty of the Person, and liberty of Estate: which consists properly in the propriety of their goods, and a disposing power of their possessions."

These principles of self-propriety and a natural right to liberty entail the right of the individual to freely dispose of his person, his labor, and his legitimately acquired goods. In contrast to Locke some decades later, Overton nowhere developed a theory of how to legitimately acquire property, although he seems to have embraced what later would be called a labor theory of acquisition. In his pamphlet *A Defiance against All Arbitrary Usurpations* (1646), he states that self-propriety is a principle by which one

> would do as you would be done unto, that would have your neighbour injoy the fruit of his own labour, industry, and sweat of his brow, the freedom of his Conscience and estate, his own naturall right, and property, and have none to invade or intrench upon the same, more than you would have upon your own.

Overton further embraced what might be called the sanctity of contract. He held that contracts entail mutual obligations, and that when a relationship entered into by consent is broken by one party, the other party is relieved from fulfilling his part of the contract. As Overton wrote in *An Appeale* (1647): "All betrusted powers if forfeit, fall into the hands of the betrusters, as their proper centure: and where such a forfeit is committed, there is disoblegeth from obedience."

This theoretical foundation of natural law and natural rights is somewhat similar to the contractarianism of Thomas Hobbes and John Locke, although in certain respects more radical in its conclusions. In all our relationships, Overton maintained, we must respect the laws of nature, specifically the rights of individuals to life, liberty, and property, and only those institutions based on voluntary relationships can be considered to be legitimate. Government is legitimate only if it is consensual, and its only proper purpose is to protect the rights of citizens. If government were to overstep these limits, citizens had both a right and a duty to rebel.

The Levellers translated this philosophy into a general demand for a new social contract, a new "agreement of the people." In *A Remonstrance* (1646), Overton insisted that the Parliament should limit government so as to secure the people against arbitrary invasions of their freedom: "The Lawes of this Nation are unworthy a Free-People, and deserve from first to last, to be considered, and seriously debated, and reduced to an agreement with common equity and right reason, which ought to be the Forme and Life of every Government." This idea again later led the Levellers to set out the first statement of principles for a constitutional government ever written, namely in the *Certaine Articles* of 1647, which later was expanded in three proposed "Agreements."

The Levellers' political program emerges most clearly in their pamphlet *An Agreement of the People* (1649), which shows them as precursors of what later came to be known as liberalism. Here the Levellers identified three—and only three—positive tasks of government for which there was no need for further consent: (a) to secure peace and free trade with other nations; (b) to protect life, liberty, and property; and (c) to engage in such activities as were evidently conducive to these two ends and the prosperity of the Commonwealth.

More specifically, the Levellers advocated legal equality and opposed all privileges, among them peerages and exceptions from legislation. In constitutional matters, this philosophy led them to advocate strict limits on the powers of government, as set out in Magna Carta, an extension of the franchise, a freely elected Parliament as the supreme political authority, and annual or biennial elections to Parliament. They were opposed to a hereditary executive and a hereditary second chamber. In addition, they sought a number of procedural rights and a strict observance of the rule of law, among them the right of the people to directly elect judges, the right of the accused to be presumed innocent until proven guilty, the right to trial by a jury of one's peers, the right not to be forced to incriminate oneself, and the right not to be imprisoned without warrant and/or trial. Indeed, Overton insisted on restitution rather than retribution as a general principle in criminal matters and, accordingly, opposed imprisonment for crimes other than those involving violence. He strongly disapproved of imprisonment for debt. The death penalty was to be reserved solely for murder, and prisoners were not to be subjected to cruel and unfair treatment.

The Levellers not only embraced a large number of procedural rights, but they also strongly condemned conscription and other forms of slavery. They argued against going to war, at least without the explicit consent of the people, protested the existence of a state Church, and opposed all restrictions on religious freedom and all censorship and other violations of freedom of expression. Similarly, with respect to property, they demanded an end to the confiscation and expropriation of private property, as well as to tithes and high taxes, tariffs, privileges in commerce, and other forms of protectionism and mercantilism.

There is no basis for concluding that the Levellers advocated government redistribution of wealth, as some theorists have claimed, nor were they early forerunners of social democracy, socialism, or communism. With the possible exception of Walwyn, whose writings reflect some communitarian leanings, they clearly felt uncomfortable with the term *Leveller* because it suggested support for some species of economic leveling. It was Cromwell and the group's other opponents who named the movement Levellers with this aim in mind. The label was, in fact, originally employed to describe those who, in 1607, protested the enclosures of previously common land by a literal leveling of the fences. From 1649 to 1652, the label was associated with the "Diggers," a pantheistic, communitarian, and utopian movement led by Gerrard Winstanley that called itself "The True Levellers" and advocated the abolishment of private property in land and other economic inequalities by communalizing property and organizing a money-free economy. Overton and his collaborators dismissed the label as unjust and slander, and in *A Manifestation* (1649), they explicitly stated their opposition to "Levelling, for which we suppose is commonly meant an equalling of mens estates, and taking away the proper right and Title that every man has to what is his own." Rather than forerunners of socialism, the Levellers had a profound influence on Whig ideology, especially as it took shape in the second half of the 17th century, and particularly in the works of John Locke.

PKK

See also Contractarianism/Social Contract; English Civil Wars; Equality; Republicanism, Classical; Whiggism

Further Readings

Aylmer, Gerald E., ed. *The Levellers in the English Revolution.* Ithaca, NY: Cornell University Press, 1975.

Dow, F. D. *Radicalism in the English Revolution, 1640–1660.* Oxford: Basil Blackwell, 1985.

Haller, William, ed. *Tracts on Liberty in the Puritan Revolution, 1638–1647: Vols. I–III.* New York: Columbia University Press, 1934.

Haller, William, and Godfrey Davies, eds. *The Leveller Tracts, 1647–1653.* New York: Columbia University Press, 1944.

Hampsher-Monk, Iain. "The Political Theory of the Levellers: Putney, Property and Professor Macpherson." *Political Studies* 24 no. 4 (December 1976): 397–422.

Kurrild-Klitgaard, Peter. "Self-ownership and Consent: The Contractarian Liberalism of Richard Overton." *Journal of Libertarian Studies* 15 no. 1 (Fall 2000): 43–96.

Macpherson, C. B. *The Political Theory of Possessive Individualism: Hobbes to Locke.* Oxford: Oxford University Press, 1962.

Sharp, Andrew, ed. *The English Levellers.* Cambridge: Cambridge University Press, 1998.

Watner, Carl. "The Proprietary Theory of Justice in the Libertarian Tradition." *Journal of Libertarian Studies* 6 nos. 3–4 (Summer–Fall 1982): 289–316.

Wolfe, Don M., ed. *Leveller Manifestoes of the Puritan Revolution.* New York: Thomas Nelson and Sons, 1944.

LIABILITY

The topic of liability is vast; it includes damages to person, property, and reputation. The range of issues that arise in a given case include, at the least, the identification of some culpable conduct by the defendant, some causal connection between that conduct and the harm to the injured person, and some account of whether, and if so how, the injured party contributed to his own loss or assumed the risk of that injury.

Structuring a sound set of liability rules is of profound importance for anyone who believes in both the importance of individual liberty and the need to provide redress for, or a deterrence of, force and fraud practiced by other individuals. Several traditional distinctions, imperfectly realized at common law, are critical for the implementation of this scheme. The first of these distinctions is the line between harms that occur between strangers and those harms that occur among individuals who stand in some special relationship with each other (e.g., physician–patient, host–guest, employer–employee). The key point here is that, in the former cases, the libertarian desire to protect both person and property tends to lead toward the adoption of strict rules of liability that afford the defendant little breathing room when his actions injure other parties. In its classical formulation, the principle of strict liability says that, once the defendant strikes the plaintiff or creates a trap that causes him injury, he can be held liable even if the defendant had no intention to cause harm and had exercised all due care in order to avoid the harm in question. This rule still allows for defenses vital to a libertarian framework. It permits the owner of land to escape liability for harm to trespassing plaintiffs, except, sensibly, if his conduct is willful and wanton. It also allows for defenses based on the plaintiff's misconduct to either eliminate liability (which was the earlier preference) or to divide it in accordance with fault, which is the dominant view today.

Many jurisdictions do not afford this high level of protection, particularly in cases of personal injury, holding actors responsible for accidental harms only if they have failed to exercise reasonable care. The differences between the strict liability and liability based on negligence are not that critical to the libertarian program because even if they have profound consequences in a few cases, the vast majority of actions between strangers entail some negligence in leading up to the accident, so that the level of legal protection turns out to be quite high in both systems. In highway accidents, for example, a party is virtually always negligent whenever he or she violates the rule of the road, except perhaps in cases of sudden heart attacks or epileptic fits—hardly major sources of concern.

The key libertarian concern stems from the reluctance to impose any duty of rescue for strangers whom a person has not injured. Although there are strong moral reasons to assist those in need, the libertarian view, which retains much vitality in modern case law, is that the concern with individual autonomy precludes any legal obligation to behave as a Good Samaritan. The fears here are multiple; they include the risk that one person will simply be able to commandeer the ability or resources of another, that omissions will be found everywhere, and that, for example, a crowd of people on the beach could all be held liable if no one of them rescues.

Liability is much more complicated in those cases where the parties have entered into some kind of consensual arrangement. In those cases where the agreement is explicit about the allocation of risk between the parties, that contract should be respected to the same extent as any other agreement. This view is in contrast to the modern one, which, either by legislation or judicial decision, overrides clear clauses that limit or exclude liability for personal injury or property damages on supposed grounds of public policy or of supposed inequality of bargaining power. This approach should be regarded as a direct effort to impose judicial regulation on private contracting authority.

Most libertarians would condemn this view simply because it undermines the scope of individual choice. But the harmful systematic consequences of this approach should be noted as well. Any decision to allow unlimited damages works to the benefit of an injured party in an individual case, but in the long term no supplier of goods or services will remain in business if he or she knows that the potential liability, whether or not insured, exceeds its anticipated revenue. Reductions in medical service and product innovation often originate in well-intended but misguided efforts to protect consumers, patients, tenants, and employees from their opposite number. This constant effort to design a legal regime in which tort dominates contract is perhaps the single most important development of the modern law, where most of the litigation explosion arises in these consensual cases and not in the random interactions among strangers. The central task of liability reform is to secure an inversion where contract once again dominates tort.

RE

See also Externalities

Further Readings

Coleman, Jules L. *Markets, Morals, and the Law*. Cambridge: Cambridge University Press, 1988.

Epstein, Richard A. *Simple Rules for a Complex World*. Cambridge, MA: Harvard University Press, 1998.

———. *A Theory of Strict Liability*. San Francisco: Cato Institute, 1980.

LIBERAL CRITIQUE OF LIBERTARIANISM

Liberal critiques of libertarianism matter because libertarians claim to be liberals. Indeed, they often claim to be the only true liberals in a world of imposters. As libertarians interpret it, liberalism confers on individuals an absolute right to conduct their lives as they choose as long as they respect the equal rights of others to do the same. They contend that this principle justifies state power only when used to enforce rights against force, fraud, and theft, and that it precludes almost all public interference in the free market, the redistribution of wealth, and any form of welfare state. On this view, those who today defend such redistributive practices in the name of liberalism betray, rather than fulfill, basic liberal ideals.

Not surprisingly, such claims have not gone unchallenged. Many see no difficulty in justifying the redistribution of wealth and at least a modest welfare state on liberal grounds. Both libertarians and *welfare liberals* (as I refer to them) claim impeccable liberal credentials. But this dispute is not just over labels: What is at stake are different conceptions of what it means to take individual liberty seriously and of how political institutions can best do so. Welfare liberals offer a variety of reasons for rejecting libertarian conclusions regarding their commitment to further individual liberty.

To understand these objections, it is important to specify libertarian assumptions a little more sharply. Libertarians accord overriding importance to basic rights, but they also characterize these individual rights in a distinctive way. They interpret them as involving self-ownership. To say that a person is a self-owner is to say that decisions about how his or her unique bundle of personal assets, resources, and capacities are to be invested over the course of his or her lifetime is ultimately up to him or her. As long as others' rights are not at risk, self-owners have the final determination over their own affairs.

Libertarians believe that this idea has far-reaching implications for the rightful acquisition of property in external goods. According to them, it is both possible and likely that, starting from a position in which the external resources of the world are unowned, self-owners will quite legitimately acquire unequal holdings in these external assets. Furthermore, they contend that the right to decide how these acquisitions should be used carries over from the original ownership of personal assets. A self-owner's legitimate acquisitions are no less their own than the bundle of personal resources (talents, skills, and energy) they used to obtain them. Therefore, the confiscation of these acquisitions through redistributive taxation, even when inspired by noble causes (human equality, the common good, and social justice), must violate basic liberal rights, for it denies self-owners the final say over how the fruits of their labors are to be used. It is an act of aggression not fundamentally different from theft.

Critics like G. A. Cohen, Will Kymlicka, Richard Arneson, and others deny that these libertarian conclusions automatically follow even if we accept the premise of self-ownership. They counter that the inference holds only if the world (other than persons) is initially "unowned," so that external resources (land, fuel, food, etc.) belong to no one until self-owners invest their labor in acquiring them. But by itself, the thesis of self-ownership does not rule out the possibility that these external resources are initially owned by humankind in common. If we accept this view (like many natural rights theorists, including Aquinas and Locke), there need not be a straightforward move from ownership of one's person to a right to the unlimited accumulation of external wealth. For the community as a whole would retain a right to place limits on the legitimate acquisition of wealth by individuals because it, too, has rightful claims that require enforcement.

This line of argument allows welfare liberals to defend redistributive taxation without denying self-ownership. If the state is the agent of the whole political community, as liberals have traditionally thought, under this argument, it presumably has at least a limited right to dictate the terms on which self-owners can draw on the common stock of resources owned by that community. On this view, redistributive taxation enforces limits on private appropriation and makes available funds that the community can then deploy to ensure that access to the common stock of resources is not unfairly denied to any of its members. Thus, public redistribution need not be on a par with theft, but rather is a device for balancing the entitlement of individual self-owners to accumulate wealth and the residual right of the whole community to a fair share of the resources of the world and their fruits.

Libertarians vigorously contest this argument and deny its compatibility with the self-ownership principle. They insist that it effectively eviscerates that principle by licensing the communal exploitation of personal assets. It is misleading, they say, to depict public redistribution as a restoration of resources wrongly expropriated from a common pool. Rather, it directly confiscates acquisitions that reflect the personal skill, talent, and energy of producers and denies them what self-ownership requires: a right to the full fruits of their efforts and their contributions. Libertarians often support this counterargument by seizing on an unfortunate phrase used by John Rawls in his famous defense of a welfare liberal position presented in *A Theory of Justice*. There Rawls argued that a just society should regard "the distribution of natural talents" as a "collective asset" (p. 87). According to libertarian critics, this notion gives the game away. Welfare liberalism institutes communal ownership of personal assets; therefore, it must be inconsistent with self-ownership.

But this description is not a fair construal of the position taken by Rawls and by welfare liberals more generally. As many welfare liberals point out, among them Jeremy Waldron in *The Right to Private Property*, Rawls does not treat talents themselves, but rather their distribution, as a collective asset. This formulation is regrettably obscure, but Rawls's point follows. The question of how far individuals may personally benefit from the natural distribution of skills and talents depends ultimately on the scheme of legal rules and conventions in place. Different sets of legal rules and conventions allow distributive outcomes to be determined by the natural distribution of personal assets to greater or lesser degrees. Because these conventions form an alterable public framework of rules, the state can consider imposing rules that require those favored by the natural distribution of personal assets to transfer some of their acquired wealth to those relatively ill favored.

Rawls argued that such rules are required as a matter of basic justice. But whatever else might be said against his position, it seems compatible with the thesis of self-ownership. The presence of rules placing limits on external acquisition need not imply that people are not owners of their original personal assets. Therefore, the bare thesis of self-ownership leaves open the possibility of rules requiring redistribution of acquired assets.

But suppose these welfare liberal counterarguments fail and we grant that libertarian conclusions do follow from the thesis of self-ownership. What about the thesis of self-ownership? Many welfare liberals are troubled by the fact that, in the minds of some libertarians, self-ownership rights are fully alienable. Hence, self-owners may, among other things, sell themselves into slavery. These libertarians accept this idea on the grounds that property rights imply the right to use and abuse. Although it may be foolish for self-owners to enslave themselves or engage in other forms of self-abuse, they have the right to do so. But, as even John Stuart Mill saw, there is something paradoxical about a theory that claims to take individual liberty seriously and yet permits slavery under certain conditions. If any conclusion seems illiberal, surely this one does.

This concern raises deeper doubts about the liberal credentials of libertarian premises. What makes the thesis of self-ownership true? Why should liberals accept it? The answer depends on the form the statement regarding self-ownership takes. Libertarians sometimes suggest, as David Boaz does, that self-ownership is rationally self-evident. However, this view is hard to accept. As we have seen, one possible implication of the self-ownership thesis is that slavery can be morally legitimate under some circumstances, but many will think it self-evident that slavery is never legitimate under any circumstances.

Furthermore, it is inconvenient for the self-evidence claim that Locke (often treated as a libertarian hero) rejected self-ownership in the form proposed by contemporary libertarians and that Kant (also regularly recruited by contemporary libertarians to their cause) repudiated self-ownership in any form.

An alternative and better answer is that the thesis of self-ownership provides an interpretation of individual freedom and its value. On this view, liberals should endorse self-ownership because it is the best available characterization of what it means to respect individuals' equal rights to freedom and independence. This idea seems plausible up to a point. Self-ownership implies that my personal concerns are my own business, that I am ultimately responsible for my life, and that I may lead my life as I choose. These notions certainly sound like fundamental liberal desiderata, and respecting self-ownership rights may often coincide with respecting people as independent and free. Still, there are several reasons to doubt that self-ownership is an adequate characterization of the kind of liberty that liberals should care about. Here are two.

First, welfare liberals can insist that respecting self-ownership rights, or indeed any scheme of rights and entitlements, cannot be an end in itself. The value of respecting such entitlements ultimately depends on deeper requirements. To be fully consistent with liberal principles, they often argue, we must establish that respecting these entitlements can guarantee everyone access to adequate opportunities to fully enjoy their liberty. A society that fails to provide this guarantee cannot really claim to be showing equal respect to the freedom of all its citizens. Welfare liberals deny that societies that do no more than rigidly respect self-ownership rights (as libertarians interpret them) could pass this test. They argue that even if self-ownership rights are consistently respected, there will still be many individuals who, through no fault of their own, find themselves in disadvantaged social circumstances, deprived of resources necessary for a minimally rewarding pursuit of their personal projects and conceptions of the good. These individuals lack an adequate opportunity to make the most of their liberty. As Rawls might put it, their freedom is effectively surrendered to arbitrary contingencies.

Welfare liberals conclude that the state should be prepared to redistribute wealth to prevent this outcome. The possibility that redistribution of this sort might violate self-ownership rights need not trouble proponents of this argument. They can deny that self-ownership is the form of freedom that ultimately matters. To them, the rights that should be of fundamental concern to liberals are not self-ownership rights, but rather rights guaranteeing everyone adequate opportunities to exercise their liberty in personally fulfilling ways.

Second, the libertarian stress on self-ownership rights encourages the view that violations of such rights are the main, and perhaps only, interferences in individual liberty that call for public action or remedy. Now infractions of liberty can count as violations of someone's rights only if we can identify agents to hold morally or legally responsible for violating them. Earthquakes and tornadoes may interfere with individuals' liberty and deprive them of property, but it obviously makes no sense to regard them as agents whom we might blame for violating their victims' rights. Libertarians think that what goes for earthquakes and tornadoes also goes for the aggregate effects of free exchange: Even if a person is rendered penniless by those effects, his rights are not violated unless he can hold a specific agent responsible for a violation, and this ability to find a morally culpable agent usually will be lacking. On these grounds, libertarians deny the need for a public remedy in such cases.

But welfare liberals counter that this view of the infringements of liberty that should trigger remedial action by the state is unduly narrow. Why should the test be that of whether an agent responsible for a violation can be found, rather than that of whether the relevant interferences and the costs to their victims are humanly preventable? Economic deprivation and social disadvantage are not unpredictable natural events that human agents are powerless to stop, like tornadoes and earthquakes. Rather, they are the predictable results of voluntary human actions that have adverse consequences for the liberty of some. Even if specific individuals cannot be held morally responsible for such infringements of liberty, we might still expect a liberal state to assume responsibility for preventing or compensating for them. This suggestion opens up another possible pathway leading from liberal assumptions to nonlibertarian conclusions.

CoB

See also Conservative Critique of Libertarianism; Locke, John; Rawls, John; Welfare State

Further Readings

Arneson, Richard J. "Lockean Self-Ownership: Towards a Demolition." *Political Studies* 39 no. 1 (March 1991): 36–54.
Bird, Colin. *The Myth of Liberal Individualism*. Cambridge: Cambridge University Press, 1999.
Boaz, David. *Libertarianism: A Primer*. New York: Free Press, 1997.
Buchanan, Allen. *Ethics, Efficiency and the Market*. Totowa, NJ: Rowman & Littlefield, 1985.
Cohen, G. A. *Self-Ownership, Freedom and Equality*. Cambridge: Cambridge University Press, 1995.
Freeman, Samuel. "Illiberal Libertarianism: Why Libertarianism Is Not a Liberal View." *Philosophy and Public Affairs* 30 no. 2 (Spring 2001): 105–151.
Johnston, David. *The Idea of a Liberal Theory*. Princeton, NJ: Princeton University Press, 1994.
Kymlicka, Will. *Contemporary Political Philosophy: An Introduction*. 2nd ed. Oxford: Oxford University Press, 2002.
Mill, John Stuart. "On Liberty." *Utilitarianism, on liberty and Considerations on Representative Government*. H. B. Acton, ed. London: J. M. Dent & Sons, 1972.
Nozick, Robert. *Anarchy, State and Utopia*. New York: Basic Books, 1974.
Rawls, John. *A Theory of Justice*. Rev. ed. Cambridge, MA: Harvard University Press, 1999.
Waldron, Jeremy. *The Right to Private Property*. Oxford: Oxford University Press, 1988.

LIBERALISM, CLASSICAL

Liberalism is a political ideology distinguishable from other ideologies by its assignment of a much greater political importance and value to human liberty, understood as a condition of being subject to as few constraints and restraints imposed by others as possible. All liberals agree that human beings will suffer deliberate constraint and restraint at each others' hands if there is no system of law limiting their powers over each other. Accordingly, liberals regard laws that prohibit these constraints as being conducive to, rather than destructive of, liberty.

Liberalism only acquired its name in the early 19th century, well over a century after the ideology began to take shape. Classical liberalism is the original version of the ideology. It received its qualifying adjective only in relatively recent times from the felt need to distinguish the original version from later forms of liberalism that differ from it significantly.

The principal doctrinal difference separating classical liberalism from other later variants of the ideology pertains to the role government must play to achieve and preserve liberty and justice. Classical liberalism regards justice and liberty as requiring a much more limited role for government than do modern forms of liberalism. Indeed, apart from the provision of a limited range of goods that benefit all but that, most argue, society seems unable to secure save by governmental provision (so-called public goods, such as roads and harbors and, more controversially, relief of destitution), the only role for government that classical liberalism considers consistent with human liberty and justice is that of restraining individuals from constraining others, plus protecting individuals in the possession of whatever lawful property is theirs. Depending on the context, libertarianism can be seen as either the contemporary name for classical liberalism, adopted to avoid confusion in those countries where liberalism is widely understood to denote advocacy of expansive government powers, or as a more radical version of classical liberalism.

Although earlier writers and political activists advanced what were later understood as liberal ideas, notably the Levellers in England and the Scholastic thinkers of the School of Salamanca, liberalism—and, hence, classical liberalism—received its first canonical articulation in the writings of the English philosopher John Locke. In his *Two Treatises of Government*, published in 1689, Locke for the first time systematically described the features of a political order necessary to secure and uphold human liberty, as well as the merits of its doing so.

The immediate occasion of the publication of Locke's work was the so-called Glorious Revolution of the preceding year. In that bloodless revolution, James II was forced to abdicate to make way for two new monarchs, William of Orange and his wife, Mary, to whom Parliament had offered the throne. That offer was subject to certain formal constitutional assurances that were specifically designed to enhance Parliament's status and power over the monarchy, as well as to enshrine in law certain qualified liberties of the subject—notably, freedom of religion and expression—that were previously without formal legal recognition. Although

we now know that the major portion of Locke's essay was written as a call for revolution several years earlier, its purpose in being published in 1689 was to vindicate that revolution and constitutional settlement.

The essence of Locke's case for human liberty rests on two major postulates. The first is the alleged fundamental equal moral standing of all human beings, from which it is inferred that no one possesses a just claim to any greater degree of liberty or power over anyone else. The second has reference to the alleged universal benefits of several, that is, private, property. Those benefits are held to obtain, notwithstanding substantial inequalities in holdings, because the holdings that result from appropriation of unowned resources render no one less well off than they would be were private appropriation not allowed. Private property benefits all. By enabling people to enjoy the fruits of their labor, of their savings, and of the property they invest, it thereby creates favorable conditions for the creation of wealth and the material improvement of the human condition. When augmented by the division of labor and exchange, the activities encouraged by private property make possible a much larger return to labor than otherwise would be possible and from which all are beneficiaries.

Government, for Locke, is a human artifice created by the consent of those subject to it for the protection of their basic rights to life, liberty, and any goods they have lawfully acquired. As Locke put it, governments are instituted by persons

> for the mutual *Preservation* of their Lives, Liberties and Estates, which I call by the general Name, *Property*. The great and *chief end* therefore, of Men uniting into Commonwealths, and putting themselves under Government, *is the Preservation of their Property*.

Accordingly, for Locke, not only must the scope of legitimate governmental activity be confined to the protection of the rights of the governed, no one may claim legitimate political power over others save on the basis of their consent. From the ultimate moral equality of all human beings, Locke also infers the need for a set of political procedural rules and institutions, including the rule of law, due process, the separation of powers, and some element of democratic accountability through regular elections. Such institutions are held to minimize the risk of abuse of political power by those in whom it has been invested.

The influence of Locke's ideas on subsequent classical liberal thought can hardly be exaggerated. That is so despite later waning of enthusiasm for the theological framework in which Locke mounts some of his arguments for liberty. Locke dwelt mainly on the moral case for, as well as the constitution of, a liberal political order. He paid only relatively scant attention to the character and material benefits of the economic order likely to grow up within one. It was the French physiocrats (among them Anne-Robert-Jacques

Turgot and Pierre Samuel Dupont de Nemours) and the thinkers of the Scottish Enlightenment, notably Adam Smith, who delineated those matters in detail. That is one reason—the other being the challenge to liberalism posed by the socialists, who argued that economic benefits could be obtained by abolishing the market—that liberals came to be closely associated with economic reasoning and economic policy, despite the fact that they also called for liberty in religion, association, and speech, and their steadfast advocacy of peace and their opposition to militarism and imperialism.

The greater emphasis on utilitarian arguments associated with the classical liberal Jeremy Bentham, who had become prominent by the mid-19th century, opened the way for later generations of utilitarians to seek a role for government that went well beyond the limits advocated by earlier classical liberals. Succeeding generations of utilitarians after Bentham thereby helped transmute the early utilitarian classical liberal case for strictly limited government into the modern liberal case for extensive government, empowered to override liberties when they believed that doing so would increase utility. Although utilitarian arguments can be used in support of empowering government to seek greater utility, many classical liberals continued either to question the efficiency of government interventions to enhance human well-being or emphasized other benefits of liberty, such as the effect of freedom on human character. Although their arguments are not neatly distinguished and often overlap, the former includes such figures as Thomas Hodgskins and Herbert Spencer in England and Jean-Baptiste Say and Frédéric Bastiat in France, whereas the latter include Wilhelm von Humboldt in Prussia, Benjamin Constant in France, and John Stuart Mill in England.

It was partly in reaction to the calls by socialists and even by self-styled 20th-century liberals for ever greater government that authors such as Ludwig von Mises and Friedrich A. Hayek initiated a revival of classical liberal thought in the early part of the 20th century. Their case for liberty remained firmly within the broad utilitarian tradition of classical liberalism. Both drew heavily on the economic insights of Adam Smith, Jean-Baptiste Say, Carl Menger, Frédéric Bastiat, and other classical liberal economists. The revival of classical liberalism in the second half of the 20th century, which their writings were to inspire, also led to a renewed appeal to natural rights, especially among classical liberal thinkers in the United States.

From its inception, classical liberalism has always been intensely and intimately bound up with the great political happenings of its day. Born in 17th-century England from the parliamentary struggles against absolute monarchy, it became the inspiration for both the American and French Revolutions, as well as for the movement toward economic liberalization in Europe in the first 70 years of the 19th century. Owing to political rivalries among the European powers, the trend toward economic liberalization was reversed in the last third of the 19th century, until intensifying

economic and political rivalries erupted into the First World War. That war triggered the Russian Revolution of 1917 and the subsequent Soviet socialist experiment, which, in its initial stages at least, convinced many Western observers that collectivism was the shape of things to come. The subsequent worldwide economic depression of the 1930s and the virtual collapse of classical liberal ideology made possible the rise of Fascism in Italy, National Socialism in Germany, and other collectivist movements in many countries.

All those 20th-century developments reinforced the endogenous collectivist political tendencies that had been in the ascendant in Europe and America during the first half of the 20th century and that, for a long time, had seen the almost total eclipse of classical liberal thought. For much of the 20th century, only a few lone authentically classical liberal voices, such as those of Mises and Hayek, could be heard amid the clamor for ever more state intervention. A major step in the reinvigoration of classical liberalism was taken in 1947, when, under the aegis of F. A. Hayek, the Mont Pelerin Society was formed with the initial intention of reviving liberal thought at the highest levels. Thirty-nine participants from 10 countries took part in the first meeting. The 1950s, 1960s, and 1970s saw a growing band of classical liberal authors, such as Milton Friedman, Ayn Rand, Murray Rothbard, and Robert Nozick, emerge as prominent advocates of classical liberal ideas. Together they sounded a growing note of dissent against the collectivist consensus that had dominated public life for a generation after the end of the Second World War. Doubtless the prestige of their ideas received a boost from the collapse of Soviet communism at the end of the 1980s, which had long been foretold by Mises and Hayek to a largely incredulous Western intellectual establishment.

Since the collapse of Soviet communism, recognition of the superiority of markets over state planning, and of competition over monopolistic public provision, has become fairly ubiquitous. Similarly, faith in the ability of even democratically legitimated governments to provide welfare or actively manage social processes has diminished substantially. There has been a corresponding increase understanding of both the limits of power and the merits of individual rights, toleration, and limited government. Classical liberal or libertarian ideals still remain quite imperfectly realized and will require much more education, research, and advocacy for them to become the dominant themes of political life. F. A. Hayek concluded his influential 1949 essay "The Intellectuals and Socialism" with a challenge:

> Unless we can make the philosophic foundations of a free society once more a living intellectual issue, and its implementation a task which challenges the ingenuity and imagination of our liveliest minds, the prospects of freedom are indeed dark. But if we can regain that belief in the power of ideas which was the mark of liberalism at its best, the battle is not lost. The intellectual revival of liberalism is already underway in many parts of the world. Will it be in time?

The growth of modern libertarianism since Hayek issued his challenge is a testament to the power of ideas.

DC

Entry reprinted from David Conway, *In Defence of the Realm: The Place of Nations in Classical Liberalism*. Aldershot, UK: Ashgate Publishing, 2004. Reprinted with permission.

See also Bastiat, Frédéric; Locke, John; Mill, John Stuart; Say, Jean-Baptiste; Smith, Adam; Whiggism

Further Readings

Bastiat, Frédéric. *Selected Essays on Political Economy*. Irvington-on-Hudson, NY: Foundation for Economic Education, 1995.

Bentham, Jeremy. *The Theory of Legislation*. Bombay and New York: Tripathi and Oceana, 1975.

Bramsted, E. K., and K. J. Melhuish, eds. *Western Liberalism: A History in Documents from Locke to Croce*. London: Longman Group, 1978.

Constant, Benjamin. *Political Writings*. Biancamaria Fontana, ed. Cambridge, MA: University Press, 1988.

Conway, David. *Classical Liberalism: The Unvanquished Ideal*. Basingstoke, UK, and New York: Macmillan and St. Martin's Press, 1995.

Friedman, Milton. *Capitalism and Freedom*. Chicago and London: University of Chicago Press, 1962.

Hayek, Friedrich. *The Constitution of Liberty*. London and Henley, UK: Routledge, 1960.

Humboldt, Wilhelm von. *The Limits of State Action*. J. W. Burrow, ed. Cambridge: Cambridge University Press, 1969.

Locke, John. *Two Treatises of Government*. Cambridge: Cambridge University Press, 1965.

Mises, Ludwig von. *Liberalism in the Classical Tradition*. New York and San Francisco: Foundation for Economic Education and Cobden Press, 1985.

Robbins, Lionel. *The Theory of Economic Policy in English Classical Political Economy*. 2nd ed. London and Basingstoke, UK: Macmillan, 1978.

Say, Jean-Baptiste. *A Treatise on Political Economy*. New York: A. M. Kelley Publishers, 1971.

Smith, Adam. *An Inquiry into the Nature and Causes of the Wealth of Nations*. Indianapolis, IN: Liberty Classics, 1981.

LIBERALISM, GERMAN

Classical liberalism in Germany can look back on a proud but also at times tragic history. With strong roots in the legal traditions of the old empire, prior to 1806, which offered strong safeguards against centralized power, liberalism began to flourish during the Enlightenment period of the late 18th century. Inspired by the American and, more important, the French Revolution, German thinkers like Immanuel Kant and Johann Gottlieb Fichte were strong supporters of the rights of man and unhindered freedom of opinion and press. Fichte especially, although he was later to change his views in favor of a nationalistic socialism, interpreted the idea of a "social contract" in so radical a manner that it appeared consistent with each citizen's ability to secede from the state. His book *Contribution to the Rectification of the Public's Judgment of the French Revolution* (1792) presaged much of what today would be viewed as an anarcho-capitalist version of libertarianism.

One of the greatest works bearing the imprint of classical liberalism of this period—if not of German liberalism as a whole—was written by Wilhelm von Humboldt (1767–1835). In his book *The Limits of State Action*, written in 1792, he defined *self-education* as the true end of man to which a minimal state was a necessary precondition.

The poor military performance of the German states during the Napoleonic Wars made thoroughgoing reforms necessary, and intellectuals and enlightened bureaucrats often combined in their efforts to introduce the principles of local autonomy and the rule of law. This collaboration was especially evident in Prussia under the leadership of Baron vom Stein. However, by far the most important of the liberal reforms was the foundation of the *Zollverein* (customs union) in 1834, which established free trade among the German states and contributed much to the rise of Germany's industrial revolution.

As bureaucratic reformism began to wane, liberalism became increasingly an oppositional creed, if not a revolutionary one. Liberal thinkers, the most important of whom were Karl von Rotteck and Karl Theodor Welcker, paved the way for the Revolution of 1848. Rotteck and Welcker were both historians and politicians from the southwest who together edited the 15-volume *Staatslexikon*, which immediately became the manual of constitutionalism throughout Germany. Even more radical was the philosophy put forward by Max Stirner in his *The Ego and Its Own* (1844), who advocated nothing short of an individualist anarchist philosophy.

By the time of the Revolution of 1848, and its subsequent failure to overthrow the old regime, a combination of constitutionalism and nationalism was predominated through the German states. Liberals joined the movement for national unity because it appeared a promising strategy to overthrow the autocratic regimes that governed the various smaller states into which Germany was then divided. It eventually became evident that linking liberal reforms with the movement for a united Germany was counterproductive because liberal politicians began to sacrifice liberal political goals on the altar of national unity. Many liberals abandoned their liberalism as they became convinced that Prussian hegemony, under the leadership of conservatives like Bismarck, was the best way to achieve unity. In the 1860s, the liberals split on this issue, bifurcating into a National Liberal Party, whose primary interest was a strong united German state, and a Progressive Party, which continued to retain its liberal links.

Following the 1848 revolution, the various German governments reinstituted strict limits on political freedoms. However, surprisingly, economic liberalism flourished, and a policy of internal and external free trade was vigorously pursued. The intellectual force behind this tendency was the *Congress of German Economists*, founded in 1858. Intellectuals, businessmen, and politicians joined in emulating the British free trade movement of Richard Cobden and John Bright. The German "Manchester-Men," as they were pejoratively dubbed by both socialists and nationalists, have often been depicted as heartless advocates of greed without any trace of concern for the poor. However, the "Manchesterites" strongly believed in the social advancement of workers; what they questioned was whether this goal could be accomplished through state coercion. This group, including Hermann Schulze-Delitzsch, embraced voluntarism and free trade. In fact, Schultze-Delitzsch was the founding father of the German self-help and cooperative movement.

Immediately following German unification in 1871, Bismarck turned on the liberals because they opposed his attempts to centralize power. In 1878, he adopted protectionist economic policies while introducing elements of the modern welfare state. The effect of these policies was to cause enormous disunity within liberal ranks.

Among the leading liberals who opposed Bismarck was Ludwig Bamberger, a radical from the 1848 revolution, who earlier had been Bismarck's economic advisor and the creator of German monetary union of 1876. In 1880, Bamberger broke with Bismarck and with the National Liberal Party, for which he sat in the Reichstag, over the issue of protectionism and social reform. Bismarck's primary opponent in the Reichstag was Eugen Richter, leader of the Progressive Liberals, who was to prove the last classical liberal of influence in Germany and whose warnings against socialism on the left and militarism on the right were, alas, confirmed by subsequent events.

World War I marked the effective end of classical liberalism as a major political movement in Germany until the late 1940s. It was not able to recover during the Weimar Republic and dismally failed to stop Hitler's advance to power. The period after World War II, however, saw a remarkable revival of liberalism. The German Constitution of 1949 was in part designed by liberals, and even during the war economists such as Walter Eucken and Wilhelm Röpke had made plans for a liberal postwar economy. With the creation of West Germany in 1949, Ludwig Erhard, who became minister of economic affairs in the first ministry of Konrad Adenauer, established the "social market economy," thus creating the "economic miracle" in the 1950s.

Since then, liberalism seems to have eroded. In the 1970s, Keynesianism and welfare statism became more and more prevalent in economic policy. The ever-increasing and costly welfare state today is the biggest challenge to German liberals.

DD

See also French Revolution; Humboldt, Wilhelm von; Interventionism; Liberalism, Classical; Stirner, Max

Further Readings

Humboldt, Wilhelm von. *The Limits of State Action*. John Wyon Burrow, trans. London: Cambridge University Press, 1969.
Raico, Ralph. *The Party of Liberty: Studies in the History of German Liberalism*. Jorg Guido Hulsmann, trans. Stuttgart, Germany: Lucius & Lucius, 1999.
Richter, Eugen. *Pictures of the Socialistic Future (Freely Adapted from Bebel)*. Henry Wright, trans. London: Swann Sonnenschein, 1907.
Sheehan, James J. *German Liberalism in the Nineteenth Century*. London: Methuen, 1982.
Sweet, Paul R. *Wilhelm von Humboldt. A Biography*. Cleveland: Ohio State University Press, 1978.

LIBERTY, PRESUMPTION OF

A "presumption of X" signifies that X is taken to be the case without requiring argument or evidence to support it. The burden of its rebuttal is on the challenger of the presumption.

The presumption of liberty signifies that an individual is taken to be free to perform any feasible act without having to show that there is no sufficient reason that he should not perform it. The burden of showing sufficient cause against the act (or against this particular individual performing it) is on the challenger. The latter is characteristically the political authority, or the plaintiff in juridical disputes, but may be anybody with access to public rule-making and administration. Sufficient cause may consist of an applicable rule prohibiting the act or in enough probability that the act, if committed, would significantly harm another person or persons.

Conventions, customs, and laws make up the rule system intended to guide social behavior. A rule system that runs in terms of prohibitions is favorable to the presumption of freedom: "everything that is not expressly prohibited is (liable to be) free." A rule system that runs in terms of permissions, such as bills of rights, favors the presumption of unfreedom: "everything that is not expressly authorized is (liable to be) prohibited." However, although the nature of the rule system may favor one presumption or the other, it does not logically establish or exclude either.

It is both widely held and widely contested that the presumption of liberty is the most solid foundation one can find for the edifice of classical liberal or libertarian theses.

One sharp criticism of the foundational role of the presumption of liberty, which dismisses it as "an implausible doctrine," condemns it mainly on the ground that it is undiscriminating and gives the same weight to vitally important as to trivially unimportant freedoms. Condemning it on this ground is like condemning the umbrella on the ground that it protects indiscriminately from the rain not only the great and the good, but the ordinary plodders as well. There may be a case for ranking liberties in a hierarchical order of greater and lesser, as was done notably by John Rawls and his followers, but it is not a liberal case if only because it must invest someone with the power of deciding which liberty is greater than another.

The other, more weighty, attack against the presumption of liberty holds that it depends on the love of liberty or, more precisely, on the imputation of a value to liberty. This dependence makes the presumption of liberty doubly vulnerable. It may be argued that liberty as such has no value and that those who claim a preference for it really like not liberty, but other values they think it would bring, but that can be obtained more directly and more safely without recourse to the presumption of freedom. It also can be argued, reasonably enough, that, although freedom may be valuable, it is not the sole value we pursue. Many believe, rightly or wrongly, that other values in effect compete with freedom, with more freedom causing less equality or security. Hence, the presumption of freedom, far from being a firm foundation, hinges precariously on the tradeoffs that happen to prevail among these competing values.

This line of argument is a mistake. The presumption of freedom in no way depends on the love of freedom. It is a pure product of logic and epistemology. Suppose opinion is divided over whether a certain act is (or should be treated as) free. The actor who wishes to perform it contends that it is free, whereas challengers contend that it is not. Propositions that have descriptive meaning are either verifiable or falsifiable or sometimes both. Take the proposition that the act is not free. There may be indefinitely many potential reasons for believing this notion, having mostly to do with the meanings of rules and with putative harms to various interests. The would-be actor can falsify some of them by showing that they are groundless or of insufficient force. But as he falsifies some, others can always be advanced because such reasons are numberless, and although the actor may falsify any large number, he cannot falsify all. Therefore, the actor cannot bear the burden of proof, and, in logic, it would be nonsensical to place it on him.

The challenger, however, is in an altogether different, we may say asymmetrical, position. Any specific reason against the act in question that he thinks is sufficient can be verified by argument and evidence bearing on that reason. If he fails to verify his first reason, he can find a second and marshal evidence supporting that until he either finally succeeds in his challenge or runs out of verifiable arguments. There is nothing logically nonsensical or epistemologically unfeasible about the task of verifying his proposition that the act should not be free. Consequently, he can carry the burden of proof. Until he succeeds in discharging it, the presumption of liberty prevails, as it were, by default.

The presumptions of innocence and property are twin sisters of the presumption of liberty, in that they spring from the same asymmetry between verification and falsification. "You have committed a crime" and "your title to this property is invalid" are unfalsifiable, but verifiable, statements open to proof, but not to disproof. The presumption of innocence does not depend on the "rights" of the accused nor the presumption of property on the economic case for the owner's security of tenure. Like liberty, they owe their status to the nature of the means the mind possesses for telling true from false.

AdJ

See also Freedom; Individualism, Political and Ethical; Rights, Theories of

Further Readings

Benn, S. I., and R. S. Peters. *The Principles of Political Thought.* New York: Free Press, 1959.

de Jasay, A. "Freedom from a Mainly Logical Perspective." *Philosophy* 80 no. 314 (October 2005): 565–584.

———."Freedoms, Rights and Rights." *Il Politico* 66 (2001): 3.

Feinberg, J. *Social Philosophy.* Englewood, NJ: Prentice Hall, 1973.

Raz, J. *The Morality of Freedom.* Oxford: Clarendon Press, 1986.

LIBERTY IN THE ANCIENT WORLD

Posterity's debt to the great civilizations of antiquity is enormous, but this legacy can hardly be regarded as consistently libertarian. Students of the centralized managerial autocracies of Egypt and Persia, for example, or of the rigid caste system of India will examine the records of these societies in vain for ideas and institutions specifically favorable to liberty. In the case of India, Buddhist criticism of violence and of caste distinctions never developed into a full-fledged critique of political power, perhaps because Buddhist teachings emphasized renouncing the world, rather than reforming it. Several ancient civilizations, however, did make substantial contributions to the libertarian tradition.

The first known use of a word meaning "liberty" (*amagi*) occurs on a 24th-century B.C. clay tablet from the

Sumerian city-state of Lagash. According to the cuneiform document, the people of Lagash had long been languishing under oppressive bureaucrats and rapacious tax collectors when a reformer named Urukagina became king, apparently by coup, and "established liberty." Urukagina's regime was short-lived, however, because Lagash was conquered by a neighboring state less than a decade later. The *amagi* symbol enjoys some popularity among libertarians today.

In the 11th century B.C., the political organization of Hebrew Palestine was transformed from a loose confederation under charismatic nonhereditary leaders called *judges* into a much more centralized and powerful hereditary monarchy. Although in institutional terms this change was a loss for liberty, by provoking critical reflection on political power it may have helped to advance liberty as an idea. By contrast with the adulatory literature of other Near Eastern monarchies, Hebrew scriptures are a sustained critical commentary on their kings. The inception of kingship is described as a rejection of God, and the prophet Samuel is portrayed as warning the Hebrews against the taxation and conscription that monarchy will inevitably bring. Over the succeeding centuries, the Hebrew prophets continued to denounce the errors of their rulers; more than the specific content of their criticisms, the prophets' chief libertarian legacy was the idea of a transcendent standard of conduct to which political rulers are answerable and to which their subjects can appeal.

In China, the effective collapse of the Chou dynasty in the 8th century B.C. fragmented the region into many smaller independent states, inaugurating five centuries of decentralization. Scholars, deprived of their former positions in the administrative hierarchy, competed vigorously for posts as political advisors to these states' *parvenu* rulers. This intellectual competition stimulated a flourishing and diverse culture of political thought, much of it favorable to liberty. One thinker, Mo-tzu (c. 5th B.C.), condemned military conquest as equivalent to murder on the grounds that rulers should be held to the same moral standards as private individuals. The followers of Lao-tzu (c. 3rd B.C.) emphasized the advantages of spontaneous order over forcibly imposed order. Most influential of all, the Confucians (e.g., Mencius, Hsün-tzu, and Ssu-ma Ch'ien) developed an ethics of reciprocity; they praised entrepreneurship, the reciprocal gains from trade, and the self-regulating character of the price system and denounced harsh punishments and heavy taxation. Equally significant, they maintained that when the king's rule is unjust he loses the "mandate of Heaven." At that point, the ruler becomes a king in name only and so may be legitimately overthrown.

Decentralization ended in 221 B.C. when the Ch'in dynasty gained supremacy over China. This brutal and totalitarian regime was quickly overthrown, however, giving way to the milder Han dynasty in 206 B.C. Revulsion against

Ch'in excesses created a favorable political climate for limitations on the state. Although the new dynasty's initial promise to eliminate all laws except those against murder, theft, and personal injury was not kept, the early Han emperors, relying heavily on Confucian and Taoist advisors, implemented many libertarian reforms—lowering taxes, moderating punishments, and repealing censorship laws (this last step on the ground that, without free discussion, the emperor "has no way to learn of his errors"). The reforms were short-lived, however; by 81 B.C., Confucians were complaining that laws had once again grown "profuse as autumn tendrils" and "thick as congealed tallow." Confucian scholars were soon co-opted into the privileged imperial bureaucracy, whereupon Confucianism began to lose much of its antistatist radicalism.

The Greek and Roman contribution to the libertarian tradition has been much debated. In his 1816 essay "The Liberty of the Ancients Compared with That of the Moderns," the French libertarian Benjamin Constant famously argued that the meaning of *liberty* in classical antiquity did not refer to a guaranteed private sphere of personal discretion, but rather to the freedom to participate in the direct and collective exercise of sovereignty—a form of liberty compatible with severe constraints on individual choice. For Constant, ancient liberty was suitable to warlike societies with small populations, but not to an advanced commercial civilization, and he looked with alarm at the willingness of contemporary collectivist thinkers to sacrifice the modern variety of liberty to recover the ancient. In fact, one can find aspects of both kinds of liberty in Greco–Roman civilization.

The Greek world, including the Greek colonies in Italy and Asia Minor, benefited from political decentralization and a geographical situation favorable to trade. During the 10th through 6th centuries B.C., trade brought new wealth and new ideas—both destabilizing forces—into the Greek city-states, undermining the traditional warrior nobility and bolstering the power of an artisan class. The ensuing class warfare gradually transformed most Greek city-states from aristocracies into mixtures of oligarchy and democracy, with the proportions of each varying from state to state.

This partial shift from a military to a commercial mode of social organization was celebrated by Hesiod, whose poem *Works and Days* praised productive effort, condemned the predatory behavior of "bribe-eating kings," and contrasted the hateful effects of military competition with the beneficent effects of economic competition. Later Greek writers were consciously proud of their distinctive institutions; in his history of the Greco–Persian Wars, Herodotus emphasized the contrast between Persian autocracy and Greek liberty.

The Greek city-state about which we know the most, Athens, also is the one Constant acknowledges as in part an exception to his thesis. During its democratic period, from about 508 to 338 B.C., adult male citizens exercised collective sovereignty in the manner of his description of ancient liberty, but Athenians also enjoyed substantial personal and economic freedom in the private sphere—what we in the modern world understand as liberty. Democratic ideology defined liberty as, in private matters, "living as one pleases," and, in public matters, "ruling and being ruled in turn."

Athenian society had many libertarian aspects. Its economic and intellectual freedom attracted merchants and philosophers from all over the Greek world. Although the execution of Socrates reminds us of the limits to Athenian free speech, Demosthenes' remark that one could freely praise the Spartan constitution in Athens, but not vice versa, also was true. Dispute resolution was a competitive field, with disputants having a choice among private arbitrators, public arbitrators, and public courts. Unlike many Greek city-states, the Athenian state exercised no control over education. The Athenian banking system, likewise unregulated, was quite sophisticated, and women exercised considerable *de facto* authority in commerce and trade. The Athenian system was never purely majoritarian; magistrates were selected by sortition (thus ensuring proportional representation), while decisions of the democratic assembly could, in some instances, be overturned by judicial review. Literary works (e.g., Sophocles' *Antigone*) and political speeches (e.g., Pericles' Funeral Oration) alike acknowledged the authority of unwritten laws to which human edicts were answerable. Critics of Athenian democracy point to its tendency to break down in civil strife, but nearly all this civil strife was confined to a single decade (413–403) in the aftermath of the disastrous and demoralizing Peloponnesian War.

The two chief Athenian philosophical movements that were to emerge were the Socratics (e.g., Plato, Xenophon, Aristotle) and the Sophists; each embraced libertarian conclusions, although seldom with regard to the same issue. The Socratics saw human interests as naturally harmonious, inferred that social cooperation under law was the natural human condition, and concluded that the state should take an active role in shaping the moral character of its citizens. The Sophists, by contrast, saw society as an artificial construct, a mutual nonaggression pact among potentially hostile egoists, and concluded that states should confine themselves to minimal defensive functions. (Arguably both groups failed to grasp the distinction between society and state, despite living in a community that largely exemplified that distinction.) The Socratics tended to favor a mixture of democracy and aristocracy to prevent the minority from tyrannizing over the majority and vice versa. Although the Socratics were sometimes suspicious of commerce as an ignoble pursuit, Aristotle did defend private property both on economic grounds—public ownership creates incentives for mismanagement—and moral ones— the virtues of generosity presuppose private property. Some

Socratics questioned the legitimacy of sexual inequality; some Sophists questioned the legitimacy of slavery.

As the age of the independent city-states gave way to the age of empires—first the Macedonian, later the Roman— the Stoic and Epicurean schools came to predominate. The Stoics, adapting the Socratic tradition to new political circumstances, stressed the individual's self-command and superiority to circumstances and proclaimed a universal Natural Law to which all human laws were answerable. The Epicureans described the spontaneous, unplanned evolution of human institutions, developed a social contract theory fusing Socratic and Sophistic elements, and advocated the pursuit of individual happiness outside of politics.

The Roman Republic, which gave way to the Empire in 31 B.C., combined a bicameral popular assembly, an elective dual executive, and a partly hereditary and partly elective Senate. The historian Polybius, who wrote during the 2nd century B.C., attributed Rome's success to this constitutional form, arguing that the balance of powers served to check abuses. Cicero added that the Roman system benefited from having evolved gradually over time, drawing on collective human experience, rather than having been designed by a single mind. Rome's greatest libertarian legacy is Roman law, a decentralized precedent-based system emphasizing private property and contract. Cicero saw Roman law as an embodiment of the universal Natural Law of the Stoics and described the state's proper function as defense of property. Despite these philosophical conclusions, personal freedom in republican Rome was arguably subject to heavier—but also more predictable—constraints than in Athens. Territorial expansion led to an inability to maintain civilian control of the military, while a series of ambitious generals advanced themselves by exploiting class conflict. This loss of civilian control led to a century of civil war culminating in the establishment of the Empire and the continuing erosion of personal and economic liberty.

The imperial period witnessed the rising influence of Christianity, on the one hand, and the increasing success of the Germanic tribes on Rome's borders, on the other hand. If Christianity represented a synthesis of Hebrew and Greco–Roman values, the Germanic ethos has been credited (e.g., by Constant's contemporary François Guizot) with infusing an ideal of personal independence. The early Christians generally counseled submission to existing political authority, except on religious matters, thus laying the philosophical foundations for the notion that church and state should be separated. Many Christians preached religious tolerance during the period when Christians were out of power and persecuted by pagans. Once imperial power passed from pagans to Christians, however, the Church's enthusiasm for religious tolerance quickly waned. The otherworldly aspect of Christian teaching fostered a suspicion of commerce, but St. Augustine defended commerce as a legitimate human activity. Echoing both Stoic and Hebrew ideas, Augustine also denied that unjust laws had the authority of law and compared governments to robber bands, but he regarded submission to government as a necessity in light of humanity's fallen nature. Also, it can be argued that the Christian emphasis on the sacred value of the individual soul laid the foundation for the development of theories of individual rights.

RL

See also Aristotle; Cicero; Epicureanism; Religion and Liberty; Republicanism, Classical; Stoicism

Further Readings

Cohen, Edward E. *Athenian Economy and Society: A Banking Perspective*. Princeton, NJ: Princeton University Press, 1992.

Constant, Benjamin. "The Liberty of the Ancients Compared with That of the Moderns." *Benjamin Constant: Political Writings.* Biancamaria Fontana, ed. and trans. Cambridge: Cambridge University Press, 1988.

Finley, M. I. *Politics in the Ancient World*. Cambridge: Cambridge University Press, 1994.

Forrest, W. G. *The Emergence of Greek Democracy: 800–400 BC*. New York: McGraw-Hill, 1975.

Hansen, Mogens H. *Polis and City-State: An Ancient Concept and Its Modern Equivalent. Acts of the Copenhagen Polis Centre*. Vol. 5. Copenhagen: Royal Danish Academy of Sciences and Letters, 1998.

Hunter, Virginia J. *Policing Athens: Social Control in the Attic Lawsuits, 420–320 B.C.* Princeton, NJ: Princeton University Press, 1994.

Leoni, Bruno. *Freedom and the Law*. 3rd ed. Indianapolis, IN: Liberty Press, 1991.

Long, Roderick T. "Austro-Libertarian Themes in Early Confucianism." *Journal of Libertarian Studies* 17 no. 3 (Summer 2003): 35–62.

Miller, Fred D., Jr., ed. *A History of Philosophy of Law from the Ancient Greeks to the Scholastics*. Dordrecht: Kluwer Academic, forthcoming.

Muller, Herbert J. *Freedom in the Ancient World*. New York: Harper & Row, 1961.

LIMITED GOVERNMENT

Limited government is one of the central tenets of modern libertarianism. However, it is one libertarians share with many of their political opponents. The idea of limited government, although seldom explicitly defended, is in principle one that few will explicitly argue against. Put simply, the notion of limited government implies that political power should be used only for a number of specific or defined purposes and that the scope of government activity and legislation should be limited to what is necessary for those purposes. In other words, government should only be concerned with a specific part of human life while the rest is left to the sphere of private action. Additionally, it commonly includes the idea that the scope of government action should be limited by a basic law or constitution that sets out the "rules of the game" for the political process and is not itself subject to everyday politics. In many cases, this constitution is an actual document—as, for example, in the United States or Germany—but it can be a matter of informal understandings and tradition as much as written text, as in the United Kingdom and Israel. Limited government also is intimately connected to the idea of the rule of law—that political power must be bound and limited by explicit and known rules and can be exercised only in a rule-defined way, rather than an arbitrary and unpredictable one.

However, the concept of limited government says nothing about how extensive the scope of government concern and activity should be, only that it should be limited. Thus, limited government is not necessarily the same as small government, which depends on how tightly the limits are drawn. For libertarians, limited government means small government because it is augmented by a second argument—that the constraints on government activity should be drawn tightly and restrictively. The antithesis of limited government is totalitarian government, where every aspect of human life is, or has the potential to be, the concern of the state and, as such, subject to the process of collective political decision making, rather than personal and private choice. This view of politics was theorized most explicitly by Benito Mussolini and Giovanni Gentile in *The Doctrine of Fascism* in 1932, but it also is a central feature of communist regimes at least in theory. Libertarians argue that contemporary social democratic regimes, while in theory disavowing this unrestricted view of legitimate government activity, have an inherent tendency in this direction. Just as the notion of limited government is associated with that of the rule of law, so the totalitarian concept of government is linked with the idea of the need for those with political power to have wide or even unlimited discretion and freedom of action and decision.

Historically, the idea of limited government has been formulated independently in a number of times and places, and it appears to be a common response by political thinkers to the reality of political power. In imperial China, Confucian thinkers argued for both natural and legal limits on the scope of politics and government in opposition to the views of the Legalists that all life should be subject to laws and political power. Classical Islamic thinkers argued that the scope of government should be limited by both the demands of piety and a clear distinction between the public and private, that is, with regard to government enforcement of moral rules. The most significant example of limited government, however, both in theory and practice (because of subsequent developments), took place in medieval Europe.

Europe during the Middle Ages saw the development of a theory of the limits to political power and its embodiment in the formal institutions and laws then established. This development was not the product of design or philosophy, but was rather the result of real-life political disputes, above all the conflict between the Holy Roman Empire and papacy over the apparently trivial issue of clerical investiture and in the disputes between monarchs and their more powerful subjects and between aristocrats and associations of peasants and the inhabitants of towns. From the early 13th century onward, a series of documents and political settlements, starting with Magna Carta in 1215, made explicit the idea that the power of rulers was limited and defined. This view was challenged during the 16th and 17th centuries with the rise of the doctrine of political absolutism. However, even theories of absolute monarchy of the kind that appeared in Europe at this time were quite different from modern defenses of totalitarian government, a difference even greater in practice. Rather, the claims associated with absolute monarchy regarding the nature and origin of political power had implications that were dangerous for the idea of limiting the sphere of government. Opponents of the rise of absolutism initially relied on conservative arguments about the need to preserve existing institutions, but were increasingly driven to produce principled arguments based on ideas about the nature and origin of political power, which, it was claimed, ultimately derived from the consent of the governed and implied that government was a delegated power exercised over a specific and delimited area of life.

However, the question that more than anything else led to the explicit articulation of a doctrine of the limited scope of government was that of religious division and the need for toleration. The divisions created in most parts of Europe by the Reformation led to a series of devastating wars and political unrest. The solution that was eventually arrived at was that, although only one denomination was established within each state, religious pluralism should exist in Europe as a whole. A minority argued that the solution to religious dissension was to make religious belief an essentially private matter and so take religious belief and observance out of the public sphere of government responsibility. This view was first formulated in the Dutch Republic and Britain (and in other parts of Europe where absolutism had been fought off) by thinkers such as Baruch Spinoza and John Locke. However, to argue for this position, these thinkers first had to develop a theory about the proper sphere and limits of government and its nature as a necessarily limited activity.

Throughout the 18th and 19th centuries, classical liberals and their progenitors argued the case for limited and rule-bound government. They argued for the primacy, both moral and practical, of personal choice and judgment concerning how we live our lives as opposed to public and collective decisions. This conclusion was grounded in the view that people were, in general, the best judges of their own interests and that truly moral behavior required the person involved to make decisions for themselves, for which they would bear the consequences, for good or ill. This precept implied strict limits on the scope of government. Limited government was thus intimately connected to the concepts of personal development and flourishing and grounded in the belief that only by limiting the scope of government could individual choice and self-development be maximized. This argument had its clearest and purest exposition in the work of Wilhelm von Humboldt in his *The Limits of State Action*. He maintained that a limited constitutional government also was a government of laws and not of men, the *Rechtsstaat* as it was known in Germany. The most prominent and historically significant example of a document expressing this view was, of course, the U.S. Constitution. However, it was only one of a number of such documents, the Belgian Constitution of 1830 being another influential example. The American constitution also showed a tactical division among classical liberals over how best to define the limits of government in constitutional rules. One method, found in the main body of the constitution, set out what the specific and enumerated areas of government power and responsibility were. The other, found in the Bill of Rights and looking back to earlier examples such as the Levellers' *Agreement of the People*, listed those activities that governments were explicitly excluded from concerning themselves with or doing. Experience suggests that the latter strategy has been more successful.

There were of course divisions among classical liberals over exactly where the limits of government should be drawn. Many were not as strict or rigorous as Humboldt and thus, for example, regarded education as a legitimate area of government responsibility. Thinkers who embraced the views associated with limited government also found themselves having to argue not only against others who wished these limits to be considerably broader, but also against those who rejected the idea of limits entirely. Among the first were advocates of what became known as the *Polizeistaat* (literally police state, but more accurately general welfare state) who claimed that governments had a responsibility to improve the moral and physical well-being of the public. A wider view of government's scope also was taken by many traditional conservatives, particularly in the Catholic and Lutheran parts of Europe. The more radical opposition came from followers of Rousseau. For them government was the embodiment of the General Will of society, which, by definition, sought the best interests of society as a whole. As such, providing government was correctly constituted so that it did indeed act in accord with the General Will, there were no theoretical limits to what it might choose to concern itself with. This radical view held that, once governments were freed from dependence on a particular minority, they could become the instrument through which society as a whole acted to achieve its collectively willed ends and, as such, should not be limited. One response to both this and a perceived threat to personal independence and judgment from social, as opposed to government, pressure and action was John Stuart Mill's *On Liberty*, which restated Humboldt's view of a limited sphere for politics, but placed it on a different foundation.

In the first two-thirds of the 19th century in particular, the classical liberal argument for limited government tended to carry the day. Reviews of Mill's work were, on the whole, favorable and even went so far as to contend that, because Mill was clearly right, his ideas required no extended argument in their support. However, the latter part of the 19th century saw, first, a decisive shift in the direction of a looser and wider understanding of limited government in the shape of "New Liberal" and social democratic thought, and, second, in the rise of explicitly totalitarian politics. This tendency remained a minority before 1914, but the disruption brought about by World War I paved the way for more totalitarian political philosophies, such as fascism in Italy and Germany and communism in Russia. World War II led to the spread of the communist totalitarian ideologies beyond their original base in the Soviet Union. Faced with this challenge, a de facto alliance emerged during the cold war between the different varieties of politics that espoused some version of limited government against these totalitarian and comprehensive theories of politics. In the latter part of the 20th century, the explicit argument against limited government—of the kind put forward by Mussolini and Gentile—seemed to have been defeated, and the debate now became one between libertarians arguing for a strictly defined and limited government and social democrats and conservatives who put the case for a limited but more extensive one.

In recent years, the debate has begun to move back onto the kind of grounds that it occupied in the later 18th and early 19th centuries. Increasingly, social democracy, the dominant tendency in contemporary democratic politics, has become defined by state intervention not only in the nation's economic life, but by intervention in many aspects of what were formerly thought to be purely private areas of life, such as diet and personal habits. In other words, we are seeing a revival of the idea of the police power and the associated general welfare state of the kind that was advocated by Prussian cameralists 200 years ago. Currently, the debate increasingly centers on where to draw the division between private matters subject to personal choice and public matters where choice is exercised by some form of collective decision-making process. This notion is clearly relevant to the more general argument of how extensive government should be. Libertarians consistently argue that giving government a large role is bad in and of itself

because it reduces the extent of individual autonomy, which is necessary for the practice of virtue; further, it is dangerous because the larger the area of government concern, the more a logic of expansion applies, which will ultimately approach a totalitarian state.

SD

See also Civil Society; Constitutionalism; Judiciary; Rule of Law; Separation of Church and State

Further Readings

Bastiat, Frédéric. "The State." *Selected Essays on Political Economy.* Seymour Cain, trans. George B. de Huszar, ed. Irvington-on-Hudson, NY: Foundation for Economic Education, 2006.

Hayek, F. A. *Constitution of Liberty.* Chicago: University of Chicago Press, 1960

Hobbes, Thomas. *Leviathan.* Richard Tuck, ed. Cambridge: Cambridge University Press, 1996.

Humboldt, Wilhelm von. *Limits of State Action.* J. W. Burrows, ed. Indianapolis, IN: Liberty Fund, 1993.

Locke, John. "Second Treatise on Government." *Two Treatises on Government.* Peter Laslett, ed. Cambridge: Cambridge University Press, 2005.

Madison, James. "Federalist No. 10." *The Federalist.* Clinton Rossiter and Charles R. Kesler, eds. New York: Signet Classics, 2003.

Mill, John Stuart. *On Liberty.* London: J. W. Parker and Son, 1859.

Rand, Ayn. "The Nature of Government." *Capitalism: The Unknown Ideal.* New York: Signet, 1986.

Spooner, Lysander. *No Treason: The Constitution of No Authority.* Boston: L. Spooner, 1867.

LOCKE, JOHN (1632–1704)

John Locke was perhaps the most influential and paradigmatic of classical liberal thinkers. Locke studied and taught at Oxford from 1652 to 1667, at which point he joined the household of Lord Ashley (later the Earl of Shaftesbury) as his personal physician. As a member of Shaftesbury's circle, Locke was deeply involved in political opposition to Charles II and James II throughout the 1670s and early 1680s. Locke went into exile in Holland shortly after Shaftesbury's death in 1683 and only returned to England after the Glorious Revolution. His early works in political philosophy include the *Essays on the Law of Nature* (1663–1664), and the pro-tolerance *An Essay on Toleration* (1667). His major and mature works in political philosophy were *Two Treatises of Government* (written 1680–1683, published in 1689) and the *Letter Concerning Toleration* (written 1685, published 1689, with the subsequent letters published in 1690 and 1692). Locke established his reputation as a major figure in philosophy with the publication of his treatise in epistemology, *An Essay Concerning Human Understanding* (1689). After his return to England, Locke was an influential advisor to the postrevolutionary regime. His most important later work was *The Reasonableness of Christianity* (1695).

The core of Locke's classical liberalism is presented in the *Second Treatise of Government*. Here Locke laid out his famous doctrines of natural rights, property rights, the consensual creation of government, and the conditions under which individual and collective resistance to government is justified. According to Locke, to understand the purpose, justification, and limits of political authority, we should inquire into the condition that people would find themselves in were all political authority absent. Such an investigation reveals what problems, if any, would exist if we lacked all political institutions and, hence, reveals what type of political authority rational individuals have reason to create. A major aspect of this inquiry into the state of nature is an investigation into what rights individuals possess in the state of nature. Such natural rights, if they exist, are possessed by individuals on the basis of yet more fundamental features of human existence.

Locke argued that the facts that each of us should engage in self-preserving actions and that none of us can reasonably view another person as existing for the sake of our own self-preserving actions support the conclusion that each of us has a right to dispose of ourselves as we judge best. Each of us possesses a right against others' disposing of us to advance their own purposes. Because we are all natural moral equals, any individual who rationally claims certain rights for himself must acknowledge that all other individuals have the same rights. Because what we each rationally claim against others is a right to freedom (i.e., a right to depose of our lives and liberty as we see fit), we each must grant that all other individuals have a like claim to freedom. Similarly, Locke argued that the way for each person to take cognizance of the facts that we are all, by nature, of equal moral standing and that each of us is directed by reason to preserve ourselves (and promote our happiness) is for each person to pursue his own self-preservation and happiness in ways that do not preclude others from comparably pursuing their own self-preservation and happiness.

In the state of nature, each individual has rights over his own life, limb, and liberty. The law of nature, which Locke held governs the state of nature, requires that we all are bound to respect each other's natural rights. For each of us, these rights also include a right over our own labor. We acquire rights to particular external objects by mixing our labor with some previously unowned material. Having so mixed our labor, we cannot be deprived of the transformed object without being deprived of our rightfully held labor. Hence, we now have a right to the transformed object. But it is crucial that the material labored on not already be the property of anyone else. This exception raises a complication; for Locke asserted that God has given the earth to all mankind in common. Thus, it may seem that no man may labor upon any part of nature without the prior consent of mankind. Locke argued, however, that God gave the earth to all mankind in the way that a father presents a cut of meat to his children: Each child may cut a slice of the meat for himself—which thereby becomes that child's property—without the prior consent of all the others. However, at least initially, two restrictions apply to the individual's acquisition of natural material. The individual may not acquire so much that a portion of what he takes spoils, and the individual must leave "enough and as good" natural material for others.

These initial provisos on individual acquisition are, however, transcended through the invention of money. Once value attaches to bits of silver or gold, individuals are able to exchange what will otherwise spoil for coins that will not spoil. The ability to preserve value indefinitely gives individuals much more incentive to produce exchangeable objects and much more incentive to discover new and better ways to produce such objects. At this point, Locke argued, failing "to leave enough and as good" of the world's natural material for others becomes morally permissible. It has become morally permissible because this eventuality is a consequence to which people agree by virtue of the introduction of money. If we ask ourselves why everyone would agree to the introduction of money when substantial economic inequalities are likely to result, the answer is that this inequality is beneficial to all. According to Locke, the introduction of money and the incentives and productivity gains engendered by money leads to a substantial expansion of the total wealth. So enormous is this expansion that even individuals who anticipate ending up with less than an equal share correctly expect that their portion will be much larger than would possess were money not introduced.

Beyond the rights to life, limb, liberty, and elaborate forms of property, individuals in the state of nature also possess rights to enforce the law of nature—to defend against violations of their rights and to enforce reparations and punish. The inconveniences of the state of nature arise from people's individual, nonstandardized, and uncoordinated attempts to enforce the law of nature. Especially as forms of property become more complex, there is a need for a clear public articulation of who owns what. In addition, the demand for known laws and reliable and impartial judges becomes increasingly important. At the same time, the need for reliable power to enforce known law and judicial decisions increases. For these reasons, directly or indirectly, individuals waive their private rights to act as executors of the law of nature. They vest this right in political society, which, in turn, entrusts a particular government with the task of articulating and enforcing the law of nature.

Government is assigned the task of securing individuals the enjoyment of their rights to life, limb, liberty, and property. These rights retain their full and original force so that any actions by government that infringe on them are criminal. If an individual correctly judges that the government or its agents has infringed on his rights, he may rightfully resist—although it is likely that things will not go well for him if he alone resists. If, in contrast, the government generally infringes on the rights of its citizens or systematically fails to protect their rights, it loses its claim to authority and may be replaced—by force if necessary. The bloodshed that accompanies a just revolution is to be blamed not on the revolutionaries, but rather on the monarch or legislators who have rebelled against justice by using force without right.

EM

See also Contractarianism/Social Contract; Hobbes, Thomas; Hume, David; Jefferson, Thomas; Private Property; Shaftesbury, Third Earl of

Further Readings

Ashcroft, Richard. *Revolutionary Politics and Locke's Two Treatises of Government*. Princeton, NJ: Princeton University Press, 1986.

Buckle, Stephen. *Natural Law and the Theory of Property: Grotius to Hume*. Oxford: Oxford University Press, 1993.

Grant, Ruth. *John Locke's Liberalism*. Chicago: University of Chicago Press, 1987.

Locke, John. *A Letter Concerning Toleration*. James Tully, ed. Indianapolis, IN: Hackett, 1990.

———. *Political Essays*. Mark Goldie, ed. Cambridge: Cambridge University Press, 1997.

———. *Two Treatises of Government* (A critical edition with introduction and notes by Peter Laslett). 2nd ed. Cambridge: Cambridge University Press, 1967.

Seliger, Martin. *The Liberal Politics of John Locke*. London: George Allen & Unwin, 1968.

Simmons, A. John. *The Lockean Theory of Rights*. Princeton, NJ: Princeton University Press, 1992.

———. *On the Edge of Anarchy*. Princeton, NJ: Princeton University Press, 1993.

MACAULAY, THOMAS BABINGTON (1800–1859)

Thomas Babington Macaulay was arguably the most influential of all the British classical liberals and a renowned historian, noted for his powerful prose. His magisterial history of England, a sensation when it first appeared, soon established itself as the standard work on its subject while his critical and historical essays were models of persuasive writing. Both commanded a worldwide mass readership long after his death and influenced the noted American journalist and essayist H. L. Mencken, among many others. Among the major themes of Macaulay's work were the cruelties and follies of arbitrary government, the harm wrought by religious strife and the persecuting spirit, and the transformative power of scientific advance and economic freedom.

Macaulay's major work, his multivolume *History of England from the Accession of James the Second*, concentrates on the events surrounding the Glorious Revolution of 1688, chronicling with unrivaled narrative grip the long struggle between "court" and "country"—between the forces of royal and governmental prerogative and those who sought for the people of England a right to govern themselves. Although unapologetically celebrating the triumph of freedom, Macaulay had little patience for abstract theories about the proper role of government. Instead, he understood English liberty to have grown hardy under constant assault, built up over long agonies like a mass of scar tissue through a succession of abuses and the resistance to them. Its extent and solidity was explainable by which bad officeholder had tried and failed to get away with which encroachment on the public during which reign.

The history's immense popularity with readers owed much to its vividly drawn individual portraits: the vain and foolish Stuart kings, vindictive Judge Jeffreys of the "Bloody Assizes," and many more. Although the standard critique of Macaulay was as an implacable partisan who was unfair to his opponents, many strokes of his characterization portray upright and admirable figures on the Tory side, as well as rogues and incompetents in his own Whig camp.

An unabashed believer in economic freedom, Macaulay in his history demonstrates the extent to which commercial and civil liberty grew up intertwined. The battle against arbitrary taxation accounted for many gains in the struggle against arbitrary government in general, while the fight to restrict unlimited search and seizure owed much to the popular resistance to tariffs and royal grants of monopoly. Few writers have dealt more effective blows to the notion that life for the English masses was worse after the Industrial Revolution than it had been before. In the famous chapter from his history on the condition of the nation in 1685—one of the great panoramic set pieces of the English language—he hammers away, page upon page, at the wretchedness of the food, the lodgings, the roads, the communications, the sanitation, the depravity of governance, and the prevalence of disorder and crime.

Turning to the controversies of his own time, in his essays Macaulay defended free trade and the new factory system. Then as now, critics assailed the increased division of labor and export-driven economic globalization, which, they argued, had impoverished ordinary workers and dissolved traditional ties of community into a mere cash nexus. Industrial advances had, they contended, replaced romantic, older farm-and-cottage landscapes with ungainly modern construction and raised a new class, the vulgar bourgeoisie, to cultural dominance. In his response, Macaulay cited vital statistics to demonstrate that the parts of England where the new manufacturing economy had penetrated furthest were the same parts where rates of poverty and mortality had plunged fastest.

He further rejected the notion that the newly affluent English urban populace—accused by some of being pleasure-obsessed and lacking in public spirit—exemplified some sort of decline in national character that a paternalistic government should seek to remedy. "The duties of government," he wrote,

> would be . . . paternal, if a government were necessarily as much superior in wisdom to a people as the most foolish father, for a time, is to the most intelligent child, and if a government loved a people as fathers generally love their children. But there is no reason to believe that a government will have either the paternal warmth of affection or the paternal superiority of intellect.

Macaulay also took issue with Christian conservatives who deplored the essentially secular turn that government had taken by the time Victoria had ascended the throne and who argued that religion should be regarded as the basis of civil government. He replied that because unbelievers, like everyone else, showed as keen a concern for not having their goods stolen or homes invaded, "we are at a loss to conceive in what sense religion can be said to be the basis of government, in which religion is not also the basis of the practices of eating, drinking, and lighting fires in cold weather." Among the most basic themes of his *History* is the almost unending series of calamities that religious intolerance brought upon the English nation; all the major sides (High Church, Low Church, and Catholics) embraced persecution as an instrument of policy and practiced it when they could, but at length no faction could summon a majority for its designs, at which point religious tolerance emerged as a kind of exhausted last resort.

Macaulay's extensive parliamentary and official career is best remembered for his role in defending adherents of minority religions, helping rid the West Indies of the slave trade, establishing modern copyright law, and reforming the government of India, which he endowed with a rational criminal code and a system of elite education based on the English language. Although he won a huge American readership, he took surprisingly little interest in American matters.

For many readers, one's first encounter with Macaulay begins a lifelong love affair with the writer. "He is always in a storm of revolt and indignation against wrong, craft, tyranny," Thackeray wrote on his death. "How he cheers heroic resistance; how he backs and applauds freedom struggling for its own; how he hates scoundrels, ever so victorious and successful; how he recognizes genius, though selfish villains possess it!"

WO

See also Free Trade; Glorious Revolution; Liberalism, Classical; Whiggism

Further Readings

Gabb, Sean. "Thomas Babington Macaulay (1800-1859): Rediscovering a Victorian Liberal." Libertarian Heritage no. 21 (Pamphlet). London: Libertarian Alliance, 2001.

Macaulay, Thomas Babington. *Miscellaneous Works in Five Volumes.* Lady Trevelyan, ed. New York: Harper & Bros., 1880.

Powell, Jim. *Thomas Babington Macaulay: Extraordinary Eloquence for Liberty.* Irvington-on-Hudson, NY: Freeman, 1996.

MacBride, Roger Lea (1929–1995)

Roger Lea MacBride was an author and the 1976 U.S. Libertarian Party presidential nominee. Roger MacBride was involved in classical liberal scholarship and activism virtually his entire life. As a child, he became close to Rose Wilder Lane, the daughter of Laura Ingalls Wilder, and he absorbed her libertarian philosophy. He graduated from Harvard Law School, practiced law in Vermont, served in the legislature, ran for governor, and published two books on constitutional law, *The American Electoral College* and *Treaties versus the Constitution.* After Lane's death, he inherited the rights to the Wilder books and turned *Little House on the Prairie* into a popular TV series. In 1972, living in Virginia, he was selected as a Republican elector. He refused to vote for Richard Nixon and cast his vote instead for the brand-new Libertarian Party ticket of philosopher John Hospers and journalist Tonie Nathan, who thus became the first woman in American history to receive an electoral vote. The Libertarian Party then chose MacBride to be its presidential nominee in 1976; his modest wealth helped the party to afford a professional campaign for the first time. He came in fourth, receiving about 173,000 votes. His campaign book *A New Dawn for America* presented libertarian principles and policies in a readable, commonsense manner. Later he returned to the Republican Party, chaired the Republican Liberty Caucus, and wrote several young-adult historical novels about Lane's childhood on a Missouri farm, including *Little House on Rocky Ridge.* MacBride put the Libertarian Party on the map with his electoral vote in 1972 and his vigorous and well-received campaign in 1976.

DB

See also Hospers, John; Lane, Rose Wilder; Nathan, Tonie

Further Readings

Doherty, Brian. *Radicals for Capitalism: A Freewheeling History of the Modern Libertarian Movement.* New York: Public Affairs, 2007.

Kelley, John L. *Bringing the Market Back In: The Political Revitalization of Market Liberalism.* New York: New York University Press, 1997. 191–192.

MacBride, Roger L. *The American Electoral College.* London: Caxton, 1952.

———. *A New Dawn for America.* Ottawa, IL: Green Hill, 1976.

MADISON, JAMES (1750–1836)

James Madison is probably best known as the "father of the constitution," but he also had a distinguished career in politics both before and after the Constitutional Convention of 1787. As leader of the House of Representatives in the first years under the new U.S. Constitution, he authored and secured the passage of the Bill of Rights; he went on to become Secretary of State in the Jefferson administration, and he succeeded Jefferson as president in 1809. Nonetheless, his fame and lasting importance rest largely on the political analyses and innovations that he developed at the time of the movement for a new constitution and Bill of Rights.

Madison thought of the foundations and ends of politics in the terms captured in the Declaration of Independence. In his role as "father of the Bill of Rights," he proposed as a first amendment to the Constitution

> that there be prefixed to the document a declaration, that all power is originally vested in, and consequently derived from, the people. That government is instituted and ought to be exercised for the benefit of the people; which consists in the enjoyment of life and liberty, with the right of acquiring and using property, and generally of pursuing and obtaining happiness and safety. That the people have an indubitable, unalienable, and indefeasible right to reform or change their government, whenever it be found adverse or inadequate to the purposes of its institution.

Madison here invokes a Lockean social contract theory of political authority. Political power traces back to the people, who are thus sovereign. Rulers possess what are, in effect, delegated powers meant to procure the good of the people, not the good of the rulers. The exercise of political power is thus to be judged according to whether it serves the public good. Like Locke, Madison understood that good as consisting of the security of preexisting (i.e., natural) rights or the objects of preexisting rights—"the enjoyment of life and liberty, with the right of acquiring and using property; and generally of pursuing and obtaining happiness and safety." Finally, Madison capped his list of first principles with the "indubitable, unalienable, and indefeasible right to reform or change their government," which is a close echo of Jefferson's parallel "right to alter or abolish" governments that fail to secure the end (rights securing) for which they exist.

Madison believed that these principles of political right had clear implications for the organization of political power. He called himself one "of those who [believe] in the doctrine that mankind are capable of governing themselves and [hate] hereditary power as an insult to the reason and an outrage to the rights of man." The "rights of man," Madison maintained, imply that only "republican government" is legitimate. If, as the social contract theory says, political authority derives exclusively from the people, then no set of rulers can claim any share or piece of it that does not derive from the people. That disqualified all hereditary and other forms of self-appointed political authority. Earlier adherents of a social contract did not draw similar conclusions, but accepted as legitimate that a part of government rest in the hands of hereditary ruling groups. When Madison and the other Americans rejected this element of earlier political philosophy, they set the terms for the task to which Madison's political science was most emphatically directed: to build a wholly republican system, what we would today call a democracy, that successfully achieves the task for which all governments rightly exist—to secure the rights we all possess.

Like Locke, Madison identified all rights as property, which he explains to be a "dominion which one man claims . . . in exclusion of every other individual." There are thus two elements to rights: dominion and exclusivity. The rights holder has a kind of control over that to which he has a right, coupled with an immunity from the intrusions of others on that to which he has a right. Madison recognized that the more usual meaning of the term *property* involves "the external things of the world," but he also identified a broader meaning: "In its larger and juster meaning, [property] embraces everything to which a man may attach a value and have a right, and *which leaves to everyone else the like advantage.*" He included in property in this broad sense "safety and liberty of person," "the free use of . . . faculties, and free choice of the objects on which to employ them," the rights Locke, and after him Jefferson, included in the catalog of rights as "life" and "liberty." In summary, Madison maintained, "as a man is said to have a right to his property, he may be equally said to have a property in his rights."

Madison asserted that "government is instituted to protect" this broad kind of property. "That alone is a *just* government which *impartially* secures to every man whatever is his *own.*" Just government, in order to secure property in external goods, must not invade property in personal rights, must not seize the property that a man has in "his personal safety and personal liberty," nor may men be denied "the free use of their faculties and free choice of their occupations" because of "arbitrary restrictions, exemptions, and monopolies." Just governments neither "invade the domestic sanctuaries of the rich" nor "grind the faces of the poor." We all equally have rights, and we all have an equal right to have our property secured, but the task of just governance is rendered difficult by the fact that some people have more (sometimes much more) of the external things of the world than do others. Although we all have equal rights (and, therefore, equal property in one sense), we all do not have equal property in the other sense; in one form or another, property tends to translate into political power, and the holders of political power are seldom neutral or fair-minded in the way they wield it. Rather, they use it to favor their own interests. How then can government act impartially and justly?

Madison's political philosophy poses three especially difficult problems that must be solved: (1) How can one combine republican government with a system that secures rights? (2) How can one impartially secure property in both the narrow and extended senses of the term? and (3) How can one navigate the narrow passage between a too strong government and too much liberty? Madison's greatness as a political scientist lay, in part, in his recognition that all previous models, including those most widely accepted in the American colonies, were inadequate to the challenge posed by these three problems. This recognition drove him to a series of political inventions intended to provide a set of novel solutions.

The years immediately following the American victory in the Revolutionary War were economically and politically difficult ones for the new nation. Madison was one of the first to see that the root of the problem was the inadequacy of political arrangements both within the new states and at the level of the union of the states. The government of the union under the Articles of Confederation was built on the model of "government of the states, by the states and for the states." The citizens of the union were the member states; the congress or assembly of the states made recommendations to its members that did or did not carry out these recommendations (more often not). Madison quickly realized that this system of essentially voluntary cooperation had serious and insoluble problems centering on collective action. He saw that coercive power was needed at the center if the union was ever to become a successful government. However, unlike many other American leaders, he realized that coercion could not be used against the member states as states because, in that case, every effort to enforce the law would be an invitation to civil war. Much better, he realized, would be for the central government to attempt to enforce its laws directly on individuals. Yet if the government of the union is to operate directly on its citizens, then the citizens must have direct involvement in its composition and operation. Thus was born the entirely new kind of federal system that entered the world with the American Constitution.

Madison's new federalism meant that, for certain purposes (those entrusted to the central government), the United States would constitute one large republic, which was regarded by contemporary political theorists as quite dangerous. Republics, it was held, must be small, and the people must be able to keep their rulers on a "short leash." Madison's analysis overturned that judgment. The commitment to small republics, he argued, not only stood in the way of an effective federal union of the states, but also stood behind the sorry record of injustice and instability within the states. Short-leash republics facilitated the formation of majorities that threatened the rights of minorities and hampered the construction of governments capable of acting effectively to accomplish the tasks for which governments were established. Large and diverse republics, such as would exist in the union, would be less likely to produce oppressive majorities. Moreover, institutions constructed on principles of greater independence for office holders would, paradoxically, secure both more effective and safer governance. Power and liberty, Madison demonstrated, are, within limits, not enemies, but could be mutually supportive.

Madison went on to explain the principles of his new political science in *The Federalist*, the series of essays he coauthored to further the Constitution's chances for ratification. These essays, especially the famous Federalist no. 10, remain the best source for understanding Madison's political innovations.

MZ

See also Bill of Rights, U.S.; Constitution, U.S.; Federalists Versus Anti-Federalists; Limited Government; Separation of Church and State

Further Readings

Banning, Lance. *The Sacred Fire of Liberty*. Ithaca, NY: Cornell University Press, 1995.

Diamond, Martin. *As Far as Republican Principles Will Admit*. Washington, DC: AEI Press, 1992.

Epstein, David F. *The Political Theory of the Federalist*. Chicago: University of Chicago Press, 1984.

Hamilton, Alexander, James Madison, and John Jay. *The Federalist Papers*. Charles R. Kesler, ed. New York: Signet Classics, 2003.

Ketcham, Ralph. *James Madison*. Charlottesville: University Press of Virginia, 1990.

Matthews, Richard. *If Men Were Angels: James Madison and the Heartless Empire of Reason*. Lawrence: University Press of Kansas, 1995.

McCoy, Drew. *The Last of the Fathers: James Madison and the Republican Legacy*. Cambridge: Cambridge University Press, 1989.

Sheldon, Garrett Ward. *The Political Philosophy of James Madison*. Baltimore: Johns Hopkins University Press, 2001.

Zuckert, Michael P. "Federalism and the Founding." *Review of Politics* 48 no. 2 (Spring 1986): 166–210.

———. "The Political Science of James Madison." *History of American Political Thought*. Bryan Paul Frost and Jeffrey Sikkenga, eds. Landham, MD: Lexington Books, 2003.

MAGNA CARTA

Magna Carta (Great Charter) was originally a peace agreement between King John and a number of rebel feudal lords (barons), signed and agreed at a meadow at Runnymede in Surrey in 1215. It addressed a number of grievances arising from the government and policy of both King John and his brother Richard I—discontents that had come to a head as a result of John's dispute with the Church and his military defeat at the hands of Philip II of France. However, the terms of the agreement dealt with these issues by articulating general principles, rather than by settling specific concrete disputes, and it was this generality that made it a historic document of permanent importance. There were precedents for royal charters of this nature, notably the Coronation Charter of Henry I of 1101, but this was the first time that specific grievances over the misuse of power led to a general statement of principles of government.

Magna Carta contains 61 clauses. Some deal with apparently trivial issues, such as the banning of fish weirs (no. 33), or with extremely specific abuses of royal power. The central clauses of the Charter, however, articulated a series of principles that the Angevin Kings and their servants had violated. The first clause recognized the freedom of the Church, stipulating that it was not under royal control. Other important principles included limitations on royal powers of taxation and appropriation and the insistence that these limits be exercised according to known and established laws (e.g., clauses 2, 3, 4, 9, 55, and 56); that general tax levies (aids) could only be raised after the King had gained consent through the calling of a general council, according to precise rules (clauses 12 and 14); that no movable goods could be taken by royal officers without payment (clause 28); and that punishment should be proportional to the offense and should not take away a man's means of livelihood (clause 20). The most important, both at the time and for later developments, were clauses 39 and 40. These clauses stated: "No freeman shall be arrested or imprisoned, or disseized, or outlawed, or banished, or in any way molested; nor will we set forth against him, nor send against him, unless by the lawful judgment of his peers and by the law of the land" (clause 39) and "To no one will we sell, to no one deny or delay right or justice." These articulated what would later be called the principle of "due process of law."

The crucial importance of Magna Carta, at the time and since, was that it limited royal power by establishing the principle that such power had to be exercised in an orderly and rule-bound fashion in accordance with known and recognized law and not simply according to the arbitrary will or interests of its holder. In other words, it was one of the first formal statements of the principle of the rule of law. An important point to note is that it did not simply limit royal power while leaving noble or ecclesiastical power unchecked. Clause 15 limited the power of barons to levy charges on their tenants in the same way that the King's power of taxation was restrained. Clause 60 stated, "All these customs and liberties that we have granted shall be observed in our kingdom insofar as concerns our own relations with our subjects. Let all men of our kingdom, whether clergy or laymen, observe them similarly in their relations their own men." Thus, Magna Carta established the principle of the rule of law as a check on power in general, at least in England.

However, Magna Carta was only the first of several such concessions by European rulers. Among the more important were the Golden Bull of Hungary (1222), the Danish Great Charter or Handfaestning (1282), the Aragonese Privileges of Union (1287), and the Statute of Piotrkow (1496). All of these concessions, like Magna Carta, laid down constitutional rules establishing a set of principles governing the way political institutions were required to operate and limiting their rule-making and enforcement powers. Magna Carta itself had great importance in later English history. Indeed, its real significance for many historians lies in the way subsequent generations came to see it as the basic constitution or law of the realm and to hold to it as a protection against the growth of arbitrary power. This interpretive shift occurred soon after its signing when Simon De Montfort, in his disputes with John's son, Henry III, demanded that Magna Carta's principles be upheld. This demand led, among other things, to the summoning of the first "Model" Parliament in 1261. Later, opponents of the Stuarts' attempts to establish absolute monarchy in England, such as Coke, Pym, and Hampden, all appealed to the symbol and authority of Magna Carta. As late as the mid-19th century, as, for example, in the Chartist movement, radicals made use of the Charter to support their demands against what they regarded as arbitrary government. The principles of constitutional government and the rule of law first articulated in Magna Carta were thus passed down and developed by later generations, including the American colonists, who also looked back to it as the first statement of the principles they held dear.

SD

See also Immigration; Limited Government; Rule of Law; Taxation

Further Readings

Adams, John. "Dissertation on the Canon and Feudal Law." *The Revolutionary Writings of John Adams* (selected by C. Bradley Thompson). Indianapolis, IN: Liberty Fund, 2000.

Brooks, David, ed. *From Magna Carta to the Constitution: Documents in the Struggle for Liberty.* San Francisco: Fox & Wilkes, 1993.

Coke, Edward. "Petition of Right." *The Selected Writings and Speeches of Sir Edward Coke*. Vol. 3. Steven Sheppard, ed. Indianapolis, IN: Liberty Fund, 2003.

Holt, J. C. *Magna Carta*. Cambridge: Cambridge University Press, 1992.

———. *Magna Carta and the Idea of Liberty*. London: Wiley, 1972.

Pallister, Anne. *Magna Carta: The Heritage of Liberty*. Oxford: Oxford University Press, 1971.

Turner, Ralph. *Magna Carta*. London: Longman, 2003.

MAINE, HENRY SUMNER (1822–1888)

Sir Henry Sumner Maine was one of the most important legal academicians of the 19th century. He was born near Leighton, Scotland, educated at Cambridge, and, toward the end of his career, became Whewell Professor of International Law at Cambridge. His seminal work, *Ancient Law* (1861), is the product of lectures he delivered during the 1850s on Roman law and jurisprudence at London's Inns of the Court. Soon after its publication, he left the academic world to accept an appointment as the law member of the Council of Governor-General of India, charged with the responsibility of reforming and codifying Indian law. His experiences in this capacity reinforced his belief, evident in *Ancient Law*, that the evolution of societies—both institutionally and philosophically—can be most thoroughly understood through the historical and comparative study of law. Following up on his work in India, he was named Corpus Professor of Jurisprudence at Oxford, thereby becoming the first professor of comparative and historical jurisprudence in the history of that university. The lectures he delivered there formed the basis for his later works, *Village Communities in East and West* (1871), *Lectures on the Early History of Institutions* (1875), and *Dissertations on Early Law and Custom* (1883).

Maine is best known for the proposition advanced in *Ancient Law* that "the movement of the progressive societies has hitherto been a movement from status to contract." As he explained, the ancient law recognized and dealt with the relationships among extended families, not individuals. Individual members of a family were subject to the control of the family head. As he points out, under the Roman legal conception, *Pater Potestas*, the head of the family possessed virtually complete power, including those of life and death, over members of the family. Consequently, the laws did not recognize individuals qua individuals because they only had status within the realm of this patriarchal authority. The gradual erosion of the notion of *Pater Potestas* was marked by a movement to contract, wherein law recognized the capacity of individuals to assume powers, responsibilities, and authority. Progressive societies, as Maine shows,

are those where this "emancipation" or "liberation" of the individual had taken place—"static" societies, those whose legal systems still adhere to "status."

Although Maine regarded Western societies as "progressive" principally because this evolution to contract resulted in greater individual liberty, initiative, and responsibility, he also was one of the more trenchant Victorian critics of a growing and seemingly inevitable movement toward democratic government. So much is clear from his *Popular Government* (1885), in which the influence of Edmund Burke and Herbert Spencer is particularly evident. The work consists of four somewhat disjointed essays that deal with major difficulties underlying both the theory and practice of democracy. He finds grave faults with Rousseau's teachings, which, he believed, fueled the notion of an omnipotent democratic state that could dispose of "everything which individual men value, their property, their persons, and their independence." In the same way, he was critical of Jeremy Bentham for supporting the desirability of "a priori" constitutions—those "founded on speculative assumptions remote from experience." Thus, he maintained that the relative success of the American Constitution could be attributed to its incorporation of the accepted and proven modes of governance. In all, Maine's contributions to the history of law and the evolution of free societies placed him in the highest rank of legal theoreticians.

GWC

See also Burke, Edmund; Liberalism, Classical; Liberty in the Ancient World; Spencer, Herbert

Further Readings

Feaver, George. *From Status to Contract: A Biography of Sir Henry Maine, 1822–1888*. London: Longmans Green, 1969.

Maine, Henry Sumner. *Ancient Law: Its Connection with the Early History of Society, and Its Relation to Modern Ideas*. London: John Murray, 1861.

MANDEVILLE, BERNARD (1670–1733)

Bernard Mandeville, a Dutch physician who settled in London shortly after earning his degree in medicine at the University of Leyden, is best known as the controversial author of *The Fable of the Bees: or, Private Vices, Publick Benefits* (6th ed., 1729). This work exhibits a number of themes, such as the role of self-interest in generating a prosperous spontaneous order, that would play a crucial role in later libertarian thought.

Mandeville had good reason to characterize *The Fable of the Bees* as "a rhapsody void of order or method." Written over a period of 24 years, it began as a brief poem, "The Grumbling Hive: or, Knaves Turn'd Honest" (1705). In later years (beginning in 1714), Mandeville appended a number of essays, remarks, and dialogues to subsequent editions until what began as a poem of 433 lines came to fill two substantial volumes. This later material includes two important theoretical essays, "An Enquiry into the Origin of Moral Virtue" and "A Search into the Nature of Society." Six dialogues that comprise the second volume are extended commentaries on the themes presented in "The Grumbling Hive."

"The Grumbling Hive" is an allegory extolling the social benefits of self-interested actions, such as avarice, greed, and other traditional vices. It is not always clear, however, what Mandeville is claiming when he notes that "private vices" produce "public benefits." He depicts the hive as a limited monarchy in which the King's power "was circumsrib'd by Laws." In the "Moral" of the poem, Mandeville states:

So Vice is beneficial found,

When it's by Justice lopt and bound

This couplet suggests that Mandeville regarded as socially beneficial only those vices that do not violate the rules of justice. This interpretation was given by F. B. Kaye in his definitive edition of the *Fable*, which was published in 1924. Kaye writes:

Vices are to be punished as soon as they grow into crimes, says Mandeville. . . . [T]he real thesis of the book is not that all evil is a public benefit, but that a certain useful proportion of it (called vice) is such a benefit (and . . . is on that account not really felt to be evil, though still called vicious).

This interpretation is somewhat problematic, however, because Mandeville also discusses the social benefits of unjust actions, such as theft and fraud, which provide employment for those in the criminal justice system, as well as for those artisans and laborers who are needed to replace goods that have been destroyed or stolen.

The ambiguities in Mandeville's poem (which also appear in his explanatory essays) partially account for the hostile reception the work later received even from those who sympathized with its defense of self-interest. For example, in *The Theory of Moral Sentiments*, Adam Smith notes that Mandeville's arguments "in some respects bordered upon the truth" despite "how destructive this system may appear."

Although Kaye and other commentators have described Mandeville as an early proponent of free trade, he is more accurately described as a mercantilist inasmuch as he believed that a government should ensure a favorable balance of trade. Whatever his position on the issue of trade, however, it is generally accepted that Mandeville was an early sympathizer to the tenets of laissez-faire.

One of Mandeville's most influential arguments was his defense of "luxury," which had been widely condemned for its supposedly enervating effects on social mores. Many of Mandeville's comments about the economic benefits of luxury, as well as his criticism of this concept as being excessively vague, would later reappear in the writings of David Hume, Edward Gibbon, Adam Smith, and other liberal individualists.

Less popular was Mandeville's psychological egoism, that is, his claim that all actions, even those virtuous actions that appear altruistic or disinterested, are ultimately motivated by self-interest. It was largely owing to this thesis that Mandeville (like Thomas Hobbes before him) was widely condemned as an enemy of morality. Mandeville responded to these charges by claiming that he was observing human behavior as it really is, not prescribing how it should be.

GHS

See also Capitalism; Civil Society; Ferguson, Adam; Natural Harmony of Interests; Republicanism, Classical; Smith, Adam

Further Readings

Hundert, E. J. *The Enlightenment's Fable: Bernard Mandeville and the Discovery of Society.* Cambridge: Cambridge University Press, 2005.

Mandeville, Bernard, and E. J. Hundert. *The Fable of the Bees: And Other Writings.* New York: Hackett, 1997.

Primer, I. *Mandeville Studies: New Explorations in the Art and Thought of Dr. Bernard Mandeville.* New York: Springer, 1975.

MARKET FAILURE

Market failure arguments lie at the root of a number of arguments supporting government intervention in the economy. A claim of market failure, by its nature, suggests some reason that voluntary, private institutions cannot produce valuable goods and services to the appropriate extent. These arguments fall into several categories, but most commonly center on the issues of public goods and externalities. Sometimes the phrase "collective action problems" serves as a more general rubric for what are perceived as failures of the market to deal with specific issues.

There are two aspects to the problem of public goods. The first, "nonrivalry," suggests that an additional person can consume a good without infringing on the consumption of others. For instance, if a movie theater is not full, another viewer can be admitted at little or no social cost. "Nonexcludability" suggests that it is hard to charge individuals for a particular good or service. For instance, imagine that nuclear defense against foreign attack were privatized. An individual who did not contribute to its provisioning could still enjoy the benefits of living under a nuclear umbrella. For this reason, it is likely that too few individuals would purchase the service, with the result that markets would fail to provide an adequate national defense.

In today's world, nonexcludability is regarded as the more important and more fundamental problem that economics and political science must address. Nonrivalry is less formidable because private suppliers of public goods have a strong incentive to gather as many paying customers as possible. If inefficient exclusion is indeed a problem, monopoly is the likely culprit. At one point or another, virtually every good or service has been labeled a public good. National defense, the rule of law, and police protection are the most universally accepted examples, but the list often includes, among many examples, roads, fire protection, social welfare insurance, health care, a clean environment, and subsidies to science and the arts.

The issue surrounding externalities is closely related to that of public goods and nonexcludability. A positive externality occurs when the action of one person confers a benefit on another when the second person does not pay for the benefit in some form or another. The externality is potentially significant when the people involved cannot conduct the appropriate trades. For instance, it may benefit my neighbors if I clean up my yard. If I do not take these benefits into account, my yard might remain excessively sloppy. Furthermore, my neighbors may be reluctant to pay me to clean my yard knowing that otherwise I might be sloppy simply in order to charge them for having a neighbor with a clean yard. Positive externalities therefore tend to be underprovided.

Negative externalities occur when the actions of a person harm another and the two cannot contract so that the one harmed is compensated for the damage suffered. Pollution is a classic case of a negative externality, but crime and traffic congestion are equally common examples. Externalities, whether positive or negative, constitute another, more general way of talking about nonexcludable public goods. In both cases, individual actions create benefits and costs for others, which cannot be traded in ordinary markets.

It is often the case that the problem of externalities can be solved by a better definition of property rights. If, for example, a lake or river is privately owned, the owner may have a personal incentive to keep the resource clean and flowing as it should. A publicly owned resource, in contrast, often is one where no one has a strong incentive to maintain its value. This situation has been dubbed "the tragedy of the commons." Many pollution problems, rather than illustrating the failures of markets, are more accurately seen as failures of government to adequately define property rights.

Well-defined property rights also can solve many local public goods problems. Proprietary communities, for instance, are able and often do provide water and electricity services, crime prevention, and numerous other public goods. Private contractors are willing to build new roads and freeway extensions provided they have the right to charge for their investments. Other public goods are produced by "tying" arrangements, such as when a private shopping mall provides security services, roads, and street lamps, all to encourage consumers to visit the mall.

Many solutions to public goods and externality problems are technological in nature. New technologies can help us identify and penalize polluters, thus improving property rights protection. We also can better define property rights, such as using electronic tags by which private owners can own or harvest wild herds of animals. The owners then have an incentive to maintain the value of those animals, rather than overhunting them. New technologies also might help us decentralize the supply of electricity and water, making those services less of a natural monopoly. Cable and satellite technologies have made TV less of a public good. In other instances, technologies lower transaction costs and allow people to trade in new ways. The Internet has proved enormously successful in finding and mobilizing relevant customers, and new securities markets can lower the cost of making transactions.

Market innovations have eased the production of health care and social welfare insurance. The Internet, for instance, now gives customers better access to health care information. HMOs simplify the purchase of health care, especially for cost-conscious individuals, and new and better insurance contracts make it easier for individuals to spread risk. The notion of catastrophic health care insurance, for instance, did not have wide currency until the 20th century.

Sometimes nonmonetary incentives also contribute to solving public goods problems. Altruism and the desire to feel good about oneself encourage individuals to give to charities and to behave well toward their neighbors. Social norms for reciprocity often develop, thereby allowing smaller initial amounts of altruism to develop into more systematic chains of assistance. The quest for fame encourages many artists, scientists, and donors. Einstein did not become rich, but his name will live in history, and many individuals help fund museums and artistic institutions, in part, to receive reflected glory. Public goods theories often take an excessively simple view of human motivations. Complex motivations imply that private entrepreneurs have access to many different ways of putting together "a deal" to produce public goods. Pecuniary incentives are just one part of a broader package of available instruments.

Indeed, there are occasions when it is arguable whether a public good or externality constitutes a significant dilemma at all. For instance, education is commonly described as a public good, but this notion is questionable. It does not suffice to cite stale clichés about the benefits of an educated population. Education yields significant enjoyment and pecuniary returns to those who seek it. The private incentive to become educated may well suffice to generate high levels of educational investment. Not surprisingly, some theories of market failure (signaling theories) say we have "too much" education, whereas other theories say we have "too little" education.

Perhaps most important, any given market failure must be compared to what is likely to occur if the government were to attempt to rectify the problem. It is not enough to establish that markets fail to provide a perfect outcome. All policy analysis is comparative, and we must consider whether markets or politics, in a given instance, will lead to greater imperfections. Politics brings in its wake bureaucracies, poorly informed voters, high discount rates, and special interest groups, among other imperfections. Once government starts intervening to support the production of public goods, it is likely to overstep its bounds and create new problems that were not initially present. It is absurd to point to market failures and to totally ignore political failures.

Market failure theories should be evaluated within the broader context of problems centering on the lack of or the difficulty of acquiring the relevant knowledge. In many cases, it is difficult to determine just how much of a good or service should be produced. For this reason, it is almost impossible to second-guess market provision. This uncertainty does not prove that market provision is always the correct one, but it does make us more skeptical about fine-tuning the economy. Often the best the economist can do is analyze the general properties of differing regimes and ask which does best at serving consumer welfare, keeping the peace, and encouraging innovation. Here the record of a market economy and the rule of law is a relatively strong one. We may wish to strengthen markets, rather than intervening each and every time we think we can improve on them. Such discretionary interventions may erode the long-run economic, political, and cultural foundations of a market order.

In summary, market failure is a broad and complex area. It potentially encompasses the entirety of our economy and involves many disparate policy issues. Few economists would argue that public goods and externalities can never justify government intervention. Nonetheless, the public goods and externalities arguments are often overrated in their force. Public goods and externalities do exist, but they provide incentives for new ways to generate and capture gains from trade.

TC

See also Externalities; Free-Market Economy; Regulation; Voluntary Contract Enforcement

Further Readings

Cowen, Tyler, ed. *Public Goods and Market Failures: A Critical Examination*. New Brunswick, NJ: Transaction, 1992.

Cowen, Tyler, and Eric Crampton, eds. *Market Failure or Success: The New Debate*. Cheltenham, UK: Edward Elgar, 2003.

Klein, Daniel, and Fred Foldvary, eds. *The Half-Life of Policy Rationales: How New Technology Affects Old Policy Issues*. New York: New York University Press, 2003.

MARRIAGE

Marriage is a socially sanctioned union that imposes rights and obligations on the parties. Although it can consist of a variety of combinations of men and women, the most common form has been a monogamous relationship between a man and a woman. Although libertarians would permit individuals to make the decisions that are most likely to increase their welfare, subject to limitations if there are effects on third parties, seldom have people been free to make their own decisions about marriage—and especially their spouse. For most of history, decisions about whom someone would marry were controlled by others, especially the spouses' families. As the ability of individuals to choose their own spouse has increased, familial restrictions have been replaced by legal ones imposed by the state. The most important restrictions on whom one may marry are on the ability to determine the basis on which a marriage will be dissolved and on the financial and custodial arrangements that will follow. Restrictions on the right of multiracial couples to marry have been removed, yet these restrictions remain in place in most states for same-sex couples. Most industrial nations have instituted a system that permits unilateral divorce and combined this system with limited compensation to a divorced spouse, which often results in less desirable outcomes than those that people could agree to on their own.

Throughout most of history, the rights and obligations of marriage were informal, enforced by family or clan members. With the introduction of the Justinian Code in the 6th century, laws were established to regulate marriage. Nevertheless, for most couples in Europe, marriage continued as an informal arrangement. However, in 1563, the Council of Trent required that all valid Catholic marriages had to be celebrated in a Catholic church by a priest and before two witnesses. The Reformation effectively introduced civil marriage, regulated by the civil authorities, although it did not preclude marriage being solemnized in a religious ceremony.

Legally, marriage is a contractual relationship that vests the parties involved with a new legal status. Just as with other binding contracts, marriage requires that the parties have the capacity to enter into contracts and that they be free of duress. However, marriage, unlike other contractual relationships, imposes a legal status that cannot be terminated at the will of both parties, but requires the intercession of a court. With few exceptions, a marriage contracted in one place is regarded as valid everywhere. The earlier British and American laws of marriage were characterized chiefly by the view that husband and wife are one legal entity for whom the husband acts. Starting with the "married women's property" statutes at the end of the 19th century, however, women have for the most part obtained equal rights and obligations within marriage.

Courts today are generally unwilling to address the ongoing marital relationship; as a consequence, legal regulations limit themselves to addressing the formation and dissolution of marriage. The major restriction on who may marry in the United States is the constraint on the right of same-sex couples to marry or receive any of the benefits of marriage. Although one state currently allows same-sex couples to marry, the federal Defense of Marriage Act permits, indeed encourages, other states not to recognize marriages between same-sex couples. At the same time, the federal government restricts the numerous federal benefits of marriage to heterosexual couples only.

The laws governing the dissolution of a marriage and the financial and custodial arrangements that might follow prevent many couples from arriving at some voluntary arrangement. Between 1969 and 1985, all the states either replaced their laws respecting the grounds necessary for a divorce—adultery, desertion, cruelty, and so on—with no-fault divorces or added no-fault divorces to the grounds in place previously. In effect, these no-fault laws permit either spouse to dissolve a marriage unilaterally. During the earlier era, most unsuccessful marriages failed for reasons other than the fault of one of the parties. The result was that couples often negotiated the dissolution of their marriage using fabricated testimony to establish fault. In these negotiations, they could effectively ignore the statutes controlling the financial and custodial arrangements at divorce. The no-fault divorce laws not only changed the grounds for divorce, but they increased the importance of the statutes governing the financial and custodial arrangements at divorce. These laws usually provide for an equal division of legally recognized property, short-term rehabilitative spousal support, and child support. The courts continue to favor mothers in the case of physical custody of children while generally providing for joint legal custody.

The current divorce laws in the United States tend to reduce social benefits relative to the outcomes that would have occurred had voluntary agreements between spouses been permitted. Current laws permit a party who initiates a divorce to ignore some of the costs of divorce. First, current law does not adequately compensate a spouse who has limited his or her career in order to provide household services to the partner. Second, divorced spouses may still be strongly attracted to their spouse and children and suffer accordingly, a suffering uncompensated by the courts. Third, the marriage in the process of being dissolved was potentially the result of a long and costly search, for which the divorced spouse will remain uncompensated. Last, the quality of life of the divorced couple's children could well deteriorate relative to what might have prevailed in the absence of the divorce. It is often impossible to negotiate a superior agreement than that imposed by the courts because of the heterogeneous and limited resources of the spouses and because of high transaction costs.

In summary, from a libertarian perspective, social welfare could be improved by permitting people more freedom to choose their spouse and to determine the grounds under which their marriage can be dissolved, together with associated financial and custodial arrangements. For many people, welfare would be increased by choosing mutual consent as the basis for a divorce—especially for established marriages—because then it is more likely that a divorce would only occur when the net benefits are positive. For both married and unmarried parents, laws that require parents to protect and support their children are appropriate because of the external effects of the parents' actions on their children.

AMP

See also Children; Civil Society; Family; Feminism and Women's Rights; Separation of Church and State; Sexuality

Further Readings

Becker, Gary S. *A Treatise on the Family*. Cambridge, MA: Harvard University Press, 1991.

Dnes, Antony W., and Robert Rowthorn. *The Law and Economics of Marriage and Divorce*. Cambridge: Cambridge University Press, 2002.

Parkman, Allen M. *Good Intentions Gone Awry*. Lanham, MD: Rowman & Littlefield, 2000.

Posner, Richard A. *Sex and Reason*. Cambridge, MA: Harvard University Press, 1992.

Marxism

Marxism purports to offer a scientific account of human history based on the economic and material conditions through which societies pass. Marxism is a species of communism in that it holds that the best society is one in which all property is held in common. Specifically, Marxism holds industrial communism to be the highest and final stage of social development. Its founder, Karl Marx (1818–1883), believed that this final stage of history was rapidly approaching, and he worked tirelessly to advance both his social theories and the revolution that they entailed. Many others had argued for communal property, but the enormous influence of Marx's thought guaranteed that modern communism will always be most closely associated with him and his system, especially in light of the fact that his economic theory of social ownership was predicated on the prior development of an industrial society.

Marxism is an intellectual descendant of German idealism, and particularly of Hegelian thought, which held that history is the story of the gradual development of man's spirit through a series of stages, each one more advanced than the last. Hegel viewed man's mind or spirit as progressing through a series of conflicts and resolutions, and he viewed the outward manifestation of this process as identical with "history" in its more conventional sense. Hegel argued that inner conflicts, present within the leading men and leading societies of any age, were ultimately the driving force of economic, political, and cultural change. These conflicts within the life of the mind in turn produced the various stages of human history, complete with their governments, beliefs, arts, and economics. Marx, however, argued that the conflicts of intellectual and social life found their ultimate origin in conflicts over scarce resources and over the ownership of the means of production for any given epoch.

History, in other words, was fundamentally an economic phenomenon, not an intellectual one, and economics provided the key to understanding all the rest. In a famous phrase of Marx's, "The hand-mill gives you society with the feudal lord; the steam-mill society with the industrial capitalist." More precisely, Marxist thought holds that the feudal system was predicated on the ownership of land and the extraction of agricultural land rent as the most important means of economic production. Because this form of extraction was the most profitable one available given the stage of material development at the time, it necessarily benefited the landlords, whose tastes, cultural values, and ideas, shaped, as they were, by economic circumstances, also were the ones that determined the culture of the era. To a Marxist, feudal forms of government, religion, philosophy, and art all reflected this basic economic reality.

The end of the feudal period, Marx held, was marked by revolution, as was the end of any stage of economic development. Marx believed that this revolution had occurred in England in the 1640s and in France beginning in 1789. Marx and his followers explained this transformation as essentially a transfer of power from the old ruling class to a new one, the bourgeois or capitalist class. With the advent of a new stage of economic development, the bourgeoisie became the chief owners of the means of production of the new era, and it was their values that predominated in all other areas of life. Bourgeois government, religion, philosophy, art—and even science—were held to be the results of this system of property ownership. As the

Communist Manifesto put it, "The modern bourgeois society that has sprouted from the ruins of feudal society has not done away with class antagonisms. It has but established new classes, new conditions of oppression, new forms of struggle in place of the old ones."

Capitalism, for Marx, like all stages, contained the seeds of its own destruction. In support of this conclusion, Marx had recourse to the labor theory of value—the notion that the value of a product is ultimately reducible to the amount of labor required to produce it. Although in the end Marx viewed capitalism as destructive, it had at least shown to the world the nature of this relationship: "Man is at last compelled to face with sober senses his real conditions of life, and his relations with his kind," he claimed. These relations, under capitalism, were merely pecuniary and increasingly exploitative. Capitalism was based on the theft of the value of goods, produced by labor, a value exploited from laborers.

The proletariat, or the working class, Marx believed, would face ever-increasing poverty and more onerous working conditions. Capitalists, who held ever more economic, cultural, and political power, would oppress them until they reached a breaking point—and then would come a communist revolution. In this final phase of history, the proletariat would appropriate the means of production, namely the entire industrial capital of the world. It would thereby crush the capitalist class, ending the capitalist phase of history. At that point, the workers would set up a socialist society, which would spread the benefits of industry to all.

The benefits of communism were said to be enormous. For example, the Soviet revolutionary Leon Trotsky offered the following grandiose vision of human enrichment under communism:

It is difficult to predict the extent of self-government which the man of the future may reach or the heights to which he may carry his technique. Social construction and psychophysical self-education will become two aspects of one and the same process. All the arts—literature, drama, painting, music and architecture will lend this process beautiful form. . . . Man will become immeasurably stronger, wiser and subtler; his body will become more harmonized, his movements more rhythmic, his voice more musical. The forms of life will become dynamically dramatic. The average human type will rise to the heights of an Aristotle, a Goethe, or a Marx.

These are noble-sounding ideals, yet, despite Marx's voluminous writings, it is never quite clear how they are to be achieved. Marx disdained incremental reforms; he scoffed at the so-called Fabian socialists, who advocated achieving socialism through gradual legal reforms. He likewise mistrusted those labor unions that negotiated peacefully with employers for improved working conditions and wages. For Marx, these half-measures did not advance industrial society toward socialism; on the contrary, they simply temporarily propped up the tottering capitalist edifice. There must be a revolution, Marx argued, and it must be entirely radical in its aims. It could be violent, but it could never be piecemeal. Yet just what should follow after the revolution is a mystery that Marx never cared to elucidate.

For example, the place of central planning in Marxist thought is a thoroughgoing puzzle. Marx famously declared that, under communism, the state would "wither away" and that fully self-realized individuals, capable as they would be in all walks of life, would have no need of anyone to direct them in their spontaneous, freely undertaken labor— a labor they would view with joy, not drudgery. Real-world Marxists who have faced the task of running a state, however, have not been able to achieve or even vaguely approach this end. Instead, they have adopted extensive central planning, including quotas, fixed prices, forced labor, and an astonishing array of directives about the minutiae of economic life. Impartial observers might well suspect that Marx would have repudiated these efforts.

As with any such all-encompassing system, Marxism has been subject to a number of criticisms. Many of the sharpest critiques have come from those closely associated with the libertarian or classical liberal tradition. Indeed, because classical liberalism champions private property and commerce and because Marxism disdains them, the two have been inveterate ideological enemies.

Karl Popper, for instance, argued that, even by Marx's own admission, ideas, emotions, and freely adopted values clearly influence political and social structures. After all, someone must devise the technologies that so profoundly shape human societies, and someone else must take it into his head to rise up in revolution or else to refrain from doing so. These determinations cannot easily be reduced to economic necessity. It may be arguing *tu quoque* to complain that Marx was not a proletarian, but rather of bourgeois stock, yet Marxism invites this critique in that it champions the importance of class struggle, rather than ideology.

Thus, Popper argued, economics is a profoundly important part of human history, but it is not the sole constitutive factor of all political and social life. Marx admitted, and indeed proclaimed, that communist revolutionaries had the power to change history through their own efforts, yet, by the tenets of his own system, it is by no means clear that they *should* have this power if the means of production really do determine our social and political capacities.

Popper further argued that the scientific pretensions of Marxism were simply a window dressing and that the core of the theory lay merely in the idea that a certain favored class should rule over all others, by violence if necessary. This notion is neither new nor particularly helpful; indeed, it amounts to little more than tyranny in fancy language.

Marx's predictions of a future communistic society are fantasies—albeit particularly dangerous and irresponsible ones because so often they seem to entail violence. To Popper, Marxism is neither systematic nor scientific; it is incomplete and prophetic.

One of the most telling and intellectually sophisticated challenges to Marxism came from the Austrian School of Economics, a movement that stressed the radically personal and subjective nature of all economic choice and the fundamental impossibility of centrally managing or directing any economy. Collective ownership of all means of production would mean an end to the free market, and Marxists candidly acknowledged this fact. Yet destroying the free market also would mean destroying the price system, which Austrians emphasize is a necessary means of transmitting information about economic wants from consumers to producers and back again. Without a functioning free-market price system, no one would be able to determine the value of goods, which would mean not limitless wealth for all, but unending dearth.

The Austrians argued that price fluctuations were neither arbitrary, as some naive observers believed, nor pernicious, as Marxists have often claimed. On the contrary, as Ludwig von Mises argued in his landmark book *Socialism*, prices transmit information that is necessary for economic prosperity. Under a Marxist system, in which the means of production are all collectively owned, this information becomes impossible to garner.

A final critique of Marxism often advanced by libertarians is simply to note that virtually none of Marx's predictions have come to pass in the roughly 150 years since he advanced them. Instead, workers in capitalist nations have seen a steady advance in their standard of living: salaries have increased, working conditions have improved, hours have grown shorter, and unemployment has not increased in any permanent way. Socialist revolutions insofar as they have been attempted, have neither achieved communism nor have managed to improve the lot of the worker. Most of them, of course, have since been abandoned, and former Marxist states now outnumber actual ones. This empirical or consequentialist critique of Marxism, when put into a more general form, tends to stress that, under any system of economic redistribution, individual incentives toward productivity vanish. Only capitalism, which rewards individual efforts, is capable of motivating individuals.

Supporters and critics alike agree that Marxism has never been fully put into practice, and it remains to this day an almost wholly theoretical system. Admirers and detractors alike have advanced differing reasons for why this should be so, but one fact is incontrovertible: In all historical cases, attempting simply to create a socialist society based on Marxist ideology has proved a horrific failure.

JTK

See also Collectivism; Communism; Industrial Revolution; Popper, Karl; Socialism; Socialist Calculation Debate

Further Readings

Marx, Karl. *Karl Marx: The Essential Writings*. Frederic L. Bender, ed. Boulder, CO: Westview Press, 1986.

Mises, Ludwig von. *Socialism*. J. Kahane, trans. Indianapolis, IN: Liberty Fund, 1981.

Popper, Karl. *The Open Society and Its Enemies*. New York: Routledge Classics, 2003 [1945].

Rand, Ayn, Nathaniel Branden, and Alan Greenspan. *Capitalism: The Unknown Ideal*. New York: New American Library, 1967.

Sciabarra, Chris Matthew. *Marx, Hayek, and Utopia*. New York: SUNY Press, 1995.

Trotsky, Leon. *Literature and Revolution*. New York: Russell & Russell, 1957 [1924].

MASON, GEORGE (1725–1792)

George Mason was a Virginia planter and statesman of the American revolutionary era. He was a firm proponent of limited government who used his influence as the holder of government offices to reduce its reach.

Elected in 1759 to Virginia's House of Burgesses, he proposed measures to resist Britain's 1765 Stamp Act, which he considered a usurpation of the colonists' right to elect the officials authorized to tax them. He joined with George Washington to write the 1774 Fairfax Resolves, which protested Britain's Coercive Acts, asserted colonial rights, criticized the slave trade, and called for a boycott of British goods. In 1775, he turned down a seat in the second Continental Congress and instead assumed the place vacated by Washington in Fairfax County's delegation to the Virginia Convention.

It was in this capacity that in June 1776 Mason authored the Virginia Declaration of Rights, which served as a model for other state rights declarations and later the national Bill of Rights. He also wrote an early draft of a constitution for Virginia, calling for a governor with severely limited powers, elected annually by a bicameral legislature.

Mason then worked as a member of the General Assembly and turned his attention to a series of other projects, including a revision of Virginia's legal code and agitating for passage of Thomas Jefferson's bill establishing religious freedom. Jefferson, who later lauded Mason's "expansive mind" and "profound judgment," found a key ally in Mason, who helped James Madison to secure the bill's 1786 adoption while Jefferson represented the United States in France.

A year later, as a Virginia delegate to the Constitutional Convention in Philadelphia, Mason occasionally bickered with Madison's proposals for a more robust national government. Like Jefferson, he considered the office of president under the proposed constitution too powerful and balked at the absence of a declaration of specific rights retained by states and individuals. Here, in his only appearance on the national stage, he opposed the creation of a truly national government and joined two other delegates in refusing to sign the finished draft of the constitution. In 1788, as a member of Virginia's ratifying convention, he opposed its adoption and had already published an influential essay detailing his objections. Although Virginia's convention agreed to the new plan of government, it made clear its support for the inclusion of a bill of rights.

Mason was pleased when the states adopted the first 10 amendments to the constitution in December 1791, and so indeed was Madison, who had come to embrace Mason's belief that Americans needed written safeguards against the potential encroachments of national power. Like Jefferson's Declaration of Independence, which reflected the principles of Mason's earlier Declaration of Rights, the constitution fathered by Madison owed much to Mason, who led the movement for the inclusion of prohibitions against unwarranted and unintended encroachments on the authority of states and the rights of individuals.

RMD

See also Bill of Rights, U.S.; Constitution, U.S.; Federalists Versus Anti-Federalists; Jefferson, Thomas; Madison, James

Further Readings

Miller, Helen Hill. *George Mason: Gentleman Revolutionary*. Chapel Hill: University of North Carolina Press, 1975.

Rutland, Robert A. *George Mason: Reluctant Statesman*. New York: Holt, Rinehart, & Winston, 1961.

MATERIAL PROGRESS

Were one asked, "If one were to use a time machine to transport Julius Caesar from 44 B.C. to George Washington's time, what would most impress the Roman general?" I suspect that what Caesar would find most impressive was gunpowder, and perhaps equally the discovery that entire continents existed about which he and other ancient Romans knew nothing. He would likely be astonished at the relatively low-cost printed materials made possible by the printing press and at improved harnesses for draft animals, improved sails for seagoing ships, and looms powered by water.

Despite these changes, however, Caesar would nevertheless recognize the world of the 18th century and be familiar with its basic shapes and rhythms. He would not be surprised by the fact that the vast majority of people lived and worked on farms and that a portion of the population were enslaved. He would know that sailing ships take weeks to travel great distances, and he would realize that infant mortality was high and that many women died as a result of giving birth. Just as in the Rome of 1,800 years earlier, no houses would be lit artificially; no cars, planes, or even bicycles would zip by; and the only human voices to be heard would be those coming from persons standing within earshot. Dysentery would be a familiar major killer, and everyday skin cuts would—as in Caesar's time—pose major risks of fatal infections.

Compare this scenario to the differences in life from 1776 to the early 21st century. Although the time separating George Washington's early America from modern America is only a small fraction of the time separating Caesar's Rome from 1776, Washington would surely be far more stunned and confused by our world than would Caesar be of Washington's world.

Only a tiny fraction of today's population works on farms. Most people live in suburbs or in cities with buildings that appear to scrape the sky and whose streets are free of horse dung and swarms of flies. Airplanes fly overhead and automobiles zoom around at speeds completely outside 18th-century experience. Nearly every home has indoor plumbing, artificial lighting, and dozens of electrical appliances that perform tasks that Washington's household slaves did for him, in addition to a host of other appliances such as TVs, cameras, and computers, which perform services that Washington never dreamed possible. Ordinary people regularly vacation thousands of miles from their homes, often on other continents. They frequently hold little plastic devices to their ears in order to talk in real time to people hundreds of miles away.

Today, antibiotics, refrigeration, plastics, and modern cleansers dramatically reduce risks posed by bacteria. Most children are born in hospitals, and impressively large numbers of them grow up and graduate from college. Few will ever need dentures, and those unlucky few will not have their dentures made of wood. Nearly all of these people will bathe daily for their entire lives. Americans' life expectancy at birth is today at 77.8 years, well more than double what it was (35 years) during Washington's time. Indeed, 21st-century American society would be almost beyond recognition to a resurrected George Washington.

There can be little doubt that standards of living for the bulk of the inhabitants of those parts of the globe that embrace commerce and industry are today hugely better than they were for nearly everyone who existed prior to the industrial revolution.

With respect to more recent trends, some analysts have argued that the standard of living of the average American has stagnated since the mid-1970s. However, the evidence is overwhelming that this determination is incorrect. Although the median wage rate paid to nonsupervisory workers, when adjusted for inflation using the Consumer Price Index (CPI), shows little increase since 1973, this fact is too weak to support the conclusion that Americans' living standards have stagnated. This essay is not the place to discuss the challenges of analyzing economic data. It is sufficient to note that the CPI likely overstates inflation, especially by poorly accounting for improvements in product quality, and that if policy or economic changes enable the workforce to employ greater numbers of low-skilled (and, hence, lower paid) workers, the median wage can be pulled down even though everyone's wages are rising. In addition, wage-rate data ignore income received from nonemployment sources, such as investments and government. Finally, median inflation-adjusted total compensation for nonsupervisory workers has indeed risen steadily, even since the mid-1970s. (Total compensation is a measure of wages plus the dollar value of fringe benefits, such as employer-provided health insurance and employer contributions to workers' retirement funds.)

We can avoid parsing such data and look at other empirical indicators of recent trends in living standards. At least two such alternative indicators were used by W. Michael Cox and Richard Alm in their 1999 book *Myths of Rich and Poor*. One of these indicators is to look at what people consume. Data on household consumption show that, in 1994, the percentage of *poor* households in the United States that have appliances such as washing machines, clothes dryers, automatic dishwashers, microwave ovens, and air conditioners was greater than the percentage of *all* U.S. households that had such appliances in 1971. This improvement in consumption occurred despite the failure of CPI-adjusted median wage rates to rise significantly during that same time period.

Relatedly, simply listing many of the new or immensely improved products widely available today, compared with the mid-1970s, strongly suggests that today's living standards are significantly higher than they were 30 years ago. Such a list might include:

- camcorders
- disposable diapers
- home computers
- high-speed (and increasingly wireless) Internet connectivity
- overnight delivery
- antilock brakes
- MP3 players
- e-mail
- high-definition TV
- microwave ovens
- satellite radio
- GPS navigation
- cell phones
- Aspartame
- availability of different varieties of coffees, teas, wine, and beer

- soft and disposable contact lenses
- LASIK surgery
- home copiers and fax machines
- digital cameras
- ATMs
- pharmaceuticals to treat high-blood pressure, depression, allergies, and impotence

This list can, of course, be extended much further.

A second alternative way to assess empirically recent trends in the material standard of living of Americans since the mid-1970s is to look at how long a worker earning the median nominal wage back then had to work to buy a sample selection of basic consumer goods, compared with how many hours of work today are required to purchase these same goods. (It is worth keeping in mind that, when adjusted for inflation using the CPI, today's median wage appears to be barely higher than was the real median wage in 1973, suggesting that a worker earning the median wage today would have to work about the same number of hours as did his counterpart 35 years earlier to buy the same goods.) Comparing the time needed to work at each of these two different points of time avoids the need to adjust wages and prices for inflation.

Cox and Alm performed this exercise in their 1999 book. For example, they found that, according to the most up-to-date data available when they wrote their book:

- a gallon of milk today (in the late 1990s) costs about 30% less work time than in the 1970s;
- a loaf of bread costs about 13% less work time;
- oranges cost 40% less work time;
- a coast-to-coast telephone call costs about 92% less work time; today, of course, such calls are practically free;
- chicken costs about 36% less work time;
- a McDonald's Big Mac costs 20% less work time; and
- 100 miles of air travel costs about 39% less work time.

A similar exercise using nominal hourly wage data and a 1975 Sears catalog suggests similar conclusions. If one checks a few items from that catalog that are reasonably—although hardly fully—comparable to similar items in January 2008 and then divides the average hourly nominal earnings of production workers in 1975 ($4.87 in December of that year) into the price of each of these (more or less) randomly selected items, these are the results:

- Sears' lowest-priced 10-inch table saw: 52.35 hours of work required in 1975; 5.63 hours of work required in 2008.
- Sears' lowest-priced gasoline-powered lawn mower: 13.14 hours of work required in 1975 (to buy a lawn mower that cuts a 20-inch swathe); 8.44 hours of work required in 2008 (to buy a lawn mower that cuts a 22-inch swathe; Sears no longer sells a power mower that cuts a swathe smaller than 22 inches).

- Sears Best side-by-side refrigerator-freezer: 139.62 hours of work required in 1975 (to buy a unit with 22.1 cubic feet of storage capacity); 61.9 hours of work required in 2008 (to buy a comparable unit with 25.0 cubic feet of storage capacity).
- Sears' lowest-priced answering machine: 20.43 hours of work required in 1975; 1.4 hours of work required in 2008 (and the 2008 machine comes with a telephone; Sears no longer sells stand-alone answering machines).
- A 1/2-horsepower garbage disposer: 20.52 hours of work required in 1975; 4.22 hours of work required in 2008.
- Sears' lowest-priced garage-door opener: 20.1 hours of work required in 1975 (to buy a 1/4-horsepower opener); 7.6 hours of work required in 2008 (to buy a 1/2-horsepower opener; Sears no longer sells garage-door openers with less than 1/2 horsepower).
- Sears' only drip coffee maker (nonprogrammable, 10 cups): 7.47 hours of work required in 1975; 1.57 hours of work required in 2008 (although the 2008 model brews 12 cups).
- Sears' highest-priced work boots: 11.49 hours of work required in 1975; 9.0 hours of work required in 2008.
- Sears Best automobile tire (with specs 165/13, and a tread life warranty of 40,000 miles): 8.37 hours of work required in 1975; 2.53 hours of work required in 2008 to buy Sears most expensive tire of this size (although in 2008 the warranty is not specified).

Still, close inspection of a 1975 Sears catalog alongside products for sale today at Sears.com makes clear four facts: (1) the range of products is larger today, (2) the range of different varieties of each type of product is larger today, (3) the inflation-adjusted prices are generally lower today, and (4) the quality of the products is much higher today.

Of course, these facts do not prove, in any rigorous way, that ordinary Americans' material well-being is higher today than it was in the recent past. But they are strongly suggestive of a higher standard of living. The strength of this suggestion increases when it is considered in light of the fact that today Americans' life expectancy is at an all-time high and that Americans' rate of homeownership is also at an all-time high. The global market economy that began to sprout immediately after World War II continues to improve living standards.

DJB

See also Civil Society; Natural Harmony of Interests; Simon, Julian; Smith, Adam

Further Readings

Cox, W. Michael, and Richard Alm. *Myths of Rich & Poor*. New York: Basic Books, 1999.

Fogel, Robert William. *The Escape from Hunger and Premature Death, 1700-2100: Europe, America, and the Third World*. New York: Cambridge University Press, 2004.

Goklany, Indur. *The Improving State of the World*. Washington, DC: Cato Institute, 2007.

Lebergott, Stanley. *Pursuing Happiness.* Princeton, NJ: Princeton University Press, 1996.

Simon, Julian L., ed. *The State of Humanity.* Boston: Wiley-Blackwell, 1995.

MENCKEN, H. L. (1880–1956)

Born in Baltimore, Maryland, Henry Louis (H. L.) Mencken, "The Sage of Baltimore," left school in 1899 to become a reporter for the city's *Morning Herald* and later served as drama critic, city editor, and then managing editor of the *Evening Herald.* So famous and influential was he in the age before TV that a prominent contemporary, the journalist Walter Lippmann, called him "the most powerful influence on this whole generation of educated people." Indeed, most Mencken admirers today may not be libertarians, but are instead appreciators of his impressive literary and journalistic skills. Soon after the *Herald* folded in 1906, he joined the Baltimore *Sun,* where he served as editor, columnist, or contributor for most of his career. His association with the *Sunpapers* was sometimes rocky, as during both world wars, when Mencken, himself German American and an admirer of German culture but certainly no Nazi, vigorously opposed American intervention in those conflicts, a position embarrassingly antithetical to that taken by his newspaper. From 1914 to 1923, he edited *The Smart Set,* a satirical magazine, and from 1924 to 1933, he edited *American Mercury,* an influential cultural magazine for a "civilized minority." As an editor, he championed the work of many authors, including Theodore Dreiser, Sinclair Lewis, and Sherwood Anderson.

A prolific writer with broad intellectual interests, he wrote more than two dozen books, many collections of journalism, and other products of laborious, painstaking scholarship, most notably, *The American Language,* originally published in 1919, tracing the development of a distinctive American idiom. His admiration for the work of Irish author and dramatist George Bernard Shaw led to a study published in 1905 called *George Bernard Shaw—His Plays,* and his admiration for the thought and values of German philosopher Friedrich Nietzsche led to both a study published in 1908 called *The Philosophy of Friedrich Nietzsche* and a translation in 1920 of the philosopher's *Der Antichrist.* It makes sense that Mencken's sensibilities should have attracted him to Nietzsche's thought, which calls for a "transvaluation" or reversal of values traditionally prized by Christians. Both men believed that meekness, humility, and a dependence on faith in God are part of a "slave morality" unworthy of self-respecting and self-reliant high achievers. Both saw Christianity as reflecting a scheme of values by which the envious and resentful masses try to pull the elite down to their own level.

Although Mencken was deeply interested in religion, his attitude toward organized religion is not central to libertarianism more generally.

Mencken's political views were close to what might be called Jeffersonian classical liberalism or, in today's language, libertarianism, although he had less confidence in the wisdom of the ordinary citizen than Jefferson did. In September 1927, Mencken wrote in *American Mercury,*

> I believe in liberty. In any dispute between a citizen and the government, it is my instinct to side with the citizen. . . . I am against all efforts to make men virtuous by law. . . . I do not have [Jefferson's] confidence in the wisdom of the common man, but I go with him in his belief that the very commonest of common men have certain inalienable rights.

Mencken believed that respect for persons requires defining and supporting clear limits on governmental power and that a recognition of reality requires accepting some differences in wealth and social status as ineradicable. Although he rejected hereditary aristocracies and special legal or economic privileges bestowed on groups, he believed that differences in intelligence, drive, and self-discipline will inevitably result in economic and social classes. Accordingly, he wrote in a *Smart Set* editorial dated October 1918,

> The simple fact is that there must always be underdogs so long as there are any dogs at all, and that nothing human volition can achieve will ever be better for them than throwing them a few bones. Christianity was launched as a scheme for uplifting them. Has it succeeded? Science was to do it. Has it done so? Socialism was to perform the trick. Turn to Russia for the result. What . . . sentimentalists constantly overlook is that the underdog is by no means a mere victim of external justice. Part of his underdoggishness, perhaps nine-tenths, is congenital and inalienable.

Like Jefferson, Mencken held that, although some government is necessary to preserve peace and perform a few other duties individuals cannot easily perform for themselves, government beyond that minimum would likely be exploiting citizens, advantaging one group by disadvantaging another. In an editorial dated January 19, 1926, for the *Evening Sun* of Baltimore, he wrote cynically about persons in favor of an expansive role for government: "A Progressive is one who is in favor of more taxes instead of less, more bureaus and jobholders, more paternalism and meddling, more regulation of private affairs and less liberty. In general, he would be inclined to regard the repeal of any tax as outrageous." His libertarian convictions also were well expressed in an editorial for the *Chicago Tribune* called "Why Liberty?" published on January 30, 1927:

> I believe that liberty is the only genuinely valuable thing that men have invented, at least in the field of government,

in a thousand years. I believe that it is better to be free than to be not free, even when the former is dangerous and the latter safe. I believe that the finest qualities of man can flourish only in free air—that progress made under a policeman's club is false progress, and of no permanent value.

Even in the 1920s he lamented that government in America had expanded far beyond what was desired by Jefferson. His passion for freedom later put him at odds with Franklin Delano Roosevelt's contributions to the welfare state and call to self-sacrifice, which Mencken regarded as a plea for governmental tyranny. His strong belief in individual liberty, esteem for reason and science, and contempt for authoritarian systems of thought made him critical—and at times contemptuous—of organized religion, especially Christianity. Although he had respect for achievement-oriented values such as hard work and self-discipline, he delighted in iconoclastic attacks on middle-class "booboisie," prudery, and organized religion.

Although thoroughly secular and this-worldly, he was interested in religion and enjoyed writing about it, often producing an equal measure of data and derision, as in the 1930 book *Treatise on the Gods* (Mencken's personal favorite) and the 1934 book *Treatise on Right and Wrong*. Both works are deftly written and irreverent, revealing at least as much about their author as their subjects. In 1925, he took a keen interest in and reported on what became known as the Scopes Monkey Trial, in which Clarence Darrow defended and William Jennings Bryan prosecuted a schoolteacher arrested for teaching Darwin's theory of evolution. Mencken's real-life role as a journalist at the trial was depicted in the 1960 movie *Inherit the Wind*, which was adapted from the Jerome Lawrence–Robert E. Lee play.

In the 1920s, Mencken also wrote about Prohibition, which he viewed as an indefensible and self-defeating violation of personal liberty. In December 1924, he wrote the following as part of an editorial for *American Mercury*:

> None of the great boons and usufructs that were to follow the passage of the Eighteenth Amendment has come to pass. There is not less drunkenness in the Republic, but more. There is not less crime, but more. There is not less insanity, but more. The cost of government is not smaller, but vastly greater. Respect for law has not increased, but diminished.

His criticism of Prohibition sounds a great deal like current criticism of the drug war, about which he would probably write with equal disdain.

Besides being one of America's most famous curmudgeons and talented journalists, Mencken is important to libertarianism because of his esteem for liberty and contempt for moralism and paternalism. His brave stance against wartime censorship, for example, marks him as a consistent defender of liberty even under adversity.

RoE

See also Censorship; Nietzsche, Friedrich; Peace and Pacifism; Prohibition of Alcohol; Rand, Ayn; Separation of Church and State

Further Readings

Bode, Carl. *Mencken*. Carbondale: Southern Illinois University Press, 1969.
Douglas, George H. *H. L. Mencken: Critic of American Life*. Hamden, CT: Archon, 1978.
Mencken, H. L. *The Gist of Mencken: Quotations from America's Critic*. Mayo DuBasky, ed. Metuchen, NJ: Scarecrow Press, 1990.
———. *A Mencken Chrestomathy*. New York: Knopf, 1949.
———. *My Life as Author and Editor*. Jonathan Yardley, ed. New York: Knopf, 1993.
———. *Prejudices: First Series*. New York: Knopf, 1919.
———. *Prejudices: Second Series*. New York: Knopf, 1920.
———. *Treatise on the Gods*. New York: Knopf, 1930.
———. *Treatise on Right and Wrong*. New York: Knopf, 1934.
Stenerson, Douglas C. *H. L. Mencken: Iconoclast from Baltimore*. Chicago: University of Chicago Press, 1971.

MENGER, CARL (1840–1921)

Carl Menger was a professor of economics at the University of Vienna and the founder of the Austrian School of economic thought. Among economists, he ranks as the 19th century's greatest contributor to the theory of spontaneous order—the social-scientific tradition supporting the libertarian view that a free society can generate beneficial and sophisticated institutions without state involvement. Menger's highly original approach to the formation of market prices and institutions marked an important advance over the classical economics of Adam Smith and laid the foundation for later contributions by the Austrian economists Eugen von Böhm-Bawerk, Ludwig von Mises, and Friedrich A. Hayek.

Menger's revolutionary book on economic theory, *Grundsätze der Volkswirthschaftslehre* [*Principles of Economics*], was published in 1871. Menger traveled with the Austrian prince Rudolf in 1876–1878 as his tutor in economics. *Carl Menger's Lectures to Crown Prince Rudolf of Austria*, translated and published in 1994, show much more clearly than his other works Menger's commitment to classical liberalism in the manner of Adam Smith. In 1879, Menger attained a full professorship in economics at the University of Vienna, and early in his professorship, in 1883, he published an essay defending theoretical economics, *Untersuchungen über die Methode der Socialwissenschaften und der Politischen Oekonomie insbesondere* [*Investigations into the Method of the Social Sciences with Special Reference to Economics*]. Menger was appointed to an Austrian state commission on currency reform in 1892; while there he wrote an essay, "Geld" [Money], part of which appeared in English translation as an article in the *Economic Journal* of the same year. The entire essay was translated and published in 2002 as part of the volume *Carl Menger and the Evolution of Payments Systems.*

Historians of economic thought commonly mention Menger as an independent codiscoverer (along with William Stanley Jevons and Léon Walras) of "marginal utility" as the key principle for explaining relative prices. Of the three economists, Menger's *Principles*, in the minds of many historians of economics, was the most readily understood and influential of their nearly contemporaneous publications. The marginal-utility theorists overthrew the prevailing "labor theory of value," according to which commodities receive their market value (or price) from the labor costs needed for their production. Menger emphasized that the creation of value in fact ran the opposite way: Labor services and other inputs are valued only insofar as they are expected to produce valuable consumer goods. Consumer goods have market value only insofar as consumers expect them to satisfy wants that are subjectively important. Menger's subjective value theory thus demolished the notion that labor bestows value, a linchpin of Marxian economics.

Menger provided (first in the *Principles*, again in the *Investigations*, and in more detail in "Money") the first satisfactory explanation of the origin of money. He demonstrated that the institution of money is a spontaneous outgrowth of market trading. In a nutshell, Menger noted that commodities differ in marketability (the ease with which they can be brought to market and sold). A barterer who comes to market with hard-to-sell commodities (say, turnips) will often find it easier to trade indirectly. He will accept a more marketable commodity (say, silver) when it is offered and then will employ it as a medium of exchange, trading the silver later for the commodities he wants to take home. An alert trader will prefer to accept a commodity as a medium of exchange that a larger network of other traders will accept and, by accepting that commodity, will further enlarge the network. Therefore, traders will spontaneously converge on a single good as a commonly accepted medium or money. In his 1892 monograph, Menger concluded: "Money was not created by law; in its origin it is not a governmental but a social phenomenon. Government sanction is foreign to the general concept of money." Yet surprisingly, Menger nonetheless thought that money had been "perfected . . . by government recognition and regulation" of coinage. Citing a doubtful account of private coinage during the several American gold rushes, he thought that laissez-faire would produce harmful "multiformity" rather than

uniformity of coins. Despite his comments regarding coinage, however, Menger's account of the origin of money serves as a particularly apt example for the case that a free society can generate its own institutions without state guidance.

In the *Investigations*, Menger posed an important research question for social scientists: How can it be that institutions that serve the common welfare and are extremely significant for its development come into being without a common will directed toward establishing them? He referred not only to money, but also to law, morals, trade customs, and cities. Menger's analytic program of building a methodologically individualistic understanding of institutions had a strong influence on the writings of Mises and Hayek, and it lives on in modern Austrian and "new institutional" economics.

LHW

See also Böhm-Bawerk, Eugen von; Economics, Austrian School of; Hayek, Friedrich A.; Mises, Ludwig von; Spontaneous Order

Further Readings

Menger, Carl. *Carl Menger's Lectures to the Crown Prince Rudolf of Austria.* Erich W. Streissler and Monika Streissler, eds. Aldershot, UK: Edward Elgar, 1994.
———. *Investigations in the Method of the Social Sciences with Special Reference to Economics.* New York: New York University Press, 1985.
———. "Money." *Carl Menger and the Evolution of Payments Systems: From Barter to Electronic Money.* Michael Latzer and Stefan W. Schmitz, eds. Cheltenham, UK: Edward Elgar, 2002.
———. *Principles of Economics.* New York: New York University Press, 1981.

MERCANTILISM

Mercantilism refers both to the economic policies of European nation-states from roughly the mid-16th to mid-18th centuries and to the constellation of economic theories that were used to justify those policies. The term *mercantilism*, although not employed by Adam Smith, derives from his discussion and critique of the "mercantile system" in the *Wealth of Nations* (1776). Characterized by Smith as "in its nature and essence a system of restraint and regulation," this system was called the mercantile (or commercial) system because Smith believed it served the special interests of domestic merchants and manufacturers at the expense of laborers, landowners, and consumers generally.

According to Smith, merchants and manufacturers frequently opposed free markets because their rate of profit was systematically lowered by unfettered competition.

They therefore attempted to maintain their profits at artificially high levels by persuading their government to enact tariffs, bounties, and other special privileges that benefited the commercial classes at the expense of everyone else. It is through mercantilist policies that commercial interests are able to impose "an absurd tax upon the rest of their fellow citizens."

Whereas Adam Smith viewed mercantilism as a self-serving ideology promoted by merchants and manufacturers, modern historians have provided a broader perspective. Many agree with Eli Heckscher—whose two-volume work, *Mercantilism* (1931), remains the definitive work in its field—that the primary purpose of mercantilist policies was to unify economic activity under state control. Mercantilism, according to Heckscher, "concentrated on the *power* of the state."

Owing to the fierce and often violent competition among nation-states, it was commonly argued in the 17th and 18th centuries that a country must constitute a self-contained economic unit to remain strong and that essential economic activities must be subordinated to the state's authority. This economic nationalism (as mercantilism is sometimes called) is required if a state is to successfully wage war, just as colonies must be established to ensure a reliable supply of raw materials.

These military and colonial ventures required enormous amounts of wealth, which in turn presupposed an economic system capable of producing it. As a leading German mercantilist put it in 1696, a "prince must first procure for his subjects a good livelihood if he will take anything from them."

Before the term *mercantilism* was coined in the 19th century, this approach was sometimes called *Colbertism* after Jean Baptiste Colbert, minister of finance under Louis XIV from 1663 to 1683. Colbert undertook to systematically implement a mercantilist agenda in France. Foreign trade, which often was regarded as a type of warfare, was heavily regulated to ensure a surplus of exports over imports. Manufacturing industries deemed essential to the welfare of the state, especially those necessary for the waging of war, were heavily regulated, and royal monopolies and other privileges were granted to private companies and entrepreneurs. Meanwhile, an earlier prohibition on the export of precious metals was allowed to remain in effect. The basic purpose of these regulations was succinctly expressed by Colbert: "Trade is the source of finance and finance is the vital nerve of war."

According to an early version of mercantilism (known as *bullionism*), the wealth of a nation consists of its precious metals. This doctrine, which led to a ban on the export of bullion and even coined money in some countries, was criticized by later mercantilists, such as Thomas Mun, who pointed to the detrimental effects of such prohibitions on foreign trade. In *England's Treasure by Foreign Trade* (1664), Mun argued that, given the absence of mines in England, "we have no means to get treasure but by foreign trade." He further maintained that this enrichment can be accomplished "by making our commodities which are exported yearly to over balance in value the foreign wares which we consume."

This balance of trade doctrine, according to which the total amount of a nation's wealth can be increased only when the value of its exports exceeds that of its imports (because payments for the difference will result in a net gain of specie), was a key component of later mercantilist theory. Although there were other facets to mercantilist policy, among them governmental manipulation of currency, maximum wage rates, a system of mandatory labor, and the regulation of interest, it was the balance of trade doctrine that received the most attention and the one that was the object of sustained criticism from Dudley North, David Hume, Adam Smith, and other critics of mercantilism.

Inasmuch as the nation was viewed as a single economic unit, it followed that a nation's gain from international trade was measured in terms of a net gain in specie, or coined money. Domestic trade, which circulated money and commodities within a nation, was regarded as advantageous to private interests, but not to the nation as a whole, because it did nothing to augment the total amount of wealth. Wealth could be increased only through foreign trade and only when the total value of a nation's exports exceeded the value of its imports, thereby resulting in a net gain of specie through payments from other countries.

It is important to keep this point in mind if we are to appreciate Adam Smith's devastating critique of mercantilism in Book IV of the *Wealth of Nations*. Smith has been widely criticized for supposedly misrepresenting his mercantilist adversaries. We are told that, contrary to Smith's inaccurate caricature, the more sophisticated mercantilists did not commit the crude fallacy of equating wealth with money. Smith, however, was not guilty of this misrepresentation. On the contrary, he expressly noted that, according to some of the better mercantilists, "the wealth of a country consists, not in its gold and silver only, but in its land, houses, and consumable goods of all different kinds." But as Smith goes on to point out, and this notion is the core of his critique, this more sophisticated theory of wealth is inconsistent with the balance of trade doctrine. According to this latter theory, a favorable balance of trade is required for a net increase in a nation's wealth, but there is no way to measure this favorable balance except in terms of money.

It follows, as Smith pointed out, that mercantilists cannot have it both ways. They cannot repudiate the crude theory that identifies wealth with money while insisting that a nation can increase its wealth only through the importation of money attained through a favorable balance of trade.

GHS

See also Free Trade; Globalization; Imperialism; Physiocracy; Smith, Adam; War; Wealth and Poverty

Further Readings

Cole, Thomas Woolsey. *Colbert and a Century of French Mercantilism*. 2 vols. New York: Columbia University Press, 1939.

Ekelund, Robert B., and Robert D. Tollison. *Politicized Economies: Monarchy, Monopoly, and Mercantilism*. College Station: Texas A&M University Press, 1997.

Heckscher, Eli. *Mercantilism*. Mendel Shapiro, trans. 2 vols. New York: Macmillan, 1962.

Mun, Thomas. "England's Treasure by Foreign Trade." *The Western Tradition*. Vol. 2. 4th ed. Eugen Weber, ed. Lexington: D.C. Heath, 1990.

Smith, Adam. *The Wealth of Nations*. Book V. Indianapolis, IN: Liberty Fund, 1981.

METHODOLOGICAL INDIVIDUALISM

See INDIVIDUALISM, METHODOLOGICAL

MEYER, FRANK S. (1909–1972)

Frank Straus Meyer was a writer, a founding editor of *National Review*, and an advocate of "fusionism"—a political theory uniting libertarianism with strands of modern conservatism that shaped the American political right during the cold war.

Born in Newark, New Jersey, Meyer attended Princeton University before transferring to Balliol College, Oxford, where he earned a B.A. in 1932. He then attended the London School of Economics and was elected president of the students' union, an office for which he campaigned as a communist. Expelled from England on account of his political activities, Meyer returned to the United States and settled in Chicago, where he met and later married another avowed communist, Elsie Brown.

Meyer and his wife grew increasingly disenchanted with the political beliefs he had embraced during the 1940s, and by the early 1950s, he began contributing regularly to periodicals popular on the political right, including the *American Mercury* and the *Freeman*. In 1955, he joined with William F. Buckley, Jr. to found *National Review*, the most influential magazine of the postwar conservative movement.

Although Meyer rejected the term, the theory that would later became known as *fusionism* reflected Meyer's conscious effort to combine Russell Kirk's traditional conservatism, which celebrated tradition and moral order, with the libertarian movement, which was grounded in reason. Meyer's most important work was *In Defense of Freedom: A Conservative Credo*, published in 1962, which fleshed out many of the ideas and themes that Meyer had been espousing for years in his columns and book reviews.

Meyer elevated the principle of human freedom to the highest order. He saw the preservation of man's freedom to be the "central and primary end of political society." Although Meyer incurred the wrath of traditional conservatives who saw in his elevation of freedom a recipe for disorder, chaos, and libertinism, Meyer perceived that order would derive from free individuals exercising choices informed by reason, even if such choices were unencumbered by the conservatives' notions of rights and duties.

Meyer regarded the state as necessary, but believed that the government should be carefully defined and its powers limited. He limited its functions to the use of military power in defense of its citizens from foreign threats, to the exercise of judicial power to resolve disputes involving competing rights, and to the protection of citizens against domestic violence.

Although Meyer was skeptical of cultural conventions and norms, after having abandoned his early communist sympathies, his views on religion softened, and he became far more sympathetic to organized Christianity. He saw in the virtuous, free-thinking individual the essence of moral man in God's image. Born into Judaism, he converted to Roman Catholicism shortly before his death on April 1, 1972.

CP

See also Conservatism; Conservative Critique of Libertarianism; Fusionism

Further Readings

Meyer, Frank S. *In Defense of Freedom: A Conservative Credo*. Chicago: Regnery, 1962.

Rothbard, Murray N. "Frank S. Meyer: The Fusionist as Libertarian Manqué." *Freedom and Virtue: The Conservative/Libertarian Debate*. George W. Carey, ed. Wilmington, DE: Intercollegiate Studies Institute, 1984.

Smant, Kevin J. *Principles and Heresies: Frank S. Meyer and the Shaping of the Modern Conservative Movement*. Wilmington, DE: Intercollegiate Studies Institute, 2002.

MILITARY-INDUSTRIAL COMPLEX

The term *military-industrial complex* refers to the loose political alliance of industrial and military interests that has contributed to the growth and persistence of the welfare–warfare state. The term was popularized in President Dwight D. Eisenhower's farewell address of January 17, 1961, when he warned his countrymen to be on guard "against the acquisition of unwarranted influence . . . by the military-industrial complex."

Scholars who have studied the workings of this alliance between industry and the military have concluded that this intimate relationship did not originate in the mid-20th century. Many trace the development of interlocking political and economic interests among the military and leading industrialists to World War I, when the Council of National Defense and its successor, the War Industries Board (WIB), mobilized billions of dollars for the war effort. The pattern of cooperation between the military and industry expanded during the 1930s as both parties began developing re-armament plans that were put into effect after the outbreak of World War II.

The image of the WIB as a band of well-meaning industrialists who sacrificed for the good of the country was shattered, however, during the Senate Munitions Inquiry hearings of 1934–1936. Chaired by North Dakota Senator Gerald P. Nye, the hearings focused on the motives driving the WIB members, aware that President Woodrow Wilson's decision to enter World War I was promoted by the so-called "merchants of death" who subverted American interests and wasted thousands of American lives.

Similar sentiments emerged during the mid- to late 1960s when the antiwar movement repeated Eisenhower's warnings about the dangers the military posed to criticize the Vietnam War and the U.S. cold war policy. However, the class-based analysis popular on the left traced the military-industrial complex to capitalists and senior military officers, who, they argued, created international crises to accumulate power and wealth. In other words, the left maintained that capitalism and militarism went hand in hand, with both ideologies collectively thwarting the will of the people. The solution to this state of affairs, at times explicit, but most of the time unstated, was the nationalization of war industries and the elimination of the profit motive.

The libertarian critique of the military-industrial complex is informed by elements of leftist scholarship, but leans toward Eisenhower's original concern that the true danger of the intimate relationship between the military and certain segments of industry arises from its tendency to corrupt the political process by increasing the power of government. Libertarians see war as occasionally but rarely necessary and then, at best, an evil that should be restricted to those instances where the survival of liberal democracy is directly threatened. Mobilization for war, however, should and must be guided by private actors seeking their own benefit in the market because that is the most efficient mechanism for marshalling resources in society.

The actual political and social effects of the military-industrial complex are far more subtle, and also more insidious, than scholars on the left realize. Wedded to their class-based critique, the left has ignored labor's role in the growth and persistence of this alliance; defense workers are by far the largest, and therefore the most powerful, constituency driving the military-industrial complex because they and their representatives have exerted substantial influence in the political realm. This corporate welfare, dispensed by politicians, flows unevenly to select geographic regions, with the result that defense workers fight to protect their jobs by supporting politicians who steer money to their employers and by punishing those who do not.

Combating this alliance of the military with segments of industry poses a great challenge to libertarians who are intent on reforming the modern welfare–warfare state inasmuch as defense spending has served as a thinly veiled jobs program that has created powerful, entrenched political constituencies who oppose reductions in military spending in peacetime.

CP

See also Corruption; Foreign Policy; Peace and Pacifism; War; War on Terror

Further Readings

Cooling, Benjamin F., ed. *War, Business, and American Society: Historical Perspectives on the Military Industrial Complex.* Port Washington, NY: Kennikat Press, 1977.
Higgs, Robert, ed. *Arms, Politics, and the Economy: Historical and Contemporary Perspectives.* New York: Holmes and Meier, 1990.
Koistinen, Paul A. C. *The Military-Industrial Complex: A Historical Perspective.* New York: Praeger, 1980.
Pursell, Carroll W., Jr., ed. *The Military-Industrial Complex.* New York: Harper & Row, 1972.

MILL, JOHN STUART (1806–1873)

John Stuart Mill was educated by his father James Mill and received training in a variety of disciplines, including classics, philosophy, history, economics, mathematics, and logic. His father was a close associate of Jeremy Bentham, who was one of the earliest exponents of utilitarian ethics. As a result, the younger Mill was exposed to these ideas at an early age. However, his learning ranged over many areas. He was able to read Greek at age 3 and Latin at age 8. For 35 years, he worked for the East India Company, but managed to write on a variety of topics. Among his most important books are *A System of Logic* (1843), *Principles of Political Economy* (1848), *On Liberty* (1859), *Considerations on Representative Government* (1861), *Utilitarianism* (1863), *Auguste Comte and Positivism* (1865), *The*

Subjection of Women (1869), and his *Autobiography* (1873). In 1851, he married Harriet Taylor, with whom he had had a close intellectual and possibly romantic relationship for some 20 years.

Mill is remembered primarily for his contributions to moral and political philosophy and logic. In later years, Mill developed strong sympathies for certain sorts of government intervention, both in the economy and socially, but for a good portion of his life he can reasonably be described as a libertarian. Utilitarianism and libertarianism are typically not allies, but Mill's conception of both was unique, and his attempt to synthesize the two yielded interesting insights into both. Although Mill was influenced by the moral theories of his father and Bentham, Mill's utilitarianism departs from Benthamism in at least two clearly identifiable ways. First of all, when Bentham argues that our actions should bring about the greatest good for the greatest number, he identifies *good* as pleasure, pain being the corresponding evil. Pleasures and pains differ only in quantitative measures such as intensity, duration, likelihood of recurring, and so on. But "[q]uantity of pleasure being equal, pushpin is as good as poetry." Mill, in contrast, argued that pleasures could differ in qualitative as well as quantitative ways. Pleasures associated with the exercise and development of the higher faculties were, he maintained, intrinsically more valuable. In a much-quoted passage, Mill says: "[I]t is better to be a human being dissatisfied than a pig satisfied; better to be Socrates dissatisfied than a fool satisfied. And if the fool, or the pig, are of a different opinion, it is because they only know their own side of the question. The other party to the comparison knows both sides." In other words, men are capable of appreciating the sorts of things that might bring a pig pleasure (food, sleep, sex), but the pig is incapable of comprehending distinctly human pleasures such as love, drama, or intellectual growth. Pushpin, a relatively mindless children's game, is not as good as poetry, even if one plays for hours, because it neither exercises nor develops the higher faculties.

Aristotle made precisely this point about the human good being categorically different from the good for other creatures. Thus, when Mill endorses the slogan "greatest good for the greatest number," he does so with a particular understanding of "good"—namely, a distinctly human good, one connected to the development of man, the "permanent interests of man as a progressive being."

The second major departure from Benthamism reflects the distinction that contemporary moral philosophers make between act utilitarianism and rule utilitarianism. Bentham argued that actions were good only insofar as they brought about the "greatest good for the greatest number." A critical objection to this formulation is that it is difficult to know all the future consequences of an action. It may be impossible to know in a given situation whether something will bring about the greatest overall good, inasmuch as one cannot predict all future consequences. Mill suggested that, rather than evaluate each individual action on the basis of utility, we should try to derive rules or policies that, taken as a whole, bring about the greatest good for the greatest number. For example, one might decide on an ad hoc basis to ban a certain demonstration, say a group of Nazis marching in a largely Jewish community, because it is likely to have a net painful effect. Mill's analysis is somewhat more subtle. For Mill, whether one decides to ban such demonstrations rests on the question of which social policy is likely to bring about the greatest good for the greatest number, a policy of freedom of expression or a policy whereby majorities can silence dissident minorities? Given Mill's understanding of the good as tied to the exercise and development of the higher faculties, it is clear that permitting the march is the more moral, utilitarian, decision.

Mill's defense of liberty as a political principle follows from his understanding of utilitarian morals. A necessary condition of social well-being, Mill argues, is individual liberty. This notion is made clear in another frequently quoted passage. In *On Liberty*, he writes that

> the object of this essay is to assert one very simple principle . . . that the sole end for which mankind are warranted, individually or collectively, in interfering with the liberty of action of any of their number is self-protection. That the only purpose for which power can be rightfully exercised over any member of a civilized community, against his will, is to prevent harm to others. His own good, either physical or moral, is not a sufficient warrant.

The antipaternalist position asserted here is an integral part of libertarian thought. The general principle that conduct that does not harm others should not be legally proscribed virtually defines libertarianism, although other theorists and activists have defended or expanded on it in many different ways.

Mill argued for a specific set of liberties being especially crucial to the development of the good: liberty of conscience, including freedom of thought and expression, and of the press; liberty of tastes and pursuits, including lifestyle and career choice (provided of course that one's choice does not infringe on the liberty of others); and liberty to associate with and unite with others for any purpose that does not violate the rights of others. These liberties are necessary for the discovery of truth and for the development of culture. To deny these liberties not only inhibits our humanity, but is most likely to lead to erroneous doctrines in morals, religion, and science, doctrines that once established are almost impossible to correct. Even if the views we seek to prohibit are clearly false, they constitute effective criticisms against which we can test and strengthen our true beliefs.

In his writings on political economy, Mill embraced free markets, with some notable exceptions. He recognized that the bureaucracy of a centralized economy would not be productive and that competitive markets were more likely to produce greater wealth. However, he did not extend this view to all aspect of economic life. He assumed that roads and basic utilities should be owned and administered by the government. He supported worker-owned firms on the grounds that this form of association was most likely to minimize class hostility and enhance productivity. Mill also was an early proponent of equal political rights for women.

By grounding his defense of liberty in terms of his understanding of utilitarianism, Mill differed significantly from proponents of natural-rights liberalism such as Locke and is an ancestor to a variety of consequentialist approaches to libertarianism. However, by conceiving of utility in terms of specifically human values, and with reference to man's full potentialities, Mill's views also foreshadow the neo-Aristotelian defenses of liberty that gained prominence in the 1990s.

AeS

See also Bentham, Jeremy; Rights, Theories of; Spencer, Herbert; Utilitarianism

Further Readings

Anschutz, R. P. *The Philosophy of John Stuart Mill*. Oxford: Oxford University Press, 1953.

Britton, Karl. *John Stuart Mill*. London: Penguin Books, 1953.

Capaldi, Nicholas. *John Stuart Mill: A Biography*. Cambridge: Cambridge University Press, 2004.

Hart, H. L. A. *Law, Liberty, and Morality*. Stanford, CA: Stanford University Press, 1963.

Himmelfarb, Gertrude. *On Liberty and Liberalism: The Case of John Stuart Mill*. New York: Knopf, 1974.

Lyons, David. *Rights, Welfare, and Mill's Moral Theory*. Oxford: Oxford University Press, 1994.

Mill, John Stuart. *On Liberty*. New York: W. W. Norton, 1975 [1859].

———. *Principles of Political Economy*. Harmondsworth, Middlesex, UK: Pelican, 1970 [1848].

———. *Utilitarianism*. Indianapolis, IN: Hackett, 1979 [1863].

Ryan, Alan. *The Philosophy of John Stuart Mill*. London: Macmillan, 1970.

MILTON, JOHN (1608–1674)

John Milton was one of the iconic figures of English literature. He is most familiar for his epic poem *Paradise Lost* and, in particular, his depiction of Satan. However, his legacy extends far beyond that one monumental work and indeed beyond poetry: He was a forceful and courageous writer on matters political and theological. In the turmoil preceding the English Civil War, he lent intellectual support

to the republican cause and, upon the establishment of the Commonwealth, was employed to write tracts defending Oliver Cromwell's actions, in particular his execution of the king. Following the Restoration of the monarchy, he was threatened with hanging and briefly jailed before influential friends secured his release. The remainder of his life was spent in the construction of his great epics.

True to his Puritan upbringing, Milton took as his central theme the inviolability of the individual conscience—a precept that, when applied to his personal affairs, often brought him strife. As early as his university days, a clash with a tutor forced him to leave Cambridge for a short time; he also abandoned his intended goal of entering the clergy because "tyranny had invaded the church" through the bishops who governed it. A visit to Rome saw him nearly jailed after he ran afoul of the Jesuits for speaking freely of religious dissent. When his first wife deserted him soon after their honeymoon, Milton took the opportunity to call for a liberalization of the divorce laws in his *Doctrine and Discipline of Divorce*.

Pulpits around the country thundered with condemnations of Milton's no-fault divorce doctrine; preachers before the Houses of Parliament advocated official censure. The Stationers' Company of London, representing the city's publishers, complained that the pamphlet had been published in violation of the recently passed "Printing Ordinance," which required all publications to be approved by government censors and licensed by the Stationers. Milton responded with his *Areopagitica*, a searing attack on censorship addressed directly to Parliament and written, he said, "in order to deliver the press from the restraints with which it was encumbered . . . that the power of determining what was true and what was false, what ought to be published and what to be suppressed, might no longer be entrusted to a few illiterate and illiberal individuals." Milton did not favor complete freedom of the press—he would in particular disallow "popery," a stance he was encouraged to employ in his stint as a censor in the Commonwealth—but his statement gave much-needed support to the ideal of religious tolerance at a time when England risked throwing off Episcopacy only to replace it with an equally tyrannical Presbyterian order.

This threat was underlined by the alliance of Royalist and Presbyterian forces in the Second Civil War, brought about through a secret treaty between King Charles and the Scots. But that alliance was smashed by Oliver Cromwell's men, one of whom was praised for his valor in Milton's "Sonnet to [Thomas] Fairfax." Following the trial and execution of the king, Milton, who since reconciling with his wife had kept apart from public discourse, returned to the fray with his *Tenure of Kings and Magistrates*, "proving that it is lawful, and hath been held so in all ages . . . to call to account a Tyrant or wicked King, and, after due conviction, to depose and put him to death." At times, Milton's language often anticipates that of the American revolutionaries. "The power of Kings and Magistrates," he wrote,

> is nothing else but what is only derivative, transferr'd and committed to them in trust from the People, to the Common good of them all, in whom the power yet remains fundamentally, and cannot be tak'n from them, without a violation of their natural birthright. . . .

Milton believed that the king served as an agent of the people, that he was charged with protecting them in their persons and property and could be removed by them when and how they deemed fit.

The unlooked-for defense of republicanism to the point of regicide earned Milton Cromwell's high esteem, as well as a position as secretary of foreign tongues. In this post, he was charged with continuing the defense of Cromwell's fledgling Commonwealth by banishing the martyr cult then forming around the dead king. He set about the task with vigor, undertaking a series of responses "on behalf of the English people" to continental scholars of varying levels of esteem. But as Milton was propounding the virtues of republican government, Cromwell was transforming the powers of the Protector into a dictatorship. Although in one sonnet Milton referred to the Lord Protector as "our chief of men," privately he grew concerned with the antirepublican implications of such a title, the more so as he saw Cromwell move to revive the House of Lords and, worse, reestablish a state-run, state-controlled Church of England.

Thus, at Cromwell's death, Milton revised and republished his first defense of the Commonwealth and followed it with a new work emphasizing the importance of separating church and state, in the hope of seeing the nation return to a republican form of government. He even went so far as to advocate, in *The Ready and Easy Way to Establish a Free Commonwealth*, a federal structure of local governments largely independent of a much-weakened Parliament. However, it soon became apparent that restoration of the monarchy was inevitable, and with it would come a purge of republican sympathizers. As a consequence, Milton was forced into hiding. Although in the end he was arrested, several influential friends managed to remove his name from the list of those marked for death, and he was soon released. In the eyes of many, he emerged "nothing more than an infamous outcast . . . who had, by too great clemency, been left unhanged," but he was already hard at work on the poem that would redeem his reputation.

Although it is his Satan that exerts the greatest influence over the modern-day imagination, Milton's stated purpose in writing *Paradise Lost* was to "justify the ways of God to men." Fresh from the bitter setback of Restoration, Milton must have felt he was due some justification of God's ways; it is hard to escape the image of Adam and Eve banished from Eden as an acknowledgment

that England's revolutionary moment was now past. In his final years, Milton produced a history of England, a Latin grammar, and an anti-Catholic pamphlet. His last great poetic work was *Samson Agonistes*: a tragic setting of the tale of the Israelite judge whose individual salvation was assured at the moment of his death as his nation lay in ruins about him.

AF

See also Censorship; Contractarianism/Social Contract; English Civil Wars

Further Readings

Armitage, David, Armand Himy, and Quentin Skinner, eds. *Milton and Republicanism*. Cambridge: Cambridge University Press, 1995.

Corns, Thomas N. *John Milton: The Prose Works*. New York: Twayne, 1998.

Hill, Christopher. *Milton and the English Revolution*. London: Faber & Faber, 1977.

Hughes, Merritt Y., ed. *John Milton: Complete Poems and Major Prose*. New York: Prentice Hall, 1957.

Knoppers, Laura, Lunger Semenza, and Gregory M. Colón, eds. *Milton in Popular Culture*. New York: Palgrave Macmillan, 2006.

Lieb, Michael. *Theological Milton: Deity, Discourse and Heresy in the Miltonic Canon*. Pittsburgh, PA: Duquesne University Press, 2006.

Parker, William Riley. *Milton: A Biography*. 2nd ed. New York: Oxford University Press, 1996.

Patrides, C. A. *Milton and the Christian Tradition*. London: Oxford University Press, 1966.

MINIMAL STATE

Libertarianism, and the classical liberalism from which it sprang, supports a strictly limited state, if indeed its adherents recognize the legitimacy of the state at all. The minimal state is a notion found within a particular variant of the limited-government variety of libertarianism. In the conception offered here, it was introduced by Robert Nozick, whose *Anarchy, State, and Utopia* is the most influential work supporting libertarianism by an American philosopher. Although Nozick criticized individualist anarchism, he did hold that the minimal state was the form of government that was morally justifiable.

Nozick's starting point is a society in which no government exists. In this situation, he maintained, people largely, although not entirely, respect the rights of others. Among these rights are self-ownership and the right to acquire property. In addition, individuals may use force against those who violate one's rights. This starting point is the same as that of most libertarian anarchists, such as Murray Rothbard. However, what Nozick attempted to show was that, from this initial position, persons would find it to their advantage to take a series of steps that would eventuate in a state—steps that would violate no rights. If Nozick's argument is successful, then he would have shown that the libertarian anarchist view embraced by Rothbard and others undermines itself. Nozick's aims were not limited to the refutation of anarchism. Because individuals in his view do possess the rights he allots them at the start, he intends his argument as a direct justification of the state.

In what sense is the minimal state a state? Nozick understood the state as possessing two main attributes: It must have a monopoly, or close to a monopoly, of legitimate force in a territory, and it must provide protective services for everyone in that territory. It cannot limit its protective services to paying customers, as a private protection agency would do. Nozick argued that the state-like entity that would inevitably result from his starting point met these requirements and thus qualified as a state.

Nozick's argument takes the following form. He begins by assuming that most individuals would join protection agencies to enforce their rights. In choosing an agency, persons would seek an agency that would be expected to win in disputes with other agencies or persons if these disputes could not be peacefully resolved. In brief, persons would seek the most powerful agency available to them. If an agency were somewhat stronger than any of its rivals, customers would shift their patronage to it. Such shifts would make it even more powerful. This movement, in turn, would elicit further shifts of business to it. The culmination of this process would be that most people in society would be protected by a single protection agency.

The market for protective services, Nozick contended, differs in a crucial respect from most other goods and services that the market provides. Like other supporters of a free-market economy, Nozick held that there is no general tendency toward monopoly in the market. Large firms do not always drive out their smaller rivals: The optimal size of a firm depends on particular circumstances. In the market for protection, however, the value of a firm to consumers depends on whether it is stronger than its rivals. In this circumstance, competition among many firms is unstable.

If Nozick's argument is correct, a dominant protection agency would arise from his starting point. This agency is not a state: It provides protection only to those who pay for its services. In the most original part of his argument, Nozick tried to show that the dominant agency would be able to transform itself into a state through morally legitimate means.

Nozick's argument depends on his views about how individuals may respond to someone who violates rights. Like nearly all libertarians, Nozick maintains that persons

are entitled to compensation from rights violators. Thus, for example, if someone steals one's car, one is entitled to the return of the item or its monetary value from the thief. Nozick understands compensation to include payment for expenses of capture and trial of the thief and also payment for any personal losses, including psychological distress occasioned by the theft.

In certain cases, however, this sort of compensation is not sufficient. If people know that they face certain or likely physical harm, they will suffer anxiety. However, although it might be the case that someone who is assaulted can receive compensation for this anxiety after his assailant is convicted, others in the anxiety-provoking situation who are not assaulted will receive no compensation. To deal with this circumstance, Nozick suggests that those who induce this sort of anxiety can be prohibited from engaging in their criminal activities. Here *prohibition* is being used in a technical sense: Nozick means that these people may be subjected to additional penalties beyond compensation to their victims. These penalties will, if successful, deter the anxiety-provoking activities.

Protection agencies can engage in anxiety-provoking activities by subjecting people to risky decision procedures. For example, if a protection agency imposes the death penalty on murderers and uses methods of trial that clients of other agencies deem unreliable, people may become anxious about the possibility of being wrongly found guilty of murder and executed. To cope with this anxiety, a protection agency may attempt to prohibit other agencies or independents operating without an agency from imposing risky decision procedures on its clients.

Any protection agency or independent may attempt to prohibit others from imposing risky procedures, but not all such attempts will be successful. Each agency considers its own procedures reliable, and it has no obligation to accept the opinion of others who disagree. It may forcibly resist such prohibitions. The upshot of such conflicts, Nozick thinks, is that the dominant agency will get its way. It will successfully prohibit others from imposing risky decision procedures on its clients, and other agencies will not be able to resist the dominant agency's use of its procedures on their clients.

If the dominant agency acts in this way, it comes close to meeting Nozick's first requirement for a state. The agency by its prohibitions can prevent any procedures against its clients that it does not recognize as legitimate. The dominant agency in effect has final authority over the application of legitimate force. Nozick terms a dominant agency that acts in this way an *ultraminimal state*. It does not prohibit other agencies from applying risky procedures to their own clients, but no state, Nozick thinks, may rightly do so.

The ultraminimal state does not meet Nozick's second requirement for a state. It provides protective services only to its clients, not to independents living in its territory. However, this condition, Nozick claims, is unstable, such that the dominant agency would find itself morally required to immediately transform itself into a minimal state that offers protective services to everyone in its territory.

Of course someone who uses a decision procedure that others consider risky has not acted in a morally wrong way. Nozick is prepared to concede that there are legitimate differences of opinion about such procedures. However, if someone is prohibited from using a procedure he considers acceptable, he is disadvantaged. His ability to defend his rights has been impeded. The dominant agency, Nozick holds, must therefore compensate those independents who are disadvantaged by its prohibition of risky procedures. This compensation may take the form of offering low-cost protection services to the disadvantaged independents. No one is required to buy these services, so Nozick's proposal is not a form of taxation. The independents will find it to their advantage to purchase the protection services, however, because otherwise they will find it difficult to protect their rights. In addition, the dominant agency may be required to provide protective services without fee to independents unable to pay. Thus, the dominant agency meets the second of Nozick's requirements for a state: The ultraminimal state has become a minimal state.

Nozick's argument has received extensive criticism, both from libertarian anarchists and others. Rothbard questioned whether a dominant agency would in fact emerge from Nozick's initial position. Would it not be more likely that agencies would reach agreements on resolving disputes rather than fight over them? If so, there is no tendency toward a monopoly protection agency, at least for the reasons Nozick suggests. Nozick takes agencies involved in such an agreement to constitute a single agency, but Rothbard thinks this view is implausible.

Eric Mack contends that an agency could circumvent the dominant agency's prohibition of risky decision procedures by using only procedures the dominant agency deemed acceptable. By carefully crafting services to its clients, an indefinite number of competitive agencies can be expected to persist in a free-market society.

What if anarchists viewed the emergence of a dominant agency as undesirable? Nozick argues that they would be unable to block its emergence; but, David Miller contends, it does not follow that they would regard the outcome as acceptable. If so, Nozick has not met his own requirement that each step of his procedure is an improvement for those who take it. One may safely anticipate that controversy over Nozick's argument will continue.

DG

See also Anarchism; Anarcho-Capitalism; Limited Government; Nozick, Robert; Rule of Law

Further Readings

Barnett, Randy. "Wither Anarchy? Has Robert Nozick Justified the State?" *Journal of Libertarian Studies* 1 no. 1 (1977): 15–21.

Childs, Roy A. "The Invisible Hand Strikes Back." *Journal of Libertarian Studies* 1 no. 1 (1977): 23–33.

Mack, Eric. "Nozick's Anarchism." *Nomos XIX: Anarchism.* J. R. Pennock and J. W. Chapman, eds. New York: New York University Press, 1978.

Miller, David. "The Justification of Political Authority." *Robert Nozick.* David Schmidtz, ed. Cambridge: Cambridge University Press, 2002.

Nozick, Robert. *Anarchy, State, and Utopia.* New York: Basic Books, 1974.

Rothbard, Murray N. *The Ethics of Liberty.* New York: New York University Press, 1998.

Sanders, John T. "The Free Market Model versus Government; A Reply to Nozick." *Journal of Libertarian Studies* 1 no. 1 (1977): 35–44.

Steiner, Hillel. "Can a Social Contract Be Signed by an Invisible Hand?" *Democracy, Consensus, and Social Contract.* P. Birnbaum, J. Lively, and G. Parry, eds. London: Sage, 1978.

Mises, Ludwig von (1881–1972)

Ludwig von Mises was the leading Austrian economist of his generation. He received several honorary doctorates and the distinction of a ceremonial 50th-anniversary renewal of his earned doctorate. The same occasion produced a *Festschrift* in his honor; another, in two volumes, celebrated his 90th birthday. The American Economic Association named him a Distinguished Fellow in 1969. The editors of *Liberty* magazine chose him in their January 2000 issue as "Libertarian of the Century."

Mises was born in Lemberg in Austrian-ruled Poland (now Lviv, Ukraine) and died in New York City. His father was a railroad engineer in the civil service; his younger brother, Richard, became an eminent professor of applied mathematics and related fields. Mises entered the University of Vienna in 1900, where he earned a doctorate in law and economics in 1906. He attended the seminar of the eminent economist Eugen von Böhm-Bawerk until qualifying in 1913 as a university lecturer. From 1913 to 1934, he taught as a Privatdozent, paid by the students rather than by the university, and in 1918, he attained the title of Ausserordentlicher Universitätsprofessor (sometimes translated as associate professor). From 1909 to 1938, he was economic advisor at the Vienna Chamber of Commerce, a quasi-governmental organization. During World War I, he served as an artillery officer, and at war's end, he briefly held the post of director of the Austrian Reparations Commission at the League of Nations. After returning from a 1926 tour of the United States on a Rockefeller fellowship, he founded the Austrian Institute for Business Cycle

Research. While at the Chamber of Commerce, he conducted a biweekly seminar, many of whose participants subsequently became prominent economists or legal and political philosophers in their own right, among them Friedrich A. Hayek, Fritz Machlup, Gottfried Haberler, Oskar Morgenstern, Alfred Schütz, Felix Kaufmann, Erich Voegelin, Georg Halm, and Paul Rosenstein-Rodan.

In 1934, Mises accepted a teaching position at the Graduate Institute of International Studies in Geneva. He kept his position at the Chamber of Commerce in Vienna, occasionally returning to work there and accepting only a partial salary. He was summarily dismissed after Hitler occupied Austria in 1938. In the summer of 1940, with Hitler's victory over France, Mises and his wife Margit (whom he had married in 1938) settled in New York City, where they lived until their deaths. He became a U.S. citizen in January 1946. After Leonard Read established the Foundation for Economic Education at Irvington-on-Hudson in 1946, Mises also became one of its staff members, lecturing there until 1972. In his early years in New York, Mises managed to get by on a fellowship at the National Bureau of Economic Research, small foundation grants, consulting for the National Association of Manufacturers, and occasional lecturing positions (including a visiting professorship at the National University of Mexico in 1942). From 1945 until retiring in May 1969, he served as Visiting Professor at New York University (NYU). Three years later, he revived his famous Vienna seminar at NYU, which met for 2 hours each Thursday evening, first at the graduate school in lower Manhattan and later at Washington Square. Prominent participants included Murray Rothbard, Israel Kirzner, Henry Hazlitt, Bettina Bien Greaves, George Reisman, Ralph Raico, Laurence Moss, and Hans Sennholz.

Mises's teaching at NYU was paid for almost entirely from foundation grants, rather than by the university. The fact that Mises never attained a regular full-time professorship, either in Austria or the United States, has aroused conjectures. One, advanced by himself, involves a bias against classical free-market liberals. Another involves anti-Semitism. Reluctance to leave New York restricted his options. Although some have reported that he could be difficult to get along with, intolerant of peers whom he thought to be compromising with error, those who heard him lecture and conduct seminars note that he was gentle in encouraging students to speak out without worry over possible mistakes because all serious errors in the field had already been committed by famous economists.

In 1947, under the leadership of F. A. Hayek, Mises joined in founding the Mont Pelerin Society, along with Wilhelm Röpke, Walter Eucken, Frank Knight, Milton Friedman, Frank D. Graham, Henry Hazlitt, Karl Popper, Michael Polanyi, and other eminent scholars. Named for its original meeting place in Switzerland, the Society is an international association of classical liberals and economic conservatives. In its early years, it was a focus of mutual moral support for adherents of a then-misunderstood and rather rare philosophy.

Mises's earliest academic writings include two works of economic history. He published *The Theory of Money and Credit* in 1912. The book sought to apply supply-and-demand theory (i.e., a cash-balance approach) to money. The work deepened economists' understanding of the quantity theory of money and the purchasing-power-parity theory of exchange rates, and it explained the wasteful consequences of inflationary policies.

Nation, State, and Economy (1919) warned against an excessively harsh peace after World War I, as well as against revanchism on the part of the vanquished. It examined the background of the war, including linguistic-ethnic conditions in Austria-Hungary and Germany that had hampered the flourishing of democracy in those empires. The book reveals Mises as a true classical liberal and democrat, not a conservative: He lauded the ideals of the French Revolution and of the ultimately frustrated German national assembly that convened in Frankfurt in 1848–1849; he scorned hereditary rule and privilege.

In 1922, Mises published *Socialism* (not translated until 1936), an expansion of a 1920 article on "Economic Calculation in the Socialist Commonwealth." He explained why central planners would be unable to meaningfully estimate the values of inputs and outputs and so could not allocate resources rationally. Although F. A. Hayek later joined in elaborating this analysis, most economists who discussed it seemed to misunderstand it as if with willful stubbornness until the collapse of the Soviet Union finally made them recognize that Mises had been right.

Liberalism appeared in 1927, *A Critique of Interventionism* in 1929. Three books followed on the methodology of economics: *Epistemological Problems of Economics* in 1933, whose arguments were elaborated in *Theory and History* (1957), and *The Ultimate Foundation of Economic Science: An Essay on Method* (1962). Mises there explored the rationale of what is sometimes scorned as "armchair theory." These works attempt to lay bare the differences between economic theory, on the one hand, and historical and statistical research, on the other hand. *Bureaucracy*, which came out in 1944, is no mere condemnation of bureaucracy, but rather a trenchant analysis of the unavoidably bureaucratic character of governmental and some other organizations. Mises here explained how the managements of nonprofit and profit-oriented organizations necessarily differ. This short book is, in fact, a capsule presentation of the logic of a market economy. *Omnipotent Government: The Rise of the Total State and Total War*, also from 1944, warns of the dangers in its title and demonstrates that Nazism and fascism, far from being creatures of capitalism, are variants of socialism.

Mises expanded his 1940 *Nationalökonomie* into his English-language magnum opus, *Human Action* (1949, revised in 1963 and 1966). Extending his treatment of the epistemology and methods of the social sciences, this massive work covers the whole range of economics and beyond. *The Anti-Capitalistic Mentality* (1956) explores the psychological sources of hostility to markets and the profit motive. Although a complete survey of Mises's writings and collections of articles is not possible here, one also should mention *Profit and Loss* (1951), *Planning for Freedom* (1952), *The Historical Setting of the Austrian School of Economics* (1969), and *Money, Method, and the Market Process* (1990). German and translated versions of Mises's *Notes and Recollections,* not published until 1978, reflect the globally and personally stressful time when he actually wrote them—1940.

One need not agree with every detail of Mises's economic teachings to be awed by his accomplishment. He presented economic theory in a comprehensive and integrated way as but one aspect, although the major aspect, of the broader science of human action that he called *praxeology*. Mises championed reason against mere intuition and emotion and unmasked the absurdity of polylogism, which is the notion that different brands of logic and rationality and truth exist for different nations, races, and classes (and genders, as we might nowadays add). He resisted the trivialization of academic economics into mathematical descriptions of imaginary static equilibria or optimal positions corresponding to the maximization of known functions subject to known restraints. He recognized that economics for the real world deals with uncertainty, change, saving, capital formation, entrepreneurial discovery and the creation of opportunities, and the constructive discipline of profit and loss. Economics explains the harmonious coordination of radically decentralized decisions and actions taken by individuals pursuing their own diverse goals. *Social cooperation* is Mises's term for the framework of peaceful and productive interaction that enables individuals to reap gains from trade in the broadest sense of the term. Its requirements serve as the basis of Mises's ethical theory, which is a version of utilitarianism immune to standard criticisms.

In policy, Mises championed laissez-faire and hard money. He showed that misconceived, but perennially popular, economic interventions tend to work against their avowed purposes, creating disorders that seem to call for still further interventions. He warned against excessive government power and imperialistic nationalism. But he was no anarchist: He recognized the necessity of government, properly restrained. Nor was he an apologist for big business or the wealthy and the privileged. On the contrary, the sincerity of his overriding concern for the interests of ordinary people shines through his writings.

Mises continues to inspire new generations of Austrian economists and scholars associated with several institutes and journals. He would be appalled by the efforts of some of his disciples—fortunately, only a small minority—to drive a posthumous wedge between him and F. A. Hayek, who, after all, had learned much from him, respected him, and worked creatively in the same tradition.

Finally, Mises deserves honor for his courage, even at heavy cost to his own career, in pursuing research, teaching, and writing with uncompromising concern that correct understanding should prevail in the long run. Although he did not live to fully see the outcome of his efforts, he and his ideas are beginning to win the recognition they deserve.

LY

See also Böhm-Bawerk, Eugen von; Economics, Austrian School of; Hayek, Friedrich A.; Hazlitt, Henry; Kirzner, Israel M.; Money and Banking; Rothbard, Murray; Socialist Calculation Debate

Further Readings

Ebeling, Richard M. "'Editor's Introduction' to Ludwig von Mises." *Money, Method, and the Market Process*. Essays selected by Margit von Mises. Auburn, AL: Ludwig von Mises Institute and Norwell, MA: Kluwer, 1990. ix–xxvi.

Hartwell, R. M. *A History of the Mont Pelerin Society*. Indianapolis, IN: Liberty Fund, 1995.

Hayek, F. A., Henry Hazlitt, Leonrad R. Read, Gustavo Velasco, and Floyd Arthur Harper. *Toward Liberty*. Festschrift for Ludwig von Mises. 2 vols. Menlo Park, CA: Institute for Humane Studies, 1971.

Herbener, Jeffrey M., ed. *The Meaning of Ludwig von Mises*. Auburn, AL: Ludwig von Mises Institute; Norwell, MA: Kluwer, 1993.

Mises, Margit von. *My Years with Ludwig von Mises*. New Rochelle, NY: Arlington House, 1976.

Moss, Laurence S., ed. *The Economics of Ludwig von Mises: Toward a Critical Reappraisal*. Kansas City, MO: Sheed & Ward, 1976.

Sennholz, Hans F. "Postscript." *Notes ad Recollections*. Hans F. Sennholz, trans. South Holland, IL: Libertarian Press, 1978. 145–176.

Sennholz, Mary, ed. *On Freedom and Free Enterprise*. Festschrift for Ludwig von Mises. Princeton, NJ: Van Nostrand, 1956.

Molinari, Gustave de (1819–1912)

Gustave de Molinari, the leading representative of the laissez-faire school of classical liberalism in France in the second half of the 19th century, continued to campaign against protectionism, statism, militarism, colonialism, and socialism into his 90s on the eve of the First World War. As he said shortly before his death, his classical liberal views had remained the same throughout his long life, but the world around him had managed to turn full circle in the meanwhile.

Molinari became active in liberal circles when he moved to Paris from his native Belgium in the 1840s to pursue a career as a journalist and political economist. He quickly became active in promoting free trade, peace, and the abolition of slavery. His liberalism was based on a theory of natural rights, especially the right to property and individual liberty, and he advocated a completely laissez-faire economic policy and an ultraminimal state. During the 1840s, he joined the Society for Political Economy and was active in the Association for Free Trade, which was inspired by Richard Cobden and supported by Frédéric Bastiat. During the 1848 revolution, he vigorously opposed the rise of socialism and shortly thereafter published two rigorous defenses of individual liberty, in which he pushed to its ultimate limits his opposition to all state intervention in the economy, including the state's monopoly of security. He published a small book called *Les Soirées de la rue Saint-Lazare* in 1849, in which he defended the free market and private property through a dialogue among a free-market political economist, a conservative, and a socialist. He extended his radical anti-statist ideas, which he had first presented in his "Eleventh Soirée," in an even more controversial article "De la Production de la Sécurité" in the *Journal des Économistes* in October 1849, where he argued that private companies, such as insurance companies, could provide police and even national security services more cheaply, more efficiently, and more in keeping with acceptable morality than could the state.

During the 1850s, he contributed a number of significant articles on free trade, peace, colonization, and slavery to the *Dictionnaire de l'économie politique* (1852–1853) before going into exile in his native Belgium to escape the authoritarian regime of Napoleon III. He became a professor of political economy at the Musée royale de l'industrie belge and published a significant treatise on political economy, the *Cours d'économie politique* (2nd ed., 1863). He also wrote a number of articles opposing state education at this time. In the 1860s, Molinari returned to Paris to work on the *Journal des Débats*, becoming editor from 1871 to 1876. Between 1878 and 1883, Molinari published two of his most significant historical works in the *Journal des Économistes* in serial and then in book form. *L'Évolution économique du dix-neuvième siècle: Théorie du progrès* (1880) and *L'Évolution politique et la révolution* (1884) were works of historical synthesis that attempted to show how modern free-market industrial societies emerged from societies in which class exploitation and economic privilege predominated and what role the French Revolution had played in this process.

Toward the end of his long life, Molinari was appointed editor of the leading journal of political economy in France, the *Journal des Économistes* (1881–1909). Here he continued his crusade against all forms of economic interventionism, publishing numerous articles on natural law, moral theory, religion, and current economic policy. At the end of the century, he wrote a prognosis of the direction in which society was heading. In *The Society of the Future* (1899), he still defended the free market in all its forms, conceding only that the private protection companies he had advocated 50 years earlier might not prove viable. Nevertheless, he continued to maintain that privatized, local geographic monopolies might still be preferable to nation-wide, state-run monopolies. Perhaps it was fortunate that he died just before the First World War broke out, and thus he was spared from seeing just how destructive such national monopolies of coercion could be.

In the 20 or so years before his death, between 1893 and 1912, Molinari published numerous works attacking the resurgence of protectionism, imperialism, militarism, and socialism, which he believed would hamper economic development, severely restrict individual liberty, and ultimately lead to war and revolution. The key works from this period of his life are *Grandeur et décadence de la guerre* (1898), *Ésquisse de l'organisation politique et économique de la Société future* (1899), *Les Problèmes du XXe siècle* (1901), *Théorie de l'évolution: Économie de l'histoire* (1908), and his aptly titled last work *Ultima Verba: Mon dernier ouvrage* (1911), which appeared when he was 92 years of age.

Molinari's death in 1912 severely weakened the classical liberal movement in France, and only a few members of the "old school" remained to teach and write—including the economist Yves Guyot and the antiwar campaigner Frédéric Passy, who both survived into the 1920s. By the time of Molinari's death, the academic posts and editorships of the major journals had fallen into the hands of the "new liberals," socialists who spurned the laissez-faire liberalism of the 19th century.

DMH

See also Anarcho-Capitalism; Free Trade; Imperialism; Liberalism, Classical; Nationalism; Peace and Pacifism; Socialism; War

Further Readings

Hart, David M. "Gustave de Molinari and the Anti-statist Liberal Tradition." *Journal of Libertarian Studies* 5 no. 3 (Summer 1981): 263–290; 5 no. 4 (Fall 1981): 399–434; 6 no. 1 (Winter 1982): 83–104.

Molinari, Gustave de. *Cours d'économie politique.* 2nd rev. ed. Paris: Guillaumin, 1863. [1855]

———. "De la production de la sécurité." *Journal des Économistes* 21 (1849): 277; "The Production of Security." *Occasional Paper Series no. 2.* J. Huston McCulloch, trans. New York: Center for Libertarian Studies, 1977.

———. *Les Soirées de la rue Saint-Lazare; entretiens sur les lois économiques et défense de la propriété.* Paris: Guillaumin, 1849.

Money and Banking

Throughout history, the state has typically monopolized the issuance of money. The various royal mints were once the exclusive sources of silver and gold coins, whereas today the national central banks alone are empowered to issue fiat currency. As private banks have developed alternatives to state-issued money (banknotes, transferrable account balances), the state has typically placed them under considerable restrictions. Many otherwise free-market economists have taken state control over money and banking for granted or, in some particulars, justified it; to the extent they recommend altering these monopolies, it is merely to limit their abuses. Those who have rejected "state tampering with money and banks," as Herbert Spencer titled his essay, have been far from unanimous about what a libertarian monetary and banking system would look like.

Classical economists like Adam Smith understood that money was originally not a creature of the state, but was rather a spontaneous institution that had emerged without explicit design. As Carl Menger concluded, "Money was not created by law; in its origin it is not a governmental but a social phenomenon." Markets in the ancient world converged on silver coins as the most commonly accepted medium of exchange. This silver coin standard prevailed across national borders without any global government. Why then did ancient and medieval monarchs insist on exclusive control over the business of producing coins? If their concern was to improve the quality of coins, they failed miserably: Royal mints were notorious for repeatedly debasing the coinage by reducing their silver content with a mix of copper and other base metals. If, however, their real concern was to raise state revenue, they succeeded. The difference between the low price paid for raw silver—for which the official mint was typically the only legal buyer—and the higher price imposed on coined silver made the mint a major source of income for the monarchy. The technical term for this profit is *seigniorage* inasmuch as it was considered the prerogative of the feudal lord or *seigneur.*

Most 19th-century classical liberals took this state monopoly for granted. Only the most radical of these writers—Thomas Hodgskin, William Leggett, Herbert Spencer, and William Brough—argued for the privatization of coinage. In the 20th century, F. A. Hayek reintroduced the idea of the "denationalization of money" in the context of fiat (unbacked) monetary standards. Hayek argued that competition among private producers of fiat money would keep its purchasing power more stable. Other libertarian monetary economists endorse Hayek's call for an end to legal restrictions against private money, but they question his predictions that dozens of distinct monetary units would circulate in parallel in the same economy or that the public would prefer unbacked private money to the more traditional

sort of commodity-backed private money. A long line of free-market economists has endorsed silver or gold as a market-chosen monetary standard that makes a laissez-faire monetary system feasible.

The issuance of money by banks, even were these notes secured by some metallic backing, is yet more controversial among libertarian monetary theorists. Perhaps because early banks often operated under exclusive state charters, some classical liberal thinkers, such as Thomas Jefferson and William Gouge, condemned bank-issued money that rested on fractional reserves as per se illegitimate. They called for a return to "hard money," a system that relied only on coins made of precious metals or on certificates fully backed by precious metals. Others such as Leggett, Spencer, and Ludwig von Mises called for *free banking*, or the complete separation of banking and the state. In their view, governments should neither shelter banks from market competition nor restrict the sorts of contractual arrangements, including fractional reserves that banks may make with their customers. Central banking is prone to causing either an oversupply or undersupply of money, the effects of which are business cycles. Competition would better regulate the supply of money. British "Free Banking School" economists in the 19th century sharply criticized Parliament for protecting the Bank of England against failure and for giving it a monopoly of banknote issue, privileges that turned it from a commercial bank into a central bank. In the United States, Jeffersonian and Jacksonian classical liberals opposed the special privileges of the first and second Banks of the United States.

The well-known monetary historian and free-market economist Milton Friedman had argued early in his career that negative external effects associated with free banking justified a state monopoly of coin and paper currency. Under free entry, he maintained, sharp operators would find it too easy to get their notes into circulation and then abscond before they could be called on to redeem these notes. Later in his career, Friedman reconsidered and endorsed competitive note issue in light of new findings by Hugh Rockoff and others that bad results under so-called free banking in the United States were due to poorly conceived regulations, whereas a relatively free market in other countries showed good results.

In principle, Friedman supported a well-managed state fiat money over a gold standard on grounds of lower resource costs, but emphasized that—in practice, at least—fiat money has been badly managed. As the leading monetarist critic of the Keynesian argument in support of an activist monetary policy, Friedman advocated a monetary rule that would commit the U.S. Federal Reserve System to slow and steady growth in the stock of money. Later, recognizing that central bank officials have no incentive to follow such a rule, he suggested effectively abolishing the Fed by freezing the stock of Fed liabilities and sending the monetary policymakers home.

Friedman's diagnosis of the Federal Reserve System's contribution to the Great Depression differed from that of the Austrian economists Mises and Hayek. The Austrians regarded the Fed's overly expansive policy in the mid- to late 1920s as fostering an unsustainable investment boom and thereby sowing the seeds of the 1929 downturn. Friedman and his co-investigator Anna Schwartz emphasized the damage done by the Fed's failure to stem bank runs and the consequent contraction in the stock of bank-issued money after 1930. Having nationalized the functions formerly played by private bank clearinghouses, the Fed failed to act as the "lender of last resort," a role played by the clearinghouses in previous monetary panics.

The leading libertarian theorist Murray Rothbard and his followers have taken the position that fractional reserve banking is illegitimate and that only "100% reserve" or warehouse banking is consistent with a libertarian legal code. Rothbard argued that a bank that promises to redeem its banknotes on demand in gold that it does not presently possess is defrauding its customers. His followers have argued that even if the customer knowingly agrees to the arrangement, the bank and the customer are conspiring to defraud third parties. In their view, "fiduciary media" (i.e., fractionally backed notes and deposit), prevail through a combination of bank trickery and legal restrictions against legitimate 100% reserve money warehouses.

In opposition to this view, modern free-banking theorists argue that fractionally backed notes and deposits have passed the market test: They have predominated over warehouse receipts because they offer customers a better deal. No fraud is committed by a bank that issues fiduciary media without misrepresenting them, and banks have typically not misrepresented them. Indeed, nothing on the face of the typical banknote proclaims it to be a warehouse receipt. Banks' customers have not been duped for centuries, but have preferred to use money free of warehousing fees despite the slightly greater risk of default.

Apart from the fraud question, 100% reservers differ from free bankers on the question of the practical effects of fractional reserve banking. Following Smith and Mises, those who support free banking maintain that fractional reserve banking beneficially economizes on the labor and capital devoted to extracting precious metals that will only be tied up in bank vaults. Following Rothbard, the 100% reservers argue that such savings are trivial in comparison to the economic damage associated with the business cycles caused by the instability of fractional reserve banking. In Hans-Herman Hoppe's view, "any injection of fiduciary media must result in a boom-bust cycle." The free bankers counter that monetary disturbances and consequent business cycles are due to central bank monetary policy and interventions that weaken the banking system, not to fractional reserves. They argue that a competitive free-banking system permits "expansion of the stock of fiduciary media only to an extent consistent with the preservation of monetary equilibrium and the avoidance of the credit-expansion-induced business cycle."

The leading argument against laissez-faire banking in recent years holds that unregulated banks are naturally prone to harmful runs and panics and that government deposit insurance offers a low-cost remedy. Defenders of unregulated banking, in contrast, have provided strong historical evidence that runs and panics are not natural: The problem has arisen only in systems, as was true of United States in the late 19th century, where government regulations have seriously weakened banks. Systems closer to a free market in banking have been more stable, whereas government deposit insurance has imposed costs in excess of its benefits.

LHW

See also Assurance and Trust; Banking, Austrian Theory of; Capitalism; Great Depression

Further Readings

Friedman, Milton, and Anna J. Schwartz. "Has Government Any Role in Money?" *Journal of Monetary Economics* 17 (1986): 37–62.

Hayek, F. A. *The Denationalisation of Money.* 2nd ed. London: Institute of Economic Affairs, 1978.

Hoppe, Hans-Hermann, with Jörg Guido Hülsmann and Walter Block. "Against Fiduciary Media." *Quarterly Journal of Austrian Economics* 1 (1998): 19–50.

Rothbard, Murray N. *What Has Government Done to Our Money?* 4th ed. Auburn, AL: Ludwig von Mises Institute, 1990.

Selgin, George, and Lawrence H. White. "In Defense of Fiduciary Media." *Review of Austrian Economics* 9 (1996): 83–107.

Smith, Vera C. *The Rationale of Central Banking and the Free-Banking Alternative.* Indianapolis, IN: Liberty Press, 1990.

Timberlake, Richard H. *Monetary Policy in the United States.* Chicago: University of Chicago Press, 1993.

MONTAIGNE, MICHEL DE (1533–1592)

Michel de Montaigne was a leading writer of the French Renaissance. Montaigne was the originator and chief popularizer of the essay as a self-conscious literary form; his most important work, his collected *Essais*, was tremendously influential in shaping Western thought and letters for the last 400 years. In his essays, Montaigne attempted not only to understand the world around him, but also to understand himself, the nature of man in general, and the peculiarities that made him who he was. His focus on the individual spirit, and the individual voice, was characteristic of Renaissance humanism. Montaigne's intense originality and devotion to the study of the self place him in the first rank of individualist thinkers.

Montaigne's individualism did not drift into a dogmatic egotism, however, and he developed both a humility about mankind's limitations and a cosmopolitan attitude toward the various modes of life he encountered during his travels throughout Europe. "If it were up to me to train myself in my own fashion," he wrote,

> there is no way so good that I should want to be fixed in it and unable to break loose. Life is an uneven, irregular, and multiform movement. We are not friends to ourselves . . . we are slaves, if we follow ourselves incessantly and are so caught in our inclinations that we cannot depart from them or twist them about.

Nor was this an idle boast. Montaigne strongly mistrusted easy certitudes. Although he was a devout Catholic, he steadfastly worked for peace between Catholics and Protestants, a view that set him apart from the vast majority of his contemporaries. He even went so far as to attempt, during the worst of the French Wars of Religion, a mediation between Henri de Guise, leader of the Catholic League, and Henri de Navarre, the future King Henri IV, who was still a Protestant. Montaigne was skeptical of the supernatural in general and particularly of the divine mandate of government, yet he remained loyal to his faith and to the French state for fear, he explained, that innovations would prove worse than the established institutions. In this he was both a new kind of conservative and a skeptic concerning the power of human knowledge.

Although he was traditional in his faith and allegiance, Montaigne abhorred cruelty, torture, and arbitrary rule. He seldom, if ever, sought to excuse these vices in rulers, and he often sided with the victims of persecution against their oppressors. Libertarians are apt to see Montaigne as an intellectual cousin, and nowhere is this kinship more evident than in his essay "Of Sumptuary Laws," where he writes,

> The way in which our laws try to regulate . . . expenditures for the table and for clothes seems to be opposed to their purpose. . . . For to say that none but princes shall eat turbot, or shall be allowed to wear velvet and gold braid, and to forbid them to the people, what else is this but to give prestige to these things and increase everyone's desire to enjoy them?

Our lack of insight into the minds of others poses a serious obstacle to any straightforward, systematic attempt to regulate the conduct of others.

Libertarians are apt to fault Montaigne in one significant respect—namely, his view of economics. He held that, in any exchange, one party must gain while another loses. He appears not to have considered the idea that exchanges might be mutually beneficial. Ludwig von Mises went so far as to term this notion the "Montaigne dogma," and he devoted a section of his seminal work *Human Action* to refuting it. Yet the Montaigne dogma was and remains so ubiquitous that it may not be wholly fair to assign it to one individual except insofar as a pervasive fallacy requires a convenient name.

Although he often appears to be a thinker well ahead of his time, Montaigne's upbringing and surroundings seem to have done much to shape, or at least suggest, his character. He was born near Bordeaux to a mother of Jewish *converso* heritage; three of his siblings would later convert to Protestantism. A member of the minor nobility, his father had served in the French army in Italy and developed an appreciation for humanistic learning. His son Michel was given peasant godparents and a tutor who spoke no French; the younger Montaigne spoke only Latin until he was 6 years old. He later made a career in the Parlement of Bordeaux, where he befriended Étienne de La Boétie and was among the first to read La Boétie's *Treatise of Involuntary Servitude*, which impressed him deeply. Montaigne struck up a close friendship with La Boétie, which ended only at La Boétie's death.

Considered as a whole, Montaigne's work presents something of a paradox. Although he was deeply skeptical about the ability of any one man or group of men to grasp absolute truth, still, he manifestly valued the more pedestrian work of simply trying to understand what one could. He exhibited remarkable insight into human character at the individual level, while, by libertarian lights, his understanding of economic interactions was simplistic. However, the fact that he had missed the mark might not have greatly surprised him. Much would always remain unknown, Montaigne believed, and this fact was to be accepted with a fortitude that he drew from ancient Stoic sources.

Libertarians still appreciate Montaigne's views on the limits of understanding, inasmuch as many libertarians tend to view society as a complex interplay of local knowledges and practices, beyond the ability of any one person or government to comprehend. In addition, libertarians, following Montaigne, tend to reject the more ambitious system-builders and planners who believe that they can fully master anything as complex as social institutions or even as complex as another individual. "I do not see the whole of anything," Montaigne wrote, "nor do those who promise to show it to us."

JTK

See also Humanism; La Boétie, Étienne de; Liberty in the Ancient World; Republicanism, Classical; Skepticism; Stoicism

Further Readings

Langer, Ulrich. *The Cambridge Companion to Montaigne.* Cambridge: Cambridge University Press, 2005.

Montaigne, Michel de. *The Complete Essays of Montaigne.* 3 vols. Donald A. Frame, trans. New York: Doubleday, 1960.

Starobinski, Jean. *Montaigne in Motion.* Arthur Goldhammer, trans. Chicago: University of Chicago Press, 1985.

MONTESQUIEU, CHARLES DE SECONDAT DE (1689–1755)

Charles de Secondat, Baron de Montesquieu was a leading legal and social philosopher of the French Enlightenment. He is best known for the theory of separation of powers, which he advanced as a safeguard against arbitrary rule. Montesquieu's ideas deeply impressed the American Founders, particularly James Madison, and the U.S. Constitution owes much to Montesquieu's analysis of the nature of good government.

Montesquieu inherited great wealth and a magistracy in the *parlement* of Bordeaux—a regional law court, rather than a legislative body. In the 18th century, the *parlements* of France represented one of the few independent authorities in the French state, and Montesquieu learned much about government from firsthand experience. Often the *parlements* feuded with the monarchy; Montesquieu was to witness arbitrary power in the person of Louis XIV, whom he later lampooned in his writings. The *parlements* regularly demanded that religious prisoners be set free and that no taxes be approved without their assent; the struggles over these issues are often reflected in Montesquieu's political writings.

In 1721, Montesquieu published the *Persian Letters*, a fictional compilation of letters exchanged by and about two Persians traveling throughout Europe. The visitors ridicule not only the vanity and folly of Europe, but also its despotic governments, oppressive laws, religious intolerance, and hypocrisy. They also ridiculed the sale of offices, monetary devaluation, and even the idea that war could enrich a country.

What elevates the *Persian Letters* above mere satire is the way in which the letters' fictional authors failed to recognize their own illiberality; one of them, Usbek, both owns eunuchs and keeps a harem, over which he extends a cruel and despotic rule. The work therefore makes the point that, although the principles of liberty may be easy to understand when applied to someone else, it is far more difficult to restrain one's own impulses toward tyranny. The *Persian Letters* was published anonymously to avoid imprisonment for its author, yet his identity was sufficiently well known that, with only a handful of minor works to his name, Montesquieu was elected to the Académie Française.

Montesquieu's greatest work, *The Spirit of the Laws,* was far more ambitious. Published in 1748, it aimed to explain in purely natural terms the various systems of government encountered throughout the world, how they grew and developed, and how they declined and ultimately collapsed. The result is a digressive and omnivorous work, containing observations about climate, agriculture, technology, history, economics, and philosophy. Some of its ideas, particularly those about climate and geography, are now merely of historical interest and have little value except as curiosities. Others, however, continue to exert a profound influence on modern politics.

One notion that runs throughout *The Spirit of the Laws* is the idea that we must judge all laws by their actual effects, not by their intentions or by the wickedness of the crime they are meant to suppress. In this regard, Montesquieu can be seen as a predecessor of libertarian consequentialism. In a particularly insightful passage, he wrote, "Among us, three crimes stand out: magic, heresy, and the crime against nature. We may say of the first, that it does not exist; of the second, that it is subject to infinite distinctions and interpretations; and of the third, that it is very often secretive. Yet all three are punished by burning at the stake." Montesquieu argued that laws of this type were bad because they augmented arbitrary power and that the evil they did far outweighed any possible good that they might achieve. The vagueness of a law, Montesquieu argued, leads directly to tyranny.

Montesquieu contended that the legitimacy of a law required not only its predictability, but strict limits on the powers of government. Anticipating the words of Lord Acton, he wrote, "Eternal experience shows that all men who have power come to abuse it, and this they will do to the limits of their power." The great question of political thought now becomes how to prevent the abuse of power, and Montesquieu supplied an answer that would have far-ranging consequences in the modern world.

The most important contribution of *The Spirit of the Laws* was the claim that government power can be effectively limited by dividing it into a legislative power, whose function was to write the laws, an executive power, which enforces the laws, and a judicial power, empowered to interpret the laws and settle disputes arising under them.

Montesquieu proposed that each of these three powers should be assigned to a separate agency or individual within the state and that these powers should be constituted in such a way that they will act as restraints on one another. "So that none can abuse power, we must arrange, by the disposition of things, that power shall check power," Montesquieu wrote.

The aims of his system were personal security and personal liberty, which Montesquieu regarded as nearly the same thing: "The government must be such that one citizen will not live in fear of another," he wrote. Montesquieu cited only two significant examples of governments that agreed with his theories: Britain and the Roman Republic. He argued that Rome lost its liberty when it abandoned the separation of powers, but that Britain retained a significant share of its own liberty owing to the separation of the King, the Parliament, and the court system.

Montesquieu had relatively little impact in France; the political theories of Jean-Jacques Rousseau were far more evident in the era of the French Revolution. Yet he achieved a remarkable posthumous success in the United States. As James Madison wrote in Federalist no. 47, "the oracle who is always consulted and cited on this subject is the celebrated Montesquieu." *The Spirit of the Laws* comported well with the colonists' understanding of government both because they were accustomed to the British system, which Montesquieu praised, and because they had come through experience to share Montesquieu's suspicion of arbitrary power. Montesquieu offered powerful arguments in favor of a three-branch system containing checks and balances on the power of each branch of government, and Madison noted how both the state constitutions and the proposed federal one were in keeping with Montesquieu's design.

A vigorous debate exists today among libertarians regarding Montesquieu's ideas on state power. Some argue that the separation of powers and checks and balances derived from Montesquieu's thought can indeed form the basis of a limited government, and that, aided by further insights about the nature of government, we can erect effective checks on its power that will prevent it from violating any individual rights. Those who share this opinion tend to describe themselves as minarchists, and they tend to work within existing systems of law with a view toward limiting, but not eliminating the state.

Others, however, observe that no government has ever fully respected individual liberty and that all limitations on government power have tended to break down over time. They tend to view Montesquieu's system and others like it as well-intentioned failures, and they note that theories of limited government have prevented neither the tyrannical regimes of the 20th century nor the advance of socialism within Britain and the United States. Thinkers of this persuasion tend to reject Montesquieu's theories of government and instead favor various systems of libertarian anarchy.

JTK

See also Constitution, U.S.; Constitutionalism; Enlightenment; Judiciary; Separation of Church and State

Further Readings

Hamilton, Alexander, James Madison, and John Jay. *The Federalist.* Maria Hong, ed. New York: Pocket Books, 2004.

Lacouture, Jean. *Montesquieu: les vendanges de la liberté.* Paris: Seuil, 2003.

Lutz, Donald S. "The Relative Influence of European Writers on Late Eighteenth-Century American Political Thought." *American Political Science Review* 78 no. 1 (March 1984): 189–197.

Montesquieu, Charles de Secondat, baron de. *The Persian Letters.* George R. Healy, trans. Indianapolis, IN: Hackett, 1999.

———. *The Spirit of the Laws.* Anne M. Cohler et al., eds. and trans. New York: Cambridge University Press, 1989.

Shackleton, Robert. *Essays on Montesquieu and on the Enlightenment.* David Gilson and Martin Smith, eds. Oxford: Voltaire Foundation at the Taylor Institution, 1988.

MONT PELERIN SOCIETY

Most of the 20th century proved a disaster for classical liberalism. By 1945, the cumulative result of the two world wars and the Great Depression was that most people, especially academics and other intellectuals, had abandoned their belief in the efficacy of limited government, the rule of law and open, competitive markets. They had arrived at the conclusion that governments had to actively intervene in private affairs, especially in the economy, to ensure public peace, prosperity, and harmony. The effect was the abandonment of classical liberalism, which had embraced the free unconstrained interaction of individuals in both social and economic affairs. Indeed, in the United States, by the early part of the 20th century, the word *liberalism* had come to denote something quite different from its 19th-century meaning; it now meant that extensive intervention in the economic life of the community was essential to stave off cycles of boom and bust, mass unemployment, and economic chaos. It seemed likely that true liberalism would soon become an odd relic of a benighted past.

In 1944, F. A. Hayek published *The Road to Serfdom*, wherein he argued that even well-intentioned interventions in private affairs, even by democratically elected governments, inexorably led to more and more intervention, increasing centralization of power, and a loss of individual liberty. Although the authoritarian powers were about to be defeated, interventionism, Hayek argued, would gradually lead to future tyrannies that were likely to be just as bad. Serfdom was already the fate of the people of the Soviet Union, and after 1945 it oppressed most of Eastern Europe.

Hayek thought that the only way that this descent to serfdom could be halted and reversed was if the principles of classical liberalism were kept alive, nurtured, developed, widely disseminated, and, eventually, widely adopted. That small remnant of intellectuals who still supported classical liberalism was widely dispersed and often isolated. Hayek thought it would be useful to form an organization that would make it possible for these thinkers to regularly come together for mutual encouragement and assistance to continue to fight the battle of ideas with interventionists and to keep liberalism alive. To discuss the possibility of forming such an organization, Hayek convened a meeting of 39 classical liberals from Western Europe and the United States that was held at Mount Pelerin, Switzerland, in April 1947. The participants at that conference came from 10 different countries and included academics from the disciplines of economics (the majority), law, history, political science, and philosophy, as well as three journalists. Among those joining Hayek at the meeting were Milton Friedman, George Stigler, Aaron Director, Ludwig von Mises, Leonard Read, Karl Popper, and Wilhelm Ropke. They agreed to form an organization that they named the Mont Pelerin Society, dedicated to reviving, sustaining, and spreading classical liberalism. Hayek became its first president, a post that he held until 1960. Hayek and most of the founding members were opposed to the Society involving itself in direct political action and advocacy. In Hayek's words, the purpose of the Society:

> is not to spread a given doctrine, but to work out in continuous effort, a philosophy of freedom which can claim to provide an alternative to the political views now widely held. . . . Our goal . . . must be the solution not of the practical task of gaining mass support for a given programme, but to enlist the support of the best minds in formulating a programme which has a chance of gaining general support.

The Mont Pelerin Society (MPS) was conceived as and remains a voluntary community of individuals who share a dedication to the principles of a free society. Its activities consist of developing the principles of liberty and helping its individual members more effectively articulate those principles. There is no central headquarters, and there is no paid permanent staff. There are no official MPS publications except for a small quarterly newsletter designed to keep members informed of future meetings and changes of membership. The Society takes no official position on political issues or on public policy. The external face of the MPS is what its members, as individuals, write, say, and do.

Although all MPS members share a dedication to the concept of a free society, its members differ on many of the details. For example, they all believe in limited government, but they disagree on what those limits should be. A few members are confident in the power of the market to generate voluntary solutions to all problems, whereas others embrace the view that governments should be limited to the protective functions of the classical night watchman state (national defense, police, and a judiciary). Still others add some "productive" functions (such as the provision of roads and the financing of some educational services) to the list of acceptable government activities. Among the more contentious issues are those centering on money and banking, monetary policy, and foreign exchange. Some members argue in favor of a return to a strict gold standard, whereas others hold that gold is simply a commodity like any other and that a country can have sound money without gold playing any monetary role. Some oppose fractional reserve banking and others support it. Although all of its members endorse free trade, some favor fixed exchange rates, whereas others advocate flexible exchange rates. These and other points of disagreement are sometimes explored at the Society's various meetings.

By the first decade of the new century, membership had grown to approximately 500 people from North America, Western Europe, Eastern Europe, Central and South America, Hong Kong, Taiwan, Japan, India, Australia, New Zealand, South Africa, and Turkey. Among its members are academics in the disciplines of economics (still a majority), history, philosophy, political science, law, and sociology. Others are business people, associates of private research institutions, lawyers, judges, journalists, clergy, and even a few politicians.

The Society is now well known and widely respected even by those who differ with its goals. Its individual members are even better known and respected for their own accomplishments. Eight of its members have won the Nobel Prize in Economic Science: F. A. Hayek (1974), Milton Friedman (1976), George Stigler (1982), James Buchanan (1986), Maurice Allais (1988), Ronald Coase (1991), Gary Becker (1992), and Vernon Smith (2002).

Membership in the Society is by invitation on the recommendation of two members and the approval of the Board of Directors. There is no formal ceiling on total membership, but the Board attempts to assure that membership does not get so large that the intimate nature of the Society's meetings is lost.

With the collapse of communism in the Soviet Union and eastern Europe, which Hayek lived to see, it certainly can be said that classical liberalism did not die in the 20th century. To the contrary, it is alive and well, especially in formerly subjugated countries such as the Czech Republic. Much of the credit for this revival must go to F. A. Hayek and many of the Society's other members.

ChB

See also Buchanan, James M.; Coase, Ronald H.; Friedman, Milton; Hayek, Friedrich A.; Popper, Karl; Read, Leonard E.

Further Readings

Hartwell, R. M. *A History of the Mont Pelerin Society*. Indianapolis, IN: Liberty Fund, 1995.

Hayek, F. A. *The Road to Serfdom*. Chicago: University of Chicago Press, 1944.

———. "Why I Am Not a Conservative." Postscript to *The Constitution of Liberty*. Chicago: University of Chicago Press, 1960. 397–411.

MURRAY, CHARLES (1943–)

Charles Murray, an American political scientist and nonacademic researcher, received his doctorate in political science from the Massachusetts Institute of Technology in 1974, but is unusual among influential American social scientists in having done all his work outside academia, from berths at private think tanks. He has worked for the American Institutes for Research (1974–1981) and the Manhattan Institute (1982–1990). He was a resident fellow and has been the W. H. Brady Scholar at the American Enterprise Institute (2003–present). Murray has written on a variety of topics, including the successes and failures of the welfare state, the conditions under which government can aid its citizens in the pursuit of happiness, and the implications of a growing social stratification in the United States based on how intelligent one is thought to be. He also has written on the practical political implications and potential benefits of applying libertarian insights to the modern American state.

Losing Ground, Murray's first widely read work, contained data and analysis that questions the wisdom and efficacy of what many consider the American government's most significant success in the late 20th century—the array of welfare programs associated with the "Great Society" and the years following. Murray demonstrated that, by most available measures, the income transfer programs that characterized the late 1960s—among them greatly loosened eligibility standards for Aid to Families with Dependent Children and massive programs for job training and funding for disadvantaged elementary and secondary school students—did not improve the lives of the poor and, in most cases, made them worse off. He used trendline analyses to show that any improvement in the lives of the poor that occurred after these programs went into effect was merely a continuation of progress that had begun long before more liberal federal efforts and that this progress, in most cases, halted in the 1970s. Crime and unemployment among the poor increased since the welfare state grew in the 1960s, whereas income and educational achievement dropped.

Murray has not relied on the "welfare cheat" rhetoric that welfare supporters think characterized the antiwelfare arguments of the Reagan years. He maintained that incentives for the poor created by the modern welfare state made it more likely that children would be born illegitimate and that men would feel less need to work or to provide for their children. Murray recommended the elimination of all racial preference programs and the issuance of educational vouchers. He also advocated the repeal of all income transfer programs. In their place, he supported the reinstatement of short-term unemployment insurance.

In the 1980s, *Losing Ground* initiated a lively debate over the future of federal welfare programs and is credited with influencing Reagan administration policy. However, the most significant steps leading to a drop in the welfare rolls along the lines suggested by Murray did not occur until the Clinton administration in the 1990s.

Murray's late 1960s stint as a Peace Corps volunteer in Thailand informed his next book, *In Pursuit: Of Happiness and Good Government*. Murray decided that, despite the relative destitution of life in the Thai villages he knew, the strength of the communities there allowed him to imagine he could have lived a quite happy life there, much happier than with greater wealth in an unsafe, atomized American inner city. This book tried to answer the following question: What does it take to be happy, and how can government social policy help or hinder that attempt?

Murray concluded that human beings need self-respect born of satisfaction with their own achievements to be happy, and that the modern state too often deprives people of the opportunity to do things for themselves and their communities. Murray argued that what Edmund Burke called the "little platoons"—the ways that humans join together to solve their own problems—are vital to social happiness. "I am proposing," he wrote,

> that there is nothing mysterious about why people become atomized in modern urban settings. Individuals are drawn to community affiliations and attach themselves to them in direct proportion to the functional value of those organizations. As people attach themselves to individual community institutions the aggregate intangible called "community" itself takes on a life and values that are greater than the sum of the parts. Take away the functions, and you take away the community. The cause of the problem is not a virus associated with modernity, it is a centralization of functions that shouldn't be centralized, and this is very much a matter of political choice, not ineluctable forces.

Murray specifically roots his political vision in the American Founding Fathers, particularly Jefferson, and has stated his preconceptions about man as a social being thusly: "Man acting in his private capacity—*if restrained from the use of the force*—is resourceful and benign, fulfilling his proper destiny; while man acting as a public and political creature is resourceful and dangerous, inherently destructive of the rights of his fellows."

In 1994, Murray collaborated with Harvard psychometrician Richard J. Herrnstein on his highly controversial analysis of intelligence testing and its effects on stratifying Americans. In *The Bell Curve*, Murray and Herrnstein expressed concern regarding how important intelligence was becoming in a highly meritocratic America. They presented data that they regarded as proving that no less than 40% to 80% of a person's IQ was attributable to heredity. They predicted a growing stratification in American culture along the lines of intelligence, which social policy would be unable to ameliorate because such a large portion of one's intelligence was not amenable to environmental influence.

Even more controversial, Murray and Herrnstein discussed how the distribution of intelligence across races seemed to be different, with blacks on average having a lower IQ than whites and whites lower than Asians. They also found that intelligence correlated inversely with various social pathologies, such as crime and illegitimacy. The book was fiercely attacked as racist, and their conclusion that racial IQ differences existed was used to discredit them and their research. In reality, the book was far less focused on race than most of its criticisms, and Murray denies any racial animus behind his reporting, pointing out that he had simply repeated the conclusions of widely known IQ test results. Murray argued that in reality there does not exist a single intelligence that IQ tests measure well except in the popular press and that no expert psychometrician has ever claimed this. Nor, he argued, does a lower score on IQ tests imply that one is inferior and should therefore be treated as such, as the public seemed to believe.

Murray wrote a popular summation of the libertarian position he had come to embrace over his decades of research in the social sciences. In *What It Means to Be a Libertarian: A Personal Interpretation*, he presents a minimal-government libertarian vision, explaining why he thinks all government regulation of business should be eliminated. At a minimum he argued that all unregulated products and services should be legally permitted to compete with regulated ones. Among his policy recommendations are that government should make no laws respecting race or restricting free association; end the regulation of education and fund it through vouchers; eliminate laws against the use and sale of drugs and those prohibiting prostitution; regulate environmental standards, rather than the methods used to meet those standards; and end all government social service and income transfer programs. Murray summed up his libertarian views in the following language:

> Libertarianism is a vision of how people should be able to live their lives—as individuals, striving to realize the best

they have within them; together, cooperating for the common good without compulsion. It is a vision of how people may endow their lives with meaning—living according to their deepest beliefs and taking responsibility for the consequences of their actions.

Despite huge reductions in the welfare rolls during the 1990s that might ordinarily have been expected to cheer the author of *Losing Ground*, Murray still worries that the rising rate of illegitimate births and the burgeoning crime rate, which is only being dealt with by increasing periods of incarceration, suggest a grim future unless we give serious consideration to complete elimination of all welfare programs. To that end, Murray has advocated a negative income tax similar to the one proposed by economist Milton Friedman. Murray's 2006 book *In Our Hands: A Plan to Replace the Welfare State* made the case for this proposal.

BDo

See also Civil Society; Urban Planning; Welfare State

Further Readings

Murray, Charles. *A Behavioral Study of Rural Modernization: Social and Economic Change in Thai Villages*. New York: Praeger, 1977.

———. *Income Inequality and IQ*. Washington, DC: AEI Press, 1998.

———. *In Pursuit of Happiness and Good Government*. New York: Simon & Schuster, 1988.

———. *Losing Ground: American Social Policy, 1950–1980*. New York: Basic Books, 1984.

———. *The Underclass Revisited*. Washington, DC: AEI Press, 1999.

———. *What It Means to Be a Libertarian: A Personal Interpretation*. New York: Broadway Books, 1997.

Murray, Charles, and Richard J. Herrnstein. *The Bell Curve: Intelligence and Class Structure in American Life*. New York: Free Press, 1994.

NATHAN, TONIE (1923–)

Theodora (Tonie) Nathan was the first woman and first Jewish person to receive an electoral vote. Nathan was a radio-TV producer in Eugene, Oregon, when she attended the first presidential nominating convention of the Libertarian Party in 1972. She was selected to run for vice president with presidential candidate John Hospers. Although the ticket received only 3,671 official votes, Virginia elector Roger L. MacBride chose to vote for Hospers and Nathan, rather than Nixon and Agnew, making Nathan the first woman in American history to receive an electoral vote. Nathan remained active in the Libertarian Party and founded the Association of Libertarian Feminists in 1973.

DB

See also Hospers, John; MacBride, Roger Lea

Further Readings

Doherty, Brian. *Radicals for Capitalism: A Freewheeling History of the Modern Libertarian Movement.* New York: Public Affairs, 2007.
Kelley, John L. *Bringing the Market Back In: The Political Revitalization of Market Liberalism.* New York: New York University Press, 1997. 191–192.

NATIONALISM

Nationalism hinges on a clear definition of the word *nation*, about which sociologists and political philosophers have often disagreed. A nation is neither a race nor a culture because there are multiracial and multicultural nations, as is the United States. Nor is a nation synonymous with a particular geographic territory, for an American living in Europe will probably still feel himself a member of the American nation and indeed may be more conscious of his Americanism there than at home. Nor, finally, can a nation be equated with specific allegiance to a state because many national identities lack independent states, as is the case today with the Kurds and Tibetans. A better definition than these, therefore, must be found.

Perhaps the best definition of *nation* comes from political theorist Benedict Anderson, who defines a nation as an "imagined community" of people that can transcend race, language, geography, and political distinctions and that understands itself, in some sense, to be traveling through history together. Anderson's imagined community is limited by the further understanding that by no means all people are, or may aspire to be, part of the nation. A nation is an in-group defined by the general agreement of those within it; also, by custom and consent, the members of a nation may select or alter the criteria for membership over time. Thus, some nationalities, in some times and places, may be based on race, language, or religion; others may be based on a shared set of political or ethical values or on common cultural practices regarding food, dress, and manners. A nation may, over time, move from one set of criteria to another, and this change may occasionally be quite radical. Whereas in the medieval era, the Cornish were not considered members of the English nation, nowadays they generally are. The French Protestants following the revocation of the Edict of Nantes officially did not exist within the nation of France and were generally regarded as aliens, whereas today French national identity certainly encompasses the Protestant religion.

However its boundaries may be constituted, a nation also is a presumptive locus of sovereignty, and it has functioned in this way for much of world history, particularly during the modern era. Nations are said to have the "right" to secure their own borders, the "right" to govern themselves as they see fit, and even—rather mystically—the "right" to determine their own destinies, as philosopher G. W. F. Hegel contended. Hegel's tremendously influential *Philosophy of Right* argued that a nation was morally obliged to consummate its own destiny through the creation of a nation-state—that is, a state that encompassed all of the members of a nation and the territory that they traditionally occupied. Hegel argued that such an entity embodies the collective will of the nation and, hence, would be authorized to act on its behalf. The nation-state, he maintained, was a manifestation of both national will and the impersonal workings of history, and it thus would necessarily command obedience from its members.

The nation-state, Hegel argued, both would and should make war against its fellows for the sake of its own greatness: "The state in and by itself is the ethical whole, the actualisation of freedom. . . . The march of God in the world, that is what the state is." Or, in his usual and impenetrable style, "The nation to which is ascribed a moment of the Idea in the form of a natural principle is entrusted with giving complete effect to it in the advance of the self-developing self-consciousness of the world mind." Thus, in the final analysis, nationalism is the belief that our own imagined community, our own nation, is the one that occupies a special place in history, and that a state must be established—and armed—to achieve it. Nationalism declares that one's particular nation has rights and interests superior to those of other nations and that these rights are to be attained by force.

Yet the sovereignty of a nation—that is, of a collective—raises profound problems for libertarians, who overwhelmingly regard the individual as the only morally salient element of society and who place individual rights ahead of group rights or group obligations. Indeed, libertarians tend strongly to deny that collective rights or obligations exist at all. Thus, many libertarians regard nationalism as a profound curse on humanity. Although libertarians are by no means immune to national self-identification, and although many may feel patriotic or even nationalistic allegiance to various nations, they also recognize that nationalism can be a profoundly dangerous force and that individual rights are universal, not national.

The pernicious consequences of nationalism have ranged from something as comparatively benign as tariffs against foreign products all the way to genocide, and they are far too extensive to summarize in one essay. When the members of a nation have determined that their national identity—that is, their national group membership—is consequent on religion, then religious persecution has often followed. Likewise, persecutions based on language, custom, and race have repeatedly arisen through essentially nationalist impulses. Because the state has so often been

seen as the achiever of national greatness, state agents have been particularly apt to disregard limits to their authority whenever nationalism has so impelled them. Almost inevitably, states have been the agents of nationalist-inspired persecution.

Those who administer actual states also have done much to encourage nationalism. This proclivity is perhaps because, under the logic of nationalism, it quickly becomes difficult to determine precisely whose will constitutes the national will—but the state, as a well-organized entity with force readily to hand, typically gets there first. As Ludwig von Mises put it, "Unfortunately there are, say the Nazis, Germans who do not think in a correct German way. . . . This would suggest the infallibility of a majority vote. However, the Nazis rejected decision by majority vote as manifestly un-German." The only way for one to assert one's proper Germanness was never to assert anything at all, but only to wait for a state directive.

Nor has the United States been immune to nationalist sentiments. Throughout its history, one may observe that nationalism has tended to corrode even the strongest limits on state power. The Alien and Sedition Acts, passed in 1798 during the quasi-war with France, are early examples; these set strong restrictions on foreigners living within the country and made it a crime to speak or write critically of the president. To offer a more recent example, the USA-PATRIOT Act of 2001 was clearly motivated by a desire for national self-preservation, even at the expense of liberty. Similar measures have almost always been implemented whenever the United States has gone to war; to this list we might add wartime censorship, military conscription, and constraints on civil liberties of all sorts—most notoriously the internment of Japanese-American citizens during World War II.

Such measures raise a puzzling question: If the United States is a nation conceived in liberty, then American nationalism would seem to entail more liberty, not less, as the path toward the American nation's particular historical destiny. Opponents of expanded state power have indeed raised this challenge, and it is worth noting that other nationalisms, too, can sometimes serve as forces of liberation. Polish, Czech, and Hungarian nationalisms, for example, were particularly prominent during the cold war as the freedom-loving members of each of these nations struggled to shake off Soviet domination. Yet the desire for national greatness is at root a collectivist desire, and the dangers of even well-intentioned nationalism can perhaps never be fully expunged.

The point is well illustrated by what is arguably the most well-intentioned nationalist enterprise ever undertaken, the 1919 Treaty of Versailles. The treaty was designed to end the First World War, which itself was unquestionably a nationalist undertaking. As a safeguard against future wars, the treaty promised national self-determination to all of the peoples of Europe, and it endeavored to give many of them a national homeland. Moreover, the treaty sought to punish the nations that lost the Great War—a view consistent with the ideology of nationalism, which demands collective winners and losers. Finally, it called for a League of Nations, a supranational governing entity that would formally instantiate the nation as a political actor endowed with rights and prerogatives beyond those of the individual. Historians generally agree that the treaty was a colossal failure: The punitive measures against Germany only embittered the German people and exacerbated German nationalism, leading to the rise of Nazism as the most murderously nationalistic political movement yet known. Impelled by a sense that they had a score to settle, the Nazis soon overran all the fragile new national homelands created by the Versailles Treaty, an act that the League of Nations was completely powerless to stop.

Nationalism, on the whole, represents one of the key forces inimical to liberalism in the modern world. Even those nationalisms that profess liberty or peace as the key to national identity are rooted in ethical collectivism. Thus, individualist philosophies have always been skeptical of nationalism, and libertarianism particularly so, occasional truces or tactical allegiances notwithstanding.

JTK

See also Collectivism; Mercantilism; Racism; State; War

Further Readings

Anderson, Benedict. *Imagined Communities: Reflections on the Origin and Spread of Nationalism.* New ed. New York: Verso, 1991.

Hegel, G. W. F. *Philosophy of Right.* S. W. Dyde, trans. Mineola, NY: Dover, 2005.

Lieven, Anatol. *America Right or Wrong: An Anatomy of American Nationalism.* New York: Oxford University Press, 2004.

Mises, Ludwig von. *Human Action.* Chicago: Contemporary Books, 1966.

———. *Nation, State, and Economy.* New York: New York University Press, 1983.

NATURAL HARMONY OF INTERESTS

The notion of a natural harmony of interests plays a significant role in libertarian thought. It is predicated on the idea that individual interests are harmonious insofar as acting in one's own interest furthers the interests of the community. Improving the general welfare is an unintended consequence of self-interested behavior. This unintended consequence is based on what Jacob Viner calls the "coordinating, harmonizing, and organizing function of free competition."

The main points of contention regarding this doctrine concern the question as to how widespread and extensive this harmony is and the question of whether state action is required to put in place the right institutional framework to ensure that interests are harmonious.

The idea that the interests of a large group of individuals could be naturally harmonious became prominent in the late 17th and early 18th centuries through the work of Richard Cumberland and was taken up by the Physiocrats in France. It received a highly detailed and systematic exposition by Adam Smith. What is probably the most well-known description of the harmony of interests can be found in the *Wealth of Nations*, where Smith claims that "It is not from the benevolence of the butcher, the brewer, or the baker, that we expect our dinner, but from their regard to their own interest." It is this harmony that underlies and explains Smith's famous "invisible hand." The coordination of the desires of a disparate group of people is possible because there is at work an invisible hand, a function of individual interests being harmonious. There is no need for intervention, no need for a conscious intelligence to bring about beneficial results. The general welfare will naturally improve as an unintended consequence of everyone acting according to his or her own self-interest. The key exponent of this idea in the 19th century was Frédéric Bastiat, who wrote a book titled *Economic Harmonies* in which he discusses many instances of this general harmony. In the 20th century, it was primarily the work of Ludwig von Mises that provided a detailed description of the way in which interests are harmonious and of the principle that we serve ourselves best by serving others. This notion is closely related to what Mises calls the *sovereignty of the consumer*—the idea that producers in a market system have to please the consumers if they are to be able to compete. Those who serve the consumers best will benefit the most. The key debate at the end of the 20th and beginning of the 21st centuries regarding the harmony of interests concerns whether state action is required to put into place an institutional framework that allows for mutually beneficial voluntary exchanges or whether the gains from trade can be realized without third-party enforcement through various self-enforcing mechanisms.

The harmony of interests leads to beneficial results by means of voluntary exchanges. A voluntary exchange is only performed if it is in the interests of all parties involved, allowing everyone to realize the mutual gains from trade that derive from the division of labor and from comparative advantage. This stricture obviously applies to both intra- and international trade. The interests of different individuals and nations are essentially harmonious, and thus there should be freedom of exchange inside and among nations. The harmony also generalizes beyond the relationship between producers and consumers and encompasses all voluntary economic interactions, such as those between employers and employees. This scalability highlights the idea that trade and other economic interactions more generally do not amount to a zero-sum game, but are mutually beneficial. There is no fixed pie that is to be divided and shared in such a way that one person's gain causes a loss to someone else.

The natural harmony of interests strongly supports a system of free markets, or what Smith called a *system of natural liberty*. If left alone, he argued, the economy will naturally develop for the better. As Smith noted, "Little else is required to carry a state to the highest degree of affluence from the lowest barbarism but peace, easy taxes, and a tolerable administration of justice; all the rest being brought about by the natural course of things." The interests of various people are harmonious, and, hence, no interference is required. Serving others is an unintended consequence of serving ourselves. Because people will take care of their own good, there is no need for the state to look after the public good. All we need for the common good to flourish is that men act in their own self-interest, which they are by nature inclined to do without any external assistance, guidance, or direction.

The harmony of interests is a general feature that holds with only few exceptions, such as in cases of natural or government-created monopolies. Such exceptions are rare, however, and the vast majority of voluntary human interactions are such that the interests of the parties involved are not essentially at odds, but can be furthered jointly. This fact supports a strong presumption in favor of liberty and against government interference. Most conflicts of interests that actually exist are the result of interventions by the state, such as the establishment of barriers to entry or exit that bring about artificial monopolies. State intervention often produces artificial and unnecessary conflicts of interest. The state shifts the strategic structure of agency from one of cooperation to one of competition for rents. People then are no longer competing to serve their own interests by serving the interests of the consumers, but are instead competing for limited and fixed benefits handed out by the government. The result is a battle for political power and political favors. Rent seeking rather than production becomes the strategy that self-interested individuals will follow given that the state has put into place an antagonistic incentive structure. Bastiat nicely captured this phenomenon when he described the state as "the great fiction by which everybody tries to live at the expense of everybody else." As opposed to the artificial conflicts produced by the state, we can describe the market as the great mechanism by which everybody manages to benefit everyone else by benefiting himself.

Another question that arises concerns the nature and kind of interest that is at issue. The interests that are harmonious are what Tocqueville and Mises classify as "interests rightly understood." That is, we are concerned with long-term interests, rather than with what counts as an agent's immediate interest. Although spoliation and aggressive behavior may be advantageous in the short run, long-run interest clearly dictates peaceful cooperation and productive behavior. As regards the kinds of ends that are harmonious, some qualification also is required. Obviously in a just society the interests of murderers and thieves, as well as of those who wish to live at the expense of others, are and should be frustrated. However, it is not these kinds of interests that are at issue when we claim that there is a natural harmony of interests. Rather, we are concerned with material ends broadly understood and the interest that all have in attempting to better their material condition. It is long-term self-interest that is harmonious, not some kind of perverse interest that essentially involves the suffering of others.

The fact that short-term interests can conflict and that it is long-run interests that are harmonious implies that certain background conditions for a stable and coordinated society must be met. Long-run interests must be taken into serious consideration, and the present and immediate future must not fully absorb the consideration of individuals. For long-run interests to become salient, individuals must be able to interact in a secure and peaceful setting. Property must be protected and contracts upheld, otherwise long-term planning will be useless and repeated reciprocal cooperative interactions will be impossible. When living in a Hobbesian state of nature and when immediate survival is the issue, the harmony of long-run interests will largely be ignored and will thus be ineffective. Consequently, peace and security are preconditions of the harmony of interests.

The idea of a natural harmony of interests underscores the importance of an adequate system of incentive structures. We can understand human actions as falling somewhere on a spectrum ranging from peaceful, productive, and cooperative behavior, on the one hand, to spoliation, on the other hand. Individuals will act in one way or the other. The relevant question is whether they will act in a peaceful and cooperative manner or one that involves conflict and antagonism. Where on the spectrum between production and spoliation a society finds itself is at least partly determined by the incentive structures that individuals face in making their decisions. To the extent that people do act in accordance with their own interest, the incentive structure directly influences their behavior. By altering the incentive structure, one alters self-interested behavior. State intervention often shifts or modifies the incentive structure, such that opportunism and spoliation, rather than production and cooperation, become the optimal strategy in some cases. As has been extensively argued by libertarians, the right incentives to ensure a socially beneficial outcome are provided by the institution of private property. Clearly defined and enforced private property rights ensure the best allocation of scarce resources and allow for the coordination of the actions of vast numbers of individuals. That is, to achieve this optimal allocation, there is a need for the right kind of framework within which humans act and interact.

Once it is accepted that the harmony of interests requires some form of institutional framework, the question arises as to what status this institutional framework possesses in the theory of the natural harmony of interests. It would appear that this framework is in some sense "unnatural" and the product of human action. Accordingly, it becomes questionable whether the harmony of interests can be classified as being "natural" in a meaningful sense. Two different approaches can be identified with respect to the question of the role and status of these apparently unnatural frameworks within which human action and interaction take place. Some theorists have put forward a moderate account of the natural harmony of interests according to which state action is required to put in place and maintain the required institutional framework. Provided that such a framework is in place, the interests of different individuals will be harmonious. Interests are harmonious when private property rights are respected, and therefore there is a need for state action to put into place the required background conditions. Although state action is required, however, it should be noted that such action on the part of the state should be of a general and rather abstract nature. That is, the state should look after the protection of private property rights and the enforcement of contracts. There is no need for specific interventions or interferences. All we need is the establishment and maintenance of the rule of law. The state only has to set up the right institutional framework, rather than micromanage human interactions. To put it differently, the state should set the general rules of the game, rather than dictate particular outcomes.

The more radical approach takes the harmony of interests to be natural in the sense that the gains from trade can be realized through voluntary means without any need to have recourse to government action. This more radical version of the natural harmony of interests is often defended by anarcho-capitalists. According to this view, self-enforcing institutions will and do emerge spontaneously. Although certain frameworks are required, these frameworks naturally arise and do not need to be deliberately imposed and enforced by government. They are endogenous and do not have to be imposed exogenously. The harmony of interests is a natural harmony in that the institutions and frameworks that allow this harmony to become fully effective are the result of a natural process. Rather than requiring political institutions, various social norms, rules, and mechanisms are available to achieve successful cooperation among strangers without requiring third-party enforcement, including signaling, selection, exclusion, inclusion, and reputation mechanisms.

RMB

See also Bastiat, Frédéric; Civil Society; Ferguson, Adam; Free Trade; Laissez-Faire Policy; Smith, Adam

Further Readings

Bastiat, Frédéric. *Economic Harmonies*. Irvington-on-Hudson, NY: Foundation for Economic Education, 1996.

Friedman, David. *The Machinery of Freedom: Guide to a Radical Capitalism*. La Salle, IL: Open Court, 1989.

Mises, Ludwig von. *Human Action: A Treatise on Economics*. Auburn, AL: Ludwig von Mises Institute, 1998.

Smith, Adam. *An Inquiry into the Nature and Causes of the Wealth of Nations*. Indianapolis, IN: Liberty Fund, 1982.

Stringham, Edward, ed. *Anarchy, State and Public Choice*. Cheltenham, UK: Edward Elgar, 2005.

Viner, Jacob. "Adam Smith and Laissez Faire." *The Journal of Political Economy* 35 no. 2 (April 1927): 198–232.

NATURAL LAW

Theories of natural law hold that there is a single law, or body of laws, based on nature, that all human societies should obey. This tradition, embraced by philosophers and legal theorists for more than 2,500 years, has been highly adaptable and multifarious.

The idea of natural law originated with the Greek philosopher Heraclitus (circa 500 B.C.), who declared, "All the laws of human beings are nourished by the one divine [law]." This universal principle was independent of human opinion or agreement, but rather was regarded as the justification for human laws. The corollary—that human ordinances are invalid if they conflict with the higher law—was asserted by the heroine of *Antigone*, where Sophocles has the heroine defy an edict on the grounds that "mortal man cannot transgress the gods' unwritten and unfailing laws." The Sophists too recognized this conflict when they pitted law (*nomos*) against nature (*phusis*). Law, they argued, was the result of human custom, agreement, and belief, and was therefore contingent, variable, and relative; but nature manifested itself in invariant instincts such as self-interest. Responding to this challenge, Plato contended that law was grounded in nature. He explicated this law in terms of his theory of Forms, the eternal principles of goodness and justice apprehended by reason rather than sense experience. Aristotle in the *Rhetoric* discussed the "law of nature" as an eternal, immutable principle, which was commonly invoked in Greek legal arguments. He elsewhere defended a notion of "natural justice," variable but grounded in universal human nature.

The theory of natural law was expounded more fully by the Stoics, whose views were summarized by the Roman Cicero. "True law," Cicero writes,

is right reason in agreement with nature, diffused among all men; constant and unchanging, it should call men to their duties by its precepts and deter them from wrongdoing by its prohibitions; and it never commands or forbids upright men in vain, while its rules and restraints are lost upon the wicked. . . . There will not be one law at Rome and another law at Athens, nor will there be a different law tomorrow than it is today; but one and the same law, eternal and unchangeable will bind all peoples and ages.

Natural law was divine in origin, but discoverable by human understanding: "This reason, when firmly fixed and fully developed in the human mind, is law." This doctrine was endorsed by the early Christian writers, among them Lactantius.

Natural law was embraced by medieval philosophers, especially Thomas Aquinas, in his treatise on law (*Summa Theologiae* I-II, QQ. 90–97). He defined law (*lex*) generally as "an ordinance of reason for the common good which is made by the person who has care of the community, and which is promulgated." Aquinas distinguished four principal types of law. Eternal law is the principle by which God rationally governs the universe. Natural law is "the sharing in the eternal law by rational creatures." They can employ their reason to serve their God-given natural ends. Human or positive law is rationally derived from natural law. "If at any point it deflects from the law of nature, it is no longer a law but a perversion of law." Finally, divine (positive) law is laid down by God, but, unlike eternal law, it is revealed through faith, rather than by reason. Aquinas held that natural law, apprehended by reason, concurs with divine law, as revealed to the Christian church. This concord remained the core of traditional natural law theory, although it was elaborated by later Scholastic and neo-Thomist thinkers.

Many modern philosophers repudiated this scholastic tradition, including Baruch Spinoza. "Nothing is absolutely prohibited by the law of nature," Spinoza maintained, "unless it is physically impossible." However, there have been modern advocates of natural law, the most important of which were Hugo Grotius (1583–1645) and Samuel Pufendorf (1632–1694). Grotius argued that natural law was the foundation for international law and the law of war and peace. It was "a dictate of right reason, which posits that an act, according as it is or is not in conformity with rational nature, has in it a quality or moral baseness or moral necessity, and that, in consequence, such an act is either forbidden or enjoined by the author of nature, God." Grotius claimed that his theory would be valid, "even if we concede what which cannot be conceded without the utmost wickedness, that there is no God, or that the affairs of men are of no concern to Him."

The most influential modern theorist, John Locke, declared in his *Second Treatise of Government* that "the State of Nature has a Law of Nature to govern it, which obliges every one: And reason, which is that law, teaches all mankind, who will but consult it, that being all equal and independent, no one ought to harm another in his life, health, liberty, or possessions." Locke affirmed the divine origin of natural law: "For all men being all the workmanship of one omnipotent, and infinitely wise maker; all the servants of one sovereign master, sent into the world by his order and about his business, they are his property, whose workmanship they are, made to last during his, not another's pleasure." According to the law of nature,

> Every one as he is bound to preserve himself, and not to quit his station willfully; so by the like reason when his own preservation comes not in competition, ought he, as much as he can, to preserve the rest of mankind, and may not unless it be to do justice on an offender, take away, or impair the life, or what tends to the preservation of the life, liberty, health or goods of another.

Natural law is thus the foundation of man's rights to life, liberty, and property. The positive laws of governments "are only so far right as they are founded on the Law of Nature, by which they are to be regulated and interpreted." Locke influenced the American founders, who invoked "the Laws of Nature and of Nature's God" in the American Declaration of Independence.

Aquinas and Locke represent opposing poles of natural law theory: traditionalist versus modernist. Traditional theorists emphasize moral duties and obedience to political authorities. They condemn abortion, homosexual unions, and contraception as unnatural acts, and they support governmental enforcement of morality. Modernist theorists are generally more libertarian and advocate revolution to protect natural rights. For Locke, the right to liberty was "the foundation of all the rest" and "liberty is to be free from restraint and violence from others." For traditionalists like Lord Acton and Pope John Paul II, "freedom consists not in doing what we like, but in having the right to do what we ought." Twentieth-century theorists also have disagreed over whether democratic capitalism or socialism is more in accord with natural law. Recent proponents of natural law jurisprudence include Lon Fuller, John Finnis, and Michael Moore.

FM

See also Aquinas, Thomas; Aristotle; Cicero; Locke, John; Rights, Natural; Stoicism

Further Readings

Finnis, John. *Natural Law and Natural Rights*. Corr. ed. Oxford: Clarendon Press, 1988.

Fuller, Lon. *The Morality of Law*. Rev. ed. New Haven, CT: Yale University Press, 1969.

George, Robert P., ed. *Natural Law Theory*. Oxford: Clarendon Press, 1992.

Hittinger, Russell. *A Critique of the New Natural Law Theory*. Notre Dame, IN: University of Notre Dame Press, 1987.

Lisska, Anthony J. *Aquinas's Theory of Natural Law: An Analytic Reconstruction*. Oxford: Clarendon Press, 1996.

Miller, Fred D., Jr. "Aristotle on Natural Law and Justice." *A Companion to Aristotle's Politics.* David Keyt and Fred D. Miller, Jr., eds. Oxford: Blackwell, 1991.

Moore, Michael. "A Natural Law Theory of Interpretation." *Southern California Law Review* 58 (1985): 277–398.

Paul, Ellen, Fred D. Miller, Jr., and Jeffrey Paul, eds. *Natural Law and Modern Moral Philosophy.* Cambridge: Cambridge University Press, 2001.

Rommen, Heinrich A. *The Natural Law: A Study in Legal and Social History and Philosophy.* Thomas R. Hanley, trans. Indianapolis, IN: Liberty Press, 1998. [orig. German 1936]

Veatch, Henry B. *Human Rights: Fact or Fancy?* Baton Rouge: Louisiana State University Press, 1985.

NEW DEAL

The New Deal was a package of economic policies adopted in the United States during the 1930s under President Franklin Roosevelt and his political allies in Congress in response to the Great Depression. These policies involved a massive expansion in the size and scope of government, especially at the federal level. Roosevelt identified the New Deal's goals as the three Rs—relief, recovery, and reform—although we should not ignore a fourth R—reelection. Relief efforts comprised massive government-run "emergency work" programs and direct transfers to the poor, elderly, and unemployed. Recovery efforts hoped to bring the economy back to its potential, although they did not prevent the Depression from lingering until the arrival of World War II. In a survey of economic historians, about half agreed that, despite many policies that helped to correct the economy, "taken as a whole, government policies of the New Deal served to lengthen and deepen the Great Depression." Reform efforts created a range of important regulatory agencies and redistributive programs—from the Securities Exchange Commission and the Federal Deposit Insurance Corporation to social security, the minimum wage, and the National Labor Relations Board—that have persisted into the 21st century.

When Franklin Roosevelt was inaugurated in March 1933, the economy was flat on its back. In less than 4 years following its peak in the summer of 1929, real GDP (the value of all final goods and services produced in the economy) had fallen about 27%, industrial output was down 45%, and housing starts plummeted more than 80%, as did the value of stocks comprising the Dow Jones Industrial Average. Simultaneously, the unemployment rate soared from about 3% to almost 25%, overall wholesale prices fell by nearly 37%, agricultural prices fell by more than 50%, and more than 9,000 banks failed—more than a third of the total.

Although economic historians have now concluded that this international catastrophe was caused primarily by the flawed policies of central banks, including the Federal Reserve, in response to a malfunctioning international gold standard, the policymakers of the New Deal did not have the benefit of this hindsight. The varied and sometimes contradictory lessons that were collectively drawn from the Great Depression framed the New Deal. The primary point of agreement shared by the New Deal's designers was that, although the capitalistic system worked fairly well, it could be unstable and was subject to excesses and inequities. Accordingly, government needed to expand its scope to fix these problems.

The first important New Deal policy was to declare a brief nationwide banking "holiday" and to arrange emergency loans from the government to struggling banks. This step ended the banking panic and was followed in June 1933 by the creation of the Federal Deposit Insurance Corporation (FDIC) to insure individual depositors' accounts, thereby virtually eliminating the problem of bank runs. Simultaneously, Roosevelt prohibited the export of gold, which effectively took the country off the gold standard. This prohibition was made explicit in June 1933 by legislation that nullified all contractual promises—public or private, past or future—denominated in gold. Abandoning the gold standard and putting an end to bank panics apparently removed the primary factors—a shrinking money supply, deflation, and collapsing consumer and investor confidence—that had been pulling the economy down, paving the way for recovery.

During the First New Deal (the "hundred days" of legislative activity from March 9 to June 16, 1933), Congress also began significant relief activities. The Federal Emergency Relief Administration (FERA) was established to distribute relief funds to the states, much of them in the form of matching grants. During its existence from mid-1933 to the end of 1935, the FERA spent almost $2.7 billion (in an economy whose GDP was $66 billion in 1934), with an average case load exceeding 4 million cases.

The Civilian Conservation Corps (CCC) was established in March 1933, almost immediately putting 250,000 young men to work on reforestation, road construction, national parks, and other projects. By 1940, the CCC had employed about 2.5 million people. In November 1933, the Civil Works Administration was established, but was replaced in July 1935 by the largest of the "emergency work" agencies, the Works Progress Administration (WPA). During its existence, the WPA spent more than $6.2 billion on projects, including construction of more than 650,000 miles of roadway and work on 124,000 bridges, 125,000 public buildings, more than 8,000 parks, and more than 850 airports. The number of federal emergency workers hired by these and other agencies rose from 2.1 million in 1933 to a peak of 3.7 million in 1936—and remained above 2 million until 1941. At its peak, about 7% of the labor force was in these jobs, whose average pay for unskilled workers was only a little below that in the private sector.

New Deal critics complained that spending on these programs was uneven and had a large political component. For example, New Deal outlays per capita were over six times higher in first-place Nevada—a low-population swing state in which electoral votes could be "purchased" cheaply—than in last-place North Carolina—which, like other poorly funded Southern states, was not likely to vote Republican regardless of federal expenditures. Economic historians have closely investigated where funds from these programs were spent, concluding that the major relief programs roughly followed Roosevelt's three Rs—with money more likely to go to places harder hit by the Depression—but that spending for political advantage in upcoming elections was a significant factor.

The most widely criticized components of the First New Deal were two related recovery measures designed to boost prices. Many New Dealers argued that excessive and wasteful competition was the cause of falling agricultural and industrial prices and proposed a vast program of national planning and coordination to boost prices largely by reducing supply. The federal government's economic coordination and planning agencies of World War I served as their templates, and veterans of World War I agencies staffed many key positions.

The Agricultural Adjustment Administration, established in May 1933, calculated the output needed to push agricultural prices up to the relatively high "parity" level of 1909–1914 and converted that quantity into acreage and herd-size estimates. Each state was then allotted its share of output. Farmers who voluntarily reduced acreage or production to the target level were directly compensated by the government, using proceeds from taxes on processors of agricultural commodities. The list of crops thus regulated began with wheat, cotton, corn, rice, tobacco, hogs, milk, and milk products and was expanded in later years. Under 1934 legislation, a degree of compulsion was added as tobacco and cotton farmers faced a punitive tax for exceeding their individual quotas. The act also established subsidized loans for farmers. After the act was declared unconstitutional in 1935, the program was reformulated with continued programs to reduce acreage ("soil conservation") and establish price floors via government purchases. These policies are credited with boosting farmers' incomes (at the expense of consumers), but they also led to the displacement of many tenant farmers, especially black sharecroppers in the South.

The second attempt to rein in competition came through the National Industrial Recovery Act of June 1933. Almost immediately, more than 2 million employers signed a preliminary "blanket code," pledging to pay minimum wages ranging from around $12 to $15 per 40-hour week. About 16 million workers were covered, out of a nonfarm labor force of 25 million. Share-the-work provisions called for limits of 35 to 40 hours per week for most employees. Over the next year and a half, the blanket code was superseded by over 500 codes of "fair competition" negotiated by trade groups within individual industries that employed almost 80% of nonfarm workers. Although the codes gave employees the right to organize unions and bargain collectively, the carrot held out to induce participation was exemption from antitrust laws, effectively allowing businesses to form cartels that substantially increased prices. Within months, however, there was widespread dissatisfaction with the National Recovery Administration (NRA) codes and a lack of compliance by many, so it is not surprising that they were not resurrected after the Supreme Court declared the act unconstitutional in 1935. The NRA appears to have derailed the economic recovery. The jump in prices and wages from late 1933 to early 1934 led to a drop in sales that is estimated to have caused manufacturing output to fall around 10%, prompting significant layoffs.

Fearful that the intermingling of commercial banking and investment banking had played a role in speculation, the stock market crash, and the banking meltdown, the Banking Act of 1933 (the Glass–Steagall Act) banned banks from acting as both lenders and investors in companies and giving them 1 year to decide whether they would specialize in commercial or investment banking. Critics argue that these provisions were an overreaction designed to punish Wall Street for its perceived sins, but this provision remained in place until 1999. To lessen competition among banks, the act also forbade payment of interest on checking deposits and authorized a cap on savings deposit interest rates—policies that stayed in place for decades. Following the grilling of Wall Street insiders by the Senate's Pecora Commission, the Securities and Exchange Commission was established in 1934 with the goal of eliminating abuses such as insider trading and stock price manipulation. In 1935, control of the Federal Reserve and its monetary policy was moved out of the hands of bankers into those of political appointees, and autonomy by the regional Federal Reserve Banks was essentially ended.

Other important early New Deal programs were designed to take the place of markets that were seen as underperforming, including agencies like the Tennessee Valley Authority (1933–present), the Home Owners' Loan Corporation (1933–1936), and the Rural Electrification Administration (1935–present).

The Second New Deal under the more radical 74th Congress enacted a sweeping array of more extensive "reform" measures. The most important of these reforms almost certainly was the Social Security Act, which established the Old Age Insurance program popularly called Social Security and that soon became a pay-as-you-go system, using payroll taxes to pay benefits to elderly retirees. In 1939, amendments added a program to provide dependents' and survivors' benefits—akin to private-sector life insurance—and the program was renamed Old Age and

Survivors Insurance. The Social Security Act also established the federal-state unemployment insurance system and federal welfare aid to the poor and blind.

Perhaps more important at the time was the Wagner Act, which created a federal agency, the National Labor Relations Board (NLRB), with the power to investigate and decide on charges of unfair labor practices and to conduct elections in which workers would decide whether they wanted to be represented by a union. If the workers voted in favor of a union, it became the workforce's collective bargaining agent, and the employer was required to bargain with it "in good faith." Organized labor became a key component of the New Deal coalition, and, under the encouragement of the openly pro-union NLRB, its ranks grew rapidly, rising from about 3 million in 1934 to almost 9 million in 1940 (about 27% of the nonfarm labor force). Although the organizing effort sparked some violence, basic industries such as automobiles and steel were soon largely unionized. Placing a right to collective bargaining above private property rights, in 1936 and 1937, New Deal–supporting governors and other elected officials in Michigan, Ohio, Pennsylvania, and elsewhere refused to send police to evict sit-down strikers who had ignored court injunctions by seizing control of factories. These actions by some states allowed the minority of workers who actively supported unionization to use force to overcome the passivity of the majority of workers and the opposition of the employers.

The New Deal philosophy had a clear element of class warfare, seemingly wresting power and resources from the rich and giving them to those with fewer resources in the form of collective bargaining rights, government transfers, and, under the Fair Labor Standards Act of 1938, minimum wages and overtime premiums. The New Deal coalition attacked "economic royalists" and threatened to "soak the rich" as the top federal income tax rate climbed from 25% in 1931 to 79% in 1936. Critics complained that the government's rhetoric and actions caused investors to fear for the security of their property rights, pointing to the 60% jump in investment after electoral defeats for the New Deal coalition in 1938.

The most important legacy of the New Deal is probably the substantial expansion of the scope of government that it brought. Economic historian Robert Higgs has argued convincingly that this response to the Great Depression brought with it accommodative court rulings, ideological changes within the electorate, bureaucratic self-interest in maintaining programs, loss of understanding of what can be accomplished in the private sector, and simple inertia that together permanently ratcheted up the size of the government.

RoW

See also Great Depression; Interventionism; Labor Unions; Price Controls; Social Security

Further Readings

Alexander, Barbara. "National Recovery Administration." Robert Whaples, ed. *EH.Net Encyclopedia*, 2001.

Bordo, Michael D., Claudia Goldin, and Eugene N. White, eds. *The Defining Moment: The Great Depression and the American Economy in the Twentieth Century*. Chicago: University of Chicago Press, 1998.

Couch, Jim, and William F. Shughart II. *The Political Economy of the New Deal*. Cheltenham, UK: Edward Elgar, 1998.

Fearon, Peter. *War, Prosperity and Depression: The U.S. Economy, 1917–45*. Lawrence: University Press of Kansas, 1987.

Fishback, Price V. *Government and the American Economy: A New History*. Chicago: University of Chicago Press, 2007.

———, Shawn Kantor, and John Wallis. "Can the New Deal's Three R's Be Rehabilitated? A Program-by-Program, County-by-County Analysis." *Explorations in Economic History* 40 no. 3 (October 2003): 278–307.

Higgs, Robert. *Crisis and Leviathan: Critical Episodes in the Growth of American Government*. New York: Oxford University Press, 1987.

Rosen, Elliot. *Roosevelt, the Great Depression and the Economics of Recovery*. Charlottesville: University of Virginia Press, 2005.

Weinstein, Michael. *Recovery and Redistribution under the NIRA*. Amsterdam: North-Holland Publishing, 1980.

NIETZSCHE, FRIEDRICH (1844–1900)

Friedrich Nietzsche was one of the most controversial writers of the 19th century. He left a remarkably ambiguous legacy for political thought, and his sweeping and often cryptic denunciations of existing institutions inspired a wide variety of thinkers, including both libertarians and many others who were profoundly hostile to libertarianism. His own views on liberty and the state are subject to a wide variety of interpretations. In his early account of Nietzsche's philosophy, H. L. Mencken interprets him as a sort of anarchist. There is certainly some reason to see Nietzsche in that way; he refers to himself repeatedly as "antipolitical," which must be rather different from being merely "apolitical," and he has blisteringly caustic things to say about the state in his *Thus Spoke Zarathustra*. However, in virtually all the writings of his mature period, he describes his own standard of value as the "Will to Power," a view that might be paraphrased as viewing power as a good or possibly the highest good. However, Walter Kaufmann, writing in the early 1950s, read that notion to mean that power over others is relatively unimportant, with true power being mastery over one's self. Undeniably, Nietzsche does have a high regard for people who have self-mastery, but his admiration is consistent with advocating power over others as well, and Nietzsche does describe his ideal human beings as molding humanity according to their own will. Accordingly, in recent decades, there has been a reaction in Nietzsche scholarship against Kaufmann's interpretation. Many interpreters, including Strong and Detwiler, now understand Nietzsche as advocating authoritarian or even totalitarian governments. Such interpretations, however, are difficult to reconcile with the sweepingly categorical nature of his denunciations of the state. Indeed, this apparent contradiction can be resolved by understanding Nietzsche as claiming that the power wielded by his heroes is, for the most part, the power of ideas and the force of personality. In his ideal world, a few exemplary individuals would hold power, but, in that scheme, the state would play at most a subordinate role.

Neitzsche's writings continue to attract interest among people who are dissatisfied with existing political and social arrangements, but the implications of his approach are contested.

LH

See also Foucault, Michel; Mencken, H. L.; Virtue

Further Readings

Detwiler, Bruce. *Nietzsche and the Politics of Aristocratic Radicalism.* Chicago: University of Chicago Press, 1990.

Hunt, Lester H. *Nietzsche and the Origin of Virtue.* New York: Routledge, 1991.

Kaufmann, Walter. *Nietzsche: Philosopher, Psychologist, Antichrist.* New York: Meridian, 1956.

Mencken, H. L. "Introduction to Friedrich Nietzsche." *The Antichrist.* H. L. Mencken, trans and ed. New York: Knopf, 1923.

———. *The Philosophy of Nietzsche.* Port Washington, NY: Kenikat Press, 1964.

Strong, Tracy. *Friedrich Nietzsche and the Politics of Transfiguration.* Berkeley: University of California Press, 1975.

Nock, Albert Jay (1870–1945)

Albert Jay Nock was one of the most thoroughgoing critics of using "political means" to achieve social ends in the American literary tradition. Libertarians have embraced Nock's often virulent antistatism, but his possession of the traits he ascribed to Jefferson—"radical principles and ideals combined with Tory manners"—have made Nock's contributions broader and more far reaching. From his first article in 1908 until his death in 1945, exploring "the quality of civilization in the United States" animated his social criticism, hopes, and scorn. He was, as his friend Bernard Iddings Bell described him, "[O]ne of the most gracious but pitiless of American social analysts in our time." More recently, Jacques Barzun praised his writings as "social and intellectual criticism at its best."

Nock was an intensely private man. While he was working as editor of *The Freeman* in New York City in the 1920s, the story is told that the only way to contact him after work was to leave a message under a certain rock in Central Park. An only child, Nock was born in Scranton, Pennsylvania, and grew up in Brooklyn and rural Michigan. His father came from a family of Dissenters and was an Episcopal minister, while his mother, with whom he was very close, was a descendant of French Huguenots and of John Jay. He attended St. Stephen's (now Bard) College between 1887 and 1892, where he received a "grand old fortifying classical curriculum." In 1897, Nock became an Episcopal minister and held several parish posts. Then, for reasons he kept to himself, in late 1909, at the age of 39, Nock made an abrupt change in his life. He left the ministry, his wife, and two sons and moved to New York City.

He joined the staff of the *American Magazine*, a gathering place for muckrakers and progressives, and later joined the staff of the liberal, antiwar periodical *The Nation* when Oswald Garrison Villard became its editor and owner. He served as an associate editor from mid-1918 until nearly the end of 1919. Nock was a forceful critic and an articulate voice dissenting from the modern liberal tenor of the magazine during his short stint there. Although many were quick to embrace an extension of war collectivism after World War I, Nock gained a heightened awareness of the destructive nature of statism and the progressive politicization of society. Nock took up Randolph Bourne's battle cry when he died in December 1918: "War is the health of the State."

The result was *The Freeman*, a weekly magazine that Nock and B. W. Huebsch published from March 17, 1920, to March 5, 1924. Nock wrote as much as 20% of the material in a 24-page tabloid-size issue. He edited and wrote for all but 8 of the 208 issues. A remarkable group of staff members and contributors joined Nock to produce a stunning periodical of individualist radicalism that Van Wyck Brooks described as "a paper that was generally known as the best written in the country." In 1964, a scholar echoed the almost universal opinion that it "was one of the important and influential journals of this century [and] must surely constitute one of the most massive monuments of journalistic excellence ever produced in so short a period."

Exhausted by the work, Nock was on board a ship bound for Europe before the last issue of *The Freeman* was off the presses. Thereafter, Nock made a meager but sufficient living as an essayist. He settled into nearly 20 years of immensely productive writing spanning the period between the two world wars. He was a regular contributor to the *Atlantic Monthly, American Mercury, Harpers,* and the *New Freeman.* Along the way, he completed several collections of essays; wrote his still respected *Jefferson,* a "study in conduct and character"; as well as several books on Rabelais. Nock also briefly taught American history and politics at Bard College (1931–1933). In 1931, he delivered the Page–Barbour lectures at the University of Virginia, which were later turned into *The Theory of Education in the United States*, an important critique of modern education.

The strongly antipolitical and antistatist flavor that runs throughout Nock's writing is most evident in his influential 1935 work *Our Enemy, the State:* "Taking the State wherever found, striking into its history at any point, one sees no way to differentiate the activities of its founders, administrators, and beneficiaries from those of a professional-criminal class." Shortly before his death, Nock criticized F. A. Hayek for not being a "whole-hogger" in his *The Road to Serfdom*. Indeed, the starting point of Nock's legacy to libertarianism is elegantly summarized in Walter E. Grinder's 1973 introduction to an edition of *Our Enemy, the State*: "It is a natural rights philosophy of self-responsibility, of inviolable individualism, and a social philosophy of unequivocal voluntarism. . . . It is a political philosophy of anti-Statism." Although conservative publisher Henry Regnery thought "he contributed substantially to the development of modern conservatism," most conservatives abandoned both his political and social warnings. Some, however, like his friend Frank Chodorov, tried to maintain the Old Right tradition.

In 1943, Nock published *The Memoirs of a Superfluous Man*, which summarized his "philosophy of intelligent selfishness, intelligent egoism, intelligent hedonism . . . they amount merely to a philosophy of informed common sense." The *Memoirs* touched on some of the influences on his thinking, including the writers of classical liberalism and the American Founding, as well as thinkers as diverse as Herbert Spencer, Henry George, Franz Oppenheimer, and Ralph Cram. The book also was, in part, a summary lament about his own intellectual journey: the necessity of disinterested thought in social criticism, and the struggle between hope for and scorn for his fellow humans. Nock did not complain because he joyfully acknowledged he had more than he deserved: "So while one must be unspeakably thankful for all the joys of existence, there comes a time when one feels that one has had enough." Maintaining his sense of privacy and perfectionism, he destroyed a number of manuscripts before his death.

Albert Jay Nock's larger legacy to the American scene and to libertarianism goes well beyond his important critique of statism. One must consider his work as a whole and remember that he saw his job as a commentator on human possibilities and foibles. There was a more positive side to his work that emphasized the essentially nonpolitical nature of civilization, but it came across to many as weak and incomplete because he refused to offer any pat solutions of his own. He distrusted hacks with solutions to sell. He saw that he was simply taking on "Isaiah's job"—to encourage and brace up a remnant of individuals in building a "substratum of right thinking and well-doing." As he noted often, "What matters is that, for life to be truly fruitful, life must be felt as a joy, and that where freedom is not, there can be no joy. . . ."

CH

See also Anarchism; Hayek, Friedrich A.; Liberalism, Classical; Voluntarism

Further Readings

Crunden, Robert M. *The Mind and Art of Albert Jay Nock*. Chicago: Henry Regnery Company, 1964.

Nock, Albert Jay. *Jefferson*. New York: Harcourt, Brace, 1926.

———. *Memoirs of a Superfluous Man*. New York: Harper & Brothers, 1943.

———. *Our Enemy, the State* (Introduction by Walter E. Grinder). New York: Morrow, 1935; New York: Free Life Editions, 1973.

———. *The State of the Union: Essays in Social Criticism*. Charles H. Hamilton, ed. Indianapolis, IN: Liberty Press, 1991.

Wreszin, Michael. *The Superfluous Anarchist*. Providence, RI: Brown University Press, 1971.

NONAGGRESSION AXIOM

The nonaggression axiom is an ethical principle often appealed to as a basis for libertarian rights theory. The principle forbids "aggression," which is understood to be any and all forcible interference with any individual's person or property except in response to the initiation (including, for most proponents of the principle, the *threatening* of initiation) of similar forcible interference on the part of that individual.

The axiom has various formulations, but two especially influential 20th-century formulations are those of Ayn Rand and Murray Rothbard, who appear to have originated the term. Ayn Rand maintained that "no man may *initiate* the use of physical force against others. . . . Men have the right to use physical force *only* in retaliation and *only* against those who initiate its use." This quote is similar to Murray Rothbard's thesis that "no man or group of men may aggress against the person or property of anyone else."

Some libertarians use the term *coercion* as synonymous with *aggression*, whereas others use *coercion* more broadly to designate all use of force, including legitimate defensive use. Hence, under the former formulation, but not the latter, the nonaggression axiom would prohibit all coercion. Although the ordinary sense of coercion arguably involves getting somebody to *do* something—so that simply assaulting somebody would not count as coercion—conformity with this usage is the exception, rather than the rule, in libertarian theory.

The axiom is often regarded as virtually equivalent to Herbert Spencer's *law of equal freedom* ("Every man has freedom to do all that he wills, provided he infringes not the equal freedom of any other man"), or to the principle of *self-ownership*, or both inasmuch as all three principles specify protected boundaries around each individual, ordinarily understood to include not just the individual's mind and body, but also legitimately acquired external property. Within these boundaries, people are to be allowed complete liberty from forcible interference by others, the extent of one individual's boundary being limited only by the similar boundaries of others.

Actions that might otherwise ordinarily count as aggression against an individual become permissible if the individual *consents*, although libertarian theorists disagree among themselves as to whether and under what circumstances such consent can be irrevocable (e.g., is a contract to alienate one's rights over oneself legitimate?). To say that an action is permissible under the axiom, it should be noted, is simply to say that the action is not a rights violation and so may not legitimately be obstructed by force. The nonaggression axiom does not rule out such an action's possible moral wrongness on other grounds or the possible appropriateness of attempting to combat it by peaceful means. The nonaggression axiom is intended as a rule specifically for actions involving force, not as a guide to the whole of moral conduct.

This axiom is intended, however, to govern the actions not only of private citizens, but of government officials. Hence, the enforcement of laws or regulations requiring anything more from individuals than their bare abstention from aggression counts as aggression and so is prohibited under the principle. The entire range of libertarian rights to personal and economic liberty is thus taken to follow from the nonaggression axiom.

The nonaggression axiom is not to be confused with a call to minimize the total amount of aggression—first, because the axiom is purely prohibitory and does not call for positive action of any kind; and, second, because the axiom does not countenance, as a minimization requirement might, the inflicting of a small amount of aggression to prevent a greater amount (e.g., conscripting citizens to deter foreign invasion). The prohibition on aggression thus counts, in Robert Nozick's terminology, as a *side constraint* to be respected, rather than a goal to be promoted. To be sure, adherents of the nonaggression axiom unsurprisingly tend to favor the overall reduction of aggression in society—so long as such reduction can be accomplished without violating the axiom—but the nonaggression axiom per se calls for no such commitment.

Some formulations of the nonaggression axiom make specific reference to external property while others do not, but it is widely agreed that the application of the axiom requires some additional principle to determine when the use of a person's possessions without permission counts as aggression. Unless such use does count as aggression,

forcibly preventing unpermitted use will violate the axiom. How, then, must one be related to an external object so that another's appropriation of that object constitutes an illegitimate appropriation of the possessor? Many attempts to answer this question draw on or develop John Locke's theory that one acquires just ownership by either mixing one's labor with previously unclaimed resources or acquiring resources by consent from already legitimate possessors. Samuel Wheeler, for example, argues that external property is an artificial extension of one's body and so entitled to the same protection as bodily integrity, whereas Nozick maintained that seizing the products of another person's labor is tantamount to forcing that person to labor for one's own benefit. Thus, theft is condemned as an indirect form of force, whereas fraud is typically condemned as an indirect form of theft (inasmuch as a transfer of property to which consent is obtained under false pretenses is tantamount to taking property without consent).

Although the nonaggression axiom prohibits initiatory force, it does not specify what forms of retaliatory force, if any, are permissible, and so is in principle compatible with a variety of conclusions on this issue. These conclusions include Rothbard's view that the victim may inflict on the aggressor an amount of force proportionate to that which the aggressor had inflicted; Randy Barnett's milder view that aggressors may be coerced only insofar as it is necessary to restrain their aggression and secure restitution to the victim; and Robert LeFevre's belief that all force, whether initiatory or retaliatory, is morally impermissible. Thus, the nonaggression axiom by itself does not specify whether its own enforcement is permissible, although it does specify that no other principle could be permissibly enforced because to enforce anything other than nonaggression is a form of aggression.

Proponents of the principle differ as to the basis of its justification, and a variety of defenses have been offered. For example, Nozick upholds nonaggression as an application of the duty to treat persons as ends in themselves, rather than as mere means. Rothbard argued that to aggress against another person is to treat that person as one's property, thus introducing an asymmetry of rights inconsistent with the requirement that ethical norms be universalizable. Jan Narveson has maintained that a mutual rejection of nonaggression would be endorsed by rationally self-interested contractors. Ayn Rand condemned aggression as a form of parasitism inconsistent with the independent mindset needed for an individual's successful living. Utilitarian libertarians argue, often on economic grounds, that a general commitment to nonaggression will tend to maximize social welfare. Douglas Den Uyl and Douglas Rasmussen regard the prohibition of aggression as part of a "metanormative" framework to protect the conditions within which individuals can pursue their own Aristotelian flourishing. Hans-Hermann Hoppe holds that inasmuch as the justification of any proposition presupposes a context of uncoerced interpersonal dialogue, no assertion of the right to aggress can be justified without self-contradiction. Less theoretically, the nonaggression axiom is often held to be simply a consistent application of the commonsense norms that govern ordinary personal morality; that we usually deal with our neighbors through persuasion rather than compulsion.

Other controversies over the axiom include what exceptions, if any, may be made to the axiom in emergencies, and whether the axiom permits the use of force against innocent shields. This question arises when collateral damage to bystanders cannot be avoided in the course of self-defense against an aggressor. A further question concerns so-called innocent threats; that is, the actions of those who aggress through no fault of their own, and whether these threats are to be considered aggression and, therefore, illegitimate.

The nonaggression axiom has "a long past but a short history." In some form, a prohibition on aggression recurs frequently throughout human history—as one might expect if it is indeed a generalization of commonsense moral norms. For example, the principle of *ahimsa* (nonviolence, noninjury) is central to Hinduism, Buddhism, and Jainism, while the notion of justice as a mutual nonaggression pact is put forward by the Greek philosophers Lycophron and Epicurus, as well as by the character Glaucon in Plato's *Republic*. The *Institutes* of the Byzantine Emperor Justinian define the essence of legal obligation as "to live honestly, to injure no one, and to give every man his due," whereas in China, Kao-tsu, the founder of the Han dynasty, announced that the only valid laws were those against murder, theft, and personal injury. But in practice the actual content of legislation generally far outstripped these suggested limits; more broadly, the invocation of a nonaggression principle was seldom applied consistently, having usually been coupled with the endorsement of institutions and practices (e.g., slavery) that seem strikingly inconsistent with it.

It is in the 17th century that the prohibition on aggression began to bear radical political fruit. Precursors of the nonaggression axiom were employed in support of revolutionary liberalism by writers like Richard Overton, who wrote that "every man by nature [is] a king, priest and prophet in his own natural circuit and compass, whereof no second may partake but by deputation, commission, and free consent from him whose natural right and freedom it is." John Locke wrote similarly that "being all equal and independent, no one ought to harm another in his life, health, liberty or possessions." With the classical liberals and individualist anarchists of the 19th century, the axiom became the foundation of a thoroughgoing libertarian political program; American anarchist Benjamin R. Tucker, for example, described his fundamental political principle as "the greatest amount of liberty compatible with equality of liberty; or, in other words, as the belief in every liberty except the liberty to invade."

There are a small group of libertarians who do not accept the nonaggression axiom. Its critics, including some libertarians, charge that it offers too simplistic an approach to the complexities of social life and ignores context; that it is illegitimately absolutistic, disallowing uses of force that might bring beneficial consequences; or that it cannot be unambiguously applied without appeal to additional ethical principles. Not all proponents of the axiom regard this last comment as an objection.

Another objection focuses on the term *axiom*, which is sometimes taken to imply that the prohibition of aggression enjoys a special epistemic status analogous to that of the law of noncontradiction (e.g., that it is self-evident or knowable a priori, or a presupposition of all knowledge, or that it cannot be denied without self-contradiction). Although some proponents of the prohibition do indeed claim such a status for it, many do not. Accordingly, it is sometimes suggested that *nonaggression principle* or *zero aggression principle* is a more accurate label than *nonaggression axiom*.

Nevertheless, an axiom also can denote a foundational presupposition of a given system of thought even if it rests on some deeper justification outside that system. For example, Isaac Newton described his fundamental laws of motion as axioms within his deductive system of mechanics, yet regarded them as grounded empirically. In this sense, nonaggression might legitimately be regarded as an axiom of libertarian rights theory, regardless of what one takes its ultimate justification to be.

The nonaggression principle must be distinguished from a number of popular moral principles easily confused with it. The golden rule ("Do unto others as you would have them do unto you"), unlike the nonaggression axiom, does not distinguish between negative and positive obligations. Again unlike the axiom, it does not clearly rule out paternalistic legislation because paternalists might sincerely prefer that they be coerced should they, in the future, stray from what they presently regard as the true path. The nonaggression axiom also should not be confused with John Stuart Mill's "harm principle," which specifies that "the only purpose for which power can be rightfully exercised over any member of a civilized community, against his will, is to prevent harm to others." Despite their similarity, the two principles are arguably not equivalent. First, *harm* seems to be a broader concept than *aggression:* outcompeting an economic or romantic rival is not aggression, but might count as harm. Second, Mill's principle does not specify that the person to be coerced in order to prevent harm must be the author of the harm to be prevented. The nonaggression axiom also should be distinguished from Immanuel Kant's categorical imperative that persons are to be treated as ends in themselves and never as mere means. Kant's requirement is broader because it forbids *all* forms of manipulative and degrading treatment (even when those so treated consent) and not aggression alone. Finally, the nonaggression axiom is distinct from John Rawls's principle that each person is to have an equal right to the most extensive basic liberty compatible with similar liberty for others because Rawls explicitly excludes from his notion of "basic liberty" the freedom to do as one likes with one's property.

RL

See also Individual Rights; Nozick, Robert; Rand, Ayn; Rothbard, Murray

Further Readings

Hoppe, Hans-Hermann. *The Economics and Ethics of Private Property*. 2nd ed. Auburn, AL: Ludwig von Mises Institute, 2006.

Nozick, Robert. *Anarchy, State, and Utopia*. New York: Basic Books, 1974.

Rand, Ayn. *The Virtue of Selfishness: A New Concept of Egoism*. New York: Signet, 1964.

Rothbard, Murray N. *The Ethics of Liberty*. New York: New York University Press, 2003.

———. *For a New Liberty: The Libertarian Manifesto*. Rev. ed. New York: Collier, 1978.

NOZICK, ROBERT (1938–2002)

Robert Nozick was a writer, a philosopher, and, at one time, a leading supporter of libertarian thought. Two Harvard professors resuscitated political philosophy in the American academy where interest had languished for decades under the sway of analytic philosophy. John Rawls, a distinguished academician, came to press first in 1971 with his somewhat ponderous tome, *A Theory of Justice*, which employed a variant of the "state of nature" argument to justify the liberal welfare state. In defending both individual liberty and redistribution, Rawls's arguments ignited a torrent of responses that have not abated in the ensuing decades. These critiques were written overwhelmingly by his fellow liberals or those further to the left who thought Rawls had not gone far enough toward collectivism. Surprisingly, however, Rawls's most enduring challenge came from one of his own colleagues, a younger philosopher with an engaging writing style who accomplished something extraordinary. Robert Nozick's book, *Anarchy, State, and Utopia*, published in 1974, had the unpredictable effect of transforming libertarianism from a political philosophy that had been taken seriously by only a few academics into an obligatory topic of discussion among American philosophers and their students. After Nozick, libertarian views have been routinely considered in introductory texts in political philosophy, typically as an ideology to be disputed, but one that must be given serious consideration.

Prior to *Anarchy, State, and Utopia*, Nozick had published two papers in political philosophy, one on "Coercion" and another, for which he was best known in libertarian circles, "On the Randian Argument," in which he discussed Ayn Rand's moral argument for natural rights, the bedrock of her defense of capitalism. Although he shared Rand's support for free markets as well as her commitment to grounding capitalism on natural rights rather than utility or a social contract, he argued that Rand's derivation of natural rights was flawed.

Emerging from the academy of the 1970s, almost uniformly hostile to and uninformed about libertarian ideas, *Anarchy, State, and Utopia* was a bombshell, challenging from its first sentence the hoary truths of the contemporary liberal professoriate. "Individuals have rights," Nozick declared, "and there are things no person or group may do to them (without violating their rights)." To the liberals' wholehearted embrace of the welfare state, Nozick responded that the justification of any state, even a minimal one, is problematic. To their fondness for redistribution, Nozick offered a blistering argument against "patterned theories" of justice that require constant intervention by the state to prevent deviations that voluntary acts cause. To utopians of various sorts, Marxists included, Nozick offered his own vision of a libertarian framework that would allow voluntary communities of all sorts to flourish under its minimalist wing. Coming from a professor at Harvard University's highly ranked philosophy department, such heretical thoughts could not be easily ignored, especially after Nozick's book received the 1975 National Book Award.

The 1970s were a time of great intellectual ferment in libertarian circles. A heady debate flourished, sometimes acrimoniously, but most often in good spirit, between advocates of a minimal state and their anarchist adversaries who argued that any state would necessarily violate individual rights. The minimalists took their inspiration from such figures as Ayn Rand, Milton Friedman, Friedrich Hayek, and Ludwig von Mises. The anarchists' champion, economist Murray Rothbard, a student of Mises and arguably the preeminent libertarian of his day, eagerly embraced the individualist anarchist tradition of Benjamin R. Tucker and Lysander Spooner. Nozick attempted, in the first part of *Anarchy, State, and Utopia*, to refute the anarchists and justify a minimal state "limited to the narrow functions of protection against force, theft, fraud, enforcement of contracts, and so on."

The imprint of John Locke's *Second Treatise* (1690) is present throughout Nozick's book. Nozick begins by assuming Locke's state of nature and then by reprising his account of its moral foundation in natural law and natural right. Nozick concedes that he has no defense of this moral theory and notes that providing that foundation is "a task for another time. (A lifetime?)." Locke's state of nature is a state of perfect freedom, yet it suffers from certain defects for which natural law, imprinted in each man's heart, is an insufficient remedy. When men are judges in their own cause, they will often overvalue their own harm and not judge impartially. Where there is no common judge on earth, this partiality in enforcing the natural law leads to feuds and retaliation. Justice suffers as well when someone in the right lacks the power to enforce his rights and to exact compensation because the rights violator is more powerful. To remedy these and other defects, Locke envisioned a voluntary agreement—a social contract—between people desirous of leaving the state of nature and forming into a civil society. Nozick followed a similar scenario, but jettisoned the social contract. His minimal state emerges as the unintended consequence of individuals' acts. Borrowing from Adam Smith, Nozick calls this account an "invisible-hand explanation" because the state is not designed, but rather evolves.

Nozick explained how many "protective associations" might form to remedy these Lockean defects in enforcing rights in the state of nature. But a multiplicity of agencies would cause problems, too, including warfare, resulting in a tendency for one agency to become dominant over a particular territory. Thus, from anarchy and only from voluntary acts, "mutual-protection associations, division of labor, market pressures, economies of scale, and rational self-interest there arises something very much resembling a minimal state or a group of geographically distinct minimal states."

The market for protection, Nozick maintained, is essentially different from other markets and will, by the nature of the service offered, result in a "virtual monopoly" because the "maximal product" (a monopoly) is the most efficient way to eliminate violent conflicts between competing agencies. Therefore, the appeal of less than maximal protection agencies declines "disproportionally with the number who purchase the maximal product," and these weaker companies are caught in a "declining spiral." (It is an argument similar to the one given by economists for the existence of so-called natural monopolies.)

A necessary condition for a state is that it "claims a monopoly on deciding who may use force" within its territory and the consequent right to punish anyone who uses force without its "express permission." Nozick tries to show how a dominant protection agency may come to exercise this defining quality of a state and do so by not violating any individual's rights. He considers the case of those who choose not to join a protection agency and insist on judging for themselves as well as the case of those who cannot afford protection from any protective agency. The latter case is important because states claim to protect everyone within their borders, which would seemingly require that the minimal state must tolerate some redistribution to provide coverage for everyone. Nozick proceeds by a two-step analysis,

first showing how an "ultraminimal state" would emerge from private protection agencies, and, second, how this ultraminimal state would be morally obligated to transform itself into a minimal state with some "redistribution" to protect everyone's rights. Neither in its inception nor in its operation does this minimal state violate anyone's rights so conceived. Nozick thinks of rights as "side constraints" on action—constraints that preclude (in Kantian terms) using others as a means toward one's own ends.

Through an intricate argument about compensation and risk, Nozick arrives at a "principle of compensation" that serves as his vehicle for moving from a dominant protection agency to the endpoint of a minimal state: "those imposing a prohibition on risky activities . . . [must] compensate those *disadvantaged* through having these risky activities prohibited to them." A dominant protection agency is the only agency that can offer its clients the assurance that risky procedures will not be used against them in judging their guilt or innocence, and it will thereby evolve into a de facto monopoly. At that point, it is morally compelled to offer protection to everyone within its domain. Independents must be compensated when the dominant agency prohibits them from punishing the agency's clients, leaving these independents vulnerable to harm. Thus, the minimal state emerges via compensation, rather than coercion and rights violations, because the dominant agency's clients are morally obligated to compensate the independents. In addition, Nozick contends, the minimal state avoids the charge of exercising coerced redistribution because the minimal state is not taxing some to benefit others, but merely insisting that its clients honor the principle of compensation by paying compensation to those deprived of a valuable good: their ability to choose their "unreliable or unfair" enforcement techniques (as assessed by the minimal state).

Critics, particularly those of a libertarian orientation, have found Nozick's justification of the minimal state suspect. They argue that the principle of compensation only masks the violation of rights of those forced to give up self-help in enforcement in favor of the monopolist's sole and unimpeachable judgment about risk to their clients.

Anarchy, State, and Utopia goes on to argue that no state more extensive than the minimal state can be justified. Nozick's target shifts from the individualist anarchists he had earlier discussed to analysis of the position embraced by Rawlsian liberals. He dismisses "end-result" principles of distributive justice such as Rawls's "difference principle," in which any economic inequality is justified only if it benefits the least well off. Nozick points out that any patterned principle must continually interfere with the results of individuals' voluntary choices. Here he offers the example of Wilt Chamberlain to demonstrate how wealth can be accumulated by voluntary transfer from basketball fans to a noted basketball star, transfers that would upset any original egalitarian distribution, but seem in each instance legitimate. In contrast to end-result principles, Nozick propounds a historical theory of distributive justice, which he calls the *entitlement theory*. Property holdings, he contends, are justified only when based on three principles: the legitimacy of original acquisition, transfer by voluntary exchange, or the rectification for transfers that depart from the first two principles.

Nozick's arguments against redistribution and the welfare state have garnered much criticism, predominantly from liberals who contend that he does not give an adequate defense of original acquisition. Also, they abhor his principle of property transfer by voluntary exchange because they find its inegalitarian results reprehensible. Nozick never could decide what justified original acquisition, thereby leaving himself vulnerable to the former charge (although he did seem to defer to Locke's mixing-one's-labor theory). As for the latter charge, liberals could not accept Nozick's entitlement theory without conceding that laissez-faire was the morally preferable economic system, an unpalatable conclusion.

After *Anarchy, State, and Utopia*, Nozick wrote three books, two of which received considerable attention in the philosophical community: *Philosophical Explanations* (on knowledge and skepticism, personal identity, value theory, and free will) and *The Nature of Rationality* (in which he introduced the notion of *symbolic utility*). *The Examined Life: A Meditation*, published in 1989, ponders matters of life, death, parenthood, and love, and it was generally ignored by philosophers. It contains one chapter, "The Zigzag of Politics," that departs radically from *Anarchy, State, and Utopia*. "The libertarian position I once propounded," Nozick wrote, "now seems to me seriously inadequate, in part because it did not fully knit the humane considerations and joint cooperative activities it left room for more closely into its fabric." The symbolic significance of democratic politics as social solidarity and humane concern, he argued, is completely ignored by libertarian theory. Remarkably, he opined that taxation to help the needy is preferable to voluntary contributions because the latter "would not constitute the society's solemn markings and symbolic validation of the importance and centrality of those ties of concern and solidarity." He followed this claim with an endorsement of antidiscrimination laws in employment, public accommodations, and housing. He no longer

considered freedoms of speech and assembly as absolute rights, and he held that they can be overridden to prevent Ku Klux Klan or Nazi marches through black or Jewish neighborhoods. This chapter constitutes a stunning rejection of the younger Nozick's ringing endorsement of individualism, his rejection of the notion of a common good, and his embrace of natural rights.

Nozick began a collection of his essays, *Socratic Puzzles*, with the admission that "it is disconcerting to be known primarily for an early work." He followed this admission with an explanation of why he had not responded to the "sizable literature" on *Anarchy, State, and Utopia*. Had he attempted to do so, it would have required that he spend the remainder of his life writing "'The Son of Anarchy, State, and Utopia,' 'The Return of the Son of . . ,' etc.," an unappealing task. Yet however disconcerting *Anarchy, State, and Utopia* may have been to the mature Nozick, his reputation will forever be tied to this work.

EFP

See also Anarchism; Anarcho-Capitalism; Minimal State; Private Property; Rawls, John; Welfare State

Further Readings

Cohen, G. A. *Self-Ownership, Freedom, and Equality* (*Studies in Marxism and Social Theory*). Cambridge: Cambridge University Press, 1995.
Nozick, Robert. *Anarchy, State, and Utopia*. New York: Basic Books, 1974.
———. "Coercion." *Philosophy, Science, and Method*. S. Morgenbesser, P. Suppes, and M. White, eds. New York: St. Martin's, 1969.
———. *The Examined Life: Philosophical Meditations*. New York: Simon & Schuster, 1989.
———. *The Nature of Rationality*. Princeton, NJ: Princeton University Press, 1993.
———. "On the Randian Argument." *The Personalist* 52 no. 2 (Spring 1971): 282–304.
———. *Philosophical Explanations*. Cambridge, MA: Harvard University Press, 1981.
———. *Socratic Puzzles*. Cambridge, MA: Harvard University Press, 1997.
Paul, Jeffrey, ed. *Reading Nozick: Essays on Anarchy, State, and Utopia*. Totowa, NJ: Rowman & Littlefield, 1981.
Wolff, Jonathan. *Robert Nozick: Property, Justice, and the Minimal State*. Stanford, CA: Stanford University Press, 1991.

OBJECTIVISM

Objectivism is the term that Ayn Rand coined to describe her system of ideas. The central themes of Objectivism are that individuals should regard their own happiness as an end in itself; that reason is their only source of knowledge and moral guidance; that people should deal with each other on the basis of mutually beneficial trade, rather than sacrifice; and that the ideal political and legal system is laissez-faire capitalism, in which a strictly limited government protects individuals' rights to life, liberty, and property. Thus, Objectivism includes aspects of libertarianism as a political doctrine, but it grounds that doctrine in the broader context of an entire philosophical system.

Rand articulated those ideas in her best-selling novels *The Fountainhead* and *Atlas Shrugged* and in nonfiction works such as *The Virtue of Selfishness* and *Capitalism: The Unknown Ideal*. She was among the most influential authors in launching the modern libertarian movement. Some previous writers had defended the morality of free exchange and the many benefits it creates, but Rand's distinctive contribution to the defense of capitalism was to portray it as a moral ideal. Her ethical theory revolves around the love of achievement, and she saw capitalism as the only economic and social system that consistently fostered and rewarded productive work and achievement. With the failure of some socialist communities, some intellectuals had argued that man was not good enough for socialism. Rand argued that socialism was not good enough for man.

Every philosophical system rests on a basic worldview regarding the nature of reality and man's place in it. Objectivism holds that there is no higher realm beyond the natural world perceivable by the senses, that nature is governed by a causal order discoverable by science, and that man is an animal who, like other animals, is part of that order. It denies the existence of God and of any life hereafter. It holds that reason is man's only means of knowledge—not only in science, but in morality and other humanistic areas—and thus denies the validity of faith, revelation, and other nonrational sources of knowledge.

Unlike many secular thinkers, however, Rand did not reduce human nature to conditioned reflexes, evolutionary drives, or economic interests. Objectivism holds that man's faculty of reason, while dependent on the evidence of the senses for its data, allows us to go beyond what is directly given, integrating sensory data into abstract concepts and principles, using logic to derive inferences from observations, and developing comprehensive theories to explain what we observe. Reason allows us to live by production, rather than by scavenging or plunder. As a volitional faculty, reason also gives rise to the need for morality and for other nonmaterial goods, such as art and love.

A philosophical system also must address issues of good and evil, values and virtues, and justice and rights—in short, the nature and standards of morality. Rand was an advocate of ethical egoism, the moral principle that a person should pursue his own self-interest. She was a vehement opponent of altruism, the ethical principle that prescribes self-sacrifice and service to others as the highest or primary good. Challenging both the religious tradition of subservience to God and the collectivist call for subordinating the individual to the collective, she argued that altruism is irrational and that it stifles everything good in human nature. The purpose of morality, Rand held, "is to teach you, not to suffer and die, but to enjoy yourself and live."

Objectivist ethics is a form of enlightened egoism. It does not define *self-interest* in terms of subjective desire, nor of exclusively material goods such as wealth. Rather, as Rand put it, *self-interest* is defined by "the terms, methods, conditions and goals required for the survival of a rational being through the whole of his lifespan." As a living being, man must survive by the exercise of his mind, with happiness as the emotional barometer of success.

Thus, the ultimate value for any individual is his own life and happiness. That ultimate value, together with the fact that humans have a definite nature and definite needs, gives morality an objective basis. To live successfully and achieve happiness, according to Objectivism, we must cultivate and use our minds; have productive purposes in our lives; take pride in our achievements and character; and act with independence, integrity, and justice. The difference between the Objectivist and the conventional ethic emerges most clearly in Rand's novels, where the heroes she portrays as the highest expressions of human potential are not warriors, saints, or charismatic leaders, but creative producers in business, science, and the arts.

The ideal society for Objectivism is based on trade—in products and services, ideas and information, and emotional goods like affection and esteem—in which the initiation of force is prohibited and individuals are otherwise free to act according to their own judgment, choosing how and on what terms to cooperate with others. Trade is an exchange of value for value, by mutual consent and to mutual advantage, a positive-sum game in which interests are harmonious. Both self-sacrifice and the use of force to pursue one's own interest at others' expense are negative-sum games that create conflicts of interest. To achieve a society of trade, Objectivism advocates a political structure of individual rights, limited government, and the rule of law (i.e., a system in which the government protects the populace against violations of their rights and provides courts to settle disputes over rights, but does not otherwise interfere with business enterprise, censor ideas, provide welfare benefits, administer schools or hospitals, etc.).

Rand was conscious that her political philosophy drew on the classical liberal tradition of John Locke and Thomas Jefferson, but she wanted to purge that tradition of any reliance on religion or altruism. According to Objectivists, a religious defense of liberty involves an arbitrary act of faith and gives collectivism unearned title to the mantle of reason. Defending liberty by appeal to the altruist standard of the public interest, or good of society, is at best derivative—there is no good for society apart from the good of individuals—and at worst an invitation to sacrifice individuals to the state. Objectivism also denies that liberty can be supported by arguing that values are subjective, purely the expression of individual desires, and that political authorities are thus not justified in imposing any values on people. Objectivists hold that values are not in fact subjective and that in any case a subjectivist theory offers no bulwark against the subjective desires of those who want power over others. Objectivism likewise rejects the appeal to skepticism, on which Hayek and others have relied in challenging the doctrinaire claims of socialism. Rather, Objectivists hold that rational certainty is in fact possible and that the skeptical attack on certainty undermines every political principle, including the principles of rights on which liberty depends.

The critics of Objectivism, for their part, have raised important issues about the philosophical soundness of Rand's defense of liberty. They have questioned whether certainty is achievable, whether values can be derived objectively from facts, and whether principles of rights can be derived from individual self-interest without relying on intrinsic duties toward others. Those questions are currently topics of research by Objectivist intellectuals. Nevertheless, it is fair to say that many, if not most, libertarians share the core Objectivist values: reason, the pursuit of happiness, production and wealth, and mutually beneficial exchange and cooperation, rather than power, are the bases for human relationships.

DK

See also Branden, Nathaniel; Capitalism; Individualism, Political and Ethical; Minimal State; Rand, Ayn

Further Readings

Branden, Nathaniel. *Taking Responsibility*. New York: Simon & Schuster, 1996.

Peikoff, Leonard. *Objectivism: The Philosophy of Ayn Rand*. New York: Penguin, 1991.

Rand, Ayn. *Atlas Shrugged*. New York: Penguin, 1957.

———. *Capitalism: The Unknown Ideal*. New York: New American Library, 1967.

———. *For the New Intellectual*. New York: Random House, 1961.

———. *Philosophy: Who Needs It*. New York: Bobbs-Merrill, 1984.

———. *The Virtue of Selfishness*. New York: Penguin, 1964.

Rasmussen, Douglas, and Douglas Den Uyl, eds. *The Philosophic Thought of Ayn Rand*. Champaign: University of Illinois Press, 1987.

Thomas, William, and David Kelley. *The Logical Structure of Objectivism*. Forthcoming.

Oppenheimer, Franz (1864–1943)

Franz Oppenheimer, a German sociologist, practiced as a physician in Berlin for many years, after which he took up the study of economics while supporting himself by writing articles. In 1909, he became a *privatdozent* (an unsalaried lecturer who received only students' fees) of economics at the University of Berlin. Ten years later, he became a full professor of economics and sociology at the University of Frankfurt, where he taught until ill health forced him to retire in 1929.

Oppenheimer disagreed with those neo-Kantians who claimed that the science of sociology should eschew value judgments and deal only with facts. Oppenheimer, while acknowledging the difference between facts and values, argued that some evaluations can be objectively justified, and this position enabled him to employ the concept of justice in his sociological and historical investigations.

Oppenheimer was influential in shaping modern libertarian thought through his book *Der Staat* (*The State*, 1914). An expanded version of this book later appeared in the second volume of his four-volume magnum opus, *System der Soziologie* (1922–1929). This treatise offers a detailed description of the origins of the state, which Oppenheimer claimed began in conquest. According to Oppenheimer, "the State grew from the subjection of one group of men by another. Its basic justification, its raison d'être, was and is the economic exploitation of those subjugated."

Oppenheimer identifies six stages in the development of the state. The first was marked by roving tribes of herdsmen who periodically attacked, looted, and killed sedentary peasants. These victorious herdsmen then realized that more could be gained by enslaving the conquered peasants than from their wholesale slaughter. There followed a system of economic exploitation that became institutionalized through the payment of regular tributes (later known as taxes) by the vanquished to their rulers. Various factors accounted for the two classes, rulers and ruled, to occupy the same territory, thereby bringing about some degree of social integration. As quarrels arose between neighboring villages and clans, the ruling class claimed the exclusive right to adjudicate disputes. Finally, as a sense of national identity developed among the residents of a territory, the ruling class (the descendants of the original conquerors) developed a system of law and other formal trappings of a sovereign government. That the state originated in conquest reflects the most significant fact about its nature.

Oppenheimer distinguishes between two methods of acquiring wealth: the economic and the political. "These are work and robbery, one's own labor and the forcible appropriation of the labor of others." Oppenheimer continues:

> I propose in the following discussion to call one's own labor and the equivalent exchange of one's own labor for the labor of others, the "economic means" for the satisfaction of needs, while the unrequited appropriation of the labor of others will be called the "political means."

Oppenheimer's distinction between state and society became a crucial aspect of libertarian philosophy. The state, he contended, is "the fully developed political means," whereas society, based on voluntary relationships, is "the fully developed economic means." He attributed the growth of individual freedom to the development of cities in late medieval Europe and to the emergence of a money economy. Industrial cities, which developed spontaneously by economic means, offered freedom and economic opportunity. They drew serfs from feudal estates, thereby diminishing the power and wealth of the landed aristocracy.

Some of Oppenheimer's ideas were transmitted to libertarian thinkers through the work Albert J. Nock, especially his influential essay, *Our Enemy, the State* (1935). Nock embraced much of Oppenheimer's interpretation of politics in his own work and regarded him as one of the "Galileos" who had deprived the state of all moral prestige. Moreover, because Nock largely agreed with the views of Henry George in regard to land and that the only legitimate tax was on the natural (unimproved) value of land, he was attracted to Oppenheimer's contention that land rent originated in unjust expropriation by the original exploiter. More recently, Oppenheimer's insights have been employed by Austrian economists, among them Murray Rothbard, who rejects the Georgist theories of land ownership and rent.

GHS

See also Cities; Nock, Albert Jay; Rothbard, Murray; Sociology and Libertarianism; State; Voluntarism

Further Readings

Heimann, Eduard. "Franz Oppenheimer's Economic Ideas." *Social Research* 11 no. 1 (February 1944): 27–39.
Nock, Albert Jay. *Our Enemy, the State*. New York: Morrow, 1935; New York: Free Life Editions, 1973 (Introduction by Walter E. Grinder).
Oppenheimer, Franz. *The State*. New York: Free Life Editions, 1975.

ORTEGA Y GASSET, JOSÉ (1883–1955)

José Ortega y Gasset was a Spanish philosopher and an essayist. Ortega was born in Madrid and became a teacher to an entire generation of writers in Spain and Latin America. He was the author of a number of essays known for their elegant and witty style. Ortega's best-known work, *The Revolt of the Masses*, was published in 1930. In it he describes a new sort of human being, which he calls the *Mass Man*. The Mass Man is the product of the unprecedented material abundance that European civilization had achieved during the 19th century. This prosperity brought with it a sudden increase in population, which in turn produced two effects that, when combined, led to devastating results. First, the Mass Man has by sheer numbers attained considerable political and social power. Second, it has proven impossible to educate so many people in the traditional manner, to subject their minds to the discipline of abstract standards, including those of tradition, logic, facts, or science. The mind of this new human type does not measure its internal experiences by any standard superior to itself. In politics, this unconstrained frame of mind expresses itself in the form of direct action. Its characteristic literary expression is the insult. Above all, the Mass Man has a powerful affinity for the state because the state promises to provide two things on which the new human type places great value: security and results without effort. The Mass Man treats the material abundance that created him as if it were the fruit of an Edenic tree, his for the plucking. He neither knows nor cares about the institutional framework that makes this abundance possible. Eventually, his indifference will kill this abundance at its root.

Another persistent Ortegean theme is his fascination with liberalism, by which he meant the classical liberalism of the 19th century, an idea that he both admired and criticized. One of his distinctive critiques centers on his conviction that this sort of liberalism, even in its relatively freedom-friendly variety, has always been too indulgent and optimistic in its view of the state.

> Liberalism [he says in the essay "Concord and Liberty"] has never been quite capable of grasping the significance of the fierce nature of the state. . . . Let us admit that societies cannot exist without government and state authority; that government implies force (and other things, more objectionable but which it would take too long to enumerate); and that for this reason "participation in government is fundamentally degrading," as Auguste Comte *whose political theory was authoritarian,* said.

Fundamentally, in Ortega's view, the state is necessary, but it is a necessary evil.

The political views and legacy of the mature Ortega probably cannot fully satisfy either conservatives or libertarians. It is true that *The Revolt of the Masses* had an aristocratic flavor that leftists and democratic readers intensely disliked and that he held a hostile view of the state. However, there is no indication that Ortega had read libertarian theorists and economists or for that matter Jefferson or the pamphlets of the Federalists and the Anti-Federalists. As a project that presumably would energize Western civilization, of which Ortega was a staunch defender, he proposed the unification of Europe. Reflecting this perspective, he chose the name *Revista de Occidente* (*The Journal of the West*) for his most important journalistic endeavor. Yet the project of European unity has led to the growth of a hyperstate that, it has been argued, strangles local differences and autonomies, subordinating them to centralized and enormous bureaucracies—all of which runs against conservative and libertarian principles.

DMF and LH

See also Burke, Edmund; Collectivism; Conservatism; Whiggism

Further Readings

Bonilla, Javier Zamora. *Ortega y Gasset.* Barcelona: Plaza & Janés, 2002.

Ferrater-Mora, José. *Ortega y Gasset: An Outline of His Philosophy.* New Haven, CT: Yale University Press, 1963,

Marías, Julián Ortega. *Ortega y Gasset: Circumstance and Vocation.* Norman: University of Oklahoma Press, 1970.

Ortega y Gasset, José. *Concord and Liberty.* New York: W. W. Norton, 1946.

———. *Invertebrate Spain.* London: Allen & Unwin, 1937.

———. *The Modern Theme.* New York: W. W. Norton, 1933.

———. *The Revolt of the Masses.* New York: W. W. Norton, 1932.

ORWELL, GEORGE (1903–1950)

George Orwell was a British novelist, essayist, and social analyst. His writings, especially *Animal Farm* and *1984,* had the effect of combating socialism, yet he was a committed socialist who never explicitly questioned socialism in the years immediately before his death at a comparatively young age. From the mid-1930s on, Orwell became increasingly preoccupied with the rise of totalitarianism. Orwell saw totalitarianism as a new slave state that would abolish capitalism, would be far worse than capitalism, and would not institute anything he would choose to call *socialism.*

Orwell was born Eric Arthur Blair in 1903 in India, where his father was an official in the British imperial administration. He was raised in England and won a scholarship to Eton, Britain's most prestigious private school. On leaving Eton in 1921, he did not go to Oxford or Cambridge, as might have been expected, but signed up for the imperial police force in India. Administratively, Burma was then part of India, and Blair was assigned to the Burmese police, where he served for 5 years. Home on leave in 1927, he abruptly resigned his position in Burma and announced his intention of becoming a writer.

In the tradition of Jack London, he began to spend days at a stretch posing as a "tramp" and making notes on his experiences. He then moved to Paris, quickly ran out of money, and worked as a dishwasher in Paris restaurants. On his return to England, he continued his forays into the life of the underclass. In 1933, he published his first book, *Down and Out in Paris and London*, under the carelessly assumed name George Orwell. The book was praised by respected literary authorities, but did not enjoy big sales. From then on, new acquaintances of Blair's tended to know him as Orwell, whereas his earlier friends continued to know him as Blair. The rather bizarre theory, developed when little biographical information was available, that Orwell and Blair are two distinct personae has turned out to be baseless.

In 1934, Orwell published his powerful novel *Burmese Days*, which, like his previous work, was not an immediate success. It is difficult to be certain of Orwell's precise political views prior to 1936. For example, *Burmese Days* is fiercely anti-empire, but we do not know exactly how Orwell's attitudes toward the empire evolved during his stint in Burma and immediately afterward. In 1936, Orwell visited the poverty-stricken North of England, quickly wrote up his experiences and his extended comments, and produced *The Road to Wigan Pier*, which had good sales. In this and subsequent writings, Orwell's views are starkly spelled out. He favored a socialist state in which the government owned nearly everything, and everyone was paid an equal wage. These opinions were standard of many British leftists at the time. He also was critical of the habits and outlooks of many of his fellow socialists, which he described in colorful terms. Orwell despised vegetarianism, feminism, effeminate dress for men, aspirin, birth control, and the soft living encouraged by machine technology. He favored tough, virile men, and women who had many babies (Orwell was sterile and later adopted a child, to whom he was devoted).

In 1936, Orwell had contacts with the Independent Labour Party (ILP), a socialist faction of the Labour Party, but soon regarded the Labour Party as having sold out its socialist commitments. While *Wigan Pier* was at the printers, Orwell went to Spain where the civil war was in progress. The war was regarded by the Left throughout Europe and America as a fateful battle between progressive forces and fascism. Orwell was unable to join the International Brigades, which were controlled by the communists, but instead used his ILP connections to enlist in the militia of the *Partido Obrero de Unificación Marxista* (POUM), a group of anti-Stalinist Marxists that had some strength in the province of Catalonia. While engaged in trench warfare, he was wounded by a bullet in the throat and invalided back to Barcelona. Here he observed the fighting between supporters of the communists and the POUM in May 1937, and he was able to compare what he had seen with the mendacious accounts successfully planted by the communists in the world's media. Soon Orwell and his wife, who had joined him in Barcelona, made their escape into France. Their names had been placed on a list of Trotskyists marked down for liquidation by the communists despite the fact that Orwell was never strictly a Trotskyist nor indeed a Marxist.

Back in England, Orwell joined the ILP and quickly wrote *Homage to Catalonia*, his account of the events in Spain. The book sold poorly for many years while the communist version of events predominated, with moderate leftists holding the opinion that, whatever vile deeds the communists had been responsible for in Spain, the Left's main enemy was fascism and, given that fact, the Left's dirty linen should not be washed in public. A strong mutual hostility developed between Orwell and the communists that facilitated Orwell's friendship with another anticommunist leftist, Arthur Koestler. Their views on politics were almost identical, except that Orwell opposed Zionism, which he saw as one more example of oppression of the people of Asia and Africa by European colonizers.

Despite his military service in the doomed Spanish republic, Orwell, like many on the Left, saw the coming world war as a Tweedledum–Tweedledee struggle between rival imperialisms. He maintained that the British Empire was just as brutal as the Third Reich. He even contemplated forming an underground antiwar organization. Orwell abruptly changed his mind in August 1939 and from then on became an outspoken supporter of the war against Nazi Germany and a ferocious critic of antiwar leftists. For the first few years of the war, he attributed Germany's military successes to its socialist economy and maintained that Britain could not effectively fight Germany unless the British ruling classes were removed from power in a socialist revolution. He came to see that this idea was mistaken, and he acknowledged his error. During the war, he worked for a time as an organizer of broadcasts to India for the British Broadcasting Corporation, which later provided some of the material he was to use in describing Winston Smith's job at the Ministry of Truth in *1984*.

He completed his short satire on the Russian Revolution, *Animal Farm*, in 1944, but at first did not find a publisher, in part because of the prevailing sentiment that the Soviet Union, as a valuable ally bearing the brunt of the struggle against Germany, should not be offended. When *Animal Farm* appeared, it was an immediate success. Because of its vivid final scene, *Animal Farm* is often misconstrued as holding that the communist system was becoming just like the West. In fact, Orwell held that life for the workers in Soviet Russia was considerably worse than under Western capitalism, just as it was worse for the animals in the pig-ruled *Animal Farm* than under human farmers.

Orwell's last years were dominated by ill health and his struggle to write *1984*. When this terrifying novel was published, it was widely seen as a repudiation of socialism. Orwell publicly insisted that he continued to embrace socialism and supported the new Labour Party government. In fact, he objected to the Labour government's compromises and failure to enact more sweeping socialization.

A key to understanding Orwell's position is that he was convinced capitalism simply could not survive much longer. Despite his rather favorable review of Hayek's *Road to Serfdom*, Orwell never abandoned his view that "the trouble with competitions is that somebody wins them." Inexorable trends within capitalism would soon lead to its abolition. He believed that the choice for the future lay between totalitarianism and democratic socialism. Thus, the horrors of totalitarianism constituted for Orwell an argument for democratic socialism, which he perceived as the only feasible alternative to totalitarianism.

DRS

See also Collectivism; Communism; Socialism

Further Readings

Angus, Ian, and Sonia Orwell, eds. *My Country Right or Left, 1940–1945: The Collected Essays Journalism and Letters of George Orwell.* New York: Harcourt, Brace, 1968.

Davison, Peter, ed. *The Complete Works of George Orwell.* London: Secker & Warburg, 1998.

Hitchens, Christopher. *Why Orwell Matters.* New York: Basic Books, 2003.

Orwell, George. "Review of the Road to Serfdom by F. A. Hayek." *The Complete Works of George Orwell: Vol. 16. I Have Tried to Tell the Truth.* Peter Davison, ed. London: Secker & Warburg, 1998.

Widmer, Kingsley. "Other Utopian Anti-Utopians: Huxley, Orwell, and Lawrence." *Literature and Liberty: A Review of Contemporary Liberal Thought* 4 no. 10 (Winter 1981): 5–62.

Woodcock, George. *The Crystal Spirit: A Study of George Orwell.* London: Black Rose Books, 2005.

OSTROM, VINCENT AND ELINOR (1919– AND 1933–)

Vincent and Elinor Ostrom were the founders and dominant figures of the Bloomington School of Institutional Analysis at the University of Indiana. The Bloomington School has a special relevance for libertarianism due to its theoretical and empirical contributions to the study of government and its optimism regarding the capacity of human beings to self-govern. The Ostroms have challenged the numerous social scientists and decision makers who have assumed that social order needs centralized coordination and control. Due to this assumption, claim the Ostroms, these social scientists have been unable to see the many self-organized governance systems that operate. An important part of the work of the Bloomington School is aimed at analyzing the nature and functions of those self-regulating, self-governance systems. We need not think of government or governance as something provided by states alone. Rather than looking only to states and "the elite decision makers of government," we need to pay much greater attention to "the basic institutional structures that enable people to find ways of relating constructively to one another and of resolving problems in their daily lives."

The Ostroms were initial contributors to the public choice movement, but broke with what they considered an excessively statecentric approach. Subsequently, they started to extend the principles of choice to the choice of institutions. When certain conditions of self-governance and decentralization are ensured, people are able to select and fashion their institutions. Thus, individual choice is not limited to choice on the basis of price in a market, but "involves a broader range of calculations extending to the choice of terms on which alternatives become available under diverse institutional arrangements and the institutional arrangements themselves."

The Ostroms elaborated Michael Polanyi's concept of *polycentricity* to analyze the conditions that lead to the emergence of a social order that combines the greatest degree of individual freedom with structural resilience and adaptability. Polycentric systems are complex institutional systems without one dominating central authority; they consist of multiple governing authorities and private arrangements. Each unit exercises considerable independence to make and enforce rules within a circumscribed authority. Because polycentric systems are nested and have overlapping units, information about what has worked well in one setting can be transmitted to other units. In experimenting with institutional arrangements within the smaller scale units of a polycentric system, citizens have access to local knowledge, obtain rapid feedback from their own policy changes, and can learn from the experience of other parallel units. When small systems fail, there are larger systems to call on, and vice versa. By challenging the state-centered paradigms in political science and by developing an entire research program focused on self-governance, the Ostroms have made a critical contribution to libertarian ideas in the social sciences.

PDA

See also Civil Society; Public Choice Economics; Spontaneous Order

Further Readings

McGinnis Michael, D. *Polycentricity and Local Public Economies: Readings from the Workshop in Political Theory and Policy Analysis.* Ann Arbor: University of Michigan Press, 1999.

Ostrom, Elinor. *Governing the Commons: The Evolution of Institutions for Collective Action.* New York: Cambridge University Press, 1990.

P

PAINE, THOMAS (1737–1809)

Thomas Paine was an agitator and a political pamphleteer with strong anarchist leanings. Paine enthusiastically participated in the American and French Revolutions as an advocate of individual rights and minimal government. He authored several of the most popular and influential works of the age, including *Common Sense*, *The Crisis*, *Rights of Man*, *Age of Reason*, and *Agrarian Justice*.

Paine based his political philosophy on the belief that the central dynamic of domestic politics was the conflict between what he called *state* and *society*. He argued that society consisted of the "productive classes," which included laborers, farmers, artisans, small merchants, and small manufacturers not holding government-chartered monopolies. The state, in contrast, consisted of government officials, standing armies, blue-water navies, aristocrats, established clergy, and holders of government-chartered monopolies, the "plundering classes" who used state power to live off the productive classes through taxation. Domestic politics, Paine believed, could be best explained as the conflict between these "two classes of men in the nation, those who pay taxes, and those who receive and live upon them."

This domestic antagonism extended into foreign affairs as well. In Paine's view, war was, in part, an attempt by the plundering classes to increase revenue through the conquest of territories whose productive members could be exploited. At the same time, these wars of conquest served to distract a nation's own productive classes, with the aim of shifting their attention from internal exploitation to the enemy abroad. Finally, war was an attempt by the plundering classes to increase taxation in the territories already under their control by creating a crisis in which national humiliation or annihilation might result should increased taxes be resisted. In summary, war was perpetrated by the plundering classes at the expense of the productive classes to further their exploitation.

Paine urged societies to rebel against their states and set up republics. His conception of republicanism adumbrated the classical liberal vision of a self-ordering, commercial society consisting largely of self-interested individuals. Government's role was confined to presiding over the clashing interests that occur in advanced commercial societies and not to attempting to promote virtue. Paine attributed social order not primarily to virtuous citizenry or a benign government, but to the "mutual and reciprocal interest" of individuals in society. He claimed that, during the American Revolution,

> there were no established forms of government. The old governments had been abolished, and the country was too much occupied in defense, to employ its attention to establishing new governments; yet during this interval, order and harmony were preserved as inviolate as in any country in Europe.

In this spontaneously generated order, virtue was highly desirable, but was not necessary to preserve civil peace. The danger to public order came not from individuals bereft of virtue, but from excessive governmental power. Because liberal governments would have minimal coercive power, it was not crucial that their politicians be particularly virtuous.

Liberal republics, Paine argued, are held together by commerce, rather than status or virtue. Commerce was beneficial to both the citizens and the state; it contributed to the wealth of nations and helped protect liberal governments from internal counterrevolution and invasions by despotic powers. International trade has a "civilizing effect" on all who participate in it; additionally, it would "temper the human mind" and help people "to know and understand each other." Commerce encourages peace by drawing the world together into mutual dependency. Because consumer goods "cannot be procured by war so cheaply or so commodiously as by commerce," liberal republics make every effort to avoid war because "war never can be in the interest of a trading nation." Commerce encourages the establishment of a "pacific system, operating to unite mankind by rendering nations, as well as individuals, useful to each other." Its salutary effects are substantial inasmuch as universal commerce would "extirpate the system of war" and go beyond the interests of particular states to serve the interests of humankind.

Despite Paine's suspicions regarding the benefits of government intrusion into social relationships, he later advocated that it play a more active role in society. He called for a system of public education and supported the division and redistribution of large landed estates. However, he attributed the need for such reforms to previous abuses of state power in Europe and believed that they were unnecessary in the United States. The main thrust of his political philosophy remained a classical liberal one, and his life and writings consistently reflect that tradition in the nature of his support for the French and American Revolutions.

DMF

See also American Revolution; Declaration of the Rights of Man and of the Citizen; French Revolution; Peace and Pacifism; Revolution, Right of; Rights, Natural

Further Readings

Aldridge, A. Owen. *Thomas Paine's American Ideology.* Newark: University Press of Delaware, 1984.

Claeys, Gregory. *The Political Thought of Thomas Paine.* Winchester, UK: Unwin Hyman, 1989.

Fruchtman, Jack. *Thomas Paine: Apostle of Freedom.* New York: Four Walls Eight Windows, 1994.

Keane, John. *Tom Paine: A Political Life.* Boston: Little, Brown, 1995.

PATERNALISM

Paternalism refers to the practice of interfering with a person's freedom and personal autonomy for his or her own good. The term evokes the idea of a family led by a benevolent father who looks after his wife and children, even if that should involve sometimes defying their desires and forcing them to do what he knows will best secure their welfare. Although individuals may treat one another paternalistically, such as a doctor who lies to a patient about a life-threatening illness to save her from grief, the term is typically applied to government legislation aimed at forcing people to make certain choices for their own good. Laws against drug use, mandating the use of seat belts, and

the prohibition against voluntary euthanasia are generally intended to keep individuals from harming themselves, whether they like it or not. The view that such laws are legitimate is called *legal paternalism* or *narrow paternalism* to distinguish it from *broad paternalism*, which includes the private application of paternalistic coercion.

Legal or narrow paternalism comes in a number of varieties; *soft paternalism* is often distinguished from what has been called *hard paternalism*. The hard paternalist supports laws that prohibit or mandate that individuals make certain choices. The soft paternalist leaves open some space for choice, but deploys coercion more subtly, manipulating behavior through propaganda, by encouraging and discouraging choices through subsidies and taxes, and by throwing up impediments to voluntary action, such as the requirement to acquire a license or undergo a waiting period before undertaking a certain activity.

Another distinction within legal paternalism centers on the way one conceives of where the good or the interest of an individual is located. Torquemada, the Spanish Inquisitor, may be said to have acted paternalistically in torturing individuals to confess their sins insofar as he did this intending to save them from damnation to eternal hellfire, which he believed to be infinitely worse than the pain of the rack. For Torquemada, the true nature of the interests of the individual had been revealed by religious texts and authorities. This kind of religious paternalism, based on a theological conception of the individual good, exists today in a number of theocratic Islamic societies and occasionally rears its head even in relatively secular societies. This view is often closely related, although not identical, to *moral paternalism*. Pornography, for example, is often banned to protect both its producers and consumers from its allegedly harmful effects on moral character. *Welfare paternalism* concerns itself with well-being as understood more broadly. Laws banning certain fatty foods may be intended to protect the individual's physical welfare by keeping them from making imprudent dietary choices, and this preference may or may not be considered a moral matter.

Until the emergence of liberal political sentiments in the 17th century, legal paternalism was a rarely questioned feature of political organization. Throughout recorded history, slaves have been considered much like older children, without the full capacity for self-governance. This deficit required, and therefore allegedly justified, paternalistic regard from their masters. Aristotle notoriously argued that, because some individuals lacked a full rational capacity, they were "natural" slaves and, therefore, required paternalistic guidance. Aristotle regarded most women as falling between natural slaves and fully rational men. Although women were able to reach a complete rational capacity, for the most part they were too emotional to exercise it reliably and, therefore, needed paternalistic guidance from fathers and husbands. This view was common in the West until the end of the 20th century and continues to be common in most of the world.

Liberalism, which developed in part as a reaction against the often explicit paternalism of monarchical, aristocratic, and slave-holding societies, has generally sought to minimize the state's paternalistic interference with individual liberty and autonomy. However, although liberal views of natural equality developed, not everyone was seen as equally capable of self-rule. Not only was legal paternalism regarding slaves and women maintained in countries with explicitly liberal constitutions, such as the United States, but also the idea that some people were limited in developing their full capacities. This view was widely considered a justification for colonial rule by otherwise liberal governments. It was thought to be in the interests of "backward" people to submit to the paternal rule of "civilized" states.

Rights-based classical liberal thinkers such as Immanuel Kant ruled out legal paternalism on principle as being inconsistent with the autonomous exercise of practical reason, which he regarded as intrinsically valuable. According to Kant, the individual's right to develop and act on one's own conception of the good was essential to one's dignity as a person. To override this right was to treat the individual with ultimate disrespect:

> A government might be established on the principle of benevolence towards the people, like that of a father towards his children. Under such a paternal government, the subjects, as immature children who cannot distinguish what is truly useful or harmful to themselves, would be obliged to behave purely passively and to rely upon the judgment of the head of state as to how they ought to be happy, and upon his kindness in willing their happiness at all. Such a government is the greatest conceivable despotism. . . .

Utilitarian liberals, such as Jeremy Bentham and John Stuart Mill, argued that allowing legal paternalism would have bad consequences for human well-being and should be opposed on those grounds. The locus classicus of liberal antipaternalism is Mill's masterpiece *On Liberty*, in which he lays out his "harm principle" for legitimate government coercion: "The only purpose for which power can be rightfully exercised over any member of a civilized community, against his will, is to prevent harm to others. His own good, either physical or moral, is not sufficient warrant."

Mill argued that the individual is more likely than not to be the best judge of his or her own good. In any case, when another individual (or assembly) substitutes their judgment for someone else's, that individual is denied the chance to cultivate his capacities of choice and learn from his mistakes. Generally, judgment improves through practice; thus, people should be left free to use their own judgment even if they sometimes do themselves harm. Finally, truth is hard to come by, and none of us can be fully certain we have arrived at what is unalterably true—especially when it comes to questions of value. Allowing people to act on diverse opinions about human well-being broadens the search for truth about good lives by allowing experiments in living that may succeed or fail in plain view. Paternalistic interference too often assumes a contentious conception of welfare and short-circuits this useful process of cultural discovery. So unless an action harms another, individuals should be left at liberty to act according to their own judgment, whether it is saintly or sinful, coolly rational or impulsively emotional.

Legal paternalism is straightforwardly inconsistent with 20th-century libertarian philosophies, which are grounded on a prohibition against the initiation of coercion; if individuals cannot be coerced for any reason, then obviously they cannot be coerced for their own good. However, even libertarians who embrace this principle of noncoercion recognize that legal paternalism may be legitimate when individuals, such as children, the senile, or the mentally handicapped, lack the capacity to act responsibly in their own interests. Difficult line-drawing questions are therefore unavoidable. What capacities are necessary for autonomous behavior? Under what conditions are individuals expected to effectively exercise them? Must one have a coherent conception of one's interests? Must one's deliberations be free of distorting emotion?

Recent work in so-called behavioral economics has created a fresh interest in the issues relating to paternalism. One recent argument, going by the name of *libertarian paternalism*, has caused some controversy due, in part, to the seeming oxymoron embodied in the name. The authors draw on recent work in psychology to demonstrate that individuals do not act as the standard interpretation of microeconomic theory would predict. Because this theory is supposed to set out certain necessary conditions for rational behavior, empirical divergence with the theory is taken as a failure of rationality. This alleged failure then motivates a kind of soft paternalist intervention.

One much-discussed example of a libertarian paternalist policy is a government mandate that employers must enroll new employees in a savings or investment program under which some portion of their pay is withheld and deposited in a designated account. Employees may choose to opt out of the program, but, if they do nothing, the employer must enroll them by default. This kind of policy is said to be libertarian because it leaves the employee free to choose either to participate or not. However, the standard libertarian view is that individuals and firms must be free to negotiate the terms of labor contracts. If employee and employer are not free to enter into a contract that does not include the opt-out savings program, then the policy is hardly libertarian in the standard sense. Nor is this paternalism *soft*, as it is sometimes claimed. Rather, this intervention in the labor market is what is known as *impure paternalism*, in which some individuals are coerced to protect the welfare of other individuals, as is the case, for example, when the manufacture of cigarettes is made illegal to protect the welfare of the people who might smoke were cigarettes available. In the case of the savings program, workers are paternalistically prevented from entering into alternative labor contracts by the virtue of coercive government regulations of employers. Indeed, a great deal of labor regulation is paternalistic in just this way and is meant to prevent workers from harming themselves by entering into unacceptable labor contracts.

More generally, the recent intellectual revival of paternalism predicated on new psychological findings appears to confuse economic models of rationality for a theory of the minimal conditions under which individuals are capable of acting effectively on their own behalf and according to their own conceptions of the good. As a consequence, when it is discovered that the models do not fit real people, some writers have concluded that there is some kind of problem with the rational capacity of real people, whom they then place in something like the category in which Aristotle had placed women: rational in principle, but unable to exercise rationality without paternalistic supervision. However, because the relevant psychological findings are general, we seem to be left without a fully rational class of paternal supervisors. The agents of government are as limited as the rest of us. But if our rational capacities are good enough to trust politicians and bureaucrats with the welfare of millions of citizens, then it would seem that they also are good enough to trust the citizens to look after themselves.

WW

See also Aristotle; Evolutionary Psychology; Interventionism; Utilitarianism

Further Readings

Aristotle. *Politics.* Book I.

Camerer, Colin, Samuel Issacharoff, George Loewenstein, Ted O'Donoghue, and Matthew Rabin. "Regulation for Conservatives: Behavioral Economics and the Case for 'Assymetric Paternalism.'" *University of Pennsylvania Law Review* 151 no. 3 (January 2003): 1211–1254.

Dworkin, Gerald. "Moral Paternalism." *Law and Philosophy* 24 (May 2005): 305–319.

Glaeser, Edward. "Paternalism and Psychology." *University of Chicago Law Review* 76 (Winter 2006): 133–156.

Husak, Douglas. "Legal Paternalism." *The Oxford Handbook of Practical Ethics.* Hugh LaFollette, ed. New York: Oxford University Press, 2003.

Kant, Immanuel. "On the Common Saying: 'This May Be True in Theory, but Does Not Apply in Practice.'" *Political Writings.* New York: Cambridge University Press, 1970.

Mill, John Stuart. *On Liberty.* New York: Longman Library of Primary Sources in Philosophy, 2006.

Sunstein, Cass R., and Richard H. Thaler. "Libertarian Paternalism." *American Economic Review* 93 no. 2 (May 2003): 175–179.

Paterson, Isabel (1886–1961)

Isabel Paterson was an early and consistent exponent of the ideas that now define radical libertarianism. She advocated minimal government, laissez-faire capitalism, and absolute individual rights in both the social and economic spheres. She thought through the implications of these ideas, argued for them over the course of many years, and embodied them in a powerful theory of history and society.

Paterson's life acquainted her with economic and social problems of many kinds. Born Isabel Bowler, on Manitoulin Island, Ontario, she was one of nine children in a family that moved several times during her girlhood, arriving at last at a ranch on the Alberta frontier. As she recalled, "There never was any money in the family." She attended school briefly and reluctantly—because her independent reading put her far ahead of her class. After leaving home, she held such jobs as a waitress and a stenographer. In 1910, she married Kenneth Birrell Paterson, of whom little is known, and she quickly separated from him. She became an editorial writer and critic for Western newspapers, and from 1916 to 1940, she published eight novels, some of them bestsellers. Of her novels, *The Singing Season* and *The Golden Vanity* are especially relevant to libertarian ideas. From 1924 to 1949, she wrote a literary column for *New York Herald Tribune Books*, a nationally influential journal. The column became an instrument of her political and literary thoughts. In 1943, she published *The God of the Machine*, a fundamental statement of her political and historical theories.

Paterson was a cultivated person with wide literary interests. She was famous for her wit and her vigorously colloquial style, which lent her arguments unique charm and emphasis. The disciple of no one, she formed her political and economic ideas before the New Deal provoked others to oppose big government on libertarian grounds. She called her philosophy "individualism," "classical Americanism," or simply "liberalism," distinguishing it sharply from the "pseudoliberalism" of the welfare state. She insisted on a complete separation of government from both economic management and moral surveillance, attacking the whole range of government intervention, from victimless crime laws to social planning. In opposition to demands for redistribution of wealth, she noted that "destitution is easily distributed. It's the one thing political power can insure you."

Collectivist theory attributes the existence of oppressive social classes to the operation of the marketplace; Paterson, a pioneer of libertarian social analysis, traces them to government manipulation. She was an independent discoverer of many economic arguments now commonly used against the welfare state. In *The God of the Machine*, she advanced an original historical theory that focused on the generation and organization of energy. She described the individual, creative mind as a "dynamo" and commerce as the means by which "circuits" are formed for the application of energy across time and space. Surveying history from ancient Carthage to modern America, she analyzed the philosophical assumptions and political devices that have enabled people to create and maintain "the long circuit" of energy, by which the work of the modern world is done. She described the devices by which governments short-circuit innovation and the dynamic creation of wealth.

The God of the Machine characterizes the engineering principles of a free society as utterly different from the principles of social engineering, which assumes that people can be treated as if they were machines. To Paterson, it is clear that "a machine economy cannot run on a mechanistic philosophy." The great example of correct engineering principles is America's original constitutional system, in which government functions mainly as a brake on invasions of liberty. The constitutional system allowed for the existence of laissez-faire capitalism, which includes its own self-controlling features and which has produced the greatest extension of the long circuit of energy. Subsequent progress depends on people's willingness to understand the principles of a liberal society and the errors of its conscious or unconscious opponents—errors that *The God of the Machine* relentlessly exposes. The book's most famous chapter, "The Humanitarian with the Guillotine," argues that "most of the harm in the world is done by good people," people willing to violate both rights and reason to realize their allegedly "high ideals." As she had said in her column, "The power to do things for people is also the power to do things to people—and you can guess for yourself which is likely to be done."

Paterson influenced many leaders of the emerging anticollectivist movement, such as her friends John Chamberlain, Rose Wilder Lane, and Ayn Rand. Rand apparently derived much of her knowledge of American history and political philosophy from her close association with Paterson from 1941 to 1948. But Paterson's uncompromising individualism was too far in advance of its time to permit her to retain her wider public influence. In 1949, she was "retired" from her job at the *Herald Tribune*. She contemptuously rejected payments from the "'Social Security' Swindle" and showed that she could manage to live comfortably without them. She spent the remainder of her life thinking, writing (another novel, still unpublished, and occasional published articles), and indulging her taste for books.

SC

See also Capitalism; Collectivism; Lane, Rose Wilder; Rand, Ayn

Further Readings

Cox, Stephen. *The Woman and the Dynamo: Isabel Paterson and the Idea of America*. New Brunswick, NJ: Transaction, 2004.
Paterson, Isabel. *The God of the Machine*. Introduction by Stephen Cox. New Brunswick, NJ: Transaction, 1993.

———. *The Golden Vanity*. New York: Morrow, 1934.
———. *The Singing Season*. New York: Boni & Liveright, 1924.

PAUL, RON (1935–)

Ron Paul is a member of Congress and was the 1988 U.S. Libertarian Party presidential nominee. For much of the period from 1976 onward, Paul, a physician from Texas, has been the only consistent libertarian in the U.S. Congress. He served briefly in 1976, from 1979 to 1985, and returned to Congress in 1996. He has always insisted that he never votes for anything that is not authorized by the U.S. Constitution, and he never votes for any bill that would increase taxes or government spending. He is an outspoken opponent of the Federal Reserve Bank, the United Nations, and most foreign wars. In 1979, he prodded Congress to create the U.S. Gold Commission to study the feasibility of a gold standard. As a member of the commission, he coauthored with Lewis Lehrman a minority report that was published as *The Case for Gold*. In 1988, he was the Libertarian nominee for president, receiving 432,000 votes, about half of 1%. Back in Congress after 1996, he has been a leading opponent of a national identification card, the proposed "Know Your Customer" banking regulations, the hastily passed USA-PATRIOT Act of 2001, and the war in Iraq. In May 2007, Representative Paul announced his candidacy for the 2008 Republican nomination for president. He participated in the presidential debates held during 2007 and generated a surprisingly strong level of fundraising and intense support on the Internet and in other venues.

DB

See also Constitution, U.S.; Money and Banking; War on Terror

Further Readings

Doherty, Brian. *Radicals for Capitalism: A Freewheeling History of the Modern Libertarian Movement*. New York: Public Affairs, 2007.
Kelley, John L. *Bringing the Market Back in: The Political Revitalization of Market Liberalism*. New York: New York University Press, 1997. 191–192.

PEACE AND PACIFISM

Although relatively few libertarians are pacifists, libertarians tend to be substantially less bellicose than the average citizen. Modern libertarianism has deep roots in classical liberalism, an ideology that looks at war as a reactionary undertaking at odds with the social progress that springs, in large part, from the unhampered movement of goods, capital, and labor across national borders and from international scientific and cultural cooperation. Moreover, libertarians strongly support individualism, which flourishes during peacetime, but clashes with the collectivism, regimentation, and herd mentality that war fosters. They favor reduction in the size, scope, and power of government, an objective that cannot be attained during wartime. They favor private enterprise, but war, the biggest socialist venture of all, fetters or displaces private enterprise, bringing high taxes, many kinds of economic controls, and sometimes the conscription of labor. If "war is the health of the state," as writer Randolph Bourne famously declared, then peace is a necessary condition for individual freedom to flourish.

Preeminent classical liberals, such as Adam Smith, Richard Cobden, John Bright, William Graham Sumner, and Ludwig von Mises, condemned war as fatal to economic and social progress. Smith famously taught that "little else is requisite to carry a [society] to the highest degree of opulence from the lowest barbarism but peace, easy taxes, and a tolerable administration of justice: all the rest being brought about by the natural course of things." Mises observed that

> the [classical] liberal . . . is convinced that victorious war is an evil even for the victor, that peace is always better than war. . . . The progressive intensification of the division of labor [the process at the heart of sustained economic development] is possible only in a society in which there is an assurance of lasting peace.

Although most people, including many professional economists, now dispute these classical liberal tenets, having been misled by Keynesian fallacies, ill-constructed national-income-and-product accounts, and a mistaken economic interpretation of World War II, libertarians generally still subscribe to these timeless maxims. If they support a war, they do so only because in the prevailing circumstances they perceive it to be the lesser evil, not because they perceive any positive good in it.

Libertarians who oppose the state's very existence, such as Lysander Spooner and Murray N. Rothbard, also naturally oppose war and view it not only as the most menacing of all state projects, but also as, at root, the product of con artists. Soon after the U.S. Civil War, Spooner wrote that

> on the part of the North, the war was carried on, not to liberate slaves, but by a government that had always perverted and violated the Constitution, to keep the slaves in bondage; and was still willing to do so, if the slaveholders could be thereby induced to stay in the Union.

He maintained that northern businessmen had supported the war for self-serving economic reasons, a claim that modern scholarship has confirmed. Similarly, Rothbard held that "the objective of the libertarian is to confine any existing State to as small a degree of invasion of person and property as possible. And this means the total avoidance of war." He argued that war depends on the state's inculcation of the false belief that the state is defending the people, whereas in reality they are defending it, at the cost of their own lives, liberties, and treasure, for the profit of the munitions makers, financiers, and other special interests that constitute the state's critical supporting coalition. For Rothbard, the military-industrial complex comprises not patriotic enterprises whose operations are necessary for the people's defense, but "boondoggles . . . every bit as wasteful but infinitely more destructive than the vast pyramid building of the Pharaoh."

In U.S. history, opposition emerged before or during almost every war, although it assumed much greater proportions on some occasions than on others. These historical episodes serve as lessons for contemporary libertarians, nourishing their pacific proclivities and inspiring their resistance to the unnecessary wars that the state continues to launch with distressing frequency.

As early as the War of 1812, war resisters gave strong voice to their opposition, especially in New England. In December 1814, delegates to the Hartford Convention from the New England states considered actions as extreme as secession from the union. Soon afterward, news of the U.S. victory at New Orleans and the signing of the Treaty of Ghent took the wind out of the dissidents' sails, and nothing substantial came of their proposals, except possibly the demise of the Federalist Party.

Three decades later, during the Mexican-American War, the many opponents included a young congressman from Illinois named Abraham Lincoln and most of his fellow Whigs, joined by such strange bedfellows as a Democratic senator from South Carolina, John C. Calhoun, who agreed with Lincoln that the war was unnecessary and unconstitutional and that it had been undertaken under false pretenses. A memorable upshot of the dissent on this occasion was that of Henry David Thoreau, who, after being briefly jailed for refusing to pay a tax in support of the war, was inspired to write his famous essay *Civil Disobedience*, to which libertarians still pay homage.

The U.S. Civil War gave rise to considerable resistance on both sides, and opposition grew as the war dragged on, causing hundreds of thousands of casualties on each side. Implementation of conscription in the Union provoked tremendous outrage and sparked riots in many places. The largest draft riot, in New York City in July 1863, was violently suppressed only with the aid of 4,000 troops drawn from the battlefield at Gettysburg. Partisan opposition to the war by northern Democrats, whom war supporters smeared as "Copperheads," prompted the Lincoln administration to censor the mails and the telegraph, to suppress hundreds of newspapers, and to arrest and imprison thousands of civilians, denying them access to the writ of habeas corpus. In 1864, northern Democrats nominated George B. McClellan as their candidate for the presidency on a platform that called for immediate negotiation of an armistice and restoration of "the Union as it was."

In the South, civilian and military authorities often used the imposition of martial law and other harsh measures to suppress war resisters. According to historian Jeffrey Rogers Hummel,

> only military force, mass arrests, and several executions for sabotage held the strongly Unionist eastern part of Tennessee in the Confederacy. In other sections bordering upon the North, the authorities imposed loyalty oaths and arrested those who refused to comply.... Fed up with inflation, impressments, conscription, and arbitrary arrests, secret peace societies flourished.... The German areas of Texas, the mountains of Appalachia and the Ozarks, and the swamps of Louisiana and Florida became centers for deserters and other armed opponents of the war.

The Spanish-American War prompted the creation, in June 1898, of the Anti-Imperialist League, an organization that included many notable classical liberals. Former president Grover Cleveland; businessmen Edward Atkinson and Andrew Carnegie; writers Mark Twain, Ambrose Bierce, and William Dean Howells; philosophers William James and John Dewey; and sociologist and economist William Graham Sumner were members. In 1899, Sumner wrote a tract called "The Conquest of the United States by Spain" to show how the U.S. embrace of imperialism undermined the nation's best traditions as a limited-government republic and presaged higher taxes, bigger armed forces, conscription, and conquest. As if to demonstrate the accuracy of Sumner's warning, the government immediately undertook to defeat the Filipinos who sought self-rule, savagely suppressing their insurgency during the Philippine-American War (1899–1902).

The outbreak of war in Europe in 1914 shocked most Americans, who wanted nothing to do with it. Afterward, as President Woodrow Wilson moved steadily closer to seeking direct U.S. engagement in the war, many sorts of opposition were expressed. Millions of Americans and resident aliens of Irish and German ethnicity ardently opposed U.S. actions to assist the Allies—on whose side alone the Wilson administration, saturated with Anglophile sensibilities and English connections, might conceivably enter the fray militarily. Most socialists and many liberals joined the opposition, including such notable classical liberals as Oswald Garrison Villard of the *Nation* and writers Randolph Bourne, Albert Jay Nock, and H. L. Mencken. A small group of Progressives led by Wisconsin Senator Robert A. LaFollette spearheaded the opposition in Congress, where LaFollette risked his good relations with congressional colleagues, his influence with the executive branch, and his political future by waging a heroic stand against the folly of U.S. entry. Despite his valiant efforts, only 6 senators and 50 representatives ultimately voted against the declaration of war.

Once the war had begun, the Wilson administration created a draconian, multifaceted system to repress resisters, based, in large part, on the draft laws and on the Espionage Act of 1917 and its notorious amendment, the Sedition Act of 1918. Under its oppressive statutes, practically any form of resistance to or any criticism of the government, its actions, or its symbols exposed the critic to felony prosecution. The government summarily deported more than 1,000 alien critics and arrested thousands of persons, alien and citizen alike, who ventured to speak or act against the war or were suspected of doing so. Frequent presidential candidate and Socialist leader Eugene V. Debs was sentenced to 10 years in prison for making a speech whose content the government disapproved. State and local authorities and vigilante groups joined forces with the national government in effecting a virtual reign of terror against antiwar and radical organizations and individuals. This officially generated "patriotic" hysteria during and immediately after the war ranks as one of the most shameful episodes in U.S. history.

Not long after the war ended, disillusionment set in; as a result, the interwar period witnessed perhaps the greatest mass dedication to peace in U.S. history. Popular writers condemned the "merchants of death" and the international investment bankers, especially those connected with the House of Morgan, and blamed them for propelling the country into the war solely for their own profit. Authors such as Ernest Hemingway and John Dos Passos gave a literary gloss to the disillusionment, and revisionist historians such as Harry Elmer Barnes and Charles Callan Tansill debunked the war's official story line in heavily footnoted treatises. In the mid-1930s, North Dakota Senator Gerald P. Nye convened extensive hearings on responsibility for U.S. engagement in the war, and a major upshot was the passage of important neutrality acts in 1935, 1936, and 1937 aimed at prohibiting international transactions that might entangle the country in a future war, as U.S. loans and arms sales to the Allies were believed to have done in the Great War. In 1938, the proposed Ludlow Amendment to the U.S. Constitution, which required approval in a national referendum before the government went to war, except in case of an actual invasion of the United States, came close to passage in the House of Representatives before being rejected under heavy pressure by President Franklin D. Roosevelt.

After war broke out in Europe in September 1939, a fierce debate ensued between those who supported and those who opposed U.S. involvement in the war. According to public opinion surveys and other evidence, the great majority of Americans favored well-armed neutrality. The Roosevelt administration, however, as Anglophile as the

Wilson administration had been, ardently desired U.S. entry to aid Great Britain, and the president worked relentlessly, if often deviously, to bring about conditions that would justify entry—for example, by carrying out a series of increasingly stringent economic warfare measures against Japan in hopes that a war provoked with Japan might open a "back door" for U.S. entry into the European conflagration. Opposing the government's maneuvers, the leading pro-peace organization was the America First Committee (AFC), formed in September 1940. A broad coalition of ideologically diverse antiwar people, the AFC included such notable proto-libertarians as writer John T. Flynn, who headed its New York City chapter and whose 1944 book, *As We Go Marching*, is a libertarian classic.

After the Japanese attack on Pearl Harbor, antiwar sentiment practically disappeared. Isolated individuals who persisted in opposing or speaking critically about the war were not only investigated by the FBI, but also shunned, fired, blacklisted, and otherwise rendered impotent for purposes of public debate and often for purposes of earning a living. The only notable war resisters who stood firm were the members of certain small religious sects, such as the Jehovah's Witnesses. When the young men in these groups refused to obey the draft laws, they were rewarded for their dedication to the Prince of Peace with long terms in prison and with especially vile treatment while they resided there.

After the early 1950s, the bipartisan commitment to the cold war, the further decline of classical liberalism, and the smearing of formerly antiwar people and organizations as isolationists and appeasers pushed pro-peace activity onto the outer fringes of politics and ideological debate. In 1965, escalation of the U.S. military engagement in Vietnam revived mass antiwar activity, but New Left, religious, and left-liberal organizations led the way, notwithstanding attempts by Rothbard and a few other libertarians to nudge the antiwar movement in a libertarian direction.

Opposition to the Vietnam War, however, did create a diverse coalition of people dedicated to seeking peace, and libertarians, whose own modern movement sprang from the turmoil of the 1960s, have continued, for the most part, to treat peace as the proper default setting for international relations and to oppose the U.S. government's persistent efforts to remake the world at gunpoint. When U.S. forces invaded and occupied Iraq in 2003, most libertarians opposed the action, and as the occupation dragged on amid increasing sectarian violence, some libertarians who had initially supported the action came to oppose it and to regret their previous support.

Libertarian insistence on every individual's right of self-defense does not require anyone to exercise that right, of course, if religious or other scruples go against a resort to violence, even in self-defense. Of the relatively few libertarians who also were pacifists, perhaps the most notable was the great Russian writer Leo Tolstoy. A former soldier who had seen a great deal of combat, he came to oppose violence. He also came to understand that governments consist of stationary bandits who induce their subjects to submit to robbery and other crimes by a combination of threats and propaganda. "Governments," he wrote,

> not only are not necessary, but are harmful and most highly immoral institutions, in which a self-respecting, honest man cannot and must not take part, and the advantages of which he cannot and should not enjoy. And as soon as people clearly understand that, they will naturally cease to take part in such deeds—that is, cease to give the governments soldiers and money. And as soon as a majority of people ceases to do this the fraud which enslaves people will be abolished.

RoH

See also Collectivism; Conscription; Imperialism; Nationalism; War; War on Terror

Further Readings

Cole, Wayne S. *America First: The Battle against Intervention.* Madison: University of Wisconsin Press, 1953.

Ekirch, Arthur A., Jr. *The Civilian and the Military: A History of the American Antimilitarist Tradition.* New York: Oxford University Press, 1956.

Hummel, Jeffrey Rogers. *Emancipating Slaves, Enslaving Free Men: A History of the American Civil War.* Chicago: Open Court.

"Lyoff N. Tolstoy." *Liberty and the Great Libertarians.* Charles T. Sprading, ed. San Francisco: Fox and Wilkes, 1995 [1913]. 204–217.

Mises, Ludwig von. *Liberalism: In the Classical Tradition.* 3rd ed. Irvington-on-Hudson, NY: Foundation for Economic Education, 1985 [in German, 1927].

———. *Nation, State, and Economy: Contributions to the Politics and History of Our Time.* New York: New York University Press, 1983 [in German, 1919].

Radosh, Ronald. *Prophets on the Right: Profiles of Conservative Critics of American Globalism.* New York: Simon & Schuster, 1975.

Richman, Sheldon. "New Deal Nemesis: The 'Old Right' Jeffersonians." *The Independent Review* 1 no. 2 (Fall 1996): 201–248.

Rothbard, Murray N. "War, Peace, and the State." *Egalitarianism as a Revolt against Nature, and Other Essays.* 2nd ed. Auburn, AL: Ludwig von Mises Institute, 2000 [1974].

Stromberg, Joseph P. "Imperialism, Noninterventionism, and Revolution: Opponents of the Modern American Empire." *The Independent Review* 11 no. 1 (Summer 2006): 79–113.

PHILOSOPHIC RADICALS

John Stuart Mill once said of Jeremy Bentham that he "has been in this age and country the great questioner of things established." To Bentham more than to any other source "might be traced the questioning spirit, the disposition to demand the *why* of everything." It was largely owning to Bentham's influence that "the yoke of authority has been broken" among thinking people, and "innumerable opinions, formerly received on tradition, as incontestable, are put upon their defense, and required to give an account of themselves."

In a polemical flourish that overlooked Thomas Paine (among others), Mill went on to ask: "Who, before Bentham . . . , dared to speak disrespectfully, in express terms, of the British Constitution or the English law? He did so; and his arguments and his example together encouraged others." Mill also notes that Bentham's works, which in many cases were densely written and difficult to understand, had "never been read by the multitude." His influence on political events, such as the Reform Bill of 1832, which extended the franchise and corrected some of the more egregious injustices of the "rotten borough" system in Britain, was exerted not through his own writings, but "through the minds and pens which those writings fed,—through men in a more direct contact with the world, into whom his spirit passed."

Those "men in a more direct contact with the world" became known as Philosophic Radicals. Some of these men, such as James Mill, the father of John Stuart and Bentham's most influential disciple, were accomplished intellectuals in their own right, whereas others, such as John Romilly, were practical politicians who fought for Radical causes in the House of Commons. The jurist John Austin forged many of Bentham's ideas into a highly influential theory of legal positivism, while his brother Charles defended them at Cambridge, the source of many recruits.

In 1824, Bentham and John Bowring, who would later edit a collected edition of Bentham's works, founded the *Westminster Review* to serve as the official organ of Philosophic Radicalism, just as the *Edinburgh Review* served this purpose for Whigs and the *Quarterly Review* for Tories. Subscriptions for the *Westminster Review* reached the respectable number of 3,000 within a few months. In 1828, James Mill and Henry Brougham were among the founders of the University of London, now University College London, and Bentham was instrumental in securing the appointment of John Austin as its first Professor of Jurisprudence. True to the democratic sentiments of Philosophic Radicalism, the University of London was open to all qualified students regardless of social class. Other Philosophic Radicals included the Unitarian physician Thomas Southwood Smith, a strong advocate of governmental regulation in the sphere of public health, and Edwin Chadwick, a proponent of administrative centralization.

The Benthamites were radical reformers, not revolutionaries. Indeed, a young Bentham, who then had Tory sympathies, condemned the American Declaration of Independence as so much "jargon." In his *Anarchical Fallacies*, Bentham undertook a minute criticism of the French Declaration of Rights (1791). To say that "all men are born free," he wrote, is "absurd and miserable nonsense." The doctrine of natural rights is "simple nonsense," and the doctrine of inalienable rights is "rhetorical nonsense—nonsense upon stilts." In place of these "fictions," Bentham proposed an empirical theory of utility. "Nature," wrote Bentham in *An Introduction to the Principles of Morals and Legislation* (1789), "has placed mankind under the governance of two sovereign masters, *pain* and *pleasure*." All pains are intrinsically evil; because governments impose coercive sanctions against those who disobey their laws, it follows that "All government is in itself one vast evil." The only justification for a law is to apply an evil in order to prevent an evil that is even worse. This moral theory occasioned the need for Bentham's felicific calculus, a method whereby legislators can estimate the effects of a given piece of legislation on the greatest happiness of the greatest number. Later, in an unpublished manuscript, Bentham conceded that his felicific calculus was little more than a "fiction" because the units of happiness in different individuals are not susceptible to cardinal measurement and so cannot be added up into a total sum. Nevertheless, this fiction was "useful" because it provided legislators with a reliable guide.

In the final analysis, Bentham's theory tended to fall back on the doctrine that individuals are generally the best judges of their own interests, so they should be left free to make decisions and to act on their own judgments so long as they do not coerce or harm other people. There can be no doubt that Bentham, despite his mania for governmental efficiency—which led him to reject many traditional safeguards, including a system of checks and balances, and even juries—had strong libertarian sentiments. Among his earlier works, for example, we find *Defence of Usury*, which calls for the abolition of all regulation of interest rates, and a lengthy criticism of laws against homosexuality—the first of its kind.

The Philosophic Radicals are best known for their support of democratic reforms. They called for universal male suffrage (Bentham was even sympathetic to female suffrage, although this issue never became a plank of Philosophic Radicalism), annual elections, and the secret ballot. The idea behind this democratic theory was essentially a simple one. Rulers, like all other people, act to further their own interests. Thus, so long as there is nothing to restrain their activities, they will form special interest groups—which Bentham was fond of calling *sinister interests*—that work against the greatest happiness for the greatest number of people. Bentham's solution to the problem of sinister interests was to establish a democracy. This democracy would give each citizen an interest in ensuring that government confined its activities to those measures that furthered the greatest good for the greatest number. Only in a democracy will the interests of rulers coincide with the interests of the ruled.

In the third volume of *History of the English People*, Élie Halévy said of Benthamite utilitarianism that it "was not solely, nor even perhaps fundamentally, a liberal system; it was at the same time a doctrine of authority which looked to the deliberate and in a sense the scientific interference of Government to produce a harmony of interests." Halévy was not the first person to observe that utilitarianism conflicted with many of the tenets of an earlier individualism. Thomas Hodgskin vigorously criticized Benthamism, especially for its rejection of natural rights, in *The Natural and Artificial Right of Property Contrasted* (1832). In 1851, Herbert Spencer launched a similar attack in *Social Statics*. Although both of these libertarians agreed with many of the reforms advocated by the Philosophic Radicals—state education was a notable exception—they also believed that Bentham's substitution of the principle of utility for the principle of natural rights had seriously undercut the philosophical foundations of a free society and would ultimately, if unintentionally, be pressed into service to justify the extension of governmental power far beyond anything Bentham had intended. Indeed, when, in 1919, the distinguished legal philosopher and historian A. V. Dicey published *Law and Public Opinion in England during the Nineteenth Century*, he included a chapter on "The Debt of Collectivism to Bentham." Dicey noted "the tendency of Benthamite teaching to extend the sphere of State intervention," and he maintained that its rejection of natural rights had deprived liberty "of one of its safeguards."

GHS

See also Bentham, Jeremy; Dicey, Albert Venn; Hodgskin, Thomas; Interventionism; Mill, John Stuart; Utilitarianism

Further Readings

Bentham, Jeremy. *In Defence of Usury*. London: Payne & Foss, 1818.
———. *An Introduction to the Principles of Morals and Legislation*. Laurence J. Lafleur, ed. New York: Hafner, 1948.
Chase, Malcolm. *Chartism: A New History*. Manchester, UK: Manchester University Press, 2007.
Dicey, A. V. *Lectures on the Relation between Law and Public Opinion in England during the Nineteenth Century*. New York: Macmillan, 1962.
Hamburger, Joseph. *Intellectuals in Politics: John Stuart Mill and the Philosophic Radicals*. New Haven, CT: Yale University Press, 1965.
Harrison, Ross. *Bentham*. London: Routledge & Kegan Paul, 1983.

PHYSIOCRACY

Physiocracy has reference to a school of economic thought that flourished in France during the second half of the 18th century. The physiocrats did not call themselves by this label, but referred to themselves simply as *les économistes*. However, as the term *economist* acquired a broader meaning in the 18th century, it became customary to distinguish these economists from others by dubbing them *physiocrats*.

The word *physiocracy*, coined in 1767 by Pierre Samuel du Pont de Nemours, means "the rule of nature." This meaning suggests that economic phenomena are governed by natural laws that operate independently of human will and intention, including the decrees of legislators. "The most important idea of the Physiocrats," notes the historian Scott Gordon, "was that economic processes are governed by laws of nature in such a way that the economic world, like the natural world, is, or can be, a system of *spontaneous* order."

Most historians agree with the assessment of Henry Higgs, who wrote at the end of the 19th century that "the Physiocrats were the first scientific school of political thought." This is not to say that they were the first true economists because this appellation can be applied to many of their predecessors. Rather, in referring to physiocracy as the first school of economic thought, we mean that the physiocrats were a loosely organized group of individuals who shared a common theoretical perspective and worked together to bring about economic and political reforms.

These reforms focused on liberating agriculture, manufacturing, and commerce from onerous mercantilist regulations and restrictions that had crippled the French economy. The physiocrats generally advocated a policy of free trade in both domestic and foreign commerce—a view that was reflected in the physiocratic motto, *Laissez-faire, laissez-passer*. Although the physiocrats were not the first to use the expression *laissez-faire* to refer to free trade—previous writers, among them two French economists, Pierre Le Pesant, Sieur de Boisguillebert and Marc-Pierre de Voyer de Paulmy, Comte d'Argenson, had used it as well—they were largely responsible for popularizing it.

The founder of physiocracy was François Quesnay, physician to Madame de Pompadour and Louis XV. Having gained an international reputation in medicine with the publication of five books, Quesnay acquired his interest in economic theory late in life, publishing his first articles on the subject in Diderot's *Encyclopedia* at age 62. The publication, in 1758, of Quesnay's *Tableau Économique* signaled the beginning of the physiocratic movement.

The *Tableau* traces the circular flow of wealth among three economic classes. It focuses on the *produit net*, which refers to the surplus value created by the "productive class" of agricultural workers—among them not only tenant farmers, but also workers in other primary industries, such as mining, fishing, and forestry. According to Quesnay, only this productive class is capable of producing new wealth (i.e., a "net product" that exceeds the expense of maintaining workers and other costs of production).

The two other classes in Quesnay's schema are proprietors (i.e., landowners) and the "sterile class" of artisans, merchants, manufacturers, professionals, servants, and so on. Quesnay's use of the word *sterile* was destined to become one of the most controversial aspects of physiocratic theory. Adam Smith writes in the *Wealth of Nations* that the physiocratic notion of a "barren or unproductive class" was an attempt to "degrade" merchants, manufacturers, and other nonagricultural workers with a "humiliating appellation."

Some commentators disagree with Smith's assessment. They maintain that Quesnay and his disciples worked from a purely physical conception of productivity, and that in using the word *sterile* they did not mean to deny that members of this class provided goods and services that possessed economic utility. Rather, they meant only that its members did not create new wealth per se, but could only transform or exchange preexisting wealth produced from the bounty of nature.

Despite the exaggerated rhetoric of one of Quesnay's enthusiastic admirers, according to whom the *Tableau* ranks with the invention of writing and the introduction of money as one of the three most beneficial social inventions in the history of mankind, the particulars of the *Tableau* are of little value or interest today except to historians of ideas.

The theoretical significance of the *Tableau* lies not in its details, but in what it represents. It is widely regarded as the first explicit theoretical model of an economic system operating under a condition of perfect competition— a self-regulating market that, in Quesnay's words, is "as constant in its principles and as susceptible of demonstration as the most certain physical sciences." The *Tableau* depicts a law-governed economic system in which, as du Pont de Nemours put it, nothing stands alone and all things hang together. This organic conception of an interdependent market order—the physician Quesnay may have been influenced by William Harvey's writings on the circulation of blood—would become a mainstay of later economic thinking.

GHS

See also Cantillon, Richard; Classical Economics; Mercantilism; Spontaneous Order; Turgot, Anne-Robert-Jacques

Further Readings

Chinard, Gilbert. *The Correspondence of Jefferson and Du Pont de Nemours. With an Introduction on Jefferson and the Physiocrats.* Baltimore: Johns Hopkins University Press, 1931.

du Pont de Nemours, Pierre Samuel. "On the Origin and Progress of a New Science." *Commerce, Culture, and Liberty: Readings in Capitalism before Adam Smith.* Henry C. Clarke, ed. Indianapolis, IN: Liberty Fund, 2003.

Gordon, Scott. *The History and Philosophy of Social Science.* New York: Routledge, 1991.

Higgs, Henry. *The Physiocrats: Six Lectures on the French Economistes of the 18th Century.* New York: Macmillan, 1897.

Mirabeau, Victor Riquetti, Marquis de. *François Quesnay: The Economic Tables (Tableau Economique).* New York: Gordon Press, 1973.

POLITICAL PARTIES

A party within the context of political science is a political organization that seeks to influence government through shaping the views of its personnel. Parties are endemic to democracy. E. E. Schattschneider maintained that "parties created democracy and . . . modern democracy is unthinkable save in terms of the parties."

Although parties are universal, their number, structure, and degree of institutionalization vary considerably from country to country. This diversity reflects the fact that parties are not part of the formal apparatus of democracy, nor do most democratic constitutions articulate a role for parties.

Nevertheless, parties play a central role in representative democracies. Three problems requiring collective action prompt the creation of parties: the need to choose candidates from among rivals, the need to take positions on issues from among competing alternatives, and the need to organize campaigns to compete for votes in elections. Hence, parties simplify and regularize the process of collective decision making for both voters and governments following elections.

Parties perform a number of important functions. According to Edmund Burke, "Party divisions are things inseparable from free government." Most important, parties serve as a link between the governed and the governors. Other functions include policy education and formulation, the aggregation and articulation of multiple group interests, and the organization of government.

In democratic theory, parties serve the purpose of making democratic institutions effective. An essential function of parties is to transmit popular preferences into policy. As Benjamin Disraeli noted, "Party is organized opinion." Parties also bring stability to legislative politics through the natural advantages of party organization.

In the modern era, parties' additional electoral functions center on connecting voters to politics: candidate recruitment and selection, campaign management, campaign communications, fundraising, voter mobilization, and the gauging of public opinion.

The modern political party is an American invention. In the American context, parties were originally perceived as collective expressions of the passions and prejudices of specific factions of the public. As a consequence, parties threatened to stand between government and political actions aimed at the general welfare, rather than particular groups. This connection between parties and government responsiveness remains unresolved.

In the early 20th century, Moisie Ostrogorski and Robert Michels, the founding fathers of the study of political parties, criticized parties on the grounds that they were inherently antidemocratic. Ostrogorski characterized party organizations as inevitably corrupt, and Michels deemed the internal party organization inevitably authoritarian. Max Weber's study of the internal organizational dynamics of political parties led him to conclude that the consequence that followed the inevitable bureaucratization of parties was the rationalization of politics.

There have been few real differences of political principle between the various American parties. Emphasis has been on a party's electoral function, and, therefore, partisan activity is geared to the electoral cycle, a brand of party politics more pragmatic than programmatic. In the European context, parties had their origin in the formation of groups of ideologically like-minded people who sought power to execute their favored policy programs. Partisan loyalties tended to be based on social cleavages, principally those of class, religion, and region. During the 20th century, this situation was the norm throughout the democratic world, with the important exceptions of the United States, Germany, Italy, and, arguably, France. Indeed, one of the crucial weaknesses of parities in parliamentary democracies is that, regardless of the personal voting records of particular representatives, voters are constrained to support the specific candidates affiliated with the party they wish to form the next government. The effect is to encourage mediocrity and blind obedience to party orders among backbenchers.

Most political scientists view the major European parties not only as chronologically newer, but also as more modern than American parties. This difference results from their traditional, national, and electoral orientations; their large dues-paying memberships; their high degrees of parliamentary discipline; and their relatively authoritarian internal organizations and unified, formal policy commitments.

Minor parties frequently play a vital role in politics. In many countries, the votes garnered by minor parties have been a crucial factor in electoral outcomes. The issues emphasized by minor parties are often absorbed into the platforms of the major parties. Libertarian parties exist in many countries, although all are minor parties. In the voting booth, most libertarians support major parties broadly and rhetorically sympathetic to limited government, such as the U.S. Republicans, the German Free Democrats, and the British Conservatives.

By the 1960s and 1970s, most major parties in the Western democracies have become less determinative of political attitudes and behavior, less highly regarded, and less likely to influence voters. Increased social and geographic mobility has weakened parties at the grassroots level, and TV has replaced the political party as the mediating force between politicians and voters.

Over the past two decades, political parties have responded to these new pressures by deemphasizing their ideological commitments and increasing the power of party leaders. This notion has been reflected in a decline of activist members, an increase in the importance of interest groups, and the recognition of marketing research and techniques as essential campaigning tools. Generally, political parties have responded effectively to ensure their survival as newly professionalized, relevant political actors while diminishing the role of forthrightness and principle in political life.

PB

See also Campaign Finance; Corruption; Democracy; Public Choice Economics

Further Readings

Bogdanor, Vernon. *Parties and Democracy in Britain and America.* New York: Praeger, 1984.

Key, V. O., Jr. *Politics, Parties, and Pressure Groups.* New York: Crowell, 1964.

Michels, Robert. *Political Parties.* New York: Free Press, 1962.

Ostrogorksi, Moisie. *Democracy and the Organization of Political Parties.* New York: Andover, 1964.

Webb, Paul D. "Are British Political Parties in Decline?" *Party Politics* 1 (1995): 299–322.

Yanai, Nathan. "Why Do Political Parties Survive? An Analytical Discussion." *Party Politics* 5 (1999): 5–17.

POPPER, KARL (1902–1994)

Karl Popper, an eminent philosopher and social theorist, was born in Vienna, but subsequently became a British subject. When young, Popper was intellectually precocious and had a keen interest in science, psychology, and, subsequently, philosophy. He became interested in socialism when in his mid-teens, and he briefly flirted with Marxism, working as a volunteer in the offices of the Austrian Communist Party. He soon abandoned his early socialist sympathies and became immersed in more purely philosophical questions, during which he developed a particular interest in what characterized scientific knowledge. Popper was influenced by the psychologists Karl Buehler and Otto Selz and by a distinctive kind of Kantianism favored by the German philosopher Leonard Nelson. His interest in science in part reflected the concerns of the logical positivists of the Vienna Circle.

Popper's theory of knowledge is distinctive in several respects. He emphasized the criterion of falsification as the distinctive mark of science (although he was prepared to accept certain unfalsifiable ideas as having influenced the development of science). More generally, he developed a unique approach to epistemology, in which he rejected induction as the sole criterion for determining the value of scientific statements and in its place underscored the importance of such statements to resolve problems and survive tests and criticism. For Popper, the scientific character of a work depended not solely on its logical character, but also on how its proponents dealt with it (e.g., how they reacted to criticism). This schema added up to a strongly antiauthoritarian view of knowledge that placed a premium on bold ideas and held even the most venerable expert open to challenge. Popper was not a relativist, but he emphasized the fallibility of our knowledge. He was a realist, with a firm belief in the existence of an external world and in the legitimacy of the attempt to undercover its truths.

In addition to his work in the philosophy of science, Popper developed several unique insights of a more general philosophical nature. These insights offered a systematic view of mankind and of the universe in which we live. Popper believed that the world was objectively indeterministic, and he developed a metaphysic of indeterministic propensities or dispositions. Although he concluded that attempts at scientific reduction were methodologically fruitful, he was skeptical about the success of most such reductions and, indeed, embraced a form of mind–body interaction. (Popper favored a biological approach to psychology and to the mind, by which he conceived the mind as playing a significant role as an intermediary between the physical world and the realm of abstract ideas.) He had a strong interest in science, and his philosophical ideas led him to undertake work on scientific issues, such as offering arguments for a realist understanding of such abstruse concepts as the arrow of time and the nature of quantum theory.

Popper also is well known for his writings on social philosophy. His books *Open Society and Its Enemies* and *The Poverty of Historicism*, both written during the Second World War, were powerful attacks on Plato, Marx, and their arguments in favor of historical inevitability as enemies of an open society. The open society that Popper favored was characterized by ethical individualism—in opposition to the moral collectivism of his day—and was influenced by Kantian ideas about the significance of intersubjective criticism. Popper supported a political regime under which government was charged with the protection of the freedom of the individual—not only in the sense favored by classical liberals, but also a protection that extended to being free from economic exploitation. He favored a policy of piecemeal social engineering, in which governmental initiatives were to address problems that were responsible for suffering and injustice about which there was general agreement. Popper noted that such actions would have unintended consequences and that consequently governments should be open to critical feedback from citizens regarding the results of these actions.

When living in Vienna, Popper was a socialist, and *The Open Society* reflected its radical character. Nevertheless, both he and F. A. Hayek were struck by strong similarities between some of its features and Hayek's *Road to Serfdom*. In later years, Popper's views became closer to those of Hayek, and he became convinced that the political pursuit of equality was a danger to liberty. However, occasional comments about the burdens of taxation notwithstanding, Popper's political views did not change substantially, and he consistently saw liberty as ultimately depending on government intervention. Although he recognized free markets as useful, he did not share Hayek's optimism about the self-coordinating characteristics of a market-based social order.

JSh

See also Freedom; Liberty, Presumption of; Marxism

Further Readings

Hacohen, Malachi. *Karl Popper—The Formative Years, 1902–1945: Politics and Philosophy in Interwar Vienna.* Cambridge: Cambridge University Press, 2000.

Miller, David. *Critical Rationalism: A Restatement and Defence.* Chicago: Open Court, 1994.

Popper, Karl. *The Open Society and Its Enemies.* 2 vols. London: Routledge, 1945.

———. *The Poverty of Historicism.* 2nd ed. London: Routledge, 1961.

Schilpp, P. A., ed. *The Philosophy of Karl Popper.* 2 vols. La Salle, IL: Open Court Press, 1974.

Shearmur, Jeremy. *Political Thought of Karl Popper.* London & New York: Routledge, 1996.

PORNOGRAPHY

Pornography refers to the graphic depiction of human sexuality whose purpose is to sexually arouse. Such depictions have existed throughout recorded history and have crossed all cultural boundaries. However, our current understanding of pornography, at least in the West, is rooted in the Victorian Era (i.e., from 1837 to 1901), when the legal control of sexual images took on the attributes of a political and moral crusade. Prior to that period, it was more common for the law to regulate sexual acts rather than sexual depictions. Defining pornography and determining its legal status is controversial because of the moral and social claims surrounding sexuality, as well as the political importance of freedom of speech.

During the first half of the 20th century, the two extremes of the debate over pornography consisted, on the one hand, of religious opponents, who called for its prohibition on moral grounds, and, on the other hand, of supporters of freedom of speech, who demanded tolerance of pornographic materials despite the fact that they might be offensive. In the United States, free speech advocates often appealed to the 1st Amendment protections of the constitution and to the abuses of censorship that often and quickly targeted political or literary works.

The sexual revolution of the 1960s permitted pornography to enter the mainstream. Publications like *Playboy* were no longer sold from under the counter at a few downtown newsstands, but were displayed on the racks of corner stores. The widespread use of birth control and liberal feminism's celebration of "the liberated woman" contributed to a period of sexual freedom, during which the line between pornography and mainstream art, especially movies, became blurred.

The rise of radical or gender feminism in the mid-1970s, however, gave rise to a new and different criticism of pornography. Radical feminists argued that pornography exploited women and acted as a linchpin of the dominant patriarchy—the white, male culture through which men as a class were said to oppress women as a class. In short, pornography was redefined as a tool of male oppression. The counterposition within feminism was and is that the principle "a woman's body, a woman's right," also found in the debate over abortion, applies with equal force to the right of women to consume or create pornography. That position remains a minority one.

The radical feminist attack circumvented the objections to the procensorship forces based on freedom of speech by claiming that pornography had a direct cause-and-effect link with violence against women, especially rape. Its primary champions, Andrea Dworkin and Catharine MacKinnon, maintained that pornography had no connection whatever to issues of free speech, but was in itself an act of violence and an act of sexual terrorism that must be prohibited to protect women.

This call to censor pornography due to its social consequences was not new. The definition of a pornographic magazine as an act of violence, however, was. The contention was immediately countered by women who openly worked in the pornography industry not only as actresses, but also behind the camera. They maintained that their experiences clearly indicated that engaging in pornography was freely chosen.

The radical feminist position also came under criticism for its attempt to distinguish pornography from erotica. A common dividing line between the two rests on the notion that erotica uses sexually arousing depictions primarily for artistic purposes, rather than for sexual ones. Radical feminists wished to define graphic depictions of lesbian sex and of sexual situations that empowered women as erotica. In short, they considered the political or social purposes of the depiction to be a defining factor. As Jill Ridington stated in the anthology *Confronting Pornography*, "If the message is one that equates sex with domination, or with the infliction of pain, or one that denies sex as a means of human communication, the message is a pornographic one. . . . Erotica, in contrast, portrays mutual interaction."

This confusion in identifying what is pornography is not limited to radical feminist writing. It was famously captured in the statement of U.S. Supreme Court Justice Potter Stewart in his opinion in the obscenity case of *Jacobellis v. Ohio* (1964): "I shall not today attempt further to define [pornography] . . . and perhaps I could never succeed in intelligibly doing so. But I know it when I see it. . . ."

Various attempts have been made to draw lines that would allow the censorship of pornography without the suppression of nonporn. For example, procensorship crusaders in the mid-20th century were aware that sexual discussion was necessary to spread public awareness of important matters, such as sexually transmitted diseases. Thus, the law made an exception for graphic sexual depictions that had "socially redeeming value." This exemption also was intended to allow the circulation of recognized works of literature, such as D. H. Lawrence's *Lady Chatterley's Lover*, although a significant portion of the novel is graphically sexual and clearly intended to arouse.

To those who argue for freedom of speech, the solution to where lines should be drawn is less complicated. There should be no legal lines that attempt to distinguish acceptable words and images from those open to censorship. Freedom to access words and images is a prerequisite to the individual's ability to think independently. Control of words and images is a prerequisite of social control. George Orwell described the latter process in his book *1984*, which described a totalitarian and dystopian future in which Newspeak severely restricted the use of words. The ultimate goal of Newspeak was to make it impossible to utter politically incorrect statements.

Some free speech advocates maintain that pornography is an unpleasant side effect of freedom and must be tolerated to ensure that other ideas and images can circulate. Others argue that pornography provides benefits to both men and women. For example, various studies have suggested that pornography may act as a catharsis, releasing sexual energy that might otherwise be expressed in violence. Other postulated benefits included the idea that pornography is a form of information that offers a panoramic view of the world's sexual possibilities, and that pornography is a species of sexual therapy. Moreover, legitimizing pornography and other forms of sex work is seen as an important step toward protecting women engaged in these occupations.

As the debate continues, an independent factor exerting a powerful influence on both pornography and society's acceptance of it is technology. It has been said that in the 1970s, pornography was instrumental in driving the development of the home video market. Today, pornography is available to the point of being ubiquitous on the Internet. The ultimate impact of having Internet pornography immediately, on demand, and in the privacy of one's own home is not yet clear. A new generation may cease to consider pornography between adults to be an issue worthy of controversy. For those people who currently argue for and against censorship, the moral and political arguments may remain constant, but they also may become irrelevant.

WME

See also Censorship; Feminism and Women's Rights; Sexuality

Further Readings

Harvey, Philip D. *The Government vs. Erotica: The Siege of Adam & Eve.* Amherst, NY: Prometheus Books, June 2001.

McElroy, Wendy. *XXX: A Woman's Right to Pornography.* New York: St. Martin's Press, 1995.

Stoller, Robert J. *Porn: Myths for the Twentieth Century.* New Haven, CT: Yale University Press, 1991.

Strossen, Nadine. *Defending Pornography: Free Speech, Sex and the Fight for Women's Rights.* New York: New York University Press, 1995.

POSITIVE LIBERTY

Although Isaiah Berlin is often credited with distinguishing positive from negative liberty, this view was, in fact, put forward in the 19th century by, among others, the English political philosopher T. H. Green, who provided a particularly cogent analysis of what positive liberty, or freedom, implies. Green put the matter this way:

> We shall probably all agree that freedom, rightly understood, is the greatest of blessings; that its attainment is the true end of all our efforts as citizens. But when we thus speak of freedom, we should consider carefully what we mean by it. We do not mean merely freedom from restraint or compulsion. We do not mean merely freedom to do as we like irrespective of what it is that we like. We do not mean a freedom that can be enjoyed by one man or one set of men at the cost of a loss of freedom to others. When we speak of freedom as something to be so highly prized, we mean a positive power or capacity of doing or enjoying something worth doing or enjoying, and that, too, something that we do or enjoy in common with others. We mean by it a power which each man exercises through the help or security given him by his fellow-men, and which he in turn helps to secure for them. When we measure the progress of a society by its growth in freedom, we measure it by the increasing development and exercise on the whole of those powers of contributing to social good with which we believe the members of the society to be endowed; in short, by the greater power on the part of the citizens as a body to make the most and best of themselves.

There are formidable defenders of the idea of positive liberty among contemporary political philosophers, among them Amartya Sen, Martha Nussbaum, Cass Sunstein, Ronald Dworkin, and Henry Shue. All of them conclude from their somewhat diverse approaches that the freedom or liberty to make progress (or advance, develop, or flourish) in one's life is even more important to respect, secure, and protect than is negative liberty. Negative liberty, in the tradition of Locke's natural rights theory, is the condition of not being interfered with or intruded on in one's person and estate. This liberty is dubbed *negative* because it requires that everyone abstain from acting aggressively—that they refrain from invasive or intrusive conduct. Positive liberty or rights involve securing, for those in need, the capabilities to achieve the ends they seek.

The understanding of human nature underlying these two schools of political thought is markedly different. In the Lockean tradition of negative liberty—or the right to it—human beings are taken to have the capacity and responsibility to advance in their lives once a condition of negative freedom has been secured for them. In other words, (negatively) free persons can and should strive to flourish in their lives, and, to this end, they may only make use of provisions from others that are given or voluntarily exchanged. Social cooperation—in such areas as education, industry, science, philanthropy, and the like—is deemed quite likely (although not guaranteed) as a function of the self-responsible conduct in which everyone is expected to engage.

With respect to the conception of human nature that underlies the notion of positive liberty, it is generally held that those who are indigent, poor, or otherwise importantly lacking in provisions needed for their lives to flourish require support mandated from others so that they will become capable or enabled. Without such support, they will likely languish in their deprived situations and will ultimately suffer the indignity of helplessness.

Implicit in the position of those who embrace the idea of positive liberty is an emphasis on the right of all citizens to take part in political decision making. "Put in the simplest terms, one might say that a democratic society is a free society because it is a self-determined society, and that a member of that society is free to the extent that he or she participates in its democratic process." Furthermore, "there are also individualist applications of the concept of positive freedom. For example, it is sometimes said that a government should aim actively to create the conditions necessary for individuals to be self-sufficient or to achieve self-realization."

The basic idea here is that, by enjoying this kind of positive political liberty—namely, the liberty to take part in the determination and configuration of laws and public policy—citizens are capable of securing for themselves the conditions that are needed for their flourishing. They are able to vote into law the appropriate and necessary distribution of society's resources.

Champions of negative liberty, who argue that laws and public policy should concentrate on extirpating social conduct that invades persons and properties of citizens (i.e., that violate our negative rights), object to this idea on the grounds that voting for laws and public policies that involve distribution of society's resources amounts to unjust rights violations and discourage self-responsible behavior. Supporters of a political theory predicated on positive liberty reject this notion on the grounds that, without such mandated provisions, too many individuals will remain poor, ignorant, and helpless in innumerable ways.

The debate between the two schools hinges on numerous features of their respective positions. Are men and women who are forced to work for objectives to which they haven't given their consent being treated unjustly? Will these laws undermine the productivity of those being forced to work in this way? In a society where resources are conceived of as commonly owned, will this inevitably lead to what has been called the *tragedy of the commons*? Alternatively, is the self-motivation that negative liberty appears to require simply a myth? Are those who are deprived indeed capable of choosing to advance, thus moving from their deprived condition toward one where their goals can be fulfilled? Is the protection of negative liberty or rights going to favor those who are well endowed to start with so that they will necessarily be advantaged while their fellow citizens will be left deprived? Will this create a class of privileged citizens?

Both negative and positive liberty (or rights) can be defended on either deontological or utilitarian grounds. The deontological approach—or something akin to this, such as a self-perfectionist or neo-Aristotelian position— implies that what is crucial in a human community is that the dignity of persons be respected and protected and thus they may guide their lives by their own decisions, for better or for worse. Thus, it does not matter so much how well off members of the community are—what is crucial is whether justice, predicated on a conception of negative liberty, or rights, prevails. Some go on to argue that a regime of purely negative liberty is more likely than not to also secure widespread well-being, but that is not its most crucial objective.

The utilitarian approach focuses on actual well-being and how prevalent it is in a society that respects and protects either negative or positive liberty or rights. If, in fact, one of these approaches to community life—to the laws and public policies of the society—is most likely to produce widespread well-being, over the long run, it will be deemed superior to the other.

Among those who argue for positive liberty or rights, some hold that these are the only kind that, in fact, exist. For example, in his book *Basic Rights*, Henry Shue maintains that, because negative liberty or rights are ineffective without being protected and their protection amounts to providing a service to others, negative liberty or rights actually amount to positive ones. Everyone is owed the protection of his or her negative liberty, but this protection is something positive—something that needs to be provided so as to be practically useful, even meaningful.

A similar line of reasoning has been advanced by Cass Sunstein and Stephen Holmes in their work *The Cost of Right, Why Liberty Depends on Taxation*. Without being dependent on taxes, which others owe as a reflection of one's positive right (or, in Sen's terminology, an enablement), no one can enjoy negative liberty—it will go unsecured and unprotected. In contrast, supporters of the notion of negative liberty or rights argue in response that unless the negative liberty or right exists, unless individuals have them, it is conceptually odd to speak of the need to secure or protect them.

We can be sure that this discussion will continue for some time because many deem it central to the issue of whether a robust welfare state or a society of limited government is the truly just political order, at least within the framework of the Western liberal political tradition. For example, the philosopher James P. Sterba has argued in several of his books, and is indeed planning several works, in support of welfare or positive liberty or rights, whereas the philosophers Jan Narveson, Eric Mack, Douglas B. Rasmussen, and others have argued, instead, for negative liberty or rights.

Of course, it also is possible to argue that this entire discussion rests on the mistaken notion that individuals have rights. Communitarians, among them Auguste Comte, object to this view. Comte argued, as far back as the early 19th century, as follows:

> . . . Everything we have belongs then to Humanity. . . . Positivism never admits anything but duties, of all to all. For its social point of view cannot tolerate the notion of *right,* constantly based on individualism. We are born loaded with obligations of every kind, to our predecessors, to our successors, to our contemporaries. Later they only grow or accumulate before we can return any service. On what human foundation then could rest the idea of right, which in reason should imply some previous efficiency? Whatever may be our efforts, the longest life well employed will never enable us to pay back but an imperceptible part of what we have received. And yet it would only be after a complete return that we should be justly authorized to require reciprocity for the new services. All human rights then are as absurd as they are immoral. This ["to live for others"], the definitive formula of human morality, gives a direct sanction exclusively to our instincts of benevolence, the common source of happiness and duty. [Man must serve] Humanity, whose we are entirely.

Contemporary communitarians, such as Charles Taylor, also hold that human beings actually belong to some community or other, and their conduct and pursuit of various goals are contingent on gaining the sanction of the community— they have no right to act on their own initiative unless they gained the community's permission to do so. Any notion of individualism that takes it that people are independent agents is a false atomism.

Critics of communitarianism claim, however, that there are conceptual problems with denying some notion of individualism because in advancing their views communitarians are conducting themselves individualistically. They are assuming that they have the right to voice their views, that they need no permission from the community to disagree with the community, which is, at least in large portions of the West, individualistic.

Another source of support for the idea of positive liberty is a deterministic view of human behavior, which is increasingly popular. Those people who do not fare well may not be regarded as having failed, but more as incapable of doing what needs to be done for them to get ahead in their lives. As John Rawls puts the matter, the assertion that we "deserve the superior character that enables us to make the effort to cultivate our talents is . . . problematic; for such character depends in good part upon fortunate family and social circumstances in early life for which we can claim no credit." Thus, having more or less (or a higher or lower quality) of what others have is of no moral significance, but a matter of the various impersonal forces that shape a person's life. Hence, it may be inferred that all who are disadvantaged are victims of circumstances and do not deserve their lot. This view counters the conception of negative liberty that libertarians embrace—namely, that once adult men or women are free from interference from others, their flourishing or lack thereof in life must be largely their own achievement.

In any case, despite the attempt to dismiss the debate between advocates of negative and positive liberty, the issue appears to have staying power because political philosophers will continue to affirm certain kinds of liberties or rights for human beings. Which are the proper kind is something that will remain both theoretically and practically significant.

Libertarians embrace the view that only negative liberty is consistent with a free society, believing as they do that individual goals are attainable without involving government and without mandating what libertarians deem to amount to involuntary servitude from others. They support this position from a variety of perspectives, but it is central to all these that individual human beings are sovereign and must not be used against their will by others, including the government.

TM

See also Constant, Benjamin; Freedom; Liberty in the Ancient World; Rights, Individual; Welfare State

Further Readings

Berlin, Isaiah. *Four Essays on Liberty*. London: Oxford University Press, 1969.
Constant, Benjamin. *Political Writings*. Biancamaria Fontana, ed. and trans. Cambridge: Cambridge University Press, 1988.
Conway, David. *Classical Liberalism: The Unvanquished Ideal*. New York: St. Martin's Press, 1995.
Mill, John Stuart. *On Liberty*. London: J. W. Parker and Son, 1859.
Narveson, Jan. *The Libertarian Idea*. Philadelphia: Temple University Press, 1988.
Rousseau, Jean-Jacques. *"The Social Contract" and Other Later Political Writings*. Victor Gourevitch, ed. Cambridge: Cambridge University Press, 1997.

POSNER, RICHARD A. (1939–)

Richard A. Posner is a judge and a legal theorist. Posner is a judge of the U.S. Court of Appeals for the Seventh Circuit, a senior lecturer at the University of Chicago Law School, and the leader of the modern law and economics movement.

Posner held a variety of positions in the Johnson administration and taught at Stanford University before joining the Chicago faculty in 1969. At Chicago, he participated in George Stigler's famous Industrial Organization Workshop, and he developed close ties with many members of the economics department. He soon began using the tools of neoclassical economics to analyze legal issues, and in 1973, Posner published his textbook, *Economic Analysis of Law*. That book has become a classic and is now in its sixth edition.

In the opening chapter of *Economic Analysis of Law*, Posner writes: "Many lawyers still think that economics is the study of inflation, unemployment, business cycles, and other mysterious macroeconomic phenomena remote from the day-to-day concerns of the legal system. Actually, the domain of economics is much broader." Economics, he argues, "is the science of rational choice in a world—our world—in which resources are limited in relation to human wants. The task of economics, so defined, is to explore the implications of assuming that man is a rational maximizer of his ends in life, his satisfactions—what we shall call his 'self-interest.' " Such a statement may seem obvious to most economists. However, as Posner notes, it will be quite surprising to many students of the law, as will the implications that follow from applying economics to legal issues.

Many legal theorists have charged that the law and economics approach ignores issues of "justice." But if one equates justice with efficiency—as Posner often seems to do—then such criticism is without merit. After all, efficiency eliminates waste, and "in a world of scarce resources waste should be regarded as immoral," Posner writes. From this viewpoint, a whole host of socially disapproved—and currently unlawful actions—cannot automatically be deemed unjust. Posner notes:

It is not obviously inefficient to allow suicide pacts; to allow private discrimination on racial, religious, or sexual grounds; to permit killing and eating the weakest passenger in the lifeboat in circumstances of genuine desperation; to force people to give self-incriminatory testimony; to flog prisoners; to allow babies to be sold for adoption; to allow the use of deadly force in defense of a pure property interest; to legalize blackmail; or to give convicted felons a choice between imprisonment and participation in dangerous medical experiments.

Posner's unorthodox and often controversial approach to the law is not limited to his academic writings. As a judge, he demonstrates much less reverence for legal precedent than most of his colleagues. Instead, Posner tries to reach "pragmatic" decisions—decisions that are the "most reasonable, all things considered, where 'all things,' include both case-specific and systemic consequences." In a series of books beginning in the early 1990s, Posner has made the case for pragmatism, concluding that it is the "best guide to the improvement of judicial performance."

Posner has written more than 30 books on a huge variety of topics. Some have argued that the substantial number of publications that Posner has produced comes at the expense of precision. For instance, his 2001 book on public intellectuals was widely criticized for employing sloppy methodology. But it seems that Posner is more interested in raising interesting questions than in providing airtight answers—and, in this regard, few can doubt his success. Posner is the most frequently cited living legal theorist.

The University of Chicago Law School sponsors two highly regarded journals—the *Journal of Legal Studies* and the *Journal of Law and Economics*—that often feature recent scholarship in the field of law and economics, including some of Posner's more famous papers. In addition, several of Posner's colleagues at the University of Chicago Law School also work within the law and economics tradition, including William Landes, Kenneth Dam, and Ronald Coase. Indeed, this approach to law is now almost half a century old. Posner has written that the modern law and economics movement began with Guido Calabresi's famous 1961 article on tort law and Coase's seminal 1960 paper on social cost.

AS

See also Coase, Ronald H.; Economics, Chicago School of; Law and Economics

Further Readings

MacFarquhar, Larissa. "The Bench Burner." *The New Yorker* 10 (December 2001): 78–89.
Posner, Richard A. *Antitrust Law: An Economic Perspective.* Chicago: University of Chicago Press, 1976.
———. *Economic Analysis of Law.* 6th ed. New York: Aspen, 2002.
———. *The Economics of Justice.* Cambridge, MA: Harvard University Press, 1981.
———. *Law, Pragmatism, and Democracy.* Cambridge, MA: Harvard University Press, 2003.

POUND, ROSCOE (1870–1964)

Roscoe Pound was a towering figure in jurisprudence during the first half of the 20th century. Pound was the son of a Nebraska judge. Although his father wanted him to follow a career in the law, the young Pound was originally more interested in botany and even completed a monograph on Nebraska plant life before attaining his fame as a legal educator. A talented and brilliant lawyer, Pound had some judicial experience as commissioner of appeals for the Nebraska Supreme Court and served as a commissioner on uniform state laws for Nebraska from 1904 to 1907. He taught law at the University of Nebraska and then moved on to teach first at Northwestern University School of Law in Chicago and then at the University of Chicago. In 1910, Pound became Professor of Law at Harvard and proceeded to serve as the dean of the law school for two decades, from 1916 to 1936, giving him the then most prestigious podium in the legal academy. Pound's early botanical work influenced his theories about the nature of law, and he never abandoned the idea that law developed organically, as social needs changed. He was an astonishingly prolific scholar, and his two masterpieces were a five-volume work titled *Jurisprudence*, which surveyed the history of the subject in a dazzling comparative treatment of European and American law, and a shorter monograph called *The Formative Era of American Law*, in which he explored the manner in which 19th-century American judges had altered the English common law to meet the needs of a young commercial and industrial republic.

Pound was the intellectual father of what he called "sociological jurisprudence," designed to clear away outdated legal rules to make the law more efficient and to make "the law in the books" come closer to what was actually being done by "the law in action." Pound's early efforts to reform the law and its procedures were widely regarded as progressive, perhaps even radical in nature, but his defense of the inherent wisdom and fairness of American contract and commercial law in the 1930s made him a target of more radical academics in the late 20th century. Toward the end of his life, he wrote passionately in defense of the received wisdom in the common law, and its furthering of human liberty, and against those who sought to dismantle its ancient doctrines and institutions. He believed in the wisdom of systematically undertaking research on how the law worked and could be improved, but never lost his disdain for those who would replace the legal rules that favored private property, commerce, and freedom of contract with socialistic schemes of regulation and redistribution.

SBP

See also Common Law; Judiciary; Sociology and Libertarianism

Further Readings

Hull, N. E. H. *Roscoe Pound and Karl Llewellyn: Searching for an American Jurisprudence*. Chicago: University of Chicago Press, 1997.

Pound, Roscoe. *The Formative Era of American Law*. Boston: Little, Brown, 1938.

———. *Jurisprudence*. 5 vols. St. Paul, MN: West Publishing, 1959.

PRAXEOLOGY

Praxeology is the "science of human action." Although this term was coined in 1890, it came into widespread use by modern Austrian economists following the publication of Ludwig von Mises's seminal treatise on economics, *Human Action*.

Misesian praxeology, which is concerned with the formal relationship between means and ends in human action, is a comprehensive discipline that subsumes not only economics, but all the social sciences. Despite general agreement about the subject matter of economics, Mises contended that we could not draw a clear line between economic actions and other types of goal-directed behavior. Because "choosing determines all human decisions," we must base our analysis of economic activity on a "general theory of choice and preference."

Mises thus rejects the classical conception of "economic man" as unduly narrow. Economics is concerned with the logical implications of human action—specifically, the necessity of choosing among scarce means in pursuit of our goals. But this necessity describes all human actions, not merely those that are ordinarily classified as "economic." Thus, there is nothing unique about economic choices that fundamentally set them apart from other kinds of choices. Mises concludes:

> The economic or catallactic problems are embedded in a more general science, and can no longer be severed from this connection. No treatment of economic problems proper can avoid starting from acts of choice; economics becomes a part, although the hitherto best elaborated part, of a more universal science, praxeology.

We can better appreciate this effort to ground economics in a universal science of human action if we view praxeology from a historical perspective. There is a sense in which Misesian praxeology was a definitive, if delayed, solution to the 19th-century *Methodenstreit* between Austrian economists, principally Carl Menger, and the Prussian Historical School. Proponents of historicism, according to Mises, "tried to deny the value and usefulness of economic theory. Historicism aimed at replacing it by economic history."

Despite his dislike of historicism, Mises shared its repudiation of positivism, which "recommended the substitution of an illusory social science which should adopt the logical structure and pattern of Newtonian mechanics." Mises insisted that economics must take into account value judgments, purposes, choices, and other subjective aspects of human action. Therefore, he joined his historicist adversaries in rejecting the "unity of science" that positivism sought to achieve by gutting the human sciences of everything that is distinctively human. Instead, he advocated a "methodological dualism" that posits "two separate realms: the external world of physical, chemical, and physiological phenomena and the internal world of thought, feeling, valuation, and purposeful action."

Mises was profoundly influenced by the historicist theory of *Verstehen*, especially the version that Max Weber integrated into this theory of ideal types. *Verstehen*, which can be understood as a type of empathy, is the distinctive methodology of the historical disciplines. It is the mental tool that enables the historian to understand the subjective meaning of singular historical actions and the motives of individual human beings.

This partial alliance with historicism left Mises with a potentially serious problem. If, as many historicists claimed, *Verstehen* was the appropriate method for dealing with the subjective aspects of human action, then it should be used not only in history, but in every human science, including economics. But this methodological shift would transform economics into what the philosopher Wilhelm Windelbandt called an "idiographic" science (i.e., a discipline that is limited to the study of unique particulars from which no general explanations can be developed). If Mises accepted *Verstehen* as the primary method of economic reasoning, then economics would be compelled to abandon the quest for universal laws of the sort found in the "nomothetic" sciences. This abandonment is what Mises meant when he said that historicism sought to replace economic theory with economic history.

Thus, Mises faced the problem of charting a course between the Scylla of historicism and the Charybdis of positivism. Historicism offered a subjectivist methodology that was unable to formulate universal laws, whereas positivism offered to bestow on economics the status of a universal, nomothetic science, but only at the cost of robbing economics of its subjectivist orientation. Mises found a solution to this problem in praxeology, a nomothetic science that arrives at general principles by abstracting the universal form of human action from its material content. As Mises puts it, "Praxeology is not concerned with the changing content of action, but with its pure form a categorical structure. The study of the accidental and environmental features of human action is the task of history."

Closely related to Mises's formalism of praxeology is his claim that economic science begins with a priori categories, forms, and concepts, after which it arrives at theorems and conclusions by purely deductive reasoning, without the need to appeal to experiential data. "Human knowledge is conditioned by the structure of the human mind." Working within this Kantian paradigm, Mises says of praxeology: "Its statements and propositions are not derived from experience. They are, like those of logic and mathematics, a priori. . . . They are both logically and temporally antecedent to the comprehension of [empirical] facts." Moreover, "no experience, however rich, could disclose [praxeological theorems] to a being who did not know a priori what human action is. The only way to a cognition of these theorems is logical analysis of our inherent knowledge of the category of action."

A priorism is unquestionably the most controversial aspect of praxeology. Although Mises emphatically disagreed with the contention that a priori reasoning is unable to generate factual knowledge, so deeply ingrained is this belief that many economists, convinced that an a priori method would completely strip their discipline of all empirical relevance and authority, tend to rule praxeology out of court without giving it the consideration it deserves. Even some avid defenders of praxeology have expressed their disagreement with its Misesian foundations. For example, Murray Rothbard has argued that praxeology can dispense with a priorism without suffering any detrimental effects. Praxeological reasoning is equally secure when based on Aristotelian empiricism. This epistemological theory explains how, through a process of abstraction, we can mentally separate the "essence" of human action from our observations of particular actions and thereby isolate a pure conception of action for the purpose of analysis. After this process of abstraction, if the Aristotelian follows the deductive method proposed by Mises, he will arrive at the same conclusions, and he will be able to justify those conclusions with the same degree of certitude.

GHS

See also Economics, Austrian School of; Individualism, Methodological; Mises, Ludwig von

Further Readings

Kant, Immanuel. *Critique of Pure Reason.* New York: Dover, 2003.

Mises, Ludwig von. *Epistemological Problems of Economics.* George Reisman, trans. Princeton, NJ: Van Nostrand, 1960.

———. *Human Action: A Treatise on Economics.* Indianapolis, IN: Liberty Fund, 2007.

Rothbard, Murray. "Praxeology: A Reply to Mr. Schuller." *American Economic Review* (December 1951): 943–946.

———. "Praxeology and the Method of Economics." *Phenomenology and the Social Sciences.* vol. 2. M. Natanson, ed. Evanston, IL: Northwestern University Press, 1973. 311.

White, Lawrence H. *The Methodology of the Austrian School Economists.* Auburn, AL: Ludwig von Mises Institute, 1988.

PRICE, RICHARD (1723–1791)

Richard Price was a British moral and political philosopher and statistician. His most important work in the area of ethics was *A Review of the Principal Questions in Morals,* in which he argued that morality is inherent within actions and can be discerned through the use of reason. Price also was a dissenting minister and a founding member of the Unitarian Society in 1791. He is best known to history, however, for staunchly defending the American and French Revolutions.

The son of a Calvinist Congregational minister, Price was born on February 23, 1723, in Wales and was educated at a dissenting academy in London. In 1758, Price became a chaplain in the London district of Stoke Newington. The English Dissenters with whom Price identified objected to state interference into religious matters, especially to the status of Anglicanism as the established Church of England. Their critique of authority on this crucial matter naturally inclined them toward nonconformity in other areas.

His earliest book, *The Question of Morals,* published in 1758, was critical of the views set forth by his Scottish contemporary Francis Hutcheson and is often referred to as a precursor of Kant's statements on morality. This work established Price's reputation as an iconoclastic intellectual who was able to effectively criticize his peers without alienating them. Throughout his life, Price formed deep friendships with the leading intellectuals of his day, both in England and in America. He corresponded extensively with the British philosopher David Hume and the British Whig statesman the Earl of Shelburne, as well as with Benjamin Franklin and Thomas Jefferson.

As a result of his friendship with the British mathematician Thomas Bayes, Bayes's family asked Price to review the mathematician's unpublished papers upon his death. The resulting essay, written in 1763, "An Essay Towards Solving a Problem in the Doctrine of Chances," was submitted to the Royal Society and dealt with the question of probability. Price's presentation of Bayes's work introduced what is now known as Bayes's Theorem, a mathematical method of calculating the likelihood of an event recurring based on its past performance. The essay proved to be a breakthrough in probability theory.

On the basis of this work, in 1765, Price was admitted to the Royal Society. In the following year, he published his *Four Dissertations*—a collection of sermons—which dealt with his conclusions regarding the rational foundations of morality. The fourth dissertation, "On the Importance of Christianity and the Nature of Historical Evidence, and Miracles," disputed Hume's famous essay on miracles and in its place argued that they were in fact probable. Nevertheless, Price continued in the liberal religious tradition by rejecting such concepts as original sin. In 1767, the

University of Aberdeen conferred an honorary doctorate of divinity upon him.

In addition to his work in these areas, Price established a reputation as an original economic thinker, especially in the area of insurance and finance. In 1769, he published a pioneering work on life expectancy in the *Philosophical Transactions*, a scientific journal published by the Royal Society. A later work, "Observations on Reversionary Payments" (1771), laid the foundation for today's system of pensions and life insurance and underscored the inadequacy of the calculations then being used. At the request of William Pitt the Younger, later prime minister of Britain, Price published a pamphlet in 1772 titled "Appeal to the Public on the Subject of the National Debt," in which he decried the surging public debt and prescribed a program for eliminating it. The program became so widely respected that, in 1778, the U.S. Congress asked Price to advise the fledging United States on finance. He also wrote "Essay on the Population of England" (1780), which influenced the economic theorist Robert Malthus.

Price's support for American independence was first expressed in print in his "Observations on the Nature of Civil Liberty, the Principles of Government, and the Justice and Policy of the War with America." Price favored American independence on the principle of self-determination, and he argued that no social contract could alienate that principle. Within a few days, the "Observations" sold several thousand copies, prompting the release of a cheaper second edition that circulated widely in both Britain and America. The work sparked furious debate. In 1777, Price wrote a second pamphlet, "Additional Observations," to clarify his position in the face of severe opposition.

Considered a hero by the American revolutionaries, Price was offered American citizenship, which he declined. However, he did address Congress in 1778 and was awarded a degree by Yale in 1781. His final work on American independence was "Observations on the Importance of the American Revolution and the Means of Rendering It a Benefit to the World," and in it extended his arguments in support of the colonists' claims against the British crown.

Price also championed the French Revolution. Shortly after the fall of the Bastille, he delivered a sermon, "Discourse on the Love of Our Country," that was meant to commemorate the 101st anniversary of England's Glorious Revolution of 1688, through which the short reign of King James II had come to a bloodless end. In supporting the events of 1688, Price praised what he called the "two other Revolutions"—the American and French. In rebuttal, the British statesman Edmund Burke penned his famous antirevolutionary work, *Reflections on the Revolution in France*.

A fiery public debate followed the appearance of Price's pamphlet and Burke's response, which lasted years and had such wide-ranging implications that the historian Thomas W. Copeland referred to it as "the most crucial ideological debate ever carried on in English." Burke's arguments inspired responses not merely from Price, but also from Thomas Paine's *The Rights of Man* in 1792 and Mary Wollstonecraft's *A Vindication of the Rights of Men* in 1790.

Price died on April 19, 1791. His intimate friend and associate Joseph Priestley preached at his funeral service. Although they disagreed on many points of theory, the two men had been leading voices for "rational dissent" for decades. With Priestley, Price had written the influential work *A Free Discussion of the Doctrines of Materialism and Philosophical Necessity* (1778), which took the form of a debate. Perhaps it was in his openness to civil debate that Price most contributed to British intellectual history.

WME

See also Assurance and Trust; Burke, Edmund; Classical Economics; Enlightenment

Further Readings

Cone, Carl B. *Torchbearer of Freedom: The Influence of Richard Price on Eighteenth Century Thought.* Lexington: University of Kentucky Press, 1952.

Laboucheix, Henri. *Richard Price as Moral Philosopher and Political Theorist.* Oxford: Voltaire Foundation, 1982.

Peach, Bernard. *Richard Price and the Ethical Foundations of the American Revolution: Selections from His Pamphlets, with Appendices.* Durham, NC: Duke University Press, 1979.

Thomas, David Oswald, *Richard Price, 1723–1791.* Cardiff, UK: University of Wales Press, 1976.

PRICE CONTROLS

Price controls are said to exist whenever government mandates a maximum price ("price ceiling") above which a good or service cannot legally be sold or a minimum price ("price floor") below which a good or service cannot legally be sold.

Price ceilings attempt to lower the cost to the consumer of acquiring the price-ceilinged product, whereas a price floor attempts to increase the return received by sellers of the product in question. Both schemes achieve outcomes opposite of their objectives.

In markets without price controls, prices are determined by the interaction of the voluntary purchase and use decisions of buyers ("demand") with the voluntary production and sales decisions of sellers ("supply"). If, for whatever reason, buyers demand a product more intensely than had previously been the case—meaning that, at a specific price, they are prepared to buy greater quantities of it today than they were willing to buy yesterday—the result will be that the price will go up.

Although the precise process through which this higher price is achieved varies from market to market, the result is unambiguously desirable. If consumers want to use a product more intensely than before, it is appropriate that the economy produce more of it. Because increased production of a product requires that resources be drawn away from other productive enterprises, the cost per unit of producing any product will generally rise as that product is produced at a higher rate of output. In short, producers will increase the quantity they supply only if they can fetch a higher price for it.

This constraint also holds true for changes in supply. For example, if a hurricane inflicts unexpected damage to oil rigs and refineries, the price of gasoline will rise to reflect its now-greater scarcity. Thus, market prices reflect a multitude of deeper market conditions—conditions summarized by the terms *demand* and *supply*. They also prompt buyers and sellers to act in ways consistent with these underlying conditions. If the demand for apples increases, the resulting higher price for apples reflects this reality and prompts producers to supply more apples.

Price controls generate a distorted report of reality, causing buyers and suppliers to act in ways inconsistent with it. Suppose the market price of apples were $4 per pound if not for a government-enforced price ceiling of $3 per pound. This price ceiling misinforms consumers about the relative scarcity of apples, signaling them that apples are more abundant than they really are. The result is that consumers attempt to consume apples at too great a rate. This problem is compounded by the fact that the same price ceiling leads producers to ignore the real, higher value of apples and instead act as if consumers valued apples at only $3 per pound, thus supplying fewer apples than they would were the price $1 higher. The consequence is an apple shortage.

By itself, a shortage is bad enough. But shortages always are accompanied by subtler, less visible problems. One such problem is the extra expenditure of time and other nonmonetary resources on efforts to acquire the product. For example, when lines form, people spend extra time attempting to purchase a product in short supply. What determines how much of these nonmonetary resources consumers spend in such efforts?

The answer is the product's market value. The higher the market value, the greater is the value of time and other nonmonetary resources that consumers will spend attempting to acquire the product. Because a price ceiling causes suppliers to bring to market fewer units of the product than otherwise—making the product scarcer—the market value of the product rises above the value that would prevail without price controls. Consequently, a price ceiling increases the value of total resources (money plus nonmonetary resources) that are spent on the price-ceilinged product. The cost of the product rises, rather than falls.

One particular nonmonetary resource warrants specific mention. Those people with political and commercial connections are better able to acquire the price-ceilinged good through nonmarket means. The effect is to allocate such products in a more arbitrary manner than would be the case if government had not attempted to regulate prices.

A similar economic analysis applies to the consequences of price floors. By arbitrarily raising the price of a good or service above its market level, a price floor creates a surplus (a willingness of suppliers to supply greater quantities than consumers are willing to buy). Also like price ceilings, price floors reduce the quantities of the product that consumers actually acquire. Price ceilings do so by reducing the quantities supplied, whereas price floors do so by reducing the quantities consumers buy. This condition also creates advantages for certain parties. When a product is in surplus and its price is prevented from falling, sellers who have special connections with buyers are better able to sell their products than are sellers who enjoy no such advantages.

A final similarity worth mentioning is that, just as price ceilings cause the market value of products to be higher than otherwise, price floors cause the market value of products to be lower than otherwise (although the aim is to raise this value). By enticing suppliers to bring more to market than they would bring at the lower (uncontrolled) price, the market is flooded with more units of the product than consumers wish to buy—and more units than would be supplied at the uncontrolled price.

Market prices are not arbitrary figures. They reflect a deep and complex underlying reality. This reality—whether good or bad, improving or deteriorating—is best dealt with when it is revealed as accurately as possible. Price controls distort consumers' and producers' views of reality, leading them to act in harmful ways.

DJB

See also Free Trade; Interventionism; Wealth and Poverty

Further Readings

Becker, Gary. *Economic Theory*. Piscataway, NJ: Aldine Transaction, 2007.

Friedman, Milton; with Friedrich Hayek, George J. Stigler, Bertrand de Jouvenel, F. W. Paish, F. G. Pennance, E. O. Olsen, Sven, Rydenfelt, and M. Walker. *Rent Control: A Popular Paradox*. Montreal: Fraser Institute, 1975.

Friedman, Milton, and Steven Medema. *Price Theory*. Piscataway, NJ: Aldine Transaction, 2007.

Privacy

The term *privacy* has a wide range of connotations for libertarians as for scholars generally. In a broad sense, privacy refers to the condition obtained when one's intimate or personal life is inviolate. In political discourse, libertarians argue, as did the classical liberal theorists who preceded them, that one's personal life is bounded by property or contract rights. As with other liberties, libertarians are particularly concerned about the government's singular powers to violate privacy rights, particularly through the use of its police powers. Although a private actor might invade a person's privacy, libertarian analysis generally treats most such instances as trespasses, whereas the surveillance of workers by their employers is treated under contract law. Thus, for most libertarians, *privacy* refers to rights threatened by government surveillance or by the abuse of the police powers of search and seizure—types of informational privacy. Using the term more broadly, other state invasions of privacy would include laws against some types of consensual sexual relations between adults, such as prostitution, polygamy, or sodomy. Some libertarians also describe regulation of intimate sexual or family conduct as a privacy issue.

In the realm of informational privacy, threats to privacy emanating from government are essentially of two types. The first involves the state's misuse of information it has gathered about individuals, whereas the second relates to the misuse of its powers to gather information. An apt example of the first is the use of census data by National Socialists in Germany, Romania, and other countries to identify Jews and other targets of the Holocaust. Census data also were used by the U.S. government to identify Japanese Americans for relocation to concentration camps.

An example of the second is the "general warrant" used by British and Canadian law enforcement between 1662 and 1766 to conduct searches of private homes at any time of the day or night without notice. These warrants also could be used to arrest previously unspecified persons. To control the threat to human rights from the unique powers of government to arrest, try, and imprison members of the public, libertarians have consistently supported strict limits on the powers of government to collect information. Historically, most such limits have been procedural rather than substantive. That is, to the extent that governments submitted to restrictions in this area, the restrictions governed the means used to collect information (e.g., the requirement that the police obtain a warrant signed by a judge), but not on how long the information could be retained or on the type of information that could be kept.

Some of the best-known limits are those set out in the 4th Amendment in the Bill of Rights to the U.S. Constitution. Although not an invention of modern libertarians, the 4th Amendment was developed by their classical liberal intellectual forebears and is of central importance to libertarian constitutional theories in the United States. It reads,

The right of the people to be secure in their persons, houses, papers and effects, against unreasonable searches and seizures, shall not be violated, and no Warrant shall issue, but upon probable cause, supported by Oath or affirmation, and particularly describing the place to be searched, and the persons or things to be seized.

The 18th-century revolutionaries who drafted the 4th Amendment tailored it to prevent the use of the "general warrant" described earlier by requiring "probable cause" before a search and requiring the object of the search be described with particularity. But it also provides a powerful general model for controlling threats to privacy: It makes one branch of government, the executive, accountable to another, the judiciary, for proper exercise of its powers. Accountability is buttressed by the warrant requirement, which creates a "paper trail."

In 1998, libertarian science fiction writer David Brin published an interesting work of nonfiction, *The Transparent Society: Will Technology Force Us to Choose between Privacy and Freedom?* In it he offered a new analysis of privacy in modern society, pointing out that high costs now follow from anonymous and concealed antisocial behavior. Because of these costs, he argued that freedom of information and openness are ultimately preferable to privacy. Governments would best be restrained by laws and technology exposing authorities' conduct to public scrutiny. The impact of videotapings of incidents of police brutality offers an example of how this openness might work in practice. Although controversial, Brin's work offers an important challenge to some libertarian concerns that a modern world of information technology and databases is inherently harmful. He joins those, libertarian and otherwise, who have noted that broad notions of privacy can conflict with freedom, particularly freedom of speech.

For the most part, libertarians' concerns for privacy parallel those of civil libertarians or left liberals. There is, however, a substantial difference. Libertarians remain true to the conceptual and historical origin of privacy rights in property rights. As a corollary, they recognize the many advantages to using information about individuals and consumers voluntarily collected in the course of trade. The most familiar example is the form that credit reporting has taken in the United States. Credit reporting firms are free to collect both positive and negative information about who pays their bills. As a result, firms can make better informed lending decisions, keeping the costs of credit in the United States low compared with many other countries. Consumer data also are widely used for direct marketing in the United States, which tends to benefit consumers by forcing businesses to compete in offering more favorable terms.

By contrast, some left liberals or civil libertarians do not distinguish between the government's use or misuse of information and the collection of information by businesses or corporations. This view is widespread in Europe, where trade in consumers' personal information is restricted by data-protection laws. Somewhat ironically, although the earliest data-protection laws in Germany and Sweden were motivated by concerns with the growing power of the welfare state, the rules largely exempt the collection of information by government where the power to tax or pursue criminal prosecutions is concerned.

Advancing technology has affected the debate about privacy in two ways. First, modern encryption techniques allow those in the private sector to encode their messages in a manner unintelligible to the police (as they could in Thomas Jefferson's day). Second, modern surveillance technologies give the police access to information not available through traditional searches. For decades following the end of World War II, the U.S. government sought to control and prevent the spread of encryption technology to the private sector or other countries. Notably, libertarian computer scientist Dorothy Denning shared the view that encryption was so great a threat to the state's police powers that it should be built with hidden access for law enforcement. The majority of libertarian technologists opposed this view. Although encryption can be used by criminals, it also is useful to dissidents and vital to securing business communications. Strong encryption programs such as Phil Zimmerman's Pretty Good Privacy became widely available around the world, while U.S. export controls on encryption software weakened the position of the U.S. software industry. The U.S. government began to abandon its controls in the 1990s. However, the debate over encryption may well revive again as Internet telephony comes into wider use.

At the same time, advances in surveillance have reduced the traditional sphere of privacy. Two centuries ago, a conversation in the middle of a plowed field would have been completely private. Today, tiny electronic bugs, satellite cameras, and other devices have changed that. Infrared cameras and other devices allow the police to see into homes through closed doors and walls. In the United States, constitutional decisions have provided some protection in the case of wiretapping (*Katz v. United States*, 389 U.S. 347, 1967) and infrared devices (*Kyllo v. United States*, 533 U.S. 27, 2001). From a libertarian perspective, these cases are not entirely satisfactory because they depend on a circular theory of privacy expectations or custom, rather than a property rights theory. It is unclear, for example, why police wiretapping without a warrant violated expectations of privacy in 1967 given that the police (and others) had been actively engaged in wiretapping since the late 19th century. Yet these cases show how difficult it is to adapt a property rights theory of privacy to modern technology as technological advances tend to blur property lines. Who, for example, owns an e-mail or a telephone call as it traverses wires owned by the phone company?

The terrorist attacks on the World Trade Center on September 11, 2001, brought about a new phase in the debate about privacy that is likely to have global implications. With respect to surveillance within the United States, Congress passed the USA PATRIOT Act, which reduced the role of the courts in overseeing law enforcement and intelligence surveillance. The police were given somewhat broader authority to track Internet messages and tap phones and potentially broad access to business records in intelligence investigations. Globally, the United States pressed other countries to step up their own intelligence activities, especially in tracing financial transactions.

Perhaps the most significant shift in the debate, however, was in the renewed attention given to security methods that would have a considerable impact on privacy. The government again raised the issue of national identity cards, the use of a host of biometric devices including facial recognition scanners, and, increasingly, began the development of a variety of remote sensing devices. Most significant, the magnitude of the 9/11 attacks shifted the focus of law enforcement from the after-crime pursuit of those who were suspected of committing crimes to preventing future attacks, the "never again" mandate. This emphasis on identifying future risks has led to proposals from the Defense Department and other quarters to compile vast databases from which patterns of normal and risky behavior would emerge statistically, as with credit reporting. Such a project would represent a fundamental shift in law enforcement methods. So far, this shift has not happened. Most libertarians would oppose such proposals.

SS

See also Bioethics; Civil Society; Family; Sexuality; War on Terror

Further Readings

Brin, David. *The Transparent Society: Will Technology Force Us to Choose between Privacy and Freedom*. New York: Perseus, 1999.

Denning, Dorothy. *Information Warfare and Security*. Upper Saddle River, NJ: Pearson Education, 1998.

Epstein, Richard. "Deconstructing Privacy: And Putting It Back Together Again." *Social Philosophy and Policy* 17 no. 2 (2000): 1–24.

———. "HIPAA on Privacy: Its Unintended and Intended Consequences." *Cato Journal* 22 no. 1 (2002): 13–31.

Kahn, David. *The Codebreakers: The Story of Secret Writing*. New York: Scribner, 1996.

Klein, Daniel B. *Reputation*. Ann Arbor: University of Michigan Press, 1997.

Klein, Daniel B., and Jason Richner. "In Defense of the Credit Bureau." *Cato Journal* 12 no. 2 (1992): 393–412.

Singleton, Solveig. "Privacy versus the First Amendment: A Skeptical Approach." *Fordham Law Journal* 11 (2000): 97.

Volokh, Eugene. "Freedom of Speech and Information Privacy: The Troubling Implications of a Right to Stop People from Speaking About You." *Stanford Law Review* 52 (2000): 1049.

PRIVATE PROPERTY

Of the different configurations of property rights, only private property provides a workable basis for a free society, a productive economy, and justice. In the 18th century and earlier, the single word *property* was customarily used because it was understood intuitively that only private property provided the incentive to work hard. Treatises such as Adam Smith's *An Inquiry into the Nature and Causes of the Wealth of Nations* did not specify that private property was the indispensable foundation of political economy because hardly anyone championed an alternative. Private property was "sacred" and, therefore, needed no intellectual defense. By the 19th century, however, and particularly in the *Communist Manifesto* (1848), the phrase *private property* began to be used pejoratively. Aristotle had defended it in passing, but the incentives and disincentives of the different configurations of property had, by the 19th century, not yet been systematically analyzed. It could be said that private property was attacked before it was fully defended. Karl Marx gave no indication of understanding why private property was essential to economic life.

Private property restricts government power and decentralizes decision making. It confers on an individual the right to use and dispose of some good and to prevent others from doing so. In a free society, there will be thousands or millions of such owners. They can sell their rights to specific property to the highest bidder and retain the proceeds. With communal property, in contrast, the rights to some good are shared in an undefined fashion by a definite or indefinite number of people. A good portion of the U.S. landmass was communal before the arrival of Europeans. Within a family, many goods also are treated as communal. As for state property, the managers who control access to it are employed by the state and cannot legally profit from the sale of such assets. Normally, state property is not for sale at all. If it is, the proceeds are expected to go into the public treasury, not into the pockets of state employees.

Since the time of the Roman Republic, it has been understood that some goods are naturally managed by the state—those that are needed to provide for the common defense, for example, or for administering justice and enforcing the rule of law. The provision of these goods runs into the difficulty that nonpayers cannot easily be excluded from sharing in their benefits. But most goods, as the Romans agreed, are best owned privately. It is assumed that the economic analysis of private property also embraces the freedom of contract.

From about 1870 to 1990, nonetheless, a majority of Western intellectuals viewed private property critically. Given that it may have been first acquired by force and inherited by heirs of no necessary merit, how could it then be justified? To this question, David Hume offered an answer: The "stability of possession" was so important, he wrote, that dispossession was unwise in cases where the origin of the title had become "obscure through time." If we can only say that it may originally have been acquired by force, the injustice involved in seizing it is far greater than that involved in tolerating the mere possibility that remote ancestors were thieves. A distant and possible injustice would be "corrected" by a present and certain one.

Under the Stuart kings, Sir Robert Filmer had argued that all English law owed its existence to the royal will, and kings could therefore redistribute property as they saw fit. Replying in his *Two Treatises of Government*, John Locke located the right to property in labor. For every man, he argued,

> the labour of his body and the work of his hands, we may say, are properly his. Whatsoever then he removes out of the state that Nature hath provided, and left it in, he hath mixed his labour with, and joyned it to something that is his own, and thereby makes it his Property.

It is a measure of the unpopularity of private property among intellectuals in recent decades that a dozen academic works have been issued that attack Locke's defense, using arguments that the apologists for the Stuart tyranny might have admired, among them those written by, for example, Jeremy Waldron, Alan Ryan, Andrew Reeve, and G. A. Cohen. But all such arguments were futile inasmuch as the case for private property depends not on the ingenuity of philosophers, but on intractable features of human nature. The need for private property would be just as great if no philosophical defense of it had ever been written. The simplest argument for it is the minimal one. Property rights have to be assigned somehow if chaos is to be avoided, and the only known alternatives to private ownership—communal or state ownership—do not and will never work.

Communal property has this great defect. If the members of a commune have the right to equal shares in the overall product, those who work hard will subsidize those who do little. Idleness is thereby encouraged and industry discouraged. This phenomenon is generally known as the "free rider problem." It was restated in 1968 by Garrett Hardin in an influential article, "The Tragedy of the Commons." If an attempt is made to circumvent this problem by apportioning reward to effort, the commune has already moved halfway toward privatization.

The free rider problem is encountered when a group goes to a restaurant and shares the tab equally or in a "master-metered" apartment building where the utilities bill is divided equally among tenants. The solution—separate checks, individual utility meters—is the equivalent of "converting" from communal to private property. When such a conversion is made, efficiency increases—utility companies report that electricity consumption may decline by 20%— but, more important, justice is introduced. Heavy electricity users and expensive eaters will pay more, whereas the frugal will pay less. In short, each person is given his due.

This notion corresponds to the classical definition of *justice* found in Aristotle and Thomas Aquinas. Private property is comparable to a set of mirrors that reflects back on individuals the consequences of their acts, thereby, in an approximate way, institutionalizing justice in society. That is probably the single most important argument in favor of a private property system. The pilgrims who came to Plymouth Colony on the Mayflower in 1620 at first tried communal property and were on the point of starvation when they shifted to private ownership. "This had very good success," William Bradford reported, "for it made all hands very industrious, so as much more corn was planted than otherwise would have been." As for the "common course" or communal arrangement, it "was thought injustice."

Under stringent conditions, communes can be made to work. They must be small enough that members know one another, and they must be imbued with religious zeal or enthusiasm that imparts a spirit of self-sacrifice. This system would not be stable if its members were permitted to have children and to divide into families. Catholic, Orthodox, and Buddhist monasteries with communal property have survived for hundreds of years. The Israeli kibbutz attempted to preserve families and do away with private property, but was unable to do so. By 1989, the 3% of the population then living on kibbutzim had accumulated debts of $4 billion, which were paid by the state.

As for state ownership, the lengthy experiment in Soviet Russia proved that it could not be the basis of a productive economy. Central planners did not have enough information to know what commands to give, and the planning system reduced the people to a form of slavery. They had no incentive to do more than the minimum required to avoid punishment. The failure of this experiment was disguised for a long time by the Western acceptance of Soviet statistics. Both the Central Intelligence Agency and Paul Samuelson's best-selling textbook, *Economics*, reported for decades that the Soviet economy was growing twice as fast as the U.S. economy. In the year the Berlin Wall fell, the *Statistical Abstract of the United States* maintained that the per capita income in East Germany was higher than in West Germany. It also was hoped that the abolition of private property would promote a change in human nature. But "New Soviet Man" stubbornly refused to appear.

A kind of taboo surrounded the discussion of property in the Western world while the Soviet experiment was underway. After it was over, books favorable to private property began to appear. Long obscured and almost forgotten, private property at once appeared as a kind of lens through which history could be reviewed. Empires that had succeeded in the past, such as the Roman and the British, were shown to have legal systems that gave security to property and so encouraged the accumulation of wealth. Countries that have conspicuously failed in our own day, often referred to as the Third World, have been shown to have lacked secure, transferable private property rights. Against all post–World War II predictions, the West has widened its economic lead, and the most important reason was that it had retained the institution whose importance Western elites had failed to grasp: private property.

In the decades ahead, the pressure to privatize property where it has not already occurred will grow stronger as the population increases.

TB

See also Externalities; Free-Market Economy; Privacy; Rule of Law

Further Readings

Bethell, Tom. *The Noblest Tiumph: Property and Prosperity through the Ages.* New York: St. Martin's Press, 1998.

Bradford, William. *Of Plymouth Plantation.* Samuel Eliot Morison, ed. New York: Knopf, 1952.

Cohen, G. A. *Self-ownership, Freedom and Equality.* Cambridge: Cambridge University Press, 1995.

Hume, David. *A Treatise of Human Nature, 1739–1740.* Oxford: Oxford University Press, 2000.

Locke, John. *Two Treatises of Government.* Peter Laslett, ed. Cambridge: Cambridge University Press, 1960.

Pipes, Richard. *Property and Freedom.* New York: Knopf, 1999.

Reeve, Andrew. *Property.* London: Macmillan Education, 1986.

Ryan, Alan. *Property.* Milton Keynes: Open University Press, 1987.

———. *Property and Political Theory.* Oxford: Basil Blackwell, 1984.

Waldron, Jeremy. *The Right to Private Property.* Oxford: Clarendon Press, 1998.

PRIVATIZATION

Privatization refers to the shift of functions and responsibilities, in whole or in part, from the public to the private sector. Its best-known form is the transfer of state-owned assets and enterprises to private hands, while another takes the form of the granting of long-term franchises or concessions by government, under which the private sector finances, builds, and operates major infrastructure. The best-known American form of privatization is the outsourcing or competitive contracting of public services. Some theorists also consider the issuance of government vouchers as a form of privatization, in which government provides the purchasing power to an eligible subset of citizens, who are then free to select their own service provider.

Although the specific application of privatization dates back to the 18th century (with franchised British turnpikes), the term dates to 1969, when the management expert Peter Drucker coined the term *reprivatize* in predicting that Europe's nationalized industries would one day be returned to ownership of private investors. Shortened to *privatize*, the term was later used in the United States primarily in the context of urging governments to seek private bidders to deliver municipal services. The term was employed in Great Britain in the latter part of the 1970s, again initially in the context of municipal service delivery and later in Drucker's original sense, meaning the divestiture of state-owned enterprises, as put into practice by Prime Minister Margaret Thatcher beginning in the early 1980s.

A useful typology for identifying various forms of privatization can be produced by separating the questions of which party—the public or private sector—is responsible for the funding for an activity and its delivery. If government acts as the purchasing agent for the citizenry as a whole, by selecting a firm to produce a service or operate a facility, we call this *outsourcing* or *competitive contracting*. But if government gives the purchasing power and decision making to each individual making up a category of eligible citizens (e.g., low-income renters), we call that form *vouchers*.

We do not have many examples of the private sector paying for a function while the government produces it, but private parties do sometimes purchase services from government (e.g., police crowd control at sports events). Additionally, there are important cases in which both the funding and the production of traditional governmental functions are carried out by the private sector. This private production of traditionally state-provided goods is certainly the case when government sells a state-owned enterprise, which then becomes a private enterprise. But it also is the case where government sees to it that a major infrastructure project—a wastewater plant, railroad, airport, or toll road—is developed and operated, by granting a long-term franchise whose terms are such that the winning franchisee can finance, build, and operate the project as business.

The sale of state-owned enterprises became one of the trademark issues of the government of Margaret Thatcher in the United Kingdom during the 1980s. Initially limited to selling off formerly nationalized companies such as British Airways, British Petroleum, British Steel, and eventually British Rail, the policy expanded to utilities and infrastructure that had always been in the public sector, including British Telecom, the British Airports Authority, and the electric, gas, and water industries. Thatcher's motivation was partly economic—to modernize and improve the efficiency of costly and bureaucratic state enterprises. But it was partly political and ideological, which is why it emphasized widespread public stock offerings to create a "share-owning democracy" in which average people owned equity stakes in companies.

These rapid and largely successful privatizations gave the idea considerable credibility as well as provided exportable expertise for British law firms, investment bankers, and consultants. During the 1980s, similar divestitures spread to France and several other parts of Europe, as well as to Australia and New Zealand. Both the idea and practice became far more widespread in the 1990s as privatization by divestiture spread to developing countries in Latin America, southern and eastern Europe, and Southeast Asia. By the end of 1999, the two decades of privatization had shifted more than $1 trillion of asset value from the public to the private sector. Even Russia—where privatization was plagued with corruption and insider dealing—shifted more than half of its productive enterprises out of state ownership by the end of the decade.

The United States participated in the divestiture wave to a limited degree. During the Reagan administration, Congress privatized Conrail for $1.6 billion, but efforts to sell other federal assets and enterprises languished until the Clinton years. Then the combination of New Democrat influences in the administration and Republican control of Congress led to the sale of the National Helium Reserve, the Elk Hills Naval Petroleum Reserve, the uranium-processing United States Enrichment Corporation, the Alaska Power Administration, and tens of billions of dollars' worth of electromagnetic frequency spectrum—all ideas proposed during the Reagan years, but considered politically impossible then. However, the decade ended with a long list of proposed divestiture candidates—Amtrak, air traffic control, the U.S. Postal Service, the Tennessee Valley Authority—still more talked about than seriously considered. At the state and local levels, despite many billions of dollars' worth of government-owned businesses (parking structures, electric and gas utilities, water and sewer systems, airports) that were being divested in other countries, only a handful of such enterprises were transferred to private ownership.

The idea of governments granting charters or franchises under which investors can develop and operate major infrastructure dates back to early toll roads, canals, and railroads in both the United States and Britain. Often, especially when some degree of monopoly power was judged to be present, such franchises provided for government regulation of rates or profits, or both. It was under this model that the United States—almost unique in the world—developed a largely investor-owned electricity and telephone industry. Interestingly, in the case of water supply, the United States instead generally opted for the European model of government enterprise. The original New York subway systems, as well as most trolley systems, also were developed and operated by private firms under long-term franchises and were generally taken over by government only after decades of price controls had driven them into bankruptcy.

The idea of long-term infrastructure franchises was revived in France and Italy in the 1950s to encourage the building of intercity toll-road networks. It later spread to

Spain and Portugal, and it may have served as the inspiration for what became the $15 billion Channel Tunnel in the 1980s, the largest privately financed project to date. During the 1990s, it spread rapidly to the developing countries in the form of numerous toll road, electricity, railroad, and water/wastewater projects in Latin America and Southeast Asia. Many of these projects actually aimed at the expansion and modernization of run-down and inadequate state-owned infrastructure, rather than the construction of entirely new facilities.

In the United States, the 1990s brought a modest revival of the infrastructure franchise idea. Some 15 states passed enabling legislation for private toll roads, although only a handful of projects had been built by the end of the decade. A small number of new water and wastewater treatment plants also had been developed by private firms using this model. In addition, a $1.2 billion international airport terminal was under construction at New York's Kennedy airport under a 25-year franchise agreement.

The United States leads the world in outsourcing public service delivery to private firms. Tens of thousands of such contracts are in effect at the municipal level, for everything from ambulance service to zoning inspection. The practice began in the 1960s and 1970s, generally in newly incorporated cities in the Sunbelt with populations less than 100,000. During the 1980s, it spread to larger and more-established cities and to a wider range of services. By the 1990s, competitive contracting was being practiced even in large, heavily unionized cities like Chicago, Cleveland, Milwaukee, Philadelphia, and New York. Some mayors used outsourcing selectively, in part, to threaten unionized workforces. But others used it systematically, as a basic change in modus operandi. A case in point is two-term Indianapolis mayor Steve Goldsmith, who put more than 75 city services through the competitive process, saving taxpayers some $400 million in the process. Many state governments became practitioners of outsourcing in the 1990s, in areas ranging from inventory management to highway maintenance to prison operation.

Outsourcing has gradually spread to other countries. The Thatcher government mandated outsourcing for certain local public services, and reforms that encouraged outsourcing were adopted in Australia and New Zealand. In selected public service fields (e.g., water supply, jails and prisons, and garbage collection), outsourcing can be found in cities in other European countries and, increasingly, in Latin America.

The final broad category of privatization is vouchers, in which government designates a certain subset of the population as eligible and provides those people with a piece of paper that they can use to purchase the service in question. Food stamps are a classic example: Recipients can make their own selection from a large variety of private providers. For several decades, the federal Department of Housing and Urban Development has provided housing vouchers as a partial alternative to providing a larger supply of public housing projects. Ever since the end of World War II, the federal government has offered higher education vouchers to veterans under the GI bill and its successors. Additionally, a growing number of counties and states make use of vouchers for a variety of social services, where a variety of providers make it more likely that individual clients can find a match that meets their needs.

It was only in the 1990s, when serious efforts were made to implement vouchers for K–12 education, that vouchers became highly controversial. Pilot voucher programs were established in Milwaukee, Cleveland, and Florida—in every case subject to court challenges on a variety of grounds. The underlying idea of injecting competition into the delivery of K–12 schooling expanded into the charter school movement, under which nominally public schools are largely deregulated and, in some cases, can be operated by private (nonprofit and for-profit) organizations.

RWP

See also Civil Society; Education; Private Property; Socialism; Welfare State

Further Readings

Donohue, John D. *The Privatization Decision: Public Ends, Private Means.* New York: Basic Books, 1989.

Drucker, Peter F. *The Age of Discontinuity.* New York: Harper & Row, 1969.

Eggers, William D., and John O'Leary. *Revolution at the Roots.* New York: Free Press, 1995.

Goldsmith, Stephen. *The Twenty-First Century City.* Washington, DC: Regnery, 1997.

Hudson, Wade, ed. *Privatization 1999.* Los Angeles: Reason Public Policy Institute, 1999.

Pirie, Madsen. *Dismantling the State: The Theory and Practice of Privatization.* Dallas, TX: National Center for Policy Analysis, 1985.

Poole, Robert W., Jr. *Cutting Back City Hall.* New York: Universe Books, 1980.

Savas, E. S. *Privatization and Public–Private Partnerships.* New York: Seven Bridges Press/Chatham House, 2000.

Vickers, John, and George Yarrow. *Privatization: An Economic Analysis.* Cambridge, MA: MIT Press, 1988.

Walker, Michael A. *Privatization: Theory and Practice.* Vancouver, BC, Canada: Fraser Institute, 1980.

Progress

According to the eminent historian J. B. Bury, the idea of human progress "is based on an interpretation of history which regards men as slowly advancing . . . in a definite and desirable direction, and infers that this progress will continue indefinitely." Bury contends that progress, in this sense, is a distinctively modern notion—one that does not begin to take shape until the 16th and 17th centuries, whereas other historians, such as Robert Nisbet, attribute the idea to Greek, Roman, and Christian writers long before the advent of the modern era.

A libertarian theory of progress is one that stresses the role of liberty in the progressive improvement of humankind. Whatever position we may take in the historical controversies about the origin of the idea of progress and its relationship to other ideas (such as the belief in an Arcadian golden age, original sin, and divine providence), there can be little doubt that the link between individual freedom and progress was forged by post-Renaissance philosophers, historians, economists, and social theorists.

In *The Idea of Progress*, Bury divides modern theories of progress into two types, which he characterizes as socialist and liberal. The socialist version he describes as "a symmetrical system in which the authority of the state is preponderant, and the individual has little more value than a cog in a well-oiled wheel: his place is assigned; it is not his right to go his own way." Liberalism, in contrast, views individual freedom and social diversity as essential to progress. Unlike the closed system of socialism, in which the ultimate goal of progress is foreseeable, having been mapped out in advance by central planners, classical liberalism was historically affiliated with a theory known as "indefinite progress." In this approach, no limits can be set to progress, nor can we predict the exact path or form that progress will take. "Individual liberty is the motive force" of indefinite progress, and this decentralized, spontaneous process generates rapid innovations that cannot be predicted or controlled by any individual, group, or institution, including government.

Theories of progress are typically concerned with three spheres of human activity: intellectual, moral, and economic.

Libertarian theories of intellectual progress emerged during the 17th century, as John Milton, Benedict Spinoza, and John Locke, among others, argued that freedom of thought, discussion, and publication are essential to the advancement of knowledge. Often grouped under the collective label of "liberty of conscience," these freedoms came to be widely accepted as indispensable to the pursuit of truth in religion, science, and other spheres, and they played a crucial role in the struggle for religious toleration.

We do not find this near-unanimity, even among libertarian thinkers, on the subject of moral progress. It has often been pointed out that knowledge can be used for good or evil purposes, and some liberals, such as Adam Ferguson and Joseph Priestley, warned against the enervating effects of luxury and other vices, which they believed would lead to the corruption of those moral virtues necessary to sustain a free society. Other liberals disagreed. In the writings of David Hume, Edward Gibbon, Adam Smith, and others, we see various arguments in defense of luxury and other personal vices (i.e., those that do not violate the rights of others) based largely on their unintended, but beneficial, consequences to society as a whole. Many of these arguments are variations on a theme first presented by the Dutch philosopher Bernard Mandeville in his notorious book, *The Fable of the Bees: Or, Private Vices, Publick Benefits*, first published in 1705 as *The Grumbling Hive* and greatly expanded in subsequent editions.

Another internal debate among classical liberals addressed the possibility of moral progress, a topic that received a good deal of attention during the 19th century. W. E. H. Lecky, J. S. Mill, Herbert Spencer, and many other liberals maintained that progress in the moral sphere (especially the "sentiment of justice") is as evident in the historical record as any other kind of progress, and they point to advances in religious toleration, the repudiation of torture, and the abolition of slavery to buttress their case. But other liberals, most notably H. T. Buckle and others influenced by the positivistic sociology of Auguste Comte, presented a different analysis.

In the first volume of his best-selling *Introduction to the History of Civilization in England* (1857), Buckle defends the thesis that moral sentiments and motives, unlike knowledge, are "stationary" and do not progress from one generation to the next. As Buckle put it, "the sole essentials of morals . . . have been known for thousands of years, and not one jot or tittle has been added to them by all the sermons, homilies, and text-books which moralists and theologians have been able to produce." True progress occurs in the realm of knowledge as people become more cognizant of the long-range consequences of their decisions and actions.

Perhaps the most important contribution of libertarian thinkers was in the sphere of economic progress. The growth of commerce, or what was sometimes called the *commercial spirit*, was widely regarded by liberals as a lynchpin of socioeconomic progress.

In Book III of *The Wealth of Nations*, Adam Smith discusses "the natural progress of opulence." The motive of self-interest, when confined within the sphere of justice, naturally leads to a division of labor that is "advantageous to all the different persons employed in the various occupations." This natural economic order—which develops spontaneously, without foresight or central planning—is called *natural* because it is "promoted by the natural inclinations of men" in a "system of natural liberty," in which the equal rights of every individual to life, liberty, and property are secured by a just system of law and government.

Free-market liberals agreed with Montesquieu that the "natural effect of commerce is to lead to peace" because trade creates a mutual dependence among nations, and "all unions are founded on mutual needs." Progress, in this view, is best achieved during periods of peace.

Although many liberals—such as the physiocrats Turgot, David Hume, and Adam Smith in the 18th century and H. T. Buckle, Frédéric Bastiat, Richard Cobden, and John Bright in the 19th century—emphasized the connection between free trade and peace and the resulting progress these made possible, the most systematic exposition of this theme appears in the voluminous writings of Herbert Spencer. Elaborating on a distinction made by H. S. Maine between societies based on status as opposed to those based on contract, Spencer dubbed two basic types of social organization *militant* and *industrial*.

According to Spencer, it is primarily due to the growth of commerce that the despotism and "compulsory cooperation" of a militant social structure evolve into the individual freedom and "voluntary cooperation" that characterize industrial society. The contractual relationships of commerce, "in which the mutual rendering of services is unforced and neither individual subordinated becomes the predominant relationship throughout society," as its perceived benefits are extended to other forms of social relationships. "Right of private judgment in religious matters gradually establishes itself along with the establishment of political rights," and coercive uniformity gives place to "a varied non-conformity maintained by willing union." Hence, the growth of commerce naturally tends to generate progress "through stages of increasing freedom," and this progress is accompanied by an ideological development of "sentiments and ideas," such as the principles of individual rights and limited government. Certainly if mankind's progress is causally related to the extension of individual liberty, there is less reason today to believe that this progress is, over the long term, inevitable. There appears no reason to accept the view that individual autonomy will inexorably flourish and expand and that the free and peaceful interactions among people will play an increasingly greater role in social life. Indeed, given the history of the 20th century, there is ample evidence to point to the fragility of free and peaceful societies.

GHS

See also Development, Economic; Enlightenment; Industrial Revolution; Mandeville, Bernard; Spencer, Herbert; Wealth and Poverty

Further Readings

Baillie, John. *The Belief in Progress*. London: Oxford University Press, 1950.

Bury, J. B. *The Idea of Progress: An Inquiry into Its Growth and Origins*. New York: Dover Publications, 1955.

Condorcet, J. A. N. de Caritat. *Selected Writings*. Keith Baker, ed. New York: Macmillan, 1976.

Nisbet, Robert. *History of the Idea of Progress*. New York: Basic Books, 1980.

Spadafora, David. *The Idea of Progress in Eighteenth-Century Britain*. New Haven, CT: Yale University Press, 1990.

Spencer, Herbert. *Essays: Scientific, Political, and Speculative. Library Edition, containing Seven Essays Not before Republished, and Various Other Additions*. 3 vols. London: Williams & Norgate, 1891.

PROGRESSIVE ERA

At the close of the Civil War in 1865, the United States was still primarily a rural and agricultural society. Business was conducted in local or regional markets by family farms, and small firms were owned and operated by single individuals or small groups of partners. The scale of production was modest, consumption for most was limited to little beyond life's necessities, and, among white Americans, wealth, with some notable exceptions, was distributed without great gaps separating rich from poor. But by 1890, huge manufacturing corporations employing a succession of revolutionary new machines and processes had begun to create the modern American economy of mass production and consumption. Millions of farm workers had left the countryside for the cities to labor for the new industrial giants, and vast quantities of material wealth were being produced by American businesses and consumed by ordinary people across the country. With these rapid economic changes came an array of new conditions and problems that alarmed and confused Americans of the time: unprecedented disparities in the distribution of newly created wealth; the transformation of previously independent, entrepreneurial artisans and merchants into wage-earning workers in large, hierarchical organizations; a growing industrial proletariat increasingly composed of immigrants crowded into urban slums; and the disproportionate, often corrupting influence of wealthy industrialists in the political system. The political reaction provoked by these economic and social changes in the years between 1890 and the First World War defines the Progressive Era, a quarter century of reform in which Americans attempted to adjust their traditional system of political economy to the new realities of the industrial age.

The first and most important of these reforms was the Sherman Act, passed in 1890 in the midst of an impassioned national debate over whether and how government should be used to rein in the trusts, as the huge corporations came to be called. Some, pointing to the ever lower cost at which the trusts could produce enormous quantities of goods, argued that they were the inevitable outcome of technological progress and should be allowed to grow as large as necessary to efficiently meet the demand of consumers in the market. Others cited the growing market power accumulated by the trusts as they swallowed smaller firms, the deadening effects of hierarchical corporate planning on individual autonomy and initiative, the closing of entrepreneurial opportunity in now highly capital-intensive industries, and the corruption bred by the infusion of great private wealth into democratic politics, and called for strict government regulation or the outright destruction of firms that had grown too big. Unable to reconcile these sharply divergent positions that ushered in an array of different policies, Congress avoided resolving the issue by passing a terse, vague statute that made the restraint or monopolizing of commerce a criminal offense and leaving it to the federal courts to decide what this actually meant, thus placing in the hands of the courts the task of defining what American policy toward the trusts was to be. After more than 20 years of uncertain interpretation, during which both positions had their moments in the judicial sun and the nation endured a major economic depression and a wave of industrial consolidation, in 1911 the Supreme Court at last decided in favor of large companies only if their size was a function of fair competition. In dismantling John D. Rockefeller's Standard Oil Company because of its "unreasonable" competitive behavior, the Court held that the mere size or market power of a corporation, no matter how great, would not violate the Sherman Act unless, like Standard Oil's, it was achieved through unfair or abusive means. This ruling was the pivotal political outcome of the Progressive Era; once the decision for efficient wealth creation in large, hierarchical firms had been made, all that remained was to create the political machinery needed to administer the policy and ameliorate the harsher economic and social consequences of large-scale industrial organization.

Given the original Framers' distrust of a strong federal government, the movement to achieve this adjustment began in the states and municipalities and was pursued on several fronts. The judicial acceptance of bigness was complemented by local legislation to regulate the rates and operation of public utilities. The settlement house movement, led by Jane Addams of Hull House in Chicago, addressed the problem of urban poverty by attempting to meet the everyday needs of the poor through close contact with sympathetic social workers. It and the Social Gospel preached by religiously inspired progressives moved others to successfully press for state laws limiting hours of work and enforcing changes in working environments aimed at making them safer and healthier in a broad range of industries. Many of these, however, were struck down by the Supreme Court for infringing on the "liberty of contract" that had been read into the 14th Amendment in 1897. To progressives, these new government responsibilities also seemed to require an extension of democracy, a political process more open and receptive to the public's needs and less responsive to the partisan maneuverings and patronage characteristic of local politics. In several states, procedural reforms such as direct party primaries, public referenda and ballot initiatives, and the recall of public officials were instituted, and cities began to

replace unsystematic government by party politicians with what was regarded as scientific administration by nonpartisan, expert city managers and commissions. The movement for women's suffrage gained strength throughout the period, culminating in the ratification of the 19th Amendment in 1920. On the national level, the 17th Amendment, ratified in 1913, moved the election of U.S. senators from the state legislatures to the voters. The protective tariff, the federal government's chief source of revenue, but seen by many as a device primarily aimed at enriching the trusts, was significantly lowered, and the nation's finances were revolutionized by the introduction of the income tax in 1913. The spectacle of Theodore Roosevelt imploring J. P. Morgan to save the nation's financial system during the Panic of 1907 eased the way for the creation of the Federal Reserve System 6 years later.

The moralistic tone of many progressive reformers encouraged an element of coercion and social control in their proposals, illustrated by the temperance movement that succeeded in imposing Prohibition in 1920. For many, progressivism also entailed a commitment to racial purity and cultural homogeneity and with it a large measure of racism. Progressives, facing resistance from southerners fearful that a national government powerful enough to regulate industry also would be powerful enough to enforce racial integration, bought Southern cooperation by turning away from the plight of African Americans. Several leading progressives traced the nation's problems and the frightening specters of socialism and anarchism directly to the influx of immigrants from eastern and southern Europe, increasing sentiment for closing the borders that led to the sharp restrictions on immigration enacted early in the 1920s. After the easy victory over Spain in 1898, the nation flirted with what supporters saw as a benevolent imperialism until a revolt in the Philippines exposed its costs and contradictions.

Indeed, the ideological primacy of the public interest has been the most important and permanent legacy of the Progressive Era. Before the Civil War, Americans generally understood political order in Lockean terms. Legitimate authority was the product of an agreement among free individuals whose validity depended on the continuing consent of those it bound. The state had neither life nor purposes of its own, but was simply an organizational device with limited powers created by individuals to promote their own welfare. But by 1900, through the efforts of such progressive intellectuals as John Bates Clark, Lester Ward, Richard T. Ely, and the young Woodrow Wilson, this view had largely been supplanted by a democratic collectivism in which, like the German model that inspired its proponents, the individual was but a cell within the larger organism of society, and the authority of the democratic state to articulate and act on the interests of the collective was unbounded. The success of the great corporations in harnessing the labors of thousands and turning them to the achievement of a single purpose drew progressive reformers to a distinctively American ideal of scientifically informed control of social and political life in the service of a collectively defined public interest. Politics, as Wilson put it in 1887, could now be separated from administration. Just as scientifically trained managers could rationally pursue profit in the interest of the corporation, the institutions of democratic government could be devoted to identifying the interests of the social organism, and a corps of disinterested, expert administrators, equipped with the conceptual tools of the emerging social sciences, charged with furthering them. It was this commitment to what was understood to be nonpartisan, scientific administration in the public interest that united the many strands of progressive reform, and if many of the specific reforms of the period have proved ephemeral, the influence of the managerial vision through the 20th century has been continuous and profound.

RA

See also Antitrust; Genetics; Interventionism; New Deal; Prohibition of Alcohol; Urban Planning; Welfare State

Further Readings

Cooper, John Milton. *Pivotal Decades: The United States, 1900–1920.* New York: W. W. Norton, 1990.

Diner, Steven J. *A Very Different Age: Americans of the Progressive Era.* New York: Hill & Wang, 1998.

Eisenach, Eldon J. *The Lost Promise of Progressivism.* Lawrence: University Press of Kansas, 1994.

Ekirch, Arthur A. *Progressivism in America: A Study of the Era from Theodore Roosevelt to Woodrow Wilson.* New York: New Viewpoints, 1974.

Gilbert, James. *Designing the Industrial State: The Intellectual Pursuit of Collectivism in America, 1880–1940.* Chicago: Quadrangle Books, 1972.

Gould, Lewis L. *America in the Progressive Era, 1890–1914.* Harlow, UK: Longman, 2001.

Hofstadter, Richard. *The Age of Reform: From Bryan to F. D. R.* New York: Knopf, 1956.

Rodgers, Daniel T. *Atlantic Crossings: Social Politics in a Progressive Age.* Cambridge, MA: Harvard University Press, 1998.

Sklar, Martin J. *The Corporate Reconstruction of American Capitalism, 1890–1916: The Market, the Law, and Politics.* New York: Cambridge University Press, 1988.

Tariello, Ralph. *The Reconstruction of American Political Ideology, 1865–1917.* Charlottesville: University Press of Virginia, 1982.

PROHIBITION OF ALCOHOL

America's discomfort with alcohol developed in the mid-19th century. Previously, alcoholic beverages were an established facet of American society: George Washington operated a whiskey distillery, Thomas Jefferson dabbled in viticulture, and Samuel Adams had his brewery. Hard cider and rum enjoyed mass appeal, and rum was a common barter item in the cash-strapped New World. Even religiously rigid groups such as the Puritans and the Quakers stressed moderation rather than abstinence.

Following the Revolution, the expanding western frontier contributed to turning the nation's tastes from cider and rum to whiskey and beer. Isolated western farmers found it easier to transport whiskey rather than raw grain to urban markets. In the 1840s, immigrants introduced German yeast strains and brewing methods, resulting in lager beers that kept better than British-style ales and porters, while the post–Civil War railroad boom allowed distillers and brewers to dispense their products nationally.

The resulting abundance of alcoholic beverages—and the saloons that served them—horrified the nation's first prohibitionists. By the mid-1800s, abstinence from alcohol had become an intrinsic element of many evangelical movements, which saw alcohol as an enslaver of men and insisted that one of the functions of government was to foster a moral society. Therefore, prohibitionist groups such as the Anti-Saloon League adopted a strategy of driving brewers and distillers out of business through government action. They did so by making drinking culturally and politically opprobrious and by vilifying politicians who opposed alcohol's opponents. The result of these efforts was that, by the end of 1919, 33 states had either full or partial prohibition.

Entry into World War I gave the federal government great control over the country's agricultural production and provided utilitarian ammunition to prohibitionists, who ticked off the pounds of grain lost to brewing and the man-hours wasted in saloons that could be spent making bullets and bayonets. Various acts and measures whittled down alcohol production, including the Wartime Prohibition Act of 1918, which was signed into law 10 days *after* the November 11 armistice in Europe. It was in this wartime atmosphere of privation, sobriety, and xenophobia toward all things German (including German American brewers and their products) that Congress passed a constitutional amendment prohibiting the manufacture, sale, and transportation of intoxicating liquors and sent it to the states for ratification. On January 16, 1919, Nebraska became the 36th state to ratify the 18th Amendment; of the 48 states, only Connecticut and Rhode Island declined their approval.

The amendment went into effect exactly 1 year later. The National Prohibition Enforcement Act, introduced by Representative Andrew Volstead (R–Minn.), but written by the Anti-Saloon League's general counsel Wayne Wheeler, gave teeth to the amendment by banning any beverage with an alcohol content of 0.5% or greater and establishing a Bureau of Prohibition within the Internal Revenue Service responsible for enforcement.

Prohibition, of course, did not stop drinking in the United States. Although per capita alcohol consumption did drop sharply during the early years of Prohibition, by the latter half of the 1920s, it had rebounded to 60% to 70% of its pre-Prohibition level and remained steady before and after repeal. Certainly crime did not decrease. According to one study, crime in 30 major cities increased 24% between 1920 and 1921. In Philadelphia alone, drunkenness-related arrests nearly tripled from 20,443 in 1920 to 58,517 in 1925. The national homicide rate climbed from about 7 per 100,000 people in 1919 to nearly 10 per 100,000 by 1933, and then it dropped sharply after repeal.

Domestic moonshine and industrial alcohol provided the majority of the alcohol consumed during Prohibition. Moonshiners would distill neutral grain spirits in hidden stills and then attempt to mimic the color and flavor of whiskey or gin with additives called *congeners*. Industrial alcohol, denatured by government order to make it undrinkable, was typically repassed through a still to remove the poisons, but not always successfully. Thus, between 1925 and 1929, 40 out of every 1 million Americans died from toxic liquor.

The rest of the booze was smuggled over land or by sea. Scarcity of alcohol meant it could be sold in the United States for anywhere between two to five times its purchase price in Canada, Mexico, or the West Indies. In the early 1920s, vessels formed "rum rows" off the American coast. After 1924, however, most freelance entrepreneurs—tramp merchant marines or fishermen seeking an easy profit—were muscled out by crime syndicates.

Public disenchantment with Prohibition grew throughout the 1920s and into the next decade. In 1930 and 1931, polls by the National Economic League found that the top three concerns of Americans related to Prohibition and its consequent lawlessness, ahead of issues regarding unemployment and the economy. Another 1930 poll revealed that almost 70% of Americans favored repeal or modification of the Volstead Act. Repeal groups formed, and their memberships swelled. In January 1931, a majority of the 11 panelists of the National Commission on Law Observation and Enforcement, appointed by President Herbert Hoover 2 years earlier to review Prohibition's effects, favored total repeal or alteration of the Volstead Act. Yet Hoover, a hardline dry, instead interpreted the Wickersham Report as an affirmation of Prohibition and did nothing.

By hitching the administration so closely to the dry cause, Hoover and the Republicans sealed their doom in the 1932 presidential election. The Democrats made repeal a part of their platform, whereas the Republicans adopted an ambiguous "moist" plank that endeared them to no one, further crippling a president already blamed for mishandling the economy. Proposed remedies such as alcohol taxes, jobs relating to alcohol manufacture and service, reopening legal markets to grain farmers, and eliminating the Bureau of

Prohibition further incited politicians to act for repeal. After the election, the Democratic majority in both houses passed the 21st Amendment, with Utah becoming the 36th state to ratify the amendment on December 5, 1933.

Decades after repeal, both state and federal government sustain control over the manufacture, sale, and consumption of alcohol. Eighteen states currently hold partial or full monopolies on the sale of alcoholic beverages, while most others have blue laws (often for protectionist purposes) limiting where and when alcohol may be sold. The National Minimum Drinking Age Act of 1984, which withholds federal highway funds to states that allow the sale of alcohol to people under 21 years old, effectively nationalized what had been a state-level decision. Meanwhile, private prohibitionist groups continue to agitate for increasingly strict or arbitrary blood-alcohol limits for drivers (e.g., at their discretion, police in Washington, D.C., may arrest drivers with any amount of alcohol in their systems) and for legislation criminalizing parents who serve alcohol to their children at home.

JaK

See also Black Markets; Drug Prohibition; Illicit Drugs

Further Readings

Cashman, Sean Dennis. *Prohibition: The Lie of the Land*. New York: Free Press, 1981.

Kerr, K. Austin. *Organized for Prohibition: A New History of the Anti-Saloon League*. New Haven, CT: Yale University Press, 1985.

Lerner, Michael A. *Dry Manhattan: Prohibition in New York City*. Cambridge, MA: Harvard University Press, 2007.

Miron, Jeffrey A., and Jeffrey Zwiebel. "Alcohol Consumption during Prohibition." *American Economic Review* 81 no. 2 (May 1991): 242–247.

Thornton, Mark. *Alcohol Prohibition Was a Failure*. Washington, DC: Cato Institute, 1991.

Willing, Joseph K. "The Bootlegger." *The Twenties: Fords, Flappers, and Fanatics*. George E. Mowry, ed. Englewood Cliffs, NJ: Prentice Hall, 1963.

PROUDHON, PIERRE-JOSEPH (1809–1865)

Pierre-Joseph Proudhon was a French writer and an anarchist. Proudhon is widely considered to be the first author to describe himself as an anarchist, although many before him had considered both the possibility and desirability of structuring a society without the state. Proudhon's most important contribution to modern libertarianism is arguably his influence on Benjamin R. Tucker, the founder of the individualist anarchist journal *Liberty*. Tucker noted that *Liberty* was "brought into existence almost as a direct consequence of the teachings of Proudhon" and "lives principally to emphasize and spread them." Tucker translated and published a number of Proudhon's writings, including *What Is Property?* arguably his best-known book, although Tucker considered Proudhon's greatest work to be *The General Idea of the Revolution in the Nineteenth Century*, which was translated into English by John Beverley Robinson in 1923. It contains one of the most radical and stirring critiques of the state ever penned. Proudhon wrote:

> To be governed is to be kept in sight, inspected, spied upon, directed, law-driven, numbered, enrolled, indoctrinated, preached at, controlled, estimated, valued, censured, commanded, by creatures who have neither the right, nor the wisdom, nor the virtue to do so. To be governed is to be, at every operation, every transaction, noted, registered, enrolled, taxed, stamped, measured, numbered, assessed, licensed, authorized, admonished, forbidden, reformed, corrected, punished. It is, under pretext of public utility, and in the name of the general interest, to be placed under contribution, trained, ransacked, exploited, monopolized, extorted, squeezed, mystified, robbed; then, at the slightest resistance, the first word of complaint, to be repressed, fined despised, harassed, tracked, abused, clubbed, disarmed, choked, imprisoned, judged, condemned, shot, deported, sacrificed, sold, betrayed; and, to crown all, mocked, ridiculed, outraged, dishonored. That is government; that is its justice; that is its morality.

Proudhon was not a systematic thinker. Indeed, his economics, like those of most anarchists of the 19th and early 20th centuries, were confused. He believed in the labor theory of value and argued against the payment of interest on money. (On the latter issue, he debated the great classical liberal economist Frédéric Bastiat, a debate that was translated by Tucker and published in the *Irish World* of New York.) He favored the creation of a "People's Bank," which would provide credit at cost, an idea later popularized both by Tucker and by the American anarchist William B. Greene. In his *History of Economic Analysis*, Joseph Schumpeter wrote that Proudhon's arguments were "absurd," but "instead of inferring from this that there is something wrong with his methods, [he] infers that there must be something wrong with the object of his research so that his mistakes are, with the utmost confidence, promulgated as results."

Proudhon considered himself a socialist, although Marx and his followers chastised him as "petty bourgeois" for his limited defense of private property, his opposition to strikes and armed revolution, and his general ambivalence toward class conflict. Indeed, although libertarians today will find many of Proudhon's specific arguments foreign, they will recognize in his writings a deep and instinctual love of liberty that is certainly not present in the works of contemporary state socialists such as Marx, nor even other continental anarchists such as Mikhail Bakunin and Peter Kropotkin. Proudhon was an individualist—a libertarian—first and a socialist second.

AS

See also Anarchism; Marxism; Private Property; Socialism; Tucker, Benjamin R.

Further Readings

Avrich, Paul. *Anarchist Portraits*. Princeton, NJ: Princeton University Press, 1988.
Edwards, Stewart, ed., and Elizabeth Fraser, trans. *Selected Writings of Pierre-Joseph Proudhon*. Garden City, NY: Anchor Books, 1969.
Ritter, Alan. *The Political Thought of Pierre-Joseph Proudhon*. Princeton, NJ: Princeton University Press, 1969.
Woodcock, George. *Pierre-Joseph Proudhon: A Biography*. London: Routledge, 1956.

PSYCHIATRY

Psychiatry appears at first to be like any other medical specialty, but on closer examination it deviates significantly from the practice of "normal" medicine, such as orthopedics or urology. Normal physicians are trained in explaining the workings of the body and in what to do if a disease is identified. Psychologists are trained in the study of mental processes and behavior, whereas psychiatrists are trained in mental health and mental disease. Controversy arises over to whom "mental illness" belongs, whether to psychologists or psychiatrists. Economic interest plays no small part in turf wars of this sort: Psychology, psychiatry, and medicine are trade professions, and, like all businesses, the seller seeks to convince consumers to buy his product rather than that of his competitor.

Politically speaking, people supporting state-sanctioned psychiatric practices such as involuntary commitment to mental hospitals and the insanity defense tend to be on the left, favoring a therapeutic (paternalistic) state. Civil libertarians have been at times conspicuously silent regarding these practices, although some have argued that liberty is for mentally competent people only. Psychiatrist Thomas Szasz is the lone exception. As a staunch defender of classical liberalism and a critic of state entanglement with psychiatry, he has consistently held that mental illness is a metaphor and coercive psychiatric practices are inconsistent with libertarian principles and the rule of law. His seminal work, *The Myth of Mental Illness* (1961), changed the world of psychiatry forever. To this day, people still blame "deinstitutionalization" and "the problem of the homeless mentally ill" on Szasz's writings (despite the fact that "deinstitutionalization" was implemented for economic reasons, not out of concern for the rights of those labeled "mentally ill"). To the extent that civil libertarians believe in mental illness and support involuntary commitment and the insanity defense, they appear to be guilty of an a priori contradiction when it comes to the liberty of self-ownership and coercive psychiatry: If they truly believed that a person owned his body, then surely they would oppose government efforts to coercively prevent suicide and to incarcerate in mental hospitals those who fail in their attempts to end their lives. The proper role of the state is to protect us from one another. The state has no place protecting a person from himself. Nowhere is this principle truer than with respect to a right to suicide.

Differences between psychiatry and normal medicine include how we define and treat a person labeled as a *patient*, how diseases are defined and diagnosed, and how psychiatry and the state interact, particularly in terms of whom the psychiatrist serves. Is a psychiatrist his patient's agent and advocate? Or is a psychiatrist first an agent of the state, feigning patient advocacy, disregarding the sacred medical ethic of *primum non nocere* by placing the interests of society over those of the patient? In the normal practice of medicine, most people assume that the doctor acts with the patient's welfare in mind. However, this assumption is not always clear in the case of psychiatry.

The psychiatric relationship can be contractual (i.e., one based on consent and mutual respect between doctor and patient [client]) or institutional (i.e., one based on coercion and paternalism). Contractual psychiatry is like any other medical practice in terms of the doctor–patient relationship. A person chooses to purchase a psychiatrist's services, the choice is mutual, and the patient as consumer can terminate the relationship at any time. This notion is referred to as "psychiatry between consenting adults." A person with cancer or severe osteoarthritis can choose not to have chemotherapy or radiation treatment for his cancer or choose not to have a knee replacement. People may try to persuade him to do otherwise, but ultimately his right of refusal must be accepted. In either case, choosing to reject medical advice will likely result in harm to oneself. Although a person may choose to purchase an institutional psychiatrist's services, there may come a point when the patient cannot terminate the relationship. He is held in treatment against his will because the psychiatrist asserts that he poses a threat to himself or others.

Further, psychiatric and normal medicine differ in several aspects, among them the way diseases are defined, diagnosed, classified, and treated. In psychiatry, behavior is considered a disease. Psychiatric diseases are classified by how much a behavior or symptom deviates from the norm; the duration, intensity, and frequency of mental and emotional discomfort; and behavioral and social maladjustment.

Psychiatric disorders are not found in standard textbooks on pathology and cannot be located in a cadaver at autopsy. To differentiate, behavior is something that a person does, whereas disease is something that a person has. Behaviors are the expression of a person's values. Diseases are value-free; they refer to alteration and destruction of tissue.

Psychiatry is deeply involved with the law, particularly in the courtroom, where a psychiatrist's expert testimony is often given tremendous latitude. This fact is most obviously true with respect to the insanity defense and involuntary commitment to a mental hospital. Psychiatric opinion regarding insanity bears heavily on how we understand justice, whereas psychiatric opinion regarding involuntary commitment bears heavily on our understanding of liberty. According to Szasz, the theocratic state (i.e., the union of church and state) has metamorphosed into the therapeutic state, the union of medicine and state. Institutional psychiatry functions as legal fiction in court, and the psychiatric examination of a defendant—with or without his consent—is used to circumvent basic constitutional protections regarding due process. Innocent persons are deprived of liberty and guilty persons of justice on the basis of psychiatric notions of mental illness and its legal corollary "insanity." In addition, any otherwise legally binding contract can be declared invalid based on psychiatric examination and testimony, and a person can be declared incompetent to stand trial and detained in perpetuity although other legal criteria for competency to stand trial are met. Psychiatry's dependence on its involvement with the law is so extensive that, were psychiatrists to be forbidden to testify in court, the profession would likely cease to exist.

Although in normal medicine a patient is free to refuse medical advice even to his own detriment, this freedom is not allowed when it comes to the opinion of an institutional psychiatrist. Moreover, the courts and others believe that psychiatrists can ascertain whether a person is likely to be a threat to others, although there is no hard scientific evidence to support the idea that we can predict, with an accuracy beyond that expected by chance, who is likely to be dangerous to others and who is not. Thus, a person who is normally regarded as innocent until proven guilty is deprived of liberty without due process of law, and the deprivation of liberty is applied in an arbitrary manner.

Although psychiatrists diagnose behavior as a disease, in normal clinical medicine, based on the sciences of pathology and nosology, diseases are marked by cellular abnormalities, lesions, and changes in physical tissue. These observational characteristics are the gold standard for disease definition as established by German pathologist Rudolf Virchow. In psychiatric medicine, a person is diagnosed with a putative disease based on a patient's symptoms alone, not signs. In cases of brain disease, there are signs of brain disease, but in cases of mental disease, there are no bodily signs (i.e., no physiological markers). Contrary to a widespread impression, there is no way to tell who is and is not mentally ill by taking pictures of the brain or by drawing blood and assessing levels of neurotransmitters. Because psychiatrists diagnose mental illness on the basis of behavior, and behavior is the expression of a person's values, the diagnosis of mental illness inevitably involves moral judgments. A person's values, morality, and ethics have nothing to do with the nature of cancer, and so the diagnosis of cancer has nothing to do with the values of the person discovering or diagnosing cancer.

Ordinarily, treatment for real disease may proceed without a person's consent only when one of three conditions is met. When a person is literally unconscious, he does not have the capacity to refuse treatment, so medical personnel err in the direction of saving a person's life by administering medical treatment. Similarly, when a person is literally a child, treatment is coerced because a child does not have the mental capacity to comprehend the consequences of refusing treatment. Finally, treatment may be forced when someone has a contagious disease, but the person is then quarantined and treated to protect others, not to help the diseased person. Institutional psychiatrists modify these three conditions to justify treatment without consent in the following ways. A person who refuses treatment for a mental illness is said to be metaphorically unconscious when he is literally conscious. The symptoms of metaphorical unconsciousness are "lack of insight" into the nature and course of mental illness when a patient disagrees with a psychiatrist's diagnosis. For example, one symptom of schizophrenia or depression is when the patient denies that he is schizophrenic or depressed. Thus, a person who is mentally ill is treated as if he is a child when he is literally an adult because the metaphorical child is allegedly incapable of being responsible for himself and is thus a danger to himself. *Contagious* is changed to *danger to others*.

The crucial factor for psychiatrists in determining mental illness is abnormal behavior. Behavior is considered abnormal when it deviates from the norm and is viewed as unacceptable. In addition, behavior is viewed as abnormal when there is a persistent experience of subjective discomfort beyond that established within a normal range. Everyone feels depressed at one time or another, but depression becomes clinical depression when the experience goes on "too long"—that is, beyond that considered normal. Finally, behavior is considered abnormal when a person has a difficult time adjusting to some major life change, in the sense that his adjustment again deviates significantly from the norm.

Contractual and institutional psychiatry have particular consequences for libertarians for policy in four areas: legal, clinical, public, and social. Depending on how mental illness is defined and explained, consequences for legal policy may vary based on the extent to which legal authorities hold a person responsible for his behavior. If he commits a crime, and the criminal behavior is attributed to mental illness, he may be exculpated or forced into a mental institution, with an indeterminate sentence. If he has committed no crime, but his mental illness is interpreted as posing a threat to himself or others, he may be deprived of his freedom and placed in a mental institution for the rest of his life. With respect to the clinical area, someone may or may not choose to receive treatment depending on whether contractual or institutional psychiatrists are involved. If the psychiatrist believes that the behavior of the person he is treating is not the result of a disease and if a psychological theory offers the most logical explanation for the client's behavior, he may engage in conversation called *psychotherapy*. If the psychiatrist believes in a biological explanation for mental illness, the client may receive any number of drugs that change the way neurons communicate with one another, or he may receive electroconvulsive therapy, where electricity is passed through his brain for a few seconds, causing seizures and then short-term memory loss, which may assist in his not being able to remember what was bothering him.

Institutional psychiatry is most likely to flourish in the area of public policy. "Mental health screening" days, sponsored by the federal and state governments, held at public schools and through federally subsidized businesses and organizations help to gather up people for diagnosis and treatment. When psychiatrists and other "mental health professionals" participate in these state activities, we have institutional psychiatry functioning within the context of formal social control—that is, control by the state.

Psychiatry also plays an important role in shaping social policy, where the control is more self-imposed and where people are left to their own devices. It is in this area that contractual psychiatry is most at home. For example, currently drug prohibition is a function of formal social controls. However, if these laws were to be repealed, informal social controls, in the form of relational and self-controls, would replace state control of drugs. Institutional psychiatric sanctions will have been removed, and at that point contractual psychiatric relationships would replace them or die depending on demand.

True libertarians are not "antipsychiatry," but seek to expand contractual relationships in psychiatry while ultimately eliminating the coercive elements that mark institutional psychiatry.

JAS

See also Foucault, Michel; Szasz, Thomas; Voluntarism

Further Readings

Kumar, Vinay, Abdul K. Abbas, and Nelson Fausto. *Robbins and Cotran's Pathologic Basis of Disease*. 7th ed. Philadelphia: Saunders, 2004.

Sarbin, Theodore R. "Toward the Obsolescence of the Schizophrenia Hypothesis." *The Journal of Mind and Behavior* 11 nos. 3 and 4 (Summer and Autumn 1990): 259–284.

Schaler, Jeffrey A. "Moral Hygiene." *SOCIETY* 39 no. 4 (May/June 2002): 63–69.

———, ed. *Szasz under Fire: The Psychiatric Abolitionist Faces His Critics*. Chicago: Open Court, 2004.

Szasz, Thomas. *The Ethics of Psychoanalysis: The Theory and Method of Autonomous Psychotherapy*. New York: Basic Books, 1965.

———. *Law, Liberty, and Psychiatry: An Inquiry into the Social Uses of Mental Health Practices*. New York: Macmillan, 1963.

———. *The Myth of Mental Illness: Foundations of a Theory of Personal Conduct*. New York: Paul B. Hoeber, 1961.

Szasz, Thomas, and Marc Hollender. "A Contribution to the Philosophy of Medicine: The Basic Models of the Doctor–Patient Relationship." *A.M.A. Archives of Internal Medicine* 97 (May 1956): 585–592.

Virchow, Rudolf. *Die Cellularpathologie in ihrer Begrundung auf physiologische und pathologische Gewebelehre* [*Cellular Pathology as Based upon Physiological and Pathological Histology*]. Berlin: August Hirschwald, 1858.

PUBLIC CHOICE ECONOMICS

Public choice refers to that area of economics devoted to the study of politics using the methods supplied by economic science. As in other applications of economics, a representative individual is the basic building block of public choice analysis—in this case, a representative voter, politician, bureaucrat, regulator, or lobbyist. The individual is assumed to face a choice among alternatives, to have a preference among those alternatives, and to choose the alternative that is most consistent with his (or her) preference. Thus, the objective of public choice analysis is to explain the aggregate outcomes of individuals making choices in specific political settings.

A common criticism of public choice should be dealt with at the start: The assumption that people make political choices in pursuit of private ends has led to a charge that public choice analysis is inherently "cynical." Maybe so. A more perceptive observation is that economics brings the same model of human behavior to analyze the choices among commercial products, jobs, neighborhoods, social relations, and political alternatives. Public choice assumes that the same person who makes those other choices is not customarily transformed to pursue some concept of the public interest when he enters the voting booth, runs for office, or contributes to a political campaign. The perspective offered in high school civics classes, for example, is that a person runs for office to pursue some policy agenda. By contrast, public choice analysis characteristically assumes that a candidate chooses some policy agenda to increase his prospects for winning the election. For that reason, James

Buchanan, a leading public-choice scholar, has described public choice as "politics without romance." Public choice should be judged by whether the hypotheses about the aggregate consequences of political behavior are more consistent with the evidence, not whether the characteristic behavioral assumptions of this analysis are cynical, realistic, or otherwise.

From the beginning, scholars from a range of disciplines made important contributions to the type of analysis now termed *public choice*. The first formal analyses of voting rules were offered by the French mathematicians Jean-Charles de Borda (1781) and the Marquis de Condorcet (1785), followed by the English mathematician (and fabulist) Charles Dodgson (1873). Condorcet was apparently the first to discover that majority rule may not lead to a clear choice when there are more than two alternatives. Candidate (or position) A, for example, may be preferred to B, and B to C, but C to A; this circularity may make the outcome of majority rule dependent on the order by which the alternatives are addressed and when the voting stops. The first significant insights into the theory and structure of a compound republic were made by James Madison, and the first important contributions by economists appear in the works of John Stuart Mill (1861), Knut Wicksell (1896), Harold Hotelling (1929), Joseph Schumpeter (1942), and Howard Bowen (1943). These contributions, however, had little influence on other scholars for many years.

Public choice became an independent discipline only after World War II, following several major publications by economists. Among them was Kenneth Arrow, who, in *Social Choice and Individual Values* (1951), studied the outcomes of various voting procedures, including majority rule, to determine whether they displayed characteristics that were consistently desirable, such as being invariant to the order of voting, efficient, and nondictatorial. Arrow's conclusion to those inquiries was negative, which stimulated a long and generally unproductive exploration by economists and mathematicians to determine whether Arrow was correct. Arrow was later awarded the Nobel Prize largely for that work. Duncan Black, in two 1948 articles and *The Theory of Committees and Elections* (1958), developed his own theory of voting in committees before he discovered that it largely replicated the work of Condorcet and other mathematicians many decades ago.

Anthony Downs, in *An Economic Theory of Democracy* (1957), inspired by Schumpeter and using Hotelling's spatial model of a two-candidate election, developed a rich set of hypotheses about democratic elections. Because the probability that any one individual vote determines the winner is only $1/n$, where n is the expected difference in the votes for the two candidates, voters have little incentive to invest in political information. In fact, most of the information they bring to their vote is likely to be a by-product of work, social relations, and entertainment. For the same reason, potential voters have little incentive to go to the polls. Indeed, G. W. F. Hegel made a similar observation many decades ago. Turnout is likely to be high only when the election is expected to be close, or when a lot is at stake, and the weather is nice. In that sense, most potential voters are both rationally ignorant and rational abstainers. The most important of Downs's hypotheses is that the decisive voter in a two-candidate election is the median voter because that voter must be part of any winning coalition; both candidates have an incentive to choose a policy agenda that appeals to the median voter, creating a perception that there is little difference between the two candidates. Careful analysis, creative graphics, and good writing made this the most influential of all public choice books, although several of Downs's hypotheses have been challenged by later analyses.

James Buchanan and Gordon Tullock, in *The Calculus of Consent* (1962), formulated what proved to be the seminal analysis in the area of constitutional choice, building on Wicksell's voluntary exchange model of government. The authors addressed such questions as the powers of government, the structure of government, and the voting rules that might command unanimous consent of people at the constitutional stage (or, in the powerful metaphor of John Rawls, "behind the veil of ignorance"). Their answers are much like those given by James Madison, as reflected in the U.S. Constitution. Buchanan and Tullock continued to be among the most productive public choice scholars, and Buchanan was awarded the Nobel Prize for his many contributions. Mancur Olson, in *The Logic of Collective Action* (1965), developed a model of comparative transaction costs to explain how small interest groups can have a disproportionate influence on political outcomes when the benefits of political action are concentrated, but the costs are diffused.

Although most of the founders of modern public choice are economists, scholars from other disciplines also made important contributions. William Riker, in *The Theory of Political Coalitions* (1962), explained why grand coalitions tend to devolve into minimum winning coalitions; Riker became the leading proponent of public choice among political scientists. James Coleman, a leading sociologist, made important early contributions to the questions first raised by Kenneth Arrow. By the end of the 1960s, public choice was a recognized subdiscipline of economics and political science with its own new journal and professional society. The range of questions addressed by public choice, however, was still quite narrow, and almost all the early contributions were theoretical.

Beginning in the 1970s, however, the scope of public choice expanded rapidly to address new questions, use new techniques, and include a large number of empirical studies. Most of the founders of modern public choice continued to be productive, and they trained a rapidly growing number of second-generation scholars. Many of them have continued to develop and test the theory of rent seeking, building on

the seminal 1967 article by Gordon Tullock. These studies explain and document that the costs of acquiring and defending the rents created by private monopolies, economic regulation, and trade protection are much higher than the allocative costs that had previously been the focus of microeconomic analysis. Other studies developed the implications of a budget-maximizing bureau faced by a passive political sponsor, building on prior analyses by Ludwig von Mises, Gordon Tullock, and Anthony Downs. In response to criticism leveled at their conclusions, these economists have adopted a modified model based on maximization of the bureau's discretionary budget. Contributions that have yet to have their full impact include the development of voting rules that reflect the intensity of voter preferences and the theory of expressive (as distinct from instrumental) voting. Important new techniques include the use of experimental economics to address the interaction of people in small groups and evolutionary game theory to address the development of constitutional rules. Vernon Smith, one of the founders of experimental economics, won the Nobel Prize for that work.

Despite these continuing contributions, some major puzzles remain. There is still no adequate explanation for why people vote or, if voting is only expressive, what the effects of this expressive voting are. More important, there are not yet any satisfactory explanations of the major political developments of the 20th century, among them the massive expansion of government budgets, the erosion of the economic constitution, and the progressive spread and recent collapse of communism.

Public choice has now become a recognized field of academic study. Many departments of economics and political science now contain one or more public choice scholars. Public choice articles are accepted in increasing numbers in a host of journals, and new public choice societies have been organized in Europe and Japan. Evaluating public choice, however, can best be done by investigating its effect on the larger community; on that basis, however, it is yet too early to determine its overall worth. One judgment rests on the fact that the most important contribution of public choice has been to provide a theory of government failure to counterbalance the theory of market failure put forward by welfare economics, the singularly most important rationale for continued government expansion. In evaluating proposed changes in government institutions and policies, we now have the opportunity to compare imperfect markets with imperfect government and thus avoid the biases inherent in assuming perfection in either institution. Thus, public choice often strengthens the case for a libertarian political economy, but from a different perspective. Normative public choice is better described as contractarian rather than libertarian because it seeks the potential for consent to rules, rather than concentrating on individual actions. For public choice to be a more effective counterbalance to welfare economics, however, those who work in this area must sort out its most important outstanding puzzles, undertake more thorough empirical tests of its hypotheses, and develop better ways to communicate its findings to the broader community.

WAN

See also Buchanan, James M.; Democracy; Economics, Chicago School of; Ostrom, Vincent and Elinor; Tullock, Gordon

Further Readings

Buchanan, James M., and Gordon Tullock. *The Calculus of Consent: The Logical Foundations of Constitutional Democracy*. Ann Arbor: University of Michigan Press, 1962.

Downs, Anthony. *An Economic Theory of Democracy*. New York: Harper & Row, 1957.

Mitchell, William C., and Randy T. Simmons. *Beyond Politics: Markets, and the Failure of Bureaucracy*. Boulder, CO: Westview Press, 1994.

Mueller, Dennis C., ed. *Perspectives on Public Choice: A Handbook*. Cambridge: Cambridge University Press, 1997.

Niskanen, William. *Bureaucracy and Representative Government*. Chicago: Aldine, Atherton, 1971.

Olson, Mancur. *The Logic of Collective Action: Public Goods and the Theory of Groups*. Cambridge, MA: Harvard University Press, 1965.

Tullock, Gordon. "The Welfare Costs of Tariffs, Monopolies, and Theft." *Western Economic Journal* 5 (1967): 224–232.

PURITANISM

Puritanism refers to the 16th- and 17th-century religious movement in England and Scotland that was based on the doctrines of French theologian John Calvin and adapted by the radical Scottish reformer John Knox. The movement attempted to reform Christianity and simplify church government along lines perceived to be in stricter conformity with biblical texts and the original teachings of Christ. Without Pope or prelates, Puritans expected, like other Protestants, to rely on the authority of scripture and the direct experience of grace. Their project was a part of the larger Reformation movement taking place in Europe under Martin Luther. Puritanism had far-reaching consequences for both the United Kingdom and North America. It was the driving force behind the English Revolution and Civil War of 1642–1649, and it formed part of the motivation for the settlement of New England in the New World as Puritans fleeing persecution sought to create a model Christian community free of external intimidation and internal dissent. As a political and institutional movement, Puritanism grew out of two initially separate developments in England and Scotland.

In the early 16th century, Henry VIII initiated the schism between his kingdom and the Roman Church for purely personal and practical considerations. The Pope not only refused to approve Henry's divorce from Catherine of Aragon, but the papacy stood as a challenge to Henry's assertion of independent regal authority. To effectuate this institutional maneuvering, however, he had to avail himself of support from a movement that was already gaining strength in the kingdom. Indeed, throughout the borderlands of the north and in the Scottish lowlands, itinerant preachers, heavily indebted to Calvin, had already made deep inroads, structuring their congregations on lines closer to Presbyterianism with a greater degree of decentralization. The official split with Rome merely widened the gap as calls for reform and greater freedom of worship increased. With Mary Tudor's ascension in 1553, draconian measures were employed to return the English Church to the Catholic fold, but the ultimate effect was to harden Protestant resolve. Reformers interpreted Mary's brutal reign as divine punishment for their failing to take reforms far enough, but with her death and the reign of her sister Elizabeth, the Reformation was once again ascendant.

Over this same period, John Knox in Scotland championed the doctrines of Calvin in support of a decentralized Church authority and adherence to practices founded on scripture rather than papal authority. With the expulsion and eventual execution of Mary, Queen of Scots, Elizabeth's cousin and a confirmed Catholic, Presbyterianism was given official recognition throughout Scotland, paving the way for the later unification of the two kingdoms under the English monarchy. Elizabeth was initially heralded by all Protestants as the defender of the faith. However, the independent Church of England was showing signs of strain.

Presbyterians clashed with conservative Anglicans who sought to preserve the hierarchy of bishops, priests, and deacons, much like the old Roman organization. Presbyterians supported more independent congregations, with organization and worship determined by local councils of laity and clergy. In England, these Presbyters differed not only over the question of church organization, but also on clerical vestments and liturgy. As a consequence, the Archbishop of Canterbury, Matthew Parker, attempted to enforce uniformity in dress and worship, but many refused and came to be called Puritans for their stubbornness on what were thought by the Anglicans to be minor issues. Eventually, a sort of uneasy compromise was reached where large numbers of Puritans practiced "Presbyterianism in episcopacy," which amounted to unofficial bible studies composed of laity and sympathetic clergy. Elizabeth grew increasingly suspicious of these groups, however, correctly suspecting that they had close ties with certain members of Parliament critical of the monarchy. With Elizabeth's death, James VI of Scotland became James I of England and the first monarch to rule over a united kingdom. However, new tensions quickly surfaced.

While preserving the independence of the English Church, James admired Rome's structured hierarchy and cultivated financial assistance from the Pope's leading supporter, Spain. James favored the more bureaucratized and regulatory governments of the Counter Reformation countries, which put him at odds with the rising number of Puritans in Parliament. Separatists, Congregationalists, and Independents especially (i.e., those Puritans who had given up on the idea that the Church of England could be reformed from within and insisted on gathering and worshipping separately and according to their own lights) were targeted for persecution. Many of these people fled to the Netherlands, which had instituted religious toleration in the 16th century. Some of these people journeyed to the New World aboard the *Mayflower* in 1620, forming a community that would become a beachhead for the settlement of Massachusetts and other New England colonies.

Conditions in England, however, did not reach a boiling point until Charles I ascended the throne. His intransigence eventually led to the English Civil War, the Westminster Assembly, the execution of the King, and the dictatorship of Oliver Cromwell. These developments profoundly shaped the English understanding of sovereignty, the rights of subjects, and the nature of constitutional government, paving the way for the Glorious Revolution at the end of the century. They also revealed the profound differences among Puritan factions with respect to religious freedom, toleration, and political government. Most Puritans continued to support a church establishment, but of a reformed, Presbyterian sort. Although Puritans in England called for toleration of their own beliefs, these demands were made on prudential grounds, as opposed to a principled adherence to religious liberty. Given the power of their opponents in the established church, toleration was a reasonable strategy for survival. In America, however, where Puritan divines felt safe from immediate threat by English authorities, they had little patience for dissenting opinions. The formation of Rhode Island can be seen, in large measure, as the result of New England intolerance. In both Old and New England, only a small group of radicals embraced disestablishment and freedom of conscience. Most of these people were drawn from the ranks of the Separatists and Enthusiasts and had support from the lower ranks of army officers and regular troops. Men such as William Walwyn, a wealthy merchant, and John Lilburne, the pamphleteer, produced powerful arguments for equal rights, free trade, republican government, and church disestablishment. They were often designated Levellers because they championed equality before the law of all citizens and an end to aristocratic privileges.

HLE

See also English Civil Wars; Levellers; Religion and Liberty; Separation of Church and State

Further Readings

Ahlstrom, Sydney E. *A Religious History of the American People.* New Haven, CT: Yale University Press, 1972.

Haller, William. *The Rise of Puritanism.* New York: HarperTorch Books, 1957.

Lutz, Donald S., ed. *Colonial Origins of the American Constitution: A Documentary History.* Indianapolis, IN: Liberty Fund, 1998.

Richardson, Glen. *Renaissance Monarchy: The Reigns of Henry VIII, Francis I and Charles V.* New York: Oxford University Press, 2002.

Simpson, Alan. *Puritanism in Old and New England.* Chicago: University of Chicago Press, 1955.

Sommerville, J. P. *Politics and Ideology in England, 1603–1640.* New York: Longman Group Limited, 1986.

Trevor-Roper, Hugh. *The Crisis of the Seventeenth Century: Religion, the Reformation, and Social Change.* Indianapolis, IN: Liberty Fund, 1967.

Walwyn, William. *The Writings of William Walwyn.* Jack R. McMichael and Barbara Taft, eds. Athens: University of Georgia Press, 1989.

PURSUIT OF HAPPINESS

The term *pursuit of happiness*, which occurs in the second sentence of the Declaration of Independence, has attracted the attention of countless scholars over the past two centuries. The phrase differs from the triad of rights put forward by John Locke in his *Two Treatises of Government* (1690), where he defended the rights of Englishmen to their "Life, Liberty, and Estates." Whigs had traditionally included estates or property as an essential element of the liberties of Englishmen, which was classified among the natural rights that all men possessed. So why did Jefferson change the formula from "Life, Liberty, and Estates" to "Life, Liberty, and the Pursuit of Happiness"? The question has produced a distinctive subcategory to the general study of the Declaration.

The oldest view is that the locution, as used by Jefferson, was meant as "words of art," used to dress up, but not significantly alter, the older Lockean formula. The similarity of the phrase with its earlier expression, the philosophy of government then current, and the importance of property to the cause of American independence lends solid historical support to this interpretation. The security of property was at the center of the colonists' dispute with England. Inasmuch as no American was represented in the British Parliament, how could this body levy taxes against Americans? This interpretation of the traditional Lockean view has been made most forcefully by Carl Becker and Ronald Hamowy.

Others, however, have argued that the "pursuit of happiness" should be accorded a more original place in the formation of modern democratic theory. The phrase, according to this view, was meant to encompass all the preconditions that make the pursuit of happiness possible. Rather than merely negative rights, the phrase supposedly imposes on government the political obligation to ensure all of the conditions essential to the happiness of each member of society be met. As understood in this way, the "pursuit of happiness" requires that government accommodate the modern desire for increased social welfare and environmental and cultural regulation. Garry Wills, Scott Gerber, and Richard K. Matthews are among the leading exponents of this interpretation.

Both the traditional and modern interpretations fall short of conveying the richness of the idea of happiness as it was used in the late 17th and 18th centuries. Because government is expected to do so much today, the distinction between government and nonpolitical social institutions has been blurred, and what is "social" and "public" is typically associated with government. Thus, the traditional Lockean interpretation is liable to be misunderstood as devoid of social concern and narrowly economic. The modern interpretation, in contrast, while providing a sense of the social dimension suggested by the term, makes an assumption about the primacy of government that was no part of the original understanding.

The distinction between government and society was fundamental to English and American Whigs, who argued against monarchical absolutism and an intrusive government. For these libertarian forebears, happiness had a specific meaning tied closely to freedom of association. It referred to a flourishing of society in which voluntary organizations formed and throve for all manner of purposes. Such a society was thought to entail a limited government based on consent, with strong protections for the right to own property as a precondition for liberty. Only then could individuals follow their natural inclinations and their rational faculties to pursue the widest range of personal objectives: commercial, philanthropic, religious, and social. Thus, the premier Whig essayists of the Atlantic world, John Trenchard and Thomas Gordon, could write that "True and impartial liberty is . . . the right of every man to pursue the natural, reasonable, and religious dictates of his own mind." Observing that such "liberty is the divine source of all human happiness," they contended that "countries are generally peopled in proportion as they are free, and are certainly happy in that proportion." Free association, for all sorts of reasons, was the basis for happiness in civil society. This notion was commonplace among Americans of the 18th century.

In 1766, Richard Bland of Williamsburg wrote that Virginians were not obliged to remain in submission to "the publick Authority of the State . . . longer than they find it will conduce to their Happiness, which they have a natural Right to promote." Daniel Shute of Boston remarked in 1768 that "Civil government among mankind is not a resignation of

their natural privileges, but that method of securing them to which they are morally obliged as conducive to their happiness." George Mason noted in his draft of the Declaration of Rights for Virginia in June of 1776 that

> all men are by nature equally free and independent, and have certain inherent rights, of which, when they enter into a state of society, they cannot by any compact deprive or divest their posterity; namely, the enjoyment of life and liberty, with the means of acquiring and possessing property, and pursuing and obtaining happiness and safety.

Many have viewed Jefferson's composition as a more effective revision of this earlier text. There are other possible influences.

A number of scholars have pointed to the important place of the Scottish moralists in Jefferson's thought. These Scottish thinkers, each in their own way, postulated an inborn moral sense or sentiment beyond mere self-interest that gave to individuals an immediate experience of the good. Individuals could be trusted to govern themselves because human motivation embraced a capacity for empathizing with the plight of others and associating for reasons other than just material gratification. Acts of faith and philanthropy had their own rewards. Perhaps the most significant source for this view comes from a work highly recommended by Jefferson and one that he read with care long before he composed the Declaration: Henry Home, Lord Kames's *Essays on Morality and Natural Religion*. In writing of the Creator and his work, Kames notes:

> What various and complicated machinery is here! and regulated with what exquisite art! While man pursues happiness as his chief aim, thou bendest self-love into the social direction. Thou infusest the generous principle, which makes him feel for sorrows not his own . . . and by sympathy linked man to man; that nothing might be solitary in thy world, but all tend to mutual association.

This idea was endorsed by Jefferson, who remarked that a "moral sense was as much a part of man as his leg or arm." The moral sense formed an important reason for Jefferson's confidence in the ability of individuals to exercise personal self-government. The pursuit of happiness was thus broader than the right to own property, but it was in no way opposed to it. From the ultimate right of self-ownership, individuals possessed the capacity to pursue their aspirations in association with others who might hold similar convictions. Thus, the pursuit of happiness was social and public, but not primarily or even essentially political. Politics entered the picture only to the extent that a limited government maintained the peace and enforced the rules of just conduct. The result, Jefferson doubtless thought, would be a flourishing associational life.

HLE

See also Cato's Letters; Declaration of Independence; Jefferson, Thomas; Locke, John

Further Readings

Becker, Carl. *The Declaration of Independence: A Study in the History of Ideas.* New York: Harcourt, Brace, 1922; New York: Vintage Books, 1970.

Gerber, Scott Douglas. *To Secure These Rights: The Declaration of Independence and Constitutional Interpretation.* New York: New York University Press, 1995.

Gordon, Thomas, and John Trenchard. "Cato's Letter No. 62: An Inquiry into the Nature and Extent of Liberty." *Cato's Letters.* Vol. 1. Ronald Hamowy, ed. Indianapolis, IN: Liberty Fund, 1995.

Hamowy, Ronald. "Jefferson and the Scottish Enlightenment: A Critique of Garry Wills' *Inventing America: Jefferson's Declaration of Independence.*" *William and Mary Quarterly* 3rd Series (October 1979): 503–523.

Hyneman, Charles S, and Donald S. Lutz, eds. *American Political Writing during the Founding Era 1760–1805.* Vol. 1. Indianapolis, IN: Liberty Fund, 1983.

Jayne, Allen. *Jefferson's Declaration of Independence: Origins, Philosophy, and Theology.* Lexington: University Press of Kentucky, 1998.

Maier, Pauline. *American Scripture: Making the Declaration of Independence.* New York: Knopf, 1997.

Matthews, Richard K. *The Radical Politics of Thomas Jefferson: A Revisionist View.* Lawrence: University Press of Kansas, 1986.

Mayer, David N. *The Constitutional Thought of Thomas Jefferson.* Charlottesville: University Press of Virginia, 1994.

Robbins, Caroline. "The Pursuit of Happiness." *America's Continuing Revolution: An Act of Conservation.* Irving Kristol, ed. Washington, DC: American Enterprise Institute, 1975.

Wills, Garry. *Inventing America: Jefferson's Declaration of Independence.* New York: Vintage Books, 1979.

R

RACISM

Racism refers to the belief that certain groups, based on their race, ethnicity, or color, possess characteristics that are in some way inferior or superior to those of other groups or otherwise entitle them to special burdens or benefits. Racism is closely related to other concepts: *bigotry*, the hatred or loathing of certain groups on the basis of racism; *prejudice* or *stereotyping*, the assignment of qualities to individual members of a group based on racial generalizations; and *discrimination*, the differing treatment of groups or individuals on the basis of race, ethnicity, or color.

Racism is antithetical to individualism, in which people are judged on the basis of individual attributes without regard to race, ethnicity, or color. The philosopher Ayn Rand states,

> Racism is the lowest most crudely primitive form of collectivism. It is the notion of ascribing moral, social, or political significance to a man's genetic lineage—the notion that a man's intellectual and characterological traits are produced and transmitted by his internal body chemistry. Which means, in practice, that a man is to be judged, not by his own character and actions, but by the characters and actions of his ancestors.

Racism has manifested itself in myriad ways, such as Hitler's plan to exterminate Jews and glorify the "Aryan race" in Nazi Germany, tribal genocide in Africa, oppression of the Indians in the Americas, the "ethnic cleansing" campaign in Bosnia, Jim Crow laws in the United States, and the massacres of Chinese and Korean people by the Japanese Empire, to name only a few from a depressingly long list of examples.

The United States was created on the principle of individual sovereignty. The Declaration of Independence professes the belief that "All men are created equal." The Rev.

Martin Luther King, Jr. declared that what "ultimately distinguishes . . . our form of government from all of the totalitarian regimes that emerge in history" is that our system "says that each individual has certain basic rights that are neither conferred by nor derived from the state." Because of its official attachment to individualism and its multiracial population, the struggle over racism took on special prominence in American life.

Of course, the same young nation that embraced individualism also gave official sanction to human slavery. Although slavery has existed for millennia and was not originally tied to race, over time, racism came to be employed as the most prominent rationale for slavery. After abolition of slavery in the United States, racism was used to justify the "separate but equal" laws that followed it. Racist ideology persists today and is a motivating factor in ethnic conflicts around the globe, from Rwanda (Hutus and Tutsis) to Malaysia (Malays and Chinese) to Guatemala (Indians and Ladinos) and elsewhere. Race has often proved itself a useful and convenient foundation for conflict by providing criteria for deciding who is on which side of a struggle for power or resources.

For many years, racism was explicitly sustained in American law. In 1857, the U.S. Supreme Court ruled in *Dred Scott v. Sanford* that emancipated blacks could not sue in the courts because they were not members of the political community. Chief Justice Roger Taney concluded that at the time of the American founding, blacks were

> considered as a subordinate and inferior class of beings, who had been subjugated by the dominant race, and whether emancipated or not, yet remained subject to their authority, and had no rights or privileges but such as those who held the power and government might choose to give them.

Antislavery advocates rejected those premises. Senator Charles Sumner declared about the Negro: "he is a MAN—the equal of all his fellow men." Former slave Frederick

411

Douglass declared that the goal of the abolitionists was that "all distinctions, founded on complexion, ought to be repealed, repudiated, and forever abolished—and every right, privilege, and immunity, now enjoyed by the white man, ought to be as freely granted to the man of color."

Following the American Civil War, Congress appeared to have embraced this view by enacting the Civil Rights Act of 1866, which guaranteed to all persons, regardless of color, the "full and equal benefit of all laws [for] the security of persons and property." That was followed by the 14th Amendment to the U.S. Constitution, which guaranteed to all the privileges and immunities of citizens and the equal protection of the laws. However, those promises were not fully honored in the United States. Jim Crow laws, constructed on the ideology of racism, discriminated in access to jobs, businesses, education, and public accommodations. Blacks also were denied full voting rights despite the legal guarantees afforded by the 15th Amendment.

In 1896, in *Plessy v. Ferguson*, the Supreme Court upheld a Louisiana law under which a man was denied access to a first-class railroad car because one of his great-grandparents was African. The majority of the Court concluded that the law was "reasonable." The sole dissenter, however, Justice John Harlan, declared that, "in the view of the Constitution, in the eye of our law, there is in this country no superior, dominant, ruling class of citizens. There is no caste here. Our Constitution is color-blind, and neither knows nor tolerates classes among citizens." The civil rights movement of the 1950s and 1960s demanded the abolition of state-sanctioned discrimination. In his argument against the "separate but equal" doctrine in *Brown v. Board of Education* (1954), Thurgood Marshall declared, "That the Constitution is color blind is our dedicated belief." Martin Luther King envisioned "a land where men no longer argue that the color of a man's skin determines the content of his character." Those aspirations were vindicated in the decision to that case, which abolished "separate but equal" laws. Several years later, the Civil Rights Act of 1964 was enacted, forbidding discrimination in employment, education, housing, and public accommodations. Since that time, numerous Supreme Court decisions have struck down laws and practices that discriminated against blacks and other groups.

Libertarians believe that, in general, the market is the best way to eradicate racism. Refusing irrationally to deal with certain individuals is costly to the discriminator. For instance, consigning blacks to second-class public facilities places the discriminator at a competitive disadvantage. Only when discrimination is enshrined in law can discriminators indulge their irrational prejudices without economic penalty. For that reason, private companies and colleges were at the forefront of the fight against Jim Crow laws.

Today, reverse racism is ubiquitous in American law and policy in the form of minority preferences in education, employment, and public contracting. Some assert that racism, to the extent that groups are discriminated against, can occur only if its benefits accrue to those groups that possess power, and that, consequently, reverse discrimination in support of minorities cannot be tarnished as racist, either in intent or effect. However, anyone who views people in terms of race and seeks to assign benefits or burdens on that basis fits the more common definition of *racist*. Some advocates of racial classifications, such as law professor Lani Guinier, even question whether black dissenters from ideological orthodoxy can be considered "authentically" black. Many who claim to have been victimized by racism today embrace much of the rhetoric and ideology of racial difference once employed by white supremacists.

Racism is found in one form or another in virtually every society. As a form of collectivism, it is at war with the individualism that undergirds libertarianism. When institutionalized in law, it licenses coercion and violations of fundamental individual rights. Libertarians hold that racism is most dangerous when combined with government power and that it is rendered less virulent when deprived of coercive sanction. The extent to which racism continues to inflict harm on people will likely depend on the vitality of the individualist libertarian credo in the years to come.

CB

See also Affirmative Action; Collectivism; Nationalism; Slavery in America

Further Readings

Bolick, Clint. *Changing Course: Civil Rights at the Crossroads.* New Brunswick, NJ: Transaction, 1988.

Myrdal, Gunnar. *An American Dilemma.* New York: Harper & Brothers, 1944.

Rand, Ayn. "Racism." *The Virtue of Selfishness.* New York: New American Library, 1989.

Sniderman, Paul M., and Thomas Piazza. *The Scar of Race.* Cambridge, MA: Belknap Press of Harvard University Press, 1993.

Steele, Shelby. *The Content of Our Character: A New Vision of Race in America.* New York: St. Martin's Press, 1990.

Thernstrom, Stephan, and Abigail Thernstrom. *America in Black and White: One Nation, Indivisible.* New York: Simon & Schuster, 1997.

Washington, James M., ed. *A Testament of Hope: The Essential Writings and Speeches of Martin Luther King, Jr.* San Francisco: Harper, 1991.

RAND, AYN (1905–1982)

Ayn Rand, a controversial novelist and philosopher, was born in Russia, but emigrated to the United States when she was 21. "For the record," she declared in her monthly periodical, *The Objectivist,* "I disapprove of, disagree with, and have no connection with, the latest aberration of some conservatives, the so-called 'hippies of the right.'" These "libertarians," she emphasized in *Philosophy: Who Needs It*, "subordinate reason to whims, and substitute anarchism for capitalism." They undermine individual rights by attacking the government's legitimate monopoly on the retaliatory use of force and by failing to recognize the dependence of politics on broader philosophical foundations. The realization of human freedom requires, in Rand's view, a simultaneous commitment to reason, egoism, and individualism. Absent any of these prerequisites, freedom cannot long survive.

Despite her antipathy to this anarchic brand of libertarianism, however, Rand profoundly inspired a generation of individuals to pursue the goal of a libertarian society. Some of her closest followers have occupied positions in government, among them Martin Anderson, who served in the Reagan administration, and Alan Greenspan, who served as chairman of the Federal Reserve Board. Others have challenged contemporary politics from without, forming such organizations as the Cato Institute, the Reason Foundation, and the Libertarian Party. Various aspects of the position she put forward have found their way into the works of libertarian-minded academic philosophers, among them Douglas Den Uyl, John Hospers, Tibor Machan, Eric Mack, Douglas Rasmussen, David Kelley, and Tara Smith. She also has played a crucial role in shaping the views of psychologist Nathaniel Branden.

Born Alissa Zinovievna Rosenbaum in St. Petersburg during the Russian Silver Age, Rand was inspired by the heroic ideals embodied in the philosophy of Friedrich Nietzsche and the Romantic fiction and drama of such writers as Victor Hugo, Edmond Rostand, and Friedrich Schiller. Educated under the Soviets, she embraced the Russian dialectical tendency toward transcending the dualisms of mind and body, theory and practice, morality and prudence. Yet she adamantly rejected that culture's altruist religious and moral traditions and statist politics. An avowed atheist, she maintained that the communists had merely substituted subordination of the individual to the collective and the state for subordination of the individual to God. Her profoundly negative personal experience with communism had long-term effects; she immigrated to America in 1926, determined to inform the world of the barbarity of totalitarian dictatorship. Her first novel, *We the Living*, published in 1936, focused on the conflict between the individual and the state, and it attempted to show how totalitarianism created an "airtight" environment that destroyed society's best men and women.

Around this time, Rand began corresponding with several leading American proponents of individualism. In the early 1930s, she wrote to H. L. Mencken, whom she regarded "as the foremost champion of individualism" in America, and she quickly identified herself as "a young and very humble brother-in-arms" of Mencken's libertarian

cause. Rand hoped to translate the remarkable success of her next novel, *The Fountainhead*, into a broad antistatist political movement of the leading conservatives and libertarians of the day with whom she had become acquainted, including Rose Wilder Lane, Albert Jay Nock, and Isabel Paterson. The coalition never materialized, however, owing to the ideological disparity of its prospective members, many of whom Rand regarded as traditionalists and religionists.

Her relationship with Paterson—whose *God of the Machine* was published in 1943, the same year as both *The Fountainhead* and Lane's *Discovery of Freedom*—probably had the deepest impact on Rand's growing individualist sensibility. Paterson had introduced Rand to many key libertarian works in economics, history, philosophy, and politics. She also publicized Rand's writings in her New York *Herald Tribune* column. Both women were headstrong, however, and their differences—primarily their disparate views of religion—eventually undermined their friendship. Nonetheless, Rand characterized *God of the Machine* as among the most "brilliant," "extraordinary," "invaluable," "sparkling," "heroic," and "illustrious" political tracts of its time—a virtual antidote to Marx's *Das Kapital*, and "the greatest defense of capitalism" she had "ever read."

Rand also had dealings with other libertarian writers, such as Leonard Read and Henry Hazlitt. Hazlitt introduced her to Ludwig von Mises, the leading economist of the Austrian School. Although Rand objected to certain aspects of Mises's "praxeological" approach to the human sciences and to his views of morality, she respected his economic defense of free markets, and, in later years, she championed his writings in her various publications. Mises, in turn, is said to have greatly respected Rand's ideological courage.

By contrast, Rand did not take well to the writings of F. A. Hayek. Hayek, a student and associate of Mises and an eventual Nobel laureate in economics, had published *The Road to Serfdom* in 1944. In her *Marginalia*, Rand expressed the conviction that Hayek's work was "real poison" because it compromised the case for freedom with various "collectivist" and "altruist" justifications. For Rand, such compromises made Hayek a "pernicious enemy" of the individualist movement; nothing less than a full, moral defense of unadulterated laissez-faire capitalism would do.

In the 1940s, while laboring on her next novel, *Atlas Shrugged*, Rand worked in Hollywood as a screenwriter. During those years, she became a vocal critic of communist propaganda in film—a conviction she shared with conservative members of the Motion Picture Alliance for the Preservation of American Ideals, such as Gary Cooper, Walt Disney, Adolphe Menjou, Robert Taylor, and John Wayne. For the alliance, Rand authored a "Screen Guide for Americans," and she also testified as a friendly witness before the House Un-American Activities Committee.

By the time *Atlas Shrugged* was published in 1957, Rand had achieved worldwide fame for offering a controversial, integrated, secular defense of capitalism. In *Atlas Shrugged*, she presented the rudiments of a systematic philosophy that she later termed *Objectivism*. Her philosophy rested on the premise that reality is what it is, independent of what human beings think or feel, and that reason is the only means of knowing it. Rand defended objective values, viewing human life as the standard by which to judge good and evil. Essential to her ethical egoism is the doctrine that human beings can and should exist as independent equals, neither sacrificing others to themselves nor themselves to others. For Rand, the "trader principle," giving value for value, is the only appropriate social maxim. Because human beings must be free to pursue the values that sustain their own lives, the doctrine of individual rights is indispensable to ensure freedom within a social context. Rand shared with many classical liberals and modern libertarians this commitment to individual rights and the rule of objective law. She argued that, to protect the individual's rights to life, liberty, property, and the pursuit of happiness, a government monopoly on the coercive use of force was necessary—through the establishment of courts, the police, and the military. Because capitalism, in her view, was based on the "trader principle" and on the principle of nonaggression (i.e., that no human being should attain values by initiating the use of force against others), she maintained that it was the only social system consonant with a genuinely human existence.

In the years after *Atlas Shrugged*, Rand worked with her closest associate, Nathaniel Branden, who organized the Nathaniel Branden Institute to disseminate the principles of Objectivism. After a bitter personal break with Rand in 1968, Branden established himself as an independent psychologist and a pioneer of the "self-esteem movement." However, in its heyday, Branden's institute was to influence a large number of students, offering live and taped lecture courses dealing with every aspect of Rand's thought—from her epistemology to her esthetics. Many of these students were potential libertarians who were discontented with both modern "liberalism," which advocated government regulation of economic life, and modern "conservatism," which advocated government regulation of people's mores. Objectivism offered a politics that contrasts sharply with the "welfare–warfare" mentality promulgated on both ends of the political spectrum. Rand's vehement opposition to John F. Kennedy's "fascist" New Frontier and Lyndon B. Johnson's Great Society matched her intense disdain for the military draft and the Vietnam War. Her rejection of Supreme Court decisions on obscenity and pornography, and her repudiation of the Religious Right, inspired many libertarian activists and writers, who applauded her call for "free minds and free markets"—a slogan that *Reason*, the libertarian magazine, later adopted as its credo.

One of these writers, Murray Rothbard, who is widely credited as the leading libertarian thinker of the late 20th century, enjoyed a brief period of intellectual engagement with Rand and her inner circle in the late 1950s. Despite their common Aristotelian premises, Rand and Rothbard differed in their views on the role of government—a difference that contributed to an irreparable break between them. Years later, Rand wrote in her *Letters* that the anarchistic Rothbard and his "so-called libertarians" were her "avowed enemies," who sought "to cash in on [her] name" and philosophy. Rothbard, who often denigrated the "cult" that surrounded Rand, voiced his distress over the intolerance of religious faith that Randians brought to the libertarian movement. Still, he credited Rand with having had a significant impact on that movement. Individualist feminists within libertarianism also have drawn strength from Rand's writings. In *Feminist Interpretations of Ayn Rand*, libertarian writers such as Joan Kennedy Taylor, Wendy McElroy, and Sharon Presley have applauded Rand's contribution to the cause of women's rights. It is a paradoxical contribution, they admit, because Rand repudiated the collectivist Women's Lib movement of the 1970s and because her fiction depicts heroines seeking masochistic fulfillment in male hero worship. But these works of fiction also present autonomous female characters, undeterred by stultifying cultural traditions and social norms, pursuing careers as engineers, journalists, and industrial executives. The idea that women should not be sacrificed on the altar of perennial motherhood, that they can be independent, self-defining, and self-motivating, finds great support in Rand's work. An ardent defender of the right of women to have abortions and of a woman's right to her own life, Rand put forth an alternative vision for those libertarian feminists who sought to reclaim the women's movement as an outgrowth of classical liberalism and individualism.

Although Rand died in 1982, her legacy lives on in many segments of the libertarian intellectual movement. That her legacy has finally sparked the interest of scholars worldwide is proof of its enduring quality.

CMS

See also Branden, Nathaniel; Capitalism; Mises, Ludwig von; Objectivism; Paterson, Isabel

Further Readings

Bradford, R. W., Stephen Cox, and Chris Matthew Sciabarra, eds. *The Journal of Ayn Rand Studies.* Vols. 1– . Port Townsend, WA: The Journal of Ayn Rand Studies Foundation, Fall 1999– .

Branden, Barbara. *The Passion of Ayn Rand.* Garden City, NY: Doubleday, 1986.

Cox, Stephen. *The Woman and the Dynamo: Isabel Paterson and the Idea of America.* New Brunswick, NJ: Transaction, 2004.

Den Uyl, Douglas J., and Douglas B. Rasmussen, eds. *The Philosophic Thought of Ayn Rand.* Urbana and Chicago: University of Illinois Press, 1984.

Gladstein, Mimi Reisel, and Chris Matthew Sciabarra, eds. *Feminist Interpretations of Ayn Rand*. University Park: Pennsylvania State University Press, 1999.

Rand, Ayn. *Atlas Shrugged*. New York: Random House, 1957.

———. "Brief Summary." *The Objectivist* 10 no. 9 (September 1971): 1–4.

———. *Capitalism: The Unknown Ideal*. New York: New American Library, 1967.

———. *Letters of Ayn Rand*. Michael S. Berliner, ed. Introduction by Leonard Peikoff. New York: Dutton, 1995.

———. *Philosophy: Who Needs It*. New York: Bobbs-Merrill, 1982.

———. *The Virtue of Selfishness: A New Concept of Egoism*. New York: New American Library, 1964.

Sciabarra, Chris Matthew. *Ayn Rand: The Russian Radical*. University Park: Pennsylvania State University Press, 1995.

———. *Ayn Rand: Her Life and Thought*. An Atlas Society Publication. Poughkeepsie, NY: The Objectivist Center, 1999.

RAWLS, JOHN (1921–2002)

John Rawls was perhaps the most prominent and broadly influential American political philosopher of the 20th century. Rawls is best known for his 1971 work, *A Theory of Justice*, which argues in favor of the institutions of the modern liberal-democratic welfare state against egalitarian socialism, on the one hand, and classical liberalism, on the other hand.

After teaching for a time at Cornell University and the Massachusetts Institute of Technology, Rawls joined the philosophy department at Harvard University in 1962 and remained there for the rest of his long career. During the 1950s, Rawls's work eschewed a straightforward analysis of moral concepts, then popular among philosophers, but instead attempted to describe a general procedure for moral decision making along Kantian lines. His work also was informed by contemporary writings in the theory of rational choice. From the late 1950s to the late 1960s, Rawls published a series of influential papers that would become the basis of his most celebrated work, *A Theory of Justice*.

A Theory of Justice declares that justice is the "first virtue of social institutions" and seeks to identify those principles of social organization that will create a "realistic utopia" in which individuals are free to pursue their ends as they wish, subject only to constraints that everyone has reason to accept. According to Rawls, the subject matter of a theory of justice is the "basic structure" of a society—the system of interlocking legal, political, economic, and social institutions that assigns to citizens their fundamental rights and duties and that determines the terms of social cooperation and the resulting distribution of opportunities and economic holdings.

Rawls's conception of justice, which he dubbed "justice as fairness," consists of two related principles of justice.

The "first principle," intended to set constitutional limits on democratic government, is essentially a restatement of J. S. Mill and Herbert Spencer's principles of equal liberty, which holds that "each person has an equal right to the most extensive liberties compatible with similar liberties for all." Crucially, however, the liberties Rawls has in mind do not include those relating to property and contract. The "second principle," intended to guarantee the "value" of the basic liberties he posits, concerns the distribution of opportunities: wealth, the "social bases of self-respect," and other social advantages. He divides this principle into two parts. The first part, known as the "difference principle," requires that "social and economic inequalities are to be arranged so that they are to be of the greatest benefit to the least-advantaged members of society." The second part requires that "inequalities attached to offices and positions open to all under conditions of fair equality of opportunity." According to Rawls, the first principle is "lexically prior" to the second, in that inequalities of opportunity and outcome may not be addressed before a maximally extensive system of equal liberties has been established and that the "rearrangement" of these inequalities must take place within the constraints of the system of liberty.

Rawls attempts to justify his view of "justice as fairness" and to rule out competing alternatives by recourse to a kind of "social contract" thought experiment in the tradition of Hobbes, Locke, and Rousseau. However, unlike the neo-Hobbesian models of rational agency embodied in standard economic models, Rawls, heavily influenced by the moral philosophy of Immanuel Kant, depicts people as distinctly moral agents possessing a "sense of justice" or "moral capacity" that provides both judgments about moral matters and motivation to act in accordance with moral rules, even when this entails the sacrifice of narrow self-interest. People are understood as rational, in the economist's sense, but also as "reasonable." Rawls's thought experiment of choice from the "original position" is meant to model the way our sense of justice moderates rational maximization. In the original position, agents are conceived as maximizing "primary goods"—goods necessary for the achievement of most any end. But agents also are conceived as choosing their terms of association from behind a "veil of ignorance" regarding their talents, opportunities, economic class, social connections, and so on, which is meant to model the impartiality and fairness of reasonable moral beings.

Rawls argues that his two principles of justice are what agents—so idealized—would choose in the original position. However, within Rawls's larger argument, this stands as only a preliminary justification of his notion of "justice as fairness." Principles of justice also must prove stable, and stability requires that real people would be able to affirm and comply with them under realistic conditions. The principles of justice must be in "reflective equilibrium" with our "considered moral judgments" (i.e., the output of the sense of justice after deliberation) for two reasons. First, if proposed principles of justice clash with the moral judgments of individuals, we will not be inclined to accept them or a theory that proposes them. If we do not accept them, we will not willingly act on them, and therefore they will fail to guide our behavior and determine the character of the social order. The principles of a just society must be self-reinforcing. As a result, Rawls spends the last third of *A Theory of Justice* arguing that individuals brought up in a society ordered by "justice as fairness" will develop a personal conception of the good congruent with the demands of justice.

In his second major work, *Political Liberalism*, published in 1993, Rawls acknowledged that his prior argument for the stability of "justice as fairness" rested on the assumption that we all are raised in a society unified under a single, heavily Kantian "comprehensive conception" of moral personhood and the good. This unity, he argues, can be maintained only though coercion and is inconsistent with the permanent diversity in moral outlooks characteristic of a free society. So *Political Liberalism* attempts to recast "justice as fairness" as a relatively neutral "political" doctrine that rests on no single metaphysical or moral view, but that can be constructed as the content of an "overlapping consensus" of many competing "reasonable" comprehensive moral views. Thus, it can be rendered consistent with "the fact of reasonable pluralism." Rawls's last major work, *The Law of Peoples*, attempts a theory of international relations that, in opposition to some of his followers, resists applying the notion of "justice as fairness" worldwide.

Rawls's work is notable for dominating Anglo-American political philosophy in the latter third of the 20th century, in part, by inspiring other works such as Robert Nozick's *Anarchy, State, and Utopia*, which was, to a large extent, written as a response to *A Theory of Justice*. Nozick argued that Rawls's difference principle would require constant, invasive government intervention in voluntary activities to maintain the prescribed pattern of distribution, thus running afoul of the priority of liberty in Rawls's own scheme. Rawls's denigration of economic liberties and his defense of redistribution have inspired a number of critical analyses by libertarian and classical liberal thinkers. F. A. Hayek and James M. Buchanan, like Nozick, were sharply critical of the centrality of distributive patterns in Rawls's account of justice. However, both Hayek and Buchanan endorsed Rawls's general methodological framework, arguing that it generates classical liberal conclusions when joined to an adequate understanding of the principles of political economy.

WW

See also Contractarianism/Social Contract; Nozick, Robert; Welfare State

Further Readings

Buchanan, James M. *Why I, Too, Am Not a Conservative: The Normative Vision of Classical Liberalism.* Cheltenham, UK: Edward Elgar, 2005.

Epstein, Richard A. "Rawls Remembered." *National Review Online,* http://www.nationalreview.com/comment/comment-epstein112702.asp.

Hayek, Friedrich A. *Law, Legislation, and Liberty: Volume 2. The Mirage of Social Justice.* Chicago: University of Chicago Press, 1976. 100.

Lomasky, Loren. "Libertarianism at Twin Harvard." *Social Philosophy and Policy* 22 no. 1 (Winter 2005): 178–199.

Nozick, Robert. *Anarchy, State, and Utopia.* New York: Free Press, 1976.

Rawls, John. *The Law of Peoples.* Cambridge, MA: Harvard University Press, 1999.

———. *Political Liberalism.* New York: Columbia University Press, 1993.

———. *A Theory of Justice.* Cambridge, MA: Harvard University Press, 1971.

READ, LEONARD E. (1898–1983)

Leonard E. Read, an activist, a fundraiser, and an administrator, is best known for originating the oldest existing free-market nonprofit in the world, the Foundation for Economic Education (FEE). At the time of its founding, FEE was "[t]he only organization that introduces newcomers to the idea of the free market as a moral institution, not just as a means of efficient production." Read also was known for his writings in moral philosophy and as a gourmet chef and curling enthusiast, all of which he pursued avidly.

Not surprisingly, statists disparaged him. Eleanor Roosevelt even commented that she was "struck" by FEE's insinuation that there was some similarity between the welfare state and communism. But even with those who ordinarily allied with him against the welfare state, Read was uncompromising in his defense of the truth. When J. Howard Pew, a generous benefactor who was troubled by the organization's stand against tariffs, asked that FEE rethink its position, Read stood firm. He even went so far as to refuse to publish an article submitted by former president Herbert Hoover, a long-time acquaintance. Years later, he allowed Ralph Nader to write an article critical of federal housing projects.

The Rev. Edmund Opitz once described Read's philosophy as:

. . . basically, that of the Declaration of Independence, to which he added a dash of mysticism, some hard-nosed free market economics, spiced by a dash of native American go-getter spirit. Leonard has always shunned argument and debate, preferring instead to win over his readers by striking illustrations, parables, and stories. . . . The methodology he stressed was based on self-improvement—let each person work on himself and present society with one improved unit.

Born Leonard Edward Read on a farm in rural Michigan, his father died when he was 11. To support the family, he helped his mother start a boarding house and worked odd jobs after school. When the United States entered World War I, Read enlisted in the American Expeditionary Force. On the way to Europe, his ship, the *Tuscania*, was torpedoed, but he survived to become a mechanic in the 158th Aero Squadron. At the conclusion of the war, Read returned to Michigan and soon started his own business, the Ann Arbor Produce Company. He also found time to marry Gladys "Aggie" Cobb and have two sons.

With the advent of the chain stores, Read found his independent wholesale business floundering and decided to move 2,000 miles to California. It was there that he embarked on an 18-year career with the Chamber of Commerce, first reviving a chapter in Burlingame and then in Palo Alto. Eventually, Read was chosen to direct the Chamber's entire western operation, where he became a spokesman for the Chamber on commercial issues and forged relationships with businessmen all over the region. In 1933, Read crossed paths with businessman W. C. Mullendore. It was through discussions with Mullendore that Read recalls beginning to examine the world through "freedom-tinted glasses."

In 1937, he wrote *The Romance of Reality*, which emphasized education over politics as the key to combating socialism. His book and lectures persuaded the Los Angeles Chamber of Commerce, the nation's largest, to oppose all collectivist programs, and 2 years later, Read became the general manager of the L.A. Chamber. Read discovered that he could not share his thoughts to the extent that he wished within the Chamber apparatus. So he started Pamphleteers, Inc., through which he hoped to disseminate works that unequivocally supported freedom, such as Rose Wilder Lane's *Give Me Liberty* and Ayn Rand's *Anthem*.

After encountering Frédéric Bastiat's booklet "Communism versus Free Trade," Read worked with R. C. Hoiles, publisher of the *Orange County Register*, to reprint three more of Bastiat's works. The lack of interest in these works was disappointing. Read surmised that "the rather archaic British prose of the translation must have prevented others from sharing his enthusiasm." Later, with the founding of FEE, he commissioned Dean Russell to do a modern translation of *The Law*, which eventuated in some 500,000 copies being sold. The success of the edition prompted Read to have more of Bastiat's works translated into modern English.

Hoping to focus more on the prevention of socialism, Leonard Read moved to New York and took a job as the executive vice president of the National Industrial Conference Board, where he sought to replicate on a national scale what he had accomplished in Los Angeles. Unfortunately, "the NICB . . . wanted to present 'both sides' of every issue." After 8 exasperating months, Read resigned.

In 1946, he acquired property in Irvington-on-Hudson, a suburb of New York City, and he set up FEE. It was to be an organization that would inform people about the consequences of government meddling. By now Read, 47, was a firm believer that government should go no further than protecting everyone equally against aggression, both domestic and foreign. He also believed that, in addition to pointing out the perils of socialism, FEE should present "the positive free market alternative."

FEE's first monograph was "Roofs or Ceilings?" a now-classic essay on the calamitous effects of rent controls written by two future Nobel Prize–winning economists Milton Friedman and George Stigler. What followed was a steady stream of high-quality and accessible works on economics, political philosophy, and history—all showing the market's indispensable role in creating prosperity and protecting liberty. Read learned that one of the most effective ways to bring the philosophy of freedom to people was through personal contact. The give and take of discussion, combined with the opportunity to pose questions, had been invaluable not only for him, but for the others who had joined with him over the years. So in the 1950s, FEE began holding seminars in Irvington and around the country. Although most seminars were aimed at a general audience, there also were seminars targeted at specific groups, such as secondary school teachers, college students, journalists, and ministers. Eschewing a mass-market approach, Read used to say, "You can't sell freedom like soap."

By 1956, FEE had officially acquired *The Freeman*, a publication started by Albert Jay Nock in the 1920s that had gone in and out of print over the following years, having been edited by such leading libertarians as Henry Hazlitt, John Chamberlain, and Frank Chodorov. Read wrote his most famous article for long-time *Freeman* editor Paul Poirot in 1958. "I, Pencil" is a simple but powerful argument against those who clamor for more government control of the economy. In it, Read argued that no single person has all the knowledge necessary to make a pencil, and yet there are pencils in abundance because the free market encourages cooperation in the worldwide division of knowledge and labor. In his most popular book, *Anything That's Peaceful* (1964), Read concluded that people may engage in any peaceful activity and have the moral right to use force only to protect themselves and their property from coercion by others.

In addition to traveling more than 3 million miles, Leonard Read lectured on hundreds of occasions a year, maintained correspondence with everyone from union members to Ayn Rand to captains of industry, and still found time to author a small library of material. In his final book, *The Path of Duty* (1982), he reemphasized the "power of attraction . . . [and how libertarians must] become so proficient in understanding and explaining freedom that others will seek [their] tutorship." Leonard Read died at Irvington-on-Hudson in May 1983 in his 85th year.

DJB and NS

See also Chodorov, Frank; Hazlitt, Henry; Nock, Albert Jay; Rand, Ayn

Further Readings

Barger, Melvin D. "From Leonard Read: A Legacy of Principles." *The Freeman* (May 1996): 355–359.

Greaves, Bettina Bien. "FEE and the Climate of Opinion." *The Freeman* (May 1996): 337–345.

———. "Leonard E. Read, Crusader." *The Freeman* (September 1998): 522–526.

Opitz, Edmund A. "Leonard E. Read: A Portrait." *The Freeman* (September 1998): 518–521.

Read, Leonard E. *Anything That's Peaceful.* Irvington-on-Hudson, NY: Foundation for Economic Education, 1998.

———. "The Essence of Americanism." *The Freeman* (September 1998): 527–534.

———. "I, Pencil." *The Freeman* (December 1958): 32–37.

———. *In Memoriam: Leonard E. Read 1898–1983.* Irvington-on-Hudson, NY: Foundation for Economic Education, 1983.

———. *The Path of Duty.* Irvington-on-Hudson, NY: Foundation for Economic Education, 1982.

Sennholz, Hans. "Onward Still." *The Freeman* (May 1996): 332–336.

Sennholz, Mary. *Leonard E. Read: Philosopher of Freedom.* Irvington-on-Hudson, NY: Foundation for Economic Education, 1993.

REGULATION

Scarcely anyone interests himself in social problems without being led to do so by the desire to see reforms enacted. In almost all cases, before anyone begins to study the science, he has already decided on definite reforms that he wants to put through. Only a few have the strength to accept the knowledge that these reforms are impracticable and to draw all the inferences from it. Most men endure the sacrifice of the intellect more easily than the sacrifice of their daydreams. They cannot bear that their utopias should run aground on the unalterable necessities of human existence. What they yearn for is another reality different from the one given in this world. . . .

They wish to be free of a universe of whose order they do not approve.

(Ludwig von Mises, *Epistemological Problems of Economics*)

The idea of *controlling* citizens is as old as government. But the notion of *regulating* citizens and markets is comparatively recent. Regulation can best be understood as the imposition of a set of rules or standards that direct or restrict conduct, with provisions for punishing violators. To be legitimate, regulators must stipulate some utopian benchmark that displays the gap between the real world and the optimal activities of certain groups. For the libertarian, regulation presents two sets of questions raised by scholars as diverse as Milton Friedman, Murray Rothbard, George Stigler, and Ludwig von Mises. First, even if this gap exists, can government close it or is regulation likely to make things worse? To ascertain whether this gap may be closed, we need a theory that allows us to determine "government success," in addition to "market failure," before regulation could be justified. Second, even if government were able, in principle, to improve the performance of the economy, should it be given the power to try?

A regulated market economy differs from socialism, where government owns the means of production. Metaphorically, supporters of regulation concede that private activity is the locomotive that moves the economy. But government regulators, they argue, should direct the train and keep it from overheating or breaking down. This notion raises the key issue in understanding regulation: By what right can government use its coercive power to restrict the private activity of some citizens for the benefit of "society"? To understand the argument supporters of regulation make for this right, we need to examine the utopian point of reference: perfect competition.

In perfectly competitive markets, prices accurately signal the relative scarcity of all valuable resources, including inputs such as labor and capital and outputs such as consumer goods and services. Wherever price exceeds the marginal cost of production, resources flow into that industry until the price is driven down, and all producers earn zero profits at the margin. "Price equals production cost" is the hallmark of perfectly competitive markets because it means all parties accept the pattern of transactions.

This perfectly competitive outcome is efficient because it implies zero waste. More technically, for the advocate of regulation, an efficient outcome is the idealized benchmark where no feasible reallocation of resources could result in higher total output of goods and services. The alternative to perfect competition, and the associated concept of efficiency, lies at the core of the rationale behind support for regulation. Inefficiency or market failure implies that regulation is needed even when the ideal of efficiency is actually unattainable.

There are three primary categories of ostensible market failure: information asymmetry, natural monopoly, and externalities.

Information asymmetry holds where citizens are unaware of the nature of products or services in advance of their purchase. There are many examples of regulation in this setting. Licensing requirements, for example, ensure that airplane pilots can fly (and land) planes. Likewise, drug regulations require that products are safe and effective before they can be marketed.

But where should the line be drawn? Why not regulate all activities where quality is unknown? After all, some restaurants are not good. Why not establish a "Federal Bureau of Indian Restaurants" and close down those that serve bad curries? In point of fact, the problem of information asymmetry is not really a market failure at all. Markets can handle this problem quite well. If you go to a restaurant and gag on the curry, you do not go back. You tell your friends or write a newspaper review. People stay away, and the restaurant closes.

Reputation and brand names are powerful and spontaneous market-generated answers to information asymmetry. If you are traveling in another city, or even another country, and you see a chain restaurant you recognize, you might eat there because you know that the quality will be of a certain level. Natives may not choose to eat there because they have local knowledge of better restaurants, but brand names can solve the information problem fairly well for people who lack such knowledge.

Concerning the issue of natural monopolies, perfect competition implies that all market participants are "price takers," whose activities are so small that their impact on price is negligible. But what if some market participants are not price takers? The problem of natural monopoly occurs when an activity, such as the supply of electricity or sewer services, requires enormous up-front costs. The result is that only one producer can supply the efficient level of the good or service. A common example of the up-front costs occurs with respect to electrical generation facilities, with its associated delivery infrastructure that includes wires, switches, and transformers. What prices should be charged by such enterprises? If their charges are set at marginal cost—that is, the cost of generating electricity once the infrastructure is in place—then they are unable to pay for the costs of the infrastructure. But if they divide the cost over all the units of output, then price greatly exceeds marginal cost. Further, the cost per unit actually falls as production goes up, meaning that one large firm can produce at lower cost than two smaller firms with the same total capacity.

Local governments can either accept the higher costs of many inefficient firms competing or suffer the higher costs (and deadweight losses) of monopoly overpricing. The third possibility is to regulate the monopoly by mandating rates to be charged and the return that can be earned on investment.

However, strong arguments have been put forward that regulation of utilities, although pervasive, is unnecessary and costly. If long-term contracts with private firms are bid competitively, the terms of the contract can easily include price and performance criteria. If the firm violates the contract, it forfeits the value of investments it has made in the long-term arrangement. The most important argument for this position was made by Harold Demsetz in 1968, but this view has lately been given more credence by a number of states' public utilities commissions.

With respect to the problem of externalities, the model of a perfectly competitive economy assumes that all consequences of consumption and production choices are internal, meaning they only affect those involved in the exchange. If there are other effects, for which no compensation is made, then individual incentives may be distorted.

Suppose, for example, someone dumps raw toxic wastes into a river. This scenario is an example of an externality, where one's action affects others, but those affected have no voice. The dumper considers only his own small costs of tipping barrels into the river, while he ignores the "social" costs of his actions—downstream poisoning and cancer. This ability to ignore a real cost appears to be a particularly apt example of market failure.

It is important to step back and ask again why it is that government action is necessary. What, in the case of the toxic waste dumper, is the source of the externality? Is it really a failure of the market or is it, as Ronald Coase has suggested, a failure to specify property rights and to provide a system of legal recourse based on torts, class action suits, and compensation for damages?

In fact, the libertarian answer to most market failures is to specify property rights more clearly and make it less costly for people to arrive at accurate prices on their own. As Ludwig von Mises noted in *Human Action:*

> It is true that where a considerable part of the costs incurred are external costs from the point of view of the acting individuals or firms, the economic calculation established by them is manifestly defective and their results deceptive. But this is not the outcome of alleged deficiencies inherent in the system of private ownership of the means of production. It is on the contrary a consequence of loopholes left in the system. It could be removed by a reform of the laws concerning liability for damages inflicted and by rescinding the institutional barriers preventing the full operation of private ownership.

Regulation often makes the problem of market failure worse because regulated markets always, by design, transmit biased or noisy price signals. Robbed of the organizing principle of accurate prices directing resource allocation, some other kind of judgment—in this case, that of a bureaucrat or regulator—must be substituted for private investment. Regulated markets generally beget more regulation, but perform no better, and often worse, than the failed market process that regulation was designed to correct in the first place.

Prices give signals about the value of resources, commodities, and activities. The unregulated market is the most efficient and impartial animating principle the world has ever known. It does not discriminate, and it directs resources to their highest valued use. The problem with regulation as a response to market failures, even with the best of intentions, is that government rarely "gets prices right."

Without the "best of intentions," regulation may even exacerbate the problem. As George Stigler (1971) points out,

> As a rule, regulation is acquired by the industry and is designed and operated primarily for its benefit. . . . The state has one basic resource which in pure principle is not shared with even the mightiest of its citizens: the power to coerce. . . . These powers provide the possibilities for the utilization of the state by an industry to increase its profitability. . . . The state—the machinery and power of the state—is a potential resource or threat to every industry in the society. With its power to prohibit or compel, to take or give money, the state can and does selectively help or hurt a vast number of industries.

Equally important, if market failures having to do with industry structure, information asymmetry, or externalities are regulated, the regulations may be designed by precisely those industries ostensibly bound by the new rules. Thus, regulation often sets the wolf to guard the henhouse.

In real markets, it may simply be impossible to regulate or redirect the forces that lead investors, producers, and consumers to act the way that they do. Even if one could imagine an alternative, ideal system, regulation is at least as likely to lead away from that goal as toward it. But the chimerical ideal of efficiency is what motivates much of what regulators do. If actual policy falls short (and it always will) of the idealized vision of the regulator, it is tempting to try to reform government agencies, revise organization charts, pass new regulations, and create new agencies and scrap old ones. This temptation should be resisted.

MM

See also Externalities; Interventionism; Rent Seeking; Taxation; Welfare State

Further Readings

Coase, Ronald H. "The Problem of Social Cost." *Journal of Law and Economics* (October 1960): 1–44.

Demsetz, Harold. "Why Regulate Utilities?" *Journal of Law and Economics* 11 (1968): 55–65.

Mises, Ludwig von. *Bureaucracy*. New York: Libertarian Press, 1994 [1944].

———. *Epistemological Problems of Economics*. New York: New York University Press, 1981 [1933].

———. *Human Action*. New York: Fox & Wilkes Press, 1997 [1949].

Niskanen, William. *Bureaucracy and Representative Government*. Chicago: Aldine-Atherton, 1971.

Rothbard, Murray N. *Power and Market: Government and the Economy*. Menlo Park, CA: Institute for Humane Studies, 1970.

Stigler, George. "The Theory of Economic Regulation." *Bell Journal of Economics and Management Science* 2 (1971): 3–21.

RELIGION AND LIBERTY

The 19th-century historian Henry Thomas Buckle expressed the view of many of his liberal contemporaries when he called religious persecution "unquestionably the greatest evil men have ever inflicted on their own species." W. E. H. Lecky also found fertile soil in the history of persecution for his extensive investigations into the influence of ideas on the course of Western civilization. As he wrote, "the burnings, the tortures, the imprisonments, the confiscations, the disabilities, the long wars" precipitated by religious intolerance were chiefly due to men of unimpeachable character, "whose lives were spent in absolute devotion to what they believed to be true."

Lord Acton was another classical liberal for whom the history of religious freedom provided a case study in the development of individual freedom in general. "Liberty of conscience is the first of liberties," according to Acton. This liberty is the "underlying principle" of individual freedom, and it "was in the strife for liberty that conscience came to the front."

Religious institutions played a key role in Acton's history of freedom in European civilization. For centuries after the fall of the Western Roman Empire, the church was the only institution with the authority to challenge the power of feudal lords, monarchs, and emperors. Church and state contended for power, and if either had achieved total victory, "all Europe would have sunk down under a Byzantine or Muscovite despotism."

A consistent principle of freedom was never upheld by either church or state, according to Acton, but while competing for allies, they granted sundry immunities and privileges to towns, parliaments, universities, guilds, and other corporations. These institutions were eventually able to resist the power of both church and state, so there evolved a decentralized system of power unknown to the ancient world and the East. Institutional barriers to arbitrary and absolute power, long advocated in theory, now existed in fact. Individual liberty was a fortunate by-product of this system of decentralized power.

If these institutional factors may be said to have produced freedom as an unintended consequence, it also is true that religious freedom was defended with various theoretical arguments and from different ideological perspectives. Tertullian, an important figure in the early Latin church, called freedom of conscience "a fundamental human right." One's religion "neither harms nor helps another man," so governments should not interfere. Moreover, Tertullian contended that "free-will and not force" is the proper basis for religious belief. Similar arguments were proposed by Christian apologist Lactantius, according to whom "religion cannot be imposed by force," but "must be carried on by words rather than by blows, that the will may be affected." This argument, which maintains that religious faith cannot be meritorious unless freely given, would later play a major role in the Christian case for toleration.

Christian pleas for toleration became less common after Constantine issued the Edict of Milan (313), which established religious liberty as a fundamental principle of public law. Constantine then bestowed special favors on the Christian church, effectively renouncing certain sections of the Edict. His Christian successors continued to extend a degree of religious freedom until Theodosius totally revoked the Edict of Milan during his despotic reign. This emperor established orthodox Christianity as the official religion, outlawed pagan worship and rituals, and decreed severe penalties for heresy. Thus, in the words of Lord Acton: "Christianity, which in earlier times had addressed itself to the masses, and relied on the principle of liberty, now made its appeal to the rulers, and threw its mighty influence into the scale of authority."

Even after the church abandoned the notion of liberty of conscience, it sometimes functioned as a protective buffer between the state and the people. "Render unto Caesar the things that are Caesar's, and unto God the things that are God's"—these words of Jesus suggested a sphere in which the church reigns supreme, a sphere immune to state power. Ambrose, Bishop of Milan from 374 to 397, fiercely defended this principle. No friend of religious liberty, Ambrose nevertheless believed in the independence of the church: "Palaces belong to the emperors, churches to the priesthood." He also believed that the church could call secular rulers to account. "Thou art a man," said Ambrose to Theodosius after this despot had ordered a brutal massacre in Thessalonica. Threatened with excommunication, Theodosius submitted to Ambrose's demand for public penance. As this astonishing story was recalled in later centuries, it did more to limit state power than volumes of theory.

The most influential arguments for persecution were put forward by St. Augustine, who defended "righteous persecution," a policy he deemed necessary "in order that men may attain eternal life and escape eternal punishment." Although Augustine conceded that a person cannot be compelled to believe something in the absence of sufficient evidence, he contended that coercion is able to change a heretic's mental attitude and make him more receptive to receive the truth by contravening the influence of bad habits, indifference, and sloth.

Arguments for religious freedom began to reappear after the Protestant Reformation shattered the religious unity of Europe. Although many of the great Reformers opposed toleration, especially for Catholics and Anabaptists, the appearance of a bewildering array of Protestant sects generated civil wars and other political problems that could only be solved with pragmatic concessions to toleration. These practical solutions were accompanied by new arguments for toleration, which gained momentum after Michael Servetus was burned at the stake for heresy in 1533. John Calvin, who had engineered this execution of a fellow Protestant, was condemned by the French Protestant Sebastian Castellio. In *Concerning Heretics*, Castellio quoted extensively from church fathers and later theologians who had defended toleration.

At this time, Basel was a center of the movement for religious toleration, thanks largely to the influence of the Catholic humanist Erasmus, who had lived there for 7 years. It was while living in Basel that Castellio influenced a number of people who would later carry the torch of toleration throughout Europe. The Italian scholar Jacobus Acontius, who was strongly influenced by Castellio's views, wrote *Satan's Stratagems*, a remarkable indictment of persecution, and Mino Celso quoted liberally from Castellio in his defense of toleration. Benardino Ochino, a friend of Castellio's and a former Franciscan monk, argued that "it is not needful to use sword or violence" when driving Satan from the hearts of men. Castellio's writings also influenced Faustus Socinus, a founder of Unitarianism and a strong voice for toleration in Poland, which became the first country to adopt an official policy of toleration during the 1570s.

It was in 17th-century England that the theoretical case for religious freedom was most fully developed. Various radicals challenged the religious and political status quo during the 1640s, a decade of religious ferment and civil war that produced hundreds of controversial tracts. The case for toleration was broadened and placed on firmer ground as radicals proclaimed freedom of conscience to be a natural right that should fall beyond the reach of government. This libertarian trend is especially evident in the tracts and political platforms of the Levellers, who advocated religious freedom for everyone, including atheists and Catholics. This proposal was so unusual that even other proponents of toleration, such as John Milton and John Locke, who wrote several decades later did not endorse it.

The Levellers viewed religious freedom as a corollary of one's "self-propriety," or "property in one's person," as John Locke later called it. This theory of self-ownership became the foundation of later libertarian treatments of what James Madison and many of his contemporaries dubbed "property in one's conscience." This argument from natural rights became the standard rejoinder to the Augustinian case for "righteous persecution." Natural rights establish boundaries to coercive interference by others even when it is motivated by good intentions.

GHS

See also Acton, Lord; Buckle, Henry Thomas; Levellers; Locke, John; Separation of Church and State

Further Readings

Acontius, Jacobus. *Satan's Stratagems*. R. E. Field, trans. Delmar, NY: Scholars' Facsimiles and Reprints, 1978.

Acton, John Emerich Edward, First Baron. *The History of Freedom and Other Essays*. John Neville Figgis and Reginald Vere Laurence, eds. London: Macmillan, 1907.

———. *Lectures on Modern History*. John Neville Figgis and Reginald Vere Laurence, eds. London: Macmillan, 1906.

Augustine. *The City of God*. Harry Bettenson, trans. New York: Penguin, 2003.

Buckle, Henry Thomas. *The History of Civilization in England*. New York: Ungar, 1964.

Castellion, Sebastien. *Concerning Heretics*. Ronald H. Bainton, trans. New York: Octagon Books, 1965.

Lecky, W. E. H. *History of the Rise and Influence of the Spirit of Rationalism in Europe*. 2 vols. London: Longman, Green, Longman, Roberts, & Green, 1865.

Locke, John. "A Letter Concerning Toleration," *The Works of John Locke in Nine Volumes*. Vol. 5. 12th ed. London: Rivington, 1824.

———. "Second Treatise of Government." *Two Treatises of Government*. Peter Laslett, ed. Cambridge: Cambridge University Press, 1988.

Milton, John. *Areopagitica and Other Political Writings of John Milton*. John Alvis, ed. Indianapolis, IN: Liberty Fund, 1999.

Sharp, Andrew, ed. *The English Levellers*. Cambridge: Cambridge University Press, 1998.

RENT SEEKING

A *rent* can be defined as a payment to the owner of any input that is used in production, such as a building in which a company operates its business, over and above what is necessary to bring forth its supply. Here the building is considered a fixed input because it will not vary in the short run as the value of the company's business rises and falls. Thus, any payment to the building's owner beyond its value in its next-most valuable use (i.e., its opportunity cost) would be considered a rent. Payment for an input that covers the opportunity cost but not more, such as a worker's wage that compensates only for the value of his lost leisure time, is therefore not rent (e.g., a person's superior in-born skills or the superior location of a parcel of land that can earn its owner surpluses over cost). Thus, rent is often associated with factors that are relatively fixed in supply.

In addition to being a regular feature of unhampered markets, however, rents also can be created through acts of government intervention that block free access to markets, limit the availability of inputs, or restrict the supplies of various products. It can do this, for example, by requiring official approval. Because such restrictions can create valuable rents, they also give agents an incentive to spend scarce resources—such as time, labor, and capital—in order to acquire the favor or other inputs needed to capture them.

This phenomenon is called *rent seeking*, a term coined by Anne Krueger in 1974. It has become a highly useful analytical tool in the study of interventionism as practiced by the so-called public choice school of political economy. For example, if a government-created rent is worth $500,000 to a single agent, he would be willing to spend up to $500,000 worth of resources on the essential input (such as a grant of special privilege) in order to capture it. Competition by multiple agents also will tend to raise the cost of the input, and, under certain assumptions (i.e., risk neutrality and perfect knowledge), the total value of the resources they expend will exactly equal the value of the rent.

Normatively, these resources represent a pure waste from the viewpoint of economic efficiency because the output of such an investment has no economic value. There is, for example, no net value added by artificially limiting the supply of taxis or from lobbying for a tariff against foreign imports. Whoever gains rents this way may be better off, but others, consumers as well as potential competitors who could provide the service more cheaply, will be made decidedly worse off. The result is typically higher prices, poorer quality, or fewer choices owing to the effectiveness of political means in discouraging potential rival entrepreneurs. In a more dynamic context, rent seeking also can stifle the competitive discovery process so that, over time, consumers will be less likely to become aware of more efficiently produced goods, and producers will be less likely to provide them.

It is important to note, however, that whether an action is rent seeking has less to do with an agent's motive than with what actions the existing social institutions or rules effectively constrain or permit. If these rules limit agents to voluntary exchanges, which can provide a good or service that others would be willing to pay more for than the cost of the resources used to produce it, then doing so will increase wealth. Rents generated in this way have a positive value insofar as creating wealth is considered desirable. Thus, acquiring rents on land or other assets through voluntary exchange is not rent seeking, but profit seeking, in which entrepreneurs transfer resources from where they are valued less to where they are valued more.

In contrast, if the rules permit the use of the government's authority to initiate aggression (i.e., "political means") to contrive rents by preventing competition or forcibly redistributing wealth, then agents have an incentive to spend valuable resources in attempting to gain access to such means. Rent seeking is therefore the rational response of agents operating under interventionism.

Another aspect of rent seeking concerns the possible effect on social norms inasmuch as rent seeking tends to encourage growing numbers of ordinary people to engage in it as they attempt to acquire political power for themselves, either to gain special privileges or to redress the mounting privileges of others. It can thereby set into motion a dynamic that progressively erodes respect for limited government, private property, and the rule of law. In particular, according to F. A. Hayek, the rule of law is supposed to bind government by rules that are fixed and announced beforehand and that are not intended to benefit or harm any particular person or group. For example, a rule that forbids anyone from engaging in fraudulent advertising is in accord with the rule of law, whereas a rule that grants a monopoly privilege to a particular agent is not. The rule of law serves to protect individuals against arbitrary government interventions, and, with private property and limited government, it is one of the pillars of personal liberty and the free market.

Rules and institutions that beget rent seeking are clear violations of the rule of law because, by their nature, they privilege some at the expense of others. This privilege, in turn, gives agents an incentive to spend resources either to associate themselves with the winners or distance themselves from the losers. The desire to capture politically generated rents is a fundamental motive for interventionist breaches of the rule of law. At the same time, rent seeking tends to prevail to the extent that violations of the rule of law are tolerated. A politico-economic system that strictly observes the rule of law would necessarily serve to severely constrain rent seeking.

SI

See also Laissez-Faire Policy; Public Choice Economics; Regulation

Further Readings

Hayek, F. A. *The Road to Serfdom.* Chicago: University of Chicago Press, 1944.

Krueger, Anne. "The Political Economy of the Rent-Seeking Society." *American Economic Review* 64 (1974): 291–303.

Mueller, Dennis. *Public Choice III.* Cambridge: Cambridge University Press, 2003.

Niskanen, William. *Bureaucracy and Representative Government.* Chicago: Aldine-Atherton, 1971.

Tullock, Gordon. "The Welfare Costs of Tariffs, Monopolies, and Theft." *Western Economic Journal (Economic Inquiry)* 5 (1971): 224–232.

Tullock, Gordon, Gordon Brady, and Arthur Seldon. *Government Failure.* Washington, DC: Cato Institute, 2002.

REPUBLICANISM, CLASSICAL

Liberty has had many different meanings over the course of the history of the term. However, from the Renaissance through the Enlightenment, it commonly appeared as an element in the intellectual tradition that scholars now term *classical republicanism.* The classical republican tradition flourished throughout Europe from the 16th to the 18th centuries, and among its most notable exponents were Niccolò Machiavelli, Algernon Sidney, James Harrington, and Jean-Jacques Rousseau. Classical republicans drew heavily on ancient models and authorities, but they matched these models with new concerns and examples drawn from the world around them to create a distinct ideology that can be recognized in various forms throughout the history of European political thought.

Liberty in the classical republican context must be distinguished from both its modern and ancient meanings; when reading texts of the early modern era, it is important to remember that liberty did not always mean what we may take it to mean today. Nonetheless, the liberty of the classical republicans is in some ways an ancestor of the modern libertarian tradition. At the same time, ironically, it also has played a role in shaping modern collectivist ideologies. Therefore, classical republicanism is of crucial importance in the development of modern political thought.

Despite its name, classical republicanism did not oppose all monarchies. A "republic" denoted for its adherents what we might today call *constitutional government, the rule of law,* or simply *good government,* and this notion was thought consistent with monarchy as one of its components. The classical republicans concerned themselves far more intensely with the proper forms and duties of government, and they were always critical of both monarchs and other government actors who overstepped their prerogatives. This concern for limited government is a feature that classical republicans share with the later classical liberal tradition and with modern libertarians. Yet a fuller account of the classical republican worldview reveals differences as well as similarities to the modern libertarian view.

Classical republicans did not emphasize or even write often about the natural rights of individuals, yet they overwhelmingly agreed that good government was exceedingly fragile and that the vicissitudes of history could sweep it away for no foreseeable reason. Classical republicans often invoked the medieval image of the Wheel of Fortune to describe capricious historical change. Moreover, the reinvigorated study of history that came with the Renaissance convinced them that polities often suffered good and bad turns of fortune. For example, Machiavelli's most famous work, *The Prince,* was written to address the proper rule of a state whose republic had lately been overthrown and in which the key question was how best to save what could be preserved. No classical republican would view the collapse of a republic as surprising; for them, republics tended to do just that.

For classical republicans, the real question lay in how to prevent republics from declining. Therefore, they offered a number of strategies to stave off the threat. Modern libertarians still champion some of these methods, whereas others are rarely encountered or else have been abandoned. Classical republicans held that successful republics, although rare, typically owed their continued existence to a political or civic virtue. The public exercise of civic virtue made for good government and ensured the liberty of the citizens. In turn, civic virtue had several components.

Above all, citizens were expected to be self-sacrificing for the good of the political community, which was usually conceived of as a local city-state. Far-flung empires tended overwhelmingly toward despotism, classical republicans noted, and they generally disparaged empires for just this reason. To keep vigilant in defense of the republic, citizens were to refrain from luxury, effeminate living, and corruption; classical republicans held all three to be closely related to each other and ultimately fatal to a republic. As Machiavelli wrote in his *Discourses on Livy*, "no ordinance is of such advantage to a commonwealth, as one which enforces poverty on its citizens." In the same work, he praised Lycurgus, the ruler of Sparta, for decreeing that all money should be made of leather, the better to discourage trade and manufacturing.

Participation in a civic militia was highly prized. Wealthy states might be tempted to hire mercenaries to defend them, but this was a bad idea according to classical republican thought. As Algernon Sidney noted in the *Discourses Concerning Government*,

> The business of mercenaries is so to perform their duty, as to keep their employments, and to draw profit from them; but that is not enough to support the spirits of men in extreme dangers. The shepherd who is a hireling, flies when the thief comes; and this adventitious help failing, all that a prince can reasonably expect from a disaffected and oppressed people is, that they should bear the yoke patiently in the time of his prosperity; but upon the change of his fortune, they leave him to shift for himself, or join with his enemies to avenge the injuries they had received.

No government should be wealthy enough to hire an independent military force, and all polities should rely on their citizens alone for self-defense. In this way, the liberty of the subject would prove consistent with the success of the state, and citizens would be inclined to defend their governments.

Often agrarian life was valued above the urban because those who owned a piece of land could always make at least a meager living without becoming dependent on others for their livelihood. City life fostered dependence on others,

and to classical republicans, this dependence was the first step toward corruption. The capital cities of large empires were especially dangerous because here money, political power, servility, and commerce converged. Imperial Rome was the paradigmatic example of this type of danger. By contrast, one figure much admired by classical republicans was Cincinnatus, a quasi-legendary Roman farmer who was chosen as dictator to repel an invasion. After his triumph, Cincinnatus surrendered all his power and returned to his farm.

Last, and anticipating much later political thought, classical republicans often advocated a mixed constitution. Machiavelli wrote in his *Discourses on Livy* that "where we have a monarchy, an aristocracy, and a democracy existing together in the same city, each of the three serves as a check upon the other."

Perhaps the remarkable thing about classical republican thought, however, is that it viewed the abuse of government as a ubiquitous problem, one amenable—perhaps—to human solutions. In an age when many other political thinkers proclaimed the divine right of kings and the notion that the forms of government were absolute, immutable, and God-given, classical republicans were in many respects the most realistic as well as the most libertarian voices to be found. For them, government was fundamentally a human affair, and it was subject to all of the many faults that plagued other human creations. Understandably, they viewed the state with constant anxiety.

There is much here that a libertarian can admire, but also much with which to take issue. The classical republicans' admiration for small, mixed republics and their mistrust of empires are consonant with later libertarian thought, as is their love for a citizen militia, which finds expression in the 2nd Amendment's right to keep and bear arms. The suspicion of standing armies, a key feature of early classical liberalism, comes directly from the classical republican tradition, and modern libertarians likewise wish the military force to be no larger than is necessary for the defense of individuals and their property.

Yet modern libertarianism embraces money, commerce, and self-interest, and herein lies a key difference between libertarianism and classical republicanism. Classical republicanism viewed self-interest and the desire for wealth as a danger to the public weal. Subsequent social thought overturned this notion and, in the process, altered the meaning of liberty, reconciling individual freedom with commerce where once they had been thought natural enemies.

Partly in response to classical republicanism and to the rising commercial society around them, thinkers including Bernard de Mandeville and Adam Smith argued that self-interest could motivate individuals toward knowledge, industry, honesty, charity, and peaceful relations with their neighbors, as well as material plenty. It is this later view that modern libertarians champion. Although libertarians do see governmental corruption as a danger, they reject the notion that corruption is an inevitable consequence of wealth or commerce.

The twilight years of classical republicanism were spent in attempting to counter this relatively new idea, which lies at the heart of 18th- and 19th-century classical liberalism. Understood in this light, the political thought of Jean-Jacques Rousseau was not a radically new contrarian position, but rather a throwback to some old ideas about the nature of commerce in a political community. Libertarians find Rousseau's account of liberty unconvincing, in part, for just this reason.

Other areas of classical republican thought are objectionable to libertarians as well, most obviously the notion of the need for self-sacrifice in the interests of the state. The idea of a citizen militia has had a darker side as well—namely, conscription. To most modern libertarians, conscription makes a "mercenary" army seem perfectly honorable, whereas classical republicans would not have agreed.

Self-sacrifice in the interests of the state is problematic for theoretical reasons as well. Social contract theory holds that we citizens create, alter, or abolish states to preserve our own security and liberty, and that we create states to serve us, not the other way around. Meanwhile, individualist libertarianism draws somewhat different borders around the entire question. Objectivism, for example, mistrusts self-sacrifice for philosophical reasons, yet Ayn Rand held that a man who voluntarily dies fighting for his own freedom is not sacrificing himself because he is working for freedom, and this may just be one of his own highest values.

One question in the history of classical republican scholarship is of particular interest to libertarians—namely, the degree to which classical republicanism influenced the founding of the United States. When the United States was founded, classical republicanism still had powerful defenders, but a new appreciation for money and commerce also was gaining a foothold, and America was already a notably commercial republic. Additionally, theories of individual rights, social contract theory, and the somewhat amorphous political thought of Montesquieu clearly played important roles in America's founding.

Yet the founding reflects elements of classical republican thought as well. We observe it when Franklin famously answered that the Constitutional Convention had given Americans "a republic, if you can keep it." It also can be seen in how Jefferson envisioned a nation of small freehold farmers. Voting rights were denied to the residents of the capital city lest they become too powerful. It was a singularly classical republican gesture when Washington returned—with evident pride—to his farm, first after fighting in the American Revolution and then after two terms as president.

JTK

See also English Civil Wars; Enlightenment; Rousseau, Jean-Jacques; Sidney, Algernon; Whiggism

Further Readings

Hamowy, Ronald. "*Cato's Letters,* John Locke, and the Republican Paradigm." *John Locke's* Two Treatises of Government: *New Interpretations.* Lawrence: University of Kansas Press, 1992.
Machiavelli Niccolò. *Chief Works, and Others.* Allan Gilbert, trans. Durham, NC: Duke University Press, 1965.
Pocock, J. G. A. *The Machiavellian Moment: Florentine Political Thought and the Atlantic Republican Tradition.* Princeton, NJ: Princeton University Press, 1975.
———. *Virtue, Commerce, and History: Essays on Political Thought and History, Chiefly in the Eighteenth Century.* Cambridge: Cambridge University Press, 1985.
Sidney, Algernon. *Discourses Concerning Government.* Thomas G. West, ed. Indianapolis, IN: Liberty Classics, 1990.
Skinner, Quentin. *Liberty before Liberalism.* Cambridge: Cambridge University Press, 1998.

RESPONSIBILITY

Most of us believe that people normally possess free will, the fundamental capacity to choose their actions. It also is commonly held that people are responsible for acquiring the skills necessary to earn a living that would allow them to take care of themselves and their families. We believe further that most people are responsible for the direction their lives take and should receive the benefits of their industry and bear the costs of their decisions and mistakes. To use a cliché, we believe that the world does not owe anyone a living.

It is a central tenet of libertarianism that the values of personal freedom and responsibility are indivisible. A corollary to that proposition is the view that respect for one of those values implies and requires a respect for the other. The notion of limited government defended by Madison and Jefferson arguably takes for granted the indivisibility of freedom and responsibility. Friedrich Hayek, a Nobel laureate in economics, explained in his 1960 work, *The Constitution of Liberty*, "a free society will not function or maintain itself unless its members regard it as right that each individual occupy the position that results from his action and accept it as due to his own action."

Modern American culture is commonly criticized because many of its members appear to have increasingly lost a sense of personal responsibility. The causes for this decline may be difficult to isolate, but symptoms of the decline are easily recognizable. Throughout the 20th century, but especially since the 1960s, Americans have come to expect more from government and demand less from themselves. That trend is evident not only in the growth of paternalistic laws, but also in the growth of the welfare state. Many, if not most, Americans have come to believe that all citizens are entitled to food, shelter, jobs, education, and medical care, whether through their own efforts or, failing that, through those of government. In his penetrating 1998 critique of the welfare state, *A Life of One's Own*, philosopher David Kelley argues:

> The premise of the welfare state—the sprawling network of programs for transferring wealth from taxpayers to recipients—is that the world *does* owe us a living. . . . [The welfare state] confers entitlements to goods independent of the process of earning them. It elevates needs and downplays responsibility. The result is a public morality at odds with our personal standards.

Libertarian critics argue that, by treating goods and services as things to which citizens are entitled, the welfare state not only violates property rights, but also erases the traditional distinction between duty and charity and attacks personal responsibility. David Kelley clarifies:

> A right is something an individual can demand as his due without apology for asking and without gratitude for receiving. When that concept is extended to the provision of social welfare, the necessary result is to empower those who make claims on public provision and silence those who do the providing. Since the New Deal, and especially during the three decades since the creation of the Great Society programs, the legal framework of entitlements has given rise to a public *spirit* of entitlement, a sense that the world does owe us a living.

Many critics theorize that this spirit of entitlement is both a symptom and a cause of expansive government. In any event, it is an obstacle to limiting government and an impediment to nourishing personal responsibility because a spirit of entitlement encourages people to depend on others rather than on themselves and to hold others rather than themselves accountable for their circumstances. Critics of the welfare state argue that when governments become involved in forcibly redistributing money, they not only violate property rights, but they also force citizens to be responsible for other citizens in ways that citizens are not expected to be responsible for themselves. In short, the critics assert that the welfare state violates any defensible notion of personal responsibility because it holds taxpayers varyingly responsible for strangers, but never fully responsible for themselves.

Henry Hazlitt explained what he describes as the essence of the welfare state as follows:

> In this state nobody pays for the education of his own children, but everybody pays for the education of everybody else's children. Nobody pays for his own medical bills, but everybody pays everybody else's medical bills. Nobody

helps his own old parents but everybody else's old parents. . . . The welfare state . . . is the great fiction by which everybody tries to live at the expense of everybody else.

Critics argue that the welfare state requires many citizens to carry not only their burdens but also those of others, relieving many people of the responsibility for their actions and circumstances. Accordingly, economist Walter Williams, in his 1999 book, *More Liberty Means Less Government*, wrote,

> If we say that one person has a government-guaranteed right to food or housing, it means that another person must have less of something in order for government to make good on that "right." In other words, government does not have any resources of its own. For government to give one person something, it must first take it from another person, usually through taxes. Thus, one person's "right" to food or housing imposes a burden on another person requiring him to have less of something.

Critics also argue that private charities and private businesses are responsible in ways that governments are not. Unlike welfare states, private charities can and often do distinguish between the deserving and undeserving poor, between the unfortunate and imprudent or lazy. Further, neither charities nor private businesses can afford to operate when their expenses exceed their resources. Governments, however, can continue to raise taxes and deficit-spend, creating a spiral that generates ever-greater burdens on current and future taxpayers.

Another major impediment to developing and exercising personal responsibility is the readiness with which many people see their circumstances as due principally, if not entirely, to factors outside their control. To the extent that people see themselves not as free agents, but as victims of their environments, genetic heritage, or some mental illness, they may view themselves as incapable of exercising personal responsibility. It follows that if people believe that they are incapable of changing their lives, they will, in fact, be unable to do so. Although there are psychologists and psychiatrists who highly value personal responsibility, the direction of psychiatry today is to regard the actions of people as determined by forces outside their control. An official classification of mental illness and mental disorders, the *Diagnostic and Statistical Manual of the American Psychiatric Association* has tended to expand over the years to include as mental disorders simply self-defeating assumptions, such as the belief that one is hopelessly unattractive. Although the psychiatrist Thomas Szasz has spent decades arguing against the classification of aberrant behavior as disease, that proposition is uncritically accepted by most people.

In addition to the many cultural influences that discourage people from believing in and taking responsibility for themselves, many people have personal incentives for rejecting responsibility. There are those people who find it frightening to think that their success or failure, happiness or unhappiness, may depend largely, if not principally, on their own actions. Many find it easier not to take charge of their lives and instead to blame others or the circumstances in which they are placed. Admitting that one is principally responsible for one's life takes courage, and making major changes in one's life can require a great deal of work, belief in oneself, and discipline.

RoE

See also Individualism, Political and Ethical; Paternalism; Virtue; Welfare State

Further Readings

Hayek, Friedrich A. *The Road to Serfdom*. Chicago: University of Chicago Press, 1944.
Kelley, David. *A Life of One's Own: Individual Rights and the Welfare State*. Washington, DC: Cato Institute, 1998.
Magnet, Myron. *The Dream and the Nightmare: The Sixties' Legacy to the Underclass*. New York: Morrow, 1993.
Olasky, Marvin. *The Tragedy of American Compassion*. Elgin, IL: Crossway, 1992.
Steele, Shelby. *The Content of Our Character*. New York: St. Martin's Press, 1990.
Sykes, Charles J. *A Nation of Victims: The Decay of the American Character*. New York: St. Martin's Press, 1992.
Szasz, Thomas. *The Myth of Mental Illness: Foundations of a Theory of Personal Conduct*. New York: Harper, 1961.
Williams, Walter E. *Do the Right Thing: The People's Economist Speaks*. Stanford, CA: Hoover Institution Press, 1995.

RESTITUTION FOR CRIME

Crime, which is defined as offenses against public law and punishable under that law, is a creation of government. Many actions currently defined as crimes were illegal before the advent of criminal law, but were offenses against private law; successful prosecution resulted in victim compensation. By designating an act to be a crime, the state replaces the victim as the focal concern of the legal system, which has a number of significant ramifications. First, making the victim whole through restitution ceases to be a primary concern of the law. As a consequence of replacing restitution with retribution, victims often lose much of their incentive to seek justice and to cooperate with the legal system. Second, the legal code comes to be increasingly populated by victimless crimes, understood as crimes for which there is no complaining victim. Examples include drinking alcohol (under Prohibition), smoking marijuana, or engaging in certain sexual activities with a willing partner.

Some libertarians believe that the category of crime should be replaced in its entirety by an alternative category, intentional tort, which focuses entirely on the victim. Others believe that the state should criminalize only those acts that involve harm to others. All argue that victimless crimes should be decriminalized.

The history of Anglo-Saxon law is illustrative of how our current concept of crime has developed. Anglo-Saxon law was concerned with the protection of individuals and their property. Every freeman's house had a "peace"; if it was broken, the violator had to pay damages minutely detailed by the *wergeld* system. The primary legal institutions were voluntary organizations called *tithings* and *hundreds*. When a theft occurred, for example, the men of the several tithings that made up a hundred, and who had a reciprocal duty to pursue the thief, were informed. The hundreds were further organized into shires, and together they performed the function of adjudicating disputes. Refusal to abide by the law or to accept a judgment (e.g., to pay restitution) resulted in outlawry (ostracizing the wrongdoer and endowing victims and their supporters with the right of victims to exact revenge). Early codes also provided that "the ealdorman," and the king at need, may be called in if the plaintiff is not strong enough himself. When the king was prepared to support the decision of the hundred, even the most powerful offenders had incentives to recognize and follow the law. Should a victim have to request such assistance, the cost to the offender included restitution (*wer*) and a payment (*wite*) to the individual called on to exercise his power to secure compliance. Although kingship evolved primarily due to external conflict (warfare), rather than as an institution to exercise power to resolve internal disputes, warfare was costly, and kings seeking additional revenue began to use the justice process as a source of funds. The institutionalization of *wite* was one of the first steps in the evolution of the revenue-generating role of law enforcement. More significant, certain offenses began to be designated as violations of the "king's peace," with fines paid to the king.

Initially, the king's peace referred simply to the peace of the king's house. Yet as royal power expanded, kings declared that their peace extended to places where they traveled, then to churches, monasteries, highways, and bridges. Eventually, it became "possible for royal officers such as sheriffs to proclaim the king's peace wherever suitable." The expansion of the notion of the king's peace produced increases in royal revenue, but at the cost of victims of injustices, because payments went to the king rather than to the victims. Thus, "there is a constant tendency to conflict between the old customs . . . and the newer laws of the State."

It is true that power became increasingly concentrated under the Saxon kings, but the Norman Conquest of England greatly accelerated this centralization. As

Pollock and Maitland note: "The chief result of the Norman Conquest in the history of law is to be found not so much in the subjection of race to race as in the establishment of an exceedingly strong kingship." One of the earliest and most significant changes made in English law by the Normans was replacing the *wergeld* with a system of fines and confiscations to the king, along with corporal and capital punishment. This change substantially reduced the incentives that citizens had to maintain their reciprocal arrangements for pursuit and prosecution and to participate in the local courts. Apparently many of the hundreds ceased functioning altogether under William the Conqueror. Thus, Norman kings were forced to attempt to establish new incentives for law enforcement and a new judicial apparatus in order to collect their profits from the administration of justice.

In the 12th century, the large number of offenses designated as violations of the king's peace came to be known as *crimes*. Those cases that were designated as criminal referred to offenses that generated revenues for the king and sheriffs, rather than compensation to a victim. Furthermore, "the king got his judicial profit whether the accused was found guilty or innocent," because a verdict of innocence meant that the plaintiff was heavily amerced ("at mercy," or fined) for false accusation. That further reduced the incentives of victims and other members of the community to report crimes. By 1168, circuit tax collectors, who also were itinerant justices, were conducting royal inquests regarding issues of justice. They also amerced communities that failed to fulfill their policing duties. The earliest development of misdemeanors involved offenses of this type. Pollock and Maitland have suggested that

> A very large part of the justices' work will indeed consist of putting in mercy men and communities guilty of neglect of police duties. This, if we have regard to actual results, is the main business of the eyre . . . the justices collect in all a very large sum from hundreds, boroughs, townships and tithings which have misconducted themselves by not presenting, or not arresting criminals . . . probably no single "community" in the county will escape without amercement.

Coercive efforts to induce victims and communities to pursue and prosecute criminals were not adequate, however, and state institutions gradually took over those tasks. The subsequent evolution of public policing, prosecution, and ultimately punishment can all be traced to the incentives set in motion at that time. Over the next several centuries, the system changed from one that generated revenues for the royal treasury into one that involved tremendous taxpayer costs, as interest groups sought the criminalization of certain noncoercive activities, the public bureaucracies expanded and increased their budgets, and the public demanded greater protection from criminals.

Most people would agree that criminals should not be allowed to impose costs on victims, and when they do so criminals should be held accountable for these costs. Justice demands that action be taken to "reflect those negative consequences of harm and injury back onto the criminal," as Bidinotto maintains. The historical roots of criminal law indicate that it did not evolve because of a "public-good" market failure, as some have contended. In fact, the development of criminal law actually deprived victims of crimes of a significant property right—the right to restitution—which had encouraged private enforcement of law. Indeed, when a criminal violates another person's rights, the costs should be reflected back onto the criminal. However, doing so through publicly imposed punishment (rather than restitution) "reflects negative consequences" to taxpayers and, more significantly, fails to compensate the victim for the harm and injury he or she has suffered. Under a system of criminal law as it is currently understood, victims suffer the costs of the crime, along with additional costs that arise as a result of the efforts of the police and prosecutors to convict the offender.

Libertarians have argued that restitution is a fundamental right; it is part of the "structure of liberty." Murray Rothbard derived the right to receive restitution from the right to punish, which in turn derives from the right to self-defense. Indeed, he contended that the fundamental right of the victim is to exact proportional punishment, so restitution arises only if the victim is willing to accept payment in lieu of punishment. Although Rothbard's arguments apply in a theoretical world wherein only the victim and the offender are involved in a dispute, every restitution-based system that has existed probably evolved from a situation such as the one Rothbard envisioned, where individuals exacted punishment and some found themselves willing to forgo punishment in exchange for an economic payment. However, individuals also found that unilateral exactions of punishment were either risky or impossible because of differences in the relative capacities for violence of victim and offender. Thus, reciprocal mutual support groups, such as the Anglo-Saxon tithings and hundreds and later thief-catching societies and posses, evolved to assist its membership in the pursuit of justice. Under those circumstances, legal issues no longer involved only the victim and the offender, but other members of the community who sought peace and security as well. Because violent extraction of retribution (or restitution) can be quite costly to other members of such groups, rules that emphasized public legal procedures emerged out of the peaceful resolution of disputes through restitution. In early medieval England, Iceland, and Ireland, and in a number of primitive societies, victims did not have the right to exact physical punishment unless and until the offender refused to pay fair restitution. Indeed, victims who extracted retributive punishment before giving the offender a chance to pay were law-breakers. Thus, functioning legal systems placed primary emphasis on the right to restitution, rather than to retribution.

In a fully restitution-based system, there would be no crimes. Their place in the legal order would be filled by intentional torts (i.e., intentional acts involving the initiation of force, fraud, or coercion). Only such acts would justify pursuing restitution from the offender. Such a system would eliminate from the legal system prosecution of all "victimless" or "consensual" crimes, such as sodomy, prostitution, drug consumption, gambling (that is not fraudulently rigged), and so on. The legal system would no longer systematically victimize those whose actions do not violate the rights of others.

Even if the moral and jurisprudential justifications for restitution offered in Rothbard, Barnett, and Benson are rejected, there are other reasons that libertarians have traditionally supported restitution over retribution. Systems of criminal law tend to generate police abuse and corruption, whereas the vast majority of crimes against persons go unreported. Even when reported, most of these crimes remain unsolved, and a substantial portion that are solved do not entail punishment that victims find to be satisfactory or that lead to the rehabilitation of the criminal. Many of those problems could be alleviated by refocusing the system on the victim's right to restitution and the offender's responsibility to pay compensation. Relatively cost-effective (efficient) deterrence would arise as victim reporting increased, resources were shifted from prosecuting and punishing victimless crimes, and offenders were more vigorously pursued and prosecuted. Incentives for actual rehabilitation of offenders would increase as offenders would respond to incentives to work off their debts and debt collectors would seek ways to support that effort. Libertarians generally believe that liberty, justice, and efficiency are complementary objectives if the legal system focuses on the rights of innocent persons not to be victimized and, should they be, to again be made whole.

BLB

See also Common Law; Judiciary; Liability; Retribution for Crime

Further Readings

Barnett, Randy E. *The Structure of Liberty: Justice and the Rule of Law*. Oxford: Clarendon Press, 1998.

Benson, Bruce L. *The Enterprise of Law: Justice without the State*. San Francisco: Pacific Research Institute for Public Policy, 1990.

———. *To Serve and Protect: Privatization and Community in Criminal Justice*. New York: New York University Press, 1998.

Bidinotto, Robert J., ed. *Criminal Justice? The Legal System vs. Individual Responsibility*. Irvington-on-Hudson, NY: The Foundation for Economic Education, 1994.

Byock, Jesse L. *Viking Age Iceland*. New York: Penguin, 2001.

Friedman, David. "Private Creation and Enforcement of Law: A Historical Case." *Journal of Legal Studies* 8 (March 1979): 399–415.

Lyon, Bruce. *A Constitutional and Legal History of Medieval England*. 2nd ed. New York: W. W. Norton, 1980.

Peden, Joseph R. "Property Rights in Celtic Irish Law." *Journal of Libertarian Studies* 1 (1977): 81–95.

Pollock, Sir Frederick, and Frederick W. Maitland. *The History of English Law*. Washington, DC: Lawyers' Literary Club, 1959.

RETRIBUTION FOR CRIME

Retributive punishment refers to punishment for a crime that is carried out for retributive reasons and is justified if there really are good retributive reasons for punishing crime. To get a clear sense of this notion, we need to explain what is meant by *crime*, *punishment*, and *retribution*. *Crime* has reference to socially disfavored actions, especially those that violate rights. *Punishment*, whether it is spontaneous or part of a system of law, refers to the imposition of a net loss on some agent in response to that agent's performance of some disfavored action. Punishment is to be distinguished from the extraction of compensation. If our agent has imposed a loss on some other party and has in consequence been required to pay compensation to that party to make up for that loss, he has not (yet) been subjected to punishment. Punishment is that additional whack on the head to which our agent is subjected beyond the extraction of restitution. However, to explain what *retribution* is, we need to distinguish between different sorts of justifications for punishment.

Most of these justifications can be classified as either *consequentialist* or *retributivist*. Consequentialists hold that punishment is justified by its desirable social results—most saliently, that punishment acts as a deterrent. Although the infliction of punishment may be socially undesirable, inflicting punishment on those who perform criminal actions may so extensively deter these sorts of actions that the net consequences of the punishment will be socially optimal. For the consequentialist, particular punishments or systems of punishment are justified if, but only if, they tend to be productive of better overall social outcomes than would be generated by other punishments or systems of punishment or would obtain if punishment were abandoned.

In contrast, retributivists insist that, if punishment is justified, it is justified by considerations of justice, rather than by its desirable results. Retributivists argue that if the rationale for punishment is weighed in terms of its socially optimal results, both punishment of the innocent and markedly disproportionate punishment of the guilty can be justified because sometimes punishment of the innocent or disproportionate punishment of the guilty will have the optimal social outcome. According to advocates of retribution, nothing but a primary focus on justice can explain the fundamental requirements that only the guilty may justifiably be punished and that all legitimate punishment must fit the crime. To endorse retributive punishment is, then, to endorse punishment of crime that is based on principles of justice, rather than on the punishment's desirable consequences. For the retributive punishment of crime to be actually justified, there must be principles of justice that actually vindicate punishment.

The retributivist critique of the consequentialist justification of punishment resonates with the common libertarian insistence that there are principles of justice that must be respected in the treatment of individuals even if violations of those principles were socially expedient. Retributivism seems to be most consistent with the characteristic libertarian insistence that individuals, their just claims, and their rights must be respected and that this respect precludes treating individuals as resources to be utilized in programs of social optimization. Hence, if libertarian doctrine is to embrace punishment, it looks like it must embrace retributive punishment. However, a more detailed examination might well reveal fatal flaws in each of the claims about justice that might be invoked in attempting to build a positive case for retributive punishment. If that turns out to be correct, then libertarian doctrine that duly incorporates sound claims of justice may end up rejecting all punishment and limiting itself to the endorsement of the practice of restitution. This sort of endorsement of restitution, combined with a rejection of punishment, is the position staked out in Randy Barnett's well-known essay, "Restitution: The New Paradigm of Criminal Justice."

A more detailed examination of the prospects for retributive punishment requires that we distinguish between the different sorts of claims about justice to which a retributivist theorist may appeal. The two main sorts of claims about justice are claims about desert and claims about rights. Some retributivists hold that what justifies that extra whack on the head is that the agent who has performed a disfavored action thereby deserves the whack on the head. The whack is his just desert, and the morality of a system of just deserts allows—or even requires—that the whack be delivered. Other retributivists hold that what justifies that extra whack on the head is that the agent has violated another's rights and that the only way to acknowledge that a right has been violated and, at least in this sense, annul the violation is to deliver the whack. A morality based on rights allows—or even requires—the retributive whack. Quite often retributivists do not attend carefully to which of these two sorts of claims about justice claims they are invoking.

Both the desert and the rights defenses of punishment require that we look backward to determine whether a given agent may be punished, rather than looking forward to the possible desirable consequences of punishing him. We must determine whether the agent actually performed the wrongful act that would make him deserving of the whack or whether he actually engaged in the violation of a right that would, in some sense, be annulled by delivering the whack. In either case, the guilt of the agent is essential to the justification of the punishment. Moreover, the magnitude of the justified whack will track the magnitude of the wrongful or rights-violating action by the guilty party. Thus, these forms of retributivism seem to limit justified punishment to the proportionate punishment of the guilty. Of course, it is this backward-looking feature of retributivism that leads its consequentialist critics to charge that retributivism is merely pointless vengefulness.

How well do these two forms of retributivism—desert and rights—fit within the general libertarian perspective? It is clear that the desert form does not accord well with libertarian doctrine inasmuch as it is predicated on rejecting the proposition that it is the role of political and legal institutions to employ their coercive powers to ensure that individuals get what they deserve. The dutiful son deserves his father's estate, whereas the prodigal son does not; yet that does not, from the libertarian perspective, justify the use of coercive means to deliver the estate to the dutiful son. The armchair fan of mass murder who revels in the news of some monstrous attack in which he plays no part more deserves to suffer than the petty thief; yet that does not, on the libertarian perspective, justify coercively imposing the greater suffering on the fan of mass murder. Indeed, it would violate the rights of the prodigal son to deprive him of the estate that his foolish father has bequeathed to him. Similarly, it would violate the rights of the devotee of mass butchery to inflict on him the suffering he so richly deserves. Libertarians do not believe that desert-based theories of morality are subject to coercive enforcement; indeed, desert is part of the moral domain, the coercive enforcement of which violates people's rights. Hence, no libertarian embrace of retributive punishment can be founded on justice as desert.

It is justice based on a respect for rights that is the crux of libertarianism. But does even this notion of justice really support retribution—as opposed to supporting only restitution? One common argument against the belief that justice demands rights-based retributive punishment depends on a false belief in the rights of the king or—in more modern contexts—the rights of society or "the people." The picture that the opponent of retribution presents is this: Extracting restitution from an agent who has inflicted a loss on some individual is based on our correct belief in that individual's rights; but any accompanying punishment of the agent will be based on our incorrect belief that the king or society or "the people" also have some right that the agent's actions have violated. The additional whack of retribution is based on this belief in additional rights held by the king, society, or "the people." According to the antiretribution argument, because these additional rights do not exist, any defense of retribution that depends on them must be unsound. Indeed, many friends of retribution quite willingly embrace the idea that, whereas restitution vindicates the rights of the individual, punishment per se vindicates the rights of the state or "the people."

Opponents of retribution take this admission to be evidence that belief in retributive punishment is inherently statist and antilibertarian.

Can a rights-oriented advocate of retributive punishment escape the charge that his doctrine depends on an antilibertarian belief in the rights of the collectivity? This advocate of retribution can escape this charge if, but only if, he can explain how the extra whack of punishment is part of the justified response to the violation of the rights of individuals. The rights-oriented retributivist seeks to provide such an explanation—an explanation that is grounded in a view about the nature of individual rights and, hence, of what constitutes a violation. According to this view, an individual's right to a particular object involves more than a right to the amount of utility or welfare that is derived from possessing or utilizing that object. The individual's right also and crucially involves the moral authority to determine by one's choice of what will be done with that rightfully held object. Hence, when one's rightful holding is taken, the holder undergoes two distinguishable losses. The victim loses the utility or welfare (if any) that would be derived from a continued possession and use of the object. This loss is the harm that is engendered by the violation. However, that individual also is deprived of the choice about what will be done with that object. This loss is the wrong that is engendered by the violation. The violation of the victim's right both harms and wrongs the victim. Restitution is responsive to the harm; it seeks to annul the harm by bringing the victim back to the level of utility or welfare that would have been attained if one's right to the object had not been violated. But, the retributivist argues, restitution is not at all responsive to the wrong that is inflicted on the victim. The restitution-only stance, in effect, treats a right to an object as nothing beyond a claim to the amount or utility or welfare that the rights holder will derive from possessing or utilizing that object. In this respect, the restitution-only stance is like the doctrine of eminent domain; all that an individual's property right requires is that he be compensated after his property is seized.

In contrast, according to the advocate of retribution, a policy of restitution *and* retributive punishment is responsive to both sorts of losses that are imposed when rights are violated; it responds to both the harm and the wrong. Just as the harming of the victim opens up the rights violator to enforced compensation payments, the wronging of the victim opens up the rights violator to retributive punishment. According to rights-oriented retributivists, the infliction of the punishment annuls the wrong in a way that is comparable to the way in which the extraction of compensation annuls the harm. However, this simply points to the hardest task for defenders of retributive punishment, namely, the task of providing a satisfactory account of how punishment for a wrongful act annuls the wrong. Of course, even restitution does not annul the harm in the sense of rolling the clock back and fully compensating for the harm inflicted.

Thus, retribution cannot be faulted for not rolling back the clock and making it false that a wrong was inflicted. What the retributivist is able to say is that the punishment annuls the wrong in the sense that the punishment vindicates the victim's status as a rights holder. The punishment reaffirms the moral inviolability of the victim in the face of her all-too-actual violability. This vindication is the annulment of the wrong that the victim or the victim's family commonly sees in the conviction and punishment of the wrongdoer. The reason that the failure to convict and punish the wrongdoer is so disturbing is that this failure leaves the wrong in place; it leaves the wrong un-nullified. As the retributivist sees it, when the wrongdoer goes unpunished, the only route to the mitigation of the wrong is foregone.

Such a rights-oriented vindication of retributive punishment seems to be the only sort of justification of punishment that fits comfortably within the libertarian perspective. However, that perspective also reminds us of the complexity of the world of human interaction, the fallibility of our factual judgments, and the mistrust that is so richly deserved by institutions that present themselves to us as vindicators of our rights. Therefore, there is more than a considerable gap between the theoretical justification of retributive punishment and the endorsement of the practice of punishment as it actually exists.

EM

See also Coercion; Common Law; Judiciary; Nonaggression Axiom; Restitution for Crime

Further Readings

Acton, H. B., ed. *The Philosophy of Punishment*. London: Macmillan, 1969.

Barnett, R. E. "Restitution: A New Paradigm of Criminal Justice." *Ethics* 87 (1976/1977): 279–301.

Barton, C. K. B. *Getting Even: Revenge as a Form of Justice*. Peru, IL: Open Court, 1999.

Jacoby, Susan. *Wild Justice: The Evolution of Revenge*. New York: HarperCollins, 1983.

Miller, W. I. *Eye for an Eye*. Cambridge: Cambridge University Press, 2006.

Murphy, J. G. *Retribution Reconsidered*. Dordrecht, Germany: Kluwer Academic, 1992.

Pilon, Roger. "Criminal Remedies: Restitution, Punishment, or Both?" *Ethics* 88 (1977/1978): 348–357.

Primoratz, Igor. *Justifying Legal Punishment*. Atlantic Highland, NJ: Humanities Press International, 1989.

REVOLUTION, RIGHT OF

The right of revolution, according to classical liberal thinkers, is derived from the natural right of self-preservation. Because the purpose of government is to protect individuals against assaults on their lives, liberty, and property, governments lack legitimacy if either they fail to offer such protection or attack the individuals they were created to safeguard. In such cases, individuals owe their government no loyalty, have no obligation to bow to its unjust measures, and may choose to dissolve the old regime in order to create a new government that performs its legitimate role. Thomas Jefferson stated this argument most famously when, in the Declaration of Independence, he wrote, echoing Locke, that "governments are instituted" to secure "inalienable rights." If a government "becomes destructive of these ends," he asserted, "it is the right of the people to alter or abolish it, and to institute new government, laying its foundation on such principles, and organizing its powers in such form . . . most likely to effect their safety and happiness."

The ancestors of classical liberalism writing in the 17th and 18th centuries frequently cited historical instances in which people exercised the right of revolution. In his *Discourses Concerning Government*, Englishman Algernon Sidney mentioned Greek and Roman revolutionaries such as Epaminondas, Publicola, Valerius, and Marcus Brutus, as well as biblical figures such as Moses, Gideon, David, and the Maccabees. In his famous outburst against George III's sanction of the 1765 Stamp Act, American statesman Patrick Henry proclaimed before Virginia's House of Burgesses that "Caesar had his Brutus, Charles the First his Cromwell, and George the Third may profit by their example."

Henry might have added that England's King John had his Magna Carta. Forced to sign the document when noblemen, clerics, and commoners united in protest of his disregard for the customary obligations of the monarchy, John agreed in 1215 to strict limits on his power to tax, incarcerate, and dispense unequal justice. He also agreed that, were he or his heirs to violate these rules and ignore subsequent complaints, a council elected by barons had the right, "by taking our castles, lands and possessions," to "oppress us in every way in their power."

Such historical precedents exemplify the theoretical basis of the right of resistance, which is predicated on the idea of a social contract entered into to achieve certain ends. Writers such as Sidney and Locke developed their ideas within a tradition that included the political philosophies of Thomas Aquinas, Marsilius of Padua, William of Ockham, Juan de Mariana, and Richard Hooker, all of whom maintained that government, authorized by either the governed or their ancestors, exists for specific purposes. They shared the belief that governments existed for the purpose of permitting individuals to collectively secure the safety that was lacking when all lived independently in—as they described it—a state of nature.

Locke wrote that the fundamental "Law of Nature" proscribed anyone from harming another "in his Life, Health, Liberty, or Possessions." Yet solitary individuals found themselves open to murder, injury, enslavement, and theft when confronted with superior force. Thus, reasonable, self-interested people joined together and formed governments to protect themselves. As Thomas Gordon, coauthor of *Cato's Letters*, explained, "What is Government, but a Trust committed by All, or the Most, to One, or a Few, who are to attend upon the Affairs of All, that every one may, with the more Security, attend upon his own?"

Proponents of the right of revolution had their critics. Thomas Hobbes had a particularly negative view of the anarchic state of nature and was prepared to support even the most absolutist of governments provided they imposed order. Once an individual entered into a society, Hobbes maintained, he could rightfully defy the orders of the sovereign only in defense of his life. In contrast, David Hume rejected the idea of a social contract, although he acknowledged "the agreement by which savage men first associated and conjoined their force." Hume contended that in nearly every instance this agreement was "so ancient" as to have been "obliterated by a thousand changes of government and princes"—in other words, "it cannot now be supposed to retain any authority." Regimes, he said, were founded on conquest far more often than consent.

Those who posited that governments rested on the consent of the governed, but denied that a right to revolution existed, rebuked their opponents by pointing out the problems faced by those who accepted an alternative theory. Men could no more permanently give away their liberty, Locke asserted, than they could take their own lives. People who question the right of revolution, he thought, might as well cast doubt on the propriety of men who "oppose Robbers or Pirates, because this may occasion disorder or bloodshed." In other words, without such checks on political authority, the wolves of government might feed freely on the sheep they governed. In such a scenario, Sidney asserted, "forests would be more safe than cities." Both Locke and Sidney identified themselves with the opposition to the Stuart depredations on English liberties, and Locke was a firm supporter of the post-1688 establishment. In that year, members of Parliament had deposed James II, who on several occasions had overreached his authority, and installed as monarchs William and Mary. In the tradition of King John, they agreed to new limits on the power of the monarchy. They also recognized a number of civil rights, all of which bolstered the protection of the natural rights to life, liberty, and property.

Advocates of the right of revolution emphasized that governments could not be dissolved, as Jefferson wrote in the Declaration of Independence, "for light and transient causes." The American Revolution against British rule, he maintained, was a case in which "repeated petitions" for reform had been "answered only by repeated injuries." Jefferson assured the world that the American revolutionaries had met the tests of Sidney, Locke, and John Milton, who believed that the overthrow of governments required significant justification, requiring "a long train of Abuses, Prevarications, and Artifices," as Locke wrote. In such instances, he maintained, people have as much right to overturn their government as a ship's passengers do to mutiny when the captain of their vessel, despite contrary winds, leaks, and low supplies, steers them into a hurricane.

Because neither ruler nor ruled should be subject to arbitrary action, singular instances of government injustice should be met with personal resistance instead of revolution. Good governments listen to the governed and revise unjust laws. Political authorities "who know the frailty of human nature will always distrust their own," Sidney contended, "and desiring only to do what they ought, will be glad to be restrained from that which they ought not to do." Likewise, people tend to restrain themselves from rash action. "*Revolutions happen* not upon every little mismanagement in publick affairs," Locke maintained, for even "*great mistakes*" of rulers will be endured by the people "without mutiny or murder." Only when regimes ignore or outlaw all criticism, public protest, and other forms of resistance may the people turn to violent resistance.

If these theorists are correct, then one of the most powerful safeguards of individual rights—as well as of law and order—is a society's recognition of the right of revolution. The public's willingness to exercise this right discourages government officials from ignoring their most basic obligations to the governed.

RMD

See also American Revolution; Glorious Revolution; Jefferson, Thomas; Locke, John; Secessionism

Further Readings

Bailyn, Bernard. *The Ideological Origins of the American Revolution*. Cambridge, MA: Harvard University Press, 1967.

Brooks, David L., ed. *From Magna Carta to the Constitution: Documents in the Struggle for Liberty*. San Francisco: Fox & Wilkes, 1993.

Locke, John. *Two Treatises of Government*. Cambridge: Cambridge University Press, 1988.

Rossiter, Clinton. *Seedtime of the Republic: The Origin of the American Tradition of Political Liberty*. New York: Harcourt, Brace, 1953.

Sidney, Algernon. *Discourses Concerning Government*. Indianapolis, IN: Liberty Fund, 1990.

Trenchard, John, and Thomas Gordon. *Cato's Letters or Essays on Liberty, Civil and Religious, and Other Important Subjects*. Indianapolis, IN: Liberty Fund, 1990.

Tuck, Richard. *Natural Rights Theories: Their Origin and Development*. Cambridge: Cambridge University Press, 1979.

RICARDO, DAVID (1772–1823)

David Ricardo was a brilliant classical economist. His policies of free trade and hard money helped propel Britain into its role as "workshop of the world" and as an industrial giant, yet his labor theory of value and antagonistic model of capitalism proved misguided and gave unexpected support to the Marxists and socialists.

Born in London to a large Jewish family, Ricardo made his fortune when a relatively young man as a stockbroker on the London Stock Exchange. He was a speculator par excellence, allegedly making a million pounds sterling in 1 day following the Battle of Waterloo. In 1815, he purchased a large estate called Gatcomb Park in Gloucestershire and devoted the remainder of his life to intellectual interests. In 1819, he was elected to Parliament. Four years later, at the age of 51, he died suddenly of an ear infection.

In the 1810s, Ricardo wrote a series of essays and books promoting laissez-faire. He argued that England's raging inflationary price spiral was caused by the Bank of England issuing excessive bank notes to pay for the war against France. Ricardo's hard-money views eventually led to England adopting the classical gold standard and 100% reserve gold backing of its currency, with the Peel Act of 1844. He vigorously attacked the Corn Laws, England's notorious high tariff wall on wheat and other agricultural goods, which was ultimately repealed in 1846. He made profound contributions to economics, including the laws of comparative advantage, diminishing returns, and the quantity theory of money.

He is considered the inventor of abstract model building in economics, creating a mathematical model with a few simple variables, a technique used later by such diverse economists as Karl Marx, John Maynard Keynes, Paul Samuelson, and Milton Friedman.

But it was this abstract reasoning that also has been called the "Ricardian Vice." In his work *On the Principles of Political Economy and Taxation* (1817), Ricardo created an oversimplified "corn" model that led to an antagonistic view of capitalism, where values are determined by labor inputs and where wages can only increase at the expense of profits. His analysis of the nature of production concluded that wages tend toward subsistence levels, known as the iron law of wages. Ricardo thought that over time, as the population grew, an increased demand for food would have the natural effect of raising its price, which would lead to an increase in the value of labor. Yet any increase in the value of labor, Ricardo concluded, must invariably lead to a fall in profits. Ricardo's dismal science, together with the doctrines of his friend, Thomas Malthus, moved economics away from Adam Smith's invisible hand with its harmony of interests and onto a path of class antagonism and exploitation, giving ammunition to socialist and Marxist causes.

MaS

See also Classical Economics; Free Trade; Money and Banking; Smith, Adam; Socialism

Further Readings

Ricardo, David. *On the Principles of Political Economy and Taxation*. Piero Sraffa, ed. Cambridge: Cambridge University Press, 1951 [1817].

Rothbard, Murray N. *Classical Economics*. Hants, UK: Edward Elgar, 1995.

Skousen, Mark. *The Making of Modern Economics*. New York: M. E. Sharpe, 2001.

St. Clair, Oswald. *A Key to Ricardo*. New York: A. M. Kelley, 1965.

RIGHTS, INDIVIDUAL

See INDIVIDUAL RIGHTS

RIGHTS, NATURAL

Natural rights are rights that individuals possess by nature rather than by law or convention. Rights belonging to all human beings universally also are termed *human rights*, a phrase often interchangeable with *natural rights*. Many political and legal theorists claim that individuals have such rights against other individuals and against the state. Libertarians appeal to natural rights to argue that the power of government should be strictly limited, and anarchists contend that the very existence of the state is inimical to individual natural rights. Such theorists have the burden of demonstrating that individuals, in fact, have natural rights and of explaining what precisely they have rights to.

Jurists as well as political philosophers have made important contributions to the understanding of natural rights. In the law, natural rights are treated as a species of constitutional rights, as distinguished from political and civil rights, which are created and circumscribed by legal codes. Political rights are rights related to citizenship and government (e.g., to vote or hold office), and civil rights are other rights belonging to citizens or legal residents (e.g., to marry or to make contracts). Natural rights, in contrast, are regarded as innate, as growing out of human nature, or as required by one's natural ends (e.g., rights to life, liberty, privacy, etc.).

The legal theorist W. N. Hohfeld showed that a right is a legal relation involving three terms, and that this relation takes different forms. The most common right is a claim of an individual against another individual to a performance (e.g., to be repaid a debt). Such a right entails a correlative duty of the other individual to perform (e.g., to repay the debt). But there are other important kinds of rights. One has a right in the sense of liberty (or privilege) when one has no duty to another person to act in a particular way (e.g., the right to use one's own property as one sees fit). One has a right in the sense of power (or authority) over others when one is able to create legal relations involving rights and duties (e.g., the right to make promises or contracts). One has a right in the sense of immunity when one is not subject to a specific power (e.g., the right against self-incrimination). In general, an ordinary right (e.g., ownership of a house) is analyzable into bundles of such relations.

Hohfeld's analysis implies that the distinction drawn from Roman law between rights *in personam* (against a person) and *in rem* (to a thing) disguises the fact that both rights involve three terms: A right *in personam* is a claim against a particular individual, whereas a right *in rem* (e.g., a right to property) is a claim against other persons generally. This distinction also helps to clarify a basic political controversy over rights. According to many libertarian (or classical liberal) theories, the only claims individuals have against all other individuals are rights not to be harmed or threatened with harm by others. Such rights entail "negative" duties—that is, duties on the part of others to refrain from harming them. Libertarians allow that individuals also may acquire rights to benefits through voluntary interactions (e.g., contracts). According to welfare liberal theories, however, individuals also have claims to their well-being against all others. Such rights entail "positive" duties—that is, duties on the part of others, and hence the state, to provide them with welfare.

The task of a theory of natural rights, then, is to demonstrate that individuals have certain rights (claims, liberties, etc.) on the basis of human nature, rather than of prevailing laws or conventions, and to determine the scope of such rights. The attempt to provide a philosophical justification for rights may be traced to antiquity. Arguably, the idea was already recognized in nascent form by even earlier thinkers such as Aristotle, who reasoned that citizens who are equal by nature have the same natural right (i.e., just claim) to political office. In the late Middle Ages, the concept of natural rights began to emerge in a more recognizably modern form. A controversy arose among canon lawyers, philosophers, and theologians over whether the right to private property was conventional—Franciscans like William of Ockham—or natural—Dominicans like John of Paris. Some (e.g., Henry of Ghent) asserted a natural right of self-ownership. Late medieval natural rights theorists assumed the existence of natural law laid down by God, the divine legislator.

Natural rights were theorized by a series of early modern thinkers, including Hugo Grotius, Thomas Hobbes, Samuel Pufendorf, and, most influentially, John Locke, who argued that natural rights exist in the state of nature:

> The State of Nature has a Law of Nature to govern it, which obliges every one: And reason, which is that law,

teaches all mankind, who will but consult it, that being all equal and independent, no one ought to harm another in his life, health, liberty, or possessions.

The natural rights of individuals consist primarily in self-ownership and, by extension, in property rights:

Though the Earth, and all inferior creatures be common to all men, yet every man has a property in his own person. This no body has any right to but himself. The labour of his body, and the work of his hands, we may say, are properly his. Whatsoever then he removes out of the state that nature hath provided, and left in it, he hath mixed his labour with, and joined to it something that is his own, and thereby makes it his property.

According to Locke, men leave the state of nature to form governments to preserve their *property*, which Locke understood to encompass "life, liberty, and estate." The positive laws of political society "are only so far right as they are founded on the Law of Nature, by which they are to be regulated and interpreted." A ruler who flouts the law of nature and the natural rights of his subjects may be removed. Locke's *Second Treatise of Government* was originally written to justify a revolution against James II, which eventuated in the Glorious Revolution of 1688, by which the King was deposed and replaced.

The revolutionary implications of Locke's theory also were manifest in the American Declaration of Independence (1776):

We hold these truths self-evident, that all men are created equal, that they are endowed by their Creator with certain unalienable rights, that among these are life, liberty, and the pursuit of happiness—that to secure these rights, governments are instituted among men, deriving their just powers from the consent of the governed, that whenever any form of government becomes destructive of these ends, it is the right of the people to alter or to abolish it, and to institute new government. . . .

The explicit basis for these rights is "the laws of nature and of nature's God."

Those who embrace a natural rights theory are faced with a problem: If natural rights derive from natural law, how is this law to be validated? Following tradition, Locke identified the law of nature with "the law of reason," which was laid down by God for his creatures. Locke's critics, most notably David Hume, questioned whether it was possible to prove that God exists or that God (if his existence could be demonstrated) would lay down such a law of nature. But is a purely secular theory of natural rights defensible? Hume also doubted whether it is possible to deduce a moral conclusion from purely factual premises— that is, a statement about what one "should" do from premises about what merely "is" the case. Natural rights

theories became less fashionable with the rise of utilitarianism in the 19th century. Jeremy Bentham's quip that natural rights were "nonsense on stilts" seemed to have driven the nail in the coffin.

The end of the 20th century, however, witnessed a remarkable revival of natural rights theory, especially among libertarian theorists. A significant influence was Ayn Rand's argument that "the source of rights is man's nature." Eschewing Locke's theistic principle of natural law, Rand based natural rights on a principle of rational self-interest. The basic principle of her "Objectivist ethics" is that life is the ultimate standard of value: "The fact that a living entity *is*, determines what it *ought* to do." From this determination she derived the basic social principle that "just as life is an end in itself, so every living human being is an end in himself, not the means to the ends or the welfare of others— and, therefore, that man must live for his own sake, neither sacrificing himself to others nor sacrificing others to himself." Thus, from the same principle, Rand deduced both ethical egoism (individuals must treat themselves as ends in themselves) and respect for persons (individuals must treat others as ends in themselves). Rand offered the following derivation of rights:

Rights are conditions of existence required by man's nature for his proper survival. If man is to live on earth, it is *right* for him to use his mind, it is right to act on his own free judgment, it is *right* to work for his values and to keep the product of his work. If life on earth is his purpose, he has a *right* to live as a rational being: nature forbids him the irrational.

Rand used the theory of rights to defend private property, limited government, and capitalism.

Robert Nozick criticized Rand's theory of rights, objecting that even if a person's life is his own highest value, an argument needs to be given that others should not forcibly intervene in his life when it is in their apparent interest to do so. He questioned her claim that there are no conflicts of interest among rationally self-interested individuals. Nozick also defended a neo-Lockean theory, contending that individuals are ends in themselves and are thus entitled to life, liberty, and private property. But he offered little by way of argument for his claim that individuals have rights in the sense of inviolable side constraints on the morally permissible actions of other individuals and political states, so that his theory was, fairly or not, criticized as "libertarianism without foundations." Subsequently, other theorists entered the controversy, some seeking to vindicate Rand's original theory and others striking out in new directions. Three distinctive approaches are mentioned briefly here.

Tibor Machan argues that ethical egoism should be understood along neo-Aristotelian lines as conducing to man's flourishing, rather than his mere survival. Hence, when rational persons interact, they need to recognize one another as moral agents: "free and equally morally responsible who require 'moral space' for living their lives in line with their natures." Thus, argues Machan, enlightened self-interest entails respect for rights:

> If, then, egoism requires that one be rational, and rationality produces a recognition of the equal moral nature of others . . . this justifies anticipating their choice to resist intrusion upon them. Their choice to live a life of rationality also commits them to a system of enforceable principles that protects and preserves the requirement that all persons obtain the moral space for their moral nature.

Tara Smith argues for a similar theory of rights.

Eric Mack argues that ethical egoism could be derived from a theory of objective functions. He infers that moral goodness is "the successful performance of those actions that sustain his existence as a living thing." Mack understands this imperative as a principle of impersonal ethical egoism (i.e., the principle that all persons should act in their own interest). In his earlier work, he argued that this principle entails not only that they should act in their own interest, but also that they should not forcibly prevent others from acting in their own interests.

Taking a somewhat different line, Mack's later writings develop a theory of moral individualism that affirms two distinct, but interrelated, forms of reasons for action: those based on the value of their outcomes for agents, and those based on the moral status of other persons. Mack maintains that individuals should respect others' rights because "there is a type of incoherence in perceiving another as a being with rational ends of his own and not perceiving that other person as having a right of self-ownership."

Douglas Den Uyl and Douglas Rasmussen have argued that "self-directedness or autonomy is nothing less than the very form, the only form, of the natural end of man." An important contribution is their insight that rights are "meta-normative principles." That is, unlike ordinary interpersonal legal or moral relations, rights are higher order principles governing constitutional arrangements. Thus, there is no need to demonstrate that it is invariably in one's rational self-interest to respect others' rights. Rather, they argue, rational egoists will recognize that it is in their mutual interest to establish a political framework of rights that protects the self-directedness—autonomy or liberty—of each and every individual.

Each of the foregoing approaches, along with others, has critics and defenders. Vigorous debate continues over whether a theory of natural rights can be successfully defended and whether such a theory would provide a philosophical foundation for libertarianism.

FM

See also Hume, David; Jefferson, Thomas; Locke, John; Nozick, Robert; Rand, Ayn; Rights, Theories of

Further Readings

Machan, Tibor R. *Individuals and Their Rights*. La Salle, IL: Open Court, 1989.

Mack, Eric. "Egoism and Rights." *The Personalist* 54 (1973): 5–33.

———. "Moral Individualism: Agent-Relativity and Deontic Restraints." *Social Philosophy & Policy* 7 (1989): 81–111.

Miller, Fred D., Jr. *Nature, Justice, and Rights in Aristotle's Politics*. Oxford, UK: Clarendon Press, 1995.

Nozick, Robert. *Anarchy, State, and Utopia*. New York: Basic Books, 1974.

———. "On the Randian Argument." *The Personalist* 52 (1971): 282–304.

Paul, Ellen F., Fred D. Miller, Jr., and Jeffrey Paul, eds. *Natural Rights Liberalism from Locke to Nozick*. Cambridge: Cambridge University Press, 2005.

Rand, Ayn. *Capitalism: The Unknown Ideal*. New York: New American Library (Signet), 1966.

———. *The Virtue of Selfishness*. New York: New American Library (Signet), 1964.

Rasmussen, Douglas B., and Douglas J. Den Uyl. *Liberty and Nature: An Aristotelian Defense of Liberal Order*. La Salle, IL: Open Court, 1991.

Smith, Tara. *Moral Rights and Political Freedom*. Lanham, MD: Rowman & Littlefield, 1995.

Tierney, Brian. *The Idea of Natural Rights: Studies on Natural Rights, Natural Law, and Church Law, 1150–1625*. Grand Rapids, MI: Eerdmans, 1997.

Tuck, Richard. *Natural Rights Theories: Their Origin and Development*. Cambridge: Cambridge University Press, 1979.

RIGHTS, THEORIES OF

Some advocates of libertarianism do not accord to individual rights a fundamental or even central role in justifying libertarian positions. Examples include Ludwig von Mises, F. A. Hayek, and David Friedman. Nonetheless, libertarianism is generally understood as the political expression of the idea that individuals have a basic, negative, moral right to liberty. *Right* is used here to refer to a claim or entitlement that individuals have on how others should treat them. These rights are "moral" in the sense that they direct that men *should* be accorded this treatment, not that it necessarily is accorded to them. *Negative* refers to the fact that persons are prohibited from initiating, or threatening to initiate, physical force in any or all of its forms against other persons. These rights are considered basic in the sense that they are not founded on any other right and are the source for other, derivative rights (e.g., contractual rights).

An individual's right to liberty also is understood to entail two corollary rights: the right to life and the right to private property. So understood, that implies that the lives and resources, as well as the conduct of individuals, may not be directed to purposes to which they have not consented. Those rights apply to every human person, but they also require a legal system for their actual implementation.

The most important and controversial feature about individual rights is that they override all other moral claims. If individuals have a right to liberty, then they may not be physically compelled or coerced to take actions merely because those actions are morally worthwhile. Individuals may not be compelled or coerced to engage in actions that, for example, constitute virtuous behavior, fulfill their moral obligations to others, achieve the political common good, or promote the greatest good for the greatest number. Further, individuals may not be coercively prohibited from doing what is morally wrong but to which they have a right. People should be free to choose the morally wrong course of action provided that it does not entail violation of the rights of others. Physical compulsion and coercion may be used only in defense against or in response to the exercise of physical force or coercion, which is generally understood to include extortion and fraud.

The central problem faced by contemporary libertarian theorists is how to justify giving the right to liberty such fundamental importance. Why is the right to liberty more important than being virtuous, fulfilling our obligations to others, achieving the common good, or promoting the greatest good for the greatest number? The answers to that question take different forms and provide a way to classify various theories of individual rights. What follows is a short summary of the various positions.

Moral skepticism holds that there is no moral knowledge and, therefore, there is no problem faced by the advocate of the right to liberty. Because we do not know what actions are morally worthwhile, we do not have to show why liberty is more important than these other allegedly worthwhile actions. Of course, the problem with this approach is that it is too sweeping. If no one knows what is morally right or wrong, then one also does not know that people have a moral right to liberty or that it is wrong to initiate physical force or coercion.

Intuitionism contends that the right to liberty is a self-evident moral truth and impossible to reject if one has any moral insight at all. Yet is that so? What do we say to those people who have moral insight but do not grasp the right to liberty as a fundamental truth? That right may indeed have some kind of basic status, but it certainly seems to be something that needs to be demonstrated, not merely intuited.

Contractarianism argues that individuals either actually do, or hypothetically would, agree to respect the liberty of each other in order to live together, and that that agreement, which may be explicit or tacit, is the ultimate source of their right to liberty. Nothing is more ethically basic than social agreement. The central issue here is, however, whether this approach is based on what people agree to or to what they should agree to. If it is the former, what happens to the right to liberty if people do not agree? What follows if they do not accord fundamental social importance to the right to liberty? Would there be no basic right to liberty? If it is the latter, then why should persons agree to respect each other's liberty? What is the basis for that claim? Is social agreement not ethically basic after all?

Utilitarianism holds that people have the right to liberty only if that right promotes the greatest good for the greatest number. Liberty is valuable only because of the good consequences it produces. Because a society based on the right to liberty tends to produce the greatest good for the greatest number, people have that right as a rule. Of course, it may not be true that protecting an individual's liberty promotes general social utility, and when following that rule does not promote overall utility, then there is no justification for following it. Utilitarian advocates of rights frankly admit that possibility, but see no alternative. Their critics believe that it is precisely in those cases where protecting an individual's liberty does not promote the general good that an individual's right to liberty is most needed. Such critics claim that the utilitarian approach cannot capture the nonconsequentialist character of individual rights.

Deontologism, or duty ethics, holds that an individual's right to liberty is not based on producing good consequences in any sense. Rather, that right is based on the insight that individual human beings are ends in themselves and not merely means to the ends of others. Thus, it is morally wrong to use people for purposes to which they have not consented. However, one can ask, why are people ends in themselves? What makes them so, and exactly how does that require that their liberty be respected? Further, does their status as ends in themselves require only that their liberty be respected? Could it not also require the fulfillment of other moral obligations?

Virtue ethics claims that the aim of life is the human flourishing of the individual, and the development of an individual's moral character is central to that activity. Yet the dispositions that constitute such character cannot be morally worthwhile unless they are the result of human choice. Physical compulsion and coercion deny human choice. Thus, liberty is necessary for the exercise of individual choice and the achievement of virtue. Nevertheless, important issues remain. What happens when people do not choose virtuously? What happens when people choose courses of action that are personally and socially destructive? Do people have a right to choose what is morally wrong? How can an individual's right to liberty be based on what is necessary to choose virtue? Is something more than liberty required to support the choice of virtue? What if someone's flourishing depends on violating someone else's rights?

However, it has been contended that many of these issues are the result of failing to see that rights are an irreducible moral concept. Rights do not exist for the sake of achieving human flourishing (or virtue), nor are they some ultimate moral duty. They are not like any other moral concept. Rather, rights exist for solving a uniquely political/legal problem. This problem stems from the highly individualized, profoundly social, and self-directed character of human flourishing. It is the problem of finding an appropriate solution to the political issue of integrated diversity: How is the appropriate political/legal order—the order that provides the overall structure to the social/political context—to be determined? How is it possible to have an ethical basis for an overall or general social/political context—a context that is open ended or cosmopolitan—that will not require, as a matter of principle, that one form of human flourishing be preferred to another? It is argued that only the right to liberty reconciles the moral propriety of individualism and the need for sociality. It seeks not to guide human conduct in moral activity, but rather to regulate conduct so that conditions will be obtained whereby the *pursuit* of human flourishing is possible. The right to liberty is a metanormative principle—the link between ethics and politics.

The legitimacy of the metanormative conception of individual rights depends on human flourishing being highly individualized and thus plural, profoundly social, and self-directed. Yet the notion of human flourishing is philosophically problematic. Can we really say what human flourishing is? Further, might not the social nature of human flourishing require the political/legal order to implement more than the right to liberty? What exactly does it mean to be self-directed? Finally, what is the connection among metanorms, norms, and ethics? Must metanorms always hold liberty paramount? This metanormative conception must address these critical questions.

DBR

See also Contractarianism/Social Contract; Freedom; Individualism, Political and Ethical; Rights, Natural; Utilitarianism; Virtue

Further Readings

Friedman, David. *The Machinery of Freedom*. La Salle, IL: Open Court, 1989.
Hazlitt, Henry. *The Foundations of Morality*. Irvington-on-Hudson, NY: Foundation for Economic Education, 1998.
Lomasky, Loren. *Persons, Rights and the Moral Community*. New York: Oxford University Press, 1987.
Machan, Tibor R. *Individuals and Their Rights*. La Salle, IL: Open Court, 1989.
Machan, Tibor R., and Douglas B. Rasmussen. *Liberty for the 21st Century*. Lanham, MD: Rowman & Littlefield, 1995.
Mack, Eric. "In Defense of the Jurisdiction Theory of Rights." *The Journal of Ethics* 4 nos. 1–2 (2000): 71–98.
———. "Moral Individualism: Agent Relativity and Deontic Restraints." *Social Philosophy & Policy* 7 (Autumn 1989): 81–111.
Narveson, Jan. *The Libertarian Idea*. Philadelphia: Temple University Press, 1988.
Nozick, Robert. *Anarchy, State and Utopia*. New York: Basic Books, 1974.
Paul, Jeffrey. "Substantive Social Contracts and the Legitimate Basis for Political Authority." *The Monist* 66 (October 1983): 517–528.
Rand, Ayn. *Capitalism: The Unknown Ideal*. New York: New American Library, 1967.
Rasmussen, Douglas B., and Douglas J. Den Uyl. *Norms of Liberty: A Perfectionist Basis for Non-Perfectionist Politics*. University Park: Pennsylvania State University Press, 2005.
Rothbard, Murray. *The Ethics of Liberty*. New York: New York University Press, 1998.

RIGHT TO BEAR ARMS

The central principle of classical liberal thought is that every human being has an inalienable right to self-preservation. One corollary is that citizens should have a right to the tools they need to defend themselves against threats to their lives, which may arise either from a failure of the government to protect them or from the government itself. Yet some restrictions on civilian access to weapons are manifestly necessary, especially in a world where the most lethal weapons have truly awesome destructive power. America's federal Constitution and most of the state constitutions have formalized a right to arms in general terms. The scope and nature of the right, however, have been subject to considerable controversy and doubt.

The 2nd Amendment to the U.S. Constitution provides that "A well regulated Militia, being necessary to the security of a free State, the right of the people to keep and bear Arms, shall not be infringed." Recent debates about the meaning of this provision have focused on whether it protects a right of individuals to keep and bear arms, or rather a right of the states to maintain military organizations like the National Guard. The lower courts have been sharply divided on the issue, and as of press time, the U.S. Supreme Court will shortly be ruling on a pending case, *District of Columbia vs. Heller*. The stronger legal arguments favor the individual rights interpretation, but even if the Supreme Court accepts those arguments, it could recognize a right too narrow in scope to contribute meaningfully to the preservation of civil liberty.

The American decision to constitutionalize a right to arms has deep roots in British history. In the early British militia system, ordinary civilians were required to arm themselves and submit to part-time, unpaid military training. This system of in-kind taxation developed primarily because the Crown could not easily afford to keep large numbers of professional troops except when Parliament was willing to provide funds for European wars. The taxpayers naturally resented these militia obligations, and kings just as understandably desired to acquire more tractable and efficient tools of royal policy. During the 17th century, the British people lived through a civil war in which they got firsthand experience of life with professional troops in their midst, and they saw how kings could use military power—including the power to regulate the militia—against their political opponents. In 1689, the Crown was forced to accept a Bill of Rights that included a provision guaranteeing the right of Protestants to "have arms for their defense suitable to their Conditions and as allowed by Law."

English history and its own colonial experience had taught America's founding generation that central governments are prone to use military power to oppress the people. Nevertheless, experience during our Revolutionary War also convinced America's most important leaders that the traditional, decentralized militia system was inadequate to protect the nation's security. Accordingly, the Constitutional Convention decided that Congress must be given virtually unfettered authority to raise and keep armies, during war and peace alike, and to strengthen the existing state militias by imposing a uniform system of regulations, training, and command on them.

Anti-Federalists strenuously objected to this massive shift of military authority from the states to the national government, which they thought would leave individual states and their people vulnerable to the kind of oppression that was then common in Europe. Supporters of the proposed constitution responded that the new governmental structure had effective safeguards against capture by abusive politicians, and that Americans, unlike Europeans, would in any event be almost impossible for a despot to subdue because they were an armed people.

The 2nd Amendment was undoubtedly meant to respond to Anti-Federalist fears. Together with the 2nd Amendment's prefatory allusion to a well-regulated militia, this consideration has led many courts and commentators to believe that the amendment guarantees a right of the states to maintain a military counterweight to the federal government. There are, however, far more powerful reasons in the text to interpret the amendment to guarantee individual citizens a private right to keep and bear arms. First, the 2nd Amendment protects a "right of the people." Identical language is used in the 1st and 4th Amendments to refer to rights that indubitably belong to individuals, and the term *the people* is never used in the Constitution to refer to any government. Second, the 2nd Amendment's prefatory phrase is grammatically absolute, and the operative clause is a command. Absolute phrases do not limit or qualify any word in an operative clause to which they are appended. If a dean announces, "The teacher being ill, class is cancelled," the class is cancelled regardless of whether the teacher is actually ill. Third, the organized militia is and always has been a small subset of "the people." Fourth, the "states' right" interpretation implies that the 2nd Amendment silently repealed or amended two separate clauses of the original Constitution: a provision giving the federal government virtually plenary authority over the militia and a provision forbidding the states to keep troops without the

consent of Congress. There is no evidence suggesting that anyone thought the 2nd Amendment would have this effect. Indeed, there is no evidence that anyone alive at the time of its framing thought that the 2nd Amendment protected a right of states rather than of individuals.

Like the rest of the Bill of Rights, the 2nd Amendment occasioned little controversy. Its effect was primarily to confirm that the original Constitution did not empower the new federal government to disarm the citizenry under the pretense of regulating the militia. What we think of as "gun control" today was a matter reserved to the state governments. Some states had provisions in their own constitutions protecting a right to arms and some did not, and the nature of weapons regulations varied from place to place. Adoption of the 2nd Amendment had no effect on the authority of state governments to make their own decisions about civilian access to guns.

For well over a century after the founding, the federal government imposed virtually no regulatory control on firearms, and federal regulations even today impose only limited restrictions on the access of most Americans to ordinary small arms like pistols, rifles, and shotguns. Some states and localities have adopted much more restrictive rules, and a few jurisdictions come close to denying their citizens any right to have effective tools for self defense against criminal violence. Because the 2nd Amendment does not confine the discretion of state and local governments, the most practically important questions about the federal right to arms arise under a different provision of the Constitution.

The 14th Amendment, adopted in the aftermath of the Civil War, forbids state and local governments to abridge "the privileges or immunities of citizens of the United States" or to deprive any person of life, liberty, or property without "due process of law." Historical evidence strongly indicates that the Privileges or Immunities Clause had as one of its objects to protect individuals from being disarmed. It is less clear whether this clause was meant to protect against all forms of unreasonable regulation or only to protect against discriminatory schemes, such as the efforts of some state governments to disarm the recently freed black population. In any event, the U.S. Supreme Court long ago rendered this debate academic by interpreting the Privileges or Immunities Clause to protect only a few rights peculiar to federal citizenship, such as the rights to interstate travel and to petition Congress.

During the 20th century, however, the Supreme Court made most provisions of the Bill of Rights applicable to the states through the 14th Amendment's Due Process Clause, using a doctrine under which the Court assesses for itself whether various governmental restrictions on individual liberty are permissible. But the Court has not yet decided whether to make the 2nd Amendment applicable to the states. This fact, combined with the absence of meaningful

Supreme Court doctrine about the scope of the 2nd Amendment, has made the status of the right to keep and bear arms one of the most important unresolved issues in American constitutional law.

Until recently, the lower federal courts had uniformly refused to recognize any meaningful individual right to keep and bear arms. That has now changed. In 2001, a federal court of appeals upheld a challenged federal gun control statute, but adopted the individual right interpretation of the 2nd Amendment. In the case that is now before the Supreme Court, another court of appeals held that the District of Columbia's firearms regulations—which are technically federal laws and which prohibit virtually all civilians from keeping handguns or operable rifles and shotguns in the home—are unconstitutional under the 2nd Amendment. As of November 2007, the Supreme Court has agreed to review this decision, and it now seems likely that a new era of constitutional jurisprudence will soon begin.

Whether in this case or some other, the Supreme Court is bound eventually to resolve several major issues. The Court could adopt the discredited states' right theory and thereby effectively render the 2nd Amendment a dead letter. Even if it adopts the individual right interpretation, it could conclude that only the federal government is affected, thereby insulating state and local infringements on the right to arms from constitutional challenge. Assuming, however, that the justices do not exercise either of these options, the most important initial decisions are likely to involve the stringency with which the Court requires governments to provide reasoned justifications for their regulations. The approach most favorable to civil liberty, and most consistent with classical liberal principles, is exemplified by much existing doctrine under the 1st Amendment's Free Speech Clause. Under this approach, courts would require governments to demonstrate that significant restrictions on civilians' access to weapons are narrowly tailored to serve a compelling public interest. Many gun control schemes that disarm law-abiding citizens and leave them vulnerable to criminal violence would be unable to survive judicial scrutiny under this approach, especially in cases where the regulation's contribution to public safety is speculative or implausible. An alternative model, exemplified by the Court's treatment of most economic regulations, would defer almost completely to legislative judgments about the utility of gun control regulations. All regulations, no matter how ineffective or counterproductive, would be upheld under this approach if a court could imagine some legitimate goal that the legislature might have been trying to achieve. Between these two poles, of course, there are intermediate possibilities.

The future of the right to arms is in considerable doubt as a matter of constitutional doctrine. American courts, including the Supreme Court, have generally shown little inclination to develop robust protections for this right, although we may hope for that to change. Interestingly, the trend among legislatures has been much more favorable to liberty. Congress has never tried to disarm the civilian population and has not enacted any truly onerous gun control measures in many years. At the state level, where the most aggressive restrictions have appeared, many jurisdictions have significantly liberalized their laws in recent years. Most notably, a large majority of states now permit almost all law-abiding adults to obtain a license to carry a concealed weapon in public. This measure was widely regarded as a dangerous experiment, especially in states with large urban populations, but misuse of this right has proved to be virtually nonexistent. Individual citizens have often used their weapons to save lives and stop crimes, and the mere existence of these armed civilians may be having a significant deterrent effect on violent crime. Here, as in so many other areas of human life, free men and women have proved that it is easy to underestimate the beneficent power of individual responsibility and to overestimate the ability of governments to improve our lives by curtailing our liberty. Perhaps it is not too much to hope that the Supreme Court will recognize this enduring truth when it next interprets our Constitution's guarantee of the right to keep and bear arms.

NL

See also American Revolution; Bill of Rights, U.S.; Revolution, Right of

Further Readings

Kates, Don B., Jr. "Handgun Prohibition and the Original Meaning of the Second Amendment." 82 *Michigan Law Review* 204 (1983).

Levy, Leonard W. *Origins of the Bill of Rights*. Chapter 6. New Haven, CT: Yale University Press, 1999.

Lund, Nelson. "A Primer on the Constitutional Right to Keep and Bear Arms." Policy Paper No. 7, Virginia Institute for Public Policy, June 2002. Available from http://www.virginiainstitute.org/publications/primer_on_const.php

———. "The Second Amendment, Political Liberty, and the Right to Self Preservation" 39 *Alabama Law Review* 103 (1987).

Malcolm, Joyce Lee. *To Keep and Bear Arms: The Origins of an Anglo-American Right*. Chapters 1–7. Cambridge, MA: Harvard University Press, 1994.

Reynolds, Glenn Harlan. "A Critical Guide to the Second Amendment." 62 *Tennessee Law Review* 461 (1995).

Röpke, Wilhelm (1899–1966)

Wilhelm Röpke, economist and author, was an economist of the Austrian School and a key influence on Ludwig Erhard, the economic minister of West Germany following World War II.

Röpke was a professor of economics at the University of Marburg when Adolf Hitler became chancellor of Germany in 1933. An outspoken critic of the Nazis, Röpke left his native Germany that same year to accept a position at the University of Istanbul. He remained in Turkey until 1937, when he joined the faculty of the Graduate Institute of International Studies in Geneva, a post he held until his death in 1966.

Röpke's early writings were on business cycle theory. His views on the causes of economic downturns were largely consistent with the writings of F. A. Hayek and other Austrian economists of the period. However, he was more sanguine than many of his Austrian colleagues about using credit expansion to help an economy recover from a depression. Still he was highly critical of John Maynard Keynes's "pump-priming" theories, which he argued "followed the banner of 'full employment' right into permanent inflation."

While at Geneva, Röpke was a colleague of economist Ludwig von Mises, who left Geneva in 1940 for the United States. Röpke, too, had employment opportunities in the United States, but he declined offers from the New School for Social Research, a haven for many continental scholars during World War II, and opted to stay in Europe instead. In 1947, he joined Hayek, Mises, and others at the founding meeting of the Mont Pelerin Society, and he served as president of that organization from 1961 to 1962.

In the 1950s, Röpke turned his attention away from strictly economic issues to problems of political and social theory. Although remaining a steadfast proponent of the market economy, he emphasized the importance of social norms and religion. In his most famous book, *A Humane Economy: The Social Framework of the Free Market*, Röpke argued,

> In the place of God we have set up the cult of man, his profane or even ungodly science and art, his technical achievements, and his State. We may be certain that some day the whole world will come to see, in a blinding flash, what is now clear to only a few, namely, that this desperate attempt has created a situation in which man can have no spiritual and moral life, and this means that he cannot live at all for any length of time, in spite of television and speedways and holiday trips and comfortable apartments.

Röpke also was skeptical of some of the effects of industrialization. In particular, he feared that large corporations compromised the spirit and humanity of their employees. Although such industrial powers "may become the source of grave perils to free society," Röpke insisted that "the most immediate and tangible threat is the state itself. I want to repeat this because it cannot be stressed too much." Along with Walter Eucken, Alexander Rüstow, and others, Röpke advised Ludwig Erhard on how to reform the West German economy following World War II. This group of *Ordoliberals*, as they came to

be known, pushed for a substantially more market-oriented system than that which preceded it, along with a modest system of transfer payments consistent with modern welfare state goals. Röpke was later quite critical about the growth of such transfer programs.

Ultimately, Röpke's liberalism must be viewed in light of his commitment to decentralization—political, social, and economic. In *A Humane Economy*, Röpke described the "natural order" as having the following characteristics:

> [W]ealth would be widely dispersed; people's lives would have solid foundations; genuine communities, from the family upward, would form a background of moral support for the individual; there would be counterweights to competition and the mechanical operation of prices; people would have roots and would not be adrift in life without anchor; there would be a broad belt of an independent middle class, a healthy balance between town and country, industry and agriculture.

It is not surprising, then, that Röpke has been viewed favorably by both libertarians and social conservatives, such as Russell Kirk, who deemed Röpke his favorite economist. Indeed, Röpke can be viewed as a major figure in the fusionist project championed by *National Review* editor Frank S. Meyer.

AS

See also Economics, Austrian School of; Fusionism; Liberalism, German; Meyer, Frank S.

Further Readings

Ebeling, Richard M. "Wilhelm Röpke: A Centenary Appreciation." *The Freeman: Ideas on Liberty* 49 no. 10 (October 1999): 19–24.
Pongracic, Ivan. "How Different Were Röpke and Mises?" *Review of Austrian Economics* 10 no. 1 (1997): 125–132.
Röpke, Wilhelm. *Against the Tide.* Chicago: Regnery, 1969.
———. *The Economics of the Free Society.* Chicago: Regnery, 1963.
———. *A Humane Economy: The Social Framework of the Free Market.* Chicago: Regnery, 1960.
Zmirak, John. *Wilhelm Röpke: Swiss Localist, Global Economist.* Wilmington, DE: ISI Books, 2001.

ROTHBARD, MURRAY (1926–1995)

Murray Rothbard, a libertarian economist, political philosopher, historian, and activist, strove throughout his life to craft a systematic approach to liberty covering all the disciplines of the humane sciences. He was of central importance to the American libertarian movement because of both his writing and scholarship and his personal outreach to young libertarians. Many young libertarian writers and activists from the

1960s and 1970s credit Rothbard as a key influence, both intellectually and personally. He combined in one body of writing most of the intellectual concerns and approaches that defined the modern American libertarian movement: anarchism based in an Aristotelian natural law ethic, an Austrian/Misesian approach to economics, the promotion and extension of the 19th-century American anarchist tradition as exemplified in the writings of Lysander Spooner and Benjamin R. Tucker, and the use of historical analysis to demonstrate the damaging effects of state actions. For his coverage of the full range of libertarian philosophy and application in his writings, and his near ubiquitousness through most institutions of the libertarian movement from the 1960s to the 1980s, he was often thought of as having shaped modern American libertarian thought, although his thoroughgoing anarchism, cultural conservatism, and tendency to feud with former associates made him a controversial figure in the libertarian movement.

Rothbard received his doctorate in economics at Columbia University in 1956. His doctoral dissertation was later published as *The Panic of 1819*—a reinterpretation of the first economic depression in American history, which he determined was the fault of the Bank of the United States. The Bank of the United States was an early precursor of the Federal Reserve, which Rothbard blamed for a good portion of the 20th century's economic ills in America. Rothbard taught economics at Brooklyn Polytechnic University and at the University of Nevada at Las Vegas.

In the 1950s, Rothbard had been a regular attendee at Ludwig von Mises's New York University seminars. In addition to writing and scholarship, he regarded building an activist movement as particularly important to the spread of libertarianism, and in the mid-1950s he was the key member of a libertarian social group in New York City known as the Circle Bastiat, which also included such later libertarian writers, historians, and scholars as Ralph Raico, Leonard Liggio, Robert Hessen, George Reisman, and Ronald Hamowy. Rothbard also met Ayn Rand in this period and briefly became part of her circle before departing amid mutual recriminations. Rothbard's Aristotelian natural rights arguments for libertarianism, based on the natural right of self-ownership and a Lockean theory of how people homestead elements of the natural world as their property, are largely similar to Rand's. Rothbard's entire political philosophy is best described as *propertarian*; he reduced all human rights to rights of property, beginning with the natural right of self-ownership.

Rothbard's writing career began in the late 1940s, and from then through the 1950s most of his essays and reviews appeared in small libertarian and right-wing journals such as Frank Chodorov's *analysis, Faith and Freedom*, and the early *National Review*. In the late 1950s, Rothbard worked with and for the Volker Fund, a foundation then dedicated to the support of classical liberal and libertarian scholarship.

He reviewed manuscripts for them, judging whether they were worthy of support, and searched academic journals and books for scholars worth cultivating. The fund supported Rothbard's writing of his major economic work, *Man, Economy, and State*, which he published in 1962. This book was a full exposition of the entire body of economic thinking from first principles in the spirit of his mentor Mises's *Human Action*. The book is in the Misesian tradition, building up economics as a deductive science starting from the fact that men act using scarce means to achieve subjectively valued ends. Rothbard's 1970 book, *Power and Market*, which was originally intended as the final segment of *Man, Economy, and State*, extended his analysis of the economics of the free market to lay bare the effects of state interference in the workings of the market. Rothbard divided state intervention into three categories—singular, binary, and triangular—and analyzed their differing effects. Most of the essay involved an analysis of the effect of taxation on the economy. Rothbard concluded that there is no such thing as a neutral tax on an economy, and that to minimize taxation's ill effects it is most important to worry about its total amount and less important to worry about the method of incidence.

In 1963, Rothbard published *America's Great Depression*, applying Misesian business cycle theory to the depression of 1929. His thesis was that a credit inflation in the 1920s, caused by the Federal Reserve and unnoticed by many because it did not manifest itself in higher consumer goods prices, created malinvestments that made the initial crash inevitable. He further argued that the various government interventions of the Hoover administration exacerbated and extended the depression. The Federal Reserve and central banking were a particular bête noire of Rothbard's. He wrote various essays, pamphlets, and a book, *The Mystery of Banking*, analyzing the inflationary effects of central banking. Rothbard advocated a 100% gold monetary standard, the only true defense against inflation, he maintained, and argued that fractional reserve banking was inherently fraudulent. His analysis was often specifically historical, rather than merely economic, relying on what Rothbard called *power elite analysis*, which some commentators condemned as conspiracy theory. In assessing the actions of the major participants in American banking, Rothbard considered the possible personal motivations of specific individuals behind the changes that have occurred in American banking policy.

In the mid-1960s, Rothbard entertained the possibility of creating a mass fusion movement with the growing student antiwar movement, reviving the Old Right (the anti-Rooseveltian right) and its anti-imperialist tradition in a new context, and winning over a new movement to a libertarian message. He and Leonard Liggio launched a journal called *Left and Right* to further forging such a movement. That journal lasted from 1965 to 1968. In the following year, Rothbard began a smaller newsletter called *Libertarian*

Forum, which he edited and largely wrote semiregularly until 1984. This newsletter served as a home for his writings on libertarian movement strategy and for more casual cultural commentary. In the earliest days of *Libertarian Forum*, Rothbard joined Karl Hess in enthusiastically embracing the radical student movement of the time. However, he soon became disenchanted with what he perceived as the antireason and antimarket aspects of the New Left; by the early 1970s, he no longer saw fusion with campus radicals as key to the libertarian movement growth.

In 1973, Rothbard published *For a New Liberty*, a manifesto of libertarianism. That book presented an overview of his complete political vision, explaining how a strictly rights-based anarchist society could function and still meet all the social needs that are now met by government, from roads to defense to justice. (Rothbard credited the 19th-century Belgian author Gustave de Molinari as the intellectual father of this individualist anarchist view, which encompassed justice and defense.) Rothbard rejected Mises's utilitarian ethics as an insufficient basis for a consistent libertarianism. In 1982, he published a defense of his entire intellectual edifice. *The Ethics of Liberty* presented and defended the moral philosophical case for a rights-based anarchism and criticized the various defenses of minimal-state libertarianism that had been put forward by Robert Nozick and F. A. Hayek. During the mid-1970s, he also was a key figure in a series of Institute for Humane Studies–sponsored conferences on Austrian economics, which were vital to the revival of that body of thought. From 1975 to 1979, Rothbard also published a four-volume popular history of the early United States, from North America's earliest colonization through the adoption of the Constitution, interpreting the early history of America from a libertarian perspective. A projected fifth volume was never published.

Rothbard thought work toward real-world political change was vital to the libertarian intellectual movement. As a consequence, he became involved with the Libertarian Party. When the party was first launched in 1972, he had determined that conditions in the United States were still premature for such a move. However, by 1975, he became an enthusiastic participant, writing position papers and helping shape the party's platform. In the late 1970s, as a result of his partnership with Kansas oil billionaire Charles Koch, Rothbard helped found various libertarian educational and advocacy organizations and think tanks, most significantly the Cato Institute and the Center for Libertarian Studies (CLS). He was the founding editor of the center's journal, *The Journal of Libertarian Studies*, and remained so until his death. In the aftermath of the 1980 Libertarian presidential campaign, Rothbard broke with Koch and Cato president Ed Crane, and his involvement with any Koch-financed organizations ceased. In the meantime, the CLS was taken over by coin dealer Burt Blumert, and Rothbard continued working with it. In 1982, Rothbard

became vice president for academic affairs at the Ludwig von Mises Institute, formed by former Ron Paul staff member Llewellyn Rockwell, Jr. The Mises Institute became Rothbard's main berth for activism and movement education during the remainder of his life. Under the auspices of the Mises Institute, in 1985 Rothbard founded and edited an academic journal dedicated to Austrian economics research, *The Review of Austrian Economics*, which he edited until his death.

In 1989, Rothbard ended his involvement with the Libertarian Party and most other aspects of the libertarian movement. He and Rockwell of the Mises Institute attempted to launch a paleolibertarian movement, a combination of libertarian political ideology with cultural conservatism. To this end, Rothbard helped found the John Randolph Club, an alliance of the Mises Institute and its associates with the conservative Rockford Institute. With the cold war over and the right no longer obsessed with anticommunism, Rothbard thought the time was right for a fuller revival of the Old Right combination of antistate and antiwar politics. He flirted with support for the protectionist Republican presidential candidate Pat Buchanan because of his antiforeign interventionism. Alliance with the dominant antiwar political movement was the common thread that made sense of many of Rothbard's seemingly erratic changes of political partnership throughout his life.

Rothbard died in 1995. Posthumously published were volumes one and two of a projected three-volume history of economic thought that had been his main concern in the last decade of his life. The last volume, projected to deal with economic thought in the 20th century, was never completed. The first two volumes advanced Rothbard's non-Whig history of economic thought, emphasizing that the history of economics was not a continual progression from error to greater truth. Rothbard argued instead that even such free-market icons as Adam Smith represented regressions from largely forgotten previous advances in economic thinking, especially in the area of value theory.

BDo

See also Anarchism; Anarcho-Capitalism; Banking, Austrian Theory of; Economics, Austrian School of; Great Depression; Nonaggression Axiom; Private Property

Further Readings

Gordon, David. *The Essential Rothbard*. Auburn, AL: Ludwig von Mises Institute, 2007.

Rothbard, Murray. *America's Great Depression*. Princeton, NJ: Van Nostrand, 1963.

———. *Conceived in Liberty*. 4 vols. New Rochelle, NY: Arlington House, 1975–1979.

———. *For a New Liberty: The Libertarian Manifesto*. New York: Macmillan, 1973.

———. *Man, Economy, and State: A Treatise on Economic Principles.* 2 vols. Princeton, NJ: Van Nostrand, 1962.

———. *The Panic of 1819: Reactions and Policies.* New York: Columbia University Press, 1962.

———. *Power and Market: Government and the Economy.* Menlo Park, CA: Institute for Humane Studies, 1970.

———. *What Has Government Done to Our Money?* Colorado Springs, CO: Pine Tree Press, 1963.

Rousseau, Jean-Jacques (1712–1778)

Jean-Jacques Rousseau was a French Enlightenment philosopher and polymath who wrote on a wide variety of topics, including education, economics, psychology, drama, and music, for which he developed a new system of notation. His best-known works, however, are in political thought. He remains one of the most important theorists of what is now termed *positive liberty*, the notion that individuals must be encouraged or even coerced into being free.

Rousseau was born in Geneva, then a small but independent city-state, and throughout his life he prided himself on his Genevan citizenship. That city would remain an ideal for him throughout his political writings, particularly for its austere virtues, military prowess, and classical republican spirit. He built his political thought around two ideas that were common to many Enlightenment writers: the state of nature and the social contract. Yet Rousseau differed from, for example, Hobbes and Locke, in that he believed the state of nature to have been a happy one and civilization to be considerably less so. In *Discourse on the Arts and Sciences* and *Discourse on the Origin of Inequality*, Rousseau argued that civilization and material progress separated man from the state of nature, causing vanity, jealousy, luxury, effeminacy, and vice. In the state of nature, Rousseau argued, all are equal. Tragically, civilization and commerce divide us from one another and render us unequal.

There were few solutions to this problem, as Rousseau saw it, and often he looked on the advance of civilization with dread. As many theorists in the ancient world had argued, liberty could only be preserved under conditions of austerity. Rousseau agreed, and he rejected the notions of modern liberty that were then coalescing around commerce, material progress, and self-interest. Instead, he argued that only a rigorous program of civic education and communal moral life could delay the encroachment of civilization and the vices that followed in its wake. Rousseau's search for alternatives to modern liberty led him to both praise the ancients and write his most important political text, *The Social Contract*, first published in 1762.

This work argued that individuals enter into a social contract in an attempt to conserve what they can of their natural goodness. The Rousseauan social contract is not an agreement to form a government, but an agreement to form a civil society of a particularly moralistic bent, encompassing religion, education, manners, family life, and economics. "In order then that the social compact may not be an empty formula," Rousseau wrote, "it tacitly includes the undertaking, which alone can give force to the rest, that whoever refuses to obey the general will shall be compelled to do so by the whole body. This means nothing less than that he will be forced to be free."

The general will is one of the most difficult of Rousseau's concepts, but also perhaps the most central. The general will is not to be identified with the totality of individual wills of those comprising society, but the will of the community as a whole. The notion may be likened to a wise parent, ultimately internalized in each of us, under whose tutelage the child is not more limited, but freer to achieve. So it is, Rousseau argued, with the individual and society. Each of us must seek to understand its lessons. When we as individuals discover that our desires conflict with the general will, we are obliged to alter them, and when our fellows discover improper desires in us, it is their duty to correct us. Even an aristocracy of the wisest people should be obliged to obey the general will, rather than their own lights, Rousseau claimed, for the general will is to be the master of us all.

The problem with all of these considerations, from a libertarian standpoint, is that society is not in any sense analogous to a parent, and what holds for the latter—an individual—may not hold for the former. Nowhere is it clearly explained how one is to recognize an opinion or a course of action as representative of the general will, and the notion of the general will has served as an invitation to the power hungry and the unscrupulous ever since. This tendency was particularly the case during the French Revolution, when Rousseau's ideas were invoked incessantly not only to dismantle the tyranny of the Old Regime, but to supplant it with an even more bloodthirsty, although short-lived, tyranny of its own. Subsequent advocates of nationalism also would find Rousseau's notion of the general will appealing, although Rousseau mistrusted all polities larger than the city-state and would certainly not have approved of mass nationalistic projects.

Moving from the abstract to the particular, Rousseau's prescriptions in social policy strike libertarians as abhorrent, particularly when they are combined with Rousseau's incessant invocations of liberty. In the name of liberty, Rousseau would censor the press and forbid the theater; he would institute both sumptuary laws and a state religion. Limits to government power were in vain, Rousseau taught, for virtue alone should guide the people who would serve—undivided—as the legislators. "The laws are but registers of what we ourselves desire," Rousseau wrote, and limits were therefore unnecessary.

Rousseau's clear, affective style made him deeply influential, and his invocations of liberty inspired many, despite the contrarian nature of many of his ideas. The opening lines of the *Social Contract* are a striking example: "Man was born free, and everywhere he is in chains. Those who think themselves the masters of others are indeed greater slaves than they." This ringing endorsement of freedom brought courage to many who were suffering under the Old Regime, as well as great fame to its author. Although he quarreled and broke ties with Enlightenment liberals such as Diderot and Voltaire, the educated public read Rousseau's books in record numbers. His novel *La nouvelle Héloise* was a great commercial success, as was his book-length treatise *Emile*, which proposed a system of education that would inculcate Rousseauan philosophy. Ironically, *Emile* was burned at both Paris and Geneva for its subversive section on natural religion, the "Confession of Faith of a Savoyard Vicar."

Rousseau's life was as paradoxical and tempestuous as his philosophy: The author of the best-selling educational and moral tracts of his era also fathered five illegitimate children and placed all of them in an orphanage. He wrote plays and ferociously attacked the theater. An advocate of unfeigned sincerity, Rousseau came to mistrust all around him, including the philosopher David Hume, who had offered him refuge in England. Rousseau's *Confessions*, published posthumously, were scandalous enough that certain of his admirers claimed that they were forgeries. Attempts to make sense of it all are likely to be futile, and Rousseau is chiefly known today for his works, which are among the most ready of all to invoke liberty as a word—and among the most ready of all to betray liberty as an ideal.

JTK

See also Enlightenment; French Revolution; Material Progress; Positive Liberty; Virtue; Wealth and Poverty

Further Readings

Cranston, Maurice. *The Noble Savage: Jean-Jacques Rousseau.* Chicago: University of Chicago Press, 1991.

Damrosch, Leo. *Jean-Jacques Rousseau: Restless Genius.* New York: Houghton Mifflin, 2005.

Rousseau, Jean-Jacques. *Confessions.* Angela Scholar, trans. New York: Oxford University Press, 2000.

———. *The Discourses and Other Early Political Writings.* Victor Gourevitch, trans. Cambridge: Cambridge University Press, 1997.

———. *Émile: Or, Treatise on Education.* William H. Payne, trans. Amherst, NY: Prometheus Books, 2003.

———. *Politics and the Arts: Letter to M. d'Alembert on the Theatre.* Allan Bloom, trans. and ed. Ithaca, NY: Cornell University Press, 1960.

———. *The Social Contract.* Maurice Cranston, trans. London: Penguin, 1968.

RULE OF LAW

The political and philosophical doctrine of the rule of law is an integral feature of the classical liberal theory. It is a necessary, if not sufficient, element to a well-rounded theory of what constitutes a proper liberal society and, in a practical sense, provides the carapace within which individualism, the market and private property, as well as personal or moral liberties flourish. Its connection with liberty was well described by Albert Venn Dicey, the English jurist, who wrote: "Liberty is not secure unless the law, in addition to punishing every kind of interference with a man's lawful freedom, provides adequate security that everyone who, without legal justification, is placed in confinement shall be able to get free."

The rule of law is a guarantee against arbitrariness inasmuch as everyone, including and especially government, is subject to its constraints. Unlike in communist regimes, where the government acts entirely on the whim of the Party, in regimes characterized by the rule of law, politicians are not exempt from legal rules. To quote Dicey again: "With us [the United Kingdom] every official, from the Prime Minister down to a constable or collector of taxes, is under the same responsibility for every act done without legal justification as any other citizen."

The rule of law is often presented as an important mechanism to ensure limited government because under it, if governments have to go through an enormously complex process of law-making and judicial action and to overcome restraints against the arbitrary seizure of property, there is likely to be less of it. One illustration of this constraint is the writ of habeas corpus, which requires that a charge be leveled against a person before he can be held in police custody against his will. The rule of law may be called an end-independent doctrine, which dictates that whatever the ends of government, it must follow certain procedures if its actions are to be regarded as legitimate. This notion derives from the general skepticism that liberals hold regarding the ends of government. Because there are innumerable disputes about the good life, it is wise to tolerate a certain kind of pluralism in which rival versions of the good compete with each other under the rule of law. It also accords with the antirationalist reservations that are a strong feature of the liberal arguments of someone like F. A. Hayek.

In contrast, a much stronger argument for limited government derives from the claim that a set of morally and economically certain purposes of government are demonstrable from first principles. This approach is reflected in those constitutions that have bills of rights attached to them, such as the first 10 amendments to the U.S. Constitution or the European Convention on Human Rights. Although these two approaches to limited government may reach the same conclusion on many issues, it is important to remember their distinct philosophical foundations.

The features of the purely formal, procedural rule of law are best expressed by Hayek. In *The Constitution of Liberty*, Hayek noted that laws should be perfectly general, name no one person or group, and be nondiscriminatory. This generality requirement is consistent with the operations of the market, which is indifferent to the sexual, racial, or religious origins of its participants. Thus, any law embodying such criteria for market action would be alien to the rule of law on grounds of both efficiency and morality. To be fully consistent with the rule of law, a putative statute should name no person or group or confer any type of privilege.

The major difficulty with this feature of the rule of law is that it does not invariably protect people potentially targeted by government because it is easy to demonstrate how a perfectly general law could be written that does nevertheless discriminate against a minority. The majority Protestant province of Northern Ireland in the United Kingdom once had its own legislative assembly—now restored—which at one point passed a law forbidding the playing of sport in public parks on a Sunday. Without mentioning Catholics, this group was the losers because it was their habit to play sports on Sunday, whereas Protestants did not. Yet this law would have passed muster under Hayek's standards. Indeed, the wholesale nationalization of the economy would be consistent with Hayek's rule of law, but seizing little bits would be discriminatory. It seems clear that if liberty is to be guaranteed, something more than the formally correct wording of a rule is required. Perhaps only a list of rights, a rationalistic, un-Hayekian approach, can properly protect liberty.

The same problem arises with respect to Hayek's position on taxes. He quite rightly sees the progressive income tax as a breach of the rule of law because it treats high earners unequally, but his preferred solution, a proportionate income tax, raises as many problems for libertarians. After all, this tax could in principle raise as much money as does a progressive tax. Yet perhaps there should be an absolute limit on the state's taxing powers, rationalistically determined. Although the rule of law prohibits retrospective legislation, and although a market could not work if what were legal today became illegal and subject to punishment tomorrow, are not all tax laws retrospective?

Even more important is the question of sovereignty. Almost all English proponents of the rule of law saw the final authority of law lying in the sovereign: first in the King and later in Parliament. They did not see, as the American revolutionaries later did, that sovereignty, however formulated and wherever located, was a threat to liberty and the rule of law. Dicey, the leading authority on the rule of law, was a fierce spokesman for both doctrines, sovereignty and the rule of law. Yet at the time he was writing, in the late 19th and early 20th centuries, the powers of an unlimited Parliament posed serious problems for liberty and the rule of law. The major victim of such regimes has been the individual

property holder. It is true that in the period from 1945 to 1951, when Britain was governed by a socialist administration, all of its reforms were enacted within the confines of the rule of law. Yet the difference between mere legality and the rule of law had been noticed by a near contemporary of Dicey's, Lord Hewart, in his prophetic 1929 work, *The New Despotism*.

In modern political thought, the theory of the rule of law is best understood in the context of democratic theory. Of course, there are many types of *democracy*, the most promiscuous word in political language: Almost all political doctrines profess their intimate connection with democracy. For the sake of convenience, the great variety of democratic theories may be reduced to two: direct and representative. The former, which derives from the politics of ancient Greece, envisages a direct role for citizens in political decision making. Traditionally, this form of direct democracy was reflected in the fact that citizens attended and voted in legislative assemblies. Outside the city-states of ancient Greece, however, this proved to be impractical, and in modern democracies the citizens take part by directly voting on issues through referenda. In representative democracies, the citizens' political role is limited to the choice of representatives who have the time and leisure to debate issues. Proponents of the rule of law on the whole favor representative democracy. Under direct democracy, the great mass of people are likely to be moved by passion rather than reason, and the democratic system disintegrates into straight mob rule. The transient decisions of direct democracies, at least superficially, appear in conflict with the rule of law, which requires the security of longevity for rules to provide the stability that the market transactors need. Edmund Burke became the most eloquent spokesman for this point of view in his famous speech to the electorate of Bristol, where he maintained,

> Your Representative owes you, not his industry only, but his judgement; and he betrays, instead of serving you, if he sacrifices it to your opinion. . . . You chuse a Member indeed; but when you have chosen him, he is not Member of Bristol, but he is a Member of *Parliament*.

However, there is reason to doubt Burke's wisdom in this regard because the main threat to the rule of law may come not from the mob, but from a myriad of interest groups that dominate modern representative assemblies. Public choice theory tells us that the modern representative is as self-interested as any market trader and cannot be relied on to act altruistically or to seek the public good. In attempting to gain government favors, they damage the rule of law. As Mancur Olson maintained,

> It does not follow that the results of pressure group activity would be harmless . . . even if the balance of power equilibrium kept any one group getting out of line. Even if

such a pressure group system worked with perfect fairness to every group it would still tend to work inefficiently.

All of this pressure group activity is in breach of the rule of law as Hayek understands it.

However, there are examples from modern politics that show that direct democracy can produce classical liberal, or at least conservative, results. Perhaps the best of these is Switzerland, where the regular use of the referendum at the cantonal and federal levels has insulated the country from the advance of European socialist programs. Even today the combined spending of the cantons is still more than that of the federal government: a situation that has not obtained in the United States since the early part of the 20th century. In 2005, the electorates in the Netherlands and France rejected by referendum the proposed heavily centralist European constitution. In Japan, former Prime Minister Junichiro Koizumi conducted the 2005 general election as if it were a referendum on his plan to privatize the postal system: a market scheme that had been held up by a previous Parliament riddled with pressure groups.

Despite the depredations that it has suffered from communism, socialism, and, more surreptitiously, unlimited democracy, the rule of law remains an essential building block in the framework of a free society. Indeed, there are encouraging signs in the United States that some traditional values with respect to property are being reasserted. Over the past 20 years, the Supreme Court has delivered several decisions favorable to property owners in disputes involving the several legislatures' use of the takings power (eminent domain). If transactors are to be secure in their dealings, they need a reliable set of rules and not the creative activity of politically motivated judges. In a world of uncertainty about science, religion, and art, in a genuinely liberal society, these ultimate questions must be left to the individual conscience and not placed in the public domain, where government can use coercion to enforce its beliefs.

However, as Hayek has pointed out, there is a distinction between law and legislation. The former encompasses private actions, especially economic ones, and the rules that enable people to conduct their aims peacefully. The latter refers to those public actions that the state undertakes; legislation is not a series of guidelines, but a structure of commands. People are ordered to do things that they would not do or to refrain from doing things they otherwise would do were governments effectively restrained by the rule of law. In the modern world, there is too much legislation and not enough genuine liberty-enhancing law.

The rule of law is a necessary condition for a free society. However, it must be supplemented by other protections, notably constitutionalism and the absolute guarantee of private property. Only if these are realized will we really have a society governed by the rule of law and not the rule of men.

NB

See also Constitutionalism; Hayek, Friedrich A.; Hobbes, Thomas; Locke, John; Republicanism, Classical; Whiggism

Further Readings

Barnett, Randy. *The Structure of Liberty: Justice and the Rule of Law*. New York: Oxford University Press, 2000.

Hayek, F. A. *Constitution of Liberty*. Chicago: University of Chicago Press, 1960.

Hobbes, Thomas. *Leviathan*. Richard Tuck, ed. Cambridge: Cambridge University Press, 1996.

Locke, John. *Two Treatises on Government*. Peter Laslett, ed. Cambridge: Cambridge University Press, 2005.

Madison, James. "Federalist No. 10." *The Federalist*. Clinton Rossiter and Charles R. Kesler, eds. New York: Signet Classics, 2003.

Olson, Mancur. *Power and Prosperity: Outgrowing Communist and Capitalist Dictatorships*. New York: Basic Books, 2000.

S

SAY, JEAN-BAPTISTE (1767–1832)

Jean-Baptiste Say was the leading French political economist in the first third of the 19th century. Before becoming an academic economist quite late in life, Say had worked at a broad range of occupations, including, following in the family tradition, an apprenticeship in a commercial office. He later was employed by a life insurance company and then took on a series of disparate occupations: journalist, soldier, politician, cotton manufacturer, and writer. His constantly changing careers were in large part due to the political and economic upheavals that his generation had to endure: the French Revolution, the Revolutionary Wars, the rise of Napoleon Bonaparte, economic warfare with Britain, and eventually the fall of the Empire and the Restoration of the Bourbon monarchy. Only after a quarter century of turmoil could Say occupy his first position teaching political economy in Paris in 1815, an activity he was to continue in until his death in 1832.

Say made his name with the publication of the *Traité d'économie politique* (1803), which went through many editions and revisions during his lifetime. The ideas that are most closely associated with his name include "Say's law" of markets—crudely formulated sometimes as "supply creates its own demand" or more broadly understood as the idea that nations and individuals benefit from each other's rising level of wealth as it provides increased opportunities for mutually beneficial trade. In addition, Say emphasized the vital role played by the entrepreneur in economic activity and the contribution of "nonmaterial" goods, such as services, human capital, and institutions, to the creation of wealth. He also provided an early formulation of the theory of rent seeking.

Say was a keen popularizer of economic ideas, writing several works in dialogue form in order to reach a broader audience with his liberal views at a time when economic nationalism and socialism were becoming increasingly popular. One of his last major works, the *Cours complet d'économie politique pratique* (1828–1829), attempted to broaden the scope of political economy, away from its earlier preoccupation with the production of wealth, by examining the moral, political, and sociological requirements of a free society and how they are interrelated with the study of political economy. In other words, he wished to return political economy to its Smithian roots.

Say's family originated in Nîmes, but they were forced to flee to Geneva in the late 17th century when the state ended its policy of toleration toward Protestants. They returned to Lyon in the mid-18th century, where Say's father became a merchant. The family intended Say and his brother Horace to continue in the family business, and, to this end, the two brothers were sent to London to learn about modern commerce. There they became proficient in English; when Say came across a copy of Smith's *Wealth of Nations*, which had not yet been translated into French, he was able to absorb its contents.

When the French Revolution broke out, Say was swept up in events. He stopped working for the Comte de Mirabeau's journal, the *Courrier de Provence*, to volunteer to fight and saw service in Champagne in 1792–1793. He got married only to find his family's moderate wealth had made him a target of the terror before hyperinflation wiped out most of what they had saved. Finally, he was appointed editor of the journal of the liberal-minded "Idéologues," *La Décade philosophique, littéraire, et politique*, for which he wrote articles on political economy from 1794 to 1799. Say's practical business experience and his knowledge of current economic policy led to his appointment in 1799 to the Tribunat, where he served on the finance committee. It was in this context that the idea of a *Treatise on Political Economy* was hatched, and the first of six editions appeared in 1803. Say's *Treatise* even came to the attention of the

First Consul, Napoleon, who, over dinner with Say, suggested that a new edition should be published that would more explicitly support the government's unpopular fiscal policies. Say's blunt refusal to serve the interests of Napoleon and his constant opposition to the profligate spending of the government in the finance committee led to his dismissal from the Tribunat.

The next stage of Say's career was a return to the commercial world after a stint as an editor and a politician. Say relocated his family to Auchy in Pas-de-Calais, where he set up a cotton-spinning plant using the latest machinery from England. After 8 successful years as a businessman, in which he employed between 400 and 500 people in his factory, Say sold the enterprise and returned to Paris in 1813. He was convinced that French economic policy would result in economic collapse. The continental system, which placed an embargo on British goods trying to enter the Continent, the proliferation of government licenses needed to enter business, the increasing tariffs on imported cotton, in addition to the difficulties of trading in wartime, were stifling French industry.

The publication of the second edition of the *Treatise on Political Economy* in 1814 once again brought Say to the attention of the government. At this point, he was employed to travel to England on a fact-finding mission for the purpose of discovering the secret of English economic growth and to examine the impact of the revolutionary wars on the British economy. Say also took advantage of his visit to England to make contact with British philosophical radicals and political economists such as James Mill, Jeremy Bentham, and David Ricardo. Part of his report was published in the pamphlet *De l'Angleterre et des Anglais* (1814), which contains a devastating critique of the economic impact of war on ordinary British working people, including the inflationary policies employed to finance the conflict.

Only after the defeat of Napoleon and the Restoration of the Bourbon monarchy was Say, then the preeminent French political economist of his day, able to obtain a position teaching economics in Paris, first at the Athénée and then at the Conservatoire des Arts et Métiers. The expression "political economy" was still regarded as somewhat radical and subversive; however, he was finally offered the first chair in political economy at the Collège de France. Although he was a notoriously bad lecturer, reading directly from his manuscripts, he published a considerable amount in his remaining 17 years. Numerous popular works on political economy appeared, along with several revised editions of the *Treatise on Political Economy*, a series of polemical letters written to Thomas Malthus, and a lengthy and unjustly neglected *Cours complet d'économie politique pratique* in 1828–1829.

DMH

See also Classical Economics; French Revolution; Ricardo, David; Smith, Adam

Further Readings

Forget, Evelyn. "Jean-Baptiste Say and Adam Smith: An Essay in the Transmission of Ideas." *Canadian Journal of Economics* 26 no. 1 (1993): 121–133.

Hart, David M. *Class Analysis, Slavery and the Industrialist Theory of History in French Liberal Thought, 1814–1830: The Radical Liberalism of Charles Comte and Charles Dunoyer.* Unpublished doctoral dissertation, King's College, Cambridge, 1994.

Say, Jean-Baptiste. *Cours complet d'économie politique pratique; ouvrage destiné à mettre sous les yeux des hommes d'état, des propriétaires fonciers et les capitalistes, des savans, des agriculteurs, des manufacturiers, des négocians, et en général de tous les citoyens, l'économie des sociétés.* 6 vols. Paris: Rapilly, 1828–1829.

———. *Oeuvres diverses contenant: Catéchisme d'économie politique, fragments et opuscules inédits, correspondance générale, Olbie, Petit Volume, Mélanges de morale et de litérature' précédées d'une Notice historique sur la vie et les travaux de l'auteur, Avec des notes par Ch. Comte, E. Daire et Horace Say.* Paris: Guillaumin, 1848.

———. *Traité d'économie politique, ou simple exposition de la manière dont se forment, se distribuent et se consomment les richesses.* Paris: Deterville, 1803.

———. *A Treatise on Political Economy; or the Production, Distribution, and Consumption of Wealth.* C. R. Princep, trans. Philadelphia: Grigg and Elliott, 1832.

Sowell, Thomas. *Say's Law: An Historical Introduction.* Princeton, NJ: Princeton University Press, 1972.

Weinburg, Mark. "The Social Analysis of Three Early 19th Century French Liberals: Say, Comte, and Dunoyer." *Journal of Libertarian Studies* 2 no. 1 (1978): 45–63.

SCHOLASTICS/SCHOOL OF SALAMANCA

Medieval Scholasticism encompassed some seven centuries, from 800 A.D. to 1500 A.D. In theological and philosophical studies, the activity of the period from 1350 to 1500 is known as Late Scholasticism. In social sciences, Late Scholasticism reaches until the end of the 17th century.

St. Thomas Aquinas (1225–1274) was the foremost Scholastic writer. His influence was so widespread that nearly all Late Scholastics studied, quoted, and commented on his remarks. Their works analyzed issues that later proved relevant to libertarian political and economic philosophy. Francisco de Vitoria (c. 1480–1546), often called the Father of the Hispanic Scholastics, is regarded as the great figure in Late Scholasticism. He belonged to the Dominican order and studied and taught at the Sorbonne, where he helped to edit one of the editions of Aquinas's *Summa Theologica* and of the *Summa* of Saint Antonino of Florence (1389–1459). From 1522 to 1546, he taught at the University of Salamanca.

From a pure libertarian perspective, the major contributions of the Late Scholastics are their focus on each person as an individual being distinguished by his freedom; their emphasis on the importance of private property for a peaceful, productive, and ethical social order; and their conclusions about the importance of the right to trade, both nationally and internationally. In addition, the Scholastics wrote much about the relevance of sound money, in its role of both preserving private property and promoting trade. Although these thinkers were prepared to access the notion of a "just" price, their analysis tended to equate a just price with market prices that were devoid of fraud, monopoly, or coercion. In addition, they treated wages, profits, and rents as a reflection of commutative justice (on which contracts were based), rather than of distributive justice, which only dealt with justice in the provision and distribution of goods held in common by a family or political body. Finally, their careful distinction between legal and moral obligations and punishments proved an essential aspect of what later became classical liberal theory.

Lord Acton wrote that, "the greater part of the political ideas of Milton, Locke, and Rousseau, may be found in the ponderous Latin of Jesuits who were subjects of the Spanish Crown, of Lessius, Molina, Mariana, and Suárez." The Jesuits mentioned by Lord Acton owed many of their views to the Late Scholastics of other religious orders who helped build the foundations of a political order based on libertarian principles. Late Scholastic contributions were not circumscribed to any one religious group or to a particular school or nation.

Scholastic authors from the 14th to the 16th centuries, including St. Bernardino of Siena (a Franciscan); St. Antonino of Florence, Francisco de Vitoria, and Domingo de Soto (all Dominicans); and Luis de Molina, Juan de Mariana, and Francisco Suárez (all Jesuits) all presented arguments that were later to serve as the foundation of a market order based on freedom and property. Bede Jarrett, a Dominican priest and a historian of thought, wrote that, for these authors,

> the right to property was an absolute right which no circumstances could ever invalidate. Even in case of necessity, when individual property might be lawfully seized or distrained—in the name of another's hunger or of the common good—yet the owner's right to property remained and endured. The right was inviolable even when the exercise of the right might have to be curtailed.

Saint Antoninus, like most of those who wrote after him, worked to place moral philosophy and moral theological studies on a respectable footing, treating them as sciences to be founded on an analysis of the nature of human action. A thorough study of human action was the starting point of Late Scholastic moral theology. Scholastic and Late Scholastic thought, based on the primacy of the individual, also is relevant to today's debates on environmental issues.

Although conflicts between man and nature were seldom discussed in their treatises, whenever the topic did arise, their approach was similar to that applied by libertarians of the 20th and 21st centuries. They used the example of common grazing lands to prove that when property is held in common it is abused. They argued that private property is used more responsibly than common property and that the individual rather than "nature" should form the locus of discussions of these issues. Everything was created by God, and everything, in that sense, was "good," but there existed an order in creation in which individuals were extended domain over the land, the seas, and even the stars.

On the issue of trade, several authors have credited the Late Scholastics, and especially Vitoria, as being the first to defend the right to trade across borders. It is worthy of note that Samuel von Pufendorf (1632–1694), who as a Protestant served in many ways as a bridge between the writings of the Late Scholastics and the Scottish enlightenment, criticized Vitoria for stating that the Laws of Nations allowed all men to trade, even in foreign territories.

Although Aquinas to Oresme and Copernicus (who apart from being an astronomer was a doctor in canon law) all commented on the nature and role of money, no one wrote better and with more consistency than did Juan de Mariana. Mariana's treatise on money and inflation, first published in the late 16th century, anticipated most, if not all, libertarian analyses of monetary policy. However, with respect to the issue of interest rates, the Scholastics almost invariably reached conclusions contrary to libertarian principles. Anne-Robert-Jacques Turgot (1727–1781), who was educated in a seminary and whose views were largely consistent with Scholastic teachings, was correct in criticizing their condemnation of levying a charge for the lending of money.

The economic contributions of the Late Scholastics were recognized by F. A. Hayek and especially Murray N. Rothbard. Their political analyses have been studied by Bernice Hamilton, Quentin Skinner, and, more recently, Annabelle S. Brett. All these commentaries help us to understand the important legacy of Late Scholastic thought. Brett's work provides us with a careful analysis of two of Vitoria's followers: Domingo de Soto and Fernando Vázquez de Menchaca. According to Brett, Vázquez "represents a major step in the development of a radical legal tradition the analysis of right of which is based on a preoccupation with fact, or what escapes juridical determination." Vázquez, he notes, made a distinction between power, *potentia*, as based on position and wealth, and power, *potestas*, based on law and right. Vázquez's distinction might serve to improve the arguments of libertarians who see no middle ground between power and markets. Vázquez argued that the consent of previous generations did not bind future citizens. This principle continued to influence leading Catholic theologians, such as the 19th-century Jesuit Mateo Liberatore, who in his defense of private property wrote that common ownership could be imposed only by the unanimous consent of individuals (e.g., shipwrecked people on an island). However, according to him, the children and grandchildren of this original group would not be obliged to obey because they received their right to property from nature and not from their progenitors.

Late Scholasticism shared with the great classical liberal authors the notion that any discussion of rights disconnected from the Creator made no sense. However, they were keenly aware of the differences among the theological, economic, and political aspects of man's rights. Vitoria and Soto emphasized the theological and economic, whereas Vázquez emphasized the voluntaristic and legal foundations of right.

The Late Scholastics equated market prices with the just price, a price predicated on a theory of value that was determined by subjective elements. As a consequence, they tended to oppose government intervention in prices. Although they recognized the right of the authorities to fix prices, they questioned its convenience. They thought taxation a more radical constraint on property than regulation, and they shared the view that taxes should be moderate. Profits, wages, and rents were all analyzed in a manner similar to their examination of the nature of prices.

Late Scholastic analysis differentiated between moral violations, such as prostitution or betrayals, and violations of positive law. Despite the baseness of their acts, prostitutes and even Judas had the right to claim what was freely offered to them. Although there was latitude in the price that one could charge without committing a moral violation, they gave even more latitude before one could be legally charged for abusing a customer or fooling a seller.

The Late Scholastics were not libertarians, and they believed that liberty, to be enjoyed by all, needed order and that order needed to be based on respect for human nature and imposed by the state. Their analysis of economic issues within the context of broader questions of man's role in the universe was made to complement what they had learned through grace and revelation. Although their conclusions cannot invariably be taken as consonant with classical liberalism, as Hayek and Rothbard have noted, aspects of it also can provide the basis for true liberty.

AlC

See also Aquinas, Thomas; Aristotle; Rothbard, Murray; Spontaneous Order; Turgot, Anne-Robert-Jacques

Further Readings

Acton, John Dalberg. *The History of Freedom and Other Essays.* New York: Classics of Liberty Library, 1993 [1907].

Brett, Annabelle S. *Liberty, Right and Nature: Individual Rights in Later Scholastic Thought.* Cambridge: Cambridge University Press, 1997.

Jarrett, Fr. Bede. *The Social Theories of the Middle Ages.* Westminster, MD: The Newman Bookshop, 1942 [1926].

Mariana, Juan de. "A Treatise on the Alteration of Money." *Markets & Morality* 5 no. 2 (Fall 2002): 533–593 [c. 1599].

Rothbard, Murray N. *Economic Thought before Adam Smith.* Cheltenham, UK: Edward Elgar, 1995.

Skinner, Quentin. *The Foundations of Modern Political Thought.* Cambridge: Cambridge University Press, 1978.

Vitoria, Francisco de Antony Pagden, and J. Lawrance, eds. *Vitoria: Political Writings.* Cambridge: Cambridge University Press, 1991.

Schumpeter, Joseph (1883–1950)

A giant among 20th-century economists, Joseph Schumpeter is best known for his path-breaking work on capitalism, innovation, entrepreneurship, and growth. He coined the phrase *creative destruction* to describe capitalistic growth as the ceaseless killing off of old ways of doing business by the new. He is not often thought of as a libertarian. Nevertheless, with his love of free markets; his stress on human freedom, initiative, and drive to succeed as the mainspring of growth; his belief in capitalism as the best, arguably the only, system capable of continuously raising the living standards of all (especially the poor); his focus on the lone-wolf entrepreneur who against all odds creates the new products, markets, technologies, and organizations that propel the economy forward; his opposition to government regulation of economic and business activity; his public choice views of democracy; and his hatred of war, Schumpeter has much in common with libertarians.

Born in Triesch, Moravia, Schumpeter was a high achiever. By the time he was 31 years old, he had earned a PhD from the University of Vienna, had been appointed professor at the Universities of Czernowitz and Graz, amassed a substantial fortune as a lawyer and financial advisor to an Egyptian princess in Cairo, published three books and numerous papers, and received an honorary doctorate from Columbia University. After stints as Minister of Finance for a post–World War I Austrian socialist government and president of a Viennese private bank that collapsed in 1924, leaving Schumpeter bankrupt, he returned to academia, holding a chair at the University of Bonn (1925–1932) and then moving to Harvard in 1932, where he taught for the rest of his life.

Schumpeter pushed one big idea all his life: that capitalism means growth and growth requires innovation. His most original book, *The Theory of Economic Development* (1912), states for the first time his view that capitalism is the system that delivers faster growth and higher living standards than any other system, albeit in a disruptive, jerky, anxiety-producing fashion. Like a perpetual motion machine, capitalism generates its own momentum internally without the need of outside force. Even technological change, seen by some as an exogenous propellant, is treated by Schumpeter as a purely endogenous matter, the product of economically motivated human ingenuity.

Upon the static, steady-state equilibrium, circular-flow model of the neoclassical marginal utility/marginal productivity school, Schumpeter erects a dynamic disequilibrium theory of cyclical growth. His key building blocks are profits, entrepreneurs, bank credit creation, and innovation. Profits (supplemented perhaps with a desire to create a business dynasty) motivate entrepreneurs, who, financed by bank credit, innovate new goods, new technologies, and new methods of management and organization. These innovations fuel growth and generate cycles.

Why cycles? Schumpeter maintained that they start with a mass of potential innovations seeking to override the forces of habit, custom, and tradition blocking their realization. When the first successful entrepreneur overcomes the stubborn resistance of incumbent interests and eases the path for other entrepreneurs, the ensuing wave of innovation boosts aggregate investment spending. The extra spending bids prices above costs and raises profit margins, thereby triggering the upswing or prosperity phase of the cycle. The high profit margins then attract swarms of imitators and would-be competitors into the innovating sectors. Output overexpands relative to the demand for it, prices fall to or below costs, thus eliminating profit margins, and a downswing or recession phase begins. The recession continues, weeding out inefficient firms (including traditional ones whose customers desert them for their innovating rivals) as it goes, until the economy absorbs the innovations and consolidates the attendant gains, thus clearing the ground for a fresh burst of innovation. If the upswing has been accompanied by speculative excesses nonessential to innovation, the downswing may overshoot the new postinnovation equilibrium. Then the cycle enters its depression phase, where the excesses are expunged and the economy returns via a recovery phase to equilibrium. Schumpeter stressed that the latter two phases and the phenomena that generate them are unnecessary for growth and could be prevented by properly designed policy. It is not speculative bubbles, Schumpeter argued, but rather the discontinuous clustering of innovations in time plus their slow diffusion across and assimilation into the economy that produces real cycles of prosperity and recession.

Profits, entrepreneurs, bank credit, and innovation are all essential to the growth of per capita real income in Schumpeter's model. Remove any one and the growth process stops. Innovation, for instance, is abortive in the absence of bank credit creation necessary to effectuate it. Cash-strapped entrepreneurs cannot create new products and technologies from thin air. They require real resource inputs and loans with which to hire those resources away from outmoded firms and uses. Schumpeter noted that resource transfer is facilitated by price inflation generated by newly created money. Inflation cuts into the real purchasing power of consumers and noninnovating firms, thus reducing their command over productive resources that are freed for employment by the innovating sector. In highlighting these points, Schumpeter effectively abandoned the so-called classical dichotomy according to which loan-created money is a mere sideshow, a neutral veil that, together with metallic money, determines the nominal or absolute price level while leaving real economic variables unaffected. Not so, said Schumpeter. For him, money and credit are integral to the process of real economic growth and so have real effects.

As the leading defender and apostle of capitalism, Schumpeter was a severe critic of the dominant Keynesian thinking of the 1930s, 1940s, and 1950s, thinking preoccupied with stagnation rather than with growth. He accused Keynes of assessing capitalism on the basis of a short-run, depression-oriented model when only a long-run growth-oriented one would do. He noted Keynes's neglect of innovation, the mainspring of capitalistic growth. He scorned Keynes's claim that mature capitalistic economies tend to be perpetually underemployed and in need of massive government deficit spending to shore them up. He attacked the "secular stagnation" notion that capitalists face vanishing investment opportunities and slowing rates of technological progress when the opposite is true. He rejected the contention that income must be redistributed from the rich (who save too much) to the poor (who cannot afford to save) in order to boost consumption spending and aggregate demand. Nonsense, said Schumpeter. The insatiability of human wants ensures that income, regardless of who receives it, will be spent in one way or another. Schumpeter's criticisms, although valid, penetrating, and correct, had little impact on a profession sold on Keynesian stabilization policies.

Even so, Schumpeter evidently erred when he opined that the Keynesian-style permanently mixed economy or public sector–private sector partnership was unsustainable and could not last. The private sector, Schumpeter reasoned, would become addicted to government expenditure stimulus and demand it in ever-increasing amounts. Furthermore, labor unions would demand increasingly frequent and aggressive intervention to equalize incomes. In these ways, the public sector would expand relative to the private one, and the economy would gravitate to socialism. Time has proved Schumpeter wrong. Private and public sectors have coexisted in a fairly stable ratio in most developed countries for the past 60 years.

Schumpeter voiced politically controversial opinions in the 1930s when New Deal activism and populist antibusiness sentiments were on the rise. He opposed President Roosevelt's New Deal reforms on the ground that they hampered entrepreneurship and growth. Similarly, he opposed Keynesian macro demand-management policies designed to tame the trade cycle. In his view, because growth is inherently cyclical, flattening the cycle comes at the cost of eliminating growth. Other controversial opinions, all corollaries of his work on innovation and creative destruction, flowed from his pen.

On income inequality, he wrote that the gap between rich and poor is a prerequisite to and a relatively harmless byproduct of growth in a capitalistic economy. The rich are necessary because it is they and not the poor who save and invest in the innovation-embodied capital formation that lifts the living standards of all. Besides, high incomes provide both incentive and reward for the entrepreneurs who propel growth. No one needs fear that an unequal distribution will condemn them to poverty. The notion of the "circulation of the elites" ensures that. The ceaseless rise and fall of entrepreneurs into and out of the top income bracket means that it will be occupied over time by different groups of people, many of them drawn from the ranks of the poor. The poor replace the rich, and the rich the poor in never-ending sequence.

In assuming a high degree of mobility across income groups, Schumpeter may have overlooked an education barrier. He failed to acknowledge that a superior education, increasingly a prerequisite to entrepreneurship and wealth in today's high-tech world, is more affordable by the rich, extending to the offspring of the rich somewhat of an advantage.

As for monopolistic firms and monopoly profits, they bothered Schumpeter not at all. He thought that monopolies, unless protected by government, are short-lived, inherently self-destroying, and require no antitrust legislation. Their high profits attract the very rivals and producers of substitute products that undercut them. For the same reason, he regarded antitrust laws aimed at breaking up large, non-monopolistic firms as ill-advised. Not only are big firms often more efficient than small ones, but their research and development (R&D) departments house teams of specialists functioning collectively—and routinely—as innovating entrepreneurs. Indeed, the very existence of R&D departments indicates that big firms realize they must continually innovate to stay alive.

Schumpeter's politically contentious opinions continued into the wartime years of the 1940s. He distrusted Roosevelt, suspecting him of trying to establish a dictatorship. He had mixed emotions about the Axis nations, Germany and Japan. He despised their military establishments, leaders, advisors, and social policies, but he admired the people and cultures of the two countries and feared that the United States would impose punitive reprisals at war's end. Most of all, he saw the United States' wartime ally, the Soviet Union, as its chief long-term foe, and thought that America would need Germany and Japan to serve as buffers against the communist nation. These views found little sympathy among Schumpeter's friends and associates in the ultrapatriotic environment of the early 1940s, a circumstance that caused him much unhappiness.

Some have seen similarities between Schumpeter and Karl Marx (an economist much admired by Schumpeter). Both sung hymns of praise to capitalism's prodigious accomplishments, and both predicted the system's death. Whereas Marx prophesized that capitalism's failures and internal contradictions would be the cause of capitalism's destruction, Schumpeter, in his *Capitalism, Socialism and Democracy* (1942), predicted that the system's successes would mark its end. These successes will produce social forces—the routinization and depersonalization of innovation, the puncturing of the image of the entrepreneur as romantic hero, and the creation of a class of intellectuals hostile to capitalism—that undermine the system and lead to its demise. Capitalism will give way to socialism, which will take the form of a democratic welfare state that seeks not growth, but distributional equality. The transition to socialism will be easier, Schumpeter noted, if capitalism has created wealth in such abundance that further growth, rendered impossible by socialism's hobbling of entrepreneurs, is unnecessary.

Schumpeter viewed democracy as a political market in which politicians compete for the votes of the electorate just as producers compete for consumers' dollars in markets for goods and services. But Schumpeter, always skeptical of consumer rationality, believed that market power resides more with vote seekers than with the electorate, whose apathy, ignorance, and lack of foresight enable politicians to set the policy agenda and to manipulate voter preferences. Even so, he felt that capitalism, provided it operated within a proper legal framework, is largely self-regulating. Thus, it constrains politicians' market power more than does socialism where such constraint is absent. These ideas mark Schumpeter as a forerunner of the modern public choice school.

The triumph of global capitalism disproves or at least renders premature Schumpeter's predictions of capitalism's death and the inevitable march into socialism. Schumpeter's work is valuable today not for its predictions, but for its seminal and lasting insights into the nature of capitalism, innovation, entrepreneurship, and creative destruction.

TMH

See also Antitrust; Entrepreneurship

Further Readings

Harris, S. E., ed. *Schumpeter: Social Scientist*. Cambridge, MA: Harvard University Press, 1951.

McCraw, Thomas K. *Prophet of Innovation: Joseph Schumpeter and Creative Destruction*. Cambridge, MA: Harvard University Press, 2007.

Schumpeter, Joseph A. *Capitalism, Socialism and Democracy*. New York: Harper, 1942.

———. *The Theory of Economic Development*. Cambridge, MA: Harvard University Press, 1934.

Stolper, W. F. *Joseph A. Schumpeter, 1883–1950: The Public Life of a Private Man*. Princeton, NJ: Princeton University Press, 1994.

SECESSIONISM

Secession has reference to the withdrawal of a people and the territory they occupy from the sovereignty of an existing government and the establishment of a new government with sovereignty over the seceding group and its territory. Secession has held enduring interest for libertarians for several reasons. First, libertarian moral theory holds that individuals enjoy a right to secede without penalty from political institutions to which they have not previously consented. Second, secession is a method by which large, intrusive governments may be reduced to smaller, more consensual units. Third, secessionism as a political strategy encourages central governments to shift power to a more local level. Finally, even if secession, in a particular instance, might have harmful consequences, "legalizing secession" may be the best way to tame ethnic and nationalist movements that might otherwise resort to violence.

Following John Locke, natural rights libertarians hold that any infringements on the individual's natural rights to life, liberty, and property are presumptively illegitimate. Thus, any government actions that regulate individuals' bodies or seize their legitimately acquired property without those individuals' consent are unjustified, except perhaps under emergency circumstances. Because all existing independent states assert a plenary legislative power over the fate of those individuals residing within their borders, and virtually none of them have acquired the unanimous consent of these individuals to such power (Vatican City may be an exception), libertarians who embrace a theory of natural rights generally hold that existing states are to varying degrees illegitimate. Philosopher A. John Simmons has termed this view *empirical anarchism*. Empirical anarchists do not hold that all governments are necessarily illegitimate, merely that governments act illegitimately whenever they assume powers beyond the scope assigned to them through the express consent of those they govern.

The immediate implication of this view is that any individual who has not consented to an actual contract with the government may secede at any time, and it would be unjust for any government to restrict this right of secession. Secession also might be an appropriate remedy if governments that were once legitimate came to violate the terms of the social contract. In addition, libertarian theorist Murray Rothbard argues that the natural right of liberty implies that individuals cannot be held to specific performance of contractual obligations, but could be held liable for damages from breach of contract. If Rothbard is correct, then even those individuals who have consented to the authority of the government under which they live enjoy a basic right to withdraw consent, perhaps by paying a penalty.

Theories of individual secession are abstract and may lack relevance for a world in which actual secessionist movements typically claim to speak for many thousands or even millions of people. If Quebec secedes from Canada, the new state will inevitably take with it thousands, possibly millions, of people who would rather Quebec had remained a part of Canada. Secession violates their rights. Therefore, libertarian moral theory gives us no clear guidelines on how to treat messy, real-world secessions that take place without unanimous consent. Some theorists of secession hold that the "least bad" solution is to allow a group of people to secede whenever a majority of voters in the group endorse secession. If this principle were followed, then territorially contiguous communities of Quebec opposed to Quebec's secession from Canada could themselves secede from Quebec and rejoin Canada, an act known as "recursive secession." As attractive as this solution appears, it raises several problems, not least of which occurs when the seceding group pursues separation from another in order to violate the rights of a minority within its midst. The historical example of the Confederacy is often cited as an example of this scenario. Additionally, if the minority is territorially dispersed, then recursive secession is not an option for them.

Because in the real world secession almost always violates the rights of some people, some libertarians have turned to consequentialist criteria to assess the desirability and permissibility of secession. A world of small countries might be freer and more prosperous than a world of large countries: if so, then widespread secessions could lead to a freer and more prosperous world. Economists have found that smaller countries tend to embrace free trade to a greater extent than do larger ones because autarky is a more costly policy for them. However, political borders seem to pose a restraint on trade via such subtle hindrances as currency exchange and customs delays, and secession would multiply international borders. Political scientists have found that smaller countries tend to be more democratic than larger ones perhaps because when people are allowed to vote on the matter, they tend to prefer smaller jurisdictions that permit better access to officials. Nevertheless, they also have found that ethnic homogeneity in countries increases the size of their welfare states, confirming the preference of Lord Acton, one of the greatest classical liberal thinkers, for multinational empires over homogeneous nation-states. Because secession is usually motivated by ethnic or national differences, widespread secession would create smaller countries that are more ethnically homogeneous than those that exist at present, causing welfare spending to increase worldwide.

One consequence of secessionism is not ambiguous, however. In advanced democracies, regions with secessionist parties tend to receive more autonomy than regions without such parties. As a result, governance has become significantly more decentralized in democracies with strong secessionist parties. The United Kingdom, Belgium, Italy, and Spain are excellent examples of this trend. Libertarians see several advantages in local governance or federalism: the ability of individuals to move to jurisdictions with policy regimes more to their liking, the creation of competitive constraints on governments' overtaxing and overregulatory tendencies (businesses flee big government and seek free markets), and the strengthening of voters' control over their elected officials. Thus, the fact that secessionist movements create pressure on central governments to grant more autonomy to lower level regions is a positive byproduct of such campaigns.

Libertarians are wary of nationalist ideologies that often motivate secessionist movements. However, constitutionalizing secession does not imply endorsing it. If American states enjoyed the right to secede, it is unlikely that any of them actually would do so. Yet the mere existence of such a right would create a "threat point" for the federal government, potentially constraining federal attempts to usurp powers properly left to the states and the people under the 9th and 10th Amendments to the U.S. Constitution. In multinational countries such as Ethiopia, Britain, India, and Iraq, a right of secession might actually be used, but countries that already recognize such a right, formally or informally, see far less of the violence often associated with secessionist movements. By ruling in 1998 that the Canadian federal government must negotiate "in good faith" with any province that votes to secede "by a clear majority on a clear question," the Canadian Supreme Court helped to set an emerging international precedent: that secession should be negotiated rather than ruled out automatically.

In the United States, the status of secession remains unclear. The Supreme Court ruled in 1869 in *Texas v. White* that unilateral secession was unconstitutional. Although scholars continue to debate the merits of that decision, it is noteworthy that it does not rule out negotiated secession approved by Congress. The United States are, strictly speaking, not indivisible—unlike Spain and France, whose constitutions proscribe secession, and who, perhaps as a result, continue to suffer secessionist violence.

Just as libertarians support legalizing drugs in order to reduce the social ills associated with drug use, but not to encourage drug use, so libertarians may well support legalizing secession in order to encourage decentralization and reduce the risks of violence.

JSo

See also Civil War, U.S.; Constitutionalism; Revolution, Right of

Further Readings

Buchanan, Allen. *Justice, Legitimacy, and Self-Determination.* Oxford, New York: Oxford University Press, 2004.

Gordon, David, ed. *Secession, State, and Liberty.* New Brunswick, NJ: Transaction, 1998.

Macedo, Stephen, and Allen Buchanan, eds. *Secession and Self-Determination.* New York: New York University Press, 2003.

Simmons, A. John. *Moral Principles and Political Obligations.* Princeton, NJ: Princeton University Press, 1979.

Sorens, Jason. "Globalization, Secessionism, and Autonomy." *Electoral Studies* 23 no. 4 (2004): 727–752.

Walter, Barbara. "Information, Uncertainty, and the Decision to Secede." *International Organization* 60 (2006): 105–135.

Self-Interest

The idea of self-interest has played an extremely important role in theories and ideologies that advocate liberty. Advocates of freedom have frequently contended that liberty would benefit all people, thus claiming that it is to each person's benefit to enact policies that enhance freedom. In this way, they have appealed to the self-interest of their audience. Sometimes, however, they have appealed to the altruistic impulses of those whom they are addressing, arguing that they should embrace liberty because it is good for their neighbors. In that case, the argument is that one should support a free society because it is in one's neighbor's self-interest. For either sort of argument, the idea of self-interest is an important one and raises similar issues. In particular, it raises the issue of what self-interest is: What is it for something to be good for a person?

To this question, libertarian thinkers have offered two broadly different sorts of answers, two families of theories that are separated not only by their content, but also by their widely different historical ancestries, each located in different intellectual disciplines. On the one hand, for several centuries, there has been a strong tendency to define the interests of the individual in terms of the facts about the individual's own motivation: what is in one's interest. The motivation involved, depending on the form one's theory takes, might either be *ex ante* or *ex post*: One can say that what is in your interest is getting whatever it is you want before you managed to get it or, more plausibly, that it consists in possessing those things you have gotten and that you are satisfied with once having experienced the consequences of having gotten them. This approach has its roots in the innovations in psychology introduced by British philosophers of the post-Renaissance period, especially Thomas Hobbes and the empiricists. Its appeal is further enhanced by the influence of Immanuel Kant, who was in these matters strongly influenced by the British. The view is extremely widespread among economists.

This approach, which might be called "the desire or preference satisfaction view," has been rejected by other theorists, among them many philosophers. They point out that it is easy to want or prefer things that are not good for the person who wants or prefers them. People who are satisfied with what they have may therefore be living in a fool's paradise. What suggests that this view is plausible is that the pain of unsatisfied desires is not the only thing that can spoil a person's well-being. It also can be spoiled by the fact that one's general level of functioning has been damaged or degraded in some way. Plato asks his readers whether they would be willing to be transformed into so many fully contented oysters. If not, then maybe well-being, as they understand it, does not consist simply in the pleasure of satisfied desires or preferences.

The alternative approach takes as its starting point the notion that there is a mode of functioning that is appropriate to human beings, which in most versions of the theory includes thinking and/or acting rationally. What is really in one's interests is, most crucially, to function in this way as well as one can. The most frequently cited instance of this sort is no doubt Aristotle's notion of *eudaimonia*, variously translated as "happiness" or "flourishing." The historical roots of this tradition are to be found in the tradition of ancient Greek philosophy that includes Plato, Aristotle, and the Stoics.

Many libertarian thinkers have been suspicious, with good reason, of the visionary view, as this approach might be called. Historically, many of the defenders of this perspective, including Plato, Aristotle, Thomas Aquinas, and Karl Marx, have failed to be sympathetic to individual freedom. We can see one likely reason for this lack of sympathy by contrasting this view with the subjective preference view. If we suppose that people should, as far as possible, attain what is in their interests, then the desires or preferences view seems to immediately create a presumption in favor of liberty. After all, desires and preferences are likely to differ from one person to the next. Individuals are likely to know more about their own wants and preferences than is some master-mind who wishes to plan their lives. The most likely route to their getting what is good for them would seem to be to leave them free to act on their own impulses. Suppose, in contrast, that a major component of well-being is to carry out a mode of functioning that is appropriate to human beings in general. That supposition does not seem to have the same libertarian implications: If there is an "appropriate" mode of functioning, then it does seem to be the sort of thing that some philosopher might have a better grasp of than would people who have no outstanding knowledge or mental skills. At least on the face of it, it would appear that this view could be used to empower the philosopher to force this mode of functioning on everyone. Some people will not like it, but one's likes and dislikes are not, according to the visionary view, the whole story concerning whether

something is in one's best interests. Whether one's way of living is suitable to a human being is more important.

Still, it is not easy to say that libertarians should simply drop the visionary view altogether in favor of the subjective preference view. To the extent that the case for liberty rests on an appeal to people's understanding of what is in their interests, the latter view suffers from an obvious rhetorical disadvantage. To promise people that they will get what they want, regardless of what it is that they want, seems less inspiring; indeed, it seems positively ignoble, compared with the promise that they will be able to live in a way that is commensurate with their standing as human beings. It is perhaps for this reason that the proponents of liberty who have had large followings, who have influenced numbers of people outside the narrow confines of some academic specialty (such as economics)—proponents like John Stuart Mill, Henry David Thoreau, and Ayn Rand—have all to one extent or other made use of the visionary conception of self-interest.

LH

See also Aristotle; Individualism, Political and Ethical; Rand, Ayn; Thoreau, Henry David; Virtue

Further Readings

Aristotle. *The Nicomachean Ethics*. H. Rackham, trans. Cambridge, MA: Harvard University Press, 1926.

Mill, John Stuart. "On Liberty." *The Philosophy of John Stuart Mill: Ethical, Political, and Religious*. Marshall Cohen, ed. New York: Modern Library, 1961.

Rand, Ayn. *The Virtue of Selfishness: A New Concept of Egoism*. New York: Signet, 1964.

Rasmussen, Douglas, and Douglas J. Den Uyl. *Liberty and Nature: An Aristotelian Defense of Liberal Order*. La Salle, IL: Open Court, 1991.

Schlick, Moritz. *Problems of Ethics*. David Rynin, trans. New York: Dover, 1939.

Smith, Tara. *Ayn Rand's Normative Ethics: The Virtuous Egoist*. New York: Cambridge University Press, 2006.

SENIOR, NASSAU WILLIAM (1790–1864)

Nassau William Senior was a noted economist who also held several government commissions. He was appointed to the first endowed chair of political economy at Oxford in 1825. After the first edition of *An Outline of the Science of Political Economy* was published in *Encyclopedia Metropolitana* in 1836, a revised and expanded edition appeared as a separate volume in 1850. Senior defined *political economy* as the science that investigates the nature, production, and distribution of wealth. He employs the term *wealth* as a synonym for *value*, and, like the economists before him, includes *utility* as one of the three causes of value. Utility is "the power, direct or indirect, of producing pleasure, including under that term gratification of every kind, or of preventing pain, including under that term every species of discomfort." This subjective notion of utility reflects the influence of the French economists, such as Condillac and especially J.-B. Say.

Senior is widely regarded as one of the forerunners of marginal utility theory. The satisfaction that we derive from a class of goods, he maintained, "diminishes in a rapidly increasing ratio" as the supply of those goods increases. "Two articles of the same kind will seldom afford twice the pleasure of one. In proportion, therefore, as any article is abundant . . . the additional supply loses all, or nearly all, its utility." In his *History of Economic Analysis*, Joseph Schumpeter calls Senior one of the first "pure" economic theorists, while adding that, in this regard "his performance is clearly superior to that of Ricardo." This applies to Senior's attempt to base economic theory on four basic postulates or axioms, on which all of economic reasoning is based. This deductive method led the Austrian economist Murray N. Rothbard to hail Senior as "the most important praxeologist" of his era.

Perhaps Senior's most important contribution to the science of economics was his theory of time preference, which he called *abstinence*, as the source of the interest accruing to capital. Senior, wrote Eugen von Böhm-Bawerk in *History and Critique of Interest Theories*, "is infinitely superior to his predecessors in the study of interest, in point of profundity, systematic organization and scientific seriousness of purpose."

Another important feature of Senior's work was his insistence that economics should be a value-free discipline—a point he emphasized not only in his book *Political Economy*, but also in his lecture on "Statistic Science," which he delivered before the British Association for the Advancement of Science in 1860. "We cease to be scientific as soon as we advise or dissuade, or even approve or censure," he wrote. "Whenever [the economist] gives a precept, whenever he advises his reader to do anything, or to abstain from doing anything, he wanders from his science into art, generally into the art of morality, or the art of government."

GHS

See also Classical Economics; Liberalism, Classical; Praxeology

Further Readings

Senior, Nassau William. *An Outline of the Science of Political Economy*. Richard Whately, ed. New York: A. M. Kelley, 1965.
———. *Three Lectures on the Rate of Wages*. New York: A. M. Kelley, 1966.

SEPARATION OF CHURCH AND STATE

The separation of church and state is an aspect of the general separation that political philosophers have argued should exist between the state and private life. Although the state has generally retreated from religion in the modern West, controversy endures on a variety of church–state issues: By no means have all European state churches been disestablished, entanglements between church and state may endure even without a formally constituted state church, and many non-Western states both openly support state religions and impose high barriers against disfavored groups. Generally speaking, however, the separation of church and state is an area where classical liberal principles have achieved considerable success. In the developed world, the issue has in most respects been settled in favor of privatized religious institutions, practices, and beliefs. Libertarians applaud this development.

It is difficult to appreciate the degree to which church and state were conjoined in premodern Europe. Although practices varied from region to region, church offices typically conveyed a set of political and social prerogatives that far exceeded those of any other profession. These prerogatives were upheld not only by custom, but by the force of law. Churches, clergy, and their property were commonly not only immune from taxation, but also were the beneficiaries of compulsory taxes of their own, known as tithes. The higher church offices conferred feudal estates and honors to their possessors. Candidates to these positions were usually recommended, if not chosen outright, by the king or the high temporal nobility of the realm.

With the support of the temporal governments, the churches of that era operated state-approved courts to try cases involving the clergy and certain crimes arising out of purely religious law. Throughout the continent, church courts arrested, imprisoned, tortured, and executed religious dissidents, blasphemers, and so-called witches usually with the support or at least the acquiescence of the civil authority. Sporadic expulsions of those who did not share the state religion were a common feature in the histories of all European nations from the medieval era to the modern. Jews, Catholics, Muslims, and all of the various Protestant sects were at times subject to these expulsions in virtually any territory where they constituted a minority. Churches exercised censorship both prior and subsequent to publication, and church attendance was often compulsory.

At times, as in Old Regime France, the church and state were so closely fused that it became difficult to determine where one began and the other ended. The cardinal ministers Richelieu and Mazarin, for example, served simultaneously in both hierarchies. The clergy held one of the three votes in the Estates General, France's traditional legislature. In both France and England, the king's touch was said, by the grace of God, to cure scrofula, a skin disease nicknamed "the king's evil." (The double entendre does not, however, persist in French.)

During the Reformation, Western Europe's always tenuous religious unity finally disintegrated, and rulers faced the question of which religious faction they, and in turn their governments, should support. For example, from 1491 to 1558, England vacillated from Catholicism, to Protestantism, to Catholicism, and then to Protestantism once more during the reigns of Henry VIII, Edward VI, Mary I, and Elizabeth I. It would endure further disruptions during the English Civil Wars, the Interregnum, and the Glorious Revolution of the 17th century.

Yet few contemporaries questioned the idea that civil peace required religious unity. Paradoxically, almost everyone imagined that, without state intervention in matters of faith, constant warfare would result. This belief persisted despite more than a century of actual religious civil war, when governments tried in vain to enforce the state's religion. Perhaps most surprisingly, religious minorities did not notably favor the separation of church and state. Instead, they usually aspired to take over the state apparatus and set up their own sect as the official, privileged church. Judaism was one of the few religions to renounce temporal power of this sort, but the Jews had almost no influence on their Christian contemporaries in this regard.

Early social contract theorists like Thomas Hobbes and John Locke were thought controversial not chiefly because they would have limited state power, but because they argued that neither spiritual nor temporal governments were ordained of God, and that humans had created them both. Locke also argued that the power of churches could not legitimately include compulsion. Locke's insights implied religious toleration and even supported the full disestablishment of the state church.

Other classical liberals were of like mind. Little appreciated during its author's lifetime, Baruch Spinoza's *Tractatus Theologico-Politicus* (1670) argued that the state should have almost no role in religious life. The *Tractatus* was outlawed even in the relatively tolerant Dutch Republic. However, its key political ideas slowly gained ground. In the next century, Voltaire, David Hume, and Thomas Jefferson all promoted disestablishment as a pragmatic compromise among competing faiths and a way of creating public peace over questions that could not readily be resolved without supernatural insight.

The 17th century saw the gradual introduction of religious tolerance in several European states, including Britain, the Dutch Republic, and, to a limited extent, even France, beginning with the Edict of Nantes in 1598. No European state, however, disestablished its church during this era; toleration took hold well before disestablishment,

and religious tolerance coexisted with special privileges for members of the officially favored religions. Even in ostensibly liberal England, Protestants enjoyed considerable advantages from the state. For example, the Test Act of 1673 barred Roman Catholics from holding office. It was not repealed until 1829, and the Church of England remains an established church to this day.

The first practical act of disestablishment came in the American colonies. In Massachusetts, the Baptist dissident Roger Williams contended that the civil power had no authority to try or punish religious crimes and that all people should enjoy freedom of conscience—what Williams termed *soul liberty*. The other colonists disagreed and exiled him. In 1636, Williams and a small group of like-minded settlers founded the city of Providence in what became the state of Rhode Island. For years, Williams worked to secure a royal charter protecting his colony, and when it finally arrived in 1663, it constituted the first formal separation of church and state in Western history.

The charter proclaimed Rhode Island a "livlie experiment." Charles II, no stranger to religious strife, admitted that

> inhabitants of the same colonie cannot, in theire private opinions, conform to the publique exercise of religion . . . or take or subscribe the oaths and articles made and established in that behalfe, [therefore] our royall will and pleasure is, that noe person within the sayd colonye . . . shall bee any wise molested, punished, disquieted, or called in question, for any differences in opinie in matters of religion.

Other British colonies followed a range of different courses, from disestablishment and religious liberty to a fully established church with compulsory public funding and laws against religious dissidents, atheists, and blasphemers. This pattern continued in the states of the early American republic, although the movement was distinctly toward disestablishment. For example, one of Thomas Jefferson's proudest achievements was his authorship of the 1786 Virginia Statute for Religious Freedom. The Statute termed established religion a "dangerous fallacy" and forbade public support for any church. By contrast, Massachusetts was a relative latecomer: Following his return to private life, Jefferson's friend and sometime political rival John Adams worked to disestablish his home state's official church. Yet disestablishment came only in 1833, 7 years after the long-lived Adams had died.

On the federal level, the U.S. Constitution protects the separation of church and state in a variety of ways. Most explicitly, the 1st Amendment declares that no established federal Church can ever exist and that no federal law can abridge the freedom of religion. Further, Article VI section 3 declares that "no religious test shall ever be required as a qualification to any office or public trust under the United States." Given the tumultuous history of England and the great religious diversity of the early republic, this step may appear virtually forced. Yet other clues reiterate the founders' intent: The text of the Constitution nowhere invokes the protection of any one church, creed, or deity. Similarly, the oath required of government officials may be either sworn or affirmed—a speech act that does not require referencing God.

The American founders were justly proud of their achievement. On January 1, 1802, Thomas Jefferson endorsed the separation of church and state with the following words: "I contemplate with sovereign reverence that act of the whole American people which declared that their legislature should make no law respecting an establishment of religion, or prohibiting the free exercise thereof, thus building a wall of separation between Church and State." James Madison, the chief architect of the U.S. Constitution, declared that "practical distinction between Religion and Civil Government is essential to the purity of both, and [is] guaranteed by the Constitution of the United States." Yet state support for religion endures in the modern world, both abroad and even at home.

In most European countries, religious groups must register with the state and submit to monitoring; those religions that refuse to register lose the tax exemption that registered religions typically enjoy, and they may face a variety of other penalties, as with the Church of Scientology, which is outlawed in Greece. Several European countries still maintain state churches, including England, Denmark, Norway, Iceland, and Malta. Although the Church of England no longer receives taxpayer subsidy, and although most religious tests for office have been removed in the United Kingdom, the holder of the highest political post, the monarch, must still be a professed member of this Church.

The world's remaining totalitarian and one-party states are generally either hostile to all religions or else have established official state churches. The latter is the case, for example, in Myanmar, whose government actively promotes Buddhism; and in Saudi Arabia and Iran, which forbid the public practice of any religion other than Islam. Islamic religious law is strictly enforced by the Saudi state among others, often with beatings and public executions.

The situation in communist China is highly peculiar. The government has established multiple official religious organizations, which aim to supplant the private but now illegal faiths on which they are modeled. For example, China has a state-run version of Catholicism, whereas the Roman Catholic Church is illegal. The Roman Catholic Church, for its part, declares the Chinese Patriotic Catholic Association to be schismatic. Likewise, the official version of Tibetan Buddhism has even promulgated communist-sponsored regulations on how souls are to be reincarnated. In response, the Dalai Lama, the highest authority in traditional Tibetan Buddhism, has publicly declared that his soul will never be reborn under the Chinese communists' authority.

Even in the United States, many issues persist regarding the separation of church and state. Several of these issues are symbolic: The U.S. motto "In God We Trust" and the phrase "under God" in the pledge of allegiance have both been subject to unsuccessful Supreme Court challenges. Under current Court doctrine, the state-sanctioned display of the Ten Commandments now depends strongly on the surrounding context: Is the display intended to make a religious statement? Or is the depiction in question merely part of a larger display showing the value of written law in the Western tradition? If it is the former, the Establishment Clause prohibits the display. The latter, however, is permitted.

However, some church–state issues in the United States are quite substantive. For example, some groups would institute compulsory or instructor-led prayer in public schools. Others would institute the teaching of biblical creationism. During the last several decades, U.S. courts have tended to reject these initiatives. Libertarians overwhelmingly find proposals of this type improper. Not only do state-sanctioned prayers run contrary to all of classical liberal tradition, but most libertarians would add that the mere existence of public schools is problematic in itself.

Controversies still exist. Since the early modern era, however, it has become increasingly clear that the separation of church and state can serve as a model to guide efforts to roll back state authority in other areas of life. If the state should not interfere in these most important of matters, then it faces high hurdles in other areas as well. Therefore, the separation of church and state is of the highest interest to libertarians for reasons of history, philosophy, and public policy alike.

JTK

See also Bill of Rights, U.S.; Constitution, U.S.; English Civil Wars; Jefferson, Thomas; Levellers; Locke, John; Religion and Liberty

Further Readings

Brenner, Lenni, ed. *Jefferson and Madison on the Separation of Church and State*. Fort Lee, NJ: Barricade Books, 2004.

Feldman, Noah. *Divided by God: America's Church-State Problem—and What We Should Do about It*. New York: Farrar, Straus & Giroux, 2005.

Gaustad, Edwin, S., ed. *Liberty of Conscience: Roger Williams in America*. Grand Rapids, MI: Eerdmans, 1991.

Jacoby, Susan. *Freethinkers: A History of American Secularism*. New York: Holt, 2004.

Spinoza, Baruch. *Tractatus Theologico-Politicus*. Boston: Brill Academic, 1997.

U.S. Senate. *U.S. Committee on International Religious Freedom: Findings on Russia, China, and Sudan; and Religious Persecutions in the World*. Hearing Before the Committee on Foreign Relations, June 2000.

Sexuality

Combining physical, psychic, and spiritual dimensions, sexuality ranks as one of the core aspects of the human personality. In the past, human sexuality has been regarded as instrumental, that is, subordinate to some other aim, usually procreation. Yet just as there is sex without procreation, so—thanks to advances in medical technology—offspring can be conceived without sexual contact. Sexuality is not tethered to procreation.

For centuries, Western society sought to confine sexual congress within the bounds of marriage. In this context, commercial arrangements (prostitution) and homosexuality were discouraged or proscribed. Today, a broader understanding of sexual freedom prevails.

From a libertarian perspective, all forms of sexual expression are permitted, provided that both parties give informed consent. This provision would exclude sex with animals and children. In keeping with the "harm" principles that almost all libertarians embrace, those who are HIV-positive would be required to engage in sex only after providing their partner with proper notice. Some situations, as when the initiator of sexual relations is a prison guard or a priest, would appear to be instances where full consent could not ordinarily be given inasmuch as the intended partner is so clearly vulnerable. However, consensual sado-masochistic (s/m) relations fall within the compass of voluntarily agreed-on acts and would be permitted, as would polyamory, which is love and relations among three or more persons. A good maxim to follow is, "Do it if you wish, but cause no harm."

Libertarians favor elimination of all laws limiting sexual freedom among consenting adults as representing a needless intrusion of the state into the business of the individual. Moreover, libertarians do not support legislation (which exists in some European countries) providing penalties sanctioning speech and writing that demeans sexual minorities. Lack of sympathy for other human groups is regrettable, but freedom of expression mandates that it be tolerated unless specific acts of incitement to violence are involved.

Full enjoyment of sex requires adequate information. Unchecked by correctives, the circulation of popular sex mythology is an obstacle to sexual maturity among young people. Access to sex education is therefore essential. This principle also entails toleration of erotic writings and images, sometimes termed *pornography*. Contraceptives must be available because sexual freedom should not be obtained at the cost of unwanted pregnancy. Evidence from European countries indicates that ready access to contraceptives reduces rates of abortion—surely a goal embraced by most people.

Just as a wide range of sexual activities should be permitted to flourish, by the same token, there should be no attempt to disparage chastity as an individual decision. The overarching goal is maximizing choice, and choosing not to have sex is a legitimate option. It need hardly be added that one should not have to marry in order to engage in sex. But what obligations does marriage entail? Does each partner agreeing to marry have the right to expect sex? In the past, annulments have been granted on the grounds of nonconsummation. However, as marriage moves closer to centering on agreed-on arrangements, it would seem that such expectations should be stipulated in advance. Provided that it is understood that this will be the case, there is no reason that the partners in a marriage should not remain chaste.

Some libertarians argue that copulation should be performed in private, but ultimately, from a libertarian perspective, the determination of whether sexual activities can take place hinges on the decision of the owner of the property where it is to occur. Public displays of affection are a different matter. Homosexuals are surely correct in arguing that they should have the same rights in this regard as heterosexuals. Moreover, if sexual self-affirmation is to be provided for all, solicitation must be accepted.

Some scholars have posited a fundamental division between sex-positive and sex-negative societies. Ancient Greece, medieval Islam, and traditional Japan have been classified as sex-positive, whereas Christian polities figure as sex-negative. This contrast seems too stark. Medieval Islam, for example, was indeed relatively sex-positive for men, even as it drastically restricted the range of women's sexuality. Western Europe has evolved over time from a situation in which the Christian churches exercised a large role to a more secular orientation. During the 18th century, a group of libertine writers emerged, especially in France—among them Jean-Baptiste Boyer d'Argens, Jean-Charles Gervaise de Latouche, and the Marquis D. A. F. de Sade—who vividly highlighted the positive value of sexual expression. Working in a different realm, the Italian legal theorist Cesare Beccaria for the first time advocated discarding laws against homosexuality, which he regarded as ineffectual. The idea that, in the absence of express justification, repressive laws should be pruned from the statute books proved influential. In the following century, feminists and others stressed the need for access to sexual information, including methods of contraception. It was not until the early 20th century, however, that Kurt Hiller, in his book *Das Recht über sich selbst* (1908; *The Right Concerning Oneself*), defended sexual freedom as part of the right to control one's own body. On a comparative basis, he dealt with such subjects as suicide, abortion, incest, and homosexuality.

Historically, the range of sexual freedom has been quite variable. The boundaries of what is permissible have been affected by theological concepts, by the promotion of state interests, and by concerns within the family unit—often centering on the importance of determining paternity. In the early 21st century, however, many of these concerns have become less salient—at least in advanced, industrialized societies.

The outlook for Western societies is continued affirmation of the expressive dimension of sex as something that should be available to every adult. In many Third World countries, however, the picture is more clouded. In some regions of the world, female genital mutilation, causing a permanent impairment of women's sexual functioning, remains prevalent. There too homophobia is rife, leading to imprisonment and even execution of those found to have engaged in same-sex behavior. Libertarians insist that these repressive acts must be opposed and not simply excused on grounds of cultural difference.

WD

See also Abortion; Bioethics; Children; Family; Feminism and Women's Rights; Marriage

Further Readings

Bullough, Vern. *Sexual Variance in Society and History*. New York: Wiley, 1976.
McElroy, Wendy. *Liberty for Women: Freedom and Feminism in the Twenty-First Century*. Chicago: Ivan R. Dee, 2002.
Posner, Richard A. *Sex and Reason*. Cambridge, MA: Harvard University Press, 1992.
Sciabarra, Chris Matthew. *Ayn Rand, Homosexuality and Human Liberation*. Cape Town: Leap Publishing, 2003.

Shaftesbury, Third Earl of (1671–1713)

The third earl of Shaftesbury, Anthony Ashley Cooper, was the leading opponent of Stuart absolutism, chief organizer of the Whig political movement, and John Locke's patron and collaborator. The third earl was the grandson of the first earl, who held the position of Lord Chancellor under Charles II until having fallen from favor when he was implicated in Monmouth's Rebellion. The third earl thus came from a family noted for its opposition to tyranny.

One of Locke's tasks was to supervise the education of the young Shaftesbury, who was fluent in Greek and Latin by age 11. Although Shaftesbury shared the political views of his grandfather (known as Real, or Radical, Whiggism) and served for a number of years in Parliament, his first loves were philosophy and literature. Rather than writing formal treatises in philosophy, Shaftesbury preferred personal essays of the sort that had been popularized by Montaigne. Five lengthy essays, which cover a wide variety of subjects, including moral and social philosophy, were

published in 1711 under the title, *Characteristics of Men, Manners, Opinions, Times*.

Shaftesbury's *Characteristics* was one of the most influential works of the 18th century. Its theory of a moral sense would influence Bishop Butler, Francis Hutcheson, David Hume, and other liberal thinkers, and its defense of freedom of speech, religious toleration, and personal liberty made it a key work of the early Enlightenment.

From a libertarian perspective, perhaps the Shaftesbury's most significant contribution was the emphasis he placed on the natural sociability of human beings and the natural harmony of interests among individuals in society. Although a severe critic of Thomas Hobbes's psychological egoism, which reduced all motives to selfish desires, Shaftesbury maintained that the pursuit of rational self-interest (which he called *self-love*) is not only compatible with the public good, but absolutely essential to it. As Henry Sidgwick wrote in *Outlines of the History of Ethics* (1886), Shaftesbury initiated a line of thought that seeks to demonstrate a harmony between man's "social affections" and his "reflective self-regard." According to Sidgwick, "no moralist before Shaftesbury had made this the cardinal point in his system." In light of these conclusions regarding the harmony of interests that marked most social interaction, Shaftesbury may be viewed as the pioneer of a tradition that culminated, decades later, in Adam Smith's famous theory of the "invisible hand."

GHS

See also Hume, David; Locke, John; Self-Interest; Whiggism

Further Readings

Hume, David. *Enquiry Concerning the Principles of Morals*. J. B. Schneewind, ed. Indianapolis, IN: Hackett, 1983.
Shaftesbury, Anthony Ashley Cooper, Earl of. *Characteristics of Men, Manners, Opinions, Times*. Lawrence Eliot Klein, ed. Cambridge: Cambridge University Press, 1999.
Smith, Adam. *The Theory of Moral Sentiments*. New York: Oxford University Press, 1976.

Sidney, Algernon (1623–1683)

Algernon Sidney was a statesman and philosopher. Sidney is best known for conspiring to rebel against Charles II of England and for his subsequent beheading for his participation in activities against the king. However, his primary significance lies in the political theory he offered in his book *Discourses Concerning Government*, published posthumously, which was of tremendous influence in the American colonies.

Sidney was born to an aristocratic family. His father, the Earl of Leicester, served as England's ambassador to France during the 1630s, and Sidney entered politics as a young man. He was elected to Parliament in 1646, before being expelled by Oliver Cromwell in 1653. He resumed his seat in Parliament in 1659, but his second term in government also was short-lived. In 1660, the English Commonwealth collapsed, and Charles II was restored to the throne. Sidney refused to recant his earlier actions under the republic and to beg for the king's forgiveness, and thus began a 20-year period of exile that took him throughout Europe.

Sidney was finally granted permission to return to England in the late 1670s. Soon after his return, he and other Whigs determined that Charles II wished to turn England into an absolute monarchy in which Parliament would play little role and Catholicism would replace the Church of England as the state religion. Sidney, a committed republican and Protestant who repeatedly warned against what he believed to be the dangers of monarchy and "Popery," was appalled and began to plot against the regime. His execution made him a martyr for the republican cause, and the *Discourses*, written from 1680 to 1683 and published in 1698, soon became influential throughout the English-speaking world.

The *Discourses*, like James Tyrrell's *Patriarcha non Monarcha*, published in 1681, and John Locke's *Two Treatises of Government*, published in 1689, were written largely in response to Robert Filmer's promonarchical tract *Patriarcha: A Defence of the Natural Power of Kings against the Unnatural Liberty of the People*. In contrast to Filmer, Sidney believed that men were naturally free and thus had the right to choose their rulers, who were as much under the law as were the subjects. If those conditions were not met, Sidney argued, revolution was justified.

Sidney's liberalism, however, was tempered by his belief that government should help people lead good, virtuous lives. "If the publick safety be provided, liberty and propriety secured, justice administered, virtue encouraged, vice suppressed, and the true interest of the nation advanced, the ends of government are accomplished," Sidney wrote. In addition, Sidney believed it important that the most virtuous men assume positions of political power.

Sidney's concern for liberty and representative government, on the one hand, and his support for a state that promoted virtue through the rule of its most outstanding citizens, on the other hand, may seem contradictory. However, Sidney believed that well-informed citizens would elect the most deserving of their fellows to government posts, and thus there would be no such contradiction in practice. In Sidney's view, a natural aristocracy, one that would rise by merit rather than birth, would assume rightful power in a free and just system of government.

Sidney's writings inspired many American revolutionaries. Thomas Jefferson, for instance, called the *Discourses*

"a rich treasure of republican principles . . . probably the best elementary book of principles of government, as founded in natural right which has ever been published in any language." According to one study, Sidney's *Discourses Concerning Government* was the third most common political book in colonial libraries, behind only John Trenchard and Thomas Gordon's *Cato's Letters* and John Locke's *Two Treatises of Government*.

Sidney defended his republican principles all his life, writing the following passage while imprisoned and awaiting execution: "I had from my youth endeavored to uphold the common rights of mankind, the laws of this land, and the true Protestant religion, against corrupt principles, arbitrary power, and Popery, and I do now willingly lay down my life for the same."

AS

See also Cato's Letters; English Civil Wars; Republicanism, Classical; Whiggism

Further Readings

Baker, Chris. "Algernon Sidney: Forgotten Founding Father." *The Freeman: Ideas on Liberty* 47 no. 10 (October 1997): 625–628.

Houston, Alan Craig. *Algernon Sidney and the Republican Heritage in England and America*. Princeton, NJ: Princeton University Press, 1991.

Scott, Jonathan. *Algernon Sidney and the English Republic, 1623–1677*. New York: Cambridge University Press, 1988.

———. *Algernon Sidney and the Restoration Crisis, 1677–1683*. New York: Cambridge University Press, 1991.

Sidney, Algernon. *Discourses Concerning Government*. Thomas G. West, ed. Indianapolis, IN: Liberty Fund, 1996.

Simon, Julian (1932–1998)

Julian Simon was one of the most underappreciated economists of the 20th century. Born in New Jersey, Simon earned his BA in experimental psychology from Harvard University and, in 1961, his PhD from the University of Chicago's Graduate School of Business. He died on February 8, 1998.

Although Simon wrote on an unusually wide range of topics—including statistical methods and mental depression—Simon's greatest contribution to economics is his refinement of the idea that humans are "the ultimate resource." Simon argued there are no resources without human creativity to figure out how to use them and human effort to actually do so.

Petroleum, for example, is certainly not, by its nature, a resource. If it were, Native Americans would long ago have put it to good use. But they did not. Petroleum did not become a resource until creative people determined how it could be used to satisfy some human desires and other people determined how it could be cost-effectively extracted from the ground.

An implication of this realization, that humans are "the ultimate resource," leads to the conclusion that a high and growing population—at least in societies with sufficient freedom to allow individuals to experiment and create—is desirable.

Simon, of course, understood that human beings, unlike tungsten and petroleum, also consume goods and services. The question thus arises in free societies whether greater numbers of human beings produce more than they consume or whether their consumption outruns their production. Most people simply assume that humans are net consumers—an assumption that explains the common hysteria over immigration and population growth that has seized so many people. But Simon, having carefully analyzed the data, found that growing human populations in free societies produce net increases in resource supplies. His books presenting much of these data are *The Ultimate Resource* (1981), *The Ultimate Resource 2* (1996), *The State of Humanity* (1995), and *Population Matters* (1990).

Population researcher Paul Ehrlich found Simon's optimism about population growth to be so absurd that he famously accepted a bet offered by Simon in 1980. Ehrlich had authored *The Population Bomb*, a book foretelling disaster from population growth. The essence of Simon's position in the bet was that, despite the population growth that was sure to occur during the 1980s, the effective supply of natural resources would increase during this decade because human beings would figure out how to find, extract, and use resources more efficiently. The surest measure of this increased supply would be lower inflation-adjusted resource prices.

Convinced that higher population would prove a curse, Ehrlich accepted the $1,000 bet. He chose a bundle of copper, chromium, nickel, tin, and tungsten and bet Simon that the real price of this bundle of resources would be higher in 1990 than in 1980. The prices of September 1990 were compared to those of September 1980, and Simon won convincingly. The real price of each of these five resources fell over the course of that decade, indicating that their supplies grew despite—or because of—growing human population.

Julian Simon's legacy is profound. Free people are net producers—they are "the ultimate resource." Thus, controls on production, creativity, and industry designed to "conserve" resources are likely to have the opposite effect in the long term. Simon's work demonstrates that those people who value continued abundance for future generations should support the free market, which rewards both efficiency and creativity in developing new resources.

DJB

Further Readings

Simon, Julian. *The State of Humanity*. Hoboken, NJ: Wiley-Blackwell, 1996.
———. *The Ultimate Resource*. Princeton, NJ: Princeton University Press, 1983.
———. *The Ultimate Resource 2*. Princeton, NJ: Princeton University Press, 1998.

SLAVERY, WORLD

Slavery was a near-universal feature of human societies from the emergence of agriculture until its near disappearance between 1770 and 1880. As such, it has played an essential role for millennia, and its complete loss of legitimacy and disappearance in practice is one of the most significant of the changes that mark the advent of modernity. Before the later 18th century, many thinkers defended slavery as a natural institution that was beneficial, at least for some people. Aristotle held this view, for example. Many Christian and Muslim thinkers defended it on scriptural grounds. Others deprecated slavery and saw it as regrettable or tried to limit its extent. Thus, some Christian and Muslim thinkers tended to argue that, although slavery as such was legitimate, it was not proper to enslave one's coreligionists. However, even these thinkers believed that slavery, although regrettable, was an unavoidable feature of human society.

The image that most people have of slavery today is taken largely from the experience of plantation slavery in the New World. However, this case was extreme, and the form taken by slavery historically has varied considerably. The essential element of slavery is completely unfree labor. Slaves possess no control over their labor, over what they do or how and when they do it. Even more significantly, they have no property right of any kind in the product of their labor. They do not own it as a self-employed artisan or free farmer would, and they do not receive monetary compensation or payment as in the case of wage laborers. Instead, all of the benefits of the work accrue to another party, the slaveowner, who exercises the full range of property rights over the slave's labor, including the crucial power of alienation—that is, the owner can sell the ownership of the slave's labor to another party. As such, slavery is at the extreme end of a spectrum of unfree labor, with such phenomena as serfdom or debt bondage and indentured labor being less extreme or thoroughgoing varieties. However, there is considerable variation historically in both the kind of work slaves are normally expected to do and the range of legal rights that they may have. In the extreme cases, such as New World plantation slavery, the slave is simply an object with no more rights or legal status than an animal or other kind of chattel, and thus has his humanity radically denied. In other forms of slavery, the slave enjoyed some legal recognition as a person and had certain rights, although these rights were never as extensive as those possessed by free persons. For most of the history of the Islamic world, slaves were not used in large-scale production or plantation agriculture, but in domestic slavery and (uniquely) as soldiers. Elsewhere, slave labor was common in agriculture, whereas the use of slaves in commercial plantation agriculture and mining became a significant feature of some parts of the world economy after the 1460s.

In the ancient world, slavery was a near universal institution. Slave labor was used for the whole range of productive tasks, from agriculture to manufacturing, including the few cases of large-scale manufacture such as brick making. Most slaves worked in agriculture, hardly surprising given that these were overwhelmingly agricultural economies where the economics of large-scale agricultural holdings, as in ancient Rome, made slavery most profitable. Although there was an active trade in slaves, the main source of slaves was war—with the enslavement of all or part of the defeated population a common feature. Another important source of slaves was debt, debtors being taken into slavery if they could not service their debts. In the ancient world, slavery was found around the world and was not associated with either particular kinds of work or with specific ethnic groups—anyone could become a slave if they were unfortunate enough to fall into certain categories.

During the early part of the Middle Ages, this pattern continued. The Islamic Middle East became the main center of demand for slaves, which, together with the central role played by Islam in the creation of a system of interlinked trading circuits that connected the various parts of the Old World, led to the appearance of a fully organized trade in slaves. The major sources of slaves at this time were Central Asia, Africa (particularly Eastern Africa), and the Slavic lands of Eastern and Central Europe—the term *slave* actually derives from the word *Slav*. During the 8th century, large-scale plantation agriculture began to develop in the Middle East, particularly in southern Iraq. This system came to an abrupt halt with the massive slave uprising of 869–879 known as the *Zanj* revolt (in the Arabic of the time, *zanj* meant black and referred both to African slaves and the part of Africa from which most of them came, the Eastern littoral down to Zanzibar). Following this upheaval, large plantations using slave labor were abandoned in that part of the world because of the risks of another rebellion.

The central and later Middle Ages saw a gradual decline of slavery in most parts of the world, apart from the Islamic world and Africa, a decline most marked in China but also true of Europe. By the 15th century, outright slavery seemed to be about to disappear in most parts of the world. However, at this point, it underwent both a revival and a transformation. There occurred a growth in demand for both domestic slaves and slave soldiers in the Islamic world following the consolidation of that area into a small number of large states, notably the Ottoman and Safavid Empires. Of equal importance, a system of large-scale plantation agriculture appeared in the New World following its conquest by the Spanish and Portuguese. These plantations produced a range of cash crops such as indigo, rice, cotton, and, above all, sugar. In addition, large-scale mining was introduced in places such as Potosi in Bolivia and Zacatecas in Mexico. All of these activities involved the use of slave labor on a massive scale and with an unprecedented degree of harshness. Slavery here was a response to the need for a captive labor force that could guarantee sustained production of cash crops and metals for sale not in their place of origin, but on a worldwide market. A paid labor force was not a realistic option at this time given the depopulation of the New World by diseases brought by the Europeans and the need to keep a labor force in place for a prolonged period of time for sustained production of cash crops and commodities. However, a slave revolt did not pose the kind of threat to European states that the Zanj revolt had to the Abbasid Caliphate inasmuch as the plantations were located a long way from the main urban centers. The result was the creation of the world's largest-ever slave labor system.

Initially the demand for a captive labor force in the Americas was met by attempts to enslave the surviving indigenous populations plus the importation of Europeans, mainly convicts. However, Native Americans found it too easy to escape, and Europeans tended to die too rapidly due to their susceptibility to tropical illnesses. The solution was to turn to what now became the main supplier of slaves to both the Atlantic and Islamic world, Africa. European convicts remained a significant source of both slaves and indentured labor, particularly in North America, but in the Americas and Caribbean as a whole, they were vastly outnumbered by those brought over from Africa. Africa became the main source of slaves for a number of reasons. One simple reason was its geographical location—in the tropics (so that its population was relatively less susceptible to tropical diseases) and halfway between both the New World and the Middle East, the two major areas with a demand for slaves. The main reason, however, was that slavery was a long-established institution within Africa, organized in much the way it had been in the entire world during antiquity, with the losers in wars being taken as slaves. Hence, there was an infrastructure already in place to capture and supply slaves to the increasingly eager Europeans and Arabs.

It was this development that led to the other major change in slavery at this time, its acquiring a distinctive racial identity. Before the 15th century, the institution of slavery was not associated with any specific ethnic group, but from that time onward it became associated in both the

Christian and Islamic worlds with Africans. It became a racial institution and was increasingly linked with a racial ideology that justified the enslavement of Africans in particular as opposed to other racial groups. At this point, the ideological rationale for this institution did not yet involve the kind of pseudoscientific arguments that were developed later. Instead it tended to rely on scriptural exegesis, particularly the biblical legend of the Curse of Ham, and arguments derived from classical philosophy that some people (now assumed to be Africans) were born to be slaves, which was both their destiny and what was best for them. By the time the plantation complex was fully established in the later 17th century, slavery had become inextricably intertwined with this racial ideology.

During the 16th and early 17th centuries, large organized slave trades appeared that connected Africa to other parts of the world trade system, with literally millions of Africans being taken and sold as slaves in many parts of the world. The first was the trans-Saharan trade, which connected central Africa to the ports of the Maghreb and to the Nile valley and Cairo and the Middle East in general via the great slave market in Cairo. The second was the Indian Ocean trade, which connected East Africa to the Middle East and all of the lands around the Indian Ocean. The third was the transatlantic trade, which linked West Africa from Senegal down to Angola to the Americas and the Caribbean. In addition, pirates from the Barbary Coast states regularly raided the coastlines of Western Europe to capture slaves. This method of acquiring slaves, however, was different from the others, in that it was a survival of the older medieval and ancient traditions of acquiring slaves by raiding and warfare, rather than commercial exchange.

The critical feature of these three main slave trades was that they were indeed trades. Arabs and Europeans did not in general acquire slaves by raiding. Instead they bought slaves from Africans who had gone into the business of slave-taking precisely to sell them to the external market represented by the Europeans and Arabs. The slaves were paid for with a number of commodities, but above all with firearms. This exchange gave the Africans who supplied the slaves an enormous military advantage over other Africans. The result was the creation of a set of damaging incentives for Africans. Essentially, they had the choice of becoming slave-takers or slaves. One result was the appearance of large empires based on the supplying of slaves such as Asante, Dahomey, Lunda, and Oyo. These then supplied slaves in ever larger numbers to external traders. Some were marched across the Sahara in great slave caravans, whereas others were taken long distances to the coasts, where they were then held in forts before being put on ships to be taken over the Indian or Atlantic Oceans to their final destinations. There were significant differences between the Atlantic slave trade and the other two. In particular, the Europeans were mainly interested in male slaves because they wanted

them for heavy manual labor, whereas the Arabs had a higher demand for female domestic slaves—most of the male slaves taken to the Middle East were castrated.

By the mid-18th century, slavery had once again become a major part of the world trade system. The various slave trades were highly profitable, as were the plantations and mines that slaves worked in the New World. However, it was at this point that the whole institution came under attack. In late 18th-century Europe, for the first time people started to articulate a fundamental critique of both the theory and practice of slavery. This viewpoint derived, in part, from the 18th-century notion of humanitarianism and "sympathy" with Africans and slaves, who were now seen as fellow human beings whose situation and suffering inspired sympathy and identification, rather than indifference. Antislavery arguments also had their origin in the increasingly influential idea of universal human rights that applied to all human beings regardless of their status or ethnicity. The result was the appearance of an organized campaign against slavery in general and the slave trade in particular. The campaigners faced formidable obstacles in the shape of entrenched and powerful special interests and centuries of practice and intellectual tradition.

Nevertheless, a great intellectual and popular movement opposed to slavery was created and went on to gain a series of victories. The first victory was the famous *Somerset's Case* of 1772, in which Lord Mansfield held that slavery could not be justified by natural law and so could only exist in Britain if it had been authorized by positive law (i.e., Parliamentary enactment), which it had not. After several attempts, the British Parliament abolished the slave trade in 1807, following a campaign that had begun with the formation of the British Committee for the Abolition of the Slave Trade in 1787 and featuring such figures as Thomas Clarkson, Granville Sharpe, Oloudah Equiano, and William Wilberforce. Similar organizations were set up in other countries, most notably the *Société des Amis des Noirs* in France, led by Brissot and the Abbé Gregoire. After a prolonged struggle, slavery was finally abolished in the British Empire in 1834. It was then abolished in one part of the world after another, with the final significant event being its abolition in Brazil in 1888.

At the same time, there also was a series of large-scale slave rebellions, particularly in the Caribbean and Brazil. The most famous and significant rebellion was the successful revolt in the French colony of Santo Domingue in 1791, led by Toussaint Louverture, which was the first successful slave rebellion in history and led to the appearance of Haiti as an independent state. There also were major uprisings in Jamaica in 1831–1832, Demerara (modern Guyana) in 1795 and 1823, Surinam in 1765–1793, Barbados in 1816, and Bahia in Brazil in 1822–1830 and 1835. These uprisings all made the institution much more difficult to sustain, not least because they raised the cost of maintaining it for the slaveholders. However, the revolts by themselves would not have been enough to destroy the institution had there not been a fundamental shift in attitudes and beliefs about slavery brought about by the campaigns of the antislavery movement. Had the antislavery movement not happened, ruthless force would still have been used to sustain colonial slavery, but thanks to the abolitionists' efforts, force alone no longer commanded enough legitimacy to make such action possible.

One of the most impressive features of the abolition of slavery was its mostly peaceful nature. In all but two cases, the institution was abolished peacefully, with compensation being paid to the owners or a "free womb" provision being applied by which although existing slaves remained enslaved, their children were born into freedom. The two exceptions were Haiti and the United States. In the American case, slavery's abolition was uniquely costly, happening only after a terrible war and more than half a million deaths. The obvious question to ask is why this was. The explanation lies in the nature and history of slavery in North America, both before and after 1776.

Slavery existed in all of the American colonies before 1776 and the American Revolution. However, it was a central economic institution only in some of the southern colonies, most notably South Carolina, but also Georgia and Virginia. One aspect of the Revolution was the spread of opposition to both the slave trade and slavery among many (but not all) of the founders. When the Constitutional Convention met in Philadelphia, the status of both slavery and the slave trade was one of the controversial issues facing the delegates. The outcome was a series of compromises. The Constitution provided for the prohibition of the importation of slaves after 1808. However, it also contained a fugitive slave clause, which effectively spread the cost of sustaining slavery in the face of attempted escapes over the entire Union, rather than leaving it to be borne by the slave owners. There also was the notorious "three fifths" clause of the Constitution, by which slaves were to count as three fifths of a person for the purposes of allocating seats in the House, a provision that significantly increased the voting weight of white southerners.

The institution of slavery was to divide the various states in the 1780s, and over the next 70 years, those divisions became more profound. There were increasing differences between various sections of the nation over the question, which reflected conflicts of both political and economic interest. However, the major division was an ideological one, and this division was one of the unique features of the American situation. The years after 1820 in particular saw the emergence of two intellectual and political ideologies. The northern states and New England saw the appearance of an increasingly radical Abolitionist movement, led by figures such as William Lloyd Garrison, William Ellery Channing, Lydia Maria Child, and

Frederick Douglass. They argued against the institution of slavery on the grounds of universalist human rights—in other words, on the basis of the common humanity of all human beings and the basic rights that they all shared. Although more radical and thoroughgoing, these arguments were essentially the same as those made by antislavery activists elsewhere since the 1770s.

However, uniquely, the United States witnessed the appearance and articulation of a systematic proslavery ideology. After the 1820s, the slaveholding interest in the southern states, particularly in South Carolina, increasingly defended the "peculiar institution." Although in this argument they were no different than were such groups as plantation owners in the British and French empires, they went considerably further than defending slavery on pragmatic and self-interested grounds. Americans such as George Fitzhugh and John C. Calhoun supported the institution of slavery as a positive good, at least for people of African descent. This proslavery ideology came to connect the defense of slavery to a more general critique of capitalist modernity as it was taking shape at the time. Their views were not anticapitalist in all respects because they favored free trade and private property. However, they advocated a different kind of capitalism, one in which racial slavery was a prominent institution. Those who embraced this position also connected the defense of slavery to arguments about the nature of the original constitutional compact and, thus, of the relationship between the states and the federal government and the nature of the United States as a political entity.

There are two reasons that this ideological division did not occur elsewhere. These reasons centered on the actual physical location of both slaves and slave owners and the nature of the racial ideology of most white Americans, compared with that held by, for example, Brazilians. In the case of European colonial empires, although plantation owners were a powerful interest, they were located a considerable distance from the metropolitan country and so did not form part of the national elite of a nation such as Britain or France in the way that southern planters did in the United States. In addition, the slaves were geographically far removed and so their emancipation had only limited implications for the population of the colonial power. This isolation was not the case in such places as the United States or Brazil, where large numbers of slaves of African descent lived among slaveholders and free whites. Here emancipation had radical implications for relations between people of African and European descent.

It was here that the nature of the racial ideology of North Americans as opposed to Latin Americans came into play. In Brazil and the former Spanish Empire, relations between the races were organized by a hierarchy that ranked Europeans above Asians, who were above Africans, who in turn were superior to Amerindians. The result was a complex hierarchy of defined subgroups produced by sexual relations among the four primary groups. This social stratification was not significantly threatened by emancipation. In North America, however, the idea of *whiteness* came to be defined in a strict and exclusive way according to the "one drop" rule so that anyone not of pure European descent who had some known African ancestors counted as African or black. This rule also was linked to the idea, shared by most Americans—including many who opposed slavery—that a mixed or multiracial society was impossible unless one racial group was in a position of clear superiority. This perspective made the prospect of emancipation, in the minds of man, fraught with serious difficulties, unless it could somehow be combined with the physical removal of the freed slaves, as many advocated. Thus, the question of slavery in the United States was much more polarizing and intractable than elsewhere, and it came to be intimately connected to other political conflicts, above all the continuing and increasing disagreement over the nature of the United States as an entity. Even so, it is plausible to argue that the actual outcome of a bloody Civil War could have been avoided through an expedient such as the compensated manumission of the slave population, which might have been instituted had people realized just how bloody the war would be. It also has been argued that allowing the Gulf States to secede in 1860 would have precipitated the collapse of slavery due to impossibly high enforcement costs for the slaveowners given that the fugitive slave provision would no longer have been effective. All of this, however, is pure speculation, as opposed to the reality of the Civil War and its aftermath.

Slavery and its abolition are the subject of a number of historiographical debates. Libertarians tend to adopt a clear position on some of these, but are divided over others. One relates to the arguments put forward originally by Eric Williams in *Capitalism and Slavery*. In this work, he makes two arguments that libertarians have generally rejected. He argues first that the abolition of slavery was not produced by humanitarian sentiment, but rather by the self-interest of property owners in the emergent capitalist economy, given the greater economic efficiency of free, compared with slave, labor. This notion has been rebutted by authors such as Seymour Drescher and Roger Anstey, who argue that, in fact, slavery and the slave trade were still highly profitable at the time of their abolition and that therefore the antislavery movement needs to be given greater credit for abolition. Williams's second argument centers on the fact that it was the profits of the slave trade and the slave plantations that provided the funding for the early stages of industrialization. This claim also has been criticized, most notably by Patrick O'Brian, who has argued that, although the profits of slavery were considerable, the bulk of the capital formed in 18th-century Europe derived from the profits of other trades and domestic agriculture.

The major division among libertarians over the historiography of slavery relates to the vexed question of the American Civil War. A minority tradition among contemporary libertarians regards the war as the disastrous turning point in American history and in the growth of the federal government and trend toward a position that is broadly pro-Confederate as a result. Others see the war as a price that had to be paid to remove the terrible curse of slavery. The more nuanced position, articulated by authors such as Jeffrey Rogers Hummel, sees the war as unnecessary, but neither favors the South nor supports its case. All libertarians, however, agree in seeing the general campaign against slavery after 1770 as one of the great movements for human liberty and its success as perhaps the greatest victory for the cause of freedom.

Slavery and its abolition are important issues for libertarians for a number of reasons. Slavery is the diametric opposite of freedom, and so slavery, by contrast, negatively defines what freedom actually is. Given that, the abolition of slavery in most of the world is one of the great victories for the cause of liberty. Moreover, the way in which it was achieved remains a model for all subsequent campaigns to extend or defend freedom. The most important aspect is the way that the campaigners focused on the transformation of public attitudes and beliefs, and it is this transformation that has made their victory permanent. So complete was their ideological victory that no one, no matter how opposed to liberty, would now dare to articulate an argument in defense of slavery. Their victory also established the absence of slavery as a central feature of modernity and is one of the things that most clearly distinguishes modernity from previous historical periods. The analysis and arguments used and developed in the fight against slavery also have been applied to other issues by libertarians. Thus, they are employed to analyze the historic status of women, hence the historically close connection between antislavery and individualist feminism. Radical libertarians have extended the general critique of unfree labor to include wage labor as a form of relation that, although freer than slavery or serfdom, is still not completely free.

However, the most important aspect of slavery and antislavery for libertarians is the following: Given the nature of slavery in the post-Renaissance world and its nature as a racially defined institution, the campaign against it and its successful definition as a terrible wrong involved the extension of the notions of human rights and liberty to all human beings by virtue of their essential common nature as humans. It is this universalism, the idea of freedom as something that pertains to all human beings, rather than to one sex or to a particular group or race, that is a central and defining feature of modern libertarianism, and the fight against slavery was crucial for its appearance.

SD

See also Abolitionism; Civil War, U.S.; Imperialism; Liberty in the Ancient World; War

Further Readings

Anstey, Roger. *The Atlantic Slave Trade and British Abolition, 1760–1810*. London: Macmillan, 1975.

Brown, Christopher Leslie. *Moral Capital: Foundations of British Abolitionism*. Chapel Hill: University of North Carolina Press, 2006.

Bush, Michael L. *Servitude in Modern Times*. London: Polity Press, 2000.

Davis, Robert C. *Christian Slaves, Muslim Masters: White Slavery in the Mediterranean, the Barbary Coast, and Italy, 1500–1800*. London: Palgrave Macmillan, 2004.

Drescher, Seymour. *From Slavery to Freedom: Comparative Studies in the Rise and Fall of Atlantic Slavery*. New York: New York University Press, 1999.

Drescher, Seymour, and Stanley Engerman, eds. *A Historical Guide to World Slavery*. Oxford: Oxford University Press, 1998.

Engerman, Stanley, Seymour Drescher, and Robert Paquette, eds. *Slavery*. Oxford: Oxford University Press, 2006.

Geneovese, Eugene. *The Political Economy of Slavery: Studies in the Economy and Society of the Slave South*. Middletown, CT: Wesleyan University Press, 1988.

Gould, Philip. *Barbaric Traffic: Commerce and Antislavery in the Eighteenth-Century Atlantic World*. Cambridge, MA: Harvard University Press, 2003.

Hochschild, Adam. *Bury the Chains: The British Struggle to Abolish Slavery*. Basingstoke, UK: Pan Macmillan, 2005.

Segal, Ronald. *Islam's Black Slaves: The Other Black Diaspora*. New York: Farrar, Straus & Giroux, 2002.

Thomas, Hugh. *The Slave Trade: The Story of the Atlantic Slave Trade: 1440–1870*. London: Phoenix Press, 2006.

Wise, Steven M. *Though the Heavens May Fall: The Landmark Trial That Led to the End of Human Slavery*. London: Pimlico, 2006.

SLAVERY IN AMERICA

Servitude has taken many forms throughout history, but the essential quality of American slavery is the total ownership of one human being by another. The slave has virtually no enforceable property rights because they all reside with the slaveowner. Title to the slave's body is so complete that the master can utilize it, sell it, or otherwise dispose of it in any way he chooses, just as he would with any other chattel, whether inanimate objects or animals. Moreover, the human chattel's status arises involuntarily and can cease only at the will of the master. A free person, in contrast, owns himself.

Of course, governments have imposed all sorts of restrictions on nominally free laborers. Even those of us who enjoy the liberty attained in modern societies usually suffer some coercive attenuation of our self-ownership, as through income taxes and other legal restrictions. A free person also may voluntarily transfer rights through contract. However, the slaveholder's power over human chattel was sometimes limited slightly within the antebellum South by unenforceable state laws preventing murder and mutilation and setting minimum standards for subsistence.

Therefore, we can visualize a spectrum running all the way from unqualified self-ownership at one end to absolute slavery at the other. This spectrum helps us to distinguish strict *chattel* slavery from other forms of unfree labor. Under serfdom, the lord's property claim was not as complete. The serfs generally had some rights in land, some control over their time and labor, and some independent obligations to the prince or central state. Indentured servitude, apprenticeship, and contract labor, unlike slavery, were forms of bondage that were most often voluntarily assumed and always for a defined period; all of these institutions could likewise be found in the American colonies and the early republic. Military conscription and convict labor generally have fixed terms as well, and moreover the title holders to these forms of compulsory service are not usually private individuals or organizations, who can trade their claims with others, but instead government bureaucracies, with numerous legal regulations on the labor's use and no obvious residual claim to its output. For this reason, we can likewise distinguish the forced labor of Nazi Germany and the Soviet Union from American chattel slavery, although the slave soldiers of the Ottoman Empire do occupy a more similar position because in that case the government was the Sultan, who presumably could exercise all the personal prerogatives of a private owner of human property.

Even in this restricted sense, chattel slavery has been a source of forced labor since the dawn of civilization. People have owned slaves on every continent and for every conceivable task. Although one of the most universal of all human institutions, slavery became a predominant mode of production in only five slave societies: classical Greece (excluding Sparta), classical Rome, the Caribbean, Brazil, and the American South. In the American case, black Africans were compelled to serve as farm laborers, servants, or concubines. Even when not directly satisfying their masters' desires, many slaves in the medieval and ancient worlds engaged in household production only. New World slavery, in contrast, produced tobacco, sugar, rice, cotton, and other commodities for world markets.

Historically, slaves have been produced in three primary ways: debt default, capture, and breeding. Only the latter two, however, are significant to American slavery. Of all three sources for slaves, raising them may have been responsible for the greatest number overall, but has rarely proved sufficient to perpetuate the institution. Such slaves were almost always the offspring of slave parents, although there have been instances of nonslave parents so destitute that they sold their own children, as well as instances of raising orphans and foundlings for slavery. Breeding did not figure prominently in ancient or medieval slavery, and among New World economies, only in North

America was the slave population reproducing itself by the mid-18th century. Virtually everywhere else, the persistence of human bondage depended on continued importation of captured slaves.

Servile rebellions faced severe free rider problems, and the only successful slave insurrection was in Haiti, ending in 1804. A more frequent and efficacious form of slave resistance was running away. As a result, slavery has never thrived unless some combination of geographical, political, or cultural barriers curtailed flight—barriers like the U.S. Constitution's fugitive slave clause. The freeing of slaves by their owners, in contrast, has been common. These manumissions would often take the form of skilled slaves buying their own liberty in mutually beneficial transactions. Only in the British Caribbean and the southern United States did governments deprive masters of the right to free individual slaves, a policy that rendered American slavery significantly worse for the slaves.

Slavery always required an array of legal, political, and military safeguards, yet it endured well into the 19th century. Although no one enjoyed being a slave, only a few thinkers—primarily early classical liberals—had challenged the institution's legitimacy or necessity before Quakers organized the world's first antislavery society in Philadelphia in 1775. Western Europe had already experienced a receding of this most extreme form of bondage, and small-scale emancipations began in the northern United States. Then starting with British colonies in 1833 and finishing with Brazil in 1888, more than 6 million slaves achieved some kind of freedom in the Western Hemisphere. The international abolitionist movement—despite being a small minority in many countries—eliminated in a little over a century a labor system that had been ubiquitous for millennia. Today we live in a world where slavery may still persist clandestinely, but no ruler, no matter how vile or ruthless, would dare get up and publicly endorse owning another human being. Thus, the abolition of chattel slavery stands as the most impressive and enduring of all classical liberalism's triumphs.

DT

See also Abolitionism; Douglass, Frederick; Garrison, William Lloyd; Racism; Slavery, World; Spooner, Lysander

Further Readings

Davis, David Brion. *Slavery and Human Progress*. New York: Oxford University Press, 1984.
Hummel, Jeffrey Rogers. *Emancipating Slaves, Enslaving Free Men: A History of the American Civil War*. Chicago: Open Court, 1996.
Patterson, Orlando. *Slavery and Social Death: A Comparative Study*. Cambridge, MA: Harvard University Press, 1982.
Sowell, Thomas. "The Economics of Slavery." Thomas Sowell, ed. *Markets and Minorities*. New York: Basic Books, 1981.

SMITH, ADAM (1723–1790)

Both a philosopher and political economist, Adam Smith was one of the principal thinkers of 18th-century Scotland, whose name is intimately associated with the early history of economic science. He was born in Kirkcaldy, Fife, in the late spring of 1723—the exact date is unknown—and was baptized on June 5, 1723. The son of the comptroller of the customs at Kirkcaldy, who died 5 months before his birth, Adam was educated in the grammar school there. At the age of 15, he was sent to the University of Glasgow, where he studied moral philosophy under Francis Hutcheson, one of Scotland's greatest thinkers, and in 1740, he entered Balliol College, Oxford, as an exhibitor (i.e., as a student possessed of a scholarship). Smith's interest in the philosophical system put forward by his fellow Scotsman David Hume, whose *Treatise of Human Nature* was published in 1739–1740, clashed with the Aristotelian epistemological and metaphysical presuppositions that dominated Oxford thinking, and Smith soon determined to leave England.

In 1746, he relinquished his scholarship and embarked on a series of public lectures at Edinburgh under the patronage of Henry Home, Lord Kames, Scottish attorney and philosopher. Kames, who was already regarded as an important scholar in the history of law and theoretical history, was impressed with Smith and undertook to sponsor Smith's lectures on rhetoric and belles-lettres. The lectures were well received and led to Smith being offered the chair of logic at the University Glasgow in 1751. In the following year, Smith was appointed to the more remunerative professorship of moral philosophy, a post earlier held by Hutcheson, in which he remained for the next 13 years. During his tenure at Glasgow, Smith published his first work, *A Theory of Moral Sentiments*, which appeared in 1759.

In *A Theory of Moral Sentiments*, Smith addresses the following question: From whence springs our ability to condemn certain intentions and actions as immoral and approve others as morally worthy? This problem is especially vexing inasmuch as we are able to judge our own behavior as either moral or immoral despite the fact that we are strongly motivated to act in our own self-interest. Smith maintained that our ability to form moral judgments is a function of our being possessed of a basic moral faculty that motivates us to act as an impartial spectator of our own and others' actions. This moral sense, which Smith labeled *sympathy* and which is not reducible to our rational faculties, allows us to see ourselves as others see us and, thus, permits us to live harmoniously with others despite our being self-regarding and passionate in our own interests. It serves not only to promote our own well-being, but to bring our actions into line with a society of other moral individuals, thus contributing to the happiness of mankind. Adumbrating his discussion of the economic benefits that follow from individuals acting in their own self-interest in *Wealth of Nations*, Smith notes in the *Theory of Moral Sentiments* that even those members of society who have profited most from their selfishness act as if "they are led by an invisible hand ..., without intending it, without knowing it, [to] advance the interests of society."

Smith left academic life in 1764, at the age of 41, to assume the position of tutor to the young Duke of Buccleugh. He accompanied the Duke on a Grand Tour of the Continent, which provided him with the opportunity of meeting some of the greatest minds in Europe. During a 2-month stay in Geneva, Smith conversed at length with Voltaire. Thanks in large part to his friendship with David Hume, who was at that time secretary to the British Embassy in Paris, Smith was able to gain access to the various salons, where he was able to meet the leading minds of the French Enlightenment, among them Jean-Jacques Rousseau, the Physiocrat economist François Quesnay, and Anne-Robert-Jacques Turgot. In addition, while traveling through Europe, Smith had the leisure to begin work on what would eventually become his most important book, the *Wealth of Nations*. On their return to London in October 1766, Smith worked with Lord Charles Townsend, the stepfather and guardian of the Duke of Buccleugh and future chancellor of the exchequer. It was during this period that Smith expanded his circle of acquaintances to include Edward Gibbon, Edmund Burke, and Samuel Johnson and was elected to the Royal Society.

As a result of his service to the Duke, Smith was granted a generous life pension of £300 per year, on which, in 1767, he retired to his birthplace of Kirkcaldy, just across the Firth of Forth from Edinburgh. There Smith spent the following 6 years working on *Wealth of Nations*. In 1773, he moved to London, where he completed his monograph on the production and distribution of wealth for which he is now famous. On March 9, 1776, *An Inquiry into the Nature and Causes of the Wealth of Nations* was published in two volumes by William Strahan and Thomas Cadell. Although originally the work was regarded as an important one only among a small group of readers, several decades after its publication, it established itself as a classic and came to be regarded as one of the most important books to appear during an age that had given birth to some of the greatest achievements of the human intellect.

In *Wealth of Nations*, Smith succeeds in laying bare the intellectual framework of economic science while marrying his theoretical discussions to a substantial amount of empirical data. Smith's analysis of the benefits that follow from the division of labor, the fallacies of mercantilism, and the destructive effects of almost all restrictions on market forces are comprehensive and accompanied by a mass of illustrations that trace the operation of the laws of economics. Indeed, so extensive is his commentary and so intense his defense of free trade and unrestricted markets—despite his few reservations—that it is no surprise that the work

was eventually hailed as a classic of promarket literature. However, despite the reputation the book was to achieve, it was not the first treatise in economics. The *Principles of Political Oeconomy* by Sir James Steuart, published in 1767, although it espoused a particularly toxic form of mercantilism, predates *Wealth of Nations*, as does Richard Cantillion's *Essai sur la nature du commerce en général*, published in 1755, but written some 25 years earlier. The fact is that most of Smith's insights into the mechanisms by which societies produce and distribute wealth had been reached by other thinkers prior to the publication of the *Wealth of Nations*, among them Cantillion, Quesnay, Turgot, David Hume, and, above all, his own teacher, Francis Hutcheson. Nevertheless, Smith has been accorded the honor of being the founder of economic science largely, it has been suggested, because he was able to build on and coordinate the various strains of economic analysis that had appeared before him and map this vast field of enquiry within the context of a sea of illustrative material.

Beyond affirming the benefits of free, unrestricted markets, *Wealth of Nations* probably offers the clearest statement that seemingly undirected market forces are in fact given coherence and direction by the existence of a spontaneously generated order that is the result of human action but not the product of human design. The notion that complex social arrangements take their shape as the unanticipated consequences of a myriad of uncoordinated human actions pervades Smith's social theory and forms the philosophical underpinning of his economic theory. Wealth is produced and distributed, Smith argued, by virtue of the fact that the market constitutes a self-regulating mechanism producing complex patterns without the need of an orderer. It is as if, he maintains, economic interactions were directed by an invisible hand, by which men, seeking their own private gain, benefit society and thus promote an end that was no part of their intention. Indeed, the notion of an unfettered market is predicated on the idea that a socially beneficial ordered arrangement is likely to emerge out of the free actions of countless individuals, each aiming at the satisfaction of his own private ends. Equally important, intervening in the self-coordinating process that is the market thwarts it in his function of maximizing production and wealth. Smith writes,

> By pursuing his own interest, he frequently promotes that of the society more effectually than when he really intends to promote it. I have never known much good done by those who affected to trade for the public good. It is an affectation, indeed, not very common among merchants and very few words need be employed in dissuading them from it.

Smith's analysis of the laws governing economic interaction develops within the context of a broader discussion dealing with the evolution of social institutions that encourage the production of wealth, the foremost of which is private property. Societies, he wrote, naturally evolve through several stages, each marked by the primary method whereby wealth is produced, from an age of hunters to one of shepherds, from there to an age of agriculture, and finally to one of commerce. These changes come about as the unplanned result of innumerable individuals actions each having far more limited ends, the total effect of which is to transform the primary mode of production by which men live. With each change in the mode of production there follow changes in our moral rules and the laws that relate to property that structure our notions of private possessions, indeed the very framework of our political institutions. Thus, history is a progression from the primitive to the civilized and from the most rudimentary notions of property to those that prevail in modern society, which alone allow for the production of sufficient amounts of wealth to permit general prosperity.

Scholars have long argued over the seeming inconsistency between Smith's argument in *A Theory of Moral Sentiments* and in *Wealth of Nations*, pointing to the fact that the first work is devoted to a discussion of the importance of a moral sensibility without which pacific human interaction would be impossible, whereas the second underscores that the most sensible economic policy, the one most likely to produce social wealth, is one that is predicated on the assumption that everyone acts in their own self-interest. A careful reading of the two works, however, indicates that there exists no real contradiction between them. *Wealth of Nations* is largely a treatise on economic policy and, as such, tends to discuss motivation in terms of self-interest. This focus on self-interest does not mean, as some seem to have concluded, that Smith abandoned benevolence as a fundamental motive force in human action in favor of an egoistic theory. Indeed, there is nothing contradictory in claiming that sympathy lies at the root of moral judgment and that men are motivated to act by, among other things, self-love. Nor should self-love, which, properly understood, refers to a regard for one's personal happiness, be confused with selfishness, which precludes a concern for the welfare of others. In summary, the difference between Smith's discussions in the two works is solely one of emphasis.

Following the publication of *Wealth of Nations*, Smith was honored with appointments both as commissioner of customs and commissioner of salt duties for Scotland, sinecures that brought him an additional £600 per year. This income, added to his pension from the Duke of Buccleugh, made Smith a wealthy man. Smith apparently enjoyed his newfound affluence inasmuch as he wrote nothing following the release of *Wealth of Nations*. He spent his final years in Edinburgh in quiet retirement, secure in the reputation as one of the leading figures of the Scottish Enlightenment. His health began to decline following the death of his mother in 1784, and he died in July 1790, the victim of a painful ailment. He is buried in the Canongate Churchyard in Edinburgh.

RH

See also Cantillon, Richard; Classical Economics; Enlightenment; Self-Interest; Spontaneous Order; Virtue

Further Readings

Campbell, R. H., and A. S. Skinner. *Adam Smith*. New York: St. Martin's Press, 1982.
Fay, C. R. *Adam Smith and the Scotland of His Day*. Cambridge: Cambridge University Press, 1956.
Haakonssen, Knud. *Science of a Legislator: The Natural Jurisprudence of David Hume and Adam Smith*. Cambridge: Cambridge University Press, 1981.
Rae, John. *Life of Adam Smith*. London: Macmillan, 1895.
Scott, William Robert. *Adam Smith as Student and Professor*. New York: A. M. Kelley, 1965.
Stewart, Dugald. *Biographical Memoir of Adam Smith*. Vol. X of the *Collected Works*. Edinburgh: T. Constable and Co., 1958.

Social Contract

See Contractarianism/Social Contract

Social Darwinism

Standard accounts of Social Darwinism often link it to the "rugged individualism" of 19th-century libertarian thought. Social Darwinism has been characterized as an unsavory doctrine that supposedly advocated "survival of the fittest" in matters of social policy, and two sociologists, the Englishman Herbert Spencer and the American William Graham Sumner, are commonly portrayed as its intellectual fathers. Our discussion concentrates on their views.

Neither Spencer nor Sumner held the positions commonly attributed to them. For one thing, Spencer's approach to evolution (which he developed independently of Darwin) was essentially Lamarckian. Unlike Darwin, Spencer believed that acquired characteristics are genetically transmitted from one generation to the next, and he placed relatively little emphasis on the process of natural selection. This Lamarckian approach, whatever its shortcomings as a biological theory, is a better model of social development than its Darwinian counterpart. Humans do "inherit" and build on the adaptations and acquired characteristics of their progenitors—as we see in language, the transmission of knowledge, technology, capital investment, social institutions, and so forth.

Although both Spencer and Sumner used the phrase "survival of the fittest" (it was Spencer, not Darwin, who coined the term), both had cause to regret it, in light of how vulnerable this expression was to misrepresentation. "I have had much experience in controversy," Spencer wrote in later life, "and my impression is that in three cases out of four the alleged opinions of mine condemned by opponents, are not opinions of mine at all, but are opinions wrongly ascribed by them to me." Sumner became so frustrated by the same problem that he stopped using the phrase "survival of the fittest" altogether, so it never appears in his later writings and lectures.

Because of the "survival of the fittest" doctrine, Spencer and Sumner have been labeled (and condemned) as Social Darwinists. We are told that they and their followers were infused with a stern and implacable contempt for the poor, disabled, and disadvantaged—those "unfit" persons who, by an inexorable law of nature, should give way in the struggle for existence to those who are more fit.

This allegation may seem strange to those who have firsthand knowledge of the voluminous writings of Spencer and Sumner. Like Adam Smith and many other classical liberals before them, both men maintained that the poor are among the greatest victims of state interference, and both men argued that free, dynamic markets offer the best prospects for economic betterment.

If *Social Darwinism* is an inappropriate label for the ideas of Spencer and Sumner, who never used it themselves, what about the expression *survival of the fittest*, which they did use? What did they mean by this expression? Spencer repeatedly emphasized that, in using the terms *fit* and *fittest*, he was not expressing a value judgment, nor was he referring to a particular characteristic, such as strength or intelligence, nor was he expressing any kind of approval or disapproval. In his article "Mr. Martineau on Evolution," Spencer noted that this doctrine "is expressible in purely physical terms, which neither imply competition nor imply better and worse." Moreover, "survival of the fittest is not always the survival of the best."

> The law [of survival of the fittest] is not the survival of the "better" or the "stronger." . . . It is the survival of those which are constitutionally fittest to thrive under the conditions in which they are placed; and very often that which, humanly speaking is inferiority, causes the survival.

If an organism is to survive and prosper, it must adapt to its external environment. This ability to adapt is what Spencer means by *fitness*. If an organism is unfit in this sense—if, in other words, it fails to adapt to its environment—then it will live in a diseased or unhealthy condition and perhaps even die. In short, to be *fit* is to be able to adapt to the conditions necessary to its survival, whatever those requirements may be.

In a social context, the fittest are those persons who are able to adapt to the survival requirements of their society. Suppose a government were to decree that all those with red hair shall be executed. It follows that the persons best fitted for survival in this society would be those without red hair or those who naturally possess red hair who adapt by changing their hair color or shaving their heads. We can state this survival of the fittest principle without condoning the penalty against people with red hair and without regarding those without red hair as superior people. It is a simple, inescapable fact that if a government determines to kill all people with red hair, then (other things being equal) you have a better chance to survive you are more fit—if you do not have red hair. This interpretation, which treats survival of the fittest as a value-free description of what in fact *does* occur, rather than as a prescription or approval of what should occur, also was maintained by Sumner. According to Sumner, the common misapprehension that "survival of the fittest" means "survival of the best" lies at the root of "all disputes about evolution and ethics."

When Spencer and Sumner applied their survival of the fittest principle to a free, industrial society, they reached conclusions that differ radically from the position supposedly taken by Social Darwinists. True, the sacrifice of one individual for the benefit of another is the general rule for lower life forms. It is equally true of the lower forms of human society—militaristic, authoritarian societies that Spencer and Sumner, following the legal historian H. S. Maine, called *regimes of status*. But as the regime of status gradually gives way to regimes of contract, as voluntary cooperation replaces coercion as the dominant mode of social interaction, there occurs a fundamental change in the conditions of social survival and in the corresponding standard of fitness.

People in a free society are able to pursue their own interests as they wish provided they respect the equal rights of others. Cooperation in a regime of contract replaces the exploitation that prevails in a regime of status, and the fittest survive not by coercing or exploiting others, but by assisting them through the mutual exchanges that mark a market economy. Survival here is achieved by providing others in society with desired goods and services. Hence, here as elsewhere, survival of the fittest is an iron law of social existence, but the standard of fitness is far removed from that suggested by the specter of Social Darwinism. Voluntary cooperation, not coercive exploitation, is the standard of fitness in a free society.

Spencer, Sumner, and other classical liberals insisted that market competition differs radically from biological competition. Unlike the latter, in which one organism preys on another to survive, market competition is able to produce additional wealth through the division of labor, capital accumulation, and so on, thereby making it possible for many people to survive and prosper who otherwise could not.

Moreover, the complex division of labor that evolves in a market economy generates specialization, and this specialization generates social interdependence, a condition in which every person must rely on the cooperation and assistance of others for essential goods and services. The solitary individual cannot produce everything he needs or wants in a market economy, so he must persuade many others to assist him. This condition of survival cultivates the character traits or virtues necessary for peaceful interaction—those civilizing mores, as Sumner called them, that make social interaction not only productive, but pleasant as well.

To associate market competition with the biological competition of Darwinian evolution is to misunderstand how classical liberals viewed the free market. Biological competition, where one individual survives at the expense of another, is a zero-sum game, whereas market competition is a positive-sum game, a process in which all participants gain from their voluntary transactions with others. It is precisely in a free society that Social Darwinism does not apply. In a complex society marked by an advanced division of labor, where we must give others what they want in order to get what we want, the fit are those who can enlist the voluntary cooperation of others. Where success depends on persuasion rather than coercion, the standard of social fitness is measured by one's ability to influence and persuade others voluntarily by offering them something of value.

GHS

See also Evolutionary Psychology; Genetics; Liberalism, Classical; Spencer, Herbert; Spontaneous Order

Further Readings

Bannister, Robert C. *Social Darwinism: Science and Myth in Anglo-American Social Thought*. Philadelphia: Temple University Press, 1989.
Long, Roderick "Herbert Spencer: Libertarian Prophet." *The Freeman* 7–8 (July/August 2004): 25–28.
Smith, George H. *Atheism, Ayn Rand, and Other Heresies*. Amherst, NY: Prometheus Books, 1991.
Spencer, Herbert. *The Principles of Ethics*. Tibor Machan, ed. Indianapolis, IN: Liberty Fund, 1978.
———. *Social Statics: The Conditions Essential to Human Happiness Specified, and the First of Them Developed*. New York: Robert Schalkenbach Foundation, 1970.

SOCIALISM

Socialism is traditionally considered a political-economic system that aspires to replace the institutions of a market capitalist economy with social ownership of the means of production, comprehensive economic planning, and an egalitarian distribution of wealth. Nineteenth-century debates over socialism focused on the issue of whether a socialist system should be instituted through reforms or revolution. A second controversy centered on whether the political mechanism that effected these changes should be decentralized or centralized. The Marxist position favored revolution and centralization and became dominant in certain parts of Europe and Asia by the 20th century, whereas most of the world adopted a nonrevolutionary brand of socialism. The Austrian School criticism of socialism from the 1920s to the 1940s, combined with the experiences of socialist regimes during the course of the 20th century, encouraged a whole series of offshoots from the traditional vision as conceived by socialism's early proponents. These offshoots took the form of market socialism, participatory socialism, libertarian socialism, anarcho-communism, and vague modifications on welfare statism.

To the extent that socialism aspires toward social ownership and comprehensive planning, it faces a fatal epistemological flaw, articulated most clearly by Mises in 1920. By destroying private ownership of the means of production, and therefore eliminating the markets for those means of production, the socialist economy abolishes the prices of capital goods, which are the measures of their relative scarcity. But by doing so, the knowledge about relative values and alternative economic uses of scarce capital goods also is unwittingly destroyed. Without this information, as Mises keenly observed, the central planning board would have no basis on which to engage in rational economic calculation. Even if the planners strove to serve the public interest, they would be left in the dark over how to best serve those interests. Although they might be awash in technical data and information regarding current availability of resources, planners would have no criteria to calculate the benefits and opportunity costs of alternative plans of action. They would find it impossible, in practice, to devise a coordinated set of production, consumption, and distribution plans that would match the levels of wealth and complexity generated by market economies.

Mises's conclusions led to the great socialist calculation debate of the 1930s and 1940s, between Austrian School economists and proponents of market socialism, discussed in great detail by Steele and Lavoie. Market socialism, exemplified by the 1936 work of Oskar Lange, conceded to the Austrians that markets are necessary—advanced economies cannot coordinate millions of independent plans without the information signals generated by market prices—which encouraged Lange and his followers to devise abstract economic models that combined social ownership of the means of production with what amounted to capitalist-like markets for consumer goods. Informed alone by these consumer goods prices, Lange believed, central economic planners would possess the kind of knowledge necessary to calculate the values of all the scarce resources and capital goods needed to produce consumer goods and services. He, and market socialists in general, failed to understand, however, that the prices of consumer goods are like the tip of a huge iceberg. Possessing these data provides almost no relevant information regarding what is unseen below the surface. The problem of economic calculation focuses on coordinating the rest of the capital structure that lies below the surface, the structure that supports the production of consumer goods and services. Trapped in an overly formal and empirically empty model of markets and equilibrium prices, market socialists failed to understand the brunt of the Austrian case against socialism; effective coordination requires not merely markets for consumer goods, but markets for all the means used to produce consumer goods. However, markets for the means of production can only come about with private property rights to capital goods, something that socialism had consistently fought to destroy since it treads too close to capitalism.

Not only had market socialists failed to appreciate the Austrian argument, but the bulk of the economics profession, while not praising market socialism, felt that Lange provided at least a theoretically satisfying answer to Mises's critique, and that the socialist calculation debate had finally been settled in socialism's favor. Only after the collapse of existing socialist regimes in the late 1980s and early 1990s has the economics profession begun to appreciate the conclusions arrived at by Austrian economists more than half a century earlier. Private ownership and markets for the means of production are a necessary element of advanced society.

Despite the stunning collapse of the socialist regimes in the East, new and quite divergent visions of socialism—alternatives to both central planning of the Soviet variety and market socialism of the Langean variety—have gained rapid currency among the radical left. Michael Albert and Robin Hahnel, for example, have championed a decentralized, council-based model of socialism. Although their notion of participatory socialism purports to have solved all the problems and contradictions of centrally planned and market-based socialism, Albert and Hahnel ignore the calculation problem and fail to answer the charge raised by Mises in 1920.

Of similar influence is the work of Murray Bookchin, who is the anarcho-communists' answer to Mises's anarcho-capitalist student, Murray Rothbard. Arguably the most important left-wing anarchist since Kropotkin, Bookchin's anarcho-communist visions of libertarian municipalism and social ecology have enjoyed remarkable growth among a younger generation of anarchists, radical environmentalists, and socialists, evidenced, among others, by the work of David Goodway's Anarchist Research Group. Not only is the work of Bookchin and his disciples totally ignorant of the socialist calculation debate, but Bookchin, like Marx, dogmatically denies that economics has any valid claims regarding the organization of society.

Most people who still embrace socialism, however, have turned to the modern welfare state almost by default. Some people, such as Joseph Stiglitz and Hilary Wainwright, have given serious consideration to the criticisms of socialism raised by Mises, Hayek, and the younger generation of Austrian School economists. They have capitulated to the necessity of private property and markets in the means of production, but call for a greater role of the welfare-regulatory state in correcting what they consider inherent failures in the incentive structures and the knowledge-disseminating properties of a free-market system.

The collapse of socialism in eastern Europe has surely reinvigorated much theoretical speculation over alternative models to traditional socialism. More concretely, it also has raised the problem of economic transition toward a market economy. Although libertarians and classical liberals have a general understanding of the institutions of a free society, they have engaged in a lengthy debate over the specific kinds of reforms needed and the speed at which these reforms should be introduced in the postcommunist countries.

Some people, such as Boettke, have argued for a shock therapy approach that calls for a rapid dismantling of the state bureaucracy and regulations and a swift conversion of state property into private property. This approach should be accompanied by a credible move to a legal constitutional framework that encourages the development and enforcement of private property rights and free trade among the means of production. The metaphor of a dope addict has been used to illustrate the transition problems under socialism: Cold turkey is the most effective route to a heroin addict's recovery, as painful as it is, rather than a gradual withdrawal over time. So, too, it is maintained, the dependents of the crumbling socialist societies should be brought into a market capitalist system as rapidly as possible. Gradual reform provides too many incentives to bring the state back in.

Gradualists such as Svetozar Pejovich respond that, although we in the West might know what the "right" institutions that comprise a free society are, we do not know exactly what the citizens of the eastern European nations want. They appear fiercely loyal to destructive nationalist sentiments and often regard institutions introduced by state fiat as illegitimate. Therefore, it may take a great deal of time before radical institutional change works to bridge the gap between a new political-economic order and its legitimacy.

Socialism, in its traditional dimensions, is an abject failure. The collapse of socialism does not necessarily imply that free-market capitalism will win by default. Markets, profit and loss, entrepreneurship, and competition are indeed necessary features of advanced societies. But these institutions require trust and legitimacy to function. Furthermore, market institutions are quite capable of supporting a parasitic welfare-regulatory state. However, the utter collapse of socialism as an economic system accounts for the fact that the bulk of socialist thought in our post-communist era has finally acknowledged the necessity of basic market institutions.

DLP

See also Communism; Interventionism; Marxism; Socialist Calculation Debate; Welfare State

Further Readings

Albert, Michael, and Robin Hahnel. *The Political Economy of Participatory Economics.* Princeton, NJ: Princeton University Press, 1991.

Boettke, Peter J. *Calculation and Coordination: Essays on Socialism and Transitional Political Economy.* New York: Routledge, 2001.

Bookchin, Murray. *Post-Scarcity Anarchism.* 2nd ed. Montreal: Black Rose Books, 1986.

Goodway, David, ed. *For Anarchism: History, Theory, and Practice.* New York: Routledge, 1989.

Lange, Oskar. "On the Economic Theory of Socialism." *On the Economic Theory of Socialism.* Benjamin Lippincott, ed. New York: McGraw-Hill, 1964.

Lavoie, Don. *Rivalry and Central Planning: The Socialist Calculation Debate Reconsidered.* New York: Cambridge University Press, 1985.

Pejovich, Svetozar. "Institutions, Nationalism, and the Transition Process in Eastern Europe." *The Economic Foundations of Property Rights: Selected Readings.* Pejovich, ed. Cheltenham, UK: Edward Elgar, 1997.

Prychitko, David L. "Marxism and Decentralized Socialism." *Critical Review* 2 no. 4 (Fall 1988): 127–148.

Steele, David Ramsay. *From Marx to Mises: Post-Capitalist Society and the Challenge of Socialist Calculation.* LaSalle, IL: Open Court, 1992.

Stiglitz, Joseph. *Whither Socialism?* Cambridge, MA: MIT Press, 1994.

Wainwright, Hilary. *Arguments for a New Left: Answering the Free Market Right.* Cambridge, MA: Blackwell, 1994.

SOCIALIST CALCULATION DEBATE

The socialist calculation debate revolves around the question of whether central planners can, at least in principle, make the economic calculations necessary to achieve the rational, efficient allocation of society's economic resources. In 1920, Ludwig von Mises argued powerfully that such economic calculation cannot be made; economic theory demonstrates that rational central planning is simply impossible. This situation set off a vigorous interwar debate, in which a number of German, British, and other economists attempted to refute Mises's argument and in which Mises and others, particularly F. A. Hayek, sought to rebut these attempts. After World War II, mainstream economic literature

uncritically assumed that Mises's thesis had been definitively refuted. However, in the 1980s, Don Lavoie challenged this orthodoxy and, on the basis of insights central to the newly resurgent tradition of Austrian economics, demonstrated how mainstream literature, operating without appreciation of these insights, had failed to grasp the subtlety of the Misesian argument. The following text examines the central elements of the history of this debate in 20th-century economic discussion and briefly explores its relevance for libertarian thought.

In 1920, Mises published an article challenging the possibility of rational central planning. Two years later, he published an influential book-length critical analysis of socialism. In this book, Mises reproduced, in substantially unchanged form, his earlier paper. We can summarize Mises's argument as follows.

For economic efficiency in any decision to be achieved, it is necessary for the decision maker to calculate the benefits and costs of alternative courses of action. In a market economy, the entrepreneurs are able to make such calculative decisions (and thus to seek efficiency in their operations) by using present and prospective market prices to represent the values of inputs and outputs. But the central planning authority under socialism is, by the very definition of *socialism*, unable to make calculations based on market prices of inputs—because no market (and therefore no market prices) exists for resource services. Without a market for resource services, no indicators of relative resource values exist. Decision making by would-be central planners, therefore, cannot be made in a manner that systematically aims at efficiency.

Mises's challenge to the possibility of rational central planning was not the first critique of socialism as an economic system. In 1935, F. A. Hayek edited a volume (including an English translation of Mises's 1920 paper) in which he republished several earlier pioneering analyses of socialism and, in particular, an important 1902 critique by the Dutch economist N. G. Pierson. But these earlier treatments had hardly been noticed by the economics profession. It was Mises's paper, published at a time when socialism was seriously contemplated in Austria and elsewhere, that placed the issue—and his provocative challenge—squarely at the center of the professional attention. It set off a series of counterarguments seeking to refute the Misesian thesis. During the 1920s and 1930s, a large literature emerged in which these arguments and counterarguments were debated. This literature was at the outset mainly in German, with an astonishing variety of defenses of the possibility of socialist planning being offered by, among others, Eduard Heimann, Otto Leichter, Klare Tisch, Herbert Zassenhaus, and Carl Landauer. By the 1930s, defenses of socialist economic efficiency were advanced in the main in British economic literature by a number of authors, among them Henry Dickinson, Evan Durbin,

Maurice Dobb, Oskar Lange, and Abba Lerner. Among the statements reaffirming the validity of Mises' thesis and criticizing the various attempted refutations of it were those of Lionel Robbins, Friedrich Hayek, and Mises himself. The literature up until shortly before the outbreak of World War II was extensively surveyed in a 1938 Norwegian-language book by Trygve J. B. Hoff (published in English translation in 1949). With the benefit of hindsight, it is clear that the most influential among the defenses of socialist efficiency was that advanced by the Polish economist Oskar Lange in two articles published in the United Kingdom in 1936 and 1937. Lange's position is generally bracketed with that of Abba P. Lerner, who published an attack on Mises at about the same time. It was apparently the Lange–Lerner line of argumentation that convinced post–World War II economists that the Mises's thesis had been definitively refuted.

Lange credited Mises with having clearly formulated the economic problem facing socialism, an important contribution in itself. But his understanding of Mises's critique of socialism was such as to convince him that Mises was quite wrong in declaring economic calculation to be impossible under socialism. Lange understood Mises as claiming that the achievements of a market economy cannot be duplicated under attempted central planning. But Lange quite incorrectly interpreted Mises as seeing the achievements of a market economy as consisting strictly in attaining an approximation to the pattern of resource allocation that would emerge in a perfectly competitive market economy in Walrasian general equilibrium. A perfectly competitive market economy is one in which many industries each consisting of a large number of relatively small firms find themselves confronting an "equilibrium" market price for their product; these firms are unable to change this price and must therefore treat it as a given. Such an equilibrium price enables each firm to successfully produce and sell the amount it wishes to sell at the equilibrium price. Thus, although these firms have no control over the price at which their good or service sells, they do have complete control over the amount they produce and put forward for sale. The array of such equilibrium prices across the entire market economy constitutes the set of market prices making up "Walrasian general equilibrium."

Lange understood Mises to argue that, because no money market prices for resource services could exist under socialism, it followed that a "general equilibrium" (for which resource prices would be an important ingredient) in a socialist economy is a logical impossibility. Lange then proceeded to show that, although market prices for resources would indeed not exist under socialism, the more general sense of prices (referring to the "terms on which alternatives are available") does, of course, still hold for a centrally planned economy. So the logical possibility of a socialist system being in a state of general equilibrium certainly does exist. Moreover, Lange proceeded to devise a system of trial and error through which an actual socialist economy might, in fact, seek to approach a pattern of (non-market) prices that would constitute the state of general equilibrium, and thus be consistent with the same pattern of efficient resource allocation generally associated with Walrasian equilibrium under capitalism.

As we have noted, Lange's critique of Mises was, during the mid-20th century, uncritically accepted in the mainstream literature. The economic calculation debate appeared to have ended with the successful refutation of the Mises–Hayek position. It is true that not all economists believed Mises to have been refuted. In 1969, James Buchanan offered an interpretation that rendered the Lange–Lerner critique harmless. But this interpretation did not challenge the mainstream perception (from which Lange had proceeded) that Mises had shared the Walrasian understanding of what a market economy consists in. It was the late 20th-century resurgence of Austrian economics that finally revealed the error in Lange's interpretation of Mises (and thus the error in his practical proposals for socialist central planning). Only then was the social calculation debate resumed in earnest.

In 1985, Don Lavoie published his *Rivalry and Central Planning.* This book carefully reexamined the entire socialist calculation debate, sharply disagreeing with the mainstream account of this debate (and particularly with its conclusion that the Lange–Lerner position constituted a definitive refutation of Mises's critique of the possibility of socialist planning). The mainstream literature (including Lange and Lerner) had not grasped the Austrian understanding of how the dynamic rivalry of competing entrepreneurs (totally absent in perfectly competitive equilibrium) drives the beneficial coordinating market process of capitalism.

From the perspective of the Austrian competitive market *process,* the logical possibility of an array of nonmarket but equilibrium prices, under socialism, is almost completely irrelevant to the central issue. The central issue is how, under socialism, resource values can be revealed for the planners to engage in economic calculation. Under capitalism it is the rivalrous, entrepreneurial activity of market participants that generates such values (in the form of [nonequilibrium] market prices). Such rivalrous entrepreneurial activity is, by definition in a socialist system, ruled out in a centrally planned economy. The consequent impossibility of centralized economic calculation means that central planners necessarily lack the knowledge needed for the efficient allocation of resources.

There occurred a gradual erosion of the earlier mainstream unanimity in regard to the possibility of socialist calculation in the economic literature of the closing decades of the 20th century. With the award of the Nobel Prize in economics to Hayek in 1974, interest renewed in the earlier Austrian critique regarding rational calculation under socialism. Economists had, by the end of the century, again become aware of the problems and complications introduced by human ignorance. The downfall of socialist regimes in eastern Europe generated new doubts (even among socialists) concerning the possibility of efficient socialist planning. The debates concerning socialist economics became more unorthodox, more intellectually open. Some of the literature of the debate within socialism is discussed in the 1993 book *Market Socialism: The Current Debate*, edited by P. K. Bardhan and J. E. Roemer. A late 20th-century survey of the calculation debate from an Austrian perspective appears in a 1998 paper by Peter Boettke. The socialist calculation debate lives on. Let us turn to the relevance of this debate for libertarian thought. Two strands of relevance can be identified.

The first area of relevance is straightforward. Clearly the case for classically liberal political arrangements rests, at least in part, on the circumstance that economics demonstrates, as libertarians claim, that such political arrangements tend to generate relative prosperity. Were it shown that a centrally planned economy could be relied on to produce a similar or better economic outcome, the case for a libertarian society would be correspondingly weakened. Indeed Mises's critics in fact claimed that a socialist economy can be more efficient than a capitalist system. Precisely because it is centrally planned, the socialist economy can, the critics held, aim at an efficiency that the "anarchy of production" under capitalism cannot, in its haphazardness, be expected to achieve. Rational socialist planning, they argued, is not only possible, but can accomplish targeted social objectives (deliberately planned rates of growth, economic equality, full employment stability, etc.) absent under capitalism, thus providing its critics with rhetorical ammunition. The provocative aspect of Mises's challenge consisted largely in that he had not merely questioned the supposed superiority of socialist planning; he had gone further and asserted that no rational planning, no systematic pursuit of efficiency, was possible under socialism at all.

Where libertarianism confronts not the central planning of complete socialism, but (as so often is the case in our modern experience) the interventionist policies of proactive governments of "mixed" economies, the socialist calculation debate has quite similar relevance for libertarian concerns. The truth is, as I have argued in "The Perils of Regulation: A Market-Process Approach," the same Misesian insights that demonstrate the overwhelming calculational problems challenging complete socialism also demonstrate the hazards of piecemeal planning or interventionism. Once we understand the discovery procedure of which the market process consists, it becomes clear that interventionist policies, so far from being precise measures aimed at specific social problems, are likely to stifle or inhibit the desirable discovery process that the free market would, in the absence of these measures, have tended to

generate. Imposed price ceilings, price floors, impeded industrial mergers, and imposed safety measures that are not justified by consumer demand tend not merely to constrain market activity away from perceived opportunities, but, more important, to obscure possibly profitable entrepreneurial opportunities that may now remain forever undiscovered. The libertarian case against such interventions is substantially strengthened by the Austrian understanding of the capitalist entrepreneurial discovery process that underlies the Mises–Hayek side of the calculation debate. We are now ready for the second, less direct strand of relevance for libertarian thought.

This aspect draws attention to the essential nature of individual freedom in the free-market system advocated by libertarians. A narrow conception of individual freedom sees each individual, in a free market, as at liberty to choose between perceived alternatives. The economic analysis of a market system defined in terms of this narrow conception of freedom allows no place to the entrepreneurial role. To find a place for this role, it is necessary to broaden one's concept of individual freedom. In its broader conception, individual freedom includes not only the capacity to choose between already perceived alternatives but also the creative freedom of identifying, in the face of the initial absolute ignorance of what alternatives are in fact available, the arrays of alternatives from among which one may choose. Once one has broadened one's conception of freedom to include this creative, entrepreneurial dimension, one has attained a perspective from which one can recognize the free-market process as one of active, dynamic, entrepreneurial competition. The active rivalry of entrepreneurs is then seen as the source for the basic ability of the market to generate market prices for consumer goods and for resource services on the basis of which economic calculation by market participants may proceed.

The socialist calculation debate is highly relevant to these insights concerning the entrepreneurial dimension of individual freedom in the operation of the free-market economy. As previously noted, what permitted Oskar Lange to believe that he had solved the problem posed for socialism by Mises was his narrow (neoclassical) understanding of the scope of the economic analysis of the market economy. That analysis had, in effect, no room whatsoever for the dynamic, innovative activity of market entrepreneurs.

It was the socialist calculation debate that forced the economics profession to recognize the active, entrepreneurial element in individual liberty and the crucial role that this element must play in our understanding of how a society structured on libertarian principles will operate.

IK

See also Collectivism; Economics, Austrian School of; Free-Market Economy; Hayek, Friedrich A.; Marxism; Mises, Ludwig von; Socialism

Further Readings

Bardhan, P. K., and Roemer, J. E., eds. *Market Socialism: The Current Debate*. New York: Oxford University Press, 1993.

Boettke, Peter J. "Economic Calculation: The Austrian Contribution to Political Economy." *Calculation and Coordination: Essays on Socialism and Transitional Political Economy*. Peter J. Boettke, ed. London and New York: Routledge, 2001.

Buchanan, James M. *Cost and Choice: An Inquiry in Economic Theory*. Chicago: Markham, 1969. 96–98.

Hayek, Friedrich A. *Collected Works, Volume X: Socialism and War: Essays, Documents, Reviews*. Bruce Caldwell, ed. Chicago: University of Chicago Press, 1997.

———, ed. *Collectivist Economic Planning: Critical Studies on the Possibilities of Socialism*. London: Routledge & Son, 1935.

Hoff, Trygve J. B. *Economic Calculation in the Socialist Society*. London, Edinburgh and Glasgow, UK: William Hodge, 1949.

Kirzner, Israel M. "The Perils of Regulation: A Market-Process Approach." *Discovery and the Capitalist Process*. Israel M. Kirzner, ed. Chicago: University of Chicago Press, 1985.

Lavoie, Don. *Rivalry and Central Planning: The Socialist Calculation Debate Reconsidered*. Cambridge: Cambridge University Press, 1985.

Lippincott, Benjamin E., ed. *On the Economic Theory of Socialism: Oskar Lange, Fred M. Taylor*. New York: McGraw-Hill, 1964 [1938].

Mises, Ludwig von. "The Organization of Production under Socialism." *Socialism, an Economic and Sociological Analysis*. J. Kahane, trans. London: Jonathan Cape, 1936 [1922]. 128–150.

SOCIAL SECURITY

Social security, also known as social insurance, refers to a wide range of government policies designed to redistribute income. Such policies are generally justified as collective protection against various hazards of life, including illness, old age, disability, unemployment, and poverty. In the United States, the term *social security* refers specifically to a program of taxing those who are currently working to support senior citizens and the disabled.

Government programs to alleviate economic hardship have deep historical roots. The English Poor Law of 1601 required localities to impose taxes to fund almshouses and other forms of poor relief, and similar poor laws were adopted by English-speaking colonies in North America. Modern social insurance, at least as it is understood today, arose in Imperial Germany under the chancellorship of Otto von Bismarck. Over the course of the 1880s, the German Reichstag passed legislation to enact health, accident, and old age and invalid insurance. Although these programs were styled as *insurance* and featured payments by current workers to fund the benefits that were currently paid out, they were by no means actuarially sound, but instead consisted of a "pay as you go" redistribution of wealth from workers to beneficiaries. Bismarckian social insurance provided the basic model for welfare state policies adopted around the world during the 20th century. In the United States, the Social Security Act, which provided for unemployment insurance, old-age pensions, and aid to families with dependent children, was signed into law by Franklin D. Roosevelt in 1935 as a crucial element of his extensive "New Deal" programs.

Libertarians oppose social security programs because they usurp functions that more properly belong to those areas that should be private and voluntary. First, private commercial enterprises are fully capable of providing many of the benefits of the contemporary welfare state. Insurance companies can protect against the risks of accident and illness, while company pension plans and investment firms can provide for retirement security. In addition, there exists a whole range of both private profit-seeking enterprises in addition to nonprofit institutions and initiatives designed to further a wide range of shared purposes, including protection against risk.

In the absence of government social security programs, it is true that some people—whether through lack of foresight, lack of resources, or extraordinary misfortune—would fail to provide adequately against various risks and consequently would face economic hardship. Libertarians contend that such cases would be marginal and could be addressed either through private charity or government "social safety net" programs.

Social insurance goes far beyond the limited redistribution provided by a social safety net, in which the goal is only to guarantee some minimum standard of living for those in dire need. Instead, it sweeps everyone into a monolithic, compulsory program, the burdens of which (in the form of heavy payroll taxes) make it difficult or impossible for many people to pursue private alternatives. Such full-blown, all-embracing collectivism is against all libertarian principles.

Social security programs around the world are currently experiencing serious and deepening financial problems. In richer countries, populations are aging, which means that the number of beneficiaries is growing at a faster rate than the number of current workers who are financing the costs involved. Therefore, older people are becoming a progressively heavier burden on the worker. The effect is that, at some point, benefits must be reduced substantially if the collapse of the system is to be avoided. In 1950, there were 16 workers in the United States for every retiree; today that ratio is only 3 workers to each social security recipient, and in 20 years this ratio will have fallen to 2 to 1.

Programs in less developed countries also are in distress despite their having much younger populations. These countries typically have large informal sectors or underground economies—a fact that triggers a vicious circle. Because many people work in the informal sector, payroll taxes (collected only in the formal sector) have to be higher than would otherwise be necessary. These high payroll taxes, however, create incentives for even more people to retreat into the informal sector, necessitating even higher rates, which push more people into tax evasion, and so forth.

Libertarians take differing approaches in proposing alternatives to the social security status quo. Some libertarians oppose all forms of coercive income redistribution as illegitimate, and they call for the complete abolition of social insurance and safety net programs, arguing that there is every reason to believe that the marketplace and private charity will fill the void. Other libertarians, such as F. A. Hayek and Milton Friedman, distinguish between social insurance and safety net policies. Hayek, writing in *The Constitution of Liberty*, endorsed public assistance for the indigent; as a corollary, he accepted the propriety of requiring people to purchase insurance and save for retirement so that they would not become public charges. In *Capitalism and Freedom*, Friedman opposed compulsory saving, but did propose a "negative income tax" that would serve as a safety net.

A number of countries, the first of which was Chile in 1981, have moved away from pay-as-you-go public pension systems toward compulsory private retirement savings. The merits of some form of social security privatization are now under intense debate in the United States.

BL

See also Charity/Friendly Societies; Family; Interventionism; Privatization; Welfare State

Further Readings

Ferrara, Peter J., and Michael Tanner. *A New Deal for Social Security*. Washington, DC: Cato Institute, 1998.
Friedman, Milton. *Capitalism and Freedom*. Chicago: University of Chicago Press, 1982 [1962].
Hayek, F. A. *The Constitution of Liberty*. Chicago: University of Chicago Press, 1960.
Lindsey, Brink. *Against the Dead Hand: The Uncertain Struggle for Global Capitalism*. New York: Wiley, 2002.
World Bank. *Averting the Old Age Crisis: Policies to Protect the Old and Promote Growth*. New York: Oxford University Press, 1994.

Sociology and Libertarianism

Sociology, properly defined, is the analytical, comparative, and historical study of societies. As such, it is an essential part of a libertarian's education because it can provide an empirical basis for assessing the kinds of institutional arrangements that allow liberty to flourish in contrast to those institutions that are inimical to its development. Whereas an economist or a philosopher might reasonably predict on a priori grounds that liberty is not going to thrive in a socialist society where all productive property is owned collectively (whether by the state or cooperatives), a sociologist can confirm that by direct observation of a large number of socialist and capitalist societies. "Compare, compare, compare"—that is the basis of a sound sociology.

It is immediately evident that capitalism is a necessary, although not sufficient, condition for the existence and exercise of liberty. The more socialist a state is, the less liberty its people enjoy. In the most extreme cases, such as the Soviet Union, Maoist China, and communist Ethiopia and Cambodia, millions of people were deliberately slaughtered for no other reason than the social position they or their ancestors held. Socialism is affirmative action through main force. It was enough to have been the son or daughter of a prosperous peasant, to wear spectacles, or to collect foreign stamps to be killed. Socialism is the antithesis of what libertarianism stands for. The core of libertarianism is the right to live free of the state; socialism, at least in its most virulent form, commonly involves death at the hands of the state. Traditional authoritarian societies also are known for their capacity for brutal murder, but rarely on that scale or extended to people other than political opponents of the government. The other cases of that kind of mass murder in the 20th century have occurred for the most part in countries such as National Socialist Germany or Ba'athist socialist Iraq, which also combined stratification by party with a zeal for social transformation. The wages of socialism are death. Sociology can tell us why, ironically enough, because of that same obsession with stratification that has distorted sociologists' perceptions of how capitalist societies work.

Sociology enables us to understand the malign consequences of a socialistic society that is stratified in terms of differential access to the coercive powers of the state, rather than by differences in income, wealth, or social status. All societies are stratified; the question is how. In the libertarian evolutionary sociology of Herbert Spencer, societies based on the free market and on contract were praised because they superseded earlier military societies stratified by ownership of or access to the means of force, a power then also used to enforce social distinctions that had some of the qualities of a caste. Spencer dominated late 19th-century thinking in the English-speaking countries and particularly the United States because of the wealth of empirical and historical data he brought to the justification of liberty. Those who are libertarians as a matter of absolute principle may feel uneasy at seeing liberty justified in utilitarian terms, but in a pragmatic world the tradition established by Spencer is vital. It enables us to understand the modern version of closed stratification, stratification by party that is the essence of socialism and the antithesis of a libertarian capitalist society. It also explains other restrictions on freedom to be found in socialist societies, such as the exceptionally savage persecution of male homosexuals in the former Soviet Union, Maoist China, or Cuba. Such persecution is an inevitable outgrowth of a society in which the dominant institution is a party hierarchy subject to strict central control and fearful of any independent links between its members (particularly those at different levels in the chain of command) or between its members and outsiders that it cannot control.

It has to be said that most of the sociologists of the last half of the 20th century neither appreciated nor propagated these essential insights into how society works. There are few libertarian sociologists, and most sociologists are, either directly or indirectly, hostile to individual liberty. In socialist societies, they were often servants of the state and may have adhered to the ruling ideology because of the psychological as well as material rewards that brings. Such a state can, after all, provide them a privileged position as prophets of an inevitably triumphant socialist future or participants in the great plan. In a milder version, the same is true of many sociologists in Western societies because the state offers them privileged positions, funds their ideologically loaded research, and allows them the satisfying delusion that they are molding society. Self-interest goes some way toward explaining why so many sociologists fear the contraction and diminishment of state power and state intervention. Social democracy often means jobs in the public sector for sociologists who would otherwise be unemployable. Sociologists opposed to liberty employed in education, race relations, welfare, or criminology have exercised great influence in free-market-based societies and have inflicted great damage on those societies.

However, the main reason that so many sociologists in free societies are hostile to libertarianism and unable to appreciate either its virtues or benefits is because they are committed egalitarians. For many reasons, societies based on freedom of speech, freedom to own property, freedom of contract, free trade, and a free labor market tend to produce marked inequalities of outcome. Some individuals are far more successful than others. Although there are high rates of individual social mobility in capitalist societies, it is in the nature of things that the inheritance of property, skills, contacts, a work ethic, and indeed general intelligence and specific talents mean that the children of the successful are more likely to succeed. It is a society that is unequal, but on the whole fair. As such, it is anathema to the professional egalitarians who dominate the ranks of the sociologists and who support massive state intervention that curbs liberty with the aim of producing greater equality of outcome as well as of opportunity. For the same reasons, modern sociologists typically resent and distance themselves from psychology and economics, both of which demonstrate that inequality is often a natural condition. The central theme of sociology is the denial of these realities; they must be denied, hidden, and suppressed by state action.

Sociologists in Western societies are often to be found in opposition to the very societies that grant them freedom of speech, subsidize their research, and employ them in sinecures. One could say that taxpayers are paying for the rope that will be used to hang them. Marxism appeals to sociologists (even after the collapse or transformation of the major socialist economies), and Marxist works, as David Marsland has pointed out, often dominate their college reading lists. By contrast, few of them read, or encourage their students to read, the founding father of sociology, Adam Smith, who recognized that market forces lead to social and economic progress, a progress that cannot be attained in any other way. Sociology lost that insight when increasing specialization cut it loose from economics and indeed psychology, which emphasize individual human autonomy and responsibility.

Most sociologists have no knowledge of either neoclassical or Austrian economics. Instead of cooperating with economists to solve the sociological problems highlighted by economic analysis, they sit on the margins and grumble about equality. Libertarians may be divided over the uses of the nation state and its armed forces, but they are likely to sympathize with the economist's demonstration of the superiority of a volunteer over a conscript army. Those sociologists who accept the need for armies typically also advocate compulsion and conscription because it equalizes the chances of being shot at. The sociologists' response to the marked rise in living standards and indeed in longevity in capitalist societies has been to invent the concepts of permanent poverty and relative deprivation and accordingly to demand ever greater state intervention. Most sociologists have become openly hostile to freedom. Even when they appear to be libertarians as, say, when they favor the legal sale of recreational drugs, they only do so because those who use and trade them are seen as underprivileged. They are quite unable to see that high taxes on tobacco—imposed in the name of coercive health improvement—are an infringement of freedom and an incitement to smuggling, illicit trading, and organized crime in exactly the same way as restrictions on other recreational drugs. The central weakness of sociology is the unwillingness of sociologists to understand the importance of prices and to work with them in the way economists do.

There is a broader relationship between deviant behavior and social change that sociologists refuse to acknowledge. During the late 19th century, the era of the growth of mutual aid organizations and stable families, the incidence of both violent and acquisitive crimes fell to low levels in most Western societies. Individuals chose not to attack the persons and property of others not because the state prevented them, but because this spontaneous order created by free individuals had a law-abiding ethos. The massive rise in crime of all kinds that has come to be seen as a general characteristic of modern societies only began in the mid-1950s after the establishment of the welfare state. It is what a libertarian would expect but is utterly contrary to the predictions of sociological collectivism. In the light of such contrary evidence, many sociologists have begun a long retreat away from their claim to be scientists into the vacuousness of postmodernism; if we can't be right, then nobody can be.

The tragedy of sociology is that it began with Adam Smith, Herbert Spencer, and William Graham Sumner as a vehicle for libertarian thought. The discipline was then captured by socialists and collectivists, often followers of Comtean and Marxist authoritarian traditions. In America, Britain, and Europe today there are many libertarian economists, legal scholars, psychologists, historians, and philosophers, but libertarian sociologists are rare indeed, and this lack of ideological diversity within the discipline has rendered it futile. I have tried above to interpret sociology from a libertarian perspective and to describe the state of the discipline. The challenge for libertarians is to change it.

CD

See also Collectivism; Marxism; Paternalism; Racism

Further Readings

Andreski, Stanislav. *The Uses of Comparative Sociology*. Berkeley: University of California Press, 1965.

Davies, Christie. *The Strange Death of Moral Britain*. New Brunswick, NJ: Transaction, 2004.

Marsland, David. *Seeds of Bankruptcy: Sociological Bias against Business and Freedom*. London: Claridge, 1988.

Rummel, R. J. *Death by Government*. New Brunswick, NJ: Transaction, 1994.

———. *Lethal Politics: Soviet Genocide and Mass Murder since 1917*. New Brunswick, NJ: Transaction, 1990.

Saunders, Peter. *Unequal but Fair?* London: I.E.A., 1996.

Smith, Adam. *An Enquiry into the Nature and Causes of the Wealth of Nations*. Indianapolis, IN: Liberty Classics, 1981 [1776].

Spencer, Herbert. *The Man versus the State with Six Essays on Government, Society and Freedom*. Indianapolis, IN: Liberty Classics, 1992 [1884].

———. *Principles of Sociology*. Abridged ed. Stanislav Andreski, ed. London: Macmillan, 1969 [1876–1896].

Sumner, William Graham. *On Liberty, Society and Politics, the Essential Essays of William Graham Sumner*. Indianapolis, IN: Liberty Classics, 1992.

SOWELL, THOMAS (1930–)

Thomas Sowell is an economist, a social theorist, and a writer. In an age in which many black leaders argue that racial identity determines political ideology, Thomas Sowell has challenged us to reexamine many widely accepted assumptions about identity and ideology. In so doing, his writings offer valuable insights into the divisions that polarize our political culture. In evaluating popular perceptions about the role of oppression and discrimination in limiting the success of certain groups, Sowell integrates history and economics to show how the best opportunities for all people—including blacks and women—come through hard work and applied effort in a free and open market. Although well known for his writings on race and culture, Sowell's emphasis on free and open markets shows up consistently in his writings, which span economics, history, and social policy. In each, he characteristically transforms complex, emotional issues into readily understandable examinations within a global and historical perspective.

Born into poverty during the Great Depression and raised in Harlem, Sowell learned the nature of responsibility and self-effort firsthand. Although he initially left home before completing high school, Sowell eventually received his bachelor's degree in economics (magna cum laude) from Harvard in 1958, his master's degree in economics from Columbia University in 1959, and his PhD in economics from the University of Chicago in 1968. He is the author of several books on economics, including *Basic Economics: A Citizen's Guide to the Economy*. In this book, Sowell explains why people are hungry in countries where there are vast amounts of rich farmland, why homeless people abound in New York City amid abandoned apartment buildings, and why unemployment reached 25% during the Great Depression. In explaining these realities, Sowell illustrates how a gap between knowledge and decisions led to unintended and often tragic consequences. This same theme is developed in many of Sowell's publications, perhaps most notably in *Knowledge and Decisions*. Crossing over between economic theory and social philosophy, this work parallels F. A. Hayek's discussions about the role of knowledge in society. In it, he describes how knowledge is embodied in the judgments and perceptions of millions of people, and how that in turn affects decisions that impact our economic, political, legal, and other social institutions.

In addition to using economics to teach us how the world works, Sowell also seeks to understand how and why ideas polarize our culture. In the area of the history of ideas, he has written *Marxism* (1985) and *Conflict of Vision* (1987). In the latter work, Sowell presents an analysis of the conflicting visions of human nature and how they have shaped moral, legal, and economic institutions.

Race and culture are perhaps the most polarizing topics that Sowell has dealt with head on. His writings have contributed vastly to our understanding of issues relating to race, culture, discrimination, and civil rights. Sowell reminds us that many incendiary statements about race, culture, and even intelligence can, and should, be boiled down to empirical questions, rather than foregone conclusions. The facts that he unearths in his many publications have shown how public policies based on false assumptions have often proved detrimental to the very people they are intended to help. He demonstrates this notion with civil rights legislation, education policy, and other policies that undermine the value of individual responsibility and self-effort. More often than not, Sowell's approach leads to findings that prove contrary to the conventional wisdom. But just as important, they illustrate how such views have become orthodox.

In addition to his many books, Sowell's writings have appeared in economics, law, and other scholarly journals. He also is a popular political commentator, appearing in newspapers, magazines, and online articles, as well as in his nationally syndicated column, which appears in more than 150 newspapers across the country. Sowell, who received the American Enterprise Institute's Francis Boyer Award, is currently a senior fellow at the Hoover Institution in Stanford, California.

JK

See also Affirmative Action; Cities; Culture; Racism; Responsibility

Further Readings

Sowell, Thomas. *Knowledge and Decisions*. New York: Basic Books, 1980.
———. *A Personal Odyssey*. New York: Free Press, 2002.
———. *The Quest for Cosmic Justice*. New York: Free Press, 1999.

SPENCER, HERBERT (1820–1903)

Although Herbert Spencer has been rightly regarded as the most influential libertarian theoretician of the 19th century, he was much more than that. He also was a founding father of modern sociology, a pioneer in the theory of evolution—his theories were developed prior to those of Charles Darwin—an important figure in progressive education—his name still adorns the education building at Stanford University—and a philosopher of distinction whose work in ethics and epistemology gained the respect of J. S. Mill and other notable contemporaries. He was, moreover, an early proponent of the rights of children, of equal rights for women, and of other civil liberties that have since gained widespread acceptance in Western democracies.

Spencer lived during a period that coincided with the rise and fall of political liberalism—or what Spencer called *true liberalism*, what today is known as *classical liberalism*. This political philosophy, which had made great strides in bringing about greater individual freedom in religion, commerce, speech, and other areas, had suffered a setback during the Napoleonic Wars. After this conflict ended in 1815, England experienced a revival of liberal ideas. Peace brought with it not only a resurgence of these views, but also the development of a form of social organization, "voluntary cooperation" founded on a "regime of contract," that supplanted much of an older form of social organization based on "compulsory cooperation" that characterized a "regime of status."

Unfortunately, things had changed for the worse by the time Spencer published *The Man versus the State* in 1884. In the first of four essays that comprise this work, "The New Toryism," Spencer noted that "most of those who now pass themselves off as Liberals are Tories of a new type." This new liberalism had abandoned its original central principle that "habitually stood for individual freedom *versus* State-coercion." Instead, it embraced the Tory principle of unlimited state authority with a slight difference: Whereas the Tories prior to the Glorious Revolution had vested unconditional authority in the monarch, a theory that was opposed to the Whig doctrine of conditional authority, modern liberalism, riding the wave of democratic sentiments, vested unconditional authority in "the people." Spencer viewed this disagreement as a distinction without an essential difference: "the real issue is whether the lives of citizens are more interfered with than they were; not the nature of the agency which interferes with them." A person is no less coerced and his rights are no less violated merely because unjust restrictions on his liberties are imposed by a majority, rather than by a single ruler.

Spencer offered several reasons for the transformation of what had been a philosophy of individual liberty into a new type of statism. The most interesting of these reasons, from a philosophical point of view, is one that he had cautioned against decades earlier. While in his early 20s, Spencer published a series of 12 letters (1842–1843) in Edward Miall's periodical, *The Nonconformist*. Collectively titled "The Proper Sphere of Government," these articles address a central problem of political philosophy, viz: "Is there any boundary to the interference of government? and, if so, what is that boundary?"

Spencer responded with the classical Lockean doctrine that the fundamental purpose of government was "to defend the natural rights of man—to protect person and property—to prevent the aggressions of the powerful upon the weak—in a word, to administer justice." He contrasts this conception with the common belief that the purpose of government is to promote the "general good." The "general good," Spencer noted, lacks a determinate meaning, so it cannot serve as a standard, or criterion, of legislation. Its vagueness gives to government a blank check on power. Has not every law, no matter how tyrannical, been justified by appealing to the general good? Spencer concluded that the "general good" cannot serve to define the duties of government because the purpose of any definition is "to mark out the boundaries of the thing defined," and "that cannot be a definition of the duty of a government, which will allow it to do anything and everything."

Spencer expanded on this theme in his first book, *Social Statics* (1851). Here he focuses his criticism on the principle of utility defended by Jeremy Bentham and his followers. He there stated that a government should promote the greatest happiness for the greatest number of people. Spencer noted that standards of happiness are "infinitely variable," so the principle of utility, although it may serve as a general formulation of the purpose of government, cannot serve as a determinate standard of legislation; an appeal to social utility does not tell us which measures a government should, and should not, enact. Hence, doctrines of expediency—whether expressed in terms of utility or the general good—"afford not a solitary command of a practical character. Let but rulers think, or profess to think, that their measures will benefit the community, and your philosophy stands mute in the presence of the most egregious folly, or the blackest misconduct." *Social Statics* contained Spencer's first extended justification of his celebrated "law of equal freedom," according to which "every man may claim the fullest liberty to exercise his faculties compatible with the possession of like liberty by every other man." The young Spencer, having been raised in a tradition of Protestant dissent, which he once described as "an expression of antagonism to arbitrary control," grounded this principle in a divinely ordained duty to pursue happiness, which in turn requires the freedom to exercise one's faculties according to one's own judgments. He further defends a version of the moral sense theory that had been developed by Francis Hutcheson and other luminaries of the Scottish Enlightenment.

Spencer later abandoned these doctrines, replacing them with an ethical theory that was thoroughly positivistic and more attuned to his theory of evolution. The "establishment of rules of right conduct on a scientific basis is a pressing need," wrote Spencer in 1879, and he published his two-volume *Principles of Ethics* to fill this need. These volumes constitute the final volumes of his massive *Synthetic Philosophy*, a project that took 38 years to complete. Spencer's efforts to deduce moral rules, including the law of equal freedom, from the "laws of life" and thereby achieve "results which follow . . . in the same necessary way as does the trajectory of a cannon-shot from the laws of motion and atmospheric resistance" had mixed results. Some critics, including those who were otherwise sympathetic to Spencer's ideas, have claimed that this scientistic approach to ethics undermined the earlier humanistic tradition of natural rights. However one may appraise Spencer's "scientific" system of ethics, there can be little doubt it later became discredited as the Larmarckian theory of evolution on which it was based (which upheld the inheritability of acquired characteristics) fell into disfavor.

Spencer's sociological insights almost certainly were to influence later libertarian thinkers such as Albert J. Nock more than did his ethical theories. In *The Study of Sociology*, Spencer pointed to instances of short-sighted political thinking by persons who have but a rudimentary grasp of social causation and who accordingly propose simplistic political solutions for complex social problems. Many people are ignorant of physical causation, he observed, so it is perhaps no surprise that many more are ignorant of social causation, "which is so much more subtle and complex." Where there is little or no appreciation of social causation, "political superstitions" flourish. Among these false notions is the belief that government has a special efficacy "beyond that naturally possessed by a certain group of citizens subsidized by the rest of the citizens." In addition, the "ordinary political schemer is convinced that out of a legislative apparatus, properly devised and worked with due dexterity, may be had beneficial State-action, without any detrimental reaction."

In addition to his other contributions to libertarian theory, such as his detailed typology of the militant and industrial forms of social organization, Spencer made seminal contributions to the theory of spontaneous order. In *The Principles of Sociology*, Spencer likened social development to a "rolling snowball or a spreading fire" where there is "compound accumulation and acceleration." An intricate social network evolves as in a market economy that is so interdependent that any considerable change in one activity "sends reverberating changes among all the rest." Society, in other words, is an unplanned spontaneous order, one that "grows" rather than is "made." A major function of sociology—which in Spencer's conception subsumed economics—is to explain the evolution of this order that is the result of human action, but not of human design. The difficulty of this task is why Spencer displayed such contempt for social planners: "A fly seated on the surface of the body has about as good a conception of its internal structure, as one of the schemers has of the social organization in which he is embedded."

GHS

See also Liberalism, Classical; Limited Government; Sociology and Libertarianism; Spontaneous Order

Further Readings

Caneiro, Robert L. "Herbert Spencer as an Anthropologist." *Journal of Libertarian Studies* 5 no 2 (Spring 1981): 153–210.

Francis, Mark. *Herbert Spencer and the Invention of Modern Life.* Ithaca, NY: Cornell University Press, 2007.

Smith, George H. "Herbert Spencer's Theory of Causation." *Journal of Libertarian Studies* 5 no. 2 (Spring 1981): 113–153.

Spencer, Herbert. *The Man versus the State; with Six Essays on Government, Society, and Freedom.* Indianapolis, IN: Liberty Classics, 1981.

———. "The Proper Sphere of Government." *Political Writings.* John Offer, ed. Cambridge: Cambridge University Press, 1994.

———. *Social Statics.* New York: Robert Schalkenbach Foundation, 1954.

Spontaneous Order

Spontaneous order theory is properly located in the history of social science. Indeed, the only part of social theory that can genuinely be said to be scientific derives from it. This scientific nature is seen in microeconomics, where the theory of the market describes how the voluntary actions of discrete individuals produce a predictable order from which we explain all the paraphernalia of modern economics. The main features of such an order are not designed by any one person or institution, but emerge spontaneously once individuals are left to pursue their private interests. Attempts to design an economic order, as in socialism, are condemned by Hayek as constructivist rationalism.

The theory of spontaneous order goes beyond economics because it seeks to explain how a range of phenomena, including law, emerged in a similar manner. There is little the government needs to do because essential institutions have been provided, seemingly by nature. The theory derives, however, from a novel distinction between nature and convention. Certain phenomena, like the weather, are purely natural and unalterable, whereas others are conventional and readily changeable, as is a statute. But there is a third range of phenomena, like the market, that are not entirely natural, but are by no means conventional and cannot be easily cast aside.

What is particularly significant for spontaneous order theory is its economical use of reason. Its theorists are antirationalists in that they explain effective social order not as a result of conscious planning, but by reference to instincts, habits, experience, and, most important, evolution. These theorists argue that traditional ways of doing things, which have developed gradually, are superior to any schemes conceived a priori. A key element of the theory is the conceptual distinction between law and the state. Law develops spontaneously, whereas the state is entirely artificial. The theory of spontaneous order does not depend on any special qualities of the person for the production of social stability and predictability. Whereas classical republicanism asks individuals to subordinate their private interests to the common good, spontaneous order theory concludes that the common good emerges from self-interested motives: It is an unintended consequence of human actions. These unintended consequences, which emerge almost by accident, are beneficial and are then imitated.

Although freedom is of great social significance, it has no necessary moral value. In spontaneous order theory, liberty is a mechanism through which the coordination of divergent human purposes is achieved. The same holds for individualism, which also is a mechanism for achieving divergent human purposes. Thus, although spontaneous order theory embraces individualism, it remains methodologically rigorous in that it is neither arbitrary nor nihilistic.

The theory of spontaneous order resolves all social action into individual action. Concepts such as *society* are shorthand expressions for multiple individual actions. Thus, although the doctrine does explain social aggregates, these aggregates are reducible to individual volitions. Although all libertarians accept the theory of spontaneous order, disagreement exists about the extent of this theory's explanatory power and whether at times its antirationalism may undercut the natural law tradition, which requires the use of reason to determine which actions are morally permissible and which are not.

The origins of the doctrine of spontaneous order are commonly thought to lie in the 18th-century Scottish Enlightenment and the beginnings of modern market economics, but the earliest reflections on the idea that a society could be conceived of as a natural process that required little in the way of central direction long predate this era. The ancient Chinese philosopher Chuang Tzu was perhaps the first to write of such a possibility. He said that "Each individual should pursue his own predilections. . . . One is led to the ideal of non-governing and to the method of letting the world alone."

In ancient Greece and Rome, the political was considered the highest human achievement, and the emphasis on the public sphere as the realization of liberty precluded their social theories from meeting the standards of spontaneous order. Indeed, much of spontaneous order theory involves a rejection of the classical ideal of "public spirit."

In the late medieval period, the first sophisticated expressions of the idea of spontaneous order were suggested in the writings on economics from the school of Salamanca. These 16th-century Jesuit priests, although Aristotelian in intellectual origin, were able to adapt that unpromising doctrine to the features of a market economy. Their theory of spontaneous order derives almost entirely from an understanding of a market economy, characterized by the price mechanism, subjective value, and supply and demand. Against the prevailing cost-of-production, or labor, theory of value, derived from Christian natural law, the Salamanca school was convinced that all economic value emanated from subjective choice and concluded that cost-of-production theories of value provided a bogus rationale for raising prices above market clearing levels. Writers like Molina identified the "just" price with the competitive price. Although there is no notion of the margin among these writers, their theories had enough basic market economics to explain, and evaluate favorably, the spontaneous self-correcting processes of free exchange.

A major achievement of the Salamanca school was its discovery of the quantity theory of money. Sixteenth- and 17th-century Spain had experienced a massive inflation, a result of the influx of gold and silver from the New World. Molina and other Salamanca writers developed a theory of inflation that, in turn, led to their justifying banking; profits on exchange dealings were not usurious, they argued, because they contributed to production and were not against natural law—despite the fact that both canon and civil law forbade usury.

It has always been a strong theme of spontaneous order that the automatic coordinating and self-correcting mechanisms in society extended not just to economics, but to other areas. In the 17th century, it was extended to a theory of common law by Sir Matthew Hale, who concluded that law did not derive from abstract reason, but rather required a kind of practical reasoning. Law depended on the application of general principles to particular cases, and this elaboration was largely a function of experience. It is better to rely on a body of stable and known rules "though the particular reason for them appear not." Hale attacked Hobbes's theory of sovereignty. While conceding that the final authority of law rested on the King or Parliament, he did not think that they should be unconstrained. He was writing in an English tradition that regarded common law as superior to statue, a battle that the judiciary eventually lost after 1688 when the British constitution became associated with the unlimited power of a sovereign Parliament. It is, of course, true that the common law system has survived, but that raises a fundamental problem regarding spontaneous order theory—namely, whether it simply celebrates the unaided survival of a social order or whether it also protects the liberty of the individual. It might not prove sufficient to ensure a free society to solely rely on institutions that are the result of social evolution. It is possible that a written constitution determined by an abstract reason may be needed for the preservation of the spontaneous order. Moreover, was not the sovereignty of Parliament the result of spontaneous order inasmuch as it was established in Britain by a series of common law decisions that are consistent with Hale's jurisprudence?

Spontaneous order theory proposed that orderly societies could emerge from the self-interested actions of decentralized individuals who had no direct concern with the common good. Yet political philosophy had always assumed that the pursuit of the common good depends on the suspension of self-interest. Therefore, what is needed is a theory that makes self-interest consistent with socially valuable action. The foundations for that approach were laid down by Bernard Mandeville. He was the author of the "amoral" "Fable of the Bees," published in 1714. Mandeville was writing at a time of moral fervor when egoism was condemned and people were urged to act altruistically by sacrificing their self-interest in favor of the public interest. Mandeville contended that this

endeavor was vain and pointless and that self-interest unintentionally generated social well-being. The "bees," when acting egoistically, he observed, produced the division of labor, the free market, and international trade. This object lesson led him to contrast virtue and commerce and to praise egoism: "Thus every part was full of vice/ Yet the whole mass a paradise." The actions of the vilest contributed something valuable. "The worst of all the multitude/ Did something for the common good."

However, Mandeville did not offer a broader explanation of how self-interest could generate social harmony in economics and society. That problem was solved by David Hume, who, while destroying the rational foundations of ethics, was yet able to produce a compelling morality and one appropriate for spontaneous order. His claim was to "whittle" down the claims of reason. He maintained that "it is not contrary to reason to prefer the destruction of the world to the scratching of my finger," but this paradox did not preclude a demonstration of spontaneous order. Further, Hume conceived of self-interest as more or less constant: "As it is impossible to change or correct anything material in our nature, the utmost we can do is to change our circumstances and situation and render the observance of the laws of justice our nearest interest and their violation the most remote."

Hume observed that we learn the laws of justice by constant interaction, often through trading with others, which quickly leads to the establishment of three social rules whose origins are in convention—the stability of ownership, its transference by consent, and the performance of contract. Whereas Hobbes saw the social game as a once-and-for-all experience in which desperate people surrender all their rights to a sovereign, Hume envisaged repeat games in which people learn the advantages of cooperation. However, the nature of these rules does not change; they are derived from "the confined generosity of man, along with the scant provision nature has made for his wants." The conventions that develop through repeated social interaction are artificial, but still natural to man. Men also develop the capacity for reciprocity by which selfish men can advance their interests by occasionally acting generously: "I learn to do a service for another," he wrote, "without bearing any real kindness because I foresee that (the other) will return my service."

Adam Smith, like Hume, was highly skeptical of the role of reason in human affairs, especially of attempts to make society conform to an abstract plan divorced from experience: The legislator, he maintained, would not have the knowledge of time and place that individuals, with their natural liberty, employ to coordinate human actions. Most valuable social institutions are not the product of reason. The division of labor is not the effect of human wisdom, but is the necessary consequence of "a certain propensity to truck, barter and exchange one thing for another." In general, if people are permitted to exercise their natural liberty, a social order will emerge that is far more complex than anything deliberately designed. Indeed, Smith was alert to the fact that social well-being was the product of unintended action. He famously wrote of man that "by pursing his own interest . . . he frequently promotes that of society more effectually than when he really intends to promote it." He observed that the market coordinated human action spontaneously and the state could not improve on its efficiency: "No regulation of commerce can increase the quantity of industry in any part of society beyond what its capital can maintain."

However, spontaneity—without conscious intervention—was not sufficient for Smith. He thus offered an elementary theory of public goods, those it would not profit any private agent to produce. Smith also modified his antirepublican individualism when he suggested that an obsessive concern with commerce might undermine communal loyalty and produce antisocial effects. People might become alienated and fail to internalize those rules that are necessary for the maintenance of spontaneous order. In addition, Smith never saw the advantages of certain spontaneously generated commercial institutions, such as the joint stock company. Yet, despite the qualifications set forth, Smith presented a compelling case for spontaneous order.

In addition to Hume and Smith, the Scottish social philosopher Adam Ferguson wrote firmly in the antirationalist tradition. He viewed society as coterminous with man and its bonds arising "from the instincts, not the speculations of men." Societies, he noted, progress by a process of evolution, and "nations stumble upon establishments, which are indeed the result of human action, but not the execution of any human design." An especially important factor in the evolutionary process was the development and protection of private property. After Smith and Ferguson, the Scottish school declined in significance for spontaneous order theory partly because they became associated with the labor theory of value, which found its fullest expression in the work of David Ricardo and, ultimately, Karl Marx.

Among more recent writers, the notion of spontaneous order was taken up by many modern economists, most notably among the writers of the Austrian School. Carl Menger's *Problems in Sociology and Economics* sought to refute the claims of the German historicists who denied the validity of abstract, universal laws of economics, claiming that economics concerned itself with historical truths limited by time and circumstance. Menger employed spontaneous order theory to support his conclusions regarding the universal laws of economics. He used the method of abstraction to explain the emergence of money, markets, language, and law. They were what Menger called *organic phenomena* because they were the results of almost natural processes. He contrasted them with pragmatic institutions that are the result of human deliberation: "Markets, competition, money and numerous other social structures are already met with in epochs of history where we cannot properly speak of purposive activity of the community . . . directed towards establishing them," he wrote. In one example, money, Menger showed how actions that resulted from self-interest led to the establishment of one good (e.g., gold, as a medium of exchange, which was useful in many transactions and had none of the inefficiencies of barter).

Menger, however, never dogmatically claimed that organic institutions were superior to pragmatic ones. Explaining common law, for example, he wrote that it "proved harmful to the common good often enough . . . and legislation has just as often changed common law in a way benefiting the common good." Still Menger provided the methodological materials with which Friedrich A. Hayek constructed a systematic normative theory of spontaneous order.

Hayek's theory of spontaneous order derives from his philosophical assaults on rationalism and scientism. Hayek rejected the idea that the social world was governed by laws analogous to physical laws and that reason can uncover them, thus allowing society to be reorganized according to rational principles. We lack the knowledge to make the predictions on which such planning depends. The future is unknowable because knowledge is dispersed across possibly millions of actors and is not available to any one person or institution, but has to be coordinated by the market. Hayek describes a spontaneous market order as a *catallaxy*. Unlike an economy, which has a designed purpose, a catallaxy has none. It is simply a network of individual agents, households, and firms each pursuing its own ends and purposes. However, their decentralized actions are coordinated through the exchange system. A catallaxy rests on "the reconciliation of different purposes for the mutual benefit of the participants." Such an order produces a tendency to equilibrium primarily through competition and entrepreneurship.

The postwar period became dominated by Keynesian economics, which held, in sharp contrast to the idea that there existed a spontaneous economic order, that a properly functioning economic system required substantial government intervention. It was the inflation of the 1970s that eventually brought some kind of change to views of the market. The gradual reduction of government intervention in many areas of the economy and the adoption of a tighter monetary policy that slowed inflation gave the idea of the spontaneous market order some respectability.

During the Second World War, Hayek realized that the case for a free society could not be made on the basis of economics alone, and in *The Road to Serfdom* he extended the theory of spontaneous order to cover law, politics, and the constitutional structure of nations. He maintained that, under the rules of just conduct, a complex social order will be generated by free action. He described these rules in two major works, *The Constitution of Liberty* and the three-volume *Law, Legislation and Liberty*. In *The Constitution of Liberty*, Hayek suggested that, although it was possible that a deliberately designed code of law could provide rules for a free society, evolution was a most appropriate mechanism for the formation of these laws. This evolutionary development was the case with the English common law, which was never consciously designed, but developed in a case-by-case manner with no purpose beyond meeting the immediate needs of the contending parties. The result was an unintended order that was compatible with a free society. The design of a code, he contended, was an example of constructivist rationalism, doomed to failure inasmuch as men did not possess sufficient knowledge to formulate such rules.

The theory of spontaneous order serves as a crucial underpinning to any libertarian theory of society because it dictates that ordered arrangements and cooperative endeavors do not require an orderer and that, in fact, such attempts to plan social institutions, such as the economy, are doomed to failure.

NB

See also Common Law; Ferguson, Adam; Hayek, Friedrich A.; Hume, David; Mandeville, Bernard; Menger, Carl; Smith, Adam

Further Readings

Barry, Norman, P. "The Tradition of Spontaneous Order." *Literature of Liberty* 5 (Summer 1982): 7–58.

Constant, Benjamin. *The Principles of Politics Applicable to All Governments*. Dennis O'Keeffe, trans. Indianapolis, IN: Liberty Fund, 2003.

Ferguson, Adam. *An Essay on Civil Society*. Edinburgh: Edinburgh University Press, 1966.

Grice Hutchinson, Marjorie. *Early Economic Thought in Spain*. London: Allen & Unwin, 1993.

Hamowy, Ronald. *The Scottish Enlightenment and the Theory of Spontaneous Order*. Carbondale: Southern Illinois University Press, 1984.

Hayek, Friedrich A. *The Constitution of Liberty*. Chicago: University of Chicago Press, 1960.

———. *The Counter-Revolution of Science: Studies in the Abuse of Reason*. Indianapolis, IN: Liberty Classics, 1979.

———. *The Mirage of Social Justice*. Chicago: University of Chicago Press, 1976.

———. *Monetary Theory and the Trade Cycle*. New York: A. M. Kelley, 1933.

———. *Rules and Order*. Chicago: University of Chicago Press, 1973.

———. *Studies in Philosophy, Politics and Economics*. Chicago: University of Chicago Press, 1964.

Hume, David. *A Treatise of Human Nature*. L. Selby Brigg, ed. Oxford: Clarendon Press, 1987.

Mandeville, Bernard. *The Fable of the Bees*. F. B. Kaye, ed. London: Oxford University Press, 1924.

Menger, Carl. *Investigations into the Methods of the Social Sciences with Special Reference to Economics*. New York: New York University Press, 1985.

Smith, Adam. *An Enquiry into the Nature and Causes of the Wealth of Nations*. R. H. Campbell and A. S. Skinner, eds. London: Oxford University Press, 1976.

Spooner, Lysander (1808–1887)

Lysander Spooner was a political and legal theorist, a writer, and an abolitionist. Born in rural New England, he was raised as one of nine children and left home to live in Worcester, Massachusetts, where, in 1833, he began studying law. He served his apprenticeship in the offices of John Davis, a prominent Massachusetts politician who shortly thereafter served as governor and then senator. In Davis's absence, Spooner also studied with Charles Allen, a state senator who eventually served as Chief Justice of the Massachusetts Supreme Court.

At the time, the rules governing Massachusetts courts required a student to study in a lawyer's office before admission to the bar. College graduates were required to study for 3 years, whereas nongraduates were required to do so for 5 years. Spooner's first act as a lawyer was to challenge what he thought was a rule that discriminated against the poor. After just 3 years of study, with encouragement from both Davis and Allen (who had graduated from Yale and Harvard, respectively), Spooner set up his practice in Worcester in open defiance of the rules. In 1835, Spooner published a petition "To the Members of the Legislature of Massachusetts" in the local newspaper and sent copies of it to each member of the state legislature. He argued that "no one has yet ever dared advocate, in direct terms, so monstrous a principle as that the rich ought to be protected by law from the competition of the poor." In 1836, the legislature abolished the restriction.

Spooner's writing career began at about the same time as his legal one, with essays criticizing Christianity from a deistic perspective. Possibly in part for this reason, his law practice did not flourish. In 1836, he left Massachusetts to make his fortune in "the West"—in this case, Ohio. While there, Spooner vied with other speculators to buy land where future cities would spring up. He purchased a tract along the Maumee River for a town called Gilead, which today is named Grand Rapids, Ohio. But Gilead lost out to better-connected rivals and a general real estate collapse, so that by 1840, Spooner returned to his father's farm.

After writing about how the banking system should be reformed to avoid the kind of speculative collapse he had experienced, Spooner struck out in an entirely new direction. In 1844, he founded the American Letter Mail Company to contest the U.S. Post Office's monopoly on the delivery of first class mail. Postal rates in that period were notoriously high, and several companies arose to challenge the government's monopoly. As he had when he confronted restrictions on entering the Massachusetts bar, Spooner vigorously defended his action with a lengthy pamphlet titled "The Unconstitutionality of the Laws of Congress, Prohibiting Private Mails" (1844).

Unfortunately, this time he was up against a more intransigent foe. Although Spooner's mail company was successful commercially, legal challenges by the government soon exhausted his financial resources, and by July 1844, his business was all but defunct without his ever having the opportunity to fully litigate his constitutional claims.

It was after this dispiriting experience that Spooner turned his attention to the issue of slavery. With financial assistance from wealthy New York philanthropist and abolitionist Gerrit Smith, Spooner produced the first volume of his book *The Unconstitutionality of Slavery* in 1845. In this fascinating work, Spooner argued that, because the Constitution did not receive the express consent of those on whom it was imposed, it can only be based on presumed or "theoretical" consent. Because no one can be presumed to have consented to a violation of their natural rights, the Constitution cannot legitimately be interpreted as having this effect. From this conclusion he derived the following interpretive principle:

> 1st, that no intention, in violation of natural justice and natural right . . . can be ascribed to the constitution, unless that intention be expressed in terms that are legally competent to express such an intention; and 2d, that no terms, except those that are plenary, express, explicit, distinct, unequivocal, and to which no other meaning can be given, are legally competent to authorize or sanction anything contrary to natural right.

In short, "all language must be construed 'strictly' in favor of natural right." By this standard, he contended, the oblique references in the Constitution to slavery were not explicit enough to sanction this practice if there existed an innocent meaning to these passages at the time of the founding. The bulk of his essay is devoted to a search, sometimes strained but always clever and interesting, for that innocent original meaning.

To be sure, Spooner's arguments drew criticism, especially from abolitionist Wendell Phillips, to which in 1847 he responded in a second, entirely new volume of the book that was appended to the first. The entire work runs nearly 300 pages. Together they persuaded Frederick Douglass to abandon his Garrisonian opposition to the Constitution as "a covenant with death and an agreement with hell" and embrace Spooner's abolitionist reading.

The passion of Spooner's opposition to slavery is evidenced by his conspiratorial efforts to free the captured John Brown. He had met Brown shortly before Brown's ill-fated raid on Harper's Ferry, and afterwards he attempted to implement a plan in which radical abolitionists would kidnap the governor of Virginia and hold him hostage for Brown's release. The plan was never acted on, although Spooner's associates had gone as far as to locate a boat and crew.

Spooner also provided legal arguments to aid abolitionists charged with violating the Fugitive Slave Act, and his work on behalf of such defendants led him in 1854 to publish another book, *Trial by Jury*, in which he defended as essential to a free society the jury's role as triers of both fact and law—the position sometimes referred to as *jury nullification*.

Despite its having resulted in the abolition of slavery, the Civil War and its forcible suppression of the South seems to have greatly radicalized Spooner. Whereas his earlier works on the unconstitutionality of the postal monopoly and of slavery implicitly assumed the legitimacy of the Constitution, or appeared to, after the war Spooner explicitly rejected the Constitution in what is today probably regarded as his best and most libertarian essay, *No Treason: The Constitution of No Authority* (1870). He began this monograph with these words:

> The Constitution has no inherent authority or obligation. It has no authority or obligation at all, unless as a contract between man and man. And it does not so much as even purport to be a contract between persons now existing. It purports, at most, to be only a contract between persons living eighty years ago. . . . Furthermore, we know, historically, that only a small portion even of the people then existing were consulted on the subject, or asked, or permitted to express either their consent or dissent in any formal manner. Those persons, if any, who did give their consent formally, are all dead. . . . And the Constitution, so far as it was their contract, died with them.

Until his death in 1887 at the age of 79, Spooner eked out an impoverished existence as a writer, activist, and legal theorist. His writings were extensive, including a lengthy, although never completed, book defending intellectual property and an essay titled "Vices Are Not Crimes." His reputation as an individualist anarchist and his opposition to all forms of oppression and injustice have made him a hero to all libertarians. At a memorial service in his honor, the following resolution was passed:

> Resolved: That while he fought this good fight and kept the faith, he did not finish his course, for his goal was in the eternities; that, starting in his youth in pursuit of truth, he kept it up through a vigorous manhood, undeterred by poverty, neglect, or scorn, and in his later life relaxed his energies not one jot; that his mental vigor seemed to grow as his physical powers declined; that although, counting his age by years, he was an octogenarian, we chiefly mourn his death, not as that of an old man who has completed his task, but as that of the youngest man among us,—youngest because, after all that he had done, he still had so much service that the best we can do in his memory is to take up his work where he was forced to drop it, carry on with all that we can summon of his energy and indomitable will, and as old age creeps upon us, not lay the harness off, but following his example and Emerson's advice, "obey the voice at eve obeyed at prime."

He is buried in Forest Hill Cemetery in Boston, where a monument to him was erected by his admirers in 1999.

REB

See also Abolitionism; Constitution, U.S.; Contractarianism/Social Contract; Individualist Anarchism; Secessionism; Slavery in America

Further Readings

Barnett, Randy E. "Was Slavery Unconstitutional Before the Thirteenth Amendment?: Lysander Spooner's Theory of Interpretation." *Pacific Law Journal* 28 (1997): 997–1014.

Cover, Robert M. "Formal Assumptions of the Antislavery Forces." *Justice Accused: Antislavery and the Judicial Process.* New Haven, CT, and London: Yale University Press, 1975. 149.

Martin, James J. "Lysander Spooner: Dissident among Dissidents." *Men against the State.* Colorado Springs, CO: Ralph Myles Publisher, 1970. 167–201.

Phillips, Wendell. *Review of Lysander Spooner's "Essay on the Unconstitutionality of Slavery."* Boston: Andrews, 1847 [1969].

Shively, Charles, ed. *The Collected Works of Lysander Spooner.* 6 vols. Weston, MA: M & S Press, 1971.

Smith, George H., ed. *The Lysander Spooner Reader.* San Francisco: Fox & Wilkes, 1992.

Weicek, William M. "Radical Constitutional Antislavery: The Imagined Past, the Remembered Future." *The Sources of Antislavery: Constitutionalism in America, 1760–1848.* Ithaca, NY: Cornell University Press, 1977. 249–275.

STATE

Definitions of the state vary depending on the political theory or political philosophy inspiring the definition. However, there is a common element to all of them. The state is an organization monopolizing the legitimate use of force or claiming a monopoly on the use of coercion in a given geographic area and over a political entity, and possessing internal and external sovereignty. Recognition of the state by other states, and thus its ability to enter into international agreements, is often considered a crucial element of its nature. When not conceptually specified, the term *state* is typically defined ostensibly by pointing out the political structure that emerged after the Peace of Westphalia and that currently constitutes the dominant form of political organization in the world. The terms *country*, *nation*, and *land* are sometimes used as synonymous with *state*. In addition, the term also is used to describe the territorial and politico-administrative divisions within a federal system. Many authors have emphasized the distinction between the state and the government—the second referring to the group of people who make decisions for the state and/or their specific decision-making

institutional arrangements; however, this distinction is not universal in common parlance.

Theories about the origins of the state fall into two categories. On the one hand are the consensual theories, which regard the state as having evolved from a stateless society through the consent of the governed. Under this notion, the state is a mechanism that expresses the public interest and acts on its behalf. Realizing that they need a state-like mechanism, the members of a society agree to create it. This mechanism is both a producer and provider of public goods while ensuring that individuals do not free ride (i.e., do not overconsume these public or common goods) and that all contribute to the costs of their production. This benign view of the origin of the state contrasts with a different set of theories that hold that the state is born in conflict. These theories trace the state's origins to the application of force applied by a victorious (or stronger) group on a defeated (or weaker) group. The purpose of the resulting institution is to regularize the dominion of the stronger group over the weaker. It ensures against revolt from within and attacks from abroad, and it functions in a more or less explicit way as an instrument of exploitation by one group of another.

Although at the normative level libertarians may have disagreements regarding the justification for a minimal state, their views on the origins of the state and its historical nature tend to embrace conflict-based interpretations. The libertarian theory is an outgrowth of the distinction between economic and political behavior, voluntary exchange and coercion, monocentriciy and polycentricity, catallaxy and hierarchy, and market processes and government processes. Irrespective of which dichotomy is employed, libertarians consider that there are two basic organizing principles of social order. One is peaceful and based on one's own labor and voluntary exchange. The other is based on coercion, domination, and the administration of force. The state emerges from society when people utilize force against others and when an entire institutional structure is established on the basis of this relationship. Many libertarians reject the standard view that the state's origin is natural, created by people who have voluntarily surrendered their sovereignty, or the view that the state grew organically, as a consequence of economic surplus and the division of labor. "Force, and not enlightened self-interest, is the mechanism by which political evolution has led, step by step, to the state." When robbery, expropriation, and conquest become institutionalized, the state takes shape. At that point, the voluntarism of market exchange is overwhelmed by the coercive apparatus of the state. It is for this reason that the analogy between the state and a criminal gang is so popular in libertarian literature again and again, and it is why so many libertarians embrace the view that those who use the state to advance their objectives are a professional criminal class.

Libertarian literature is especially preoccupied with the problem of the state's unchecked growth—that apparently once set in motion, the state has a propensity to expand until it penetrates and controls both the market and all other spheres of social life. The concern is particularly pronounced in F. A. Hayek's *The Road to Serfdom*, which provides the most frightening description of the process. The growth in size and the scope of government has been almost continuous during the past century. The question is whether this evolution is contextual and accidental or whether unchecked growth is inherent in the nature of government. There appear to be two mechanisms at work that account for this unrestrained expansion. First, the internal dynamics of state bureaucracies are self-enlarging. Second, states grow in massive leaps in supposed response to alleged national crises. As Robert Higgs explained in his study of the state, *Crisis and Leviathan*, these crises can either be real, as were World Wars I and II, the Great Depression, or invented, as is the war on drugs. Irrespective of the nature of the crisis, the government assumes new functions with each problem and creates new agencies that endure long after each emergency has passed. The more the government grows—incrementally or in radical leaps—the more autonomous it becomes. Thus, it becomes increasingly immune to the efforts to decrease its size and scope and more able to resist those opposing its further attempts to enlarge its reach.

A normative discussion regarding the justification of the state should not, of course, be confused with an analysis of its origins, nature, and growth. One may consider that currently existing states are mechanisms whose main function is pillage, yet hope for sufficient structural reform so that they become transmuted into noncoercive, voluntary institutions. The arguments used to allow theoretical justification of the state are of two types: teleological and emergent. Teleological arguments justify the state by showing that it is in fact what it ideally should be or that it accomplishes the purposes for which it was created. Some states might possibly develop in accordance with a set of normative principles. A state that in fact develops in this manner would be justified because, by its very functioning, it embodies these objectives. Hobbes's account of the state, based as it is on a "social contract" and justified either "by obtaining the consent of [its] citizens" or by "being the kind of state that rational agents would consent to," falls in this category. Emergent arguments, in contrast, offer a totally different approach. The state is justified by virtue of reflecting the emergent properties embedded in its evolutionary history. Inasmuch as the state emerged as a consequence of a spontaneous order, that is, through an invisible hand mechanism, it is therefore legitimate. The classic example of this argument for a state is provided by Robert Nozick in his discussion of the rise of a minimal state. For Nozick, the minimal state is justified by the fact that, by their very

decisions, uncoerced individuals have set into motion an invisible hand process.

Libertarians have made use of both emergent and teleological arguments, but have generally applied them to governance systems rather than to government, on voluntary forms of association rather than on the state. Yet when they discuss the state, libertarians tend to divide on its size and role. Moderates, often referred to as *minarchists*, argue for a small or minimal state that simply protects property rights and enforces individual contracts. However, in the view of radical libertarians, people do not need nonvoluntary institutional arrangements to protect and enforce their rights. They argue that the institutions through which individuals can provide for all social services, including arbitration and police services, are more naturally based on voluntary contracts. Although moderate libertarianism has adjusted and adapted the standard teleological and emergence theories to support the idea of a minimal state, the radicals, also called *anarcho-capitalists*, reject the state in its totality. Those theorists who have rejected the legitimacy of the state in all its aspects have sometimes relied on the notion of self-ownership, coupled with an unlimited right to private property and a sweeping prohibition against coercion. Murray Rothbard offers the clearest example of this type of approach, which is inspired by a theory of natural rights. In contrast, David Friedman, also an anarcho-capitalist, has argued that there is no need for either moral arguments or an appeal to a theory of natural rights to demolish the legitimacy and justification of the state. Rather, his arguments are based on issues of economic efficiency. Utilitarian ethics and economic reasoning are sufficient, he maintains, to justify a libertarian social order.

Irrespective of interpretive nuances and schools of thought, the libertarian ideal remains that of a contractual society, one based exclusively on voluntary action and exchange. Such a society evolves naturally, emerging out of countless individual decisions and freely entered contracts between individuals. The aggregate result is the emergence of an institutional structure and social order difficult to predict. Chances are that it will differ from place to place depending on the individuals' preferences and how those preferences are manifested in their contracts. Any institutional system would be regarded as acceptable as long as it were formed on the basis of voluntary contracts among individuals. The results are likely to be complex and diverse systems, with many overlapping and competing authorities and a large variety of governance arrangements. In other words, it will be a polycentric system. One of the most difficult problems radical libertarians have to deal with is the issue of collective defense of individual liberty in polycentric arrangements. Yet from their standpoint, the principle of voluntarism holds here as well. Collective defense, some libertarians argue, should be seen as an industry like any other, and its organization should not differ from that of other industries. They point out that private systems of arbitration, justice, and defense already exist and that history is replete with examples of these private institutions before the rise of the modern national state. In summary, their ideal, regardless of whether it is reachable, is a contractual society based on voluntarism.

PDA

See also Anarchism; Anarcho-Capitalism; Hobbes, Thomas; Minimal State; Nozick, Robert

Further Readings

Friedman, David. *The Machinery of Freedom: Guide to a Radical Capitalism.* La Salle, IL: Open Court, 1989.

Hampton, Jean. *Hobbes and the Social Contract Tradition.* Cambridge and New York: Cambridge University Press, 1988.

Hayek, Friedrich August von. *The Road to Serfdom.* Chicago: University of Chicago Press, 1994.

Higgs, Robert. *Crisis and Leviathan: Critical Episodes in the Growth of American Government.* New York: Oxford University Press, 1987.

Mises, Ludwig von. *Omnipotent Government: The Rise of the Total State and Total War.* New Rochelle, NY: Arlington House, 1969.

Nozick, Robert. *Anarchy, State, and Utopia.* New York: Basic Books, 1974.

Oppenheimer, Franz. *The State.* New York: Free Life Editions, 1975.

Rand, Ayn. *Capitalism, the Unknown Ideal.* New York: New American Library, 1966.

Rothbard, Murray N. *For a New Liberty: The Libertarian Manifesto.* Lanham, MD: University Press of America, 1978.

Schmidtz, David. "Justifying the State." *Ethics* 101 (October 1990): 89–102.

STIGLER, GEORGE J. (1911–1991)

George J. Stigler was one of the central figures of the Chicago School of Economics. He was awarded the Nobel Prize in 1982 for "his seminal studies of industrial structures, functioning of markets and causes and effects of public regulation."

Stigler was born and raised near Seattle. He earned his undergraduate degree from the University of Washington and then moved to Northwestern University, where he received his MBA. In 1933, he enrolled in a PhD program in economics at the University of Chicago and studied under the three scholars most closely identified with what some have called the "first" Chicago School of Economics: Henry Simons, Jacob Viner, and Frank Knight. Stigler wrote his dissertation on the history of economic thought under Knight and was awarded his doctoral degree in 1938. He also was influenced by Viner's neoclassical approach to microeconomic questions, an approach that Stigler would use profitably throughout his career. At Chicago, Stigler became lifelong friends with two fellow graduate students, Milton Friedman and W. Allen Wallis.

Stigler's first teaching position was at Iowa State. He moved from there to Minnesota and then Brown, before settling at Columbia from 1947 to 1958. In 1958, Stigler returned to Chicago, where he rejoined his old friends Friedman and Wallis and where he would spend the rest of his life.

Stigler's belief in the power of markets to solve social problems—and the often negative consequences of government intervention—can be seen in two of his earliest publications. In 1945, he examined the effects of the minimum wage in a paper published in the *American Economic Review*, arguing that it does little to alleviate poverty and distorts the allocation of resources. The following year, in *Roofs or Ceilings? The Current Housing Problem*, Stigler and Friedman critiqued the policy of rent control, arguing that it led to shortages in the housing supply and higher prices for most consumers. The pamphlet was published by the newly founded Foundation for Economic Education, which would become one of the libertarian movement's most venerable institutions. In 1947, Stigler traveled to Europe with Friedman and Aaron Director, Friedman's brother-in-law and one of the early leaders in the economic study of the law, to attend the inaugural meeting of the Mont Pelerin Society. Stigler would serve as president of the society from 1976 to 1978.

After Stigler returned to Chicago for good in 1958, he and Friedman became the almost universally acknowledged leaders of what has been called the "second" Chicago School of Economics, which also would count Gary Becker, Robert Lucas, Ronald Coase, Harold Demsetz, Arnold Harberger, Sherwin Rosen, and Sam Peltzman, among others, as its members. Many of these economists would hold positions in multiple departments in the university, including the Law School, the Graduate School of Business, and the Department of Sociology. In addition, within the Graduate School of Business, a distinguished group of financial economists, including Merton Miller, James Lorie, and Eugene Fama, made their mark on the profession. It also is true that the Chicago School of Economics extended beyond the physical domain of the university. Economists trained at Chicago or sympathetic to the Chicago tradition would help to shape the direction of the economics departments at the University of Rochester (where Wallis would eventually become president), the University of California at Los Angeles, and the University of Minnesota.

Stigler's contributions to economic theory were numerous and wide ranging. His textbook on price theory, built on the insights he had learned from Viner, would help define the way Chicago School economists tackled microeconomic questions. In the early 1960s, Stigler's attention turned in large measure to examining economic regulation. He was skeptical of the view held by many political scientists that most regulations were, quite simply, necessary and rational responses to problems with a relatively unfettered market system. Through a number of careful empirical studies, on the electricity and securities industries, for example, he found that regulations often reduced consumer welfare rather than enhanced it. If true, then, why had the number and power of regulatory agencies expanded so greatly in the 20th century? In answer, Stigler came up with his "capture theory." Business leaders urged the regulation of their industries to restrict competition and thus benefit incumbent firms. Regulatory capture led Stigler to conclude:

> And so we face an embarrassing problem if we wish to return to a freer, more traditionally liberal society: the business community does not wish to be released from the public interventions to which it is subject. The merchant marine does not want unregulated, unsubsidized cargo ships; the steel industry does not want free imports; the construction industry does not want competitive interest rates. Each industry will agree on the desirability of making *other* industries freer and more competitive, but will assert that its own industry would become disorganized and perhaps even non-viable if the state withdrew. There are mavericks in many industries—entrepreneurs and firms that are eager to take their chances in the freer winds of competition—but they are seldom in a majority.

Hence, Stigler often took a pessimistic view when considering the viability of market-oriented reforms. "[T]he persistence of the vast array of regulations is evident—and it is inevitable." Some economists have gone further to assert that Stigler also maintained that whatever we observe is not only inevitable, it also is efficient. However, it is difficult to find direct evidence for such a claim in Stigler's written work.

Stigler considered his most important contribution in economics to be his work on information theory. Economists had a hard time reconciling how similar, or even identical, products could fetch different prices from one seller to another. This diversity of price, some argued, was an example of market failure. But Stigler made the case that it was the result of rational decisions by consumers. Attaining information about products is costly, so in many cases it simply does not make sense to acquire "perfect information." Consumers will search until the marginal expected gain is equal to the marginal cost of additional searching. For some consumers—those whose time is worth a lot—this differential could mean that little searching will be done. For others, whose time is less valuable, we should expect more effort to be expended in seeking information. Stigler's work in this area, although seemingly

intuitive, was groundbreaking and has sparked a vast literature in information theory.

Stigler wished to see a return to a more liberal society with far less government intervention. But he was first and foremost an economist. His understanding of the nature of freedom differed from the conventional libertarian view. Freedom, to Stigler, did not mean merely the absence of coercion. It also had a positive dimension. A "widening range of choices due to the growth of income and education" amounted to an effective increase in freedom in Stigler's eyes. Capitalism, even in the case of the modern mixed economy, enhanced people's abilities to direct their lives as they wished, and this enhancement, in Stigler's view, should be seen as enhancing their liberty.

George Stigler was one of the most eminent economists of his generation. Although his work was often highly technical and quantitative, he also was a gifted writer who paid great attention to his prose. Many of his most important professional papers can be found in a volume titled *The Essence of Stigler.* His highly readable autobiography, *Memoirs of an Unregulated Economist*, published just a few years before his death, discusses not only his own life and work but also the development of the Chicago School and economic theory more generally.

AS

See also Economics, Chicago School of; Friedman, Milton; Price Controls

Further Readings

Friedman, Milton, and George J. Stigler. *Roofs or Ceilings? The Current Housing Problem.* Irvington-on-Hudson, NY: Foundation for Economic Education, 1946.
Leube, Kurt R., and Thomas Gale Moore, eds. *The Essence of Stigler.* Stanford, CA: Hoover Institution, 1986.
Stigler, George J. *The Citizen and the State: Essays on Regulation.* Chicago: University of Chicago Press, 1975.
———. *Essays in the History of Economics.* Chicago: University of Chicago Press, 1965.
———. *Memoirs of an Unregulated Economist.* New York: Basic Books, 1988.
———. *The Pleasures and Pains of Modern Capitalism.* Occasional Paper 64. London: Institute of Economic Affairs, 1982.
———. *The Theory of Price.* New York: Macmillan, 1946.

STIRNER, MAX (1806–1856)

Johan Caspar Schmitt, who wrote under the name Max Stirner, was a German intellectual associated with the "Young Hegelians" and best known as the author of *The Ego and Its Own (Der Einzige und sein Eigenthum),* an idiosyncratic case for a radical form of egoism that was influential in the development of American individualist anarchism.

The overriding thrust of *The Ego and Its Own* is that the best life is one totally free of constraint or obligation. "Owness [*Eigenheit*]" is incompatible with any surrender of individual judgment. "I am my own," Stirner wrote, "only when I am master of myself, instead of being mastered . . . by anything else." Stirner therefore rejected the existence of any legitimate obligation to others or to the laws of the state. According to Stirner, "every state is a despotism, be the despot one or many." Even one's own promises are not binding because the truly free individual cannot permit his present will to be limited by past choices. Although Stirner maintained that society is, for the most part, a source of ego-suffocating constraint, it is possible to build purely instrumental and conditional alliances that are aimed at mutual advantage through a union of egoists. The peculiar structure and style of *The Ego and Its Own* reflects Stirner's view that even reason and language are oppressive constructs to which the individual owes no deference.

The first American edition of the English translation of *The Ego and Its Own* was published in 1907 by the American individualist anarchist Benjamin Tucker. In the pages of Tucker's magazine, *Liberty,* the main conduit of Stirner's ideas to America, Tucker and others, among them James L. Walker, defended Stirnerite antinomian egoism as the correct grounds for rejecting the legitimacy and authority of the state against those anarchists who embraced natural rights. Stirner's emphasis on liberation from unchosen obligations is reflected in contemporary works such as *How I Found Freedom in an Unfree World* by two-time Libertarian Party presidential nominee Harry Browne.

WW

See also Individualism, Political and Ethical; Individualist Anarchism; Tucker, Benjamin R.

Further Readings

McElroy, Wendy. "Benjamin Tucker, *Liberty,* and Individualist Anarchism." *The Independent Review* 2 no. 3 (Winter 1998): 421–434.

Stirner, Max. *The Ego and Its Own.* David Leopold, ed. New York: Cambridge University Press, 1995.

STOICISM

Stoicism is the term applied to a philosophical movement that dominated Greek and Roman thought from the 3rd century B.C. to the 3rd century A.D. Its central doctrines include self-discipline, natural law, resistance to tyranny, and an unconditional commitment to duty.

The name *Stoic* derives from the *Stoa Poikilé*, the colonnade in Athens where the movement was founded. The most important of the early Stoic philosophers are Zeno, the school's founder—usually called Zeno of Citium to avoid confusion with Zeno of Elea, author of the famous paradoxes of motion—and Chrysippus, a logician who so thoroughly reworked Stoic doctrine as to earn the title of "second founder." Unfortunately, the writings of these and other early Stoics are lost and must be reconstructed from ancient reports and quotations. Stoicism has thus had an influence on later thinkers primarily through the surviving writings of the later Stoics, particularly the Roman statesman Marcus Tullius Cicero, the playwright and imperial advisor Lucius Annaeus Seneca, and the Greek freedman Epictetus. Cicero, an adherent of the skeptical outlook of the New Academy, did not unconditionally accept the tenets of Stoic philosophy, but he is in substantial agreement with Stoic ethical and political doctrine, much of which he borrowed from the now-lost writings of Panaetius and Poseidonius. Seneca and Epictetus, by contrast, are fairly orthodox Stoics. Another influential Stoic author was the Roman Emperor Marcus Aurelius. Stoic philosophy also draws heavily on the views of such earlier thinkers as Heraclitus, Socrates, and the Cynics.

The central teaching of Stoic ethics is that nothing is desirable or valuable except virtue; hence, a Stoic will be unruffled by the vicissitudes of fortune so long as his personal honor remains intact. For example, a courageous warrior will concern himself with doing the best he can to save his city because that is his duty and because it is in his power, but will not really care about actually saving his city because that ultimately depends on fortune and is not his responsibility. Several arguments were offered for this position.

First, a wise person, it was felt, could be trusted never to be tempted away from virtue; but if anything other than virtue were valuable, such a good would be a potential rival to virtue and so the wise person's commitment to virtue would not be reliable after all.

Second, our happiness is vulnerable to bad luck so long as we allow ourselves to care about things outside our power, whereas those who care only about their own attitudes and choices can never have their happiness frustrated. Third, each of us should attempt to be like a good stage actor, performing without complaint the part that has been assigned to us by God or Fate, regarded by the Stoics as a living and intelligent cosmic fire pervading and controlling the universe. Finally, although human beings start off with an instinctual attachment to their own self-preservation and natural functioning, and initially value reason only as an instrumental means to these more fundamental goals, should we develop and mature properly and become habituated to the use of reason, we will come to value reason as an end rather than as a means. The result is that our rational activity in orderly harmony with other people and with nature will entirely supersede our earlier concerns.

The Stoic ethical position entails a negative attitude toward the emotions. Emotions are not mere feelings, but involve cognitive judgments; in experiencing love, fear, anger, and so forth, we are committing ourselves to the judgment that certain external objects are good or bad. These judgments, however, are false because nothing is good but virtue, or bad but vice. Because a wise person will not endorse false judgments, in order to become wise, we must overcome all such emotions and be governed by reason alone. (The apparently unrealistic character of this advice is mitigated by the Stoics' clarification that the emotions are to be identified not with our initial involuntary impressions, but with our assent to them as true judgments and as guides to action.)

In politics, the Stoics embraced the cosmopolitan doctrine that all human beings were citizens of a single natural community, governed by the natural law of reason that superseded local man-made statutes. In Cicero's memorable formulation in *On the Republic*: "There will not be a different law at Rome and at Athens, or a different law now and in the future, but one law, everlasting and immutable, will hold good for all peoples and at all times." Although Zeno seems to have interpreted this doctrine in an antinomian fashion, envisioning a utopian society free from such conventional institutions as law courts, temples, money, or constraints on sexual freedom, the later Stoics made a greater accommodation to traditional mores. Stoic writings in the Roman period defended private property and market exchange, holding that the protection of property rights was the central function of the state. Among Stoics, Roman law came to be interpreted as a reflection of natural law and Roman imperialism as the realization of the universal human community.

Nevertheless, the emergence of the Roman Empire from what had been a republic did not meet with Stoic approval. Although the Stoic conception of freedom is primarily a psychological one, Stoicism was nonetheless hostile to autocratic despotism and looked back with nostalgia to the pre-imperial days of participatory republicanism and the rule of law. Adherents of Stoicism are numbered among the assassins of Julius Caesar and the would-be assassins of the Emperor Nero.

Stoicism cast a long shadow on later thought. The apostle Paul came from Tarsus, a center of Stoic learning, and he frequently cited Stoic authors favorably. A forged correspondence between Paul and Seneca ensured the latter's popularity among the early Christians, and such writers as Augustine and Boethius were responsible for incorporating a great deal of Stoic thought into Christian theology. In later centuries, Stoicism exercised a powerful influence on the development of classical liberalism through such works as John Locke's *Two Treatises of Government*, Jean-Jacques Rousseau's *Discourses*, Adam Smith's *Theory of Moral Sentiments*, and the ethical writings of Immanuel Kant.

Of particular significance for the liberal tradition is the Stoic statesman Cato the Younger, whose intransigent defense of republican ideals earned him the enmity of Julius Caesar. To his 18th-century admirers, Cato was an apt symbol of resistance to despotism. George Washington had Joseph Addison's play *Cato* performed at Valley Forge to inspire his troops. Anonymous tracts hostile to governmental power were often signed with the pseudonym *Cato*, among the most famous of which were *Cato's Letters* by John Trenchard and Thomas Gordon and several Anti-Federalist pamphlets (criticizing the proposed U.S. Constitution) attributed to New York Governor George Clinton.

RL

See also Cato's Letters; Cicero; Cosmopolitanism; Kant, Immanuel; Natural Law

Further Readings

Cicero, Marcus Tullius. *On Duties*. E. M. Atkins and Miriam Griffin, eds. Cambridge: Cambridge University Press, 1991.
———. *The Republic and the Laws*. Jonathan Powell and Niall Rudd, eds. Oxford: Oxford University Press, 1998.
Epictetus. *The Discourses as Reported by Arrian. Fragments. Encheiridion*. 2 vols. W. A. Oldfather, ed. Cambridge, MA: Harvard University Press, 1998.
Erskine, Andrew. *The Hellenistic Stoa: Political Thought and Action*. Ithaca, NY: Cornell University Press, 1990.
Long, A. A., and D. N. Sedley. *The Hellenistic Philosophers: Volume I. Translations of the Principal Sources with Philosophical Commentary*. Cambridge: Cambridge University Press, 1987.
Schofield, Malcolm. *The Stoic Idea of the City*. Cambridge: Cambridge University Press, 1991.
Seneca. *Moral and Political Essays*. John M. Cooper and J. F. Procopé, eds. Cambridge: Cambridge University Press, 1995.

SUBSIDIARITY

Subsidiarity is the term used to describe the principle that decisions should be taken at the lowest possible level, beginning with the individual, through the family, local voluntary associations, and then to government (local, national, and global). This decision-making approach has been characterized as decentralist or bottom–up. The principle has both libertarian and collectivist interpretations. The origins of the doctrine can be found in Aristotle and Thomas Aquinas, and it was most developed in Roman Catholic social doctrine. The idea was formally documented as "a most weighty principle" in article 79 of Pope Pius XI's encyclical *Quadragesimo Anno*:

> Just as it is gravely wrong to take from individuals what they can accomplish by their own initiative and industry and give it to the community, also it is an injustice and at the same time a grave evil and disturbance of right order to assign to a greater and higher association what lesser and subordinate organizations can do.

The libertarian case for decentralism is predicated on the principle that if a decision cannot be taken by the individual (e.g., when rights are claimed to be violated), the lower the level of decision making, the better. First, the individual is sovereign and may delegate responsibilities upward, in contrast to national sovereignty, which places sovereignty in the hands of government. Second, subsidiarity provides for competition between jurisdictions, rather than monopolies at each jurisdictional level. Competition leads to greater efficiency. Third, fragmented decision-making structures provide an opportunity to leave an unwelcome jurisdiction in favor of another, more conducive to one's values. Fourth, subsidiarity provides for the existence of a wide variety of communities, which can be closest to the diverse preferences of individuals. Fifth, subsidiarity provides for a system of checks and balances against what would otherwise be the overwhelming power of any jurisdiction. Finally, it recognizes that efficiency is not always the most important value and might be regarded by many as subsidiary to liberty.

The collectivist or republican interpretation emphasizes the values of effectiveness, efficiency, and the common good. It draws sustenance from article 80 of Pius XI's encyclical that "the State will more freely, powerfully and effectively do all those things that belong to it alone: directing, watching, urging, restraining, as occasion requires and necessity demands." Although the lower level may be the best for all three values, it is not always. In these circumstances, the higher body has the legitimacy to act.

The idea of subsidiarity plays a central role in the debate over the European Union (EU). That the principle of subsidiarity should be formally incorporated in the treaties by which states acceded to the EU is a reflection of the fear some Europeans felt regarding the overcentralization of power. The resistance was led by Bavaria, which was Catholic, localist, and fearful that its powers as a constituent German state would be usurped by the EU. The notion was then embraced by Anti-Federalist governments, among them the United Kingdom. However, collectivists claimed that the nation-state was unable to carry out a number of its legitimate functions in an increasingly complex Europe, such as protection of the environment or security, and that these decisions should be relocated at the higher pan-European level.

This concern led to the adoption in the Treaty of European Union of 1992 of this ambiguous statement:

> In areas which do not fall within its exclusive competence, the Community shall take action, in accordance with the principle of subsidiarity, only if and insofar as the objectives of the proposed action cannot be sufficiently achieved by the Member States.

Although the inclusion of this principle was perceived as a victory for the decentralists, the actual wording favored a collectivist interpretation. The criteria for the allocation of powers were to be determined by whether the objectives were perceived as being achieved (i.e., by their apparent effectiveness). The statement contained no reference to the values of liberty or to the strength of subsidiary institutions, both of which are central to the doctrine.

Whenever the principle of subsidiarity is invoked, it is vital to note whether it is based on libertarian values—the individual, liberty, voluntary association, and decentralism—or on collectivist claims of effectiveness, efficiency, and the common good.

NA

See also Decentralism; Federalism

Further Readings

Beabout Gregory R. "The Principle of Subsidiarity and Freedom in the Family, Church, Market, and Government." *Journal of Markets and Morality* 1 no. 2 (October 1998).

Begg, David, ed. *Making Sense of Subsidiarity: How Much Centralization for Europe?* London: Center for Economic Policy Research, 1993.

de Noriega, Antonio Estella. *The EU Principle of Subsidiarity and Its Critique*. Oxford: Oxford University Press, 2002.

Pope Pius XI. *Quadragesimo anno: On the Reconstitution of the Social Order*. Washington, DC: United States Catholic Conference, 1931.

Sumner, William Graham (1840–1910)

William Graham Sumner was an economist, a sociologist, and a leading defender of individualism and the free market. He opposed most of the reforms that coalesced in the progressivist program after 1900, and he also denounced American imperialism. His *Folkways* (1907) is one of the most important works in early American sociology.

Sumner was born in Paterson, New Jersey, the son of an English-born artisan, from whom he inherited a lifelong dislike of social causes. After the death of his mother in 1848, his experience in an emotionally starved household under the care of a penurious stepmother reinforced a keen sense of the gap that separates emotion and fact, a major theme in his work. Sumner came to social science by way of religion. After graduating from Yale in 1863, he studied languages and theology in Europe before returning to New Haven as a classics tutor and Episcopalian minister (1866–1869). After 2 years at a church in Morristown, New Jersey, he returned to Yale as a professor of political economy in the fall of 1872, where he remained throughout his career.

In more than 100 articles and almost a dozen books, Sumner supported sound currency, attacked labor unions as unjustified monopolies, and championed free trade. In *What Social Classes Owe to Each Other* (1883), he reduced "most schemes of philanthropy" to the formula: "A and B put their heads together to decide what C shall be made to do for D." "C" he called the "forgotten man." Writing in the *Independent* in the late 1880s, he argued that "civil liberty" does not derive from abstract "rights," but consists of "the chance to fight the struggle for existence [against nature] for one's self," as guaranteed by "institutions" and "laws." Although references to the "struggle for existence" earned him a reputation as a ruthless "social Darwinist," some scholars have argued that this label misrepresents both the sources and substance of his views, which drew heavily on the work of Thomas Malthus and other classical British economists.

In "The Conquest of the United States by Spain" (1899), a speech delivered in the aftermath of the Spanish-American War, Sumner denounced American expansionism. The war began in political struggles in Washington and was fueled by reports of Cuba "we now know to be false." In annexing the Philippines, the United States was adopting the values for which it criticized Spain.

In *Folkways* (1907), Sumner defined *folkways* as the methods that were discovered through trial and error to best satisfy basic human needs. Mores are folkways grown moral, reflective, and coercive. They have the "authority of fact," in that there are no appeals to right or wrong beyond them. Legislation not rooted in these mores can do little to effect social change. His conclusions respecting the role of custom and tradition in shaping laws and institutions evoked the institutional conservatism of such predecessors as Edmund Burke and adumbrated the notion of spontaneous order put forward by F. A. Hayek.

In his discussion of minimalist government, especially in economic matters, Sumner provided a link between classical liberalism and present-day libertarianism. However, Sumner's thought was complex, and he qualified the anarchist implications of his libertarian conclusions with a strong emphasis on well-disciplined civil liberty.

RoB

See also Imperialism; Progressive Era; Sociology; War

Further Readings

Bannister, Robert C., ed. *On Liberty, Society, and Politics: The Essential Essays of William Graham Sumner*. Indianapolis, IN: Liberty Fund, 1992.

Curtis, Bruce. *William Graham Sumner*. Boston: Twayne, 1981.

Starr, Harris E. *William Graham Sumner*. New York: Henry Holt, 1925.

Szasz, Thomas (1920–)

Thomas Stephen Szasz was born in Budapest, Hungary, and is currently a Professor Emeritus of Psychiatry at the State University of New York Health Sciences Center in Syracuse. Although many of his colleagues regard Dr. Szasz as a bird that fouls its own nest, he is highly esteemed among many humanists, libertarians, and critics of psychiatry, including an increasingly growing number of attorneys. Libertarians are often especially attracted to him because of what they would describe as his unremitting defense of personal freedom and responsibility, two values he regards as indivisible. He has received numerous national awards, including Humanist of the Year in 1973. His "passion against coercion" has led him to oppose involuntary mental hospitalization (as well as all other involuntary treatment), and his esteem for personal responsibility has led him to oppose the insanity defense. If people commit crimes, they should, according to Dr. Szasz, be punished, "not treated." If they do not commit crimes, they should be left alone regardless of how bizarre their behavior is. Should they want help increasing their self-knowledge and understanding of others with whom they have contact, psychiatrists and other health care professionals can legitimately help them, provided that the relationship is contractual and educational and free of coercion and domination.

After emigrating from Budapest, Hungary, to the United States in 1938, Dr. Szasz attended the University of Cincinnati from 1939 to 1944, earning an undergraduate degree in physics and a medical degree. In 1956, he went to Syracuse, where he took a position as a professor of psychiatry at the Upstate Medical Center at the State University of New York, from which he retired in 1990. Besides teaching and writing, he has had a private practice throughout most of his career.

A prolific writer, he has written more than 700 articles and two dozen books (the number increases almost yearly). His most famous and most controversial book is his second one, *The Myth of Mental Illness: Foundations of a Theory of Personal Conduct*, published in 1961. He had been thinking about many ideas in that book since the 1950s, and he presented them in an address at the annual meeting of the Southern California Psychiatric Society in the fall of 1960. The central thesis of the book, crucial to understanding Dr. Szasz's point of view, is that the expression *mental illness* and its relatives are metaphors not for problems special to medicine, but for problems of living concerned with internal and external conflict involving roles or games. In his 1990 book *The Untamed Tongue*, he describes how he believes the concept of mental illness is connected to social norms or expectations:

> When a person fails to follow rules of conduct—that is, the rules most people follow—we say that he is mentally ill, and when he does not respond to conventional rewards and punishments as we want him to respond—we say he is seriously mentally ill.

He holds that, although real illness is physical and defined by such bodily criteria as lesions and organic malfunctions, what qualifies as mental illness can be almost any behavior that is perceived as unpleasant, obnoxious, or threatening to its author, others, or both. Historically, behavior classified as *mental illness* or a form of *mental disorder* has been wide ranging, including refusal to support oneself through work, reckless gambling, drug habits, unconventional sexual practices, dissatisfaction with one's physical appearance, impulsive violence, and political nonconformity (as in the former Soviet Union).

"Classifying thoughts, feelings, and behaviors as diseases is a logical and semantic error, like classifying the whale as a fish," he writes on his Web site (www.szasz .com). For him, *mental illness* no more describes a species of illness than *decoy duck* describes a species of duck. He would contend, however, that although everybody knows that decoy ducks are not ducks, people commonly think that mental illness describes a species of illness. The unquestioning belief in mental illness has profound social consequences because it provides the justification for what Dr. Szasz would describe as state-sponsored social control, as when people labeled *mentally ill* are involuntarily hospitalized. Although Dr. Szasz never denies that people can have real problems coping with life and dealing with others, he denies that those problems are properly regarded as a form of illness. What is more, although he acknowledges that some organic conditions, such as Alzheimer's disease, can influence thought and behavior, he argues that the behavior is never a disease.

By asserting that the concept of mental illness is a myth, Dr. Szasz intends, among other things, to reject a medical frame of reference for describing, understanding, and attempting to control people's actions and habits. When people regard actions and habits as illness, they are, he insists, rejecting the conception of people as free and responsible moral agents and accepting instead the conception of people as patients and victims needing the intervention, at times forced, of medical professionals. Because most people have uncritically accepted the appropriateness of applying medical concepts to disapproved behavior, we, as a society, have replaced a moral-theological outlook with a therapeutic one. By treating habits, actions, and complex social performances as illnesses, we increase the power of psychiatrists and other health care professionals while we devalue personal freedom and responsibility. (Dr. Szasz's influential writings on drug prohibition illustrate his central thesis well.)

Because of his work and the actions of civil libertarians and other social critics, there has been a growing uneasiness about coercive psychiatry, leading to legal reforms that have made it more difficult to hospitalize involuntarily those labeled *mentally ill*. His writings are important not only because they require people to question foundational definitions in psychiatry, but also because they provide a point of view for defending personal freedom and responsibility against therapeutic paternalism.

RoE

See also Coercion; Drug Prohibition; Foucault, Michel; Psychiatry

Further Readings

Szasz, Thomas. *Ceremonial Chemistry: The Ritual Persecution of Drugs, Addicts, and Pushers.* Rev. ed. Holmes Beach, FL: Learning Publications, 1985 [1974].
———. *Cruel Compassion: Psychiatric Control of Society's Unwanted.* New York: Wiley, 1994.
———. *The Myth of Mental Illness: Foundations of a Theory of Personal Conduct.* New York: Harper, 1961.
———. *Our Right to Drugs: The Case for a Free Market.* New York: Praeger, 1992.
———. *The Untamed Tongue: A Dissenting Dictionary.* LaSalle, IL: Open Court, 1990.
Vatz, Richard, and Lee Weinberg. *Thomas Szasz: Primary Values and Major Contentions.* Buffalo, NY: Prometheus Books, 1982.

T

TAFT, ROBERT A. (1889–1953)

Robert Alfonso Taft was a U.S. Senator and a prominent conservative. Taft was called "Mr. Republican" during his terms in the Senate, where he represented Ohio from 1939 until his death 14 years later. The grandson of an attorney general and the son of a president of the United States, Robert Taft was an assistant to Herbert Hoover during the First World War. At that time, Hoover was the director of the American Food Administration, which oversaw the supply and conservation of food for the duration of the war. Taft accompanied Hoover to Paris to attend the Versailles Conference, and, along with Hoover, he left the Wilson delegation on the grounds that the conference's policies were creating the conditions for another European war.

Serving in the Ohio legislature, Taft gained national stature when, in the Supreme Court, he argued against President Franklin Roosevelt's decision to criminalize all private domestic transactions in gold. In the 1938 elections, after the Congress rejected the president's attempt to pack the U.S. Supreme Court, Taft was elected to the U.S. Senate.

Taft was greatly distrustful of big government; when the Republicans gained a majority in Congress in 1946, he led the fight against continuing government controls. As chairman of the Senate Labor Committee, he managed passage of the Taft–Hartley Labor Relations Act, which outlawed "closed shops"—those that required, as a condition of employment, that a worker be a member in good standing of the union. It also permitted the states to outlaw compulsory union membership for all new employees—the so-called "Right to Work." Taft spoke extensively in the 1940s in favor of international law and an effective World Court as a solution to international problems and opposed the United Nations. As an advocate of international law and of constitutionalism, Taft opposed Harry Truman's intervention in Korea in 1950 without a declaration of war by the Congress, as he opposed Truman's seizure of the steel industry under the president's power as commander in chief. Taft barely lost the 1952 Republican presidential nomination to Dwight D. Eisenhower; despite his losing the nomination, Eisenhower later adopted Taft's principles in his Morningside Heights program of September 1952. Taft became majority leader of the U.S. Senate when the Republicans regained the majority in that body in the 1952 elections. He died in July 1953.

LL

See also Conservatism; Foreign Policy; Labor Unions; Peace and Pacifism; War

Further Readings

De John, Samuel, Jr. *Robert Taft, Economic Conservatism, and Opposition to United States Foreign Policy, 1944–1951.* Unpublished doctoral dissertation, University of Southern California, August 1976.

Patterson, James T. *Mr. Republican: A Biography of Robert A. Taft.* Boston, Houghton Mifflin, 1972.

———. "Robert A. Taft and American Foreign Policy, 1939–1945." *Watershed of Empire: Essays in New Deal Foreign Policy.* Leonard P. Liggio and James J. Martin, eds. Colorado Springs, CO: Ralph Myles, 1976.

Taft, Robert A. *A Foreign Policy for Americans.* New York: Doubleday, 1952.

TAXATION

Above the entrance to the headquarters of the Internal Revenue Service on Constitution Avenue is chiseled this quotation from Oliver Wendell Holmes: "Taxation is the price we pay for civilization." It is easy enough to see why government officials would want to put that quotation on display because it counsels people to be pleased with the taxes they pay. It is not so easy, however, to determine the accuracy or moral force of the sentiment expressed there. Taxation represents the replacement of the handshakes of commerce with the threat of force as an instrument for human governance. Although some libertarians think this threat is unnecessary to human governance, others think some modest use, although unfortunate, is unavoidable. This second position makes taxation a form of Faustian bargain: Some modest use of force is thought necessary to promote peaceful social order, but mere possession of the power to employ force will almost inevitably expand its use beyond its necessary limits.

In their treatise *A History of Taxation and Public Expenditure in the Western World*, Carolyn Webber and Aaron Wildavsky observe that all political cultures are uneasy mixtures of individualist and collectivist sentiments and orientations. In individualist cultures, human relationships are governed primarily by principles rooted in private property and freedom of contract. In collectivist cultures, contractual governance becomes rooted in common or collective property. Taxation is an instrument in a continuing war over how human relationships are to be constituted. As taxation recedes, handshakes and promises become more prominent in human governance. As taxation expands, duress, threats, and force take on greater significance.

Economists distinguish between private and common or collective property. Budgetary operations transform private property into collective property, thereby changing the governance relationships that operate within a society. An average tax rate of 40%, for instance, means that approximately 60% of the economy is organized through private property relationships, with the remaining 40% organized through collective property. This disjunction between private and collective property has a number of significant implications. One is that private property generally secures greater economic efficiency than collective property because, with private property, those who make economic decisions bear the consequences of their decisions. By contrast, with collective property, these consequences are diffused throughout the polity. Another significant implication concerns differences in the character of human relationships. When these relationships are grounded in private property, economic relationships occur in some sense among equals, in that any kind of joint activity must be mutually agreeable. In contrast, relationships grounded in collective property are those of rulership, with grantors on the one side and supplicants or petitioners on the other.

Some taxation is almost surely necessary to secure an economic order grounded in private property, and such taxation would be likely to command close to universal support. Actual levels of taxation, however, are surely significantly higher than whatever this minimal level might

be. The primary line of justification that has been advanced for the power to tax is the problem of free ridership. If taxes were replaced by voluntary contributions, it would be impossible for anyone to claim that the state was involved in expropriating private property. At the same time, it is argued, people would have strong incentives to take free rides on the contributions of others. As a result, services such as civil order and national security, which we all value, are likely to be underfunded.

Thus, taxation represents a type of *forced exchange*, as Richard Epstein explains in *Takings*. This term might appear oxymoronic at first glance, but it conveys an important truth. Government, by its nature, is not limited to purely voluntary exchanges, and, as a consequence, the problem posed by free riding might make some modicum of taxation nearly universally acceptable. Under this idealized image of taxation, taxes should mirror the voluntary payments that people would have made were it not for free riding.

The difficulty, of course, is that there is no way to truly know what the pattern of those voluntary contributions would have been. In actual tax systems, forced carrying, whereby people pay to support activities they do not value, also is a significant feature. The principle of forced exchange treats taxation as a means of pricing state-supplied services to citizens. To speak of taxes as prices, however, also has its problematical side because this simile is easily corruptible. In some cases, the forced exchanges that taxation makes possible might be beneficial to all. But in other cases, taxation will be used as an instrument for the deprivation and abridgement of property. The dark side of the Faustian bargain is that the power to tax also can be used to expropriate property, which would never occur with truly voluntary contributions. Among three adjoining neighbors, two might steal asparagus from a patch owned by the third. Should the three neighbors comprise a government and the majority support a tax on asparagus, what otherwise would have been theft will have been converted into tax policy. The best tax, after all, is always one that someone else pays, and governments offer plenty of scope to do just this.

The central feature that enables government to abridge property rights through taxation is its ability to practice tax discrimination. Consider a state that possesses an unlimited power to tax, compared with one whose power to tax is limited by a constitutional requirement of generality or nondiscrimination in taxation. If all income is taxed at, say, 10%, there is no scope for government to discriminate among taxpayers by their sources or uses of income, or by any other personal characteristic. The range of political controversy regarding taxation is limited to its rate alone.

The opportunity to practice political price discrimination greatly expands the scope for venality in politics. The possession of an unlimited power to tax increases the value of holding political office for two reasons, both of which are politically related to bribery and extortion. Economists call the political cousin to bribery *rent seeking*. If tax discrimination is a permissible outcome of tax legislation, interest groups will seek to secure favorable tax treatment. These policies will take the form of exemptions, deductions, or exclusions from the tax base, the consequences of which are to generate higher rates of tax applied to a narrower base. Should legislators be able to tax discriminate, it seems clear that there will be a market for tax legislation in which interest groups lobby for particularly desired tax provisions.

Economists label the political cousin to extortion *rent extraction*. Rent extraction is manifested in threats to tax should the tax target not respond to the demands of the threatening politician. A possible change in a tax provision can be announced and a hearing scheduled, only later to be canceled if sufficient opposition materializes, with opposition being signified by such things as campaign contributions. In this case, money is being paid for nothing but a continuation of the present tax status. In contrast, with rent seeking, money is being paid to secure some change in tax status.

A central tenet of democratic ideology is the belief that taxation is something we do to ourselves for our common benefit. Thus, it becomes reasonable to speak of taxing ourselves, in contrast to speaking of the victors as taxing the vanquished. The principle of generality in taxation, however, leads naturally to support for broad-based taxation. Although broad-based taxation would not eliminate all possible claims of tax discrimination, it would severely restrict the practice. A broad-based tax on income, where the entire base is taxed at the same rate, would conform to reasonable notions of generality in taxation. There would be no scope for one's political position to influence one's tax liability. The same rate of tax would apply to everyone, and each person's tax liability would simply depend on his own income or consumption, in conjunction with the tax rate that was enacted through the political process.

Broad-based, nondiscriminatory taxation impedes efforts to use taxation to reward or punish certain forms of activity. The principle of nondiscrimination is based on the notion that the state is neutral to all kinds of activities. Yet a great deal of tax legislation rewards or punishes specific forms of activity. Once a government acquires the power to reward or punish particular types of activity, the principle of broad-based, nondiscriminatory taxation quickly evaporates under the heat of politics. The result is an unlimited power to tax, where the only limit on the reach of the tax collector is the pragmatic one of political pressure and votes.

RW

See also Rent Seeking; State; Voluntarism

Further Readings

Adams, Charles. *For Good and Evil: The Impact of Taxes on the Course of Civilization*. London: Madison Books, 1993.

Blum, Walter J., and Harry Kalven, Jr. *The Uneasy Case for Progressive Taxation*. Chicago: University of Chicago Press, 1953.

Buchanan, James M., and Roger D. Congleton. *Politics by Principle, Not Interest: Toward Nondiscriminatory Democracy*. Cambridge: Cambridge University Press, 1998.

Epstein, Richard A. *Takings: Private Property and the Power of Eminent Domain*. Cambridge, MA: Harvard University Press, 1985.

Foldvary, Fred. *Public Goods and Private Communities*. Hants, UK: Edward Elgar, 1994.

McChesney, Fred. *Money for Nothing: Politicians, Rent Extraction, and Political Extortion*. Cambridge, MA: Harvard University Press, 1997.

Shughart, William F., II, ed. *Taxing Choice: The Predatory Politics of Fiscal Discrimination*. New Brunswick, NJ: Transaction, 1997.

Wagner, Richard E. *Fiscal Sociology and the Theory of Public Finance*. Cheltenham, UK: Edward Elgar, 2007.

Webber, Carolyn, and Aaron Wildavsky. *A History of Taxation and Expenditure in the Western World*. New York: Simon & Schuster, 1986.

TAX COMPETITION

Globalization has significantly reduced the cost of cross-border economic activity. This cost reduction has been responsible for large increases in worldwide commerce and also a dramatic expansion of international capital flows. These developments have greatly benefited consumers and the overall global economy, but they also have yielded important indirect advantages. Governments, for instance, must now compete to attract jobs and capital (or to keep jobs and capital from fleeing to jurisdictions with better policy), and this scarcity is encouraging politicians to lower tax rates and reform tax systems.

This process, known as *tax competition*, has led to sweeping changes in tax policy. Personal income tax rates have dropped, corporate tax rates have plummeted, and more than 20 governments have adopted flat tax systems. With a few exceptions, these reforms were not implemented because politicians had read economists such as Milton Friedman and Friedrich Hayek. Instead, progrowth policies were adopted to attract the geese that lay the golden eggs (or to discourage them from escaping).

The economic analysis of this process is straightforward: Monopolies are bad, competition is good. This concept is well understood in the private sector. Consumers benefit when banks, grocery stores, or pet supply stores compete for their business. The notion of tax competition simply extends the analysis to political decision making when more than one government is involved. In the absence of any constraints, there is a tendency among politicians to raise tax rates because it is in their self-interest to increase the size of government. The expansion of the public sector and the concomitant rising tax rates during most of the 20th century are certainly consistent with this public choice view of political behavior, which focuses on incentives to accumulate power and attract votes.

Globalization, however, has imposed constraints on politicians, and the process became especially important following the elections of Margaret Thatcher and Ronald Reagan. In 1979, when Margaret Thatcher became prime minister of the United Kingdom, the top personal income tax rate was 83%, and England was in terrible shape. During her tenure, she reduced the top tax rate to 40% and implemented other free-market reforms. The economy of the United Kingdom, not surprisingly, recovered, and the nation prospered.

Similarly, in 1980, Ronald Reagan was elected president in the United States. The top tax rate was then 70% and America was suffering from stagflation—a debilitating combination of inflation, stagnation, and unemployment. To restore America's economy, President Reagan slashed the top tax rate to 28%. Along with other reforms to reduce the burden of government, this tax reduction helped to restore America's economy. However, what is really interesting about the Thatcher and Reagan tax cuts is that nations all over the world have been forced to play follow-the-leader. Average top tax rates in the developed world have since dropped from more than 65% to about 40%. This shift toward better tax policy is dramatic, and it explains, at least in part, why the global economy is much stronger today than it was in the 1970s.

It is crucial to realize that politicians in other nations almost invariably cut their tax rates because of competitive pressure, not because of a philosophical belief in smaller government or lower tax rates. This strong motivational effect is why tax competition is such an important force for good policy. Even statist policymakers are compelled to do the right thing when they fear that the neighboring nations will reap advantages at their expense.

Nor is it just the personal tax rate that is at issue. Corporate tax rates have dropped, on average, by more than 20 percentage points since Thatcher and Reagan took office. Indeed, Ireland deserves the lion's share of the credit by slashing its corporate rate from 50% to 12.5%. Irish leaders turned their economy from the sick man of Europe into the Celtic Tiger. The global effect is even bigger. To compete, nations all over Europe and around the globe are racing to lower their corporate tax rates. Last, but not least, tax competition also is playing a role in the global flat tax revolution. Fifteen years ago, the only flat-tax jurisdictions were the little British territories of Hong Kong, Jersey, and Guernsey. Today, there are nearly two dozen flat-tax jurisdictions, including Russia, Slovakia, Iceland, and Estonia.

Not surprisingly, politicians from high-tax nations do not like tax competition and resent being forced to lower tax rates. Much like the owner of a town's only gas station, they want captive customers who have no choices. They prefer "tax harmonization," policies aimed at preventing taxpayers from benefitting from better tax policy in other jurisdictions. There are two forms of tax harmonization.

Explicit tax harmonization occurs when nations agree to set minimum tax rates or decide to tax at the same rate. The European Union (EU), for instance, requires that member nations impose a value-added tax (VAT) of at least 15%. The EU also has harmonized tax rates for fuel, alcohol, and tobacco, and there have been many proposals to harmonize the taxation of personal and corporate income. Under this *direct* form of tax harmonization, taxpayers are unable to benefit from better tax policy in other nations, and governments are insulated from market discipline.

Implicit tax harmonization occurs when governments tax the income their citizens earn in other jurisdictions. This policy of worldwide taxation requires governments to collect financial information on nonresident investors and to share that information with tax collectors from foreign governments. This information exchange system tends to be a one-way street because jobs and capital generally flow from high-tax to low-tax nations. Under this *indirect* form of tax harmonization, just as under the direct form, taxpayers are unable to benefit from better tax policy in other nations, and governments are insulated from market discipline.

Working through the Organisation for Economic Cooperation and Development (OECD), an international bureaucracy based in Paris, politicians seek to hinder the flow of jobs and investment from high-tax to low-tax nations. Indeed, the OECD has a "harmful tax competition" project. It even put together a blacklist of low-tax jurisdictions and threatened them with financial protectionism if they did not help high-tax nations enforce their tax laws.

Although some divisions of the OECD are more market-oriented, the bureaucrats in charge of the anti-tax competition project have an openly statist orientation. In its 1998 report, it reported that "no or only nominal" taxes are the primary reason for being identified as tax havens. The OECD also complained in various reports that low-tax policies "unfairly erode the tax bases of other countries"; tax competition is "re-shaping the desired level and mix of taxes and public spending," and tax competition hampers "the application of progressive tax rates and the achievement of redistributive goals."

The OECD's antitax competition project is bad policy, and it also is a threat to America's economic interests. According to the OECD's definition, the United States is a tax haven, and these favorable tax rules for foreign investors have helped attract more than $10 trillion of capital. But the antitax competition campaign also could have a direct impact on U.S. taxpayers because, for all intents and purposes, America would not be able to adopt a flat tax or a national sales tax if the OECD's wish-list policies became global tax rules.

Tax competition issues also have been addressed by academics. Charles Tiebout published a famous article in 1956 that introduced what became known as the Tiebout Hypothesis, which shows that tax competition is desirable because it allows people to choose jurisdictions that best match their preferences for spending and taxes. However, there also have been a number of academics who are hostile to tax competition. Advocates of this approach start with the theoretical assumption of a world with no taxes. They then hypothesize, quite plausibly, that people will allocate resources in that world in ways that maximize economic output.

They then introduce real-world considerations to the theory, such as the existence of different jurisdictions with different tax rates. These different tax rates presumably lead some taxpayers to change the allocation of their resources. However, because those resources are being reallocated on the basis of tax considerations, rather than on the underlying economic merit of various options, critics of tax competition assert that people make less efficient choices in a world with multiple tax regimes when compared with a hypothetical world with no taxes. To maximize economic efficiency, proponents of what is called capital export neutrality believe taxpayers should face the same tax rates regardless of where they work, save, shop, or invest.

Critics respond, however, by explaining that capital export neutrality (CEN) is based on several highly implausible assumptions. The CEN model, for instance, assumes that taxes are exogenous—meaning that they are independently determined. Yet the real-world experience of tax competition shows that tax rates are dependent on what is happening in other jurisdictions. Another glaring mistake in this analysis is the assumption that the global stock of capital is fixed—and, more specifically, the assumption that the capital stock is independent of the tax treatment of savings and investment. Needless to say, these are grossly unrealistic conditions.

In the real world, tax competition has played a critical role in promoting more efficient tax policy. Not only has it stimulated reductions in personal and corporate income tax rates, but it also has encouraged nations to reduce capital gains tax rates, death tax rates, wealth tax rates, and tax rates on capital income. These reforms have significantly improved incentives for productive behavior.

The existence of varying tax rates does not mean that competing tax systems automatically generate economically efficient choices. Indeed, there are even some forms of tax competition—such as special tax breaks for specific companies and specific behaviors—that almost certainly encourage suboptimal decisions. But tax competition generally encourages the right kind of tax reforms, which is an additional reason that multilateral bureaucracies, among them the OECD, the European Commission, and the United Nations, should not be permitted to hinder this liberalizing process.

The tax competition debate largely revolves around economics, but there are other important issues, particularly the role of financial privacy as a protector of human rights. Financial privacy laws are important in the tax-haven fight because they make it difficult for governments to achieve the implicit forms of tax harmonization. If a Venezuelan puts money in a New York bank or a Swede puts money in a Swiss bank, for instance, they can choose whether to report any interest earnings to their home-country tax collectors. This activity puts pressure on governments to lower tax rates. But the existence of financial privacy (thanks especially to nations with strict bank secrecy laws) means that people can shield their assets for nontax reasons as well.

Financial privacy laws have important implications because a majority of the world's population still resides in nations with governments that oppress at least some segment of the citizenry. Financial privacy laws mean that real or potential victims of ethnic, religious, sexual, and/or political persecution can shield at least some of their activities and assets from a hostile government. Likewise, there are governments that do not have the capacity to provide adequate protection against corruption, crime, and mismanagement. So-called offshore banking and fund management is a way from people in these nations to protect their assets.

Politicians from high-tax nations resent tax competition, but competition among governments has been good for taxpayers and the global economy. Tax rates have been reduced, tax reforms have been implemented, and global commerce has expanded. Along with indirect benefits, such as providing individual protection against venal or incompetent governments, low-tax jurisdictions play a valuable and desirable role.

DM

See also Globalization; Spontaneous Order; Taxation

Further Readings

Bessard, Pierre. *The European Tax Cartel and Switzerland's Role*. Lausanne, Switzerland: Institut Constant de Rebecque, 2007.

Edwards, Chris, and Veronique de Rugy. "International Tax Competition: A 21st-Century Restraint on Government." *Policy Analysis No. 431*. The Cato Institute, April 12, 2002.

McGinnis, John O. "The Political Economy of Global Multilateralism." *Chicago Journal of International Law* 1 no. 2 (2000): 381.

Mitchell, Daniel J. "The Economics of Tax Competition: Harmonization vs. Liberalization." *2004 Index of Economic Freedom*. Marc A. Miles, Edwin J. Feulner, and Mary Anastasia O'Grady, eds. Washington, DC: The Heritage Foundation and Dow Jones & Company, 2004.

———. "The Moral Case for Tax Havens." Occasional Paper No. 24, Friedrich Naumann Stiftung, December 3, 2005.

Mitchell, Daniel J., and Chris Edwards. *Global Tax Revolution: The Rise of Tax Competition and the Battle to Defend It*. Washington, DC: Cato Institute, 2008.

Rohac, Dalibor. "Evidence and Myths about Tax Competition." *New Perspectives on Political Economy* 2 no. 2 (2006): 86–115.

Teather, Richard. *The Benefits of Tax Competition*. London: Institute for Economic Affairs, 2005.

Tiebout, Charles. "A Pure Theory of Local Expenditures." *The Journal of Political Economy* 64 no. 5 (1956): 416–424.

TERM LIMITS

Rotation in office was a central feature of early American government. Under the Articles of Confederation, newly independent Americans limited delegates to Congress to no more than "three years in any term of six years."

In 1777, for instance, 7 of the 10 new state constitutions limited the terms of the executive. The Declaration of Rights in the Massachusetts Constitution of 1780, for instance, required "public officers to return to private life" so as "to prevent those, who are vested with authority, from becoming oppressors." Pennsylvania required rotation of legislators and executives to obviate "the danger of establishing an inconvenient aristocracy." Rotation in office was a venerable principle of republican governments long before the American Revolution. Political scientist Mark Petracca has outlined the importance of rotation in the ancient Republics of Athens, Rome, Venice, and Florence. The Renaissance city-state of Venice required rotation because "human nature is such that men cannot be trusted with long continuance in office of great power." This background influenced the English authors of *Cato's Letters*, which was "the most popular, quotable, esteemed source of political ideas in the colonial period," according to historian Clinton Rossiter. *Cato's Letter* No. 61 makes the case that men may well be just and represent their constituents when first in power,

> But the possession of power soon alters and vitiates their hearts, which are at the same time sure to have leavened and puffed up to an unnatural size, by the deceitful incense of false friends and the prostrate submission of parasites. First they grow indifferent to all their good designs, then drop them. Next, they lose their moderation: Afterwards, they renounce all measures with their old acquaintances and old principles, and seeing themselves in magnifying glasses, grow in conceit, a different species from their fellow subjects. And so, by sudden degrees become insolent, rapacious and tyrannical, ready to catch all means, often the vilest and most oppressive, to raise their fortunes as high as their imaginary greatness. . . . A rotation, therefore, in power and magistracy, is essentially necessary to a free government.

However, the constraining effect of real term limits on politicians created opposition. By the mid-1780s, six popular governors had been rotated out of office. In 1784, the Republican Society in Pennsylvania argued against rotation on democratic grounds: "the privilege of the people in elections, is so far infringed as they are thereby deprived of the right of choosing those persons whom they would prefer."

Despite these doubts, the Virginia plan presented by Edmund Randolph to the Constitutional Convention in the summer of 1787 included a limit of one 2-year term for members of the House; in addition, no incumbent could be reelected. But the measure was dropped because most delegates believed that short terms and voluntary rotation would ensure adequate representation.

Rotation was a frequent topic of debate at the state-ratifying conventions. At the New York convention, Alexander Hamilton maintained that term limits in the Articles of Confederation were an understandable overreaction to British usurpations: "The zeal for liberty," he argued, "became predominant and excessive." Rather, the absence of term limits would provide "a principle of strength and stability in the organization of our government, and vigor in its operation." Gilbert Livingston countered that incumbents would become entrenched and have "nearly an appointment for life." Although the rotation amendment prevailed in New York, it was not sent to the states by the first Congress, and, as a result, the Republic was launched with no term limits on national officeholders.

For over a century, the optimists were right about voluntary rotation. Stints of one or two terms prevailed in the House of Representatives, and George Washington's example of a two-term limit for the presidency was followed until 144 years later, when Franklin Roosevelt, breaking precedent, won a third term in 1940. Two years after Roosevelt died during his fourth term in 1945, Congress reported out the 22nd Amendment, which was ratified in 1951, limiting the time a president could serve. But Congress was in no hurry to address careerism in Congress. The arguments put forward on both sides in the modern term limits movement echo those of the founding period.

In addition, U.S. Term Limits board member Ed Crane argued that the careerist Congress and its seniority system create "adverse preselection." Those people who are successful in the private sector "might be willing to spend some time in Congress as a public service, but not if their time has no impact." That attitude makes them "precisely the kinds of men and women who should be in Congress," wrote Crane. Instead, the field is left to the aspiring careerist, someone unrepresentative from the first day in office. Moreover, political scientist James Payne, among others, has demonstrated that a "culture of spending" exists in Congress, in which members begin to view state intervention more favorably as they spend time in office—even those members who were initially elected on promarket agendas.

Behind the arguments on term limits lie questions regarding whether Congress is in fact representative. Most term limit supporters believe that Congress does not represent the American people; most opponents of term limits disagree. Incumbent entrenchment and adverse preselection create a dilemma: Even when Congress is unpopular, incumbents are almost always easily reelected. Mandatory term limits would, it was felt, break this cycle. In 1990, the term limits movement became increasingly popular. Government had grown ever-more expensive and imposing, while the approval of government and politicians declined to historic lows. The last third of the 20th century saw a sharp erosion in the belief that government is representative of the people. Over two-thirds of the electorate believed that Congress primarily benefited the government and big special interests. This public disapproval of the federal government was not reflected in elections, however; a record 98.3% of House incumbents were reelected in 1988.

These trends set the stage for the first serious push for congressional term limits in 200 years. Incumbents were not about to surrender power by limiting their own terms. But 22 states had a viable initiative process, and in 1990, activists in California, Oklahoma, and Colorado organized petition drives to propose term limits directly to the voters. Oklahoma's state limits passed easily, without organized opposition. The California effort was launched by antitax leader Lee Phelps, joined by libertarian activist Mike Ford, and Lew Uhler of the National Tax Limitation Committee, with former legislator Pete Schabarum providing vital support. They were successful in getting two propositions on the California ballot in 1990. Proposition 140 combined lifetime limits of 6 years in the House and 8 years in the Senate with a cut in legislative budgets and an end to legislative pensions. Proposition 131 coupled 12-year term limits with campaign regulation and government funding of campaigns. Pro-term limits forces gathered $700,000 for radio ads and squeaked by with 52%; Proposition 131 failed with 37%.

Colorado overwhelmingly approved term limits: The limits also applied to the Colorado congressional delegation. Authored by state legislator Terry Considine, the measure sailed through with 71% of the vote. The legislature "rewarded" Considine by putting him on the Agriculture Committee—his farm-free district was in suburban Denver—and taking away his good parking place.

California's victory against strong opposition and Considine's creative approach in Colorado convinced a number of people around the country that there was an effective way to limit the emergence of a professional political class. Most states, however, could not vote on an equivalent initiative until 1992. The exception was Washington State, which alone decided the question in 1991. The issue of term limits was amplified by the details of the initiative: It imposed retroactive term limits of 6 years for the House.

Polls throughout the state indicated that opponents of term limits were unlikely to succeed in overcoming 70% support for the measure. As a consequence, they were able to recast the nature of the debate by claiming that, without the protection of senior members of Congress, California would divert water from the northwest, and Congress would allow oil drilling close to Washington's coast. They also charged that some backers supported the initiative as a way to help abolish the Environmental Protection Agency. Meanwhile, House Speaker Tom Foley of Washington argued that term limits would seriously compromise the power of the state delegation in Congress if they were to lose their seniority in Congress.

The result was that term limits lost with 46% of the vote, which stunned the term limits movement. Rather than retrenching, however, the movement to limit terms of office at the federal level adopted an aggressive strategy and managed to introduce initiatives in no less than 14 states in 1992—a national record for any issue. The result was an astounding victory in support of term limits, with all 14 states voting to approve these measures, with an average victory margin of two to one. Voters enacted the biggest legislative reform since women's suffrage. The initiatives followed the Colorado example of combining congressional term limits with state legislative term limits. Even voters in Washington reversed ground, imposing term limits on Foley and his fellow Congressmen. In 1994, this success was duplicated; initiatives were introduced in nine states and passed in eight of them. The sole defeat was in Utah, where the legislature had imposed softer term limits to preempt the popular vote. Unfortunately, these victories at the congressional level were overturned by a decision of the Supreme Court in 1995. In a case hinging on the constitutionality of setting term limits of Arkansas members of Congress, the Court ruled in *U.S. Term Limits v. Thornton* that states had no authority to impose such limitations. Subsequently, term limits for state legislators have been ruled unconstitutional in four states: Massachusetts, Oregon, Washington, and Wyoming.

Still, term limits are in effect in 15 state legislatures, with 268 legislators termed out in the 2006 elections. The effects of term limits in these states have been widely studied by political scientists. There is disagreement about whether term limits have affected the influence of lobbyists. Some have claimed that citizen legislators are less prone to listen to lobbyists, whereas others have argued that lobbyists have become an increasingly important source of information for newcomers. Most people agree that power has shifted from the lower to the upper bodies of state legislatures, as term-limited house members obtain office in their states' senates, bringing with them political experience and ambition for federal office. Also, the executive branch seems to have gained influence relative to the legislative branch in term-limited states.

There is much evidence that term limits have increased diversity in state legislatures along racial, ethnic, gender, and party lines. Minorities and women have experienced unprecedented electoral success since term limits were enacted. Moreover, term limits have ended virtual one-party rule in some states. For instance, in Arkansas, the Democratic Party continued its post-Reconstruction domination of state politics well into the 1990s, despite a significant increase in registered Republican voters. Democratic legislators, who had held office for decades, were finally forced out due to term limits, giving Republican candidates realistic chances to win those seats and introducing party competition to the state.

Although the courts and Congress have blocked federal term limits, they have not restored confidence in government. Term limits remain popular with the American public and with most libertarians, who have been at the forefront of efforts to restore citizen legislatures. The momentum to limit legislative terms, however, has slowed dramatically since its peak in the mid-1990s, leaving the future of the movement, especially at the federal level, much in doubt.

EO

See also Constitutionalism; Corruption; Democracy; Rent Seeking

Further Readings

Carey, John M., Richard G. Niemi, and Lynda W. Powell. *Term Limits in State Legislatures.* Ann Arbor: University of Michigan Press, 2000.

Crane, Edward H., "Reclaiming the Political Process." *Market Liberalism: A Paradigm for the 21st Century.* David Boaz and Edward H. Crane, eds. Washington, DC: Cato Institute, 1993.

Erickson, Stephen C. "The Entrenching of Incumbency: Reelections in the U.S. House of Representatives, 1790–1994." *The Cato Journal* 14 no. 3. Available from http://www.cato.org.

Hummel, Marta. "The Empire Strikes Back: A History of Political and Judicial Attacks on Term Limits." *U.S. Term Limits Foundation Outlook Series* 6 no. 2 (January 1998).

Kull, Steven, Principal Investigator. "Expecting More Say: The American Public on Its Role in Government Decisionmaking." Center on Policy Attitudes, Washington, DC, May 10, 1999.

Malbin, Michael J. "Federalists v. Antifederalists: The Term-Limitation Debate at the Founding." *Limiting Legislative Terms.* Benjamin and Malbin, eds. Washington, DC: CQ Press, 1992.

O'Keefe, Eric. *Who Rules America.* Spring Green, WI: Citizen Government Foundation, 1999.

Petracca, Mark P. "Rotation in Office: The History of an Idea." *Limiting Legislative Terms.* Gerald Benjamin and Michael J. Malbin, eds. Washington, DC: CQ Press, 1992.

THOREAU, HENRY DAVID (1817–1862)

Henry David Thoreau was an American naturalist, a lecturer, and an abolitionist. Thoreau was the author of perhaps the most radical and influential essay in the history of American political philosophy, "Civil Disobedience." This series of reflections on a night Thoreau spent in the Concord, Massachusetts, jail for tax resistance proclaimed "that government is best which governs not at all" and urged its readers to "withdraw their support, both in person and property" from governments that make and enforce unjust laws. The essay had a profound impact on two of the 20th century's greatest political activists—Mohandas K. Gandhi and Martin Luther King, Jr.

Thoreau's tax resistance, which led to his being jailed in Concord in 1846, was occasioned by his opposition to slavery. Thoreau was an abolitionist, as was his father, and there is some evidence that both the Thoreau family home in Concord and Henry's famous cottage on Walden Pond, a short distance outside the village, were stops on the Underground Railroad that carried escaped slaves to freedom. A lifelong resident of Concord, Thoreau and his antislavery views were well known to his neighbors and were not regarded as either shocking or scandalous.

Thoreau, in contrast, was both shocked and scandalized when he visited the village from Walden one day in 1846 and found his neighbors enthusiastically preparing for the newly declared Mexican War. Thoreau regarded this war as nothing but an ignoble effort on the part of proslavery forces in Congress to build up their voting strength by annexing Texas. When asked for payment of his annual poll tax—much needed this year, he was told, because of the war effort—he refused. The constable, a longtime friend, told Thoreau he had no interest in locking him up and would pay the tax for him if Thoreau could not raise the necessary funds. Again Thoreau refused, and this time he was jailed. Within 24 hours, his tax had been paid against his will by members of his family, so he spent only one night in prison. That one night was sufficient time, however, for him to gather his thoughts on the proper relationship of the individual to the state.

Two years later, he committed these thoughts to paper for a lecture he called "The Rights and Duties of the Individual in Relation to Government," which was subsequently published as "Resistance to Civil Government" (1849) and finally as "Civil Disobedience" (1866), the title under which we know it today. Thoreau begins his famous essay by inquiring into the nature and justification of the state.

> I heartily accept the motto,—"That government is best which governs least"; and I should like to see it acted up to

more rapidly and systematically. Carried out, it finally amounts to this, which I also believe,—"That government is best which governs not at all"; and when men are prepared for it, that will be the kind of government which they will have.

In the interim, Thoreau argued, until such time as we are fully prepared for a government that "governs not at all," we should live peaceably with the state—unless and until it adopts policies that require us to participate in or assist with the perpetration of injustice. At that point, Thoreau asserts, it is incumbent on every moral person to refuse cooperation with the state. So, in light of the persistence of slavery and the waging of the Mexican War, "[h]ow does it become a man to behave toward this American government today? I answer that he cannot without disgrace be associated with it." As for Thoreau, not only did he refuse to pay his taxes; not only did he write that "I cannot for an instant recognize that political organization as my government which is the slave's government also"; in addition, he recorded in his journal that "[m]y thoughts are murder to the State; I endeavor in vain to observe nature; my thoughts involuntarily go plotting against the State. I trust that all just men will conspire."

Although not all just men have rallied to Thoreau's call for support and solidarity, many have. His political views were not influential during his lifetime, yet they have steadily grown in influence over the decades. Two of the most important figures in the history of philosophical anarchism, Leo Tolstoy and Emma Goldman, learned much from Thoreau's brief excursion into political philosophy. Still others were forced to acknowledge the power of his ideas after Mohandas K. Gandhi used them to bring the British Empire to its knees and after Martin Luther King, Jr. used them to effect a civil rights revolution in Thoreau's native land.

JR

See also Abolitionism; Anarchism; Individualist Anarchism; Slavery in America; State

Further Readings

Dahlberg, Edward. "Thoreau and Walden." *The Edward Dahlberg Reader*. Paul Carroll, ed. New York: New Directions, 1967.

Parrington, Vernon Louis. "Henry Thoreau: Transcendental Economist." *Main Currents in American Thought*. New York: Harcourt, Brace, 1930.

Stevenson, Robert Louis. "Henry David Thoreau: His Character and Opinions." *Familiar Studies of Men and Books*. New York: Charles Scribner's Sons, 1925.

Thoreau, Henry David. *Political Writings*. Nancy L. Rosenblum, ed. Cambridge: Cambridge University Press, 1996.

TOCQUEVILLE, ALEXIS DE (1805–1859)

Alexis de Tocqueville was one of the foremost scholars of the French Revolution and of the early American republic. Although he was a member of both the Académie Française and the Chamber of Deputies, Tocqueville is best remembered for his work as a political theorist. His observations on monarchical and representative government, commerce, and individual liberty make him perhaps the most influential of all modern social commentators. Tocqueville emphasized that healthy societies develop naturally from the free pursuit of legitimate ends; he mistrusted both aristocracy and centralized government, and he stressed the limits of any government's ability to enact social change.

Paradoxically, for a thinker with libertarian sympathies, Tocqueville also mistrusted what he termed *individualism*. He argued that only under liberty could individuals construct the social bonds that constituted a fully mature and developed community and that intense communal activity was the natural outcome of liberty. Tocqueville argued that, without liberty, individuals would either embrace a hostile, isolated individualism, largely bereft of morality, or else they would become servile creatures of the state. Unsurprisingly, he disdained both of these outcomes. In a similar vein, Tocqueville mistrusted great concentrations of wealth. He feared the undue influence that extraordinary wealth could exert on governments, and he held that concentrated wealth was one of the chief evils produced by a government that grew beyond its proper bounds. Without unfair government privilege, Tocqueville thought, competition among individuals and the vicissitudes of ordinary life would exert a broadly leveling influence, enriching the poor and reining in the wealthy.

These themes run throughout his political works. Tocqueville's unfinished masterpiece *L'Ancien Régime et la Révolution* argued that the French Old Regime improperly individualized and atomized French society. As the central government grew in power, it obliterated the private communal bonds that could otherwise have brought the citizens a more equitable and enriching social life. Each person was instead brought into a relationship of dependence on the state, in which the individual sought to extract state privileges from those around him, rather than living through peaceful exchange. Tocqueville documented how old, local forms of justice and administration were progressively vitiated, and how Paris, the capital city, had grown enormously in population and concentrated wealth. Tocqueville ascribed all of these developments to the state's inordinate and unchecked power.

When the government was no longer able to keep up with the many demands on its finances, it collapsed. Yet

Tocqueville was no friend of the French Revolution: Although his work was never finished, it is clear from his notes and from indications in his extant work that Tocqueville intended to argue that the Revolution actually systematized and reinforced the Old Regime's centralization of political power. "When they envisaged all the social and administrative reforms subsequently carried out by our Revolutionaries, the idea of free political institutions never crossed their minds," Tocqueville acidly wrote. Vigorous yet arbitrary rules of administration prevailed instead, coupled with a fierce insistence on national unity, of which the state was the only guarantor. Tocqueville found all of this inimical to liberty.

Once a minority view, Tocqueville's analysis of the French Revolution has in recent years become the consensus among academic historians. These historians have for the most part rejected Marx's interpretation that the Revolution was a symptom of class warfare. Yet Tocqueville's critique of state power is more far-reaching than many historians and political thinkers are prepared to acknowledge; far from being a conservative, he condemned Old Regime paternalism even where it seemed the most harmless or well intentioned. As Tocqueville wrote, "Paradoxically enough, what made things worse was that the King and his Ministers were inspired by purely altruistic ideals; for by showing that methods of violence can be employed with good intentions by people of good will, they set a dangerous precedent." Indeed, Tocqueville explicitly likened the Old Regime to socialism, in that both held property to a revocable privilege, not an inherent right: "This idea is basic to our modern socialism, and it is odd to find it emerging for the first time in France under a despotic monarchy." The idea that the Old Regime and socialism had much in common was a frequent theme among such 19th-century French liberals as Charles Comte and Charles Dunoyer, and it remains influential among libertarian historians today.

Tocqueville is best known for *De la démocratie en Amérique*, a sprawling analysis of American political and social life in the age of Andrew Jackson that was first published in 1835–1840. Europeans of his own day admired Tocqueville for the depth of his firsthand knowledge. From 1831–1832, Tocqueville had traveled extensively throughout the United States and interviewed people in every stratum of society, including Native Americans, slaves, merchants, clergy, and the president. Tocqueville's analysis is commonly cited even today by academics and popular pundits alike, and it is without a doubt one of the most important political texts of the modern era.

Tocqueville's understanding of American society emphasized the liberty, egalitarianism, and entrepreneurship of the new republic. He found that, in contrast to Europeans of the same period, Americans tended to discount social rank and mixed freely with different social classes. He argued that this social egalitarianism was only natural in a flourishing commercial society and that liberty had tended on the whole to strengthen rather than weaken Americans' virtue. Freedom of the press had never been as widespread as it then was in America. American newspapers illustrated to Tocqueville American entrepreneurship and the American love of liberty, and these qualities positively astonished him.

His relationship to American egalitarianism was more complex. He admired the notion that no one should possess arbitrary governmental power. He despised slavery and condemned the laws and mores supporting it. Yet he also feared that equality of rank and condition might paradoxically lead to despotism: "As conditions become more equal among people," he wrote, "individuals seem of less and society of greater importance . . . every citizen, having grown like the rest, is lost in the crowd, and nothing stands out conspicuously but the great and imposing image of the people itself." Tocqueville knew all too well that tyrants might easily appropriate this image, as they had done in France. Thus, one strongly libertarian reading of *De la démocratie en Amérique* is that it is a story of American decline—from Jeffersonian liberty, to Jacksonian equality, to an all-powerful state that will one day emerge as the avatar of the common man. "The idea of rights inherent in certain individuals is rapidly disappearing . . . the idea of the omnipotence and sole authority of society at large is coming to fill its place," Tocqueville worried, with barely a pause for genuine liberty.

There are inconsistencies in Tocqueville's defense of liberty, which are manifest in his approach toward the French colonies. Tocqueville wrote about Algeria first as a private citizen and then as a commissioned representative of the Chamber of Deputies. As Tocqueville scholar Jennifer Pitts has written, "Tocqueville's writings on Algeria imply . . . that nation-building legitimated the suspension of principles of human equality and self-determination, and that French glory justified any aggression the nation could muster." In 1841, he wrote, "Any people that easily gives up what it has taken and chooses to retire peacefully to its original borders proclaims that its age of greatness is over. It visibly enters the period of its decline." Although few were as frank as Tocqueville about the massive costs, the violence, and the difficulties of colonialism, he nonetheless supported these endeavors and spent much of the 1840s defending this policy before the Chamber of Deputies. To his credit, however, Tocqueville always urged the immediate and unconditional abolition of slavery in all French territories. Perhaps naively, he often hoped that colonialism could be achieved without violence, a notion that history has abundantly falsified.

JTK

See also Civil Society; Democracy; Entrepreneurship; Equality; French Revolution; Liberalism, Classical

Further Readings

Aron, Raymond. *Main Currents in Sociological Thought: I. Montesquieu, Comte, Marx, Tocqueville, the Sociologists and the Revolution of 1848.* Richard Howard and Helen Weaver, trans. New York: Basic Books, 1965.

Epstein, Joseph. *Alexis de Tocqueville: Democracy's Guide.* New York: HarperCollins, 2006.

Tocqueville, Alexis de. *Democracy in America.* George Lawrence, trans., J. P. Mayer, ed. New York: Harper & Row, 1988.

———. *The Old Regime and the French Revolution.* Stuart Gilbert, trans. New York: Anchor Doubleday, 1955.

———. *Writings on Empire and Slavery.* Jennifer Pitts, ed. and trans. Baltimore: Johns Hopkins University Press, 2001.

TRACY, DESTUTT DE (1754–1836)

Antoine-Louis-Claude Destutt de Tracy was an economist and a political theorist. Destutt de Tracy was a *philosophe* and one of the founders in the 1790s of the classical liberal republican group known as the *Idéologues*, which included Condorcet, Constant, Say, and Madame de Staël. He was active in politics under several regimes spanning the Revolution and the Restoration, and he was an influential author during his lifetime. When the Estates-General were called to meet in 1789, although a member of an aristocratic family that had been ennobled twice (hence his name), he joined the Third Estate and renounced his title. He was later elected to the Constituent Assembly and served in the army under the Marquis de Lafayette in 1792. During the Terror, he was imprisoned and escaped execution only because Maximilien Robespierre beat him to the scaffold. It was during his period of imprisonment that he read the works of Etienne Condillac and John Locke and began working on his theory of *idéologie*. During the Directory, Tracy was active in educational reform, especially in creating a national system of education. His membership in the Senate during the Consulate and Empire gave him many opportunities to express his ideological opposition to Napoleon's illiberal regime, which culminated in 1814 with Tracy's call for the removal of the Emperor. He was rewarded later that year with the restoration of his noble title by Louis XVIII. Nevertheless, he continued to support the liberal opposition during the restoration of Louis XVIII and Charles X. Although Tracy was active in bringing to power a more liberal, constitutional monarchy during the July Revolution of 1830, he quickly became disillusioned with the results.

Tracy coined the term *ideology* shortly after his appointment to the *Institut National* in 1796 to refer to his "science of ideas," which attempted to create a secure foundation for all the moral and political sciences by closely examining our sensations and ideas as these interacted with our physical environment. His deductive methodology for the social sciences was to have much in common with that of the Austrian School of Economics, which emerged after 1870. For Tracy, *ideology* referred to a liberal social and economic philosophy that provided the basis for a strong defense of private property, individual liberty, the free market, and constitutional limits to the power of the state, preferably a republic modeled on that of the United States. For Napoleon, *ideology* was a term of abuse that he directed against his liberal opponents in the *Institut National.* It was this negative sense of the term that Marx had in mind in his writings on ideology. (He called Tracy a *fischblütige Bourgeoisdoktrinär*—a fish-blooded bourgeois doctrinaire.)

The impact of Tracy's political and economic ideas was considerable. His *Commentary and Review of Montesquieu's Spirit of Laws* (1811) was much admired by Thomas Jefferson, who translated it and had it published in America at a time when a French edition was impossible due to Napoleon's censorship. In the *Commentary*, Tracy criticized Montesquieu's defense of monarchy and supported an American-style republic that operated in the context of an economic order based on free markets. Tracy's multivolume work, *Elements of Ideology* (1801–1815), is his magnum opus, the fourth volume of which appeared in 1815 and dealt with political economy. This volume also was translated and published by Jefferson in 1817. The whole work was quickly translated into the major European languages and influenced a new generation of Italian, Spanish, and Russian liberals who were involved in revolutionary activity in the early 1820s—the Carbonari in France and Italy and the Decembrists in Russia. One of Tracy's most significant economic insights was that "society is purely and solely a continual series of exchanges," and his broader social theory is based on working out the implications of this notion of free exchange. Within France, Tracy's work influenced the thinking of the novelist Stendhal, the historian Augustin Thierry, and the political economists and lawyers Charles Comte and Charles Dunoyer.

DMH

See also Comte, Charles; Dunoyer, Charles; French Revolution; Liberalism, Classical; Montesquieu, Charles de Secondat de

Further Readings

Destutt de Tracy, Antoine-Louis-Claude. *A Commentary and Review of Montesquieu's Spirit of Laws.* Thomas Jefferson, trans. New York: Burt Franklin, 1969 [1811].

———. *A Treatise on Political Economy.* Thomas Jefferson, trans. Georgetown: Joseph Milligan, 1817. New York: A. M. Kelley, 1970.

Head, Brian. *Ideology and Social Science: Destutt de Tracy and French Liberalism.* Dordrecht: M. Nijhoff. Boston: Hingham, 1985.

Kennedy, Emmet. "'Ideology' from Destutt de Tracy to Marx." *Journal of the History of Ideas* 40 no. 3 (1979): 353–368.

———. *A Philosophe in the Age of Revolution: Destutt de Tracy and the Origins of "Ideology."* Philadelphia: American Philosophical Society, 1978.

Klein, Daniel, "Deductive Economic Methodology in the French Enlightenment: Condillac and Destutt de Tracy." *History of Political Economy* 17 no. 1 (1985): 51–71.

Welch, Cheryl B. *Liberty and Utility: The French Idéologues and the Transformation of Liberalism.* New York: Columbia University Press, 1984.

TRANSPORTATION

The transportation policy of a government constrained by libertarian principles would aim to establish the institutional framework that would enable private entities to supply all the services that transportation users would be prepared to pay for, taking into account characteristics such as safety, frequency, and comfort. In some circumstances, government might have to assist in the provision of the services that users were not prepared to pay for—for example, roads that were specifically needed for national defense but have little other use—but these exceptions are almost certainly rare.

The movement of people and goods is critically important to interaction among individuals and to the development of social and commercial activities. It can take place on land, on water, and in the air. People have a propensity to travel. They may do so to obtain more suitable employment, better housing, and better shopping selections or to enjoy their leisure. As incomes rise, the proportion of income spent on transportation increases. In all countries, the rich tend to rely on motorized mobility—two-wheelers and automobiles—to travel more than the poor. Wealthy individuals only rarely use their increased income to reduce their own travel (e.g., by persuading others to travel to them). In all areas of the world, increases in wealth (or decreases in poverty) are associated with increased travel.

Travelers use their legs, animal power, wheeled vehicles, ships, or aircraft, all of which can be individually owned and controlled. But their movement is facilitated by infrastructure—roads, ports, and air traffic control—that is generally provided and controlled by government. The main transportation problems today arise out of the inadequacy or misuse of infrastructure. However, the safety and regulation of vehicles also pose intractable problems.

Safety on the world's roads is so poor that over a million people a year are estimated to be killed on them. This huge toll is associated with poor management of roads, which, in turn, can be associated with a lack of effective property rights. Safety probably could be improved if—as in maritime transportation—insurers were responsible for the testing and licensing of the drivers and vehicles insured by them. But it is beyond the capability of most governments even to enforce laws requiring road users to be insured against claims from those they may injure.

Vehicle regulation impacts not only safety, but also the provision of public transportation. In Western countries, it has generally been accepted that public transportation must be supplied by a government-supported monopoly and that it cannot be operated at a profit. Yet Robert Cervero has identified many profitable private systems outside the United States that provide frequent reliable service, among them those in Belfast, Buenos Aires, Manila, Singapore, and a few within the country, such as the legal jitney services in Atlantic City and the illegal ones in New York City. Many of these successful systems have the following characteristics: Their ownership is private, the vehicles and operating systems are small, and private "route associations" coordinate the operations of privately owned vehicles.

Unfortunately, the managers of public transport in most Western cities, which tend to be more responsive to labor unions than to users, prefer public ownership, large vehicles, large systems using fixed rails, and centralized management. The resulting services do not respond to the travel needs of modern, decentralized cities, and these public transport systems are generally unable to cover their operating costs out of revenues, much less their capital costs.

Land transportation involves the movement of people or goods by rail or road. Railroads are generally operated as commercial entities, but most roads are in the public sector and operate, like public parks, outside the market economy. This divergence makes it difficult to compare and coordinate road and rail services.

In the 19th century, before the advent of motorized road transportation, railroads were alleged to have substantial monopoly power and were economically regulated. At the beginning of the 21st century, railroads in most countries are subject to keen competition from road and air travel, and this competition should provide sufficient regulation. Railroads are particularly suitable for carrying freight over large distances and thus are particularly appropriate in Canada, China, India, Russia, and the United States. Railroads, however, are much less competitive for passenger transport, where their main strength is in dense urban areas and in linking large urban areas 100 to 300 miles apart. Inasmuch as railroads are commercially operated, they pose no significant policy problems to a government, which would expect them to pay their way or go out of business.

Most publicly owned roads are run socialistically by politically appointed officials with scant regard to costs, profit, or loss. Road users are not required to pay the costs arising out of their use of roads, and road providers spend taxpayers' funds without regard to market criteria. As a result, road problems include excessive congestion, waste, and, in some countries, massive deterioration because providing new roads is politically more attractive than maintaining existing ones. The application of private ownership and commercial principles to roads would almost certainly make them more responsive to the wishes of road users. Only governments are in a position to establish the necessary institutional arrangements for such reforms, which could include regulations to protect the public from possible abuse by private owners.

However, governments do not willingly surrender the kind of power involved in the ownership and control of roads. When considering the transition to the free-market provision of roads, it is useful to distinguish between local roads, giving access to properties, and long-distance roads, designed to connect different areas.

Local roads are generally regarded as public goods that have to be provided by government to protect residents from being exploited by monopolistic road owners. But it is more useful to regard them as part of community infrastructure, like sewerage or street lighting. So long as these facilities are controlled by local residents, either by property associations or local government, the fears of exploitation seem far-fetched. Building owners do not exploit guests or tenants who use the elevators. All in a community have an interest in the existence of high-quality services if only to protect the value of their properties.

Users of long-distance roads do not share these common interests, so the roads have to be provided by outside entities. Such roads were privately provided in the United Kingdom from the 17th to the 19th centuries and in the United States from the 18th to the 19th centuries. In Britain there were more than 1,100 "Turnpike Trusts" providing over 22,000 miles of road, whereas in the United States more than 3,000 companies financed, built, and operated more than 30,000 miles. All were toll roads. Many were put out of business in the 19th century by the superior performance of the railroads. The beginning of the 20th century coincided with the prevalence of "Progressivism," a collectivist ideology based on European socialist movements. In that period, it seemed appropriate for governments to provide long-distance "free" roads, and most road tolls were abolished in both the United Kingdom and the United States.

In 1909, the British government established a "Road Fund," fed mainly by special duties on motor fuel, to enable "owners of motor vehicles in combination and under state guidance to spend money on roads for their mutual benefit." This idea crossed the Atlantic; the first U.S. dedicated road fund was established in Oregon in 1919, and others quickly followed. It was believed then that these funds would enable road users to get, under state guidance, the roads for which they were prepared to pay. However, this goal did not happen in either the United Kingdom or the United States because these funds could not be targeted on specific roads, and their allocation to different projects became politicized.

In the 21st century, there are electronic means of charging for road use without vehicles even having to stop at toll booths. In the United States, road users are able to set up "EZPass" accounts with road providers and have these accounts automatically debited when passing electronic "readers." Similar arrangements can be made in Australia, France, Spain, and other countries. In Singapore, motorists may purchase plastic "Cash Cards" that lose value as they pass designated "pricing points." Special fees can be imposed to charge for the use of congested roads. These systems have been in operation in Singapore since 1975, in Scandinavia since 1986, and in London since 2003. There are no longer technical difficulties in charging for the use of most roads, which can be done by direct tolling, manual or electronic, or, in the case of government-owned roads, by imposts on items associated with their use, such as motor fuel or tires.

There are other obstacles to the private provision of roads, but they are by no means insuperable. Among them is acquiring the necessary land—the right of way. This acquisition constitutes a special problem for those who are opposed to governments using their power of eminent domain to take land from private owners. However, these difficulties can be dealt with in a variety of ways. For example, it is often possible to find space for additional road lanes within existing road rights of way. Such surplus land has been recently used for road expansion in both Virginia and California. It also is sometimes possible to convert to road use underutilized railway rights of way, which exist in many areas. The Pennsylvania Turnpike and the Port-of-Spain "busway" in Trinidad were built on abandoned railway rights of way. Furthermore, private road providers do not have to advertise their intentions and can assemble rights of way in secret, as is done for the construction of pipelines.

Another obstacle to private ownership of the roads is the competition they must face from so-called free roads. However, under a regime of *shadow tolls*, road providers can be reimbursed an agreed amount for each vehicle kilometer "produced" on their roads, the payments being based on traffic counts. This method of payment would require no toll booths. Such contracts between government and private road owners already exist in Britain, Finland, Portugal, and Uruguay. Payments can be out of the government's general funds or out of dedicated road funds.

Thus, there is no problem in providing new toll roads by private owners, as is currently happening in Japan, France, Spain, and many other countries. Privatizing existing roads is much more difficult because of opposition to paying for the use of a facility that has appeared to have been free. However, privatization has been successfully done in Singapore, London, and Scandinavia. The politically easiest way to introduce private ownership to the road sector may be to allow the private sector to provide additional priced lanes, with the charges being varied electronically to ensure congestion-free travel on these lanes at all times. Such lanes were first introduced on State Route 91 in California in 1995 and have since been successfully copied in San Diego (1996), Minneapolis (2005), and Denver (2006). But even roads remaining in the public sector could be substantially improved by applying to them the familiar principles used by commercial entities: accountability, charges that cover costs, and investment for profitability. These commercial principles are used in public utilities all over the world and in the operation of toll roads, such as the state-owned New Jersey Turnpike.

As with railroads and some roads, shipping services have been privately provided since the dawn of the market economy. Indeed, Phoenician, Arab, and Dutch traders, among numerous others, provided a major impetus to their development. The design, construction, and operation of vessels can be carried out by private entities, which also can ensure vessels and their cargoes against the risks inherent in transportation on water.

The private sector may be less suited to protect trade routes against pirates and to facilitate services (such as lighting, marking, and dredging) that are required for safe passage, especially in coastal areas and in the vicinity of ports. These duties are often left to government agencies, which attempt to recover the costs by the imposition of port dues. However, there is nothing inherent in these services that prevents them from being supplied by private firms.

Government agencies, or government-approved monopolies, operate most major ports despite the fact that ports have been privately operated throughout history. There are several factors that account for this government involvement in controlling port facilities. First, most governments have chosen to follow the Roman legal tradition of arrogating to themselves jurisdiction over the beaches and foreshores surrounding their territories, ostensibly to make these areas freely accessible to all. From this practice evolved the idea that port facilities should be available to all users on equal terms, which led to the concept of "Trust Ports" run by public bodies in the public interest. Second, the control of ports is generally regarded as important for purposes of defense. Third, governments throughout the ages have attempted to control trade entering and leaving their territories to enable tariffs to be levied and to control the importation of substances deemed dangerous. Finally, the control of ports permits government to impose port dues, which, it is argued, are necessary to keep the shipping channels safe.

Since 1910, the United States has developed the concept of the *landlord port*, which enables government to carry out public functions, such as dredging and import tariff collection, while leaving to the private sector such activities as warehousing and cargo handling, which can be carried out competitively, even within a single port.

A government that operated more in keeping with libertarian principles would encourage the private and competitive provision of port facilities, relying on competition and free entry to protect the interests of shippers and traders. Where a single port has a dominant influence over a small territory, as, say, in Singapore, government might possibly have to impose regulations to ensure that port users are not harmed by monopoly power exerted by port managers or labor unions.

Most of the discussion on shipping and ports applies equally to air transportation and to airports. There are no convincing reasons for aircraft to be operated by government agencies, for governmental control of fares and timetables, or even of safety, a matter that could probably be handled by the industry and private insurers, as is maritime safety. It might be thought that a possible problem could exist with respect to the licensing and approval of international service. But there is no reason that a government would not open its borders to all air carriers meeting the obligations imposed on local carriers.

Airports have been privately owned and operated since the early days of aviation. The Burbank airport was owned and operated by Lockheed at the time it served as the main airport for the Los Angeles area. Atlanta's Hartsfield–Jackson Airport may be worth as much as $5.5 billion, and selling it to a private operator could benefit each Atlanta resident by as much as $13,500. London's main airports are owned and commercially operated by the British Airport Authority, which now participates in the provision of airport services outside Britain, including the management of Indianapolis International Airport in the United States. Airport services also have been privatized in Canada, Africa, Asia, Australasia, and Latin America.

However, no airport, whether governmentally or privately owned, applies market principles to allocate landing and take-off "slots." The result is excessive delays at runways at many of the world's largest airports. It is sensible to encourage airports to vary landing and take-off charges to both dampen the demand for scarce slots and attract finance for commercial expansion.

Air traffic control (ATC) is another weak link in the air transportation systems of Europe and the United States, where it is regularly responsible for serious delays during peak travel periods and for an increasing numbers of near misses. ATC is already owned and operated by nonprofit corporations independent of government in Australia, Canada, Germany, New Zealand, Switzerland, and Great Britain. The Canadian system, *Nav Canada*, is controlled by major aviation stakeholders such as airlines, pilots, and air traffic controllers. It has been operating since 1996 and claims that its operations save airlines $100 million each year. However, unless a major accident brings home the urgency of reforming ATC in the United States, agreement on appropriate reform is unlikely in the foreseeable future.

GR

See also Capitalism; Cities; Free Trade; Globalization; Immigration

Further Readings

Cervero, Robert. *Paratransit in America: Redefining Mass Transportation*. Westport, CT: Praeger, 1997.

Estache, Antonia, and José Carbajo. "Competing Private Ports—Lessons from Argentina." *The Private Sector in Infrastructure*. Washington, DC: World Bank, 1997.

Hakim, Simon, Paul Seidenstat, and Gary W. Bowman, eds. *Privatizing Transportation Systems*. Westport, CT: Praeger, 1996.

Heggie, Ian, and Piers Vickers. *Commercial Management and Financing of Roads*. Technical Paper 409. Washington, DC: World Bank, 1998.

Klein, Dan B., Adrian T. Moore, and Binyam Reja. *Curb Rights: A Foundation for Free Enterprise Urban Transit*. Washington, DC: Brookings Institution Press, 1998.

Mohring, Herbert, and Mitchell Harwitz. *Highway Benefits: An Analytical Framework*. Evanston, IL: Northwestern University Press, 1962.

Poole, Robert W., Jr., and Viggo Butler. *Reinventing Air Traffic Control: A New Blueprint for a Better System*. Policy Study No. 206. Los Angeles: Reason Foundation, 1996.

Roth, Gabriel. *Roads in a Market Economy*. Aldershot, UK: Ashgate, 1996.

———, ed. *Street Smart: Competition, Entrepreneurship and the Future of Roads*. New Brunswick, NJ: Transaction, 2006.

Roth, Gabriel, and Anthony Shephard. *Wheels within Cities—Private Alternatives to Public Transport*. London: Adam Smith Institute, 1984.

Utt, Ron. "FAA Reauthorization: Time to Chart a Course for Privatizing Airports." *Heritage Backgrounder*. No. 1289. Washington, DC: Heritage Foundation, June 1999.

World Business Council for Sustainable Development. *Mobility 2001*. Conches-Geneva: Author, 2001. 2–6.

World Health Organization. *World Report on Road Traffic Injury Prevention*. Geneva: Author, 2004.

Tucker, Benjamin R. (1854–1939)

Benjamin R. Tucker was a writer, an editor, and a publisher. Tucker is arguably the most significant figure in American individualist anarchism. Through his periodical *Liberty: Not the Daughter but the Mother of Order*, published from 1881 to 1908, Tucker made the case for a stateless society in clear and uncompromising prose. In addition to Tucker's writings, *Liberty* published articles by such notable libertarians as Lysander Spooner, Auberon Herbert, and Wordsworth Donisthorpe. It also featured pieces by Irish literary critic George Bernard Shaw and Italian economist Vilfredo Pareto, as well as early translations of the work of German philosopher Friedrich Nietzsche.

Tucker's views, like those of most 19th-century individualist anarchists, seem somewhat eclectic—if not odd—to modern libertarians. The principal reason lies in Tucker's self-identified socialism. In perhaps his most famous essay, "State Socialism and Anarchism: How Far They Agree, and Wherein They Differ," originally published in March 1886,

Tucker argued that individualist anarchism should be viewed as part of the broader socialist movement. But he was quick to draw the distinction between Marxian socialism, which he defined as "the doctrine that all the affairs of men should be managed by the government, regardless of individual choice," and his own view, "the doctrine that all the affairs of men should be managed by individuals or voluntary associations, and that the State should be abolished."

Like Marx, Tucker was a proponent of the labor theory of value. But he did not believe that socialism could be achieved through greater state action. In fact, Tucker maintained that socialism required breaking government monopolies in four areas: money, land, tariffs, and patents. Such a program, Tucker argued, would put labor "in possession of its own." One can trace many of Tucker's economic theories to his association with Josiah Warren, the author of *The Emancipation of Labor*, who introduced Tucker to anarchism in his teens. Tucker also drew from the writings of William B. Greene, Ezra Heywood, and Stephen Pearl Andrews.

In addition to discussions of economic reform, Tucker devoted much space in *Liberty* to debates over natural rights. In its early years, *Liberty* published many intellectuals who were strongly influenced by the English philosopher Herbert Spencer, such as Henry Appleton, Gertrude Kelly, and M. E. Lazarus, who argued that natural rights provided the proper foundation for libertarian anarchism. Eventually, however, proponents of natural rights theory virtually disappeared from the pages of *Liberty* as Tucker became more enamored with the egoism of German writer Max Stirner. In fact, in 1907, Tucker, who also owned a bookstore, published the first English translation of Stirner's *The Ego and His Own*.

A fire destroyed Tucker's offices in January 1908, and with it *Liberty*, which ceased publication with the April 1908 issue. Tucker moved to Europe shortly thereafter, eventually settling in Monaco, where he died on June 22, 1939. In his later years, Tucker became more pessimistic about the chances for libertarian reform. Indeed, according to Wendy McElroy, who has written extensively about individualist anarchism, "It was no longer clear to Tucker that a free market alone could overcome the problems created by a government monopoly."

AS

See also Anarchism; Herbert, Auberon; Individualist Anarchism; Marxism; Socialism; Spooner, Lysander

Further Readings

Brooks, Frank H., ed. *The Individualist Anarchists: An Anthology of Liberty (1881-1908)*. New Brunswick, NJ: Transaction, 1994.

Martin, James J. *Men against the State: The Expositors of Individualist Anarchism in America, 1827–1908*. Colorado Springs, CO: Ralph Myles Publisher, 1970.

McElroy, Wendy. "Benjamin Tucker, Individualism, and *Liberty: Not the Daughter but the Mother of Order." Literature of Liberty* 4 no. 3 (Autumn 1981): 7–39.

Tullock, Gordon (1922–)

Gordon Tullock is an economist and a sociologist. Although he explicitly rejects the notion of being a libertarian, his work has a special relevance for 20th-century libertarianism. His studies on bureaucracies, rent seeking, economic theory of anarchy, and constitutional governance have questioned the "disastrous orthodoxies" of the day regarding the nature, role, and functioning of the state and have challenged what he called the *terrible superstition* that the government should operate the economy. At the same time, he advanced the frontiers of political economy by creating the intellectual tools that are today used to bolster libertarian arguments and a libertarian agenda. Tullock and his 1962 coauthor, James M. Buchanan, are credited with founding the Public Choice school in economics, a discipline that analyzes the political behavior of voters, special interests, bureaucrats, and legislators on the assumption that each actor is pursuing not so much the public interest but his own. In systematically applying the rational choice approach of economics to the analysis of political phenomena, they contrast Adam Smith's "invisible hand," which associates self-interest in the private marketplace with the wealth of a nation, with the "visible boot" of government, a process specific to political markets that more often than not results in economic ruin.

Gordon Tullock was born in Rockford, Illinois, of Scottish ancestry; his mother was Pennsylvania Dutch. Tullock received a JD from the University of Chicago in 1947, and, after practicing as an attorney and working in the U.S. Department of State, Tullock taught at several universities, including the University of Virginia, Virginia Tech, the University of Arizona, and George Mason University. He was the founder of the Public Choice Society, served as its president, and was honored as a distinguished fellow of the American Economic Association. Among his formative intellectual influences were Henry Simons at the University of Chicago, and Karl Popper, whom he assisted in writing the postscript to *The Logic of Scientific Discovery*, an experience that marked his approach to scientific inquiry. Tullock also has acknowledged the strong influence of Ludwig von Mises. He noted that, as a young scholar, he read *Human Action* three times and that his first book, *The Politics of Bureaucracy*, used Mises's methods extensively.

From the first reviews of his work, it was noted that he "writes in the ideological tradition of Hayek and Mises, contrasting the market with politics as a co-ordinating mechanism to the denigration of the latter." He had a decisive contribution in destroying the idea that we can expect government to be a benevolent mechanism that can be used to remedy market failures. Most of the major themes in his work are an extension and continuation of this line of argument: State intervention, like the market, he maintained, should respond to the preferences of individual persons. If the market does not provide perfect responses, neither does the state. Some individuals are usually hurt regardless of whether public intervention occurs; compensation may be theoretically possible, but in actuality it will rarely be undertaken. Politicians act on behalf of ill-informed voters or special interest lobbies, neither of whom can be expected to press for economically rational solutions. These conditions generate "rent seeking"—a search for gains not through productive activity, but through manipulation of the legal, regulatory, and political environment. Information and bargaining costs are of much greater importance than are generally considered when considering the desirability of public intervention. His conclusions pointed toward the desirability of the division of government into small jurisdictions and "a sizeable reduction in the total amount of activities attempted by the governmental apparatus," while at the same time inspired him to explore the possibility of developing an economic theory of anarchy.

Despite having what some critics labeled a "visceral preference for the market," by viewing government as a mechanism for responding to individual preferences, he placed it on a par with the market. That is why his work could ultimately be seen as a search for means of comparing private market exchanges with public (governmental) decisions in an effort to identify the mechanisms for getting meaningful indications from individuals of their preference on specific issues involving state intervention.

PDA

See also Buchanan, James M.; Mises, Ludwig von; Popper, Karl; Public Choice Economics

Further Readings

Buchanan, James M., and Gordon Tullock. *The Calculus of Consent, Logical Foundations of Constitutional Democracy*. Ann Arbor: University of Michigan Press, 1965.
Tullock, Gordon. *Explorations in the Theory of Anarchy*. Blacksburg, VA: Polytechnic Institute and State University, 1972.
———. *The Politics of Bureaucracy*. Washington, DC: Public Affairs Press, 1965.
———. *Private Wants, Public Means; An Economic Analysis of the Desirable Scope of Government*. New York: Basic Books, 1970.
———. *Toward a Mathematics of Politics*. Ann Arbor: University of Michigan Press, 1972.

Turgot, Anne-Robert-Jacques (1727–1781)

Anne-Robert-Jacques Turgot was an economist and a states-man. Turgot was associated with the Physiocratic school of economics and was a strong supporter of reforms during his political career. He came from an old Norman family, but seldom used his title, Baron d'Aulne. His family wanted him to become a priest, so he was educated at the college of Louis-le-Grand before taking a degree in theology at the seminary of St. Sulpice and at the Sorbonne. It was while studying theology that Turgot discovered political economy and wrote his first essays on economics and history, most notably, "A Philosophical Review of the Successive Advances of the Human Mind" (1750), in which he made the first of several contributions to the development of the "four stages theory," also called the stadial theory, of economic and social development from hunter gatherers, to pastoral society and herding, to settled agriculture, and to the peace and prosperity made possible by commercial society. In 1751, he decided not to enter the priesthood, preferring instead a career in royal administration. In December 1752, he was appointed a councilor to the Paris *parlement*, where he served from 1753 to 1761; in 1753, he purchased the office of *maître des requêtes* (or legal advisor).

Turgot's early writings included a defense of religious toleration (in *Lettres sur la tolérance*, 1753) and several articles written for Denis Diderot's *Encyclopédie* in 1755 (including "Fairs and Markets" and "Foundations"). Although Turgot was forced to withdraw from any further formal association with the Encyclopedists because of his official position, he was able to maintain contact with enlightened circles through the salon of Madame Geoffrin. It was during the mid-1750s that Turgot came into contact with members of the French free-market school of economics known as the Physiocrats. He met Dr. François Quesnay and Pierre Samuel du Pont de Nemours and traveled extensively with Jacques-Claude-Marie Vincent de Gournay (who was then the Intendant for Commerce) on his tours of inspection around the country during 1753–1756. Gournay is reputed to have coined the expression "laissez faire, laissez passer" when asked what government economic policy should be. When Gournay died in 1759, Turgot wrote a lengthy "Eloge de Gournay" in which he defended Gournay's laissez-faire economic policies with an eloquence often lacking in other members of the Physiocratic school.

Turgot had two opportunities to put free-market reforms into practice: on a local scale when he was appointed Intendant of Limoges in 1761–1774 and on a national level when the new King Louis XVI made him Minister of Finances. During the first period, Turgot combined economic and legal reform with a concerted propaganda effort to defend his reforms in a series of memoirs, memos, and formal opinions that were disseminated both within the government and publicly. Turgot's attempted reforms were extensive and comprise a veritable "revolution in government." Had they succeeded, the French Old Regime might well have opened up its economy, overcome its internal economic problems, and thus averted the Revolution that was to break out in 1789. Turgot aimed to make taxation more equitable, spend tax revenue on roads and other infrastructure, replace forced labor obligations (such as the *corvée*) with paid labor, end military requisitioning of goods and transport, and make service in the local militia voluntary. Those reforms were accompanied by the publication of his most important economic works, the *Mémoire sur les prêts d'argent* (*Memoir on Lending Money*) (1770); and the *Lettres sur la liberté du commerce des grains* (*Letters on Free Trade in Grain*) (1770), which were addressed to the Abbot Terray in an effort to prevent the free trade regulations that had been promulgated in 1764 from being revoked. His major work, *Réflexions sur la formation et la distribution des richesses* (1766), offers one of the clearest statements of the Physiocratic position. What emerges from those works is a clearly articulated and impassioned defense of individual and economic liberty. One distinguishing feature of Turgot's approach is that he did not share his fellow Physiocrats' faith in enlightened despotism, preferring more extensive political liberty (such as constitutional limits on royal power and strong regional government), more in keeping with Montesquieu's ideas. When the American Revolution broke out, he followed events there with a keen interest.

The death of King Louis XV in May 1774 gave Turgot his second opportunity to introduce free-market reforms to France. Louis XVI appointed Turgot first as minister of the navy and then as finance minster in 1774–1776. As finance minister, Turgot attempted to reproduce on a larger scale the reforms he had pioneered at Limoges. In his Six Edicts of 1776, Turgot tried to bring an end to official corruption and military requisitioning, abolish many local monopolies, introduce reforms in banking and taxation, and return to internal free trade in grain. Unfortunately, his efforts failed due to the political inexperience of the new king, the ability of the vested interests who were being harmed by reform to organize against it, and the food riots that broke out as a consequence of a food shortage and rising prices (the famous "guerre des farines"). Turgot was forced to resign in May 1776, and France's experiment in free-market reform came to an abrupt end.

DMH

See also Cantillon, Richard; Enlightenment; Montesquieu, Charles de Secondat de; Physiocracy; Smith, Adam

Further Readings

Dakin, Douglas. *Turgot and the Ancien Régime in France*. London: Methuen, 1939.

Faure, Edgar. *La Disgrâce de Turgot*. Paris: Gallimard, 1961.

Kaplan, Steven L. *Bread, Politics and Political Economy in the Reign of Louis XV*. 2 vols. The Hague, Netherlands: Martinus Nijhoff, 1976.

Turgot, A. R. J. *The Economics of R. J. Turgot*. P. D. Groenewegen, trans. The Hague, Netherlands: Martinus Nijhoff, 1977.

———. *Ecrits économiques*. Bernard Cazes, ed. Paris: Calmann-Levy, 1970.

———. *Eloge de Vincent de Gournay*. Henry Clark, ed. Indianapolis, IN: Liberty Fund, 2003 [1759].

———. "Lettres sur la liberté du commerce des grains." *Oeuvres de Turgot*. 2 vols. Nouv, ed. Paris: Guillaumin, Collection des principaux economists, 1844.

———. *Réflexions sur la formation et la distribution des richesses*. New York: A. M. Kelley, 1979.

———. *Turgot on Progress, Sociology and Economics*. R. L. Meek, ed. Cambridge: Cambridge University Press, 1973.

Weulersse, Georges. *La Physiocratie sous les ministères de Turgot et de Necker, 1774–1781*. Paris: Presses Universitaires de France, 1950.

Urban Planning

The term *urban planning* refers to the attempt to control the character and location of housing, industry, and recreational developments according to a preconceived pattern or design. Such designs are thought necessary in the context of urban development because of the externalities or third-party effects associated with the close contiguity of urban life. In densely populated areas, for example, the location of major industrial developments close to the places in which people live may result in objectionable pollution. Urban planning is considered necessary to ensure the appropriate separation of different land uses in order to improve the quality of urban life.

Traditionally arguments of this nature are invoked in the context of theories of market failure, which suggest that without governmental oversight unregulated market processes will result in a suboptimal pattern of land use. Within this context, governmental urban planning can take the form of either direct ownership of land with the state acting as the developer of different sites or the more common form of regulatory restrictions on the property rights of private individuals and organizations. In this latter case, it remains the prerogative of private agents to bring forward proposals for the development of land, but these proposals must conform to the principles laid down in some form of land use plan prepared by the public authorities.

With its emphasis on the importance of competition and spontaneous order, libertarianism is often thought to be hostile to the design mentality that appears inherent in this notion of urban planning. Libertarians, however, tend not to question the need for urban planning per se, but governmental attempts to monopolize the process of land use control. Libertarians do not oppose hierarchies and organizations such as firms, which engage in planning activities. What they question are attempts to replace a diversity of competing private plans with a unitary structure of government control.

The planning activities of firms within a market do not constitute a unitary hierarchy of control because they are embedded in a wider process of competitive experimentation as workers, investors, and consumers may select from a range of competing organizations in pursuit of their personal goals. Seen in this light, competition is a process that may operate at multiple levels, including competition between different organizational forms and between different sets of rules for ordering social behavior.

The case of shopping malls has often been invoked in this context to illustrate the manner in which private planning may perform most, if not all, of the major functions often ascribed to governmental land-use controls. The proprietors of malls do not allow a free-for-all on their premises, but define a set of rules that govern the behavior of retailers and shoppers alike in order to internalize potential externalities and, thus, to benefit all who use the mall. Competition in such a context occurs on at least two different levels. On the one hand, the various retailers compete for customers within the boundaries of the mall. On the other hand, the proprietors of the mall compete for consumers to patronize their mall, rather than those owned by competitors. In the latter instance, the rules of conduct, such as regulations on shop frontages, smoking, animals, and skateboarding supplied by the proprietor, and the environmental characteristics of the mall, such as access to car parking, landscaping, and architectural design, are subject to competition from alternative proprietors who offer different arrangements.

Seen in this light, the libertarian approach to urban planning focuses on the importance of competition between different types of control or, to put it differently, on the importance of a "market in regulation." In one of his few published statements on the topic, Friedrich Hayek put the issue very well:

> Most of what is valid in the argument for town planning is in effect an argument for making the planning unit for certain

purposes larger than the size of individually owned property. Some of the aims of planning could be achieved by a division of the content of property rights in such a way that certain decisions could rest with the holder of the superior right. . . . Estate development in which the developer retains some permanent control over the use of individual plots provides at least one alternative to the exercise of control by political authority. There is also the advantage that the larger planning unit will be one of many and that it will be constrained in the exercise of its powers by the necessity of competing with other similar units.

Libertarians have cited historical evidence to illustrate the practical successes that have been achieved by such private forms of proprietary urban planning. Stephen Davies, for example, has shown that a large part of the urban infrastructure developed during and after the Industrial Revolution in Britain was the product of private planning and was responsible for what are now some of the most sought-after residential areas in England. Covenants and estate development models provided a wide range of public goods, such as street lighting, roads and sewage facilities, as well as aesthetic controls, and housed the vast majority of the middle and working classes in affordable accommodation, whereas the unsanitary and shabby housing developments that are the stuff of Dickensian imagery were the exception and not the rule.

More recently, the growth of innovations such as homeowners' associations, condominium developments, and private communities have been cited in support of a libertarian approach. In the United States, for example, the most recent data suggest that there are approaching a quarter of a million private associations involving 50 million people that use contractual forms of land-use control such as restrictive covenants. Developers compete by providing different packages of contractual restrictions tied to the purchase of property on the assumption that people are willing to pay a premium to live in an area where there are limits on what their neighbors can do with their property. These groupings range from relatively small-scale associations working at the level of an individual neighborhood or street to much larger developments such as Reston, Virginia, with a population of 50,000, where entire towns have developed on the basis of private contractual planning.

From a libertarian perspective, the advantages of private urban planning are similar to those of competitive processes in general. They facilitate a higher level of experimentation in discovering public preferences for different types of land-use control than possible under governmental alternatives, and they provide more powerful incentives for planners to improve the quality of their performance over time.

MP

See also Cities; Eminent Domain/Takings; Jacobs, Jane; Transportation

Further Readings

Davies, S. "Laissez Faire Urban Planning." *The Voluntary City*. D. Beito, P. Gordon, and A. Tabarrok, eds. Ann Arbor: University of Michigan Press/The Independent Institute, 2002.

Hayek, F. A. *The Constitution of Liberty*. London: Routledge, 1960.

Jacobs, Jane. *The Death and Life of Great American Cities*. New York: Vintage, 1961.

Nelson, R. "Privatising the Neighbourhood." *The Voluntary City*. D. Beito, P. Gordon, and A. Tabarrok, eds. Ann Arbor: University of Michigan Press/The Independent Institute, 2002.

UTILITARIANISM

Consequentialist ethical theories, including utilitarianism, judge the rightness or wrongness of an action solely on the basis of the consequences it produces. Utilitarianism asserts that the moral quality of an action is determined exclusively by its usefulness, its utility, in producing good consequences for the parties it affects. Under utilitarianism, there is only one binding moral principle, the principle of utility, which holds that one should always act so as to maximize the good consequences resulting from one's action.

There are as many versions of utilitarianism as there are theories of the good. Jeremy Bentham and John Stuart Mill, who first articulated the modern utilitarian theory, believed that the good was identifiable as pleasure and, thus, that moral action required one to act so as to maximize the amount of pleasure in the world. Preference utilitarians, who believe that the good consists of the satisfaction of rational desires, judge actions as right on the basis of their tendency to maximize the ability of human beings to realize their rational desires. Eudaimonic utilitarians, who identify the good with human happiness, assert that proper moral actions are those that maximize the sum total of happiness experienced by human beings. Because this version of utilitarianism is the most widely discussed, the principle of utility is often referred to as the greatest happiness principle.

Utilitarianism is not an altruistic theory in that it does not require individuals to ignore their own interests. Under utilitarianism, the moral quality of an action depends on its consequences for all the parties it affects, including the actor. Utilitarianism is an egalitarian theory, however, because the interests of everyone count equally. The actor's own good counts as much as, but no more than, anyone else's.

The essential nature of utilitarian ethics may be captured by the claim that the point of morality is the promotion of overall human welfare by maximizing benefits and minimizing harms or, more colloquially, the promotion of the greatest good for the greatest number. Utilitarianism is inconsistent with all natural or contractual rights-based ethical theories, and hence, it is inconsistent with any version of libertarianism based on such theories. Yet it is by no means incompatible with libertarianism per se. However, because utilitarianism implies that the principle of utility is the only binding moral principle, individual rights can possess no independent moral authority. One can have no duty to respect individual rights as such, but may have a duty to violate rights if doing so would increase the sum total of human happiness. Thus, utilitarianism is incompatible with any version of libertarianism that is based on or demands a strict adherence to individual rights.

Whether utilitarianism is inconsistent with all versions of libertarianism, however, turns on a question of empirical fact. If maximizing human freedom is, in fact, the most effective way to maximize the sum total of human happiness, then utilitarianism would prescribe that human freedom be maximized. In such a case, utilitarianism would not only be consistent with, but would require a libertarian political structure. Thus, libertarian economists such as Ludwig von Mises (1881–1973), Friedrich Hayek (1899–1992), and Milton Friedman (1912–2006), who argue that this is indeed the way the world works, may be characterized as utilitarian libertarians.

JoH

See also Bentham, Jeremy; Consequentialism; Mill, John Stuart; Rights, Theories of

Further Readings

Bentham, Jeremy. *The Works of Jeremy Bentham*. John Bowring, ed. London: Simpkin, Marshall, 1838–1843 [1962].

Mill, John Stuart. *On Liberty*. London: J. W. Parker and Son, 1859.

Paul, Ellen Frankel. "J. S. Mill: The Utilitarian Influence in the Demise of Laissez-Faire." *Journal of Libertarian Studies* 2 no. 2 (1978): 135–149.

Rosen, Frederick. *Classical Utilitarianism from Hume to Mill*. London and New York: Routledge, 2003.

V

VIRTUE

The term *virtue* is often used equivocally in both scholarly and ordinary discourse. The term is sometimes employed to mean whatever is morally good or appropriate. However, it has traditionally been used more precisely to mean certain qualities of character, or dispositions to choose actions, that are essential to living the right kind of life. As Aristotle defined it in the *Nicomachean Ethics*, virtue "is a settled disposition toward actions by deliberate choice." According to Aristotle and those who have followed him, one acquires virtues by engaging in virtuous acts: "A man becomes just by doing just actions and temperate by doing temperate actions; and no one can have the remotest chance of becoming good without doing them." He ridicules those who, "instead of doing virtuous acts, resort to merely talking about them and think that they are philosophizing and that by doing that they will become virtuous."

If one uses the term to refer to certain dispositions of a person's character that both produce and express moral excellence, which is the traditional meaning of *virtue* and the one used here, then there is no easy or direct connection between libertarianism and virtue, either theoretically or particularly. With respect to libertarian political theory, the idea of using the state to directly promote virtuous conduct would violate its central principles. Practically speaking, the pluralism embedded in libertarianism would appear to leave no room for using force to promote the "right kind of life" or the "right sort of character," although libertarians have no problem with individuals or groups achieving or promoting those things through voluntary means, such as education, persuasion, and example.

There is a general tension in classical liberalism between the concern with procedural rights, which specify limits, constraints, and procedures rather than goals or ends, and the traditionally nonprocedural and substantively specified characteristics of virtue found in much of traditional moral theory. Indeed, a central element of classical liberal theories of social order is the observation that individuals can interact for mutual benefit without any real knowledge or concern about each others' characters.

Although virtuc and liberty are not directly linked, a number of connections between the two may nonetheless be identified. Libertarianism implies free and open markets, and it has been a common view, at least since Adam Smith, that such markets promote certain widely appreciated virtues, such as honesty, thrift, civility, probity, temperance, tolerance, and prudence. Having to please others in order to be successful in the market, rather than being able to use force to accumulate wealth, provides a certain discipline that engenders the habits just mentioned.

Free-market competition among providers of goods and services tends to reward those who exhibit such traits and to encourage others to emulate them. But can free-market competition emerge if such virtues are absent? In recent years, there has been substantial interest in the issue of whether markets are dependent on preexisting moral dispositions. The question has become especially acute since the fall of the Soviet empire because markets in a number of formerly communist countries have had difficulty taking root, although no state appears to have been systematically and deliberately preventing them from doing so. The issues and problems are complex, and their study offers many opportunities for advancing our knowledge of how self-ordering systems emerge and sustain themselves. It may be that the rule of law and well-defined property rights are more central to the development of markets than is any given set of moral dispositions. At the same time, the establishment of the rule of law and well-defined property rights may be dependent in some important way on moral beliefs and attitudes. It is not obvious which must precede the other.

Similarly, a culture of scientific inquiry and progress may generate certain intellectual virtues, such as willingness to listen to criticism, toleration of alternative hypotheses, willingness to consult reason and evidence, and so forth. Yet such a culture may require the preexistence of the virtues it fosters for it to emerge at all. Once virtue-generating institutions are established, they may well continue to generate and sustain the virtue necessary for their perpetuation. Even so, two questions would still remain: Are all or the most important virtues sustained by the market order? Are the dispositions engendered by such practices and institutions truly virtues in any recognizable classical sense, that is, are they goods pursued for their own sake and not because they contribute to some other end, such as successful generation of wealth? Libertarians have not written a great deal about either of those questions perhaps because they do not apparently need to be answered for free societies to exist. They would be relevant, instead, to the important question of whether such societies are good.

If the establishment and maintenance of free societies are dependent on the prior presence of at least some virtues, then presumably libertarians would need to be concerned about the generation of those virtues where they do not now exist. That would presuppose a common moral framework or foundation for libertarianism. Inasmuch as libertarianism is a political theory and does not aspire to be a more widely embracing moral theory, a variety of moral theories might be compatible with it. Those theories might have different approaches to the virtues. For example, the classical liberal writer Wilhelm von Humboldt, who exercised a great influence over John Stuart Mill's work *On Liberty*, identified "the true end of man" as "the highest and most harmonious development of his powers to a complete and consistent whole" and argued that "the evil results of a too extensive solicitude on the part of the state are . . . shown in the suppression of all active energy, and the necessary deterioration of the moral character." The key concept for Humboldt is *Bildung*, which, rendered into English, carries the sense of education or formation of character.

Ayn Rand articulated another perspective associated with libertarianism that openly professes the importance of virtue. In her essay, "The Objectivist Ethics," she identifies certain qualities of character as being necessary for living the right kind of life. Those virtues include rationality, productiveness, and pride. Although Rand believed that if these virtues were widely possessed society would certainly be better, her justification of them was not based on their effects on social life and interaction. In this particular regard, her position is akin to that of von Humboldt, in that she defends these virtues as constituents of a good or fully human life.

For Rand, free-market exchange is a reflection of the virtues she championed. Yet that again raises a version of the problem mentioned previously. It would seem that traditional methods of moral education would be needed to generate the virtues she admires and, in turn, the social order that would be sustained by them. Yet her ethical philosophy stands in some contrast to what she regards as the altruistic and virtue-destroying bias of the dominant philosophical and educational traditions and institutions. Presumably, then, the right ideas about ethics and markets are needed to inform a new tradition of moral education, which will in turn support the market order as well as make possible morally virtuous lives that are good in and for themselves. If Rand is right, without the replacement of those traditions by more suitable ideas, the market framework would overlay a substratum unsuitable to its support, making the collapse of the free society inevitable.

In general, libertarian thinkers believe that virtues must be voluntarily self-realized to be virtues at all, that force and virtue are generally incompatible. Libertarianism is by no means unique or original in wondering about the connection between virtue and social order. That problem is as old as Socrates. But by leaving the state out of the definition and direct promotion of virtue, libertarianism offers a unique perspective on virtue—one that separates it from politics as other approaches do not. That separation may serve not to diminish virtue, but to give it an added focus or importance.

DDU

See also Aristotle; Freedom; Mill, John Stuart; Positive Liberty; Rand, Ayn

Further Readings

Aristotle. *Nicomacheaon Ethics*. Hippocrates G. Apostle, trans. Grinnell, IA: Peripatetic Press, 1984.

Buchanan, James. *The Logical Foundations of Constitutional Liberty*. Vol. 1. Chap. 5. Indianapolis, IN: Liberty Fund, 1999.

Den Uyl, Douglas J. "Liberalism and Virtue." *Public Morality, Civic Virtue, and the Problem of Modern Liberalism*. T. William Boxx and Gary M. Quinlivan, eds. Grand Rapids, MI: Wm. B. Eerdmans Publishing, 2000.

Humboldt, Wilhelm von. *The Limits of State Action*. Indianapolis, IN: Liberty Fund, 1993 [1854].

Macedo, Stephen. *Liberal Virtues*. New York: Oxford University Press, 1991.

Mueller, John. "Democracy, Capitalism, and the End of Transition." *Post-Communism: Four Perspectives*. Michael Mandelbaum, ed. New York: Council on Foreign Relations Books, 1996.

North, Douglas. *Institutions, Institutional Change and Economic Performance*. Cambridge: Cambridge University Press, 1990.

Rand, Ayn. *The Virtue of Selfishness*. New York: Signet Books, 1964.

Smith, Adam. *The Theory of Moral Sentiments*. Indianapolis, IN: Liberty Fund, 1979.

VOLTAIRE (1694–1778)

François Marie Arouet, also known as Voltaire, was a writer, historian, and philosopher, and almost certainly the most important figure of the French Enlightenment. The impact of this French author and philosopher on Western thought was so profound that he is simply known as "Voltaire"—the name he adopted in 1718. With a philosophy based on both skepticism and rationalism, on both tolerance and scientific curiosity, he intellectually straddled the France of his birth—a superstitious, class-bound society under the absolute monarchy of Louis XIV—and the France of his death—a society on the brink of demanding "Liberty, Equality, Fraternity" through revolution. His plays lampooning society and his nonfiction works on history, politics, religion, and philosophy made him the best-known intellectual of his day, with such prominent admirers and correspondents as Catherine the Great of Russia and Frederick the Great of Prussia. The Enlightenment is sometimes referred to as "The Age of Voltaire" because of his tireless advocacy of religious tolerance and of the application of natural laws discoverable through science to the improvement of men's lives.

Born into comfortable circumstances, Voltaire studied law before deciding to devote himself entirely to writing, specializing in attacks on government, the church, and social mores. In 1717, as result of satirical verses aimed at the aristocracy, he spent 11 months in the Bastille. His brilliant and irreverent wit made Voltaire a prized presence in the elite intellectual salons of Paris, but led to another threat of imprisonment in 1726, when he insulted a powerful aristocrat. Voltaire avoided a second stay at the Bastille through self-exile in England, where he lived for 3 years, absorbing the best that Britain had to offer, from the classical liberalism of philosopher John Locke to the scientific optimism of mathematician Sir Isaac Newton.

Returning to France, Voltaire produced poetry and plays, most notably *La Henriade* (1728) and *Zaire* (1732), as well as historical and scientific treatises. Two nonfiction works have particular significance: His *Charles XII* (1731)—an acclaimed biography of the King of Sweden—rejected a role for divine intervention in the course of history and had to be printed surreptitiously; and his *Philosophical Letters*, which appeared in France in 1734, was promptly banned and burned. However, the English edition quickly became a best seller, both in Britain and throughout the Continent. The book contrasted the French system of government unfavorably with that of England. He praised England's religious tolerance, individual freedom, constitutional monarchy, and comparatively modest barriers to economic advancement. Once more, Voltaire had to flee Paris, arriving at the chateau of Cirey in the independent duchy of Lorraine.

During his lengthy stay, Voltaire studied physics and chemistry, prodigiously writing novels, satires, and verse. The *Elements of Newton's Philosophy* (1738), coauthored with the Marquise du Châtelet, brought Newton's ideas to the attention of the general public in continental Europe. In 1750, Voltaire accepted a longstanding invitation from Frederick II, known as Frederick the Great, the King of Prussia, and this decision led to his journeying to the Prussian court at Berlin. It was there that Voltaire wrote the historical study *The Age of Louis XIV* (1751), which is widely credited with having established a new approach to historical analysis. Rather than dwell exclusively on political and military accomplishments, Voltaire credited philosophers, writers, artists, inventors, scientists, and other "producers" with having a defining influence on their age. Despite the importance of this work and his international reputation, Voltaire soon clashed with crucial German aristocratic egos and departed the Prussian court. Voltaire was not to know a settled home until he moved to Ferney, near Geneva, in 1758. In the interim, he completed his *Essay on General History and on the Customs and the Character of Nations* (1756), in which he decried the impact of traditional religion and the clergy on the progress of mankind.

Ferney became not only a magnet for the most celebrated European intellectuals and political figures, but also a haven from which Voltaire produced some of his greatest literary works and political tracts. The most celebrated of these works of literature was the novel, *Candide* (1759), a satiric response to Leibniz's solution to the "problem of evil," against which Voltaire argued for a practical philosophy of common sense and political optimism. His *Philosophical Dictionary* (1764) included, among others, the articles Voltaire had contributed to Diderot's famed *Encyclopédie*—a massive reference work of approximately 72,000 articles on the arts and sciences through which Enlightenment ideas were propagated. The *Philosophical Dictionary* reflected Voltaire's vigorous anti-ecclesiastical convictions and cemented his reputation as the most widely read of the *philosophes*—the name given to those French intellectuals who stressed human progress through reason and respect for natural law.

The elderly Voltaire continued to be persecuted by authorities. Indeed, the *Dictionary* met such condemnation that at one point he was forced to deny authorship and seek refuge in Switzerland for several weeks. Before his death, however, he was heralded in the streets of Paris as a hero.

Voltaire left a legacy of over 14,000 letters and more than 2,000 books and pamphlets. The brightest light of the French Enlightenment, he became a spark of the French Revolution whose name is ever associated with religious tolerance, freedom of speech, and the love of reason.

WME

See also Censorship; Cosmopolitanism; Diderot, Denis; Enlightenment

Further Readings

Aldridge, A. Owen. *Voltaire and the Century of Light*. Princeton, NJ: Princeton University Press, 1975.

Durant, Will, and Ariel Durant. *The Age of Voltaire: A History of Civilization in Western Europe from 1715 to 1756*. New York: Simon & Schuster, 1965.

Gay, Peter. *Voltaire's Politics: The Poet as Realist*. 2nd ed. New Haven, CT: Yale University Press, 1988.

Knapp, Bettina Liebowitz. *Voltaire Revisited*. New York: Twayne, 2000.

Voluntarism

Voluntarism—sometimes called philanthropy or charity—is the donation of money, goods, and time either to those in need or an otherwise worthy cause.

A question that confronts every society and every political philosophy concerns our obligations to the poor and unfortunate and how we are to extend them help. Probably the most common answer involves an appeal to government to supply them welfare benefits and other entitlements financed through taxation. But free-market advocates maintain that coercing people to assist others is wrong, both pragmatically and in that it violates others' rights. Instead, they appeal to private organizations to provide the necessities for those in need.

Pragmatically, free-market advocates argue that a taxed and regulated society is less prosperous with less upward mobility and thereby experiences poverty; the redistribution of wealth can be a strong disincentive for people to earn and so increases the number of people who need help. Moreover, people who are taxed to underwrite the costs of welfare are less likely to give voluntarily. The rise of the welfare state is commonly viewed as the turning point at which the large-scale philanthropy that marked 19th-century society disappeared. If government services were removed, free-market advocates maintain that people would be far more likely to voluntarily contribute to charity and other community causes and in larger amounts. As evidence, they point to the wide variety of private organizations that currently exist even in competition with free—that is, government—assistance.

Those who defend the free market further maintain that, regardless of whether government best provides for the poor, coercing such assistance violates individual rights. As Robert Nozick phrased it, no one has "an enforceable right"—that is, a legal claim—to assistance from another. Even a drowning man should not be able to legally compel aid from people on the shore. Rendering assistance may be a moral duty, but this notion should not be taken as equivalent to a legal duty. In many instances, acting within your rights may be immoral. For example, lying to a friend does not violate rights, but by most standards is immoral. Equally, indifference to human suffering does not violate rights, but may be immoral. Concluding that an action is moral or immoral does not automatically translate into a call for the state to either require or punish that action. Indeed, to demand that all moral duties become legal obligations would so constrict our lives as to deprive us of all freedom.

Thus, although free-market advocates agree that caring for the needy is both proper and necessary, they hold on pragmatic, ethical, and rights-based grounds that these decisions are ultimately private and must rest with each individual and his or her conscience.

WME

See also Coercion; Taxation; Welfare State

Further Readings

Machan, Tibor. "Does Libertarianism Imply the Welfare State?" *Res Publica* 3 no. 2 (1997): 131–148.

Nozick, Robert. *Anarchy, State, and Utopia*. New York: Basic Books, 1974.

Rand, Ayn. "Government Financing in a Free Society." *The Virtue of Selfishness*. New York: Signet Books, 1964.

Voluntary Contract Enforcement

Most people believe that a market economy requires that governments enforce private contracts. Although some people may recognize that simple face-to-face trades are possible without external enforcement, most people argue that government enforcement is necessary when contracts are complicated, include commitments over time, or involve large groups. In many real-world situations, however, enforcement of contracts by public courts is too costly—government courts are not perfect, after all—or impossible, inasmuch as government courts often lack jurisdiction across political boundaries or the desire to enforce contracts in sectors not sanctioned by law. The private sector, in contrast, has found numerous ways to promote contractual performance even when government enforcement is absent. From the discipline of continuous dealings in small groups, to reputation mechanisms or more formal private tribunals for large groups, numerous devices have emerged that have made possible contractual performance independent of government. Recognizing that private parties can overcome the potential problem of contractual performance brings into question whether government enforcement of contracts is necessary. This topic is of growing interest to libertarians.

Private contract enforcement has occurred in many historical and contemporary cases. The argument for government enforcement rests on the fact that, although both parties gain from trade, they have an incentive to cheat after having contracted with each other. Many economists point out, however, that the Prisoner's Dilemma conditions are not ubiquitous and that the private sector often finds ways to eliminate them. In addition to morality having guided certain people to keep their word, private parties have profited by devising mechanisms to prevent even egoists from cheating.

If two parties know each other and have had repeated dealings, it may be in both of their interests to cooperate rather than cheat. Parties can gain more by establishing a trusting relationship over the long run than by cheating and thus ending a fruitful trading relationship. Thus, contracts can be honored with or without government courts. Adam Smith called this the *discipline of continuous dealings*, and modern economists have elaborated on additional mechanisms to make contracts self-enforcing. Relying on the discipline of continuous dealings is easiest among small groups of people in which everyone has repeated interactions. However, contracts may be self-enforcing even if parties do not expect to interact again. When parties are able to share information about the reputations of others, a breach may result in damage to one's reputation in the wider community. Others will be less willing to deal with a known cheat, so it can be in everyone's best interest to keep their word.

Recent research in law and economics has documented how the private sector has overcome the problem of fraud, all the way from small and homogenous to large and heterogeneous groups. In the diamond industry, for example, much is at stake, and transaction costs would be extremely high if people had to go to government courts after each transaction. The New York diamond industry has solved this problem by organizing trade in a small and homogenous group, as has been demonstrated by scholars. The New York Diamond Dealers Club has traditionally comprised members of the orthodox Jewish community. Disputes between members are submitted to the club's arbitration system, which has many advantages, including speed of resolution, privacy, and judges who are industry insiders and can rely on custom rather than overly formal rules. Reputation and social sanctions enforce arbitration decisions without any use of coercion. Social sanctions take place in connection with Jewish religious and civic activities; in addition, dealers are required to have a reputation for abiding by the arbitration network's decisions if they wish to conduct business. A party that does not abide by decisions will be ostracized and may even be removed from the trading community. Thus, a trader's reputation serves as a bond that would be forfeited unless one is reliable. By requiring everyone to be a member of a tight-knit group,

the potential problem of fraud among diamond traders has been solved.

Reputation mechanisms can enforce relatively sophisticated contracts among less homogenous groups as well. An analysis of the world's first stock market in 17th-century Amsterdam, which by the end of the century included hundreds of traders who were fairly diverse socially and religiously, has demonstrated that such enforcement was possible. The government then considered most financial contracts as forms of gambling that could be used to manipulate markets, so it refused to enforce contracts for all but the simplest types of transactions. Although traders' contracts were not sanctioned by law, parties to these contracts developed relatively sophisticated ones, including forward contracts, options, and short sales. The market was able to function because traders were able to share information about each other and boycott those who were unreliable. This multilateral reputation mechanism enabled sophisticated contracts with payments over time to occur although no formal rules existed.

As markets increase in size, mechanisms of enforcement that rely on the personal reputation of the participants often become more difficult. At the end of the 17th century and throughout the 18th century, England developed its own stock market, which expanded in speed and complexity to the point where stockbrokers had a difficult time tracking who was reliable. Brokers solved the potential problem of fraud by congregating in coffeehouses and transforming them into private clubs to create and enforce rules. One of their original solutions was to write the names of defaulters on a blackboard in Jonathan's Coffeehouse so that others were informed that in was unwise to deal with them. Eventually, brokers contracted with the owners of the coffeehouse to make Jonathan's a private club to exclude the unreliable. After a few iterations, the brokers successfully created a self-policing club referred to as New Jonathan's, which later became formally known as the London Stock Exchange. Only the more reliable traders were allowed to join, and those traders defaulting on contracts were expelled, thus creating an atmosphere of trust. Individuals may have had a hard time investigating the reliability of all of their trading partners, but the club's ability to enforce rules for members and exclude nonmembers enabled brokers to mitigate the problem of fraud.

As the scope of trade expands, requiring that everyone involved in the trade fall inside the confines of a self-policing club may become impossible. Authors such as Douglas North have argued that government enforcement has become necessary as trade moves outside of small groups, but state enforcement in fact has proved useless if a trader's local jurisdiction lacks the ability to enforce rules on traders abroad. Bruce Benson has extensively documented how parties have solved this problem in the past and continue to do so today. In medieval Europe, for example, merchants who could not rely on civil law to adjudicate disputes developed the Law Merchant, a network of law and of arbitrators to which merchants could voluntarily submit if they wished to conduct business. By opting into this system, merchants who refused to commit themselves to following the agreed-on set of privately developed laws and those who ignored the law merchant courts were boycotted by everyone else. The system has many similarities to arbitration today. Private enforcement will be effective even without government enforcement if the relationship is structured so that anyone attempting to ignore the judgment will lose. Requiring a party to post a surety bond or even to have a reputational bond are two ways to encourage parties to follow a private set of rules.

Many of these examples exist as pockets of privately enforced rules, although the state lurks in the background. Could private enforcement of contracts occur in the absence of government laws securing property rights or outlawing acts like violent theft? Many historical examples of order without law exist. Two examples of private enforcement mechanisms that functioned without any state enforcement that prevented violent theft of property are worth examining.

Peter Leeson has studied trade between European caravans and local producers in the West African interior in the late 19th century. The mobile European caravans were possessed of greater force than the largely immobile native producers of ivory, rubber, and wax. If the natives possessed a stock of desired goods, the Europeans' superior power meant that they had the ability to raid rather than trade with the natives. This situation created a potential problem because if the natives knew their goods for trade would be stolen, they would have no incentive to produce these goods in the first place. Market participants recognized this problem and solved it by separating payment from exchange by a system of credit. Leeson explains that natives did not hold stocks of goods that the Europeans could plunder, should they choose. Instead, European traders paid for the goods in advance, after which the natives harvested the resources to be traded. When the Europeans returned, only the goods for which they had already paid were available, so there was nothing to steal. The use of credit allowed for self-enforcing contracts between weaker and stronger parties even without government to enforce property rights and prevent violent theft.

Present-day Somalia also presents a unique opportunity to look at contract and property rights enforcement in a large stateless society. Since the fall of Siad Barre in 1991, Somalia has had no national government. Yet a fairly developed nonstate legal system exists. Law enforcement is provided by a decentralized clan elder network. When a dispute arises, participants turn to a clan elder for a resolution. In cases where the parties are from different clans, both elders mediate or turn to an elder from a third-party clan. Decisions are based on the Somali customary law, Xeer. The clans are not de facto governments. They have no geographic monopoly, and individuals are free to secede and join another clan without moving. Once decisions are rendered, enforcement is achieved through community action. Each Somali is a member of an insurance-paying group; if a guilty party does not pay the required restitution, the other members of his insurance group are liable. Thus, they have an incentive to encourage the guilty party to make good on his debts. Enforcement also is achieved by a form of expulsion. Troublesome insurance group members can be expelled from their clan and insurance-paying group. These members are not required to physically move, but they are no longer under the protection of the law, and thus others are free to steal from or even maim them. The threat of expulsion from the protective group helps ensure compliance with Somali law. Private solutions to the problem of contractual compliance surround us. Although we have mentioned several examples of nonstate contract enforcement, many different private solutions exist. Scholars have uncovered and documented more examples in recent years, yet much work is left to be done. Libertarians can be encouraged by this research. Although limited government libertarians have claimed that government enforcement of contracts is an absolute necessity, recent research has shown that this view is overly pessimistic and that market solutions are far more robust.

BP and ES

See also Anarcho-Capitalism; Assurance and Trust; Law Merchant; Privatization

Further Readings

Benson, Bruce. *The Enterprise of Law: Justice without the State*. San Francisco: Pacific Research Institute for Public Policy, 1990.

Bernstein, Lisa. "Opting Out of the Legal System: Extralegal Contractual Relations in the Diamond Industry." *Journal of Legal Studies* 21 no. 1 (1992): 115–157.

Caplan, Bryan, and Edward Stringham. "Privatizing the Adjudication of Disputes." *Theoretical Inquiries in Law* 9 no. 2 (2008).

Friedman, David. *Law's Order*. Princeton, NJ: Princeton University Press, 2000.

Klein, Daniel. *Reputation*. Ann Arbor: University of Michigan Press, 1997.

Leeson, Peter. "Trading with Bandits." *Journal of Law and Economics* 50 no. 2 (2007): 303–321.

Powell, Benjamin, Ryan Ford, and Alex Nowrasteh. "Somalia after State Collapse: Chaos or Improvement?" *Independent Institute Working Paper* no. 64 (November 30, 2006).

Stringham, Edward, ed. *Anarchy and the Law: The Political Economy of Choice*. Somerset, NJ: Transaction, 2007.

———. "The Emergence of the London Stock Exchange as a Self-Policing Club." *Journal of Private Enterprise* 17 no. 2 (2002): 1–19.

———."The Extralegal Development of Securities Trading in Seventeenth-Century Amsterdam." *Quarterly Review of Economics and Finance* 43 (2003): 321–344.

Telser, L. G. "A Theory of Self-Enforcing Agreements." *Journal of Business* 53 (1980): 27–44.

WAR

War is the quintessential undertaking of the state, especially the modern centralized nation-state of the past five or six centuries. Indeed, the relationship between the two is encapsulated in the aphorism, "War made the state, and the state made war." Because libertarians distrust the state and fear its capacity to diminish or destroy individuals' rights to life, liberty, and property, they have taken a special interest in war. "War is the health of the state," writer Randolph Bourne famously declared during World War I. For the most part, libertarians have taken that declaration to heart as a warning against ill-founded support for the state's war-making, whatever its announced rationale.

No single libertarian position exists on war. Anarchist libertarians, who oppose the state's very existence, naturally oppose its war-making, too. Pacifist libertarians, who oppose violence in general, even when defensive, clearly disapprove of war. Although most libertarians are neither anarchists nor pacifists, even within this larger group, many tend to be highly skeptical of state claims that war-making is necessary or desirable in any particular case. Others take a less skeptical, more ad hoc approach, preferring to judge each case within the context of the libertarian values and goals they embrace. On the whole, and notwithstanding their differences, libertarians tend to differ from the bulk of the population with respect to war in some readily identifiable ways.

As individualists, libertarians take much less pleasure in their nation's victories (or its heroic defeats) in war than do most others. Even when libertarians conclude that a particular war is justified and should be fought, they are inclined to view it as a regrettable necessity, a cost that must be borne to achieve some overriding benefit, such as national survival. Whereas nationalists and conservatives are apt to react to war by pledging their allegiance to "my country right or wrong," libertarians are more likely to march under a banner such as "peace and free trade." Not for them is the common cry for "national greatness" attained on the field of battle. Instead, libertarians find greatness in the nation that fosters great individual achievements in industry, commerce, charity, science, and the arts. The idea that people should seek "the moral equivalent of war," in the words of William James, rings hollow in libertarian ears because the subjugation to a single group purpose that such a quest bespeaks has no appeal to them.

More than the adherents of other ideologies, libertarians recognize that war, whether fought for good reasons or bad, augments the size, scope, and power of the warring governments. Hence, war creates, often long after the belligerents have ceased their violence, a heightened threat to individual rights. Having surveyed the Western world during the past 500 years, political scientist Bruce Porter concluded in *War and the Rise of the State* that

> a government at war is a juggernaut of centralization determined to crush any internal opposition that impedes the mobilization of militarily vital resources. This centralizing tendency of war has made the rise of the state throughout much of history a disaster for human liberty and rights.

James Madison, one of the many sages who appreciated the enduring adverse effects of war, and writing from personal experience as well as a wide knowledge of history, observed in 1795, "Of all the enemies to public liberty, war is, perhaps, the most to be dreaded, because it comprises and develops the germ of every other."

War brings higher taxes, greater regimentation of the population (and often conscription), increased public debt, diminished civil liberties, political repression, and other ill effects too numerous to catalog here. War substitutes a herd mentality and blind obedience for the normal propensity to question authority and to demand good and proper reasons for government actions. Even in democratic nations, war often brings violence against inoffensive dissenters. In these ways, among others, war promotes collectivism at the expense of individualism, force at the expense of reason, and coarseness at the expense of sensibility. Libertarians regard all of those tendencies with sorrow.

Much of the growth and centralization of government during the past several centuries has been traced to war and its various consequences. Although in this regard all great wars present certain common aspects, the world wars of the 20th century offer the starkest examples.

World War I caused not only the deaths of some 9 million combatants and the serious wounding of some 21 million others, but also vast suffering among the civilian populations of Germany, Russia, France, and other countries. Each of the major belligerents mobilized millions of men, for the most part by means of conscription, and exercised sweeping economic controls—what contemporaries called *war socialism.* Many industries were nationalized outright. Taxes, government spending, and public debt soared to unprecedented heights. The gold standard was abandoned, and vast amounts of fiat paper currency were issued, giving rise to rapid price inflation in each country. International trade and finance suffered great disruption and diminution. So great was the damage done by the conflict that not even a series of international reconstruction efforts during the 1920s could restore the North Atlantic economy to a flourishing condition, and ultimately, if indirectly, the Great Depression of the 1930s became one of the delayed effects of the Great War.

Other effects included the destruction of four great empires—Austro-Hungarian, German, Russian, and Ottoman—and the creation of an ill-fated house-of-cards arrangement of new nations in their place in Europe and the Middle East, not to speak of the Bolshevik house of horrors in Russia. Thus, besides the death, devastation, misery, and disruption of civilized life, the aftermath of World War I included communism, fascism, and, after a short interlude, national socialism. Small wonder that Britain's wartime Prime Minister David Lloyd George wrote in his postwar memoirs, "War has always been fatal to Liberalism." In many ways, World War I can be seen as the fount from which nearly all the great horrors of the 20th century flowed.

Nevertheless, World War II wreaked destruction so vast that it made the catastrophe of 1914–1918 pale by comparison: more than 60 million deaths, most of them of civilians; countless scores of millions seriously wounded or sickened; and property destruction on an unimaginable scale stretching from England to Japan. Again, wartime collectivism prevailed, this time with concentration camps for persons of Japanese ancestry in the United States and death camps for Jews in German-occupied Europe. The suppression of civil liberties, conscription, rationing, government takeovers and economic controls, huge taxes and public debts, gigantic currency issues, and price inflation—all the proven means by which governments mobilize resources for war and despoil normal life—came into play, in most

places even more extensively than in the previous war. When the madness finally ended, in the lingering smoke of the scores of thousands of civilians incinerated at Hiroshima and Nagasaki, the world could only look on in dazed astonishment and wonder at what had been done.

Oddly, however, the lesson that Americans and many western Europeans carried away from the experience of world war was one of heightened trust in the ability of governments to provide for the public welfare. Especially after World War II in the victorious nations, the opponents of active government intervention in economy and society emerged greatly weakened. Democratic socialism, New Dealism, and other so-called third-way systems of political economy—"welfare states"—took hold all over the Western world, and in many cases elsewhere in the world as well. Collectivism was at its zenith, and individualism was everywhere in retreat. Economist and political philosopher F. A. Hayek feared that the Western world had set forth on a "road to serfdom" because no one seemed to value highly the liberties cherished by classical liberals anymore. In the aftermath of depression and war, the great mass of people wanted not liberty, but security, and they had become convinced that their governments could provide it.

Since 1945, the world has avoided a repetition of warfare on the scale of the World Wars, but lesser wars aplenty have raged, and their effects have continued to confirm the worst fears of libertarians. Thus, for example, the cold war gave rise to massive civil rights violations even in the United States as the government sought to clamp down on groups and individuals who opposed its foreign policy. Between 1948 and 1989, some 7.5% of the U.S. gross national product, on average, was channeled into military spending, consuming many trillions of dollars that otherwise might have gone into the maintenance and adornment of life for the general public. American military adventures in Korea, Vietnam, Panama, Serbia, Iraq, and many other places around the globe continued to divide the polity and deplete the public treasury. Ultimately, the Soviet Union fell apart, ending the cold war and its cumulating adverse consequences for the United States and the other nations that had opposed the Soviets. However, the world continues to endure new wars and to stagger under heavy military burdens even during peacetime, and libertarians continue to regard this situation with deep regret.

RoH

See also Collectivism; Foreign Policy; Imperialism; Military-Industrial Complex; Peace and Pacifism

Further Readings

De Jouvenel, Bertrand. *On Power: The Natural History of Its Growth.* Indianapolis, IN: Liberty Fund, 1993 [in French, 1945].

Denson, John V., ed. *The Costs of War: America's Pyrrhic Victories.* New Brunswick, NJ: Transaction, 1997.

Ebeling, Richard M., and Jacob G. Hornberger, eds. *The Failure of America's Foreign Wars*. Fairfax, VA: Future of Freedom Foundation.

Higgs, Robert. *Crisis and Leviathan: Critical Episodes in the Growth of American Government*. New York: Oxford University Press, 1987.

———. *Depression, War, and Cold War: Studies in Political Economy*. New York: Oxford University Press, 2006.

Hummel, Jeffrey Rogers. *Emancipating Slaves, Enslaving Free Men: A History of the American Civil War*. Chicago: Open Court, 1996.

Leebaert, Derek. *The Fifty-Year Wound: The True Price of America's Cold War Victory*. Boston: Little, Brown, 2002.

Mises, Ludwig von. *Nation, State, and Economy: Contributions to the Politics and History of Our Time*. New York: New York University Press, 1983 [in German, 1919].

Porter, Bruce D. *War and the Rise of the State: The Military Foundations of Modern Politics*. New York: Free Press, 1994.

Rothbard, Murray N. "War, Peace, and the State." *Egalitarianism as a Revolt against Nature, and Other Essays*. 2nd ed. Auburn, AL: Ludwig von Mises Institute, 2000.

Van Creveld, Martin. *The Rise and Decline of the State*. New York: Cambridge University Press, 1999.

WAR ON TERROR

The "war on terrorism" was launched by the administration of George W. Bush in the wake of the September 11, 2001, terrorist attacks on the United States. The word *war* was applied in the metaphoric sense, as in the "war on drugs" and the "war on poverty," and the campaign has embraced a variety of policies and governmental efforts focused on dealing with the problem of terrorism. These efforts have included military ventures, policing efforts—both international and domestic—and policies designed to make the country more secure and less vulnerable to terrorist attack.

The chief military venture of the "war" was the invasion of Afghanistan in late 2001. It was established that the 9/11 terrorists were linked to and apparently trained by Osama bin Laden's al-Qaeda, a group of foreign terrorists based in Afghanistan. The United States actively threw its considerable military support to the efforts of anti-Taliban forces in the civil war that had been going on for years in that country. It did so bolstered by an outraged domestic public, favorable resolutions passed in NATO and Congress, and crucial aid from Pakistan, which had previously supported the Afghan Muslim fundamentalist Taliban regime.

Special Forces teams and agents from the Central Intelligence Agency entered the country armed with large metal suitcases packed with U.S. currency. The Americans hired platoons of combatants and supplied leadership, tactical direction, and the coordination of precision, and sometimes massive, bombardment from the air. After 8 years of chaotic and often brutal rule, the Taliban had become deeply unpopular, and its poorly trained forces

mostly disintegrated under the air and ground onslaught, although many al-Qaeda members did stand and fight. A later operation undertaken to dislodge residual al-Qaeda elements from bases in remote mountainous terrain was only a qualified success because many of the most important al-Qaeda and Taliban leaders were able to escape.

In the wake of the war, a new, somewhat broadly based government was set up, many Afghans returned to their tortured country, and foreign aid and assistance contributions were sent in by a large number of countries. A fair amount of security was established, particularly in the capital, Kabul, but much of the country continued to be run or plagued by warlords following traditional modes of conduct. After a few years, Taliban fighters and terrorists regrouped and, apparently working from bases and training camps in tribal areas of neighboring Pakistan, began an increasingly effective campaign against the new government and its foreign supporters.

A second military venture connected to the war on terror involved an invasion, this time without international approval, of Iraq in March 2003. Efforts to tie Iraq directly to international terrorism mostly proved futile, but fears that Iraq's dictator, Saddam Hussein, could develop weapons of mass destruction remained high, now embellished by the argument that he might palm them off to dedicated terrorists to explode in the United States.

As expected, the Iraqi military disintegrated under the onslaught. The victors then sought to build a viable national government out of the rubble that remained after Saddam. However, severe economic sanctions and the war had taken their toll. Although many Iraqis were glad to see Saddam's tyranny ended, the invaders often found the population resentful and humiliated, rather than grateful. Moreover, bringing order to the situation was vastly complicated by the fact that the government-toppling invasion had effectively created a failed state, which permitted widespread criminality and looting. In addition, some people— including some foreign terrorists drawn opportunistically to the area—were dedicated to sabotaging the victors' peace and to killing the policing forces, and the occupation became increasingly costly in lives and treasure. In late 2004, some elements in the insurgency linked themselves with al-Qaeda, and this connection seems to have helped further in attracting recruits and in generating financial and logistical support.

The international policing of terrorism—including the sharing and coordinating of intelligence—has been enhanced by heightened concerns about terrorism around the world in the wake of the 9/11 attacks. No matter how much they might disagree on other issues (most notably on America's war on Iraq), there is a compelling incentive for states—including Arab and Muslim ones—to cooperate in dealing with international terrorism. These cooperative international policing efforts may not have prevented a large number of attacks, but more than 3,000 "suspects" have been arrested around the world, and doubtless at least some of these were dangerous.

In addition, continuing and perhaps accelerating a long-range trend, state sponsorship of terrorism (at least against countries other than Israel) seems to be distinctly on the wane after 9/11. Moreover, a key result among a great many jihadists and religious nationalists was a vehement rejection of al-Qaeda's strategy and methods.

The post-9/11 willingness of governments around the world to take on international terrorism has been much reinforced and amplified by subsequent, if sporadic, terrorist activity overseas. For example, a terrorist bombing in Bali in 2002 galvanized the Indonesian government into action. When terrorists attacked Saudis in Saudi Arabia in 2003, that country seemed, for self-interested reasons, to have become considerably more serious about dealing with terrorism. In addition, al-Qaeda–linked explosions in Jordan in 2005 resulted in outrage, causing the number of Jordanians expressing a lot of confidence in bin Laden to "do the right thing" in polls to plunge from 25% to less than 1%.

The war on terror also has embraced massively enhanced police and intelligence efforts within the United States. After 9/11, for example, fully 67% of those people working on criminal investigations in the FBI were reassigned to counterterrorism activities. Between 2000 and 2006, Justice Department funds devoted to counterterrorism programs tripled while organized crime prosecutions dropped 38%. State and local policing efforts also have been extensively enhanced, as have intelligence-gathering efforts at bureaus like the National Security Agency.

The results of this preoccupation and effort thus far seem to have been rather limited. In 2002, intelligence estimates concluded that there were up to 5,000 people loose in the country who were "connected" to al-Qaeda. However, a secret FBI report in 2005 noted that, after years of intense and well-funded hunting, the agency had not been able to identify a single true al-Qaeda sleeper cell anywhere in the country.

Since 9/11, a dozen or two apparent plots or enterprises put together by local or "home-grown" terrorists have been uncovered. Only a handful of people picked up on terrorism charges have thus far been convicted, and almost all of these charges have been for other infractions, particularly immigration violations. At least some of these have clearly been mental cases or simply flaunting jihadist bravado—rattling on about taking down the Brooklyn Bridge with a blowtorch or conducting a "full ground offensive" against the United States.

In the meantime, thousands of people in the United States have had their overseas communications tapped under a controversial warrantless surveillance program. Of these people, fewer than 10 U.S. citizens or residents per year have aroused enough suspicion to impel the agencies spying on them to seek warrants to carry out surveillance of their domestic communications as well, and little, of any, of this activity, it appears, has led to indictments on any charges whatever. Meanwhile, 80,000 Arab and Muslim immigrants have been subjected to fingerprinting and registration, another 8,000 have been called in for FBI interviews, and more than 5,000 foreign nationals have been imprisoned in initiatives designed to prevent terrorism. This activity has resulted in few, if any, convictions for a terrorist crime. There also have been massive eavesdropping and detention programs, as well as the yearly issuance, without judicial review, of 30,000 "national security letters," in which businesses and institutions are forced to disclose information about their customers and are forbidden from telling anyone they have done so—a process that has generated thousands of leads that, when pursued, seem in almost all cases to have led nowhere. Monumental amounts of personal data have been accumulated, and there has been an incredible number of false positives.

In addition to much enhanced policing and intelligence efforts, the war on terror has inspired (and funded) extensive efforts to protect the country, to make it more secure and less vulnerable to terrorist attack. Most of this activity has been carried out under the auspices of the newly created Department of Homeland Security (DHS). A senior economist in the DHS candidly acknowledged in 2006 that "We really don't know a whole lot about the overall costs and benefits of homeland security." Nonetheless, hundreds of billions of dollars have been spent on the program—airline security alone is approaching $10 billion a year, far greater than total airline profits in a good year—with results that have often been questionable.

Because terrorism can be committed by any single person or small group that takes a notion to do so and is willing to make the effort and to take the risks, there is no way to make everything completely safe from terrorists any more than every store can be protected against shoplifting or every street can be made permanently free of muggers. Nor is it possible to secure every border or have perfect or, for that matter, semiperfect port security—a particular vulnerability, among billions, that has attracted the focused attention of many in the homeland security business, if not so far of any actual terrorists.

To get some idea of the magnitude of this issue, the DHS sought to list potential terrorist targets in the United States, and by 2005 it had enumerated 80,000—a tally that apparently has become much larger since. Although the list has remained secret, there have been a number of leaks indicating that miniature golf courses are included, as well as Weekee Wachee Springs, a roadside water park in Florida. An additional problem for this exercise is this: If one tempting target becomes less vulnerable, an inventive terrorist could simply move on to other ones.

Any coherent exercise in target protection is likely, then, to prove close to impossible as well as expensive and disruptive. For example, the Pentagon extrapolated from 9/11 to conclude that "it is unsafe to have employees in urban office buildings" and is in the process of moving tens of thousands of people in its more obscure agencies to a remote area with little consideration about how they will manage to get to work on highways that are already congested.

An alternative policy—but one probably politically unacceptable—to seeking to make everything (or even a lot of things) safe would be to stress resilience: Be prepared to absorb the (probably limited) damage terrorism is likely to inflict and then use the money saved to repair any terrorist damage and to compensate any victims. That is, one would focus preventive efforts on only a few especially dangerous concerns—nuclear weapons and the power grid, perhaps—and then wait for the event to take place, fixing problems as they arise.

In approaching a terrorism policy, three key issues set out by risk analyst Howard Kunreuther require careful consideration:

1. How much should we be willing to pay for a small reduction in probabilities that are already extremely low?

2. How much should we be willing to pay for actions that are primarily reassuring, but do little to change the actual risk?

3. How can certain other social measures, which some think provide broader protection than counterterrorism, get greater attention?

Without such an approach, and given the extreme vagaries of estimating risks and vulnerabilities—there are an infinite number of potential targets, and the likelihood that any single one will be hit approaches zero—protection measures have often been dictated by political infighting and outbidding. The result has been such spending as $180,000 for a port that receives less than 20 ships a year, $30,000 to buy a defibrillator for use at a high school basketball tournament, $100,000 to fund a summer-jobs program in Washington, D.C., and $100,000 for a child pornography tip line. A 2006 congressional report pointed to $34 billion worth of projects that have "experienced significant overcharges, wasteful spending, or mismanagement."

There also have been efforts by people with political agendas to fold them into the war on terror. The gun control lobby, for example, wants "to deny weapons to terrorists and to actively prevent private citizens from providing them," whereas the National Rifle Association asserts that people would rather face the terrorist threat "with a firearm than without one."

In all these efforts, there are opportunity costs as other important societal needs may go underaddressed. As risk analyst David Banks puts it, if resources are directed away from apparently sensible programs and future growth to pursue "unachievable but politically popular levels of domestic security," the terrorists have won "an important victory that mortgages our future."

JM

See also Foreign Policy; Islam; Privacy; War; War Powers

Further Readings

Cole, David, and Jules Lobel. *Less Free, Less Safe: Why America Is Losing the War on Terror*. New York: New Press, 2007.

Ellig, Jerry, Amos Guiora, and Kyle McKenzie. *A Framework for Evaluating Counterterrorism Regulations*. Mercatus Policy Series, Mercatus Center, George Mason University, September 2006.

Flynn, Stephen E. *The Edge of Disaster: Building a Resilient Nation*. New York: Random House, 2007.

Healy, Gene. "The Imperial Presidency and the War on Terror." *Cato Policy Report*, March/April 2006.

Lustick, Ian S. *Trapped in the War on Terror*. Philadelphia: University of Pennsylvania Press, 2006.

Mueller, John. *Overblown: How Politicians and the Terrorism Industry Inflate National Security Threats, and Why We Believe Them*. New York: Free Press, 2006.

Schneier, Bruce. *Beyond Fear: Thinking Sensibly about Security in an Uncertain World*. New York: Copernicus, 2003.

Simon, Jeffrey D. 2001. *The Terrorist Trap: America's Experience with Terrorism*. 2nd ed. Bloomington: Indiana University Press.

Sunstein, Cass R. "Terrorism and Probability Neglect." *Journal of Risk and Uncertainty* 26 no. 2/3 (March–May 2003), 121–136.

WAR POWERS

Classical liberals and libertarians view war as a terrible engine of destruction, oppression, and government growth, holding with James Madison that "Of all the enemies to public liberty, war is, perhaps, the most to be dreaded, because it comprises and develops the germ of every other." But libertarianism does not imply pacifism. Most libertarians have recognized that war, although evil, is at times a necessary evil. For the libertarian, then, the issue of war powers presents two questions: When is going to war justified? Who should have the authority to decide?

The first question is harder to answer than the second. Although libertarianism proscribes the initiation of force, it approves of self-defense. Because the legitimate state is an organization for collective self-defense, made necessary in part by the existence of other, aggressive states, few libertarians have been willing to rule out war in all cases.

But the issue of collective self-defense is morally more complicated than individual self-defense. As the historian Jeffrey Rogers Hummel has pointed out, when a state commits itself to armed conflict, it is actually declaring war on three fronts: against the other state, against the people of the other state, and against its own dissenting citizens who do not want to contribute to the war effort. Seeking to minimize the rights violations inherent in such an enterprise, libertarians have generally looked to the tradition of the "just war" to determine when war is legitimate. That ethical tradition, developed over the centuries by figures such as Cicero, St. Thomas Aquinas, and Hugo Grotius, holds that a nation may make war only when it is undertaken in a just cause, with right intention, as a last resort, and with a reasonable chance of success. Further, the means used must be proportional to the ends sought. According to the criteria set down by the notion of the just war, self-defense is the only indisputably legitimate justification for the use of force.

Of course, there is plenty of room for debate over what constitutes self-defense. Some libertarians hold that a country must wait until it is attacked before responding militarily. For others, preemptive war—attacking an enemy that is about to attack you—is permissible. A few libertarians have gone even further, arguing that preventive war can occasionally be justified—that in order to protect its citizens, a country can attack an avowed enemy before it grows strong enough to present a serious threat. But the farther one goes along the scale toward preventive attacks, the more speculative the threat, and the less clear it is that the war is truly a defensive one.

What branch of government should be empowered to resolve these issues and decide when war is necessary? In the British constitutional tradition, the decision at one time belonged to the monarch. Thus, in *Commentaries on the Laws of England*, Blackstone noted that,

> the king has also the sole prerogative of making war and peace. For it is held by all the writers on the law of nature and nations, that the right of making war, which by nature subsisted in every individual, is given up by all private persons that enter into society, and is vested in the sovereign power: and this right is given up not only by individuals, but even by the intire body of people, that are under the dominion of a sovereign.

Libertarians reject this allocation of powers, holding that a decision as momentous as declaring war cannot safely be left to one man. Hence, they follow the American constitutional tradition. Wary of the executive's propensity to wage war, the Constitution's framers explicitly rejected the British model and granted the power to declare war to Congress. James Madison's notes of the constitutional convention in 1789 report that only one delegate, South Carolina's Pierce Butler, spoke in favor of granting the executive the authority to initiate war. His proposal was not warmly received. "Mr. [Elbridge] Gerry [of Massachusetts said he] never expected to hear in a republic a motion to empower the Executive alone to declare war." For his part, George Mason of Virginia "was aghast at giving the power of war to the Executive, because [he could] not . . . be trusted with it. . . . He was for clogging rather than facilitating war."

Accordingly, the Constitution specifies that the president lacks the authority to initiate military action. Article I, section 8 gives Congress the power "to declare War." In the Framers' view, in the absence of a congressional declaration of war, the president's war powers would be restricted to being purely reactive. If the territory of the United States or American forces were attacked, the president was empowered to respond. Except for his power to "repel sudden attacks," in Madison's phrase, the president could not act without congressional authorization. As delegate James Wilson explained,

> This system will not hurry us into war; it is calculated to guard against it. It will not be in the power of a single man, or a single body of men, to involve us in such distress; for the important power in declaring war is vested in the legislature at large.

For the first century and a half of our history, this constitutional allocation of war powers held. Large-scale wars— even nondefensive ones, such as the Mexican-American War of 1846—were declared by Congress; smaller wars were generally preceded by statutory authorization. But by the latter half of the 20th century, presidential wars small and large became a disturbingly common feature of the American political landscape. From President Harry Truman's 300,000 troop "police action" in Korea to President William Jefferson Clinton's 1999 air war over Kosovo, the decision to make war has increasingly been a unilateral one made by the president.

In fact, today the principle that the decision to initiate force belongs to the legislature is arguably healthier in Europe than in America. When NATO launched air strikes on Serbia in 1999, President Clinton refused to go to Congress for approval. However, other NATO countries made the decision to go to war legislatively: the Italian parliament had to authorize the strikes, and the German Bundestag had to be called into session to approve the participation of German forces.

In the United States throughout the 20th century, congressional control over the war power eroded, not simply as a result of executive aggrandizement, but also in part due to congressional complicity. The imperial presidency continues to grow largely because many legislators wish to avoid their responsibility to decide questions of war and peace. By delegating that responsibility to the president, they reserve their right to criticize him should military action go badly. For example, the use-of-force resolution passed by Congress immediately after 9/11 contains a sweeping delegation of authority to the president, authorizing him to make war on "those nations, organizations, or persons *he determines* planned, authorized, committed, or aided the terrorist attacks that occurred on September 11, 2001, or harbored such organizations or persons" [italics added]. In plain unambiguous language, the resolution leaves in the hands of the president the decision regarding when the evidence that a target nation has cooperated with al-Qaeda justifies war. Such broad delegations of legislative authority are constitutionally suspect in the domestic arena; surely they are no less so when it comes to questions of war and peace. As Madison put it: "Those who are to conduct a war cannot in the nature of things, be proper or safe judges, whether a war ought to be commenced, continued, or concluded."

The war on terror presents special challenges for those who wish to restore the war power to Congress. Congress's eagerness to shirk its deliberative responsibility, combined with a growing executive predilection for preventive war, will make it far more difficult to correct the constitutional balance of power, but ever more vital if we are to avoid unnecessary wars.

GH

See also Foreign Policy; Imperialism; Limited Government; Peace and Pacifism; War; War on Terror

Further Readings

Fisher, Louis. *Presidential War Power.* Lawrence: University Press of Kansas, 1995.
Walzer, Michael. *Just and Unjust Wars: A Moral Argument with Historical Illustrations.* New York: Basic Books, 1977.
Wormuth, Francis D., and Edwin B. Firmage. *To Chain the Dog of War.* Dallas, TX: Southern Methodist University Press, 1986.

WASHINGTON, GEORGE (1732–1799)

George Washington was the first president of the United States and the "father of his country." Washington fought for the Virginia colony early in the French and Indian War, and he later commanded the Continental Army in America's fight for independence. He presided over the Constitutional Convention and served for two terms as president under the new Constitution of the United States. Washington was fervently committed to the cause of republicanism, which embraced the view that political liberty was an inalienable right. Indeed, he played leading roles in nearly every major event of America's founding. As such, a number of historians have regarded his role as indispensable in delivering liberty to America.

Washington was born in 1732 at Wakefield Plantation, Virginia, to Augustine Washington and his second wife, Mary Ball Washington. Theirs was a gentry, planter family. Augustine died in 1743 when George was just 11. George then went off to live with his older brother Lawrence, who served as his mentor and a surrogate father. Lawrence had married into the Fairfax family, who were prominent in Virginia. The Fairfaxes helped launch George Washington's career as a land surveyor, and it was on behalf of Lord Thomas Fairfax that Washington surveyed the Shenandoah Valley.

In need of someone with a strong knowledge of Virginia's geography west of the Blue Ridge Mountains, Robert Dimwittie, acting governor of Virginia, appointed George, then 22 years old, to lead an expedition to challenge the French, who had claimed American territories in the Allegheny River Valley. The French and Indian War emerged out of this and similar disputes.

Washington faced major setbacks early in his military career. The French defeated his forces at Fort Necessity, Pennsylvania, in 1754. In the following year, as the war between Britain and France continued, General Edward Braddock commanded Washington, now a colonel, on another expedition to the forks of the Ohio. Braddock's forces were defeated at the Battle of the Monongahela, where the general was critically wounded and died shortly thereafter. George Washington, reputed to have been fearless in battle, was nearly killed there.

In 1758, under the command of Brigadier General John Forbes, Washington finally achieved victory against the French at Fort Duquesne. During the 5 years that he was involved in the French and Indian War, Washington honed his military skills, learned the intricacies of British and French warfare, and became a war hero in America and Great Britain.

Convinced that the French no longer threatened the Virginia frontier, in 1758, Washington left the army and returned to his home at Mount Vernon. In 1759, he married Martha Dandridge Custis, who was recently widowed and left with two young children whom Washington raised as his own. George and Martha would have no biological children of their own. In the same year, Washington first entered politics by being elected to Virginia's House of Burgesses, where he served until 1774. There he first became embroiled in Virginia's struggle against Great Britain's heavy-handed colonial policies. In part because of the vast expenses of the French and Indian War, Britain had levied a string of new taxes on the American colonies, which angered the colonists. In 1774–1775, Washington served as a delegate to the First and Second Continental Congresses, and in June 1775, Congress unanimously chose him as Commander and Chief of the Continental Army. On July 3, 1775, Washington assumed command of the American army that had surrounded British-occupied Boston. He then devoted his time and effort to training and disciplining his troops and securing much-needed supplies in order to prosecute the war for America's independence.

The war's early years were difficult ones for the American forces, particularly for Washington. In November 1776, British General William Howe was successful in driving Washington's forces from New York. However, his luck soon turned; on Christmas night, 1776, Washington crossed the Delaware to surprise Hessian forces and capture Trenton. Less than 2 weeks later, he secured Princeton. This good fortune did not last, however. In September and October 1777, Washington lost Brandywine and Germantown, Pennsylvania. The result was that Washington and his troops were forced to suffer a brutal winter in 1777 at Valley Forge, Pennsylvania.

A crucial reversal of fortune came in 1778 when France entered the war in support of America's independence. The Prussian Baron von Steuben trained Washington's troops at Valley Forge, and with the help of the Marquis de Lafayette, Washington snatched at least a draw from the jaws of defeat at the battle of Monmouth. The French army arrived in 1780 to help Washington secure victory over British Lord Charles Cornwallis at the Battle of Yorktown and ensure America's ultimate victory in the war. Britain formally recognized America's independence in the 1783 Treaty of Paris. After the war, some of Washington's officers wanted to make him king, but Washington declined the position for both personal and ideological reasons. Instead, he determined to retire to Mount Vernon. If he did that, King George III said Washington would be the "greatest man in the world." And indeed, he did.

Washington reentered politics when, in 1787, he was unanimously elected presiding officer at the Constitutional Convention, meeting in Philadelphia. The prestige that Washington lent to Constitutional deliberations helped ensure that the states would ratify the product of the Convention's proceedings. The delegates at the Convention desired Washington to be the first president under the new Constitution. Indeed, in retrospect, some historians have concluded that the office was created with him in mind.

Somewhat reluctantly, Washington assumed the presidency in New York City on April 30, 1789. Although he wanted to retire after his first term, the Electoral College unanimously reelected him in 1792. After completing his second term in 1797, Washington voluntarily relinquished power, establishing the precedents of the two-term presidency and the peaceful transfer of power between administrations. He died on December 14, 1799, at Mount Vernon, Virginia.

In politics, Washington was, like his fellow Whig American founders, fervently committed to the cause of republicanism. Harvard professor and historian Bernard Bailyn traces the ideological origins of America's founding-era republican thought to the following principal sources: Classical Greco-Roman antiquity; Biblical theology; English common law; Enlightenment rationalism, and the writings of British Whig theorists like Algernon Sidney, John Locke, and Joseph Priestly.

Although not as well read or well spoken as Hamilton, Jefferson, or Madison, Washington had embraced the republican philosophy of the founding era. His 1783 *Circular to the States* captured this "Whig" ideology, a synthesis of classical, biblical, common law, and rationalistic thought. "The foundation of our Empire," he wrote,

> was not laid in the gloomy age of Ignorance and Superstition, but at an Epocha when the rights of mankind were better understood and more clearly defined, than at any former period, the researches of the human mind, after social happiness, have been carried to a great extent, the Treasures of knowledge, acquired by the labours of Philosophers, Sages and Legislatures, through a long succession of years, are laid open for our use, and their collected wisdom may be happily applied in the Establishment of our forms of Government; the free cultivation of Letters, the unbounded extension of Commerce, the progressive refinement of Manners, the growing liberality of sentiment, and above all, the pure and benign light of Revelation, have had a meliorating influence on mankind and increased the blessings of Society.

Washington, like the authors of *The Federalist Papers*, had a particular affinity for ancient Rome. His favorite play was Joseph Addison's 1713 work about the implacable enemy of tyranny, *Cato the Younger*, and throughout his life, he saw the play numerous times. He commonly quoted from it and had it performed before his troops at Valley Forge. The play concerns the Roman Senator who committed suicide rather than submit to the tyranny of Julius Caesar. Washington's stoic sense of honor developed, in large part, from the profound influence this play had on his character.

As did the other republicans of his day, Washington ardently believed in the cause of political liberty. To our founders, liberty, in its broad and abstract sense, had a metaphysical quality to it, a God-given, inalienable right. As Washington put it in his first inaugural address, liberty was a "sacred fire" that the American people were entrusted to preserve.

The notion that men had an inalienable right to political liberty was one of the hallmarks of Whig ideology and Enlightenment thought. In his Farewell Address, Washington asserted that "public opinion should be enlightened," and that "[i]t will be worthy of a free, enlightened, and at no distant period a great nation to give to mankind the magnanimous and too novel example of a people always guided by an exalted justice and benevolence."

Enlightenment writers also contributed to Washington's belief that men of all religions—Christian or non-Christian, orthodox or heterodox—should possess full and equal rights under the laws of the United States. That religious liberty was granted to all Americans, at least at the federal level, was unprecedented. As Washington wrote on January 27, 1793, to the New Church in Baltimore, whose founder,

Emanuel Swedenborg, taught novel doctrines not in accord with prevailing Christian orthodoxy:

> We have abundant reason to rejoice that in this land the light of truth and reason has triumphed over the power of bigotry and superstition and that every person may here worship God according to the dictates of his own heart. In this enlightened Age & in this Land of equal liberty it is our boast, that a man's religious tenets, will not forfeit his protection of the Laws, nor deprive him of the right of attaining & holding the highest offices that are known in the United States.

As president, Washington governed largely in accord with his republican ideals. In his biography of Washington, *Realistic Visionary: A Portrait of George Washington*, Peter Henriques identifies Washington's presidential goals as "national unity, social stability, sound money, and flourishing commerce." Faced with the task of building a nation out of a collection of states, Washington sought to unify the separate states under a new Constitution that granted the central government far more power and authority than had prevailed under the Articles of Confederation. A number of founders, most notably Patrick Henry, regarded the expanded, centralized powers of the Constitution as betraying the spirit of the Revolution. However, Washington thought a stronger national government was necessary to preserve individual and states' rights.

During his presidency, he cautioned against America's becoming involved in foreign entanglements. The advice Washington gave in his Farewell Address underscored his presidential policies of neutrality and diplomacy:

> The nation which indulges toward another an habitual hatred or an habitual fondness is in some degree a slave. It is a slave to its animosity or to its affection, either of which is sufficient to lead it astray from its duty and its interest. . . . The great rule of conduct for us in regard to foreign nations is, in extending our commercial relations to have with them as little political connection as possible. So far as we have already formed engagements let them be fulfilled with perfect good faith. Here let us stop.

In part because of differences over foreign policy, organized political parties had begun to emerge during Washington's administration. This development disturbed Washington, who, in his Farewell Address, admonished the parties to put aside their differences and unite for the common good.

Perhaps the most important precedent Washington established as president was his decision to step down after completing his second term. Thereafter, power would be transferred peacefully from one administration to the next, and no president would serve more than two terms. No American president violated this precedent until Franklin Roosevelt in 1940. The 22nd Amendment, ratified in 1951, which states "[n]o person shall be elected to the office of the President more than twice . . . ," effectively enshrined Washington's precedent into law.

JoR

See also American Revolution; Constitution, U.S.; Liberalism, Classical; Republicanism, Classical; Term Limits; Whiggism

Further Readings

Bailyn, Bernard. *The Ideological Origins of the American Revolution.* Cambridge and London: Harvard University Press, 1967, 1992.

Brookhiser, Richard. *Founding Father: Rediscovering George Washington.* New York: Free Press, 1996.

Fitzpatrick, John C., ed. *The Writings of George Washington from the Original Manuscript Sources 1745–99.* Washington, DC: U.S. Government Printing Office, 1937.

Flexner, James Thomas. *Washington: The Indispensable Man.* New York: Signet, 1984.

Freeman, Douglas Southall. *George Washington: A Biography.* 7 vols. New York: Charles Scribner's Sons, 1948–1957.

Henriques, Peter R. *Realistic Visionary: A Portrait of George Washington.* Charlottesville and London: University of Virginia Press, 2006.

McCullough, David G. *1776.* New York: Simon & Schuster, 2005.

McDonald, Forrest. *Novus Ordo Seclorum: The Intellectual Origins of the Constitution.* Lawrence: University Press of Kansas, 1985.

WEALTH AND POVERTY

Wealth results from producing things that consumers value most by sacrificing the least valuable combinations of labor and resources. The best place to begin a discussion of wealth is with the division of labor (or specialization), which Adam Smith discusses in the first chapter of *Wealth of Nations*. Understanding the conditions that create wealth also provides useful insight into those conditions that result in poverty.

Dividing workers' tasks into narrow productive specialties increases the amount that can be produced by increasing one's skills in that activity, reducing the time spent shifting from one activity to another, and increasing the amount of capital that one can effectively employ. If most workers had to make more than a small contribution to the production of the goods they were involved in producing, only a fraction of us would long survive, and those who did would live in extreme poverty, as most of what we now consume would be prohibitively costly. However, although specialization is necessary for producing the abundance of goods and services that constitute wealth, it is not sufficient. Specialization cannot be fully productive without freedom and coordination—the freedom of each individual to use his specialized skills in accordance with his knowledge of local conditions while somehow making sure that his actions are coordinated with countless others with the same freedom.

In an unfree economy, the decisions of remote planners lacking relevant information on local conditions are substituted for the decisions of those who have this information. As Hayek eloquently explained, centralizing economic decisions inevitably substitutes ignorance for the local knowledge essential for making choices fully consistent with the production of wealth.

Without overall coordination, each individual could be competent at what he is doing and could be adjusting well to local conditions, but is likely to fail to combine his activities with those of others to produce goods, much less the combination and quality of goods most valued by consumers. People often believe that this supposed inability to coordinate action over a distance suggests a trade-off between freedom and coordination. More freedom reduces coordination, and more coordination can be achieved only by reducing freedom. Thus, the best possibility seems to be some compromise between making decisions that fully utilize local information and coordinating the decisions that are made in the most productive way. Fortunately, this situation is one of the few where economists do not see a trade-off. Adam Smith's fundamental insight, as developed in *Wealth of Nations*, is that the wealth-producing advantages of specialization can be realized—indeed, more fully realized—when there are no authorities attempting to coordinate private decisions. Coordination is best achieved without a coordinator. As Smith stated,

> The statesman who should attempt to direct private people in what manner they ought to employ their capitals [including human capital embodied in labor], would not only load himself with a most unnecessary attention, but assume an authority which could safely be trusted, not only to no single person, but to no council or senate whatever, and which would nowhere be so dangerous as in the hands of a man who had folly and presumption enough to fancy himself fit to exercise it.

But how can decisions based on local knowledge be coordinated without central direction? Explaining how this coordination occurs under the right set of economic institutions has been a central achievement of economic analysis since Adam Smith. Critical to this achievement is understanding how countless people, each pursuing their own interests, collectively communicate information on how everyone can use their individual talents and resources to best serve the interests of others, and to do so in a way that motivates each to do exactly that. The institutions that make this communication and coordination possible are those associated with a market economy. In general terms, these institutions consist of private property, a stable currency,

and a legal system that protects property rights and enforces mutually agreed-on contracts, all of which facilitate voluntary exchanges.

The market prices that result from these exchanges allow people to communicate both the information vital to coordinating their actions and the incentives for them to do so. This "information economy" and its wealth-enhancing productivity are not new. Indeed, the "information economy" is as old as economies based on voluntary exchange and market prices, as a discussion of the major types of market communication and coordination easily illustrate.

Making the most valuable use of a fixed supply of a consumption good requires communication and coordination between consumers. When some consumers decide they want more of a good, they communicate that information to other consumers through the higher prices resulting from their increased demand. The other consumers respond to this information by reducing their consumption of the good, which has the effect of sharing more of the good with those who now value it more. Those consumers who reduce their consumption need not know why the price has increased, nor need they care about those consumers whose demand has increased, but the higher price motivates them to act as if they did. Collectively, they will reduce their consumption by just enough for those with the higher demands to increase their consumption by the extra amount they desire at the higher price. This process represents a truly impressive amount of coordination, and it happens with countless goods without anyone being in charge.

Creating wealth by using resources and labor in their highest valued employment requires communication and coordination between consumers and producers. The first to respond to the price communication of increased demand from some consumers are other consumers. But these higher prices for a good also inform producers that the value gained from producing more of the good is now greater than the cost. Given a little time, this information will motivate a shift in labor and resources from the production of less valued goods to the production of the now more valued one. This shift will continue as long as the value of producing additional units of the good is greater than the value sacrificed by having fewer other goods. This coordination between producers and consumers keeps labor and resources constantly moving toward employments where they are worth more and away from employments where they are worth less.

The price communication between consumers and producers goes both ways. If the cost of producing a good increases for any reason, its price will go up, informing consumers that the same value of labor and resources in the production of other goods now creates less value in the production of this particular good than had been the case. Consumers respond to this information by reducing their consumption of this good, thus allowing its producers to create more value by shifting some of the labor and resources being used in its production to the production of other goods. This shift will continue to be motivated by further changes in market prices until no additional value results. In like manner, productive resources would move in the opposite direction in response to price communication if the cost of producing the good decreases. In either case, the spontaneous coordination between producers and consumers, informed and motivated by market prices, creates wealth by directing resources into their highest valued uses.

Producing something as simple as an ordinary wooden pencil is beyond the ability of any one person and requires extensive communication between producers. As one economist has explained, pencil production requires the coordinated efforts of highly specialized workers from all over the world, employed by a long chain of firms and using a large variety of widely dispersed resources and sophisticated capital equipment. Yet wooden pencils are conveniently available at prices so low that they are commonly given away as advertisements. Coordination among the many producers that are needed to produce a wooden pencil, not to mention far more complex goods, at the lowest possible cost would be impossible without the information communicated by market prices. Market prices inform producers which part of the productive process is most profitable for them to specialize in—that is, that part of the productive process where the most net value is added. When a producer has added as much net value as possible, the result is that it becomes more profitable to sell this output to another specialist, rather than to continue production. This market-motivated coordination results in far more wealth creation than would be possible were central planners to attempt to impose coordination.

The tremendous wealth from the freedom and coordination of the market does come at a price. Markets make freedom possible by imposing discipline on the use of freedom—discipline necessary for the coordination of markets. Those whose decisions are inconsistent with the desires of others, who are not using their labor and resources to serve others as well as possible, will have their jobs and personal wealth competed away by those who create more wealth by making decisions more consistent with the decisions and well-being of others. This discipline takes the form of bankruptcies, layoffs, and other types of financial losses. Such discipline is painful and commonly blamed on the harshness of market economies. Although it is easy to see the pain imposed by markets, it is difficult to make the connection between the information and discipline causing the pain and the wealth and freedom that result. As Machiavelli observed in another context, "Thoughtless writers admire [the] achievement . . . , yet condemn the main reason for it."

The freedom and economic coordination made possible by market information and discipline constantly expands wealth by unleashing the creativity of entrepreneurship. Entrepreneurs are interested not just in making the best use of existing knowledge and resources, but in discovering new knowledge and resources by pursuing what most people have not thought about and might consider impossible if they had. Many, probably most, entrepreneurial ventures fail to create wealth, but without the freedom to try those that fail, there will be far fewer discoveries that succeed. Only when entrepreneurial freedom is guided by the information and ruthless discipline communicated and imposed by market prices will the entrepreneurial ventures that do not increase wealth be quickly identified and terminated, with resources redirected into the expansion of those that expand wealth. This process of entrepreneurial discovery explains not just the wealth of a market economy at any moment, but the growth in wealth that turns one generation's luxuries into the next generation's necessities and finds the goods limited to the wealthy of one generation widely available to the nonwealthy of the next. As Joseph Schumpeter pointed out, "Queen Elizabeth owned silk stockings. The capitalist achievement does not typically consist in providing more silk stockings for queens but in bringing them within the reach of factory girls in return for steadily decreasing amounts of effort."

Unfortunately, although few recognize the connection between the discipline of the market and the wealth of the economy, we all are perfectly aware that our personal wealth would be increased if we were exempted from that discipline. If our jobs were protected, if our firms did not have to face competition, or if compassionate and well-intended policies were enacted to reduce the economic pain inflicted on us, we would be wealthier. More accurately, we would be wealthier if we were among the favored few who received such exemptions while everyone else had to continue coordinating their actions for the benefit of others even when that coordination required losing their jobs, going out of business, or giving up on their entrepreneurial dreams. However, any serious attempt by government to universalize these safeguards, to protect everyone from the discipline of the marketplace, would quickly convert wealth into poverty by suppressing the communication, coordination, and freedom of the market.

DRL

See also Classical Economics; Division of Labor; Free Trade; Globalization; Kleptocracy; Smith, Adam

Further Readings

Buchanan, James M., and Yoon, Yong J. *The Return to Increasing Returns*. Ann Arbor: University of Michigan Press, 1994.

Hayek, Friedrich A. "The Use of Knowledge in Society." *The American Economic Review* 35 (1945): 519–530.

Machiavelli, Niccolò, Quentin Skinner, and Russell Price, eds. *The Prince*. Cambridge: Cambridge University Press, 1988.

Read, Leonard. "I, Pencil." *The Freeman* 8 (1958): 32–37.

Schumpeter, Joseph A. *Capitalism, Socialism and Democracy.* New York: HarperTorch Books, 1950.

Smith, Adam. *An Inquiry into the Nature and Causes of the Wealth of Nations.* Indianapolis, IN: Liberty Fund, 1981.

WELFARE STATE

The welfare state denotes the wide array of social welfare services provided by modern governments. It can be differentiated from socialism or Marxism in that the means of production are not owned by the state. Rather, the state undertakes—through a variety of tax and spending initiatives—to redistribute wealth and shield citizens from many of the normal risks of life.

As a designation of a particular type of polity, *welfare state* appears to have first been used by William Temple, Archbishop of Canterbury, who argued in his 1942 book *Christianity and Social Order* that it was the Christian duty of modern states like Britain to provide all citizens with a minimum standard of living. Temple contrasted his vision of the beneficent *welfare state* with the evils of the German *warfare state.* The term was later popularized by British social reformers and explicitly became part of the Labor Party's platform in 1945.

Although the name is relatively modern, the concept is not. Indeed, it could be said that nearly all states have been involved in providing some level of social welfare services, going back at least to the free grain provided to the poor in ancient Rome and Egypt. The Caliphate under Umar ibn al-Khattab offered a wide variety of welfare benefits, including old-age pensions and government-paid physicians. In 19th-century France, government welfare programs became so extensive that they were ridiculed by opponents as the "providence state."

However, the welfare state in its modern sense can probably best be dated to imperial Germany under Otto von Bismarck in the 1880s. Under Bismarck, the state began to offer not just assistance to the poor, but benefits that were extended to all citizens, such as accident and health insurance and old-age pensions—so-called social insurance programs. In fact, it was a particularly significant innovation of Bismarck's that government social assistance should not be provided just to the "deserving poor," as was the custom with most charities, or even the poor more generally, but to all citizens without regard to need, employment, or family situation. By the start of the 20th century, social expenditures by the German government were already in excess of 3% of the GDP.

There is no doubt that Bismarck's ideas provided the basis for the modern welfare state. For example, Lloyd George and William Beveridge, the architects of welfare statism in Britain, visited Germany in the early years of the 20th century. Indeed, the central ideas of Bismarck's "social state"—universality, social insurance, redistribution of wealth, and government-funded charity—became the linchpins of the welfare state worldwide.

During the first 150 years of U.S. history, both tradition and the Constitution limited government involvement in providing social welfare programs, particularly at the federal level. In 1794, while debating a proposed welfare bill, James Madison rose on the floor of the House to declare, "I cannot undertake to lay my finger on that article of the Constitution which granted a right to Congress" to pass such a bill. However, the rise of modernism and progressivism at the end of the 19th century was accompanied by a change in Americans' attitudes toward government. Progressive reformers, drawing on doubtful conclusions of the emerging field of social science, believed that the problems wrought by urbanization, industrialization, and the aftermath of the Civil War were too overwhelming for average citizens. These reformers concluded that "experts" were needed to deal with such important issues, and only government could provide the needed expertise. Whereas previously the purpose of government had been seen as protecting individual rights, the government was now seen as a more universal problem solver. By 1920, Owen Lovejoy, president of the National Conference of Social Work, was writing that government workers were "social engineers" imposing "a divine order on earth as it is in heaven."

Government was already growing rapidly when the United States experienced one of the most traumatic and transforming events in the nation's history—the Great Depression. At its worst point in 1933, nearly 13 million Americans were unemployed—almost one quarter of the labor force. Among nonfarm workers, unemployment was even worse, reaching a high of 37.6%. The nation's real gross national product declined by half between 1929 and 1933. One third of the nation's banks suspended operations. Businesses went bankrupt, and mortgage foreclosures were widespread, particularly on farms. Both traditional, private, charitable organizations and state and local governments were overwhelmed by the sudden demands placed on them.

With Americans frightened and insecure, President Franklin Roosevelt responded with a massive expansion of the federal role in social welfare and in regulating the economy. The administration regulated prices, set labor standards, and subsidized commodities. Indeed, virtually no area remained exempt from federal control. At the same time, the government undertook to construct a vast new welfare state in the Bismarckian mode. When the Supreme Court tried to hold the government to constitutionally imposed boundaries, Roosevelt threatened to pack the Court with pro–New Deal judges until it capitulated.

To provide some idea of how vast and rapid the expansion of government was, consider that in 1932 just 2.1% of all government social welfare spending was at the federal level. By 1939, the federal government accounted for 62.5% of social welfare spending, and this new larger slice was from a much larger pie. Over that same period, welfare programs increased from 6.5% of all government expenditures (federal, state, and local) to 27.1%. Most important, Roosevelt established both unemployment insurance and social security, thus creating the first broad-based social insurance programs in the country.

Scholars dispute whether Roosevelt's measures had any role in bringing America out of the Depression. Unemployment in 1939, for example, was nearly as high as it was in 1932, and many observers believe it was World War II that actually broke the cycle. However, Roosevelt received the credit, and in the prosperity following the end of the war, there was little interest in challenging the programs he introduced. From Roosevelt on, there was broad bipartisan support for the welfare state, which expanded rapidly regardless of the party or professed ideology of his successors.

Today, Western welfare states have grown to enormous proportions. In some European countries, such as Denmark, France, Germany, and Sweden, social welfare spending consumes more than a quarter of the GDP. By comparison, the U.S. welfare state remains relatively small, amounting to just 15% of the GDP. Even so, the U.S. federal government spends more than $477 billion on some 80 different programs to fight poverty. This figure amounts to $12,892 for every poor man, woman, and child in the country. Social insurance programs are even larger. The cost of the two largest, Medicare and social security, providing health care and pensions to the elderly, has risen from just 0.3% of the GDP in 1950 to nearly 10% today. Government health care programs now account for roughly half of all U.S. health care spending. Some estimates suggest that if the current growth rate of the U.S. welfare state continues unchecked, government spending could consume an astounding 50% to 70% of the GDP by the end of the century.

Libertarians have objected to the welfare state on several grounds. The most pragmatic of these objections is that these welfare programs perform poorly. They have not eliminated or even significantly reduced poverty, nor have they made our health care or retirement systems better. They have not improved education. They have not solved any of the myriad problems society faces. Indeed, more often than not, they have made those problems worse.

For example, despite nearly $9 trillion in total welfare spending since Lyndon Johnson declared war on poverty in 1964, the poverty rate is perilously close to where it was when the war began more than 40 years ago. Social security systems in all Western countries provide recipients with rates of return below what could be earned through privately investing the same funds. National health insurance programs have yielded rationing and massive waiting lists.

Moreover, the welfare state comes at a huge cost that is most obviously manifested in reduced economic growth, fewer jobs, reduced take-home pay, and less overall prosperity. In an era of globalization when countries must compete on an international basis, taxation and regulation act as anchors on productivity and competitiveness. The resources that the government extracts from the private sector to pay for itself are resources that are not available for the private sector to use in producing more goods and services. When the government takes money out of workers' pockets, these workers have less money to spend or save; when the government takes money from business, it has less money to use for investment, research, or to pay workers.

Taxation is a penalty on the activity being taxed. Thus, taxing an activity, any activity, will reduce the level of that activity. This logic is behind policies such as raising cigarette taxes to discourage smoking, but it applies equally to the impact of taxes on business decisions. Once investment is taxed, investment will decline. Tax employment and there will be fewer employees. Tax corporate profits and businesses will be fewer.

Third, the welfare state distracts government from those functions that most libertarians accept as legitimate, such as defense. Every Western nation spends far more on the welfare state than it does on national defense. Even in the United States, with its relatively smaller welfare state, social welfare spending is three times larger than defense spending. Many libertarians note with disapproval that when the United States was attacked on September 11, President Bush was in a Florida schoolroom promoting a federal government reading program.

Fourth, the welfare state undermines many of the "bourgeois virtues" that undergird a democratic and civil society. When government assumes greater responsibility for our lives, less reason exists for us to act virtuously. We are, in effect, protected from the consequences of our nonvirtuous behavior. The results are readily apparent. As government has grown, we have become less likely to work and save, more intemperate, and less concerned with the consequences of our actions, less self-reliant, and even less compassionate toward others. Studies show that as government welfare spending increases, donations to private charities decline. Other studies have demonstrated that social security programs reduce private savings. Of course, for years we have known that welfare programs reduce work effort and increase out-of-wedlock births.

Finally, and most importantly, libertarians believe that the welfare state is antithetical to freedom. Every new government program reduces our freedom just a little bit more. We are less free to manage our own lives, decide how to spend our money, go into business, plan for our retirement, take care of our health, or educate our children. Social welfare, libertarians believe, is properly the realm of the family and civil society, institutions that are not only more effective, but also are based on voluntary social interaction. As a result, most libertarians favor rolling back or eliminating most aspects of the current welfare state.

MT

See also Freedom; Interventionism; Murray, Charles; New Deal; Wealth and Poverty

Further Readings

Bartholomew, James. *The Welfare State We're In*. London: Politico's Publishing, 2006.

Murray, Charles. *In Pursuit: Of Happiness and Good Government*. Oakland, CA: ICS Press, 1994.

Paul, Ellen, Fred Miller, and Jeffrey Paul, eds. *The Welfare State*. Cambridge: Cambridge University Press, 1997.

Pierson, Chris. *Beyond the Welfare State?* University Park: Pennsylvania State University Press, 1991.

Tanner, Michael. *The End of Welfare: Fighting Poverty in the Civil Society*. Washington, DC: Cato Institute, 1996.

WHIGGISM

The term *Whiggism* refers to the philosophical principles of the British Whig party, the name attached to the reformist political party that, by the mid-19th century, had come to be called the Liberal party. The term *Whig* appears to be Scots Gaelic, a derogatory term for horse thief, that was used to describe adherents of the Presbyterian cause in Scotland in the early 17th century. The Tory Party, the traditional political opposition to the Whigs, fared no better in its designation, "Tory" having derived from an Irish term for those associated with the Papist outlaws loyal to the deposed James II.

Following the Restoration of the Stuarts to the English throne in 1660, the House of Commons found itself divided between a Country party, who regarded themselves as representing the interests of the people, and a Court party, whose primary loyalty was to the King and Court. To those groups, the names Whig and Tory were attached in 1679, during the bitter struggle between the two parties over the succession of the Roman Catholic Duke of York (later James II) to the throne. The Whig party supported the supremacy of Parliament and toleration for Protestant dissenters and was adamantly opposed to a Catholic on the throne. The Glorious Revolution of 1688, which deposed James II and replaced him with his Protestant daughter Mary and her husband William of Orange, was an unqualified triumph for Whig party principles. The Revolution permanently settled the issue of constitutional sovereignty in England and ushered in a period of Whig domination of British politics, which, with the exception of a period of 4 years when Anne was on the throne, lasted until the mid-18th century. Throughout that period, the Whigs tended to be the party of the nation's great landowners and of its merchants and tradesmen, whereas the Tories more often represented the interests of the smaller landowners and the rural clergy.

The principal influence on Whig thought following the Revolution settlement was that of John Locke. Locke's political views, as set down in his *Two Treatises of Government*, underpinned Whig ideology and shaped its notions regarding the nature and scope of government. Locke and the radical Whig political writers who followed him affirmed that all men in the state of nature are equal and that the basis of all legitimate government is the consent of the governed; that all men are possessed of certain natural, inalienable rights; and that the civil magistrate is bound by the terms of the original contract by which he holds authority to govern. Should the sovereign violate the terms of that contract, as had James II, men had a right to resist him and to substitute in his place a sovereign prepared to adhere to the terms under which men surrendered their original power to judge and punish their fellow men. Those conclusions were in sharp contrast to the claims of James II and the Tories who supported him—namely, that the sovereign was the bearer of hereditary indefeasible rights and the final arbiter of all things affecting the governance of the nation. With the success of the Revolution of 1688, however, the Tories were forced to abandon their earlier extravagant monarchist views and to come to terms with the revolutionary settlement and the relationship between Crown and Parliament.

In the years following the Revolution, a large number of political tracts and dissertations were written by a host of authors in an effort to secure its benefits and to extend its influence. Among those writers were Matthew Tindal, Benjamin Hoadly, and, more important, Robert Molesworth. Molesworth, who had been forced into exile during the reign of James II, wrote *An Account of Denmark* in 1693 in an attempt to warn his fellow Englishmen of the dangers to individual liberty that can follow from an ignorance or indifference to political affairs. Molesworth's essay underscored the need for constant vigilance and for an electorate that actively participates in public life. That theme was reiterated by a number of Whig authors, whose tracts combined elements of classical republicanism with a Lockean theory of rights and of the legitimacy of resistance to tyranny.

Perhaps the best example of the political language of post-Lockean Whig thought appears in the writings of John Trenchard and Thomas Gordon, whose *Cato's Letters* were published between 1720 and 1723. The letters are a splendid example of the literature of political opposition during the first half of the 18th century and over the next 50 years were to serve as an important source of revolutionary inspiration in the colonial struggle against the British. While *Cato's Letters* embraced a Lockean conception of rights, it also borrowed from the language of English republican thought, which emphasized the temptations of political corruption, the dangers in gratifying the private passions at the public expense, and the need for an active electorate as guardians of the polity.

Like most Whigs, Trenchard and Gordon strongly supported the removal of the civil disabilities under which religious dissenters then suffered. John Locke in his *Letter Concerning Toleration* had earlier called for the removal of restrictions on religious practice. Indeed, toleration for religious dissidents was a cardinal principle of Whig ideology. But the arguments put forward in *Cato's Letters* were even more forceful than those in Locke's writings. In one of the most impassioned defenses of freedom of conscience published during the 18th century, Trenchard and Gordon maintained that our consciences constitute the most integral part of our being and, as such, are exempt from all regulation by the civil magistrate. Those exhortations for religious toleration did not go unheeded by the various Whig governments, and a number of disabilities were repealed over the course of the first 50 years of the 18th century. Unfortunately, the easing of disabilities did not extend to Roman Catholicism, which many regarded as combining the most primitive elements of superstition with political oppression.

Although no formal Whig or Tory parties existed as such during the early part of the reign of George III, who ascended the throne in 1760, they emerged in the Commons following the appointment of William Pitt the Younger as first minister and head of the Tory Party in 1783. At that point, a revived Whig party, representing religious dissenters, entrepreneurs, and other reformist elements, coalesced around the leadership of Charles James Fox. The name finally fell into disuse after the turn of the century when the more radical members of the reformist party began to call themselves Liberals and employed "Whig" as a term of opprobrium for those members they regarded as too conservative.

RH

See also English Civil Wars; Glorious Revolution; Levellers; Liberalism, Classical; Limited Government

Further Readings

Hamowy, Ronald. "'Cato's Letters,' John Locke, and the Republican Paradigm." *History of Political Thought* 11 (Summer 1990): 273–294.

Robbins, Caroline. *The Eighteenth-Century Commonwealthman.* New York: Atheneum, 1968.

Stephen, Sir Leslie. *History of English Thought in the Eighteenth Century.* 2 vols. New York: Harcourt, Brace & World, 1962 [1876].

Williams, Basil. *The Whig Supremacy, 1714–1760.* 2nd ed. Oxford: Clarendon Press, 1962.

Wootton, David, ed. *Republicanism, Liberty, and Commercial Society, 1649–1776.* Stanford, CA: Stanford University Press, 1994.

WICKSELL, KNUT (1851–1926)

Knut Wicksell was a Swedish economist. In any ranking of economists who were active in the 100 years following Wicksell's birth, his name would surely appear in the top 10. Wicksell's work included substantial contributions both to the Austrian theory of the business cycle and the theory of public choice. Wicksell followed Eugen von Böhm-Bawerk in treating production as a sequence of stages, where the production of consumer goods was supported by a hierarchical structure of capital goods. To this structure of production, Wicksell attached the idea of two distinct rates of interest: a natural rate and a loan rate. A divergence between the natural rate and the loan rate would induce a change in the structure of production. For instance, a fall in the natural rate of interest through a decline in time preference would lead to a more capital-intensive structure of production. In contrast, a rise in interest and time preference would lead to a less capital-intensive structure of production.

Wicksell's work on capital and money centered on securing macrolevel coordination among savers and investors, and Wicksell's significance to contemporary theorizing about coordination was stressed especially strongly by Axel Leijonhufvud in 1981. Among other things, Wicksell's coordinationist orientation set the stage for the Austrian theory of the business cycle that subsequently was developed by Ludwig von Mises and F. A. Hayek. Wicksell maintained that an expansion in bank credit would drive the loan rate below the natural rate. This initial effect of the credit expansion is identical to a fall in time preference and will produce an economic expansion, the first manifestation of which would be an expansion in capital goods. Because time preferences will not have fallen, however, voluntary saving will be insufficient to sustain this lengthened structure of production. Hence, the credit-financed boom will subsequently bust.

In 1896, Wicksell published his *Investigations in the Theory of Public Finance.* The core of this work emphasized consensus and unanimity in place of majority rule as a standard of governance and became the guiding framework for the theory of public choice and constitutional economics, particularly as illustrated by James Buchanan and Gordon Tullock's *Calculus of Consent.* In this work, Wicksell asked what kind of institutional framework for parliamentary governance would make it possible for people in their capacities as taxpayers reasonably to say that their tax monies were directed as they wished. Wicksell assumed that, through proportional representation, it would be possible to select a parliament that would serve reasonably well as a miniature model of the Swedish population. If this parliament were then bound by a rule of unanimity, its decisions would conform closely to unanimity within the underlying population.

Wicksell subsequently relaxed this principle of unanimity to something approximating unanimity, three quarters or seven eighths of the total. Wicksell recognized that this shift to approximate unanimity involved a trade-off. True unanimity would ensure that people would not have to pay taxes for activities they were not willing to support. But it also would prove too costly to any effort of trying to work out arrangements for collective support. Some modest movement away from unanimity might, Wicksell thought, be a reasonable compromise to expediency.

RW

See also Banking, Austrian Theory of; Buchanan, James M.; Democracy; Public Choice Economics; Tullock, Gordon

Further Readings

Buchanan, James M., and Gordon Tullock. *The Calculus of Consent.* Ann Arbor: University of Michigan Press, 1962.

Gardlund, Torsten. *The Life of Knut Wicksell.* Stockholm: Almqvist & Wiksell, 1958.

Leijonhufvud, Axel. "The Wicksell Connection: Variations on a Theme." *Information and Coordination.* New York: Oxford University Press, 1981. 131–201.

Wagner, Richard E. "The Calculus of Consent: A Wicksellian Retrospective." *Public Choice* 56 (February 1988): 153–166.

Wicksell, Knut. *Lectures on Political Economy.* 2 vols. London: Routledge, 1901, 1906.

WILBERFORCE, WILLIAM (1759–1833)

William Wilberforce was a philanthropist, politician, social activist, and the leading figure in the British abolitionist movement. He convinced Parliament to put a stop to the slave trade in 1807 and to end slavery within the British Empire in 1833. He was elected to Parliament in 1780 at the age of 21 and served there for 45 years, until his retirement in 1825. Although his elected position gave him the platform and visibility to promote the antislavery cause for which he is best known, he also devoted considerable time and energy to a second cause he termed "the reformation of manners." The latter cause led him to champion an eclectic range of efforts, including "free" education, sobriety, charity schools, penal reform, child labor, moral instruction, Christian mission work in India, and an end to cruelty toward animals. His work against slavery clearly raises him to the highest

ranks in the annals of libertarianism, but some of his other activities evidenced a willingness to deploy state power to advance a whole range of social objectives.

Wilberforce never had the physical presence one might expect of someone so eager to take on entrenched interests. James Boswell, the famous biographer of Samuel Johnson, called Wilberforce a "shrimp." Thin and short, Wilberforce compensated with vision, eloquence, and willpower. As a newly minted Tory Parliamentarian, he spoke out against the war with America, labeling it "cruel, bloody and impractical," clearly a minority view in the midst of the war. But he drifted from issue to issue without a central focus until a religious awakening sparked a lifelong calling to the nascent antislavery movement. Repulsed by the hideous barbarity of the slave trade then prevalent, he determined in October 1787 to work for its abolition. His allies included Thomas Clarkson, John Newton, Hannah More, Granville Sharp, Charles Fox, and close friend and prime minister, William Pitt the Younger.

Ending slavery seemed an unlikely prospect in the 1780s. Viewed widely as integral to British naval and commercial success, slavery was a huge business, enjoying broad political support, as well as widespread (through essentially racist) intellectual justification. For 75 years before Wilberforce set about to end the trade in slaves, indeed, the slave trade, while lucrative for British slavers, was savagely merciless for its millions of victims.

Wilberforce assisted the Society for the Abolition of the Slave Trade and other organizations to spread the word about the inhumanity of one man owning another. "Our motto must continue to be perseverance," he once told followers. He endured and overcame just about every obstacle imaginable, including ill health, derision from his colleagues, death threats, and defeats almost too numerous to count.

He rose in the House of Commons to give his first abolition speech in 1789. It would take 18 years before the slave trade would be ended by law. He introduced an abolition measure in every session, only to lose time after time. On at least one occasion, some of his own allies deserted him for reasons as petty as the opposition having given them free tickets to attend the theater during a crucial vote. The war with France that began in the 1790s often put the slavery issue on the back burner, and those who opposed Wilberforce's argued persuasively that if Britain ended its trade in slaves, it would simply hand a profitable enterprise over to a mortal enemy, the French. He was often ridiculed and condemned as a traitorous rabble-rouser.

Abolition of the slave trade finally won Parliament's approval on February 23, 1807. Biographer David J. Vaughan reports that,

> as the attorney general, Sir Samuel Romilly, stood and praised the perseverance of Wilberforce, the House rose to its feet and broke out in cheers. Wilberforce was so overcome

with emotion that he sat head in hand, tears streaming down his face.

Although the trade in slaves was officially over, an end to slavery remained the biggest prize. To bring it about, Wilberforce worked for another 26 years after the 1807 vote, even after retiring from nearly a half-century of service in Parliament in 1825. He was finally victorious on July 26, 1833, when Britain enacted a peaceful, compensated emancipation and became the world's first major nation to unshackle an entire race within its jurisdiction. Hailed as one of the heroes who made it possible, Wilberforce died 3 days later.

Wilberforce was born in Hull, in Yorkshire, the son of a wealthy merchant. He inherited substantial assets, which sustained him at a comfortable level for most of his life and financed his political, philanthropic, and community efforts. Unlike many social activists, he largely spent away his personal wealth on the causes he championed, leaving little behind when he died at the age of 73. A lover of animals, he helped start and substantially funded the Royal Society for the Prevention of Cruelty to Animals.

Although libertarians admire his principled stance on slavery, Wilberforce was not uniformly committed to the principle of noninitiation of force. He endorsed public education funded by taxes. He joined leading clergymen in encouraging the government to suppress vice, leading to repressive fines and prison sentences for trifling offenses and even deterring freedoms of speech and assembly. He convinced Parliament to require the British East India Company to sponsor Christian missionary work in India as a condition of its being granted a monopoly share of the spice trade. He worked against parliamentary reforms that were promoted by secular elements. Early labor union advocates saw him as an enemy of worker rights to organize for better pay, hours, and working conditions. Many libertarians might applaud his successful campaign to end the state lottery.

The most lasting legacy of William Wilberforce remains the remarkable change in world opinion and policy toward the institution of slavery. Widespread and commonly accepted throughout the world in the 1780s, slavery was virtually wiped out over the course of a century, an outcome inspired in great measure by Wilberforce, his eloquence, and his allies.

LWR

See also Abolitionism; Slavery, World; Slavery in America

Further Readings

Belmonte, Kevin. *William Wilberforce: A Hero for Humanity*. Grand Rapids, MI: Zondervan, 2007.

Furneaux, Robin. *William Wilberforce*. Vancouver, BC, Canada: Regent College Publishing, 2006.

Hochschild, Adam. *Bury the Chains: Prophets and Rebels in the Fight to Free an Empire's Slaves*. Boston: Houghton Mifflin, 2005.

Metaxas, Eric. *William Wilberforce and the Heroic Campaign to End Slavery*. New York: HarperCollins, 2007.

Tomkins, Stephen. *William Wilberforce: A Biography*. Grand Rapids, MI: Wm. B. Eerdsman Publishing, 2007.

WOLLSTONECRAFT, MARY (1759–1797)

Mary Wollstonecraft was a writer and feminist. She is one of the founders of American and British feminism, whose most famous work, *Vindication of the Rights of Woman* (1792), is widely viewed as the first great feminist treatise. In the late 18th century, Wollstonecraft became a member of a London circle of libertarian authors, among them Percy Bysshe Shelley and William Godwin, whom she later married. Wollstonecraft embraced the Enlightenment, a social revolution that celebrated reason as the core of human identity and which sought to reconstruct social institutions, such as the family, by our rational understanding. Her contributions to this approach included applying the principle of personal liberty to the sexual realm and her insistence that women were "rational creatures." She rejected the traditional methods of educating girls, demanding their education accord with those dedicated by Enlightenment views on how children should be raised. Wollstonecraft's life embraced drama and tragedy as she pursued the intellectual, financial, and sexual independence her writings promoted. She died at the age of 38, shortly after giving birth to her second child, the future Mary Shelley.

Wollstonecraft was born in London into a working-class family. In 1784, she cofounded a school in the village of Newington Green, where she befriended its radical minister Richard Price. Price was one of the leaders of a group known as the Rational Dissenters and the author of an influential book titled *Review of the Principal Questions of Morals* (1758), which argued that individual conscience and reason should determine moral choices. Through Price, Wollstonecraft became acquainted with England's leading reformers.

The radical publisher Joseph Johnson commissioned her to write the pamphlet "Thoughts on the Education of Daughters" (1787). In 1788, he published her first two books: a biographical novel, *Mary, a Fiction*, which depicted how women's social limitations oppressed them; and a children's book, *Original Stories from Real Life*. Wollstonecraft began working for Johnson as a reviewer for his monthly "Analytical Review" and as a translator, rendering Jacques Necker's *On the Importance of Religious Opinions* into English.

The French Revolution (1789) was a pivotal event for Wollstonecraft, who viewed it as a struggle for individual liberty against tyrannical monarchy. When Price publicly argued that Britain should support the rights that the French were exercising to dethrone a bad king, the statesman Edmund Burke replied with *Reflections on the Revolution in France* in which he argued in favor of the French monarchy. In turn, Wollstonecraft wrote "A Vindication of the Rights of Men" (1790) in support of Price and revolution and against social practices such as the slave trade. Wollestonescraft's pamphlet was well received by other radicals, such as Thomas Paine. Her manifesto, *Vindication of the Rights of Woman*, appeared the following year. In it, she examined women's education, the status of woman and her rights, as well as the role of private versus public life. She excoriated the educational system for keeping women in "ignorance and slavish dependence," she advocated the identical rights of women and men, and famously referred to marriage as "legal prostitution." The *Vindication* also argued against monarchy.

In 1792, Wollstonecraft moved to France to witness the revolution. Her book, *Historical and Moral View of the Origin and Progress of the French Revolution* (1794), documents her disillusionment, which sprang from the Revolution's violence, chaos, and unrealized goals. While in France, Wollstonecraft became pregnant by the American writer Gilbert Imlay, whom she did not marry and by whom she was abandoned. With her newborn daughter, Wollstonecraft followed Imlay back to London in 1795, where she twice attempted suicide over the failed romance. In 1796, her book *Letters Written during a Short Residence in Sweden, Norway, and Denmark* was published; it mixed travelogue with political theory and emotional outbursts. Recovering from Imlay, Wollstonecraft rejoined the London radicals, among whose ranks were Paine, William Blake, and William Wordsworth. She reestablished contact with Godwin—the founder of philosophical anarchism—with whom she had quarreled years before, and they soon became lovers. They married in 1797, although both had repudiated marriage in their writings. Soon thereafter, Mary gave birth to a second daughter, Mary, who would later marry Percy Bysshe Shelley and write *Frankenstein* among several other novels. Less than 2 weeks later, Wollstonecraft died of septicemia.

In 1798, a heartbroken Godwin published the *Posthumous Works of Mary Wollstonecraft,* which included her unfinished novel *Maria, or, the Wrongs of Woman: A Posthumous Fragment* and his own *Memoirs of the Author of a Vindication of the Rights of Woman. Maria* likened the life of working women to imprisonment. The *Memoirs* candidly described Wollstonecraft's struggles due to her sex, including Imlay's betrayal, her illegitimate daughter, and single motherhood. Wollstonecraft's legacy, which rests on the pioneering *Vindication of the Rights of Woman,* has been enhanced by the drama and tragedy of her life, which is often pointed to as a reminder of the high price women paid for freedom.

WME

See also Feminism and Women's Rights; French Revolution; Godwin, William; Price, Richard

Further Readings

Falso, Maria J., ed. *Feminist Interpretations of Mary Wollstonecraft.* University Park: Pennsylvania State University, 1996.

Ferguson, Moira, and Janet Todd. *Mary Wollstonecraft.* Boston: Twayne, 1984.

Flexner, Eleanor. *Mary Wollstonecraft.* New York: Putnam, 1972.

George, Margaret. *One Woman's "Situation": A Study of Mary Wollstonecraft.* Urbana: University of Illinois Press, 1970.

Godwin, William. *Memoirs of the Author of a Vindication of the Rights of Woman.* London, 1798; New York: Penguin, 1987.

Index

Entry titles and their page numbers are in **bold.**

history of, 467–468

human being ownership and, 469

indentured servitude, apprenticeship, and contract labor *vs.,* 469

Thomas Jefferson and, 263

libertarian controversy regarding, 468

manumissions and, 468, 470

military conscription and convict labor *vs.,* 469

"one drop rule" and, 468

plantation slavery and, 464–465

proslavery ideology and, 467–468

racism and, 411–412

serfdom *vs.,* 469

slave rebellions and, 470

slave societies and, 469

sources for slaves and, 469–470

The Unconstitutionality of Slavery (Spooner), 489

William Wilberforce and, 544–545

See also **Civil War, U.S.;** *specific individual*

Smiles, Samuel, xxxi

Smith, Adam, 470–472

balance of trade doctrine and, 327

Jeremy Bentham and, 31

Edmund Burke influenced by, 43, 44, 95

capital fundamentalism concept and, 248

classical liberalism of, xxix–xxx

competition beliefs of, 84

discipline of continuous dealings concept of, 525

division of labor and extent of the market relationship and, 125–126, 189, 471, 486, 537–538

economic life and public policies focus of, xxix–xxx

economic nationalism and isolation opposed by, 71

economic prosperity thoughts of, 120

Enlightenment philosophers and, 471

Adam Ferguson's influence on, 177

free movement of labor, capital, money, and goods advocated by, 71, 471

free trade and peace and economic progress and, 398

French laissez-faire school and, 72

harmony of interests concept of, 73

David Hume and, 230–231, 470, 471

Francis Hutcheson, 231

imperialism criticized by, 238

individual promoting good of society and, 93

"invisible hand" doctrine of, 71–72, 73, 95, 177, 219, 349, 361, 433, 462, 471, 491, 514

laws governing economic interaction and, 471–472

liberal class theory and, xxx

luxury defended by, 397

Robert Malthus influenced by, 72

market as self-regulating concept of, 471

mercantilism criticized by, 71, 326–327, 471

money as spontaneous institution, 338

monopolies as government-granted privileges and, 84

moral sentiment concept of, 138, 248, 315, 470–471, 472

natural harmony of interests concept and, 349

natural liberty advocated by, 71

political economy influence on, xxvii

private property concepts of, 472

rises in income projections of, 247

role of reason in human affairs and, 486

self-interest as motivator and, 424, 470–471, 472

social institution complex evolution concept and, 219, 240, 471–472

sociology founded by, 481, 482

spontaneous order work of, 138, 240, 486–487

Stoicism influence on, 495

sympathy as moral sense and, 470

"system of natural liberty" concept of, 68, 71, 350

tariffs and trade restraints denounced by, 71

"the natural progress of opulence" concept of, 397

The Theory of Moral Sentiments written by, 138, 315, 470–472, 495

Treatise of Human Nature (Hume) and, 231, 470

Ann-Robert-Jacques Turgot and, 515

Voltaire and, 471

voluntary contract enforcement and, 525

war condemned by, 374

wealth creation and distribution process and, 176, 189

The Wealth of Nations written by, 71, 120, 125, 138, 147, 189, 238, 326, 349, 379, 393, 450, 471–472, 537

Smith, Bradley, 106

Smith, Gerrit, 1, 102

Smith, Sydney, xxix

Smith, Tara, 413, 436

Smith, Thomas Southwood, 377

Smith, Vernon, 343, 406

Social Choice and Individual Values (Arrow), 405

Social contract. *See* Contractarianism/social contract

The Social Contract (Rousseau), 181, 444, 445

Social Darwinism, 472–474

cooperation of individuals and, 474

division of labor and social interdependence and, 474

fitness term and, 472

genetics and, 204–206

market *vs.* biological competition and, 473–474

regimes of status to regimes of contract progression and, 472

Herbert Spencer and, 472–473

William Graham Sumner and, 472–473, 497

"survival of the fittest" doctrine and, 472–473

Social holism, 239–240

Socialism, 474–476

Australian School criticism of, 474–475

Bookchin's anarcho-communism and, 475

capitalism *vs.,* 474

collective ownership of wealth concept and, 273

collectivism and, xxxvi, 78–79

communism and, 81–84

concept emergence and, xxvi

decentralization *vs.* centralization and, 474

decentralized, council-based model of, 475